American Institute of Real Estate Appraisers Financial Tables

Edited and compiled by
James J. Mason, MAI

American Institute of Real Estate Appraisers
of the
National Association of Realtors®
430 North Michigan Avenue
Chicago, Illinois 60611

PUBLICATION NO. 373, REVISED EDITION
COPYRIGHT, © 1981, 1982 BY
AMERICAN INSTITUTE OF REAL ESTATE APPRAISERS
WITH TABLES COMPUTED BY FINANCIAL PUBLISHING COMPANY

ISBN: 0-911780-54-8

PRINTED IN THE
UNITED STATES OF AMERICA

GREAT CARE HAS BEEN TAKEN
TO MAKE THESE TABLES CORRECT
THOUGH THERE IS NO WARRANTY
OF COMPLETE ACCURACY.

EXTENT OF TABLES

3

American Institute of Real Estate Appraisers
Tables for Financial Analysis and Valuation
Introduction

"All values are anticipations of the future." Justice Oliver Wendell Holmes

As our anticipations become increasingly sophisticated and specialized, appraisal knowledge must keep pace and education must provide the basis for knowledge. These tables were created in response to the latest evolutionary step in appraisal education and are a logical extension of the basic capitalization formulas and procedures in current use. Although the tables took form as an educational tool for appraisers, they should prove useful to other students of the mathematics of finance, as well as practicing appraisers, lenders, investment consultants, and other financial analysts.

The intended use of this book is as a reference in conjunction with presentations of the Institute's courses and required examinations. It includes a summary of the formulas studied in the various capitalization courses and nine sets of tables of financial factors with each set prefaced by its formulation, a brief explanation, and examples of use.

The reader will find that the selection and arrangement of tables is unique and that the range of rates and frequencies of compounding have been expanded over those of previous publications.

Special features of this publication are: continuous compounding and discounting factors; annuities changing in constant amount; annuities changing in constant ratio; sinking fund factors for annual payments with daily interest; part-paid-off for monthly, direct reduction loans; and straight-line J-Factors for income adjustment in mortgage/equity analysis.

In these inflationary times, the changing annuity factors should prove to be useful. In addition to assisting in the analysis and valuation of increasing incomes, the declining income factors can be used to interpret loss of purchasing power inherent in incomes that are fixed by lease or otherwise are not keeping up with inflation.

The constant ratio (exponential curve) table displays a fairly broad range of factors using 6% to 30% yield rates and $+/-$ 1% to 12% change rates by 1% increments.

The yield rates used in the constant amount (straight-line pattern) table also range from 6% to 30%, but the incremental changes are limited to $+/-$ .02, .04, .05, and .10. The scope of this table has been expanded by the inclusion of factors for slope and intercept (.00). To calculate the factor for *any* rate of change, the standard formula for a straight line can be used: $y = a + bx$; where $y =$ the desired factor, $a =$ the intercept, $b =$ the slope, and $x =$ the rate of change.

The Straight-line J-Factor should be of particular interest with respect to inflation studies. It works within the standard Ellwood formula, yet, unlike the Ellwood J-Factor, the overall rate reflects the relationship between the anticipated first year income and the present value; also, this adjustment contemplates the change in income *after* the first year. On the other hand, it is similar to the Ellwood J-Factor in that a constant overall capitalization rate will result from those situations where the rate of change in both income and value are assumed to be the same.

SUMMARY OF BASIC FORMULAE — (CAP 1)

Where:

I	= Income		
R	= Capitalization Rate	Subscript:	
V	= Value	0	= Overall Property
M	= Mortgage Ratio	M	= Mortgage
DCR	= Debt Coverage Ratio	E	= Equity
F	= Capitalization Factor (Multiplier)	L	= Land
GIM	= Gross Income Multiplier	B	= Building
EGIM	= Effective Gross Income Multiplier		
NIR	= Net Income Ratio		

Basic Income/Cap Rate/Value Formulae:

$$I = R \times V$$
$$R = I/V$$
$$V = I/R$$

Basic Value/Income/Factor Formulae:

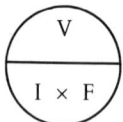

$$V = I \times F$$
$$I = V/F$$
$$F = V/I$$

Adaptations for Mortgage/Equity Components:

Band of Investment: (using Ratios):

$$R_0 = M \times R_M + [(1 - M) \times R_E]$$
$$R_E = (R_0 - M \times R_M)/(1 - M)$$

Equity Residual:

$$V_0 = [(I_0 - V_M \times R_M)/R_E] + V_M$$
$$R_E = (I_0 - V_M \times R_M)/V_E$$

Mortgage Residual:

$$V_0 = [(I_0 - V_E \times R_E)/R_M] + V_E$$

Debt Coverage Ratio:

$$R_0 = DCR \times M \times R_M$$
$$DCR = R/(M \times R_M)$$
$$M = R/(DCR \times R_M)$$

Adaptations for Land/Building Components:

Land Residual:

$$V_0 = [(I_0 - V_B \times R_B)/R_L] + V_B$$
$$R_L = (I_0 - V_B \times R_B)/V_L$$
$$R_B = (I_0 - V_L \times R_L)/V_B$$

Building Residual:

$$V_0 = [(I_0 - V_L \times R_L)/R_B] + V_L$$

Cap Rate/Factor Relationships:

$$R = 1/F$$
$$R_0 = NIR/GIM$$
$$R_0 = NIR/EGIM$$

Note:

NIR may relate to Scheduled Gross or Effective Gross Income and care should be taken to insure consistency.

6

SUMMARY OF BASIC FORMULAE — (CAP 2)

Where:

PV = Present Value
CF = Cash Flow
Y = Yield Rate
R = Capitalization Rate
Δ = Change
a = Annualizer
$1/S_{\overline{n}|}$ = Sinking Fund Factor
$1/n$ = 1/Projection Period
CR = Compound Rate of Change
V = Value

Subscript:

n = Projection Periods
0 = Overall Property
I = Income

Discounted Cash Flows/Present Value (DCF/PV):

$$PV = \frac{CF_1}{1 + Y} + \frac{CF_2}{(1 + Y)^2} + \frac{CF_3}{(1 + Y)^3} + \ldots + \frac{CF_n}{(1 + Y)^n}$$

Basic CAP Rate/Yield Rate/Value Change Formulae:

$R = Y - \Delta a$

$Y = R + \Delta a$

$\Delta a = Y - R$

$\Delta = (Y - R)/a$

Adaptations for Common Income/Value Patterns:

Pattern	Premise	Cap Rates (R)	Yield Rates (Y)	Value Changes (Δ)
Perpetuity	($\Delta = 0$)	R = Y	Y = R	
Level Annuity*	($a = 1/S_{\overline{n}|}$)	$R = Y - \Delta 1/S_{\overline{n}|}$	$Y = R + \Delta 1/S_{\overline{n}|}$	$\Delta = (Y - R)/1/S_{\overline{n}|}$
St. Line Change	($a = 1/n$)	$R = Y - \Delta 1/n$	$Y = R + \Delta 1/n$	$\Delta = (Y - R)/1/n$
Exponential Change	($\Delta_0 a = CR$)	$R_0 = Y_0 - CR$	$Y_0 = R_0 + CR$	$\Delta_0 = (1 + CR)^n - 1$

*Inwood Premise: $1/S_{\overline{n}|}$ at Y Rate; Hoskold Premise: $1/S_{\overline{n}|}$ at Safe Rate

St. Line Change* in Income:

$\$\Delta_I = V \times \Delta 1/n \times Y$

$\Delta_I = (Y \times \Delta 1/n)/(Y - \Delta 1/n)$

St. Line Change* in Value:

$\$\Delta 1/n = \$\Delta_I/Y$

$\Delta 1/n = (Y \times \Delta_I)/(Y + \Delta_I)$

Compound Rate of Change:

$CR = \sqrt[n]{FV/PV} - 1$

$CR = Y_0 = R_0$

*Δ_I in these formulae is the ratio of one year's change in income related to the first year income.

7

SUMMARY OF BASIC FORMULAE — (CAP 2)

Table Relationships:

Conversion of the Annual Constant (R_M) for a monthly payment loan to the corresponding monthly functions.

Function for Monthly Frequency:	Formula:
Amount of $1	$S^n = R_M/(R_M - I)$
Amount of $1 per month	$S_{\overline{n}\vert} = 12/(R_M - I)$
Sinking Fund Factor	$1/S_{\overline{n}\vert} = (R_M - I)/12$
Present Value of $1	$1/S^n = (R_M - I)/R_M$
Present Value of $1 per month	$a_{\overline{n}\vert} = 12/R_M$
Partial Payment	$1/a_{\overline{n}\vert} = R_M/12$

(In these formulas, I = Nominal Interest Rate)

Present Value of Increasing/Decreasing Annuities:

Straight Line Changes:

To obtain the present value of an annuity that has a starting income of **d** at the end of the first period and *increases h dollars* per period for **n** periods:

$$PV = (d + hn)a_{\overline{n}\vert} - \frac{h(n - a_{\overline{n}\vert})}{i}$$

To obtain the present value of an annuity that has a starting income of **d** at the end of the first period and *decreases h dollars* per period for **n** periods, simply treat **h** as a negative quantity in the foregoing formula.

Constant Ratio (Exponential Curve) Changes:

To obtain the present value of an annuity that starts at $1 at the end of the first period and *increases each period* thereafter at the rate **x** for **n** periods:

$$PV = \frac{1 - (1 + x)^n/(1 + i)^n}{i - x}$$

Where: **i** is the periodic discount rate and **x** is the ratio of the increase in income for any period to the income for the previous period.

To obtain the present value of an annuity that starts at $1 at the end of the first period and *decreases each period* thereafter at rate **x**, simply treat rate **x** as a negative quantity in the foregoing formula.

8

SUMMARY OF BASIC FORMULAE — (CAP 3)

Where:

r = Basic Capitalization Rate
Y = Yield Rate
M = Mortgage Ratio
C = Mortgage Coefficient
P = Ratio Paid Off — Mortgage
$1/S_{\overline{n}|}$ = Sinking Fund Factor
R = Capitalization Rate
$S_{\overline{n}|}$ = Future Value of \$1 Per Period
Δ = Change
J = J Factor (Changing Income)
n = Projection Period
NOI = Net Operating Income
B = Mortgage Balance
I = Nominal Interest Rate

Subscript:

E = Equity
M = Mortgage
P = Projection
0 = Overall Property
I = Income
1 = 1st Mortgage
2 = 2nd Mortgage

Mortgage/Equity Formulae:

Basic Capitalization Rates (r):

$r = Y_E - MC$

$r = Y_E - (M_1 C_1 + M_2 C_2)$

$C = Y_E + P\ 1/S_{\overline{n}|} - R_M$

$P = (R_M - I)/(R_{MP} - I)$

$P = 1/S_{\overline{n}|} \times S_{\overline{n}|\ P}$

Capitalization Rates (R):

Level Income:

$R = Y_E - MC - \Delta 1/S_{\overline{n}|}$

$R = r - \Delta 1/S_{\overline{n}|}$

J Factor Changing Income:

$$R_0 = \frac{Y_E - MC - \Delta_0\ 1/S_{\overline{n}|}}{1 + \Delta_I J}$$

$$R_0 = \frac{r - \Delta_0\ 1/S_{\overline{n}|}}{1 + \Delta_I J}$$

Required Change in Value (Δ):

Level Income:

$$\Delta = \frac{r - R}{1/S_{\overline{n}|}}$$

$$\Delta = \frac{Y_E - MC - R}{1/S_{\overline{n}|}}$$

J Factor Changing Income:

$$\Delta_0 = \frac{r - R_0\ (1 + \Delta_I J)}{1/S_{\overline{n}|}}$$

$$^*\Delta_0 = \frac{r - R_0}{R_0 J + 1/S_{\overline{n}|}}$$

Note: For multiple mortgage situations, insert M and C for each mortgage.

*This formula assumes Value and Income change at the same Ratio.

9

SUMMARY OF BASIC FORMULAE — (CAP 3)

Equity Yield (Y_E):

Level Income:

$$Y_E = R_E + \Delta_E \ 1/S_{\overline{n}|}$$

J Factor Changing Income:

$$Y_E = R_E + \Delta_E \ 1/S_{\overline{n}|} + \left[\frac{R_0 \ \Delta_I}{1 - M}\right] J$$

Change in Equity:

$$\Delta_E = (\Delta_0 + MP)/(1 - M) \textbf{ or}$$

$$\Delta_E = [V_0 \ (1 + \Delta_0) - B - V_E]/V_E$$

Assumed Mortgage Situation:

Level Income:

$$V_0 = \frac{NOI + BC}{Y_E - \Delta_0 \ 1/S_{\overline{n}|}}$$

J Factor Changing Income:

$$V_0 = \frac{NOI \ (1 + \Delta_I J) + BC}{Y_E - \Delta_0 \ 1/S_{\overline{n}|}}$$

Mortgage/Equity Without Algebra Format:

1. Loan Ratio × Annual Constant   =   _____

2. Equity Ratio × Equity Yield Rate   =   + _____

3. Loan Ratio × Paid Off Loan Ratio × SFF   =   − _____

          Basic Rate (r)   =   _____

4. + Dep **or** − App × SFF   = + / − _____

          Cap Rate (R)   =   _____

Note: SFF is sinking fund factor at equity yield rate for projection period. Dep/App is the change in value from depreciation/appreciation during the projection period.

SUMMARY OF BASIC FORMULAE — (CAP 3)

Where:

PV = Present Value
NPV = Net Present Value
CF = Cash Flow
i = Discount Rate in NPV Formula
n = Projection Period
IRR = Internal Rate of Return
PI = Profitability Index
MIRR = Modified Internal Rate of Return
$FVCF_j$ = Future Value of a Series of Cash Flows
i = Re-investment Rate in MIRR Formula

Subscript:

0 = At Time Zero
1 = End of 1st Period
2 = End of 2nd Period
3 = End of 3rd Period
n = End Period of Series

Net Present Value (NPV):

$$NPV = CF_0 + \frac{CF_1}{1 + i} + \frac{CF_2}{(1 + i)^2} + \frac{CF_3}{(1 + i)^3} + \ldots + \frac{CF_n}{(1 + i)^n}$$

Internal Rate of Return (IRR):

$$\text{Where: } NPV = 0; \quad IRR = i$$

Profitability Index (PI):

$$PI = PV / CF_0$$

Modified Internal Rate of Return (MIRR):

$$MIRR = \sqrt[n]{\frac{FVCF_j}{CF_0}} - 1$$

$$MIRR = \sqrt[n]{\frac{CF_1(1 + i)^{n-1} + CF_2(1 + i)^{n-2} + CF_3(1 + i)^{n-3} + \ldots + CF_n}{CF_0}} - 1$$

Note: In these formulae . . . . individual CF's may be positive or negative for PV and NPV solutions, however, CF_0 is treated as a positive value for PI and MIRR solutions.

Table 1

Compound Interest
(Future Value of $1)

Table 1 - COMPOUND INTEREST (Future Value of $1)

The amount to which an investment or deposit will grow in a given number of time periods including the accumulation of interest at the effective rate per period. This factor is also known as the *amount of one.*

$$S^n = (1 + i)^n$$

Where S^n = Future Value Factor

            i = Effective Rate of Interest

            n = Number of Compounding Periods

AND $S^n = (e)^{in}$ for Continuous Compounding

Where S^n = Future Value Factor

            i = Nominal Rate of Interest

            n = Number of Years

            e = 2.718282

This Table is used in solving problems dealing with compound growth.

Example 1:
What is the Future Value of $10,000 assuming interest at 6%, compounded annually, for 10 years?

$10,000 × 1.790848 = $17,908.48

Example 2:
What is the Future Value of $10,000 assuming interest at 6%, compounded annually, for 10 years and 7 months?

$10,000 × 1.790848 × 1.035000 = $18,535.28

(Assumes simple interest for time less than one conversion period).

Example 3:
A property sold for $135,000. Five years previously it sold for $100,000. What is the trend in sales price expressed as a monthly compound rate of growth?

$135,000/$100,000 = 1.350000 (Future Value Factor)

Scan tables of Future Value Factors, monthly frequency, for 1.350000 at 5 years. Closest match is found at 6% nominal and monthly rate of growth is therefore approximately 0.5%.

Example 4:
How long will it take prices to double assuming a 6% rate of inflation?

2.00/1.00 = 2.000000 (Future Value Factor)

Scan tables of Future Value Factors at 6% nominal interest for 2.000000.

Assuming annual frequency, the target is bracketed between the Factors for 11 and 12 years. Visual interpolation indicates an answer of slightly less than 12 years. Mathematical straight-line interpolation calculates 11.9 years:

(2.000000 − 1.898299)/(2.012196 − 1.898299) + 11 = 11.9 years

¼%

COMPOUND INTEREST
(Future Value of $1)

Base:	2.718 282	1.000 208	1.000 625	1.001 250	1.002 500	
			Frequency of Conversion			
Months	Continuous	Monthly	Quarterly	Semiannual	Annual	Months
0	1.000 000	1.000 000	1.000 000	1.000 000	1.000 000	0
1	1.000 208	1.000 208	1.000 208	1.000 208	1.000 208	1
2	1.000 417	1.000 417	1.000 417	1.000 417	1.000 417	2
3	1.000 625	1.000 625	1.000 625	1.000 625	1.000 625	3
4	1.000 834	1.000 834	1.000 833	1.000 833	1.000 833	4
5	1.001 042	1.001 042	1.001 042	1.001 042	1.001 042	5
6	1.001 251	1.001 251	1.001 250	1.001 250	1.001 250	6
7	1.001 459	1.001 459	1.001 459	1.001 459	1.001 458	7
8	1.001 668	1.001 668	1.001 668	1.001 667	1.001 667	8
9	1.001 877	1.001 877	1.001 876	1.001 876	1.001 875	9
10	1.002 086	1.002 085	1.002 085	1.002 084	1.002 083	10
11	1.002 294	1.002 294	1.002 294	1.002 293	1.002 292	11

Years						Years
1	1.002 503	1.002 503	1.002 502	1.002 502	1.002 500	1
2	1.005 013	1.005 012	1.005 011	1.005 009	1.005 006	2
3	1.007 528	1.007 527	1.007 526	1.007 523	1.007 519	3
4	1.010 050	1.010 049	1.010 047	1.010 044	1.010 038	4
5	1.012 578	1.012 577	1.012 574	1.012 571	1.012 563	5
6	1.015 113	1.015 111	1.015 108	1.015 104	1.015 094	6
7	1.017 654	1.017 652	1.017 648	1.017 643	1.017 632	7
8	1.020 201	1.020 199	1.020 195	1.020 189	1.020 176	8
9	1.022 755	1.022 753	1.022 748	1.022 741	1.022 726	9
10	1.025 315	1.025 312	1.025 307	1.025 299	1.025 283	10
11	1.027 882	1.027 879	1.027 873	1.027 864	1.027 846	11
12	1.030 455	1.030 451	1.030 445	1.030 435	1.030 416	12
13	1.033 034	1.033 030	1.033 023	1.033 013	1.032 992	13
14	1.035 620	1.035 616	1.035 608	1.035 597	1.035 574	14
15	1.038 212	1.038 208	1.038 200	1.038 188	1.038 163	15
16	1.040 811	1.040 806	1.040 798	1.040 785	1.040 759	16
17	1.043 416	1.043 411	1.043 402	1.043 388	1.043 361	17
18	1.046 028	1.046 023	1.046 013	1.045 998	1.045 969	18
19	1.048 646	1.048 641	1.048 631	1.048 615	1.048 584	19
20	1.051 271	1.051 266	1.051 255	1.051 238	1.051 206	20
21	1.053 903	1.053 897	1.053 885	1.053 868	1.053 834	21
22	1.056 541	1.056 535	1.056 522	1.056 504	1.056 468	22
23	1.059 185	1.059 179	1.059 166	1.059 147	1.059 109	23
24	1.061 837	1.061 830	1.061 817	1.061 797	1.061 757	24
25	1.064 494	1.064 488	1.064 474	1.064 453	1.064 411	25
26	1.067 159	1.067 152	1.067 137	1.067 116	1.067 072	26
27	1.069 830	1.069 823	1.069 808	1.069 785	1.069 740	27
28	1.072 508	1.072 500	1.072 485	1.072 461	1.072 414	28
29	1.075 193	1.075 185	1.075 168	1.075 144	1.075 096	29
30	1.077 884	1.077 876	1.077 859	1.077 834	1.077 783	30
31	1.080 582	1.080 574	1.080 556	1.080 530	1.080 478	31
32	1.083 287	1.083 278	1.083 260	1.083 233	1.083 179	32
33	1.085 999	1.085 989	1.085 971	1.085 943	1.085 887	33
34	1.088 717	1.088 707	1.088 688	1.088 659	1.088 602	34
35	1.091 442	1.091 432	1.091 412	1.091 383	1.091 323	35
36	1.094 174	1.094 164	1.094 144	1.094 113	1.094 051	36
37	1.096 913	1.096 903	1.096 881	1.096 850	1.096 787	37
38	1.099 659	1.099 648	1.099 626	1.099 594	1.099 528	38
39	1.102 411	1.102 400	1.102 378	1.102 344	1.102 277	39
40	1.105 171	1.105 159	1.105 136	1.105 102	1.105 033	40

COMPOUND INTEREST
(Future Value of $1)

½ %

Base:	2.718 282	1.000 417	1.001 250	1.002 500	1.005 000	
			Frequency of Conversion			
Months	Continuous	Monthly	Quarterly	Semiannual	Annual	Months
0	1.000 000	1.000 000	1.000 000	1.000 000	1.000 000	0
1	1.000 417	1.000 417	1.000 417	1.000 417	1.000 417	1
2	1.000 834	1.000 834	1.000 833	1.000 833	1.000 833	2
3	1.001 251	1.001 251	1.001 250	1.001 250	1.001 250	3
4	1.001 668	1.001 668	1.001 667	1.001 667	1.001 667	4
5	1.002 086	1.002 085	1.002 084	1.002 083	1.002 083	5
6	1.002 503	1.002 503	1.002 502	1.002 500	1.002 500	6
7	1.002 921	1.002 920	1.002 919	1.002 918	1.002 917	7
8	1.003 339	1.003 338	1.003 337	1.003 335	1.003 333	8
9	1.003 757	1.003 756	1.003 755	1.003 753	1.003 750	9
10	1.004 175	1.004 174	1.004 173	1.004 171	1.004 167	10
11	1.004 594	1.004 593	1.004 591	1.004 589	1.004 583	11

Years						Years
1	1.005 013	1.005 011	1.005 009	1.005 006	1.005 000	1
2	1.010 050	1.010 048	1.010 044	1.010 038	1.010 025	2
3	1.015 113	1.015 110	1.015 104	1.015 094	1.015 075	3
4	1.020 201	1.020 197	1.020 189	1.020 176	1.020 151	4
5	1.025 315	1.025 310	1.025 299	1.025 283	1.025 251	5
6	1.030 455	1.030 448	1.030 435	1.030 416	1.030 378	6
7	1.035 620	1.035 612	1.035 597	1.035 574	1.035 529	7
8	1.040 811	1.040 802	1.040 785	1.040 759	1.040 707	8
9	1.046 028	1.046 018	1.045 998	1.045 969	1.045 911	9
10	1.051 271	1.051 260	1.051 238	1.051 206	1.051 140	10
11	1.056 541	1.056 529	1.056 504	1.056 468	1.056 396	11
12	1.061 837	1.061 823	1.061 797	1.061 757	1.061 678	12
13	1.067 159	1.067 145	1.067 116	1.067 072	1.066 986	13
14	1.072 508	1.072 493	1.072 461	1.072 414	1.072 321	14
15	1.077 884	1.077 867	1.077 834	1.077 783	1.077 683	15
16	1.083 287	1.083 269	1.083 233	1.083 179	1.083 071	16
17	1.088 717	1.088 698	1.088 659	1.088 602	1.088 487	17
18	1.094 174	1.094 154	1.094 113	1.094 051	1.093 929	18
19	1.099 659	1.099 637	1.099 594	1.099 528	1.099 399	19
20	1.105 171	1.105 148	1.105 102	1.105 033	1.104 896	20
21	1.110 711	1.110 686	1.110 638	1.110 565	1.110 420	21
22	1.116 278	1.116 252	1.116 201	1.116 125	1.115 972	22
23	1.121 873	1.121 847	1.121 793	1.121 712	1.121 552	23
24	1.127 497	1.127 469	1.127 412	1.127 328	1.127 160	24
25	1.133 148	1.133 119	1.133 060	1.132 972	1.132 796	25
26	1.138 828	1.138 798	1.138 736	1.138 644	1.138 460	26
27	1.144 537	1.144 505	1.144 440	1.144 344	1.144 152	27
28	1.150 274	1.150 240	1.150 173	1.150 073	1.149 873	28
29	1.156 040	1.156 005	1.155 935	1.155 830	1.155 622	29
30	1.161 834	1.161 798	1.161 725	1.161 617	1.161 400	30
31	1.167 658	1.167 620	1.167 545	1.167 432	1.167 207	31
32	1.173 511	1.173 472	1.173 394	1.173 277	1.173 043	32
33	1.179 393	1.179 353	1.179 272	1.179 150	1.178 908	33
34	1.185 305	1.185 263	1.185 179	1.185 053	1.184 803	34
35	1.191 246	1.191 203	1.191 116	1.190 986	1.190 727	35
36	1.197 217	1.197 172	1.197 083	1.196 948	1.196 681	36
37	1.203 218	1.203 172	1.203 079	1.202 941	1.202 664	37
38	1.209 250	1.209 202	1.209 106	1.208 963	1.208 677	38
39	1.215 311	1.215 262	1.215 163	1.215 015	1.214 721	39
40	1.221 403	1.221 352	1.221 250	1.221 098	1.220 794	40

¾%

COMPOUND INTEREST
(Future Value of $1)

Base:	2.718 282	1.000 625	1.001 875	1.003 750	1.007 500	
			Frequency of Conversion			
Months	Continuous	Monthly	Quarterly	Semiannual	Annual	Months
0	1.000 000	1.000 000	1.000 000	1.000 000	1.000 000	0
1	1.000 625	1.000 625	1.000 625	1.000 625	1.000 625	1
2	1.001 251	1.001 250	1.001 250	1.001 250	1.001 250	2
3	1.001 877	1.001 876	1.001 875	1.001 875	1.001 875	3
4	1.002 503	1.002 502	1.002 501	1.002 500	1.002 500	4
5	1.003 130	1.003 129	1.003 127	1.003 125	1.003 125	5
6	1.003 757	1.003 756	1.003 754	1.003 750	1.003 750	6
7	1.004 385	1.004 383	1.004 381	1.004 377	1.004 375	7
8	1.005 013	1.005 011	1.005 008	1.005 005	1.005 000	8
9	1.005 641	1.005 639	1.005 636	1.005 632	1.005 625	9
10	1.006 270	1.006 268	1.006 264	1.006 259	1.006 250	10
11	1.006 899	1.006 897	1.006 893	1.006 887	1.006 875	11

Years						Years
1	1.007 528	1.007 526	1.007 521	1.007 514	1.007 500	1
2	1.015 113	1.015 108	1.015 099	1.015 085	1.015 056	2
3	1.022 755	1.022 748	1.022 733	1.022 712	1.022 669	3
4	1.030 455	1.030 445	1.030 426	1.030 397	1.030 339	4
5	1.038 212	1.038 200	1.038 176	1.038 139	1.038 067	5
6	1.046 028	1.046 013	1.045 984	1.045 940	1.045 852	6
7	1.053 903	1.053 885	1.053 851	1.053 799	1.053 696	7
8	1.061 837	1.061 817	1.061 777	1.061 717	1.061 599	8
9	1.069 830	1.069 808	1.069 763	1.069 695	1.069 561	9
10	1.077 884	1.077 859	1.077 808	1.077 733	1.077 583	10
11	1.085 999	1.085 971	1.085 915	1.085 831	1.085 664	11
12	1.094 174	1.094 144	1.094 082	1.093 990	1.093 807	12
13	1.102 411	1.102 378	1.102 311	1.102 210	1.102 010	13
14	1.110 711	1.110 674	1.110 601	1.110 493	1.110 276	14
15	1.119 072	1.119 033	1.118 954	1.118 837	1.118 603	15
16	1.127 497	1.127 455	1.127 370	1.127 244	1.126 992	16
17	1.135 985	1.135 940	1.135 849	1.135 714	1.135 445	17
18	1.144 537	1.144 489	1.144 392	1.144 248	1.143 960	18
19	1.153 153	1.153 102	1.152 999	1.152 846	1.152 540	19
20	1.161 834	1.161 780	1.161 671	1.161 508	1.161 184	20
21	1.170 581	1.170 523	1.170 408	1.170 236	1.169 893	21
22	1.179 393	1.179 332	1.179 211	1.179 029	1.178 667	22
23	1.188 272	1.188 208	1.188 080	1.187 889	1.187 507	23
24	1.197 217	1.197 150	1.197 016	1.196 814	1.196 414	24
25	1.206 230	1.206 160	1.206 019	1.205 807	1.205 387	25
26	1.215 311	1.215 237	1.215 089	1.214 868	1.214 427	26
27	1.224 460	1.224 383	1.224 228	1.223 996	1.223 535	27
28	1.233 678	1.233 597	1.233 436	1.233 194	1.232 712	28
29	1.242 965	1.242 881	1.242 712	1.242 460	1.241 95?	29
30	1.252 323	1.252 235	1.252 059	1.251 796	1.251 272	30
31	1.261 750	1.261 659	1.261 476	1.261 202	1.260 656	31
32	1.271 249	1.271 154	1.270 964	1.270 679	1.270 111	32
33	1.280 819	1.280 720	1.280 523	1.280 227	1.279 637	33
34	1.290 462	1.290 359	1.290 154	1.289 846	1.289 234	34
35	1.300 176	1.300 070	1.299 857	1.299 538	1.298 904	35
36	1.309 964	1.309 854	1.309 633	1.309 303	1.308 645	36
37	1.319 826	1.319 712	1.319 483	1.319 141	1.318 460	37
38	1.329 762	1.329 644	1.329 407	1.329 053	1.328 349	38
39	1.339 773	1.339 650	1.339 406	1.339 040	1.338 311	39
40	1.349 859	1.349 732	1.349 480	1.349 102	1.348 349	40

COMPOUND INTEREST

(Future Value of $1)

1%

Base:	2.718 282	1.000 833	1.002 500	1.005 000	1.010 000	
			Frequency of Conversion			
Months	Continuous	Monthly	Quarterly	Semiannual	Annual	Months
0	1.000 000	1.000 000	1.000 000	1.000 000	1.000 000	0
1	1.000 834	1.000 833	1.000 833	1.000 833	1.000 833	1
2	1.001 668	1.001 667	1.001 667	1.001 667	1.001 667	2
3	1.002 503	1.002 502	1.002 502	1.002 500	1.002 500	3
4	1.003 339	1.003 338	1.003 335	1.003 333	1.003 333	4
5	1.004 175	1.004 174	1.004 171	1.004 167	1.004 167	5
6	1.005 013	1.005 010	1.005 006	1.005 000	1.005 000	6
7	1.005 850	1.005 848	1.005 844	1.005 837	1.005 833	7
8	1.006 689	1.006 686	1.006 681	1.006 675	1.006 667	8
9	1.007 528	1.007 525	1.007 519	1.007 513	1.007 500	9
10	1.008 368	1.008 365	1.008 358	1.008 350	1.008 333	10
11	1.009 209	1.009 205	1.009 198	1.009 188	1.009 167	11

Years						Years
1	1.010 050	1.010 046	1.010 038	1.010 025	1.010 000	1
2	1.020 201	1.020 193	1.020 176	1.020 151	1.020 100	2
3	1.030 455	1.030 442	1.030 416	1.030 378	1.030 301	3
4	1.040 811	1.040 793	1.040 759	1.040 707	1.040 604	4
5	1.051 271	1.051 249	1.051 206	1.051 140	1.051 010	5
6	1.061 837	1.061 810	1.061 757	1.061 678	1.061 520	6
7	1.072 508	1.072 477	1.072 414	1.072 321	1.072 135	7
8	1.083 287	1.083 251	1.083 179	1.083 071	1.082 857	8
9	1.094 174	1.094 133	1.094 051	1.093 929	1.093 685	9
10	1.105 171	1.105 125	1.105 033	1.104 896	1.104 622	10
11	1.116 278	1.116 227	1.116 125	1.115 972	1.115 668	11
12	1.127 497	1.127 441	1.127 328	1.127 160	1.126 825	12
13	1.138 828	1.138 767	1.138 644	1.138 460	1.138 093	13
14	1.150 274	1.150 207	1.150 073	1.149 873	1.149 474	14
15	1.161 834	1.161 762	1.161 617	1.161 400	1.160 969	15
16	1.173 511	1.173 433	1.173 277	1.173 043	1.172 579	16
17	1.185 305	1.185 221	1.185 053	1.184 803	1.184 304	17
18	1.197 217	1.197 128	1.196 948	1.196 681	1.196 147	18
19	1.209 250	1.209 154	1.208 963	1.208 677	1.208 109	19
20	1.221 403	1.221 301	1.221 098	1.220 794	1.220 190	20
21	1.233 678	1.233 570	1.233 355	1.233 033	1.232 392	21
22	1.246 077	1.245 963	1.245 735	1.245 394	1.244 716	22
23	1.258 600	1.258 479	1.258 239	1.257 879	1.257 163	23
24	1.271 249	1.271 122	1.270 868	1.270 489	1.269 735	24
25	1.284 025	1.283 892	1.283 625	1.283 226	1.282 432	25
26	1.296 930	1.296 790	1.296 509	1.296 090	1.295 256	26
27	1.309 964	1.309 817	1.309 523	1.309 083	1.308 209	27
28	1.323 130	1.322 976	1.322 668	1.322 207	1.321 291	28
29	1.336 427	1.336 266	1.335 944	1.335 462	1.334 504	29
30	1.349 859	1.349 690	1.349 354	1.348 850	1.347 849	30
31	1.363 425	1.363 249	1.362 898	1.362 372	1.361 327	31
32	1.377 128	1.376 944	1.376 578	1.376 030	1.374 941	32
33	1.390 968	1.390 777	1.390 395	1.389 825	1.388 690	33
34	1.404 948	1.404 749	1.404 352	1.403 758	1.402 577	34
35	1.419 068	1.418 861	1.418 448	1.417 831	1.416 603	35
36	1.433 329	1.433 115	1.432 686	1.432 044	1.430 769	36
37	1.447 735	1.447 512	1.447 066	1.446 401	1.445 076	37
38	1.462 285	1.462 053	1.461 591	1.460 901	1.459 527	38
39	1.476 981	1.476 741	1.476 262	1.475 546	1.474 123	39
40	1.491 825	1.491 576	1.491 080	1.490 339	1.488 864	40

1¼%

COMPOUND INTEREST
(Future Value of $1)

Base:	2.718 282	1.001 042	1.003 125	1.006 250	1.012 500	
			Frequency of Conversion			
Months	Continuous	Monthly	Quarterly	Semiannual	Annual	Months
0	1.000 000	1.000 000	1.000 000	1.000 000	1.000 000	0
1	1.001 042	1.001 042	1.001 042	1.001 042	1.001 042	1
2	1.002 086	1.002 084	1.002 083	1.002 083	1.002 083	2
3	1.003 130	1.003 128	1.003 125	1.003 125	1.003 125	3
4	1.004 175	1.004 173	1.004 170	1.004 167	1.004 167	4
5	1.005 222	1.005 219	1.005 215	1.005 208	1.005 208	5
6	1.006 270	1.006 266	1.006 260	1.006 250	1.006 250	6
7	1.007 318	1.007 314	1.007 308	1.007 298	1.007 292	7
8	1.008 368	1.008 364	1.008 356	1.008 346	1.008 333	8
9	1.009 419	1.009 414	1.009 404	1.009 395	1.009 375	9
10	1.010 471	1.010 466	1.010 456	1.010 443	1.010 417	10
11	1.011 524	1.011 518	1.011 507	1.011 491	1.011 458	11

Years						Years
1	1.012 578	1.012 572	1.012 559	1.012 539	1.012 500	1
2	1.025 315	1.025 302	1.025 275	1.025 235	1.025 156	2
3	1.038 212	1.038 192	1.038 151	1.038 091	1.037 971	3
4	1.051 271	1.051 244	1.051 189	1.051 108	1.050 945	4
5	1.064 494	1.064 460	1.064 391	1.064 287	1.064 082	5
6	1.077 884	1.077 842	1.077 758	1.077 633	1.077 383	6
7	1.091 442	1.091 393	1.091 293	1.091 145	1.090 850	7
8	1.105 171	1.105 113	1.104 999	1.104 827	1.104 486	8
9	1.119 072	1.119 007	1.118 876	1.118 681	1.118 292	9
10	1.133 148	1.133 075	1.132 928	1.132 708	1.132 271	10
11	1.147 402	1.147 320	1.147 156	1.146 911	1.146 424	11
12	1.161 834	1.161 744	1.161 563	1.161 292	1.160 755	12
13	1.176 448	1.176 349	1.176 150	1.175 854	1.175 264	13
14	1.191 246	1.191 138	1.190 921	1.190 598	1.189 955	14
15	1.206 230	1.206 113	1.205 878	1.205 527	1.204 829	15
16	1.221 403	1.221 276	1.221 022	1.220 643	1.219 890	16
17	1.236 766	1.236 629	1.236 356	1.235 949	1.235 138	17
18	1.252 323	1.252 176	1.251 883	1.251 446	1.250 577	18
19	1.268 075	1.267 918	1.267 605	1.267 138	1.266 210	19
20	1.284 025	1.283 858	1.283 525	1.283 027	1.282 037	20
21	1.300 176	1.299 999	1.299 644	1.299 115	1.298 063	21
22	1.316 531	1.316 342	1.315 966	1.315 404	1.314 288	22
23	1.333 091	1.332 891	1.332 493	1.331 898	1.330 717	23
24	1.349 859	1.349 648	1.349 228	1.348 599	1.347 351	24
25	1.366 838	1.366 616	1.366 172	1.365 509	1.364 193	25
26	1.384 031	1.383 797	1.383 329	1.382 632	1.381 245	26
27	1.401 440	1.401 193	1.400 702	1.399 968	1.398 511	27
28	1.419 068	1.418 809	1.418 293	1.417 523	1.415 992	28
29	1.436 917	1.436 646	1.436 105	1.435 297	1.433 692	29
30	1.454 991	1.454 707	1.454 141	1.453 294	1.451 613	30
31	1.473 293	1.472 996	1.472 403	1.471 517	1.469 759	31
32	1.491 825	1.491 514	1.490 895	1.489 969	1.488 131	32
33	1.510 590	1.510 265	1.509 618	1.508 652	1.506 732	33
34	1.529 590	1.529 252	1.528 577	1.527 569	1.525 566	34
35	1.548 830	1.548 478	1.547 774	1.546 723	1.544 636	35
36	1.568 312	1.567 945	1.567 212	1.566 117	1.563 944	36
37	1.588 039	1.587 657	1.586 894	1.585 755	1.583 493	37
38	1.608 014	1.607 617	1.606 824	1.605 639	1.603 287	38
39	1.628 241	1.627 827	1.627 003	1.625 772	1.623 328	39
40	1.648 721	1.648 292	1.647 436	1.646 158	1.643 619	40

COMPOUND INTEREST
(Future Value of $1)

1½%

Base:	2.718 282	1.001 250	1.003 750	1.007 500	1.015 000	
			Frequency of Conversion			
Months	Continuous	Monthly	Quarterly	Semiannual	Annual	Months
0	1.000 000	1.000 000	1.000 000	1.000 000	1.000 000	0
1	1.001 251	1.001 250	1.001 250	1.001 250	1.001 250	1
2	1.002 503	1.002 502	1.002 500	1.002 500	1.002 500	2
3	1.003 757	1.003 755	1.003 750	1.003 750	1.003 750	3
4	1.005 013	1.005 009	1.005 005	1.005 000	1.005 000	4
5	1.006 270	1.006 266	1.006 259	1.006 250	1.006 250	5
6	1.007 528	1.007 523	1.007 514	1.007 500	1.007 500	6
7	1.008 788	1.008 783	1.008 773	1.008 759	1.008 750	7
8	1.010 050	1.010 044	1.010 033	1.010 019	1.010 000	8
9	1.011 314	1.011 306	1.011 292	1.011 278	1.011 250	9
10	1.012 578	1.012 571	1.012 556	1.012 538	1.012 500	10
11	1.013 845	1.013 836	1.013 820	1.013 797	1.013 750	11

Years						Years
1	1.015 113	1.015 104	1.015 085	1.015 056	1.015 000	1
2	1.030 455	1.030 435	1.030 397	1.030 339	1.030 225	2
3	1.046 028	1.045 998	1.045 940	1.045 852	1.045 678	3
4	1.061 837	1.061 797	1.061 717	1.061 599	1.061 364	4
5	1.077 884	1.077 834	1.077 733	1.077 583	1.077 284	5
6	1.094 174	1.094 113	1.093 990	1.093 807	1.093 443	6
7	1.110 711	1.110 638	1.110 493	1.110 276	1.109 845	7
8	1.127 497	1.127 412	1.127 244	1.126 992	1.126 493	8
9	1.144 537	1.144 440	1.144 248	1.143 960	1.143 390	9
10	1.161 834	1.161 725	1.161 508	1.161 184	1.160 541	10
11	1.179 393	1.179 272	1.179 029	1.178 667	1.177 949	11
12	1.197 217	1.197 083	1.196 814	1.196 414	1.195 618	12
13	1.215 311	1.215 163	1.214 868	1.214 427	1.213 552	13
14	1.233 678	1.233 516	1.233 194	1.232 712	1.231 756	14
15	1.252 323	1.252 147	1.251 796	1.251 272	1.250 232	15
16	1.271 249	1.271 059	1.270 679	1.270 111	1.268 986	16
17	1.290 462	1.290 256	1.289 846	1.289 234	1.288 020	17
18	1.309 964	1.309 744	1.309 303	1.308 645	1.307 341	18
19	1.329 762	1.329 525	1.329 053	1.328 349	1.326 951	19
20	1.349 859	1.349 606	1.349 102	1.348 349	1.346 855	20
21	1.370 259	1.369 990	1.369 452	1.368 650	1.367 058	21
22	1.390 968	1.390 682	1.390 110	1.389 256	1.387 564	22
23	1.411 990	1.411 686	1.411 079	1.410 173	1.408 377	23
24	1.433 329	1.433 007	1.432 365	1.431 405	1.429 503	24
25	1.454 991	1.454 651	1.453 971	1.452 957	1.450 945	25
26	1.476 981	1.476 621	1.475 904	1.474 833	1.472 710	26
27	1.499 303	1.498 923	1.498 167	1.497 038	1.494 800	27
28	1.521 962	1.521 562	1.520 766	1.519 578	1.517 222	28
29	1.544 963	1.544 543	1.543 707	1.542 457	1.539 981	29
30	1.568 312	1.567 872	1.566 993	1.565 681	1.563 080	30
31	1.592 014	1.591 552	1.590 630	1.589 254	1.586 526	31
32	1.616 074	1.615 590	1.614 624	1.613 183	1.610 324	32
33	1.640 498	1.639 991	1.638 980	1.637 471	1.634 479	33
34	1.665 291	1.664 761	1.663 703	1.662 125	1.658 996	34
35	1.690 459	1.689 905	1.688 800	1.687 151	1.683 881	35
36	1.716 007	1.715 428	1.714 275	1.712 553	1.709 140	36
37	1.741 941	1.741 337	1.740 134	1.738 337	1.734 777	37
38	1.768 267	1.767 638	1.766 383	1.764 510	1.760 798	38
39	1.794 991	1.794 335	1.793 028	1.791 077	1.787 210	39
40	1.822 119	1.821 436	1.820 075	1.818 044	1.814 018	40

1¾%

COMPOUND INTEREST
(Future Value of $1)

Base: 2.718 282   1.001 458   1.004 375   1.008 750   1.017 500

Frequency of Conversion

Months	Continuous	Monthly	Quarterly	Semiannual	Annual	Months
0	1.000 000	1.000 000	1.000 000	1.000 000	1.000 000	0
1	1.001 459	1.001 458	1.001 458	1.001 458	1.001 458	1
2	1.002 921	1.002 919	1.002 917	1.002 917	1.002 917	2
3	1.004 385	1.004 381	1.004 375	1.004 375	1.004 375	3
4	1.005 850	1.005 846	1.005 840	1.005 833	1.005 833	4
5	1.007 318	1.007 313	1.007 304	1.007 292	1.007 292	5
6	1.008 788	1.008 782	1.008 769	1.008 750	1.008 750	6
7	1.010 261	1.010 253	1.010 240	1.010 221	1.010 208	7
8	1.011 735	1.011 726	1.011 711	1.011 692	1.011 667	8
9	1.013 212	1.013 202	1.013 183	1.013 163	1.013 125	9
10	1.014 690	1.014 679	1.014 660	1.014 634	1.014 583	10
11	1.016 171	1.016 159	1.016 138	1.016 105	1.016 042	11

Years						Years
1	1.017 654	1.017 641	1.017 615	1.017 577	1.017 500	1
2	1.035 620	1.035 593	1.035 541	1.035 462	1.035 306	2
3	1.053 903	1.053 862	1.053 782	1.053 662	1.053 424	3
4	1.072 508	1.072 453	1.072 344	1.072 182	1.071 859	4
5	1.091 442	1.091 373	1.091 234	1.091 027	1.090 617	5
6	1.110 711	1.110 626	1.110 456	1.110 203	1.109 702	6
7	1.130 319	1.130 218	1.130 017	1.129 717	1.129 122	7
8	1.150 274	1.150 156	1.149 923	1.149 574	1.148 882	8
9	1.170 581	1.170 446	1.170 179	1.169 779	1.168 987	9
10	1.191 246	1.191 094	1.190 792	1.190 340	1.189 444	10
11	1.212 277	1.212 107	1.211 768	1.211 262	1.210 260	11
12	1.233 678	1.233 489	1.233 113	1.232 552	1.231 439	12
13	1.255 457	1.255 249	1.254 835	1.254 216	1.252 990	13
14	1.277 621	1.277 393	1.276 939	1.276 261	1.274 917	14
15	1.300 176	1.299 928	1.299 432	1.298 693	1.297 228	15
16	1.323 130	1.322 860	1.322 322	1.321 519	1.319 929	16
17	1.346 488	1.346 197	1.345 615	1.344 747	1.343 028	17
18	1.370 259	1.369 945	1.369 318	1.368 383	1.366 531	18
19	1.394 450	1.394 112	1.393 439	1.392 435	1.390 445	19
20	1.419 068	1.418 706	1.417 985	1.416 909	1.414 778	20
21	1.444 120	1.443 733	1.442 963	1.441 813	1.439 537	21
22	1.469 614	1.469 202	1.468 381	1.467 155	1.464 729	22
23	1.495 559	1.495 120	1.494 247	1.492 943	1.490 361	23
24	1.521 962	1.521 496	1.520 568	1.519 184	1.516 443	24
25	1.548 830	1.548 337	1.547 353	1.545 886	1.542 981	25
26	1.576 173	1.575 651	1.574 610	1.573 057	1.569 983	26
27	1.603 999	1.603 447	1.602 347	1.600 706	1.597 457	27
28	1.632 316	1.631 734	1.630 573	1.628 841	1.625 413	28
29	1.661 133	1.660 519	1.659 295	1.657 470	1.653 858	29
30	1.690 459	1.689 812	1.688 524	1.686 603	1.682 800	30
31	1.720 302	1.719 623	1.718 268	1.716 248	1.712 249	31
32	1.750 673	1.749 958	1.748 535	1.746 413	1.742 213	32
33	1.781 579	1.780 830	1.779 336	1.777 109	1.772 702	33
34	1.813 031	1.812 245	1.810 680	1.808 345	1.803 725	34
35	1.845 038	1.844 215	1.842 575	1.840 129	1.835 290	35
36	1.877 611	1.876 749	1.875 032	1.872 472	1.867 407	36
37	1.910 758	1.909 857	1.908 061	1.905 384	1.900 087	37
38	1.944 491	1.943 549	1.941 672	1.938 874	1.933 338	38
39	1.978 819	1.977 835	1.975 875	1.972 953	1.967 172	39
40	2.013 753	2.012 726	2.010 680	2.007 631	2.001 597	40

22

COMPOUND INTEREST

(Future Value of $1)

2%

Base:	2.718 282	1.001 667	1.005 000	1.010 000	1.020 000	
			Frequency of Conversion			
Months	Continuous	Monthly	Quarterly	Semiannual	Annual	Months
0	1.000 000	1.000 000	1.000 000	1.000 000	1.000 000	0
1	1.001 668	1.001 667	1.001 667	1.001 667	1.001 667	1
2	1.003 339	1.003 336	1.003 333	1.003 333	1.003 333	2
3	1.005 013	1.005 008	1.005 000	1.005 000	1.005 000	3
4	1.006 689	1.006 683	1.006 675	1.006 667	1.006 667	4
5	1.008 368	1.008 361	1.008 350	1.008 333	1.008 333	5
6	1.010 050	1.010 042	1.010 025	1.010 000	1.010 000	6
7	1.011 735	1.011 725	1.011 708	1.011 683	1.011 667	7
8	1.013 423	1.013 411	1.013 392	1.013 367	1.013 333	8
9	1.015 113	1.015 100	1.015 075	1.015 050	1.015 000	9
10	1.016 806	1.016 792	1.016 767	1.016 733	1.016 667	10
11	1.018 502	1.018 487	1.018 459	1.018 417	1.018 333	11

Years						Years
1	1.020 201	1.020 184	1.020 151	1.020 100	1.020 000	1
2	1.040 811	1.040 776	1.040 707	1.040 604	1.040 400	2
3	1.061 837	1.061 784	1.061 678	1.061 520	1.061 208	3
4	1.083 287	1.083 215	1.083 071	1.082 857	1.082 432	4
5	1.105 171	1.105 079	1.104 896	1.104 622	1.104 081	5
6	1.127 497	1.127 384	1.127 160	1.126 825	1.126 162	6
7	1.150 274	1.150 140	1.149 873	1.149 474	1.148 686	7
8	1.173 511	1.173 355	1.173 043	1.172 579	1.171 659	8
9	1.197 217	1.197 038	1.196 681	1.196 147	1.195 093	9
10	1.221 403	1.221 199	1.220 794	1.220 190	1.218 994	10
11	1.246 077	1.245 849	1.245 394	1.244 716	1.243 374	11
12	1.271 249	1.270 995	1.270 489	1.269 735	1.268 242	12
13	1.296 930	1.296 649	1.296 090	1.295 256	1.293 607	13
14	1.323 130	1.322 821	1.322 207	1.321 291	1.319 479	14
15	1.349 859	1.349 522	1.348 850	1.347 849	1.345 868	15
16	1.377 128	1.376 761	1.376 030	1.374 941	1.372 786	16
17	1.404 948	1.404 550	1.403 758	1.402 577	1.400 241	17
18	1.433 329	1.432 900	1.432 044	1.430 769	1.428 246	18
19	1.462 285	1.461 822	1.460 901	1.459 527	1.456 811	19
20	1.491 825	1.491 328	1.490 339	1.488 864	1.485 947	20
21	1.521 962	1.521 430	1.520 370	1.518 790	1.515 666	21
22	1.552 707	1.552 139	1.551 006	1.549 318	1.545 980	22
23	1.584 074	1.583 468	1.582 259	1.580 459	1.576 899	23
24	1.616 074	1.615 429	1.614 143	1.612 226	1.608 437	24
25	1.648 721	1.648 035	1.646 668	1.644 632	1.640 606	25
26	1.682 028	1.681 300	1.679 850	1.677 689	1.673 418	26
27	1.716 007	1.715 236	1.713 699	1.711 410	1.706 886	27
28	1.750 673	1.749 857	1.748 231	1.745 810	1.741 024	28
29	1.786 038	1.785 176	1.783 459	1.780 901	1.775 845	29
30	1.822 119	1.821 209	1.819 397	1.816 697	1.811 362	30
31	1.858 928	1.857 969	1.856 058	1.853 212	1.847 589	31
32	1.896 481	1.895 471	1.893 459	1.890 462	1.884 541	32
33	1.934 792	1.933 730	1.931 613	1.928 460	1.922 231	33
34	1.973 878	1.972 761	1.970 536	1.967 222	1.960 676	34
35	2.013 753	2.012 580	2.010 243	2.006 763	1.999 890	35
36	2.054 433	2.053 202	2.050 751	2.047 099	2.039 887	36
37	2.095 936	2.094 645	2.092 074	2.088 246	2.080 685	37
38	2.138 276	2.136 924	2.134 231	2.130 220	2.122 299	38
39	2.181 472	2.180 056	2.177 237	2.173 037	2.164 745	39
40	2.225 541	2.224 059	2.221 109	2.216 715	2.208 040	40

2¼%

COMPOUND INTEREST
(Future Value of $1)

Base:	2.718 282	1.001 875	1.005 625	1.011 250	1.022 500	
			Frequency of Conversion			
Months	Continuous	Monthly	Quarterly	Semiannual	Annual	Months
0	1.000 000	1.000 000	1.000 000	1.000 000	1.000 000	0
1	1.001 877	1.001 875	1.001 875	1.001 875	1.001 875	1
2	1.003 757	1.003 754	1.003 750	1.003 750	1.003 750	2
3	1.005 641	1.005 636	1.005 625	1.005 625	1.005 625	3
4	1.007 528	1.007 521	1.007 511	1.007 500	1.007 500	4
5	1.009 419	1.009 410	1.009 396	1.009 375	1.009 375	5
6	1.011 314	1.011 303	1.011 282	1.011 250	1.011 250	6
7	1.013 212	1.013 199	1.013 178	1.013 146	1.013 125	7
8	1.015 113	1.015 099	1.015 074	1.015 042	1.015 000	8
9	1.017 018	1.017 002	1.016 970	1.016 938	1.016 875	9
10	1.018 927	1.018 909	1.018 877	1.018 834	1.018 750	10
11	1.020 839	1.020 819	1.020 784	1.020 730	1.020 625	11

Years						Years
1	1.022 755	1.022 733	1.022 691	1.022 627	1.022 500	1
2	1.046 028	1.045 984	1.045 896	1.045 765	1.045 506	2
3	1.069 830	1.069 763	1.069 628	1.069 427	1.069 030	3
4	1.094 174	1.094 082	1.093 898	1.093 625	1.093 083	4
5	1.119 072	1.118 954	1.118 720	1.118 370	1.117 678	5
6	1.144 537	1.144 392	1.144 104	1.143 674	1.142 825	6
7	1.170 581	1.170 408	1.170 064	1.169 552	1.168 539	7
8	1.197 217	1.197 016	1.196 614	1.196 015	1.194 831	8
9	1.224 460	1.224 228	1.223 766	1.223 077	1.221 715	9
10	1.252 323	1.252 059	1.251 533	1.250 751	1.249 203	10
11	1.280 819	1.280 523	1.279 931	1.279 051	1.277 311	11
12	1.309 964	1.309 633	1.308 974	1.307 991	1.306 050	12
13	1.339 773	1.339 406	1.338 675	1.337 587	1.335 436	13
14	1.370 259	1.369 855	1.369 050	1.367 852	1.365 483	14
15	1.401 440	1.400 997	1.400 115	1.398 801	1.396 207	15
16	1.433 329	1.432 846	1.431 884	1.430 451	1.427 621	16
17	1.465 945	1.465 420	1.464 375	1.462 818	1.459 743	17
18	1.499 303	1.498 734	1.497 602	1.495 916	1.492 587	18
19	1.533 419	1.532 806	1.531 583	1.529 764	1.526 170	19
20	1.568 312	1.567 652	1.566 336	1.564 377	1.560 509	20
21	1.603 999	1.603 290	1.601 877	1.599 773	1.595 621	21
22	1.640 498	1.639 738	1.638 224	1.635 971	1.631 522	22
23	1.677 828	1.677 015	1.675 397	1.672 987	1.668 231	23
24	1.716 007	1.715 139	1.713 412	1.710 841	1.705 767	24
25	1.755 055	1.754 131	1.752 291	1.749 552	1.744 146	25
26	1.794 991	1.794 008	1.792 051	1.789 138	1.783 390	26
27	1.835 836	1.834 792	1.832 714	1.829 620	1.823 516	27
28	1.877 611	1.876 503	1.874 299	1.871 018	1.864 545	28
29	1.920 336	1.919 163	1.916 828	1.913 353	1.906 497	29
30	1.964 033	1.962 792	1.960 322	1.956 645	1.949 393	30
31	2.008 725	2.007 413	2.004 803	2.000 917	1.993 255	31
32	2.054 433	2.053 049	2.050 293	2.046 191	2.038 103	32
33	2.101 182	2.099 722	2.096 815	2.092 489	2.083 960	33
34	2.148 994	2.147 456	2.144 393	2.139 835	2.130 849	34
35	2.197 895	2.196 275	2.193 050	2.188 252	2.178 794	35
36	2.247 908	2.246 204	2.242 812	2.237 765	2.227 816	36
37	2.299 059	2.297 268	2.293 703	2.288 398	2.277 942	37
38	2.351 374	2.349 493	2.345 748	2.340 177	2.329 196	38
39	2.404 880	2.402 905	2.398 974	2.393 127	2.381 603	39
40	2.459 603	2.457 531	2.453 408	2.447 275	2.435 189	40

COMPOUND INTEREST

(Future Value of $1)

2½%

Base:	2.718 282	1.002 083	1.006 250	1.012 500	1.025 000	
			Frequency of Conversion			
Months	Continuous	Monthly	Quarterly	Semiannual	Annual	Months
0	1.000 000	1.000 000	1.000 000	1.000 000	1.000 000	0
1	1.002 086	1.002 083	1.002 083	1.002 083	1.002 083	1
2	1.004 175	1.004 171	1.004 167	1.004 167	1.004 167	2
3	1.006 270	1.006 263	1.006 250	1.006 250	1.006 250	3
4	1.008 368	1.008 359	1.008 346	1.008 333	1.008 333	4
5	1.010 471	1.010 460	1.010 443	1.010 417	1.010 417	5
6	1.012 578	1.012 565	1.012 539	1.012 500	1.012 500	6
7	1.014 690	1.014 675	1.014 649	1.014 609	1.014 583	7
8	1.016 806	1.016 789	1.016 758	1.016 719	1.016 667	8
9	1.018 927	1.018 907	1.018 867	1.018 828	1.018 750	9
10	1.021 052	1.021 030	1.020 990	1.020 937	1.020 833	10
11	1.023 181	1.023 157	1.023 113	1.023 047	1.022 917	11
Years						Years
1	1.025 315	1.025 288	1.025 235	1.025 156	1.025 000	1
2	1.051 271	1.051 216	1.051 108	1.050 945	1.050 625	2
3	1.077 884	1.077 800	1.077 633	1.077 383	1.076 891	3
4	1.105 171	1.105 056	1.104 827	1.104 486	1.103 813	4
5	1.133 148	1.133 001	1.132 708	1.132 271	1.131 408	5
6	1.161 834	1.161 653	1.161 292	1.160 755	1.159 693	6
7	1.191 246	1.191 029	1.190 598	1.189 955	1.188 686	7
8	1.221 403	1.221 149	1.220 643	1.219 890	1.218 403	8
9	1.252 323	1.252 030	1.251 446	1.250 577	1.248 863	9
10	1.284 025	1.283 692	1.283 027	1.282 037	1.280 085	10
11	1.316 531	1.316 154	1.315 404	1.314 288	1.312 087	11
12	1.349 859	1.349 438	1.348 599	1.347 351	1.344 889	12
13	1.384 031	1.383 563	1.382 632	1.381 245	1.378 511	13
14	1.419 068	1.418 551	1.417 523	1.415 992	1.412 974	14
15	1.454 991	1.454 424	1.453 294	1.451 613	1.448 298	15
16	1.491 825	1.491 204	1.489 969	1.488 131	1.484 506	16
17	1.529 590	1.528 914	1.527 569	1.525 566	1.521 618	17
18	1.568 312	1.567 578	1.566 117	1.563 944	1.559 659	18
19	1.608 014	1.607 220	1.605 639	1.603 287	1.598 650	19
20	1.648 721	1.647 864	1.646 158	1.643 619	1.638 616	20
21	1.690 459	1.689 536	1.687 699	1.684 967	1.679 582	21
22	1.733 253	1.732 262	1.730 289	1.727 354	1.721 571	22
23	1.777 131	1.776 068	1.773 953	1.770 808	1.764 611	23
24	1.822 119	1.820 982	1.818 720	1.815 355	1.808 726	24
25	1.868 246	1.867 032	1.864 616	1.861 022	1.853 944	25
26	1.915 541	1.914 246	1.911 670	1.907 839	1.900 293	26
27	1.964 033	1.962 654	1.959 912	1.955 833	1.947 800	27
28	2.013 753	2.012 287	2.009 371	2.005 034	1.996 495	28
29	2.064 731	2.063 175	2.060 078	2.055 473	2.046 407	29
30	2.117 000	2.115 349	2.112 065	2.107 181	2.097 568	30
31	2.170 592	2.168 843	2.165 363	2.160 190	2.150 007	31
32	2.225 541	2.223 690	2.220 007	2.214 532	2.203 757	32
33	2.281 881	2.279 923	2.276 030	2.270 242	2.258 851	33
34	2.339 647	2.337 579	2.333 466	2.327 353	2.315 322	34
35	2.398 875	2.396 693	2.392 352	2.385 900	2.373 205	35
36	2.459 603	2.457 302	2.452 724	2.445 920	2.432 535	36
37	2.521 868	2.519 443	2.514 619	2.507 450	2.493 349	37
38	2.585 710	2.583 156	2.578 076	2.570 529	2.555 682	38
39	2.651 167	2.648 480	2.643 135	2.635 193	2.619 574	39
40	2.718 282	2.715 456	2.709 836	2.701 485	2.685 064	40

2¾%

COMPOUND INTEREST
(Future Value of $1)

Base:	2.718 282	1.002 292	1.006 875	1.013 750	1.027 500	
			Frequency of Conversion			
Months	Continuous	Monthly	Quarterly	Semiannual	Annual	Months
0	1.000 000	1.000 000	1.000 000	1.000 000	1.000 000	0
1	1.002 294	1.002 292	1.002 292	1.002 292	1.002 292	1
2	1.004 594	1.004 589	1.004 583	1.004 583	1.004 583	2
3	1.006 899	1.006 891	1.006 875	1.006 875	1.006 875	3
4	1.009 209	1.009 198	1.009 182	1.009 167	1.009 167	4
5	1.011 524	1.011 511	1.011 490	1.011 458	1.011 458	5
6	1.013 845	1.013 829	1.013 797	1.013 750	1.013 750	6
7	1.016 171	1.016 152	1.016 121	1.016 073	1.016 042	7
8	1.018 502	1.018 481	1.018 444	1.018 396	1.018 333	8
9	1.020 839	1.020 815	1.020 767	1.020 720	1.020 625	9
10	1.023 181	1.023 154	1.023 106	1.023 043	1.022 917	10
11	1.025 529	1.025 499	1.025 446	1.025 366	1.025 208	11

Years						Years
1	1.027 882	1.027 849	1.027 785	1.027 689	1.027 500	1
2	1.056 541	1.056 474	1.056 342	1.056 145	1.055 756	2
3	1.085 999	1.085 896	1.085 692	1.085 388	1.084 790	3
4	1.116 278	1.116 138	1.115 858	1.115 442	1.114 621	4
5	1.147 402	1.147 221	1.146 862	1.146 327	1.145 273	5
6	1.179 393	1.179 171	1.178 727	1.178 068	1.176 768	6
7	1.212 277	1.212 010	1.211 478	1.210 688	1.209 129	7
8	1.246 077	1.245 763	1.245 139	1.244 211	1.242 381	8
9	1.280 819	1.280 457	1.279 735	1.278 662	1.276 546	9
10	1.316 531	1.316 117	1.315 292	1.314 067	1.311 651	10
11	1.353 238	1.352 769	1.351 838	1.350 452	1.347 721	11
12	1.390 968	1.390 443	1.389 398	1.387 845	1.384 784	12
13	1.429 751	1.429 166	1.428 003	1.426 273	1.422 865	13
14	1.469 614	1.468 967	1.467 680	1.465 765	1.461 994	14
15	1.510 590	1.509 877	1.508 459	1.506 350	1.502 199	15
16	1.552 707	1.551 926	1.550 371	1.548 060	1.543 509	16
17	1.595 999	1.595 146	1.593 448	1.590 924	1.585 956	17
18	1.640 498	1.639 569	1.637 722	1.634 975	1.629 570	18
19	1.686 238	1.685 230	1.683 226	1.680 246	1.674 383	19
20	1.733 253	1.732 163	1.729 994	1.726 771	1.720 428	20
21	1.781 579	1.780 402	1.778 062	1.774 583	1.767 740	21
22	1.831 252	1.829 985	1.827 465	1.823 720	1.816 353	22
23	1.882 310	1.880 949	1.878 241	1.874 217	1.866 303	23
24	1.934 792	1.933 332	1.930 428	1.926 112	1.917 626	24
25	1.988 737	1.987 174	1.984 064	1.979 445	1.970 361	25
26	2.044 187	2.042 515	2.039 191	2.034 254	2.024 546	26
27	2.101 182	2.099 398	2.095 850	2.090 580	2.080 221	27
28	2.159 766	2.157 864	2.154 083	2.148 466	2.137 427	28
29	2.219 984	2.217 959	2.213 934	2.207 955	2.196 206	29
30	2.281 881	2.279 728	2.275 448	2.269 092	2.256 602	30
31	2.345 503	2.343 217	2.338 671	2.331 921	2.318 658	31
32	2.410 900	2.408 474	2.403 651	2.396 489	2.382 421	32
33	2.478 119	2.475 548	2.470 436	2.462 846	2.447 938	33
34	2.547 213	2.544 490	2.539 077	2.531 040	2.515 256	34
35	2.618 234	2.615 352	2.609 625	2.601 122	2.584 426	35
36	2.691 234	2.688 188	2.682 133	2.673 145	2.655 498	36
37	2.766 270	2.763 052	2.756 656	2.747 161	2.728 524	37
38	2.843 399	2.840 001	2.833 249	2.823 228	2.803 558	38
39	2.922 677	2.919 093	2.911 971	2.901 400	2.880 656	39
40	3.004 166	3.000 388	2.992 880	2.981 737	2.959 874	40

COMPOUND INTEREST

(Future Value of $1)

3%

Base:	2.718 282	1.002 500	1.007 500	1.015 000	1.030 000	
			Frequency of Conversion			
Months	Continuous	Monthly	Quarterly	Semiannual	Annual	Months
0	1.000 000	1.000 000	1.000 000	1.000 000	1.000 000	0
1	1.002 503	1.002 500	1.002 500	1.002 500	1.002 500	1
2	1.005 013	1.005 006	1.005 000	1.005 000	1.005 000	2
3	1.007 528	1.007 519	1.007 500	1.007 500	1.007 500	3
4	1.010 050	1.010 038	1.010 019	1.010 000	1.010 000	4
5	1.012 578	1.012 563	1.012 537	1.012 500	1.012 500	5
6	1.015 113	1.015 094	1.015 056	1.015 000	1.015 000	6
7	1.017 654	1.017 632	1.017 594	1.017 538	1.017 500	7
8	1.020 201	1.020 176	1.020 132	1.020 075	1.020 000	8
9	1.022 755	1.022 726	1.022 669	1.022 613	1.022 500	9
10	1.025 315	1.025 283	1.025 226	1.025 150	1.025 000	10
11	1.027 882	1.027 846	1.027 783	1.027 688	1.027 500	11
Years						Years
1	1.030 455	1.030 416	1.030 339	1.030 225	1.030 000	1
2	1.061 837	1.061 757	1.061 599	1.061 364	1.060 900	2
3	1.094 174	1.094 051	1.093 807	1.093 443	1.092 727	3
4	1.127 497	1.127 328	1.126 992	1.126 493	1.125 509	4
5	1.161 834	1.161 617	1.161 184	1.160 541	1.159 274	5
6	1.197 217	1.196 948	1.196 414	1.195 618	1.194 052	6
7	1.233 678	1.233 355	1.232 712	1.231 756	1.229 874	7
8	1.271 249	1.270 868	1.270 111	1.268 986	1.266 770	8
9	1.309 964	1.309 523	1.308 645	1.307 341	1.304 773	9
10	1.349 859	1.349 354	1.348 349	1.346 855	1.343 916	10
11	1.390 968	1.390 395	1.389 256	1.387 564	1.384 234	11
12	1.433 329	1.432 686	1.431 405	1.429 503	1.425 761	12
13	1.476 981	1.476 262	1.474 833	1.472 710	1.468 534	13
14	1.521 962	1.521 164	1.519 578	1.517 222	1.512 590	14
15	1.568 312	1.567 432	1.565 681	1.563 080	1.557 967	15
16	1.616 074	1.615 107	1.613 183	1.610 324	1.604 706	16
17	1.665 291	1.664 232	1.662 125	1.658 996	1.652 848	17
18	1.716 007	1.714 851	1.712 553	1.709 140	1.702 433	18
19	1.768 267	1.767 010	1.764 510	1.760 798	1.753 506	19
20	1.822 119	1.820 755	1.818 044	1.814 018	1.806 111	20
21	1.877 611	1.876 135	1.873 202	1.868 847	1.860 295	21
22	1.934 792	1.933 199	1.930 033	1.925 333	1.916 103	22
23	1.993 716	1.992 000	1.988 589	1.983 526	1.973 587	23
24	2.054 433	2.052 588	2.048 921	2.043 478	2.032 794	24
25	2.117 000	2.115 020	2.111 084	2.105 242	2.093 778	25
26	2.181 472	2.179 350	2.175 132	2.168 873	2.156 591	26
27	2.247 908	2.245 637	2.241 124	2.234 428	2.221 289	27
28	2.316 367	2.313 940	2.309 118	2.301 963	2.287 928	28
29	2.386 911	2.384 321	2.379 175	2.371 540	2.356 566	29
30	2.459 603	2.456 842	2.451 357	2.443 220	2.427 262	30
31	2.534 509	2.531 569	2.525 729	2.517 066	2.500 080	31
32	2.611 696	2.608 570	2.602 358	2.593 144	2.575 083	32
33	2.691 234	2.687 912	2.681 311	2.671 522	2.652 335	33
34	2.773 195	2.769 667	2.762 660	2.752 269	2.731 905	34
35	2.857 651	2.853 909	2.846 477	2.835 456	2.813 862	35
36	2.944 680	2.940 714	2.932 837	2.921 158	2.898 278	36
37	3.034 358	3.030 158	3.021 817	3.009 450	2.985 227	37
38	3.126 768	3.122 323	3.113 496	3.100 411	3.074 783	38
39	3.221 993	3.217 292	3.207 957	3.194 120	3.167 027	39
40	3.320 117	3.315 149	3.305 284	3.290 663	3.262 038	40

3¼% COMPOUND INTEREST
(Future Value of $1)

Base: 2.718 282   1.002 708   1.008 125   1.016 250   1.032 500

Frequency of Conversion

Months	Continuous	Monthly	Quarterly	Semiannual	Annual	Months
0	1.000 000	1.000 000	1.000 000	1.000 000	1.000 000	0
1	1.002 712	1.002 708	1.002 708	1.002 708	1.002 708	1
2	1.005 431	1.005 424	1.005 417	1.005 417	1.005 417	2
3	1.008 158	1.008 147	1.008 125	1.008 125	1.008 125	3
4	1.010 892	1.010 877	1.010 855	1.010 833	1.010 833	4
5	1.013 634	1.013 615	1.013 586	1.013 542	1.013 542	5
6	1.016 383	1.016 360	1.016 316	1.016 250	1.016 250	6
7	1.019 139	1.019 113	1.019 069	1.019 002	1.018 958	7
8	1.021 903	1.021 873	1.021 821	1.021 755	1.021 667	8
9	1.024 674	1.024 641	1.024 574	1.024 507	1.024 375	9
10	1.027 453	1.027 416	1.027 348	1.027 259	1.027 083	10
11	1.030 240	1.030 198	1.030 123	1.030 012	1.029 792	11

Years						Years
1	1.033 034	1.032 989	1.032 898	1.032 764	1.032 500	1
2	1.067 159	1.067 065	1.066 879	1.066 602	1.066 056	2
3	1.102 411	1.102 266	1.101 977	1.101 548	1.100 703	3
4	1.138 828	1.138 628	1.138 230	1.137 639	1.136 476	4
5	1.176 448	1.176 190	1.175 676	1.174 913	1.173 411	5
6	1.215 311	1.214 991	1.214 354	1.213 408	1.211 547	6
7	1.255 457	1.255 071	1.254 304	1.253 164	1.250 923	7
8	1.296 930	1.296 474	1.295 568	1.294 222	1.291 578	8
9	1.339 773	1.339 243	1.338 190	1.336 626	1.333 554	9
10	1.384 031	1.383 423	1.382 214	1.380 420	1.376 894	10
11	1.429 751	1.429 060	1.427 687	1.425 648	1.421 643	11
12	1.476 981	1.476 202	1.474 655	1.472 358	1.467 847	12
13	1.525 771	1.524 900	1.523 169	1.520 598	1.515 552	13
14	1.576 173	1.575 204	1.573 278	1.570 419	1.564 807	14
15	1.628 241	1.627 168	1.625 036	1.621 873	1.615 663	15
16	1.682 028	1.680 846	1.678 497	1.675 012	1.668 173	16
17	1.737 592	1.736 294	1.733 717	1.729 892	1.722 388	17
18	1.794 991	1.793 572	1.790 753	1.786 570	1.778 366	18
19	1.854 287	1.852 739	1.849 666	1.845 106	1.836 163	19
20	1.915 541	1.913 859	1.910 516	1.905 559	1.895 838	20
21	1.978 819	1.976 994	1.973 369	1.967 993	1.957 453	21
22	2.044 187	2.042 212	2.038 289	2.032 472	2.021 070	22
23	2.111 714	2.109 581	2.105 346	2.099 064	2.086 755	23
24	2.181 472	2.179 173	2.174 608	2.167 838	2.154 574	24
25	2.253 535	2.251 061	2.246 149	2.238 865	2.224 598	25
26	2.327 978	2.325 320	2.320 043	2.312 219	2.296 897	26
27	2.404 880	2.402 029	2.396 368	2.387 977	2.371 546	27
28	2.484 323	2.481 269	2.475 205	2.466 217	2.448 622	28
29	2.566 389	2.563 122	2.556 634	2.547 020	2.528 202	29
30	2.651 167	2.647 675	2.640 743	2.630 471	2.610 368	30
31	2.738 746	2.735 018	2.727 619	2.716 656	2.695 205	31
32	2.829 217	2.825 243	2.817 353	2.805 665	2.782 800	32
33	2.922 677	2.918 443	2.910 039	2.897 590	2.873 241	33
34	3.019 224	3.014 718	3.005 774	2.992 526	2.966 621	34
35	3.118 961	3.114 169	3.104 659	3.090 574	3.063 036	35
36	3.221 993	3.216 901	3.206 797	3.191 833	3.162 585	36
37	3.328 428	3.323 022	3.312 294	3.296 411	3.265 369	37
38	3.438 379	3.432 643	3.421 263	3.404 415	3.371 493	38
39	3.551 962	3.545 881	3.533 817	3.515 957	3.481 067	39
40	3.669 297	3.662 854	3.650 073	3.631 154	3.594 201	40

COMPOUND INTEREST   3½%
(Future Value of $1)

Base:	2.718 282	1.002 917	1.008 750	1.017 500	1.035 000	
			Frequency of Conversion			
Months	Continuous	Monthly	Quarterly	Semiannual	Annual	Months
0	1.000 000	1.000 000	1.000 000	1.000 000	1.000 000	0
1	1.002 921	1.002 917	1.002 917	1.002 917	1.002 917	1
2	1.005 850	1.005 842	1.005 833	1.005 833	1.005 833	2
3	1.008 788	1.008 776	1.008 750	1.008 750	1.008 750	3
4	1.011 735	1.011 718	1.011 692	1.011 667	1.011 667	4
5	1.014 690	1.014 669	1.014 634	1.014 583	1.014 583	5
6	1.017 654	1.017 628	1.017 577	1.017 500	1.017 500	6
7	1.020 627	1.020 596	1.020 544	1.020 468	1.020 417	7
8	1.023 608	1.023 573	1.023 512	1.023 435	1.023 333	8
9	1.026 598	1.026 558	1.026 480	1.026 403	1.026 250	9
10	1.029 596	1.029 552	1.029 474	1.029 371	1.029 167	10
11	1.032 604	1.032 555	1.032 468	1.032 339	1.032 083	11
Years						Years
1	1.035 620	1.035 567	1.035 462	1.035 306	1.035 000	1
2	1.072 508	1.072 399	1.072 182	1.071 859	1.071 225	2
3	1.110 711	1.110 541	1.110 203	1.109 702	1.108 718	3
4	1.150 274	1.150 039	1.149 574	1.148 882	1.147 523	4
5	1.191 246	1.190 943	1.190 340	1.189 444	1.187 686	5
6	1.233 678	1.233 301	1.232 552	1.231 439	1.229 255	6
7	1.277 621	1.277 166	1.276 261	1.274 917	1.272 279	7
8	1.323 130	1.322 591	1.321 519	1.319 929	1.316 809	8
9	1.370 259	1.369 631	1.368 383	1.366 531	1.362 897	9
10	1.419 068	1.418 345	1.416 909	1.414 778	1.410 599	10
11	1.469 614	1.468 791	1.467 155	1.464 729	1.459 970	11
12	1.521 962	1.521 031	1.519 184	1.516 443	1.511 069	12
13	1.576 173	1.575 130	1.573 057	1.569 983	1.563 956	13
14	1.632 316	1.631 152	1.628 841	1.625 413	1.618 695	14
15	1.690 459	1.689 168	1.686 603	1.682 800	1.675 349	15
16	1.750 673	1.749 246	1.746 413	1.742 213	1.733 986	16
17	1.813 031	1.811 461	1.808 345	1.803 725	1.794 676	17
18	1.877 611	1.875 890	1.872 472	1.867 407	1.857 489	18
19	1.944 491	1.942 609	1.938 874	1.933 338	1.922 501	19
20	2.013 753	2.011 702	2.007 631	2.001 597	1.989 789	20
21	2.085 482	2.083 252	2.078 825	2.072 266	2.059 431	21
22	2.159 766	2.157 347	2.152 545	2.145 430	2.131 512	22
23	2.236 696	2.234 077	2.228 878	2.221 177	2.206 114	23
24	2.316 367	2.313 537	2.307 919	2.299 599	2.283 328	24
25	2.398 875	2.395 822	2.389 763	2.380 789	2.363 245	25
26	2.484 323	2.481 034	2.474 509	2.464 846	2.445 959	26
27	2.572 813	2.569 277	2.562 260	2.551 870	2.531 567	27
28	2.664 456	2.660 658	2.653 123	2.641 967	2.620 172	28
29	2.759 363	2.755 290	2.747 208	2.735 245	2.711 878	29
30	2.857 651	2.853 287	2.844 630	2.831 816	2.806 794	30
31	2.959 440	2.954 770	2.945 506	2.931 797	2.905 031	31
32	3.064 854	3.059 862	3.049 960	3.035 308	3.006 708	32
33	3.174 023	3.168 692	3.158 118	3.142 473	3.111 942	33
34	3.287 081	3.281 393	3.270 111	3.253 422	3.220 860	34
35	3.404 166	3.398 102	3.386 076	3.368 288	3.333 590	35
36	3.525 421	3.518 962	3.506 153	3.487 210	3.450 266	36
37	3.650 996	3.644 121	3.630 488	3.610 330	3.571 025	37
38	3.781 043	3.773 731	3.759 233	3.737 797	3.696 011	38
39	3.915 723	3.907 951	3.892 543	3.869 765	3.825 372	39
40	4.055 200	4.046 945	4.030 581	4.006 392	3.959 260	40

3¾%

COMPOUND INTEREST
(Future Value of $1)

Base: 2.718 282   1.003 125   1.009 375   1.018 750   1.037 500

Frequency of Conversion

Months	Continuous	Monthly	Quarterly	Semiannual	Annual	Months
0	1.000 000	1.000 000	1.000 000	1.000 000	1.000 000	0
1	1.003 130	1.003 125	1.003 125	1.003 125	1.003 125	1
2	1.006 270	1.006 260	1.006 250	1.006 250	1.006 250	2
3	1.009 419	1.009 404	1.009 375	1.009 375	1.009 375	3
4	1.012 578	1.012 559	1.012 529	1.012 500	1.012 500	4
5	1.015 748	1.015 723	1.015 684	1.015 625	1.015 625	5
6	1.018 927	1.018 897	1.018 838	1.018 750	1.018 750	6
7	1.022 116	1.022 081	1.022 022	1.021 934	1.021 875	7
8	1.025 315	1.025 275	1.025 206	1.025 117	1.025 000	8
9	1.028 524	1.028 479	1.028 389	1.028 301	1.028 125	9
10	1.031 743	1.031 693	1.031 603	1.031 484	1.031 250	10
11	1.034 973	1.034 917	1.034 817	1.034 668	1.034 375	11

Years						Years
1	1.038 212	1.038 151	1.038 031	1.037 852	1.037 500	1
2	1.077 884	1.077 758	1.077 508	1.077 136	1.076 406	2
3	1.119 072	1.118 876	1.118 486	1.117 907	1.116 771	3
4	1.161 834	1.161 563	1.161 023	1.160 222	1.158 650	4
5	1.206 230	1.205 878	1.205 177	1.204 138	1.202 100	5
6	1.252 323	1.251 883	1.251 011	1.249 716	1.247 179	6
7	1.300 176	1.299 644	1.298 588	1.297 020	1.293 948	7
8	1.349 859	1.349 228	1.347 974	1.346 114	1.342 471	8
9	1.401 440	1.400 702	1.399 238	1.397 067	1.392 813	9
10	1.454 991	1.454 141	1.452 452	1.449 948	1.445 044	10
11	1.510 590	1.509 618	1.507 690	1.504 831	1.499 233	11
12	1.568 312	1.567 212	1.565 028	1.561 791	1.555 454	12
13	1.628 241	1.627 003	1.624 547	1.620 907	1.613 784	13
14	1.690 459	1.689 076	1.686 330	1.682 261	1.674 301	14
15	1.755 055	1.753 516	1.750 462	1.745 937	1.737 087	15
16	1.822 119	1.820 415	1.817 033	1.812 024	1.802 228	16
17	1.891 746	1.889 866	1.886 136	1.880 612	1.869 811	17
18	1.964 033	1.961 967	1.957 867	1.951 796	1.939 929	18
19	2.039 083	2.036 819	2.032 326	2.025 674	2.012 677	19
20	2.117 000	2.114 526	2.109 617	2.102 349	2.088 152	20
21	2.197 895	2.195 198	2.189 847	2.181 926	2.166 458	21
22	2.281 881	2.278 947	2.273 128	2.264 516	2.247 700	22
23	2.369 076	2.365 892	2.359 576	2.350 231	2.331 989	23
24	2.459 603	2.456 154	2.449 313	2.439 191	2.419 438	24
25	2.553 589	2.549 859	2.542 462	2.531 518	2.510 167	25
26	2.651 167	2.647 140	2.639 153	2.627 340	2.604 298	26
27	2.752 474	2.748 132	2.739 522	2.726 789	2.701 960	27
28	2.857 651	2.852 976	2.843 708	2.830 002	2.803 283	28
29	2.966 848	2.961 821	2.951 856	2.937 123	2.908 406	29
30	3.080 217	3.074 818	3.064 117	3.048 297	3.017 471	30
31	3.197 918	3.192 127	3.180 647	3.163 680	3.130 627	31
32	3.320 117	3.313 910	3.301 609	3.283 430	3.248 025	32
33	3.446 985	3.440 340	3.427 171	3.407 713	3.369 826	33
34	3.578 701	3.571 594	3.557 509	3.536 700	3.496 194	34
35	3.715 451	3.707 855	3.692 803	3.670 570	3.627 302	35
36	3.857 426	3.849 314	3.833 243	3.809 507	3.763 326	36
37	4.004 825	3.996 171	3.979 024	3.953 703	3.904 450	37
38	4.157 858	4.148 630	4.130 348	4.103 357	4.050 867	38
39	4.316 738	4.306 905	4.287 428	4.258 675	4.202 775	39
40	4.481 689	4.471 219	4.450 482	4.419 872	4.360 379	40

COMPOUND INTEREST

4%

(Future Value of $1)

Base:	2.718 282	1.003 333	1.010 000	1.020 000	1.040 000	
			Frequency of Conversion			
Months	Continuous	Monthly	Quarterly	Semiannual	Annual	Months
0	1.000 000	1.000 000	1.000 000	1.000 000	1.000 000	0
1	1.003 339	1.003 333	1.003 333	1.003 333	1.003 333	1
2	1.006 689	1.006 678	1.006 667	1.006 667	1.006 667	2
3	1.010 050	1.010 033	1.010 000	1.010 000	1.010 000	3
4	1.013 423	1.013 400	1.013 367	1.013 333	1.013 333	4
5	1.016 806	1.016 778	1.016 733	1.016 667	1.016 667	5
6	1.020 201	1.020 167	1.020 100	1.020 000	1.020 000	6
7	1.023 608	1.023 568	1.023 500	1.023 400	1.023 333	7
8	1.027 025	1.026 980	1.026 901	1.026 800	1.026 667	8
9	1.030 455	1.030 403	1.030 301	1.030 200	1.030 000	9
10	1.033 895	1.033 838	1.033 735	1.033 600	1.033 333	10
11	1.037 347	1.037 284	1.037 170	1.037 000	1.036 667	11
Years						Years
1	1.040 811	1.040 742	1.040 604	1.040 400	1.040 000	1
2	1.083 287	1.083 143	1.082 857	1.082 432	1.081 600	2
3	1.127 497	1.127 272	1.126 825	1.126 162	1.124 864	3
4	1.173 511	1.173 199	1.172 579	1.171 659	1.169 859	4
5	1.221 403	1.220 997	1.220 190	1.218 994	1.216 653	5
6	1.271 249	1.270 742	1.269 735	1.268 242	1.265 319	6
7	1.323 130	1.322 514	1.321 291	1.319 479	1.315 932	7
8	1.377 128	1.376 395	1.374 941	1.372 786	1.368 569	8
9	1.433 329	1.432 472	1.430 769	1.428 246	1.423 312	9
10	1.491 825	1.490 833	1.488 864	1.485 947	1.480 244	10
11	1.552 707	1.551 572	1.549 318	1.545 980	1.539 454	11
12	1.616 074	1.614 785	1.612 226	1.608 437	1.601 032	12
13	1.682 028	1.680 574	1.677 689	1.673 418	1.665 074	13
14	1.750 673	1.749 043	1.745 810	1.741 024	1.731 676	14
15	1.822 119	1.820 302	1.816 697	1.811 362	1.800 944	15
16	1.896 481	1.894 464	1.890 462	1.884 541	1.872 981	16
17	1.973 878	1.971 647	1.967 222	1.960 676	1.947 900	17
18	2.054 433	2.051 975	2.047 099	2.039 887	2.025 817	18
19	2.138 276	2.135 575	2.130 220	2.122 299	2.106 849	19
20	2.225 541	2.222 582	2.216 715	2.208 040	2.191 123	20
21	2.316 367	2.313 134	2.306 723	2.297 244	2.278 768	21
22	2.410 900	2.407 374	2.400 385	2.390 053	2.369 919	22
23	2.509 290	2.505 454	2.497 850	2.486 611	2.464 716	23
24	2.611 696	2.607 530	2.599 273	2.587 070	2.563 304	24
25	2.718 282	2.713 765	2.704 814	2.691 588	2.665 836	25
26	2.829 217	2.824 328	2.814 640	2.800 328	2.772 470	26
27	2.944 680	2.939 396	2.928 926	2.913 461	2.883 369	27
28	3.064 854	3.059 151	3.047 852	3.031 165	2.998 703	28
29	3.189 933	3.183 786	3.171 607	3.153 624	3.118 651	29
30	3.320 117	3.313 498	3.300 387	3.281 031	3.243 398	30
31	3.455 613	3.448 495	3.434 396	3.413 584	3.373 133	31
32	3.596 640	3.588 992	3.573 846	3.551 493	3.508 059	32
33	3.743 421	3.735 213	3.718 959	3.694 974	3.648 381	33
34	3.896 193	3.887 391	3.869 963	3.844 251	3.794 316	34
35	4.055 200	4.045 770	4.027 099	3.999 558	3.946 089	35
36	4.220 696	4.210 601	4.190 616	4.161 140	4.103 933	36
37	4.392 946	4.382 147	4.360 771	4.329 250	4.268 090	37
38	4.572 225	4.560 682	4.537 836	4.504 152	4.438 813	38
39	4.758 821	4.746 492	4.722 091	4.686 120	4.616 366	39
40	4.953 032	4.939 871	4.913 826	4.875 439	4.801 021	40

4¼%

COMPOUND INTEREST
(Future Value of $1)

Base:	2.718 282	1.003 542	1.010 625	1.021 250	1.042 500	
			Frequency of Conversion			
Months	Continuous	Monthly	Quarterly	Semiannual	Annual	Months
0	1.000 000	1.000 000	1.000 000	1.000 000	1.000 000	0
1	1.003 548	1.003 542	1.003 542	1.003 542	1.003 542	1
2	1.007 108	1.007 096	1.007 083	1.007 083	1.007 083	2
3	1.010 682	1.010 663	1.010 625	1.010 625	1.010 625	3
4	1.014 267	1.014 242	1.014 204	1.014 167	1.014 167	4
5	1.017 866	1.017 834	1.017 784	1.017 708	1.017 708	5
6	1.021 477	1.021 439	1.021 363	1.021 250	1.021 250	6
7	1.025 102	1.025 057	1.024 980	1.024 867	1.024 792	7
8	1.028 739	1.028 687	1.028 598	1.028 484	1.028 333	8
9	1.032 388	1.032 330	1.032 215	1.032 101	1.031 875	9
10	1.036 051	1.035 986	1.035 871	1.035 718	1.035 417	10
11	1.039 727	1.039 656	1.039 526	1.039 335	1.038 958	11

Years						Years
1	1.043 416	1.043 338	1.043 182	1.042 952	1.042 500	1
2	1.088 717	1.088 554	1.088 229	1.087 748	1.086 806	2
3	1.135 985	1.135 729	1.135 221	1.134 468	1.132 996	3
4	1.185 305	1.184 949	1.184 242	1.183 196	1.181 148	4
5	1.236 766	1.236 302	1.235 381	1.234 016	1.231 347	5
6	1.290 462	1.289 880	1.288 727	1.287 019	1.283 679	6
7	1.346 488	1.345 781	1.344 377	1.342 298	1.338 235	7
8	1.404 948	1.404 104	1.402 430	1.399 952	1.395 110	8
9	1.465 945	1.464 955	1.462 990	1.460 082	1.454 402	9
10	1.529 590	1.528 442	1.526 165	1.522 795	1.516 214	10
11	1.595 999	1.594 682	1.592 068	1.588 201	1.580 654	11
12	1.665 291	1.663 791	1.660 817	1.656 417	1.647 831	12
13	1.737 592	1.735 896	1.732 535	1.727 563	1.717 864	13
14	1.813 031	1.811 126	1.807 349	1.801 764	1.790 873	14
15	1.891 746	1.889 616	1.885 394	1.879 153	1.866 986	15
16	1.973 878	1.971 508	1.966 810	1.959 865	1.946 332	16
17	2.059 576	2.056 949	2.051 741	2.044 045	2.029 052	17
18	2.148 994	2.146 092	2.140 340	2.131 839	2.115 286	18
19	2.242 295	2.239 099	2.232 764	2.223 405	2.205 186	19
20	2.339 647	2.336 136	2.329 180	2.318 904	2.298 906	20
21	2.441 225	2.437 379	2.429 759	2.418 505	2.396 610	21
22	2.547 213	2.543 009	2.534 681	2.522 383	2.498 466	22
23	2.657 803	2.653 218	2.644 134	2.630 723	2.604 651	23
24	2.773 195	2.768 202	2.758 313	2.743 717	2.715 348	24
25	2.893 596	2.888 170	2.877 423	2.861 564	2.830 750	25
26	3.019 224	3.013 336	3.001 676	2.984 473	2.951 057	26
27	3.150 307	3.143 927	3.131 295	3.112 661	3.076 477	27
28	3.287 081	3.280 178	3.266 511	3.246 354	3.207 228	28
29	3.429 793	3.422 333	3.407 566	3.385 790	3.343 535	29
30	3.578 701	3.570 649	3.554 712	3.531 215	3.485 635	30
31	3.734 075	3.725 393	3.708 213	3.682 886	3.633 775	31
32	3.896 193	3.886 843	3.868 341	3.841 072	3.788 210	32
33	4.065 351	4.055 290	4.035 384	4.006 052	3.949 209	33
34	4.241 852	4.231 037	4.209 641	4.178 118	4.117 050	34
35	4.426 017	4.414 401	4.391 422	4.357 575	4.292 025	35
36	4.618 177	4.605 711	4.581 054	4.544 740	4.474 436	36
37	4.818 680	4.805 312	4.778 873	4.739 943	4.664 599	37
38	5.027 888	5.013 563	4.985 235	4.943 531	4.862 845	38
39	5.246 179	5.230 839	5.200 509	5.155 864	5.069 516	39
40	5.473 947	5.457 532	5.425 078	5.377 316	5.284 970	40

COMPOUND INTEREST
(Future Value of $1)

4½%

Base:	2.718 282	1.003 750	1.011 250	1.022 500	1.045 000	
			Frequency of Conversion			
Months	Continuous	Monthly	Quarterly	Semiannual	Annual	Months
0	1.000 000	1.000 000	1.000 000	1.000 000	1.000 000	0
1	1.003 757	1.003 750	1.003 750	1.003 750	1.003 750	1
2	1.007 528	1.007 514	1.007 500	1.007 500	1.007 500	2
3	1.011 314	1.011 292	1.011 250	1.011 250	1.011 250	3
4	1.015 113	1.015 085	1.015 042	1.015 000	1.015 000	4
5	1.018 927	1.018 891	1.018 834	1.018 750	1.018 750	5
6	1.022 755	1.022 712	1.022 627	1.022 500	1.022 500	6
7	1.026 598	1.026 547	1.026 461	1.026 334	1.026 250	7
8	1.030 455	1.030 397	1.030 296	1.030 169	1.030 000	8
9	1.034 326	1.034 261	1.034 131	1.034 003	1.033 750	9
10	1.038 212	1.038 139	1.038 009	1.037 838	1.037 500	10
11	1.042 113	1.042 032	1.041 887	1.041 672	1.041 250	11

Years						Years
1	1.046 028	1.045 940	1.045 765	1.045 506	1.045 000	1
2	1.094 174	1.093 990	1.093 625	1.093 083	1.092 025	2
3	1.144 537	1.144 248	1.143 674	1.142 825	1.141 166	3
4	1.197 217	1.196 814	1.196 015	1.194 831	1.192 519	4
5	1.252 323	1.251 796	1.250 751	1.249 203	1.246 182	5
6	1.309 964	1.309 303	1.307 991	1.306 050	1.302 260	6
7	1.370 259	1.369 452	1.367 852	1.365 483	1.360 862	7
8	1.433 329	1.432 365	1.430 451	1.427 621	1.422 101	8
9	1.499 303	1.498 167	1.495 916	1.492 587	1.486 095	9
10	1.568 312	1.566 993	1.564 377	1.560 509	1.552 969	10
11	1.640 498	1.638 980	1.635 971	1.631 522	1.622 853	11
12	1.716 007	1.714 275	1.710 841	1.705 767	1.695 881	12
13	1.794 991	1.793 028	1.789 138	1.783 390	1.772 196	13
14	1.877 611	1.875 399	1.871 018	1.864 545	1.851 945	14
15	1.964 033	1.961 555	1.956 645	1.949 393	1.935 282	15
16	2.054 433	2.051 669	2.046 191	2.038 103	2.022 370	16
17	2.148 994	2.145 922	2.139 835	2.130 849	2.113 377	17
18	2.247 908	2.244 505	2.237 765	2.227 816	2.208 479	18
19	2.351 374	2.347 617	2.340 177	2.329 196	2.307 860	19
20	2.459 603	2.455 466	2.447 275	2.435 189	2.411 714	20
21	2.572 813	2.568 270	2.559 275	2.546 005	2.520 241	21
22	2.691 234	2.686 256	2.676 400	2.661 864	2.633 652	22
23	2.815 106	2.809 662	2.798 886	2.782 996	2.752 166	23
24	2.944 680	2.938 737	2.926 977	2.909 640	2.876 014	24
25	3.080 217	3.073 743	3.060 930	3.042 046	3.005 434	25
26	3.221 993	3.214 950	3.201 014	3.180 479	3.140 679	26
27	3.370 294	3.362 644	3.347 509	3.325 210	3.282 010	27
28	3.525 421	3.517 123	3.500 708	3.476 528	3.429 700	28
29	3.687 689	3.678 699	3.660 918	3.634 732	3.584 036	29
30	3.857 426	3.847 698	3.828 460	3.800 135	3.745 318	30
31	4.034 975	4.024 461	4.003 670	3.973 065	3.913 857	31
32	4.220 696	4.209 344	4.186 898	4.153 864	4.089 981	32
33	4.414 965	4.402 720	4.378 512	4.342 891	4.274 030	33
34	4.618 177	4.604 980	4.578 895	4.540 519	4.466 362	34
35	4.830 742	4.816 532	4.788 449	4.747 141	4.667 348	35
36	5.053 090	5.037 803	5.007 593	4.963 166	4.877 378	36
37	5.285 673	5.269 239	5.236 765	5.189 021	5.096 860	37
38	5.528 961	5.511 307	5.476 426	5.425 154	5.326 219	38
39	5.783 448	5.764 495	5.727 056	5.672 032	5.565 899	39
40	6.049 647	6.029 315	5.989 155	5.930 145	5.816 365	40

4¾%

COMPOUND INTEREST
(Future Value of $1)

Base:	2.718 282	1.003 958	1.011 875	1.023 750	1.047 500	
			Frequency of Conversion			
Months	Continuous	Monthly	Quarterly	Semiannual	Annual	Months
0	1.000 000	1.000 000	1.000 000	1.000 000	1.000 000	0
1	1.003 966	1.003 958	1.003 958	1.003 958	1.003 958	1
2	1.007 948	1.007 932	1.007 917	1.007 917	1.007 917	2
3	1.011 946	1.011 922	1.011 875	1.011 875	1.011 875	3
4	1.015 959	1.015 928	1.015 880	1.015 833	1.015 833	4
5	1.019 989	1.019 949	1.019 886	1.019 792	1.019 792	5
6	1.024 034	1.023 986	1.023 891	1.023 750	1.023 750	6
7	1.028 096	1.028 040	1.027 944	1.027 802	1.027 708	7
8	1.032 173	1.032 109	1.031 997	1.031 855	1.031 667	8
9	1.036 267	1.036 194	1.036 050	1.035 907	1.035 625	9
10	1.040 377	1.040 296	1.040 151	1.039 959	1.039 583	10
11	1.044 504	1.044 414	1.044 252	1.044 012	1.043 542	11

Years						Years
1	1.048 646	1.048 548	1.048 353	1.048 064	1.047 500	1
2	1.099 659	1.099 453	1.099 044	1.098 438	1.097 256	2
3	1.153 153	1.152 829	1.152 185	1.151 234	1.149 376	3
4	1.209 250	1.208 796	1.207 897	1.206 567	1.203 971	4
5	1.268 075	1.267 481	1.266 302	1.264 559	1.261 160	5
6	1.329 762	1.329 014	1.327 531	1.325 339	1.321 065	6
7	1.394 450	1.393 535	1.391 721	1.389 040	1.383 816	7
8	1.462 285	1.461 188	1.459 015	1.455 803	1.449 547	8
9	1.533 419	1.532 126	1.529 562	1.525 775	1.518 400	9
10	1.608 014	1.606 507	1.603 521	1.599 110	1.590 524	10
11	1.686 238	1.684 500	1.681 056	1.675 970	1.666 074	11
12	1.768 267	1.766 279	1.762 339	1.756 523	1.745 213	12
13	1.854 287	1.852 028	1.847 554	1.840 949	1.828 110	13
14	1.944 491	1.941 940	1.936 888	1.929 433	1.914 946	14
15	2.039 083	2.036 217	2.030 542	2.022 169	2.005 906	15
16	2.138 276	2.135 071	2.128 724	2.119 363	2.101 186	16
17	2.242 295	2.238 724	2.231 654	2.221 228	2.200 992	17
18	2.351 374	2.347 409	2.339 561	2.327 989	2.305 540	18
19	2.465 760	2.461 371	2.452 685	2.439 882	2.415 053	19
20	2.585 710	2.580 865	2.571 280	2.557 152	2.529 768	20
21	2.711 495	2.706 161	2.695 608	2.680 059	2.649 932	21
22	2.843 399	2.837 539	2.825 948	2.808 874	2.775 803	22
23	2.981 719	2.975 296	2.962 591	2.943 880	2.907 654	23
24	3.126 768	3.119 740	3.105 840	3.085 375	3.045 768	24
25	3.278 874	3.271 197	3.256 017	3.233 670	3.190 442	25
26	3.438 379	3.430 007	3.413 454	3.389 094	3.341 988	26
27	3.605 643	3.596 526	3.578 504	3.551 987	3.500 732	27
28	3.781 043	3.771 130	3.751 535	3.722 710	3.667 017	28
29	3.964 977	3.954 210	3.932 932	3.901 639	3.841 200	29
30	4.157 858	4.146 179	4.123 101	4.089 167	4.023 657	30
31	4.360 122	4.347 467	4.322 464	4.285 709	4.214 781	31
32	4.572 225	4.558 527	4.531 467	4.491 698	4.414 983	32
33	4.794 647	4.779 834	4.750 577	4.707 587	4.624 694	33
34	5.027 888	5.011 885	4.980 280	4.933 853	4.844 367	34
35	5.272 476	5.255 201	5.221 091	5.170 994	5.074 475	35
36	5.528 961	5.510 330	5.473 545	5.419 533	5.315 512	36
37	5.797 924	5.777 845	5.738 207	5.680 018	5.567 999	37
38	6.079 971	6.058 347	6.015 665	5.953 022	5.832 479	38
39	6.375 739	6.352 467	6.306 539	6.239 149	6.109 522	39
40	6.685 894	6.660 866	6.611 478	6.539 028	6.399 724	40

COMPOUND INTEREST

(Future Value of $1)

5%

Base:	2.718 282	1.004 167	1.012 500	1.025 000	1.050 000	
			Frequency of Conversion			
Months	Continuous	Monthly	Quarterly	Semiannual	Annual	Months
0	1.000 000	1.000 000	1.000 000	1.000 000	1.000 000	0
1	1.004 175	1.004 167	1.004 167	1.004 167	1.004 167	1
2	1.008 368	1.008 351	1.008 333	1.008 333	1.008 333	2
3	1.012 578	1.012 552	1.012 500	1.012 500	1.012 500	3
4	1.016 806	1.016 771	1.016 719	1.016 667	1.016 667	4
5	1.021 052	1.021 008	1.020 937	1.020 833	1.020 833	5
6	1.025 315	1.025 262	1.025 156	1.025 000	1.025 000	6
7	1.029 596	1.029 534	1.029 428	1.029 271	1.029 167	7
8	1.033 895	1.033 824	1.033 699	1.033 542	1.033 333	8
9	1.038 212	1.038 131	1.037 971	1.037 813	1.037 500	9
10	1.042 547	1.042 457	1.042 296	1.042 083	1.041 667	10
11	1.046 900	1.046 800	1.046 620	1.046 354	1.045 833	11

Years						Years
1	1.051 271	1.051 162	1.050 945	1.050 625	1.050 000	1
2	1.105 171	1.104 941	1.104 486	1.103 813	1.102 500	2
3	1.161 834	1.161 472	1.160 755	1.159 693	1.157 625	3
4	1.221 403	1.220 895	1.219 890	1.218 403	1.215 506	4
5	1.284 025	1.283 359	1.282 037	1.280 085	1.276 282	5
6	1.349 859	1.349 018	1.347 351	1.344 889	1.340 096	6
7	1.419 068	1.418 036	1.415 992	1.412 974	1.407 100	7
8	1.491 825	1.490 585	1.488 131	1.484 506	1.477 455	8
9	1.568 312	1.566 847	1.563 944	1.559 659	1.551 328	9
10	1.648 721	1.647 009	1.643 619	1.638 616	1.628 895	10
11	1.733 253	1.731 274	1.727 354	1.721 571	1.710 339	11
12	1.822 119	1.819 849	1.815 355	1.808 726	1.795 856	12
13	1.915 541	1.912 956	1.907 839	1.900 293	1.885 649	13
14	2.013 753	2.010 826	2.005 034	1.996 495	1.979 932	14
15	2.117 000	2.113 704	2.107 181	2.097 568	2.078 928	15
16	2.225 541	2.221 845	2.214 532	2.203 757	2.182 875	16
17	2.339 647	2.335 519	2.327 353	2.315 322	2.292 018	17
18	2.459 603	2.455 008	2.445 920	2.432 535	2.406 619	18
19	2.585 710	2.580 611	2.570 529	2.555 682	2.526 950	19
20	2.718 282	2.712 640	2.701 485	2.685 064	2.653 298	20
21	2.857 651	2.851 424	2.839 113	2.820 995	2.785 963	21
22	3.004 166	2.997 308	2.983 753	2.963 808	2.925 261	22
23	3.158 193	3.150 656	3.135 761	3.113 851	3.071 524	23
24	3.320 117	3.311 850	3.295 513	3.271 490	3.225 100	24
25	3.490 343	3.481 290	3.463 404	3.437 109	3.386 355	25
26	3.669 297	3.659 400	3.639 849	3.611 112	3.555 673	26
27	3.857 426	3.846 622	3.825 282	3.793 925	3.733 456	27
28	4.055 200	4.043 422	4.020 162	3.985 992	3.920 129	28
29	4.263 115	4.250 291	4.224 971	4.187 783	4.116 136	29
30	4.481 689	4.467 744	4.440 213	4.399 790	4.321 942	30
31	4.711 470	4.696 323	4.666 421	4.622 529	4.538 039	31
32	4.953 032	4.936 595	4.904 154	4.856 545	4.764 941	32
33	5.206 980	5.189 161	5.153 998	5.102 407	5.003 189	33
34	5.473 947	5.454 648	5.416 570	5.360 717	5.253 348	34
35	5.754 603	5.733 718	5.692 519	5.632 103	5.516 015	35
36	6.049 647	6.027 066	5.982 526	5.917 228	5.791 816	36
37	6.359 820	6.335 423	6.287 308	6.216 788	6.081 407	37
38	6.685 894	6.659 555	6.607 617	6.531 513	6.385 477	38
39	7.028 688	7.000 270	6.944 244	6.862 170	6.704 751	39
40	7.389 056	7.358 417	7.298 021	7.209 568	7.039 989	40

5¼%

COMPOUND INTEREST
(Future Value of $1)

Base:	2.718 282	1.004 375	1.013 125	1.026 250	1.052 500	
			Frequency of Conversion			
Months	Continuous	Monthly	Quarterly	Semiannual	Annual	Months
0	1.000 000	1.000 000	1.000 000	1.000 000	1.000 000	0
1	1.004 385	1.004 375	1.004 375	1.004 375	1.004 375	1
2	1.008 788	1.008 769	1.008 750	1.008 750	1.008 750	2
3	1.013 212	1.013 183	1.013 125	1.013 125	1.013 125	3
4	1.017 654	1.017 615	1.017 557	1.017 500	1.017 500	4
5	1.022 116	1.022 067	1.021 990	1.021 875	1.021 875	5
6	1.026 598	1.026 539	1.026 422	1.026 250	1.026 250	6
7	1.031 099	1.031 030	1.030 913	1.030 740	1.030 625	7
8	1.035 620	1.035 541	1.035 403	1.035 230	1.035 000	8
9	1.040 160	1.040 071	1.039 894	1.039 720	1.039 375	9
10	1.044 721	1.044 621	1.044 444	1.044 209	1.043 750	10
11	1.049 302	1.049 192	1.048 993	1.048 699	1.048 125	11
Years						Years
1	1.053 903	1.053 782	1.053 543	1.053 189	1.052 500	1
2	1.110 711	1.110 456	1.109 952	1.109 207	1.107 756	2
3	1.170 581	1.170 179	1.169 382	1.168 205	1.165 913	3
4	1.233 678	1.233 113	1.231 994	1.230 341	1.227 124	4
5	1.300 176	1.299 432	1.297 958	1.295 781	1.291 548	5
6	1.370 259	1.369 318	1.367 454	1.364 703	1.359 354	6
7	1.444 120	1.442 963	1.440 671	1.437 290	1.430 720	7
8	1.521 962	1.520 568	1.517 809	1.513 738	1.505 833	8
9	1.603 999	1.602 347	1.599 076	1.594 252	1.584 889	9
10	1.690 459	1.688 524	1.684 695	1.679 049	1.668 096	10
11	1.781 579	1.779 336	1.774 898	1.768 356	1.755 671	11
12	1.877 611	1.875 032	1.869 931	1.862 413	1.847 844	12
13	1.978 819	1.975 875	1.970 052	1.961 473	1.944 856	13
14	2.085 482	2.082 141	2.075 534	2.065 802	2.046 961	14
15	2.197 895	2.194 123	2.186 663	2.175 680	2.154 426	15
16	2.316 367	2.312 127	2.303 743	2.291 403	2.267 533	16
17	2.441 225	2.436 477	2.427 092	2.413 280	2.386 579	17
18	2.572 813	2.567 516	2.557 045	2.541 641	2.511 874	18
19	2.711 495	2.705 602	2.693 956	2.676 828	2.643 748	19
20	2.857 651	2.851 114	2.838 197	2.819 206	2.782 544	20
21	3.011 686	3.004 452	2.990 162	2.969 157	2.928 628	21
22	3.174 023	3.166 037	3.150 263	3.127 084	3.082 381	22
23	3.345 111	3.336 313	3.318 937	3.293 410	3.244 206	23
24	3.525 421	3.515 746	3.496 641	3.468 584	3.414 527	24
25	3.715 451	3.704 830	3.683 861	3.653 074	3.593 789	25
26	3.915 723	3.904 082	3.881 105	3.847 378	3.782 463	26
27	4.126 791	4.114 051	4.088 909	4.052 016	3.981 043	27
28	4.349 235	4.335 313	4.307 840	4.267 539	4.190 047	28
29	4.583 670	4.568 474	4.538 494	4.494 526	4.410 025	29
30	4.830 742	4.814 175	4.781 497	4.733 585	4.641 551	30
31	5.091 131	5.073 090	5.037 511	4.985 360	4.885 233	31
32	5.365 556	5.345 931	5.307 233	5.250 527	5.141 707	32
33	5.654 773	5.633 445	5.591 396	5.529 798	5.411 647	33
34	5.959 580	5.936 422	5.890 774	5.823 922	5.695 758	34
35	6.280 817	6.255 694	6.206 182	6.133 691	5.994 786	35
36	6.619 369	6.592 137	6.538 478	6.459 937	6.309 512	36
37	6.976 170	6.946 675	6.888 565	6.803 534	6.640 761	37
38	7.352 203	7.320 280	7.257 397	7.165 408	6.989 401	38
39	7.748 506	7.713 979	7.645 978	7.546 529	7.356 345	39
40	8.166 170	8.128 851	8.055 364	7.947 922	7.742 553	40

COMPOUND INTEREST

(Future Value of $1)

5½%

Base:	2.718 282	1.004 583	1.013 750	1.027 500	1.055 000	

Frequency of Conversion

Months	Continuous	Monthly	Quarterly	Semiannual	Annual	Months
0	1.000 000	1.000 000	1.000 000	1.000 000	1.000 000	0
1	1.004 594	1.004 583	1.004 583	1.004 583	1.004 583	1
2	1.009 209	1.009 188	1.009 167	1.009 167	1.009 167	2
3	1.013 845	1.013 813	1.013 750	1.013 750	1.013 750	3
4	1.018 502	1.018 460	1.018 396	1.018 333	1.018 333	4
5	1.023 181	1.023 128	1.023 043	1.022 917	1.022 917	5
6	1.027 882	1.027 817	1.027 689	1.027 500	1.027 500	6
7	1.032 604	1.032 528	1.032 399	1.032 209	1.032 083	7
8	1.037 347	1.037 260	1.037 110	1.036 919	1.036 667	8
9	1.042 113	1.042 014	1.041 820	1.041 628	1.041 250	9
10	1.046 900	1.046 790	1.046 595	1.046 337	1.045 833	10
11	1.051 709	1.051 588	1.051 370	1.051 047	1.050 417	11

Years						Years
1	1.056 541	1.056 408	1.056 145	1.055 756	1.055 000	1
2	1.116 278	1.115 998	1.115 442	1.114 621	1.113 025	2
3	1.179 393	1.178 949	1.178 068	1.176 768	1.174 241	3
4	1.246 077	1.245 451	1.244 211	1.242 381	1.238 825	4
5	1.316 531	1.315 704	1.314 067	1.311 651	1.306 960	5
6	1.390 968	1.389 920	1.387 845	1.384 784	1.378 843	6
7	1.469 614	1.468 322	1.465 765	1.461 994	1.454 679	7
8	1.552 707	1.551 147	1.548 060	1.543 509	1.534 687	8
9	1.640 498	1.638 644	1.634 975	1.629 570	1.619 094	9
10	1.733 253	1.731 076	1.726 771	1.720 428	1.708 144	10
11	1.831 252	1.828 723	1.823 720	1.816 353	1.802 092	11
12	1.934 792	1.931 877	1.926 112	1.917 626	1.901 207	12
13	2.044 187	2.040 850	2.034 254	2.024 546	2.005 774	13
14	2.159 766	2.155 970	2.148 466	2.137 427	2.116 091	14
15	2.281 881	2.277 584	2.269 092	2.256 602	2.232 476	15
16	2.410 900	2.406 057	2.396 489	2.382 421	2.355 263	16
17	2.547 213	2.541 778	2.531 040	2.515 256	2.484 802	17
18	2.691 234	2.685 154	2.673 145	2.655 498	2.621 466	18
19	2.843 399	2.836 618	2.823 228	2.803 558	2.765 647	19
20	3.004 166	2.996 626	2.981 737	2.959 874	2.917 757	20
21	3.174 023	3.165 659	3.149 146	3.124 905	3.078 234	21
22	3.353 485	3.344 227	3.325 955	3.299 138	3.247 537	22
23	3.543 093	3.532 868	3.512 690	3.483 086	3.426 152	23
24	3.743 421	3.732 149	3.709 909	3.677 290	3.614 590	24
25	3.955 077	3.942 672	3.918 201	3.882 322	3.813 392	25
26	4.178 050	4.165 069	4.138 188	4.098 785	4.023 129	26
27	4.414 965	4.400 012	4.370 526	4.327 318	4.244 401	27
28	4.664 590	4.648 207	4.615 908	4.568 593	4.477 843	28
29	4.928 329	4.910 403	4.875 067	4.823 321	4.724 124	29
30	5.206 980	5.187 388	5.148 777	5.092 251	4.983 951	30
31	5.501 386	5.479 997	5.437 854	5.376 176	5.258 069	31
32	5.812 437	5.789 112	5.743 161	5.675 932	5.547 262	32
33	6.141 076	6.115 664	6.065 610	5.992 400	5.852 362	33
34	6.488 296	6.460 635	6.406 162	6.326 514	6.174 242	34
35	6.855 149	6.825 066	6.765 835	6.679 257	6.513 825	35
36	7.242 743	7.210 053	7.145 702	7.051 667	6.872 085	36
37	7.652 252	7.616 757	7.546 896	7.444 842	7.250 050	37
38	8.084 915	8.046 402	7.970 615	7.859 938	7.648 803	38
39	8.542 041	8.500 282	8.418 123	8.298 179	8.069 487	39
40	9.025 013	8.979 765	8.890 757	8.760 854	8.513 309	40

5¾%

COMPOUND INTEREST
(Future Value of $1)

Base: 2.718 282   1.004 792   1.014 375   1.028 750   1.057 500

Frequency of Conversion

Months	Continuous	Monthly	Quarterly	Semiannual	Annual	Months
0	1.000 000	1.000 000	1.000 000	1.000 000	1.000 000	0
1	1.004 803	1.004 792	1.004 792	1.004 792	1.004 792	1
2	1.009 629	1.009 606	1.009 583	1.009 583	1.009 583	2
3	1.014 479	1.014 444	1.014 375	1.014 375	1.014 375	3
4	1.019 352	1.019 305	1.019 236	1.019 167	1.019 167	4
5	1.024 248	1.024 189	1.024 096	1.023 958	1.023 958	5
6	1.029 167	1.029 097	1.028 957	1.028 750	1.028 750	6
7	1.034 111	1.034 028	1.033 887	1.033 679	1.033 542	7
8	1.039 078	1.038 982	1.038 817	1.038 609	1.038 333	8
9	1.044 068	1.043 961	1.043 748	1.043 538	1.043 125	9
10	1.049 083	1.048 963	1.048 749	1.048 468	1.047 917	10
11	1.054 122	1.053 989	1.053 750	1.053 397	1.052 708	11

Years						Years
1	1.059 185	1.059 040	1.058 752	1.058 327	1.057 500	1
2	1.121 873	1.121 565	1.120 955	1.120 055	1.118 306	2
3	1.188 272	1.187 782	1.186 813	1.185 384	1.182 609	3
4	1.258 600	1.257 909	1.256 541	1.254 523	1.250 609	4
5	1.333 091	1.332 176	1.330 365	1.327 695	1.322 519	5
6	1.411 990	1.410 827	1.408 526	1.405 135	1.398 564	6
7	1.495 559	1.494 122	1.491 279	1.487 092	1.478 981	7
8	1.584 074	1.582 335	1.578 895	1.573 829	1.564 023	8
9	1.677 828	1.675 755	1.671 658	1.665 625	1.653 954	9
10	1.777 131	1.774 692	1.769 870	1.762 775	1.749 056	10
11	1.882 310	1.879 469	1.873 854	1.865 592	1.849 627	11
12	1.993 716	1.990 433	1.983 946	1.974 406	1.955 980	12
13	2.111 714	2.107 948	2.100 506	2.089 566	2.068 449	13
14	2.236 696	2.232 401	2.223 914	2.211 443	2.187 385	14
15	2.369 076	2.364 201	2.354 573	2.340 429	2.313 160	15
16	2.509 290	2.503 783	2.492 909	2.476 938	2.446 167	16
17	2.657 803	2.651 606	2.639 372	2.621 409	2.586 821	17
18	2.815 106	2.808 156	2.794 439	2.774 307	2.735 563	18
19	2.981 719	2.973 950	2.958 618	2.936 123	2.892 858	19
20	3.158 193	3.149 531	3.132 442	3.107 377	3.059 198	20
21	3.345 111	3.335 479	3.316 478	3.288 619	3.235 101	21
22	3.543 093	3.532 405	3.511 327	3.480 433	3.421 120	22
23	3.752 792	3.740 958	3.717 624	3.683 435	3.617 834	23
24	3.974 902	3.961 823	3.936 041	3.898 277	3.825 860	24
25	4.210 157	4.195 728	4.167 290	4.125 650	4.045 846	25
26	4.459 337	4.443 443	4.412 126	4.366 285	4.278 483	26
27	4.723 264	4.705 784	4.671 346	4.620 956	4.524 495	27
28	5.002 811	4.983 612	4.945 796	4.890 480	4.784 654	28
29	5.298 904	5.277 844	5.236 370	5.175 725	5.059 772	29
30	5.612 521	5.589 447	5.544 016	5.477 607	5.350 708	30
31	5.944 700	5.919 447	5.869 737	5.797 097	5.658 374	31
32	6.296 538	6.268 930	6.214 594	6.135 222	5.983 731	32
33	6.669 201	6.639 047	6.579 712	6.493 068	6.327 795	33
34	7.063 919	7.031 015	6.966 282	6.871 787	6.691 643	34
35	7.481 999	7.446 125	7.375 563	7.272 595	7.076 413	35
36	7.924 823	7.885 743	7.808 891	7.696 780	7.483 307	36
37	8.393 856	8.351 316	8.267 677	8.145 707	7.913 597	37
38	8.890 649	8.844 376	8.753 418	8.620 818	8.368 629	38
39	9.416 844	9.366 546	9.267 696	9.123 640	8.849 825	39
40	9.974 182	9.919 546	9.812 190	9.655 791	9.358 690	40

COMPOUND INTEREST

(Future Value of $1)

6%

Base:	2.718 282	1.005 000	1.015 000	1.030 000	1.060 000	
			Frequency of Conversion			
Months	Continuous	Monthly	Quarterly	Semiannual	Annual	Months
0	1.000 000	1.000 000	1.000 000	1.000 000	1.000 000	0
1	1.005 013	1.005 000	1.005 000	1.005 000	1.005 000	1
2	1.010 050	1.010 025	1.010 000	1.010 000	1.010 000	2
3	1.015 113	1.015 075	1.015 000	1.015 000	1.015 000	3
4	1.020 201	1.020 151	1.020 075	1.020 000	1.020 000	4
5	1.025 315	1.025 251	1.025 150	1.025 000	1.025 000	5
6	1.030 455	1.030 378	1.030 225	1.030 000	1.030 000	6
7	1.035 620	1.035 529	1.035 376	1.035 150	1.035 000	7
8	1.040 811	1.040 707	1.040 527	1.040 300	1.040 000	8
9	1.046 028	1.045 911	1.045 678	1.045 450	1.045 000	9
10	1.051 271	1.051 140	1.050 907	1.050 600	1.050 000	10
11	1.056 541	1.056 396	1.056 135	1.055 750	1.055 000	11

Years						Years
1	1.061 837	1.061 678	1.061 364	1.060 900	1.060 000	1
2	1.127 497	1.127 160	1.126 493	1.125 509	1.123 600	2
3	1.197 217	1.196 681	1.195 618	1.194 052	1.191 016	3
4	1.271 249	1.270 489	1.268 986	1.266 770	1.262 477	4
5	1.349 859	1.348 850	1.346 855	1.343 916	1.338 226	5
6	1.433 329	1.432 044	1.429 503	1.425 761	1.418 519	6
7	1.521 962	1.520 370	1.517 222	1.512 590	1.503 630	7
8	1.616 074	1.614 143	1.610 324	1.604 706	1.593 848	8
9	1.716 007	1.713 699	1.709 140	1.702 433	1.689 479	9
10	1.822 119	1.819 397	1.814 018	1.806 111	1.790 848	10
11	1.934 792	1.931 613	1.925 333	1.916 103	1.898 299	11
12	2.054 433	2.050 751	2.043 478	2.032 794	2.012 196	12
13	2.181 472	2.177 237	2.168 873	2.156 591	2.132 928	13
14	2.316 367	2.311 524	2.301 963	2.287 928	2.260 904	14
15	2.459 603	2.454 094	2.443 220	2.427 262	2.396 558	15
16	2.611 696	2.605 457	2.593 144	2.575 083	2.540 352	16
17	2.773 195	2.766 156	2.752 269	2.731 905	2.692 773	17
18	2.944 680	2.936 766	2.921 158	2.898 278	2.854 339	18
19	3.126 768	3.117 899	3.100 411	3.074 783	3.025 600	19
20	3.320 117	3.310 204	3.290 663	3.262 038	3.207 135	20
21	3.525 421	3.514 371	3.492 590	3.460 696	3.399 564	21
22	3.743 421	3.731 129	3.706 907	3.671 452	3.603 537	22
23	3.974 902	3.961 257	3.934 376	3.895 044	3.819 750	23
24	4.220 696	4.205 579	4.175 804	4.132 252	4.048 935	24
25	4.481 689	4.464 970	4.432 046	4.383 906	4.291 871	25
26	4.758 821	4.740 359	4.704 012	4.650 886	4.549 383	26
27	5.053 090	5.032 734	4.992 667	4.934 125	4.822 346	27
28	5.365 556	5.343 142	5.299 034	5.234 613	5.111 687	28
29	5.697 343	5.672 696	5.624 202	5.553 401	5.418 388	29
30	6.049 647	6.022 575	5.969 323	5.891 603	5.743 491	30
31	6.423 737	6.394 034	6.335 622	6.250 402	6.088 101	31
32	6.820 958	6.788 405	6.724 398	6.631 051	6.453 387	32
33	7.242 743	7.207 098	7.137 031	7.034 882	6.840 590	33
34	7.690 609	7.651 617	7.574 984	7.463 307	7.251 025	34
35	8.166 170	8.123 551	8.039 812	7.917 822	7.686 087	35
36	8.671 138	8.624 594	8.533 164	8.400 017	8.147 252	36
37	9.207 331	9.156 540	9.056 789	8.911 578	8.636 087	37
38	9.776 680	9.721 296	9.612 546	9.454 293	9.154 252	38
39	10.381 237	10.320 884	10.202 406	10.030 060	9.703 507	39
40	11.023 176	10.957 454	10.828 462	10.640 891	10.285 718	40

6¼%

COMPOUND INTEREST
(Future Value of $1)

Base:	2.718 282	1.005 208	1.015 625	1.031 250	1.062 500	
			Frequency of Conversion			
Months	Continuous	Monthly	Quarterly	Semiannual	Annual	Months
0	1.000 000	1.000 000	1.000 000	1.000 000	1.000 000	0
1	1.005 222	1.005 208	1.005 208	1.005 208	1.005 208	1
2	1.010 471	1.010 444	1.010 417	1.010 417	1.010 417	2
3	1.015 748	1.015 707	1.015 625	1.015 625	1.015 625	3
4	1.021 052	1.020 997	1.020 915	1.020 833	1.020 833	4
5	1.026 384	1.026 314	1.026 204	1.026 042	1.026 042	5
6	1.031 743	1.031 660	1.031 494	1.031 250	1.031 250	6
7	1.037 131	1.037 033	1.036 867	1.036 621	1.036 458	7
8	1.042 547	1.042 434	1.042 239	1.041 992	1.041 667	8
9	1.047 991	1.047 864	1.047 611	1.047 363	1.046 875	9
10	1.053 464	1.053 321	1.053 068	1.052 734	1.052 083	10
11	1.058 965	1.058 807	1.058 524	1.058 105	1.057 292	11

Years						Years
1	1.064 494	1.064 322	1.063 980	1.063 477	1.062 500	1
2	1.133 148	1.132 781	1.132 054	1.130 982	1.128 906	2
3	1.206 230	1.205 643	1.204 483	1.202 773	1.199 463	3
4	1.284 025	1.283 193	1.281 546	1.279 121	1.274 429	4
5	1.366 838	1.365 730	1.363 539	1.360 315	1.354 081	5
6	1.454 991	1.453 576	1.450 779	1.446 664	1.438 711	6
7	1.548 830	1.547 073	1.543 600	1.538 493	1.528 631	7
8	1.648 721	1.646 583	1.642 360	1.636 151	1.624 170	8
9	1.755 055	1.752 495	1.747 438	1.740 008	1.725 681	9
10	1.868 246	1.865 218	1.859 239	1.850 458	1.833 536	10
11	1.988 737	1.985 192	1.978 194	1.967 919	1.948 132	11
12	2.117 000	2.112 884	2.104 759	2.092 835	2.069 890	12
13	2.253 535	2.248 788	2.239 422	2.225 681	2.199 258	13
14	2.398 875	2.393 434	2.382 700	2.366 960	2.336 712	14
15	2.553 589	2.547 384	2.535 146	2.517 207	2.482 756	15
16	2.718 282	2.711 237	2.697 345	2.676 990	2.637 928	16
17	2.893 596	2.885 628	2.869 922	2.846 916	2.802 799	17
18	3.080 217	3.071 237	3.053 540	3.027 629	2.977 974	18
19	3.278 874	3.268 785	3.248 906	3.219 812	3.164 097	19
20	3.490 343	3.479 039	3.456 771	3.424 195	3.361 853	20
21	3.715 451	3.702 817	3.677 936	3.641 551	3.571 969	21
22	3.955 077	3.940 989	3.913 251	3.872 704	3.795 217	22
23	4.210 157	4.194 480	4.163 621	4.118 530	4.032 418	23
24	4.481 689	4.464 277	4.430 010	4.379 960	4.284 445	24
25	4.770 733	4.751 427	4.713 443	4.657 985	4.552 222	25
26	5.078 419	5.057 048	5.015 010	4.953 658	4.836 736	26
27	5.405 949	5.382 326	5.335 871	5.268 099	5.139 032	27
28	5.754 603	5.728 527	5.677 261	5.602 500	5.460 222	28
29	6.125 743	6.096 997	6.040 493	5.958 127	5.801 486	29
30	6.520 819	6.489 166	6.426 965	6.336 329	6.164 079	30
31	6.941 376	6.906 561	6.838 163	6.738 537	6.549 333	31
32	7.389 056	7.350 804	7.275 670	7.166 276	6.958 667	32
33	7.865 609	7.823 621	7.741 168	7.621 167	7.393 583	33
34	8.372 897	8.326 850	8.236 450	8.104 932	7.855 682	34
35	8.912 903	8.862 449	8.763 419	8.619 405	8.346 663	35
36	9.487 736	9.432 497	9.324 104	9.166 536	8.868 329	36
37	10.099 642	10.039 213	9.920 662	9.748 396	9.422 600	37
38	10.751 013	10.684 953	10.555 387	10.367 190	10.011 512	38
39	11.444 394	11.372 229	11.230 722	11.025 264	10.637 231	39
40	12.182 494	12.103 711	11.949 266	11.725 110	11.302 058	40

COMPOUND INTEREST

(Future Value of $1)

6½%

Base:	2.718 282	1.005 417	1.016 250	1.032 500	1.065 000	
			Frequency of Conversion			
Months	Continuous	Monthly	Quarterly	Semiannual	Annual	Months
0	1.000 000	1.000 000	1.000 000	1.000 000	1.000 000	0
1	1.005 431	1.005 417	1.005 417	1.005 417	1.005 417	1
2	1.010 892	1.010 863	1.010 833	1.010 833	1.010 833	2
3	1.016 383	1.016 338	1.016 250	1.016 250	1.016 250	3
4	1.021 903	1.021 843	1.021 755	1.021 667	1.021 667	4
5	1.027 453	1.027 378	1.027 259	1.027 083	1.027 083	5
6	1.033 034	1.032 943	1.032 764	1.032 500	1.032 500	6
7	1.038 645	1.038 538	1.038 358	1.038 093	1.037 917	7
8	1.044 286	1.044 164	1.043 952	1.043 685	1.043 333	8
9	1.049 958	1.049 820	1.049 546	1.049 278	1.048 750	9
10	1.055 661	1.055 506	1.055 232	1.054 871	1.054 167	10
11	1.061 394	1.061 224	1.060 917	1.060 464	1.059 583	11

Years						Years
1	1.067 159	1.066 972	1.066 602	1.066 056	1.065 000	1
2	1.138 828	1.138 429	1.137 639	1.136 476	1.134 225	2
3	1.215 311	1.214 672	1.213 408	1.211 547	1.207 950	3
4	1.296 930	1.296 020	1.294 222	1.291 578	1.286 466	4
5	1.384 031	1.382 817	1.380 420	1.376 894	1.370 087	5
6	1.476 981	1.475 427	1.472 358	1.467 847	1.459 142	6
7	1.576 173	1.574 239	1.570 419	1.564 807	1.553 987	7
8	1.682 028	1.679 669	1.675 012	1.668 173	1.654 996	8
9	1.794 991	1.792 160	1.786 570	1.778 366	1.762 570	9
10	1.915 541	1.912 184	1.905 559	1.895 838	1.877 137	10
11	2.044 187	2.040 246	2.032 472	2.021 070	1.999 151	11
12	2.181 472	2.176 885	2.167 838	2.154 574	2.129 096	12
13	2.327 978	2.322 675	2.312 219	2.296 897	2.267 487	13
14	2.484 323	2.478 229	2.466 217	2.448 622	2.414 874	14
15	2.651 167	2.644 201	2.630 471	2.610 368	2.571 841	15
16	2.829 217	2.821 288	2.805 665	2.782 800	2.739 011	16
17	3.019 224	3.010 235	2.992 526	2.966 621	2.917 046	17
18	3.221 993	3.211 836	3.191 833	3.162 585	3.106 654	18
19	3.438 379	3.426 938	3.404 415	3.371 493	3.308 587	19
20	3.669 297	3.656 447	3.631 154	3.594 201	3.523 645	.20
21	3.915 723	3.901 326	3.872 995	3.831 621	3.752 682	21
22	4.178 699	4.162 605	4.130 943	4.084 723	3.996 606	22
23	4.459 337	4.441 382	4.406 070	4.354 545	4.256 386	23
24	4.758 821	4.738 830	4.699 521	4.642 190	4.533 051	24
25	5.078 419	5.056 198	5.012 517	4.948 835	4.827 699	25
26	5.419 481	5.394 821	5.346 359	5.275 737	5.141 500	26
27	5.783 448	5.756 122	5.702 435	5.624 232	5.475 697	27
28	6.171 858	6.141 620	6.082 226	5.995 748	5.831 617	28
29	6.586 354	6.552 936	6.487 312	6.391 805	6.210 672	29
30	7.028 688	6.991 798	6.919 378	6.814 023	6.614 366	30
31	7.500 727	7.460 052	7.380 219	7.264 132	7.044 300	31
32	8.004 469	7.959 665	7.871 754	7.743 974	7.502 179	32
33	8.542 041	8.492 739	8.396 025	8.255 511	7.989 821	33
34	9.115 716	9.061 513	8.955 214	8.800 840	8.509 159	34
35	9.727 919	9.668 379	9.551 646	9.382 190	9.062 255	35
36	10.381 237	10.315 889	10.187 801	10.001 942	9.651 301	36
37	11.078 430	11.006 763	10.866 325	10.662 633	10.278 636	37
38	11.822 447	11.743 906	11.590 039	11.366 967	10.946 747	38
39	12.616 431	12.530 417	12.361 955	12.117 826	11.658 286	39
40	13.463 738	13.369 602	13.185 281	12.918 284	12.416 075	40

6¾%

COMPOUND INTEREST
(Future Value of $1)

Base: 2.718 282   1.005 625   1.016 875   1.033 750   1.067 500

Frequency of Conversion

Months	Continuous	Monthly	Quarterly	Semiannual	Annual	Months
0	1.000 000	1.000 000	1.000 000	1.000 000	1.000 000	0
1	1.005 641	1.005 625	1.005 625	1.005 625	1.005 625	1
2	1.011 314	1.011 282	1.011 250	1.011 250	1.011 250	2
3	1.017 018	1.016 970	1.016 875	1.016 875	1.016 875	3
4	1.022 755	1.022 691	1.022 595	1.022 500	1.022 500	4
5	1.028 524	1.028 443	1.028 315	1.028 125	1.028 125	5
6	1.034 326	1.034 228	1.034 035	1.033 750	1.033 750	6
7	1.040 160	1.040 046	1.039 851	1.039 565	1.039 375	7
8	1.046 028	1.045 896	1.045 668	1.045 380	1.045 000	8
9	1.051 928	1.051 779	1.051 484	1.051 195	1.050 625	9
10	1.057 862	1.057 695	1.057 399	1.057 009	1.056 250	10
11	1.063 829	1.063 645	1.063 313	1.062 824	1.061 875	11

Years						Years
1	1.069 830	1.069 628	1.069 228	1.068 639	1.067 500	1
2	1.144 537	1.144 104	1.143 248	1.141 989	1.139 556	2
3	1.224 460	1.223 766	1.222 393	1.220 375	1.216 476	3
4	1.309 964	1.308 974	1.307 017	1.304 140	1.298 588	4
5	1.401 440	1.400 115	1.397 499	1.393 655	1.386 243	5
6	1.499 303	1.497 602	1.494 245	1.489 314	1.479 815	6
7	1.603 999	1.601 877	1.597 688	1.591 539	1.579 702	7
8	1.716 007	1.713 412	1.708 293	1.700 781	1.686 332	8
9	1.835 836	1.832 714	1.826 554	1.817 521	1.800 159	9
10	1.964 033	1.960 322	1.953 003	1.942 274	1.921 670	10
11	2.101 182	2.096 815	2.088 205	2.075 590	2.051 383	11
12	2.247 908	2.242 812	2.232 767	2.218 056	2.189 851	12
13	2.404 880	2.398 974	2.387 337	2.370 301	2.337 666	13
14	2.572 813	2.566 010	2.552 607	2.532 997	2.495 459	14
15	2.752 474	2.744 676	2.729 318	2.706 859	2.663 902	15
16	2.944 680	2.935 782	2.918 263	2.892 656	2.843 715	16
17	3.150 307	3.140 194	3.120 289	3.091 205	3.035 666	17
18	3.370 294	3.358 840	3.336 300	3.303 382	3.240 574	18
19	3.605 643	3.592 709	3.567 265	3.530 123	3.459 312	19
20	3.857 426	3.842 862	3.814 219	3.772 428	3.692 816	20
21	4.126 791	4.110 432	4.078 269	4.031 363	3.942 081	21
22	4.414 965	4.396 633	4.360 599	4.308 072	4.208 172	22
23	4.723 264	4.702 762	4.662 474	4.603 774	4.492 223	23
24	5.053 090	5.030 205	4.985 248	4.919 773	4.795 448	24
25	5.405 949	5.380 448	5.330 366	5.257 462	5.119 141	25
26	5.783 448	5.755 077	5.699 376	5.618 329	5.464 683	26
27	6.187 307	6.155 792	6.093 932	6.003 966	5.833 549	27
28	6.619 369	6.584 407	6.515 802	6.416 073	6.227 314	28
29	7.081 601	7.042 865	6.966 877	6.856 466	6.647 657	29
30	7.576 111	7.533 245	7.449 179	7.327 087	7.096 374	30
31	8.105 153	8.057 770	7.964 870	7.830 011	7.575 380	31
32	8.671 138	8.618 816	8.516 262	8.367 456	8.086 718	32
33	9.276 645	9.218 926	9.105 825	8.941 790	8.632 571	33
34	9.924 436	9.860 821	9.736 202	9.555 547	9.215 270	34
35	10.617 462	10.547 409	10.410 218	10.211 430	9.837 300	35
36	11.358 882	11.281 804	11.130 896	10.912 333	10.501 318	36
37	12.152 076	12.067 333	11.901 464	11.661 346	11.210 157	37
38	13.000 658	12.907 556	12.725 378	12.461 770	11.966 843	38
39	13.908 498	13.806 282	13.606 329	13.317 134	12.774 605	39
40	14.879 732	14.767 585	14.548 266	14.231 209	13.636 890	40

42

COMPOUND INTEREST

(Future Value of $1)

7%

Base:	2.718 282	1.005 833	1.017 500	1.035 000	1.070 000	
			Frequency of Conversion			
Months	Continuous	Monthly	Quarterly	Semiannual	Annual	Months
0	1.000 000	1.000 000	1.000 000	1.000 000	1.000 000	0
1	1.005 850	1.005 833	1.005 833	1.005 833	1.005 833	1
2	1.011 735	1.011 701	1.011 667	1.011 667	1.011 667	2
3	1.017 654	1.017 602	1.017 500	1.017 500	1.017 500	3
4	1.023 608	1.023 538	1.023 435	1.023 333	1.023 333	4
5	1.029 596	1.029 509	1.029 371	1.029 167	1.029 167	5
6	1.035 620	1.035 514	1.035 306	1.035 000	1.035 000	6
7	1.041 678	1.041 555	1.041 346	1.041 037	1.040 833	7
8	1.047 773	1.047 631	1.047 385	1.047 075	1.046 667	8
9	1.053 903	1.053 742	1.053 424	1.053 113	1.052 500	9
10	1.060 068	1.059 889	1.059 569	1.059 150	1.058 333	10
11	1.066 270	1.066 071	1.065 714	1.065 188	1.064 167	11

Years						Years
1	1.072 508	1.072 290	1.071 859	1.071 225	1.070 000	1
2	1.150 274	1.149 806	1.148 882	1.147 523	1.144 900	2
3	1.233 678	1.232 926	1.231 439	1.229 255	1.225 043	3
4	1.323 130	1.322 054	1.319 929	1.316 809	1.310 796	4
5	1.419 068	1.417 625	1.414 778	1.410 599	1.402 552	5
6	1.521 962	1.520 106	1.516 443	1.511 069	1.500 730	6
7	1.632 316	1.629 994	1.625 413	1.618 695	1.605 781	7
8	1.750 673	1.747 826	1.742 213	1.733 986	1.718 186	8
9	1.877 611	1.874 177	1.867 407	1.857 489	1.838 459	9
10	2.013 753	2.009 661	2.001 597	1.989 789	1.967 151	10
11	2.159 766	2.154 940	2.145 430	2.131 512	2.104 852	11
12	2.316 367	2.310 721	2.299 599	2.283 328	2.252 192	12
13	2.484 323	2.477 763	2.464 846	2.445 959	2.409 845	13
14	2.664 456	2.656 881	2.641 967	2.620 172	2.578 534	14
15	2.857 651	2.848 947	2.831 816	2.806 794	2.759 032	15
16	3.064 854	3.054 897	3.035 308	3.006 708	2.952 164	16
17	3.287 081	3.275 736	3.253 422	3.220 860	3.158 815	17
18	3.525 421	3.512 539	3.487 210	3.450 266	3.379 932	18
19	3.781 043	3.766 461	3.737 797	3.696 011	3.616 528	19
20	4.055 200	4.038 739	4.006 392	3.959 260	3.869 684	20
21	4.349 235	4.330 700	4.294 287	4.241 258	4.140 562	21
22	4.664 590	4.643 766	4.602 871	4.543 342	4.430 402	22
23	5.002 811	4.979 464	4.933 629	4.866 941	4.740 530	23
24	5.365 556	5.339 430	5.288 154	5.213 589	5.072 367	24
25	5.754 603	5.725 418	5.668 156	5.584 927	5.427 433	25
26	6.171 858	6.139 309	6.075 464	5.982 713	5.807 353	26
27	6.619 369	6.583 120	6.512 041	6.408 832	6.213 868	27
28	7.099 327	7.059 015	6.979 990	6.865 301	6.648 838	28
29	7.614 086	7.569 311	7.481 565	7.354 282	7.114 257	29
30	8.166 170	8.116 497	8.019 183	7.878 091	7.612 255	30
31	8.758 284	8.703 240	8.595 434	8.439 208	8.145 113	31
32	9.393 331	9.332 398	9.213 094	9.040 291	8.715 271	32
33	10.074 425	10.007 037	9.875 138	9.684 185	9.325 340	33
34	10.804 903	10.730 447	10.584 756	10.373 941	9.978 114	34
35	11.588 347	11.506 152	11.345 366	11.112 825	10.676 581	35
36	12.428 597	12.337 932	12.160 633	11.904 336	11.423 942	36
37	13.329 772	13.229 843	13.034 484	12.752 223	12.223 618	37
38	14.296 289	14.186 229	13.971 130	13.660 500	13.079 271	38
39	15.332 887	15.211 753	14.975 081	14.633 469	13.994 820	39
40	16.444 647	16.311 411	16.051 176	15.675 738	14.974 458	40

7¼%

COMPOUND INTEREST
(Future Value of $1)

Base: 2.718 282 1.006 042 1.018 125 1.036 250 1.072 500

Frequency of Conversion

Months	Continuous	Monthly	Quarterly	Semiannual	Annual	Months
0	1.000 000	1.000 000	1.000 000	1.000 000	1.000 000	0
1	1.006 060	1.006 042	1.006 042	1.006 042	1.006 042	1
2	1.012 157	1.012 120	1.012 083	1.012 083	1.012 083	2
3	1.018 290	1.018 235	1.018 125	1.018 125	1.018 125	3
4	1.024 461	1.024 387	1.024 276	1.024 167	1.024 167	4
5	1.030 669	1.030 576	1.030 427	1.030 208	1.030 208	5
6	1.036 915	1.036 802	1.036 579	1.036 250	1.036 250	6
7	1.043 199	1.043 066	1.042 841	1.042 511	1.042 292	7
8	1.049 520	1.049 368	1.049 104	1.048 771	1.048 333	8
9	1.055 880	1.055 708	1.055 367	1.055 032	1.054 375	9
10	1.062 279	1.062 086	1.061 743	1.061 293	1.060 417	10
11	1.068 716	1.068 503	1.068 119	1.067 553	1.066 458	11

Years						Years
1	1.075 193	1.074 958	1.074 495	1.073 814	1.072 500	1
2	1.156 040	1.155 535	1.154 540	1.153 077	1.150 256	2
3	1.242 965	1.242 152	1.240 547	1.238 190	1.233 650	3
4	1.336 427	1.335 262	1.332 962	1.329 586	1.323 089	4
5	1.436 917	1.435 351	1.432 261	1.427 728	1.419 013	5
6	1.544 963	1.542 942	1.538 957	1.533 114	1.521 892	6
7	1.661 133	1.658 599	1.653 601	1.646 280	1.632 229	7
8	1.786 038	1.782 924	1.776 787	1.767 798	1.750 566	8
9	1.920 336	1.916 569	1.909 148	1.898 287	1.877 482	9
10	2.064 731	2.060 232	2.051 370	2.038 407	2.013 599	10
11	2.219 984	2.214 664	2.204 187	2.188 870	2.159 585	11
12	2.386 911	2.380 671	2.368 388	2.350 439	2.316 155	12
13	2.566 389	2.559 122	2.544 821	2.523 935	2.484 076	13
14	2.759 363	2.750 950	2.734 398	2.710 237	2.664 172	14
15	2.966 848	2.957 156	2.938 097	2.910 290	2.857 324	15
16	3.189 933	3.178 819	3.156 970	3.125 111	3.064 480	16
17	3.429 793	3.417 098	3.392 149	3.355 788	3.286 655	17
18	3.687 689	3.673 238	3.644 847	3.603 492	3.524 937	18
19	3.964 977	3.948 578	3.916 370	3.869 480	3.780 495	19
20	4.263 115	4.244 557	4.208 120	4.155 103	4.054 581	20
21	4.583 670	4.562 721	4.521 604	4.461 808	4.348 538	21
22	4.928 329	4.904 735	4.858 441	4.791 152	4.663 808	22
23	5.298 904	5.272 386	5.220 371	5.144 806	5.001 934	23
24	5.697 343	5.667 595	5.609 262	5.524 565	5.364 574	24
25	6.125 743	6.092 428	6.027 125	5.932 356	5.753 505	25
26	6.586 354	6.549 106	6.476 115	6.370 247	6.170 634	26
27	7.081 601	7.040 016	6.958 554	6.840 461	6.618 005	27
28	7.614 086	7.567 724	7.476 931	7.345 383	7.097 811	28
29	8.186 611	8.134 987	8.033 925	7.887 575	7.612 402	29
30	8.802 185	8.744 772	8.632 413	8.469 789	8.164 301	30
31	9.464 046	9.400 265	9.275 485	9.094 979	8.756 213	31
32	10.175 674	10.104 893	9.966 462	9.766 316	9.391 039	32
33	10.940 812	10.862 339	10.708 914	10.487 208	10.071 889	33
34	11.763 482	11.676 561	11.506 674	11.261 311	10.802 101	34
35	12.648 011	12.551 816	12.363 864	12.092 554	11.585 253	35
36	13.599 051	13.492 679	13.284 911	12.985 155	12.425 184	36
37	14.621 602	14.504 067	14.274 570	13.943 642	13.326 010	37
38	15.721 041	15.591 267	15.337 955	14.972 879	14.292 146	38
39	16.903 150	16.759 962	16.480 556	16.078 088	15.328 326	39
40	18.174 145	18.016 260	17.708 275	17.264 877	16.439 630	40

COMPOUND INTEREST

(Future Value of $1)

7½%

Base:	2.718 282	1.006 250	1.018 750	1.037 500	1.075 000	
			Frequency of Conversion			
Months	Continuous	Monthly	Quarterly	Semiannual	Annual	Months
0	1.000 000	1.000 000	1.000 000	1.000 000	1.000 000	0
1	1.006 270	1.006 250	1.006 250	1.006 250	1.006 250	1
2	1.012 578	1.012 539	1.012 500	1.012 500	1.012 500	2
3	1.018 927	1.018 867	1.018 750	1.018 750	1.018 750	3
4	1.025 315	1.025 235	1.025 117	1.025 000	1.025 000	4
5	1.031 743	1.031 643	1.031 484	1.031 250	1.031 250	5
6	1.038 212	1.038 091	1.037 852	1.037 500	1.037 500	6
7	1.044 721	1.044 579	1.044 338	1.043 984	1.043 750	7
8	1.051 271	1.051 108	1.050 825	1.050 469	1.050 000	8
9	1.057 862	1.057 677	1.057 311	1.056 953	1.056 250	9
10	1.064 494	1.064 287	1.063 919	1.063 438	1.062 500	10
11	1.071 168	1.070 939	1.070 528	1.069 922	1.068 750	11

Years						Years
1	1.077 884	1.077 633	1.077 136	1.076 406	1.075 000	1
2	1.161 834	1.161 292	1.160 222	1.158 650	1.155 625	2
3	1.252 323	1.251 446	1.249 716	1.247 179	1.242 297	3
4	1.349 859	1.348 599	1.346 114	1.342 471	1.335 469	4
5	1.454 991	1.453 294	1.449 948	1.445 044	1.435 629	5
6	1.568 312	1.566 117	1.561 791	1.555 454	1.543 302	6
7	1.690 459	1.687 699	1.682 261	1.674 301	1.659 049	7
8	1.822 119	1.818 720	1.812 024	1.802 228	1.783 478	8
9	1.964 033	1.959 912	1.951 796	1.939 929	1.917 239	9
10	2.117 000	2.112 065	2.102 349	2.088 152	2.061 032	10
11	2.281 881	2.276 030	2.264 516	2.247 700	2.215 609	11
12	2.459 603	2.452 724	2.439 191	2.419 438	2.381 780	12
13	2.651 167	2.643 135	2.627 340	2.604 298	2.560 413	13
14	2.857 651	2.848 329	2.830 002	2.803 283	2.752 444	14
15	3.080 217	3.069 452	3.048 297	3.017 471	2.958 877	15
16	3.320 117	3.307 741	3.283 430	3.248 025	3.180 793	16
17	3.578 701	3.564 530	3.536 700	3.496 194	3.419 353	17
18	3.857 426	3.841 254	3.809 507	3.763 326	3.675 804	18
19	4.157 858	4.139 460	4.103 357	4.050 867	3.951 489	19
20	4.481 689	4.460 817	4.419 872	4.360 379	4.247 851	20
21	4.830 742	4.807 122	4.760 803	4.693 539	4.566 440	21
22	5.206 980	5.180 311	5.128 032	5.052 155	4.908 923	22
23	5.612 521	5.582 472	5.523 587	5.438 171	5.277 092	23
24	6.049 647	6.015 854	5.949 654	5.853 681	5.672 874	24
25	6.520 819	6.482 880	6.408 585	6.300 939	6.098 340	25
26	7.028 688	6.986 163	6.902 917	6.782 370	6.555 715	26
27	7.576 111	7.528 517	7.435 380	7.300 585	7.047 394	27
28	8.166 170	8.112 976	8.008 914	7.858 396	7.575 948	28
29	8.802 185	8.742 807	8.626 689	8.458 826	8.144 144	29
30	9.487 736	9.421 534	9.292 116	9.105 134	8.754 955	30
31	10.226 680	10.152 952	10.008 871	9.800 823	9.411 577	31
32	11.023 176	10.941 152	10.780 914	10.549 667	10.117 445	32
33	11.881 707	11.790 542	11.612 509	11.355 727	10.876 253	33
34	12.807 104	12.705 873	12.508 250	12.223 376	11.691 972	34
35	13.804 574	13.692 263	13.473 085	13.157 318	12.568 870	35
36	14.879 732	14.755 228	14.512 343	14.162 620	13.511 536	36
37	16.038 627	15.900 715	15.631 765	15.244 732	14.524 901	37
38	17.287 782	17.135 129	16.837 535	16.409 525	15.614 268	38
39	18.634 226	18.465 374	18.136 313	17.663 315	16.785 339	39
40	20.085 537	19.898 889	19.535 273	19.012 903	18.044 239	40

7¾%

COMPOUND INTEREST
(Future Value of $1)

Base:	2.718 282	1.006 458	1.019 375	1.038 750	1.077 500	

Frequency of Conversion

Months	Continuous	Monthly	Quarterly	Semiannual	Annual	Months
0	1.000 000	1.000 000	1.000 000	1.000 000	1.000 000	0
1	1.006 479	1.006 458	1.006 458	1.006 458	1.006 458	1
2	1.013 000	1.012 958	1.012 917	1.012 917	1.012 917	2
3	1.019 564	1.019 500	1.019 375	1.019 375	1.019 375	3
4	1.026 170	1.026 085	1.025 958	1.025 833	1.025 833	4
5	1.032 819	1.032 711	1.032 542	1.032 292	1.032 292	5
6	1.039 511	1.039 381	1.039 125	1.038 750	1.038 750	6
7	1.046 246	1.046 094	1.045 836	1.045 459	1.045 208	7
8	1.053 025	1.052 850	1.052 547	1.052 167	1.051 667	8
9	1.059 847	1.059 649	1.059 258	1.058 876	1.058 125	9
10	1.066 714	1.066 493	1.066 099	1.065 584	1.064 583	10
11	1.073 626	1.073 381	1.072 941	1.072 293	1.071 042	11

Years						Years
1	1.080 582	1.080 313	1.079 782	1.079 002	1.077 500	1
2	1.167 658	1.167 076	1.165 928	1.164 244	1.161 006	2
3	1.261 750	1.260 808	1.258 948	1.256 221	1.250 984	3
4	1.363 425	1.362 067	1.359 389	1.355 465	1.347 936	4
5	1.473 293	1.471 458	1.467 843	1.462 549	1.452 401	5
6	1.592 014	1.589 636	1.584 950	1.578 092	1.564 962	6
7	1.720 302	1.717 304	1.711 399	1.702 764	1.686 246	7
8	1.858 928	1.855 226	1.847 938	1.837 285	1.816 930	8
9	2.008 725	2.004 225	1.995 369	1.982 434	1.957 742	9
10	2.170 592	2.165 190	2.154 563	2.139 049	2.109 467	10
11	2.345 503	2.339 083	2.326 457	2.308 037	2.272 951	11
12	2.534 509	2.526 942	2.512 066	2.490 376	2.449 105	12
13	2.738 746	2.729 888	2.712 482	2.687 119	2.638 910	13
14	2.959 440	2.949 133	2.928 888	2.899 406	2.843 426	14
15	3.197 918	3.185 987	3.162 559	3.128 464	3.063 791	15
16	3.455 613	3.441 863	3.414 873	3.375 617	3.301 235	16
17	3.734 075	3.718 290	3.687 317	3.642 296	3.557 081	17
18	4.034 975	4.016 917	3.981 497	3.930 043	3.832 755	18
19	4.360 122	4.339 527	4.299 148	4.240 523	4.129 793	19
20	4.711 470	4.688 048	4.642 140	4.575 531	4.449 852	20
21	5.091 131	5.064 559	5.012 498	4.937 005	4.794 716	21
22	5.501 386	5.471 309	5.412 403	5.327 036	5.166 306	22
23	5.944 700	5.910 726	5.844 213	5.747 880	5.566 695	23
24	6.423 737	6.385 434	6.310 473	6.201 971	5.998 114	24
25	6.941 376	6.898 268	6.813 933	6.691 937	6.462 967	25
26	7.500 727	7.452 288	7.357 559	7.220 610	6.963 847	26
27	8.105 153	8.050 804	7.944 557	7.791 050	7.503 546	27
28	8.758 284	8.697 388	8.578 386	8.406 555	8.085 070	28
29	9.464 046	9.395 901	9.262 783	9.070 686	8.711 663	29
30	10.226 680	10.150 514	10.001 783	9.787 284	9.386 817	30
31	11.050 769	10.965 732	10.799 740	10.560 495	10.114 296	31
32	11.941 264	11.846 423	11.661 361	11.394 791	10.898 154	32
33	12.903 518	12.797 845	12.591 723	12.294 997	11.742 760	33
34	13.943 312	13.825 678	13.596 310	13.266 321	12.652 824	34
35	15.066 896	14.936 060	14.681 045	14.314 381	13.633 418	35
36	16.281 020	16.135 620	15.852 322	15.445 240	14.690 008	36
37	17.592 981	17.431 520	17.117 045	16.665 438	15.828 484	37
38	19.010 662	18.831 497	18.482 670	17.982 033	17.055 191	38
39	20.542 584	20.343 911	19.957 247	19.402 642	18.376 969	39
40	22.197 951	21.977 792	21.549 467	20.935 481	19.801 184	40

COMPOUND INTEREST

8%

(Future Value of $1)

Base:	2.718 282	1.006 667	1.020 000	1.040 000	1.080 000	
			Frequency of Conversion			
Months	Continuous	Monthly	Quarterly	Semiannual	Annual	Months
0	1.000 000	1.000 000	1.000 000	1.000 000	1.000 000	0
1	1.006 689	1.006 667	1.006 667	1.006 667	1.006 667	1
2	1.013 423	1.013 378	1.013 333	1.013 333	1.013 333	2
3	1.020 201	1.020 134	1.020 000	1.020 000	1.020 000	3
4	1.027 025	1.026 935	1.026 800	1.026 667	1.026 667	4
5	1.033 895	1.033 781	1.033 600	1.033 333	1.033 333	5
6	1.040 811	1.040 673	1.040 400	1.040 000	1.040 000	6
7	1.047 773	1.047 610	1.047 336	1.046 933	1.046 667	7
8	1.054 781	1.054 595	1.054 272	1.053 867	1.053 333	8
9	1.061 837	1.061 625	1.061 208	1.060 800	1.060 000	9
10	1.068 939	1.068 703	1.068 283	1.067 733	1.066 667	10
11	1.076 089	1.075 827	1.075 357	1.074 667	1.073 333	11

Years						Years
1	1.083 287	1.083 000	1.082 432	1.081 600	1.080 000	1
2	1.173 511	1.172 888	1.171 659	1.169 859	1.166 400	2
3	1.271 249	1.270 237	1.268 242	1.265 319	1.259 712	3
4	1.377 128	1.375 666	1.372 786	1.368 569	1.360 489	4
5	1.491 825	1.489 846	1.485 947	1.480 244	1.469 328	5
6	1.616 074	1.613 502	1.608 437	1.601 032	1.586 874	6
7	1.750 673	1.747 422	1.741 024	1.731 676	1.713 824	7
8	1.896 481	1.892 457	1.884 541	1.872 981	1.850 930	8
9	2.054 433	2.049 530	2.039 887	2.025 817	1.999 005	9
10	2.225 541	2.219 640	2.208 040	2.191 123	2.158 925	10
11	2.410 900	2.403 869	2.390 053	2.369 919	2.331 639	11
12	2.611 696	2.603 389	2.587 070	2.563 304	2.518 170	12
13	2.829 217	2.819 469	2.800 328	2.772 470	2.719 624	13
14	3.064 854	3.053 484	3.031 165	2.998 703	2.937 194	14
15	3.320 117	3.306 921	3.281 031	3.243 398	3.172 169	15
16	3.596 640	3.581 394	3.551 493	3.508 059	3.425 943	16
17	3.896 193	3.878 648	3.844 251	3.794 316	3.700 018	17
18	4.220 696	4.200 574	4.161 140	4.103 933	3.996 019	18
19	4.572 225	4.549 220	4.504 152	4.438 813	4.315 701	19
20	4.953 032	4.926 803	4.875 439	4.801 021	4.660 957	20
21	5.365 556	5.335 725	5.277 332	5.192 784	5.033 834	21
22	5.812 437	5.778 588	5.712 354	5.616 515	5.436 540	22
23	6.296 538	6.258 207	6.183 236	6.074 823	5.871 464	23
24	6.820 958	6.777 636	6.692 933	6.570 528	6.341 181	24
25	7.389 056	7.340 176	7.244 646	7.106 683	6.848 475	25
26	8.004 469	7.949 407	7.841 838	7.686 589	7.396 353	26
27	8.671 138	8.609 204	8.488 258	8.313 814	7.988 061	27
28	9.393 331	9.323 763	9.187 963	8.992 222	8.627 106	28
29	10.175 674	10.097 631	9.945 347	9.725 987	9.317 275	29
30	11.023 176	10.935 730	10.765 163	10.519 627	10.062 657	30
31	11.941 264	11.843 390	11.652 559	11.378 029	10.867 669	31
32	12.935 817	12.826 385	12.613 104	12.306 476	11.737 083	32
33	14.013 204	13.890 969	13.652 830	13.310 685	12.676 050	33
34	15.180 322	15.043 913	14.778 262	14.396 836	13.690 134	34
35	16.444 647	16.292 550	15.996 466	15.571 618	14.785 344	35
36	17.814 273	17.644 824	17.315 089	16.842 262	15.968 172	36
37	19.297 972	19.109 335	18.742 409	18.216 591	17.245 626	37
38	20.905 243	20.695 401	20.287 387	19.703 065	18.625 276	38
39	22.646 380	22.413 109	21.959 720	21.310 835	20.115 298	39
40	24.532 530	24.273 386	23.769 907	23.049 799	21.724 521	40

47

8¼%

COMPOUND INTEREST
(Future Value of $1)

Base: 2.718 282   1.006 875   1.020 625   1.041 250   1.082 500

Frequency of Conversion

Months	Continuous	Monthly	Quarterly	Semiannual	Annual	Months
0	1.000 000	1.000 000	1.000 000	1.000 000	1.000 000	0
1	1.006 899	1.006 875	1.006 875	1.006 875	1.006 875	1
2	1.013 845	1.013 797	1.013 750	1.013 750	1.013 750	2
3	1.020 839	1.020 767	1.020 625	1.020 625	1.020 625	3
4	1.027 882	1.027 785	1.027 642	1.027 500	1.027 500	4
5	1.034 973	1.034 851	1.034 659	1.034 375	1.034 375	5
6	1.042 113	1.041 966	1.041 675	1.041 250	1.041 250	6
7	1.049 302	1.049 129	1.048 837	1.048 409	1.048 125	7
8	1.056 541	1.056 342	1.055 998	1.055 567	1.055 000	8
9	1.063 829	1.063 604	1.063 160	1.062 726	1.061 875	9
10	1.071 168	1.070 916	1.070 469	1.069 884	1.068 750	10
11	1.078 558	1.078 279	1.077 778	1.077 043	1.075 625	11

Years						Years
1	1.085 999	1.085 692	1.085 088	1.084 202	1.082 500	1
2	1.179 393	1.178 727	1.177 415	1.175 493	1.171 806	2
3	1.280 819	1.279 735	1.277 599	1.274 471	1.268 480	3
4	1.390 968	1.389 398	1.386 306	1.381 784	1.373 130	4
5	1.510 590	1.508 459	1.504 264	1.498 132	1.486 413	5
6	1.640 498	1.637 722	1.632 258	1.624 277	1.609 042	6
7	1.781 579	1.778 062	1.771 143	1.761 044	1.741 788	7
8	1.934 792	1.930 428	1.921 845	1.909 327	1.885 486	8
9	2.101 182	2.095 850	2.085 371	2.070 095	2.041 038	9
10	2.281 881	2.275 448	2.262 810	2.244 400	2.209 424	10
11	2.478 119	2.470 436	2.455 347	2.433 382	2.391 701	11
12	2.691 234	2.682 133	2.664 267	2.638 277	2.589 017	12
13	2.922 677	2.911 971	2.890 963	2.860 424	2.802 611	13
14	3.174 023	3.161 504	3.136 948	3.101 276	3.033 826	14
15	3.446 985	3.432 420	3.403 863	3.362 408	3.284 117	15
16	3.743 421	3.726 551	3.693 490	3.645 528	3.555 056	16
17	4.065 351	4.045 887	4.007 760	3.952 487	3.848 348	17
18	4.414 965	4.392 588	4.348 771	4.285 293	4.165 837	18
19	4.794 647	4.768 998	4.718 798	4.646 121	4.509 519	19
20	5.206 980	5.177 664	5.120 309	5.037 332	4.881 554	20
21	5.654 773	5.621 349	5.555 984	5.461 483	5.284 282	21
22	6.141 076	6.103 055	6.028 729	5.921 349	5.720 236	22
23	6.669 201	6.626 038	6.541 700	6.419 935	6.192 155	23
24	7.242 743	7.193 838	7.098 317	6.960 504	6.703 008	24
25	7.865 609	7.810 293	7.702 296	7.546 589	7.256 006	25
26	8.542 041	8.479 574	8.357 666	8.182 024	7.854 626	26
27	9.276 645	9.206 207	9.068 800	8.870 963	8.502 633	27
28	10.074 425	9.995 106	9.840 443	9.617 912	9.204 100	28
29	10.940 812	10.851 608	10.677 742	10.427 755	9.963 439	29
30	11.881 707	11.781 506	11.586 286	11.305 789	10.785 422	30
31	12.903 518	12.791 088	12.572 136	12.257 754	11.675 220	31
32	14.013 204	13.887 184	13.641 869	13.289 876	12.638 425	32
33	15.218 321	15.077 206	14.802 623	14.408 904	13.681 095	33
34	16 527 076	16.369 204	16.062 143	15.622 156	14.809 786	34
35	17.948 383	17.771 916	17.428 832	16.937 566	16.031 593	35
36	19.491 920	19.294 830	18.911 810	18.363 736	17.354 199	36
37	21.168 199	20.948 245	20.520 971	19.909 991	18.785 921	37
38	22.988 636	22.743 345	22.267 052	21.586 444	20.335 759	38
39	24.965 628	24.692 271	24.161 702	23.404 056	22.013 459	39
40	27.112 639	26.808 204	26.217 564	25.374 714	23.829 570	40

COMPOUND INTEREST
(Future Value of $1)

8½ %

Base:	2.718 282	1.007 083	1.021 250	1.042 500	1.085 000	
			Frequency of Conversion			
Months	Continuous	Monthly	Quarterly	Semiannual	Annual	Months
0	1.000 000	1.000 000	1.000 000	1.000 000	1.000 000	0
1	1.007 108	1.007 083	1.007 083	1.007 083	1.007 083	1
2	1.014 267	1.014 217	1.014 167	1.014 167	1.014 167	2
3	1.021 477	1.021 401	1.021 250	1.021 250	1.021 250	3
4	1.028 739	1.028 636	1.028 484	1.028 333	1.028 333	4
5	1.036 051	1.035 922	1.035 718	1.035 417	1.035 417	5
6	1.043 416	1.043 260	1.042 952	1.042 500	1.042 500	6
7	1.050 833	1.050 650	1.050 339	1.049 884	1.049 583	7
8	1.058 303	1.058 092	1.057 727	1.057 269	1.056 667	8
9	1.065 826	1.065 586	1.065 114	1.064 653	1.063 750	9
10	1.073 402	1.073 134	1.072 659	1.072 037	1.070 833	10
11	1.081 033	1.080 736	1.080 203	1.079 422	1.077 917	11

Years						Years
1	1.088 717	1.088 391	1.087 748	1.086 806	1.085 000	1
2	1.185 305	1.184 595	1.183 196	1.181 148	1.177 225	2
3	1.290 462	1.289 302	1.287 019	1.283 679	1.277 289	3
4	1.404 948	1.403 265	1.399 952	1.395 110	1.385 859	4
5	1.529 590	1.527 301	1.522 795	1.516 214	1.503 657	5
6	1.665 291	1.662 300	1.656 417	1.647 831	1.631 468	6
7	1.813 031	1.809 232	1.801 764	1.790 873	1.770 142	7
8	1.973 878	1.969 152	1.959 865	1.946 332	1.920 604	8
9	2.148 994	2.143 207	2.131 839	2.115 286	2.083 856	9
10	2.339 647	2.332 647	2.318 904	2.298 906	2.260 983	10
11	2.547 213	2.538 832	2.522 383	2.498 466	2.453 167	11
12	2.773 195	2.763 242	2.743 717	2.715 348	2.661 686	12
13	3.019 224	3.007 487	2.984 473	2.951 057	2.887 930	13
14	3.287 081	3.273 321	3.246 354	3.207 228	3.133 404	14
15	3.578 701	3.562 653	3.531 215	3.485 635	3.399 743	15
16	3.896 193	3.877 559	3.841 072	3.788 210	3.688 721	16
17	4.241 852	4.220 300	4.178 118	4.117 050	4.002 262	17
18	4.618 177	4.593 337	4.544 740	4.474 436	4.342 455	18
19	5.027 888	4.999 346	4.943 531	4.862 845	4.711 563	19
20	5.473 947	5.441 243	5.377 316	5.284 970	5.112 046	20
21	5.959 580	5.922 199	5.849 165	5.743 739	5.546 570	21
22	6.488 296	6.445 667	6.362 417	6.242 331	6.018 028	22
23	7.063 919	7.015 406	6.920 706	6.784 204	6.529 561	23
24	7.690 609	7.635 504	7.527 984	7.373 116	7.084 574	24
25	8.372 897	8.310 413	8.188 549	8.013 148	7.686 762	25
26	9.115 716	9.044 978	8.907 078	8.708 740	8.340 137	26
27	9.924 436	9.844 472	9.688 655	9.464 713	9.049 049	27
28	10.804 903	10.714 634	10.538 815	10.286 309	9.818 218	28
29	11.763 482	11.661 710	11.463 575	11.179 225	10.652 766	29
30	12.807 104	12.692 499	12.469 480	12.149 651	11.558 252	30
31	13.943 312	13.814 400	13.563 652	13.204 317	12.540 703	31
32	15.180 322	15.035 468	14.753 834	14.350 534	13.606 663	32
33	16.527 076	16.364 466	16.048 453	15.596 250	14.763 229	33
34	17.993 310	17.810 936	17.456 672	16.950 102	16.018 104	34
35	19.589 623	19.385 261	18.988 460	18.421 477	17.379 642	35
36	21.327 557	21.098 742	20.654 658	20.020 577	18.856 912	36
37	23.219 675	22.963 679	22.467 062	21.758 488	20.459 750	37
38	25.279 657	24.993 459	24.438 501	23.647 261	22.198 828	38
39	27.522 394	27.202 654	26.582 930	25.699 991	24.085 729	39
40	29.964 100	29.607 121	28.915 528	27.930 910	26.133 016	40

49

8¾%

COMPOUND INTEREST
(Future Value of $1)

Base:	2.718 282	1.007 292	1.021 875	1.043 750	1.087 500	
			Frequency of Conversion			
Months	Continuous	Monthly	Quarterly	Semiannual	Annual	Months
0	1.000 000	1.000 000	1.000 000	1.000 000	1.000 000	0
1	1.007 318	1.007 292	1.007 292	1.007 292	1.007 292	1
2	1.014 690	1.014 637	1.014 583	1.014 583	1.014 583	2
3	1.022 116	1.022 035	1.021 875	1.021 875	1.021 875	3
4	1.029 596	1.029 487	1.029 326	1.029 167	1.029 167	4
5	1.037 131	1.036 994	1.036 777	1.036 458	1.036 458	5
6	1.044 721	1.044 555	1.044 229	1.043 750	1.043 750	6
7	1.052 367	1.052 172	1.051 843	1.051 361	1.051 042	7
8	1.060 068	1.059 844	1.059 457	1.058 971	1.058 333	8
9	1.067 826	1.067 572	1.067 071	1.066 582	1.065 625	9
10	1.075 641	1.075 356	1.074 852	1.074 193	1.072 917	10
11	1.083 513	1.083 198	1.082 632	1.081 803	1.080 208	11

Years						Years
1	1.091 442	1.091 096	1.090 413	1.089 414	1.087 500	1
2	1.191 246	1.190 490	1.189 001	1.186 823	1.182 656	2
3	1.300 176	1.298 939	1.296 502	1.292 942	1.286 139	3
4	1.419 068	1.417 267	1.413 723	1.408 549	1.398 676	4
5	1.548 830	1.546 374	1.541 542	1.534 493	1.521 060	5
6	1.690 459	1.687 242	1.680 918	1.671 698	1.654 153	6
7	1.845 038	1.840 943	1.832 895	1.821 171	1.798 891	7
8	2.013 753	2.008 645	1.998 613	1.984 010	1.956 294	8
9	2.197 895	2.191 624	2.179 314	2.161 408	2.127 470	9
10	2.398 875	2.391 272	2.376 353	2.354 668	2.313 623	10
11	2.618 234	2.609 107	2.591 207	2.565 209	2.516 065	11
12	2.857 651	2.846 785	2.825 486	2.794 575	2.736 221	12
13	3.118 961	3.106 116	3.080 947	3.044 449	2.975 640	13
14	3.404 166	3.389 070	3.359 506	3.316 666	3.236 009	14
15	3.715 451	3.697 800	3.663 249	3.613 222	3.519 160	15
16	4.055 200	4.034 654	3.994 455	3.936 295	3.827 086	16
17	4.426 017	4.402 194	4.355 607	4.288 255	4.161 956	17
18	4.830 742	4.803 215	4.749 411	4.671 685	4.526 127	18
19	5.272 476	5.240 768	5.178 820	5.089 400	4.922 164	19
20	5.754 603	5.718 180	5.647 054	5.544 464	5.352 853	20
21	6.280 817	6.239 083	6.157 622	6.040 217	5.821 228	21
22	6.855 149	6.807 437	6.714 353	6.580 297	6.330 585	22
23	7.481 999	7.427 566	7.321 419	7.168 668	6.884 511	23
24	8.166 170	8.104 186	7.983 371	7.809 648	7.486 906	24
25	8.912 903	8.842 444	8.705 174	8.507 940	8.142 010	25
26	9.727 919	9.647 954	9.492 236	9.268 670	8.854 436	26
27	10.617 462	10.526 842	10.350 459	10.097 419	9.629 199	27
28	11.588 347	11.485 793	11.286 278	11.000 270	10.471 754	28
29	12.648 011	12.532 101	12.306 706	11.983 849	11.388 033	29
30	13.804 574	13.673 723	13.419 395	13.055 374	12.384 485	30
31	15.066 896	14.919 342	14.632 685	14.222 708	13.468 128	31
32	16.444 647	16.278 432	15.955 673	15.494 418	14.646 589	32
33	17.948 383	17.761 329	17.398 276	16.879 837	15.928 166	33
34	19.589 623	19.379 312	18.971 310	18.389 131	17.321 880	34
35	21.380 943	21.144 686	20.686 566	20.033 378	18.837 545	35
36	23.336 065	23.070 878	22.556 905	21.824 644	20.485 830	36
37	25.469 967	25.172 539	24.596 346	23.776 074	22.278 340	37
38	27.798 999	27.465 652	26.820 181	25.901 990	24.227 695	38
39	30.341 002	29.967 658	29.245 079	28.217 992	26.347 618	39
40	33.115 452	32.697 587	31.889 220	30.741 077	28.653 035	40

COMPOUND INTEREST

(Future Value of $1)

9%

Base:	2.718 282	1.007 500	1.022 500	1.045 000	1.090 000	
			Frequency of Conversion			
Months	Continuous	Monthly	Quarterly	Semiannual	Annual	Months
0	1.000 000	1.000 000	1.000 000	1.000 000	1.000 000	0
1	1.007 528	1.007 500	1.007 500	1.007 500	1.007 500	1
2	1.015 113	1.015 056	1.015 000	1.015 000	1.015 000	2
3	1.022 755	1.022 669	1.022 500	1.022 500	1.022 500	3
4	1.030 455	1.030 339	1.030 169	1.030 000	1.030 000	4
5	1.038 212	1.038 067	1.037 837	1.037 500	1.037 500	5
6	1.046 028	1.045 852	1.045 506	1.045 000	1.045 000	6
7	1.053 903	1.053 696	1.053 348	1.052 838	1.052 500	7
8	1.061 837	1.061 599	1.061 189	1.060 675	1.060 000	8
9	1.069 830	1.069 561	1.069 030	1.068 513	1.067 500	9
10	1.077 884	1.077 583	1.077 048	1.076 350	1.075 000	10
11	1.085 999	1.085 664	1.085 066	1.084 188	1.082 500	11
Years						Years
1	1.094 174	1.093 807	1.093 083	1.092 025	1.090 000	1
2	1.197 217	1.196 414	1.194 831	1.192 519	1.188 100	2
3	1.309 964	1.308 645	1.306 050	1.302 260	1.295 029	3
4	1.433 329	1.431 405	1.427 621	1.422 101	1.411 582	4
5	1.568 312	1.565 681	1.560 509	1.552 969	1.538 624	5
6	1.716 007	1.712 553	1.705 767	1.695 881	1.677 100	6
7	1.877 611	1.873 202	1.864 545	1.851 945	1.828 039	7
8	2.054 433	2.048 921	2.038 103	2.022 370	1.992 563	8
9	2.247 908	2.241 124	2.227 816	2.208 479	2.171 893	9
10	2.459 603	2.451 357	2.435 189	2.411 714	2.367 364	10
11	2.691 234	2.681 311	2.661 864	2.633 652	2.580 426	11
12	2.944 680	2.932 837	2.909 640	2.876 014	2.812 665	12
13	3.221 993	3.207 957	3.180 479	3.140 679	3.065 805	13
14	3.525 421	3.508 886	3.476 528	3.429 700	3.341 727	14
15	3.857 426	3.838 043	3.800 135	3.745 318	3.642 482	15
16	4.220 696	4.198 078	4.153 864	4.089 981	3.970 306	16
17	4.618 177	4.591 887	4.540 519	4.466 362	4.327 633	17
18	5.053 090	5.022 638	4.963 166	4.877 378	4.717 120	18
19	5.528 961	5.493 796	5.425 154	5.326 219	5.141 661	19
20	6.049 647	6.009 152	5.930 145	5.816 365	5.604 411	20
21	6.619 369	6.572 851	6.482 143	6.351 615	6.108 808	21
22	7.242 743	7.189 430	7.085 522	6.936 123	6.658 600	22
23	7.924 823	7.863 848	7.745 066	7.574 420	7.257 874	23
24	8.671 138	8.601 532	8.466 003	8.271 456	7.911 083	24
25	9.487 736	9.408 415	9.254 046	9.032 636	8.623 081	25
26	10.381 237	10.290 989	10.115 444	9.863 865	9.399 158	26
27	11.358 882	11.256 354	11.057 023	10.771 587	10.245 082	27
28	12.428 597	12.312 278	12.086 247	11.762 842	11.167 140	28
29	13.599 051	13.467 255	13.211 275	12.845 318	12.172 182	29
30	14.879 732	14.730 576	14.441 024	14.027 408	13.267 678	30
31	16.281 020	16.112 406	15.785 243	15.318 280	14.461 770	31
32	17.814 273	17.623 861	17.254 586	16.727 945	15.763 329	32
33	19.491 920	19.277 100	18.860 700	18.267 334	17.182 028	33
34	21.327 557	21.085 425	20.616 316	19.948 385	18.728 411	34
35	23.336 065	23.063 384	22.535 351	21.784 136	20.413 968	35
36	25.533 722	25.226 888	24.633 017	23.788 821	22.251 225	36
37	27.938 342	27.593 344	26.925 940	25.977 987	24.253 835	37
38	30.569 415	30.181 790	29.432 296	28.368 611	26.436 680	38
39	33.448 268	33.013 050	32.171 951	30.979 233	28.815 982	39
40	36.598 234	36.109 902	35.166 623	33.830 096	31.409 420	40

9¼%

COMPOUND INTEREST
(Future Value of $1)

Base: 2.718 282   1.007 708   1.023 125   1.046 250   1.092 500

Frequency of Conversion

Months	Continuous	Monthly	Quarterly	Semiannual	Annual	Months
0	1.000 000	1.000 000	1.000 000	1.000 000	1.000 000	0
1	1.007 738	1.007 708	1.007 708	1.007 708	1.007 708	1
2	1.015 536	1.015 476	1.015 417	1.015 417	1.015 417	2
3	1.023 394	1.023 304	1.023 125	1.023 125	1.023 125	3
4	1.031 314	1.031 192	1.031 012	1.030 833	1.030 833	4
5	1.039 294	1.039 140	1.038 898	1.038 542	1.038 542	5
6	1.047 336	1.047 150	1.046 785	1.046 250	1.046 250	6
7	1.055 441	1.055 222	1.054 854	1.054 315	1.053 958	7
8	1.063 608	1.063 356	1.062 923	1.062 380	1.061 667	8
9	1.071 838	1.071 553	1.070 992	1.070 445	1.069 375	9
10	1.080 132	1.079 813	1.079 247	1.078 509	1.077 083	10
11	1.088 490	1.088 136	1.087 503	1.086 574	1.084 792	11

Years						Years
1	1.096 913	1.096 524	1.095 758	1.094 639	1.092 500	1
2	1.203 218	1.202 365	1.200 686	1.198 235	1.193 556	2
3	1.319 826	1.318 422	1.315 662	1.311 634	1.303 960	3
4	1.447 735	1.445 682	1.441 648	1.435 766	1.424 577	4
5	1.588 039	1.585 225	1.579 698	1.571 646	1.556 350	5
6	1.741 941	1.738 238	1.730 967	1.720 385	1.700 312	6
7	1.910 758	1.906 020	1.896 721	1.883 201	1.857 591	7
8	2.095 936	2.089 997	2.078 348	2.061 425	2.029 418	8
9	2.299 059	2.291 732	2.277 367	2.256 516	2.217 139	9
10	2.521 868	2.512 939	2.495 444	2.470 071	2.422 225	10
11	2.766 270	2.755 499	2.734 404	2.703 836	2.646 281	11
12	3.034 358	3.021 471	2.996 246	2.959 725	2.891 062	12
13	3.328 428	3.313 116	3.283 161	3.239 830	3.158 485	13
14	3.650 996	3.632 911	3.597 551	3.546 445	3.450 645	14
15	4.004 825	3.983 575	3.942 047	3.882 077	3.769 829	15
16	4.392 946	4.368 086	4.319 531	4.249 473	4.118 539	16
17	4.818 680	4.789 712	4.733 162	4.651 639	4.499 503	17
18	5.285 673	5.252 035	5.186 402	5.091 866	4.915 707	18
19	5.797 924	5.758 983	5.683 043	5.573 755	5.370 410	19
20	6.359 820	6.314 864	6.227 242	6.101 250	5.867 173	20
21	6.976 170	6.924 401	6.823 552	6.678 667	6.409 887	21
22	7.652 252	7.592 773	7.476 964	7.310 730	7.002 801	22
23	8.393 856	8.325 659	8.192 946	8.002 610	7.650 560	23
24	9.207 331	9.129 286	8.977 489	8.759 970	8.358 237	24
25	10.099 642	10.010 482	9.837 159	9.589 005	9.131 374	25
26	11.078 430	10.976 736	10.779 149	10.496 500	9.976 026	26
27	12.152 076	12.036 256	11.811 342	11.489 878	10.898 809	27
28	13.329 772	13.198 045	12.942 377	12.577 270	11.906 949	28
29	14.621 602	14.471 975	14.181 717	13.767 571	13.008 341	29
30	16.038 627	15.868 870	15.539 735	15.070 521	14.211 613	30
31	17.592 981	17.400 599	17.027 794	16.496 781	15.526 187	31
32	19.297 972	19.080 177	18.658 348	18.058 021	16.962 359	32
33	21.168 199	20.921 875	20.445 040	19.767 015	18.531 378	33
34	23.219 675	22.941 341	22.402 824	21.637 746	20.245 530	34
35	25.469 967	25.155 735	24.548 081	23.685 523	22.118 242	35
36	27.938 342	27.583 871	26.898 765	25.927 098	24.164 179	36
37	30.645 934	30.246 380	29.474 546	28.380 814	26.399 365	37
38	33.615 928	33.165 886	32.296 979	31.066 748	28.841 307	38
39	36.873 753	36.367 195	35.389 685	34.006 876	31.509 128	39
40	40.447 304	39.877 508	38.778 542	37.225 255	34.423 722	40

COMPOUND INTEREST

(Future Value of $1)

9½%

Base:	2.718 282	1.007 917	1.023 750	1.047 500	1.095 000	
			Frequency of Conversion			
Months	Continuous	Monthly	Quarterly	Semiannual	Annual	Months
0	1.000 000	1.000 000	1.000 000	1.000 000	1.000 000	0
1	1.007 948	1.007 917	1.007 917	1.007 917	1.007 917	1
2	1.015 959	1.015 896	1.015 833	1.015 833	1.015 833	2
3	1.024 034	1.023 939	1.023 750	1.023 750	1.023 750	3
4	1.032 173	1.032 045	1.031 855	1.031 667	1.031 667	4
5	1.040 377	1.040 215	1.039 959	1.039 583	1.039 583	5
6	1.048 646	1.048 450	1.048 064	1.047 500	1.047 500	6
7	1.056 981	1.056 750	1.056 361	1.055 793	1.055 417	7
8	1.065 382	1.065 116	1.064 658	1.064 085	1.063 333	8
9	1.073 850	1.073 548	1.072 956	1.072 378	1.071 250	9
10	1.082 385	1.082 047	1.081 450	1.080 671	1.079 167	10
11	1.090 988	1.090 614	1.089 944	1.088 964	1.087 083	11
Years						Years
1	1.099 659	1.099 248	1.098 438	1.097 256	1.095 000	1
2	1.209 250	1.208 345	1.206 567	1.203 971	1.199 025	2
3	1.329 762	1.328 271	1.325 339	1.321 065	1.312 932	3
4	1.462 285	1.460 098	1.455 803	1.449 547	1.437 661	4
5	1.608 014	1.605 009	1.599 110	1.590 524	1.574 239	5
6	1.768 267	1.764 303	1.756 523	1.745 213	1.723 791	6
7	1.944 491	1.939 406	1.929 433	1.914 946	1.887 552	7
8	2.138 276	2.131 887	2.119 363	2.101 186	2.066 869	8
9	2.351 374	2.343 472	2.327 989	2.305 540	2.263 222	9
10	2.585 710	2.576 055	2.557 152	2.529 768	2.478 228	10
11	2.843 399	2.831 723	2.808 874	2.775 803	2.713 659	11
12	3.126 768	3.112 764	3.085 375	3.045 768	2.971 457	12
13	3.438 379	3.421 699	3.389 094	3.341 988	3.253 745	13
14	3.781 043	3.761 294	3.722 710	3.667 017	3.562 851	14
15	4.157 858	4.134 593	4.089 167	4.023 657	3.901 322	15
16	4.572 225	4.544 942	4.491 698	4.414 983	4.271 948	16
17	5.027 888	4.996 016	4.933 853	4.844 367	4.677 783	17
18	5.528 961	5.491 859	5.419 533	5.315 512	5.122 172	18
19	6.079 971	6.036 912	5.953 022	5.832 479	5.608 778	19
20	6.685 894	6.636 061	6.539 028	6.399 724	6.141 612	20
21	7.352 203	7.294 674	7.182 718	7.022 137	6.725 065	21
22	8.084 915	8.018 653	7.889 773	7.705 084	7.363 946	22
23	8.890 649	8.814 485	8.666 429	8.454 452	8.063 521	23
24	9.776 680	9.689 302	9.519 537	9.276 700	8.829 556	24
25	10.751 013	10.650 941	10.456 624	10.178 917	9.668 364	25
26	11.822 447	11.708 022	11.485 956	11.168 881	10.586 858	26
27	13.000 658	12.870 014	12.616 613	12.255 124	11.592 610	27
28	14.296 289	14.147 332	13.858 571	13.447 011	12.693 908	28
29	15.721 041	15.551 421	15.222 785	14.754 817	13.899 829	29
30	17.287 782	17.094 862	16.721 290	16.189 815	15.220 313	30
31	19.010 662	18.791 486	18.367 305	17.764 376	16.666 242	31
32	20.905 243	20.656 495	20.175 351	19.492 073	18.249 535	32
33	22.988 636	22.706 602	22.161 377	21.387 799	19.983 241	33
34	25.279 657	24.960 178	24.342 905	23.467 896	21.881 649	34
35	27.798 999	27.437 415	26.739 179	25.750 295	23.960 406	35
36	30.569 415	30.160 512	29.371 338	28.254 673	26.236 644	36
37	33.615 928	33.153 870	32.262 602	31.002 616	28.729 126	37
38	36.966 053	36.444 312	35.438 477	34.017 814	31.458 393	38
39	40.650 047	40.061 322	38.926 979	37.326 259	34.446 940	39
40	44.701 184	44.037 311	42.758 884	40.956 471	37.719 399	40

9¾%

COMPOUND INTEREST
(Future Value of $1)

Base:	2.718 282	1.008 125	1.024 375	1.048 750	1.097 500	
			Frequency of Conversion			
Months	Continuous	Monthly	Quarterly	Semiannual	Annual	Months
0	1.000 000	1.000 000	1.000 000	1.000 000	1.000 000	0
1	1.008 158	1.008 125	1.008 125	1.008 125	1.008 125	1
2	1.016 383	1.016 316	1.016 250	1.016 250	1.016 250	2
3	1.024 674	1.024 574	1.024 375	1.024 375	1.024 375	3
4	1.033 034	1.032 898	1.032 698	1.032 500	1.032 500	4
5	1.041 461	1.041 291	1.041 021	1.040 625	1.040 625	5
6	1.049 958	1.049 751	1.049 344	1.048 750	1.048 750	6
7	1.058 523	1.058 280	1.057 870	1.057 271	1.056 875	7
8	1.067 159	1.066 879	1.066 396	1.065 792	1.065 000	8
9	1.075 865	1.075 547	1.074 922	1.074 313	1.073 125	9
10	1.084 642	1.084 286	1.083 656	1.082 834	1.081 250	10
11	1.093 491	1.093 096	1.092 389	1.091 355	1.089 375	11

Years						Years
1	1.102 411	1.101 977	1.101 123	1.099 877	1.097 500	1
2	1.215 311	1.214 354	1.212 472	1.209 728	1.204 506	2
3	1.339 773	1.338 190	1.335 081	1.330 552	1.321 946	3
4	1.476 981	1.474 655	1.470 089	1.463 443	1.450 835	4
5	1.628 241	1.625 036	1.618 749	1.609 607	1.592 292	5
6	1.794 991	1.790 753	1.782 442	1.770 369	1.747 540	6
7	1.978 819	1.973 369	1.962 688	1.947 187	1.917 925	7
8	2.181 472	2.174 608	2.161 161	2.141 665	2.104 923	8
9	2.404 880	2.396 368	2.379 704	2.355 567	2.310 153	9
10	2.651 167	2.640 743	2.620 347	2.590 833	2.535 393	10
11	2.922 677	2.910 039	2.885 325	2.849 597	2.782 594	11
12	3.221 993	3.206 797	3.177 098	3.134 205	3.053 897	12
13	3.551 962	3.533 817	3.498 376	3.447 238	3.351 652	13
14	3.915 723	3.894 185	3.852 143	3.791 537	3.678 438	14
15	4.316 738	4.291 304	4.241 683	4.170 222	4.037 085	15
16	4.758 821	4.728 919	4.670 616	4.586 730	4.430 701	16
17	5.246 179	5.211 161	5.142 923	5.044 837	4.862 695	17
18	5.783 448	5.742 581	5.662 991	5.548 698	5.336 807	18
19	6.375 739	6.328 193	6.235 651	6.102 882	5.857 146	19
20	7.028 688	6.973 525	6.866 219	6.712 417	6.428 218	20
21	7.748 506	7.684 665	7.560 553	7.382 831	7.054 969	21
22	8.542 041	8.468 326	8.325 100	8.120 202	7.742 828	22
23	9.416 844	9.331 902	9.166 960	8.931 220	8.497 754	23
24	10.381 237	10.283 544	10.093 951	9.823 240	9.326 285	24
25	11.444 394	11.332 231	11.114 683	10.804 351	10.235 598	25
26	12.616 431	12.487 860	12.238 635	11.883 453	11.233 569	26
27	13.908 498	13.761 338	13.476 244	13.070 331	12.328 842	27
28	15.332 887	15.164 681	14.839 004	14.375 751	13.530 904	28
29	16.903 150	16.711 133	16.339 570	15.811 551	14.850 167	29
30	18.634 226	18.415 288	17.991 879	17.390 755	16.298 058	30
31	20.542 584	20.293 227	19.811 273	19.127 684	17.887 119	31
32	22.646 380	22.362 674	21.814 651	21.038 091	19.631 113	32
33	24.965 628	24.643 158	24.020 617	23.139 303	21.545 147	33
34	27.522 394	27.156 198	26.449 657	25.450 377	23.645 798	34
35	30.341 002	29.925 512	29.124 329	27.992 273	25.951 264	35
36	33.448 268	32.977 232	32.069 472	30.788 045	28.481 512	36
37	36.873 753	36.340 159	35.312 437	33.863 049	31.258 459	37
38	40.650 047	40.046 027	38.883 341	37.245 174	34.306 159	38
39	44.813 077	44.129 810	42.815 346	40.965 094	37.651 010	39
40	49.402 449	48.630 045	47.144 968	45.056 547	41.321 983	40

COMPOUND INTEREST

(Future Value of $1)

10%

Base:	2.718 282	1.008 333	1.025 000	1.050 000	1.100 000	
			Frequency of Conversion			
Months	Continuous	Monthly	Quarterly	Semiannual	Annual	Months
0	1.000 000	1.000 000	1.000 000	1.000 000	1.000 000	0
1	1.008 368	1.008 333	1.008 333	1.008 333	1.008 333	1
2	1.016 806	1.016 736	1.016 667	1.016 667	1.016 667	2
3	1.025 315	1.025 209	1.025 000	1.025 000	1.025 000	3
4	1.033 895	1.033 752	1.033 542	1.033 333	1.033 333	4
5	1.042 547	1.042 367	1.042 083	1.041 667	1.041 667	5
6	1.051 271	1.051 053	1.050 625	1.050 000	1.050 000	6
7	1.060 068	1.059 812	1.059 380	1.058 750	1.058 333	7
8	1.068 939	1.068 644	1.068 135	1.067 500	1.066 667	8
9	1.077 884	1.077 549	1.076 891	1.076 250	1.075 000	9
10	1.086 904	1.086 529	1.085 865	1.085 000	1.083 333	10
11	1.095 999	1.095 583	1.094 839	1.093 750	1.091 667	11
Years						Years
1	1.105 171	1.104 713	1.103 813	1.102 500	1.100 000	1
2	1.221 403	1.220 391	1.218 403	1.215 506	1.210 000	2
3	1.349 859	1.348 182	1.344 889	1.340 096	1.331 000	3
4	1.491 825	1.489 354	1.484 506	1.477 455	1.464 100	4
5	1.648 721	1.645 309	1.638 616	1.628 895	1.610 510	5
6	1.822 119	1.817 594	1.808 726	1.795 856	1.771 561	6
7	2.013 753	2.007 920	1.996 495	1.979 932	1.948 717	7
8	2.225 541	2.218 176	2.203 757	2.182 875	2.143 589	8
9	2.459 603	2.450 448	2.432 535	2.406 619	2.357 948	9
10	2.718 282	2.707 041	2.685 064	2.653 298	2.593 742	10
11	3.004 166	2.990 504	2.963 808	2.925 261	2.853 117	11
12	3.320 117	3.303 649	3.271 490	3.225 100	3.138 428	12
13	3.669 297	3.649 584	3.611 112	3.555 673	3.452 271	13
14	4.055 200	4.031 743	3.985 992	3.920 129	3.797 498	14
15	4.481 689	4.453 920	4.399 790	4.321 942	4.177 248	15
16	4.953 032	4.920 303	4.856 545	4.764 941	4.594 973	16
17	5.473 947	5.435 523	5.360 717	5.253 348	5.054 470	17
18	6.049 647	6.004 693	5.917 228	5.791 816	5.559 917	18
19	6.685 894	6.633 463	6.531 513	6.385 477	6.115 909	19
20	7.389 056	7.328 074	7.209 568	7.039 989	6.727 500	20
21	8.166 170	8.095 419	7.958 014	7.761 588	7.400 250	21
22	9.025 013	8.943 115	8.784 158	8.557 150	8.140 275	22
23	9.974 182	9.879 576	9.696 067	9.434 258	8.954 302	23
24	11.023 176	10.914 097	10.702 644	10.401 270	9.849 733	24
25	12.182 494	12.056 945	11.813 716	11.467 400	10.834 706	25
26	13.463 738	13.319 465	13.040 132	12.642 808	11.918 177	26
27	14.879 732	14.714 187	14.393 866	13.938 696	13.109 994	27
28	16.444 647	16.254 954	15.888 135	15.367 412	14.420 994	28
29	18.174 145	17.957 060	17.537 528	16.942 572	15.863 093	29
30	20.085 537	19.837 399	19.358 150	18.679 186	17.449 402	30
31	22.197 951	21.914 634	21.367 775	20.593 802	19.194 342	31
32	24.532 530	24.209 383	23.586 026	22.704 667	21.113 777	32
33	27.112 639	26.744 422	26.034 559	25.031 896	23.225 154	33
34	29.964 100	29.544 912	28.737 282	27.597 665	25.547 670	34
35	33.115 452	32.638 650	31.720 583	30.426 426	28.102 437	35
36	36.598 234	36.056 344	35.013 588	33.545 134	30.912 681	36
37	40.447 304	39.831 914	38.648 450	36.983 510	34.003 949	37
38	44.701 184	44.002 836	42.660 657	40.774 320	37.404 343	38
39	49.402 449	48.610 508	47.089 383	44.953 688	41.144 778	39
40	54.598 150	53.700 663	51.977 868	49.561 441	45.259 256	40

10¼%

COMPOUND INTEREST
(Future Value of $1)

Base: 2.718 282   1.008 542   1.025 625   1.051 250   1.102 500

Frequency of Conversion

Months	Continuous	Monthly	Quarterly	Semiannual	Annual	Months
0	1.000 000	1.000 000	1.000 000	1.000 000	1.000 000	0
1	1.008 578	1.008 542	1.008 542	1.008 542	1.008 542	1
2	1.017 230	1.017 156	1.017 083	1.017 083	1.017 083	2
3	1.025 956	1.025 845	1.025 625	1.025 625	1.025 625	3
4	1.034 757	1.034 607	1.034 386	1.034 167	1.034 167	4
5	1.043 633	1.043 444	1.043 146	1.042 708	1.042 708	5
6	1.052 586	1.052 357	1.051 907	1.051 250	1.051 250	6
7	1.061 615	1.061 346	1.060 892	1.060 229	1.059 792	7
8	1.070 722	1.070 411	1.069 877	1.069 209	1.068 333	8
9	1.079 907	1.079 555	1.078 862	1.078 188	1.076 875	9
10	1.089 171	1.088 776	1.088 077	1.087 168	1.085 417	10
11	1.098 514	1.098 076	1.097 292	1.096 147	1.093 958	11

Years						Years
1	1.107 937	1.107 455	1.106 508	1.105 127	1.102 500	1
2	1.227 525	1.226 457	1.224 359	1.221 305	1.215 506	2
3	1.360 021	1.358 246	1.354 763	1.349 696	1.340 096	3
4	1.506 818	1.504 196	1.499 055	1.491 585	1.477 455	4
5	1.669 460	1.665 830	1.658 716	1.648 390	1.628 895	5
6	1.849 657	1.844 832	1.835 382	1.821 680	1.795 856	6
7	2.049 304	2.043 069	2.030 864	2.013 187	1.979 932	7
8	2.270 500	2.262 607	2.247 166	2.224 826	2.182 875	8
9	2.515 571	2.505 736	2.486 506	2.458 715	2.406 619	9
10	2.787 095	2.774 990	2.751 338	2.717 191	2.653 298	10
11	3.087 927	3.073 177	3.044 376	3.002 840	2.925 261	11
12	3.421 230	3.403 406	3.368 625	3.318 518	3.225 100	12
13	3.790 508	3.769 119	3.727 410	3.667 383	3.555 673	13
14	4.199 645	4.174 130	4.124 407	4.052 922	3.920 129	14
15	4.652 943	4.622 662	4.563 688	4.478 992	4.321 942	15
16	5.155 170	5.119 391	5.049 755	4.949 853	4.764 941	16
17	5.711 605	5.669 496	5.587 592	5.470 214	5.253 348	17
18	6.328 100	6.278 712	6.182 713	6.045 279	5.791 816	18
19	7.011 138	6.953 392	6.841 219	6.680 798	6.385 471	19
20	7.767 901	7.700 570	7.569 860	7.383 127	7.039 989	20
21	8.606 347	8.528 036	8.376 108	8.159 290	7.761 588	21
22	9.535 293	9.444 417	9.268 227	9.017 048	8.557 150	22
23	10.564 507	10.459 268	10.255 363	9.964 979	9.434 258	23
24	11.704 812	11.583 170	11.347 637	11.012 563	10.401 270	24
25	12.968 197	12.827 841	12.556 247	12.170 276	11.467 400	25
26	14.367 950	14.206 259	13.893 582	13.449 696	12.642 808	26
27	15.918 787	15.732 794	15.373 354	14.863 616	13.938 696	27
28	17.637 018	17.423 364	17.010 733	16.426 177	15.367 412	28
29	19.540 710	19.295 594	18.822 505	18.153 004	16.942 572	29
30	21.649 882	21.369 005	20.827 244	20.061 367	18.679 186	30
31	23.986 712	23.665 214	23.045 504	22.170 350	20.593 802	31
32	26.575 773	26.208 163	25.500 024	24.501 042	22.704 667	32
33	29.444 290	29.024 365	28.215 970	27.076 753	25.031 896	33
34	32.622 427	32.143 182	31.221 185	29.923 239	27.597 665	34
35	36.143 604	35 597 132	34.546 478	33.068 966	30.426 426	35
36	40.044 847	39.422 227	38.225 940	36.545 393	33.545 134	36
37	44.367 180	43.658 348	42.297 292	40.387 284	36.983 510	37
38	49.156 053	48.349 662	46.802 274	44.633 061	40.774 320	38
39	54.461 825	53.545 082	51.787 071	49.325 181	44.953 688	39
40	60.340 288	59.298 776	57.302 787	54.510 568	49.561 441	40

COMPOUND INTEREST

(Future Value of $1)

10½%

Base:	2.718 282	1.008 750	1.026 250	1.052 500	1.105 000	

Frequency of Conversion

Months	Continuous	Monthly	Quarterly	Semiannual	Annual	Months
0	1.000 000	1.000 000	1.000 000	1.000 000	1.000 000	0
1	1.008 788	1.008 750	1.008 750	1.008 750	1.008 750	1
2	1.017 654	1.017 577	1.017 500	1.017 500	1.017 500	2
3	1.026 598	1.026 480	1.026 250	1.026 250	1.026 250	3
4	1.035 620	1.035 462	1.035 230	1.035 000	1.035 000	4
5	1.044 721	1.044 522	1.044 209	1.043 750	1.043 750	5
6	1.053 903	1.053 662	1.053 189	1.052 500	1.052 500	6
7	1.063 165	1.062 881	1.062 404	1.061 709	1.061 250	7
8	1.072 508	1.072 182	1.071 620	1.070 919	1.070 000	8
9	1.081 934	1.081 563	1.080 835	1.080 128	1.078 750	9
10	1.091 442	1.091 027	1.090 293	1.089 338	1.087 500	10
11	1.101 034	1.100 573	1.099 750	1.098 547	1.096 250	11

Years						Years
1	1.110 711	1.110 203	1.109 207	1.107 756	1.105 000	1
2	1.233 678	1.232 552	1.230 341	1.227 124	1.221 025	2
3	1.370 259	1.368 383	1.364 703	1.359 354	1.349 233	3
4	1.521 962	1.519 184	1.513 738	1.505 833	1.490 902	4
5	1.690 459	1.686 603	1.679 049	1.668 096	1.647 447	5
6	1.877 611	1.872 472	1.862 413	1.847 844	1.820 429	6
7	2.085 482	2.078 825	2.065 802	2.046 961	2.011 574	7
8	2.316 367	2.307 919	2.291 403	2.267 533	2.222 789	8
9	2.572 813	2.562 260	2.541 641	2.511 874	2.456 182	9
10	2.857 651	2.844 630	2.819 206	2.782 544	2.714 081	10
11	3.174 023	3.158 118	3.127 084	3.082 381	2.999 059	11
12	3.525 421	3.506 153	3.468 584	3.414 527	3.313 961	12
13	3.915 723	3.892 543	3.847 378	3.782 463	3.661 926	13
14	4.349 235	4.321 515	4.267 539	4.190 047	4.046 429	14
15	4.830 742	4.797 761	4.733 585	4.641 551	4.471 304	15
16	5.365 556	5.326 491	5.250 527	5.141 707	4.940 791	16
17	5.959 580	5.913 488	5.823 922	5.695 758	5.459 574	17
18	6.619 369	6.565 175	6.459 937	6.309 512	6.032 829	18
19	7.352 203	7.288 680	7.165 408	6.989 401	6.666 276	19
20	8.166 170	8.091 918	7.947 922	7.742 553	7.366 235	20
21	9.070 252	8.983 675	8.815 893	8.576 861	8.139 690	21
22	10.074 425	9.973 707	9.778 652	9.501 072	8.994 357	22
23	11.189 770	11.072 844	10.846 551	10.524 872	9.938 764	23
24	12.428 597	12.293 109	12.031 072	11.658 992	10.982 335	24
25	13.804 574	13.647 852	13.344 952	12.915 322	12.135 480	25
26	15.332 887	15.151 893	14.802 317	14.307 028	13.409 705	26
27	17.030 400	16.821 684	16.418 836	15.848 700	14.817 724	27
28	18.915 846	18.675 491	18.211 892	17.556 496	16.373 585	28
29	21.010 031	20.733 595	20.200 761	19.448 319	18.092 812	29
30	23.336 065	23.018 509	22.406 830	21.543 997	19.992 557	30
31	25.919 615	25.555 228	24.853 817	23.865 497	22.091 775	31
32	28.789 191	28.371 502	27.568 033	26.437 153	24.411 412	32
33	31.976 460	31.498 139	30.578 660	29.285 922	26.974 610	33
34	35.516 593	34.969 343	33.918 070	32.441 663	29.806 944	34
35	39.448 657	38.823 085	37.622 168	35.937 455	32.936 673	35
36	43.816 042	43.101 523	41.730 780	39.809 940	36.395 024	36
37	48.666 942	47.851 460	46.288 081	44.099 710	40.216 501	37
38	54.054 889	53.124 856	51.343 073	48.851 729	44.439 234	38
39	60.039 339	58.979 398	56.950 106	54.115 809	49.105 354	39
40	66.686 331	65.479 132	63.169 468	59.947 125	54.261 416	40

10¾%

COMPOUND INTEREST
(Future Value of $1)

Base:	2.718 282	1.008 958	1.026 875	1.053 750	1.107 500	

Frequency of Conversion

Months	Continuous	Monthly	Quarterly	Semiannual	Annual	Months
0	1.000 000	1.000 000	1.000 000	1.000 000	1.000 000	0
1	1.008 999	1.008 958	1.008 958	1.008 958	1.008 958	1
2	1.018 078	1.017 997	1.017 917	1.017 917	1.017 917	2
3	1.027 239	1.027 116	1.026 875	1.026 875	1.026 875	3
4	1.036 483	1.036 318	1.036 074	1.035 833	1.035 833	4
5	1.045 810	1.045 601	1.045 273	1.044 792	1.044 792	5
6	1.055 221	1.054 968	1.054 472	1.053 750	1.053 750	6
7	1.064 716	1.064 419	1.063 919	1.063 190	1.062 708	7
8	1.074 297	1.073 954	1.073 365	1.072 630	1.071 667	8
9	1.083 964	1.083 575	1.082 811	1.082 070	1.080 625	9
10	1.093 718	1.093 282	1.092 511	1.091 509	1.089 583	10
11	1.103 560	1.103 076	1.102 212	1.100 949	1.098 542	11

Years						Years
1	1.113 491	1.112 958	1.111 912	1.110 389	1.107 500	1
2	1.239 862	1.238 676	1.236 348	1.232 964	1.226 556	2
3	1.380 575	1.378 594	1.374 710	1.369 070	1.358 411	3
4	1.537 258	1.534 317	1.528 556	1.520 200	1.504 440	4
5	1.711 722	1.707 630	1.699 619	1.688 013	1.666 168	5
6	1.905 987	1.900 521	1.889 827	1.874 352	1.845 281	6
7	2.122 299	2.115 200	2.101 320	2.081 259	2.043 648	7
8	2.363 161	2.354 129	2.336 483	2.311 008	2.263 340	8
9	2.631 358	2.620 047	2.597 963	2.566 118	2.506 650	9
10	2.929 993	2.916 002	2.888 705	2.849 389	2.776 114	10
11	3.262 520	3.245 388	3.211 985	3.163 930	3.074 547	11
12	3.632 787	3.611 980	3.571 444	3.513 194	3.405 060	12
13	4.045 075	4.019 982	3.971 131	3.901 012	3.771 104	13
14	4.504 154	4.474 072	4.415 547	4.331 641	4.176 498	14
15	5.015 334	4.979 454	4.909 699	4.809 807	4.625 472	15
16	5.584 528	5.541 923	5.459 152	5.340 757	5.122 710	16
17	6.218 321	6.167 928	6.070 095	5.930 318	5.673 401	17
18	6.924 044	6.864 644	6.749 410	6.584 960	6.283 292	18
19	7.709 860	7.640 061	7.504 748	7.311 868	6.958 746	19
20	8.584 858	8.503 067	8.344 618	8.119 018	7.706 811	20
21	9.559 161	9.463 557	9.278 479	9.015 269	8.535 293	21
22	10.644 039	10.532 541	10.316 850	10.010 456	9.452 837	22
23	11.852 040	11.722 276	11.471 427	11.115 501	10.469 017	23
24	13.197 138	13.046 401	12.755 214	12.342 530	11.594 436	24
25	14.694 893	14.520 096	14.182 673	13.705 011	12.840 838	25
26	16.362 629	16.160 258	15.769 880	15.217 894	14.221 228	26
27	18.219 638	17.985 688	17.534 716	16.897 783	15.750 010	27
28	20.287 400	20.017 316	19.497 056	18.767 114	17.443 136	28
29	22.589 834	22.278 432	21.679 006	20.834 356	19.318 274	29
30	25.153 574	24.794 959	24.105 142	23.134 241	21.394 988	30
31	28.008 275	27.595 749	26.802 791	25.688 008	23.694 949	31
32	31.186 958	30.712 910	29.802 338	28.523 683	26.242 156	32
33	34.726 393	34.182 179	33.137 570	31.672 386	29.063 188	33
34	38.667 521	38.043 330	36.846 054	35.168 671	32.187 481	34
35	43.055 931	42.340 629	40.969 561	39.050 908	35.647 635	35
36	47.942 386	47.123 342	45.554 536	43.361 701	39.479 756	36
37	53.383 409	52.446 301	50.652 625	48.148 358	43.723 829	37
38	59.441 938	58.370 531	56.321 249	53.463 411	48.424 141	38
39	66.188 054	64.963 950	62.624 259	59.365 186	53.629 736	39
40	73.699 794	72.302 148	69.632 650	65.918 454	59.394 933	40

(Future Value of $1)

Base:	2.718 282	1.009 167	1.027 500	1.055 000	1.110 000	
			Frequency of Conversion			
Months	Continuous	Monthly	Quarterly	Semiannual	Annual	Months
0	1.000 000	1.000 000	1.000 000	1.000 000	1.000 000	0
1	1.009 209	1.009 167	1.009 167	1.009 167	1.009 167	1
2	1.018 502	1.018 417	1.018 333	1.018 333	1.018 333	2
3	1.027 882	1.027 753	1.027 500	1.027 500	1.027 500	3
4	1.037 347	1.037 174	1.036 919	1.036 667	1.036 667	4
5	1.046 900	1.046 681	1.046 337	1.045 833	1.045 833	5
6	1.056 541	1.056 276	1.055 756	1.055 000	1.055 000	6
7	1.066 270	1.065 958	1.065 434	1.064 671	1.064 167	7
8	1.076 089	1.075 730	1.075 112	1.074 342	1.073 333	8
9	1.085 999	1.085 591	1.084 790	1.084 013	1.082 500	9
10	1.095 999	1.095 542	1.094 733	1.093 683	1.091 667	10
11	1.106 092	1.105 584	1.104 677	1.103 354	1.100 833	11

Years						Years
1	1.116 278	1.115 719	1.114 621	1.113 025	1.110 000	1
2	1.246 077	1.244 829	1.242 381	1.238 825	1.232 100	2
3	1.390 968	1.388 879	1.384 784	1.378 843	1.367 631	3
4	1.552 707	1.549 598	1.543 509	1.534 687	1.518 070	4
5	1.733 253	1.728 916	1.720 428	1.708 144	1.685 058	5
6	1.934 792	1.928 984	1.917 626	1.901 207	1.870 415	6
7	2.159 766	2.152 204	2.137 427	2.116 091	2.076 160	7
8	2.410 900	2.401 254	2.382 421	2.355 263	2.304 538	8
9	2.691 234	2.679 124	2.655 498	2.621 466	2.558 037	9
10	3.004 166	2.989 150	2.959 874	2.917 757	2.839 421	10
11	3.353 485	3.335 051	3.299 138	3.247 537	3.151 757	11
12	3.743 421	3.720 979	3.677 290	3.614 590	3.498 451	12
13	4.178 699	4.151 566	4.098 785	4.023 129	3.883 280	13
14	4.664 590	4.631 980	4.568 593	4.477 843	4.310 441	14
15	5.206 980	5.167 988	5.092 251	4.983 951	4.784 589	15
16	5.812 437	5.766 021	5.675 932	5.547 262	5.310 894	16
17	6.488 296	6.433 259	6.326 514	6.174 242	5.895 093	17
18	7.242 743	7.177 708	7.051 667	6.872 085	6.543 553	18
19	8.084 915	8.008 304	7.859 938	7.648 803	7.263 344	19
20	9.025 013	8.935 015	8.760 854	8.513 309	8.062 312	20
21	10.074 425	9.968 965	9.765 034	9.475 525	8.949 166	21
22	11.245 859	11.122 562	10.884 315	10.546 497	9.933 574	22
23	12.553 506	12.409 652	12.131 889	11.738 515	11.026 267	23
24	14.013 204	13.845 682	13.522 461	13.065 260	12.239 157	24
25	15.642 632	15.447 889	15.072 422	14.541 961	13.585 464	25
26	17.461 527	17.235 500	16.800 042	16.185 566	15.079 865	26
27	19.491 920	19.229 972	18.725 684	18.014 940	16.738 650	27
28	21.758 402	21.455 242	20.872 046	20.051 079	18.579 901	28
29	24.288 427	23.938 018	23.264 426	22.317 352	20.623 691	29
30	27.112 639	26.708 098	25.931 024	24.839 770	22.892 297	30
31	30.265 244	29.798 728	28.903 271	27.647 285	25.410 449	31
32	33.784 428	33.247 002	32.216 200	30.772 120	28.205 599	32
33	37.712 817	37.094 306	35.908 861	34.250 139	31.308 214	33
34	42.097 990	41.386 816	40.024 780	38.121 261	34.752 118	34
35	46.993 063	46.176 050	44.612 471	42.429 916	38.574 851	35
36	52.457 326	51.519 489	49.726 008	47.225 558	42.818 085	36
37	58.556 963	57.481 264	55.425 666	52.563 226	47.528 074	37
38	65.365 853	64.132 929	61.778 626	58.504 185	52.756 162	38
39	72.966 468	71.554 317	68.859 770	65.116 620	58.559 340	39
40	81.450 869	79.834 499	76.752 563	72.476 426	65.000 867	40

11¼%

COMPOUND INTEREST
(Future Value of $1)

Base:	2.718 282	1.009 375	1.028 125	1.056 250	1.112 500	

Frequency of Conversion

Months	Continuous	Monthly	Quarterly	Semiannual	Annual	Months
0	1.000 000	1.000 000	1.000 000	1.000 000	1.000 000	0
1	1.009 419	1.009 375	1.009 375	1.009 375	1.009 375	1
2	1.018 927	1.018 838	1.018 750	1.018 750	1.018 750	2
3	1.028 524	1.028 389	1.028 125	1.028 125	1.028 125	3
4	1.038 212	1.038 031	1.037 764	1.037 500	1.037 500	4
5	1.047 991	1.047 762	1.047 402	1.046 875	1.046 875	5
6	1.057 862	1.057 585	1.057 041	1.056 250	1.056 250	6
7	1.067 826	1.067 500	1.066 951	1.066 152	1.065 625	7
8	1.077 884	1.077 508	1.076 861	1.076 055	1.075 000	8
9	1.088 037	1.087 609	1.086 770	1.085 957	1.084 375	9
10	1.098 285	1.097 806	1.096 959	1.095 859	1.093 750	10
11	1.108 630	1.108 098	1.107 147	1.105 762	1.103 125	11

Years						Years
1	1.119 072	1.118 486	1.117 336	1.115 664	1.112 500	1
2	1.252 323	1.251 011	1.248 439	1.244 706	1.237 656	2
3	1.401 440	1.399 238	1.394 926	1.388 674	1.376 893	3
4	1.568 312	1.565 028	1.558 600	1.549 294	1.531 793	4
5	1.755 055	1.750 462	1.741 480	1.728 491	1.704 120	5
6	1.964 033	1.957 867	1.945 817	1.928 416	1.895 833	6
7	2.197 895	2.189 847	2.174 131	2.151 464	2.109 114	7
8	2.459 603	2.449 313	2.429 234	2.400 311	2.346 390	8
9	2.752 474	2.739 522	2.714 270	2.677 941	2.610 359	9
10	3.080 217	3.064 117	3.032 751	2.987 682	2.904 024	10
11	3.446 985	3.427 171	3.388 601	3.333 250	3.230 727	11
12	3.857 426	3.833 243	3.786 205	3.718 787	3.594 183	12
13	4.316 738	4.287 428	4.230 462	4.148 917	3.998 529	13
14	4.830 742	4.795 428	4.726 847	4.628 798	4.448 364	14
15	5.405 949	5.363 619	5.281 474	5.164 183	4.948 804	15
16	6.049 647	5.999 132	5.901 180	5.761 494	5.505 545	16
17	6.769 993	6.709 945	6.593 599	6.427 892	6.124 919	17
18	7.576 111	7.504 979	7.367 264	7.171 368	6.813 972	18
19	8.478 216	8.394 214	8.231 707	8.000 837	7.580 544	19
20	9.487 736	9.388 810	9.197 580	8.926 247	8.433 355	20
21	10.617 462	10.501 252	10.276 784	9.958 692	9.382 108	21
22	11.881 707	11.745 503	11.482 618	11.110 555	10.437 595	22
23	13.296 489	13.137 180	12.829 939	12.395 647	11.611 824	23
24	14.879 732	14.693 751	14.335 349	13.829 378	12.918 154	24
25	16.651 495	16.434 754	16.017 398	15.428 940	14.371 447	25
26	18.634 226	18.382 041	17.896 811	17.213 514	15.988 235	26
27	20.853 045	20.560 054	19.996 746	19.204 499	17.786 911	27
28	23.336 065	22.996 132	22.343 078	21.425 770	19.787 938	28
29	26.114 742	25.720 850	24.964 719	23.903 961	22.014 081	29
30	29.224 284	28.768 409	27.893 972	26.668 790	24.490 666	30
31	32.704 085	32.177 061	31.166 931	29.753 411	27.245 866	31
32	36.598 234	35.989 590	34.823 925	33.194 811	30.311 025	32
33	40.956 069	40.253 850	38.910 014	37.034 258	33.721 016	33
34	45.832 800	45.023 366	43.475 548	41.317 791	37.514 630	34
35	51.290 215	50.358 001	48.576 783	46.096 774	41.735 026	35
36	57.397 457	56.324 716	54.276 574	51.428 515	46.430 216	36
37	64.231 902	62.998 403	60.645 154	57.376 946	51.653 616	37
38	71.880 139	70.462 828	67.760 996	64.013 396	57.464 647	38
39	80.439 070	78.811 682	75.711 781	71.417 446	63.929 420	39
40	90.017 131	88.149 758	84.595 476	79.677 878	71.121 480	40

COMPOUND INTEREST
(Future Value of $1)

Base:	2.718 282	1.009 583	1.028 750	1.057 500	1.115 000	
			Frequency of Conversion			
Months	Continuous	Monthly	Quarterly	Semiannual	Annual	Months
0	1.000 000	1.000 000	1.000 000	1.000 000	1.000 000	0
1	1.009 629	1.009 583	1.009 583	1.009 583	1.009 583	1
2	1.019 352	1.019 259	1.019 167	1.019 167	1.019 167	2
3	1.029 167	1.029 026	1.028 750	1.028 750	1.028 750	3
4	1.039 078	1.038 888	1.038 609	1.038 333	1.038 333	4
5	1.049 083	1.048 844	1.048 468	1.047 917	1.047 917	5
6	1.059 185	1.058 895	1.058 327	1.057 500	1.057 500	6
7	1.069 385	1.069 043	1.068 469	1.067 634	1.067 083	7
8	1.079 682	1.079 288	1.078 611	1.077 769	1.076 667	8
9	1.090 079	1.089 631	1.088 753	1.087 903	1.086 250	9
10	1.100 576	1.100 074	1.099 187	1.098 037	1.095 833	10
11	1.111 174	1.110 616	1.109 621	1.108 172	1.105 417	11

Years						Years
1	1.121 873	1.121 259	1.120 055	1.118 306	1.115 000	1
2	1.258 600	1.257 222	1.254 523	1.250 609	1.243 225	2
3	1.411 990	1.409 672	1.405 135	1.398 564	1.386 196	3
4	1.584 074	1.580 608	1.573 829	1.564 023	1.545 608	4
5	1.777 131	1.772 272	1.762 775	1.749 056	1.723 353	5
6	1.993 716	1.987 176	1.974 406	1.955 980	1.921 539	6
7	2.236 696	2.228 140	2.211 443	2.187 385	2.142 516	7
8	2.509 290	2.498 323	2.476 938	2.446 167	2.388 905	8
9	2.815 106	2.801 268	2.774 307	2.735 563	2.663 629	9
10	3.158 193	3.140 948	3.107 377	3.059 198	2.969 947	10
11	3.543 093	3.521 817	3.480 433	3.421 120	3.311 491	11
12	3.974 902	3.948 870	3.898 277	3.825 860	3.692 312	12
13	4.459 337	4.427 707	4.366 285	4.278 483	4.116 928	13
14	5.002 811	4.964 608	4.890 480	4.784 654	4.590 375	14
15	5.612 521	5.566 613	5.477 607	5.350 708	5.118 268	15
16	6.296 538	6.241 617	6.135 222	5.983 731	5.706 869	16
17	7.063 919	6.998 471	6.871 787	6.691 643	6.363 159	17
18	7.924 823	7.847 101	7.696 780	7.483 307	7.094 922	18
19	8.890 649	8.798 635	8.620 818	8.368 629	7.910 838	19
20	9.974 182	9.865 552	9.655 791	9.358 690	8.820 584	20
21	11.189 770	11.061 842	10.815 018	10.465 881	9.834 951	21
22	12.553 506	12.403 194	12.113 416	11.704 060	10.965 971	22
23	14.083 445	13.907 196	13.567 694	13.088 724	12.227 057	23
24	15.799 843	15.593 574	15.196 565	14.637 201	13.633 169	24
25	17.725 424	17.484 440	17.020 990	16.368 874	15.200 983	25
26	19.885 682	19.604 591	19.064 447	18.305 414	16.949 096	26
27	22.309 219	21.981 831	21.353 231	20.471 059	18.898 243	27
28	25.028 120	24.647 333	23.916 796	22.892 913	21.071 540	28
29	28.078 383	27.636 052	26.788 130	25.601 288	23.494 768	29
30	31.500 392	30.987 181	30.004 182	28.630 080	26.196 666	30
31	35.339 453	34.744 666	33.606 337	32.017 197	29.209 282	31
32	39.646 394	38.957 781	37.640 950	35.805 032	32.568 350	32
33	44.478 236	43.681 775	42.159 938	40.040 991	36.313 710	33
34	49.898 952	48.978 598	47.221 454	44.778 091	40.489 787	34
35	55.980 309	54.917 710	52.890 631	50.075 619	45.146 112	35
36	62.802 821	61.576 995	59.240 422	55.999 877	50.337 915	36
37	70.456 817	69.043 780	66.352 538	62.625 013	56.126 776	37
38	79.043 632	77.415 982	74.318 499	70.033 943	62.581 355	38
39	88.676 951	86.803 392	83.240 815	78.319 396	69.778 211	39
40	99.484 316	97.329 113	93.234 300	87.585 070	77.802 705	40

11¾%

COMPOUND INTEREST
(Future Value of $1)

Base:	2.718 282	1.009 792	1.029 375	1.058 750	1.117 500	
			Frequency of Conversion			
Months	Continuous	Monthly	Quarterly	Semiannual	Annual	Months
0	1.000 000	1.000 000	1.000 000	1.000 000	1.000 000	0
1	1.009 840	1.009 792	1.009 792	1.009 792	1.009 792	1
2	1.019 776	1.019 679	1.019 583	1.019 583	1.019 583	2
3	1.029 811	1.029 664	1.029 375	1.029 375	1.029 375	3
4	1.039 944	1.039 746	1.039 454	1.039 167	1.039 167	4
5	1.050 177	1.049 927	1.049 534	1.048 958	1.048 958	5
6	1.060 510	1.060 207	1.059 613	1.058 750	1.058 750	6
7	1.070 945	1.070 588	1.069 988	1.069 117	1.068 542	7
8	1.081 483	1.081 071	1.080 364	1.079 484	1.078 333	8
9	1.092 125	1.091 657	1.090 739	1.089 851	1.088 125	9
10	1.102 871	1.102 346	1.101 419	1.100 218	1.097 917	10
11	1.113 723	1.113 140	1.112 099	1.110 585	1.107 708	11

Years						Years
1	1.124 682	1.124 039	1.122 779	1.120 952	1.117 500	1
2	1.264 909	1.263 464	1.260 634	1.256 532	1.248 806	2
3	1.422 620	1.420 183	1.415 414	1.408 512	1.395 541	3
4	1.599 994	1.596 341	1.589 197	1.578 874	1.559 517	4
5	1.799 484	1.794 349	1.784 318	1.769 841	1.742 760	5
6	2.023 847	2.016 918	2.003 396	1.983 906	1.947 535	6
7	2.276 183	2.267 095	2.249 372	2.223 862	2.176 370	7
8	2.559 981	2.548 303	2.525 549	2.492 842	2.432 093	8
9	2.879 164	2.864 392	2.835 634	2.794 355	2.717 864	9
10	3.238 143	3.219 689	3.183 792	3.132 337	3.037 213	10
11	3.641 880	3.619 056	3.574 696	3.511 198	3.394 086	11
12	4.095 955	4.067 960	4.013 595	3.935 883	3.792 891	12
13	4.606 646	4.572 546	4.506 383	4.411 934	4.238 556	13
14	5.181 010	5.139 720	5.059 674	4.945 564	4.736 586	14
15	5.826 987	5.777 245	5.680 898	5.543 738	5.293 135	15
16	6.553 505	6.493 849	6.378 396	6.214 262	5.915 078	16
17	7.370 607	7.299 340	7.161 532	6.965 886	6.610 100	17
18	8.289 586	8.204 743	8.040 821	7.808 421	7.386 787	18
19	9.323 145	9.222 451	9.028 069	8.752 862	8.254 734	19
20	10.485 570	10.366 395	10.136 530	9.811 534	9.224 666	20
21	11.792 928	11.652 233	11.381 088	10.998 255	10.308 564	21
22	13.263 289	13.097 564	12.778 452	12.328 511	11.519 820	22
23	14.916 978	14.722 173	14.347 384	13.819 664	12.873 399	23
24	16.776 851	16.548 297	16.108 948	15.491 174	14.386 023	24
25	18.868 616	18.600 932	18.086 796	17.364 855	16.076 381	25
26	21.221 186	20.908 173	20.307 484	19.465 162	17.965 356	26
27	23.867 078	23.501 603	22.800 826	21.819 503	20.076 285	27
28	26.842 864	26.416 719	25.600 300	24.458 606	22.435 249	28
29	30.189 676	29.693 422	28.743 491	27.416 913	25.071 391	29
30	33.953 774	33.376 565	32.272 602	30.733 031	28.017 279	30
31	38.187 185	37.516 562	36.235 015	34.450 240	31.309 309	31
32	42.948 426	42.170 080	40.683 931	38.617 050	34.988 153	32
33	48.303 306	47.400 815	45.679 083	43.287 842	39.099 261	33
34	54.325 841	53.280 366	51.287 537	48.523 575	43.693 424	34
35	61.099 275	59.889 210	57.584 594	54.392 577	48.827 402	35
36	68.717 232	67.317 809	64.654 801	60.971 444	54.564 621	36
37	77.285 009	75.667 844	72.593 083	68.346 035	60.975 964	37
38	86.921 030	85.053 610	81.506 024	76.612 595	68.140 640	38
39	97.758 485	95.603 576	91.513 292	85.879 008	76.147 165	39
40	109.947 172	107.462 150	102.749 246	96.266 208	85.094 457	40

62

COMPOUND INTEREST

(Future Value of $1)

12%

Frequency of Conversion

Months	Continuous	Monthly	Quarterly	Semiannual	Annual	Months
0	1.000 000	1.000 000	1.000 000	1.000 000	1.000 000	0
1	1.010 050	1.010 000	1.010 000	1.010 000	1.010 000	1
2	1.020 201	1.020 100	1.020 000	1.020 000	1.020 000	2
3	1.030 455	1.030 301	1.030 000	1.030 000	1.030 000	3
4	1.040 811	1.040 604	1.040 300	1.040 000	1.040 000	4
5	1.051 271	1.051 010	1.050 600	1.050 000	1.050 000	5
6	1.061 837	1.061 520	1.060 900	1.060 000	1.060 000	6
7	1.072 508	1.072 135	1.071 509	1.070 600	1.070 000	7
8	1.083 287	1.082 857	1.082 118	1.081 200	1.080 000	8
9	1.094 174	1.093 685	1.092 727	1.091 800	1.090 000	9
10	1.105 171	1.104 622	1.103 654	1.102 400	1.100 000	10
11	1.116 278	1.115 668	1.114 582	1.113 000	1.110 000	11

Years						Years
1	1.127 497	1.126 825	1.125 509	1.123 600	1.120 000	1
2	1.271 249	1.269 735	1.266 770	1.262 477	1.254 400	2
3	1.433 329	1.430 769	1.425 761	1.418 519	1.404 928	3
4	1.616 074	1.612 226	1.604 706	1.593 848	1.573 519	4
5	1.822 119	1.816 697	1.806 111	1.790 848	1.762 342	5
6	2.054 433	2.047 099	2.032 794	2.012 196	1.973 823	6
7	2.316 367	2.306 723	2.287 928	2.260 904	2.210 681	7
8	2.611 696	2.599 273	2.575 083	2.540 352	2.475 963	8
9	2.944 680	2.928 926	2.898 278	2.854 339	2.773 079	9
10	3.320 117	3.300 387	3.262 038	3.207 135	3.105 848	10
11	3.743 421	3.718 959	3.671 452	3.603 537	3.478 550	11
12	4.220 696	4.190 616	4.132 252	4.048 935	3.895 976	12
13	4.758 821	4.722 091	4.650 886	4.549 383	4.363 493	13
14	5.365 556	5.320 970	5.234 613	5.111 687	4.887 112	14
15	6.049 647	5.995 802	5.891 603	5.743 491	5.473 566	15
16	6.820 958	6.756 220	6.631 051	6.453 387	6.130 394	16
17	7.690 609	7.613 078	7.463 307	7.251 025	6.866 041	17
18	8.671 138	8.578 606	8.400 017	8.147 252	7.689 966	18
19	9.776 680	9.666 588	9.454 293	9.154 252	8.612 762	19
20	11.023 176	10.892 554	10.640 891	10.285 718	9.646 293	20
21	12.428 597	12.274 002	11.976 416	11.557 033	10.803 848	21
22	14.013 204	13.830 653	13.479 562	12.985 482	12.100 310	22
23	15.799 843	15.584 726	15.171 366	14.590 487	13.552 347	23
24	17.814 273	17.561 259	17.075 506	16.393 872	15.178 629	24
25	20.085 537	19.788 466	19.218 632	18.420 154	17.000 064	25
26	22.646 380	22.298 139	21.630 740	20.696 885	19.040 072	26
27	25.533 722	25.126 101	24.345 588	23.255 020	21.324 881	27
28	28.789 191	28.312 720	27.401 174	26.129 341	23.883 866	28
29	32.459 722	31.903 481	30.840 262	29.358 927	26.749 930	29
30	36.598 234	35.949 641	34.710 987	32.987 691	29.959 922	30
31	41.264 394	40.508 956	39.067 522	37.064 969	33.555 113	31
32	46.525 474	45.646 505	43.970 840	41.646 200	37.581 726	32
33	52.457 326	51.435 625	49.489 568	46.793 670	42.091 533	33
34	59.145 470	57.958 949	55.700 945	52.577 368	47.142 517	34
35	66.686 331	65.309 595	62.691 904	59.075 930	52.799 620	35
36	75.188 628	73.592 486	70.560 290	66.377 715	59.135 574	36
37	84.774 942	82.925 855	79.416 228	74.582 001	66.231 843	37
38	95.583 480	93.442 929	89.383 664	83.800 336	74.179 664	38
39	107.770 073	105.293 832	100.602 102	94.158 058	83.081 224	39
40	121.510 418	118.647 725	113.228 552	105.795 993	93.050 970	40

12½%

COMPOUND INTEREST
(Future Value of $1)

Base: 2.718 282 1.010 417 1.031 250 1.062 500 1.125 000

Frequency of Conversion

Months	Continuous	Monthly	Quarterly	Semiannual	Annual	Months
0	1.000 000	1.000 000	1.000 000	1.000 000	1.000 000	0
1	1.010 471	1.010 417	1.010 417	1.010 417	1.010 417	1
2	1.021 052	1.020 942	1.020 833	1.020 833	1.020 833	2
3	1.031 743	1.031 577	1.031 250	1.031 250	1.031 250	3
4	1.042 547	1.042 322	1.041 992	1.041 667	1.041 667	4
5	1.053 464	1.053 180	1.052 734	1.052 083	1.052 083	5
6	1.064 494	1.064 150	1.063 477	1.062 500	1.062 500	6
7	1.075 641	1.075 235	1.074 554	1.073 568	1.072 917	7
8	1.086 904	1.086 436	1.085 632	1.084 635	1.083 333	8
9	1.098 285	1.097 753	1.096 710	1.095 703	1.093 750	9
10	1.109 785	1.109 188	1.108 134	1.106 771	1.104 167	10
11	1.121 406	1.120 742	1.119 558	1.117 839	1.114 583	11

Years	Continuous	Monthly	Quarterly	Semiannual	Annual	Years
1	1.133 148	1.132 416	1.130 982	1.128 906	1.125 000	1
2	1.284 025	1.282 366	1.279 121	1.274 429	1.265 625	2
3	1.454 991	1.452 172	1.446 664	1.438 711	1.423 828	3
4	1.648 721	1.644 463	1.636 151	1.624 170	1.601 807	4
5	1.868 246	1.862 216	1.850 458	1.833 536	1.802 032	5
6	2.117 000	2.108 803	2.092 835	2.069 890	2.027 287	6
7	2.398 875	2.388 043	2.366 960	2.336 712	2.280 697	7
8	2.718 282	2.704 258	2.676 990	2.637 928	2.565 785	8
9	3.080 217	3.062 345	3.027 629	2.977 974	2.886 508	9
10	3.490 343	3.467 849	3.424 195	3.361 853	3.247 321	10
11	3.955 077	3.927 048	3.872 704	3.795 217	3.653 236	11
12	4.481 689	4.447 052	4.379 960	4.284 445	4.109 891	12
13	5.078 419	5.035 913	4.953 658	4.836 736	4.623 627	13
14	5.754 603	5.702 748	5.602 500	5.460 222	5.201 580	14
15	6.520 819	6.457 884	6.336 329	6.164 079	5.851 778	15
16	7.389 056	7.313 011	7.166 276	6.958 667	6.583 250	16
17	8.372 897	8.281 371	8.104 932	7.855 682	7.406 156	17
18	9.487 736	9.377 958	9.166 536	8.868 329	8.331 926	18
19	10.751 013	10.619 750	10.367 190	10.011 512	9.373 417	19
20	12.182 494	12.025 975	11.725 110	11.302 058	10.545 094	20
21	13.804 574	13.618 407	13.260 893	12.758 964	11.863 231	21
22	15.642 632	15.421 703	14.997 837	14.403 675	13.346 134	22
23	17.725 424	17.463 783	16.962 289	16.260 398	15.014 401	23
24	20.085 537	19.776 269	19.184 051	18.356 465	16.891 201	24
25	22.759 895	22.394 964	21.696 823	20.722 728	19.002 602	25
26	25.790 340	25.360 417	24.538 725	23.394 018	21.377 927	26
27	29.224 284	28.718 543	27.752 867	26.409 653	24.050 168	27
28	33.115 452	32.521 339	31.388 004	29.814 022	27.056 438	28
29	37.524 723	36.827 686	35.499 280	33.657 236	30.438 493	29
30	42.521 082	41.704 262	40.149 060	37.995 864	34.243 305	30
31	48.182 698	47.226 576	45.407 881	42.893 768	38.523 718	31
32	54.598 150	53.480 132	51.355 514	48.423 043	43.339 183	32
33	61.867 809	60.561 760	58.082 182	54.665 076	48.756 581	33
34	70.105 412	68.581 108	65.689 926	61.711 746	54.851 153	34
35	79.439 840	77.662 348	74.294 150	69.666 776	61.707 547	35
36	90.017 131	87.946 089	84.025 376	78.647 258	69.420 991	36
37	102.002 773	99.591 562	95.031 221	88.785 382	78.098 615	37
38	115.584 285	112.779 083	107.478 639	100.230 372	87.860 942	38
39	130.974 153	127.712 843	121.556 449	113.150 694	98.843 559	39
40	148.413 159	144.624 073	137.478 204	127.736 525	111.199 004	40

COMPOUND INTEREST

13%

(Future Value of $1)

Base:	2.718 282	1.010 833	1.032 500	1.065 000	1.130 000	

Frequency of Conversion

Months	Continuous	Monthly	Quarterly	Semiannual	Annual	Months
0	1.000 000	1.000 000	1.000 000	1.000 000	1.000 000	0
1	1.010 892	1.010 833	1.010 833	1.010 833	1.010 833	1
2	1.021 903	1.021 784	1.021 667	1.021 667	1.021 667	2
3	1.033 034	1.032 853	1.032 500	1.032 500	1.032 500	3
4	1.044 286	1.044 043	1.043 685	1.043 333	1.043 333	4
5	1.055 661	1.055 353	1.054 871	1.054 167	1.054 167	5
6	1.067 159	1.066 786	1.066 056	1.065 000	1.065 000	6
7	1.078 783	1.078 343	1.077 605	1.076 537	1.075 833	7
8	1.090 533	1.090 025	1.089 154	1.088 075	1.086 667	8
9	1.102 411	1.101 834	1.100 703	1.099 613	1.097 500	9
10	1.114 419	1.113 770	1.112 627	1.111 150	1.108 333	10
11	1.126 558	1.125 836	1.124 552	1.122 688	1.119 167	11

Years						Years
1	1.138 828	1.138 032	1.136 476	1.134 225	1.130 000	1
2	1.296 930	1.295 118	1.291 578	1.286 466	1.276 900	2
3	1.476 981	1.473 886	1.467 847	1.459 142	1.442 897	3
4	1.682 028	1.677 330	1.668 173	1.654 996	1.630 474	4
5	1.915 541	1.908 857	1.895 838	1.877 137	1.842 435	5
6	2.181 472	2.172 341	2.154 574	2.129 096	2.081 952	6
7	2.484 323	2.472 194	2.448 622	2.414 874	2.352 605	7
8	2.829 217	2.813 437	2.782 800	2.739 011	2.658 444	8
9	3.221 993	3.201 783	3.162 585	3.106 654	3.004 042	9
10	3.669 297	3.643 733	3.594 201	3.523 645	3.394 567	10
11	4.178 699	4.146 687	4.084 723	3.996 606	3.835 861	11
12	4.758 821	4.719 064	4.642 190	4.533 051	4.334 523	12
13	5.419 481	5.370 448	5.275 737	5.141 500	4.898 011	13
14	6.171 858	6.111 745	5.995 748	5.831 617	5.534 753	14
15	7.028 688	6.955 364	6.814 023	6.614 366	6.254 270	15
16	8.004 469	7.915 430	7.743 974	7.502 179	7.067 326	16
17	9.115 716	9.008 017	8.800 840	8.509 159	7.986 078	17
18	10.381 237	10.251 416	10.001 942	9.651 301	9.024 268	18
19	11.822 447	11.666 444	11.366 967	10.946 747	10.197 423	19
20	13.463 738	13.276 792	12.918 284	12.416 075	11.523 088	20
21	15.332 887	15.109 421	14.681 319	14.082 622	13.021 089	21
22	17.461 527	17.195 012	16.684 965	15.972 862	14.713 831	22
23	19.885 682	19.568 482	18.962 061	18.116 820	16.626 629	23
24	22.646 380	22.269 568	21.549 926	20.548 550	18.788 091	24
25	25.790 340	25.343 491	24.490 973	23.306 679	21.230 542	25
26	29.370 771	28.841 716	27.833 401	26.435 018	23.990 513	26
27	33.448 268	32.822 810	31.631 990	29.983 258	27.109 279	27
28	38.091 837	37.353 424	35.948 995	34.007 761	30.633 486	28
29	43.380 065	42.509 410	40.855 168	38.572 452	34.615 839	29
30	49.402 449	48.377 089	46.430 915	43.749 840	39.115 898	30
31	56.260 911	55.054 699	52.767 617	49.622 162	44.200 965	31
32	64.071 523	62.654 036	59.969 126	56.282 697	49.947 090	32
33	72.966 468	71.302 328	68.153 469	63.837 242	56.440 212	33
34	83.096 285	81.144 365	77.454 776	72.405 795	63.777 439	34
35	94.632 408	92.344 923	88.025 489	82.124 463	72.068 506	35
36	107.770 073	105.091 522	100.038 849	93.147 619	81.437 412	36
37	122.731 618	119.597 566	113.691 744	105.650 359	92.024 276	37
38	139.770 250	136.105 914	129.207 930	119.831 278	103.987 432	38
39	159.174 327	154.892 951	146.841 703	135.915 631	117.505 798	39
40	181.272 242	176.273 210	166.882 060	154.158 907	132.781 552	40

13½%

COMPOUND INTEREST
(Future Value of $1)

Base: 2.718 282   1.011 250   1.033 750   1.067 500   1.135 000

Frequency of Conversion

Months	Continuous	Monthly	Quarterly	Semiannual	Annual	Months
0	1.000 000	1.000 000	1.000 000	1.000 000	1.000 000	0
1	1.011 314	1.011 250	1.011 250	1.011 250	1.011 250	1
2	1.022 755	1.022 627	1.022 500	1.022 500	1.022 500	2
3	1.034 326	1.034 131	1.033 750	1.033 750	1.033 750	3
4	1.046 028	1.045 765	1.045 380	1.045 000	1.045 000	4
5	1.057 862	1.057 530	1.057 009	1.056 250	1.056 250	5
6	1.069 830	1.069 427	1.068 639	1.067 500	1.067 500	6
7	1.081 934	1.081 458	1.080 661	1.079 509	1.078 750	7
8	1.094 174	1.093 625	1.092 683	1.091 519	1.090 000	8
9	1.106 553	1.105 928	1.104 706	1.103 528	1.101 250	9
10	1.119 072	1.118 370	1.117 134	1.115 538	1.112 500	10
11	1.131 733	1.130 951	1.129 562	1.127 547	1.123 750	11

Years						Years
1	1.144 537	1.143 674	1.141 989	1.139 556	1.135 000	1
2	1.309 964	1.307 991	1.304 140	1.298 588	1.288 225	2
3	1.499 303	1.495 916	1.489 314	1.479 815	1.462 135	3
4	1.716 007	1.710 841	1.700 781	1.686 332	1.659 524	4
5	1.964 033	1.956 645	1.942 274	1.921 670	1.883 559	5
6	2.247 908	2.237 765	2.218 056	2.189 851	2.137 840	6
7	2.572 813	2.559 275	2.532 997	2.495 459	2.426 448	7
8	2.944 680	2.926 977	2.892 656	2.843 715	2.754 019	8
9	3.370 294	3.347 509	3.303 382	3.240 574	3.125 811	9
10	3.857 426	3.828 460	3.772 428	3.692 816	3.547 796	10
11	4.414 965	4.378 512	4.308 072	4.208 172	4.026 748	11
12	5.053 090	5.007 593	4.919 773	4.795 448	4.570 359	12
13	5.783 448	5.727 056	5.618 329	5.464 683	5.187 358	13
14	6.619 369	6.549 887	6.416 073	6.227 314	5.887 651	14
15	7.576 111	7.490 939	7.327 087	7.096 374	6.682 484	15
16	8.671 138	8.567 195	8.367 456	8.086 718	7.584 619	16
17	9.924 436	9.798 082	9.555 547	9.215 270	8.608 543	17
18	11.358 882	11.205 816	10.912 333	10.501 318	9.770 696	18
19	13.000 658	12.815 805	12.461 770	11.966 843	11.089 740	19
20	14.879 732	14.657 109	14.231 209	13.636 890	12.586 855	20
21	17.030 400	16.762 961	16.251 891	15.540 004	14.286 080	21
22	19.491 920	19.171 370	18.559 488	17.708 708	16.214 701	22
23	22.309 219	21.925 805	21.194 739	20.180 069	18.403 686	23
24	25.533 722	25.075 983	24.204 168	22.996 324	20.888 184	24
25	29.224 284	28.678 761	27.640 905	26.205 605	23.708 088	25
26	33.448 268	32.799 166	31.565 622	29.862 761	26.908 680	26
27	38.282 773	37.511 568	36.047 607	34.030 295	30.541 352	27
28	43.816 042	42.901 021	41.165 986	38.779 436	34.664 435	28
29	50.149 072	49.064 802	47.011 122	44.191 349	39.344 133	29
30	57.397 457	56.114 160	53.686 205	50.358 527	44.655 591	30
31	65.693 501	64.176 330	61.309 080	57.386 375	50.684 096	31
32	75.188 628	73.396 828	70.014 322	65.395 002	57.526 449	32
33	86.056 151	83.942 077	79.955 617	74.521 283	65.292 520	33
34	98.494 430	96.002 408	91.308 471	84.921 194	74.107 010	34
35	112.730 498	109.795 500	104.273 310	96.772 477	84.111 457	35
36	129.024 202	125.570 307	119.079 019	110.277 681	95.466 503	36
37	147.672 945	143.611 551	135.986 983	125.667 621	108.354 481	37
38	169.017 118	164.244 860	155.295 699	143.205 323	122.982 336	38
39	193.446 309	187.842 648	177.346 050	163.190 521	139.584 951	39
40	221.406 416	214.830 836	202.527 317	185.964 778	158.428 920	40

(Future Value of $1)

Base:	2.718 282	1.011 667	1.035 000	1.070 000	1.140 000	
			Frequency of Conversion			
Months	Continuous	Monthly	Quarterly	Semiannual	Annual	Months
0	1.000 000	1.000 000	1.000 000	1.000 000	1.000 000	0
1	1.011 735	1.011 667	1.011 667	1.011 667	1.011 667	1
2	1.023 608	1.023 469	1.023 333	1.023 333	1.023 333	2
3	1.035 620	1.035 410	1.035 000	1.035 000	1.035 000	3
4	1.047 773	1.047 490	1.047 075	1.046 667	1.046 667	4
5	1.060 068	1.059 710	1.059 150	1.058 333	1.058 333	5
6	1.072 508	1.072 074	1.071 225	1.070 000	1.070 000	6
7	1.085 094	1.084 581	1.083 723	1.082 483	1.081 667	7
8	1.097 828	1.097 235	1.096 220	1.094 967	1.093 333	8
9	1.110 711	1.110 036	1.108 718	1.107 450	1.105 000	9
10	1.123 745	1.122 986	1.121 653	1.119 933	1.116 667	10
11	1.136 932	1.136 088	1.134 588	1.132 417	1.128 333	11

Years						Years
1	1.150 274	1.149 342	1.147 523	1.144 900	1.140 000	1
2	1.323 130	1.320 987	1.316 809	1.310 796	1.299 600	2
3	1.521 962	1.518 266	1.511 069	1.500 730	1.481 544	3
4	1.750 673	1.745 007	1.733 986	1.718 186	1.688 960	4
5	2.013 753	2.005 610	1.989 789	1.967 151	1.925 415	5
6	2.316 367	2.305 132	2.283 328	2.252 192	2.194 973	6
7	2.664 456	2.649 385	2.620 172	2.578 534	2.502 269	7
8	3.064 854	3.045 049	3.006 708	2.952 164	2.852 586	8
9	3.525 421	3.499 803	3.450 266	3.379 932	3.251 949	9
10	4.055 200	4.022 471	3.959 260	3.869 684	3.707 221	10
11	4.664 590	4.623 195	4.543 342	4.430 402	4.226 232	11
12	5.365 556	5.313 632	5.213 589	5.072 367	4.817 905	12
13	6.171 858	6.107 180	5.982 713	5.807 353	5.492 411	13
14	7.099 327	7.019 239	6.865 301	6.648 838	6.261 349	14
15	8.166 170	8.067 507	7.878 091	7.612 255	7.137 938	15
16	9.393 331	9.272 324	9.040 291	8.715 271	8.137 249	16
17	10.804 903	10.657 072	10.373 941	9.978 114	9.276 464	17
18	12.428 597	12.248 621	11.904 336	11.423 942	10.575 169	18
19	14.296 289	14.077 855	13.660 500	13.079 271	12.055 693	19
20	16.444 647	16.180 270	15.675 738	14.974 458	13.743 490	20
21	18.915 846	18.596 664	17.988 269	17.144 257	15.667 578	21
22	21.758 402	21.373 928	20.641 953	19.628 460	17.861 039	22
23	25.028 120	24.565 954	23.687 116	22.472 623	20.361 585	23
24	28.789 191	28.234 683	27.181 510	25.728 907	23.212 207	24
25	33.115 452	32.451 308	31.191 408	29.457 025	26.461 916	25
26	38.091 837	37.297 652	35.792 858	33.725 348	30.166 584	26
27	43.816 042	42.867 759	41.073 128	38.612 151	34.389 906	27
28	50.400 445	49.269 718	47.132 359	44.207 052	39.204 493	28
29	57.974 311	56.627 757	54.085 466	50.612 653	44.693 122	29
30	66.686 331	65.084 661	62.064 316	57.946 427	50.950 159	30
31	76.707 539	74.804 537	71.220 230	66.342 864	58.083 181	31
32	88.234 673	85.975 998	81.726 852	75.955 945	66.214 826	32
33	101.494 032	98.815 828	93.783 443	86.961 962	75.484 902	33
34	116.745 926	113.573 184	107.618 658	99.562 750	86.052 788	34
35	134.289 780	130.534 434	123.494 885	113.989 392	98.100 178	35
36	154.470 015	150.028 711	141.713 221	130.506 455	111.834 203	36
37	177.682 811	172.434 303	162.619 181	149.416 840	127.490 992	37
38	204.383 882	198.185 992	186.609 250	171.067 341	145.339 731	38
39	235.097 424	227.783 490	214.138 407	195.854 998	165.687 293	39
40	270.426 407	261.801 139	245.728 747	224.234 388	188.883 514	40

14½%

COMPOUND INTEREST
(Future Value of $1)

Base: 2.718 282   1.012 083   1.036 250   1.072 500   1.145 000

Frequency of Conversion

Months	Continuous	Monthly	Quarterly	Semiannual	Annual	Months
0	1.000 000	1.000 000	1.000 000	1.000 000	1.000 000	0
1	1.012 157	1.012 083	1.012 083	1.012 083	1.012 083	1
2	1.024 461	1.024 313	1.024 167	1.024 167	1.024 167	2
3	1.036 915	1.036 690	1.036 250	1.036 250	1.036 250	3
4	1.049 520	1.049 216	1.048 771	1.048 333	1.048 333	4
5	1.062 279	1.061 894	1.061 293	1.060 417	1.060 417	5
6	1.075 193	1.074 726	1.073 814	1.072 500	1.072 500	6
7	1.088 264	1.087 712	1.086 789	1.085 459	1.084 583	7
8	1.101 493	1.100 855	1.099 765	1.098 419	1.096 667	8
9	1.114 884	1.114 157	1.112 740	1.111 378	1.108 750	9
10	1.128 437	1.127 620	1.126 185	1.124 337	1.120 833	10
11	1.142 155	1.141 245	1.139 631	1.137 297	1.132 917	11

Years						Years
1	1.156 040	1.155 035	1.153 077	1.150 256	1.145 000	1
2	1.336 427	1.334 107	1.329 586	1.323 089	1.311 025	2
3	1.544 963	1.540 940	1.533 114	1.521 892	1.501 124	3
4	1.786 038	1.779 841	1.767 798	1.750 566	1.718 787	4
5	2.064 731	2.055 779	2.038 407	2.013 599	1.968 011	5
6	2.386 911	2.374 497	2.350 439	2.316 155	2.253 372	6
7	2.759 363	2.742 628	2.710 237	2.664 172	2.580 111	7
8	3.189 933	3.167 833	3.125 111	3.064 480	2.954 227	8
9	3.687 689	3.658 959	3.603 492	3.524 937	3.382 590	9
10	4.263 115	4.226 227	4.155 103	4.054 581	3.873 066	10
11	4.928 329	4.881 441	4.791 152	4.663 808	4.434 660	11
12	5.697 343	5.638 237	5.524 565	5.364 574	5.077 686	12
13	6.586 354	6.512 363	6.370 247	6.170 634	5.813 950	13
14	7.614 086	7.522 010	7.345 383	7.097 811	6.656 973	14
15	8.802 185	8.688 187	8.469 789	8.164 301	7.622 234	15
16	10.175 674	10.035 163	9.766 316	9.391 039	8.727 458	16
17	11.763 482	11.590 968	11.261 311	10.802 101	9.992 940	17
18	13.599 051	13.387 978	12.985 155	12.425 184	11.441 916	18
19	15.721 041	15.463 588	14.972 879	14.292 146	13.100 994	19
20	18.174 145	17.860 991	17.264 877	16.439 630	15.000 638	20
21	21.010 031	20.630 076	19.907 726	18.909 787	17.175 731	21
22	24.288 427	23.828 467	22.955 134	21.751 101	19.666 212	22
23	28.078 383	27.522 721	26.469 029	25.019 339	22.517 812	23
24	32.459 722	31.789 716	30.520 819	28.778 652	25.782 895	24
25	37.524 723	36.718 246	35.192 843	33.102 824	29.521 415	25
26	43.380 065	42.410 872	40.580 046	38.076 730	33.802 020	26
27	50.149 072	48.986 057	46.791 903	43.797 997	38.703 313	27
28	57.974 311	56.580 627	53.954 650	50.378 919	44.315 293	28
29	67.020 598	65.352 625	62.213 846	57.948 667	50.741 011	29
30	77.478 463	75.484 592	71.737 333	66.655 816	58.098 457	30
31	89.568 169	87.187 373	82.718 643	76.671 269	66.522 734	31
32	103.544 348	100.704 498	95.380 935	88.191 607	76.168 530	32
33	119.701 363	116.317 255	109.981 528	101.442 947	87.212 967	33
34	138.379 512	134.350 542	126.817 131	116.685 384	99.858 847	34
35	159.972 192	155.179 625	146.229 871	134.218 092	114.338 380	35
36	184.934 184	179.237 953	168.614 249	154.385 199	130.917 445	36
37	213.791 235	207.026 173	194.425 152	177.582 540	149.900 474	37
38	247.151 127	239.122 549	224.187 101	204.265 426	171.636 043	38
39	285.716 483	276.194 997	258.504 909	234.957 583	196.523 269	39
40	330.299 560	319.014 986	298.075 972	270.261 429	225.019 143	40

68

COMPOUND INTEREST

(Future Value of $1)

Base:	2.718 282	1.012 500	1.037 500	1.075 000	1.150 000	
			Frequency of Conversion			
Months	Continuous	Monthly	Quarterly	Semiannual	Annual	Months
0	1.000 000	1.000 000	1.000 000	1.000 000	1.000 000	0
1	1.012 578	1.012 500	1.012 500	1.012 500	1.012 500	1
2	1.025 315	1.025 156	1.025 000	1.025 000	1.025 000	2
3	1.038 212	1.037 971	1.037 500	1.037 500	1.037 500	3
4	1.051 271	1.050 945	1.050 469	1.050 000	1.050 000	4
5	1.064 494	1.064 082	1.063 437	1.062 500	1.062 500	5
6	1.077 884	1.077 383	1.076 406	1.075 000	1.075 000	6
7	1.091 442	1.090 850	1.089 861	1.088 438	1.087 500	7
8	1.105 171	1.104 486	1.103 316	1.101 875	1.100 000	8
9	1.119 072	1.118 292	1.116 771	1.115 313	1.112 500	9
10	1.133 148	1.132 271	1.130 731	1.128 750	1.125 000	10
11	1.147 402	1.146 424	1.144 691	1.142 188	1.137 500	11
Years						Years
1	1.161 834	1.160 755	1.158 650	1.155 625	1.150 000	1
2	1.349 859	1.347 351	1.342 471	1.335 469	1.322 500	2
3	1.568 312	1.563 944	1.555 454	1.543 302	1.520 875	3
4	1.822 119	1.815 355	1.802 228	1.783 478	1.749 006	4
5	2.117 000	2.107 181	2.088 152	2.061 032	2.011 357	5
6	2.459 603	2.445 920	2.419 438	2.381 780	2.313 061	6
7	2.857 651	2.839 113	2.803 283	2.752 444	2.660 020	7
8	3.320 117	3.295 513	3.248 025	3.180 793	3.059 023	8
9	3.857 426	3.825 282	3.763 326	3.675 804	3.517 876	9
10	4.481 689	4.440 213	4.360 379	4.247 851	4.045 558	10
11	5.206 980	5.153 998	5.052 155	4.908 923	4.652 391	11
12	6.049 647	5.982 526	5.853 681	5.672 874	5.350 250	12
13	7.028 688	6.944 244	6.782 370	6.555 715	6.152 788	13
14	8.166 170	8.060 563	7.858 396	7.575 948	7.075 706	14
15	9.487 736	9.356 334	9.105 134	8.754 955	8.137 062	15
16	11.023 176	10.860 408	10.549 667	10.117 445	9.357 621	16
17	12.807 104	12.606 267	12.223 376	11.691 972	10.761 264	17
18	14.879 732	14.632 781	14.162 620	13.511 536	12.375 454	18
19	17.287 782	16.985 067	16.409 525	15.614 268	14.231 772	19
20	20.085 537	19.715 494	19.012 903	18.044 239	16.366 537	20
21	23.336 065	22.884 848	22.029 308	20.852 374	18.821 518	21
22	27.112 639	26.563 691	25.524 267	24.097 524	21.644 746	22
23	31.500 392	30.833 924	29.573 702	27.847 702	24.891 458	23
24	36.598 234	35.790 617	34.265 582	32.181 500	28.625 176	24
25	42.521 082	41.544 120	39.701 831	37.189 746	32.918 953	25
26	49.402 449	48.222 525	46.000 543	42.977 400	37.856 796	26
27	57.397 457	55.974 514	53.298 548	49.665 758	43.535 315	27
28	66.686 331	64.972 670	61.754 385	57.394 992	50.065 612	28
29	77.478 463	75.417 320	71.551 744	66.327 087	57.575 454	29
30	90.017 131	87.540 995	82.903 458	76.649 240	66.211 772	30
31	104.584 986	101.613 606	96.056 126	88.577 778	76.143 538	31
32	121.510 418	117.948 452	111.295 470	102.362 695	87.565 068	32
33	141.174 964	136.909 198	128.952 543	118.292 890	100.699 829	33
34	164.021 907	158.917 970	149.410 917	136.702 221	115.804 803	34
35	190.566 268	184.464 752	173.115 021	157.976 504	133.175 523	35
36	221.406 416	214.118 294	200.579 791	182.561 597	153.151 852	36
37	257.237 556	248.538 777	232.401 859	210.972 746	176.124 630	37
38	298.867 401	288.492 509	269.272 510	243.805 379	202.543 324	38
39	347.234 380	334.868 983	311.992 705	281.747 591	232.924 823	39
40	403.428 793	388.700 685	361.490 478	325.594 560	267.863 546	40

15½%

COMPOUND INTEREST
(Future Value of $1)

Base:	2.718 282	1.012 917	1.038 750	1.077 500	1.155 000	

Frequency of Conversion

Months	Continuous	Monthly	Quarterly	Semiannual	Annual	Months
0	1.000 000	1.000 000	1.000 000	1.000 000	1.000 000	0
1	1.013 000	1.012 917	1.012 917	1.012 917	1.012 917	1
2	1.026 170	1.026 000	1.025 833	1.025 833	1.025 833	2
3	1.039 511	1.039 253	1.038 750	1.038 750	1.038 750	3
4	1.053 025	1.052 676	1.052 167	1.051 667	1.051 667	4
5	1.066 714	1.066 273	1.065 584	1.064 583	1.064 583	5
6	1.080 582	1.080 046	1.079 002	1.077 500	1.077 500	6
7	1.094 630	1.093 997	1.092 939	1.091 418	1.090 417	7
8	1.108 861	1.108 128	1.106 876	1.105 335	1.103 333	8
9	1.123 277	1.122 441	1.120 813	1.119 253	1.116 250	9
10	1.137 880	1.136 939	1.135 290	1.133 171	1.129 167	10
11	1.152 673	1.151 624	1.149 767	1.147 089	1.142 083	11

Years						Years
1	1.167 658	1.166 500	1.164 244	1.161 006	1.155 000	1
2	1.363 425	1.360 721	1.355 465	1.347 936	1.334 025	2
3	1.592 014	1.587 281	1.578 092	1.564 962	1.540 799	3
4	1.858 928	1.851 563	1.837 285	1.816 930	1.779 623	4
5	2.170 592	2.159 847	2.139 049	2.109 467	2.055 464	5
6	2.534 509	2.519 461	2.490 376	2.449 105	2.374 061	6
7	2.959 440	2.938 950	2.899 406	2.843 426	2.742 041	7
8	3.455 613	3.428 284	3.375 617	3.301 235	3.167 057	8
9	4.034 975	3.999 093	3.930 043	3.832 755	3.657 951	9
10	4.711 470	4.664 940	4.575 531	4.449 852	4.224 933	10
11	5.501 386	5.441 651	5.327 036	5.166 306	4.879 798	11
12	6.423 737	6.347 684	6.201 971	5.998 114	5.636 166	12
13	7.500 727	7.404 571	7.220 610	6.963 847	6.509 772	13
14	8.758 284	8.637 429	8.406 555	8.085 070	7.518 787	14
15	10.226 680	10.075 557	9.787 284	9.386 817	8.684 199	15
16	11.941 264	11.753 134	11.394 791	10.898 154	10.030 250	16
17	13.943 312	13.710 027	13.266 321	12.652 824	11.584 938	17
18	16.281 020	15.992 741	15.445 240	14.690 008	13.380 604	18
19	19.010 662	18.655 526	17.982 033	17.055 191	15.454 598	19
20	22.197 951	21.761 665	20.935 481	19.801 184	17.850 060	20
21	25.919 615	25.384 974	24.374 016	22.989 298	20.616 820	21
22	30.265 244	29.611 562	28.377 311	26.690 719	23.812 427	22
23	35.339 453	34.541 877	33.038 124	30.988 091	27.503 353	23
24	41.264 394	40.293 086	38.464 450	35.977 368	31.766 372	24
25	48.182 698	47.001 870	44.782 020	41.769 949	36.690 160	25
26	56.260 911	54.827 664	52.137 215	48.495 171	42.377 135	26
27	65.693 501	63.956 450	60.700 459	56.303 197	48.945 591	27
28	76.707 539	74.605 175	70.670 168	65.368 364	56.532 157	28
29	89.568 169	87.026 910	82.277 345	75.893 079	65.294 642	29
30	104.584 986	101.516 858	95.790 936	88.112 339	75.415 311	30
31	122.119 491	118.419 377	111.524 058	102.298 976	87.104 684	31
32	142.593 796	138.136 160	129.841 256	118.769 751	100.605 910	32
33	166.500 781	161.135 779	151.166 952	137.892 423	116.199 826	33
34	194.415 962	187.964 827	175.995 273	160.093 965	134.210 800	34
35	227.011 346	219.260 901	204.901 506	185.870 094	155.013 474	35
36	265.071 606	255.767 761	238.555 425	215.796 341	179.040 562	36
37	309.512 971	298.352 998	277.736 811	250.540 900	206.791 849	37
38	361.405 284	348.028 662	323.353 520	290.879 551	238.844 586	38
39	421.997 757	405.975 306	376.462 515	337.712 977	275.865 496	39
40	492.749 041	473.570 044	438.294 365	392.086 877	318.624 648	40

COMPOUND INTEREST **16%**
(Future Value of $1)

Base:	2.718 282	1.013 333	1.040 000	1.080 000	1.160 000	
			Frequency of Conversion			
Months	Continuous	Monthly	Quarterly	Semiannual	Annual	Months
0	1.000 000	1.000 000	1.000 000	1.000 000	1.000 000	0
1	1.013 423	1.013 333	1.013 333	1.013 333	1.013 333	1
2	1.027 025	1.026 844	1.026 667	1.026 667	1.026 667	2
3	1.040 811	1.040 536	1.040 000	1.040 000	1.040 000	3
4	1.054 781	1.054 410	1.053 867	1.053 333	1.053 333	4
5	1.068 939	1.068 468	1.067 733	1.066 667	1.066 667	5
6	1.083 287	1.082 715	1.081 600	1.080 000	1.080 000	6
7	1.097 828	1.097 151	1.096 021	1.094 400	1.093 333	7
8	1.112 563	1.111 779	1.110 443	1.108 800	1.106 667	8
9	1.127 497	1.126 603	1.124 864	1.123 200	1.120 000	9
10	1.142 631	1.141 625	1.139 862	1.137 600	1.133 333	10
11	1.157 968	1.156 846	1.154 860	1.152 000	1.146 667	11

Years						Years
1	1.173 511	1.172 271	1.169 859	1.166 400	1.160 000	1
2	1.377 128	1.374 219	1.368 569	1.360 489	1.345 600	2
3	1.616 074	1.610 957	1.601 032	1.586 874	1.560 896	3
4	1.896 481	1.888 477	1.872 981	1.850 930	1.810 639	4
5	2.225 541	2.213 807	2.191 123	2.158 925	2.100 342	5
6	2.611 696	2.595 181	2.563 304	2.518 170	2.436 396	6
7	3.064 854	3.042 255	2.998 703	2.937 194	2.826 220	7
8	3.596 640	3.566 347	3.508 059	3.425 943	3.278 415	8
9	4.220 696	4.180 724	4.103 933	3.996 019	3.802 961	9
10	4.953 032	4.900 941	4.801 021	4.660 957	4.411 435	10
11	5.812 437	5.745 230	5.616 515	5.436 540	5.117 265	11
12	6.820 958	6.734 965	6.570 528	6.341 181	5.936 027	12
13	8.004 469	7.895 203	7.686 589	7.396 353	6.885 791	13
14	9.393 331	9.255 316	8.992 222	8.627 106	7.987 518	14
15	11.023 176	10.849 737	10.519 627	10.062 657	9.265 521	15
16	12.935 817	12.718 830	12.306 476	11.737 083	10.748 004	16
17	15.180 322	14.909 912	14.396 836	13.690 134	12.467 685	17
18	17.814 273	17.478 455	16.842 262	15.968 172	14.462 514	18
19	20.905 243	20.489 482	19.703 065	18.625 276	16.776 517	19
20	24.532 530	24.019 222	23.049 799	21.724 521	19.460 759	20
21	28.789 191	28.157 032	26.965 005	25.339 482	22.574 481	21
22	33.784 428	33.007 667	31.545 242	29.555 972	26.186 398	22
23	39.646 394	38.693 924	36.903 471	34.474 085	30.376 222	23
24	46.525 474	45.359 757	43.171 841	40.210 573	35.236 417	24
25	54.598 150	53.173 919	50.504 948	46.901 613	40.874 244	25
26	64.071 523	62.334 232	59.083 646	54.706 041	47.414 123	26
27	75.188 628	73.072 600	69.119 509	63.809 126	55.000 382	27
28	88.234 673	85.660 875	80.860 049	74.426 965	63.800 444	28
29	103.544 348	100.417 742	94.594 821	86.811 612	74.008 515	29
30	121.510 418	117.716 787	110.662 561	101.257 064	85.849 877	30
31	142.593 796	137.995 952	129.459 544	118.106 239	99.585 857	31
32	167.335 370	161.768 625	151.449 356	137.759 117	115.519 594	32
33	196.369 875	189.636 635	177.174 325	160.682 234	134.002 729	33
34	230.442 183	222.305 489	207.268 901	187.419 758	155.443 166	34
35	270.426 407	260.602 233	242.475 298	218.606 406	180.314 073	35
36	317.348 329	305.496 388	283.661 803	254.982 512	209.164 324	36
37	372.411 714	358.124 495	331.844 188	297.411 602	242.630 616	37
38	437.029 195	419.818 887	388.210 764	346.900 892	281.451 515	38
39	512.858 511	492.141 422	454.151 686	404.625 201	326.483 757	39
40	601.845 038	576.923 018	531.293 237	471.954 834	378.721 158	40

16½%

COMPOUND INTEREST
(Future Value of $1)

Base:	2.718 282	1.013 750	1.041 250	1.082 500	1.165 000	

Frequency of Conversion

Months	Continuous	Monthly	Quarterly	Semiannual	Annual	Months
0	1.000 000	1.000 000	1.000 000	1.000 000	1.000 000	0
1	1.013 845	1.013 750	1.013 750	1.013 750	1.013 750	1
2	1.027 882	1.027 689	1.027 500	1.027 500	1.027 500	2
3	1.042 113	1.041 820	1.041 250	1.041 250	1.041 250	3
4	1.056 541	1.056 145	1.055 567	1.055 000	1.055 000	4
5	1.071 168	1.070 667	1.069 884	1.068 750	1.068 750	5
6	1.085 999	1.085 388	1.084 202	1.082 500	1.082 500	6
7	1.101 034	1.100 313	1.099 109	1.097 384	1.096 250	7
8	1.116 278	1.115 442	1.114 017	1.112 269	1.110 000	8
9	1.131 733	1.130 779	1.128 925	1.127 153	1.123 750	9
10	1.147 402	1.146 327	1.144 448	1.142 038	1.137 500	10
11	1.163 287	1.162 089	1.159 970	1.156 922	1.151 250	11

Years						Years
1	1.179 393	1.178 068	1.175 493	1.171 806	1.165 000	1
2	1.390 968	1.387 845	1.381 784	1.373 130	1.357 225	2
3	1.640 498	1.634 975	1.624 277	1.609 042	1.581 167	3
4	1.934 792	1.926 112	1.909 327	1.885 486	1.842 060	4
5	2.281 881	2.269 092	2.244 400	2.209 424	2.146 000	5
6	2.691 234	2.673 145	2.638 277	2.589 017	2.500 089	6
7	3.174 023	3.149 146	3.101 276	3.033 826	2.912 604	7
8	3.743 421	3.709 909	3.645 528	3.555 056	3.393 184	8
9	4.414 965	4.370 526	4.285 293	4.165 837	3.953 059	9
10	5.206 980	5.148 777	5.037 332	4.881 554	4.605 314	10
11	6.141 076	6.065 610	5.921 349	5.720 236	5.365 191	11
12	7.242 743	7.145 702	6.960 504	6.703 008	6.250 447	12
13	8.542 041	8.418 123	8.182 024	7.854 626	7.281 771	13
14	10.074 425	9.917 123	9.617 912	9.204 100	8.483 263	14
15	11.881 707	11.683 046	11.305 789	10.785 422	9.883 002	15
16	14.013 204	13.763 425	13.289 876	12.638 425	11.513 697	16
17	16.527 076	16.214 252	15.622 156	14.809 786	13.413 457	17
18	19.491 920	19.101 493	18.363 736	17.354 199	15.626 678	18
19	22.988 636	22.502 860	21.586 444	20.335 759	18.205 080	19
20	27.112 639	26.509 903	25.374 714	23.829 570	21.208 918	20
21	31.976 460	31.230 471	29.827 799	27.923 639	24.708 389	21
22	37.712 817	36.791 623	35.062 370	32.721 094	28.785 273	22
23	44.478 236	43.343 038	41.215 571	38.342 783	33.534 843	23
24	52.457 326	51.061 052	48.448 617	44.930 313	39.068 093	24
25	61.867 809	60.153 398	56.951 011	52.649 621	45.514 328	25
26	72.966 468	70.864 801	66.945 517	61.695 155	53.024 192	26
27	86.056 151	83.483 564	78.693 988	72.294 768	61.773 184	27
28	101.494 032	98.349 325	92.504 235	84.715 462	71.965 759	28
29	119.701 363	115.862 206	108.738 083	99.270 107	83.840 109	29
30	141.174 964	136.493 572	127.820 858	116.325 332	97.673 727	30
31	166.500 781	160.798 727	150.252 528	136.310 751	113.789 892	31
32	196.369 875	189.431 855	176.620 799	159.729 790	132.565 224	32
33	231.597 280	223.163 631	207.616 518	187.172 367	154.438 487	33
34	273.144 238	262.901 961	244.051 769	219.329 749	179.920 837	34
35	322.144 435	309.716 421	286.881 153	257.011 971	209.607 775	35
36	379.934 930	364.867 044	337.226 796	301.168 234	244.193 058	36
37	448.092 641	429.838 236	396.407 747	352.910 818	284.484 912	37
38	528.477 378	506.378 726	465.974 543	413.543 103	331.424 923	38
39	623.282 583	596.548 638	547.749 827	484.592 393	386.110 035	39
40	735.095 189	702.774 938	643.876 102	567.848 394	449.818 191	40

(Future Value of $1)

Base:	2.718 282	1.014 167	1.042 500	1.085 000	1.170 000	
			Frequency of Conversion			
Months	Continuous	Monthly	Quarterly	Semiannual	Annual	Months
0	1.000 000	1.000 000	1.000 000	1.000 000	1.000 000	0
1	1.014 267	1.014 167	1.014 167	1.014 167	1.014 167	1
2	1.028 739	1.028 534	1.028 333	1.028 333	1.028 333	2
3	1.043 416	1.043 105	1.042 500	1.042 500	1.042 500	3
4	1.058 303	1.057 882	1.057 269	1.056 667	1.056 667	4
5	1.073 402	1.072 869	1.072 037	1.070 833	1.070 833	5
6	1.088 717	1.088 068	1.086 806	1.085 000	1.085 000	6
7	1.104 250	1.103 482	1.102 203	1.100 371	1.099 167	7
8	1.120 005	1.119 115	1.117 599	1.115 742	1.113 333	8
9	1.135 985	1.134 969	1.132 996	1.131 113	1.127 500	9
10	1.152 193	1.151 048	1.149 046	1.146 483	1.141 667	10
11	1.168 631	1.167 354	1.165 097	1.161 854	1.155 833	11

Years						Years
1	1.185 305	1.183 892	1.181 148	1.177 225	1.170 000	1
2	1.404 948	1.401 600	1.395 110	1.385 859	1.368 900	2
3	1.665 291	1.659 342	1.647 831	1.631 468	1.601 613	3
4	1.973 878	1.964 482	1.946 332	1.920 604	1.873 887	4
5	2.339 647	2.325 733	2.298 906	2.260 983	2.192 448	5
6	2.773 195	2.753 417	2.715 348	2.661 686	2.565 164	6
7	3.287 081	3.259 747	3.207 228	3.133 404	3.001 242	7
8	3.896 193	3.859 188	3.788 210	3.688 721	3.511 453	8
9	4.618 177	4.568 860	4.474 436	4.342 455	4.108 400	9
10	5.473 947	5.409 036	5.284 970	5.112 046	4.806 828	10
11	6.488 296	6.403 713	6.242 331	6.018 028	5.623 989	11
12	7.690 609	7.581 303	7.373 116	7.084 574	6.580 067	12
13	9.115 716	8.975 441	8.708 740	8.340 137	7.698 679	13
14	10.804 903	10.625 951	10.286 309	9.818 218	9.007 454	14
15	12.807 104	12.579 975	12.149 651	11.558 252	10.538 721	15
16	15.180 322	14.893 329	14.350 534	13.606 663	12.330 304	16
17	17.993 310	17.632 089	16.950 102	16.018 104	14.426 456	17
18	21.327 557	20.874 484	20.020 577	18.856 912	16.878 953	18
19	25.279 657	24.713 129	23.647 261	22.198 828	19.748 375	19
20	29.964 100	29.257 669	27.930 910	26.133 016	23.105 599	20
21	35.516 593	34.637 912	32.990 534	30.764 439	27.033 551	21
22	42.097 990	41.007 538	38.966 698	36.216 667	31.629 255	22
23	49.898 952	48.548 485	46.025 430	42.635 166	37.006 228	23
24	59.145 470	57.476 150	54.362 837	50.191 183	43.297 287	24
25	70.105 412	68.045 538	64.210 546	59.086 316	50.657 826	25
26	83.096 285	80.558 550	75.842 147	69.557 888	59.269 656	26
27	98.494 430	95.372 601	89.580 787	81.885 284	69.345 497	27
28	116.745 926	112.910 833	105.808 152	96.397 404	81.134 232	28
29	138.379 512	133.674 202	124.975 068	113.481 434	94.927 051	29
30	164.021 907	158.255 782	147.614 030	133.593 181	111.064 650	30
31	194.415 962	187.357 711	174.353 991	157.269 233	129.945 641	31
32	230.442 183	221.811 244	205.937 837	185.141 272	152.036 399	32
33	273.144 238	262.600 497	243.243 028	217.952 934	177.882 587	33
34	323.759 190	310.890 557	287.305 974	256.579 643	208.122 627	34
35	383.753 339	368.060 758	339.350 826	302.051 970	243.503 474	35
36	454.864 694	435.744 087	400.823 490	355.583 131	284.899 064	36
37	539.153 329	515.873 821	473.431 793	418.601 351	333.331 905	37
38	639.061 057	610.738 749	559.192 933	492.787 975	389.998 329	38
39	757.482 171	723.048 553	660.489 516	580.122 324	456.298 045	39
40	897.847 292	856.011 201	780.135 756	682.934 503	533.868 713	40

17½%

COMPOUND INTEREST
(Future Value of $1)

Base:	2.718 282	1.014 583	1.043 750	1.087 500	1.175 000	

Frequency of Conversion

Months	Continuous	Monthly	Quarterly	Semiannual	Annual	Months
0	1.000 000	1.000 000	1.000 000	1.000 000	1.000 000	0
1	1.014 690	1.014 583	1.014 583	1.014 583	1.014 583	1
2	1.029 596	1.029 379	1.029 167	1.029 167	1.029 167	2
3	1.044 721	1.044 391	1.043 750	1.043 750	1.043 750	3
4	1.060 068	1.059 622	1.058 971	1.058 333	1.058 333	4
5	1.075 641	1.075 075	1.074 193	1.072 917	1.072 917	5
6	1.091 442	1.090 753	1.089 414	1.087 500	1.087 500	6
7	1.107 476	1.106 660	1.105 301	1.103 359	1.102 083	7
8	1.123 745	1.122 798	1.121 189	1.119 219	1.116 667	8
9	1.140 253	1.139 173	1.137 076	1.135 078	1.131 250	9
10	1.157 003	1.155 785	1.153 658	1.150 937	1.145 833	10
11	1.174 000	1.172 641	1.170 241	1.166 797	1.160 417	11

Years						Years
1	1.191 246	1.189 742	1.186 823	1.182 656	1.175 000	1
2	1.419 068	1.415 485	1.408 549	1.398 676	1.380 625	2
3	1.690 459	1.684 062	1.671 698	1.654 153	1.622 234	3
4	2.013 753	2.003 599	1.984 010	1.956 294	1.906 125	4
5	2.398 875	2.383 765	2.354 668	2.313 623	2.239 697	5
6	2.857 651	2.836 065	2.794 575	2.736 221	2.631 644	6
7	3.404 166	3.374 184	3.316 666	3.236 009	3.092 182	7
8	4.055 200	4.014 408	3.936 295	3.827 086	3.633 314	8
9	4.830 742	4.776 108	4.671 685	4.526 127	4.269 144	9
10	5.754 603	5.682 335	5.544 464	5.352 853	5.016 244	10
11	6.855 149	6.760 511	6.580 297	6.330 585	5.894 087	11
12	8.166 170	8.043 262	7.809 648	7.486 906	6.925 552	12
13	9.727 919	9.569 405	9.268 670	8.854 436	8.137 524	13
14	11.588 347	11.385 120	11.000 270	10.471 754	9.561 590	14
15	13.804 574	13.545 352	13.055 374	12.384 485	11.234 869	15
16	16.444 647	16.115 470	15.494 418	14.646 589	13.200 971	16
17	19.589 623	19.173 247	18.389 131	17.321 880	15.511 141	17
18	23.336 065	22.811 211	21.824 644	20.485 830	18.225 590	18
19	27.798 999	27.139 450	25.901 990	24.227 695	21.415 068	19
20	33.115 452	32.288 935	30.741 077	28.653 035	25.162 705	20
21	39.448 657	38.415 493	36.484 217	33.886 691	29.566 179	21
22	46.993 063	45.704 514	43.300 308	40.076 306	34.740 260	22
23	55.980 309	54.376 566	51.389 802	47.396 494	40.819 806	23
24	66.686 331	64.694 069	60.990 599	56.053 760	47.963 272	24
25	79.439 840	76.969 232	72.385 045	66.292 330	56.356 844	25
26	94.632 408	91.573 505	85.908 236	78.401 038	66.219 292	26
27	112.730 498	108.948 818	101.957 871	92.721 478	77.807 668	27
28	134.289 780	129.620 953	121.005 946	109.657 635	91.424 010	28
29	159.972 192	154.215 454	143.612 640	129.687 287	107.423 211	29
30	190.566 268	183.476 557	170.442 784	153.375 481	126.222 273	30
31	227.011 346	218.289 712	202.285 416	181.390 471	148.311 171	31
32	270.426 407	259.708 375	240.076 984	214.522 574	174.265 626	32
33	322.144 435	308.985 885	284.928 887	253.706 463	204.762 111	33
34	383.753 339	367.613 394	338.160 156	300.047 535	240.595 480	34
35	457.144 713	437.364 986	401.336 250	354.853 092	282.699 689	35
36	544.571 910	520.351 365	476.315 093	419.669 227	332.172 135	36
37	648.719 228	619.083 721	565.301 707	496.324 434	390.302 259	37
38	772.784 326	736.549 723	670.913 067	586.981 194	458.605 154	38
39	920.576 404	876.303 925	796.255 059	694.196 978	538.861 056	39
40	1096.633 158	1042.575 327	945.013 818	820.996 395	633.161 741	40

COMPOUND INTEREST

(Future Value of $1)

18%

Base: 2.718 282   1.015 000   1.045 000   1.090 000   1.180 000

Frequency of Conversion

Months	Continuous	Monthly	Quarterly	Semiannual	Annual	Months
0	1.000 000	1.000 000	1.000 000	1.000 000	1.000 000	0
1	1.015 113	1.015 000	1.015 000	1.015 000	1.015 000	1
2	1.030 455	1.030 225	1.030 000	1.030 000	1.030 000	2
3	1.046 028	1.045 678	1.045 000	1.045 000	1.045 000	3
4	1.061 837	1.061 364	1.060 675	1.060 000	1.060 000	4
5	1.077 884	1.077 284	1.076 350	1.075 000	1.075 000	5
6	1.094 174	1.093 443	1.092 025	1.090 000	1.090 000	6
7	1.110 711	1.109 845	1.108 405	1.106 350	1.105 000	7
8	1.127 497	1.126 493	1.124 786	1.122 700	1.120 000	8
9	1.144 537	1.143 390	1.141 166	1.139 050	1.135 000	9
10	1.161 834	1.160 541	1.158 284	1.155 400	1.150 000	10
11	1.179 393	1.177 949	1.175 401	1.171 750	1.165 000	11

Years	Continuous	Monthly	Quarterly	Semiannual	Annual	Years
1	1.197 217	1.195 618	1.192 519	1.188 100	1.180 000	1
2	1.433 329	1.429 503	1.422 101	1.411 582	1.392 400	2
3	1.716 007	1.709 140	1.695 881	1.677 100	1.643 032	3
4	2.054 433	2.043 478	2.022 370	1.992 563	1.938 778	4
5	2.459 603	2.443 220	2.411 714	2.367 364	2.287 758	5
6	2.944 680	2.921 158	2.876 014	2.812 665	2.699 554	6
7	3.525 421	3.492 590	3.429 700	3.341 727	3.185 474	7
8	4.220 696	4.175 804	4.089 981	3.970 306	3.758 859	8
9	5.053 090	4.992 667	4.877 378	4.717 120	4.435 454	9
10	6.049 647	5.969 323	5.816 365	5.604 411	5.233 836	10
11	7.242 743	7.137 031	6.936 123	6.658 600	6.175 926	11
12	8.671 138	8.533 164	8.271 456	7.911 083	7.287 593	12
13	10.381 237	10.202 406	9.863 865	9.399 158	8.599 359	13
14	12.428 597	12.198 182	11.762 842	11.167 140	10.147 244	14
15	14.879 732	14.584 368	14.027 408	13.267 678	11.973 748	15
16	17.814 273	17.437 335	16.727 945	15.763 329	14.129 023	16
17	21.327 557	20.848 395	19.948 385	18.728 411	16.672 247	17
18	25.533 722	24.926 719	23.788 821	22.251 225	19.673 251	18
19	30.569 415	29.802 839	28.368 611	26.436 680	23.214 436	19
20	36.598 234	35.632 816	33.830 096	31.409 420	27.393 035	20
21	43.816 042	42.603 242	40.343 019	37.317 532	32.323 781	21
22	52.457 326	50.937 210	48.109 801	44.336 960	38.142 061	22
23	62.802 821	60.901 454	57.371 832	52.676 742	45.007 632	23
24	75.188 628	72.814 885	68.416 977	62.585 237	53.109 006	24
25	90.017 131	87.058 800	81.588 518	74.357 520	62.668 627	25
26	107.770 073	104.089 083	97.295 825	88.344 170	73.948 980	26
27	129.024 202	124.450 799	116.027 081	104.961 708	87.259 797	27
28	154.470 015	148.795 637	138.364 453	124.705 005	102.966 560	28
29	184.934 184	177.902 767	165.002 184	148.162 017	121.500 541	29
30	221.406 416	212.703 781	196.768 173	176.031 292	143.370 638	30
31	265.071 606	254.312 506	234.649 707	209.142 778	169.177 353	31
32	317.348 329	304.060 653	279.824 140	248.482 535	199.629 277	32
33	379.934 930	363.540 442	333.695 491	295.222 099	235.562 547	33
34	454.864 694	434.655 558	397.938 081	350.753 376	277.963 805	34
35	544.571 910	519.682 084	474.548 563	416.730 086	327.997 290	35
36	651.970 946	621.341 343	565.907 988	495.117 015	387.036 802	36
37	780.550 937	742.887 000	674.855 802	588.248 526	456.703 427	37
38	934.489 135	888.209 197	804.778 097	698.898 074	538.910 044	38
39	1118.786 618	1061.959 056	959.712 850	830.360 801	635.913 852	39
40	1339.430 764	1269.697 544	1144.475 425	986.551 668	750.378 345	40

19%   COMPOUND INTEREST
(Future Value of $1)

Base:	2.718 282	1.015 833	1.047 500	1.095 000	1.190 000	
			Frequency of Conversion			
Months	Continuous	Monthly	Quarterly	Semiannual	Annual	Months
0	1.000 000	1.000 000	1.000 000	1.000 000	1.000 000	0
1	1.015 959	1.015 833	1.015 833	1.015 833	1.015 833	1
2	1.032 173	1.031 917	1.031 667	1.031 667	1.031 667	2
3	1.048 646	1.048 256	1.047 500	1.047 500	1.047 500	3
4	1.065 382	1.064 853	1.064 085	1.063 333	1.063 333	4
5	1.082 385	1.081 714	1.080 671	1.079 167	1.079 167	5
6	1.099 659	1.098 841	1.097 256	1.095 000	1.095 000	6
7	1.117 209	1.116 239	1.114 629	1.112 337	1.110 833	7
8	1.135 039	1.133 913	1.132 003	1.129 675	1.126 667	8
9	1.153 153	1.151 866	1.149 376	1.147 013	1.142 500	9
10	1.171 557	1.170 104	1.167 574	1.164 350	1.158 333	10
11	1.190 254	1.188 631	1.185 773	1.181 688	1.174 167	11

Years						Years
1	1.209 250	1.207 451	1.203 971	1.199 025	1.190 000	1
2	1.462 285	1.457 938	1.449 547	1.437 661	1.416 100	2
3	1.768 267	1.760 389	1.745 213	1.723 791	1.685 159	3
4	2.138 276	2.125 583	2.101 186	2.066 869	2.005 339	4
5	2.585 710	2.566 537	2.529 768	2.478 228	2.386 354	5
6	3.126 768	3.098 968	3.045 768	2.971 457	2.839 761	6
7	3.781 043	3.741 852	3.667 017	3.562 851	3.379 315	7
8	4.572 225	4.518 103	4.414 983	4.271 948	4.021 385	8
9	5.528 961	5.455 388	5.315 512	5.122 172	4.785 449	9
10	6.685 894	6.587 114	6.399 724	6.141 612	5.694 684	10
11	8.084 915	7.953 617	7.705 084	7.363 946	6.776 674	11
12	9.776 680	9.603 603	9.276 700	8.829 556	8.064 242	12
13	11.822 447	11.595 879	11.168 881	10.586 858	9.596 448	13
14	14.296 289	14.001 456	13.447 011	12.693 908	11.419 773	14
15	17.287 782	16.906 072	16.189 815	15.220 313	13.589 530	15
16	20.905 243	20.413 254	19.492 073	18.249 535	16.171 540	16
17	25.279 657	24.648 004	23.467 896	21.881 649	19.244 133	17
18	30.569 415	29.761 257	28.254 673	26.236 644	22.900 518	18
19	36.966 053	35.935 259	34.017 814	31.458 393	27.251 616	19
20	44.701 184	43.390 065	40.956 471	37.719 399	32.429 423	20
21	54.054 889	52.391 377	49.310 415	45.226 503	38.591 014	21
22	65.365 853	63.260 020	59.368 323	54.227 707	45.923 307	22
23	79.043 632	76.383 375	71.477 756	65.020 377	54.648 735	23
24	95.583 480	92.229 182	86.057 165	77.961 057	65.031 994	24
25	115.584 285	111.362 218	103.610 356	93.477 257	77.388 073	25
26	139.770 250	134.464 421	124.743 892	112.081 568	92.091 807	26
27	169.017 118	162.359 199	150.188 063	134.388 602	109.589 251	27
28	204.383 882	196.040 777	180.822 114	161.135 293	130.411 208	28
29	247.151 127	236.709 632	217.704 632	193.205 245	155.189 338	29
30	298.867 401	285.815 282	262.110 124	231.657 919	184.675 312	30
31	361.405 284	345.107 947	315.573 062	277.763 636	219.763 621	31
32	437.029 195	416.700 935	379.940 902	333.045 544	261.518 710	32
33	528.477 378	503.145 960	457.437 934	399.329 933	311.207 264	33
34	639.061 057	607.524 092	550.742 134	478.806 573	370.336 645	34
35	772.784 326	733.555 571	663.077 711	574.101 052	440.700 607	35
36	934.489 135	885.732 406	798.326 519	688.361 513	524.433 722	36
37	1130.030 610	1069.478 478	961.162 199	825.362 664	624.076 130	37
38	1366.489 061	1291.342 856	1157.211 682	989.630 468	742.650 594	38
39	1652.426 347	1559.233 220	1393.249 627	1186.591 671	883.754 207	39
40	1998.195 895	1882.697 708	1677.432 535	1422.753 079	1051.667 507	40

COMPOUND INTEREST
(Future Value of $1)

20%

Base:	2.718 282	1.016 667	1.050 000	1.100 000	1.200 000	
			Frequency of Conversion			
Months	Continuous	Monthly	Quarterly	Semiannual	Annual	Months
0	1.000 000	1.000 000	1.000 000	1.000 000	1.000 000	0
1	1.016 806	1.016 667	1.016 667	1.016 667	1.016 667	1
2	1.033 895	1.033 611	1.033 333	1.033 333	1.033 333	2
3	1.051 271	1.050 838	1.050 000	1.050 000	1.050 000	3
4	1.068 939	1.068 352	1.067 500	1.066 667	1.066 667	4
5	1.086 904	1.086 158	1.085 000	1.083 333	1.083 333	5
6	1.105 171	1.104 260	1.102 500	1.100 000	1.100 000	6
7	1.123 745	1.122 665	1.120 875	1.118 333	1.116 667	7
8	1.142 631	1.141 376	1.139 250	1.136 667	1.133 333	8
9	1.161 834	1.160 399	1.157 625	1.155 000	1.150 000	9
10	1.181 360	1.179 739	1.176 919	1.173 333	1.166 667	10
11	1.201 215	1.199 401	1.196 212	1.191 667	1.183 333	11

Years						Years
1	1.221 403	1.219 391	1.215 506	1.210 000	1.200 000	1
2	1.491 825	1.486 915	1.477 455	1.464 100	1.440 000	2
3	1.822 119	1.813 130	1.795 856	1.771 561	1.728 000	3
4	2.225 541	2.210 915	2.182 875	2.143 589	2.073 600	4
5	2.718 282	2.695 970	2.653 298	2.593 742	2.488 320	5
6	3.320 117	3.287 442	3.225 100	3.138 428	2.985 984	6
7	4.055 200	4.008 677	3.920 129	3.797 498	3.583 181	7
8	4.953 032	4.888 145	4.764 941	4.594 973	4.299 817	8
9	6.049 647	5.960 561	5.791 816	5.559 917	5.159 780	9
10	7.389 056	7.268 255	7.039 989	6.727 500	6.191 736	10
11	9.025 013	8.862 845	8.557 150	8.140 275	7.430 084	11
12	11.023 176	10.807 275	10.401 270	9.849 733	8.916 100	12
13	13.463 738	13.178 294	12.642 808	11.918 177	10.699 321	13
14	16.444 647	16.069 495	15.367 412	14.420 994	12.839 185	14
15	20.085 537	19.594 998	18.679 186	17.449 402	15.407 022	15
16	24.532 530	23.893 966	22.704 667	21.113 777	18.488 426	16
17	29.964 100	29.136 090	27.597 665	25.547 670	22.186 111	17
18	36.598 234	35.528 288	33.545 134	30.912 681	26.623 333	18
19	44.701 184	43.322 878	40.774 320	37.404 343	31.948 000	19
20	54.598 150	52.827 531	49.561 441	45.259 256	38.337 600	20
21	66.686 331	64.417 420	60.242 241	54.763 699	46.005 120	21
22	81.450 869	78.550 028	73.224 821	66.264 076	55.206 144	22
23	99.484 316	95.783 203	89.005 227	80.179 532	66.247 373	23
24	121.510 418	116.797 184	108.186 410	97.017 234	79.496 847	24
25	148.413 159	142.421 445	131.501 258	117.390 853	95.396 217	25
26	181.272 242	173.667 440	159.840 601	142.042 932	114.475 460	26
27	221.406 416	211.768 529	194.287 249	171.871 948	137.370 552	27
28	270.426 407	258.228 656	236.157 366	207.965 057	164.844 662	28
29	330.299 560	314.881 721	287.050 754	251.637 719	197.813 595	29
30	403.428 793	383.963 963	348.911 986	304.481 640	237.376 314	30
31	492.749 041	468.202 234	424.104 699	368.422 784	284.851 577	31
32	601.845 038	570.921 630	515.501 913	445.791 568	341.821 892	32
33	735.095 189	696.176 745	626.595 797	539.407 798	410.186 270	33
34	897.847 292	848.911 717	761.631 107	652.683 435	492.223 524	34
35	1096.633 158	1035.155 379	925.767 371	789.746 957	590.668 229	35
36	1339.430 764	1262.259 241	1125.276 025	955.593 818	708.801 875	36
37	1635.984 430	1539.187 666	1367.780 042	1156.268 519	850.562 250	37
38	1998.195 895	1876.871 717	1662.545 189	1399.084 909	1020.674 700	38
39	2440.601 978	2288.640 640	2020.834 069	1692.892 739	1224.809 640	39
40	2980.957 987	2790.747 993	2456.336 441	2048.400 215	1469.771 568	40

21%

COMPOUND INTEREST
(Future Value of $1)

Base: 2.718 282 1.017 500 1.052 500 1.105 000 1.210 000

Frequency of Conversion

Months	Continuous	Monthly	Quarterly	Semiannual	Annual	Months
0	1.000 000	1.000 000	1.000 000	1.000 000	1.000 000	0
1	1.017 654	1.017 500	1.017 500	1.017 500	1.017 500	1
2	1.035 620	1.035 306	1.035 000	1.035 000	1.035 000	2
3	1.053 903	1.053 424	1.052 500	1.052 500	1.052 500	3
4	1.072 508	1.071 859	1.070 919	1.070 000	1.070 000	4
5	1.091 442	1.090 617	1.089 337	1.087 500	1.087 500	5
6	1.110 711	1.109 702	1.107 756	1.105 000	1.105 000	6
7	1.130 319	1.129 122	1.127 142	1.124 338	1.122 500	7
8	1.150 274	1.148 882	1.146 528	1.143 675	1.140 000	8
9	1.170 581	1.168 987	1.165 913	1.163 013	1.157 500	9
10	1.191 246	1.189 444	1.186 317	1.182 350	1.175 000	10
11	1.212 277	1.210 260	1.206 720	1.201 688	1.192 500	11

Years	Continuous	Monthly	Quarterly	Semiannual	Annual	Years
1	1.233 678	1.231 439	1.227 124	1.221 025	1.210 000	1
2	1.521 962	1.516 443	1.505 833	1.490 902	1.464 100	2
3	1.877 611	1.867 407	1.847 844	1.820 429	1.771 561	3
4	2.316 367	2.299 599	2.267 533	2.222 789	2.143 589	4
5	2.857 651	2.831 816	2.782 544	2.714 081	2.593 742	5
6	3.525 421	3.487 210	3.414 527	3.313 961	3.138 428	6
7	4.349 235	4.294 287	4.190 047	4.046 429	3.797 498	7
8	5.365 556	5.288 154	5.141 707	4.940 791	4.594 973	8
9	6.619 369	6.512 041	6.309 512	6.032 829	5.559 917	9
10	8.166 170	8.019 183	7.742 553	7.366 235	6.727 500	10
11	10.074 425	9.875 138	9.501 072	8.994 357	8.140 275	11
12	12.428 597	12.160 633	11.658 992	10.982 335	9.849 733	12
13	15.332 887	14.975 081	14.307 028	13.409 705	11.918 177	13
14	18.915 846	18.440 904	17.556 496	16.373 585	14.420 994	14
15	23.336 065	22.708 854	21.543 997	19.992 557	17.449 402	15
16	28.789 191	27.964 576	26.437 153	24.411 412	21.113 777	16
17	35.516 593	34.436 678	32.441 663	29.806 944	25.547 670	17
18	43.816 042	42.406 679	39.809 940	36.395 024	30.912 681	18
19	54.054 889	52.221 252	48.851 729	44.439 234	37.404 343	19
20	66.686 331	64.307 303	59.947 125	54.261 416	45.259 256	20
21	82.269 464	79.190 541	73.562 551	66.254 545	54.763 699	21
22	101.494 032	97.518 346	90.270 365	80.898 456	66.264 076	22
23	125.210 961	120.087 925	110.772 923	98.779 037	80.179 532	23
24	154.470 015	147.880 992	135.932 102	120.611 674	97.017 234	24
25	190.566 268	182.106 467	166.805 532	147.269 869	117.390 853	25
26	235.097 424	224.253 063	204.691 057	179.820 192	142.042 932	26
27	290.034 534	276.154 038	251.181 290	219.564 950	171.871 948	27
28	357.809 242	340.066 940	308.230 567	268.094 293	207.965 057	28
29	441.421 411	418.771 800	378.237 098	327.349 834	251.637 719	29
30	544.571 910	515.692 058	464.143 787	399.702 331	304.481 640	30
31	671.826 418	635.043 475	569.561 938	488.046 539	368.422 784	31
32	828.817 511	782.017 501	698.923 072	595.917 025	445.791 568	32
33	1022.493 980	963.007 096	857.665 212	727.629 586	539.407 798	33
34	1261.428 389	1185.884 799	1052.461 488	888.453 915	652.683 435	34
35	1556.196 528	1460.345 164	1291.500 656	1084.824 442	789.746 957	35
36	1919.845 513	1798.326 448	1584.831 334	1324.597 764	955.593 818	36
37	2368.471 288	2214.529 890	1944.784 422	1617.366 985	1156.268 519	37
38	2921.931 064	2727.059 170	2386.491 463	1974.845 522	1399.084 909	38
39	3604.722 246	3358.207 877	2928.520 734	2411.335 754	1692.892 739	39
40	4447.066 748	4135.429 207	3593.657 812	2944.301 239	2048.400 215	40

78

COMPOUND INTEREST
(Future Value of $1)

22%

Base:	2.718 282	1.018 333	1.055 000	1.110 000	1.220 000	

Frequency of Conversion

Months	Continuous	Monthly	Quarterly	Semiannual	Annual	Months
0	1.000 000	1.000 000	1.000 000	1.000 000	1.000 000	0
1	1.018 502	1.018 333	1.018 333	1.018 333	1.018 333	1
2	1.037 347	1.037 003	1.036 667	1.036 667	1.036 667	2
3	1.056 541	1.056 014	1.055 000	1.055 000	1.055 000	3
4	1.076 089	1.075 375	1.074 342	1.073 333	1.073 333	4
5	1.095 999	1.095 090	1.093 683	1.091 667	1.091 667	5
6	1.116 278	1.115 167	1.113 025	1.110 000	1.110 000	6
7	1.136 932	1.135 611	1.133 430	1.130 350	1.128 333	7
8	1.157 968	1.156 431	1.153 836	1.150 700	1.146 667	8
9	1.179 393	1.177 632	1.174 241	1.171 050	1.165 000	9
10	1.201 215	1.199 222	1.195 769	1.191 400	1.183 333	10
11	1.223 440	1.221 208	1.217 297	1.211 750	1.201 667	11

Years						Years
1	1.246 077	1.243 597	1.238 825	1.232 100	1.220 000	1
2	1.552 707	1.546 532	1.534 687	1.518 070	1.488 400	2
3	1.934 792	1.923 262	1.901 207	1.870 415	1.815 848	3
4	2.410 900	2.391 763	2.355 263	2.304 538	2.215 335	4
5	3.004 166	2.974 388	2.917 757	2.839 421	2.702 708	5
6	3.743 421	3.698 938	3.614 590	3.498 451	3.297 304	6
7	4.664 590	4.599 987	4.477 843	4.310 441	4.022 711	7
8	5.812 437	5.720 528	5.547 262	5.310 894	4.907 707	8
9	7.242 743	7.114 030	6.872 085	6.543 553	5.987 403	9
10	9.025 013	8.846 983	8.513 309	8.062 312	7.304 631	10
11	11.245 859	11.002 078	10.546 497	9.933 574	8.911 650	11
12	14.013 204	13.682 146	13.065 260	12.239 157	10.872 213	12
13	17.461 527	17.015 070	16.185 566	15.079 865	13.264 100	13
14	21.758 402	21.159 883	20.051 079	18.579 901	16.182 202	14
15	27.112 639	26.314 358	24.839 770	22.892 297	19.742 287	15
16	33.784 428	32.724 445	30.772 120	28.205 599	24.085 590	16
17	42.097 990	40.696 008	38.121 261	34.752 118	29.384 420	17
18	52.457 326	50.609 416	47.225 558	42.818 085	35.848 992	18
19	65.365 853	62.937 697	58.504 185	52.756 162	43.735 771	19
20	81.450 869	78.269 105	72.476 426	65.000 867	53.357 640	20
21	101.494 032	97.335 191	89.785 583	80.087 569	65.096 321	21
22	126.469 352	121.045 710	111.228 594	98.675 893	79.417 512	22
23	157.590 516	150.532 031	137.792 724	121.578 568	96.889 364	23
24	196.369 875	187.201 119	170.701 023	149.796 954	118.205 024	24
25	244.691 932	232.802 670	211.468 636	184.564 827	144.210 130	25
26	304.904 923	289.512 604	261.972 559	227.402 323	175.936 358	26
27	379.934 930	360.036 884	324.538 064	280.182 402	214.642 357	27
28	473.428 075	447.740 637	402.045 753	345.212 738	261.863 675	28
29	589.927 708	556.808 724	498.064 190	425.336 614	319.473 684	29
30	735.095 189	692.445 423	617.014 196	524.057 242	389.757 894	30
31	915.985 010	861.122 759	764.372 395	645.690 928	475.504 631	31
32	1141.387 607	1070.889 316	946.923 366	795.555 793	580.115 650	32
33	1422.256 537	1331.754 289	1173.072 008	980.204 292	707.741 093	33
34	1772.240 776	1656.165 076	1453.230 520	1207.709 708	863.444 133	34
35	2208.347 992	2059.601 222	1800.297 792	1488.019 132	1053.401 842	35
36	2751.771 046	2561.313 031	2230.253 283	1833.388 372	1285.150 248	36
37	3428.917 868	3185.240 121	2762.892 744	2258.917 813	1567.883 302	37
38	4272.694 766	3961.153 714	3422.739 638	2783.212 638	1912.817 629	38
39	5324.105 525	4926.077 203	4240.174 236	3429.196 291	2333.637 507	39
40	6634.244 006	6126.052 753	5252.832 366	4225.112 750	2847.037 759	40

23%

COMPOUND INTEREST
(Future Value of $1)

Base:	2.718 282	1.019 167	1.057 500	1.115 000	1.230 000	
			Frequency of Conversion			
Months	Continuous	Monthly	Quarterly	Semiannual	Annual	Months
0	1.000 000	1.000 000	1.000 000	1.000 000	1.000 000	0
1	1.019 352	1.019 167	1.019 167	1.019 167	1.019 167	1
2	1.039 078	1.038 701	1.038 333	1.038 333	1.038 333	2
3	1.059 185	1.058 609	1.057 500	1.057 500	1.057 500	3
4	1.079 682	1.078 899	1.077 769	1.076 667	1.076 667	4
5	1.100 576	1.099 578	1.098 037	1.095 833	1.095 833	5
6	1.121 873	1.120 653	1.118 306	1.115 000	1.115 000	6
7	1.143 583	1.142 132	1.139 740	1.136 371	1.134 167	7
8	1.165 713	1.164 023	1.161 175	1.157 742	1.153 333	8
9	1.188 272	1.186 334	1.182 609	1.179 113	1.172 500	9
10	1.211 267	1.209 072	1.205 276	1.200 483	1.191 667	10
11	1.234 707	1.232 246	1.227 942	1.221 854	1.210 833	11

Years						Years
1	1.258 600	1.255 864	1.250 609	1.243 225	1.230 000	1
2	1.584 074	1.577 194	1.564 023	1.545 608	1.512 900	2
3	1.993 716	1.980 741	1.955 980	1.921 539	1.860 867	3
4	2.509 290	2.487 540	2.446 167	2.388 905	2.288 866	4
5	3.158 193	3.124 012	3.059 198	2.969 947	2.815 306	5
6	3.974 902	3.923 333	3.825 860	3.692 312	3.462 826	6
7	5.002 811	4.927 172	4.784 654	4.590 375	4.259 276	7
8	6.296 538	6.187 857	5.983 731	5.706 869	5.238 909	8
9	7.924 823	7.771 105	7.483 307	7.094 922	6.443 859	9
10	9.974 182	9.759 449	9.358 690	8.820 584	7.925 946	10
11	12.553 506	12.256 539	11.704 060	10.965 971	9.748 914	11
12	15.799 843	15.392 543	14.637 201	13.633 169	11.991 164	12
13	19.885 682	19.330 937	18.305 414	16.949 096	14.749 132	13
14	25.028 120	24.277 024	22.892 913	21.071 540	18.141 432	14
15	31.500 392	30.488 635	28.630 080	26.196 666	22.313 961	15
16	39.646 394	38.289 572	35.805 032	32.568 350	27.446 172	16
17	49.898 952	48.086 486	44.778 091	40.489 787	33.758 792	17
18	62.802 821	60.390 076	55.999 877	50.337 915	41.523 314	18
19	79.043 632	75.841 708	70.033 943	62.581 355	51.073 676	19
20	99.484 316	95.246 853	87.585 070	77.802 705	62.820 622	20
21	125.210 961	119.617 072	109.534 666	96.726 268	77.269 364	21
22	157.590 516	150.222 748	136.985 025	120.252 514	95.041 318	22
23	198.343 425	188.659 306	171.314 687	149.500 932	116.900 822	23
24	249.635 037	236.930 388	214.247 667	185.863 296	143.788 010	24
25	314.190 660	297.552 290	267.940 032	231.069 896	176.859 253	25
26 ·	395.440 368	373.685 140	335.088 180	287.271 872	217.536 881	26
27	497.701 251	469.297 629	419.064 250	357.143 573	267.570 364	27
28	626.406 800	589.373 890	524.085 468	444.009 818	329.111 547	28
29	788.395 604	740.173 316	655.425 934	552.004 106	404.807 203	29
30	992.274 716	929.556 851	819.681 486	686.265 305	497.912 860	30
31	1248.876 967	1167.396 771	1025.100 935	853.182 184	612.432 818	31
32	1571.836 563	1466.091 310	1282.000 321	1060.697 420	753.292 366	32
33	1978.313 514	1841.210 960	1603.280 972	1318.685 550	926.549 610	33
34	2489.905 408	2312.310 138	2005.077 402	1639.422 843	1139.656 020	34
35	3133.794 971	2903.946 528	2507.567 582	2038.171 464	1401.776 905	35
36	3944.194 382	3646.961 235	3135.986 257	2533.905 719	1724.185 593	36
37	4964.163 088	4580.086 487	3921.892 225	3150.214 937	2120.748 279	37
38	6247.895 712	5751.964 683	4904.753 199	3916.425 965	2608.520 383	38
39	7863.601 605	7223.684 053	6133.927 850	4868.998 671	3208.480 071	39
40	9897.129 059	9071.963 089	7671.144 570	6053.260 872	3946.430 488	40

80

COMPOUND INTEREST
(Future Value of $1)

24%

Base:	2.718 282	1.020 000	1.060 000	1.120 000	1.240 000	
			Frequency of Conversion			
Months	Continuous	Monthly	Quarterly	Semiannual	Annual	Months
0	1.000 000	1.000 000	1.000 000	1.000 000	1.000 000	0
1	1.020 201	1.020 000	1.020 000	1.020 000	1.020 000	1
2	1.040 811	1.040 400	1.040 000	1.040 000	1.040 000	2
3	1.061 837	1.061 208	1.060 000	1.060 000	1.060 000	3
4	1.083 287	1.082 432	1.081 200	1.080 000	1.080 000	4
5	1.105 171	1.104 081	1.102 400	1.100 000	1.100 000	5
6	1.127 497	1.126 162	1.123 600	1.120 000	1.120 000	6
7	1.150 274	1.148 686	1.146 072	1.142 400	1.140 000	7
8	1.173 511	1.171 659	1.168 544	1.164 800	1.160 000	8
9	1.197 217	1.195 093	1.191 016	1.187 200	1.180 000	9
10	1.221 403	1.218 994	1.214 836	1.209 600	1.200 000	10
11	1.246 077	1.243 374	1.238 657	1.232 000	1.220 000	11

Years						Years
1	1.271 249	1.268 242	1.262 477	1.254 400	1.240 000	1
2	1.616 074	1.608 437	1.593 848	1.573 519	1.537 600	2
3	2.054 433	2.039 887	2.012 196	1.973 823	1.906 624	3
4	2.611 696	2.587 070	2.540 352	2.475 963	2.364 214	4
5	3.320 117	3.281 031	3.207 135	3.105 848	2.931 625	5
6	4.220 696	4.161 140	4.048 935	3.895 976	3.635 215	6
7	5.365 556	5.277 332	5.111 687	4.887 112	4.507 667	7
8	6.820 958	6.692 933	6.453 387	6.130 394	5.589 507	8
9	8.671 138	8.488 258	8.147 252	7.689 966	6.930 988	9
10	11.023 176	10.765 163	10.285 718	9.646 293	8.594 426	10
11	14.013 204	13.652 830	12.985 482	12.100 310	10.657 088	11
12	17.814 273	17.315 089	16.393 872	15.178 629	13.214 789	12
13	22.646 380	21.959 720	20.696 885	19.040 072	16.386 338	13
14	28.789 191	27.850 234	26.129 341	23.883 866	20.319 059	14
15	36.598 234	35.320 831	32.987 691	29.959 922	25.195 633	15
16	46.525 474	44.795 355	41.646 200	37.581 726	31.242 585	16
17	59.145 470	56.811 341	52.577 368	47.142 517	38.740 806	17
18	75.188 628	72.050 517	66.377 715	59.135 574	48.038 599	18
19	95.583 480	91.377 477	83.800 336	74.179 664	59.567 863	19
20	121.510 418	115.888 735	105.795 993	93.050 970	73.864 150	20
21	154.470 015	146.974 937	133.565 004	116.723 137	91.591 546	21
22	196.369 875	186.399 758	168.622 741	146.417 503	113.573 517	22
23	249.635 037	236.399 964	212.882 325	183.666 116	140.831 161	23
24	317.348 329	299.812 315	268.759 030	230.390 776	174.630 639	24
25	403.428 793	380.234 508	339.302 084	289.002 190	216.541 993	25
26	512.858 511	482.229 295	428.361 063	362.524 347	268.512 071	26
27	651.970 946	611.583 346	540.795 972	454.750 541	332.954 968	27
28	828.817 511	775.635 561	682.742 455	570.439 078	412.864 160	28
29	1053.633 557	983.693 435	861.946 619	715.558 780	511.951 559	29
30	1339.430 764	1247.561 128	1088.187 748	897.596 933	634.819 933	30
31	1702.750 221	1582.209 163	1373.811 960	1125.945 593	787.176 717	31
32	2164.619 772	2006.623 789	1734.405 947	1412.386 152	976.099 129	32
33	2751.771 046	2544.884 155	2189.647 547	1771.697 189	1210.362 920	33
34	3498.186 604	3227.528 448	2764.379 578	2222.416 954	1500.850 021	34
35	4447.066 748	4093.286 471	3489.965 527	2787.799 828	1861.054 026	35
36	5653.329 824	5191.276 979	4406.001 068	3497.016 104	2307.706 992	36
37	7186.790 736	6583.794 432	5562.474 835	4386.657 001	2861.556 670	37
38	9136.201 616	8349.843 265	7022.496 319	5502.622 542	3548.330 270	38
39	11614.388 542	10589.620 207	8865.739 805	6902.489 716	4399.929 535	39
40	14764.781 566	13430.198 935	11192.792 237	8658.483 100	5455.912 624	40

25%

COMPOUND INTEREST
(Future Value of $1)

Base:	2.718 282	1.020 833	1.062 500	1.125 000	1.250 000	
			Frequency of Conversion			
Months	Continuous	Monthly	Quarterly	Semiannual	Annual	Months
0	1.000 000	1.000 000	1.000 000	1.000 000	1.000 000	0
1	1.021 052	1.020 833	1.020 833	1.020 833	1.020 833	1
2	1.042 547	1.042 101	1.041 667	1.041 667	1.041 667	2
3	1.064 494	1.063 811	1.062 500	1.062 500	1.062 500	3
4	1.086 904	1.085 974	1.084 635	1.083 333	1.083 333	4
5	1.109 785	1.108 598	1.106 771	1.104 167	1.104 167	5
6	1.133 148	1.131 694	1.128 906	1.125 000	1.125 000	6
7	1.157 003	1.155 271	1.152 425	1.148 437	1.145 833	7
8	1.181 360	1.179 339	1.175 944	1.171 875	1.166 667	8
9	1.206 230	1.203 909	1.199 463	1.195 313	1.187 500	9
10	1.231 624	1.228 990	1.224 452	1.218 750	1.208 333	10
11	1.257 552	1.254 594	1.249 441	1.242 188	1.229 167	11

Years						Years
1	1.284 025	1.280 732	1.274 429	1.265 625	1.250 000	1
2	1.648 721	1.640 273	1.624 170	1.601 807	1.562 500	2
3	2.117 000	2.100 750	2.069 890	2.027 287	1.953 125	3
4	2.718 282	2.690 497	2.637 928	2.565 785	2.441 406	4
5	3.490 343	3.445 804	3.361 853	3.247 321	3.051 758	5
6	4.481 689	4.413 150	4.284 445	4.109 891	3.814 697	6
7	5.754 603	5.652 060	5.460 222	5.201 580	4.768 372	7
8	7.389 056	7.238 772	6.958 667	6.583 250	5.960 464	8
9	9.487 736	9.270 924	8.868 329	8.331 926	7.450 581	9
10	12.182 494	11.873 565	11.302 058	10.545 094	9.313 226	10
11	15.642 632	15.206 849	14.403 675	13.346 134	11.641 532	11
12	20.085 537	19.475 891	18.356 465	16.891 201	14.551 915	12
13	25.790 340	24.943 389	23.394 018	21.377 927	18.189 894	13
14	33.115 452	31.945 785	29.814 022	27.056 438	22.737 368	14
15	42.521 082	40.913 975	37.995 864	34.243 305	28.421 709	15
16	54.598 150	52.399 819	48.423 043	43.339 183	35.527 137	16
17	70.105 412	67.110 102	61.711 746	54.851 153	44.408 921	17
18	90.017 131	85.950 026	78.647 258	69.420 991	55.511 151	18
19	115.584 285	110.078 911	100.230 372	87.860 942	69.388 939	19
20	148.413 159	140.981 536	127.736 525	111.199 004	86.736 174	20
21	190.566 268	180.559 502	162.791 173	140.736 240	108.420 217	21
22	244.691 932	231.248 253	207.465 844	178.119 303	135.525 272	22
23	314.190 660	296.166 936	264.400 555	225.432 243	169.406 589	23
24	403.428 793	379.310 342	336.959 820	285.312 683	211.758 237	24
25	518.012 825	485.794 726	429.431 475	361.098 864	264.697 796	25
26	665.141 633	622.172 638	547.280 063	457.015 750	330.872 245	26
27	854.058 763	796.836 134	697.469 759	578.410 559	413.590 306	27
28	1096.633 158	1020.533 185	888.875 911	732.050 863	516.987 883	28
29	1408.104 848	1307.029 059	1132.809 524	926.501 874	646.234 854	29
30	1808.042 414	1673.953 366	1443.685 673	1172.603 934	807.793 567	30
31	2321.572 415	2143.884 907	1839.875 353	1484.076 854	1009.741 959	31
32	2980.957 987	2745.741 063	2344.791 097	1878.284 768	1262.177 448	32
33	3827.625 821	3516.557 237	2988.270 526	2377.204 160	1577.721 810	33
34	4914.768 840	4503.765 838	3808.339 579	3008.649 015	1972.152 263	34
35	6310.688 108	5768.115 051	4853.459 625	3807.821 409	2465.190 329	35
36	8103.083 928	7387.406 991	6185.391 255	4819.273 971	3081.487 911	36
37	10404.565 717	9461.285 285	7882.843 979	6099.393 619	3851.859 889	37
38	13359.726 830	12117.366 669	10046.127 503	7719.545 050	4814.824 861	38
39	17154.228 809	15519.093 925	12803.079 455	9770.049 203	6018.531 076	39
40	22026.465 795	19875.793 382	16316.619 860	12365.218 523	7523.163 845	40

COMPOUND INTEREST
(Future Value of $1)

26%

Base:	2.718 282	1.021 667	1.065 000	1.130 000	1.260 000	

Frequency of Conversion

Months	Continuous	Monthly	Quarterly	Semiannual	Annual	Months
0	1.000 000	1.000 000	1.000 000	1.000 000	1.000 000	0
1	1.021 903	1.021 667	1.021 667	1.021 667	1.021 667	1
2	1.044 286	1.043 803	1.043 333	1.043 333	1.043 333	2
3	1.067 159	1.066 419	1.065 000	1.065 000	1.065 000	3
4	1.090 533	1.089 524	1.088 075	1.086 667	1.086 667	4
5	1.114 419	1.113 131	1.111 150	1.108 333	1.108 333	5
6	1.138 828	1.137 248	1.134 225	1.130 000	1.130 000	6
7	1.163 772	1.161 889	1.158 800	1.154 483	1.151 667	7
8	1.189 262	1.187 063	1.183 375	1.178 967	1.173 333	8
9	1.215 311	1.212 783	1.207 950	1.203 450	1.195 000	9
10	1.241 930	1.239 060	1.234 122	1.227 933	1.216 667	10
11	1.269 132	1.265 906	1.260 294	1.252 417	1.238 333	11

Years						Years
1	1.296 930	1.293 334	1.286 466	1.276 900	1.260 000	1
2	1.682 028	1.672 713	1.654 996	1.630 474	1.587 600	2
3	2.181 472	2.163 376	2.129 096	2.081 952	2.000 376	3
4	2.829 217	2.797 968	2.739 011	2.658 444	2.520 474	4
5	3.669 297	3.618 707	3.523 645	3.394 567	3.175 797	5
6	4.758 821	4.680 197	4.533 051	4.334 523	4.001 504	6
7	6.171 858	6.053 058	5.831 617	5.534 753	5.041 895	7
8	8.004 469	7.828 625	7.502 179	7.067 326	6.352 788	8
9	10.381 237	10.125 027	9.651 301	9.024 268	8.004 513	9
10	13.463 738	13.095 042	12.416 075	11.523 088	10.085 686	10
11	17.461 527	16.936 263	15.972 862	14.713 831	12.707 965	11
12	22.646 380	21.904 244	20.548 550	18.788 091	16.012 035	12
13	29.370 771	28.329 504	26.435 018	23.990 513	20.175 165	13
14	38.091 837	36.639 510	34.007 761	30.633 486	25.420 707	14
15	49.402 449	47.387 123	43.749 840	39.115 898	32.030 091	15
16	64.071 523	61.287 377	56.282 697	49.947 090	40.357 915	16
17	83.096 285	79.265 047	72.405 795	63.777 439	50.850 973	17
18	107.770 073	102.516 180	93.147 619	81.437 412	64.072 226	18
19	139.770 250	132.587 659	119.831 278	103.987 432	80.731 005	19
20	181.272 242	171.480 125	154.158 907	132.781 552	101.721 066	20
21	235.097 424	221.781 074	198.320 246	169.548 763	128.168 543	21
22	304.904 923	286.837 000	255.132 323	216.496 816	161.492 364	22
23	395.440 368	370.976 040	328.219 149	276.444 784	203.480 379	23
24	512.858 511	479.795 920	422.242 891	352.992 345	256.385 277	24
25	665.141 633	620.536 369	543.201 271	450.735 925	323.045 450	25
26	862.642 196	802.560 775	698.810 157	575.544 703	407.037 266	26
27	1118.786 618	1037.979 126	898.995 752	734.913 031	512.866 956	27
28	1450.988 025	1342.453 679	1156.527 785	938.410 449	646.212 364	28
29	1881.830 025	1736.240 965	1487.834 078	1198.256 303	814.227 579	29
30	2440.601 978	2245.539 446	1914.048 477	1530.053 473	1025.926 749	30
31	3165.290 134	2904.232 480	2462.358 959	1953.725 280	1292.667 704	31
32	4105.160 008	3756.142 566	3167.741 944	2494.711 810	1628.761 307	32
33	5324.105 525	4857.946 832	4075.193 419	3185.497 510	2052.239 247	33
34	6904.992 640	6282.947 734	5242.599 206	4067.561 770	2585.821 452	34
35	8955.292 703	8125.949 829	6744.427 468	5193.869 624	3258.135 029	35
36	11614.388 542	10509.567 073	8676.478 992	6632.052 123	4105.250 137	36
37	15063.049 938	13592.380 260	11161.998 265	8468.467 356	5172.615 172	37
38	19535.722 662	17579.487 324	14359.535 173	10813.385 967	6517.495 117	38
39	25336.466 485	22736.148 390	18473.058 811	13807.612 541	8212.043 848	39
40	32859.625 674	29405.433 396	23764.968 554	17630.940 454	10347.175 248	40

27%

COMPOUND INTEREST
(Future Value of $1)

Base: 2.718 282   1.022 500   1.067 500   1.135 000   1.270 000

Frequency of Conversion

Months	Continuous	Monthly	Quarterly	Semiannual	Annual	Months
0	1.000 000	1.000 000	1.000 000	1.000 000	1.000 000	0
1	1.022 755	1.022 500	1.022 500	1.022 500	1.022 500	1
2	1.046 028	1.045 506	1.045 000	1.045 000	1.045 000	2
3	1.069 830	1.069 030	1.067 500	1.067 500	1.067 500	3
4	1.094 174	1.093 083	1.091 519	1.090 000	1.090 000	4
5	1.119 072	1.117 678	1.115 537	1.112 500	1.112 500	5
6	1.144 537	1.142 825	1.139 556	1.135 000	1.135 000	6
7	1.170 581	1.168 539	1.165 196	1.160 538	1.157 500	7
8	1.197 217	1.194 831	1.190 836	1.186 075	1.180 000	8
9	1.224 460	1.221 715	1.216 476	1.211 613	1.202 500	9
10	1.252 323	1.249 203	1.243 847	1.237 150	1.225 000	10
11	1.280 819	1.277 311	1.271 218	1.262 688	1.247 500	11

Years						Years
1	1.309 964	1.306 050	1.298 588	1.288 225	1.270 000	1
2	1.716 007	1.705 767	1.686 332	1.659 524	1.612 900	2
3	2.247 908	2.227 816	2.189 851	2.137 840	2.048 383	3
4	2.944 680	2.909 640	2.843 715	2.754 019	2.601 446	4
5	3.857 426	3.800 135	3.692 816	3.547 796	3.303 837	5
6	5.053 090	4.963 166	4.795 448	4.570 359	4.195 873	6
7	6.619 369	6.482 143	6.227 314	5.887 651	5.328 759	7
8	8.671 138	8.466 003	8.086 718	7.584 619	6.767 523	8
9	11.358 882	11.057 023	10.501 318	9.770 696	8.594 755	9
10	14.879 732	14.441 024	13.636 890	12.586 855	10.915 339	10
11	19.491 920	18.860 700	17.708 708	16.214 701	13.862 480	11
12	25.533 722	24.633 017	22.996 324	20.888 184	17.605 350	12
13	33.448 268	32.171 951	29.862 761	26.908 680	22.358 794	13
14	43.816 042	42.018 177	38.779 436	34.664 435	28.395 668	14
15	57.397 457	54.877 839	50.358 527	44.655 591	36.062 499	15
16	75.188 628	71.673 201	65.395 002	57.526 449	45.799 373	16
17	98.494 430	93.608 784	84.921 194	74.107 010	58.165 204	17
18	129.024 202	122.257 751	110.277 681	95.466 503	73.869 809	18
19	169.017 118	159.674 735	143.205 323	122.982 336	93.814 658	19
20	221.406 416	208.543 185	185.964 778	158.428 920	119.144 615	20
21	290.034 534	272.367 825	241.491 712	204.092 095	151.313 661	21
22	379.934 930	355.725 995	313.598 347	262.916 539	192.168 350	22
23	497.701 251	464.595 933	407.235 191	338.695 659	244.053 804	23
24	651.970 946	606.785 513	528.830 914	436.316 215	309.948 332	24
25	854.058 763	792.492 213	686.733 715	562.073 456	393.634 381	25
26	1118.786 618	1035.034 447	891.784 469	724.077 078	499.915 664	26
27	1465.570 697	1351.806 730	1158.061 008	932.774 194	634.892 893	27
28	1919.845 513	1765.527 165	1503.844 646	1201.623 036	806.313 974	28
29	2514.929 373	2305.866 737	1952.875 284	1547.960 836	1024.018 748	29
30	3294.468 075	3011.577 228	2535.981 282	1994.121 848	1300.503 809	30
31	4315.636 063	3933.270 408	3293.195 994	2568.877 618	1651.639 838	31
32	5653.329 824	5137.047 777	4276.506 271	3309.292 369	2097.582 594	32
33	7405.661 098	6709.241 197	5553.421 637	4263.113 162	2663.929 895	33
34	9701.152 773	8762.604 398	7211.609 178	5491.848 953	3383.190 966	34
35	12708.165 264	11444.399 385	9364.912 363	7074.737 118	4296.652 527	35
36	16647.244 729	14946.957 701	12161.167 001	9113.853 224	5456.748 710	36
37	21807.298 798	19521.473 954	15792.350 968	11740.693 569	6930.070 861	37
38	28566.786 192	25496.020 860	20507.764 517	15124.654 973	8801.189 994	38
39	37421.474 383	33299.077 787	26631.146 074	19483.958 653	11177.511 292	39
40	49020.801 136	43490.260 207	34582.898 619	25099.722 635	14195.439 341	40

84

COMPOUND INTEREST 28%
(Future Value of $1)

Base: 2.718 282   1.023 333   1.070 000   1.140 000   1.280 000

Frequency of Conversion

Months	Continuous	Monthly	Quarterly	Semiannual	Annual	Months
0	1.000 000	1.000 000	1.000 000	1.000 000	1.000 000	0
1	1.023 608	1.023 333	1.023 333	1.023 333	1.023 333	1
2	1.047 773	1.047 211	1.046 667	1.046 667	1.046 667	2
3	1.072 508	1.071 646	1.070 000	1.070 000	1.070 000	3
4	1.097 828	1.096 651	1.094 967	1.093 333	1.093 333	4
5	1.123 745	1.122 240	1.119 933	1.116 667	1.116 667	5
6	1.150 274	1.148 425	1.144 900	1.140 000	1.140 000	6
7	1.177 429	1.175 222	1.171 614	1.166 600	1.163 333	7
8	1.205 225	1.202 644	1.198 329	1.193 200	1.186 667	8
9	1.233 678	1.230 705	1.225 043	1.219 800	1.210 000	9
10	1.262 802	1.259 422	1.253 627	1.246 400	1.233 333	10
11	1.292 614	1.288 808	1.282 212	1.273 000	1.256 667	11

Years						Years
1	1.323 130	1.318 881	1.310 796	1.299 600	1.280 000	1
2	1.750 673	1.739 446	1.718 186	1.688 960	1.638 400	2
3	2.316 367	2.294 121	2.252 192	2.194 973	2.097 152	3
4	3.064 854	3.025 672	2.952 164	2.852 586	2.684 355	4
5	4.055 200	3.990 499	3.869 684	3.707 221	3.435 974	5
6	5.365 556	5.262 992	5.072 367	4.817 905	4.398 047	6
7	7.099 327	6.941 257	6.648 838	6.261 349	5.629 500	7
8	9.393 331	9.154 689	8.715 271	8.137 249	7.205 759	8
9	12.428 597	12.073 941	11.423 942	10.575 169	9.223 372	9
10	16.444 647	15.924 085	14.974 458	13.743 490	11.805 916	10
11	21.758 402	21.001 965	19.628 460	17.861 039	15.111 573	11
12	28.789 191	27.699 083	25.728 907	23.212 207	19.342 813	12
13	38.091 837	36.531 780	33.725 348	30.166 584	24.758 801	13
14	50.400 445	48.181 053	44.207 052	39.204 493	31.691 265	14
15	66.686 331	63.545 052	57.946 427	50.950 159	40.564 819	15
16	88.234 673	83.808 330	75.955 945	66.214 826	51.922 969	16
17	116.745 926	110.533 172	99.562 750	86.052 788	66.461 400	17
18	154.470 015	145.780 046	130.506 455	111.834 203	85.070 592	18
19	204.383 882	192.266 461	171.067 341	145.339 731	108.890 357	19
20	270.426 407	253.576 488	224.234 388	188.883 514	139.379 657	20
21	357.809 242	334.437 086	293.925 541	245.473 015	178.405 962	21
22	473.428 075	441.082 553	385.276 426	319.016 730	228.359 631	22
23	626.406 800	581.735 181	505.018 802	414.594 142	292.300 327	23
24	828.817 511	767.239 190	661.976 630	538.806 547	374.144 419	24
25	1096.633 158	1011.896 811	867.716 326	700.232 988	478.904 857	25
26	1450.988 025	1334.570 978	1137.399 097	910.022 792	612.998 216	26
27	1919.845 513	1760.139 647	1490.898 199	1182.665 620	784.637 717	27
28	2540.204 834	2321.413 868	1954.263 410	1536.992 240	1004.336 278	28
29	3361.020 745	3061.667 496	2561.640 680	1997.475 115	1285.550 435	29
30	4447.066 748	4037.973 577	3357.788 383	2595.918 660	1645.504 557	30
31	5884.046 591	5325.604 634	4401.375 615	3373.655 890	2106.245 833	31
32	7785.357 462	7023.836 133	5769.305 594	4384.403 195	2695.994 667	32
33	10301.038 558	9263.600 553	7562.382 753	5697.970 392	3450.873 173	33
34	13629.611 214	12217.582 184	9912.741 139	7405.082 321	4417.117 662	34
35	18033.744 928	16113.530 971	12993.581 534	9623.644 985	5653.910 607	35
36	23860.985 542	21251.821 880	17031.934 830	12506.889 022	7237.005 577	36
37	31571.181 323	28028.613 592	22325.392 218	16253.952 973	9263.367 139	37
38	41772.771 219	36966.392 074	29264.035 040	21123.637 284	11857.109 938	38
39	55270.798 943	48754.253 880	38359.180 367	27452.279 015	15177.100 721	39
40	73130.441 833	64301.035 023	50281.060 573	35676.981 807	19426.688 922	40

29%

COMPOUND INTEREST
(Future Value of $1)

Base:	2.718 282	1.024 167	1.072 500	1.145 000	1.290 000	

Frequency of Conversion

Months	Continuous	Monthly	Quarterly	Semiannual	Annual	Months
0	1.000 000	1.000 000	1.000 000	1.000 000	1.000 000	0
1	1.024 461	1.024 167	1.024 167	1.024 167	1.024 167	1
2	1.049 520	1.048 917	1.048 333	1.048 333	1.048 333	2
3	1.075 193	1.074 266	1.072 500	1.072 500	1.072 500	3
4	1.101 493	1.100 228	1.098 419	1.096 667	1.096 667	4
5	1.128 437	1.126 816	1.124 337	1.120 833	1.120 833	5
6	1.156 040	1.154 048	1.150 256	1.145 000	1.145 000	6
7	1.184 318	1.181 937	1.178 054	1.172 671	1.169 167	7
8	1.213 287	1.210 501	1.205 852	1.200 342	1.193 333	8
9	1.242 965	1.239 755	1.233 650	1.228 013	1.217 500	9
10	1.273 370	1.269 715	1.263 463	1.255 683	1.241 667	10
11	1.304 518	1.300 400	1.293 276	1.283 354	1.265 833	11

Years						Years
1	1.336 427	1.331 826	1.323 089	1.311 025	1.290 000	1
2	1.786 038	1.773 762	1.750 566	1.718 787	1.664 100	2
3	2.386 911	2.362 343	2.316 155	2.253 372	2.146 689	3
4	3.189 933	3.146 231	3.064 480	2.954 227	2.769 229	4
5	4.263 115	4.190 233	4.054 581	3.873 066	3.572 305	5
6	5.697 343	5.580 664	5.364 574	5.077 686	4.608 274	6
7	7.614 086	7.432 476	7.097 811	6.656 973	5.944 673	7
8	10.175 674	9.898 768	9.391 039	8.727 458	7.668 628	8
9	13.599 051	13.183 441	12.425 184	11.441 916	9.892 530	9
10	18.174 145	17.558 056	16.439 630	15.000 638	12.761 364	10
11	24.288 427	23.384 283	21.751 101	19.666 212	16.462 160	11
12	32.459 722	31.143 807	28.778 652	25.782 895	21.236 186	12
13	43.380 065	41.478 147	38.076 730	33.802 020	27.394 680	13
14	57.974 311	55.241 694	50.378 919	44.315 293	35.339 137	14
15	77.478 463	73.572 350	66.655 816	58.098 457	45.587 487	15
16	103.544 348	97.985 604	88.191 607	76.168 530	58.807 859	16
17	138.379 512	130.499 821	116.685 384	99.858 847	75.862 137	17
18	184.934 184	173.803 116	154.385 199	130.917 445	97.862 157	18
19	247.151 127	231.475 590	204.265 426	171.636 043	126.242 183	19
20	330.299 560	308.285 317	270.261 429	225.019 143	162.852 416	20
21	441.421 411	410.582 546	357.580 043	295.005 722	210.079 617	21
22	589.927 708	546.824 703	473.110 379	386.759 877	271.002 705	22
23	788.395 604	728.275 613	625.967 346	507.051 868	349.593 490	23
24	1053.633 557	969.936 739	828.210 786	664.757 675	450.975 602	24
25	1408.104 848	1291.787 422	1095.796 946	871.513 931	581.758 527	25
26	1881.830 025	1720.436 682	1449.837 368	1142.576 552	750.468 500	26
27	2514.929 373	2291.323 112	1918.264 513	1497.946 424	968.104 365	27
28	3361.020 745	3051.644 771	2538.035 521	1963.845 210	1248.854 630	28
29	4491.760 512	4064.261 282	3358.047 998	2574.650 167	1611.022 473	29
30	6002.912 217	5412.890 754	4442.997 847	3375.430 735	2078.218 990	30
31	8022.456 895	7209.031 182	5878.483 537	4425.274 079	2680.902 497	31
32	10721.431 916	9601.178 548	7777.759 494	5801.644 950	3458.364 222	32
33	14328.416 324	12787.103 729	10290.671 459	7606.101 571	4461.289 846	33
34	19148.889 435	17030.203 214	13615.478 745	9971.789 312	5755.063 901	34
35	25591.102 207	22681.275 421	18014.496 157	13073.265 082	7424.032 433	35
36	34200.652 438	30207.522 968	23834.789 644	17139.377 354	9577.001 838	36
37	45706.692 026	40231.178 667	31535.558 498	22470.152 196	12354.332 371	37
38	61083.679 611	53580.948 648	41724.364 454	29458.931 283	15937.088 759	38
39	81633.908 502	71360.525 671	55205.066 028	38621.395 385	20558.844 499	39
40	109097.799 277	95039.836 966	73041.239 933	50633.614 885	26520.909 403	40

COMPOUND INTEREST
(Future Value of $1)

30%

Base:	2.718 282	1.025 000	1.075 000	1.150 000	1.300 000	

Frequency of Conversion

Months	Continuous	Monthly	Quarterly	Semiannual	Annual	Months
0	1.000 000	1.000 000	1.000 000	1.000 000	1.000 000	0
1	1.025 315	1.025 000	1.025 000	1.025 000	1.025 000	1
2	1.051 271	1.050 625	1.050 000	1.050 000	1.050 000	2
3	1.077 884	1.076 891	1.075 000	1.075 000	1.075 000	3
4	1.105 171	1.103 813	1.101 875	1.100 000	1.100 000	4
5	1.133 148	1.131 408	1.128 750	1.125 000	1.125 000	5
6	1.161 834	1.159 693	1.155 625	1.150 000	1.150 000	6
7	1.191 246	1.188 686	1.184 516	1.178 750	1.175 000	7
8	1.221 403	1.218 403	1.213 406	1.207 500	1.200 000	8
9	1.252 323	1.248 863	1.242 297	1.236 250	1.225 000	9
10	1.284 025	1.280 085	1.273 354	1.265 000	1.250 000	10
11	1.316 531	1.312 087	1.304 412	1.293 750	1.275 000	11

Years						Years
1	1.349 859	1.344 889	1.335 469	1.322 500	1.300 000	1
2	1.822 119	1.808 726	1.783 478	1.749 006	1.690 000	2
3	2.459 603	2.432 535	2.381 780	2.313 061	2.197 000	3
4	3.320 117	3.271 490	3.180 793	3.059 023	2.856 100	4
5	4.481 689	4.399 790	4.247 851	4.045 558	3.712 930	5
6	6.049 647	5.917 228	5.672 874	5.350 250	4.826 809	6
7	8.166 170	7.958 014	7.575 948	7.075 706	6.274 852	7
8	11.023 176	10.702 644	10.117 445	9.357 621	8.157 307	8
9	14.879 732	14.393 866	13.511 536	12.375 454	10.604 499	9
10	20.085 537	19.358 150	18.044 239	16.366 537	13.785 849	10
11	27.112 639	26.034 559	24.097 524	21.644 746	17.921 604	11
12	36.598 234	35.013 588	32.181 500	28.625 176	23.298 085	12
13	49.402 449	47.089 383	42.977 400	37.856 796	30.287 511	13
14	66.686 331	63.329 985	57.394 992	50.065 612	39.373 764	14
15	90.017 131	85.171 789	76.649 240	66.211 772	51.185 893	15
16	121.510 418	114.546 587	102.362 695	87.565 068	66.541 661	16
17	164.021 907	154.052 425	136.702 221	115.804 803	86.504 159	17
18	221.406 416	207.183 385	182.561 597	153.151 852	112.455 407	18
19	298.867 401	278.638 619	243.805 379	202.543 324	146.192 029	19
20	403.428 793	374.737 965	325.594 560	267.863 546	190.049 638	20
21	544.571 910	503.980 901	434.821 487	354.249 540	247.064 529	21
22	735.095 189	677.798 282	580.690 678	468.495 017	321.183 888	22
23	992.274 716	911.563 334	775.494 481	619.584 659	417.539 054	23
24	1339.430 764	1225.951 340	1035.648 948	819.400 712	542.800 770	24
25	1808.042 414	1648.768 257	1383.077 210	1083.657 442	705.641 001	25
26	2440.601 978	2217.410 002	1847.056 933	1433.136 966	917.333 302	26
27	3294.468 075	2982.169 931	2466.687 535	1895.323 638	1192.533 293	27
28	4447.066 748	4010.687 012	3294.185 082	2506.565 512	1550.293 280	28
29	6002.912 217	5393.928 140	4399.282 521	3314.932 889	2015.381 264	29
30	8103.083 928	7254.233 675	5875.106 048	4383.998 746	2619.995 644	30
31	10938.019 208	9756.137 797	7846.022 825	5797.838 341	3405.994 337	31
32	14764.781 566	13120.920 692	10478.121 359	7667.641 206	4427.792 638	32
33	19930.370 438	17646.179 602	13993.207 727	10140.455 495	5756.130 429	33
34	26903.186 074	23732.149 737	18687.497 098	13410.752 392	7482.969 558	34
35	36315.502 674	31917.102 957	24956.575 690	17735.720 039	9727.860 425	35
36	49020.801 136	42924.955 069	33328.736 689	23455.489 751	12646.218 553	36
37	66171.160 168	57729.292 354	44509.499 344	31019.885 196	16440.084 119	37
38	89321.723 361	77639.480 119	59441.062 839	41023.798 172	21372.109 354	38
39	120571.714 986	104416.469 132	79381.705 107	54253.973 082	27783.742 160	39
40	162754.791 419	140428.542 403	106011.817 501	71750.879 401	36118.864 808	40

31% COMPOUND INTEREST
(Future Value of $1)

Base: 2.718 282   1.025 833   1.077 500   1.155 000   1.310 000

Frequency of Conversion

Months	Continuous	Monthly	Quarterly	Semiannual	Annual	Months
0	1.000 000	1.000 000	1.000 000	1.000 000	1.000 000	0
1	1.026 170	1.025 833	1.025 833	1.025 833	1.025 833	1
2	1.053 025	1.052 334	1.051 667	1.051 667	1.051 667	2
3	1.080 582	1.079 519	1.077 500	1.077 500	1.077 500	3
4	1.108 861	1.107 407	1.105 335	1.103 333	1.103 333	4
5	1.137 880	1.136 015	1.133 171	1.129 167	1.129 167	5
6	1.167 658	1.165 362	1.161 006	1.155 000	1.155 000	6
7	1.198 215	1.195 467	1.190 999	1.184 837	1.180 833	7
8	1.229 573	1.226 350	1.220 992	1.214 675	1.206 667	8
9	1.261 750	1.258 031	1.250 984	1.244 513	1.232 500	9
10	1.294 770	1.290 530	1.283 301	1.274 350	1.258 333	10
11	1.328 654	1.323 869	1.315 618	1.304 188	1.284 167	11

Years						Years
1	1.363 425	1.358 069	1.347 936	1.334 025	1.310 000	1
2	1.858 928	1.844 350	1.816 930	1.779 623	1.716 100	2
3	2.534 509	2.504 754	2.449 105	2.374 061	2.248 091	3
4	3.455 613	3.401 627	3.301 235	3.167 057	2.944 999	4
5	4.711 470	4.619 643	4.449 852	4.224 933	3.857 949	5
6	6.423 737	6.273 792	5.998 114	5.636 166	5.053 913	6
7	8.758 284	8.520 239	8.085 070	7.518 787	6.620 626	7
8	11.941 264	11.571 068	10.898 154	10.030 250	8.673 020	8
9	16.281 020	15.714 304	14.690 008	13.380 604	11.361 657	9
10	22.197 951	21.341 101	19.801 184	17.850 060	14.883 770	10
11	30.265 244	28.982 678	26.690 719	23.812 427	19.497 739	11
12	41.264 394	39.360 462	35.977 368	31.766 372	25.542 038	12
13	56.260 911	53.454 205	48.495 171	42.377 135	33.460 070	13
14	76.707 539	72.594 473	65.368 364	56.532 157	43.832 692	14
15	104.584 986	98.588 268	88.112 339	75.415 311	57.420 826	15
16	142.593 796	133.889 624	118.769 751	100.605 910	75.221 282	16
17	194.415 962	181.831 283	160.093 965	134.210 800	98.539 879	17
18	265.071 606	246.939 342	215.796 341	179.040 562	129.087 242	18
19	361.405 284	335.360 547	290.879 551	238.844 586	169.104 287	19
20	492.749 041	455.442 602	392.086 877	318.624 648	221.526 616	20
21	671.826 418	618.522 261	528.507 825	425.053 246	290.199 867	21
22	915.985 010	839.995 612	712.394 466	567.031 657	380.161 826	22
23	1248.876 967	1140.771 598	960.261 800	756.434 406	498.011 991	23
24	1702.750 221	1549.245 996	1294.370 982	1009.102 409	652.395 709	24
25	2321.572 415	2103.982 218	1744.728 612	1346.167 841	854.638 378	25
26	3165.290 134	2857.352 019	2351.781 656	1795.821 554	1119.576 276	26
27	4315.636 063	3880.479 829	3170.050 012	2395.670 849	1466.644 921	27
28	5884.046 591	5269.957 501	4273.022 988	3195.884 804	1921.304 847	28
29	8022.456 895	7156.963 388	5759.759 432	4263.390 226	2516.909 349	29
30	10938.019 208	9719.646 680	7763.784 282	5687.469 146	3297.151 248	30
31	14913.170 087	13199.946 188	10465.080 545	7587.226 028	4319.268 135	31
32	20332.990 628	17926.431 392	14106.253 708	10121.549 202	5658.241 256	32
33	27722.510 068	24345.322 162	19014.320 322	13502.399 674	7412.296 046	33
34	37797.566 454	33062.615 653	25630.077 609	18012.538 725	9710.107 820	34
35	51534.151 356	44901.297 529	34547.691 799	24029.176 973	12720.241 244	35
36	70262.956 194	60979.038 711	46568.060 652	32055.522 811	16663.516 030	36
37	95798.279 068	82813.712 893	62770.742 703	42762.868 818	21829.205 999	37
38	130613.779 572	112466.696 559	84610.913 238	57046.736 075	28596.259 859	38
39	178082.107 320	152737.480 219	114050.054 701	76101.772 093	37461.100 415	39
40	242801.617 498	207427.963 809	153732.118 939	101521.666 516	49074.041 544	40

COMPOUND INTEREST

32%

(Future Value of $1)

Base:	2.718 282	1.026 667	1.080 000	1.160 000	1.320 000	

Frequency of Conversion

Months	Continuous	Monthly	Quarterly	Semiannual	Annual	Months
0	1.000 000	1.000 000	1.000 000	1.000 000	1.000 000	0
1	1.027 025	1.026 667	1.026 667	1.026 667	1.026 667	1
2	1.054 781	1.054 044	1.053 333	1.053 333	1.053 333	2
3	1.083 287	1.082 152	1.080 000	1.080 000	1.080 000	3
4	1.112 563	1.111 010	1.108 800	1.106 667	1.106 667	4
5	1.142 631	1.140 637	1.137 600	1.133 333	1.133 333	5
6	1.173 511	1.171 054	1.166 400	1.160 000	1.160 000	6
7	1.205 225	1.202 282	1.197 504	1.190 933	1.186 667	7
8	1.237 797	1.234 343	1.228 608	1.221 867	1.213 333	8
9	1.271 249	1.267 258	1.259 712	1.252 800	1.240 000	9
10	1.305 605	1.301 052	1.293 304	1.283 733	1.266 667	10
11	1.340 890	1.335 747	1.326 897	1.314 667	1.293 333	11

Years						Years
1	1.377 128	1.371 367	1.360 489	1.345 600	1.320 000	1
2	1.896 481	1.880 646	1.850 930	1.810 639	1.742 400	2
3	2.611 696	2.579 055	2.518 170	2.436 396	2.299 968	3
4	3.596 640	3.536 830	3.425 943	3.278 415	3.035 958	4
5	4.953 032	4.850 290	4.660 957	4.411 435	4.007 464	5
6	6.820 958	6.651 525	6.341 181	5.936 027	5.289 853	6
7	9.393 331	9.121 679	8.627 106	7.987 518	6.982 606	7
8	12.935 817	12.509 165	11.737 083	10.748 004	9.217 040	8
9	17.814 273	17.154 650	15.968 172	14.462 514	12.166 492	9
10	24.532 530	23.525 313	21.724 521	19.460 759	16.059 770	10
11	33.784 428	32.261 827	29.555 972	26.186 398	21.198 896	11
12	46.525 474	44.242 789	40.210 573	35.236 417	27.982 543	12
13	64.071 523	60.673 079	54.706 041	47.414 123	36.936 956	13
14	88.234 673	83.205 030	74.426 965	63.800 444	48.756 782	14
15	121.510 418	114.104 592	101.257 064	85.849 877	64.358 953	15
16	167.335 370	156.479 216	137.759 117	115.519 594	84.953 818	16
17	230.442 183	214.590 357	187.419 758	155.443 166	112.139 039	17
18	317.348 329	294.282 031	254.982 512	209.164 324	148.023 532	18
19	437.029 195	403.568 524	346.900 892	281.451 515	195.391 062	19
20	601.845 038	553.440 360	471.954 834	378.721 158	257.916 202	20
21	828.817 511	758.969 579	642.089 342	509.607 191	340.449 386	21
22	1141.387 607	1040.825 467	873.555 461	685.727 436	449.393 190	22
23	1571.836 563	1427.353 195	1188.462 560	922.714 838	593.199 010	23
24	2164.619 772	1957.424 378	1616.890 192	1241.605 086	783.022 694	24
25	2980.957 987	2684.346 251	2199.761 256	1670.703 804	1033.589 955	25
26	4105.160 008	3681.222 566	2992.750 904	2248.099 038	1364.338 741	26
27	5653.329 824	5048.305 366	4071.604 565	3025.042 066	1800.927 138	27
28	7785.357 462	6923.076 942	5539.373 060	4070.496 604	2377.223 823	28
29	10721.431 916	9494.075 908	7536.255 893	5477.260 230	3137.935 446	29
30	14764.781 566	13019.857 803	10252.992 943	7370.201 365	4142.074 789	30
31	20332.990 628	17854.997 037	13949.083 705	9917.342 957	5467.538 721	31
32	28001.125 926	24485.745 083	18977.574 383	13344.776 683	7217.151 112	32
33	38561.127 946	33578.930 932	25818.780 436	17956.731 505	9526.639 467	33
34	53103.599 918	46049.021 531	35126.165 744	24162.577 913	12575.164 097	34
35	73130.441 833	63150.086 233	47788.760 701	32513.164 839	16599.216 608	35
36	100709.961 867	86601.913 756	65016.081 346	43749.714 608	21910.965 923	36
37	138690.484 632	118762.964 766	88453.660 894	58869.615 976	28922.475 018	37
38	190994.517 036	162867.553 248	120340.229 118	79214.955 258	38177.667 023	38
39	263023.852 246	223351.109 103	163721.553 158	106591.643 795	50394.520 471	39
40	362217.449 611	306296.232 386	222741.365 586	143429.715 890	66520.767 022	40

33%   COMPOUND INTEREST
(Future Value of $1)

Base:	2.718 282	1.027 500	1.082 500	1.165 000	1.330 000	
			Frequency of Conversion			
Months	Continuous	Monthly	Quarterly	Semiannual	Annual	Months
0	1.000 000	1.000 000	1.000 000	1.000 000	1.000 000	0
1	1.027 882	1.027 500	1.027 500	1.027 500	1.027 500	1
2	1.056 541	1.055 756	1.055 000	1.055 000	1.055 000	2
3	1.085 999	1.084 790	1.082 500	1.082 500	1.082 500	3
4	1.116 278	1.114 621	1.112 269	1.110 000	1.110 000	4
5	1.147 402	1.145 273	1.142 037	1.137 500	1.137 500	5
6	1.179 393	1.176 768	1.171 806	1.165 000	1.165 000	6
7	1.212 277	1.209 129	1.204 031	1.197 038	1.192 500	7
8	1.246 077	1.242 381	1.236 256	1.229 075	1.220 000	8
9	1.280 819	1.276 546	1.268 480	1.261 113	1.247 500	9
10	1.316 531	1.311 651	1.303 363	1.293 150	1.275 000	10
11	1.353 238	1.347 721	1.338 247	1.325 188	1.302 500	11

Years						Years
1	1.390 968	1.384 784	1.373 130	1.357 225	1.330 000	1
2	1.934 792	1.917 626	1.885 486	1.842 060	1.768 900	2
3	2.691 234	2.655 498	2.589 017	2.500 089	2.352 637	3
4	3.743 421	3.677 290	3.555 056	3.393 184	3.129 007	4
5	5.206 980	5.092 251	4.881 554	4.605 314	4.161 580	5
6	7.242 743	7.051 667	6.703 008	6.250 447	5.534 901	6
7	10.074 425	9.765 034	9.204 100	8.483 263	7.361 418	7
8	14.013 204	13.522 461	12.638 425	11.513 697	9.790 686	8
9	19.491 920	18.725 684	17.354 199	15.626 678	13.021 613	9
10	27.112 639	25.931 024	23.829 570	21.208 918	17.318 745	10
11	37.712 817	35.908 861	32.721 094	28.785 273	23.033 930	11
12	52.457 326	49.726 008	44.930 313	39.068 093	30.635 127	12
13	72.966 468	68.859 770	61.695 155	53.024 192	40.744 720	13
14	101.494 032	95.355 892	84.715 462	71.965 759	54.190 477	14
15	141.174 964	132.047 292	116.325 332	97.673 727	72.073 334	15
16	196.369 875	182.856 947	159.729 790	132.565 224	95.857 535	16
17	273.144 238	253.217 334	219.329 749	179.920 837	127.490 521	17
18	379.934 930	350.651 256	301.168 234	244.193 058	169.562 393	18
19	528.477 378	485.576 170	413.543 103	331.424 923	225.517 983	19
20	735.095 189	672.418 001	567.848 394	449.818 191	299.938 917	20
21	1022.493 980	931.153 539	779.729 602	610.504 494	398.918 760	21
22	1422.256 537	1289.446 313	1070.670 020	828.591 962	530.561 951	22
23	1978.313 514	1785.604 334	1470.169 005	1124.585 725	705.647 394	23
24	2751.771 046	2472.675 911	2018.733 000	1526.315 861	938.511 035	24
25	3827.625 821	3424.121 483	2771.982 617	2071.554 045	1248.219 676	25
26	5324.105 525	4741.667 875	3806.292 179	2811.564 938	1660.132 169	26
27	7405.661 098	6566.184 742	5226.533 552	3815.926 224	2207.975 785	27
28	10301.038 558	9092.746 097	7176.709 429	5179.070 469	2936.607 794	28
29	14328.416 324	12591.487 270	9854.554 211	7029.163 917	3905.688 366	29
30	19930.370 438	17436.487 280	13531.582 916	9540.156 997	5194.565 526	30
31	27722.510 068	24145.764 687	18580.620 927	12948.139 581	6908.772 150	31
32	38561.127 946	33436.663 185	25513.605 924	17573.538 743	9188.666 960	32
33	53637.299 970	46302.548 685	35033.494 833	23851.246 120	12220.927 056	33
34	74607.774 755	64119.018 182	48105.538 820	32371.507 515	16253.832 985	34
35	103777.036 820	88790.976 077	66055.153 110	43935.419 287	21617.597 870	35
36	144350.550 683	122956.303 080	90702.304 962	59630.249 442	28751.405 167	36
37	200787.015 326	170267.893 598	124546.045 812	80931.665 299	38239.368 872	37
38	279288.338 928	235784.216 538	171017.897 879	109842.479 435	50858.360 600	38
39	388481.178 101	326510.157 574	234829.786 881	149080.959 152	67641.619 598	39
40	540364.937 247	452145.968 736	322451.798 851	202336.404 785	89963.354 066	40

COMPOUND INTEREST   **34%**
(Future Value of $1)

Base:	2.718 282	1.028 333	1.085 000	1.170 000	1.340 000	

Frequency of Conversion

Months	Continuous	Monthly	Quarterly	Semiannual	Annual	Months
0	1.000 000	1.000 000	1.000 000	1.000 000	1.000 000	0
1	1.028 739	1.028 333	1.028 333	1.028 333	1.028 333	1
2	1.058 303	1.057 469	1.056 667	1.056 667	1.056 667	2
3	1.088 717	1.087 431	1.085 000	1.085 000	1.085 000	3
4	1.120 005	1.118 242	1.115 742	1.113 333	1.113 333	4
5	1.152 193	1.149 925	1.146 483	1.141 667	1.141 667	5
6	1.185 305	1.182 506	1.177 225	1.170 000	1.170 000	6
7	1.219 369	1.216 011	1.210 580	1.203 150	1.198 333	7
8	1.254 412	1.250 464	1.243 934	1.236 300	1.226 667	8
9	1.290 462	1.285 894	1.277 289	1.269 450	1.255 000	9
10	1.327 548	1.322 328	1.313 479	1.302 600	1.283 333	10
11	1.365 699	1.359 794	1.349 669	1.335 750	1.311 667	11

Years						Years
1	1.404 948	1.398 321	1.385 859	1.368 900	1.340 000	1
2	1.973 878	1.955 302	1.920 604	1.873 887	1.795 600	2
3	2.773 195	2.734 141	2.661 686	2.565 164	2.406 104	3
4	3.896 193	3.823 207	3.688 721	3.511 453	3.224 179	4
5	5.473 947	5.346 072	5.112 046	4.806 828	4.320 400	5
6	7.690 609	7.475 526	7.084 574	6.580 067	5.789 336	6
7	10.804 903	10.453 188	9.818 218	9.007 454	7.757 711	7
8	15.180 322	14.616 915	13.606 663	12.330 304	10.395 333	8
9	21.327 557	20.439 143	18.856 912	16.878 953	13.929 746	9
10	29.964 100	28.580 488	26.133 016	23.105 599	18.665 859	10
11	42.097 990	39.964 704	36.216 667	31.629 255	25.012 251	11
12	59.145 470	55.883 496	50.191 183	43.297 287	33.516 417	12
13	83.096 285	78.143 081	69.557 888	59.269 656	44.911 998	13
14	116.745 926	109.269 132	96.397 404	81.134 232	60.182 078	14
15	164.021 907	152.793 351	133.593 181	111.064 650	80.643 984	15
16	230.442 183	213.654 193	185.141 272	152.036 399	108.062 939	16
17	323.759 190	298.757 203	256.579 643	208.122 627	144.804 338	17
18	454.864 694	417.758 551	355.583 131	284.899 064	194.037 813	18
19	639.061 057	584.160 668	492.787 975	389.998 329	260.010 669	19
20	897.847 292	816.844 287	682.934 503	533.868 713	348.414 297	20
21	1261.428 389	1142.210 741	946.450 723	730.812 881	466.875 157	21
22	1772.240 776	1597.177 574	1311.646 970	1000.409 753	625.612 711	22
23	2489.905 408	2233.367 373	1817.757 365	1369.460 910	838.321 033	23
24	3498.186 604	3122.965 101	2519.154 860	1874.655 040	1123.350 184	24
25	4914.768 840	4366.908 527	3491.192 681	2566.215 284	1505.289 246	25
26	6904.992 640	6106.341 077	4838.299 753	3512.892 103	2017.087 590	26
27	9701.152 773	8538.626 610	6705.199 808	4808.798 000	2702.897 371	27
28	13629.611 214	11939.743 205	9292.459 494	6582.763 582	3621.882 477	28
29	19148.889 435	16695.596 882	12878.035 840	9011.145 067	4853.322 519	29
30	26903.186 074	23345.808 235	17847.138 016	12335.356 482	6503.452 176	30
31	37797.566 454	32644.940 220	24733.611 500	16885.869 488	8714.625 916	31
32	53103.599 918	45648.114 267	34277.290 695	23115.066 742	11677.598 727	32
33	74607.774 755	63830.729 114	47503.481 544	31642.214 863	15647.982 294	33
34	104820.013 380	89255.866 200	65833.113 208	43315.027 927	20968.296 274	34
35	147266.625 241	124808.376 179	91235.392 728	59293.941 729	28097.517 008	35
36	206901.890 302	174522.207 084	126439.362 817	81167.476 832	37650.672 790	36
37	290686.312 263	244038.114 251	175227.091 062	111110.159 036	50451.901 539	37
38	408399.034 024	341243.685 846	242839.988 733	152098.696 704	67605.548 062	38
39	573779.238 840	477168.304 168	336541.911 246	208207.905 919	90591.434 403	39
40	806129.759 124	667234.589 084	466399.535 825	285015.802 412	121392.522 100	40

91

35%

COMPOUND INTEREST
(Future Value of $1)

Base:	2.718 282	1.029 167	1.087 500	1.175 000	1.350 000	
			Frequency of Conversion			
Months	Continuous	Monthly	Quarterly	Semiannual	Annual	Months
0	1.000 000	1.000 000	1.000 000	1.000 000	1.000 000	0
1	1.029 596	1.029 167	1.029 167	1.029 167	1.029 167	1
2	1.060 068	1.059 184	1.058 333	1.058 333	1.058 333	2
3	1.091 442	1.090 077	1.087 500	1.087 500	1.087 500	3
4	1.123 745	1.121 871	1.119 219	1.116 667	1.116 667	4
5	1.157 003	1.154 592	1.150 937	1.145 833	1.145 833	5
6	1.191 246	1.188 268	1.182 656	1.175 000	1.175 000	6
7	1.226 503	1.222 925	1.217 150	1.209 271	1.204 167	7
8	1.262 802	1.258 594	1.251 645	1.243 542	1.233 333	8
9	1.300 176	1.295 303	1.286 139	1.277 813	1.262 500	9
10	1.338 657	1.333 083	1.323 651	1.312 083	1.291 667	10
11	1.378 276	1.371 964	1.361 163	1.346 354	1.320 833	11

Years						Years
1	1.419 068	1.411 980	1.398 676	1.380 625	1.350 000	1
2	2.013 753	1.993 687	1.956 294	1.906 125	1.822 500	2
3	2.857 651	2.815 047	2.736 221	2.631 644	2.460 375	3
4	4.055 200	3.974 790	3.827 086	3.633 314	3.321 506	4
5	5.754 603	5.612 323	5.352 853	5.016 244	4.484 033	5
6	8.166 170	7.924 488	7.486 906	6.925 552	6.053 445	6
7	11.588 347	11.189 219	10.471 754	9.561 590	8.172 151	7
8	16.444 647	15.798 953	14.646 589	13.200 971	11.032 404	8
9	23.336 065	22.307 805	20.485 830	18.225 590	14.893 745	9
10	33.115 452	31.498 175	28.653 035	25.162 705	20.106 556	10
11	46.993 063	44.474 792	40.076 306	34.740 260	27.143 850	11
12	66.686 331	62.797 516	56.053 760	47.963 272	36.644 198	12
13	94.632 408	88.668 835	78.401 038	66.219 292	49.469 667	13
14	134.289 780	125.198 619	109.657 635	91.424 010	66.784 051	14
15	190.566 268	176.777 944	153.375 481	126.222 273	90.158 469	15
16	270.426 407	249.606 918	214.522 574	174.265 626	121.713 933	16
17	383.753 339	352.439 970	300.047 535	240.595 480	164.313 809	17
18	544.571 910	497.638 181	419.669 227	332.172 135	221.823 643	18
19	772.784 326	702.655 149	586.981 194	458.605 154	299.461 918	19
20	1096.633 158	992.135 002	820.996 395	633.161 741	404.273 589	20
21	1556.196 528	1400.874 759	1148.307 794	874.158 928	545.769 345	21
22	2208.347 992	1978.007 112	1606.110 329	1206.885 670	736.788 616	22
23	3133.794 971	2792.906 439	2246.427 659	1666.256 528	994.664 631	23
24	4447.066 748	3943.527 973	3142.024 015	2300.475 419	1342.797 252	24
25	6310.688 108	5568.182 543	4394.672 971	3176.093 876	1812.776 291	25
26	8955.292 703	7862.162 267	6146.722 759	4384.994 607	2447.247 992	26
27	12708.165 264	11101.215 709	8597.272 407	6054.033 180	3303.784 789	27
28	18033.744 928	15674.694 318	12024.796 910	8358.349 559	4460.109 466	28
29	25591.102 207	22132.354 547	16818.792 506	11539.746 360	6021.147 779	29
30	36315.502 674	31250.441 497	23524.038 158	15932.062 318	8128.549 501	30
31	51534.151 356	44124.997 712	32902.503 024	21996.203 537	10973.541 827	31
32	73130.441 833	62303.613 321	46019.934 925	30368.508 509	14814.281 466	32
33	103777.036 820	87971.454 596	64366.969 558	41927.522 060	19999.279 979	33
34	147266.625 241	124213.932 569	90028.523 005	57886.185 144	26999.027 972	34
35	208981.288 870	175387.585 837	125920.716 946	79919.114 364	36448.687 763	35
36	296558.565 298	247643.759 677	176122.260 224	110338.327 269	49205.728 479	36
37	420836.636 272	349668.030 463	246337.944 215	152335.853 085	66427.733 447	37
38	597195.613 793	493724.258 132	344546.922 590	210318.687 166	89677.440 154	38
39	847460.915 696	697128.767 378	481909.444 543	290371.237 468	121064.544 208	39
40	1202604.284 165	984331.861 968	674035.080 603	400893.789 730	163437.134 680	40

COMPOUND INTEREST

36%

(Future Value of $1)

Base: 2.718 282   1.030 000   1.090 000   1.180 000   1.360 000

Frequency of Conversion

Months	Continuous	Monthly	Quarterly	Semiannual	Annual	Months
0	1.000 000	1.000 000	1.000 000	1.000 000	1.000 000	0
1	1.030 455	1.030 000	1.030 000	1.030 000	1.030 000	1
2	1.061 837	1.060 900	1.060 000	1.060 000	1.060 000	2
3	1.094 174	1.092 727	1.090 000	1.090 000	1.090 000	3
4	1.127 497	1.125 509	1.122 700	1.120 000	1.120 000	4
5	1.161 834	1.159 274	1.155 400	1.150 000	1.150 000	5
6	1.197 217	1.194 052	1.188 100	1.180 000	1.180 000	6
7	1.233 678	1.229 874	1.223 743	1.215 400	1.210 000	7
8	1.271 249	1.266 770	1.259 386	1.250 800	1.240 000	8
9	1.309 964	1.304 773	1.295 029	1.286 200	1.270 000	9
10	1.349 859	1.343 916	1.333 880	1.321 600	1.300 000	10
11	1.390 968	1.384 234	1.372 731	1.357 000	1.330 000	11

Years						Years
1	1.433 329	1.425 761	1.411 582	1.392 400	1.360 000	1
2	2.054 433	2.032 794	1.992 563	1.938 778	1.849 600	2
3	2.944 680	2.898 278	2.812 665	2.699 554	2.515 456	3
4	4.220 696	4.132 252	3.970 306	3.758 859	3.421 020	4
5	6.049 647	5.891 603	5.604 411	5.233 836	4.652 587	5
6	8.671 138	8.400 017	7.911 083	7.287 593	6.327 519	6
7	12.428 597	11.976 416	11.167 140	10.147 244	8.605 426	7
8	17.814 273	17.075 506	15.763 329	14.129 023	11.703 379	8
9	25.533 722	24.345 588	22.251 225	19.673 251	15.916 595	9
10	36.598 234	34.710 987	31.409 420	27.393 035	21.646 570	10
11	52.457 326	49.489 568	44.336 960	38.142 061	29.439 335	11
12	75.188 628	70.560 290	62.585 237	53.109 006	40.037 495	12
13	107.770 073	100.602 102	88.344 170	73.948 980	54.450 994	13
14	154.470 015	143.434 542	124.705 005	102.966 560	74.053 351	14
15	221.406 416	204.503 360	176.031 292	143.370 638	100.712 558	15
16	317.348 329	291.572 891	248.482 535	199.629 277	136.969 078	16
17	454.864 694	415.713 224	350.753 376	277.963 805	186.277 947	17
18	651.970 946	592.707 655	495.117 015	387.036 802	253.338 008	18
19	934.489 135	845.059 392	698.898 074	538.910 044	344.539 690	19
20	1339.430 764	1204.852 628	986.551 668	750.378 345	468.573 979	20
21	1919.845 513	1717.831 751	1392.598 192	1044.826 807	637.260 611	21
22	2751.771 046	2449.217 321	1965.765 998	1454.816 847	866.674 431	22
23	3944.194 382	3491.998 260	2774.839 132	2025.686 977	1178.677 227	23
24	5653.329 824	4978.754 536	3916.911 890	2820.566 547	1603.001 028	24
25	8103.083 928	7098.513 483	5529.040 792	3927.356 860	2180.081 398	25
26	11614.388 542	10120.782 878	7804.692 303	5468.451 692	2964.910 702	26
27	16647.244 729	14429.816 372	11016.960 126	7614.272 136	4032.278 554	27
28	23860.985 542	20573.467 788	15551.338 312	10602.112 522	5483.898 834	28
29	34200.652 438	29332.845 678	21951.983 172	14762.381 475	7458.102 414	29
30	49020.801 136	41821.624 068	30987.015 749	20555.139 966	10143.019 282	30
31	70262.956 194	59627.635 821	43740.701 580	28620.976 889	13794.506 224	31
32	100709.961 867	85014.750 929	61743.569 959	39851.848 220	18760.528 465	32
33	144350.550 683	121210.706 679	87156.087 890	55489.713 461	25514.318 712	33
34	206901.890 302	172817.484 650	123027.930 866	77263.877 024	34699.473 449	34
35	296558.565 298	246396.410 177	173663.964 726	107582.222 368	47191.283 890	35
36	425066.114 782	351302.364 290	245140.858 927	149797.486 425	64180.146 091	36
37	609259.765 450	500873.170 461	346036.328 321	208578.020 098	87284.998 683	37
38	873269.942 927	714125.375 714	488458.517 450	290424.035 185	118707.598 209	38
39	1251683.496 049	1018172.028 997	689499.060 480	404386.426 591	161442.333 565	39
40	1794074.772 606	1451669.855 025	973284.193 886	563067.660 386	219561.573 648	40

Table 2

Reversion Factors
(Present Value of $1)

Table 2 - REVERSION FACTORS (Present Value of $1)

The present value of one to be collected at a given future time when discounted at the effective interest rate for the number of periods from now to the date of collection. This factor is reciprocal to the corresponding factor in Table 1.

$$1/S^n = \frac{1}{(1 + i)^n}$$

Where $1/S^n$ = Present Value Factor

i = Effective Rate of Interest

n = Number of Compounding Periods

AND $1/S^n = \frac{1}{(e)^{in}}$ for Continuous Compounding

Where $1/S^n$ = Present Value Factor

i = Nominal Rate of Interest

n = Number of Years

e = 2.718282

This Table is used in solving problems dealing with compound discounting.

Example 1:
What is the Present Value of $10,000 to be received in 10 years, assuming an interest rate of 6% and annual compounding?

$10,000 × .558395 = $5,583.95

Example 2:
What is the Present Value of $10,000 to be received in 10 years and 7 months, assuming an interest rate of 6% and annual compounding?

$10,000 × .558395 × .966184 = $5,395.12

(Assumes simple interest for time less than one conversion period).

Example 3:

Assuming a 6% rate and annual compounding, what is the Present Value of the following cash flows: $1,000 in 1 year; $2,000 in 2 years; and $3,000 in 3 years?

Cash Flows		Present Value Factor		Present Value
$1,000	×	.943396	=	$ 943.40
2,000	×	.889996	=	1,779.99
3,000	×	.839619	=	2,518.86
	Present Value		=	$5,242.25

Example 4:

A property sold for $100,000. Five years previously it sold for $135,000. What is the depreciation in sales price expressed as a monthly compound rate?

$100,000/$135,000 = .740741 (Present Value Factor)

Scan tables of Present Value Factors, monthly frequency, for .740741 at 5 years. Closest match is found at 6% nominal and therefore monthly rate is approximately 0.5%.

Example 5:

How long will it take $1 to be worth 50 cents assuming a 6% rate of inflation?

.50/1.00 = .500000 (Present Value Factor)

Scan tables of Present Value Factors at 6% nominal interest for .500000.

Assuming annual frequency, the target is bracketed between the Factors for 11 and 12 years. Visual interpolation indicates an answer of slightly less than 12 years. Mathematical straight-line interpolation calculates 11.9 years:

(.526788 − .500000)/(.526788 − .496969) + 11 = 11.9 years

6%

REVERSION FACTORS
(Present Value of $1)

Base: 2.718 282 1.005 000 1.015 000 1.030 000 1.060 000

Frequency of Conversion

Months	Continuous	Monthly	Quarterly	Semiannual	Annual	Months
0	1.000 000	1.000 000	1.000 000	1.000 000	1.000 000	0
1	.995 012	.995 025	.995 025	.995 025	.995 025	1
2	.990 050	.990 075	.990 099	.990 099	.990 099	2
3	.985 112	.985 149	.985 222	.985 222	.985 222	3
4	.980 199	.980 248	.980 320	.980 392	.980 392	4
5	.975 310	.975 371	.975 467	.975 610	.975 610	5
6	.970 446	.970 518	.970 662	.970 874	.970 874	6
7	.965 605	.965 690	.965 833	.966 044	.966 184	7
8	.960 789	.960 885	.961 051	.961 261	.961 538	8
9	.955 997	.956 105	.956 317	.956 526	.956 938	9
10	.951 229	.951 348	.951 559	.951 837	.952 381	10
11	.946 485	.946 615	.946 849	.947 194	.947 867	11

Years						Years
1	.941 765	.941 905	.942 184	.942 596	.943 396	1
2	.886 920	.887 186	.887 711	.888 487	.889 996	2
3	.835 270	.835 645	.836 387	.837 484	.839 619	3
4	.786 628	.787 098	.788 031	.789 409	.792 094	4
5	.740 818	.741 372	.742 470	.744 094	.747 258	5
6	.697 676	.698 302	.699 544	.701 380	.704 961	6
7	.657 047	.657 735	.659 099	.661 118	.665 057	7
8	.618 783	.619 524	.620 993	.623 167	.627 412	8
9	.582 748	.583 533	.585 090	.587 395	.591 898	9
10	.548 812	.549 633	.551 262	.553 676	.558 395	10
11	.516 851	.517 702	.519 391	.521 893	.526 788	11
12	.486 752	.487 626	.489 362	.491 934	.496 969	12
13	.458 406	.459 298	.461 069	.463 695	.468 839	13
14	.431 711	.432 615	.434 412	.437 077	.442 301	14
15	.406 570	.407 482	.409 296	.411 987	.417 265	15
16	.382 893	.383 810	.385 632	.388 337	.393 646	16
17	.360 595	.361 513	.363 337	.366 045	.371 364	17
18	.339 596	.340 511	.342 330	.345 032	.350 344	18
19	.319 819	.320 729	.322 538	.325 226	.330 513	19
20	.301 194	.302 096	.303 890	.306 557	.311 805	20
21	.283 654	.284 546	.286 321	.288 959	.294 155	21
22	.267 135	.268 015	.269 767	.272 372	.277 505	22
23	.251 579	.252 445	.254 170	.256 737	.261 797	23
24	.236 928	.237 779	.239 475	.241 999	.246 979	24
25	.223 130	.223 966	.225 629	.228 107	.232 999	25
26	.210 136	.210 954	.212 585	.215 013	.219 810	26
27	.197 899	.198 699	.200 294	.202 670	.207 368	27
28	.186 374	.187 156	.188 714	.191 036	.195 630	28
29	.175 520	.176 283	.177 803	.180 070	.184 557	29
30	.165 299	.166 042	.167 523	.169 733	.174 110	30
31	.155 673	.156 396	.157 838	.159 990	.164 255	31
32	.146 607	.147 310	.148 712	.150 806	.154 957	32
33	.138 069	.138 752	.140 114	.142 149	.146 186	33
34	.130 029	.130 691	.132 013	.133 989	.137 912	34
35	.122 456	.123 099	.124 381	.126 297	.130 105	35
36	.115 325	.115 947	.117 190	.119 047	.122 741	36
37	.108 609	.109 212	.110 414	.112 214	.115 793	37
38	.102 284	.102 867	.104 031	.105 772	.109 239	38
39	.096 328	.096 891	.098 016	.099 700	.103 056	39
40	.090 718	.091 262	.092 349	.093 977	.097 222	40

REVERSION FACTORS

(Present Value of $1)

6¼ %

Base:	2.718 282	1.005 208	1.015 625	1.031 250	1.062 500	
			Frequency of Conversion			
Months	Continuous	Monthly	Quarterly	Semiannual	Annual	Months
0	1.000 000	1.000 000	1.000 000	1.000 000	1.000 000	0
1	.994 805	.994 819	.994 819	.994 819	.994 819	1
2	.989 637	.989 664	.989 691	.989 691	.989 691	2
3	.984 496	.984 536	.984 615	.984 615	.984 615	3
4	.979 382	.979 435	.979 514	.979 592	.979 592	4
5	.974 294	.974 360	.974 465	.974 619	.974 619	5
6	.969 233	.969 312	.969 467	.969 697	.969 697	6
7	.964 198	.964 290	.964 444	.964 673	.964 824	7
8	.959 189	.959 293	.959 473	.959 700	.960 000	8
9	.954 207	.954 323	.954 553	.954 779	.955 224	9
10	.949 250	.949 378	.949 607	.949 907	.950 495	10
11	.944 319	.944 459	.944 712	.945 085	.945 813	11
Years						Years
1	.939 413	.939 565	.939 867	.940 312	.941 176	1
2	.882 497	.882 783	.883 350	.884 187	.885 813	2
3	.829 029	.829 433	.830 232	.831 412	.833 706	3
4	.778 801	.779 306	.780 308	.781 787	.784 665	4
5	.731 616	.732 209	.733 386	.735 124	.738 508	5
6	.687 289	.687 958	.689 285	.691 246	.695 067	6
7	.645 649	.646 382	.647 836	.649 987	.654 180	7
8	.606 531	.607 318	.608 880	.611 191	.615 699	8
9	.569 783	.570 615	.572 266	.574 710	.579 481	9
10	.535 261	.536 130	.537 854	.540 407	.545 394	10
11	.502 832	.503 730	.505 512	.508 151	.513 312	11
12	.472 367	.473 287	.475 114	.477 821	.483 117	12
13	.443 747	.444 684	.446 544	.449 301	.454 699	13
14	.416 862	.417 810	.419 692	.422 483	.427 952	14
15	.391 606	.392 560	.394 455	.397 266	.402 778	15
16	.367 879	.368 835	.370 735	.373 554	.379 085	16
17	.345 591	.346 545	.348 442	.351 257	.356 786	17
18	.324 652	.325 602	.327 489	.330 291	.335 799	18
19	.304 983	.305 924	.307 796	.310 577	.316 046	19
20	.286 505	.287 436	.289 287	.292 039	.297 455	20
21	.269 146	.270 065	.271 892	.274 608	.279 958	21
22	.252 840	.253 743	.255 542	.258 218	.263 490	22
23	.237 521	.238 409	.240 176	.242 805	.247 990	23
24	.223 130	.224 000	.225 733	.228 313	.233 402	24
25	.209 611	.210 463	.212 159	.214 685	.219 673	25
26	.196 912	.197 744	.199 401	.201 871	.206 751	26
27	.184 981	.185 793	.187 411	.189 822	.194 589	27
28	.173 774	.174 565	.176 141	.178 492	.183 143	28
29	.163 246	.164 015	.165 549	.167 838	.172 370	29
30	.153 355	.154 103	.155 594	.157 820	.162 230	30
31	.144 064	.144 790	.146 238	.148 400	.152 687	31
32	.135 335	.136 040	.137 444	.139 542	.143 706	32
33	.127 136	.127 818	.129 179	.131 214	.135 252	33
34	.119 433	.120 093	.121 412	.123 382	.127 296	34
35	.112 197	.112 836	.114 111	.116 017	.119 808	35
36	.105 399	.106 016	.107 249	.109 092	.112 761	36
37	.099 013	.099 609	.100 800	.102 581	.106 128	37
38	.093 014	.093 590	.094 738	.096 458	.099 885	38
39	.087 379	.087 934	.089 041	.090 701	.094 009	39
40	.082 085	.082 619	.083 687	.085 287	.088 479	40

6½%

REVERSION FACTORS
(Present Value of $1)

Base:	2.718 282	1.005 417	1.016 250	1.032 500	1.065 000	
			Frequency of Conversion			
Months	Continuous	Monthly	Quarterly	Semiannual	Annual	Months
0	1.000 000	1.000 000	1.000 000	1.000 000	1.000 000	0
1	.994 598	.994 613	.994 613	.994 613	.994 613	1
2	.989 225	.989 254	.989 283	.989 283	.989 283	2
3	.983 881	.983 924	.984 010	.984 010	.984 010	3
4	.978 566	.978 624	.978 709	.978 793	.978 793	4
5	.973 280	.973 351	.973 464	.973 631	.973 631	5
6	.968 022	.968 107	.968 275	.968 523	.968 523	6
7	.962 793	.962 892	.963 059	.963 305	.963 468	7
8	.957 592	.957 704	.957 898	.958 143	.958 466	8
9	.952 419	.952 545	.952 792	.953 036	.953 516	9
10	.947 274	.947 413	.947 659	.947 983	.948 617	10
11	.942 157	.942 309	.942 581	.942 984	.943 767	11

Years						Years
1	.937 067	.937 232	.937 557	.938 037	.938 967	1
2	.878 095	.878 404	.879 013	.879 913	.881 659	2
3	.822 835	.823 268	.824 125	.825 391	.827 849	3
4	.771 052	.771 593	.772 665	.774 247	.777 323	4
5	.722 527	.723 161	.724 417	.726 272	.729 881	5
6	.677 057	.677 770	.679 183	.681 270	.685 334	6
7	.634 448	.635 227	.636 773	.639 056	.643 506	7
8	.594 521	.595 355	.597 011	.599 458	.604 231	8
9	.557 106	.557 986	.559 732	.562 314	.567 353	9
10	.522 046	.522 962	.524 780	.527 471	.532 726	10
11	.489 192	.490 137	.492 012	.494 787	.500 212	11
12	.458 406	.459 372	.461 289	.464 129	.469 683	12
13	.429 557	.430 538	.432 485	.435 370	.441 017	13
14	.402 524	.403 514	.405 479	.408 393	.414 100	14
15	.377 192	.378 186	.380 160	.383 088	.388 827	15
16	.353 455	.354 448	.356 422	.359 350	.365 095	16
17	.331 211	.332 200	.334 166	.337 084	.342 813	17
18	.310 367	.311 348	.313 300	.316 197	.321 890	18
19	.290 835	.291 806	.293 736	.296 604	.302 244	19
20	.272 532	.273 490	.275 395	.278 226	.283 797	20
21	.255 381	.256 323	.258 198	.260 986	.266 476	21
22	.239 309	.240 234	.242 076	.244 815	.250 212	22
23	.224 249	.225 155	.226 960	.229 645	.234 941	23
24	.210 136	.211 023	.212 788	.215 416	.220 602	24
25	.196 912	.197 777	.199 501	.202 068	.207 138	25
26	.184 520	.185 363	.187 043	.189 547	.194 496	26
27	.172 907	.173 728	.175 364	.177 802	.182 625	27
28	.162 026	.162 823	.164 413	.166 785	.171 479	28
29	.151 829	.152 603	.154 147	.156 450	.161 013	29
30	.142 274	.143 025	.144 522	.146 756	.151 186	30
31	.133 320	.134 047	.135 497	.137 663	.141 959	31
32	.124 930	.125 633	.127 036	.129 133	.133 295	32
33	.117 068	.117 748	.119 104	.121 131	.125 159	33
34	.109 701	.110 357	.111 667	.113 626	.117 520	34
35	.102 797	.103 430	.104 694	.106 585	.110 348	35
36	.096 328	.096 938	.098 157	.099 981	.103 613	36
37	.090 265	.090 853	.092 027	.093 785	.097 289	37
38	.084 585	.085 151	.086 281	.087 974	.091 351	38
39	.079 262	.079 806	.080 893	.082 523	.085 776	39
40	.074 274	.074 797	.075 842	.077 410	.080 541	40

REVERSION FACTORS

(Present Value of $1)

6¾%

Base: 2.718 282   1.005 625   1.016 875   1.033 750   1.067 500

Frequency of Conversion

Months	Continuous	Monthly	Quarterly	Semiannual	Annual	Months
0	1.000 000	1.000 000	1.000 000	1.000 000	1.000 000	0
1	.994 391	.994 406	.994 406	.994 406	.994 406	1
2	.988 813	.988 844	.988 875	.988 875	.988 875	2
3	.983 267	.983 313	.983 405	.983 405	.983 405	3
4	.977 751	.977 813	.977 904	.977 995	.977 995	4
5	.972 267	.972 343	.972 465	.972 644	.972 644	5
6	.966 813	.966 905	.967 085	.967 352	.967 352	6
7	.961 390	.961 496	.961 676	.961 941	.962 117	7
8	.955 997	.956 118	.956 327	.956 590	.956 938	8
9	.950 635	.950 770	.951 037	.951 299	.951 814	9
10	.945 303	.945 452	.945 717	.946 065	.946 746	10
11	.940 000	.940 163	.940 457	.940 889	.941 730	11

Years						Years
1	.934 728	.934 905	.935 254	.935 770	.936 768	1
2	.873 716	.874 046	.874 701	.875 665	.877 535	2
3	.816 686	.817 150	.818 068	.819 421	.822 046	3
4	.763 379	.763 957	.765 101	.766 789	.770 067	4
5	.713 552	.714 227	.715 564	.717 538	.721 374	5
6	.666 977	.667 734	.669 234	.671 450	.675 760	6
7	.623 442	.624 268	.625 904	.628 323	.633 031	7
8	.582 748	.583 631	.585 380	.587 965	.593 003	8
9	.544 711	.545 639	.547 479	.550 200	.555 506	9
10	.509 156	.510 120	.512 032	.514 860	.520 381	10
11	.475 923	.476 914	.478 880	.481 791	.487 476	11
12	.444 858	.445 869	.447 875	.450 845	.456 652	12
13	.415 821	.416 845	.418 877	.421 887	.427 777	13
14	.388 680	.389 710	.391 756	.394 789	.400 728	14
15	.363 310	.364 342	.366 392	.369 432	.375 389	15
16	.339 596	.340 625	.342 670	.345 703	.351 653	16
17	.317 429	.318 452	.320 483	.323 498	.329 417	17
18	.296 710	.297 722	.299 733	.302 720	.308 587	18
19	.277 343	.278 342	.280 327	.283 276	.289 075	19
20	.259 240	.260 223	.262 177	.265 081	.270 796	20
21	.242 319	.243 283	.245 202	.248 055	.253 673	21
22	.226 502	.227 447	.229 326	.232 122	.237 633	22
23	.211 718	.212 641	.214 478	.217 213	.222 607	23
24	.197 899	.198 799	.200 592	.203 261	.208 531	24
25	.184 981	.185 858	.187 604	.190 206	.195 345	25
26	.172 907	.173 760	.175 458	.177 989	.182 993	26
27	.161 621	.162 449	.164 098	.166 557	.171 422	27
28	.151 072	.151 874	.153 473	.155 859	.160 583	28
29	.141 211	.141 988	.143 536	.145 848	.150 429	29
30	.131 994	.132 745	.134 243	.136 480	.140 917	30
31	.123 378	.124 104	.125 551	.127 714	.132 007	31
32	.115 325	.116 025	.117 422	.119 511	.123 660	32
33	.107 798	.108 473	.109 820	.111 834	.115 840	33
34	.100 761	.101 411	.102 709	.104 651	.108 516	34
35	.094 184	.094 810	.096 059	.097 929	.101 654	35
36	.088 037	.088 638	.089 840	.091 639	.095 226	36
37	.082 290	.082 868	.084 023	.085 753	.089 205	37
38	.076 919	.077 474	.078 583	.080 245	.083 564	38
39	.071 898	.072 431	.073 495	.075 091	.078 280	39
40	.067 206	.067 716	.068 737	.070 268	.073 331	40

7%   REVERSION FACTORS
(Present Value of $1)

Base: 2.718 282   1.005 833   1.017 500   1.035 000   1.070 000

Frequency of Conversion

Months	Continuous	Monthly	Quarterly	Semiannual	Annual	Months
0	1.000 000	1.000 000	1.000 000	1.000 000	1.000 000	0
1	.994 184	.994 200	.994 200	.994 200	.994 200	1
2	.988 401	.988 435	.988 468	.988 468	.988 468	2
3	.982 652	.982 702	.982 801	.982 801	.982 801	3
4	.976 937	.977 003	.977 101	.977 199	.977 199	4
5	.971 255	.971 337	.971 467	.971 660	.971 660	5
6	.965 605	.965 704	.965 898	.966 184	.966 184	6
7	.959 989	.960 103	.960 296	.960 580	.960 769	7
8	.954 405	.954 535	.954 759	.955 041	.955 414	8
9	.948 854	.948 999	.949 285	.949 566	.950 119	9
10	.943 335	.943 495	.943 780	.944 153	.944 882	10
11	.937 849	.938 024	.938 338	.938 802	.939 702	11

Years						Years
1	.932 394	.932 583	.932 959	.933 511	.934 579	1
2	.869 358	.869 712	.870 412	.871 442	.873 439	2
3	.810 584	.811 079	.812 058	.813 501	.816 298	3
4	.755 784	.756 399	.757 616	.759 412	.762 895	4
5	.704 688	.705 405	.706 825	.708 919	.712 986	5
6	.657 047	.657 849	.659 438	.661 783	.666 342	6
7	.612 626	.613 499	.615 228	.617 782	.622 750	7
8	.571 209	.572 139	.573 982	.576 706	.582 009	8
9	.532 592	.533 568	.535 502	.538 361	.543 934	9
10	.496 585	.497 596	.499 601	.502 566	.508 349	10
11	.463 013	.464 050	.466 107	.469 151	.475 093	11
12	.431 711	.432 765	.434 858	.437 957	.444 012	12
13	.402 524	.403 590	.405 705	.408 838	.414 964	13
14	.375 311	.376 381	.378 506	.381 654	.387 817	14
15	.349 938	.351 007	.353 130	.356 278	.362 446	15
16	.326 280	.327 343	.329 456	.332 590	.338 735	16
17	.304 221	.305 275	.307 369	.310 476	.316 574	17
18	.283 654	.284 694	.286 762	.289 833	.295 864	18
19	.264 477	.265 501	.267 537	.270 562	.276 508	19
20	.246 597	.247 602	.249 601	.252 572	.258 419	20
21	.229 925	.230 910	.232 868	.235 779	.241 513	21
22	.214 381	.215 342	.217 256	.220 102	.225 713	22
23	.199 888	.200 825	.202 691	.205 468	.210 947	23
24	.186 374	.187 286	.189 102	.191 806	.197 147	24
25	.173 774	.174 660	.176 424	.179 053	.184 249	25
26	.162 026	.162 885	.164 596	.167 148	.172 195	26
27	.151 072	.151 904	.153 562	.156 035	.160 930	27
28	.140 858	.141 663	.143 267	.145 660	.150 402	28
29	.131 336	.132 112	.133 662	.135 975	.140 563	29
30	.122 456	.123 206	.124 701	.126 934	.131 367	30
31	.114 178	.114 900	.116 341	.118 495	.122 773	31
32	.106 459	.107 154	.108 541	.110 616	.114 741	32
33	.099 261	.099 930	.101 264	.103 261	.107 235	33
34	.092 551	.093 193	.094 475	.096 395	.100 219	34
35	.086 294	.086 910	.088 142	.089 986	.093 663	35
36	.080 460	.081 051	.082 233	.084 003	.087 535	36
37	.075 020	.075 587	.076 720	.078 418	.081 809	37
38	.069 948	.070 491	.071 576	.073 204	.076 457	38
39	.065 219	.065 739	.066 778	.068 336	.071 455	39
40	.060 810	.061 307	.062 301	.063 793	.066 780	40

(Present Value of $1)

Base:	2.718 282	1.006 042	1.018 125	1.036 250	1.072 500	
			Frequency of Conversion			
Months	Continuous	Monthly	Quarterly	Semiannual	Annual	Months
0	1.000 000	1.000 000	1.000 000	1.000 000	1.000 000	0
1	.993 977	.993 995	.993 995	.993 995	.993 995	1
2	.987 989	.988 025	.988 061	.988 061	.988 061	2
3	.982 038	.982 092	.982 198	.982 198	.982 198	3
4	.976 123	.976 194	.976 299	.976 404	.976 404	4
5	.970 243	.970 332	.970 471	.970 677	.970 677	5
6	.964 399	.964 504	.964 712	.965 018	.965 018	6
7	.958 590	.958 712	.958 919	.959 223	.959 424	7
8	.952 816	.952 955	.953 194	.953 497	.953 895	8
9	.947 077	.947 232	.947 538	.947 839	.948 429	9
10	.941 372	.941 543	.941 848	.942 247	.943 026	10
11	.935 702	.935 889	.936 225	.936 721	.937 683	11

Years						Years
1	.930 066	.930 269	.930 670	.931 260	.932 401	1
2	.865 022	.865 400	.866 146	.867 245	.869 371	2
3	.804 528	.805 054	.806 096	.807 631	.810 603	3
4	.748 264	.748 917	.750 209	.752 114	.755 807	4
5	.695 934	.696 694	.698 197	.700 414	.704 715	5
6	.647 265	.648 112	.649 791	.652 267	.657 077	6
7	.601 999	.602 919	.604 741	.607 430	.612 659	7
8	.559 898	.560 876	.562 814	.565 675	.571 244	8
9	.520 742	.521 766	.523 794	.526 791	.532 628	9
10	.484 325	.485 382	.487 479	.490 579	.496 623	10
11	.450 454	.451 536	.453 682	.456 857	.463 052	11
12	.418 952	.420 050	.422 228	.425 452	.431 750	12
13	.389 652	.390 759	.392 955	.396 207	.402 564	13
14	.362 402	.363 511	.365 711	.368 971	.375 351	14
15	.337 058	.338 163	.340 356	.343 608	.349 978	15
16	.313 486	.314 582	.316 759	.319 989	.326 320	16
17	.291 563	.292 646	.294 798	.297 993	.304 261	17
18	.271 173	.272 239	.274 360	.277 509	.283 693	18
19	.252 208	.253 256	.255 338	.258 433	.264 516	19
20	.234 570	.235 596	.237 636	.240 668	.246 635	20
21	.218 166	.219 167	.221 160	.224 124	.229 962	21
22	.202 909	.203 885	.205 827	.208 718	.214 417	22
23	.188 718	.189 667	.191 557	.194 371	.199 923	23
24	.175 520	.176 442	.178 277	.181 010	.186 408	24
25	.163 246	.164 138	.165 917	.168 567	.173 807	25
26	.151 829	.152 693	.154 414	.156 980	.162 058	26
27	.141 211	.142 045	.143 708	.146 189	.151 103	27
28	.131 336	.132 140	.133 745	.136 140	.140 889	28
29	.122 151	.122 926	.124 472	.126 782	.131 365	29
30	.113 608	.114 354	.115 842	.118 067	.122 484	30
31	.105 663	.106 380	.107 811	.109 951	.114 205	31
32	.098 274	.098 962	.100 337	.102 393	.106 484	32
33	.091 401	.092 061	.093 380	.095 354	.099 286	33
34	.085 009	.085 642	.086 906	.088 800	.092 575	34
35	.079 064	.079 670	.080 881	.082 696	.086 317	35
36	.073 535	.074 114	.075 273	.077 011	.080 482	36
37	.068 392	.068 946	.070 055	.071 717	.075 041	37
38	.063 609	.064 138	.065 198	.066 787	.069 969	38
39	.059 161	.059 666	.060 678	.062 196	.065 239	39
40	.055 023	.055 505	.056 471	.057 921	.060 829	40

7½% REVERSION FACTORS
(Present Value of $1)

Base:	2.718 282	1.006 250	1.018 750	1.037 500	1.075 000	
			Frequency of Conversion			
Months	Continuous	Monthly	Quarterly	Semiannual	Annual	Months
0	1.000 000	1.000 000	1.000 000	1.000 000	1.000 000	0
1	.993 769	.993 789	.993 789	.993 789	.993 789	1
2	.987 578	.987 616	.987 654	.987 654	.987 654	2
3	.981 425	.981 482	.981 595	.981 595	.981 595	3
4	.975 310	.975 386	.975 498	.975 610	.975 610	4
5	.969 233	.969 327	.969 477	.969 697	.969 697	5
6	.963 194	.963 307	.963 529	.963 855	.963 855	6
7	.957 193	.957 324	.957 544	.957 869	.958 084	7
8	.951 229	.951 377	.951 634	.951 956	.952 381	8
9	.945 303	.945 468	.945 795	.946 116	.946 746	9
10	.939 413	.939 596	.939 921	.940 347	.941 176	10
11	.933 560	.933 760	.934 119	.934 648	.935 673	11

Years						Years
1	.927 743	.927 960	.928 388	.929 017	.930 233	1
2	.860 708	.861 110	.861 904	.863 073	.865 333	2
3	.798 516	.799 076	.800 182	.801 810	.804 961	3
4	.740 818	.741 510	.742 879	.744 895	.748 801	4
5	.687 289	.688 092	.689 680	.692 020	.696 559	5
6	.637 628	.638 522	.640 291	.642 899	.647 962	6
7	.591 555	.592 523	.594 438	.597 264	.602 755	7
8	.548 812	.549 837	.551 869	.554 869	.560 702	8
9	.509 156	.510 227	.512 349	.515 483	.521 583	9
10	.472 367	.473 470	.475 658	.478 892	.485 194	10
11	.438 235	.439 362	.441 596	.444 899	.451 343	11
12	.406 570	.407 710	.409 972	.413 319	.419 854	12
13	.377 192	.378 339	.380 613	.383 981	.390 562	13
14	.349 938	.351 083	.353 357	.356 725	.363 313	14
15	.324 652	.325 791	.328 052	.331 403	.337 966	15
16	.301 194	.302 321	.304 560	.307 879	.314 387	16
17	.279 431	.280 542	.282 749	.286 025	.292 453	17
18	.259 240	.260 332	.262 501	.265 722	.272 049	18
19	.240 508	.241 577	.243 703	.246 861	.253 069	19
20	.223 130	.224 174	.226 251	.229 338	.235 413	20
21	.207 008	.208 025	.210 049	.213 059	.218 989	21
22	.192 050	.193 039	.195 007	.197 935	.203 711	22
23	.178 173	.179 132	.181 042	.183 885	.189 498	23
24	.165 299	.166 227	.168 077	.170 833	.176 277	24
25	.153 355	.154 252	.156 041	.158 707	.163 979	25
26	.142 274	.143 140	.144 866	.147 441	.152 539	26
27	.131 994	.132 828	.134 492	.136 975	.141 896	27
28	.122 456	.123 259	.124 861	.127 252	.131 997	28
29	.113 608	.114 380	.115 919	.118 220	.122 788	29
30	.105 399	.106 140	.107 618	.109 828	.114 221	30
31	.097 783	.098 494	.099 911	.102 032	.106 252	31
32	.090 718	.091 398	.092 757	.094 790	.098 839	32
33	.084 163	.084 814	.086 114	.088 061	.091 943	33
34	.078 082	.078 704	.079 947	.081 810	.085 529	34
35	.072 440	.073 034	.074 222	.076 003	.079 562	35
36	.067 206	.067 773	.068 907	.070 608	.074 011	36
37	.062 349	.062 890	.063 972	.065 596	.068 847	37
38	.057 844	.058 360	.059 391	.060 940	.064 044	38
39	.053 665	.054 155	.055 138	.056 615	.059 576	39
40	.049 787	.050 254	.051 189	.052 596	.055 419	40

REVERSION FACTORS

(Present Value of $1)

7¾%

Base:	2.718 282	1.006 458	1.019 375	1.038 750	1.077 500	
			Frequency of Conversion			
Months	Continuous	Monthly	Quarterly	Semiannual	Annual	Months
0	1.000 000	1.000 000	1.000 000	1.000 000	1.000 000	0
1	.993 562	.993 583	.993 583	.993 583	.993 583	1
2	.987 166	.987 207	.987 248	.987 248	.987 248	2
3	.980 811	.980 873	.980 993	.980 993	.980 993	3
4	.974 497	.974 578	.974 698	.974 817	.974 817	4
5	.968 224	.968 325	.968 484	.968 718	.968 718	5
6	.961 991	.962 111	.962 348	.962 696	.962 696	6
7	.955 798	.955 937	.956 172	.956 518	.956 747	7
8	.949 645	.949 803	.950 076	.950 419	.950 872	8
9	.943 532	.943 708	.944 057	.944 398	.945 068	9
10	.937 458	.937 653	.937 999	.938 452	.939 335	10
11	.931 423	.931 636	.932 018	.932 581	.933 670	11
Years						Years
1	.925 427	.925 658	.926 113	.926 783	.928 074	1
2	.856 415	.856 842	.857 686	.858 926	.861 322	2
3	.792 550	.793 142	.794 314	.796 038	.799 371	3
4	.733 447	.734 178	.735 625	.737 754	.741 875	4
5	.678 752	.679 598	.681 272	.683 738	.688 515	5
6	.628 135	.629 075	.630 935	.633 676	.638 993	6
7	.581 293	.582 308	.584 317	.587 280	.593 033	7
8	.537 944	.539 018	.541 144	.544 281	.550 379	8
9	.497 828	.498 946	.501 160	.504 430	.510 792	9
10	.460 704	.461 853	.464 131	.467 497	.474 053	10
11	.426 348	.427 518	.429 838	.433 269	.439 957	11
12	.394 554	.395 735	.398 079	.401 546	.408 312	12
13	.365 131	.366 315	.368 666	.372 146	.378 944	13
14	.337 902	.339 083	.341 426	.344 898	.351 688	14
15	.312 703	.313 874	.316 200	.319 646	.326 393	15
16	.289 384	.290 540	.292 837	.296 242	.302 917	16
17	.267 804	.268 941	.271 200	.274 552	.281 129	17
18	.247 833	.248 947	.251 162	.254 450	.260 909	18
19	.229 351	.230 440	.232 604	.235 820	.242 143	19
20	.212 248	.213 308	.215 418	.218 554	.224 727	20
21	.196 420	.197 451	.199 501	.202 552	.208 563	21
22	.181 772	.182 772	.184 761	.187 722	.193 562	22
23	.168 217	.169 184	.171 109	.173 977	.179 640	23
24	.155 673	.156 606	.158 467	.161 239	.166 719	24
25	.144 064	.144 964	.146 758	.149 434	.154 728	25
26	.133 320	.134 187	.135 915	.138 492	.143 599	26
27	.123 378	.124 211	.125 872	.128 352	.133 270	27
28	.114 178	.114 977	.116 572	.118 955	.123 685	28
29	.105 663	.106 429	.107 959	.110 245	.114 789	29
30	.097 783	.098 517	.099 982	.102 173	.106 532	30
31	.090 491	.091 193	.092 595	.094 693	.098 870	31
32	.083 743	.084 414	.085 753	.087 759	.091 759	32
33	.077 498	.078 138	.079 417	.081 334	.085 159	33
34	.071 719	.072 329	.073 549	.075 379	.079 034	34
35	.066 371	.066 952	.068 115	.069 860	.073 349	35
36	.061 421	.061 975	.063 082	.064 745	.068 073	36
37	.056 841	.057 367	.058 421	.060 004	.063 177	37
38	.052 602	.053 103	.054 105	.055 611	.058 633	38
39	.048 679	.049 155	.050 107	.051 539	.054 416	39
40	.045 049	.045 500	.046 405	.047 766	.050 502	40

8%

REVERSION FACTORS
(Present Value of $1)

Base:	2.718 282	1.006 667	1.020 000	1.040 000	1.080 000	

Frequency of Conversion

Months	Continuous	Monthly	Quarterly	Semiannual	Annual	Months
0	1.000 000	1.000 000	1.000 000	1.000 000	1.000 000	0
1	.993 356	.993 377	.993 377	.993 377	.993 377	1
2	.986 755	.986 799	.986 842	.986 842	.986 842	2
3	.980 199	.980 264	.980 392	.980 392	.980 392	3
4	.973 686	.973 772	.973 899	.974 026	.974 026	4
5	.967 216	.967 323	.967 492	.967 742	.967 742	5
6	.960 789	.960 917	.961 169	.961 538	.961 538	6
7	.954 405	.954 553	.954 803	.955 171	.955 414	7
8	.948 064	.948 232	.948 522	.948 887	.949 367	8
9	.941 765	.941 952	.942 322	.942 685	.943 396	9
10	.935 507	.935 714	.936 082	.936 563	.937 500	10
11	.929 291	.929 517	.929 923	.930 521	.931 677	11

Years						Years
1	.923 116	.923 361	.923 845	.924 556	.925 926	1
2	.852 144	.852 596	.853 490	.854 804	.857 339	2
3	.786 628	.787 255	.788 493	.790 315	.793 832	3
4	.726 149	.726 921	.728 446	.730 690	.735 030	4
5	.670 320	.671 210	.672 971	.675 564	.680 583	5
6	.618 783	.619 770	.621 721	.624 597	.630 170	6
7	.571 209	.572 272	.574 375	.577 475	.583 490	7
8	.527 292	.528 414	.530 633	.533 908	.540 269	8
9	.486 752	.487 917	.490 223	.493 628	.500 249	9
10	.449 329	.450 523	.452 890	.456 387	.463 193	10
11	.414 783	.415 996	.418 401	.421 955	.428 883	11
12	.382 893	.384 115	.386 538	.390 121	.397 114	12
13	.353 455	.354 677	.357 101	.360 689	.367 698	13
14	.326 280	.327 495	.329 906	.333 477	.340 461	14
15	.301 194	.302 396	.304 782	.308 319	.315 242	15
16	.278 037	.279 221	.281 572	.285 058	.291 890	16
17	.256 661	.257 822	.260 129	.263 552	.270 269	17
18	.236 928	.238 063	.240 319	.243 669	.250 249	18
19	.218 712	.219 818	.222 017	.225 285	.231 712	19
20	.201 897	.202 971	.205 110	.208 289	.214 548	20
21	.186 374	.187 416	.189 490	.192 575	.198 656	21
22	.172 045	.173 053	.175 059	.178 046	.183 941	22
23	.158 817	.159 790	.161 728	.164 614	.170 315	23
24	.146 607	.147 544	.149 411	.152 195	.157 699	24
25	.135 335	.136 237	.138 033	.140 713	.146 018	25
26	.124 930	.125 796	.127 521	.130 097	.135 202	26
27	.115 325	.116 155	.117 810	.120 282	.125 187	27
28	.106 459	.107 253	.108 838	.111 207	.115 914	28
29	.098 274	.099 033	.100 550	.102 817	.107 328	29
30	.090 718	.091 443	.092 892	.095 060	.099 377	30
31	.083 743	.084 435	.085 818	.087 889	.092 016	31
32	.077 305	.077 964	.079 283	.081 258	.085 200	32
33	.071 361	.071 989	.073 245	.075 128	.078 889	33
34	.065 875	.066 472	.067 667	.069 460	.073 045	34
35	.060 810	.061 378	.062 514	.064 219	.067 635	35
36	.056 135	.056 674	.057 753	.059 374	.062 625	36
37	.051 819	.052 330	.053 355	.054 895	.057 986	37
38	.047 835	.048 320	.049 292	.050 754	.053 690	38
39	.044 157	.044 617	.045 538	.046 924	.049 713	39
40	.040 762	.041 197	.042 070	.043 384	.046 031	40

Base:	2.718 282	1.006 875	1.020 625	1.041 250	1.082 500	
			Frequency of Conversion			
Months	Continuous	Monthly	Quarterly	Semiannual	Annual	Months
0	1.000 000	1.000 000	1.000 000	1.000 000	1.000 000	0
1	.993 149	.993 172	.993 172	.993 172	.993 172	1
2	.986 344	.986 391	.986 436	.986 436	.986 436	2
3	.979 586	.979 655	.979 792	.979 792	.979 792	3
4	.972 875	.972 966	.973 102	.973 236	.973 236	4
5	.966 209	.966 323	.966 502	.966 767	.966 767	5
6	.959 589	.959 725	.959 992	.960 384	.960 384	6
7	.953 015	.953 172	.953 437	.953 827	.954 085	7
8	.946 485	.946 663	.946 971	.947 358	.947 867	8
9	.940 000	.940 199	.940 592	.940 977	.941 730	9
10	.933 560	.933 780	.934 170	.934 680	.935 673	10
11	.927 164	.927 404	.927 835	.928 468	.929 692	11

Years						Years
1	.920 811	.921 071	.921 585	.922 338	.923 788	1
2	.847 894	.848 373	.849 318	.850 707	.853 383	2
3	.780 750	.781 412	.782 718	.784 639	.788 345	3
4	.718 924	.719 736	.721 341	.723 702	.728 263	4
5	.661 993	.662 928	.664 777	.667 498	.672 760	5
6	.609 571	.610 604	.612 648	.615 658	.621 488	6
7	.561 300	.562 410	.564 607	.567 845	.574 123	7
8	.516 851	.518 020	.520 333	.523 745	.530 367	8
9	.475 923	.477 133	.479 531	.483 070	.489 947	9
10	.438 235	.439 474	.441 928	.445 553	.452 607	10
11	.403 532	.404 787	.407 274	.410 951	.418 112	11
12	.371 577	.372 838	.375 338	.379 035	.386 247	12
13	.342 152	.343 410	.345 906	.349 599	.356 810	13
14	.315 058	.316 305	.318 781	.322 448	.329 617	14
15	.290 109	.291 340	.293 784	.297 406	.304 496	15
16	.267 135	.268 345	.270 747	.274 309	.281 289	16
17	.245 981	.247 165	.249 516	.253 005	.259 852	17
18	.226 502	.227 656	.229 950	.233 356	.240 048	18
19	.208 566	.209 688	.211 918	.215 233	.221 753	19
20	.192 050	.193 137	.195 301	.198 518	.204 853	20
21	.176 842	.177 893	.179 986	.183 100	.189 240	21
22	.162 838	.163 852	.165 872	.168 880	.174 818	22
23	.149 943	.150 920	.152 865	.155 765	.161 495	23
24	.138 069	.139 008	.140 878	.143 668	.149 187	24
25	.127 136	.128 036	.129 831	.132 510	.137 817	25
26	.117 068	.117 930	.119 651	.122 219	.127 314	26
27	.107 798	.108 622	.110 268	.112 727	.117 611	27
28	.099 261	.100 049	.101 621	.103 973	.108 647	28
29	.091 401	.092 152	.093 653	.095 898	.100 367	29
30	.084 163	.084 879	.086 309	.088 450	.092 718	30
31	.077 498	.078 179	.079 541	.081 581	.085 651	31
32	.071 361	.072 009	.073 304	.075 245	.079 124	32
33	.065 710	.066 325	.067 556	.069 402	.073 094	33
34	.060 507	.061 090	.062 258	.064 012	.067 523	34
35	.055 715	.056 269	.057 376	.059 040	.062 377	35
36	.051 303	.051 827	.052 877	.054 455	.057 623	36
37	.047 241	.047 737	.048 731	.050 226	.053 231	37
38	.043 500	.043 969	.044 909	.046 325	.049 174	38
39	.040 055	.040 499	.041 388	.042 728	.045 427	39
40	.036 883	.037 302	.038 142	.039 409	.041 965	40

8½%

REVERSION FACTORS
(Present Value of $1)

Base: 2.718 282   1.007 083   1.021 250   1.042 500   1.085 000

Frequency of Conversion

Months	Continuous	Monthly	Quarterly	Semiannual	Annual	Months
0	1.000 000	1.000 000	1.000 000	1.000 000	1.000 000	0
1	.992 942	.992 966	.992 966	.992 966	.992 966	1
2	.985 933	.985 982	.986 031	.986 031	.986 031	2
3	.978 974	.979 048	.979 192	.979 192	.979 192	3
4	.972 064	.972 161	.972 305	.972 447	.972 447	4
5	.965 203	.965 324	.965 514	.965 795	.965 795	5
6	.958 390	.958 534	.958 817	.959 233	.959 233	6
7	.951 626	.951 792	.952 073	.952 486	.952 759	7
8	.944 909	.945 098	.945 424	.945 833	.946 372	8
9	.938 240	.938 450	.938 866	.939 273	.940 071	9
10	.931 617	.931 850	.932 263	.932 803	.933 852	10
11	.925 042	.925 296	.925 752	.926 422	.927 716	11

Years						Years
1	.918 512	.918 788	.919 331	.920 127	.921 659	1
2	.843 665	.844 171	.845 169	.846 634	.849 455	2
3	.774 916	.775 613	.776 990	.779 011	.782 908	3
4	.711 770	.712 624	.714 310	.716 789	.721 574	4
5	.653 770	.654 750	.656 687	.659 537	.665 045	5
6	.600 496	.601 576	.603 713	.606 858	.612 945	6
7	.551 563	.552 721	.555 012	.558 387	.564 926	7
8	.506 617	.507 833	.510 239	.513 787	.520 669	8
9	.465 334	.466 590	.469 078	.472 749	.479 880	9
10	.427 415	.428 698	.431 238	.434 989	.442 285	10
11	.392 586	.393 882	.396 450	.400 246	.407 636	11
12	.360 595	.361 894	.364 469	.368 277	.375 702	12
13	.331 211	.332 504	.335 068	.338 862	.346 269	13
14	.304 221	.305 500	.308 038	.311 796	.319 142	14
15	.279 431	.280 690	.283 189	.286 892	.294 140	15
16	.256 661	.257 894	.260 344	.263 977	.271 097	16
17	.235 746	.236 950	.239 342	.242 892	.249 859	17
18	.216 536	.217 707	.220 035	.223 492	.230 285	18
19	.198 891	.200 026	.202 285	.205 641	.212 244	19
20	.182 684	.183 782	.185 966	.189 216	.195 616	20
21	.167 797	.168 856	.170 965	.174 103	.180 292	21
22	.154 124	.155 143	.157 173	.160 197	.166 167	22
23	.141 564	.142 543	.144 494	.147 401	.153 150	23
24	.130 029	.130 967	.132 838	.135 628	.141 152	24
25	.119 433	.120 331	.122 122	.124 795	.130 094	25
26	.109 701	.110 559	.112 270	.114 827	.119 902	26
27	.100 761	.101 580	.103 213	.105 656	.110 509	27
28	.092 551	.093 330	.094 887	.097 217	.101 851	28
29	.085 009	.085 751	.087 233	.089 452	.093 872	29
30	.078 082	.078 787	.080 196	.082 307	.086 518	30
31	.071 719	.072 388	.073 726	.075 733	.079 740	31
32	.065 875	.066 509	.067 779	.069 684	.073 493	32
33	.060 507	.061 108	.062 311	.064 118	.067 736	33
34	.055 576	.056 145	.057 285	.058 997	.062 429	34
35	.051 047	.051 586	.052 664	.054 284	.057 539	35
36	.046 888	.047 396	.048 415	.049 949	.053 031	36
37	.043 067	.043 547	.044 510	.045 959	.048 876	37
38	.039 557	.040 010	.040 919	.042 288	.045 047	38
39	.036 334	.036 761	.037 618	.038 911	.041 518	39
40	.033 373	.033 776	.034 583	.035 803	.038 266	40

REVERSION FACTORS

(Present Value of $1)

8¾ %

Base: 2.718 282   1.007 292   1.021 875   1.043 750   1.087 500

Frequency of Conversion

Months	Continuous	Monthly	Quarterly	Semiannual	Annual	Months
0	1.000 000	1.000 000	1.000 000	1.000 000	1.000 000	0
1	.992 735	.992 761	.992 761	.992 761	.992 761	1
2	.985 522	.985 575	.985 626	.985 626	.985 626	2
3	.978 363	.978 440	.978 593	.978 593	.978 593	3
4	.971 255	.971 357	.971 509	.971 660	.971 660	4
5	.964 198	.964 326	.964 527	.964 824	.964 824	5
6	.957 193	.957 345	.957 645	.958 084	.958 084	6
7	.950 239	.950 415	.950 713	.951 148	.951 437	7
8	.943 335	.943 535	.943 880	.944 313	.944 882	8
9	.936 482	.936 705	.937 145	.937 574	.938 416	9
10	.929 678	.929 924	.930 361	.930 932	.932 039	10
11	.922 924	.923 193	.923 674	.924 382	.925 747	11

Years						Years
1	.916 219	.916 510	.917 084	.917 925	.919 540	1
2	.839 457	.839 990	.841 042	.842 586	.845 554	2
3	.769 126	.769 859	.771 306	.773 430	.777 521	3
4	.704 688	.705 584	.707 352	.709 951	.714 962	4
5	.645 649	.646 674	.648 701	.651 681	.657 436	5
6	.591 555	.592 683	.594 913	.598 194	.604 539	6
7	.541 994	.543 200	.545 585	.549 097	.555 898	7
8	.496 585	.497 848	.500 347	.504 030	.511 171	8
9	.454 981	.456 283	.458 860	.462 661	.470 042	9
10	.416 862	.418 188	.420 813	.424 688	.432 222	10
11	.381 937	.383 273	.385 921	.389 832	.397 446	11
12	.349 938	.351 273	.353 921	.357 836	.365 468	12
13	.320 620	.321 946	.324 575	.328 467	.336 062	13
14	.293 758	.295 066	.297 663	.301 508	.309 023	14
15	.269 146	.270 431	.272 982	.276 761	.284 159	15
16	.246 597	.247 853	.250 347	.254 046	.261 295	16
17	.225 937	.227 159	.229 589	.233 195	.240 272	17
18	.207 008	.208 194	.210 552	.214 056	.220 939	18
19	.189 664	.190 812	.193 094	.196 487	.203 163	19
20	.173 774	.174 881	.177 083	.180 360	.186 816	20
21	.159 215	.160 280	.162 400	.165 557	.171 785	21
22	.145 876	.146 898	.148 935	.151 969	.157 963	22
23	.133 654	.134 634	.136 586	.139 496	.145 254	23
24	.122 456	.123 393	.125 260	.128 047	.133 567	24
25	.112 197	.113 091	.114 874	.117 537	.122 820	25
26	.102 797	.103 649	.105 349	.107 890	.112 938	26
27	.094 184	.094 995	.096 614	.099 035	.103 851	27
28	.086 294	.087 064	.088 603	.090 907	.095 495	28
29	.079 064	.079 795	.081 257	.083 446	.087 811	29
30	.072 440	.073 133	.074 519	.076 597	.080 746	30
31	.066 371	.067 027	.068 340	.070 310	.074 249	31
32	.060 810	.061 431	.062 674	.064 539	.068 275	32
33	.055 715	.056 302	.057 477	.059 242	.062 782	33
34	.051 047	.051 601	.052 711	.054 380	.057 730	34
35	.046 771	.047 293	.048 341	.049 917	.053 085	35
36	.042 852	.043 345	.044 332	.045 820	.048 814	36
37	.039 262	.039 726	.040 656	.042 059	.044 887	37
38	.035 973	.036 409	.037 285	.038 607	.041 275	38
39	.032 959	.033 369	.034 194	.035 438	.037 954	39
40	.030 197	.030 583	.031 359	.032 530	.034 900	40

9%

REVERSION FACTORS
(Present Value of $1)

Base:	2.718 282	1.007 500	1.022 500	1.045 000	1.090 000	
			Frequency of Conversion			
Months	Continuous	Monthly	Quarterly	Semiannual	Annual	Months
0	1.000 000	1.000 000	1.000 000	1.000 000	1.000 000	0
1	.992 528	.992 556	.992 556	.992 556	.992 556	1
2	.985 112	.985 167	.985 222	.985 222	.985 222	2
3	.977 751	.977 833	.977 995	.977 995	.977 995	3
4	.970 446	.970 554	.970 715	.970 874	.970 874	4
5	.963 194	.963 329	.963 542	.963 855	.963 855	5
6	.955 997	.956 158	.956 474	.956 938	.956 938	6
7	.948 854	.949 040	.949 354	.949 814	.950 119	7
8	.941 765	.941 975	.942 339	.942 796	.943 396	8
9	.934 728	.934 963	.935 427	.935 880	.936 768	9
10	.927 743	.928 003	.928 464	.929 066	.930 233	10
11	.920 811	.921 095	.921 603	.922 350	.923 788	11

Years						Years
1	.913 931	.914 238	.914 843	.915 730	.917 431	1
2	.835 270	.835 831	.836 938	.838 561	.841 680	2
3	.763 379	.764 149	.765 667	.767 896	.772 183	3
4	.697 676	.698 614	.700 466	.703 185	.708 425	4
5	.637 628	.638 700	.640 816	.643 928	.649 931	5
6	.582 748	.583 924	.586 247	.589 664	.596 267	6
7	.532 592	.533 845	.536 324	.539 973	.547 034	7
8	.486 752	.488 062	.490 652	.494 469	.501 866	8
9	.444 858	.446 205	.448 870	.452 800	.460 428	9
10	.406 570	.407 937	.410 646	.414 643	.422 411	10
11	.371 577	.372 952	.375 677	.379 701	.387 533	11
12	.339 596	.340 967	.343 685	.347 703	.355 535	12
13	.310 367	.311 725	.314 418	.318 402	.326 179	13
14	.283 654	.284 991	.287 643	.291 571	.299 246	14
15	.259 240	.260 549	.263 149	.267 000	.274 538	15
16	.236 928	.238 204	.240 740	.244 500	.251 870	16
17	.216 536	.217 775	.220 239	.223 896	.231 073	17
18	.197 899	.199 099	.201 484	.205 028	.211 994	18
19	.180 866	.182 024	.184 327	.187 750	.194 490	19
20	.165 299	.166 413	.168 630	.171 929	.178 431	20
21	.151 072	.152 141	.154 270	.157 440	.163 698	21
22	.138 069	.139 093	.141 133	.144 173	.150 182	22
23	.126 186	.127 164	.129 114	.132 023	.137 781	23
24	.115 325	.116 258	.118 119	.120 898	.126 405	24
25	.105 399	.106 288	.108 061	.110 710	.115 968	25
26	.096 328	.097 172	.098 859	.101 380	.106 393	26
27	.088 037	.088 839	.090 440	.092 837	.097 608	27
28	.080 460	.081 220	.082 739	.085 013	.089 548	28
29	.073 535	.074 254	.075 693	.077 849	.082 155	29
30	.067 206	.067 886	.069 247	.071 289	.075 371	30
31	.061 421	.062 064	.063 350	.065 281	.069 148	31
32	.056 135	.056 741	.057 956	.059 780	.063 438	32
33	.051 303	.051 875	.053 020	.054 743	.058 200	33
34	.046 888	.047 426	.048 505	.050 129	.053 395	34
35	.042 852	.043 359	.044 375	.045 905	.048 986	35
36	.039 164	.039 640	.040 596	.042 037	.044 941	36
37	.035 793	.036 241	.037 139	.038 494	.041 231	37
38	.032 712	.033 133	.033 976	.035 250	.037 826	38
39	.029 897	.030 291	.031 083	.032 280	.034 703	39
40	.027 324	.027 693	.028 436	.029 559	.031 838	40

Base:	2.718 282	1.007 708	1.023 125	1.046 250	1.092 500	
			Frequency of Conversion			
Months	Continuous	Monthly	Quarterly	Semiannual	Annual	Months
0	1.000 000	1.000 000	1.000 000	1.000 000	1.000 000	0
1	.992 321	.992 351	.992 351	.992 351	.992 351	1
2	.984 702	.984 760	.984 817	.984 817	.984 817	2
3	.977 140	.977 227	.977 398	.977 398	.977 398	3
4	.969 637	.969 752	.969 921	.970 089	.970 089	4
5	.962 192	.962 334	.962 558	.962 889	.962 889	5
6	.954 803	.954 973	.955 306	.955 795	.955 795	6
7	.947 472	.947 668	.947 999	.948 483	.948 804	7
8	.940 196	.940 419	.940 802	.941 283	.941 915	8
9	.932 977	.933 225	.933 714	.934 191	.935 126	9
10	.925 813	.926 086	.926 572	.927 206	.928 433	10
11	.918 704	.919 002	.919 538	.920 324	.921 836	11
Years						Years
1	.911 649	.911 973	.912 610	.913 543	.915 332	1
2	.831 104	.831 694	.832 857	.834 561	.837 832	2
3	.757 676	.758 482	.760 074	.762 408	.766 895	3
4	.690 734	.691 715	.693 651	.696 492	.701 963	4
5	.629 707	.630 825	.633 033	.636 276	.642 529	5
6	.574 072	.575 295	.577 712	.581 265	.588 127	6
7	.523 353	.524 654	.527 226	.531 011	.538 332	7
8	.477 114	.478 470	.481 151	.485 101	.492 752	8
9	.434 961	.436 351	.439 104	.443 161	.451 032	9
10	.396 531	.397 940	.400 730	.404 847	.412 844	10
11	.361 498	.362 911	.365 710	.369 845	.377 889	11
12	.329 559	.330 965	.333 751	.337 869	.345 894	12
13	.300 442	.301 831	.304 584	.308 658	.316 608	13
14	.273 898	.275 261	.277 967	.281 973	.289 801	14
15	.249 699	.251 031	.253 675	.257 594	.265 264	15
16	.227 638	.228 933	.231 507	.235 323	.242 805	16
17	.207 526	.208 781	.211 275	.214 978	.222 247	17
18	.189 191	.190 402	.192 812	.196 392	.203 430	18
19	.172 476	.173 642	.175 962	.179 412	.186 206	19
20	.157 237	.158 357	.160 585	.163 901	.170 440	20
21	.143 345	.144 417	.146 551	.149 730	.156 009	21
22	.130 680	.131 704	.133 744	.136 785	.142 800	22
23	.119 135	.120 111	.122 056	.124 959	.130 709	23
24	.108 609	.109 538	.111 390	.114 156	.119 642	24
25	.099 013	.099 895	.101 655	.104 286	.109 513	25
26	.090 265	.091 102	.092 772	.095 270	.100 240	26
27	.082 290	.083 082	.084 664	.087 033	.091 753	27
28	.075 020	.075 769	.077 266	.079 509	.083 985	28
29	.068 392	.069 099	.070 513	.072 634	.076 874	29
30	.062 349	.063 016	.064 351	.066 355	.070 365	30
31	.056 841	.057 469	.058 728	.060 618	.064 407	31
32	.051 819	.052 410	.053 595	.055 377	.058 954	32
33	.047 241	.047 797	.048 912	.050 589	.053 963	33
34	.043 067	.043 589	.044 637	.046 216	.049 394	34
35	.039 262	.039 752	.040 736	.042 220	.045 212	35
36	.035 793	.036 253	.037 176	.038 570	.041 384	36
37	.032 631	.033 062	.033 928	.035 235	.037 880	37
38	.029 748	.030 151	.030 963	.032 189	.034 672	38
39	.027 120	.027 497	.028 257	.029 406	.031 737	39
40	.024 724	.025 077	.025 787	.026 863	.029 050	40

9½%

REVERSION FACTORS
(Present Value of $1)

Base: 2.718 282   1.007 917   1.023 750   1.047 500   1.095 000

Frequency of Conversion

Months	Continuous	Monthly	Quarterly	Semiannual	Annual	Months
0	1.000 000	1.000 000	1.000 000	1.000 000	1.000 000	0
1	.992 115	.992 146	.992 146	.992 146	.992 146	1
2	.984 291	.984 353	.984 413	.984 413	.984 413	2
3	.976 530	.976 621	.976 801	.976 801	.976 801	3
4	.968 829	.968 950	.969 129	.969 305	.969 305	4
5	.961 190	.961 340	.961 576	.961 924	.961 924	5
6	.953 610	.953 789	.954 140	.954 654	.954 654	6
7	.946 091	.946 297	.946 646	.947 156	.947 493	7
8	.938 631	.938 865	.939 268	.939 774	.940 439	8
9	.931 229	.931 490	.932 005	.932 507	.933 489	9
10	.923 886	.924 174	.924 685	.925 351	.926 641	10
11	.916 601	.916 915	.917 478	.918 304	.919 893	11

Years						Years
1	.909 373	.909 713	.910 383	.911 364	.913 242	1
2	.826 959	.827 578	.828 798	.830 585	.834 011	2
3	.752 014	.752 859	.754 524	.756 965	.761 654	3
4	.683 861	.684 885	.686 906	.689 871	.695 574	4
5	.621 885	.623 049	.625 348	.628 723	.635 228	5
6	.565 525	.566 796	.569 306	.572 996	.580 117	6
7	.514 274	.515 622	.518 287	.522 208	.529 787	7
8	.467 666	.469 068	.471 840	.475 922	.483 824	8
9	.425 283	.426 717	.429 555	.433 738	.441 848	9
10	.386 741	.388 190	.391 060	.395 293	.403 514	10
11	.351 692	.353 142	.356 015	.360 256	.368 506	11
12	.319 819	.321 258	.324 110	.328 324	.336 535	12
13	.290 835	.292 253	.295 064	.299 223	.307 338	13
14	.264 477	.265 866	.268 622	.272 701	.280 674	14
15	.240 508	.241 862	.244 549	.248 530	.256 323	15
16	.218 712	.220 025	.222 633	.226 501	.234 085	16
17	.198 891	.200 159	.202 681	.206 425	.213 777	17
18	.180 866	.182 088	.184 518	.188 129	.195 230	18
19	.164 474	.165 648	.167 982	.171 454	.178 292	19
20	.149 569	.150 692	.152 928	.156 257	.162 824	20
21	.136 014	.137 086	.139 223	.142 407	.148 697	21
22	.123 687	.124 709	.126 746	.129 784	.135 797	22
23	.112 478	.113 450	.115 388	.118 281	.124 015	23
24	.102 284	.103 207	.105 047	.107 797	.113 256	24
25	.093 014	.093 888	.095 633	.098 242	.103 430	25
26	.084 585	.085 412	.087 063	.089 534	.094 457	26
27	.076 919	.077 700	.079 261	.081 599	.086 262	27
28	.069 948	.070 685	.072 158	.074 366	.078 778	28
29	.063 609	.064 303	.065 691	.067 774	.071 943	29
30	.057 844	.058 497	.059 804	.061 767	.065 702	30
31	.052 602	.053 216	.054 445	.056 292	.060 002	31
32	.047 835	.048 411	.049 565	.051 303	.054 796	32
33	.043 500	.044 040	.045 124	.046 756	.050 042	33
34	.039 557	.040 064	.041 080	.042 611	.045 700	34
35	.035 973	.036 447	.037 398	.038 835	.041 736	35
36	.032 712	.033 156	.034 047	.035 392	.038 115	36
37	.029 748	.030 162	.030 996	.032 255	.034 808	37
38	.027 052	.027 439	.028 218	.029 396	.031 788	38
39	.024 600	.024 962	.025 689	.026 791	.029 030	39
40	.022 371	.022 708	.023 387	.024 416	.026 512	40

REVERSION FACTORS
(Present Value of $1)

9¾%

Base:	2.718 282	1.008 125	1.024 375	1.048 750	1.097 500	
			Frequency of Conversion			
Months	Continuous	Monthly	Quarterly	Semiannual	Annual	Months
0	1.000 000	1.000 000	1.000 000	1.000 000	1.000 000	0
1	.991 908	.991 940	.991 940	.991 940	.991 940	1
2	.983 881	.983 946	.984 010	.984 010	.984 010	2
3	.975 920	.976 016	.976 205	.976 205	.976 205	3
4	.968 022	.968 150	.968 337	.968 523	.968 523	4
5	.960 189	.960 347	.960 595	.960 961	.960 961	5
6	.952 419	.952 607	.952 976	.953 516	.953 516	6
7	.944 712	.944 929	.945 296	.945 831	.946 186	7
8	.937 067	.937 314	.937 738	.938 269	.938 967	8
9	.929 485	.929 759	.930 300	.930 827	.931 858	9
10	.921 963	.922 266	.922 802	.923 502	.924 855	10
11	.914 503	.914 833	.915 424	.916 292	.917 958	11

Years						Years
1	.907 102	.907 460	.908 164	.909 193	.911 162	1
2	.822 835	.823 483	.824 761	.826 632	.830 216	2
3	.746 395	.747 278	.749 018	.751 568	.756 461	3
4	.677 057	.678 125	.680 231	.683 320	.689 258	4
5	.614 160	.615 371	.617 761	.621 270	.628 026	5
6	.557 106	.558 424	.561 028	.564 854	.572 233	6
7	.505 352	.506 748	.509 505	.513 561	.521 397	7
8	.458 406	.459 853	.462 714	.466 926	.475 077	8
9	.415 821	.417 298	.420 220	.424 526	.432 872	9
10	.377 192	.378 681	.381 629	.385 976	.394 416	10
11	.342 152	.343 638	.346 581	.350 927	.359 377	11
12	.310 367	.311 838	.314 753	.319 060	.327 450	12
13	.281 535	.282 980	.285 847	.290 087	.298 360	13
14	.255 381	.256 793	.259 596	.263 745	.271 855	14
15	.231 656	.233 029	.235 755	.239 795	.247 703	15
16	.210 136	.211 465	.214 105	.218 020	.225 698	16
17	.190 615	.191 896	.194 442	.198 222	.205 647	17
18	.172 907	.174 138	.176 585	.180 222	.187 378	18
19	.156 845	.158 023	.160 368	.163 857	.170 732	19
20	.142 274	.143 400	.145 641	.148 978	.155 564	20
21	.129 057	.130 129	.132 265	.135 449	.141 744	21
22	.117 068	.118 087	.120 119	.123 150	.129 152	22
23	.106 193	.107 159	.109 087	.111 967	.117 678	23
24	.096 328	.097 243	.099 069	.101 799	.107 224	24
25	.087 379	.088 244	.089 971	.092 555	.097 698	25
26	.079 262	.080 078	.081 708	.084 151	.089 019	26
27	.071 898	.072 667	.074 205	.076 509	.081 111	27
28	.065 219	.065 943	.067 390	.069 562	.073 905	28
29	.059 161	.059 840	.061 201	.063 245	.067 339	29
30	.053 665	.054 303	.055 581	.057 502	.061 357	30
31	.048 679	.049 278	.050 476	.052 280	.055 906	31
32	.044 157	.044 717	.045 841	.047 533	.050 940	32
33	.040 055	.040 579	.041 631	.043 217	.046 414	33
34	.036 334	.036 824	.037 808	.039 292	.042 291	34
35	.032 959	.033 416	.034 336	.035 724	.038 534	35
36	.029 897	.030 324	.031 182	.032 480	.035 110	36
37	.027 120	.027 518	.028 319	.029 531	.031 991	37
38	.024 600	.024 971	.025 718	.026 849	.029 149	38
39	.022 315	.022 660	.023 356	.024 411	.026 560	39
40	.020 242	.020 563	.021 211	.022 194	.024 200	40

10%

REVERSION FACTORS
(Present Value of $1)

Base:	2.718 282	1.008 333	1.025 000	1.050 000	1.100 000	
			Frequency of Conversion			
Months	Continuous	Monthly	Quarterly	Semiannual	Annual	Months
0	1.000 000	1.000 000	1.000 000	1.000 000	1.000 000	0
1	.991 701	.991 736	.991 736	.991 736	.991 736	1
2	.983 471	.983 539	.983 607	.983 607	.983 607	2
3	.975 310	.975 411	.975 610	.975 610	.975 610	3
4	.967 216	.967 350	.967 547	.967 742	.967 742	4
5	.959 189	.959 355	.959 616	.960 000	.960 000	5
6	.951 229	.951 427	.951 814	.952 381	.952 381	6
7	.943 335	.943 563	.943 948	.944 510	.944 882	7
8	.935 507	.935 765	.936 211	.936 768	.937 500	8
9	.927 743	.928 032	.928 599	.929 152	.930 233	9
10	.920 044	.920 362	.920 925	.921 659	.923 077	10
11	.912 409	.912 756	.913 376	.914 286	.916 031	11
Years						**Years**
1	.904 837	.905 212	.905 951	.907 029	.909 091	1
2	.818 731	.819 410	.820 747	.822 702	.826 446	2
3	.740 818	.741 740	.743 556	.746 215	.751 315	3
4	.670 320	.671 432	.673 625	.676 839	.683 013	4
5	.606 531	.607 789	.610 271	.613 913	.620 921	5
6	.548 812	.550 178	.552 875	.556 837	.564 474	6
7	.496 585	.498 028	.500 878	.505 068	.513 158	7
8	.449 329	.450 821	.453 771	.458 112	.466 507	8
9	.406 570	.408 089	.411 094	.415 521	.424 098	9
10	.367 879	.369 407	.372 431	.376 889	.385 543	10
11	.332 871	.334 392	.337 404	.341 850	.350 494	11
12	.301 194	.302 696	.305 671	.310 068	.318 631	12
13	.272 532	.274 004	.276 923	.281 241	.289 664	13
14	.246 597	.248 032	.250 879	.255 094	.263 331	14
15	.223 130	.224 521	.227 284	.231 377	.239 392	15
16	.201 897	.203 240	.205 908	.209 866	.217 629	16
17	.182 684	.183 975	.186 542	.190 355	.197 845	17
18	.165 299	.166 536	.168 998	.172 657	.179 859	18
19	.149 569	.150 751	.153 104	.156 605	.163 508	19
20	.135 335	.136 462	.138 705	.142 046	.148 644	20
21	.122 456	.123 527	.125 659	.128 840	.135 131	21
22	.110 803	.111 818	.113 841	.116 861	.122 846	22
23	.100 259	.101 219	.103 135	.105 997	.111 678	23
24	.090 718	.091 625	.093 435	.096 142	.101 526	24
25	.082 085	.082 940	.084 647	.087 204	.092 296	25
26	.074 274	.075 078	.076 686	.079 096	.083 905	26
27	.067 206	.067 962	.069 474	.071 743	.076 278	27
28	.060 810	.061 520	.062 940	.065 073	.069 343	28
29	.055 023	.055 688	.057 021	.059 023	.063 039	29
30	.049 787	.050 410	.051 658	.053 536	.057 309	30
31	.045 049	.045 632	.046 799	.048 558	.052 099	31
32	.040 762	.041 306	.042 398	.044 044	.047 362	32
33	.036 883	.037 391	.038 410	.039 949	.043 057	33
34	.033 373	.033 847	.034 798	.036 235	.039 143	34
35	.030 197	.030 639	.031 525	.032 866	.035 584	35
36	.027 324	.027 734	.028 560	.029 811	.032 349	36
37	.024 724	.025 105	.025 874	.027 039	.029 408	37
38	.022 371	.022 726	.023 441	.024 525	.026 735	38
39	.020 242	.020 572	.021 236	.022 245	.024 304	39
40	.018 316	.018 622	.019 239	.020 177	.022 095	40

REVERSION FACTORS
(Present Value of $1)

10¼%

Base: 2.718 282   1.008 542   1.025 625   1.051 250   1.102 500

Frequency of Conversion

Months	Continuous	Monthly	Quarterly	Semiannual	Annual	Months
0	1.000 000	1.000 000	1.000 000	1.000 000	1.000 000	0
1	.991 495	.991 531	.991 531	.991 531	.991 531	1
2	.983 062	.983 133	.983 204	.983 204	.983 204	2
3	.974 701	.974 807	.975 015	.975 015	.975 015	3
4	.966 410	.966 551	.966 758	.966 962	.966 962	4
5	.958 191	.958 365	.958 638	.959 041	.959 041	5
6	.950 041	.950 248	.950 655	.951 249	.951 249	6
7	.941 961	.942 200	.942 603	.943 192	.943 582	7
8	.933 949	.934 220	.934 687	.935 271	.936 037	8
9	.926 006	.926 308	.926 903	.927 482	.928 613	9
10	.918 130	.918 463	.919 053	.919 821	.921 305	10
11	.910 321	.910 684	.911 334	.912 286	.914 112	11

Years						Years
1	.902 578	.902 971	.903 744	.904 874	.907 029	1
2	.814 647	.815 357	.816 754	.818 796	.822 702	2
3	.735 283	.736 244	.738 137	.740 907	.746 215	3
4	.663 650	.664 807	.667 087	.670 428	.676 839	4
5	.598 996	.600 301	.602 876	.606 652	.613 913	5
6	.540 641	.542 055	.544 846	.548 944	.556 837	6
7	.487 971	.489 460	.492 401	.496 725	.505 068	7
8	.440 432	.441 968	.445 005	.449 473	.458 112	8
9	.397 524	.399 084	.402 171	.406 717	.415 521	9
10	.358 796	.360 362	.363 460	.368 027	.376 889	10
11	.323 842	.325 396	.328 475	.333 018	.341 850	11
12	.292 293	.293 823	.296 857	.301 339	.310 068	12
13	.263 817	.265 314	.268 283	.272 674	.281 241	13
14	.238 115	.239 571	.242 459	.246 736	.255 094	14
15	.214 918	.216 326	.219 121	.223 265	.231 377	15
16	.193 980	.195 336	.198 029	.202 026	.209 866	16
17	.175 082	.176 383	.178 968	.182 808	.190 355	17
18	.158 025	.159 268	.161 741	.165 418	.172 657	18
19	.142 630	.143 815	.146 173	.149 683	.156 605	19
20	.128 735	.129 861	.132 103	.135 444	.142 046	20
21	.116 193	.117 260	.119 387	.122 560	.128 840	21
22	.104 874	.105 883	.107 896	.110 901	.116 861	22
23	.094 657	.095 609	.097 510	.100 351	.105 997	23
24	.085 435	.086 332	.088 124	.090 805	.096 142	24
25	.077 112	.077 955	.079 642	.082 167	.087 204	25
26	.069 599	.070 392	.071 976	.074 351	.079 096	26
27	.062 819	.063 561	.065 048	.067 278	.071 743	27
28	.056 699	.057 394	.058 786	.060 878	.065 073	28
29	.051 175	.051 825	.053 128	.055 087	.059 023	29
30	.046 190	.046 797	.048 014	.049 847	.053 536	30
31	.041 690	.042 256	.043 392	.045 105	.048 558	31
32	.037 628	.038 156	.039 216	.040 815	.044 044	32
33	.033 962	.034 454	.035 441	.036 932	.039 949	33
34	.030 654	.031 111	.032 030	.033 419	.036 235	34
35	.027 667	.028 092	.028 947	.030 240	.032 866	35
36	.024 972	.025 366	.026 160	.027 363	.029 811	36
37	.022 539	.022 905	.023 642	.024 760	.027 039	37
38	.020 343	.020 683	.021 366	.022 405	.024 525	38
39	.018 361	.018 676	.019 310	.020 274	.022 245	39
40	.016 573	.016 864	.017 451	.018 345	.020 177	40

10½%

REVERSION FACTORS
(Present Value of $1)

Base: 2.718 282   1.008 750   1.026 250   1.052 500   1.105 000

Frequency of Conversion

Months	Continuous	Monthly	Quarterly	Semiannual	Annual	Months
0	1.000 000	1.000 000	1.000 000	1.000 000	1.000 000	0
1	.991 288	.991 326	.991 326	.991 326	.991 326	1
2	.982 652	.982 727	.982 801	.982 801	.982 801	2
3	.974 092	.974 203	.974 421	.974 421	.974 421	3
4	.965 605	.965 752	.965 969	.966 184	.966 184	4
5	.957 193	.957 375	.957 662	.958 084	.958 084	5
6	.948 854	.949 071	.949 497	.950 119	.950 119	6
7	.940 588	.940 839	.941 261	.941 877	.942 285	7
8	.932 394	.932 678	.933 167	.933 778	.934 579	8
9	.924 271	.924 588	.925 210	.925 816	.926 999	9
10	.916 219	.916 568	.917 185	.917 989	.919 540	10
11	.908 237	.908 617	.909 298	.910 293	.912 201	11

Years						Years
1	.900 325	.900 736	.901 545	.902 726	.904 977	1
2	.810 584	.811 325	.812 783	.814 914	.818 984	2
3	.729 789	.730 789	.732 760	.735 643	.741 162	3
4	.657 047	.658 248	.660 616	.664 084	.670 735	4
5	.591 555	.592 908	.595 575	.599 486	.607 000	5
6	.532 592	.534 053	.536 938	.541 171	.549 321	6
7	.479 505	.481 041	.484 073	.488 529	.497 123	7
8	.431 711	.433 291	.436 414	.441 008	.449 885	8
9	.388 680	.390 280	.393 447	.398 109	.407 136	9
10	.349 938	.351 540	.354 710	.359 383	.368 449	10
11	.315 058	.316 644	.319 787	.324 425	.333 438	11
12	.283 654	.285 213	.288 302	.292 866	.301 754	12
13	.255 381	.256 901	.259 917	.264 378	.273 080	13
14	.229 925	.231 400	.234 327	.238 661	.247 132	14
15	.207 008	.208 431	.211 256	.215 445	.223 648	15
16	.186 374	.187 741	.190 457	.194 488	.202 397	16
17	.167 797	.169 105	.171 706	.175 569	.183 164	17
18	.151 072	.152 319	.154 800	.158 491	.165 760	18
19	.136 014	.137 199	.139 559	.143 074	.150 009	19
20	.122 456	.123 580	.125 819	.129 156	.135 755	20
21	.110 251	.111 313	.113 432	.116 593	.122 855	21
22	.099 261	.100 264	.102 264	.105 251	.111 181	22
23	.089 367	.090 311	.092 195	.095 013	.100 616	23
24	.080 460	.081 346	.083 118	.085 771	.091 055	24
25	.072 440	.073 272	.074 935	.077 427	.082 403	25
26	.065 219	.065 998	.067 557	.069 896	.074 573	26
27	.058 719	.059 447	.060 906	.063 097	.067 487	27
28	.052 866	.053 546	.054 909	.056 959	.061 074	28
29	.047 596	.048 231	.049 503	.051 418	.055 271	29
30	.042 852	.043 443	.044 629	.046 417	.050 019	30
31	.038 581	.039 131	.040 235	.041 901	.045 266	31
32	.034 735	.035 247	.036 274	.037 826	.040 964	32
33	.031 273	.031 748	.032 703	.034 146	.037 072	33
34	.028 156	.028 596	.029 483	.030 825	.033 549	34
35	.025 349	.025 758	.026 580	.027 826	.030 361	35
36	.022 823	.023 201	.023 963	.025 119	.027 476	36
37	.020 548	.020 898	.021 604	.022 676	.024 865	37
38	.018 500	.018 824	.019 477	.020 470	.022 503	38
39	.016 656	.016 955	.017 559	.018 479	.020 364	39
40	.014 996	.015 272	.015 830	.016 681	.018 429	40

Base:	2.718 282	1.008 958	1.026 875	1.053 750	1.107 500	
			Frequency of Conversion			
Months	Continuous	Monthly	Quarterly	Semiannual	Annual	Months
0	1.000 000	1.000 000	1.000 000	1.000 000	1.000 000	0
1	.991 082	.991 121	.991 121	.991 121	.991 121	1
2	.982 243	.982 321	.982 399	.982 399	.982 399	2
3	.973 483	.973 599	.973 828	.973 828	.973 828	3
4	.964 801	.964 955	.965 182	.965 406	.965 406	4
5	.956 197	.956 387	.956 688	.957 129	.957 129	5
6	.947 669	.947 896	.948 342	.948 992	.948 992	6
7	.939 217	.939 480	.939 922	.940 566	.940 992	7
8	.930 841	.931 138	.931 650	.932 288	.933 126	8
9	.922 540	.922 871	.923 522	.924 155	.925 390	9
10	.914 312	.914 677	.915 322	.916 163	.917 782	10
11	.906 158	.906 556	.907 267	.908 307	.910 298	11

Years						Years
1	.898 077	.898 506	.899 352	.900 585	.902 935	1
2	.806 541	.807 314	.808 834	.811 054	.815 291	2
3	.724 336	.725 377	.727 426	.730 423	.736 154	3
4	.650 509	.651 756	.654 212	.657 808	.664 699	4
5	.584 207	.585 607	.588 367	.592 412	.600 180	5
6	.524 663	.526 171	.529 149	.533 518	.541 923	6
7	.471 187	.472 769	.475 891	.480 478	.489 321	7
8	.423 162	.424 786	.427 994	.432 712	.441 825	8
9	.380 032	.381 673	.384 917	.389 694	.398 939	9
10	.341 298	.342 935	.346 176	.350 952	.360 216	10
11	.306 512	.308 130	.311 334	.316 063	.325 251	11
12	.275 271	.276 856	.279 999	.284 641	.293 681	12
13	.247 214	.248 757	.251 817	.256 344	.265 174	13
14	.222 017	.223 510	.226 473	.230 859	.239 435	14
15	.199 389	.200 825	.203 678	.207 909	.216 194	15
16	.179 066	.180 443	.183 179	.187 239	.195 209	16
17	.160 815	.162 129	.164 742	.168 625	.176 261	17
18	.144 424	.145 674	.148 161	.151 861	.159 152	18
19	.129 704	.130 889	.133 249	.136 764	.143 704	19
20	.116 484	.117 605	.119 838	.123 168	.129 755	20
21	.104 612	.105 669	.107 776	.110 923	.117 161	21
22	.093 949	.094 944	.096 929	.099 896	.105 788	22
23	.084 374	.085 308	.087 173	.089 964	.095 520	23
24	.075 774	.076 649	.078 399	.081 021	.086 248	24
25	.068 051	.068 870	.070 509	.072 966	.077 877	25
26	.061 115	.061 880	.063 412	.065 712	.070 317	26
27	.054 886	.055 600	.057 030	.059 179	.063 492	27
28	.049 292	.049 957	.051 290	.053 296	.057 329	28
29	.044 268	.044 886	.046 128	.047 998	.051 764	29
30	.039 756	.040 331	.041 485	.043 226	.046 740	30
31	.035 704	.036 237	.037 310	.038 929	.042 203	31
32	.032 065	.032 560	.033 554	.035 059	.038 107	32
33	.028 797	.029 255	.030 177	.031 573	.034 408	33
34	.025 861	.026 286	.027 140	.028 434	.031 068	34
35	.023 226	.023 618	.024 408	.025 608	.028 052	35
36	.020 858	.021 221	.021 952	.023 062	.025 329	36
37	.018 732	.019 067	.019 742	.020 769	.022 871	37
38	.016 823	.017 132	.017 755	.018 704	.020 651	38
39	.015 108	.015 393	.015 968	.016 845	.018 646	39
40	.013 569	.013 831	.014 361	.015 170	.016 836	40

11%

REVERSION FACTORS
(Present Value of $1)

Base:	2.718 282	1.009 167	1.027 500	1.055 000	1.110 000	
			Frequency of Conversion			
Months	Continuous	Monthly	Quarterly	Semiannual	Annual	Months
0	1.000 000	1.000 000	1.000 000	1.000 000	1.000 000	0
1	.990 875	.990 917	.990 917	.990 917	.990 917	1
2	.981 834	.981 916	.981 997	.981 997	.981 997	2
3	.972 875	.972 997	.973 236	.973 236	.973 236	3
4	.963 997	.964 158	.964 396	.964 630	.964 630	4
5	.955 201	.955 401	.955 715	.956 175	.956 175	5
6	.946 485	.946 722	.947 188	.947 867	.947 867	6
7	.937 849	.938 123	.938 585	.939 257	.939 702	7
8	.929 291	.929 602	.930 136	.930 803	.931 677	8
9	.920 811	.921 158	.921 838	.922 499	.923 788	9
10	.912 409	.912 790	.913 464	.914 341	.916 031	10
11	.904 084	.904 499	.905 242	.906 327	.908 403	11

Years						Years
1	.895 834	.896 283	.897 166	.898 452	.900 901	1
2	.802 519	.803 323	.804 906	.807 217	.811 622	2
3	.718 924	.720 005	.722 134	.725 246	.731 191	3
4	.644 036	.645 329	.647 874	.651 599	.658 731	4
5	.576 950	.578 397	.581 251	.585 431	.593 451	5
6	.516 851	.518 408	.521 478	.525 982	.534 641	6
7	.463 013	.464 640	.467 852	.472 569	.481 658	7
8	.414 783	.416 449	.419 741	.424 581	.433 926	8
9	.371 577	.373 256	.376 577	.381 466	.390 925	9
10	.332 871	.334 543	.337 852	.342 729	.352 184	10
11	.298 197	.299 846	.303 109	.307 926	.317 283	11
12	.267 135	.268 747	.271 939	.276 657	.285 841	12
13	.239 309	.240 873	.243 975	.248 563	.257 514	13
14	.214 381	.215 890	.218 886	.223 322	.231 995	14
15	.192 050	.193 499	.196 377	.200 644	.209 004	15
16	.172 045	.173 430	.176 183	.180 269	.188 292	16
17	.154 124	.155 442	.158 065	.161 963	.169 633	17
18	.138 069	.139 320	.141 810	.145 516	.152 822	18
19	.123 687	.124 870	.127 227	.130 739	.137 678	19
20	.110 803	.111 919	.114 144	.117 463	.124 034	20
21	.099 261	.100 311	.102 406	.105 535	.111 742	21
22	.088 922	.089 907	.091 875	.094 818	.100 669	22
23	.079 659	.080 582	.082 427	.085 190	.090 693	23
24	.071 361	.072 225	.073 951	.076 539	.081 705	24
25	.063 928	.064 734	.066 346	.068 767	.073 608	25
26	.057 269	.058 020	.059 524	.061 783	.066 314	26
27	.051 303	.052 002	.053 403	.055 509	.059 742	27
28	.045 959	.046 609	.047 911	.049 873	.053 822	28
29	.041 172	.041 775	.042 984	.044 808	.048 488	29
30	.036 883	.037 442	.038 564	.040 258	.043 683	30
31	.033 041	.033 558	.034 598	.036 170	.039 354	31
32	.029 599	.030 078	.031 040	.032 497	.035 454	32
33	.026 516	.026 958	.027 848	.029 197	.031 940	33
34	.023 754	.024 162	.024 985	.026 232	.028 775	34
35	.021 280	.021 656	.022 415	.023 568	.025 924	35
36	.019 063	.019 410	.020 110	.021 175	.023 355	36
37	.017 077	.017 397	.018 042	.019 025	.021 040	37
38	.015 299	.015 593	.016 187	.017 093	.018 955	38
39	.013 705	.013 975	.014 522	.015 357	.017 077	39
40	.012 277	.012 526	.013 029	.013 798	.015 384	40

Base: 2.718 282   1.009 375   1.028 125   1.056 250   1.112 500

Frequency of Conversion

Months	Continuous	Monthly	Quarterly	Semiannual	Annual	Months
0	1.000 000	1.000 000	1.000 000	1.000 000	1.000 000	0
1	.990 669	.990 712	.990 712	.990 712	.990 712	1
2	.981 425	.981 510	.981 595	.981 595	.981 595	2
3	.972 267	.972 394	.972 644	.972 644	.972 644	3
4	.963 194	.963 363	.963 611	.963 855	.963 855	4
5	.954 207	.954 415	.954 743	.955 224	.955 224	5
6	.945 303	.945 551	.946 037	.946 746	.946 746	6
7	.936 482	.936 768	.937 250	.937 952	.938 416	7
8	.927 743	.928 068	.928 625	.929 321	.930 233	8
9	.919 087	.919 448	.920 158	.920 847	.922 190	9
10	.910 510	.910 908	.911 611	.912 526	.914 286	10
11	.902 014	.902 448	.903 222	.904 354	.906 516	11

Years						Years
1	.893 597	.894 066	.894 986	.896 327	.898 876	1
2	.798 516	.799 354	.801 000	.803 402	.807 979	2
3	.713 552	.714 675	.716 884	.720 111	.726 273	3
4	.637 628	.638 966	.641 601	.645 455	.652 830	4
5	.569 783	.571 278	.574 224	.578 539	.586 813	5
6	.509 156	.510 760	.513 923	.518 560	.527 473	6
7	.454 981	.456 653	.459 954	.464 800	.474 133	7
8	.406 570	.408 278	.411 652	.416 613	.426 187	8
9	.363 310	.365 027	.368 423	.373 421	.383 089	9
10	.324 652	.326 358	.329 734	.334 708	.344 350	10
11	.290 109	.291 786	.295 107	.300 008	.309 528	11
12	.259 240	.260 876	.264 117	.268 905	.278 227	12
13	.231 656	.233 240	.236 381	.241 027	.250 092	13
14	.207 008	.208 532	.211 558	.216 039	.224 802	14
15	.184 981	.186 441	.189 341	.193 641	.202 069	15
16	.165 299	.166 691	.169 458	.173 566	.181 635	16
17	.147 711	.149 033	.151 662	.155 572	.163 267	17
18	.131 994	.133 245	.135 736	.139 443	.146 757	18
19	.117 949	.119 130	.121 481	.124 987	.131 917	19
20	.105 399	.106 510	.108 724	.112 029	.118 577	20
21	.094 184	.095 227	.097 307	.100 415	.106 586	21
22	.084 163	.085 139	.087 088	.090 005	.095 808	22
23	.075 208	.076 120	.077 943	.080 673	.086 119	23
24	.067 206	.068 056	.069 758	.072 310	.077 410	24
25	.060 055	.060 847	.062 432	.064 813	.069 582	25
26	.053 665	.054 401	.055 876	.058 094	.062 546	26
27	.047 955	.048 638	.050 008	.052 071	.056 221	27
28	.042 852	.043 486	.044 757	.046 673	.050 536	28
29	.038 293	.038 879	.040 057	.041 834	.045 425	29
30	.034 218	.034 760	.035 850	.037 497	.040 832	30
31	.030 577	.031 078	.032 085	.033 610	.036 703	31
32	.027 324	.027 786	.028 716	.030 125	.032 991	32
33	.024 416	.024 842	.025 700	.027 002	.029 655	33
34	.021 818	.022 211	.023 001	.024 203	.026 656	34
35	.019 497	.019 858	.020 586	.021 693	.023 961	35
36	.017 422	.017 754	.018 424	.019 444	.021 538	36
37	.015 569	.015 873	.016 489	.017 429	.019 360	37
38	.013 912	.014 192	.014 758	.015 622	.017 402	38
39	.012 432	.012 688	.013 208	.014 002	.015 642	39
40	.011 109	.011 344	.011 821	.012 551	.014 060	40

11½%

REVERSION FACTORS
(Present Value of $1)

Base: 2.718 282   1.009 583   1.028 750   1.057 500   1.115 000

Frequency of Conversion

Months	Continuous	Monthly	Quarterly	Semiannual	Annual	Months
0	1.000 000	1.000 000	1.000 000	1.000 000	1.000 000	0
1	.990 462	.990 508	.990 508	.990 508	.990 508	1
2	.981 016	.981 105	.981 194	.981 194	.981 194	2
3	.971 659	.971 792	.972 053	.972 053	.972 053	3
4	.962 392	.962 568	.962 826	.963 082	.963 082	4
5	.953 213	.953 431	.953 773	.954 274	.954 274	5
6	.944 122	.944 380	.944 888	.945 626	.945 626	6
7	.935 117	.935 416	.935 919	.936 650	.937 134	7
8	.926 199	.926 537	.927 118	.927 843	.928 793	8
9	.917 365	.917 742	.918 482	.919 199	.920 598	9
10	.908 615	.909 030	.909 763	.910 716	.912 548	10
11	.899 949	.900 401	.901 208	.902 387	.904 636	11

Years						Years
1	.891 366	.891 854	.892 813	.894 209	.896 861	1
2	.794 534	.795 404	.797 115	.799 611	.804 360	2
3	.708 220	.709 385	.711 675	.715 019	.721 399	3
4	.631 284	.632 668	.635 393	.639 377	.646 994	4
5	.562 705	.564 248	.567 287	.571 737	.580 264	5
6	.501 576	.503 227	.506 482	.511 253	.520 416	6
7	.447 088	.448 805	.452 193	.457 167	.466 741	7
8	.398 519	.400 269	.403 724	.408 803	.418 602	8
9	.355 226	.356 981	.360 450	.365 555	.375 428	9
10	.316 637	.318 375	.321 815	.326 883	.336 706	10
11	.282 239	.283 944	.287 321	.292 302	.301 979	11
12	.251 579	.253 237	.256 524	.261 379	.270 833	12
13	.224 249	.225 851	.229 028	.233 728	.242 900	13
14	.199 888	.201 426	.204 479	.209 002	.217 847	14
15	.178 173	.179 642	.182 561	.186 891	.195 379	15
16	.158 817	.160 215	.162 993	.167 120	.175 227	16
17	.141 564	.142 888	.145 523	.149 440	.157 155	17
18	.126 186	.127 436	.129 924	.133 631	.140 946	18
19	.112 478	.113 654	.115 998	.119 494	.126 409	19
20	.100 259	.101 363	.103 565	.106 853	.113 371	20
21	.089 367	.090 401	.092 464	.095 549	.101 678	21
22	.079 659	.080 624	.082 553	.085 440	.091 191	22
23	.071 005	.071 905	.073 704	.076 402	.081 786	23
24	.063 292	.064 129	.065 804	.068 319	.073 351	24
25	.056 416	.057 194	.058 751	.061 092	.065 785	25
26	.050 287	.051 008	.052 454	.054 629	.059 000	26
27	.044 825	.045 492	.046 831	.048 849	.052 915	27
28	.039 955	.040 572	.041 812	.043 682	.047 457	28
29	.035 615	.036 185	.037 330	.039 061	.042 563	29
30	.031 746	.032 271	.033 329	.034 928	.038 173	30
31	.028 297	.028 781	.029 756	.031 233	.034 236	31
32	.025 223	.025 669	.026 567	.027 929	.030 705	32
33	.022 483	.022 893	.023 719	.024 974	.027 538	33
34	.020 041	.020 417	.021 177	.022 332	.024 698	34
35	.017 863	.018 209	.018 907	.019 970	.022 150	35
36	.015 923	.016 240	.016 880	.017 857	.019 866	36
37	.014 193	.014 484	.015 071	.015 968	.017 817	37
38	.012 651	.012 917	.013 456	.014 279	.015 979	38
39	.011 277	.011 520	.012 013	.012 768	.014 331	39
40	.010 052	.010 274	.010 726	.011 417	.012 853	40

REVERSION FACTORS   11¾%
(Present Value of $1)

Base:	2.718 282	1.009 792	1.029 375	1.058 750	1.117 500	
			Frequency of Conversion			
Months	Continuous	Monthly	Quarterly	Semiannual	Annual	Months
0	1.000 000	1.000 000	1.000 000	1.000 000	1.000 000	0
1	.990 256	.990 303	.990 303	.990 303	.990 303	1
2	.980 607	.980 701	.980 793	.980 793	.980 793	2
3	.971 052	.971 191	.971 463	.971 463	.971 463	3
4	.961 590	.961 774	.962 043	.962 310	.962 310	4
5	.952 221	.952 448	.952 804	.953 327	.953 327	5
6	.942 942	.943 212	.943 741	.944 510	.944 510	6
7	.933 755	.934 066	.934 590	.935 351	.935 855	7
8	.924 656	.925 009	.925 614	.926 369	.927 357	8
9	.915 646	.916 039	.916 810	.917 557	.919 012	9
10	.906 724	.907 156	.907 920	.908 911	.910 816	10
11	.897 889	.898 360	.899 200	.900 427	.902 765	11

Years						Years
1	.889 141	.889 649	.890 647	.892 099	.894 855	1
2	.790 571	.791 475	.793 252	.795 841	.800 765	2
3	.702 929	.704 135	.706 507	.709 969	.716 568	3
4	.625 002	.626 433	.629 248	.633 363	.641 224	4
5	.555 715	.557 305	.560 438	.565 023	.573 802	5
6	.494 109	.495 806	.499 152	.504 056	.513 470	6
7	.439 332	.441 093	.444 569	.449 668	.459 481	7
8	.390 628	.392 418	.395 954	.401 149	.411 168	8
9	.347 323	.349 114	.352 655	.357 864	.367 936	9
10	.308 819	.310 589	.314 091	.319 250	.329 249	10
11	.274 583	.276 315	.279 744	.284 803	.294 630	11
12	.244 143	.245 823	.249 153	.254 073	.263 651	12
13	.217 078	.218 697	.221 907	.226 658	.235 929	13
14	.193 013	.194 563	.197 641	.202 201	.211 123	14
15	.171 615	.173 093	.176 029	.180 384	.188 924	15
16	.152 590	.153 992	.156 779	.160 920	.169 059	16
17	.135 674	.136 999	.139 635	.143 557	.151 284	17
18	.120 633	.121 881	.124 365	.128 067	.135 377	18
19	.107 260	.108 431	.110 766	.114 248	.121 143	19
20	.095 369	.096 466	.098 653	.101 921	.108 405	20
21	.084 797	.085 820	.087 865	.090 924	.097 007	21
22	.075 396	.076 350	.078 257	.081 113	.086 807	22
23	.067 038	.067 925	.069 699	.072 361	.077 680	23
24	.059 606	.060 429	.062 077	.064 553	.069 512	24
25	.052 998	.053 761	.055 289	.057 588	.062 203	25
26	.047 123	.047 828	.049 243	.051 374	.055 663	26
27	.041 899	.042 550	.043 858	.045 831	.049 810	27
28	.037 254	.037 855	.039 062	.040 885	.044 573	28
29	.033 124	.033 677	.034 790	.036 474	.039 886	29
30	.029 452	.029 961	.030 986	.032 538	.035 692	30
31	.026 187	.026 655	.027 598	.029 027	.031 939	31
32	.023 284	.023 713	.024 580	.025 895	.028 581	32
33	.020 703	.021 097	.021 892	.023 101	.025 576	33
34	.018 407	.018 769	.019 498	.020 609	.022 887	34
35	.016 367	.016 697	.017 366	.018 385	.020 480	35
36	.014 552	.014 855	.015 467	.016 401	.018 327	36
37	.012 939	.013 216	.013 775	.014 631	.016 400	37
38	.011 505	.011 757	.012 269	.013 053	.014 676	38
39	.010 229	.010 460	.010 927	.011 644	.013 132	39
40	.009 095	.009 306	.009 732	.010 388	.011 752	40

12%

REVERSION FACTORS
(Present Value of $1)

Base: 2.718 282   1.010 000   1.030 000   1.060 000   1.120 000

Frequency of Conversion

Months	Continuous	Monthly	Quarterly	Semiannual	Annual	Months
0	1.000 000	1.000 000	1.000 000	1.000 000	1.000 000	0
1	.990 050	.990 099	.990 099	.990 099	.990 099	1
2	.980 199	.980 296	.980 392	.980 392	.980 392	2
3	.970 446	.970 590	.970 874	.970 874	.970 874	3
4	.960 789	.960 980	.961 261	.961 538	.961 538	4
5	.951 229	.951 466	.951 837	.952 381	.952 381	5
6	.941 765	.942 045	.942 596	.943 396	.943 396	6
7	.932 394	.932 718	.933 263	.934 056	.934 579	7
8	.923 116	.923 483	.924 114	.924 898	.925 926	8
9	.913 931	.914 340	.915 142	.915 919	.917 431	9
10	.904 837	.905 287	.906 081	.907 112	.909 091	10
11	.895 834	.896 324	.897 198	.898 473	.900 901	11

Years						Years
1	.886 920	.887 449	.888 487	.889 996	.892 857	1
2	.786 628	.787 566	.789 409	.792 094	.797 194	2
3	.697 676	.698 925	.701 380	.704 961	.711 780	3
4	.618 783	.620 260	.623 167	.627 412	.635 518	4
5	.548 812	.550 450	.553 676	.558 395	.567 427	5
6	.486 752	.488 496	.491 934	.496 969	.506 631	6
7	.431 711	.433 515	.437 077	.442 301	.452 349	7
8	.382 893	.384 723	.388 337	.393 646	.403 883	8
9	.339 596	.341 422	.345 032	.350 344	.360 610	9
10	.301 194	.302 995	.306 557	.311 805	.321 973	10
11	.267 135	.268 892	.272 372	.277 505	.287 476	11
12	.236 928	.238 628	.241 999	.246 979	.256 675	12
13	.210 136	.211 771	.215 013	.219 810	.229 174	13
14	.186 374	.187 936	.191 036	.195 630	.204 620	14
15	.165 299	.166 783	.169 733	.174 110	.182 696	15
16	.146 607	.148 012	.150 806	.154 957	.163 122	16
17	.130 029	.131 353	.133 989	.137 912	.145 644	17
18	.115 325	.116 569	.119 047	.122 741	.130 040	18
19	.102 284	.103 449	.105 772	.109 239	.116 107	19
20	.090 718	.091 806	.093 977	.097 222	.103 667	20
21	.080 460	.081 473	.083 497	.086 527	.092 560	21
22	.071 361	.072 303	.074 186	.077 009	.082 643	22
23	.063 292	.064 165	.065 914	.068 538	.073 788	23
24	.056 135	.056 944	.058 563	.060 998	.065 882	24
25	.049 787	.050 534	.052 033	.054 288	.058 823	25
26	.044 157	.044 847	.046 231	.048 316	.052 521	26
27	.039 164	.039 799	.041 075	.043 001	.046 894	27
28	.034 735	.035 320	.036 495	.038 271	.041 869	28
29	.030 807	.031 345	.032 425	.034 061	.037 383	29
30	.027 324	.027 817	.028 809	.030 314	.033 378	30
31	.024 234	.024 686	.025 597	.026 980	.029 802	31
32	.021 494	.021 907	.022 742	.024 012	.026 609	32
33	.019 063	.019 442	.020 206	.021 370	.023 758	33
34	.016 907	.017 254	.017 953	.019 020	.021 212	34
35	.014 996	.015 312	.015 951	.016 927	.018 940	35
36	.013 300	.013 588	.014 172	.015 065	.016 910	36
37	.011 796	.012 059	.012 592	.013 408	.015 098	37
38	.010 462	.010 702	.011 188	.011 933	.013 481	38
39	.009 279	.009 497	.009 940	.010 620	.012 036	39
40	.008 230	.008 428	.008 832	.009 452	.010 747	40

REVERSION FACTORS

12½%

(Present Value of $1)

Base: 2.718 282   1.010 417   1.031 250   1.062 500   1.125 000

Frequency of Conversion

Months	Continuous	Monthly	Quarterly	Semiannual	Annual	Months
0	1.000 000	1.000 000	1.000 000	1.000 000	1.000 000	0
1	.989 637	.989 691	.989 691	.989 691	.989 691	1
2	.979 382	.979 488	.979 592	.979 592	.979 592	2
3	.969 233	.969 390	.969 697	.969 697	.969 697	3
4	.959 189	.959 396	.959 700	.960 000	.960 000	4
5	.949 250	.949 506	.949 907	.950 495	.950 495	5
6	.939 413	.939 717	.940 312	.941 176	.941 176	6
7	.929 678	.930 029	.930 618	.931 474	.932 039	7
8	.920 044	.920 441	.921 122	.921 969	.923 077	8
9	.910 510	.910 952	.911 818	.912 656	.914 286	9
10	.901 075	.901 561	.902 418	.903 529	.905 660	10
11	.891 738	.892 266	.893 209	.894 584	.897 196	11

Years						Years
1	.882 497	.883 068	.884 187	.885 813	.888 889	1
2	.778 801	.779 809	.781 787	.784 665	.790 123	2
3	.687 289	.688 624	.691 246	.695 067	.702 332	3
4	.606 531	.608 101	.611 191	.615 699	.624 295	4
5	.535 261	.536 995	.540 407	.545 394	.554 929	5
6	.472 367	.474 203	.477 821	.483 117	.493 270	6
7	.416 862	.418 753	.422 483	.427 952	.438 462	7
8	.367 879	.369 787	.373 554	.379 085	.389 744	8
9	.324 652	.326 547	.330 291	.335 799	.346 439	9
10	.286 505	.288 363	.292 039	.297 455	.307 946	10
11	.252 840	.254 644	.258 218	.263 490	.273 730	11
12	.223 130	.224 868	.228 313	.233 402	.243 315	12
13	.196 912	.198 574	.201 871	.206 751	.216 280	13
14	.173 774	.175 354	.178 492	.183 143	.192 249	14
15	.153 355	.154 849	.157 820	.162 230	.170 888	15
16	.135 335	.136 743	.139 542	.143 706	.151 901	16
17	.119 433	.120 753	.123 382	.127 296	.135 023	17
18	.105 399	.106 633	.109 092	.112 761	.120 020	18
19	.093 014	.094 164	.096 458	.099 885	.106 685	19
20	.082 085	.083 153	.085 287	.088 479	.094 831	20
21	.072 440	.073 430	.075 410	.078 376	.084 294	21
22	.063 928	.064 844	.066 676	.069 427	.074 928	22
23	.056 416	.057 261	.058 954	.061 499	.066 603	23
24	.049 787	.050 566	.052 127	.054 477	.059 202	24
25	.043 937	.044 653	.046 090	.048 256	.052 624	25
26	.038 774	.039 432	.040 752	.042 746	.046 777	26
27	.034 218	.034 821	.036 032	.037 865	.041 580	27
28	.030 197	.030 749	.031 859	.033 541	.036 960	28
29	.026 649	.027 153	.028 170	.029 711	.032 853	29
30	.023 518	.023 978	.024 907	.026 319	.029 203	30
31	.020 754	.021 175	.022 023	.023 313	.025 958	31
32	.018 316	.018 699	.019 472	.020 651	.023 074	32
33	.016 163	.016 512	.017 217	.018 293	.020 510	33
34	.014 264	.014 581	.015 223	.016 204	.018 231	34
35	.012 588	.012 876	.013 460	.014 354	.016 205	35
36	.011 109	.011 371	.011 901	.012 715	.014 405	36
37	.009 804	.010 041	.010 523	.011 263	.012 804	37
38	.008 652	.008 867	.009 304	.009 977	.011 382	38
39	.007 635	.007 830	.008 227	.008 838	.010 117	39
40	.006 738	.006 914	.007 274	.007 829	.008 993	40

13%

REVERSION FACTORS
(Present Value of $1)

Base:	2.718 282	1.010 833	1.032 500	1.065 000	1.130 000	
			Frequency of Conversion			
Months	Continuous	Monthly	Quarterly	Semiannual	Annual	Months
0	1.000 000	1.000 000	1.000 000	1.000 000	1.000 000	0
1	.989 225	.989 283	.989 283	.989 283	.989 283	1
2	.978 566	.978 680	.978 793	.978 793	.978 793	2
3	.968 022	.968 192	.968 523	.968 523	.968 523	3
4	.957 592	.957 815	.958 143	.958 466	.958 466	4
5	.947 274	.947 550	.947 983	.948 617	.948 617	5
6	.937 067	.937 395	.938 037	.938 967	.938 967	6
7	.926 971	.927 349	.927 984	.928 904	.929 512	7
8	.916 983	.917 410	.918 144	.919 054	.920 245	8
9	.907 102	.907 578	.908 510	.909 411	.911 162	9
10	.897 328	.897 851	.898 774	.899 969	.902 256	10
11	.887 660	.888 229	.889 243	.890 720	.893 522	11

Years						Years
1	.878 095	.878 710	.879 913	.881 659	.884 956	1
2	.771 052	.772 130	.774 247	.777 323	.783 147	2
3	.677 057	.678 478	.681 270	.685 334	.693 050	3
4	.594 521	.596 185	.599 458	.604 231	.613 319	4
5	.522 046	.523 874	.527 471	.532 726	.542 760	5
6	.458 406	.460 333	.464 129	.469 683	.480 319	6
7	.402 524	.404 499	.408 393	.414 100	.425 061	7
8	.353 455	.355 437	.359 350	.365 095	.376 160	8
9	.310 367	.312 326	.316 197	.321 890	.332 885	9
10	.272 532	.274 444	.278 226	.283 797	.294 588	10
11	.239 309	.241 156	.244 815	.250 212	.260 698	11
12	.210 136	.211 906	.215 416	.220 602	.230 706	12
13	.184 520	.186 204	.189 547	.194 496	.204 165	13
14	.162 026	.163 619	.166 785	.171 479	.180 677	14
15	.142 274	.143 774	.146 756	.151 186	.159 891	15
16	.124 930	.126 336	.129 133	.133 295	.141 496	16
17	.109 701	.111 012	.113 626	.117 520	.125 218	17
18	.096 328	.097 548	.099 981	.103 613	.110 812	18
19	.084 585	.085 716	.087 974	.091 351	.098 064	19
20	.074 274	.075 319	.077 410	.080 541	.086 782	20
21	.065 219	.066 184	.068 114	.071 010	.076 798	21
22	.057 269	.058 156	.059 934	.062 606	.067 963	22
23	.050 287	.051 103	.052 737	.055 197	.060 144	23
24	.044 157	.044 904	.046 404	.048 665	.053 225	24
25	.038 774	.039 458	.040 831	.042 906	.047 102	25
26	.034 047	.034 672	.035 928	.037 829	.041 683	26
27	.029 897	.030 467	.031 614	.033 352	.036 888	27
28	.026 252	.026 771	.027 817	.029 405	.032 644	28
29	.023 052	.023 524	.024 477	.025 925	.028 889	29
30	.020 242	.020 671	.021 537	.022 857	.025 565	30
31	.017 774	.018 164	.018 951	.020 152	.022 624	31
32	.015 608	.015 961	.016 675	.017 767	.020 021	32
33	.013 705	.014 025	.014 673	.015 665	.017 718	33
34	.012 034	.012 324	.012 911	.013 811	.015 680	34
35	.010 567	.010 829	.011 360	.012 177	.013 876	35
36	.009 279	.009 516	.009 996	.010 736	.012 279	36
37	.008 148	.008 361	.008 796	.009 465	.010 867	37
38	.007 155	.007 347	.007 739	.008 345	.009 617	38
39	.006 282	.006 456	.006 810	.007 358	.008 510	39
40	.005 517	.005 673	.005 992	.006 487	.007 531	40

Base:	2.718 282	1.011 250	1.033 750	1.067 500	1.135 000	
			Frequency of Conversion			
Months	Continuous	Monthly	Quarterly	Semiannual	Annual	Months
0	1.000 000	1.000 000	1.000 000	1.000 000	1.000 000	0
1	.988 813	.988 875	.988 875	.988 875	.988 875	1
2	.977 751	.977 874	.977 995	.977 995	.977 995	2
3	.966 813	.966 995	.967 352	.967 352	.967 352	3
4	.955 997	.956 238	.956 590	.956 938	.956 938	4
5	.945 303	.945 600	.946 065	.946 746	.946 746	5
6	.934 728	.935 080	.935 770	.936 768	.936 768	6
7	.924 271	.924 677	.925 359	.926 347	.926 999	7
8	.913 931	.914 391	.915 178	.916 155	.917 431	8
9	.903 707	.904 218	.905 219	.906 184	.908 059	9
10	.893 597	.894 159	.895 148	.896 429	.898 876	10
11	.883 601	.884 211	.885 299	.886 881	.889 878	11
Years						Years
1	.873 716	.874 375	.875 665	.877 535	.881 057	1
2	.763 379	.764 531	.766 789	.770 067	.776 262	2
3	.666 977	.668 487	.671 450	.675 760	.683 931	3
4	.582 748	.584 508	.587 965	.593 003	.602 583	4
5	.509 156	.511 079	.514 860	.520 381	.530 910	5
6	.444 858	.446 874	.450 845	.456 652	.467 762	6
7	.388 680	.390 736	.394 789	.400 728	.412 125	7
8	.339 596	.341 649	.345 703	.351 653	.363 106	8
9	.296 710	.298 730	.302 720	.308 587	.319 917	9
10	.259 240	.261 202	.265 081	.270 796	.281 865	10
11	.226 502	.228 388	.232 122	.237 633	.248 339	11
12	.197 899	.199 697	.203 261	.208 531	.218 801	12
13	.172 907	.174 610	.177 989	.182 993	.192 776	13
14	.151 072	.152 674	.155 859	.160 583	.169 847	14
15	.131 994	.133 495	.136 480	.140 917	.149 645	15
16	.115 325	.116 724	.119 511	.123 660	.131 846	16
17	.100 761	.102 061	.104 651	.108 516	.116 164	17
18	.088 037	.089 239	.091 639	.095 226	.102 347	18
19	.076 919	.078 029	.080 245	.083 564	.090 173	19
20	.067 206	.068 226	.070 268	.073 331	.079 448	20
21	.058 719	.059 655	.061 531	.064 350	.069 998	21
22	.051 303	.052 161	.053 881	.056 469	.061 672	22
23	.044 825	.045 608	.047 182	.049 554	.054 337	23
24	.039 164	.039 879	.041 315	.043 485	.047 874	24
25	.034 218	.034 869	.036 178	.038 160	.042 180	25
26	.029 897	.030 489	.031 680	.033 487	.037 163	26
27	.026 121	.026 658	.027 741	.029 386	.032 742	27
28	.022 823	.023 309	.024 292	.025 787	.028 848	28
29	.019 941	.020 381	.021 272	.022 629	.025 417	29
30	.017 422	.017 821	.018 627	.019 858	.022 394	30
31	.015 222	.015 582	.016 311	.017 426	.019 730	31
32	.013 300	.013 625	.014 283	.015 292	.017 383	32
33	.011 620	.011 913	.012 507	.013 419	.015 316	33
34	.010 153	.010 416	.010 952	.011 776	.013 494	34
35	.008 871	.009 108	.009 590	.010 334	.011 889	35
36	.007 750	.007 964	.008 398	.009 068	.010 475	36
37	.006 772	.006 963	.007 354	.007 957	.009 229	37
38	.005 917	.006 088	.006 439	.006 983	.008 131	38
39	.005 169	.005 324	.005 639	.006 128	.007 164	39
40	.004 517	.004 655	.004 938	.005 377	.006 312	40

14%

REVERSION FACTORS
(Present Value of $1)

Base:	2.718 282	1.011 667	1.035 000	1.070 000	1.140 000	

Frequency of Conversion

Months	Continuous	Monthly	Quarterly	Semiannual	Annual	Months
0	1.000 000	1.000 000	1.000 000	1.000 000	1.000 000	0
1	.988 401	.988 468	.988 468	.988 468	.988 468	1
2	.976 937	.977 069	.977 199	.977 199	.977 199	2
3	.965 605	.965 801	.966 184	.966 184	.966 184	3
4	.954 405	.954 663	.955 041	.955 414	.955 414	4
5	.943 335	.943 654	.944 153	.944 882	.944 882	5
6	.932 394	.932 772	.933 511	.934 579	.934 579	6
7	.921 579	.922 015	.922 745	.923 802	.924 499	7
8	.910 890	.911 382	.912 225	.913 270	.914 634	8
9	.900 325	.900 872	.901 943	.902 975	.904 977	9
10	.889 882	.890 483	.891 541	.892 910	.895 522	10
11	.879 560	.880 214	.881 377	.883 067	.886 263	11

Years						Years
1	.869 358	.870 063	.871 442	.873 439	.877 193	1
2	.755 784	.757 010	.759 412	.762 895	.769 468	2
3	.657 047	.658 646	.661 783	.666 342	.674 972	3
4	.571 209	.573 064	.576 706	.582 009	.592 080	4
5	.496 585	.498 601	.502 566	.508 349	.519 369	5
6	.431 711	.433 815	.437 957	.444 012	.455 587	6
7	.375 311	.377 446	.381 654	.387 817	.399 637	7
8	.326 280	.328 402	.332 590	.338 735	.350 559	8
9	.283 654	.285 730	.289 833	.295 864	.307 508	9
10	.246 597	.248 603	.252 572	.258 419	.269 744	10
11	.214 381	.216 301	.220 102	.225 713	.236 617	11
12	.186 374	.188 195	.191 806	.197 147	.207 559	12
13	.162 026	.163 742	.167 148	.172 195	.182 069	13
14	.140 858	.142 466	.145 660	.150 402	.159 710	14
15	.122 456	.123 954	.126 934	.131 367	.140 096	15
16	.106 459	.107 848	.110 616	.114 741	.122 892	16
17	.092 551	.093 834	.096 395	.100 219	.107 800	17
18	.080 460	.081 642	.084 003	.087 535	.094 561	18
19	.069 948	.071 034	.073 204	.076 457	.082 948	19
20	.060 810	.061 804	.063 793	.066 780	.072 762	20
21	.052 866	.053 773	.055 592	.058 329	.063 826	21
22	.045 959	.046 786	.048 445	.050 946	.055 988	22
23	.039 955	.040 707	.042 217	.044 499	.049 112	23
24	.034 735	.035 417	.036 790	.038 867	.043 081	24
25	.030 197	.030 815	.032 060	.033 948	.037 790	25
26	.026 252	.026 811	.027 939	.029 651	.033 149	26
27	.022 823	.023 328	.024 347	.025 899	.029 078	27
28	.019 841	.020 296	.021 217	.022 621	.025 507	28
29	.017 249	.017 659	.018 489	.019 758	.022 375	29
30	.014 996	.015 365	.016 112	.017 257	.019 627	30
31	.013 037	.013 368	.014 041	.015 073	.017 217	31
32	.011 333	.011 631	.012 236	.013 166	.015 102	32
33	.009 853	.010 120	.010 663	.011 499	.013 248	33
34	.008 566	.008 805	.009 292	.010 044	.011 621	34
35	.007 447	.007 661	.008 098	.008 773	.010 194	35
36	.006 474	.006 665	.007 057	.007 662	.008 942	36
37	.005 628	.005 799	.006 149	.006 693	.007 844	37
38	.004 893	.005 046	.005 359	.005 846	.006 880	38
39	.004 254	.004 390	.004 670	.005 106	.006 035	39
40	.003 698	.003 820	.004 070	.004 460	.005 294	40

(Present Value of $1)

Base:	2.718 282	1.012 083	1.036 250	1.072 500	1.145 000	
			Frequency of Conversion			
Months	Continuous	Monthly	Quarterly	Semiannual	Annual	Months
0	1.000 000	1.000 000	1.000 000	1.000 000	1.000 000	0
1	.987 989	.988 061	.988 061	.988 061	.988 061	1
2	.976 123	.976 264	.976 404	.976 404	.976 404	2
3	.964 399	.964 609	.965 018	.965 018	.965 018	3
4	.952 816	.953 092	.953 497	.953 895	.953 895	4
5	.941 372	.941 713	.942 247	.943 026	.943 026	5
6	.930 066	.930 470	.931 260	.932 401	.932 401	6
7	.918 895	.919 361	.920 142	.921 269	.922 013	7
8	.907 859	.908 385	.909 286	.910 400	.911 854	8
9	.896 955	.897 539	.898 683	.899 784	.901 917	9
10	.886 182	.886 824	.887 953	.889 413	.892 193	10
11	.875 538	.876 236	.877 477	.879 278	.882 677	11

Years						Years
1	.865 022	.865 774	.867 245	.869 371	.873 362	1
2	.748 264	.749 565	.752 114	.755 807	.762 762	2
3	.647 265	.648 954	.652 267	.657 077	.666 168	3
4	.559 898	.561 848	.565 675	.571 244	.581 806	4
5	.484 325	.486 434	.490 579	.496 623	.508 127	5
6	.418 952	.421 142	.425 452	.431 750	.443 779	6
7	.362 402	.364 614	.368 971	.375 351	.387 580	7
8	.313 486	.315 673	.319 989	.326 320	.338 498	8
9	.271 173	.273 302	.277 509	.283 693	.295 631	9
10	.234 570	.236 618	.240 668	.246 635	.258 193	10
11	.202 909	.204 858	.208 718	.214 417	.225 496	11
12	.175 520	.177 360	.181 010	.186 408	.196 940	12
13	.151 829	.153 554	.156 980	.162 058	.172 000	13
14	.131 336	.132 943	.136 140	.140 889	.150 218	14
15	.113 608	.115 099	.118 067	.122 484	.131 195	15
16	.098 274	.099 650	.102 393	.106 484	.114 581	16
17	.085 009	.086 274	.088 800	.092 575	.100 071	17
18	.073 535	.074 694	.077 011	.080 482	.087 398	18
19	.063 609	.064 668	.066 787	.069 969	.076 330	19
20	.055 023	.055 988	.057 921	.060 829	.066 664	20
21	.047 596	.048 473	.050 232	.052 883	.058 222	21
22	.041 172	.041 967	.043 563	.045 975	.050 849	22
23	.035 615	.036 334	.037 780	.039 969	.044 409	23
24	.030 807	.031 457	.032 765	.034 748	.038 785	24
25	.026 649	.027 234	.028 415	.030 209	.033 874	25
26	.023 052	.023 579	.024 643	.026 263	.029 584	26
27	.019 941	.020 414	.021 371	.022 832	.025 838	27
28	.017 249	.017 674	.018 534	.019 850	.022 566	28
29	.014 921	.015 302	.016 074	.017 257	.019 708	29
30	.012 907	.013 248	.013 940	.015 002	.017 212	30
31	.011 165	.011 470	.012 089	.013 043	.015 032	31
32	.009 658	.009 930	.010 484	.011 339	.013 129	32
33	.008 354	.008 597	.009 092	.009 858	.011 466	33
34	.007 227	.007 443	.007 885	.008 570	.010 014	34
35	.006 251	.006 444	.006 839	.007 451	.008 746	35
36	.005 407	.005 579	.005 931	.006 477	.007 638	36
37	.004 677	.004 830	.005 143	.005 631	.006 671	37
38	.004 046	.004 182	.004 461	.004 896	.005 826	38
39	.003 500	.003 621	.003 868	.004 256	.005 088	39
40	.003 028	.003 135	.003 355	.003 700	.004 444	40

15%

REVERSION FACTORS
(Present Value of $1)

Base:	2.718 282	1.012 500	1.037 500	1.075 000	1.150 000	

Frequency of Conversion

Months	Continuous	Monthly	Quarterly	Semiannual	Annual	Months
0	1.000 000	1.000 000	1.000 000	1.000 000	1.000 000	0
1	.987 578	.987 654	.987 654	.987 654	.987 654	1
2	.975 310	.975 461	.975 610	.975 610	.975 610	2
3	.963 194	.963 418	.963 855	.963 855	.963 855	3
4	.951 229	.951 524	.951 956	.952 381	.952 381	4
5	.939 413	.939 777	.940 347	.941 176	.941 176	5
6	.927 743	.928 175	.929 017	.930 233	.930 233	6
7	.916 219	.916 716	.917 548	.918 748	.919 540	7
8	.904 837	.905 398	.906 358	.907 544	.909 091	8
9	.893 597	.894 221	.895 438	.896 610	.898 876	9
10	.882 497	.883 181	.884 384	.885 936	.888 889	10
11	.871 534	.872 277	.873 598	.875 513	.879 121	11

Years						Years
1	.860 708	.861 509	.863 073	.865 333	.869 565	1
2	.740 818	.742 197	.744 895	.748 801	.756 144	2
3	.637 628	.639 409	.642 899	.647 962	.657 516	3
4	.548 812	.550 856	.554 869	.560 702	.571 753	4
5	.472 367	.474 568	.478 892	.485 194	.497 177	5
6	.406 570	.408 844	.413 319	.419 854	.432 328	6
7	.349 938	.352 223	.356 725	.363 313	.375 937	7
8	.301 194	.303 443	.307 879	.314 387	.326 902	8
9	.259 240	.261 419	.265 722	.272 049	.284 262	9
10	.223 130	.225 214	.229 338	.235 413	.247 185	10
11	.192 050	.194 024	.197 935	.203 711	.214 943	11
12	.165 299	.167 153	.170 833	.176 277	.186 907	12
13	.142 274	.144 004	.147 441	.152 539	.162 528	13
14	.122 456	.124 061	.127 252	.131 997	.141 329	14
15	.105 399	.106 879	.109 828	.114 221	.122 894	15
16	.090 718	.092 078	.094 790	.098 839	.106 865	16
17	.078 082	.079 326	.081 810	.085 529	.092 926	17
18	.067 206	.068 340	.070 608	.074 011	.080 805	18
19	.057 844	.058 875	.060 940	.064 044	.070 265	19
20	.049 787	.050 722	.052 596	.055 419	.061 100	20
21	.042 852	.043 697	.045 394	.047 956	.053 131	21
22	.036 883	.037 645	.039 178	.041 498	.046 201	22
23	.031 746	.032 432	.033 814	.035 910	.040 174	23
24	.027 324	.027 940	.029 184	.031 074	.034 934	24
25	.023 518	.024 071	.025 188	.026 889	.030 378	25
26	.020 242	.020 737	.021 739	.023 268	.026 415	26
27	.017 422	.017 865	.018 762	.020 135	.022 970	27
28	.014 996	.015 391	.016 193	.017 423	.019 974	28
29	.012 907	.013 260	.013 976	.015 077	.017 369	29
30	.011 109	.011 423	.012 062	.013 046	.015 103	30
31	.009 562	.009 841	.010 411	.011 290	.013 133	31
32	.008 230	.008 478	.008 985	.009 769	.011 420	32
33	.007 083	.007 304	.007 755	.008 454	.009 931	33
34	.006 097	.006 293	.006 693	.007 315	.008 635	34
35	.005 248	.005 421	.005 777	.006 330	.007 509	35
36	.004 517	.004 670	.004 986	.005 478	.006 529	36
37	.003 887	.004 024	.004 303	.004 740	.005 678	37
38	.003 346	.003 466	.003 714	.004 102	.004 937	38
39	.002 880	.002 986	.003 205	.003 549	.004 293	39
40	.002 479	.002 573	.002 766	.003 071	.003 733	40

128

REVERSION FACTORS

(Present Value of $1)

15½%

Base:	2.718 282	1.012 917	1.038 750	1.077 500	1.155 000	

Frequency of Conversion

Months	Continuous	Monthly	Quarterly	Semiannual	Annual	Months
0	1.000 000	1.000 000	1.000 000	1.000 000	1.000 000	0
1	.987 166	.987 248	.987 248	.987 248	.987 248	1
2	.974 497	.974 659	.974 817	.974 817	.974 817	2
3	.961 991	.962 230	.962 696	.962 696	.962 696	3
4	.949 645	.949 960	.950 419	.950 872	.950 872	4
5	.937 458	.937 846	.938 452	.939 335	.939 335	5
6	.925 427	.925 886	.926 783	.928 074	.928 074	6
7	.913 550	.914 080	.914 964	.916 239	.917 081	7
8	.901 826	.902 423	.903 444	.904 703	.906 344	8
9	.890 253	.890 916	.892 210	.893 453	.895 857	9
10	.878 827	.879 555	.880 832	.882 479	.885 609	10
11	.867 549	.868 339	.869 741	.871 772	.875 593	11

Years						Years
1	.856 415	.857 266	.858 926	.861 322	.865 801	1
2	.733 447	.734 904	.737 754	.741 875	.749 611	2
3	.628 135	.630 008	.633 676	.638 993	.649 014	3
4	.537 944	.540 084	.544 281	.550 379	.561 917	4
5	.460 704	.462 996	.467 497	.474 053	.486 508	5
6	.394 554	.396 910	.401 546	.408 312	.421 219	6
7	.337 902	.340 258	.344 898	.351 688	.364 692	7
8	.289 384	.291 691	.296 242	.302 917	.315 751	8
9	.247 833	.250 057	.254 450	.260 909	.273 377	9
10	.212 248	.214 365	.218 554	.224 727	.236 690	10
11	.181 772	.183 768	.187 722	.193 562	.204 927	11
12	.155 673	.157 538	.161 239	.166 719	.177 426	12
13	.133 320	.135 052	.138 492	.143 599	.153 615	13
14	.114 178	.115 775	.118 955	.123 685	.133 000	14
15	.097 783	.099 250	.102 173	.106 532	.115 152	15
16	.083 743	.085 084	.087 759	.091 759	.099 698	16
17	.071 719	.072 939	.075 379	.079 034	.086 319	17
18	.061 421	.062 528	.064 745	.068 073	.074 735	18
19	.052 602	.053 603	.055 611	.058 633	.064 706	19
20	.045 049	.045 952	.047 766	.050 502	.056 022	20
21	.038 581	.039 393	.041 027	.043 499	.048 504	21
22	.033 041	.033 771	.035 239	.037 466	.041 995	22
23	.028 297	.028 950	.030 268	.032 270	.036 359	23
24	.024 234	.024 818	.025 998	.027 795	.031 480	24
25	.020 754	.021 276	.022 330	.023 941	.027 255	25
26	.017 774	.018 239	.019 180	.020 621	.023 598	26
27	.015 222	.015 636	.016 474	.017 761	.020 431	27
28	.013 037	.013 404	.014 150	.015 298	.017 689	28
29	.011 165	.011 491	.012 154	.013 176	.015 315	29
30	.009 562	.009 851	.010 439	.011 349	.013 260	30
31	.008 189	.008 445	.008 967	.009 775	.011 480	31
32	.007 013	.007 239	.007 702	.008 420	.009 940	32
33	.006 006	.006 206	.006 615	.007 252	.008 606	33
34	.005 144	.005 320	.005 682	.006 246	.007 451	34
35	.004 405	.004 561	.004 880	.005 380	.006 451	35
36	.003 773	.003 910	.004 192	.004 634	.005 585	36
37	.003 231	.003 352	.003 601	.003 991	.004 836	37
38	.002 767	.002 873	.003 093	.003 438	.004 187	38
39	.002 370	.002 463	.002 656	.002 961	.003 625	39
40	.002 029	.002 112	.002 282	.002 550	.003 138	40

16%

REVERSION FACTORS
(Present Value of $1)

Base: 2.718 282   1.013 333   1.040 000   1.080 000   1.160 000

Frequency of Conversion

Months	Continuous	Monthly	Quarterly	Semiannual	Annual	Months
0	1.000 000	1.000 000	1.000 000	1.000 000	1.000 000	0
1	.986 755	.986 842	.986 842	.986 842	.986 842	1
2	.973 686	.973 857	.974 026	.974 026	.974 026	2
3	.960 789	.961 043	.961 538	.961 538	.961 538	3
4	.948 064	.948 398	.948 887	.949 367	.949 367	4
5	.935 507	.935 919	.936 563	.937 500	.937 500	5
6	.923 116	.923 604	.924 556	.925 926	.925 926	6
7	.910 890	.911 452	.912 391	.913 743	.914 634	7
8	.898 825	.899 459	.900 542	.901 876	.903 614	8
9	.886 920	.887 624	.888 996	.890 313	.892 857	9
10	.875 173	.875 945	.877 299	.879 044	.882 353	10
11	.863 582	.864 419	.865 906	.868 056	.872 093	11

Years						Years
1	.852 144	.853 045	.854 804	.857 339	.862 069	1
2	.726 149	.727 686	.730 690	.735 030	.743 163	2
3	.618 783	.620 749	.624 597	.630 170	.640 658	3
4	.527 292	.529 527	.533 908	.540 269	.552 291	4
5	.449 329	.451 711	.456 387	.463 193	.476 113	5
6	.382 893	.385 330	.390 121	.397 114	.410 442	6
7	.326 280	.328 704	.333 477	.340 461	.353 830	7
8	.278 037	.280 399	.285 058	.291 890	.305 025	8
9	.236 928	.239 193	.243 669	.250 249	.262 953	9
10	.201 897	.204 042	.208 289	.214 548	.226 684	10
11	.172 045	.174 057	.178 046	.183 941	.195 417	11
12	.146 607	.148 479	.152 195	.157 699	.168 463	12
13	.124 930	.126 659	.130 097	.135 202	.145 227	13
14	.106 459	.108 046	.111 207	.115 914	.125 195	14
15	.090 718	.092 168	.095 060	.099 377	.107 927	15
16	.077 305	.078 624	.081 258	.085 200	.093 041	16
17	.065 875	.067 069	.069 460	.073 045	.080 207	17
18	.056 135	.057 213	.059 374	.062 625	.069 144	18
19	.047 835	.048 806	.050 754	.053 690	.059 607	19
20	.040 762	.041 633	.043 384	.046 031	.051 385	20
21	.034 735	.035 515	.037 085	.039 464	.044 298	21
22	.029 599	.030 296	.031 701	.033 834	.038 188	22
23	.025 223	.025 844	.027 098	.029 007	.032 920	23
24	.021 494	.022 046	.023 163	.024 869	.028 380	24
25	.018 316	.018 806	.019 800	.021 321	.024 465	25
26	.015 608	.016 043	.016 925	.018 280	.021 091	26
27	.013 300	.013 685	.014 468	.015 672	.018 182	27
28	.011 333	.011 674	.012 367	.013 436	.015 674	28
29	.009 658	.009 958	.010 571	.011 519	.013 512	29
30	.008 230	.008 495	.009 036	.009 876	.011 648	30
31	.007 013	.007 247	.007 724	.008 467	.010 042	31
32	.005 976	.006 182	.006 603	.007 259	.008 657	32
33	.005 092	.005 273	.005 644	.006 223	.007 463	33
34	.004 339	.004 498	.004 825	.005 336	.006 433	34
35	.003 698	.003 837	.004 124	.004 574	.005 546	35
36	.003 151	.003 273	.003 525	.003 922	.004 781	36
37	.002 685	.002 792	.003 013	.003 362	.004 121	37
38	.002 288	.002 382	.002 576	.002 883	.003 553	38
39	.001 950	.002 032	.002 202	.002 471	.003 063	39
40	.001 662	.001 733	.001 882	.002 119	.002 640	40

REVERSION FACTORS
(Present Value of $1)

16½%

Base:	2.718 282	1.013 750	1.041 250	1.082 500	1.165 000	
			Frequency of Conversion			
Months	Continuous	Monthly	Quarterly	Semiannual	Annual	Months
0	1.000 000	1.000 000	1.000 000	1.000 000	1.000 000	0
1	.986 344	.986 436	.986 436	.986 436	.986 436	1
2	.972 875	.973 057	.973 236	.973 236	.973 236	2
3	.959 589	.959 859	.960 384	.960 384	.960 384	3
4	.946 485	.946 840	.947 358	.947 867	.947 867	4
5	.933 560	.933 997	.934 680	.935 673	.935 673	5
6	.920 811	.921 329	.922 338	.923 788	.923 788	6
7	.908 237	.908 833	.909 828	.911 258	.912 201	7
8	.895 834	.896 506	.897 652	.899 063	.900 901	8
9	.883 601	.884 346	.885 799	.887 191	.889 878	9
10	.871 534	.872 351	.873 784	.875 628	.879 121	10
11	.859 633	.860 519	.862 091	.864 363	.868 621	11

Years						Years
1	.847 894	.848 847	.850 707	.853 383	.858 369	1
2	.718 924	.720 542	.723 702	.728 263	.736 798	2
3	.609 571	.611 630	.615 658	.621 488	.632 444	3
4	.516 851	.519 181	.523 745	.530 367	.542 871	4
5	.438 235	.440 705	.445 553	.452 607	.465 983	5
6	.371 577	.374 091	.379 035	.386 247	.399 986	6
7	.315 058	.317 546	.322 448	.329 617	.343 335	7
8	.267 135	.269 548	.274 309	.281 289	.294 708	8
9	.226 502	.228 805	.233 356	.240 048	.252 969	9
10	.192 050	.194 221	.198 518	.204 853	.217 140	10
11	.162 838	.164 864	.168 880	.174 818	.186 387	11
12	.138 069	.139 944	.143 668	.149 187	.159 989	12
13	.117 068	.118 791	.122 219	.127 314	.137 329	13
14	.099 261	.100 836	.103 973	.108 647	.117 879	14
15	.084 163	.085 594	.088 450	.092 718	.101 184	15
16	.071 361	.072 656	.075 245	.079 124	.086 853	16
17	.060 507	.061 674	.064 012	.067 523	.074 552	17
18	.051 303	.052 352	.054 455	.057 623	.063 993	18
19	.043 500	.044 439	.046 325	.049 174	.054 930	19
20	.036 883	.037 722	.039 409	.041 965	.047 150	20
21	.031 273	.032 020	.033 526	.035 812	.040 472	21
22	.026 516	.027 180	.028 521	.030 561	.034 740	22
23	.022 483	.023 072	.024 263	.026 081	.029 820	23
24	.019 063	.019 584	.020 640	.022 257	.025 596	24
25	.016 163	.016 624	.017 559	.018 993	.021 971	25
26	.013 705	.014 111	.014 938	.016 209	.018 859	26
27	.011 620	.011 978	.012 707	.013 832	.016 188	27
28	.009 853	.010 168	.010 810	.011 804	.013 895	28
29	.008 354	.008 631	.009 196	.010 074	.011 927	29
30	.007 083	.007 326	.007 823	.008 597	.010 238	30
31	.006 006	.006 219	.006 655	.007 336	.008 788	31
32	.005 092	.005 279	.005 662	.006 261	.007 543	32
33	.004 318	.004 481	.004 817	.005 343	.006 475	33
34	.003 661	.003 804	.004 097	.004 559	.005 558	34
35	.003 104	.003 229	.003 486	.003 891	.004 771	35
36	.002 632	.002 741	.002 965	.003 320	.004 095	36
37	.002 232	.002 326	.002 523	.002 834	.003 515	37
38	.001 892	.001 975	.002 146	.002 418	.003 017	38
39	.001 604	.001 676	.001 826	.002 064	.002 590	39
40	.001 360	.001 423	.001 553	.001 761	.002 223	40

17%

REVERSION FACTORS
(Present Value of $1)

Base:	2.718 282	1.014 167	1.042 500	1.085 000	1.170 000	
			Frequency of Conversion			
Months	Continuous	Monthly	Quarterly	Semiannual	Annual	Months
0	1.000 000	1.000 000	1.000 000	1.000 000	1.000 000	0
1	.985 933	.986 031	.986 031	.986 031	.986 031	1
2	.972 064	.972 258	.972 447	.972 447	.972 447	2
3	.958 390	.958 676	.959 233	.959 233	.959 233	3
4	.944 909	.945 285	.945 833	.946 372	.946 372	4
5	.931 617	.932 080	.932 803	.933 852	.933 852	5
6	.918 512	.919 060	.920 127	.921 659	.921 659	6
7	.905 592	.906 222	.907 274	.908 785	.909 780	7
8	.892 853	.893 563	.894 775	.896 265	.898 204	8
9	.880 293	.881 081	.882 616	.884 085	.886 918	9
10	.867 911	.868 774	.870 287	.872 232	.875 912	10
11	.855 702	.856 638	.858 298	.860 693	.865 177	11

Years						Years
1	.843 665	.844 672	.846 634	.849 455	.854 701	1
2	.711 770	.713 471	.716 789	.721 574	.730 514	2
3	.600 496	.602 648	.606 858	.612 945	.624 371	3
4	.506 617	.509 040	.513 787	.520 669	.533 650	4
5	.427 415	.429 972	.434 989	.442 285	.456 111	5
6	.360 595	.363 185	.368 277	.375 702	.389 839	6
7	.304 221	.306 772	.311 796	.319 142	.333 195	7
8	.256 661	.259 122	.263 977	.271 097	.284 782	8
9	.216 536	.218 873	.223 492	.230 285	.243 404	9
10	.182 684	.184 876	.189 216	.195 616	.208 037	10
11	.154 124	.156 159	.160 197	.166 167	.177 810	11
12	.130 029	.131 903	.135 628	.141 152	.151 974	12
13	.109 701	.111 415	.114 827	.119 902	.129 892	13
14	.092 551	.094 109	.097 217	.101 851	.111 019	14
15	.078 082	.079 491	.082 307	.086 518	.094 888	15
16	.065 875	.067 144	.069 684	.073 493	.081 101	16
17	.055 576	.056 715	.058 997	.062 429	.069 317	17
18	.046 888	.047 905	.049 949	.053 031	.059 245	18
19	.039 557	.040 464	.042 288	.045 047	.050 637	19
20	.033 373	.034 179	.035 803	.038 266	.043 280	20
21	.028 156	.028 870	.030 312	.032 505	.036 991	21
22	.023 754	.024 386	.025 663	.027 612	.031 616	22
23	.020 041	.020 598	.021 727	.023 455	.027 022	23
24	.016 907	.017 399	.018 395	.019 924	.023 096	24
25	.014 264	.014 696	.015 574	.016 924	.019 740	25
26	.012 034	.012 413	.013 185	.014 377	.016 872	26
27	.010 153	.010 485	.011 163	.012 212	.014 421	27
28	.008 566	.008 857	.009 451	.010 374	.012 325	28
29	.007 227	.007 481	.008 002	.008 812	.010 534	29
30	.006 097	.006 319	.006 774	.007 485	.009 004	30
31	.005 144	.005 337	.005 735	.006 359	.007 696	31
32	.004 339	.004 508	.004 856	.005 401	.006 577	32
33	.003 661	.003 808	.004 111	.004 588	.005 622	33
34	.003 089	.003 217	.003 481	.003 897	.004 805	34
35	.002 606	.002 717	.002 947	.003 311	.004 107	35
36	.002 198	.002 295	.002 495	.002 812	.003 510	36
37	.001 855	.001 938	.002 112	.002 389	.003 000	37
38	.001 565	.001 637	.001 788	.002 029	.002 564	38
39	.001 320	.001 383	.001 514	.001 724	.002 192	39
40	.001 114	.001 168	.001 282	.001 464	.001 873	40

(Present Value of $1)

Base: 2.718 282   1.014 583   1.043 750   1.087 500   1.175 000

Frequency of Conversion

Months	Continuous	Monthly	Quarterly	Semiannual	Annual	Months
0	1.000 000	1.000 000	1.000 000	1.000 000	1.000 000	0
1	.985 522	.985 626	.985 626	.985 626	.985 626	1
2	.971 255	.971 459	.971 660	.971 660	.971 660	2
3	.957 193	.957 496	.958 084	.958 084	.958 084	3
4	.943 335	.943 733	.944 313	.944 882	.944 882	4
5	.929 678	.930 168	.930 932	.932 039	.932 039	5
6	.916 219	.916 798	.917 925	.919 540	.919 540	6
7	.902 954	.903 620	.904 731	.906 323	.907 372	7
8	.889 882	.890 632	.891 911	.893 480	.895 522	8
9	.876 998	.877 830	.879 449	.880 997	.883 978	9
10	.864 302	.865 212	.866 808	.868 857	.872 727	10
11	.851 789	.852 776	.854 525	.857 047	.861 759	11

Years						Years
1	.839 457	.840 519	.842 586	.845 554	.851 064	1
2	.704 688	.706 471	.709 951	.714 962	.724 310	2
3	.591 555	.593 802	.598 194	.604 539	.616 434	3
4	.496 585	.499 102	.504 030	.511 171	.524 624	4
5	.416 862	.419 504	.424 688	.432 222	.446 489	5
6	.349 938	.352 601	.357 836	.365 468	.379 991	6
7	.293 758	.296 368	.301 508	.309 023	.323 396	7
8	.246 597	.249 103	.254 046	.261 295	.275 231	8
9	.207 008	.209 375	.214 056	.220 939	.234 239	9
10	.173 774	.175 984	.180 360	.186 816	.199 352	10
11	.145 876	.147 918	.151 969	.157 963	.169 662	11
12	.122 456	.124 328	.128 047	.133 567	.144 393	12
13	.102 797	.104 500	.107 890	.112 938	.122 888	13
14	.086 294	.087 834	.090 907	.095 495	.104 585	14
15	.072 440	.073 826	.076 597	.080 746	.089 009	15
16	.060 810	.062 052	.064 539	.068 275	.075 752	16
17	.051 047	.052 156	.054 380	.057 730	.064 470	17
18	.042 852	.043 838	.045 820	.048 814	.054 868	18
19	.035 973	.036 847	.038 607	.041 275	.046 696	19
20	.030 197	.030 970	.032 530	.034 900	.039 741	20
21	.025 349	.026 031	.027 409	.029 510	.033 822	21
22	.021 280	.021 880	.023 095	.024 952	.028 785	22
23	.017 863	.018 390	.019 459	.021 099	.024 498	23
24	.014 996	.015 457	.016 396	.017 840	.020 849	24
25	.012 588	.012 992	.013 815	.015 085	.017 744	25
26	.010 567	.010 920	.011 640	.012 755	.015 101	26
27	.008 871	.009 179	.009 808	.010 785	.012 852	27
28	.007 447	.007 715	.008 264	.009 119	.010 938	28
29	.006 251	.006 484	.006 963	.007 711	.009 309	29
30	.005 248	.005 450	.005 867	.006 520	.007 923	30
31	.004 405	.004 581	.004 944	.005 513	.006 743	31
32	.003 698	.003 850	.004 165	.004 662	.005 738	32
33	.003 104	.003 236	.003 510	.003 942	.004 884	33
34	.002 606	.002 720	.002 957	.003 333	.004 156	34
35	.002 187	.002 286	.002 492	.002 818	.003 537	35
36	.001 836	.001 922	.002 099	.002 383	.003 010	36
37	.001 541	.001 615	.001 769	.002 015	.002 562	37
38	.001 294	.001 358	.001 491	.001 704	.002 181	38
39	.001 086	.001 141	.001 256	.001 441	.001 856	39
40	.000 912	.000 959	.001 058	.001 218	.001 579	40

18%

REVERSION FACTORS
(Present Value of $1)

Base:	2.718 282	1.015 000	1.045 000	1.090 000	1.180 000	
			Frequency of Conversion			
Months	Continuous	Monthly	Quarterly	Semiannual	Annual	Months
0	1.000 000	1.000 000	1.000 000	1.000 000	1.000 000	0
1	.985 112	.985 222	.985 222	.985 222	.985 222	1
2	.970 446	.970 662	.970 874	.970 874	.970 874	2
3	.955 997	.956 317	.956 938	.956 938	.956 938	3
4	.941 765	.942 184	.942 796	.943 396	.943 396	4
5	.927 743	.928 260	.929 066	.930 233	.930 233	5
6	.913 931	.914 542	.915 730	.917 431	.917 431	6
7	.900 325	.901 027	.902 197	.903 873	.904 977	7
8	.886 920	.887 711	.889 058	.890 710	.892 857	8
9	.873 716	.874 592	.876 297	.877 925	.881 057	9
10	.860 708	.861 667	.863 346	.865 501	.869 565	10
11	.847 894	.848 933	.850 773	.853 424	.858 369	11

Years						Years
1	.835 270	.836 387	.838 561	.841 680	.847 458	1
2	.697 676	.699 544	.703 185	.708 425	.718 184	2
3	.582 748	.585 090	.589 664	.596 267	.608 631	3
4	.486 752	.489 362	.494 469	.501 866	.515 789	4
5	.406 570	.409 296	.414 643	.422 411	.437 109	5
6	.339 596	.342 330	.347 703	.355 535	.370 432	6
7	.283 654	.286 321	.291 571	.299 246	.313 925	7
8	.236 928	.239 475	.244 500	.251 870	.266 038	8
9	.197 899	.200 294	.205 028	.211 994	.225 456	9
10	.165 299	.167 523	.171 929	.178 431	.191 064	10
11	.138 069	.140 114	.144 173	.150 182	.161 919	11
12	.115 325	.117 190	.120 898	.126 405	.137 220	12
13	.096 328	.098 016	.101 380	.106 393	.116 288	13
14	.080 460	.081 979	.085 013	.089 548	.098 549	14
15	.067 206	.068 567	.071 289	.075 371	.083 516	15
16	.056 135	.057 348	.059 780	.063 438	.070 776	16
17	.046 888	.047 965	.050 129	.053 395	.059 980	17
18	.039 164	.040 118	.042 037	.044 941	.050 830	18
19	.032 712	.033 554	.035 250	.037 826	.043 077	19
20	.027 324	.028 064	.029 559	.031 838	.036 506	20
21	.022 823	.023 472	.024 787	.026 797	.030 937	21
22	.019 063	.019 632	.020 786	.022 555	.026 218	22
23	.015 923	.016 420	.017 430	.018 984	.022 218	23
24	.013 300	.013 733	.014 616	.015 978	.018 829	24
25	.011 109	.011 486	.012 257	.013 449	.015 957	25
26	.009 279	.009 607	.010 278	.011 319	.013 523	26
27	.007 750	.008 035	.008 619	.009 527	.011 460	27
28	.006 474	.006 721	.007 227	.008 019	.009 712	28
29	.005 407	.005 621	.006 061	.006 749	.008 230	29
30	.004 517	.004 701	.005 082	.005 681	.006 975	30
31	.003 773	.003 932	.004 262	.004 781	.005 911	31
32	.003 151	.003 289	.003 574	.004 024	.005 009	32
33	.002 632	.002 751	.002 997	.003 387	.004 245	33
34	.002 198	.002 301	.002 513	.002 851	.003 598	34
35	.001 836	.001 924	.002 107	.002 400	.003 049	35
36	.001 534	.001 609	.001 767	.002 020	.002 584	36
37	.001 281	.001 346	.001 482	.001 700	.002 190	37
38	.001 070	.001 126	.001 243	.001 431	.001 856	38
39	.000 894	.000 942	.001 042	.001 204	.001 573	39
40	.000 747	.000 788	.000 874	.001 014	.001 333	40

(Present Value of $1)

Base:	2.718 282	1.015 833	1.047 500	1.095 000	1.190 000	
			Frequency of Conversion			
Months	Continuous	Monthly	Quarterly	Semiannual	Annual	Months
0	1.000 000	1.000 000	1.000 000	1.000 000	1.000 000	0
1	.984 291	.984 413	.984 413	.984 413	.984 413	1
2	.968 829	.969 070	.969 305	.969 305	.969 305	2
3	.953 610	.953 965	.954 654	.954 654	.954 654	3
4	.938 631	.939 096	.939 774	.940 439	.940 439	4
5	.923 886	.924 459	.925 351	.926 641	.926 641	5
6	.909 373	.910 050	.911 364	.913 242	.913 242	6
7	.895 088	.895 865	.897 159	.899 008	.900 225	7
8	.881 027	.881 902	.883 390	.885 210	.887 574	8
9	.867 188	.868 156	.870 037	.871 830	.875 274	9
10	.853 565	.854 625	.856 476	.858 848	.863 309	10
11	.840 157	.841 304	.843 332	.846 247	.851 668	11

Years						Years
1	.826 959	.828 191	.830 585	.834 011	.840 336	1
2	.683 861	.685 900	.689 871	.695 574	.706 165	2
3	.565 525	.568 056	.572 996	.580 117	.593 416	3
4	.467 666	.470 459	.475 922	.483 824	.498 669	4
5	.386 741	.389 630	.395 293	.403 514	.419 049	5
6	.319 819	.322 688	.328 324	.336 535	.352 142	6
7	.264 477	.267 247	.272 701	.280 674	.295 918	7
8	.218 712	.221 332	.226 501	.234 085	.248 671	8
9	.180 866	.183 305	.188 129	.195 230	.208 967	9
10	.149 569	.151 812	.156 257	.162 824	.175 602	10
11	.123 687	.125 729	.129 784	.135 797	.147 565	11
12	.102 284	.104 128	.107 797	.113 256	.124 004	12
13	.084 585	.086 238	.089 534	.094 457	.104 205	13
14	.069 948	.071 421	.074 366	.078 778	.087 567	14
15	.057 844	.059 150	.061 767	.065 702	.073 586	15
16	.047 835	.048 988	.051 303	.054 796	.061 837	16
17	.039 557	.040 571	.042 611	.045 700	.051 964	17
18	.032 712	.033 601	.035 392	.038 115	.043 667	18
19	.027 052	.027 828	.029 396	.031 788	.036 695	19
20	.022 371	.023 047	.024 416	.026 512	.030 836	20
21	.018 500	.019 087	.020 280	.022 111	.025 913	21
22	.015 299	.015 808	.016 844	.018 441	.021 775	22
23	.012 651	.013 092	.013 990	.015 380	.018 299	23
24	.010 462	.010 843	.011 620	.012 827	.015 377	24
25	.008 652	.008 980	.009 652	.010 698	.012 922	25
26	.007 155	.007 437	.008 016	.008 922	.010 859	26
27	.005 917	.006 159	.006 658	.007 441	.009 125	27
28	.004 893	.005 101	.005 530	.006 206	.007 668	28
29	.004 046	.004 225	.004 593	.005 176	.006 444	29
30	.003 346	.003 499	.003 815	.004 317	.005 415	30
31	.002 767	.002 898	.003 169	.003 600	.004 550	31
32	.002 288	.002 400	.002 632	.003 003	.003 824	32
33	.001 892	.001 987	.002 186	.002 504	.003 213	33
34	.001 565	.001 646	.001 816	.002 089	.002 700	34
35	.001 294	.001 363	.001 508	.001 742	.002 269	35
36	.001 070	.001 129	.001 253	.001 453	.001 907	36
37	.000 885	.000 935	.001 040	.001 212	.001 602	37
38	.000 732	.000 774	.000 864	.001 010	.001 347	38
39	.000 605	.000 641	.000 718	.000 843	.001 132	39
40	.000 500	.000 531	.000 596	.000 703	.000 951	40

20%

REVERSION FACTORS
(Present Value of $1)

Base:	2.718 282	1.016 667	1.050 000	1.100 000	1.200 000	
			Frequency of Conversion			
Months	Continuous	Monthly	Quarterly	Semiannual	Annual	Months
0	1.000 000	1.000 000	1.000 000	1.000 000	1.000 000	0
1	.983 471	.983 607	.983 607	.983 607	.983 607	1
2	.967 216	.967 482	.967 742	.967 742	.967 742	2
3	.951 229	.951 622	.952 381	.952 381	.952 381	3
4	.935 507	.936 021	.936 768	.937 500	.937 500	4
5	.920 044	.920 677	.921 659	.923 077	.923 077	5
6	.904 837	.905 583	.907 029	.909 091	.909 091	6
7	.889 882	.890 738	.892 160	.894 188	.895 522	7
8	.875 173	.876 136	.877 770	.879 765	.882 353	8
9	.860 708	.861 773	.863 838	.865 801	.869 565	9
10	.846 482	.847 645	.849 676	.852 273	.857 143	10
11	.832 491	.833 749	.835 972	.839 161	.845 070	11

Years						Years
1	.818 731	.820 081	.822 702	.826 446	.833 333	1
2	.670 320	.672 534	.676 839	.683 013	.694 444	2
3	.548 812	.551 532	.556 837	.564 474	.578 704	3
4	.449 329	.452 301	.458 112	.466 507	.482 253	4
5	.367 879	.370 924	.376 889	.385 543	.401 878	5
6	.301 194	.304 188	.310 068	.318 631	.334 898	6
7	.246 597	.249 459	.255 094	.263 331	.279 082	7
8	.201 897	.204 577	.209 866	.217 629	.232 568	8
9	.165 299	.167 769	.172 657	.179 859	.193 807	9
10	.135 335	.137 585	.142 046	.148 644	.161 506	10
11	.110 803	.112 831	.116 861	.122 846	.134 588	11
12	.090 718	.092 530	.096 142	.101 526	.112 157	12
13	.074 274	.075 882	.079 096	.083 905	.093 464	13
14	.060 810	.062 230	.065 073	.069 343	.077 887	14
15	.049 787	.051 033	.053 536	.057 309	.064 905	15
16	.040 762	.041 852	.044 044	.047 362	.054 088	16
17	.033 373	.034 322	.036 235	.039 143	.045 073	17
18	.027 324	.028 147	.029 811	.032 349	.037 561	18
19	.022 371	.023 082	.024 525	.026 735	.031 301	19
20	.018 316	.018 930	.020 177	.022 095	.026 084	20
21	.014 996	.015 524	.016 600	.018 260	.021 737	21
22	.012 277	.012 731	.013 657	.015 091	.018 114	22
23	.010 052	.010 440	.011 235	.012 472	.015 095	23
24	.008 230	.008 562	.009 243	.010 307	.012 579	24
25	.006 738	.007 021	.007 604	.008 519	.010 483	25
26	.005 517	.005 758	.006 256	.007 040	.008 735	26
27	.004 517	.004 722	.005 147	.005 818	.007 280	27
28	.003 698	.003 873	.004 234	.004 809	.006 066	28
29	.003 028	.003 176	.003 484	.003 974	.005 055	29
30	.002 479	.002 604	.002 866	.003 284	.004 213	30
31	.002 029	.002 136	.002 358	.002 714	.003 511	31
32	.001 662	.001 752	.001 940	.002 243	.002 926	32
33	.001 360	.001 436	.001 596	.001 854	.002 438	33
34	.001 114	.001 178	.001 313	.001 532	.002 032	34
35	.000 912	.000 966	.001 080	.001 266	.001 693	35
36	.000 747	.000 792	.000 889	.001 046	.001 411	36
37	.000 611	.000 650	.000 731	.000 865	.001 176	37
38	.000 500	.000 533	.000 601	.000 715	.000 980	38
39	.000 410	.000 437	.000 495	.000 591	.000 816	39
40	.000 335	.000 358	.000 407	.000 488	.000 680	40

Base:	2.718 282	1.017 500	1.052 500	1.105 000	1.210 000	
			Frequency of Conversion			
Months	Continuous	Monthly	Quarterly	Semiannual	Annual	Months
0	1.000 000	1.000 000	1.000 000	1.000 000	1.000 000	0
1	.982 652	.982 801	.982 801	.982 801	.982 801	1
2	.965 605	.965 898	.966 184	.966 184	.966 184	2
3	.948 854	.949 285	.950 119	.950 119	.950 119	3
4	.932 394	.932 959	.933 778	.934 579	.934 579	4
5	.916 219	.916 913	.917 989	.919 540	.919 540	5
6	.900 325	.901 143	.902 726	.904 977	.904 977	6
7	.884 706	.885 644	.887 200	.889 413	.890 869	7
8	.869 358	.870 412	.872 199	.874 374	.877 193	8
9	.854 277	.855 441	.857 697	.859 836	.863 931	9
10	.839 457	.840 729	.842 945	.845 773	.851 064	10
11	.824 894	.826 269	.828 692	.832 163	.838 574	11

Years						Years
1	.810 584	.812 058	.814 914	.818 984	.826 446	1
2	.657 047	.659 438	.664 084	.670 735	.683 013	2
3	.532 592	.535 502	.541 171	.549 321	.564 474	3
4	.431 711	.434 858	.441 008	.449 885	.466 507	4
5	.349 938	.353 130	.359 383	.368 449	.385 543	5
6	.283 654	.286 762	.292 866	.301 754	.318 631	6
7	.229 925	.232 868	.238 661	.247 132	.263 331	7
8	.186 374	.189 102	.194 488	.202 397	.217 629	8
9	.151 072	.153 562	.158 491	.165 760	.179 859	9
10	.122 456	.124 701	.129 156	.135 755	.148 644	10
11	.099 261	.101 264	.105 251	.111 181	.122 846	11
12	.080 460	.082 233	.085 771	.091 055	.101 526	12
13	.065 219	.066 778	.069 896	.074 573	.083 905	13
14	.052 866	.054 227	.056 959	.061 074	.069 343	14
15	.042 852	.044 036	.046 417	.050 019	.057 309	15
16	.034 735	.035 760	.037 826	.040 964	.047 362	16
17	.028 156	.029 039	.030 825	.033 549	.039 143	17
18	.022 823	.023 581	.025 119	.027 476	.032 349	18
19	.018 500	.019 149	.020 470	.022 503	.026 735	19
20	.014 996	.015 550	.016 681	.018 429	.022 095	20
21	.012 155	.012 628	.013 594	.015 093	.018 260	21
22	.009 853	.010 254	.011 078	.012 361	.015 091	22
23	.007 987	.008 327	.009 027	.010 124	.012 472	23
24	.006 474	.006 762	.007 357	.008 291	.010 307	24
25	.005 248	.005 491	.005 995	.006 790	.008 519	25
26	.004 254	.004 459	.004 885	.005 561	.007 040	26
27	.003 448	.003 621	.003 981	.004 554	.005 818	27
28	.002 795	.002 941	.003 244	.003 730	.004 809	28
29	.002 265	.002 388	.002 644	.003 055	.003 974	29
30	.001 836	.001 939	.002 155	.002 502	.003 284	30
31	.001 488	.001 575	.001 756	.002 049	.002 714	31
32	.001 207	.001 279	.001 431	.001 678	.002 243	32
33	.000 978	.001 038	.001 166	.001 374	.001 854	33
34	.000 793	.000 843	.000 950	.001 126	.001 532	34
35	.000 643	.000 685	.000 774	.000 922	.001 266	35
36	.000 521	.000 556	.000 631	.000 755	.001 046	36
37	.000 422	.000 452	.000 514	.000 618	.000 865	37
38	.000 342	.000 367	.000 419	.000 506	.000 715	38
39	.000 277	.000 298	.000 341	.000 415	.000 591	39
40	.000 225	.000 242	.000 278	.000 340	.000 488	40

22%

REVERSION FACTORS
(Present Value of $1)

Base: 2.718 282   1.018 333   1.055 000   1.110 000   1.220 000

Frequency of Conversion

Months	Continuous	Monthly	Quarterly	Semiannual	Annual	Months
0	1.000 000	1.000 000	1.000 000	1.000 000	1.000 000	0
1	.981 834	.981 997	.981 997	.981 997	.981 997	1
2	.963 997	.964 318	.964 630	.964 630	.964 630	2
3	.946 485	.946 957	.947 867	.947 867	.947 867	3
4	.929 291	.929 908	.930 803	.931 677	.931 677	4
5	.912 409	.913 167	.914 341	.916 031	.916 031	5
6	.895 834	.896 727	.898 452	.900 901	.900 901	6
7	.879 560	.880 583	.882 277	.884 682	.886 263	7
8	.863 582	.864 730	.866 674	.869 036	.872 093	8
9	.847 894	.849 162	.851 614	.853 935	.858 369	9
10	.832 491	.833 874	.836 282	.839 349	.845 070	10
11	.817 367	.818 861	.821 492	.825 253	.832 178	11

Years						Years
1	.802 519	.804 119	.807 217	.811 622	.819 672	1
2	.644 036	.646 608	.651 599	.658 731	.671 862	2
3	.516 851	.519 950	.525 982	.534 641	.550 707	3
4	.414 783	.418 102	.424 581	.433 926	.451 399	4
5	.332 871	.336 204	.342 729	.352 184	.369 999	5
6	.267 135	.270 348	.276 657	.285 841	.303 278	6
7	.214 381	.217 392	.223 322	.231 995	.248 589	7
8	.172 045	.174 809	.180 269	.188 292	.203 761	8
9	.138 069	.140 567	.145 516	.152 822	.167 017	9
10	.110 803	.113 033	.117 463	.124 034	.136 899	10
11	.088 922	.090 892	.094 818	.100 669	.112 213	11
12	.071 361	.073 088	.076 539	.081 705	.091 978	12
13	.057 269	.058 771	.061 783	.066 314	.075 391	13
14	.045 959	.047 259	.049 873	.053 822	.061 796	14
15	.036 883	.038 002	.040 258	.043 683	.050 653	15
16	.029 599	.030 558	.032 497	.035 454	.041 519	16
17	.023 754	.024 572	.026 232	.028 775	.034 032	17
18	.019 063	.019 759	.021 175	.023 355	.027 895	18
19	.015 299	.015 889	.017 093	.018 955	.022 865	19
20	.012 277	.012 776	.013 798	.015 384	.018 741	20
21	.009 853	.010 274	.011 138	.012 486	.015 362	21
22	.007 907	.008 261	.008 990	.010 134	.012 592	22
23	.006 346	.006 643	.007 257	.008 225	.010 321	23
24	.005 092	.005 342	.005 858	.006 676	.008 460	24
25	.004 087	.004 295	.004 729	.005 418	.006 934	25
26	.003 280	.003 454	.003 817	.004 397	.005 684	26
27	.002 632	.002 777	.003 081	.003 569	.004 659	27
28	.002 112	.002 233	.002 487	.002 897	.003 819	28
29	.001 695	.001 796	.002 008	.002 351	.003 130	29
30	.001 360	.001 444	.001 621	.001 908	.002 566	30
31	.001 092	.001 161	.001 308	.001 549	.002 103	31
32	.000 876	.000 934	.001 056	.001 257	.001 724	32
33	.000 703	.000 751	.000 852	.001 020	.001 413	33
34	.000 564	.000 604	.000 688	.000 828	.001 158	34
35	.000 453	.000 486	.000 555	.000 672	.000 949	35
36	.000 363	.000 390	.000 448	.000 545	.000 778	36
37	.000 292	.000 314	.000 362	.000 443	.000 638	37
38	.000 234	.000 252	.000 292	.000 359	.000 523	38
39	.000 188	.000 203	.000 236	.000 292	.000 429	39
40	.000 151	.000 163	.000 190	.000 237	.000 351	40

REVERSION FACTORS   **23%**

(Present Value of $1)

Base: | 2.718 282 | 1.019 167 | 1.057 500 | 1.115 000 | 1.230 000

Frequency of Conversion

Months	Continuous	Monthly	Quarterly	Semiannual	Annual	Months
0	1.000 000	1.000 000	1.000 000	1.000 000	1.000 000	0
1	.981 016	.981 194	.981 194	.981 194	.981 194	1
2	.962 392	.962 741	.963 082	.963 082	.963 082	2
3	.944 122	.944 636	.945 626	.945 626	.945 626	3
4	.926 199	.926 871	.927 843	.928 793	.928 793	4
5	.908 615	.909 440	.910 716	.912 548	.912 548	5
6	.891 366	.892 337	.894 209	.896 861	.896 861	6
7	.874 444	.875 555	.877 393	.879 994	.881 705	7
8	.857 844	.859 089	.861 197	.863 751	.867 052	8
9	.841 558	.842 933	.845 588	.848 095	.852 878	9
10	.825 582	.827 081	.829 686	.832 998	.839 161	10
11	.809 909	.811 526	.814 371	.818 428	.825 877	11

Years						Years
1	.794 534	.796 265	.799 611	.804 360	.813 008	1
2	.631 284	.634 037	.639 377	.646 994	.660 982	2
3	.501 576	.504 862	.511 253	.520 416	.537 384	3
4	.398 519	.402 004	.408 803	.418 602	.436 897	4
5	.316 637	.320 101	.326 883	.336 706	.355 201	5
6	.251 579	.254 885	.261 379	.270 833	.288 781	6
7	.199 888	.202 956	.209 002	.217 847	.234 782	7
8	.158 817	.161 607	.167 120	.175 227	.190 879	8
9	.126 186	.128 682	.133 631	.140 946	.155 187	9
10	.100 259	.102 465	.106 853	.113 371	.126 168	10
11	.079 659	.081 589	.085 440	.091 191	.102 576	11
12	.063 292	.064 967	.068 319	.073 351	.083 395	12
13	.050 287	.051 731	.054 629	.059 000	.067 801	13
14	.039 955	.041 191	.043 682	.047 457	.055 122	14
15	.031 746	.032 799	.034 928	.038 173	.044 815	15
16	.025 223	.026 117	.027 929	.030 705	.036 435	16
17	.020 041	.020 796	.022 332	.024 698	.029 622	17
18	.015 923	.016 559	.017 857	.019 866	.024 083	18
19	.012 651	.013 185	.014 279	.015 979	.019 580	19
20	.010 052	.010 499	.011 417	.012 853	.015 918	20
21	.007 987	.008 360	.009 130	.010 338	.012 942	21
22	.006 346	.006 657	.007 300	.008 316	.010 522	22
23	.005 042	.005 301	.005 837	.006 689	.008 554	23
24	.004 006	.004 221	.004 667	.005 380	.006 955	24
25	.003 183	.003 361	.003 732	.004 328	.005 654	25
26	.002 529	.002 676	.002 984	.003 481	.004 597	26
27	.002 009	.002 131	.002 386	.002 800	.003 737	27
28	.001 596	.001 697	.001 908	.002 252	.003 038	28
29	.001 268	.001 351	.001 526	.001 812	.002 470	29
30	.001 008	.001 076	.001 220	.001 457	.002 008	30
31	.000 801	.000 857	.000 976	.001 172	.001 633	31
32	.000 636	.000 682	.000 780	.000 943	.001 328	32
33	.000 505	.000 543	.000 624	.000 758	.001 079	33
34	.000 402	.000 432	.000 499	.000 610	.000 877	34
35	.000 319	.000 344	.000 399	.000 491	.000 713	35
36	.000 254	.000 274	.000 319	.000 395	.000 580	36
37	.000 201	.000 218	.000 255	.000 317	.000 472	37
38	.000 160	.000 174	.000 204	.000 255	.000 383	38
39	.000 127	.000 138	.000 163	.000 205	.000 312	39
40	.000 101	.000 110	.000 130	.000 165	.000 253	40

24%

REVERSION FACTORS
(Present Value of $1)

Base:	2.718 282	1.020 000	1.060 000	1.120 000	1.240 000	

Frequency of Conversion

Months	Continuous	Monthly	Quarterly	Semiannual	Annual	Months
0	1.000 000	1.000 000	1.000 000	1.000 000	1.000 000	0
1	.980 199	.980 392	.980 392	.980 392	.980 392	1
2	.960 789	.961 169	.961 538	.961 538	.961 538	2
3	.941 765	.942 322	.943 396	.943 396	.943 396	3
4	.923 116	.923 845	.924 898	.925 926	.925 926	4
5	.904 837	.905 731	.907 112	.909 091	.909 091	5
6	.886 920	.887 971	.889 996	.892 857	.892 857	6
7	.869 358	.870 560	.872 546	.875 350	.877 193	7
8	.852 144	.853 490	.855 766	.858 516	.862 069	8
9	.835 270	.836 755	.839 619	.842 318	.847 458	9
10	.818 731	.820 348	.823 156	.826 720	.833 333	10
11	.802 519	.804 263	.807 326	.811 688	.819 672	11

Years						Years
1	.786 628	.788 493	.792 094	.797 194	.806 452	1
2	.618 783	.621 721	.627 412	.635 518	.650 364	2
3	.486 752	.490 223	.496 969	.506 631	.524 487	3
4	.382 893	.386 538	.393 646	.403 883	.422 974	4
5	.301 194	.304 782	.311 805	.321 973	.341 108	5
6	.236 928	.240 319	.246 979	.256 675	.275 087	6
7	.186 374	.189 490	.195 630	.204 620	.221 844	7
8	.146 607	.149 411	.154 957	.163 122	.178 907	8
9	.115 325	.117 810	.122 741	.130 040	.144 280	9
10	.090 718	.092 892	.097 222	.103 667	.116 354	10
11	.071 361	.073 245	.077 009	.082 643	.093 834	11
12	.056 135	.057 753	.060 998	.065 882	.075 673	12
13	.044 157	.045 538	.048 316	.052 521	.061 026	13
14	.034 735	.035 906	.038 271	.041 869	.049 215	14
15	.027 324	.028 312	.030 314	.033 378	.039 689	15
16	.021 494	.022 324	.024 012	.026 609	.032 008	16
17	.016 907	.017 602	.019 020	.021 212	.025 813	17
18	.013 300	.013 879	.015 065	.016 910	.020 817	18
19	.010 462	.010 944	.011 933	.013 481	.016 788	19
20	.008 230	.008 629	.009 452	.010 747	.013 538	20
21	.006 474	.006 804	.007 487	.008 567	.010 918	21
22	.005 092	.005 365	.005 930	.006 830	.008 805	22
23	.004 006	.004 230	.004 697	.005 445	.007 101	23
24	.003 151	.003 335	.003 721	.004 340	.005 726	24
25	.002 479	.002 630	.002 947	.003 460	.004 618	25
26	.001 950	.002 074	.002 334	.002 758	.003 724	26
27	.001 534	.001 635	.001 849	.002 199	.003 003	27
28	.001 207	.001 289	.001 465	.001 753	.002 422	28
29	.000 949	.001 017	.001 160	.001 398	.001 953	29
30	.000 747	.000 802	.000 919	.001 114	.001 575	30
31	.000 587	.000 632	.000 728	.000 888	.001 270	31
32	.000 462	.000 498	.000 577	.000 708	.001 024	32
33	.000 363	.000 393	.000 457	.000 564	.000 826	33
34	.000 286	.000 310	.000 362	.000 450	.000 666	34
35	.000 225	.000 244	.000 287	.000 359	.000 537	35
36	.000 177	.000 193	.000 227	.000 286	.000 433	36
37	.000 139	.000 152	.000 180	.000 228	.000 349	37
38	.000 109	.000 120	.000 142	.000 182	.000 282	38
39	.000 086	.000 094	.000 113	.000 145	.000 227	39
40	.000 068	.000 074	.000 089	.000 115	.000 183	40

REVERSION FACTORS

(Present Value of $1)

25%

Base:	2.718 282	1.020 833	1.062 500	1.125 000	1.250 000	
			Frequency of Conversion			
Months	Continuous	Monthly	Quarterly	Semiannual	Annual	Months
0	1.000 000	1.000 000	1.000 000	1.000 000	1.000 000	0
1	.979 382	.979 592	.979 592	.979 592	.979 592	1
2	.959 189	.959 600	.960 000	.960 000	.960 000	2
3	.939 413	.940 016	.941 176	.941 176	.941 176	3
4	.920 044	.920 832	.921 969	.923 077	.923 077	4
5	.901 075	.902 040	.903 529	.905 660	.905 660	5
6	.882 497	.883 631	.885 813	.888 889	.888 889	6
7	.864 302	.865 598	.867 735	.870 748	.872 727	7
8	.846 482	.847 932	.850 381	.853 333	.857 143	8
9	.829 029	.830 628	.833 706	.836 601	.842 105	9
10	.811 936	.813 676	.816 692	.820 513	.827 586	10
11	.795 196	.797 070	.800 358	.805 031	.813 559	11

Years						Years
1	.778 801	.780 804	.784 665	.790 123	.800 000	1
2	.606 531	.609 654	.615 699	.624 295	.640 000	2
3	.472 367	.476 021	.483 117	.493 270	.512 000	3
4	.367 879	.371 679	.379 085	.389 744	.409 600	4
5	.286 505	.290 208	.297 455	.307 946	.327 680	5
6	.223 130	.226 596	.233 402	.243 315	.262 144	6
7	.173 774	.176 927	.183 143	.192 249	.209 715	7
8	.135 335	.138 145	.143 706	.151 901	.167 772	8
9	.105 399	.107 864	.112 761	.120 020	.134 218	9
10	.082 085	.084 221	.088 479	.094 831	.107 374	10
11	.063 928	.065 760	.069 427	.074 928	.085 899	11
12	.049 787	.051 346	.054 477	.059 202	.068 719	12
13	.038 774	.040 091	.042 746	.046 777	.054 976	13
14	.030 197	.031 303	.033 541	.036 960	.043 980	14
15	.023 518	.024 442	.026 319	.029 203	.035 184	15
16	.018 316	.019 084	.020 651	.023 074	.028 147	16
17	.014 264	.014 901	.016 204	.018 231	.022 518	17
18	.011 109	.011 635	.012 715	.014 405	.018 014	18
19	.008 652	.009 084	.009 977	.011 382	.014 412	19
20	.006 738	.007 093	.007 829	.008 993	.011 529	20
21	.005 248	.005 538	.006 143	.007 105	.009 223	21
22	.004 087	.004 324	.004 820	.005 614	.007 379	22
23	.003 183	.003 376	.003 782	.004 436	.005 903	23
24	.002 479	.002 636	.002 968	.003 505	.004 722	24
25	.001 930	.002 058	.002 329	.002 769	.003 778	25
26	.001 503	.001 607	.001 827	.002 188	.003 022	26
27	.001 171	.001 255	.001 434	.001 729	.002 418	27
28	.000 912	.000 980	.001 125	.001 366	.001 934	28
29	.000 710	.000 765	.000 883	.001 079	.001 547	29
30	.000 553	.000 597	.000 693	.000 853	.001 238	30
31	.000 431	.000 466	.000 544	.000 674	.000 990	31
32	.000 335	.000 364	.000 426	.000 532	.000 792	32
33	.000 261	.000 284	.000 335	.000 421	.000 634	33
34	.000 203	.000 222	.000 263	.000 332	.000 507	34
35	.000 158	.000 173	.000 206	.000 263	.000 406	35
36	.000 123	.000 135	.000 162	.000 208	.000 325	36
37	.000 096	.000 106	.000 127	.000 164	.000 260	37
38	.000 075	.000 083	.000 100	.000 130	.000 208	38
39	.000 058	.000 064	.000 078	.000 102	.000 166	39
40	.000 045	.000 050	.000 061	.000 081	.000 133	40

26%

REVERSION FACTORS
(Present Value of $1)

Base: 2.718 282   1.021 667   1.065 000   1.130 000   1.260 000

Frequency of Conversion

Months	Continuous	Monthly	Quarterly	Semiannual	Annual	Months
0	1.000 000	1.000 000	1.000 000	1.000 000	1.000 000	0
1	.978 566	.978 793	.978 793	.978 793	.978 793	1
2	.957 592	.958 035	.958 466	.958 466	.958 466	2
3	.937 067	.937 718	.938 967	.938 967	.938 967	3
4	.916 983	.917 832	.919 054	.920 245	.920 245	4
5	.897 328	.898 367	.899 969	.902 256	.902 256	5
6	.878 095	.879 315	.881 659	.884 956	.884 956	6
7	.859 275	.860 668	.862 962	.866 188	.868 307	7
8	.840 857	.842 415	.845 041	.848 200	.852 273	8
9	.822 835	.824 550	.827 849	.830 944	.836 820	9
10	.805 198	.807 064	.810 293	.814 376	.821 918	10
11	.787 940	.789 948	.793 466	.798 456	.807 537	11

Years						Years
1	.771 052	.773 195	.777 323	.783 147	.793 651	1
2	.594 521	.597 831	.604 231	.613 319	.629 882	2
3	.458 406	.462 240	.469 683	.480 319	.499 906	3
4	.353 455	.357 402	.365 095	.376 160	.396 751	4
5	.272 532	.276 342	.283 797	.294 588	.314 882	5
6	.210 136	.213 666	.220 602	.230 706	.249 906	6
7	.162 026	.165 206	.171 479	.180 677	.198 338	7
8	.124 930	.127 736	.133 295	.141 496	.157 411	8
9	.096 328	.098 765	.103 613	.110 812	.124 930	9
10	.074 274	.076 365	.080 541	.086 782	.099 150	10
11	.057 269	.059 045	.062 606	.067 963	.078 691	11
12	.044 157	.045 653	.048 665	.053 225	.062 453	12
13	.034 047	.035 299	.037 829	.041 683	.049 566	13
14	.026 252	.027 293	.029 405	.032 644	.039 338	14
15	.020 242	.021 103	.022 857	.025 565	.031 221	15
16	.015 608	.016 317	.017 767	.020 021	.024 778	16
17	.012 034	.012 616	.013 811	.015 680	.019 665	17
18	.009 279	.009 755	.010 736	.012 279	.015 607	18
19	.007 155	.007 542	.008 345	.009 617	.012 387	19
20	.005 517	.005 832	.006 487	.007 531	.009 831	20
21	.004 254	.004 509	.005 042	.005 898	.007 802	21
22	.003 280	.003 486	.003 920	.004 619	.006 192	22
23	.002 529	.002 696	.003 047	.003 617	.004 914	23
24	.001 950	.002 084	.002 368	.002 833	.003 900	24
25	.001 503	.001 612	.001 841	.002 219	.003 096	25
26	.001 159	.001 246	.001 431	.001 737	.002 457	26
27	.000 894	.000 963	.001 112	.001 361	.001 950	27
28	.000 689	.000 745	.000 865	.001 066	.001 547	28
29	.000 531	.000 576	.000 672	.000 835	.001 228	29
30	.000 410	.000 445	.000 522	.000 654	.000 975	30
31	.000 316	.000 344	.000 406	.000 512	.000 774	31
32	.000 244	.000 266	.000 316	.000 401	.000 614	32
33	.000 188	.000 206	.000 245	.000 314	.000 487	33
34	.000 145	.000 159	.000 191	.000 246	.000 387	34
35	.000 112	.000 123	.000 148	.000 193	.000 307	35
36	.000 086	.000 095	.000 115	.000 151	.000 244	36
37	.000 066	.000 074	.000 090	.000 118	.000 193	37
38	.000 051	.000 057	.000 070	.000 092	.000 153	38
39	.000 039	.000 044	.000 054	.000 072	.000 122	39
40	.000 030	.000 034	.000 042	.000 057	.000 097	40

(Present Value of $1)

Base:	2.718 282	1.022 500	1.067 500	1.135 000	1.270 000	

Frequency of Conversion

Months	Continuous	Monthly	Quarterly	Semiannual	Annual	Months
0	1.000 000	1.000 000	1.000 000	1.000 000	1.000 000	0
1	.977 751	.977 995	.977 995	.977 995	.977 995	1
2	.955 997	.956 474	.956 938	.956 938	.956 938	2
3	.934 728	.935 427	.936 768	.936 768	.936 768	3
4	.913 931	.914 843	.916 155	.917 431	.917 431	4
5	.893 597	.894 712	.896 429	.898 876	.898 876	5
6	.873 716	.875 024	.877 535	.881 057	.881 057	6
7	.854 277	.855 769	.858 225	.861 670	.863 931	7
8	.835 270	.836 938	.839 746	.843 117	.847 458	8
9	.816 686	.818 522	.822 046	.825 346	.831 601	9
10	.798 516	.800 510	.803 957	.808 309	.816 327	10
11	.780 750	.782 895	.786 647	.791 962	.801 603	11

Years						Years
1	.763 379	.765 667	.770 067	.776 262	.787 402	1
2	.582 748	.586 247	.593 003	.602 583	.620 001	2
3	.444 858	.448 870	.456 652	.467 762	.488 190	3
4	.339 596	.343 685	.351 653	.363 106	.384 402	4
5	.259 240	.263 149	.270 796	.281 865	.302 678	5
6	.197 899	.201 484	.208 531	.218 801	.238 329	6
7	.151 072	.154 270	.160 583	.169 847	.187 661	7
8	.115 325	.118 119	.123 660	.131 846	.147 765	8
9	.088 037	.090 440	.095 226	.102 347	.116 350	9
10	.067 206	.069 247	.073 331	.079 448	.091 614	10
11	.051 303	.053 020	.056 469	.061 672	.072 137	11
12	.039 164	.040 596	.043 485	.047 874	.056 801	12
13	.029 897	.031 083	.033 487	.037 163	.044 725	13
14	.022 823	.023 799	.025 787	.028 848	.035 217	14
15	.017 422	.018 222	.019 858	.022 394	.027 730	15
16	.013 300	.013 952	.015 292	.017 383	.021 834	16
17	.010 153	.010 683	.011 776	.013 494	.017 192	17
18	.007 750	.008 179	.009 068	.010 475	.013 537	18
19	.005 917	.006 263	.006 983	.008 131	.010 659	19
20	.004 517	.004 795	.005 377	.006 312	.008 393	20
21	.003 448	.003 672	.004 141	.004 900	.006 609	21
22	.002 632	.002 811	.003 189	.003 803	.005 204	22
23	.002 009	.002 152	.002 456	.002 953	.004 097	23
24	.001 534	.001 648	.001 891	.002 292	.003 226	24
25	.001 171	.001 262	.001 456	.001 779	.002 540	25
26	.000 894	.000 966	.001 121	.001 381	.002 000	26
27	.000 682	.000 740	.000 864	.001 072	.001 575	27
28	.000 521	.000 566	.000 665	.000 832	.001 240	28
29	.000 398	.000 434	.000 512	.000 646	.000 977	29
30	.000 304	.000 332	.000 394	.000 501	.000 769	30
31	.000 232	.000 254	.000 304	.000 389	.000 605	31
32	.000 177	.000 195	.000 234	.000 302	.000 477	32
33	.000 135	.000 149	.000 180	.000 235	.000 375	33
34	.000 103	.000 114	.000 139	.000 182	.000 296	34
35	.000 079	.000 087	.000 107	.000 141	.000 233	35
36	.000 060	.000 067	.000 082	.000 110	.000 183	36
37	.000 046	.000 051	.000 063	.000 085	.000 144	37
38	.000 035	.000 039	.000 049	.000 066	.000 114	38
39	.000 027	.000 030	.000 038	.000 051	.000 089	39
40	.000 020	.000 023	.000 029	.000 040	.000 070	40

28%

REVERSION FACTORS
(Present Value of $1)

Base:	2.718 282	1.023 333	1.070 000	1.140 000	1.280 000	
			Frequency of Conversion			
Months	Continuous	Monthly	Quarterly	Semiannual	Annual	Months
0	1.000 000	1.000 000	1.000 000	1.000 000	1.000 000	0
1	.976 937	.977 199	.977 199	.977 199	.977 199	1
2	.954 405	.954 917	.955 414	.955 414	.955 414	2
3	.932 394	.933 144	.934 579	.934 579	.934 579	3
4	.910 890	.911 867	.913 270	.914 634	.914 634	4
5	.889 882	.891 075	.892 910	.895 522	.895 522	5
6	.869 358	.870 758	.873 439	.877 193	.877 193	6
7	.849 308	.850 903	.853 523	.857 192	.859 599	7
8	.829 720	.831 501	.834 496	.838 082	.842 697	8
9	.810 584	.812 542	.816 298	.819 807	.826 446	9
10	.791 890	.794 015	.797 685	.802 311	.810 811	10
11	.773 626	.775 911	.779 902	.785 546	.795 756	11

Years						Years
1	.755 784	.758 219	.762 895	.769 468	.781 250	1
2	.571 209	.574 896	.582 009	.592 080	.610 352	2
3	.431 711	.435 897	.444 012	.455 587	.476 837	3
4	.326 280	.330 505	.338 735	.350 559	.372 529	4
5	.246 597	.250 595	.258 419	.269 744	.291 038	5
6	.186 374	.190 006	.197 147	.207 559	.227 374	6
7	.140 858	.144 066	.150 402	.159 710	.177 636	7
8	.106 459	.109 234	.114 741	.122 892	.138 778	8
9	.080 460	.082 823	.087 535	.094 561	.108 420	9
10	.060 810	.062 798	.066 780	.072 762	.084 703	10
11	.045 959	.047 615	.050 946	.055 988	.066 174	11
12	.034 735	.036 102	.038 867	.043 081	.051 699	12
13	.026 252	.027 373	.029 651	.033 149	.040 390	13
14	.019 841	.020 755	.022 621	.025 507	.031 554	14
15	.014 996	.015 737	.017 257	.019 627	.024 652	15
16	.011 333	.011 932	.013 166	.015 102	.019 259	16
17	.008 566	.009 047	.010 044	.011 621	.015 046	17
18	.006 474	.006 860	.007 662	.008 942	.011 755	18
19	.004 893	.005 201	.005 846	.006 880	.009 184	19
20	.003 698	.003 944	.004 460	.005 294	.007 175	20
21	.002 795	.002 990	.003 402	.004 074	.005 605	21
22	.002 112	.002 267	.002 596	.003 135	.004 379	22
23	.001 596	.001 719	.001 980	.002 412	.003 421	23
24	.001 207	.001 303	.001 511	.001 856	.002 673	24
25	.000 912	.000 988	.001 152	.001 428	.002 088	25
26	.000 689	.000 749	.000 879	.001 099	.001 631	26
27	.000 521	.000 568	.000 671	.000 846	.001 274	27
28	.000 394	.000 431	.000 512	.000 651	.000 996	28
29	.000 298	.000 327	.000 390	.000 501	.000 778	29
30	.000 225	.000 248	.000 298	.000 385	.000 608	30
31	.000 170	.000 188	.000 227	.000 296	.000 475	31
32	.000 128	.000 142	.000 173	.000 228	.000 371	32
33	.000 097	.000 108	.000 132	.000 176	.000 290	33
34	.000 073	.000 082	.000 101	.000 135	.000 226	34
35	.000 055	.000 062	.000 077	.000 104	.000 177	35
36	.000 042	.000 047	.000 059	.000 080	.000 138	36
37	.000 032	.000 036	.000 045	.000 062	.000 108	37
38	.000 024	.000 027	.000 034	.000 047	.000 084	38
39	.000 018	.000 021	.000 026	.000 036	.000 066	39
40	.000 014	.000 016	.000 020	.000 028	.000 051	40

REVERSION FACTORS

(Present Value of $1)

29%

Base:	2.718 282	1.024 167	1.072 500	1.145 000	1.290 000	
			Frequency of Conversion			
Months	Continuous	Monthly	Quarterly	Semiannual	Annual	Months
0	1.000 000	1.000 000	1.000 000	1.000 000	1.000 000	0
1	.976 123	.976 404	.976 404	.976 404	.976 404	1
2	.952 816	.953 364	.953 895	.953 895	.953 895	2
3	.930 066	.930 868	.932 401	.932 401	.932 401	3
4	.907 859	.908 903	.910 400	.911 854	.911 854	4
5	.886 182	.887 456	.889 413	.892 193	.892 193	5
6	.865 022	.866 515	.869 371	.873 362	.873 362	6
7	.844 368	.846 069	.848 857	.852 754	.855 310	7
8	.824 207	.826 104	.829 289	.833 096	.837 989	8
9	.804 528	.806 611	.810 603	.814 324	.821 355	9
10	.785 318	.787 578	.791 475	.796 379	.805 369	10
11	.766 567	.768 994	.773 230	.779 208	.789 993	11

Years						Years
1	.748 264	.750 849	.755 807	.762 762	.775 194	1
2	.559 898	.563 774	.571 244	.581 806	.600 925	2
3	.418 952	.423 309	.431 750	.443 779	.465 834	3
4	.313 486	.317 841	.326 320	.338 498	.361 111	4
5	.234 570	.238 650	.246 635	.258 193	.279 931	5
6	.175 520	.179 190	.186 408	.196 940	.217 001	6
7	.131 336	.134 545	.140 889	.150 218	.168 218	7
8	.098 274	.101 023	.106 484	.114 581	.130 401	8
9	.073 535	.075 853	.080 482	.087 398	.101 086	9
10	.055 023	.056 954	.060 829	.066 664	.078 362	10
11	.041 172	.042 764	.045 975	.050 849	.060 745	11
12	.030 807	.032 109	.034 748	.038 785	.047 089	12
13	.023 052	.024 109	.026 263	.029 584	.036 503	13
14	.017 249	.018 102	.019 850	.022 566	.028 297	14
15	.012 907	.013 592	.015 002	.017 212	.021 936	15
16	.009 658	.010 206	.011 339	.013 129	.017 005	16
17	.007 227	.007 663	.008 570	.010 014	.013 182	17
18	.005 407	.005 754	.006 477	.007 638	.010 218	18
19	.004 046	.004 320	.004 896	.005 826	.007 921	19
20	.003 028	.003 244	.003 700	.004 444	.006 141	20
21	.002 265	.002 436	.002 797	.003 390	.004 760	21
22	.001 695	.001 829	.002 114	.002 586	.003 690	22
23	.001 268	.001 373	.001 598	.001 972	.002 860	23
24	.000 949	.001 031	.001 207	.001 504	.002 217	24
25	.000 710	.000 774	.000 913	.001 147	.001 719	25
26	.000 531	.000 581	.000 690	.000 875	.001 333	26
27	.000 398	.000 436	.000 521	.000 668	.001 033	27
28	.000 298	.000 328	.000 394	.000 509	.000 801	28
29	.000 223	.000 246	.000 298	.000 388	.000 621	29
30	.000 167	.000 185	.000 225	.000 296	.000 481	30
31	.000 125	.000 139	.000 170	.000 226	.000 373	31
32	.000 093	.000 104	.000 129	.000 172	.000 289	32
33	.000 070	.000 078	.000 097	.000 131	.000 224	33
34	.000 052	.000 059	.000 073	.000 100	.000 174	34
35	.000 039	.000 044	.000 056	.000 076	.000 135	35
36	.000 029	.000 033	.000 042	.000 058	.000 104	36
37	.000 022	.000 025	.000 032	.000 045	.000 081	37
38	.000 016	.000 019	.000 024	.000 034	.000 063	38
39	.000 012	.000 014	.000 018	.000 026	.000 049	39
40	.000 009	.000 011	.000 014	.000 020	.000 038	40

30%

REVERSION FACTORS
(Present Value of $1)

Base:	2.718 282	1.025 000	1.075 000	1.150 000	1.300 000	
			Frequency of Conversion			
Months	Continuous	Monthly	Quarterly	Semiannual	Annual	Months
0	1.000 000	1.000 000	1.000 000	1.000 000	1.000 000	0
1	.975 310	.975 610	.975 610	.975 610	.975 610	1
2	.951 229	.951 814	.952 381	.952 381	.952 381	2
3	.927 743	.928 599	.930 233	.930 233	.930 233	3
4	.904 837	.905 951	.907 544	.909 091	.909 091	4
5	.882 497	.883 854	.885 936	.888 889	.888 889	5
6	.860 708	.862 297	.865 333	.869 565	.869 565	6
7	.839 457	.841 265	.844 227	.848 356	.851 064	7
8	.818 731	.820 747	.824 126	.828 157	.833 333	8
9	.798 516	.800 728	.804 961	.808 898	.816 327	9
10	.778 801	.781 198	.785 327	.790 514	.800 000	10
11	.759 572	.762 145	.766 629	.772 947	.784 314	11

Years						Years
1	.740 818	.743 556	.748 801	.756 144	.769 231	1
2	.548 812	.552 875	.560 702	.571 753	.591 716	2
3	.406 570	.411 094	.419 854	.432 328	.455 166	3
4	.301 194	.305 671	.314 387	.326 902	.350 128	4
5	.223 130	.227 284	.235 413	.247 185	.269 329	5
6	.165 299	.168 998	.176 277	.186 907	.207 176	6
7	.122 456	.125 659	.131 997	.141 329	.159 366	7
8	.090 718	.093 435	.098 839	.106 865	.122 589	8
9	.067 206	.069 474	.074 011	.080 805	.094 300	9
10	.049 787	.051 658	.055 419	.061 100	.072 538	10
11	.036 883	.038 410	.041 498	.046 201	.055 799	11
12	.027 324	.028 560	.031 074	.034 934	.042 922	12
13	.020 242	.021 236	.023 268	.026 415	.033 017	13
14	.014 996	.015 790	.017 423	.019 974	.025 398	14
15	.011 109	.011 741	.013 046	.015 103	.019 537	15
16	.008 230	.008 730	.009 769	.011 420	.015 028	16
17	.006 097	.006 491	.007 315	.008 635	.011 560	17
18	.004 517	.004 827	.005 478	.006 529	.008 892	18
19	.003 346	.003 589	.004 102	.004 937	.006 840	19
20	.002 479	.002 669	.003 071	.003 733	.005 262	20
21	.001 836	.001 984	.002 300	.002 823	.004 048	21
22	.001 360	.001 475	.001 722	.002 134	.003 113	22
23	.001 008	.001 097	.001 289	.001 614	.002 395	23
24	.000 747	.000 816	.000 966	.001 220	.001 842	24
25	.000 553	.000 607	.000 723	.000 923	.001 417	25
26	.000 410	.000 451	.000 541	.000 698	.001 090	26
27	.000 304	.000 335	.000 405	.000 528	.000 839	27
28	.000 225	.000 249	.000 304	.000 399	.000 645	28
29	.000 167	.000 185	.000 227	.000 302	.000 496	29
30	.000 123	.000 138	.000 170	.000 228	.000 382	30
31	.000 091	.000 102	.000 127	.000 172	.000 294	31
32	.000 068	.000 076	.000 095	.000 130	.000 226	32
33	.000 050	.000 057	.000 071	.000 099	.000 174	33
34	.000 037	.000 042	.000 054	.000 075	.000 134	34
35	.000 028	.000 031	.000 040	.000 056	.000 103	35
36	.000 020	.000 023	.000 030	.000 043	.000 079	36
37	.000 015	.000 017	.000 022	.000 032	.000 061	37
38	.000 011	.000 013	.000 017	.000 024	.000 047	38
39	.000 008	.000 010	.000 013	.000 018	.000 036	39
40	.000 006	.000 007	.000 009	.000 014	.000 028	40

146

Table 3

Ordinary Level Annuity
(Present Value of $1 per Period)

Table 3 - ORDINARY LEVEL ANNUITY (Present Value of $1 per Period)

The present value of a series of future installments or payments of one per period for a given number of periods when discounted at an effective interest rate. This factor is commonly referred to as the *Inwood Coefficient*.

$$a_{\overline{n}|} = \frac{1 - 1/S^n}{i}$$

Where

$a_{\overline{n}|}$ = Level Annuity Factor

$1/S^n$ = Present Value Factor

i = Rate of Interest/Yield

This Table is used in solving problems dealing with the compound discounting of cash flows that are level or effectively level.

Example 1:

What is the Present Value of an ordinary annuity of $1,000 per month for 10 years, assuming an interest rate of 6%?

$1,000 $\times$ 90.073453 = $90,073.45

Same example assuming payments in advance.

$1,000 $\times$ 90.073453 $\times$ 1.005000 = $90,523.82
$$OR$$
$1,000 $\times$ 90.073453/.995025 = $90,523.81

Example 2:

What is the Present Value of an ordinary annuity of $1,000 per month for 10 years and 7 months, assuming an interest rate of 6%?

$1,000 $\times$ 90.073453	=	$90,073.45
$1,000 $\times$ 6.862074 $\times$ .549633*	=	3,771.62
		$93,845.07

* Reversion Factor for 120 months.

Example 2 (Cont.)
Same example assuming payments in advance.

$93,845.07 × 1.005000 = $94,314.30
                OR
$93,845.07/.995025 = $94,314.28

Example 3:
What is the Present Value of an ordinary annuity consisting of the following cash flows at a 6% annual discount rate: $1,000 per year for 5 years; then $2,000 per year for 5 years; then $3,000 per year for 5 years?

$1,000 × 4.212364   = $ 4,212.36
 2,000 × (7.360087 – 4.212364)   =   6,295.45
 3,000 × (9.712249 – 7.360087)   =   7,056.49
                                                  $17,564.30

Same example assuming payments in advance.

$17,564.30 × 1.060000 = $18,618.16
                OR
$17,564.30/.943396 = $18,618.16

Example 4:
A 10-year level ordinary annuity of $1,000 per month has a Present Value of $90,000. What is the indicated interest/yield rate?

$90,000/$1,000 = 90.000000 (Present Value Factor)

Scan Ordinary Level Annuity tables at 10 years, monthly frequency, for 90.000000.

Closest match is at 6% nominal.

6%

ORDINARY LEVEL ANNUITY
(Present Value of $1 per period)

Base:	1.005 000	1.015 000	1.030 000	1.060 000	
		Frequency of Payments			
Months	Monthly	Quarterly	Semiannual	Annual	Months
1	.995 025	—	—	—	1
2	1.985 099	—	—	—	2
3	2.970 248	.985 222	—	—	3
4	3.950 496	—	—	—	4
5	4.925 866	—	—	—	5
6	5.896 384	1.955 883	.970 874	—	6
7	6.862 074	—	—	—	7
8	7.822 959	—	—	—	8
9	8.779 064	2.912 200	—	—	9
10	9.730 412	—	—	—	10
11	10.677 027	—	—	—	11
Years					Years
1	11.618 932	3.854 385	1.913 470	.943 396	1
2	22.562 866	7.485 925	3.717 098	1.833 393	2
3	32.871 016	10.907 505	5.417 191	2.673 012	3
4	42.580 318	14.131 264	7.019 692	3.465 106	4
5	51.725 561	17.168 639	8.530 203	4.212 364	5
6	60.339 514	20.030 405	9.954 004	4.917 324	6
7	68.453 042	22.726 717	11.296 073	5.582 381	7
8	76.095 218	25.267 139	12.561 102	6.209 794	8
9	83.293 424	27.660 684	13.753 513	6.801 692	9
10	90.073 453	29.915 845	14.877 475	7.360 087	10
11	96.459 599	32.040 622	15.936 917	7.886 875	11
12	102.474 743	34.042 554	16.935 542	8.383 844	12
13	108.140 440	35.928 742	17.876 842	8.852 683	13
14	113.476 990	37.705 879	18.764 108	9.294 984	14
15	118.503 515	39.380 269	19.600 441	9.712 249	15
16	123.238 025	40.957 853	20.388 766	10.105 895	16
17	127.697 486	42.444 228	21.131 837	10.477 260	17
18	131.897 876	43.844 667	21.832 252	10.827 603	18
19	135.854 246	45.164 138	22.492 462	11.158 116	19
20	139.580 772	46.407 323	23.114 772	11.469 921	20
21	143.090 806	47.578 633	23.701 359	11.764 077	21
22	146.396 927	48.682 222	24.254 274	12.041 582	22
23	149.510 979	49.722 007	24.775 449	12.303 379	23
24	152.444 121	50.701 675	25.266 707	12.550 358	24
25	155.206 864	51.624 704	25.729 764	12.783 356	25
26	157.809 106	52.494 366	26.166 240	13.003 166	26
27	160.260 172	53.313 749	26.577 660	13.210 534	27
28	162.568 844	54.085 758	26.965 464	13.406 164	28
29	164.743 394	54.813 133	27.331 005	13.590 721	29
30	166.791 614	55.498 454	27.675 564	13.764 831	30
31	168.720 844	56.144 153	28.000 343	13.929 086	31
32	170.537 996	56.752 520	28.306 478	14.084 043	32
33	172.249 581	57.325 714	28.595 040	14.230 230	33
34	173.861 732	57.865 769	28.867 038	14.368 141	34
35	175.380 226	58.374 599	29.123 421	14.498 246	35
36	176.810 504	58.854 011	29.365 088	14.620 987	36
37	178.157 690	59.305 706	29.592 881	14.736 780	37
38	179.426 611	59.731 286	29.807 598	14.846 019	38
39	180.621 815	60.132 260	30.009 990	14.949 075	39
40	181.747 584	60.510 052	30.200 763	15.046 297	40

ORDINARY LEVEL ANNUITY

6¼%

(Present Value of $1 per period)

Base:	1.005 208	1.015 625	1.031 250	1.062 500	
		Frequency of Payments			
Months	Monthly	Quarterly	Semiannual	Annual	Months
1	.994 819	—	—	—	1
2	1.984 483	—	—	—	2
3	2.969 019	.984 615	—	—	3
4	3.948 454	—	—	—	4
5	4.922 815	—	—	—	5
6	5.892 126	1.954 083	.969 697	—	6
7	6.856 416	—	—	—	7
8	7.815 709	—	—	—	8
9	8.770 032	2.908 635	—	—	9
10	9.719 410	—	—	—	10
11	10.663 869	—	—	—	11
Years					Years
1	11.603 434	3.848 503	1.910 009	.941 176	1
2	22.505 621	7.465 584	3.706 014	1.826 990	2
3	32.748 938	10.865 159	5.394 820	2.660 696	3
4	42.373 205	14.060 309	6.982 824	3.445 361	4
5	51.415 833	17.063 325	8.476 044	4.183 869	5
6	59.911 975	19.885 761	9.880 137	4.878 936	6
7	67.894 656	22.538 476	11.200 422	5.533 116	7
8	75.394 907	25.031 676	12.441 903	6.148 815	8
9	82.441 884	27.374 952	13.609 283	6.728 297	9
10	89.062 980	29.577 321	14.706 984	7.273 691	10
11	95.283 933	31.647 255	15.739 166	7.787 003	11
12	101.128 925	33.592 718	16.709 739	8.270 121	12
13	106.620 678	35.421 194	17.622 381	8.724 819	13
14	111.780 539	37.139 719	18.480 549	9.152 771	14
15	116.628 567	38.754 905	19.287 495	9.555 549	15
16	121.183 606	40.272 964	20.046 276	9.934 635	16
17	125.463 363	41.699 739	20.759 768	10.291 421	17
18	129.484 475	43.040 717	21.430 672	10.627 220	18
19	133.262 573	44.301 058	22.061 532	10.943 266	19
20	136.812 343	45.485 612	22.654 737	11.240 721	20
21	140.147 585	46.598 935	23.212 535	11.520 678	21
22	143.281 262	47.645 311	23.737 040	11.784 168	22
23	146.225 557	48.628 765	24.230 237	12.032 158	23
24	148.991 915	49.553 081	24.693 997	12.265 560	24
25	151.591 090	50.421 815	25.130 077	12.485 233	25
26	154.033 184	51.238 310	25.540 127	12.691 984	26
27	156.327 692	52.005 707	25.925 703	12.886 573	27
28	158.483 532	52.726 958	26.288 264	13.069 716	28
29	160.509 085	53.404 838	26.629 185	13.242 086	29
30	162.412 224	54.041 956	26.949 757	13.404 316	30
31	164.200 348	54.640 761	27.251 195	13.557 003	31
32	165.880 408	55.203 559	27.534 640	13.700 709	32
33	167.458 934	55.732 514	27.801 168	13.835 961	33
34	168.942 062	56.229 662	28.051 787	13.963 258	34
35	170.335 558	56.696 914	28.287 447	14.083 066	35
36	171.644 839	57.136 070	28.509 041	14.195 827	36
37	172.874 994	57.548 817	28.717 409	14.301 955	37
38	174.030 805	57.936 745	28.913 339	14.401 840	38
39	175.116 766	58.301 346	29.097 575	14.495 849	39
40	176.137 096	58.644 022	29.270 815	14.584 329	40

6½%

ORDINARY LEVEL ANNUITY
(Present Value of $1 per period)

Base:	1.005 417	1.016 250	1.032 500	1.065 000	
		Frequency of Payments			
Months	Monthly	Quarterly	Semiannual	Annual	Months
1	.994 613	—	—	—	1
2	1.983 867	—	—	—	2
3	2.967 791	.984 010	—	—	3
4	3.946 415	—	—	—	4
5	4.919 766	—	—	—	5
6	5.887 873	1.952 285	.968 523	—	6
7	6.850 765	—	—	—	7
8	7.808 469	—	—	—	8
9	8.761 014	2.905 078	—	—	9
10	9.708 426	—	—	—	10
11	10.650 735	—	—	—	11
Years					Years
1	11.587 967	3.842 635	1.906 560	.938 967	1
2	22.448 578	7.445 325	3.694 983	1.820 626	2
3	32.627 489	10.823 053	5.372 590	2.648 476	3
4	42.167 488	13.989 866	6.946 247	3.425 799	4
5	51.108 680	16.958 934	8.422 395	4.155 679	5
6	59.488 649	19.742 605	9.807 076	4.841 014	6
7	67.342 623	22.352 456	11.105 958	5.484 520	7
8	74.703 617	24.799 341	12.324 358	6.088 751	8
9	81.602 576	27.093 435	13.467 261	6.656 104	9
10	88.068 500	29.244 279	14.539 346	7.188 830	10
11	94.128 569	31.260 819	15.545 002	7.689 042	11
12	99.808 260	33.151 440	16.488 343	8.158 725	12
13	105.131 446	34.924 006	17.373 233	8.599 742	13
14	110.120 506	36.585 887	18.203 292	9.013 842	14
15	114.796 412	38.143 997	18.981 917	9.402 669	15
16	119.178 820	39.604 813	19.712 297	9.767 764	16
17	123.286 152	40.974 412	20.397 420	10.110 577	17
18	127.135 675	42.258 489	21.040 090	10.432 466	18
19	130.743 570	43.462 385	21.642 939	10.734 710	19
20	134.125 004	44.591 106	22.208 433	11.018 507	20
21	137.294 192	45.649 346	22.738 888	11.284 983	21
22	140.264 456	46.641 508	23.236 473	11.535 196	22
23	143.048 282	47.571 715	23.703 227	11.770 137	23
24	145.657 372	48.443 838	24.141 059	11.990 739	24
25	148.102 695	49.261 503	24.551 762	12.197 877	25
26	150.394 529	50.028 111	24.937 016	12.392 373	26
27	152.542 509	50.746 850	25.298 399	12.574 998	27
28	154.555 664	51.420 709	25.637 389	12.746 477	28
29	156.442 457	52.052 490	25.955 374	12.907 490	29
30	158.210 820	52.644 820	26.253 656	13.058 676	30
31	159.868 185	53.200 164	26.533 456	13.200 635	31
32	161.421 521	53.720 831	26.795 918	13.333 929	32
33	162.877 357	54.208 986	27.042 117	13.459 088	33
34	164.241 813	54.666 659	27.273 061	13.576 609	34
35	165.520 625	55.095 754	27.489 695	13.686 957	35
36	166.719 167	55.498 055	27.692 905	13.790 570	36
37	167.842 480	55.875 235	27.883 524	13.887 859	37
38	168.895 284	56.228 862	28.062 332	13.979 210	38
39	169.882 006	56.560 409	28.230 060	14.064 986	39
40	170.806 793	56.871 252	28.387 395	14.145 527	40

(Present Value of $1 per period)

Base:	1.005 625	1.016 875	1.033 750	1.067 500	
		Frequency of Payments			
Months	Monthly	Quarterly	Semiannual	Annual	Months
1	.994 406	—	—	—	1
2	1.983 251	—	—	—	2
3	2.966 564	.983 405	—	—	3
4	3.944 377	—	—	—	4
5	4.916 720	—	—	—	5
6	5.883 625	1.950 491	.967 352	—	6
7	6.845 121	—	—	—	7
8	7.801 239	—	—	—	8
9	8.752 009	2.901 527	—	—	9
10	9.697 461	—	—	—	10
11	10.637 624	—	—	—	11

Years					Years
1	11.572 529	3.836 782	1.903 122	.936 768	1
2	22.391 738	7.425 148	3.684 005	1.814 303	2
3	32.506 666	10.781 183	5.350 501	2.636 349	3
4	41.963 157	13.919 930	6.909 958	3.406 416	4
5	50.804 074	16.855 456	8.369 251	4.127 790	5
6	59.069 488	19.600 919	9.734 812	4.803 551	6
7	66.796 860	22.168 626	11.012 664	5.436 581	7
8	74.021 215	24.570 084	12.208 438	6.029 584	8
9	80.775 298	26.816 059	13.327 407	6.585 091	9
10	87.089 720	28.916 616	14.374 505	7.105 471	10
11	92.993 102	30.881 172	15.354 347	7.592 947	11
12	98.512 201	32.718 530	16.271 253	8.049 600	12
13	103.672 031	34.436 928	17.129 266	8.477 377	13
14	108.495 980	36.044 067	17.932 169	8.878 105	14
15	113.005 911	37.547 151	18.683 501	9.253 494	15
16	117.222 266	38.952 916	19.386 575	9.605 146	16
17	121.164 156	40.267 664	20.044 490	9.934 563	17
18	124.849 447	41.497 288	20.660 147	10.243 151	18
19	128.294 841	42.647 299	21.236 260	10.532 225	19
20	131.515 956	43.722 852	21.775 369	10.803 021	20
21	134.527 392	44.728 767	22.279 851	11.056 695	21
22	137.342 796	45.669 554	22.751 930	11.294 327	22
23	139.974 930	46.549 429	23.193 687	11.516 934	23
24	142.435 724	47.372 336	23.607 070	11.725 465	24
25	144.736 332	48.141 963	23.993 901	11.920 811	25
26	146.887 181	48.861 760	24.355 886	12.103 804	26
27	148.898 019	49.534 953	24.694 620	12.275 226	27
28	150.777 960	50.164 560	25.011 597	12.435 809	28
29	152.535 526	50.753 402	25.308 215	12.586 238	29
30	154.178 682	51.304 120	25.585 781	12.727 155	30
31	155.714 877	51.819 181	25.845 519	12.859 162	31
32	157.151 072	52.300 894	26.088 574	12.982 821	32
33	158.493 777	52.751 418	26.316 017	13.098 662	33
34	159.749 078	53.172 773	26.528 852	13.207 177	34
35	160.922 665	53.566 847	26.728 016	13.308 831	35
36	162.019 856	53.935 406	26.914 387	13.404 057	36
37	163.045 626	54.280 102	27.088 788	13.493 262	37
38	164.004 622	54.602 481	27.251 987	13.576 826	38
39	164.901 192	54.903 988	27.404 704	13.655 107	39
40	165.739 400	55.185 973	27.547 612	13.728 437	40

7%

ORDINARY LEVEL ANNUITY
(Present Value of $1 per period)

Base:	1.005 833	1.017 500	1.035 000	1.070 000	
		Frequency of Payments			
Months	Monthly	Quarterly	Semiannual	Annual	Months
1	.994 200	—	—	—	1
2	1.982 635	—	—	—	2
3	2.965 337	.982 801	—	—	3
4	3.942 340	—	—	—	4
5	4.913 677	—	—	—	5
6	5.879 381	1.948 699	.966 184	—	6
7	6.839 484	—	—	—	7
8	7.794 019	—	—	—	8
9	8.743 018	2.897 984	—	—	9
10	9.686 513	—	—	—	10
11	10.624 537	—	—	—	11

Years					Years
1	11.557 120	3.830 943	1.899 694	.934 579	1
2	22.335 099	7.405 053	3.673 079	1.808 018	2
3	32.386 464	10.739 550	5.328 553	2.624 316	3
4	41.760 201	13.850 497	6.873 956	3.387 211	4
5	50.501 994	16.752 881	8.316 605	4.100 197	5
6	58.654 444	19.460 686	9.663 334	4.766 540	6
7	66.257 285	21.986 955	10.920 520	5.389 289	7
8	73.347 569	24.343 859	12.094 117	5.971 299	8
9	79.959 850	26.542 753	13.189 682	6.515 232	9
10	86.126 354	28.594 230	14.212 403	7.023 582	10
11	91.877 134	30.508 172	15.167 125	7.498 674	11
12	97.240 216	32.293 801	16.058 368	7.942 686	12
13	102.241 738	33.959 719	16.890 352	8.357 651	13
14	106.906 074	35.513 951	17.667 019	8.745 468	14
15	111.255 958	36.963 986	18.392 045	9.107 914	15
16	115.312 587	38.316 807	19.068 865	9.446 649	16
17	119.095 732	39.578 934	19.700 684	9.763 223	17
18	122.623 831	40.756 445	20.290 494	10.059 087	18
19	125.914 077	41.855 015	20.841 087	10.335 595	19
20	128.982 506	42.879 935	21.355 072	10.594 014	20
21	131.844 073	43.836 142	21.834 883	10.835 527	21
22	134.512 723	44.728 244	22.282 791	11.061 240	22
23	137.001 461	45.560 539	22.700 918	11.272 187	23
24	139.322 418	46.337 035	23.091 244	11.469 334	24
25	141.486 903	47.061 473	23.455 618	11.653 583	25
26	143.505 467	47.737 344	23.795 765	11.825 779	26
27	145.387 946	48.367 904	24.113 295	11.986 709	27
28	147.143 515	48.956 190	24.409 713	12.137 111	28
29	148.780 729	49.505 036	24.686 423	12.277 674	29
30	150.307 568	50.017 087	24.944 734	12.409 041	30
31	151.731 473	50.494 809	25.185 870	12.531 814	31
32	153.059 383	50.940 504	25.410 974	12.646 555	32
33	154.297 770	51.356 319	25.621 110	12.753 790	33
34	155.452 669	51.744 258	25.817 275	12.854 009	34
35	156.529 709	52.106 188	26.000 397	12.947 672	35
36	157.534 139	52.443 854	26.171 343	13.035 208	36
37	158.470 853	52.758 882	26.330 923	13.117 017	37
38	159.344 418	53.052 790	26.479 892	13.193 473	38
39	160.159 090	53.326 994	26.618 957	13.264 928	39
40	160.918 839	53.582 815	26.748 776	13.331 709	40

ORDINARY LEVEL ANNUITY

(Present Value of $1 per period)

7¼%

Base: 1.006 042   1.018 125   1.036 250   1.072 500

Frequency of Payments

Months	Monthly	Quarterly	Semiannual	Annual	Months
1	.993 995	—	—	—	1
2	1.982 020	—	—	—	2
3	2.964 112	.982 198	—	—	3
4	3.940 306	—	—	—	4
5	4.910 637	—	—	—	5
6	5.875 142	1.946 910	.965 018	—	6
7	6.833 854	—	—	—	7
8	7.786 808	—	—	—	8
9	8.734 040	2.894 448	—	—	9
10	9.675 584	—	—	—	10
11	10.611 473	—	—	—	11

Years					Years
1	11.541 741	3.825 118	1.896 278	.932 401	1
2	22.278 661	7.385 039	3.662 206	1.801 772	2
3	32.266 882	10.698 150	5.306 743	2.612 375	3
4	41.558 610	13.781 563	6.838 235	3.368 182	4
5	50.202 413	16.651 201	8.264 453	4.072 897	5
6	58.243 472	19.321 887	9.592 632	4.729 974	6
7	65.723 817	21.807 413	10.829 511	5.342 633	7
8	72.682 548	24.120 617	11.981 368	5.913 877	8
9	79.156 037	26.273 446	13.054 046	6.446 505	9
10	85.178 120	28.277 019	14.052 988	6.943 128	10
11	90.780 276	30.141 684	14.983 262	7.406 180	11
12	95.991 786	31.877 071	15.849 590	7.837 930	12
13	100.839 890	33.492 143	16.656 366	8.240 495	13
14	105.349 929	34.995 242	17.407 684	8.615 846	14
15	109.545 477	36.394 131	18.107 356	8.965 824	15
16	113.448 464	37.696 034	18.758 933	9.292 143	16
17	117.079 291	38.907 676	19.365 721	9.596 404	17
18	120.456 934	40.035 314	19.930 797	9.880 097	18
19	123.599 051	41.084 773	20.457 031	10.144 612	19
20	126.522 063	42.061 473	20.947 091	10.391 247	20
21	129.241 249	42.970 458	21.403 464	10.621 209	21
22	131.770 823	43.816 423	21.828 467	10.835 626	22
23	134.124 007	44.603 737	22.224 254	11.035 549	23
24	136.313 100	45.336 466	22.592 835	11.221 957	24
25	138.349 544	46.018 395	22.936 080	11.395 764	25
26	140.243 984	46.653 045	23.255 730	11.557 822	26
27	142.006 323	47.243 695	23.553 407	11.708 925	27
28	143.645 771	47.793 395	23.830 622	11.849 814	28
29	145.170 898	48.304 985	24.088 781	11.981 178	29
30	146.589 676	48.781 105	24.329 195	12.103 663	30
31	147.909 521	49.224 216	24.553 082	12.217 867	31
32	149.137 331	49.636 606	24.761 579	12.324 352	32
33	150.279 524	50.020 405	24.955 744	12.423 638	33
34	151.342 071	50.377 595	25.136 563	12.516 213	34
35	152.330 525	50.710 021	25.304 951	12.602 529	35
36	153.250 052	51.019 400	25.461 765	12.683 011	36
37	154.105 460	51.307 330	25.607 799	12.758 052	37
38	154.901 219	51.575 297	25.743 795	12.828 021	38
39	155.641 489	51.824 686	25.870 443	12.893 259	39
40	156.330 138	52.056 785	25.988 384	12.954 088	40

7½%

ORDINARY LEVEL ANNUITY
(Present Value of $1 per period)

Base:	1.006 250	1.018 750	1.037 500	1.075 000	
		Frequency of Payments			
Months	Monthly	Quarterly	Semiannual	Annual	Months
1	.993 789	—	—	—	1
2	1.981 405	—	—	—	2
3	2.962 887	.981 595	—	—	3
4	3.938 273	—	—	—	4
5	4.907 600	—	—	—	5
6	5.870 907	1.945 124	.963 855	—	6
7	6.828 231	—	—	—	7
8	7.779 608	—	—	—	8
9	8.725 076	2.890 919	—	—	9
10	9.664 672	—	—	—	10
11	10.598 432	—	—	—	11
Years					Years
1	11.526 392	3.819 307	1.892 873	.930 233	1
2	22.222 423	7.365 106	3.651 384	1.795 565	2
3	32.147 913	10.656 983	5.285 072	2.600 526	3
4	41.358 371	13.713 123	6.802 796	3.349 326	4
5	49.905 308	16.550 406	8.212 787	4.045 885	5
6	57.836 524	19.184 505	9.522 694	4.693 846	6
7	65.196 376	21.629 971	10.739 620	5.296 601	7
8	72.026 024	23.900 313	11.870 165	5.857 304	8
9	78.363 665	26.008 071	12.920 461	6.378 887	9
10	84.244 743	27.964 888	13.896 204	6.864 081	10
11	89.702 148	29.781 573	14.802 686	7.315 424	11
12	94.766 401	31.468 162	15.644 824	7.735 278	12
13	99.465 827	33.033 971	16.427 185	8.125 840	13
14	103.826 706	34.487 649	17.154 011	8.489 154	14
15	107.873 427	35.837 226	17.829 245	8.827 120	15
16	111.628 623	37.090 158	18.456 549	9.141 507	16
17	115.113 294	38.253 364	19.039 326	9.433 960	17
18	118.346 930	39.333 271	19.580 735	9.706 009	18
19	121.347 615	40.335 844	20.083 714	9.959 078	19
20	124.132 131	41.266 620	20.550 990	10.194 491	20
21	126.716 051	42.130 742	20.985 097	10.413 480	21
22	129.113 825	42.932 982	21.388 391	10.617 191	22
23	131.338 863	43.677 772	21.763 057	10.806 689	23
24	133.403 610	44.369 226	22.111 129	10.982 967	24
25	135.319 613	45.011 164	22.434 493	11.146 946	25
26	137.097 587	45.607 131	22.734 904	11.299 485	26
27	138.747 475	46.160 420	23.013 992	11.441 381	27
28	140.278 506	46.674 087	23.273 268	11.573 378	28
29	141.699 242	47.150 969	23.514 141	11.696 165	29
30	143.017 627	47.593 700	23.737 916	11.810 386	30
31	144.241 037	48.004 727	23.945 807	11.916 638	31
32	145.376 312	48.386 319	24.138 941	12.015 478	32
33	146.429 801	48.740 585	24.318 366	12.107 421	33
34	147.407 398	49.069 481	24.485 054	12.192 950	34
35	148.314 568	49.374 824	24.639 911	12.272 511	35
36	149.156 386	49.658 301	24.783 776	12.346 522	36
37	149.937 560	49.921 477	24.917 429	12.415 370	37
38	150.662 457	50.165 807	25.041 594	12.479 414	38
39	151.335 133	50.392 640	25.156 946	12.538 989	39
40	151.959 350	50.603 229	25.264 110	12.594 409	40

(Present Value of $1 per period)

Base:	1.006 458	1.019 375	1.038 750	1.077 500	
		Frequency of Payments			
Months	Monthly	Quarterly	Semiannual	Annual	Months
1	.993 583	—	—	—	1
2	1.980 791	—	—	—	2
3	2.961 663	.980 993	—	—	3
4	3.936 242	—	—	—	4
5	4.904 566	—	—	—	5
6	5.866 677	1.943 341	.962 696	—	6
7	6.822 615	—	—	—	7
8	7.772 418	—	—	—	8
9	8.716 126	2.887 398	—	—	9
10	9.653 779	—	—	—	10
11	10.585 415	—	—	—	11
Years					Years
1	11.511 072	3.813 511	1.889 478	.928 074	1
2	22.166 384	7.345 254	3.640 614	1.789 396	2
3	32.029 556	10.616 048	5.263 536	2.588 767	3
4	41.159 476	13.645 173	6.767 633	3.330 642	4
5	49.610 656	16.450 486	8.161 603	4.019 157	5
6	57.433 556	19.048 524	9.453 511	4.658 151	6
7	64.674 883	21.454 601	10.650 829	5.251 184	7
8	71.377 873	23.682 900	11.760 483	5.801 563	8
9	77.582 547	25.746 558	12.788 890	6.312 355	9
10	83.325 951	27.657 739	13.742 001	6.786 409	10
11	88.642 377	29.427 709	14.625 327	7.226 365	11
12	93.563 568	31.066 901	15.443 979	7.634 678	12
13	98.118 905	32.584 979	16.202 691	8.013 622	13
14	102.335 588	33.990 891	16.905 852	8.365 310	14
15	106.238 793	35.292 925	17.557 530	8.691 703	15
16	109.851 825	36.498 755	18.161 493	8.994 620	16
17	113.196 255	37.615 491	18.721 236	9.275 750	17
18	116.292 053	38.649 714	19.239 997	9.536 659	18
19	119.157 701	39.607 523	19.720 775	9.778 802	19
20	121.810 311	40.494 562	20.166 351	10.003 528	20
21	124.265 720	41.316 060	20.579 304	10.212 091	21
22	126.538 587	42.076 860	20.962 022	10.405 653	22
23	128.642 485	42.781 448	21.316 718	10.585 293	23
24	130.589 973	43.433 976	21.645 444	10.752 012	24
25	132.392 681	44.038 290	21.950 102	10.906 740	25
26	134.061 371	44.597 954	22.232 453	11.050 338	26
27	135.606 007	45.116 266	22.494 131	11.183 609	27
28	137.035 812	45.596 281	22.736 651	11.307 293	28
29	138.359 321	46.040 830	22.961 413	11.422 082	29
30	139.584 437	46.452 533	23.169 719	11.528 614	30
31	140.718 475	46.833 816	23.362 773	11.627 484	31
32	141.768 207	47.186 927	23.541 693	11.719 243	32
33	142.739 898	47.513 948	23.707 512	11.804 402	33
34	143.639 352	47.816 807	23.861 191	11.883 436	34
35	144.471 939	48.097 288	24.003 618	11.956 785	35
36	145.242 629	48.357 046	24.135 616	12.024 858	36
37	145.956 024	48.597 610	24.257 950	12.088 036	37
38	146.616 384	48.820 401	24.371 327	12.146 669	38
39	147.227 651	49.026 730	24.476 403	12.201 085	39
40	147.793 475	49.217 814	24.573 786	12.251 587	40

8% ORDINARY LEVEL ANNUITY
(Present Value of $1 per period)

Base: 1.006 667 1.020 000 1.040 000 1.080 000

Frequency of Payments

Months	Monthly	Quarterly	Semiannual	Annual	Months
1	.993 377	—	—	—	1
2	1.980 176	—	—	—	2
3	2.960 440	.980 392	—	—	3
4	3.934 212	—	—	—	4
5	4.901 535	—	—	—	5
6	5.862 452	1.941 561	.961 538	—	6
7	6.817 005	—	—	—	7
8	7.765 237	—	—	—	8
9	8.707 189	2.883 883	—	—	9
10	9.642 903	—	—	—	10
11	10.572 420	—	—	—	11

Years					Years
1	11.495 782	3.807 729	1.886 095	.925 926	1
2	22.110 544	7.325 481	3.629 895	1.783 265	2
3	31.911 806	10.575 341	5.242 137	2.577 097	3
4	40.961 913	13.577 709	6.732 745	3.312 127	4
5	49.318 433	16.351 433	8.110 896	3.992 710	5
6	57.034 522	18.913 926	9.385 074	4.622 880	6
7	64.159 261	21.281 272	10.563 123	5.206 370	7
8	70.737 970	23.468 335	11.652 296	5.746 639	8
9	76.812 497	25.488 842	12.659 297	6.246 888	9
10	82.421 481	27.355 479	13.590 326	6.710 081	10
11	87.600 600	29.079 963	14.451 115	7.138 964	11
12	92.382 800	30.673 120	15.246 963	7.536 078	12
13	96.798 498	32.144 950	15.982 769	7.903 776	13
14	100.875 784	33.504 694	16.663 063	8.244 237	14
15	104.640 592	34.760 887	17.292 033	8.559 479	15
16	108.116 871	35.921 415	17.873 551	8.851 369	16
17	111.326 733	36.993 564	18.411 198	9.121 638	17
18	114.290 596	37.984 063	18.908 282	9.371 887	18
19	117.027 313	38.899 132	19.367 864	9.603 599	19
20	119.554 292	39.744 514	19.792 774	9.818 147	20
21	121.887 606	40.525 516	20.185 627	10.016 803	21
22	124.042 099	41.247 041	20.548 841	10.200 744	22
23	126.031 475	41.913 619	20.884 654	10.371 059	23
24	127.868 388	42.529 434	21.195 131	10.528 758	24
25	129.564 523	43.098 352	21.482 185	10.674 776	25
26	131.130 668	43.623 944	21.747 582	10.809 978	26
27	132.576 786	44.109 510	21.992 957	10.935 165	27
28	133.912 076	44.558 097	22.219 819	11.051 078	28
29	135.145 031	44.972 523	22.429 567	11.158 406	29
30	136.283 494	45.355 389	22.623 490	11.257 783	30
31	137.334 707	45.709 097	22.802 783	11.349 799	31
32	138.305 357	46.035 869	22.968 549	11.434 999	32
33	139.201 617	46.337 756	23.121 810	11.513 888	33
34	140.029 190	46.616 652	23.263 507	11.586 934	34
35	140.793 338	46.874 310	23.394 515	11.654 568	35
36	141.498 923	47.112 345	23.515 639	11.717 193	36
37	142.150 433	47.332 253	23.627 625	11.775 179	37
38	142.752 013	47.535 414	23.731 162	11.828 869	38
39	143.307 488	47.723 104	23.826 888	11.878 582	39
40	143.820 392	47.896 500	23.915 392	11.924 613	40

Base: 1.006 875   1.020 625   1.041 250   1.082 500

Frequency of Payments

Months	Monthly	Quarterly	Semiannual	Annual	Months
1	.993 172	—	—	—	1
2	1.979 562	—	—	—	2
3	2.959 218	.979 792	—	—	3
4	3.932 184	—	—	—	4
5	4.898 507	—	—	—	5
6	5.858 231	1.939 784	.960 384	—	6
7	6.811 403	—	—	—	7
8	7.758 066	—	—	—	8
9	8.698 266	2.880 376	—	—	9
10	9.632 045	—	—	—	10
11	10.559 449	—	—	—	11

Years					Years
1	11.480 521	3.801 961	1.882 722	.923 788	1
2	22.054 900	7.305 789	3.619 227	1.777 171	2
3	31.794 659	10.534 863	5.220 872	2.565 516	3
4	40.765 672	13.510 727	6.698 129	3.293 779	4
5	49.028 616	16.253 238	8.060 659	3.966 540	5
6	56.639 378	18.780 694	9.317 372	4.588 027	6
7	63.649 433	21.109 958	10.476 485	5.162 150	7
8	70.106 194	23.256 572	11.545 579	5.692 517	8
9	76.053 333	25.234 859	12.531 645	6.182 464	9
10	81.531 072	27.058 017	13.441 131	6.635 071	10
11	86.576 461	28.738 211	14.279 984	7.053 183	11
12	91.223 625	30.286 652	15.053 690	7.439 430	12
13	95.503 994	31.713 672	15.767 308	7.796 240	13
14	99.446 520	33.028 791	16.425 505	8.125 857	14
15	103.077 868	34.240 784	17.032 584	8.430 353	15
16	106.422 599	35.357 739	17.592 517	8.711 642	16
17	109.503 335	36.387 107	18.108 964	8.971 494	17
18	112.340 913	37.335 757	18.585 302	9.211 542	18
19	114.954 525	38.210 018	19.024 647	9.433 295	19
20	117.361 849	39.015 723	19.429 872	9.638 148	20
21	119.579 165	39.758 249	19.803 626	9.827 388	21
22	121.621 472	40.442 549	20.148 353	10.002 206	22
23	123.502 583	41.073 189	20.466 308	10.163 701	23
24	125.235 220	41.654 378	20.759 570	10.312 888	24
25	126.831 103	42.189 992	21.030 056	10.450 705	25
26	128.301 025	42.683 606	21.279 536	10.578 018	26
27	129.654 928	43.138 513	21.509 640	10.695 629	27
28	130.901 969	43.557 748	21.721 875	10.804 276	28
29	132.050 583	43.944 109	21.917 626	10.904 643	29
30	133.108 539	44.300 173	22.098 175	10.997 361	30
31	134.082 992	44.628 316	22.264 703	11.083 012	31
32	134.980 532	44.930 728	22.418 297	11.162 136	32
33	135.807 231	45.209 426	22.559 963	11.235 230	33
34	136.568 680	45.466 269	22.690 627	11.302 752	34
35	137.270 029	45.702 973	22.811 143	11.365 129	35
36	137.916 021	45.921 115	22.922 299	11.422 752	36
37	138.511 026	46.122 151	23.024 823	11.475 984	37
38	139.059 068	46.307 423	23.119 385	11.525 158	38
39	139.563 854	46.478 167	23.206 603	11.570 585	39
40	140.028 798	46.635 521	23.287 047	11.612 549	40

8½%

ORDINARY LEVEL ANNUITY
(Present Value of $1 per period)

Base:	1.007 083	1.021 250	1.042 500	1.085 000	
		Frequency of Payments			
Months	Monthly	Quarterly	Semiannual	Annual	Months
1	.992 966	—	—	—	1
2	1.978 949	—	—	—	2
3	2.957 996	.979 192	—	—	3
4	3.930 158	—	—	—	4
5	4.895 482	—	—	—	5
6	5.854 016	1.938 009	.959 233	—	6
7	6.805 808	—	—	—	7
8	7.750 906	—	—	—	8
9	8.689 356	2.876 876	—	—	9
10	9.621 206	—	—	—	10
11	10.546 501	—	—	—	11
Years					Years
1	11.465 289	3.796 206	1.879 360	.921 659	1
2	21.999 453	7.286 175	3.608 610	1.771 114	2
3	31.678 112	10.494 610	5.199 740	2.554 022	3
4	40.570 744	13.444 223	6.663 782	3.275 597	4
5	48.741 183	16.155 892	8.010 887	3.940 642	5
6	56.248 080	18.648 813	9.250 395	4.553 587	6
7	63.145 324	20.940 631	10.390 900	5.118 514	7
8	69.482 425	23.047 570	11.440 309	5.639 183	8
9	75.304 875	24.984 543	12.405 900	6.119 063	9
10	80.654 470	26.765 261	13.294 366	6.561 348	10
11	85.569 611	28.402 331	14.111 868	6.968 984	11
12	90.085 581	29.907 339	14.864 073	7.344 686	12
13	94.234 798	31.290 938	15.556 198	7.690 955	13
14	98.047 046	32.562 924	16.193 041	8.010 097	14
15	101.549 693	33.732 299	16.779 017	8.304 237	15
16	104.767 881	34.807 342	17.318 190	8.575 333	16
17	107.724 713	35.795 661	17.814 298	8.825 192	17
18	110.441 412	36.704 254	18.270 780	9.055 476	18
19	112.937 482	37.539 551	18.690 801	9.267 720	19
20	115.230 840	38.307 464	19.077 275	9.463 337	20
21	117.337 948	39.013 431	19.432 879	9.643 628	21
22	119.273 933	39.662 448	19.760 081	9.809 796	22
23	121.052 692	40.259 109	20.061 148	9.962 945	23
24	122.686 994	40.807 638	20.338 168	10.104 097	24
25	124.188 570	41.311 917	20.593 061	10.234 191	25
26	125.568 199	41.775 517	20.827 596	10.354 093	26
27	126.835 785	42.201 718	21.043 397	10.464 602	27
28	128.000 428	42.593 538	21.241 962	10.566 453	28
29	129.070 487	42.953 749	21.424 667	10.660 326	29
30	130.053 643	43.284 903	21.592 779	10.746 844	30
31	130.956 956	43.589 343	21.747 463	10.826 584	31
32	131.786 908	43.869 224	21.889 793	10.900 078	32
33	132.549 457	44.126 527	22.020 754	10.967 813	33
34	133.250 078	44.363 074	22.141 254	11.030 243	34
35	133.893 800	44.580 538	22.252 130	11.087 781	35
36	134.485 244	44.780 460	22.354 150	11.140 812	36
37	135.028 655	44.964 254	22.448 022	11.189 689	37
38	135.527 934	45.133 222	22.534 395	11.234 736	38
39	135.986 665	45.288 559	22.613 870	11.276 255	39
40	136.408 142	45.431 365	22.686 997	11.314 520	40

ORDINARY LEVEL ANNUITY
(Present Value of $1 per period)

8¾%

Base:	1.007 292	1.021 875	1.043 750	1.087 500	
			Frequency of Payments		
Months	Monthly	Quarterly	Semiannual	Annual	Months
1	.992 761	—	—	—	1
2	1.978 336	—	—	—	2
3	2.956 776	.978 593	—	—	3
4	3.928 133	—	—	—	4
5	4.892 459	—	—	—	5
6	5.849 804	1.936 238	.958 084	—	6
7	6.800 219	—	—	—	7
8	7.743 754	—	—	—	8
9	8.680 459	2.873 383	—	—	9
10	9.610 384	—	—	—	10
11	10.533 576	—	—	—	11
Years					Years
1	11.450 086	3.790 466	1.876 008	.919 540	1
2	21.944 202	7.266 641	3.598 043	1.765 094	2
3	31.562 162	10.454 583	5.178 741	2.542 616	3
4	40.377 117	13.378 192	6.629 702	3.257 578	4
5	48.456 109	16.059 387	7.961 575	3.915 014	5
6	55.860 585	18.518 266	9.184 134	4.519 553	6
7	62.646 859	20.773 263	10.306 352	5.075 451	7
8	68.866 545	22.841 284	11.336 463	5.586 622	8
9	74.566 949	24.737 832	12.282 027	6.056 664	9
10	79.791 425	26.477 125	13.149 983	6.488 886	10
11	84.579 708	28.072 202	13.946 702	6.886 332	11
12	88.968 217	29.535 021	14.678 030	7.251 800	12
13	92.990 328	30.876 549	15.349 333	7.587 862	13
14	96.676 632	32.106 841	15.965 540	7.896 884	14
15	100.055 165	33.235 122	16.531 171	8.181 043	15
16	103.151 625	34.269 850	17.050 377	8.442 338	16
17	105.989 560	35.218 782	17.526 970	8.682 610	17
18	108.590 555	36.089 032	17.964 445	8.903 549	18
19	110.974 393	36.887 124	18.366 015	9.106 712	19
20	113.159 204	37.619 041	18.734 626	9.293 528	20
21	115.161 604	38.290 270	19.072 983	9.465 313	21
22	116.996 823	38.905 843	19.383 570	9.623 277	22
23	118.678 820	39.470 375	19.668 665	9.768 530	23
24	120.220 386	39.988 098	19.930 360	9.902 097	24
25	121.633 247	40.462 893	20.170 577	10.024 917	25
26	122.928 148	40.898 320	20.391 078	10.137 854	26
27	124.114 937	41.297 643	20.593 481	10.241 705	27
28	125.202 641	41.663 855	20.779 272	10.337 200	28
29	126.199 532	41.999 702	20.949 814	10.425 012	29
30	127.113 192	42.307 702	21.106 359	10.505 758	30
31	127.950 571	42.590 164	21.250 055	10.580 007	31
32	128.718 037	42.849 205	21.381 957	10.648 282	32
33	129.421 427	43.086 768	21.503 034	10.711 064	33
34	130.066 091	43.304 632	21.614 173	10.768 795	34
35	130.656 932	43.504 432	21.716 190	10.821 880	35
36	131.198 443	43.687 665	21.809 834	10.870 695	36
37	131.694 743	43.855 705	21.895 792	10.915 581	37
38	132.149 608	44.009 812	21.974 695	10.956 856	38
39	132.566 495	44.151 141	22.047 123	10.994 810	39
40	132.948 576	44.280 752	22.113 605	11.029 711	40

9%

ORDINARY LEVEL ANNUITY
(Present Value of $1 per period)

Base:	1.007 500	1.022 500	1.045 000	1.090 000	
			Frequency of Payments		
Months	Monthly	Quarterly	Semiannual	Annual	Months
1	.992 556	—	—	—	1
2	1.977 723	—	—	—	2
3	2.955 556	.977 995	—	—	3
4	3.926 110	—	—	—	4
5	4.889 440	—	—	—	5
6	5.845 598	1.934 470	.956 938	—	6
7	6.794 638	—	—	—	7
8	7.736 613	—	—	—	8
9	8.671 576	2.869 897	—	—	9
10	9.599 580	—	—	—	10
11	10.520 675	—	—	—	11

Years					Years
1	11.434 913	3.784 740	1.872 668	.917 431	1
2	21.889 146	7.247 185	3.587 526	1.759 111	2
3	31.446 805	10.414 779	5.157 872	2.531 295	3
4	40.184 782	13.312 631	6.595 886	3.239 720	4
5	48.173 374	15.963 712	7.912 718	3.889 651	5
6	55.476 849	18.389 036	9.118 581	4.485 919	6
7	62.153 965	20.607 828	10.222 825	5.032 953	7
8	68.258 439	22.637 674	11.234 015	5.534 819	8
9	73.839 382	24.494 666	12.159 992	5.995 247	9
10	78.941 693	26.193 522	13.007 936	6.417 658	10
11	83.606 420	27.747 710	13.784 425	6.805 191	11
12	87.871 092	29.169 548	14.495 478	7.160 725	12
13	91.770 018	30.470 307	15.146 611	7.486 904	13
14	95.334 564	31.660 298	15.742 874	7.786 150	14
15	98.593 409	32.748 953	16.288 889	8.060 688	15
16	101.572 769	33.744 902	16.788 891	8.312 558	16
17	104.296 613	34.656 039	17.246 758	8.543 631	17
18	106.786 856	35.489 587	17.666 041	8.755 625	18
19	109.063 531	36.252 153	18.049 990	8.950 115	19
20	111.144 954	36.949 781	18.401 584	9.128 546	20
21	113.047 870	37.588 001	18.723 550	9.292 244	21
22	114.787 589	38.171 873	19.018 383	9.442 425	22
23	116.378 106	38.706 024	19.288 371	9.580 207	23
24	117.832 218	39.194 689	19.535 607	9.706 612	24
25	119.161 622	39.641 741	19.762 008	9.822 580	25
26	120.377 014	40.050 723	19.969 330	9.928 972	26
27	121.488 172	40.424 877	20.159 181	10.026 580	27
28	122.504 035	40.767 170	20.333 034	10.116 128	28
29	123.432 776	41.080 315	20.492 236	10.198 283	29
30	124.281 866	41.366 793	20.638 022	10.273 654	30
31	125.058 136	41.628 875	20.771 523	10.342 802	31
32	125.767 832	41.868 640	20.893 773	10.406 240	32
33	126.416 664	42.087 987	21.005 722	10.464 441	33
34	127.009 850	42.288 655	21.108 236	10.517 835	34
35	127.552 164	42.472 234	21.202 112	10.566 821	35
36	128.047 967	42.640 181	21.288 077	10.611 763	36
37	128.501 250	42.793 826	21.366 797	10.652 993	37
38	128.915 659	42.934 387	21.438 884	10.690 820	38
39	129.294 526	43.062 979	21.504 896	10.725 523	39
40	129.640 902	43.180 620	21.565 345	10.757 360	40

(Present Value of $1 per period)

Base:	1.007 708	1.023 125	1.046 250	1.092 500	
			Frequency of Payments		
Months	Monthly	Quarterly	Semiannual	Annual	Months
1	.992 351	—	—	—	1
2	1.977 110	—	—	—	2
3	2.954 337	.977 398	—	—	3
4	3.924 089	—	—	—	4
5	4.886 423	—	—	—	5
6	5.841 396	1.932 704	.955 795	—	6
7	6.789 063	—	—	—	7
8	7.729 482	—	—	—	8
9	8.662 707	2.866 418	—	—	9
10	9.588 793	—	—	—	10
11	10.507 796	—	—	—	11

Years					Years
1	11.419 768	3.779 028	1.869 338	.915 332	1
2	21.834 284	7.227 807	3.577 058	1.753 164	2
3	31.332 037	10.375 196	5.137 135	2.520 059	3
4	39.993 729	13.247 536	6.562 332	3.222 022	4
5	47.892 954	15.868 861	7.864 311	3.864 551	5
6	55.096 831	18.261 109	9.053 725	4.452 678	6
7	61.666 569	20.444 298	10.140 306	4.991 010	7
8	67.657 991	22.436 699	11.132 944	5.483 762	8
9	73.122 003	24.254 983	12.039 762	5.934 793	9
10	78.105 033	25.914 367	12.868 180	6.347 637	10
11	82.649 420	27.428 738	13.624 975	6.725 526	11
12	86.793 776	28.810 768	14.316 340	7.071 419	12
13	90.573 316	30.072 023	14.947 932	7.388 027	13
14	94.020 152	31.223 056	15.524 918	7.677 828	14
15	97.163 573	32.273 500	16.052 020	7.943 092	15
16	100.030 286	33.232 146	16.533 550	8.185 896	16
17	102.644 650	34.107 016	16.973 449	8.408 143	17
18	105.028 879	34.905 431	17.375 315	8.611 573	18
19	107.203 230	35.634 073	17.742 438	8.797 778	19
20	109.186 179	36.299 038	18.077 820	8.968 218	20
21	110.994 574	36.905 893	18.384 206	9.124 227	21
22	112.643 781	37.459 714	18.664 103	9.267 027	22
23	114.147 812	37.965 137	18.919 800	9.397 736	23
24	115.519 447	38.426 390	19.153 391	9.517 379	24
25	116.770 341	38.847 335	19.366 787	9.626 891	25
26	117.911 122	39.231 494	19.561 733	9.727 132	26
27	118.951 483	39.582 081	19.739 824	9.818 885	27
28	119.900 264	39.902 030	19.902 519	9.902 869	28
29	120.765 526	40.194 019	20.051 147	9.979 743	29
30	121.554 622	40.460 490	20.186 925	10.050 108	30
31	122.274 255	40.703 675	20.310 965	10.114 516	31
32	122.930 541	40.925 608	20.424 280	10.173 470	32
33	123.529 056	41.128 146	20.527 798	10.227 432	33
34	124.074 885	41.312 985	20.622 367	10.276 826	34
35	124.572 666	41.481 670	20.708 759	10.322 037	35
36	125.026 629	41.635 614	20.787 682	10.363 421	36
37	125.440 630	41.776 105	20.859 782	10.401 301	37
38	125.818 189	41.904 318	20.925 649	10.435 973	38
39	126.162 511	42.021 327	20.985 820	10.467 710	39
40	126.476 524	42.128 110	21.040 790	10.496 760	40

9½%

ORDINARY LEVEL ANNUITY
(Present Value of $1 per period)

Base: 1.007 917   1.023 750   1.047 500   1.095 000

Frequency of Payments

Months	Monthly	Quarterly	Semiannual	Annual	Months
1	.992 146	—	—	—	1
2	1.976 498	—	—	—	2
3	2.953 119	.976 801	—	—	3
4	3.922 070	—	—	—	4
5	4.883 409	—	—	—	5
6	5.837 198	1.930 941	.954 654	—	6
7	6.783 496	—	—	—	7
8	7.722 360	—	—	—	8
9	8.653 851	2.862 946	—	—	9
10	9.578 024	—	—	—	10
11	10.494 940	—	—	—	11

Years					Years
1	11.404 653	3.773 330	1.866 018	.913 242	1
2	21.779 615	7.208 506	3.566 640	1.747 253	2
3	31.217 856	10.335 834	5.116 526	2.508 907	3
4	39.803 947	13.182 902	6.529 036	3.204 481	4
5	47.614 827	15.774 825	7.816 348	3.839 709	5
6	54.720 488	18.134 469	8.989 557	4.419 825	6
7	61.184 601	20.282 649	10.058 778	4.949 612	7
8	67.065 090	22.238 317	11.033 228	5.433 436	8
9	72.414 648	24.018 725	11.921 306	5.875 284	9
10	77.281 211	25.639 578	12.730 669	6.278 798	10
11	81.708 388	27.115 177	13.468 293	6.647 304	11
12	85.735 849	28.458 537	14.140 538	6.983 839	12
13	89.399 684	29.681 510	14.753 197	7.291 178	13
14	92.732 722	30.794 884	15.311 553	7.571 852	14
15	95.764 831	31.808 482	15.820 418	7.828 175	15
16	98.523 180	32.731 244	16.284 180	8.062 260	16
17	101.032 487	33.571 311	16.706 836	8.276 037	17
18	103.315 236	34.336 095	17.092 029	8.471 266	18
19	105.391 883	35.032 341	17.443 081	8.649 558	19
20	107.281 037	35.666 192	17.763 016	8.812 382	20
21	108.999 624	36.243 240	18.054 594	8.961 080	21
22	110.563 046	36.768 574	18.320 328	9.096 876	22
23	111.985 311	37.246 830	18.562 508	9.220 892	23
24	113.279 165	37.682 226	18.783 222	9.334 148	24
25	114.456 200	38.078 604	18.984 373	9.437 578	25
26	115.526 965	38.439 459	19.167 695	9.532 034	26
27	116.501 054	38.767 976	19.334 768	9.618 296	27
28	117.387 195	39.067 052	19.487 032	9.697 074	28
29	118.193 330	39.339 326	19.625 801	9.769 018	29
30	118.926 681	39.587 200	19.752 269	9.834 719	30
31	119.593 820	39.812 860	19.867 528	9.894 721	31
32	120.200 725	40.018 298	19.972 570	9.949 517	32
33	120.752 835	40.205 324	20.068 303	9.999 559	33
34	121.255 097	40.375 590	20.155 549	10.045 259	34
35	121.712 011	40.530 598	20.235 063	10.086 995	35
36	122.127 671	40.671 714	20.307 529	10.125 109	36
37	122.505 803	40.800 184	20.373 572	10.159 917	37
38	122.849 795	40.917 140	20.433 761	10.191 705	38
39	123.162 729	41.023 616	20.488 615	10.220 735	39
40	123.447 408	41.120 549	20.538 607	10.247 247	40

ORDINARY LEVEL ANNUITY

9¾%

(Present Value of $1 per period)

Base: 1.008 125   1.024 375   1.048 750   1.097 500

Frequency of Payments

Months	Monthly	Quarterly	Semiannual	Annual	Months
1	.991 940	—	—	—	1
2	1.975 886	—	—	—	2
3	2.951 902	.976 205	—	—	3
4	3.920 052	—	—	—	4
5	4.880 399	—	—	—	5
6	5.833 005	1.929 181	.953 516	—	6
7	6.777 935	—	—	—	7
8	7.715 248	—	—	—	8
9	8.645 008	2.859 481	—	—	9
10	9.567 273	—	—	—	10
11	10.482 106	—	—	—	11

Years					Years
1	11.389 566	3.767 645	1.862 709	.911 162	1
2	21.725 139	7.189 283	3.556 271	1.741 377	2
3	31.104 256	10.296 691	5.096 045	2.497 838	3
4	39.615 427	13.118 725	6.495 998	3.187 096	4
5	47.338 973	15.681 594	7.768 824	3.815 122	5
6	54.347 780	18.009 099	8.926 069	4.387 355	6
7	60.707 990	20.122 854	9.978 228	4.908 752	7
8	66.479 625	22.042 490	10.934 843	5.383 828	8
9	71.717 152	23.785 833	11.804 591	5.816 700	9
10	76.469 997	25.369 074	12.595 360	6.211 116	10
11	80.783 012	26.806 916	13.314 321	6.570 493	11
12	84.696 900	28.112 712	13.967 996	6.897 944	12
13	88.248 596	29.298 588	14.562 312	7.196 304	13
14	91.471 617	30.375 558	15.102 660	7.468 159	14
15	94.396 379	31.353 622	15.593 941	7.715 862	15
16	97.050 483	32.241 865	16.040 610	7.941 560	16
17	99.458 976	33.048 535	16.446 719	8.147 207	17
18	101.644 586	33.781 123	16.815 949	8.334 585	18
19	103.627 939	34.446 433	17.151 651	8.505 317	19
20	105.427 753	35.050 644	17.456 869	8.660 881	20
21	107.061 011	35.599 366	17.734 371	8.802 625	21
22	108.543 127	36.097 695	17.986 674	8.931 777	22
23	109.888 088	36.550 260	18.216 066	9.049 455	23
24	111.108 586	36.961 262	18.424 628	9.156 679	24
25	112.216 138	37.334 520	18.614 250	9.254 377	25
26	113.221 198	37.673 499	18.786 654	9.343 396	26
27	114.133 249	37.981 348	18.943 402	9.424 506	27
28	114.960 898	38.260 924	19.085 916	9.498 411	28
29	115.711 957	38.514 826	19.215 489	9.565 751	29
30	116.393 513	38.745 410	19.333 296	9.627 108	30
31	117.011 997	38.954 818	19.440 405	9.683 014	31
32	117.573 247	39.144 995	19.537 788	9.733 953	32
33	118.082 558	39.317 707	19.626 328	9.780 368	33
34	118.544 738	39.474 557	19.706 828	9.822 658	34
35	118.964 147	39.617 003	19.780 018	9.861 192	35
36	119.344 744	39.746 367	19.846 561	9.896 303	36
37	119.690 121	39.863 851	19.907 062	9.928 294	37
38	120.003 536	39.970 545	19.962 069	9.957 443	38
39	120.287 948	40.067 442	20.012 082	9.984 003	39
40	120.546 041	40.155 439	20.057 552	10.008 203	40

10%   ORDINARY LEVEL ANNUITY
(Present Value of $1 per period)

Base: 1.008 333   1.025 000   1.050 000   1.100 000

Frequency of Payments

Months	Monthly	Quarterly	Semiannual	Annual	Months
1	.991 736	—	—	—	1
2	1.975 275	—	—	—	2
3	2.950 686	.975 610	—	—	3
4	3.918 036	—	—	—	4
5	4.877 391	—	—	—	5
6	5.828 817	1.927 424	.952 381	—	6
7	6.772 381	—	—	—	7
8	7.708 146	—	—	—	8
9	8.636 178	2.856 024	—	—	9
10	9.556 540	—	—	—	10
11	10.469 296	—	—	—	11

Years					Years
1	11.374 508	3.761 974	1.859 410	.909 091	1
2	21.670 855	7.170 137	3.545 951	1.735 537	2
3	30.991 236	10.257 765	5.075 692	2.486 852	3
4	39.428 160	13.055 003	6.463 213	3.169 865	4
5	47.065 369	15.589 162	7.721 735	3.790 787	5
6	53.978 665	17.884 986	8.863 252	4.355 261	6
7	60.236 667	19.964 889	9.898 641	4.868 419	7
8	65.901 488	21.849 178	10.837 770	5.334 926	8
9	71.029 355	23.556 251	11.689 587	5.759 024	9
10	75.671 163	25.102 775	12.462 210	6.144 567	10
11	79.872 986	26.503 849	13.163 003	6.495 061	11
12	83.676 528	27.773 154	13.798 642	6.813 692	12
13	87.119 542	28.923 081	14.375 185	7.103 356	13
14	90.236 201	29.964 858	14.898 127	7.366 687	14
15	93.057 439	30.908 656	15.372 451	7.606 080	15
16	95.611 259	31.763 691	15.802 677	7.823 709	16
17	97.923 008	32.538 311	16.192 904	8.021 553	17
18	100.015 633	33.240 078	16.546 852	8.201 412	18
19	101.909 902	33.875 844	16.867 893	8.364 920	19
20	103.624 619	34.451 817	17.159 086	8.513 564	20
21	105.176 801	34.973 620	17.423 208	8.648 694	21
22	106.581 856	35.446 348	17.662 773	8.771 540	22
23	107.853 730	35.874 616	17.880 066	8.883 218	23
24	109.005 045	36.262 606	18.077 158	8.984 744	24
25	110.047 230	36.614 105	18.255 925	9.077 040	25
26	110.990 629	36.932 546	18.418 073	9.160 945	26
27	111.844 605	37.221 039	18.565 146	9.237 223	27
28	112.617 635	37.482 398	18.698 545	9.306 567	28
29	113.317 392	37.719 177	18.819 542	9.369 606	29
30	113.950 820	37.933 687	18.929 290	9.426 914	30
31	114.524 207	38.128 022	19.028 834	9.479 013	31
32	115.043 244	38.304 081	19.119 124	9.526 376	32
33	115.513 083	38.463 581	19.201 019	9.569 432	33
34	115.938 387	38.608 080	19.275 301	9.608 575	34
35	116.323 377	38.738 989	19.342 677	9.644 159	35
36	116.671 876	38.857 586	19.403 788	9.676 508	36
37	116.987 340	38.965 030	19.459 218	9.705 917	37
38	117.272 903	39.062 368	19.509 495	9.732 651	38
39	117.531 398	39.150 552	19.555 098	9.756 956	39
40	117.765 391	39.230 442	19.596 460	9.779 051	40

(Present Value of $1 per period)

Base:	1.008 542	1.025 625	1.051 250	1.102 500	

Frequency of Payments

Months	Monthly	Quarterly	Semiannual	Annual	Months
1	.991 531	—	—	—	1
2	1.974 664	—	—	—	2
3	2.949 470	.975 015	—	—	3
4	3.916 021	—	—	—	4
5	4.874 386	—	—	—	5
6	5.824 634	1.925 670	.951 249	—	6
7	6.766 834	—	—	—	7
8	7.701 054	—	—	—	8
9	8.627 362	2.852 573	—	—	9
10	9.545 824	—	—	—	10
11	10.456 508	—	—	—	11

Years					Years
1	11.359 479	3.756 317	1.856 122	.907 029	1
2	21.616 761	7.151 068	3.535 679	1.729 732	2
3	30.878 791	10.219 054	5.055 465	2.475 947	3
4	39.242 135	12.991 730	6.430 680	3.152 787	4
5	46.793 994	15.497 520	7.675 075	3.766 700	5
6	53.613 104	17.762 114	8.801 096	4.323 537	6
7	59.770 564	19.808 727	9.820 003	4.828 605	7
8	65.330 572	21.658 343	10.741 985	5.286 717	8
9	70.351 099	23.329 923	11.576 263	5.702 238	9
10	74.884 490	24.840 604	12.331 178	6.079 127	10
11	78.978 010	26.205 873	13.014 281	6.420 977	11
12	82.674 341	27.439 727	13.632 404	6.731 045	12
13	86.012 022	28.554 816	14.191 726	7.012 286	13
14	89.025 850	29.562 572	14.697 843	7.267 379	14
15	91.747 251	30.473 325	15.155 814	7.498 757	15
16	94.204 596	31.296 413	15.570 220	7.708 623	16
17	96.423 509	32.040 274	15.945 206	7.898 978	17
18	98.427 122	32.712 535	16.284 520	8.071 635	18
19	100.236 328	33.320 086	16.591 557	8.228 240	19
20	101.869 988	33.869 158	16.869 386	8.370 286	20
21	103.345 136	34.365 378	17.120 787	8.499 126	21
22	104.677 152	34.813 834	17.348 272	8.615 987	22
23	105.879 924	35.219 124	17.554 118	8.721 984	23
24	106.965 992	35.585 402	17.740 383	8.818 126	24
25	107.946 680	35.916 424	17.908 929	8.905 329	25
26	108.832 214	36.215 583	18.061 441	8.984 426	26
27	109.631 824	36.485 947	18.199 446	9.056 169	27
28	110.353 850	36.730 286	18.324 323	9.121 241	28
29	111.005 818	36.951 107	18.437 321	9.180 264	29
30	111.594 527	37.150 672	18.539 570	9.233 800	30
31	112.126 113	37.331 028	18.632 092	9.282 358	31
32	112.606 121	37.494 023	18.715 813	9.326 402	32
33	113.039 554	37.641 330	18.791 570	9.366 351	33
34	113.430 931	37.774 457	18.860 120	9.402 586	34
35	113.784 334	37.894 770	18.922 150	9.435 452	35
36	114.103 446	38.003 503	18.978 278	9.465 263	36
37	114.391 595	38.101 769	19.029 068	9.492 302	37
38	114.651 785	38.190 576	19.075 026	9.516 827	38
39	114.886 730	38.270 836	19.116 612	9.539 072	39
40	115.098 878	38.343 369	19.154 243	9.559 249	40

10½% ORDINARY LEVEL ANNUITY
(Present Value of $1 per period)

Base: 1.008 750   1.026 250   1.052 500   1.105 000

Frequency of Payments

Months	Monthly	Quarterly	Semiannual	Annual	Months
1	.991 326	—	—	—	1
2	1.974 053	—	—	—	2
3	2.948 256	.974 421	—	—	3
4	3.914 008	—	—	—	4
5	4.871 384	—	—	—	5
6	5.820 455	1.923 919	.950 119	—	6
7	6.761 293	—	—	—	7
8	7.693 971	—	—	—	8
9	8.618 559	2.849 129	—	—	9
10	9.535 126	—	—	—	10
11	10.443 743	—	—	—	11

Years					Years
1	11.344 479	3.750 674	1.852 844	.904 977	1
2	21.562 858	7.132 074	3.525 455	1.723 961	2
3	30.766 918	10.180 558	5.035 363	2.465 123	3
4	39.057 344	12.928 903	6.398 396	3.135 858	4
5	46.524 827	15.406 659	7.628 840	3.742 858	5
6	53.251 057	17.640 468	8.739 595	4.292 179	6
7	59.309 613	19.654 346	9.742 301	4.789 303	7
8	64.766 771	21.469 947	10.647 469	5.239 188	8
9	69.682 229	23.106 793	11.464 588	5.646 324	9
10	74.109 758	24.582 484	12.202 223	6.014 773	10
11	78.097 792	25.912 884	12.868 104	6.348 211	11
12	81.689 957	27.112 300	13.469 212	6.649 964	12
13	84.925 549	28.193 627	14.011 848	6.923 045	13
14	87.839 962	29.168 492	14.501 699	7.170 176	14
15	90.465 078	30.047 377	14.943 901	7.393 825	15
16	92.829 614	30.839 730	15.343 087	7.596 221	16
17	94.959 437	31.554 073	15.703 443	7.779 386	17
18	96.877 844	32.198 084	16.028 745	7.945 146	18
19	98.605 822	32.778 690	16.322 404	8.095 154	19
20	100.162 274	33.302 132	16.587 498	8.230 909	20
21	101.564 226	33.774 038	16.826 804	8.353 764	21
22	102.827 014	34.199 482	17.042 833	8.464 945	22
23	103.964 453	34.583 040	17.237 847	8.565 561	23
24	104.988 985	34.928 834	17.413 891	8.656 616	24
25	105.911 817	35.240 583	17.572 811	8.739 019	25
26	106.743 045	35.521 638	17.716 272	8.813 592	26
27	107.491 762	35.775 023	17.845 778	8.881 079	27
28	108.166 158	36.003 460	17.962 686	8.942 153	28
29	108.773 611	36.209 406	18.068 222	8.997 423	29
30	109.320 766	36.395 076	18.163 493	9.047 442	30
31	109.813 607	36.562 466	18.249 495	9.092 707	31
32	110.257 527	36.713 375	18.327 132	9.133 672	32
33	110.657 382	36.849 427	18.397 217	9.170 744	33
34	111.017 546	36.972 083	18.460 485	9.204 293	34
35	111.341 958	37.082 664	18.517 598	9.234 654	35
36	111.634 167	37.182 357	18.569 155	9.262 131	36
37	111.897 371	37.272 235	18.615 697	9.286 996	37
38	112.134 448	37.353 264	18.657 712	9.309 499	38
39	112.347 992	37.426 315	18.695 640	9.329 863	39
40	112.540 338	37.492 174	18.729 879	9.348 292	40

ORDINARY LEVEL ANNUITY   10¾%
(Present Value of $1 per period)

Base: 1.008 958   1.026 875   1.053 750   1.107 500

Frequency of Payments

Months	Monthly	Quarterly	Semiannual	Annual	Months
1	.991 121	—	—	—	1
2	1.973 442	—	—	—	2
3	2.947 042	.973 828	—	—	3
4	3.911 997	—	—	—	4
5	4.868 384	—	—	—	5
6	5.816 280	1.922 170	.948 992	—	6
7	6.755 760	—	—	—	7
8	7.686 898	—	—	—	8
9	8.609 769	2.845 692	—	—	9
10	9.524 446	—	—	—	10
11	10.431 001	—	—	—	11

Years					Years
1	11.329 508	3.745 044	1.849 577	.902 935	1
2	21.509 144	7.113 157	3.515 279	1.718 225	2
3	30.655 613	10.142 275	5.015 385	2.454 380	3
4	38.873 775	12.866 519	6.366 359	3.119 079	4
5	46.257 847	15.316 573	7.583 026	3.719 258	5
6	52.892 484	17.520 034	8.678 738	4.261 181	6
7	58.853 748	19.501 720	9.665 520	4.750 502	7
8	64.209 982	21.283 954	10.554 202	5.192 327	8
9	69.022 594	22.886 809	11.354 535	5.591 266	9
10	73.346 757	24.328 340	12.075 304	5.951 482	10
11	77.232 045	25.624 784	12.724 417	6.276 733	11
12	80.723 001	26.790 743	13.308 999	6.570 414	12
13	83.859 649	27.839 351	13.835 465	6.835 588	13
14	86.677 947	28.782 419	14.309 593	7.075 023	14
15	89.210 206	29.630 568	14.736 585	7.291 217	15
16	91.485 457	30.393 353	15.121 128	7.486 426	16
17	93.529 785	31.079 365	15.467 441	7.662 687	17
18	95.366 626	31.696 331	15.779 326	7.821 840	18
19	97.017 041	32.251 201	16.060 205	7.965 544	19
20	98.499 949	32.750 224	16.313 161	8.095 299	20
21	99.832 351	33.199 022	16.540 969	8.212 460	21
22	101.029 524	33.602 649	16.746 129	8.318 248	22
23	102.105 191	33.965 652	16.930 894	8.413 768	23
24	103.071 685	34.292 119	17.097 290	8.500 016	24
25	103.940 086	34.585 728	17.247 144	8.577 893	25
26	104.720 350	34.849 785	17.382 100	8.648 210	26
27	105.421 422	35.087 266	17.503 640	8.711 702	27
28	106.051 340	35.300 845	17.613 097	8.769 031	28
29	106.617 325	35.492 927	17.711 672	8.820 796	29
30	107.125 867	35.665 677	17.800 447	8.867 536	30
31	107.582 795	35.821 040	17.880 397	8.909 739	31
32	107.993 347	35.960 766	17.952 398	8.947 845	32
33	108.362 231	36.086 429	18.017 242	8.982 253	33
34	108.693 676	36.199 444	18.075 639	9.013 321	34
35	108.991 482	36.301 084	18.128 231	9.041 373	35
36	109.259 062	36.392 494	18.175 594	9.066 703	36
37	109.499 484	36.474 705	18.218 249	9.089 574	37
38	109.715 505	36.548 640	18.256 663	9.110 225	38
39	109.909 602	36.615 135	18.291 258	9.128 871	39
40	110.083 998	36.674 937	18.322 414	9.145 707	40

11%

ORDINARY LEVEL ANNUITY
(Present Value of $1 per period)

	1.009 167	1.027 500	1.055 000	1.110 000	
		Frequency of Payments			
Months	Monthly	Quarterly	Semiannual	Annual	Months
1	.990 917	—	—	—	1
2	1.972 832	—	—	—	2
3	2.945 829	.973 236	—	—	3
4	3.909 987	—	—	—	4
5	4.865 388	—	—	—	5
6	5.812 110	1.920 424	.947 867	—	6
7	6.750 233	—	—	—	7
8	7.679 835	—	—	—	8
9	8.600 992	2.842 262	—	—	9
10	9.513 783	—	—	—	10
11	10.418 282	—	—	—	11
Years					Years
1	11.314 565	3.739 428	1.846 320	.900 901	1
2	21.455 619	7.094 314	3.505 150	1.712 523	2
3	30.544 874	10.104 204	4.995 530	2.443 715	3
4	38.691 421	12.804 573	6.334 566	3.102 446	4
5	45.993 034	15.227 252	7.537 626	3.695 897	5
6	52.537 346	17.400 797	8.618 518	4.230 538	6
7	58.402 903	19.350 826	9.589 648	4.712 196	7
8	63.660 103	21.100 326	10.462 162	5.146 123	8
9	68.372 043	22.669 918	11.246 074	5.537 048	9
10	72.595 275	24.078 101	11.950 382	5.889 232	10
11	76.380 487	25.341 475	12.583 170	6.206 515	11
12	79.773 109	26.474 931	13.151 699	6.492 356	12
13	82.813 859	27.491 829	13.662 495	6.749 870	13
14	85.539 231	28.404 155	14.121 422	6.981 865	14
15	87.981 937	29.222 662	14.533 745	7.190 870	15
16	90.171 293	29.956 999	14.904 198	7.379 162	16
17	92.133 576	30.615 821	15.237 033	7.548 794	17
18	93.892 337	31.206 893	15.536 068	7.701 617	18
19	95.468 685	31.737 183	15.804 738	7.839 294	19
20	96.881 539	32.212 941	16.046 125	7.963 328	20
21	98.147 856	32.639 775	16.262 999	8.075 070	21
22	99.282 835	33.022 715	16.457 851	8.175 739	22
23	100.300 098	33.366 276	16.632 915	8.266 432	23
24	101.211 853	33.674 508	16.790 203	8.348 137	24
25	102.029 044	33.951 042	16.931 518	8.421 745	25
26	102.761 478	34.199 140	17.058 483	8.488 058	26
27	103.417 947	34.421 724	17.172 555	8.547 800	27
28	104.006 328	34.621 419	17.275 043	8.601 622	28
29	104.533 685	34.800 579	17.367 124	8.650 110	29
30	105.006 346	34.961 315	17.449 854	8.693 793	30
31	105.429 984	35.105 521	17.524 183	8.733 146	31
32	105.809 684	35.234 899	17.590 965	8.768 600	32
33	106.150 002	35.350 972	17.650 964	8.800 541	33
34	106.455 024	35.455 108	17.704 871	8.829 316	34
35	106.728 409	35.548 536	17.753 304	8.855 240	35
36	106.973 440	35.632 356	17.796 819	8.878 594	36
37	107.193 057	35.707 557	17.835 914	8.899 635	37
38	107.389 897	35.775 024	17.871 040	8.918 590	38
39	107.566 320	35.835 554	17.902 599	8.935 666	39
40	107.724 446	35.889 859	17.930 953	8.951 051	40

ORDINARY LEVEL ANNUITY

(Present Value of $1 per period)

11¼%

Base:	1.009 375	1.028 125	1.056 250	1.112 500	
			Frequency of Payments		
Months	Monthly	Quarterly	Semiannual	Annual	Months
1	.990 712	—	—	—	1
2	1.972 222	—	—	—	2
3	2.944 617	.972 644	—	—	3
4	3.907 979	—	—	—	4
5	4.862 394	—	—	—	5
6	5.807 945	1.918 681	.946 746	—	6
7	6.744 713	—	—	—	7
8	7.672 781	—	—	—	8
9	8.592 229	2.838 839	—	—	9
10	9.503 137	—	—	—	10
11	10.405 585	—	—	—	11

Years					Years
1	11.299 650	3.733 825	1.843 073	.898 876	1
2	21.402 281	7.075 547	3.495 069	1.706 855	2
3	30.434 697	10.066 342	4.975 798	2.433 128	3
4	38.510 272	12.743 062	6.303 015	3.085 958	4
5	45.730 366	15.138 690	7.492 637	3.672 771	5
6	52.185 606	17.282 743	8.558 926	4.200 244	6
7	57.957 015	19.201 641	9.514 671	4.674 376	7
8	63.117 034	20.919 028	10.371 331	5.100 563	8
9	67.730 430	22.456 066	11.139 178	5.483 652	9
10	71.855 110	23.831 694	11.827 421	5.828 002	10
11	75.542 845	25.062 862	12.444 311	6.137 530	11
12	78.839 923	26.164 740	12.997 247	6.415 757	12
13	81.787 728	27.150 905	13.492 858	6.665 849	13
14	84.423 259	28.033 510	13.937 088	6.890 651	14
15	86.779 597	28.823 429	14.335 263	7.092 720	15
16	88.886 318	29.530 395	14.692 158	7.274 355	16
17	90.769 865	30.163 120	15.012 053	7.437 622	17
18	92.453 881	30.729 401	15.298 784	7.584 380	18
19	93.959 501	31.236 214	15.555 788	7.716 296	19
20	95.305 625	31.689 804	15.786 148	7.834 873	20
21	96.509 148	32.095 762	15.992 626	7.941 459	21
22	97.585 177	32.459 088	16.177 698	8.037 267	22
23	98.547 217	32.784 260	16.343 583	8.123 386	23
24	99.407 345	33.075 284	16.492 270	8.200 796	24
25	100.176 355	33.335 747	16.625 542	8.270 379	25
26	100.863 902	33.568 858	16.744 998	8.332 925	26
27	101.478 613	33.777 488	16.852 069	8.389 146	27
28	102.028 205	33.964 210	16.948 040	8.439 681	28
29	102.519 577	34.131 323	17.034 061	8.485 107	29
30	102.958 896	34.280 887	17.111 164	8.525 939	30
31	103.351 676	34.414 745	17.180 274	8.562 642	31
32	103.702 847	34.534 546	17.242 219	8.595 633	32
33	104.016 817	34.641 766	17.297 742	8.625 288	33
34	104.297 526	34.737 727	17.347 508	8.651 944	34
35	104.548 499	34.823 610	17.392 116	8.675 905	35
36	104.772 886	34.900 474	17.432 098	8.697 443	36
37	104.973 502	34.969 267	17.467 936	8.716 802	37
38	105.152 866	35.030 835	17.500 058	8.734 204	38
39	105.313 229	35.085 938	17.528 850	8.749 847	39
40	105.456 605	35.135 255	17.554 657	8.763 907	40

11½%

ORDINARY LEVEL ANNUITY
(Present Value of $1 per period)

Base:	1.009 583	1.028 750	1.057 500	1.115 000	
			Frequency of Payments		
Months	Monthly	Quarterly	Semiannual	Annual	Months
1	.990 508	—	—	—	1
2	1.971 613	—	—	—	2
3	2.943 405	.972 053	—	—	3
4	3.905 973	—	—	—	4
5	4.859 404	—	—	—	5
6	5.803 784	1.916 941	.945 626	—	6
7	6.739 200	—	—	—	7
8	7.665 737	—	—	—	8
9	8.583 479	2.835 423	—	—	9
10	9.492 509	—	—	—	10
11	10.392 910	—	—	—	11
Years					Years
1	11.284 764	3.728 236	1.839 836	.896 861	1
2	21.349 130	7.056 855	3.485 035	1.701 221	2
3	30.325 079	10.028 689	4.956 187	2.422 619	3
4	38.330 318	12.681 982	6.271 705	3.069 614	4
5	45.469 825	15.050 878	7.448 054	3.649 878	5
6	51.837 225	17.165 859	8.499 956	4.170 294	6
7	57.516 018	19.054 142	9.440 576	4.637 035	7
8	62.580 675	20.740 025	10.281 688	5.055 637	8
9	67.097 611	22.245 205	11.033 819	5.431 064	9
10	71.126 060	23.589 049	11.706 381	5.767 771	10
11	74.718 850	24.788 851	12.307 792	6.069 750	11
12	77.923 095	25.860 050	12.845 580	6.340 583	12
13	80.780 815	26.816 430	13.326 474	6.583 482	13
14	83.329 485	27.670 299	13.756 495	6.801 329	14
15	85.602 527	28.432 645	14.141 024	6.996 708	15
16	87.629 750	29.113 277	14.484 873	7.171 935	16
17	89.437 737	29.720 954	14.792 346	7.329 090	17
18	91.050 199	30.263 497	15.067 291	7.470 036	18
19	92.488 279	30.747 886	15.313 150	7.596 445	19
20	93.770 838	31.180 355	15.532 999	7.709 816	20
21	94.914 693	31.566 469	15.729 590	7.811 494	21
22	95.934 846	31.911 197	15.905 384	7.902 685	22
23	96.844 673	32.218 974	16.062 580	7.984 471	23
24	97.656 106	32.493 762	16.203 147	8.057 822	24
25	98.379 787	32.739 096	16.328 842	8.123 607	25
26	99.025 204	32.958 134	16.441 241	8.182 607	26
27	99.600 823	33.153 693	16.541 749	8.235 522	27
28	100.114 191	33.328 291	16.631 624	8.282 979	28
29	100.572 040	33.484 175	16.711 991	8.325 542	29
30	100.980 375	33.623 350	16.783 856	8.363 715	30
31	101.344 550	33.747 607	16.848 118	8.397 951	31
32	101.669 341	33.858 546	16.905 582	8.428 655	32
33	101.959 008	33.957 593	16.956 967	8.456 193	33
34	102.217 348	34.046 024	17.002 916	8.480 891	34
35	102.447 750	34.124 976	17.044 004	8.503 041	35
36	102.653 235	34.195 466	17.080 745	8.522 907	36
37	102.836 498	34.258 400	17.113 599	8.540 723	37
38	102.999 941	34.314 588	17.142 978	8.556 703	38
39	103.145 709	34.364 753	17.169 248	8.571 034	39
40	103.275 713	34.409 542	17.192 740	8.583 887	40

ORDINARY LEVEL ANNUITY 11¾%
(Present Value of $1 per period)

Base:	1.009 792	1.029 375	1.058 750	1.117 500	
			Frequency of Payments		
Months	Monthly	Quarterly	Semiannual	Annual	Months
1	.990 303	—	—	—	1
2	1.971 004	—	—	—	2
3	2.942 195	.971 463	—	—	3
4	3.903 969	—	—	—	4
5	4.856 416	—	—	—	5
6	5.799 628	1.915 204	.944 510	—	6
7	6.733 694	—	—	—	7
8	7.658 703	—	—	—	8
9	8.574 742	2.832 014	—	—	9
10	9.481 898	—	—	—	10
11	10.380 258	—	—	—	11

Years					Years
1	11.269 907	3.722 661	1.836 609	.894 855	1
2	21.296 166	7.038 236	3.475 047	1.695 619	2
3	30.216 016	9.991 244	4.936 696	2.412 187	3
4	38.151 550	12.621 330	6.240 632	3.053 411	4
5	45.211 389	14.963 809	7.403 872	3.627 214	5
6	51.492 166	17.050 129	8.441 597	4.140 684	6
7	57.079 852	18.908 305	9.367 352	4.600 164	7
8	62.050 930	20.563 282	10.193 216	5.011 333	8
9	66.473 444	22.037 283	10.929 969	5.379 269	9
10	70.407 928	23.350 097	11.587 226	5.708 518	10
11	73.908 238	24.519 351	12.173 565	6.003 148	11
12	77.022 284	25.560 743	12.696 637	6.266 799	12
13	79.792 692	26.488 256	13.163 269	6.502 728	13
14	82.257 381	27.314 342	13.579 551	6.713 851	14
15	84.450 090	28.050 093	13.950 916	6.902 775	15
16	86.400 830	28.705 388	14.282 210	7.071 834	16
17	88.136 304	29.289 024	14.577 758	7.223 118	17
18	89.680 267	29.808 837	14.841 415	7.358 495	18
19	91.053 851	30.271 807	15.076 624	7.479 637	19
20	92.275 859	30.684 150	15.286 453	7.588 042	20
21	93.363 017	31.051 402	15.473 642	7.685 049	21
22	94.330 205	31.378 494	15.640 633	7.771 856	22
23	95.190 663	31.669 817	15.789 606	7.849 536	23
24	95.956 169	31.929 283	15.922 504	7.919 048	24
25	96.637 200	32.160 376	16.041 062	7.981 251	25
26	97.243 079	32.366 198	16.146 828	8.036 913	26
27	97.782 098	32.549 513	16.241 182	8.086 723	27
28	98.261 636	32.712 782	16.325 355	8.131 296	28
29	98.688 256	32.858 196	16.400 445	8.171 182	29
30	99.067 798	32.987 709	16.467 434	8.206 874	30
31	99.405 458	33.103 060	16.527 194	8.238 814	31
32	99.705 856	33.205 796	16.580 506	8.267 395	32
33	99.973 105	33.297 298	16.628 065	8.292 971	33
34	100.210 862	33.378 794	16.670 493	8.315 858	34
35	100.422 383	33.451 379	16.708 343	8.336 338	35
36	100.610 562	33.516 025	16.742 109	8.354 665	36
37	100.777 976	33.573 603	16.772 231	8.371 065	37
38	100.926 915	33.624 884	16.799 103	8.385 740	38
39	101.059 419	33.670 557	16.823 076	8.398 873	39
40	101.177 300	33.711 236	16.844 462	8.410 624	40

12%

ORDINARY LEVEL ANNUITY
(Present Value of $1 per period)

Base:	1.010 000	1.030 000	1.060 000	1.120 000	
		Frequency of Payments			
Months	Monthly	Quarterly	Semiannual	Annual	Months
1	.990 099	—	—	—	1
2	1.970 395	—	—	—	2
3	2.940 985	.970 874	—	—	3
4	3.901 966	—	—	—	4
5	4.853 431	—	—	—	5
6	5.795 476	1.913 470	.943 396	—	6
7	6.728 195	—	—	—	7
8	7.651 678	—	—	—	8
9	8.566 018	2.828 611	—	—	9
10	9.471 305	—	—	—	10
11	10.367 628	—	—	—	11

Years					Years
1	11.255 077	3.717 098	1.833 393	.892 857	1
2	21.243 387	7.019 692	3.465 106	1.690 051	2
3	30.107 505	9.954 004	4.917 324	2.401 831	3
4	37.973 959	12.561 102	6.209 794	3.037 349	4
5	44.955 038	14.877 475	7.360 087	3.604 776	5
6	51.150 391	16.935 542	8.383 844	4.111 407	6
7	56.648 453	18.764 108	9.294 984	4.563 757	7
8	61.527 703	20.388 766	10.105 895	4.967 640	8
9	65.857 790	21.832 252	10.827 603	5.328 250	9
10	69.700 522	23.114 772	11.469 921	5.650 223	10
11	73.110 752	24.254 274	12.041 582	5.937 699	11
12	76.137 157	25.266 707	12.550 358	6.194 374	12
13	78.822 939	26.166 240	13.003 166	6.423 548	13
14	81.206 434	26.965 464	13.406 164	6.628 168	14
15	83.321 664	27.675 564	13.764 831	6.810 864	15
16	85.198 824	28.306 478	14.084 043	6.973 986	16
17	86.864 707	28.867 038	14.368 141	7.119 630	17
18	88.343 095	29.365 088	14.620 987	7.249 670	18
19	89.655 089	29.807 598	14.846 019	7.365 777	19
20	90.819 416	30.200 763	15.046 297	7.469 444	20
21	91.852 698	30.550 086	15.224 543	7.562 003	21
22	92.769 683	30.860 454	15.383 182	7.644 646	22
23	93.583 461	31.136 212	15.524 370	7.718 434	23
24	94.305 647	31.381 219	15.650 027	7.784 316	24
25	94.946 551	31.598 905	15.761 861	7.843 139	25
26	95.515 321	31.792 317	15.861 393	7.895 660	26
27	96.020 075	31.964 160	15.949 976	7.942 554	27
28	96.468 019	32.116 840	16.028 814	7.984 423	28
29	96.865 546	32.252 495	16.098 980	8.021 806	29
30	97.218 331	32.373 023	16.161 428	8.055 184	30
31	97.531 410	32.480 110	16.217 006	8.084 986	31
32	97.809 252	32.575 255	16.266 470	8.111 594	32
33	98.055 822	32.659 791	16.310 493	8.135 352	33
34	98.274 641	32.734 899	16.349 673	8.156 564	34
35	98.468 831	32.801 633	16.384 544	8.175 504	35
36	98.641 166	32.860 924	16.415 578	8.192 414	36
37	98.794 103	32.913 604	16.443 199	8.207 513	37
38	98.929 828	32.960 409	16.467 781	8.220 993	38
39	99.050 277	33.001 995	16.489 659	8.233 030	39
40	99.157 169	33.038 944	16.509 131	8.243 777	40

ORDINARY LEVEL ANNUITY 12½%
(Present Value of $1 per period)

Base: 1.010 417   1.031 250   1.062 500   1.125 000

Frequency of Payments

Months	Monthly	Quarterly	Semiannual	Annual	Months
1	.989 691	—	—	—	1
2	1.969 178	—	—	—	2
3	2.938 568	.969 697	—	—	3
4	3.897 965	—	—	—	4
5	4.847 470	—	—	—	5
6	5.787 187	1.910 009	.941 176	—	6
7	6.717 216	—	—	—	7
8	7.637 657	—	—	—	8
9	8.548 609	2.821 827	—	—	9
10	9.450 170	—	—	—	10
11	10.342 436	—	—	—	11

Years	Monthly	Quarterly	Semiannual	Annual	Years
1	11.225 504	3.706 014	1.826 990	.888 889	1
2	21.138 383	6.982 824	3.445 361	1.679 012	2
3	29.892 126	9.880 137	4.878 936	2.381 344	3
4	37.622 274	12.441 903	6.148 815	3.005 639	4
5	44.448 517	14.706 984	7.273 691	3.560 568	5
6	50.476 552	16.709 739	8.270 121	4.053 839	6
7	55.799 715	18.480 549	9.152 771	4.492 301	7
8	60.500 428	20.046 276	9.934 635	4.882 045	8
9	64.651 476	21.430 672	10.627 220	5.228 485	9
10	68.317 132	22.654 737	11.240 721	5.536 431	10
11	71.554 154	23.737 040	11.784 168	5.810 161	11
12	74.412 664	24.693 997	12.265 560	6.053 476	12
13	76.936 921	25.540 127	12.691 984	6.269 757	13
14	79.166 011	26.288 264	13.069 716	6.462 006	14
15	81.134 449	26.949 757	13.404 316	6.632 894	15
16	82.872 712	27.534 640	13.700 709	6.784 795	16
17	84.407 717	28.051 787	13.963 258	6.919 818	17
18	85.763 229	28.509 041	14.195 827	7.039 838	18
19	86.960 239	28.913 339	14.401 840	7.146 523	19
20	88.017 279	29.270 815	14.584 329	7.241 353	20
21	88.950 717	29.586 890	14.745 980	7.325 647	21
22	89.775 006	29.866 359	14.889 172	7.400 575	22
23	90.502 909	30.113 462	15.016 014	7.467 178	23
24	91.145 697	30.331 948	15.128 372	7.526 381	24
25	91.713 322	30.525 130	15.227 901	7.579 005	25
26	92.214 573	30.695 939	15.316 064	7.625 782	26
27	92.657 212	30.846 966	15.394 161	7.667 362	27
28	93.048 092	30.980 502	15.463 340	7.704 322	28
29	93.393 265	31.098 573	15.524 619	7.737 175	29
30	93.698 077	31.202 970	15.578 902	7.766 378	30
31	93.967 246	31.295 277	15.626 985	7.792 336	31
32	94.204 941	31.376 893	15.669 579	7.815 410	32
33	94.414 841	31.449 057	15.707 309	7.835 920	33
34	94.600 198	31.512 863	15.740 730	7.854 151	34
35	94.763 880	31.569 280	15.770 335	7.870 356	35
36	94.908 422	31.619 163	15.796 560	7.884 761	36
37	95.036 063	31.663 269	15.819 790	7.897 565	37
38	95.148 778	31.702 266	15.840 368	7.908 947	38
39	95.248 314	31.736 748	15.858 596	7.919 064	39
40	95.336 210	31.767 236	15.874 742	7.928 057	40

13%

ORDINARY LEVEL ANNUITY
(Present Value of $1 per period)

Base: 1.010 833   1.032 500   1.065 000   1.130 000

Frequency of Payments

Months	Monthly	Quarterly	Semiannual	Annual	Months
1	.989 283	—	—	—	1
2	1.967 963	—	—	—	2
3	2.936 155	.968 523	—	—	3
4	3.893 970	—	—	—	4
5	4.841 520	—	—	—	5
6	5.778 915	1.906 560	.938 967	—	6
7	6.706 264	—	—	—	7
8	7.623 674	—	—	—	8
9	8.531 253	2.815 070	—	—	9
10	9.429 104	—	—	—	10
11	10.317 333	—	—	—	11

Years	Monthly	Quarterly	Semiannual	Annual	Years
1	11.196 042	3.694 983	1.820 626	.884 956	1
2	21.034 112	6.946 247	3.425 799	1.668 102	2
3	29.678 917	9.807 076	4.841 014	2.361 153	3
4	37.275 190	12.324 358	6.088 751	2.974 471	4
5	43.950 107	14.539 346	7.188 830	3.517 231	5
6	49.815 421	16.488 343	8.158 725	3.997 550	6
7	54.969 328	18.203 292	9.013 842	4.422 610	7
8	59.498 115	19.712 297	9.767 764	4.798 770	8
9	63.477 604	21.040 090	10.432 466	5.131 655	9
10	66.974 419	22.208 433	11.018 507	5.426 243	10
11	70.047 103	23.236 473	11.535 196	5.686 941	11
12	72.747 100	24.141 059	11.990 739	5.917 647	12
13	75.119 613	24.937 016	12.392 373	6.121 812	13
14	77.204 363	25.637 389	12.746 477	6.302 488	14
15	79.036 253	26.253 656	13.058 676	6.462 379	15
16	80.645 952	26.795 918	13.333 929	6.603 875	16
17	82.060 410	27.273 061	13.576 609	6.729 093	17
18	83.303 307	27.692 905	13.790 570	6.839 905	18
19	84.395 453	28.062 332	13.979 210	6.937 969	19
20	85.355 132	28.387 395	14.145 527	7.024 752	20
21	86.198 412	28.673 422	14.292 161	7.101 550	21
22	86.939 409	28.925 102	14.421 443	7.169 513	22
23	87.590 531	29.146 557	14.535 426	7.229 658	23
24	88.162 677	29.341 419	14.635 919	7.282 883	24
25	88.665 428	29.512 881	14.724 521	7.329 985	25
26	89.107 200	29.663 752	14.802 637	7.371 668	26
27	89.495 389	29.796 506	14.871 509	7.408 556	27
28	89.836 495	29.913 317	14.932 230	7.441 200	28
29	90.136 227	30.016 101	14.985 766	7.470 088	29
30	90.399 605	30.106 542	15.032 966	7.495 653	30
31	90.631 038	30.186 123	15.074 580	7.518 277	31
32	90.834 400	30.256 146	15.111 270	7.538 299	32
33	91.013 097	30.317 761	15.143 618	7.556 016	33
34	91.170 119	30.371 977	15.172 138	7.571 696	34
35	91.308 095	30.419 682	15.197 282	7.585 572	35
36	91.429 337	30.461 658	15.219 452	7.597 851	36
37	91.535 873	30.498 593	15.238 997	7.608 718	37
38	91.629 487	30.531 093	15.256 230	7.618 334	38
39	91.711 747	30.559 691	15.271 423	7.626 844	39
40	91.784 030	30.584 854	15.284 818	7.634 376	40

ORDINARY LEVEL ANNUITY

(Present Value of $1 per period)

13½%

Base: 1.011 250   1.033 750   1.067 500   1.135 000

Frequency of Payments

Months	Monthly	Quarterly	Semiannual	Annual	Months
1	.988 875	—	—	—	1
2	1.966 749	—	—	—	2
3	2.933 745	.967 352	—	—	3
4	3.889 982	—	—	—	4
5	4.835 582	—	—	—	5
6	5.770 662	1.903 122	.936 768	—	6
7	6.695 339	—	—	—	7
8	7.609 730	—	—	—	8
9	8.513 948	2.808 340	—	—	9
10	9.408 107	—	—	—	10
11	10.292 318	—	—	—	11

Years					Years
1	11.166 693	3.684 005	1.814 303	.881 057	1
2	20.930 567	6.909 958	3.406 416	1.657 319	2
3	29.467 851	9.734 812	4.803 551	2.341 250	3
4	36.932 637	12.208 438	6.029 584	2.943 833	4
5	43.459 656	14.374 505	7.105 471	3.474 743	5
6	49.166 717	16.271 253	8.049 600	3.942 505	6
7	54.156 827	17.932 169	8.878 105	4.354 630	7
8	58.520 052	19.386 575	9.605 146	4.717 735	8
9	62.335 146	20.660 147	10.243 151	5.037 652	9
10	65.670 968	21.775 369	10.803 021	5.319 517	10
11	68.587 726	22.751 930	11.294 327	5.567 857	11
12	71.138 066	23.607 070	11.725 465	5.786 658	12
13	73.368 018	24.355 886	12.103 804	5.979 434	13
14	75.317 832	25.011 597	12.435 809	6.149 281	14
15	77.022 700	25.585 781	12.727 155	6.298 926	15
16	78.513 394	26.088 574	12.982 821	6.430 772	16
17	79.816 818	26.528 852	13.207 177	6.546 936	17
18	80.956 500	26.914 387	13.404 057	6.649 283	18
19	81.953 009	27.251 987	13.576 826	6.739 456	19
20	82.824 331	27.547 612	13.728 437	6.818 904	20
21	83.586 193	27.806 480	13.861 481	6.888 902	21
22	84.252 345	28.033 162	13.978 231	6.950 575	22
23	84.834 813	28.231 659	14.080 684	7.004 912	23
24	85.344 107	28.405 476	14.170 589	7.052 786	24
25	85.789 421	28.557 681	14.249 485	7.094 965	25
26	86.178 793	28.690 962	14.318 718	7.132 128	26
27	86.519 249	28.807 671	14.379 473	7.164 870	27
28	86.816 936	28.909 870	14.432 787	7.193 718	28
29	87.077 226	28.999 361	14.479 572	7.219 135	29
30	87.304 817	29.077 726	14.520 628	7.241 529	30
31	87.503 816	29.146 347	14.556 656	7.261 259	31
32	87.677 816	29.206 436	14.588 271	7.278 642	32
33	87.829 958	29.259 054	14.616 015	7.293 958	33
34	87.962 986	29.305 129	14.640 361	7.307 452	34
35	88.079 303	29.345 476	14.661 726	7.319 341	35
36	88.181 007	29.380 806	14.680 474	7.329 816	36
37	88.269 935	29.411 744	14.696 926	7.339 045	37
38	88.347 692	29.438 835	14.711 363	7.347 176	38
39	88.415 680	29.462 557	14.724 032	7.354 340	39
40	88.475 127	29.483 330	14.735 150	7.360 652	40

14%

ORDINARY LEVEL ANNUITY
(Present Value of $1 per period)

Base:	1.011 667	1.035 000	1.070 000	1.140 000	
			Frequency of Payments		
Months	Monthly	Quarterly	Semiannual	Annual	Months
1	.988 468	—	—	—	1
2	1.965 537	—	—	—	2
3	2.931 338	.966 184	—	—	3
4	3.886 001	—	—	—	4
5	4.829 655	—	—	—	5
6	5.762 427	1.899 694	.934 579	—	6
7	6.684 442	—	—	—	7
8	7.595 824	—	—	—	8
9	8.496 696	2.801 637	—	—	9
10	9.387 178	—	—	—	10
11	10.267 392	—	—	—	11
Years					**Years**
1	11.137 455	3.673 079	1.808 018	.877 193	1
2	20.827 743	6.873 956	3.387 211	1.646 661	2
3	29.258 904	9.663 334	4.766 540	2.321 632	3
4	36.594 546	12.094 117	5.971 299	2.913 712	4
5	42.977 016	14.212 403	7.023 582	3.433 081	5
6	48.530 168	16.058 368	7.942 686	3.888 668	6
7	53.361 760	17.667 019	8.745 468	4.288 305	7
8	57.565 549	19.068 865	9.446 649	4.638 864	8
9	61.223 111	20.290 494	10.059 087	4.946 372	9
10	64.405 420	21.355 072	10.594 014	5.216 116	10
11	67.174 230	22.282 791	11.061 240	5.452 733	11
12	69.583 269	23.091 244	11.469 334	5.660 292	12
13	71.679 284	23.795 765	11.825 779	5.842 362	13
14	73.502 950	24.409 713	12.137 111	6.002 072	14
15	75.089 654	24.944 734	12.409 041	6.142 168	15
16	76.470 187	25.410 974	12.646 555	6.265 060	16
17	77.671 337	25.817 245	12.854 009	6.372 859	17
18	78.716 413	26.171 343	13.035 208	6.467 420	18
19	79.625 696	26.479 892	13.193 473	6.550 369	19
20	80.416 829	26.748 776	13.331 709	6.623 131	20
21	81.105 164	26.983 092	13.452 449	6.686 957	21
22	81.704 060	27.187 285	13.557 908	6.742 944	22
23	82.225 136	27.365 227	13.650 020	6.792 056	23
24	82.678 506	27.520 294	13.730 474	6.835 137	24
25	83.072 966	27.655 425	13.800 746	6.872 927	25
26	83.416 171	27.773 185	13.862 124	6.906 077	26
27	83.714 781	27.875 805	13.915 735	6.935 155	27
28	83.974 591	27.965 233	13.962 560	6.960 662	28
29	84.200 641	28.043 164	14.003 458	6.983 037	29
30	84.397 320	28.111 077	14.039 181	7.002 664	30
31	84.568 442	28.170 258	14.070 383	7.019 881	31
32	84.717 330	28.221 832	14.097 635	7.034 983	32
33	84.846 871	28.266 775	14.121 439	7.048 231	33
34	84.959 580	28.305 941	14.142 230	7.059 852	34
35	85.057 645	28.340 071	14.160 389	7.070 045	35
36	85.142 966	28.369 814	14.176 251	7.078 987	36
37	85.217 202	28.395 733	14.190 104	7.086 831	37
38	85.281 792	28.418 320	14.202 205	7.093 711	38
39	85.337 989	28.438 004	14.212 774	7.099 747	39
40	85.386 883	28.455 156	14.222 005	7.105 041	40

ORDINARY LEVEL ANNUITY

(Present Value of $1 per period)

14½%

Base:	1.012 083	1.036 250	1.072 500	1.145 000	
		Frequency of Payments			
Months	Monthly	Quarterly	Semiannual	Annual	Months
1	.988 061	—	—	—	1
2	1.964 325	—	—	—	2
3	2.928 934	.965 018	—	—	3
4	3.882 026	—	—	—	4
5	4.823 739	—	—	—	5
6	5.754 209	1.896 278	.932 401	—	6
7	6.673 570	—	—	—	7
8	7.581 955	—	—	—	8
9	8.479 495	2.794 961	—	—	9
10	9.366 318	—	—	—	10
11	10.242 554	—	—	—	11
Years					Years
1	11.108 328	3.662 206	1.801 772	.873 362	1
2	20.725 634	6.838 235	3.368 182	1.636 124	2
3	29.052 051	9.592 632	4.729 974	2.302 292	3
4	36.260 850	11.981 368	5.913 877	2.884 098	4
5	42.502 042	14.052 988	6.943 128	3.392 225	5
6	47.905 507	15.849 590	7.837 930	3.836 005	6
7	52.583 688	17.407 684	8.615 846	4.223 585	7
8	56.633 938	18.758 933	9.292 143	4.562 083	8
9	60.140 540	19.930 797	9.880 097	4.857 714	9
10	63.176 466	20.947 091	10.391 247	5.115 908	10
11	65.804 893	21.828 467	10.835 626	5.341 404	11
12	68.080 518	22.592 835	11.221 957	5.538 344	12
13	70.050 696	23.255 730	11.557 822	5.710 344	13
14	71.756 425	23.830 622	11.849 814	5.860 563	14
15	73.233 202	24.329 195	12.103 663	5.991 758	15
16	74.511 757	24.761 579	12.324 352	6.106 339	16
17	75.618 698	25.136 563	12.516 213	6.206 409	17
18	76.577 058	25.461 765	12.683 011	6.293 807	18
19	77.406 782	25.743 795	12.828 021	6.370 137	19
20	78.125 136	25.988 384	12.954 088	6.436 801	20
21	78.747 069	26.200 503	13.063 687	6.495 023	21
22	79.285 522	26.384 462	13.158 970	6.545 871	22
23	79.751 701	26.544 000	13.241 806	6.590 281	23
24	80.155 306	26.682 358	13.313 821	6.629 066	24
25	80.504 738	26.802 348	13.376 429	6.662 940	25
26	80.807 267	26.906 410	13.430 858	6.692 524	26
27	81.069 189	26.996 656	13.478 178	6.718 362	27
28	81.295 954	27.074 922	13.519 316	6.740 927	28
29	81.492 281	27.142 797	13.555 081	6.760 635	29
30	81.662 256	27.201 662	13.586 173	6.777 847	30
31	81.809 416	27.252 712	13.613 204	6.792 880	31
32	81.936 824	27.296 986	13.636 704	6.806 008	32
33	82.047 130	27.335 381	13.657 134	6.817 475	33
34	82.142 630	27.368 679	13.674 896	6.827 489	34
35	82.225 312	27.397 557	13.690 337	6.836 235	35
36	82.296 896	27.422 601	13.703 761	6.843 873	36
37	82.358 871	27.444 321	13.715 432	6.850 544	37
38	82.412 528	27.463 157	13.725 578	6.856 370	38
39	82.458 982	27.479 492	13.734 399	6.861 459	39
40	82.499 201	27.493 659	13.742 067	6.865 903	40

15%

ORDINARY LEVEL ANNUITY
(Present Value of $1 per period)

Base:	1.012 500	1.037 500	1.075 000	1.150 000	
			Frequency of Payments		
Months	Monthly	Quarterly	Semiannual	Annual	Months
1	.987 654	—	—	—	1
2	1.963 115	—	—	—	2
3	2.926 534	.963 855	—	—	3
4	3.878 058	—	—	—	4
5	4.817 835	—	—	—	5
6	5.746 010	1.892 873	.930 233	—	6
7	6.662 726	—	—	—	7
8	7.568 124	—	—	—	8
9	8.462 345	2.788 311	—	—	9
10	9.345 526	—	—	—	10
11	10.217 803	—	—	—	11
Years					Years
1	11.079 312	3.651 384	1.795 565	.869 565	1
2	20.624 235	6.802 796	3.349 326	1.625 709	2
3	28.847 267	9.522 694	4.693 846	2.283 225	3
4	35.931 481	11.870 165	5.857 304	2.854 978	4
5	42.034 592	13.896 204	6.864 081	3.352 155	5
6	47.292 474	15.644 824	7.735 278	3.784 483	6
7	51.822 185	17.154 011	8.489 154	4.160 420	7
8	55.724 570	18.456 549	9.141 507	4.487 322	8
9	59.086 509	19.580 735	9.706 009	4.771 584	9
10	61.982 847	20.550 990	10.194 491	5.018 769	10
11	64.478 068	21.388 391	10.617 191	5.233 712	11
12	66.627 722	22.111 129	10.982 967	5.420 619	12
13	68.479 668	22.734 904	11.299 485	5.583 147	13
14	70.075 134	23.273 268	11.573 378	5.724 476	14
15	71.449 643	23.737 916	11.810 386	5.847 370	15
16	72.633 794	24.138 941	12.015 478	5.954 235	16
17	73.653 950	24.485 054	12.192 950	6.047 161	17
18	74.532 823	24.783 776	12.346 522	6.127 966	18
19	75.289 980	25.041 594	12.479 414	6.198 231	19
20	75.942 278	25.264 110	12.594 409	6.259 331	20
21	76.504 237	25.456 158	12.693 918	6.312 462	21
22	76.988 370	25.621 909	12.780 026	6.358 663	22
23	77.405 455	25.764 965	12.854 539	6.398 837	23
24	77.764 777	25.888 432	12.919 017	6.433 771	24
25	78.074 336	25.994 993	12.974 812	6.464 149	25
26	78.341 024	26.086 963	13.023 093	6.490 564	26
27	78.570 778	26.166 340	13.064 872	6.513 534	27
28	78.768 713	26.234 848	13.101 025	6.533 508	28
29	78.939 236	26.293 976	13.132 309	6.550 877	29
30	79.086 142	26.345 007	13.159 381	6.565 980	30
31	79.212 704	26.389 051	13.182 806	6.579 113	31
32	79.321 738	26.427 064	13.203 078	6.590 533	32
33	79.415 671	26.459 872	13.220 619	6.600 463	33
34	79.496 596	26.488 188	13.235 798	6.609 099	34
35	79.566 313	26.512 627	13.248 933	6.616 607	35
36	79.626 375	26.533 719	13.260 299	6.623 137	36
37	79.678 119	26.551 923	13.270 134	6.628 815	37
38	79.722 696	26.567 634	13.278 645	6.633 752	38
39	79.761 101	26.581 195	13.286 010	6.638 045	39
40	79.794 186	26.592 898	13.292 383	6.641 778	40

ORDINARY LEVEL ANNUITY   15½%
(Present Value of $1 per period)

Base: 1.012 917   1.038 750   1.077 500   1.155 000

Frequency of Payments

Months	Monthly	Quarterly	Semiannual	Annual	Months
1	.987 248	—	—	—	1
2	1.961 907	—	—	—	2
3	2.924 137	.962 696	—	—	3
4	3.874 096	—	—	—	4
5	4.811 942	—	—	—	5
6	5.737 828	1.889 478	.928 074	—	6
7	6.651 908	—	—	—	7
8	7.554 331	—	—	—	8
9	8.445 247	2.781 688	—	—	9
10	9.324 801	—	—	—	10
11	10.193 140	—	—	—	11

Years					Years
1	11.050 406	3.640 614	1.789 396	.865 801	1
2	20.523 538	6.767 633	3.330 642	1.615 412	2
3	28.644 529	9.453 511	4.658 151	2.264 426	3
4	35.606 374	11.760 483	5.801 563	2.826 343	4
5	41.574 525	13.742 001	6.786 409	3.312 851	5
6	46.690 816	15.443 979	7.634 678	3.734 070	6
7	51.076 835	16.905 852	8.365 310	4.098 762	7
8	54.836 819	18.161 493	8.994 620	4.414 513	8
9	58.060 124	19.239 997	9.536 659	4.687 890	9
10	60.823 352	20.166 351	10.003 528	4.924 580	10
11	63.192 173	20.962 022	10.405 653	5.129 506	11
12	65.222 881	21.645 444	10.752 012	5.306 932	12
13	66.963 738	22.232 453	11.050 338	5.460 547	13
14	68.456 114	22.736 651	11.307 293	5.593 547	14
15	69.735 477	23.169 719	11.528 614	5.708 699	15
16	70.832 231	23.541 693	11.719 243	5.808 397	16
17	71.772 440	23.861 191	11.883 436	5.894 716	17
18	72.578 449	24.135 616	12.024 858	5.969 451	18
19	73.269 413	24.371 327	12.146 669	6.034 157	19
20	73.861 752	24.573 786	12.251 587	6.090 179	20
21	74.369 545	24.747 683	12.341 955	6.138 683	21
22	74.804 857	24.897 047	12.419 791	6.180 678	22
23	75.178 036	25.025 340	12.486 833	6.217 037	23
24	75.497 949	25.135 535	12.544 577	6.248 517	24
25	75.772 200	25.230 183	12.594 314	6.275 772	25
26	76.007 306	25.311 480	12.637 153	6.299 370	26
27	76.208 854	25.381 307	12.674 052	6.319 801	27
28	76.381 634	25.441 284	12.705 833	6.337 490	28
29	76.529 752	25.492 800	12.733 207	6.352 805	29
30	76.656 729	25.537 048	12.756 785	6.366 065	30
31	76.765 582	25.575 054	12.777 093	6.377 546	31
32	76.858 898	25.607 698	12.794 585	6.387 485	32
33	76.938 894	25.635 737	12.809 651	6.396 091	33
34	77.007 473	25.659 820	12.822 628	6.403 542	34
35	77.066 262	25.680 506	12.833 805	6.409 993	35
36	77.116 661	25.698 274	12.843 432	6.415 579	36
37	77.159 866	25.713 535	12.851 724	6.420 414	37
38	77.196 904	25.726 643	12.858 866	6.424 601	38
39	77.228 655	25.737 902	12.865 018	6.428 226	39
40	77.255 875	25.747 572	12.870 317	6.431 365	40

16%

ORDINARY LEVEL ANNUITY
(Present Value of $1 per period)

Base:	1.013 333	1.040 000	1.080 000	1.160 000	
			Frequency of Payments		
Months	Monthly	Quarterly	Semiannual	Annual	Months
1	.986 842	—	—	—	1
2	1.960 699	—	—	—	2
3	2.921 743	.961 538	—	—	3
4	3.870 141	—	—	—	4
5	4.806 060	—	—	—	5
6	5.729 665	1.886 095	.925 926	—	6
7	6.641 116	—	—	—	7
8	7.540 575	—	—	—	8
9	8.428 199	2.775 091	—	—	9
10	9.304 144	—	—	—	10
11	10.168 563	—	—	—	11

Years					Years
1	11.021 609	3.629 895	1.783 265	.862 069	1
2	20.423 539	6.732 745	3.312 127	1.605 232	2
3	28.443 811	9.385 074	4.622 880	2.245 890	3
4	35.285 465	11.652 296	5.746 639	2.798 181	4
5	41.121 706	13.590 326	6.710 081	3.274 294	5
6	46.100 283	15.246 963	7.536 078	3.684 736	6
7	50.347 235	16.663 063	8.244 237	4.038 565	7
8	53.970 077	17.873 551	8.851 369	4.343 591	8
9	57.060 524	18.908 282	9.371 887	4.606 544	9
10	59.696 816	19.792 774	9.818 147	4.833 227	10
11	61.945 692	20.548 841	10.200 744	5.028 644	11
12	63.864 085	21.195 131	10.528 758	5.197 107	12
13	65.500 561	21.747 582	10.809 978	5.342 334	13
14	66.896 549	22.219 819	11.051 078	5.467 529	14
15	68.087 390	22.623 490	11.257 783	5.575 456	15
16	69.103 231	22.968 549	11.434 999	5.668 497	16
17	69.969 789	23.263 507	11.586 934	5.748 704	17
18	70.709 003	23.515 639	11.717 193	5.817 848	18
19	71.339 585	23.731 162	11.828 869	5.877 455	19
20	71.877 501	23.915 392	11.924 613	5.928 841	20
21	72.336 367	24.072 872	12.006 699	5.973 139	21
22	72.727 801	24.207 487	12.077 074	6.011 326	22
23	73.061 711	24.322 557	12.137 409	6.044 247	23
24	73.346 552	24.420 919	12.189 136	6.072 627	24
25	73.589 534	24.504 999	12.233 485	6.097 092	25
26	73.796 809	24.576 871	12.271 506	6.118 183	26
27	73.973 623	24.638 308	12.304 103	6.136 364	27
28	74.124 454	24.690 824	12.332 050	6.152 038	28
29	74.253 120	24.735 715	12.356 010	6.165 550	29
30	74.362 878	24.774 088	12.376 552	6.177 198	30
31	74.456 506	24.806 889	12.394 163	6.187 240	31
32	74.536 375	24.834 928	12.409 262	6.195 897	32
33	74.604 507	24.858 896	12.422 207	6.203 359	33
34	74.662 626	24.879 384	12.433 305	6.209 792	34
35	74.712 205	24.896 897	12.442 820	6.215 338	35
36	74.754 498	24.911 867	12.450 977	6.220 119	36
37	74.790 576	24.924 663	12.457 971	6.224 241	37
38	74.821 352	24.935 602	12.463 967	6.227 794	38
39	74.847 605	24.944 952	12.469 107	6.230 857	39
40	74.870 000	24.952 945	12.473 514	6.233 497	40

ORDINARY LEVEL ANNUITY
(Present Value of $1 per period)

16½%

Base: 1.013 750   1.041 250   1.082 500   1.165 000

Frequency of Payments

Months	Monthly	Quarterly	Semiannual	Annual	Months
1	.986 436	—	—	—	1
2	1.959 493	—	—	—	2
3	2.919 352	.960 384	—	—	3
4	3.866 192	—	—	—	4
5	4.800 190	—	—	—	5
6	5.721 519	1.882 722	.923 788	—	6
7	6.630 351	—	—	—	7
8	7.526 857	—	—	—	8
9	8.411 203	2.768 520	—	—	9
10	9.283 554	—	—	—	10
11	10.144 073	—	—	—	11

Years					Years
1	10.992 921	3.619 227	1.777 171	.858 369	1
2	20.324 232	6.698 129	3.293 779	1.595 167	2
3	28.245 091	9.317 372	4.588 027	2.227 611	3
4	34.968 691	11.545 579	5.692 517	2.770 481	4
5	40.676 001	13.441 131	6.635 071	3.236 465	5
6	45.520 636	15.053 690	7.439 430	3.636 450	6
7	49.632 991	16.425 505	8.125 857	3.979 786	7
8	53.123 753	17.592 517	8.711 642	4.274 494	8
9	56.086 877	18.585 302	9.211 542	4.527 463	9
10	58.602 117	19.429 872	9.638 148	4.744 603	10
11	60.737 172	20.148 353	10.002 206	4.930 990	11
12	62.549 508	20.759 570	10.312 888	5.090 978	12
13	64.087 904	21.279 536	10.578 018	5.228 308	13
14	65.393 767	21.721 875	10.804 276	5.346 187	14
15	66.502 246	22.098 175	10.997 361	5.447 371	15
16	67.443 176	22.418 297	11.162 136	5.534 224	16
17	68.241 881	22.690 627	11.302 752	5.608 776	17
18	68.919 860	22.922 299	11.422 752	5.672 769	18
19	69.495 360	23.119 385	11.525 158	5.727 699	19
20	69.983 873	23.287 047	11.612 549	5.774 849	20
21	70.398 545	23.429 678	11.687 128	5.815 321	21
22	70.750 538	23.551 016	11.750 772	5.850 061	22
23	71.049 327	23.654 238	11.805 085	5.879 880	23
24	71.302 953	23.742 050	11.851 434	5.905 477	24
25	71.518 243	23.816 753	11.890 988	5.927 448	25
26	71.700 991	23.880 303	11.924 743	5.946 307	26
27	71.856 116	23.934 365	11.953 548	5.962 495	27
28	71.987 794	23.980 356	11.978 131	5.976 391	28
29	72.099 568	24.019 481	11.999 109	5.988 318	29
30	72.194 447	24.052 765	12.017 011	5.998 557	30
31	72.274 985	24.081 080	12.032 289	6.007 345	31
32	72.343 350	24.105 167	12.045 326	6.014 888	32
33	72.401 381	24.125 659	12.056 452	6.021 363	33
34	72.450 640	24.143 091	12.065 947	6.026 921	34
35	72.492 454	24.157 921	12.074 050	6.031 692	35
36	72.527 947	24.170 537	12.080 965	6.035 787	36
37	72.558 076	24.181 269	12.086 866	6.039 302	37
38	72.583 650	24.190 399	12.091 901	6.042 320	38
39	72.605 359	24.198 166	12.096 199	6.044 909	39
40	72.623 787	24.204 773	12.099 866	6.047 133	40

17%

ORDINARY LEVEL ANNUITY
(Present Value of $1 per period)

Base:	1.014 167	1.042 500	1.085 000	1.170 000	
			Frequency of Payments		
Months	Monthly	Quarterly	Semiannual	Annual	Months
1	.986 031	—	—	—	1
2	1.958 289	—	—	—	2
3	2.916 965	.959 233	—	—	3
4	3.862 250	—	—	—	4
5	4.794 330	—	—	—	5
6	5.713 391	1.879 360	.921 659	—	6
7	6.619 613	—	—	—	7
8	7.513 176	—	—	—	8
9	8.394 257	2.761 976	—	—	9
10	9.263 031	—	—	—	10
11	10.119 669	—	—	—	11

Years					Years
1	10.964 341	3.608 610	1.771 114	.854 701	1
2	20.225 611	6.663 782	3.275 597	1.585 214	2
3	28.048 345	9.250 395	4.553 587	2.209 585	3
4	34.655 988	11.440 309	5.639 183	2.743 235	4
5	40.237 278	13.294 366	6.561 348	3.199 346	5
6	44.951 636	14.864 073	7.344 686	3.589 185	6
7	48.933 722	16.193 041	8.010 097	3.922 380	7
8	52.297 278	17.318 190	8.575 333	4.207 163	8
9	55.138 379	18.270 780	9.055 476	4.450 566	9
10	57.538 177	19.077 275	9.463 337	4.658 604	10
11	59.565 218	19.760 081	9.809 796	4.836 413	11
12	61.277 403	20.338 168	10.104 097	4.988 387	12
13	62.723 638	20.827 596	10.354 093	5.118 280	13
14	63.945 231	21.241 962	10.566 453	5.229 299	14
15	64.977 077	21.592 779	10.746 844	5.324 187	15
16	65.848 648	21.889 793	10.900 078	5.405 288	16
17	66.584 839	22.141 254	11.030 243	5.474 605	17
18	67.206 679	22.354 150	11.140 812	5.533 851	18
19	67.731 930	22.534 395	11.234 736	5.584 488	19
20	68.175 595	22.686 997	11.314 520	5.627 767	20
21	68.550 346	22.816 195	11.382 293	5.664 758	21
22	68.866 887	22.925 578	11.439 864	5.696 375	22
23	69.134 261	23.018 185	11.488 767	5.723 397	23
24	69.360 104	23.096 590	11.530 308	5.746 493	24
25	69.550 868	23.162 970	11.565 595	5.766 234	25
26	69.712 000	23.219 170	11.595 570	5.783 106	26
27	69.848 104	23.266 750	11.621 033	5.797 526	27
28	69.963 067	23.307 034	11.642 662	5.809 851	28
29	70.060 174	23.341 139	11.661 035	5.820 386	29
30	70.142 196	23.370 014	11.676 642	5.829 390	30
31	70.211 479	23.394 460	11.689 900	5.837 085	31
32	70.270 000	23.415 157	11.701 161	5.843 663	32
33	70.319 431	23.432 680	11.710 728	5.849 284	33
34	70.361 184	23.447 515	11.718 854	5.854 089	34
35	70.396 451	23.460 075	11.725 757	5.858 196	35
36	70.426 241	23.470 709	11.731 620	5.861 706	36
37	70.451 403	23.479 712	11.736 601	5.864 706	37
38	70.472 657	23.487 334	11.740 832	5.867 270	38
39	70.490 609	23.493 788	11.744 426	5.869 461	39
40	70.505 773	23.499 251	11.747 479	5.871 335	40

(Present Value of $1 per period)

Base: 1.014 583   1.043 750   1.087 500   1.175 000

Frequency of Payments

Months	Monthly	Quarterly	Semiannual	Annual	Months
1	.985 626	—	—	—	1
2	1.957 085	—	—	—	2
3	2.914 581	.958 084	—	—	3
4	3.858 314	—	—	—	4
5	4.788 482	—	—	—	5
6	5.705 280	1.876 008	.919 540	—	6
7	6.608 900	—	—	—	7
8	7.499 532	—	—	—	8
9	8.377 362	2.755 457	—	—	9
10	9.242 575	—	—	—	10
11	10.095 351	—	—	—	11

Years					Years
1	10.935 869	3.598 043	1.765 094	.851 064	1
2	20.127 671	6.629 702	3.257 578	1.575 373	2
3	27.853 550	9.184 134	4.519 553	2.191 807	3
4	34.347 296	11.336 463	5.586 622	2.716 432	4
5	39.805 409	13.149 983	6.488 886	3.162 921	5
6	44.393 055	14.678 030	7.251 800	3.542 911	6
7	48.249 057	15.965 540	7.896 884	3.866 307	7
8	51.490 098	17.050 377	8.442 338	4.141 538	8
9	54.214 253	17.964 445	8.903 549	4.375 777	9
10	56.503 956	18.734 626	9.293 528	4.575 129	10
11	58.428 493	19.383 570	9.623 277	4.744 791	11
12	60.046 103	19.930 360	9.902 097	4.889 184	12
13	61.405 734	20.391 078	10.137 854	5.012 071	13
14	62.548 529	20.779 272	10.337 200	5.116 657	14
15	63.509 070	21.106 359	10.505 758	5.205 665	15
16	64.316 422	21.381 957	10.648 282	5.281 417	16
17	64.995 017	21.614 173	10.768 795	5.345 887	17
18	65.565 388	21.809 834	10.870 695	5.400 755	18
19	66.044 796	21.974 695	10.956 856	5.447 451	19
20	66.447 747	22.113 605	11.029 711	5.487 192	20
21	66.786 434	22.230 649	11.091 313	5.521 015	21
22	67.071 108	22.329 268	11.143 401	5.549 800	22
23	67.310 381	22.412 363	11.187 444	5.574 298	23
24	67.511 495	22.482 378	11.224 686	5.595 147	24
25	67.680 535	22.541 371	11.256 175	5.612 891	25
26	67.822 616	22.591 078	11.282 801	5.627 992	26
27	67.942 037	22.632 961	11.305 314	5.640 845	27
28	68.042 414	22.668 250	11.324 351	5.651 783	28
29	68.126 782	22.697 985	11.340 447	5.661 092	29
30	68.197 695	22.723 038	11.354 058	5.669 014	30
31	68.257 298	22.744 148	11.365 566	5.675 757	31
32	68.307 396	22.761 935	11.375 297	5.681 495	32
33	68.349 504	22.776 922	11.383 525	5.686 379	33
34	68.384 897	22.789 550	11.390 482	5.690 535	34
35	68.414 645	22.800 190	11.396 365	5.694 072	35
36	68.439 649	22.809 155	11.401 339	5.697 083	36
37	68.460 666	22.816 709	11.405 545	5.699 645	37
38	68.478 330	22.823 074	11.409 101	5.701 826	38
39	68.493 178	22.828 437	11.412 108	5.703 681	39
40	68.505 657	22.832 956	11.414 651	5.705 261	40

18%

ORDINARY LEVEL ANNUITY
(Present Value of $1 per period)

Base: 1.015 000   1.045 000   1.090 000   1.180 000

Frequency of Payments

Months	Monthly	Quarterly	Semiannual	Annual	Months
1	.985 222	—	—	—	1
2	1.955 883	—	—	—	2
3	2.912 200	.956 938	—	—	3
4	3.854 385	—	—	—	4
5	4.782 645	—	—	—	5
6	5.697 187	1.872 668	.917 431	—	6
7	6.598 214	—	—	—	7
8	7.485 925	—	—	—	8
9	8.360 517	2.748 964	—	—	9
10	9.222 185	—	—	—	10
11	10.071 118	—	—	—	11

Years	Monthly	Quarterly	Semiannual	Annual	Years
1	10.907 505	3.587 526	1.759 111	.847 458	1
2	20.030 405	6.595 886	3.239 720	1.565 642	2
3	27.660 684	9.118 581	4.485 919	2.174 273	3
4	34.042 554	11.234 015	5.534 819	2.690 062	4
5	39.380 269	13.007 936	6.417 658	3.127 171	5
6	43.844 667	14.495 478	7.160 725	3.497 603	6
7	47.578 633	15.742 874	7.786 150	3.811 528	7
8	50.701 675	16.788 891	8.312 558	4.077 566	8
9	53.313 749	17.666 041	8.755 625	4.303 022	9
10	55.498 454	18.401 584	9.128 546	4.494 086	10
11	57.325 714	19.018 383	9.442 425	4.656 005	11
12	58.854 011	19.535 607	9.706 612	4.793 225	12
13	60.132 260	19.969 330	9.928 972	4.909 513	13
14	61.201 371	20.333 034	10.116 128	5.008 062	14
15	62.095 562	20.638 022	10.273 654	5.091 578	15
16	62.843 452	20.893 773	10.406 240	5.162 354	16
17	63.468 978	21.108 236	10.517 835	5.222 334	17
18	63.992 160	21.288 077	10.611 763	5.273 164	18
19	64.429 743	21.438 884	10.690 820	5.316 241	19
20	64.795 732	21.565 345	10.757 360	5.352 746	20
21	65.101 841	21.671 390	10.813 366	5.383 683	21
22	65.357 866	21.760 316	10.860 505	5.409 901	22
23	65.572 002	21.834 885	10.900 181	5.432 120	23
24	65.751 103	21.897 417	10.933 575	5.450 949	24
25	65.900 901	21.949 853	10.961 683	5.466 906	25
26	66.026 190	21.993 824	10.985 340	5.480 429	26
27	66.130 980	22.030 696	11.005 252	5.491 889	27
28	66.218 625	22.061 616	11.022 012	5.501 601	28
29	66.291 930	22.087 544	11.036 118	5.509 831	29
30	66.353 242	22.109 286	11.047 991	5.516 806	30
31	66.404 522	22.127 518	11.057 984	5.522 717	31
32	66.447 412	22.142 807	11.066 395	5.527 726	32
33	66.483 285	22.155 628	11.073 475	5.531 971	33
34	66.513 289	22.166 379	11.079 433	5.535 569	34
35	66.538 383	22.175 394	11.084 449	5.538 618	35
36	66.559 372	22.182 954	11.088 670	5.541 201	36
37	66.576 927	22.189 293	11.092 223	5.543 391	37
38	66.591 609	22.194 909	11.095 213	5.545 247	38
39	66.603 890	22.199 067	11.097 730	5.546 819	39
40	66.614 161	22.202 805	11.099 849	5.548 152	40

ORDINARY LEVEL ANNUITY
(Present Value of $1 per period)

Base:	1.015 833	1.047 500	1.095 000	1.190 000	
			Frequency of Payments		
Months	Monthly	Quarterly	Semiannual	Annual	Months
1	.984 413	—	—	—	1
2	1.953 483	—	—	—	2
3	2.907 449	.954 654	—	—	3
4	3.846 545	—	—	—	4
5	4.771 004	—	—	—	5
6	5.681 054	1.866 018	.913 242	—	6
7	6.576 920	—	—	—	7
8	7.458 822	—	—	—	8
9	8.326 978	2.736 055	—	—	9
10	9.181 602	—	—	—	10
11	10.022 906	—	—	—	11

Years					Years
1	10.851 097	3.566 640	1.747 253	.840 336	1
2	19.837 878	6.529 036	3.204 481	1.546 501	2
3	27.280 649	8.989 557	4.419 825	2.139 917	3
4	33.444 684	11.033 228	5.433 436	2.638 586	4
5	38.549 682	12.730 669	6.278 798	3.057 635	5
6	42.777 596	14.140 538	6.983 839	3.409 777	6
7	46.279 115	15.311 553	7.571 852	3.705 695	7
8	49.179 042	16.284 180	8.062 260	3.954 366	8
9	51.580 735	17.092 029	8.471 266	4.163 332	9
10	53.569 796	17.763 016	8.812 382	4.338 935	10
11	55.217 118	18.320 328	9.096 876	4.486 500	11
12	56.581 415	18.783 222	9.334 148	4.610 504	12
13	57.711 314	19.167 695	9.532 034	4.714 709	13
14	58.647 086	19.487 032	9.697 074	4.802 277	14
15	59.422 084	19.752 269	9.834 719	4.875 863	15
16	60.063 930	19.972 570	9.949 517	4.937 700	16
17	60.595 501	20.155 549	10.045 259	4.989 664	17
18	61.035 743	20.307 529	10.125 109	5.033 331	18
19	61.400 348	20.433 761	10.191 705	5.070 026	19
20	61.702 310	20.538 607	10.247 247	5.100 862	20
21	61.952 393	20.625 691	10.293 569	5.126 775	21
22	62.159 509	20.698 021	10.332 203	5.148 550	22
23	62.331 041	20.758 098	10.364 423	5.166 849	23
24	62.473 102	20.807 996	10.391 296	5.182 226	24
25	62.590 755	20.849 441	10.413 707	5.195 148	25
26	62.688 195	20.883 865	10.432 399	5.206 007	26
27	62.768 894	20.912 456	10.447 988	5.215 132	27
28	62.835 728	20.936 204	10.460 990	5.222 800	28
29	62.891 079	20.955 929	10.471 833	5.229 243	29
30	62.936 920	20.972 312	10.480 877	5.234 658	30
31	62.974 886	20.985 919	10.488 419	5.239 209	31
32	63.006 328	20.997 221	10.494 710	5.243 033	32
33	63.032 369	21.006 609	10.499 956	5.246 246	33
34	63.053 935	21.014 406	10.504 331	5.248 946	34
35	63.071 796	21.020 882	10.507 980	5.251 215	35
36	63.086 589	21.026 261	10.511 024	5.253 122	36
37	63.098 840	21.030 728	10.513 562	5.254 724	37
38	63.108 986	21.034 439	10.515 679	5.256 071	38
39	63.117 389	21.037 521	10.517 445	5.257 202	39
40	63.124 348	21.040 081	10.518 917	5.258 153	40

20%

ORDINARY LEVEL ANNUITY
(Present Value of $1 per period)

Base: 1.016 667   1.050 000   1.100 000   1.200 000

Frequency of Payments

Months	Monthly	Quarterly	Semiannual	Annual	Months
1	.983 607	—	—	—	1
2	1.951 088	—	—	—	2
3	2.902 710	.952 381	—	—	3
4	3.838 731	—	—	—	4
5	4.759 408	—	—	—	5
6	5.664 991	1.859 410	.909 091	—	6
7	6.555 729	—	—	—	7
8	7.431 865	—	—	—	8
9	8.293 637	2.723 248	—	—	9
10	9.141 283	—	—	—	10
11	9.975 032	—	—	—	11

Years					Years
1	10.795 113	3.545 951	1.735 537	.833 333	1
2	19.647 986	6.463 213	3.169 865	1.527 778	2
3	26.908 062	8.863 252	4.355 261	2.106 481	3
4	32.861 916	10.837 770	5.334 926	2.588 735	4
5	37.744 561	12.462 210	6.144 567	2.990 612	5
6	41.748 727	13.798 642	6.813 692	3.325 510	6
7	45.032 470	14.898 127	7.366 687	3.604 592	7
8	47.725 406	15.802 677	7.823 709	3.837 160	8
9	49.933 833	16.546 852	8.201 412	4.030 967	9
10	51.744 924	17.159 086	8.513 564	4.192 472	10
11	53.230 165	17.662 773	8.771 540	4.327 060	11
12	54.448 184	18.077 158	8.984 744	4.439 217	12
13	55.447 059	18.418 073	9.160 945	4.532 681	13
14	56.266 217	18.698 545	9.306 567	4.610 567	14
15	56.937 994	18.929 290	9.426 914	4.675 473	15
16	57.488 906	19.119 124	9.526 376	4.729 561	16
17	57.940 698	19.275 301	9.608 575	4.774 634	17
18	58.311 205	19.403 788	9.676 508	4.812 195	18
19	58.615 050	19.509 495	9.732 651	4.843 496	19
20	58.864 229	19.596 460	9.779 051	4.869 580	20
21	59.068 575	19.668 007	9.817 397	4.891 316	21
22	59.236 156	19.726 869	9.849 089	4.909 430	22
23	59.373 585	19.775 294	9.875 280	4.924 525	23
24	59.486 289	19.815 134	9.896 926	4.937 104	24
25	59.578 715	19.847 910	9.914 814	4.947 587	25
26	59.654 512	19.874 875	9.929 599	4.956 323	26
27	59.716 672	19.897 060	9.941 817	4.963 602	27
28	59.767 648	19.915 311	9.951 915	4.969 668	28
29	59.809 452	19.930 326	9.960 260	4.974 724	29
30	59.843 735	19.942 679	9.967 157	4.978 936	30
31	59.871 850	19.952 842	9.972 857	4.982 447	31
32	59.894 907	19.961 203	9.977 568	4.985 372	32
33	59.913 815	19.968 081	9.981 461	4.987 810	33
34	59.929 321	19.973 741	9.984 679	4.989 842	34
35	59.942 038	19.978 396	9.987 338	4.991 535	35
36	59.952 466	19.982 227	9.989 535	4.992 946	36
37	59.961 018	19.985 378	9.991 351	4.994 122	37
38	59.968 032	19.987 970	9.992 852	4.995 101	38
39	59.973 784	19.990 103	9.994 093	4.995 918	39
40	59.978 500	19.991 858	9.995 118	4.996 598	40

ORDINARY LEVEL ANNUITY 21%
(Present Value of $1 per period)

Base:	1.017 500	1.052 500	1.105 000	1.210 000	
		Frequency of Payments			
Months	Monthly	Quarterly	Semiannual	Annual	Months
1	.982 801	—	—	—	1
2	1.948 699	—	—	—	2
3	2.897 984	.950 119	—	—	3
4	3.830 943	—	—	—	4
5	4.747 855	—	—	—	5
6	5.648 998	1.852 844	.904 977	—	6
7	6.534 641	—	—	—	7
8	7.405 053	—	—	—	8
9	8.260 494	2.710 541	—	—	9
10	9.101 223	—	—	—	10
11	9.927 492	—	—	—	11

Years					Years
1	10.739 550	3.525 455	1.723 961	.826 446	1
2	19.460 686	6.398 396	3.135 858	1.509 460	2
3	26.542 753	8.739 595	4.292 179	2.073 934	3
4	32.293 801	10.647 469	5.239 188	2.540 441	4
5	36.963 986	12.202 223	6.014 773	2.925 984	5
6	40.756 445	13.469 212	6.649 964	3.244 615	6
7	43.836 142	14.501 699	7.170 176	3.507 946	7
8	46.337 035	15.343 087	7.596 221	3.725 576	8
9	48.367 904	16.028 745	7.945 146	3.905 434	9
10	50.017 087	16.587 498	8.230 909	4.054 078	10
11	51.356 319	17.042 333	8.464 945	4.176 924	11
12	52.443 854	17.413 891	8.656 616	4.278 450	12
13	53.326 994	17.716 272	8.813 592	4.362 355	13
14	54.044 156	17.962 686	8.942 153	4.431 698	14
15	54.626 532	18.163 493	9.047 442	4.489 007	15
16	55.099 456	18.327 132	9.133 672	4.536 369	16
17	55.483 497	18.460 485	9.204 293	4.575 512	17
18	55.795 361	18.569 155	9.262 131	4.607 861	18
19	56.048 612	18.657 712	9.309 499	4.634 596	19
20	56.254 267	18.729 879	9.348 292	4.656 691	20
21	56.421 270	18.788 688	9.380 064	4.674 951	21
22	56.556 887	18.836 613	9.406 084	4.690 042	22
23	56.667 015	18.875 667	9.427 394	4.702 514	23
24	56.756 446	18.907 493	9.444 847	4.712 822	24
25	56.829 069	18.933 428	9.459 140	4.721 340	25
26	56.888 043	18.954 564	9.470 847	4.728 380	26
27	56.935 933	18.971 787	9.480 434	4.734 199	27
28	56.974 823	18.985 822	9.488 285	4.739 007	28
29	57.006 404	18.997 260	9.494 716	4.742 981	29
30	57.032 049	19.006 581	9.499 982	4.746 265	30
31	57.052 875	19.014 176	9.504 295	4.748 980	31
32	57.069 786	19.020 366	9.507 828	4.751 223	32
33	57.083 519	19.025 410	9.510 721	4.753 077	33
34	57.094 671	19.029 521	9.513 090	4.754 609	34
35	57.103 727	19.032 871	9.515 030	4.755 875	35
36	57.111 082	19.035 600	9.516 620	4.756 922	36
37	57.117 054	19.037 825	9.517 921	4.757 786	37
38	57.121 903	19.039 638	9.518 987	4.758 501	38
39	57.125 841	19.041 115	9.519 860	4.759 092	39
40	57.129 039	19.042 319	9.520 575	4.759 580	40

22%

ORDINARY LEVEL ANNUITY
(Present Value of $1 per period)

Base:	1.018 333	1.055 000	1.110 000	1.220 000	
		Frequency of Payments			
Months	Monthly	Quarterly	Semiannual	Annual	Months
1	.981 997	—	—	—	1
2	1.946 314	—	—	—	2
3	2.893 271	.947 867	—	—	3
4	3.823 179	—	—	—	4
5	4.736 346	—	—	—	5
6	5.633 073	1.846 320	.900 901	—	6
7	6.513 656	—	—	—	7
8	7.378 386	—	—	—	8
9	8.227 548	2.697 933	—	—	9
10	9.061 421	—	—	—	10
11	9.880 283	—	—	—	11
Years					Years
1	10.684 402	3.505 150	1.712 523	.819 672	1
2	19.275 936	6.334 566	3.102 446	1.491 535	2
3	26.184 554	8.618 518	4.230 538	2.042 241	3
4	31.739 908	10.462 162	5.146 123	2.493 641	4
5	36.207 074	11.950 382	5.889 232	2.863 640	5
6	39.799 209	13.151 699	6.492 356	3.166 918	6
7	42.687 714	14.121 422	6.981 865	3.415 506	7
8	45.010 417	14.904 198	7.379 162	3.619 268	8
9	46.878 147	15.536 068	7.701 617	3.786 285	9
10	48.380 024	16.046 125	7.963 328	3.923 184	10
11	49.587 713	16.457 851	8.175 739	4.035 397	11
12	50.558 839	16.790 203	8.348 137	4.127 375	12
13	51.339 740	17.058 483	8.488 058	4.202 766	13
14	51.967 678	17.275 043	8.601 622	4.264 562	14
15	52.472 614	17.449 854	8.693 793	4.315 215	15
16	52.878 644	17.590 965	8.768 600	4.356 734	16
17	53.205 140	17.704 871	8.829 316	4.390 765	17
18	53.467 682	17.796 819	8.878 594	4.418 660	18
19	53.678 797	17.871 040	8.918 590	4.441 525	19
20	53.848 558	17.930 953	8.951 051	4.460 266	20
21	53.985 067	17.979 316	8.977 397	4.475 628	21
22	54.094 836	18.018 355	8.998 780	4.488 220	22
23	54.183 103	18.049 868	9.016 135	4.498 541	23
24	54.254 081	18.075 306	9.030 221	4.507 001	24
25	54.311 155	18.095 839	9.041 653	4.513 935	25
26	54.357 050	18.112 415	9.050 932	4.519 619	26
27	54.393 955	18.125 794	9.058 463	4.524 278	27
28	54.423 631	18.136 595	9.064 575	4.528 096	28
29	54.447 494	18.145 313	9.069 536	4.531 227	29
30	54.466 682	18.152 351	9.073 562	4.533 792	30
31	54.482 112	18.158 032	9.076 830	4.535 895	31
32	54.494 520	18.162 617	9.079 482	4.537 619	32
33	54.504 497	18.166 319	9.081 635	4.539 032	33
34	54.512 520	18.169 307	9.083 382	4.540 190	34
35	54.518 971	18.171 719	9.084 800	4.541 140	35
36	54.524 159	18.173 666	9.085 951	4.541 918	36
37	54.528 330	18.175 237	9.086 885	4.542 555	37
38	54.531 684	18.176 506	9.087 643	4.543 078	38
39	54.534 382	18.177 530	9.088 258	4.543 507	39
40	54.536 551	18.178 357	9.088 757	4.543 858	40

ORDINARY LEVEL ANNUITY

23%

(Present Value of $1 per period)

Base:	1.019 167	1.057 500	1.115 000	1.230 000	
			Frequency of Payments		
Months	Monthly	Quarterly	Semiannual	Annual	Months
1	.981 194	—	—	—	1
2	1.943 935	—	—	—	2
3	2.888 571	.945 626	—	—	3
4	3.815 441	—	—	—	4
5	4.724 881	—	—	—	5
6	5.617 218	1.839 836	.896 861	—	6
7	6.492 773	—	—	—	7
8	7.351 862	—	—	—	8
9	8.194 795	2.685 424	—	—	9
10	9.021 876	—	—	—	10
11	9.833 403	—	—	—	11
Years					Years
1	10.629 667	3.485 035	1.701 221	.813 008	1
2	19.093 696	6.271 705	3.069 614	1.473 990	2
3	25.833 304	8.499 956	4.170 294	2.011 374	3
4	31.199 816	10.281 688	5.055 637	2.448 272	4
5	35.472 979	11.706 381	5.767 771	2.803 473	5
6	38.875 549	12.845 580	6.340 583	3.092 254	6
7	41.584 895	13.756 495	6.801 329	3.327 036	7
8	43.742 252	14.484 873	7.171 935	3.517 916	8
9	45.460 079	15.067 291	7.470 036	3.673 102	9
10	46.827 924	15.532 999	7.709 816	3.799 270	10
11	47.917 090	15.905 384	7.902 685	3.901 846	11
12	48.784 355	16.203 147	8.057 822	3.985 240	12
13	49.474 928	16.441 241	8.182 607	4.053 041	13
14	50.024 806	16.631 624	8.282 979	4.108 163	14
15	50.462 655	16.783 856	8.363 715	4.152 978	15
16	50.811 299	16.905 582	8.428 655	4.189 413	16
17	51.088 911	17.002 916	8.480 891	4.219 035	17
18	51.309 965	17.080 745	8.522 907	4.243 118	18
19	51.485 981	17.142 978	8.556 703	4.262 698	19
20	51.626 137	17.192 740	8.583 887	4.278 616	20
21	51.737 739	17.232 530	8.605 753	4.291 558	21
22	51.826 603	17.264 347	8.623 341	4.302 079	22
23	51.897 362	17.289 788	8.637 488	4.310 634	23
24	51.953 705	17.310 131	8.648 867	4.317 588	24
25	51.998 569	17.326 397	8.658 020	4.323 243	25
26	52.034 293	17.339 404	8.665 382	4.327 839	26
27	52.062 739	17.349 804	8.671 304	4.331 577	27
28	52.085 389	17.358 120	8.676 068	4.334 615	28
29	52.103 424	17.364 770	8.679 899	4.337 086	29
30	52.117 785	17.370 087	8.682 981	4.339 094	30
31	52.129 221	17.374 339	8.685 460	4.340 727	31
32	52.138 326	17.377 739	8.687 454	4.342 054	32
33	52.145 576	17.380 457	8.689 058	4.343 134	33
34	52.151 349	17.382 631	8.690 348	4.344 011	34
35	52.155 946	17.384 369	8.691 386	4.344 724	35
36	52.159 607	17.385 759	8.692 220	4.345 304	36
37	52.162 522	17.386 870	8.692 892	4.345 776	37
38	52.164 842	17.387 759	8.693 432	4.346 159	38
39	52.166 690	17.388 469	8.693 866	4.346 471	39
40	52.168 162	17.389 037	8.694 216	4.346 724	40

24%

ORDINARY LEVEL ANNUITY
(Present Value of $1 per period)

Base:	1.020 000	1.060 000	1.120 000	1.240 000	
			Frequency of Payments		
Months	Monthly	Quarterly	Semiannual	Annual	Months
1	.980 392	—	—	—	1
2	1.941 561	—	—	—	2
3	2.883 883	.943 396	—	—	3
4	3.807 729	—	—	—	4
5	4.713 460	—	—	—	5
6	5.601 431	1.833 393	.892 857	—	6
7	6.471 991	—	—	—	7
8	7.325 481	—	—	—	8
9	8.162 237	2.673 012	—	—	9
10	8.982 585	—	—	—	10
11	9.786 848	—	—	—	11
Years					Years
1	10.575 341	3.465 106	1.690 051	.806 452	1
2	18.913 926	6.209 794	3.037 349	1.456 816	2
3	25.488 842	8.383 844	4.111 407	1.981 303	3
4	30.673 120	10.105 895	4.967 640	2.404 277	4
5	34.760 887	11.469 921	5.650 223	2.745 384	5
6	37.984 063	12.550 358	6.194 374	3.020 471	6
7	40.525 516	13.406 164	6.628 168	3.242 316	7
8	42.529 434	14.084 043	6.973 986	3.421 222	8
9	44.109 510	14.620 987	7.249 670	3.565 502	9
10	45.355 389	15.046 297	7.469 444	3.681 856	10
11	46.337 756	15.383 182	7.644 646	3.775 691	11
12	47.112 345	15.650 027	7.784 316	3.851 363	12
13	47.723 104	15.861 393	7.895 660	3.912 390	13
14	48.204 683	16.028 814	7.984 423	3.961 605	14
15	48.584 405	16.161 428	8.055 184	4.001 294	15
16	48.883 813	16.266 470	8.111 594	4.033 302	16
17	49.119 894	16.349 673	8.156 564	4.059 114	17
18	49.306 042	16.415 578	8.192 414	4.079 931	18
19	49.452 819	16.467 781	8.220 993	4.096 718	19
20	49.568 552	16.509 131	8.243 777	4.110 257	20
21	49.659 806	16.541 883	8.261 939	4.121 175	21
22	49.731 759	16.567 827	8.276 418	4.129 980	22
23	49.788 494	16.588 376	8.287 961	4.137 080	23
24	49.833 229	16.604 653	8.297 163	4.142 807	24
25	49.868 502	16.617 546	8.304 498	4.147 425	25
26	49.896 315	16.627 759	8.310 346	4.151 149	26
27	49.918 245	16.635 848	8.315 008	4.154 152	27
28	49.935 537	16.642 255	8.318 725	4.156 575	28
29	49.949 171	16.647 331	8.321 687	4.158 528	29
30	49.959 922	16.651 351	8.324 049	4.160 103	30
31	49.968 399	16.654 535	8.325 932	4.161 373	31
32	49.975 083	16.657 057	8.327 433	4.162 398	32
33	49.980 353	16.659 055	8.328 630	4.163 224	33
34	49.984 508	16.660 638	8.329 584	4.163 890	34
35	49.987 785	16.661 891	8.330 344	4.164 428	35
36	49.990 368	16.662 884	8.330 950	4.164 861	36
37	49.992 406	16.663 670	8.331 434	4.165 211	37
38	49.994 012	16.664 293	8.331 819	4.165 492	38
39	49.995 278	16.664 787	8.332 126	4.165 720	39
40	49.996 277	16.665 178	8.332 371	4.165 903	40

ORDINARY LEVEL ANNUITY

25%

(Present Value of $1 per period)

Base:	1.020 833	1.062 500	1.125 000	1.250 000	
		Frequency of Payments			

Months	Monthly	Quarterly	Semiannual	Annual	Months
1	.979 592	—	—	—	1
2	1.939 192	—	—	—	2
3	2.879 208	.941 176	—	—	3
4	3.800 041	—	—	—	4
5	4.702 081	—	—	—	5
6	5.585 712	1.826 990	.888 889	—	6
7	6.451 310	—	—	—	7
8	7.299 242	—	—	—	8
9	8.129 870	2.660 696	—	—	9
10	8.943 546	—	—	—	10
11	9.740 616	—	—	—	11

Years					Years
1	10.521 420	3.445 361	1.679 012	.800 000	1
2	18.736 585	6.148 815	3.005 639	1.440 000	2
3	25.151 016	8.270 121	4.053 839	1.952 000	3
4	30.159 427	9.934 635	4.882 045	2.361 600	4
5	34.070 014	11.240 721	5.536 431	2.689 280	5
6	37.123 415	12.265 560	6.053 476	2.951 424	6
7	39.507 522	13.069 716	6.462 006	3.161 139	7
8	41.369 041	13.700 709	6.784 795	3.328 911	8
9	42.822 522	14.195 827	7.039 838	3.463 129	9
10	43.957 406	14.584 329	7.241 353	3.570 503	10
11	44.843 528	14.889 172	7.400 575	3.656 403	11
12	45.535 414	15.128 372	7.526 381	3.725 122	12
13	46.075 642	15.316 064	7.625 782	3.780 098	13
14	46.497 454	15.463 340	7.704 322	3.824 078	14
15	46.826 807	15.578 902	7.766 378	3.859 263	15
16	47.083 966	15.669 579	7.815 410	3.887 410	16
17	47.284 757	15.740 730	7.854 151	3.909 928	17
18	47.441 536	15.796 560	7.884 761	3.927 942	18
19	47.563 949	15.840 368	7.908 947	3.942 354	19
20	47.659 530	15.874 742	7.928 057	3.953 883	20
21	47.734 160	15.901 715	7.943 156	3.963 107	21
22	47.792 431	15.922 879	7.955 086	3.970 485	22
23	47.837 929	15.939 486	7.964 513	3.976 388	23
24	47.873 455	15.952 517	7.971 961	3.981 111	24
25	47.901 193	15.962 741	7.977 845	3.984 888	25
26	47.922 851	15.970 765	7.982 495	3.987 911	26
27	47.939 762	15.977 060	7.986 169	3.990 329	27
28	47.952 966	15.982 000	7.989 072	3.992 263	28
29	47.963 275	15.985 876	7.991 365	3.993 810	29
30	47.971 325	15.988 917	7.993 178	3.995 048	30
31	47.977 611	15.991 304	7.994 609	3.996 039	31
32	47.982 518	15.993 176	7.995 741	3.996 831	32
33	47.986 350	15.994 646	7.996 635	3.997 465	33
34	47.989 342	15.995 799	7.997 341	3.997 972	34
35	47.991 678	15.996 703	7.997 899	3.998 377	35
36	47.993 502	15.997 413	7.998 340	3.998 702	36
37	47.994 927	15.997 970	7.998 688	3.998 962	37
38	47.996 039	15.998 407	7.998 964	3.999 169	38
39	47.996 907	15.998 750	7.999 181	3.999 335	39
40	47.997 585	15.999 019	7.999 353	3.999 468	40

26%

ORDINARY LEVEL ANNUITY
(Present Value of $1 per period)

Base:	1.021 667	1.065 000	1.130 000	1.260 000	
		Frequency of Payments			
Months	Monthly	Quarterly	Semiannual	Annual	Months
1	.978 793	—	—	—	1
2	1.936 828	—	—	—	2
3	2.874 546	.938 967	—	—	3
4	3.792 378	—	—	—	4
5	4.690 745	—	—	—	5
6	5.570 061	1.820 626	.884 956	—	6
7	6.430 728	—	—	—	7
8	7.273 143	—	—	—	8
9	8.097 693	2.648 476	—	—	9
10	8.904 757	—	—	—	10
11	9.694 705	—	—	—	11

Years					Years
1	10.467 901	3.425 799	1.668 102	.793 651	1
2	18.561 634	6.088 751	2.974 471	1.423 532	2
3	24.819 672	8.158 725	3.997 550	1.923 438	3
4	29.658 359	9.767 764	4.798 770	2.320 189	4
5	33.399 610	11.018 507	5.426 243	2.635 071	5
6	36.292 328	11.990 739	5.917 647	2.884 977	6
7	38.528 965	12.746 477	6.302 488	3.083 315	7
8	40.258 323	13.333 929	6.603 875	3.240 726	8
9	41.595 454	13.790 570	6.839 905	3.365 656	9
10	42.629 318	14.145 527	7.024 752	3.464 806	10
11	43.428 697	14.421 443	7.169 513	3.543 497	11
12	44.046 773	14.635 919	7.282 883	3.605 950	12
13	44.524 667	14.802 637	7.371 668	3.655 516	13
14	44.894 172	14.932 230	7.441 200	3.694 854	14
15	45.179 872	15.032 966	7.495 653	3.726 074	15
16	45.400 774	15.111 270	7.538 299	3.750 853	16
17	45.571 574	15.172 138	7.571 696	3.770 518	17
18	45.703 636	15.219 452	7.597 851	3.786 125	18
19	45.805 746	15.256 230	7.618 334	3.798 512	19
20	45.884 696	15.284 818	7.634 376	3.808 343	20
21	45.945 741	15.307 041	7.646 938	3.816 145	21
22	45.992 940	15.324 315	7.656 777	3.822 338	22
23	46.029 434	15.337 742	7.664 482	3.827 252	23
24	46.057 651	15.348 180	7.670 516	3.831 152	24
25	46.079 469	15.356 293	7.675 242	3.834 248	25
26	46.096 338	15.362 600	7.678 942	3.836 705	26
27	46.109 381	15.367 502	7.681 841	3.838 655	27
28	46.119 466	15.371 313	7.684 111	3.840 202	28
29	46.127 264	15.374 275	7.685 888	3.841 430	29
30	46.133 293	15.376 578	7.687 280	3.842 405	30
31	46.137 954	15.378 367	7.688 370	3.843 178	31
32	46.141 559	15.379 759	7.689 224	3.843 792	32
33	46.144 345	15.380 840	7.689 893	3.844 280	33
34	46.146 500	15.381 681	7.690 417	3.844 666	34
35	46.148 166	15.382 334	7.690 827	3.844 973	35
36	46.149 455	15.382 842	7.691 148	3.845 217	36
37	46.150 451	15.383 237	7.691 399	3.845 410	37
38	46.151 221	15.383 544	7.691 596	3.845 564	38
39	46.151 816	15.383 783	7.691 751	3.845 685	39
40	46.152 277	15.383 968	7.691 871	3.845 782	40

ORDINARY LEVEL ANNUITY

27%

(Present Value of $1 per period)

Base:	1.022 500	1.067 500	1.135 000	1.270 000	
			Frequency of Payments		
Months	Monthly	Quarterly	Semiannual	Annual	Months
1	.977 995	—	—	—	1
2	1.934 470	—	—	—	2
3	2.869 897	.936 768	—	—	3
4	3.784 740	—	—	—	4
5	4.679 453	—	—	—	5
6	5.554 477	1.814 303	.881 057	—	6
7	6.410 246	—	—	—	7
8	7.247 185	—	—	—	8
9	8.065 706	2.636 349	—	—	9
10	8.866 216	—	—	—	10
11	9.649 111	—	—	—	11
Years					Years
1	10.414 779	3.406 416	1.657 319	.787 402	1
2	18.389 036	6.029 584	2.943 833	1.407 403	2
3	24.494 666	8.049 600	3.942 505	1.895 593	3
4	29.169 548	9.605 146	4.717 735	2.279 994	4
5	32.748 953	10.803 021	5.319 517	2.582 673	5
6	35.489 587	11.725 465	5.786 658	2.821 002	6
7	37.588 001	12.435 809	6.149 281	3.008 663	7
8	39.194 689	12.982 821	6.430 772	3.156 428	8
9	40.424 877	13.404 057	6.649 283	3.272 778	9
10	41.366 793	13.728 437	6.818 904	3.364 392	10
11	42.087 987	13.978 231	6.950 575	3.436 529	11
12	42.640 181	14.170 589	7.052 786	3.493 330	12
13	43.062 979	14.318 718	7.132 128	3.538 055	13
14	43.386 701	14.432 787	7.193 718	3.573 272	14
15	43.634 565	14.520 628	7.241 529	3.601 001	15
16	43.824 346	14.588 271	7.278 642	3.622 836	16
17	43.969 655	14.640 361	7.307 452	3.640 028	17
18	44.080 914	14.680 474	7.329 816	3.653 565	18
19	44.166 101	14.711 363	7.347 176	3.664 225	19
20	44.231 326	14.735 150	7.360 652	3.672 618	20
21	44.281 266	14.753 468	7.371 113	3.679 227	21
22	44.319 504	14.767 573	7.379 233	3.684 430	22
23	44.348 782	14.778 436	7.385 537	3.688 528	23
24	44.371 199	14.786 801	7.390 430	3.691 754	24
25	44.388 363	14.793 242	7.394 229	3.694 295	25
26	44.401 504	14.798 202	7.397 177	3.696 295	26
27	44.411 567	14.802 022	7.399 466	3.697 870	27
28	44.419 271	14.804 964	7.401 243	3.699 110	28
29	44.425 170	14.807 229	7.402 622	3.700 087	29
30	44.429 687	14.808 973	7.403 693	3.700 856	30
31	44.433 145	14.810 316	7.404 524	3.701 461	31
32	44.435 793	14.811 351	7.405 169	3.701 938	32
33	44.437 820	14.812 147	7.405 670	3.702 313	33
34	44.439 372	14.812 761	7.406 059	3.702 609	34
35	44.440 561	14.813 233	7.406 360	3.702 842	35
36	44.441 471	` 14.813 597	7.406 595	3.703 025	36
37	44.442 168	14.813 877	7.406 776	3.703 169	37
38	44.442 701	14.814 092	7.406 918	3.703 283	38
39	44.443 110	14.814 259	7.407 027	3.703 372	39
40	44.443 423	14.814 386	7.407 112	3.703 443	40

28%

ORDINARY LEVEL ANNUITY
(Present Value of $1 per period)

Base:	1.023 333	1.070 000	1.140 000	1.280 000	
		Frequency of Payments			
Months	Monthly	Quarterly	Semiannual	Annual	Months
1	.977 199	—	—	—	1
2	1.932 116	—	—	—	2
3	2.865 260	.934 579	—	—	3
4	3.777 127	—	—	—	4
5	4.668 202	—	—	—	5
6	5.538 960	1.808 018	.877 193	—	6
7	6.389 863	—	—	—	7
8	7.221 365	—	—	—	8
9	8.033 907	2.624 316	—	—	9
10	8.827 922	—	—	—	10
11	9.603 832	—	—	—	11
Years					Years
1	10.362 051	3.387 211	1.646 661	.781 250	1
2	18.218 753	5.971 299	2.913 712	1.391 602	2
3	24.175 853	7.942 686	3.888 668	1.868 439	3
4	28.692 637	9.446 649	4.638 864	2.240 968	4
5	32.117 348	10.594 014	5.216 116	2.532 006	5
6	34.714 029	11.469 334	5.660 292	2.759 380	6
7	36.682 881	12.137 111	6.002 072	2.937 015	7
8	38.175 701	12.646 555	6.265 060	3.075 793	8
9	39.307 586	13.035 208	6.467 420	3.184 214	9
10	40.165 802	13.331 709	6.623 131	3.268 917	10
11	40.816 518	13.557 908	6.742 944	3.335 091	11
12	41.309 902	13.730 474	6.835 137	3.386 790	12
13	41.683 996	13.862 124	6.906 077	3.427 180	13
14	41.967 641	13.962 560	6.960 662	3.458 734	14
15	42.182 706	14.039 181	7.002 664	3.483 386	15
16	42.345 772	14.097 635	7.034 983	3.502 645	16
17	42.469 412	14.142 230	7.059 852	3.517 692	17
18	42.563 158	14.176 251	7.078 987	3.529 447	18
19	42.634 238	14.202 205	7.093 711	3.538 630	19
20	42.688 132	14.222 005	7.105 041	3.545 805	20
21	42.728 996	14.237 111	7.113 759	3.551 410	21
22	42.759 979	14.248 635	7.120 467	3.555 789	22
23	42.783 472	14.257 427	7.125 629	3.559 210	23
24	42.801 284	14.264 134	7.129 600	3.561 883	24
25	42.814 790	14.269 251	7.132 656	3.563 971	25
26	42.825 030	14.273 154	7.135 008	3.565 602	26
27	42.832 794	14.276 132	7.136 818	3.566 877	27
28	42.838 681	14.278 404	7.138 210	3.567 873	28
29	42.843 145	14.280 138	7.139 281	3.568 650	29
30	42.846 529	14.281 460	7.140 106	3.569 258	30
31	42.849 095	14.282 469	7.140 740	3.569 733	31
32	42.851 041	14.283 238	7.141 228	3.570 104	32
33	42.852 516	14.283 825	7.141 604	3.570 394	33
34	42.853 635	14.284 273	7.141 893	3.570 620	34
35	42.854 483	14.284 615	7.142 115	3.570 797	35
36	42.855 126	14.284 876	7.142 286	3.570 935	36
37	42.855 614	14.285 074	7.142 418	3.571 043	37
38	42.855 984	14.285 226	7.142 519	3.571 127	38
39	42.856 264	14.285 342	7.142 597	3.571 193	39
40	42.856 476	14.285 430	7.142 657	3.571 245	40

(Present Value of $1 per period)

Base:	1.024 167	1.072 500	1.145 000	1.290 000	
		Frequency of Payments			
Months	Monthly	Quarterly	Semiannual	Annual	Months
1	.976 404	—	—	—	1
2	1.929 768	—	—	—	2
3	2.860 636	.932 401	—	—	3
4	3.769 538	—	—	—	4
5	4.656 994	—	—	—	5
6	5.523 509	1.801 772	.873 362	—	6
7	6.369 578	—	—	—	7
8	7.195 682	—	—	—	8
9	8.002 294	2.612 375	—	—	9
10	8.789 872	—	—	—	10
11	9.558 866	—	—	—	11

Years					Years
1	10.309 714	3.368 182	1.636 124	.775 194	1
2	18.050 749	5.913 877	2.884 098	1.376 119	2
3	23.863 093	7.837 930	3.836 005	1.841 953	3
4	28.227 284	9.292 143	4.562 083	2.203 064	4
5	31.504 130	10.391 247	5.115 908	2.482 996	5
6	33.964 545	11.221 957	5.538 344	2.699 997	6
7	35.811 945	11.849 814	5.860 563	2.868 214	7
8	37.199 062	12.324 352	6.106 339	2.998 616	8
9	38.240 577	12.683 011	6.293 807	3.099 702	9
10	39.022 597	12.954 088	6.436 801	3.178 064	10
11	39.609 775	13.158 970	6.545 871	3.238 809	11
12	40.050 657	13.313 821	6.629 066	3.285 899	12
13	40.381 693	13.430 858	6.692 524	3.322 402	13
14	40.630 251	13.519 316	6.740 927	3.350 699	14
15	40.816 880	13.586 173	6.777 847	3.372 635	15
16	40.957 010	13.636 704	6.806 008	3.389 640	16
17	41.062 227	13.674 896	6.827 489	3.402 821	17
18	41.141 229	13.703 761	6.843 873	3.413 040	18
19	41.200 547	13.725 578	6.856 370	3.420 961	19
20	41.245 086	13.742 067	6.865 903	3.427 102	20
21	41.278 528	13.754 530	6.873 174	3.431 862	21
22	41.303 638	13.763 949	6.878 720	3.435 552	22
23	41.322 492	13.771 069	6.882 950	3.438 412	23
24	41.336 648	13.776 449	6.886 177	3.440 630	24
25	41.347 278	13.780 516	6.888 638	3.442 349	25
26	41.355 259	13.783 590	6.890 516	3.443 681	26
27	41.361 251	13.785 913	6.891 948	3.444 714	27
28	41.365 751	13.787 669	6.893 040	3.445 515	28
29	41.369 129	13.788 996	6.893 873	3.446 135	29
30	41.371 666	13.789 999	6.894 509	3.446 617	30
31	41.373 570	13.790 757	6.894 993	3.446 990	31
32	41.375 001	13.791 330	6.895 363	3.447 279	32
33	41.376 074	13.791 763	6.895 645	3.447 503	33
34	41.376 881	13.792 090	6.895 860	3.447 677	34
35	41.377 486	13.792 338	6.896 024	3.447 811	35
36	41.377 941	13.792 525	6.896 149	3.447 916	36
37	41.378 282	13.792 666	6.896 245	3.447 997	37
38	41.378 538	13.792 773	6.896 318	3.448 059	38
39	41.378 730	13.792 854	6.896 373	3.448 108	39
40	41.378 875	13.792 915	6.896 416	3.448 146	40

30%   ORDINARY LEVEL ANNUITY
(Present Value of $1 per period)

Base:	1.025 000	1.075 000	1.150 000	1.300 000	
		Frequency of Payments			
Months	Monthly	Quarterly	Semiannual	Annual	Months
1	.975 610	—	—	—	1
2	1.927 424	—	—	—	2
3	2.856 024	.930 233	—	—	3
4	3.761 974	—	—	—	4
5	4.645 828	—	—	—	5
6	5.508 125	1.795 565	.869 565	—	6
7	6.349 391	—	—	—	7
8	7.170 137	—	—	—	8
9	7.970 866	2.600 526	—	—	9
10	8.752 064	—	—	—	10
11	9.514 209	—	—	—	11
Years					Years
1	10.257 765	3.349 326	1.625 709	.769 231	1
2	17.884 986	5.857 304	2.854 978	1.360 947	2
3	23.556 251	7.735 278	3.784 483	1.816 113	3
4	27.773 154	9.141 507	4.487 322	2.166 241	4
5	30.908 656	10.194 491	5.018 769	2.435 570	5
6	33.240 078	10.982 967	5.420 619	2.642 746	6
7	34.973 620	11.573 378	5.724 476	2.802 112	7
8	36.262 606	12.015 478	5.954 235	2.924 702	8
9	37.221 039	12.346 522	6.127 966	3.019 001	9
10	37.933 687	12.594 409	6.259 331	3.091 539	10
11	38.463 581	12.780 026	6.358 663	3.147 338	11
12	38.857 586	12.919 017	6.433 771	3.190 260	12
13	39.150 552	13.023 093	6.490 564	3.223 277	13
14	39.368 388	13.101 025	6.533 508	3.248 675	14
15	39.530 361	13.159 381	6.565 980	3.268 211	15
16	39.650 797	13.203 078	6.590 533	3.283 239	16
17	39.740 348	13.235 798	6.609 099	3.294 800	17
18	39.806 934	13.260 299	6.623 137	3.303 692	18
19	39.856 445	13.278 645	6.633 752	3.310 532	19
20	39.893 259	13.292 383	6.641 778	3.315 794	20
21	39.920 632	13.302 669	6.647 848	3.319 842	21
22	39.940 985	13.310 372	6.652 437	3.322 955	22
23	39.956 119	13.316 140	6.655 907	3.325 350	23
24	39.967 372	13.320 459	6.658 531	3.327 192	24
25	39.975 739	13.323 693	6.660 515	3.328 609	25
26	39.981 961	13.326 115	6.662 015	3.329 700	26
27	39.986 587	13.327 928	6.663 149	3.330 538	27
28	39.990 027	13.329 286	6.664 007	3.331 183	28
29	39.992 584	13.330 303	6.664 656	3.331 679	29
30	39.994 486	13.331 064	6.665 146	3.332 061	30
31	39.995 900	13.331 634	6.665 517	3.332 355	31
32	39.996 951	13.332 061	6.665 797	3.332 581	32
33	39.997 733	13.332 380	6.666 009	3.332 754	33
34	39.998 315	13.332 620	6.666 170	3.332 888	34
35	39.998 747	13.332 799	6.666 291	3.332 991	35
36	39.999 068	13.332 933	6.666 382	3.333 070	36
37	39.999 307	13.333 034	6.666 452	3.333 131	37
38	39.999 485	13.333 109	6.666 504	3.333 177	38
39	39.999 617	13.333 165	6.666 544	3.333 213	39
40	39.999 715	13.333 208	6.666 574	3.333 241	40

Table 4

**Ordinary Annuities Changing in Constant Amount
(Present Value of Annual Payments Starting at $1
and Changing in Constant Amounts)**

Table 4 · ORDINARY ANNUITIES CHANGING IN CONSTANT AMOUNT
(Present Value of Annual Payments Starting at $1 and Changing in Constant Amounts)

$$\text{PVF} = (1 + \text{hn})a_{\overline{n}|} - \frac{h(n - a_{\overline{n}|})}{i}$$

Where   PVF = Present Value Factor

            h = Annual Increase or Decrease after 1st Year

            n = Number of Years

         $a_{\overline{n}|}$ = PVF for Ordinary Level Annuity

            i = Rate of Interest/Yield

            (h is positive for increase; negative for decrease)

This Table is used in solving problems dealing with the compound discounting of cash flows that are best represented by a straight-line pattern of change (increase/decrease).

Example 1:
Assuming a 15% interest/yield rate, what is the Present Value of an ordinary annuity of ten annual cash flows that start at $10,000 and increase $1,000 per year?

$10,000 × 6.7167 = $67,167

Same example assuming payments in advance.

$67,167 × 1.150000 = $77,242
          OR
$67,167/.869565 = $77,242

Example 2:
Assuming a 15% interest/yield rate, what is the Present Value of an ordinary annuity of ten annual cash flows that start at $10,000 and increase $300 per year?

$10,000 × (5.3584 + 5.6979)/2 = $55,282
            OR
$10,000 × (5.018769 + 16.979477 × .03) = $55,281.53

Example 3:

There are 5 years remaining on a lease that provides a level income of $1,000 per year. Inflation over this period will cause purchasing power to decline an average of 10% per year (straight-line basis). What is the value of the income expressed in constant dollars and discounted at 6%?

$1,000 × (.90 × 4.212364 − 7.934549 × .10) = $2,997.67

PROOF:

Year	Income	×	Inflation Factor	×	PVF @6%	=	Value
1	$1,000	×	.90	×	.943396	=	$ 849.06
2	1,000	×	.80	×	.889996	=	712.00
3	1,000	×	.70	×	.839619	=	587.73
4	1,000	×	.60	×	.792094	=	475.26
5	1,000	×	.50	×	.747258	=	373.63
							$2,997.68

6%

ORDINARY ANNUITIES CHANGING IN CONSTANT AMOUNT

(Present Value of Annual Payments Starting at $1 and Changing in Constant Amounts)

Base: 1.060 000

Annual INCREASE of:

Years	Slope	.00	.02	.04	.05	.10	Years
1	.000 000	.943 396	.9434	.9434	.9434	.9434	1
2	.889 996	1.833 393	1.8512	1.8690	1.8779	1.9224	2
3	2.569 235	2.673 012	2.7244	2.7758	2.8015	2.9299	3
4	4.945 516	3.465 106	3.5640	3.6629	3.7124	3.9597	4
5	7.934 549	4.212 364	4.3711	4.5297	4.6091	5.0058	5
6	11.459 351	4.917 324	5.1465	5.3757	5.4903	6.0633	6
7	15.449 694	5.582 381	5.8914	6.2004	6.3549	7.1274	7
8	19.841 581	6.209 794	6.6066	7.0035	7.2019	8.1940	8
9	24.576 768	6.801 692	7.2932	7.7848	8.0305	9.2594	9
10	29.602 321	7.360 087	7.9521	8.5442	8.8402	10.3203	10
11	34.870 197	7.886 875	8.5843	9.2817	9.6304	11.3739	11
12	40.336 860	8.383 844	9.1906	9.9973	10.4007	12.4175	12
13	45.962 928	8.852 683	9.7719	10.6912	11.1508	13.4490	13
14	51.712 840	9.294 984	10.3292	11.3635	11.8806	14.4663	14
15	57.554 551	9.712 249	10.8633	12.0144	12.5900	15.4677	15
16	63.459 246	10.105 895	11.3751	12.6443	13.2789	16.4518	16
17	69.401 076	10.477 260	11.8653	13.2533	13.9473	17.4174	17
18	75.356 921	10.827 603	12.3347	13.8419	14.5954	18.3633	18
19	81.306 155	11.158 116	12.7842	14.4104	15.2234	19.2887	19
20	87.230 445	11.469 921	13.2145	14.9591	15.8314	20.1930	20

Annual DECREASE of:

Years	Slope	.00	.02	.04	.05	.10	Years
1	.000 000	.943 396	.9434	.9434	.9434	.9434	1
2	− .889 996	1.833 393	1.8156	1.7978	1.7889	1.7444	2
3	− 2.569 235	2.673 012	2.6216	2.5702	2.5446	2.4161	3
4	− 4.945 516	3.465 106	3.3662	3.2673	3.2178	2.9706	4
5	− 7.934 549	4.212 364	4.0537	3.8950	3.8156	3.4189	5
6	− 11.459 351	4.917 324	4.6881	4.4590	4.3444	3.7714	6
7	− 15.449 694	5.582 381	5.2734	4.9644	4.8099	4.0374	7
8	− 19.841 581	6.209 794	5.8130	5.4161	5.2177	4.2256	8
9	− 24.576 768	6.801 692	6.3102	5.8186	5.5729	4.3440	9
10	− 29.602 321	7.360 087	6.7680	6.1760	5.8800	4.3999	10
11	− 34.870 197	7.886 875	7.1895	6.4921	6.1434	—	11
12	− 40.336 860	8.383 844	7.5771	6.7704	6.3670	—	12
13	− 45.962 928	8.852 683	7.9334	7.0142	6.5545	—	13
14	− 51.712 840	9.294 984	8.2607	7.2265	6.7093	—	14
15	− 57.554 551	9.712 249	8.5612	7.4101	6.8345	—	15
16	− 63.459 246	10.105 895	8.8367	7.5675	6.9329	—	16
17	− 69.401 076	10.477 260	9.0892	7.7012	7.0072	—	17
18	− 75.356 921	10.827 603	9.3205	7.8133	7.0598	—	18
19	− 81.306 155	11.158 116	9.5320	7.9059	7.0928	—	19
20	− 87.230 445	11.469 921	9.7253	7.9807	7.1084	—	20

ORDINARY ANNUITIES CHANGING IN CONSTANT AMOUNT

(Present Value of Annual Payments Starting at $1 and Changing in Constant Amounts)

Base: 1.070 000

Annual INCREASE of:

Years	Slope	.00	.02	.04	.05	.10	Years
1	.000 000	.934 579	.9346	.9346	.9346	.9346	1
2	.873 439	1.808 018	1.8255	1.8430	1.8517	1.8954	2
3	2.506 034	2.624 316	2.6744	2.7246	2.7496	2.8749	3
4	4.794 720	3.387 211	3.4831	3.5790	3.6269	3.8667	4
5	7.646 665	4.100 197	4.2531	4.4061	4.4825	4.8649	5
6	10.978 376	4.766 540	4.9861	5.2057	5.3155	5.8644	6
7	14.714 874	5.389 289	5.6836	5.9779	6.1250	6.8608	7
8	18.788 938	5.971 299	6.3471	6.7229	6.9107	7.8502	8
9	23.140 408	6.515 232	6.9780	7.4408	7.6723	8.8293	9
10	27.715 552	7.023 582	7.5779	8.1322	8.4094	9.7951	10
11	32.466 480	7.498 674	8.1480	8.7973	9.1220	10.7453	11
12	37.350 611	7.942 686	8.6897	9.4367	9.8102	11.6777	12
13	42.330 185	8.357 651	9.2043	10.0509	10.4742	12.5907	13
14	47.371 809	8.745 468	9.6929	10.6403	11.1141	13.4826	14
15	52.446 053	9.107 914	10.1568	11.2058	11.7302	14.3525	15
16	57.527 072	9.446 649	10.5972	11.7477	12.3230	15.1994	16
17	62.592 262	9.763 223	11.0151	12.2669	12.8928	16.0224	17
18	67.621 949	10.059 087	11.4115	12.7640	13.4402	16.8213	18
19	72.599 099	10.335 595	11.7876	13.2396	13.9656	17.5955	19
20	77.509 060	10.594 014	12.1442	13.6944	14.4695	18.3449	20

Annual DECREASE of:

Years	Slope	.00	.02	.04	.05	.10	Years
1	.000 000	.934 579	.9346	.9346	.9346	.9346	1
2	— .873 439	1.808 018	1.7905	1.7731	1.7643	1.7207	2
3	— 2.506 034	2.624 316	2.5742	2.5241	2.4990	2.3737	3
4	— 4.794 720	3.387 211	3.2913	3.1954	3.1475	2.9077	4
5	— 7.646 665	4.100 197	3.9473	3.7943	3.7179	3.3355	5
6	— 10.978 376	4.766 540	4.5470	4.3274	4.2176	3.6687	6
7	— 14.714 874	5.389 289	5.0950	4.8007	4.6535	3.9178	7
8	— 18.788 938	5.971 299	5.5955	5.2197	5.0319	4.0924	8
9	— 23.140 408	6.515 232	6.0524	5.5896	5.3582	4.2012	9
10	— 27.715 552	7.023 582	6.4693	5.9150	5.6378	4.2520	10
11	— 32.466 480	7.498 674	6.8493	6.2000	5.8754	—	11
12	— 37.350 611	7.942 686	7.1957	6.4487	6.0752	—	12
13	— 42.330 185	8.357 651	7.5110	6.6644	6.2411	—	13
14	— 47.371 809	8.745 468	7.7980	6.8506	6.3769	—	14
15	— 52.446 053	9.107 914	8.0590	7.0101	6.4856	—	15
16	— 57.527 072	9.446 649	8.2961	7.1456	6.5703	—	16
17	— 62.592 262	9.763 223	8.5114	7.2595	6.6336	—	17
18	— 67.621 949	10.059 087	8.7066	7.3542	6.6780	—	18
19	— 72.599 099	10.335 595	8.8836	7.4316	6.7056	—	19
20	— 77.509 060	10.594 014	9.0438	7.4937	6.7186	—	20

8%

ORDINARY ANNUITIES CHANGING IN CONSTANT AMOUNT

(Present Value of Annual Payments Starting at $1 and Changing in Constant Amounts)

Base: 1.080 000

Annual INCREASE of:

Years	Slope	.00	.02	.04	.05	.10	Years
1	.000 000	.925 926	.9259	.9259	.9259	.9259	1
2	.857 339	1.783 265	1.8004	1.8176	1.8261	1.8690	2
3	2.445 003	2.577 097	2.6260	2.6749	2.6993	2.8216	3
4	4.650 093	3.312 127	3.4051	3.4981	3.5446	3.7771	4
5	7.372 426	3.992 710	4.1402	4.2876	4.3613	4.7300	5
6	10.523 274	4.622 880	4.8333	5.0438	5.1490	5.6752	6
7	14.024 216	5.206 370	5.4869	5.7673	5.9076	6.6088	7
8	17.806 098	5.746 639	6.1028	6.4589	6.6369	7.5272	8
9	21.808 090	6.246 888	6.6830	7.1192	7.3373	8.4277	9
10	25.976 831	6.710 081	7.2296	7.7492	8.0089	9.3078	10
11	30.265 660	7.138 964	7.7443	8.3496	8.6522	10.1655	11
12	34.633 911	7.536 078	8.2288	8.9214	9.2678	10.9995	12
13	39.046 287	7.903 776	8.6847	9.4656	9.8561	11.8084	13
14	43.472 280	8.244 237	9.1137	9.9831	10.4179	12.5915	14
15	47.885 664	8.559 479	9.5172	10.4749	10.9538	13.3480	15
16	52.264 021	8.851 369	9.8966	10.9419	11.4646	14.0778	16
17	56.588 324	9.121 638	10.2534	11.3852	11.9511	14.7805	17
18	60.842 558	9.371 887	10.5887	11.8056	12.4140	15.4561	18
19	65.013 375	9.603 599	10.9039	12.2041	12.8543	16.1049	19
20	69.089 791	9.818 147	11.1999	12.5817	13.2726	16.7271	20

Annual DECREASE of:

Years	Slope	.00	.02	.04	.05	.10	Years
1	.000 000	.925 926	.9259	.9259	.9259	.9259	1
2	— .857 339	1.783 265	1.7661	1.7490	1.7404	1.6975	2
3	— 2.445 003	2.577 097	2.5282	2.4793	2.4548	2.3326	3
4	— 4.650 093	3.312 127	3.2191	3.1261	3.0796	2.8471	4
5	— 7.372 426	3.992 710	3.8453	3.6978	3.6241	3.2555	5
6	— 10.523 274	4.622 880	4.4124	4.2019	4.0967	3.5706	6
7	— 14.024 216	5.206 370	4.9259	4.6454	4.5052	3.8039	7
8	— 17.806 098	5.746 639	5.3905	5.0344	4.8563	3.9660	8
9	— 21.808 090	6.246 888	5.8107	5.3746	5.1565	4.0661	9
10	— 25.976 831	6.710 081	6.1905	5.6710	5.4112	4.1124	10
11	— 30.265 660	7.138 964	6.5337	5.9283	5.6257	—	11
12	— 34.633 911	7.536 078	6.8434	6.1507	5.8044	—	12
13	— 39.046 287	7.903 776	7.1229	6.3419	5.9515	—	13
14	— 43.472 280	8.244 237	7.3748	6.5053	6.0706	—	14
15	— 47.885 664	8.559 479	7.6018	6.6441	6.1652	—	15
16	— 52.264 021	8.851 369	7.8061	6.7608	6.2382	—	16
17	— 56.588 324	9.121 638	7.9899	6.8581	6.2922	—	17
18	— 60.842 558	9.371 887	8.1550	6.9382	6.3298	—	18
19	— 65.013 375	9.603 599	8.3033	7.0031	6.3529	—	19
20	— 69.089 791	9.818 147	8.4364	7.0546	6.3637	—	20

ORDINARY ANNUITIES CHANGING IN CONSTANT AMOUNT

(Present Value of Annual Payments Starting at $1 and Changing in Constant Amounts)

Base: 1.090 000

Annual INCREASE of:

Years	Slope	.00	.02	.04	.05	.10	Years
1	.000 000	.917 431	.9174	.9174	.9174	.9174	1
2	.841 680	1.759 111	1.7759	1.7928	1.8012	1.8433	2
3	2.386 047	2.531 295	2.5790	2.6267	2.6506	2.7699	3
4	4.511 323	3.239 720	3.3299	3.4202	3.4653	3.6909	4
5	7.111 048	3.889 651	4.0319	4.1741	4.2452	4.6008	5
6	10.092 385	4.485 919	4.6878	4.8896	4.9905	5.4952	6
7	13.374 590	5.032 953	5.3004	5.5679	5.7017	6.3704	7
8	16.887 654	5.534 819	5.8726	6.2103	6.3792	7.2236	8
9	20.571 076	5.995 247	6.4067	6.8181	7.0238	8.0524	9
10	24.372 774	6.417 658	6.9051	7.3926	7.6363	8.8549	10
11	28.248 102	6.805 191	7.3702	7.9351	8.2176	9.6300	11
12	32.158 984	7.160 725	7.8039	8.4471	8.7687	10.3766	12
13	36.073 128	7.486 904	8.2084	8.9298	9.2906	11.0942	13
14	39.963 332	7.786 150	8.5854	9.3847	9.7843	11.7825	14
15	43.806 865	8.060 688	8.9368	9.8130	10.2510	12.4414	15
16	47.584 911	8.312 558	9.2643	10.2160	10.6918	13.0710	16
17	51.282 082	8.543 631	9.5693	10.5949	11.1077	13.6718	17
18	54.885 975	8.755 625	9.8533	10.9511	11.4999	14.2442	18
19	58.386 789	8.950 115	10.1179	11.2856	11.8695	14.7888	19
20	61.776 976	9.128 546	10.3641	11.5996	12.2174	15.3062	20

Annual DECREASE of:

Years	Slope	.00	.02	.04	.05	.10	Years
1	.000 000	.917 431	.9174	.9174	.9174	.9174	1
2	— .841 680	1.759 111	1.7423	1.7254	1.7170	1.6749	2
3	— 2.386 047	2.531 295	2.4836	2.4359	2.4120	2.2927	3
4	— 4.511 323	3.239 720	3.1495	3.0593	3.0142	2.7886	4
5	— 7.111 048	3.889 651	3.7474	3.6052	3.5341	3.1785	5
6	— 10.092 385	4.485 919	4.2841	4.0822	3.9813	3.4767	6
7	— 13.374 590	5.032 953	4.7655	4.4980	4.3642	3.6955	7
8	— 16.887 654	5.534 819	5.1971	4.8593	4.6904	3.8461	8
9	— 20.571 076	5.995 247	5.5838	5.1724	4.9667	3.9381	9
10	— 24.372 774	6.417 658	5.9302	5.4427	5.1990	3.9804	10
11	— 28.248 102	6.805 191	6.2402	5.6753	5.3928	—	11
12	— 32.158 984	7.160 725	6.5175	5.8744	5.5528	—	12
13	— 36.073 128	7.486 904	6.7654	6.0440	5.6832	—	13
14	— 39.963 332	7.786 150	6.9869	6.1876	5.7880	—	14
15	— 43.806 865	8.060 688	7.1846	6.3084	5.8703	—	15
16	— 47.584 911	8.312 558	7.3609	6.4092	5.9333	—	16
17	— 51.282 082	8.543 631	7.5180	6.4923	5.9795	—	17
18	— 54.885 975	8.755 625	7.6579	6.5602	6.0113	—	18
19	— 58.386 789	8.950 115	7.7824	6.6146	6.0308	—	19
20	— 61.776 976	9.128 546	7.8930	6.6575	6.0397	—	20

10%

ORDINARY ANNUITIES CHANGING IN CONSTANT AMOUNT

(Present Value of Annual Payments Starting at $1 and Changing in Constant Amounts)

Base: 1.100 000

Annual INCREASE of:

Years	Slope	.00	.02	.04	.05	.10	Years
1	.000 000	.909 091	.9091	.9091	.9091	.9091	1
2	.826 446	1.735 537	1.7521	1.7686	1.7769	1.8182	2
3	2.329 076	2.486 852	2.5334	2.5800	2.6033	2.7198	3
4	4.378 116	3.169 865	3.2574	3.3450	3.3888	3.6077	4
5	6.861 802	3.790 787	3.9280	4.0653	4.1339	4.4770	5
6	9.684 171	4.355 261	4.5489	4.7426	4.8395	5.3237	6
7	12.763 120	4.868 419	5.1237	5.3789	5.5066	6.1447	7
8	16.028 672	5.334 926	5.6555	5.9761	6.1364	6.9378	8
9	19.421 453	5.759 024	6.1475	6.5359	6.7301	7.7012	9
10	22.891 342	6.144 567	6.6024	7.0602	7.2891	8.4337	10
11	26.396 281	6.495 061	7.0230	7.5509	7.8149	9.1347	11
12	29.901 220	6.813 692	7.4117	8.0097	8.3088	9.8038	12
13	33.377 193	7.103 356	7.7709	8.4384	8.7722	10.4411	13
14	36.800 499	7.366 687	8.1027	8.8387	9.2067	11.0467	14
15	40.151 988	7.606 080	8.4091	9.2122	9.6137	11.6213	15
16	43.416 425	7.823 709	8.6920	9.5604	9.9945	12.1654	16
17	46.581 939	8.021 553	8.9532	9.8848	10.3507	12.6797	17
18	49.639 539	8.201 412	9.1942	10.1870	10.6834	13.1654	18
19	52.582 683	8.364 920	9.4166	10.4682	10.9941	13.6232	19
20	55.406 912	8.513 564	9.6217	10.7298	11.2839	14.0543	20

Annual DECREASE of:

Years	Slope	.00	.02	.04	.05	.10	Years
1	.000 000	.909 091	.9091	.9091	.9091	.9091	1
2	− .826 446	1.735 537	1.7190	1.7025	1.6942	1.6529	2
3	− 2.329 076	2.486 852	2.4403	2.3937	2.3704	2.2539	3
4	− 4.378 116	3.169 865	3.0823	2.9947	2.9510	2.7321	4
5	− 6.861 802	3.790 787	3.6536	3.5163	3.4477	3.1046	5
6	− 9.684 171	4.355 261	4.1616	3.9679	3.8711	3.3868	6
7	− 12.763 120	4.868 419	4.6132	4.3579	4.2303	3.5921	7
8	− 16.028 672	5.334 926	5.0144	4.6938	4.5335	3.7321	8
9	− 19.421 453	5.759 024	5.3706	4.9822	4.7880	3.8169	9
10	− 22.891 342	6.144 567	5.6867	5.2289	5.0000	3.8554	10
11	− 26.396 281	6.495 061	5.9671	5.4392	5.1752	—	11
12	− 29.901 220	6.813 692	6.2157	5.6176	5.3186	—	12
13	− 33.377 193	7.103 356	6.4358	5.7683	5.4345	—	13
14	− 36.800 499	7.366 687	6.6307	5.8947	5.5267	—	14
15	− 40.151 988	7.606 080	6.8030	6.0000	5.5985	—	15
16	− 43.416 425	7.823 709	6.9554	6.0871	5.6529	—	16
17	− 46.581 939	8.021 553	7.0899	6.1583	5.6925	—	17
18	− 49.639 539	8.201 412	7.2086	6.2158	5.7194	—	18
19	− 52.582 683	8.364 920	7.3133	6.2616	5.7358	—	19
20	− 55.406 912	8.513 564	7.4054	6.2973	5.7432	—	20

ORDINARY ANNUITIES CHANGING IN CONSTANT AMOUNT

(Present Value of Annual Payments Starting at $1 and Changing in Constant Amounts)

Base: 1.110 000

Annual INCREASE of:

Years	Slope	.00	.02	.04	.05	.10	Years
1	.000 000	.900 901	.9009	.9009	.9009	.9009	1
2	.811 622	1.712 523	1.7288	1.7450	1.7531	1.7937	2
3	2.274 005	2.443 715	2.4892	2.5347	2.5574	2.6711	3
4	4.250 198	3.102 446	3.1874	3.2725	3.3150	3.5275	4
5	6.624 003	3.695 897	3.8284	3.9609	4.0271	4.3583	5
6	9.297 208	4.230 538	4.4165	4.6024	4.6954	5.1603	6
7	12.187 158	4.712 196	4.9559	5.1997	5.3216	5.9309	7
8	15.224 644	5.146 123	5.4506	5.7551	5.9074	6.6686	8
9	18.352 042	5.537 048	5.9041	6.2711	6.4546	7.3723	9
10	21.521 702	5.889 232	6.3197	6.7501	6.9653	8.0414	10
11	24.694 535	6.206 515	6.7004	7.1943	7.4412	8.6760	11
12	27.838 784	6.492 356	7.0491	7.6059	7.8843	9.2762	12
13	30.928 955	6.749 870	7.3684	7.9870	8.2963	9.8428	13
14	33.944 888	6.981 865	7.6608	8.3397	8.6791	10.3764	14
15	36.870 949	7.190 870	7.9283	8.6657	9.0344	10.8780	15
16	39.695 332	7.379 162	8.1731	8.9670	9.3639	11.3487	16
17	42.409 454	7.548 794	8.3970	9.2452	9.6693	11.7897	17
18	45.007 431	7.701 617	8.6018	9.5019	9.9520	12.2024	18
19	47.485 628	7.839 294	8.7890	9.7387	10.2136	12.5879	19
20	49.842 273	7.963 328	8.9602	9.9570	10.4554	12.9476	20

Annual DECREASE of:

Years	Slope	.00	.02	.04	.05	.10	Years
1	.000 000	.900 901	.9009	.9009	.9009	.9009	1
2	− .811 622	1.712 523	1.6963	1.6801	1.6719	1.6314	2
3	− 2.274 005	2.443 715	2.3982	2.3528	2.3300	2.2163	3
4	− 4.250 198	3.102 446	3.0174	2.9324	2.8899	2.6774	4
5	− 6.624 003	3.695 897	3.5634	3.4309	3.3647	3.0335	5
6	− 9.297 208	4.230 538	4.0446	3.8586	3.7657	3.3008	6
7	− 12.187 158	4.712 196	4.4685	4.2247	4.1028	3.4935	7
8	− 15.224 644	5.146 123	4.8416	4.5371	4.3849	3.6237	8
9	− 18.352 042	5.537 048	5.1700	4.8030	4.6194	3.7018	9
10	− 21.521 702	5.889 232	5.4588	5.0284	4.8131	3.7371	10
11	− 24.694 535	6.206 515	5.7126	5.2187	4.9718	—	11
12	− 27.838 784	6.492 356	5.9356	5.3788	5.1004	—	12
13	− 30.928 955	6.749 870	6.1313	5.5127	5.2034	—	13
14	− 33.944 888	6.981 865	6.3030	5.6241	5.2846	—	14
15	− 36.870 949	7.190 870	6.4535	5.7160	5.3473	—	15
16	− 39.695 332	7.379 162	6.5853	5.7913	5.3944	—	16
17	− 42.409 454	7.548 794	6.7006	5.8524	5.4283	—	17
18	− 45.007 431	7.701 617	6.8015	5.9013	5.4512	—	18
19	− 47.485 628	7.839 294	6.8896	5.9399	5.4650	—	19
20	− 49.842 273	7.963 328	6.9665	5.9696	5.4712	—	20

12%

ORDINARY ANNUITIES CHANGING IN CONSTANT AMOUNT

(Present Value of Annual Payments Starting at $1 and Changing in Constant Amounts)

Base: 1.120 000

Annual INCREASE of:

Years	Slope	.00	.02	.04	.05	.10	Years
1	.000 000	.892 857	.8929	.8929	.8929	.8929	1
2	.797 194	1.690 051	1.7060	1.7219	1.7299	1.7698	2
3	2.220 754	2.401 831	2.4462	2.4907	2.5129	2.6239	3
4	4.127 309	3.037 349	3.1199	3.2024	3.2437	3.4501	4
5	6.397 016	3.604 776	3.7327	3.8607	3.9246	4.2445	5
6	8.930 172	4.111 407	4.2900	4.4686	4.5579	5.0044	6
7	11.644 267	4.563 757	4.7966	5.0295	5.1460	5.7282	7
8	14.471 450	4.967 640	5.2571	5.5465	5.6912	6.4148	8
9	17.356 330	5.328 250	5.6754	6.0225	6.1961	7.0639	9
10	20.254 089	5.650 223	6.0553	6.4604	6.6629	7.6756	10
11	23.128 850	5.937 699	6.4003	6.8629	7.0941	8.2506	11
12	25.952 276	6.194 374	6.7134	7.2325	7.4920	8.7896	12
13	28.702 366	6.423 548	6.9976	7.5716	7.8587	9.2938	13
14	31.362 424	6.628 168	7.2554	7.8827	8.1963	9.7644	14
15	33.920 171	6.810 864	7.4893	8.1677	8.5069	10.2029	15
16	36.366 996	6.973 986	7.7013	8.4287	8.7923	10.6107	16
17	38.697 306	7.119 630	7.8936	8.6675	9.0545	10.9894	17
18	40.907 979	7.249 670	8.0678	8.8860	9.2951	11.3405	18
19	42.997 901	7.365 777	8.2257	9.0857	9.5157	11.6656	19
20	44.967 569	7.469 444	8.3688	9.2681	9.7178	11.9662	20

Annual DECREASE of:

Years	Slope	.00	.02	.04	.05	.10	Years
1	.000 000	.892 857	.8929	.8929	.8929	.8929	1
2	— .797 194	1.690 051	1.6741	1.6582	1.6502	1.6103	2
3	— 2.220 754	2.401 831	2.3574	2.3130	2.2908	2.1798	3
4	— 4.127 309	3.037 349	2.9548	2.8723	2.8310	2.6246	4
5	— 6.397 016	3.604 776	3.4768	3.3489	3.2849	2.9651	5
6	— 8.930 172	4.111 407	3.9328	3.7542	3.6649	3.2184	6
7	— 11.644 267	4.563 757	4.3309	4.0980	3.9815	3.3993	7
8	— 14.471 450	4.967 640	4.6782	4.3888	4.2441	3.5205	8
9	— 17.356 330	5.328 250	4.9811	4.6340	4.4604	3.5926	9
10	— 20.254 089	5.650 223	5.2451	4.8401	4.6375	3.6248	10
11	— 23.128 850	5.937 699	5.4751	5.0125	4.7813	—	11
12	— 25.952 276	6.194 374	5.6753	5.1563	4.8968	—	12
13	— 28.702 366	6.423 548	5.8495	5.2755	4.9884	—	13
14	— 31.362 424	6.628 168	6.0009	5.3737	5.0600	—	14
15	— 33.920 171	6.810 864	6.1325	5.4541	5.1149	—	15
16	— 36.366 996	6.973 986	6.2466	5.5193	5.1556	—	16
17	— 38.697 306	7.119 630	6.3457	5.5717	5.1848	—	17
18	— 40.907 979	7.249 670	6.4315	5.6134	5.2043	—	18
19	— 42.997 901	7.365 777	6.5058	5.6459	5.2159	—	19
20	— 44.967 569	7.469 444	6.5701	5.6707	5.2211	—	20

ORDINARY ANNUITIES CHANGING IN CONSTANT AMOUNT

(Present Value of Annual Payments Starting at $1 and Changing in Constant Amounts)

Base: 1.130 000

Annual INCREASE of:

Years	Slope	.00	.02	.04	.05	.10	Years
1	.000 000	.884 956	.8850	.8850	.8850	.8850	1
2	.783 147	1.668 102	1.6838	1.6994	1.7073	1.7464	2
3	2.169 247	2.361 153	2.4045	2.4479	2.4696	2.5781	3
4	4.009 203	2.974 471	3.0547	3.1348	3.1749	3.3754	4
5	6.180 243	3.517 231	3.6408	3.7644	3.8262	4.1353	5
6	8.581 836	3.997 550	4.1692	4.3408	4.4266	4.8557	6
7	11.132 199	4.422 610	4.6453	4.8679	4.9792	5.5358	7
8	13.765 318	4.798 770	5.0741	5.3494	5.4870	6.1753	8
9	16.428 397	5.131 655	5.4602	5.7888	5.9531	6.7745	9
10	19.079 692	5.426 243	5.8078	6.1894	6.3802	7.3342	10
11	21.686 669	5.686 941	6.1207	6.5544	6.7713	7.8556	11
12	24.224 434	5.917 647	6.4021	6.8866	7.1289	8.3401	12
13	26.674 408	6.121 812	6.6553	7.1888	7.4555	8.7893	13
14	29.023 203	6.302 488	6.8830	7.4634	7.7536	9.2048	14
15	31.261 673	6.462 379	7.0876	7.7128	8.0255	9.5885	15
16	33.384 117	6.603 875	7.2716	7.9392	8.2731	9.9423	16
17	35.387 604	6.729 093	7.4368	8.1446	8.4985	10.2679	17
18	37.271 413	6.839 905	7.5853	8.3308	8.7035	10.5670	18
19	39.036 565	6.937 969	7.7187	8.4994	8.8898	10.8416	19
20	40.685 428	7.024 752	7.8385	8.6522	9.0590	11.0933	20

Annual DECREASE of:

Years	Slope	.00	.02	.04	.05	.10	Years
1	.000 000	.884 956	.8850	.8850	.8850	.8850	1
2 —	.783 147	1.668 102	1.6524	1.6368	1.6289	1.5898	2
3 —	2.169 247	2.361 153	2.3178	2.2744	2.2527	2.1442	3
4 —	4.009 203	2.974 471	2.8943	2.8141	2.7740	2.5736	4
5 —	6.180 243	3.517 231	3.3936	3.2700	3.2082	2.8992	5
6 —	8.581 836	3.997 550	3.8259	3.6543	3.5685	3.1394	6
7 —	11.132 199	4.422 610	4.2000	3.9773	3.8660	3.3094	7
8 —	13.765 318	4.798 770	4.5235	4.2482	4.1105	3.4222	8
9 —	16.428 397	5.131 655	4.8031	4.4745	4.3102	3.4888	9
10 —	19.079 692	5.426 243	5.0446	4.6631	4.4723	3.5183	10
11 —	21.686 669	5.686 941	5.2532	4.8195	4.6026	—	11
12 —	24.224 434	5.917 647	5.4332	4.9487	4.7064	—	12
13 —	26.674 408	6.121 812	5.5883	5.0548	4.7881	—	13
14 —	29.023 203	6.302 488	5.7220	5.1416	4.8513	—	14
15 —	31.261 673	6.462 379	5.8371	5.2119	4.8993	—	15
16 —	33.384 117	6.603 875	5.9362	5.2685	4.9347	—	16
17 —	35.387 604	6.729 093	6.0213	5.3136	4.9597	—	17
18 —	37.271 413	6.839 905	6.0945	5.3490	4.9763	—	18
19 —	39.036 565	6.937 969	6.1572	5.3765	4.9861	—	19
20 —	40.685 428	7.024 752	6.2110	5.3973	4.9905	—	20

14%

ORDINARY ANNUITIES CHANGING IN CONSTANT AMOUNT

(Present Value of Annual Payments Starting at $1 and Changing in Constant Amounts)

Base: 1.140 000

Annual INCREASE of:

Years	Slope	.00	.02	.04	.05	.10	Years
1	.000 000	.877 193	.8772	.8772	.8772	.8772	1
2	.769 468	1.646 661	1.6620	1.6774	1.6851	1.7236	2
3	2.119 411	2.321 632	2.3640	2.4064	2.4276	2.5336	3
4	3.895 651	2.913 712	2.9916	3.0695	3.1085	3.3033	4
5	5.973 126	3.433 081	3.5525	3.6720	3.7317	4.0304	5
6	8.251 059	3.888 668	4.0537	4.2187	4.3012	4.7138	6
7	10.648 883	4.288 305	4.5013	4.7143	4.8207	5.3532	7
8	13.102 796	4.638 864	4.9009	5.1630	5.2940	5.9491	8
9	15.562 860	4.946 372	5.2576	5.5689	5.7245	6.5027	9
10	17.990 554	5.216 116	5.5759	5.9357	6.1156	7.0152	10
11	20.356 728	5.452 733	5.8599	6.2670	6.4706	7.4884	11
12	22.639 878	5.660 292	6.1131	6.5659	6.7923	7.9243	12
13	24.824 710	5.842 362	6.3389	6.8353	7.0836	8.3248	13
14	26.900 940	6.002 072	6.5401	7.0781	7.3471	8.6922	14
15	28.862 291	6.142 168	6.7194	7.2967	7.5853	9.0284	15
16	30.705 666	6.265 060	6.8792	7.4933	7.8003	9.3356	16
17	32.430 461	6.372 859	7.0215	7.6701	7.9944	9.6159	17
18	34.038 000	6.467 420	7.1482	7.8289	8.1693	9.8712	18
19	35.531 071	6.550 369	7.2610	7.9716	8.3269	10.1035	19
20	36.913 544	6.623 131	7.3614	8.0997	8.4688	10.3145	20

Annual DECREASE of:

Years	Slope	.00	.02	.04	.05	.10	Years
1	.000 000	.877 193	.8772	.8772	.8772	.8772	1
2 —	.769 468	1.646 661	1.6313	1.6159	1.6082	ꞏ1.5697	2
3 —	2.119 411	2.321 632	2.2792	2.2369	2.2157	2.1097	3
4 —	3.895 651	2.913 712	2.8358	2.7579	2.7189	2.5241	4
5 —	5.973 126	3.433 081	3.3136	3.1942	3.1344	2.8358	5
6 —	8.251 059	3.888 668	3.7236	3.5586	3.4761	3.0636	6
7 —	10.648 883	4.288 305	4.0753	3.8623	3.7559	3.2234	7
8 —	13.102 796	4.638 864	4.3768	4.1148	3.9837	3.3286	8
9 —	15.562 860	4.946 372	4.6351	4.3239	4.1682	3.3901	9
10 —	17.990 554	5.216 116	4.8563	4.4965	4.3166	3.4171	10
11 —	20.356 728	5.452 733	5.0456	4.6385	4.4349	—	11
12 —	22.639 878	5.660 292	5.2075	4.7547	4.5283	—	12
13 —	24.824 710	5.842 362	5.3459	4.8494	4.6011	—	13
14 —	26.900 940	6.002 072	5.4641	4.9260	4.6570	—	14
15 —	28.862 291	6.142 168	5.5649	4.9877	4.6991	—	15
16 —	30.705 666	6.265 060	5.6509	5.0368	4.7298	—	16
17 —	32.430 461	6.372 859	5.7243	5.0756	4.7513	—	17
18 —	34.038 000	6.467 420	5.7867	5.1059	4.7655	—	18
19 —	35.531 071	6.550 369	5.8397	5.1291	4.7738	—	19
20 —	36.913 544	6.623 131	5.8849	5.1466	4.7775	—	20

ORDINARY ANNUITIES CHANGING IN CONSTANT AMOUNT

(Present Value of Annual Payments Starting at $1 and Changing in Constant Amounts)

Base: 1.150 000

Annual INCREASE of:

Years	Slope	.00	.02	.04	.05	.10	Years
1	.000 000	.869 565	.8696	.8696	.8696	.8696	1
2	.756 144	1.625 709	1.6408	1.6560	1.6635	1.7013	2
3	2.071 176	2.283 225	2.3246	2.3661	2.3868	2.4903	3
4	3.786 436	2.854 978	2.9307	3.0064	3.0443	3.2336	4
5	5.775 143	3.352 155	3.4677	3.5832	3.6409	3.9297	5
6	7.936 781	3.784 483	3.9432	4.1020	4.1813	4.5782	6
7	10.192 403	4.160 420	4.3643	4.5681	4.6700	5.1797	7
8	12.480 715	4.487 322	4.7369	4.9866	5.1114	5.7354	8
9	14.754 815	4.771 584	5.0667	5.3618	5.5093	6.2471	9
10	16.979 477	5.018 769	5.3584	5.6979	5.8677	6.7167	10
11	19.128 909	5.233 712	5.6163	5.9989	6.1902	7.1466	11
12	21.184 888	5.420 619	5.8443	6.2680	6.4799	7.5391	12
13	23.135 223	5.583 147	6.0459	6.5086	6.7399	7.8967	13
14	24.972 496	5.724 476	6.2239	6.7234	6.9731	8.2217	14
15	26.693 019	5.847 370	6.3812	6.9151	7.1820	8.5167	15
16	28.295 990	5.954 235	6.5202	7.0861	7.3690	8.7838	16
17	29.782 805	6.047 161	6.6428	7.2385	7.5363	9.0254	17
18	31.156 492	6.127 966	6.7511	7.3742	7.6858	9.2436	18
19	32.421 267	6.198 231	6.8467	7.4951	7.8193	9.4404	19
20	33.582 173	6.259 331	6.9310	7.6026	7.9384	9.6175	20

Annual DECREASE of:

Years	Slope	.00	.02	.04	.05	.10	Years
1	.000 000	.869 565	.8696	.8696	.8696	.8696	1
2	—.756 144	1.625 709	1.6106	1.5955	1.5879	1.5501	2
3	—2.071 176	2.283 225	2.2418	2.2004	2.1797	2.0761	3
4	—3.786 436	2.854 978	2.7792	2.7035	2.6657	2.4763	4
5	—5.775 143	3.352 155	3.2367	3.1211	3.0634	2.7746	5
6	—7.936 781	3.784 483	3.6257	3.4670	3.3876	2.9908	6
7	—10.192 403	4.160 420	3.9566	3.7527	3.6508	3.1412	7
8	—12.480 715	4.487 322	4.2377	3.9881	3.8633	3.2392	8
9	—14.754 815	4.771 584	4.4765	4.1814	4.0338	3.2961	9
10	—16.979 477	5.018 769	4.6792	4.3396	4.1698	3.3208	10
11	—19.128 909	5.233 712	4.8511	4.4686	4.2773	—	11
12	—21.184 888	5.420 619	4.9969	4.5732	4.3614	—	12
13	—23.135 223	5.583 147	5.1204	4.6577	4.4264	—	13
14	—24.972 496	5.724 476	5.2250	4.7256	4.4759	—	14
15	—26.693 019	5.847 370	5.3135	4.7796	4.5127	—	15
16	—28.295 990	5.954 235	5.3883	4.8224	4.5394	—	16
17	—29.782 805	6.047 161	5.4515	4.8558	4.5580	—	17
18	—31.156 492	6.127 966	5.5048	4.8817	4.5701	—	18
19	—32.421 267	6.198 231	5.5498	4.9014	4.5772	—	19
20	—33.582 173	6.259 331	5.5877	4.9160	4.5802	—	20

16%

ORDINARY ANNUITIES CHANGING IN CONSTANT AMOUNT

(Present Value of Annual Payments Starting at $1 and Changing in Constant Amounts)

Base: 1.160 000

Annual INCREASE of:

Years	Slope	.00	.02	.04	.05	.10	Years
1	.000 000	.862 069	.8621	.8621	.8621	.8621	1
2	.743 163	1.605 232	1.6201	1.6350	1.6424	1.6795	2
3	2.024 478	2.245 890	2.2864	2.3269	2.3471	2.4483	3
4	3.681 352	2.798 181	2.8718	2.9454	2.9822	3.1663	4
5	5.585 804	3.274 294	3.3860	3.4977	3.5536	3.8329	5
6	7.638 015	3.684 736	3.8375	3.9903	4.0666	4.4485	6
7	9.760 992	4.038 565	4.2338	4.4290	4.5266	5.0147	7
8	11.896 170	4.343 591	4.5815	4.8194	4.9384	5.5332	8
9	13.999 794	4.606 544	4.8865	5.1665	5.3065	6.0065	9
10	16.039 947	4.833 227	5.1540	5.4748	5.6352	6.4372	10
11	17.994 116	5.028 644	5.3885	5.7484	5.9284	6.8281	11
12	19.847 207	5.197 107	5.5941	5.9910	6.1895	7.1818	12
13	21.589 926	5.342 334	5.7741	6.2059	6.4218	7.5013	13
14	23.217 465	5.467 529	5.9319	6.3962	6.6284	7.7893	14
15	24.728 443	5.575 456	6.0700	6.5646	6.8119	8.0483	15
16	26.124 051	5.668 497	6.1910	6.7135	6.9747	8.2809	16
17	27.407 369	5.748 704	6.2969	6.8450	7.1191	8.4894	17
18	28.582 822	5.817 848	6.3895	6.9612	7.2470	8.6761	18
19	29.655 750	5.877 455	6.4706	7.0637	7.3602	8.8430	19
20	30.632 074	5.928 841	6.5415	7.1541	7.4604	8.9920	20

Annual DECREASE of:

Years	Slope	.00	.02	.04	.05	.10	Years
1	.000 000	.862 069	.8621	.8621	.8621	.8621	1
2	—.743 163	1.605 232	1.5904	1.5755	1.5681	1.5309	2
3	—2.024 478	2.245 890	2.2054	2.1649	2.1447	2.0434	3
4	—3.681 352	2.798 181	2.7246	2.6509	2.6141	2.4300	4
5	—5.585 804	3.274 294	3.1626	3.0509	2.9950	2.7157	5
6	—7.638 015	3.684 736	3.5320	3.3792	3.3028	2.9209	6
7	—9.760 992	4.038 565	3.8433	3.6481	3.5505	3.0625	7
8	—11.896 170	4.343 591	4.1057	3.8677	3.7488	3.1540	8
9	—13.999 794	4.606 544	4.3265	4.0466	3.9066	3.2066	9
10	—16.039 947	4.833 227	4.5124	4.1916	4.0312	3.2292	10
11	—17.994 116	5.028 644	4.6688	4.3089	4.1289	—	11
12	—19.847 207	5.197 107	4.8002	4.4032	4.2047	—	12
13	—21.589 926	5.342 334	4.9105	4.4787	4.2628	—	13
14	—23.217 465	5.467 529	5.0032	4.5388	4.3067	—	14
15	—24.728 443	5.575 456	5.0809	4.5863	4.3390	—	15
16	—26.124 051	5.668 497	5.1460	4.6235	4.3623	—	16
17	—27.407 369	5.748 704	5.2006	4.6524	4.3783	—	17
18	—28.582 822	5.817 848	5.2462	4.6745	4.3887	—	18
19	—29.655 750	5.877 455	5.2843	4.6912	4.3947	—	19
20	—30.632 074	5.928 841	5.3162	4.7036	4.3972	—	20

ORDINARY ANNUITIES CHANGING IN CONSTANT AMOUNT
(Present Value of Annual Payments Starting at $1 and Changing in Constant Amounts)

Base: 1.170 000

Annual INCREASE of:

Years	Slope	.00	.02	.04	.05	.10	Years
1	.000 000	.854 701	.8547	.8547	.8547	.8547	1
2	.730 514	1.585 214	1.5998	1.6144	1.6217	1.6583	2
3	1.979 255	2.209 585	2.2492	2.2888	2.3085	2.4075	3
4	3.580 205	2.743 235	2.8148	2.8864	2.9222	3.1013	4
5	5.404 649	3.199 346	3.3074	3.4155	3.4696	3.7398	5
6	7.353 842	3.589 185	3.7363	3.8833	3.9569	4.3246	6
7	9.353 015	3.922 380	4.1094	4.2965	4.3900	4.8577	7
8	11.346 491	4.207 163	4.4341	4.6610	4.7745	5.3418	8
9	13.293 721	4.450 566	4.7164	4.9823	5.1153	5.7799	9
10	15.166 058	4.658 604	4.9619	5.2652	5.4169	6.1752	10
11	16.944 155	4.836 413	5.1753	5.5142	5.6836	6.5308	11
12	18.615 870	4.988 387	5.3607	5.7330	5.9192	6.8500	12
13	20.174 579	5.118 280	5.5218	5.9253	6.1270	7.1357	13
14	21.617 828	5.229 299	5.6617	6.0940	6.3102	7.3911	14
15	22.946 263	5.324 187	5.7831	6.2420	6.4715	7.6188	15
16	24.162 778	5.405 288	5.8885	6.3718	6.6134	7.8216	16
17	25.271 851	5.474 605	5.9800	6.4855	6.7382	8.0018	17
18	26.279 023	5.533 851	6.0594	6.5850	6.8478	8.1618	18
19	27.190 490	5.584 488	6.1283	6.6721	6.9440	8.3035	19
20	28.012 802	5.627 767	6.1880	6.7483	7.0284	8.4290	20

Annual DECREASE of:

Years	Slope	.00	.02	.04	.05	.10	Years
1	.000 000	.854 701	.8547	.8547	.8547	.8547	1
2	—.730 514	1.585 214	1.5706	1.5560	1.5487	1.5122	2
3	—1.979 255	2.209 585	2.1700	2.1304	2.1106	2.0117	3
4	—3.580 205	2.743 235	2.6716	2.6000	2.5642	2.3852	4
5	—5.404 649	3.199 346	3.0913	2.9832	2.9291	2.6589	5
6	—7.353 842	3.589 185	3.4421	3.2950	3.2215	2.8538	6
7	—9.353 015	3.922 380	3.7353	3.5483	3.4547	2.9871	7
8	—11.346 491	4.207 163	3.9802	3.7533	3.6398	3.0725	8
9	—13.293 721	4.450 566	4.1847	3.9188	3.7859	3.1212	9
10	—15.166 058	4.658 604	4.3553	4.0520	3.9003	3.1420	10
11	—16.944 155	4.836 413	4.4975	4.1586	3.9892	—	11
12	—18.615 870	4.988 387	4.6161	4.2438	4.0576	—	12
13	—20.174 579	5.118 280	4.7148	4.3113	4.1096	—	13
14	—21.617 828	5.229 299	4.7969	4.3646	4.1484	—	14
15	—22.946 263	5.324 187	4.8653	4.4063	4.1769	—	15
16	—24.162 778	5.405 288	4.9220	4.4388	4.1971	—	16
17	—25.271 851	5.474 605	4.9692	4.4637	4.2110	—	17
18	—26.279 023	5.533 851	5.0083	4.4827	4.2199	—	18
19	—27.190 490	5.584 488	5.0407	4.4969	4.2250	—	19
20	—28.012 802	5.627 767	5.0675	4.5073	4.2271	—	20

18%

ORDINARY ANNUITIES CHANGING IN CONSTANT AMOUNT

(Present Value of Annual Payments Starting at $1 and Changing in Constant Amounts)

Base: 1.180 000

Annual INCREASE of:

Years	Slope	.00	.02	.04	.05	.10	Years
1	.000 000	.847 458	.8475	.8475	.8475	.8475	1
2	.718 184	1.565 642	1.5800	1.5944	1.6016	1.6375	2
3	1.935 446	2.174 273	2.2130	2.2517	2.2710	2.3678	3
4	3.482 813	2.690 062	2.7597	2.8294	2.8642	3.0383	4
5	5.231 250	3.127 171	3.2318	3.3364	3.3887	3.6503	5
6	7.083 407	3.497 603	3.6393	3.7809	3.8518	4.2059	6
7	8.966 958	3.811 528	3.9909	4.1702	4.2599	4.7082	7
8	10.829 225	4.077 566	4.2942	4.5107	4.6190	5.1605	8
9	12.632 873	4.303 022	4.5557	4.8083	4.9347	5.5663	9
10	14.352 453	4.494 086	4.7811	5.0682	5.2117	5.9293	10
11	15.971 644	4.656 005	4.9754	5.2949	5.4546	6.2532	11
12	17.481 059	4.793 225	5.1428	5.4925	5.6673	6.5413	12
13	18.876 511	4.909 513	5.2870	5.6646	5.8533	6.7972	13
14	20.157 647	5.008 062	5.4112	5.8144	6.0159	7.0238	14
15	21.326 872	5.091 578	5.5181	5.9447	6.1579	7.2243	15
16	22.388 517	5.162 354	5.6101	6.0579	6.2818	7.4012	16
17	23.348 195	5.222 334	5.6893	6.1563	6.3897	7.5572	17
18	24.212 313	5.273 164	5.7574	6.2417	6.4838	7.6944	18
19	24.987 692	5.316 241	5.8160	6.3157	6.5656	7.8150	19
20	25.681 299	5.352 746	5.8664	6.3800	6.6368	7.9209	20

Annual DECREASE of:

Years	Slope	.00	.02	.04	.05	.10	Years
1	.000 000	.847 458	.8475	.8475	.8475	.8475	1
2	—.718 184	1.565 642	1.5513	1.5369	1.5297	1.4938	2
3	—1.935 446	2.174 273	2.1356	2.0969	2.0775	1.9807	3
4	—3.482 813	2.690 062	2.6204	2.5507	2.5159	2.3418	4
5	—5.231 250	3.127 171	3.0225	2.9179	2.8656	2.6040	5
6	—7.083 407	3.497 603	3.3559	3.2143	3.1434	2.7893	6
7	—8.966 958	3.811 528	3.6322	3.4528	3.3632	2.9148	7
8	—10.829 225	4.077 566	3.8610	3.6444	3.5361	2.9946	8
9	—12.632 873	4.303 022	4.0504	3.7977	3.6714	3.0397	9
10	—14.352 453	4.494 086	4.2070	3.9200	3.7765	3.0588	10
11	—15.971 644	4.656 005	4.3366	4.0171	3.8574	—	11
12	—17.481 059	4.793 225	4.4436	4.0940	3.9192	—	12
13	—18.876 511	4.909 513	4.5320	4.1545	3.9657	—	13
14	—20.157 647	5.008 062	4.6049	4.2018	4.0002	—	14
15	—21.326 872	5.091 578	4.6650	4.2385	4.0252	—	15
16	—22.388 517	5.162 354	4.7146	4.2668	4.0429	—	16
17	—23.348 195	5.222 334	4.7554	4.2884	4.0549	—	17
18	—24.212 313	5.273 164	4.7889	4.3047	4.0625	—	18
19	—24.987 692	5.316 241	4.8165	4.3167	4.0669	—	19
20	—25.681 299	5.352 746	4.8391	4.3255	4.0687	—	20

ORDINARY ANNUITIES CHANGING IN CONSTANT AMOUNT

(Present Value of Annual Payments Starting at $1 and Changing in Constant Amounts)

Base: 1.190 000

Annual INCREASE of:

Years	Slope	.00	.02	.04	.05	.10	Years
1	.000 000	.840 336	.8403	.8403	.8403	.8403	1
2	.706 165	1.546 501	1.5606	1.5747	1.5818	1.6171	2
3	1.892 996	2.139 917	2.1778	2.2156	2.2346	2.3292	3
4	3.389 003	2.638 586	2.7064	2.7741	2.8080	2.9775	4
5	5.065 200	3.057 635	3.1589	3.2602	3.3109	3.5642	5
6	6.825 912	3.409 777	3.5463	3.6828	3.7511	4.0924	6
7	8.601 419	3.705 695	3.8777	4.0498	4.1358	4.5658	7
8	10.342 113	3.954 366	4.1612	4.3681	4.4715	4.9886	8
9	12.013 848	4.163 332	4.4036	4.6439	4.7640	5.3647	9
10	13.594 269	4.338 935	4.6108	4.8827	5.0186	5.6984	10
11	15.069 919	4.486 500	4.7879	5.0893	5.2400	5.9935	11
12	16.433 966	4.610 504	4.9392	5.2679	5.4322	6.2539	12
13	17.684 428	4.714 709	5.0684	5.4221	5.5989	6.4832	13
14	18.822 805	4.802 277	5.1787	5.5552	5.7434	6.6846	14
15	19.853 010	4.875 863	5.2729	5.6700	5.8685	6.8612	15
16	20.780 565	4.937 700	5.3533	5.7689	5.9767	7.0158	16
17	21.611 987	4.989 664	5.4219	5.8541	6.0703	7.1509	17
18	22.354 329	5.033 331	5.4804	5.9275	6.1510	7.2688	18
19	23.014 840	5.070 026	5.5303	5.9906	6.2208	7.3715	19
20	23.600 728	5.100 862	5.5729	6.0449	6.2809	7.4609	20

Annual DECREASE of:

Years	Slope	.00	.02	.04	.05	.10	Years
1	.000 000	.840 336	.8403	.8403	.8403	.8403	1
2	—.706 165	1.546 501	1.5324	1.5183	1.5112	1.4759	2
3	—1.892 996	2.139 917	2.1021	2.0642	2.0453	1.9506	3
4	—3.389 003	2.638 586	2.5708	2.5030	2.4691	2.2997	4
5	—5.065 200	3.057 635	2.9563	2.8550	2.8044	2.5511	5
6	—6.825 912	3.409 777	3.2733	3.1367	3.0685	2.7272	6
7	—8.601 419	3.705 695	3.5337	3.3616	3.2756	2.8456	7
8	—10.342 113	3.954 366	3.7475	3.5407	3.4373	2.9202	8
9	—12.013 848	4.163 332	3.9231	3.6828	3.5626	2.9619	9
10	—13.594 269	4.338 935	4.0670	3.7952	3.6592	2.9795	10
11	—15.069 919	4.486 500	4.1851	3.8837	3.7330	—	11
12	—16.433 966	4.610 504	4.2818	3.9531	3.7888	—	12
13	—17.684 428	4.714 709	4.3610	4.0073	3.8305	—	13
14	—18.822 805	4.802 277	4.4258	4.0494	3.8611	—	14
15	—19.853 010	4.875 863	4.4788	4.0817	3.8832	—	15
16	—20.780 565	4.937 700	4.5221	4.1065	3.8987	—	16
17	—21.611 987	4.989 664	4.5574	4.1252	3.9091	—	17
18	—22.354 329	5.033 331	4.5862	4.1392	3.9156	—	18
19	—23.014 840	5.070 026	4.6097	4.1494	3.9193	—	19
20	—23.600 728	5.100 862	4.6288	4.1568	3.9208	—	20

20%

ORDINARY ANNUITIES CHANGING IN CONSTANT AMOUNT

(Present Value of Annual Payments Starting at $1 and Changing in Constant Amounts)

Base: 1.200 000

Annual INCREASE of:

Years	Slope	.00	.02	.04	.05	.10	Years
1	.000 000	.833 333	.8333	.8333	.8333	.8333	1
2	.694 444	1.527 778	1.5417	1.5556	1.5625	1.5972	2
3	1.851 852	2.106 481	2.1435	2.1806	2.1991	2.2917	3
4	3.298 611	2.588 735	2.6547	2.7207	2.7537	2.9186	4
5	4.906 121	2.990 612	3.0887	3.1869	3.2359	3.4812	5
6	6.580 611	3.325 510	3.4571	3.5887	3.6545	3.9836	6
7	8.255 101	3.604 592	3.7697	3.9348	4.0173	4.4301	7
8	9.883 077	3.837 160	4.0348	4.2325	4.3313	4.8255	8
9	11.433 531	4.030 967	4.2596	4.4883	4.6026	5.1743	9
10	12.887 081	4.192 472	4.4502	4.7080	4.8368	5.4812	10
11	14.232 961	4.327 060	4.6117	4.8964	5.0387	5.7504	11
12	15.466 684	4.439 217	4.7486	5.0579	5.2126	5.9859	12
13	16.588 251	4.532 681	4.8644	5.1962	5.3621	6.1915	13
14	17.600 776	4.610 567	4.9626	5.3146	5.4906	6.3706	14
15	18.509 453	4.675 473	5.0457	5.4159	5.6009	6.5264	15
16	19.320 771	4.729 561	5.1160	5.5024	5.6956	6.6616	16
17	20.041 943	4.774 634	5.1755	5.5763	5.7767	6.7788	17
18	20.680 481	4.812 195	5.2258	5.6394	5.8462	6.8802	18
19	21.243 896	4.843 496	5.2684	5.6933	5.9057	6.9679	19
20	21.739 493	4.869 580	5.3044	5.7392	5.9566	7.0435	20

Annual DECREASE of:

Years	Slope	.00	.02	.04	.05	.10	Years
1	.000 000	.833 333	.8333	.8333	.8333	.8333	1
2	—.694 444	1.527 778	1.5139	1.5000	1.4931	1.4583	2
3	—1.851 852	2.106 481	2.0694	2.0324	2.0139	1.9213	3
4	—3.298 611	2.588 735	2.5228	2.4568	2.4238	2.2589	4
5	—4.906 121	2.990 612	2.8925	2.7944	2.7453	2.5000	5
6	—6.580 611	3.325 510	3.1939	3.0623	2.9965	2.6674	6
7	—8.255 101	3.604 592	3.4395	3.2744	3.1918	2.7791	7
8	—9.883 077	3.837 160	3.6395	3.4418	3.3430	2.8489	8
9	—11.433 531	4.030 967	3.8023	3.5736	3.4593	2.8876	9
10	—12.887 081	4.192 472	3.9347	3.6770	3.5481	2.9038	10
11	—14.232 961	4.327 060	4.0424	3.7577	3.6154	—	11
12	—15.466 684	4.439 217	4.1299	3.8205	3.6659	—	12
13	—16.588 251	4.532 681	4.2009	3.8692	3.7033	—	13
14	—17.600 776	4.610 567	4.2586	3.9065	3.7305	—	14
15	—18.509 453	4.675 473	4.3053	3.9351	3.7500	—	15
16	—19.320 771	4.729 561	4.3431	3.9567	3.7635	—	16
17	—20.041 943	4.774 634	4.3738	3.9730	3.7725	—	17
18	—20.680 481	4.812 195	4.3986	3.9850	3.7782	—	18
19	—21.243 896	4.843 496	4.4186	3.9937	3.7813	—	19
20	—21.739 493	4.869 580	4.4348	4.0000	3.7826	—	20

ORDINARY ANNUITIES CHANGING IN CONSTANT AMOUNT

(Present Value of Annual Payments Starting at $1 and Changing in Constant Amounts)

Base: 1.210 000

Annual INCREASE of:

Years	Slope	.00	.02	.04	.05	.10	Years
1	.000 000	.826 446	.8264	.8264	.8264	.8264	1
2	.683 013	1.509 460	1.5231	1.5368	1.5436	1.5778	2
3	1.811 961	2.073 934	2.1102	2.1464	2.1645	2.2551	3
4	3.211 483	2.540 441	2.6047	2.6689	2.7010	2.8616	4
5	4.753 657	2.925 984	3.0211	3.1161	3.1637	3.4013	5
6	6.346 811	3.244 615	3.3716	3.4985	3.5620	3.8793	6
7	7.926 798	3.507 946	3.6665	3.8250	3.9043	4.3006	7
8	9.450 202	3.725 576	3.9146	4.1036	4.1981	4.6706	8
9	10.889 072	3.905 434	4.1232	4.3410	4.4499	4.9943	9
10	12.226 865	4.054 078	4.2986	4.5432	4.6654	5.2768	10
11	13.455 325	4.176 924	4.4460	4.7151	4.8497	5.5225	11
12	14.572 106	4.278 450	4.5699	4.8613	5.0071	5.7357	12
13	15.578 972	4.362 355	4.6739	4.9855	5.1413	5.9203	13
14	16.480 435	4.431 698	4.7613	5.0909	5.2557	6.0797	14
15	17.282 755	4.489 007	4.8347	5.1803	5.3531	6.2173	15
16	17.993 192	4.536 369	4.8962	5.2561	5.4360	6.3357	16
17	18.619 472	4.575 512	4.9479	5.3203	5.5065	6.4375	17
18	19.169 408	4.607 861	4.9912	5.3746	5.5663	6.5248	18
19	19.650 636	4.634 596	5.0276	5.4206	5.6171	6.5997	19
20	20.070 439	4.656 691	5.0581	5.4595	5.6602	6.6637	20

Annual DECREASE of:

Years	Slope	.00	.02	.04	.05	.10	Years
1	.000 000	.826 446	.8264	.8264	.8264	.8264	1
2	−.683 013	1.509 460	1.4958	1.4821	1.4753	1.4412	2
3	−1.811 961	2.073 934	2.0377	2.0015	1.9833	1.8927	3
4	−3.211 483	2.540 441	2.4762	2.4120	2.3799	2.2193	4
5	−4.753 657	2.925 984	2.8309	2.7358	2.6883	2.4506	5
6	−6.346 811	3.244 615	3.1177	2.9907	2.9273	2.6099	6
7	−7.926 798	3.507 946	3.3494	3.1909	3.1116	2.7153	7
8	−9.450 202	3.725 576	3.5366	3.3476	3.2531	2.7806	8
9	−10.889 072	3.905 434	3.6877	3.4699	3.3610	2.8165	9
10	−12.226 865	4.054 078	3.8095	3.5650	3.4427	2.8314	10
11	−13.455 325	4.176 924	3.9078	3.6387	3.5042	—	11
12	−14.572 106	4.278 450	3.9870	3.6956	3.5498	—	12
13	−15.578 972	4.362 355	4.0508	3.7392	3.5834	—	13
14	−16.480 435	4.431 698	4.1021	3.7725	3.6077	—	14
15	−17.282 755	4.489 007	4.1434	3.7977	3.6249	—	15
16	−17.993 192	4.536 369	4.1765	3.8166	3.6367	—	16
17	−18.619 472	4.575 512	4.2031	3.8307	3.6445	—	17
18	−19.169 408	4.607 861	4.2245	3.8411	3.6494	—	18
19	−19.650 636	4.634 596	4.2416	3.8486	3.6521	—	19
20	−20.070 439	4.656 691	4.2553	3.8539	3.6532	—	20

22%

ORDINARY ANNUITIES CHANGING IN CONSTANT AMOUNT

(Present Value of Annual Payments Starting at $1 and Changing in Constant Amounts)

Base: 1.220 000

Annual INCREASE of:

Years	Slope	.00	.02	.04	.05	.10	Years
1	.000 000	.819 672	.8197	.8197	.8197	.8197	1
2	.671 862	1.491 535	1.5050	1.5184	1.5251	1.5587	2
3	1.773 276	2.042 241	2.0777	2.1132	2.1309	2.2196	3
4	3.127 473	2.493 641	2.5562	2.6187	2.6500	2.8064	4
5	4.607 470	2.863 640	2.9558	3.0479	3.0940	3.3244	5
6	6.123 861	3.166 918	3.2894	3.4119	3.4731	3.7793	6
7	7.615 392	3.415 506	3.5678	3.7201	3.7963	4.1770	7
8	9.041 720	3.619 268	3.8001	3.9809	4.0714	4.5234	8
9	10.377 859	3.786 285	3.9938	4.2014	4.3052	4.8241	9
10	11.609 954	3.923 184	4.1554	4.3876	4.5037	5.0842	10
11	12.732 081	4.035 397	4.2900	4.5447	4.6720	5.3086	11
12	13.743 834	4.127 375	4.4023	4.6771	4.8146	5.5018	12
13	14.648 532	4.202 766	4.4957	4.7887	4.9352	5.6676	13
14	15.451 883	4.264 562	4.5736	4.8826	5.0372	5.8098	14
15	16.161 021	4.315 215	4.6384	4.9617	5.1233	5.9313	15
16	16.783 800	4.356 734	4.6924	5.0281	5.1959	6.0351	16
17	17.328 306	4.390 765	4.7373	5.0839	5.2572	6.1236	17
18	17.802 518	4.418 660	4.7747	5.1308	5.3088	6.1989	18
19	18.214 080	4.441 525	4.8058	5.1701	5.3522	6.2629	19
20	18.570 168	4.460 266	4.8317	5.2031	5.3888	6.3173	20

Annual DECREASE of:

Years	Slope	.00	.02	.04	.05	.10	Years
1	.000 000	.819 672	.8197	.8197	.8197	.8197	1
2	—.671 862	1.491 535	1.4781	1.4647	1.4579	1.4243	2
3	—1.773 276	2.042 241	2.0068	1.9713	1.9536	1.8649	3
4	—3.127 473	2.493 641	2.4311	2.3685	2.3373	2.1809	4
5	—4.607 470	2.863 640	2.7715	2.6793	2.6333	2.4029	5
6	—6.123 861	3.166 918	3.0444	2.9220	2.8607	2.5545	6
7	—7.615 392	3.415 506	3.2632	3.1109	3.0347	2.6540	7
8	—9.041 720	3.619 268	3.4384	3.2576	3.1672	2.7151	8
9	—10.377 859	3.786 285	3.5787	3.3712	3.2674	2.7485	9
10	—11.609 954	3.923 184	3.6910	3.4588	3.3427	2.7622	10
11	—12.732 081	4.035 397	3.7808	3.5261	3.3988	—	11
12	—13.743 834	4.127 375	3.8525	3.5776	3.4402	—	12
13	—14.648 532	4.202 766	3.9098	3.6168	3.4703	—	13
14	—15.451 883	4.264 562	3.9555	3.6465	3.4920	—	14
15	—16.161 021	4.315 215	3.9920	3.6688	3.5072	—	15
16	—16.783 800	4.356 734	4.0211	3.6854	3.5175	—	16
17	—17.328 306	4.390 765	4.0442	3.6976	3.5243	—	17
18	—17.802 518	4.418 660	4.0626	3.7066	3.5285	—	18
19	—18.214 080	4.441 525	4.0772	3.7130	3.5308	—	19
20	—18.570 168	4.460 266	4.0889	3.7175	3.5318	—	20

23%

ORDINARY ANNUITIES CHANGING IN CONSTANT AMOUNT

(Present Value of Annual Payments Starting at $1 and Changing in Constant Amounts)

Base: 1.230 000

Annual INCREASE of:

Years	Slope	.00	.02	.04	.05	.10	Years
1	.000 000	.813 008	.8130	.8130	.8130	.8130	1
2	.660 982	1.473 990	1.4872	1.5004	1.5070	1.5401	2
3	1.735 750	2.011 374	2.0461	2.0808	2.0982	2.1849	3
4	3.046 443	2.448 272	2.5092	2.5701	2.6006	2.7529	4
5	4.467 247	2.803 473	2.8928	2.9822	3.0268	3.2502	5
6	5.911 155	3.092 254	3.2105	3.3287	3.3878	3.6834	6
7	7.319 845	3.327 036	3.4734	3.6198	3.6930	4.0590	7
8	8.656 001	3.517 916	3.6910	3.8642	3.9507	4.3835	8
9	9.897 493	3.673 102	3.8711	4.0690	4.1680	4.6629	9
10	11.033 004	3.799 270	4.0199	4.2406	4.3509	4.9026	10
11	12.058 759	3.901 846	4.1430	4.3842	4.5048	5.1077	11
12	12.976 102	3.985 240	4.2448	4.5043	4.6340	5.2829	12
13	13.789 709	4.053 041	4.3288	4.6046	4.7425	5.4320	13
14	14.506 301	4.108 163	4.3983	4.6884	4.8335	5.5588	14
15	15.133 710	4.152 978	4.4557	4.7583	4.9097	5.6663	15
16	15.680 235	4.189 413	4.5030	4.8166	4.9734	5.7574	16
17	16.154 185	4.219 035	4.5421	4.8652	5.0267	5.8345	17
18	16.563 594	4.243 118	4.5744	4.9057	5.0713	5.8995	18
19	16.916 026	4.262 698	4.6010	4.9393	5.1085	5.9543	19
20	17.218 474	4.278 616	4.6230	4.9674	5.1395	6.0005	20

Annual DECREASE of:

Years	Slope	.00	.02	.04	.05	.10	Years
1	.000 000	.813 008	.8130	.8130	.8130	.8130	1
2	—.660 982	1.473 990	1.4608	1.4476	1.4409	1.4079	2
3	—1.735 750	2.011 374	1.9767	1.9419	1.9246	1.8378	3
4	—3.046 443	2.448 272	2.3873	2.3264	2.2959	2.1436	4
5	—4.467 247	2.803 473	2.7141	2.6248	2.5801	2.3567	5
6	—5.911 155	3.092 254	2.9740	2.8558	2.7967	2.5011	6
7	—7.319 845	3.327 036	3.1806	3.0342	2.9610	2.5951	7
8	—8.656 001	3.517 916	3.3448	3.1717	3.0851	2.6523	8
9	—9.897 493	3.673 102	3.4752	3.2772	3.1782	2.6834	9
10	—11.033 004	3.799 270	3.5786	3.3579	3.2476	2.6960	10
11	—12.058 759	3.901 846	3.6607	3.4195	3.2989	—	11
12	—12.976 102	3.985 240	3.7257	3.4662	3.3364	—	12
13	—13.789 709	4.053 041	3.7772	3.5015	3.3636	—	13
14	—14.506 301	4.108 163	3.8180	3.5279	3.3828	—	14
15	—15.133 710	4.152 978	3.8503	3.5476	3.3963	—	15
16	—15.680 235	4.189 413	3.8758	3.5622	3.4054	—	16
17	—16.154 185	4.219 035	3.8960	3.5729	3.4113	—	17
18	—16.563 594	4.243 118	3.9118	3.5806	3.4149	—	18
19	—16.916 026	4.262 698	3.9244	3.5861	3.4169	—	19
20	—17.218 474	4.278 616	3.9342	3.5899	3.4177	—	20

24%

ORDINARY ANNUITIES CHANGING IN CONSTANT AMOUNT

(Present Value of Annual Payments Starting at $1 and Changing in Constant Amounts)

Base: 1.240 000

Annual INCREASE of:

Years	Slope	.00	.02	.04	.05	.10	Years
1	.000 000	.806 452	.8065	.8065	.8065	.8065	1
2	.650 364	1.456 816	1.4698	1.4828	1.4893	1.5219	2
3	1.699 339	1.981 303	2.0153	2.0493	2.0663	2.1512	3
4	2.968 260	2.404 277	2.4636	2.5230	2.5527	2.7011	4
5	4.332 690	2.745 384	2.8320	2.9187	2.9620	3.1787	5
6	5.708 125	3.020 471	3.1346	3.2488	3.3059	3.5913	6
7	7.039 190	3.242 316	3.3831	3.5239	3.5943	3.9462	7
8	8.291 537	3.421 222	3.5871	3.7529	3.8358	4.2504	8
9	9.445 774	3.565 502	3.7544	3.9433	4.0378	4.5101	9
10	10.492 964	3.681 856	3.8917	4.1016	4.2065	4.7312	10
11	11.431 307	3.775 691	4.0043	4.2329	4.3473	4.9188	11
12	12.263 708	3.851 363	4.0966	4.3419	4.4645	5.0777	12
13	12.996 025	3.912 390	4.1723	4.4322	4.5622	5.2120	13
14	13.635 818	3.961 605	4.2343	4.5070	4.6434	5.3252	14
15	14.191 470	4.001 294	4.2851	4.5690	4.7109	5.4204	15
16	14.671 584	4.033 302	4.3267	4.6202	4.7669	5.5005	16
17	15.084 585	4.059 114	4.3608	4.6625	4.8133	5.5676	17
18	15.438 467	4.079 931	4.3887	4.6975	4.8519	5.6238	18
19	15.740 644	4.096 718	4.4115	4.7263	4.8838	5.6708	19
20	15.997 873	4.110 257	4.4302	4.7502	4.9102	5.7100	20

Annual DECREASE of:

Years	Slope	.00	.02	.04	.05	.10	Years
1	.000 000	.806 452	.8065	.8065	.8065	.8065	1
2	—.650 364	1.456 816	1.4438	1.4308	1.4243	1.3918	2
3	—1.699 339	1.981 303	1.9473	1.9133	1.8963	1.8114	3
4	—2.968 260	2.404 277	2.3449	2.2855	2.2559	2.1075	4
5	—4.332 690	2.745 384	2.6587	2.5721	2.5287	2.3121	5
6	—5.708 125	3.020 471	2.9063	2.7921	2.7351	2.4497	6
7	—7.039 190	3.242 316	3.1015	2.9607	2.8904	2.5384	7
8	—8.291 537	3.421 222	3.2554	3.0896	3.0066	2.5921	8
9	—9.445 774	3.565 502	3.3766	3.1877	3.0932	2.6209	9
10	—10.492 964	3.681 856	3.4720	3.2621	3.1572	2.6326	10
11	—11.431 307	3.775 691	3.5471	3.3184	3.2041	—	11
12	—12.263 708	3.851 363	3.6061	3.3608	3.2382	—	12
13	—12.996 025	3.912 390	3.6525	3.3925	3.2626	—	13
14	—13.635 818	3.961 605	3.6889	3.4162	3.2798	—	14
15	—14.191 470	4.001 294	3.7175	3.4336	3.2917	—	15
16	—14.671 584	4.033 302	3.7399	3.4464	3.2997	—	16
17	—15.084 585	4.059 114	3.7574	3.4557	3.3049	—	17
18	—15.438 467	4.079 931	3.7712	3.4624	3.3080	—	18
19	—15.740 644	4.096 718	3.7819	3.4671	3.3097	—	19
20	—15.997 873	4.110 257	3.7903	3.4703	3.3104	—	20

ORDINARY ANNUITIES CHANGING IN CONSTANT AMOUNT

(Present Value of Annual Payments Starting at $1 and Changing in Constant Amounts)

Base: 1.250 000

Annual INCREASE of:

Years	Slope	.00	.02	.04	.05	.10	Years
1	.000 000	.800 000	.8000	.8000	.8000	.8000	1
2	.640 000	1.440 000	1.4528	1.4656	1.4720	1.5040	2
3	1.664 000	1.952 000	1.9853	2.0186	2.0352	2.1184	3
4	2.892 800	2.361 600	2.4195	2.4773	2.5062	2.6509	4
5	4.203 520	2.689 280	2.7734	2.8574	2.8995	3.1096	5
6	5.514 240	2.951 424	3.0617	3.1720	3.2271	3.5028	6
7	6.772 531	3.161 139	3.2966	3.4320	3.4998	3.8384	7
8	7.946 936	3.328 911	3.4879	3.6468	3.7263	4.1236	8
9	9.020 678	3.463 129	3.6435	3.8240	3.9142	4.3652	9
10	9.987 046	3.570 503	3.7702	3.9700	4.0699	4.5692	10
11	10.846 039	3.656 403	3.8733	4.0902	4.1987	4.7410	11
12	11.601 953	3.725 122	3.9572	4.1892	4.3052	4.8853	12
13	12.261 660	3.780 098	4.0253	4.2706	4.3932	5.0063	13
14	12.833 407	3.824 078	4.0807	4.3374	4.4657	5.1074	14
15	13.325 988	3.859 263	4.1258	4.3923	4.5256	5.1919	15
16	13.748 200	3.887 410	4.1624	4.4373	4.5748	5.2622	16
17	14.108 488	3.909 928	4.1921	4.4743	4.6154	5.3208	17
18	14.414 733	3.927 942	4.2162	4.5045	4.6487	5.3694	18
19	14.674 140	3.942 354	4.2358	4.5293	4.6761	5.4098	19
20	14.893 195	3.953 883	4.2517	4.5496	4.6985	5.4432	20

Annual DECREASE of:

Years	Slope	.00	.02	.04	.05	.10	Years
1	.000 000	.800 000	.8000	.8000	.8000	.8000	1
2	—.640 000	1.440 000	1.4272	1.4144	1.4080	1.3760	2
3	—1.664 000	1.952 000	1.9187	1.8854	1.8688	1.7856	3
4	—2.892 800	2.361 600	2.3037	2.2459	2.2170	2.0723	4
5	—4.203 520	2.689 280	2.6052	2.5211	2.4791	2.2689	5
6	—5.514 240	2.951 424	2.8411	2.7309	2.6757	2.4000	6
7	—6.772 531	3.161 139	3.0257	2.8902	2.8225	2.4839	7
8	—7.946 936	3.328 911	3.1700	3.0110	2.9316	2.5342	8
9	—9.020 678	3.463 129	3.2827	3.1023	3.0121	2.5611	9
10	—9.987 046	3.570 503	3.3708	3.1710	3.0712	2.5718	10
11	—10.846 039	3.656 403	3.4395	3.2226	3.1141	—	11
12	—11.601 953	3.725 122	3.4931	3.2610	3.1450	—	12
13	—12.261 660	3.780 098	3.5349	3.2896	3.1670	—	13
14	—12.833 407	3.824 078	3.5674	3.3107	3.1824	—	14
15	—13.325 988	3.859 263	3.5927	3.3262	3.1930	—	15
16	—13.748 200	3.887 410	3.6124	3.3375	3.2000	—	16
17	—14.108 488	3.909 928	3.6278	3.3456	3.2045	—	17
18	—14.414 733	3.927 942	3.6396	3.3514	3.2072	—	18
19	—14.674 140	3.942 354	3.6489	3.3554	3.2086	—	19
20	—14.893 195	3.953 883	3.6560	3.3582	3.2092	—	20

26%

ORDINARY ANNUITIES CHANGING IN CONSTANT AMOUNT

(Present Value of Annual Payments Starting at $1 and Changing in Constant Amounts)

Base: 1.260 000

Annual INCREASE of:

Years	Slope	.00	.02	.04	.05	.10	Years
1	.000 000	.793 651	.7937	.7937	.7937	.7937	1
2	.629 882	1.423 532	1.4361	1.4487	1.4550	1.4865	2
3	1.629 694	1.923 438	1.9560	1.9886	2.0049	2.0864	3
4	2.819 946	2.320 189	2.3766	2.4330	2.4612	2.6022	4
5	4.079 472	2.635 071	2.7167	2.7982	2.8390	3.0430	5
6	5.329 003	2.884 977	2.9916	3.0981	3.1514	3.4179	6
7	6.519 031	3.083 315	3.2137	3.3441	3.4093	3.7352	7
8	7.620 910	3.240 726	3.3931	3.5456	3.6218	4.0028	8
9	8.620 346	3.365 656	3.5381	3.7105	3.7967	4.2277	9
10	9.512 700	3.464 806	3.6551	3.8453	3.9404	4.4161	10
11	10.299 608	3.543 497	3.7495	3.9555	4.0585	4.5735	11
12	10.986 591	3.605 950	3.8257	4.0454	4.1553	4.7046	12
13	11.581 382	3.655 516	3.8871	4.1188	4.2346	4.8137	13
14	12.092 776	3.694 854	3.9367	4.1786	4.2995	4.9041	14
15	12.529 865	3.726 074	3.9767	4.2273	4.3526	4.9791	15
16	12.901 539	3.750 853	4.0089	4.2669	4.3959	5.0410	16
17	13.216 184	3.770 518	4.0348	4.2992	4.4313	5.0921	17
18	13.481 510	3.786 125	4.0558	4.3254	4.4602	5.1343	18
19	13.704 472	3.798 512	4.0726	4.3467	4.4837	5.1690	19
20	13.891 257	3.808 343	4.0862	4.3640	4.5029	5.1975	20

Annual DECREASE of:

Years	Slope	.00	.02	.04	.05	.10	Years
1	.000 000	.793 651	.7937	.7937	.7937	.7937	1
2	—.629 882	1.423 532	1.4109	1.3983	1.3920	1.3605	2
3	—1.629 694	1.923 438	1.8908	1.8583	1.8420	1.7605	3
4	—2.819 946	2.320 189	2.2638	2.2074	2.1792	2.0382	4
5	—4.079 472	2.635 071	2.5535	2.4719	2.4311	2.2271	5
6	—5.329 003	2.884 977	2.7784	2.6718	2.6185	2.3521	6
7	—6.519 031	3.083 315	2.9529	2.8226	2.7574	2.4314	7
8	—7.620 910	3.240 726	3.0883	2.9359	2.8597	2.4786	8
9	—8.620 346	3.365 656	3.1932	3.0208	2.9346	2.5036	9
10	—9.512 700	3.464 806	3.2746	3.0843	2.9892	2.5135	10
11	—10.299 608	3.543 497	3.3375	3.1315	3.0285	—	11
12	—10.986 591	3.605 950	3.3862	3.1665	3.0566	—	12
13	—11.581 382	3.655 516	3.4239	3.1923	3.0764	—	13
14	—12.092 776	3.694 854	3.4530	3.2111	3.0902	—	14
15	—12.529 865	3.726 074	3.4755	3.2249	3.0996	—	15
16	—12.901 539	3.750 853	3.4928	3.2348	3.1058	—	16
17	—13.216 184	3.770 518	3.5062	3.2419	3.1097	—	17
18	—13.481 510	3.786 125	3.5165	3.2469	3.1120	—	18
19	—13.704 472	3.798 512	3.5244	3.2503	3.1133	—	19
20	—13.891 257	3.808 343	3.5305	3.2527	3.1138	—	20

ORDINARY ANNUITIES CHANGING IN CONSTANT AMOUNT

(Present Value of Annual Payments Starting at $1 and Changing in Constant Amounts)

Base: 1.270 000

Annual INCREASE of:

Years	Slope	.00	.02	.04	.05	.10	Years
1	.000 000	.787 402	.7874	.7874	.7874	.7874	1
2	.620 001	1.407 403	1.4198	1.4322	1.4384	1.4694	2
3	1.596 381	1.895 593	1.9275	1.9594	1.9754	2.0552	3
4	2.749 586	2.279 994	2.3350	2.3900	2.4175	2.5550	4
5	3.960 299	2.582 673	2.6619	2.7411	2.7807	2.9787	5
6	5.151 946	2.821 002	2.9240	3.0271	3.0786	3.3362	6
7	6.277 912	3.008 663	3.1342	3.2598	3.3226	3.6365	7
8	7.312 264	3.156 428	3.3027	3.4489	3.5220	3.8877	8
9	8.243 064	3.272 778	3.4376	3.6025	3.6849	4.0971	9
10	9.067 592	3.364 392	3.5457	3.7271	3.8178	4.2712	10
11	9.788 964	3.436 529	3.6323	3.8281	3.9260	4.4154	11
12	10.413 774	3.493 330	3.7016	3.9099	4.0140	4.5347	12
13	10.950 475	3.538 055	3.7571	3.9761	4.0856	4.6331	13
14	11.408 292	3.573 272	3.8014	4.0296	4.1437	4.7141	14
15	11.796 507	3.601 001	3.8369	4.0729	4.1908	4.7807	15
16	12.124 022	3.622 836	3.8653	4.1078	4.2290	4.8352	16
17	12.399 101	3.640 028	3.8880	4.1360	4.2600	4.8799	17
18	12.629 235	3.653 565	3.9062	4.1587	4.2850	4.9165	18
19	12.821 103	3.664 225	3.9206	4.1771	4.3053	4.9463	19
20	12.980 573	3.672 618	3.9322	4.1918	4.3216	4.9707	20

Annual DECREASE of:

Years	Slope	.00	.02	.04	.05	.10	Years
1	.000 000	.787 402	.7874	.7874	.7874	.7874	1
2	—.620 001	1.407 403	1.3950	1.3826	1.3764	1.3454	2
3	—1.596 381	1.895 593	1.8637	1.8317	1.8158	1.7360	3
4	—2.749 586	2.279 994	2.2250	2.1700	2.1425	2.0050	4
5	—3.960 299	2.582 673	2.5035	2.4243	2.3847	2.1866	5
6	—5.151 946	2.821 002	2.7180	2.6149	2.5634	2.3058	6
7	—6.277 912	3.008 663	2.8831	2.7575	2.6948	2.3809	7
8	—7.312 264	3.156 428	3.0102	2.8639	2.7908	2.4252	8
9	—8.243 064	3.272 778	3.1079	2.9431	2.8606	2.4485	9
10	—9.067 592	3.364 392	3.1830	3.0017	2.9110	2.4576	10
11	—9.788 964	3.436 529	3.2407	3.0450	2.9471	—	11
12	—10.413 774	3.493 330	3.2851	3.0768	2.9726	—	12
13	—10.950 475	3.538 055	3.3190	3.1000	2.9905	—	13
14	—11.408 292	3.573 272	3.3451	3.1169	3.0029	—	14
15	—11.796 507	3.601 001	3.3651	3.1291	3.0112	—	15
16	—12.124 022	3.622 836	3.3804	3.1379	3.0166	—	16
17	—12.399 101	3.640 028	3.3920	3.1441	3.0201	—	17
18	—12.629 235	3.653 565	3.4010	3.1484	3.0221	—	18
19	—12.821 103	3.664 225	3.4078	3.1514	3.0232	—	19
20	—12.980 573	3.672 618	3.4130	3.1534	3.0236	—	20

28%

ORDINARY ANNUITIES CHANGING IN CONSTANT AMOUNT

(Present Value of Annual Payments Starting at $1 and Changing in Constant Amounts)

Base: 1.280 000

Annual INCREASE of:

Years	Slope	.00	.02	.04	.05	.10	Years
1	.000 000	.781 250	.7812	.7812	.7812	.7812	1
2	.610 352	1.391 602	1.4038	1.4160	1.4221	1.4526	2
3	1.564 026	1.868 439	1.8997	1.9310	1.9466	2.0248	3
4	2.681 613	2.240 968	2.2946	2.3482	2.3750	2.5091	4
5	3.845 766	2.532 006	2.6089	2.6858	2.7243	2.9166	5
6	4.982 635	2.759 380	2.8590	2.9587	3.0085	3.2576	6
7	6.048 449	2.937 015	3.0580	3.1790	3.2394	3.5419	7
8	7.019 894	3.075 793	3.2162	3.3566	3.4268	3.7778	8
9	7.887 256	3.184 214	3.3420	3.4997	3.5786	3.9729	9
10	8.649 585	3.268 917	3.4419	3.6149	3.7014	4.1339	10
11	9.311 330	3.335 091	3.5213	3.7075	3.8007	4.2662	11
12	9.880 016	3.386 790	3.5844	3.7820	3.8808	4.3748	12
13	10.364 693	3.427 180	3.6345	3.8418	3.9454	4.4636	13
14	10.774 900	3.458 734	3.6742	3.8897	3.9975	4.5362	14
15	11.120 027	3.483 386	3.7058	3.9282	4.0394	4.5954	15
16	11.408 916	3.502 645	3.7308	3.9590	4.0731	4.6435	16
17	11.649 658	3.517 692	3.7507	3.9837	4.1002	4.6827	17
18	11.849 492	3.529 447	3.7664	4.0034	4.1219	4.7144	18
19	12.014 795	3.538 630	3.7789	4.0192	4.1394	4.7401	19
20	12.151 114	3.545 805	3.7888	4.0318	4.1534	4.7609	20

Annual DECREASE of:

Years	Slope	.00	.02	.04	.05	.10	Years
1	.000 000	.781 250	.7812	.7812	.7812	.7812	1
2	—.610 352	1.391 602	1.3794	1.3672	1.3611	1.3306	2
3	—1.564 026	1.868 439	1.8372	1.8059	1.7902	1.7120	3
4	—2.681 613	2.240 968	2.1873	2.1337	2.1069	1.9728	4
5	—3.845 766	2.532 006	2.4551	2.3782	2.3397	2.1474	5
6	—4.982 635	2.759 380	2.6597	2.5601	2.5102	2.2611	6
7	—6.048 449	2.937 015	2.8160	2.6951	2.6346	2.3322	7
8	—7.019 894	3.075 793	2.9354	2.7950	2.7248	2.3738	8
9	—7.887 256	3.184 214	3.0265	2.8687	2.7899	2.3955	9
10	—8.649 585	3.268 917	3.0959	2.9229	2.8364	2.4040	10
11	—9.311 330	3.335 091	3.1489	2.9626	2.8695	—	11
12	—9.880 016	3.386 790	3.1892	2.9916	2.8928	—	12
13	—10.364 693	3.427 180	3.2199	3.0126	2.9089	—	13
14	—10.774 900	3.458 734	3.2432	3.0277	2.9200	—	14
15	—11.120 027	3.483 386	3.2610	3.0386	2.9274	—	15
16	—11.408 916	3.502 645	3.2745	3.0463	2.9322	—	16
17	—11.649 658	3.517 692	3.2847	3.0517	2.9352	—	17
18	—11.849 492	3.529 447	3.2925	3.0555	2.9370	—	18
19	—12.014 795	3.538 630	3.2983	3.0580	2.9379	—	19
20	—12.151 114	3.545 805	3.3028	3.0598	2.9382	—	20

ORDINARY ANNUITIES CHANGING IN CONSTANT AMOUNT

(Present Value of Annual Payments Starting at $1 and Changing in Constant Amounts)

Base: 1.290 000

Annual INCREASE of:

Years	Slope	.00	.02	.04	.05	.10	Years
1	.000 000	.775 194	.7752	.7752	.7752	.7752	1
2	.600 925	1.376 119	1.3881	1.4002	1.4062	1.4362	2
3	1.532 593	1.841 953	1.8726	1.9033	1.9186	1.9952	3
4	2.615 927	2.203 064	2.2554	2.3077	2.3339	2.4647	4
5	3.735 652	2.482 996	2.5577	2.6324	2.6698	2.8566	5
6	4.820 657	2.699 997	2.7964	2.8928	2.9410	3.1821	6
7	5.829 964	2.868 214	2.9848	3.1014	3.1597	3.4512	7
8	6.742 774	2.998 616	3.1335	3.2683	3.3358	3.6729	8
9	7.551 465	3.099 702	3.2507	3.4018	3.4773	3.8548	9
10	8.256 719	3.178 064	3.3432	3.5083	3.5909	4.0037	10
11	8.864 172	3.238 809	3.4161	3.5934	3.6820	4.1252	11
12	9.382 156	3.285 899	3.4735	3.6612	3.7550	4.2241	12
13	9.820 197	3.322 402	3.5188	3.7152	3.8134	4.3044	13
14	10.188 062	3.350 699	3.5545	3.7582	3.8601	4.3695	14
15	10.495 163	3.372 635	3.5825	3.7924	3.8974	4.4222	15
16	10.750 231	3.389 640	3.6046	3.8196	3.9272	4.4647	16
17	10.961 140	3.402 821	3.6220	3.8413	3.9509	4.4989	17
18	11.134 854	3.413 040	3.6357	3.8584	3.9698	4.5265	18
19	11.277 437	3.420 961	3.6465	3.8721	3.9848	4.5487	19
20	11.394 107	3.427 102	3.6550	3.8829	3.9968	4.5665	20

Annual DECREASE of:

Years	Slope	.00	.02	.04	.05	.10	Years
1	.000 000	.775 194	.7752	.7752	.7752	.7752	1
2	−.600 925	1.376 119	1.3641	1.3521	1.3461	1.3160	2
3	−1.532 593	1.841 953	1.8113	1.7806	1.7653	1.6887	3
4	−2.615 927	2.203 064	2.1507	2.0984	2.0723	1.9415	4
5	−3.735 652	2.482 996	2.4083	2.3336	2.2962	2.1094	5
6	−4.820 657	2.699 997	2.6036	2.5072	2.4590	2.2179	6
7	−5.829 964	2.868 214	2.7516	2.6350	2.5767	2.2852	7
8	−6.742 774	2.998 616	2.8638	2.7289	2.6615	2.3243	8
9	−7.551 465	3.099 702	2.9487	2.7976	2.7221	2.3446	9
10	−8.256 719	3.178 064	3.0129	2.8478	2.7652	2.3524	10
11	−8.864 172	3.238 809	3.0615	2.8842	2.7956	—	11
12	−9.382 156	3.285 899	3.0983	2.9106	2.8168	—	12
13	−9.820 197	3.322 402	3.1260	2.9296	2.8314	—	13
14	−10.188 062	3.350 699	3.1469	2.9432	2.8413	—	14
15	−10.495 163	3.372 635	3.1627	2.9528	2.8479	—	15
16	−10.750 231	3.389 640	3.1746	2.9596	2.8521	—	16
17	−10.961 140	3.402 821	3.1836	2.9644	2.8548	—	17
18	−11.134 854	3.413 040	3.1903	2.9676	2.8563	—	18
19	−11.277 437	3.420 961	3.1954	2.9699	2.8571	—	19
20	−11.394 107	3.427 102	3.1992	2.9713	2.8574	—	20

30%

ORDINARY ANNUITIES CHANGING IN CONSTANT AMOUNT

(Present Value of Annual Payments Starting at $1 and Changing in Constant Amounts)

Base: 1.300 000

Annual INCREASE of:

Years	Slope	.00	.02	.04	.05	.10	Years
1	.000 000	.769 231	.7692	.7692	.7692	.7692	1
2	.591 716	1.360 947	1.3728	1.3846	1.3905	1.4201	2
3	1.502 048	1.816 113	1.8462	1.8762	1.8912	1.9663	3
4	2.552 432	2.166 241	2.2173	2.2683	2.2939	2.4215	4
5	3.629 748	2.435 570	2.5082	2.5808	2.6171	2.7985	5
6	4.665 629	2.642 746	2.7361	2.8294	2.8760	3.1093	6
7	5.621 827	2.802 112	2.9145	3.0270	3.0832	3.3643	7
8	6.479 953	2.924 702	3.0543	3.1839	3.2487	3.5727	8
9	7.234 350	3.019 001	3.1637	3.3084	3.3807	3.7424	9
10	7.887 193	3.091 539	3.2493	3.4070	3.4859	3.8803	10
11	8.445 179	3.147 338	3.3162	3.4851	3.5696	3.9919	11
12	8.917 321	3.190 260	3.3686	3.5470	3.6361	4.0820	12
13	9.313 524	3.223 277	3.4095	3.5958	3.6890	4.1546	13
14	9.643 693	3.248 675	3.4415	3.6344	3.7309	4.2130	14
15	9.917 206	3.268 211	3.4666	3.6649	3.7641	4.2599	15
16	10.142 628	3.283 239	3.4861	3.6889	3.7904	4.2975	16
17	10.327 591	3.294 800	3.5014	3.7079	3.8112	4.3276	17
18	10.478 762	3.303 692	3.5133	3.7228	3.8276	4.3516	18
19	10.601 887	3.310 532	3.5226	3.7346	3.8406	4.3707	19
20	10.701 861	3.315 794	3.5298	3.7439	3.8509	4.3860	20

Annual DECREASE of:

Years	Slope	.00	.02	.04	.05	.10	Years
1	.000 000	.769 231	.7692	.7692	.7692	.7692	1
2	—.591 716	1.360 947	1.3491	1.3373	1.3314	1.3018	2
3	—1.502 048	1.816 113	1.7861	1.7560	1.7410	1.6659	3
4	—2.552 432	2.166 241	2.1152	2.0641	2.0386	1.9110	4
5	—3.629 748	2.435 570	2.3630	2.2904	2.2541	2.0726	5
6	—4.665 629	2.642 746	2.5494	2.4561	2.4095	2.1762	6
7	—5.621 827	2.802 112	2.6897	2.5772	2.5210	2.2399	7
8	—6.479 953	2.924 702	2.7951	2.6655	2.6007	2.2767	8
9	—7.234 350	3.019 001	2.8743	2.7296	2.6573	2.2956	9
10	—7.887 193	3.091 539	2.9338	2.7761	2.6972	2.3028	10
11	—8.445 179	3.147 338	2.9784	2.8095	2.7251	—	11
12	—8.917 321	3.190 260	3.0119	2.8336	2.7444	—	12
13	—9.313 524	3.223 277	3.0370	2.8507	2.7576	—	13
14	—9.643 693	3.248 675	3.0558	2.8629	2.7665	—	14
15	—9.917 206	3.268 211	3.0699	2.8715	2.7724	—	15
16	—10.142 628	3.283 239	3.0804	2.8775	2.7761	—	16
17	—10.327 591	3.294 800	3.0882	2.8817	2.7784	—	17
18	—10.478 762	3.303 692	3.0941	2.8845	2.7798	—	18
19	—10.601 887	3.310 532	3.0985	2.8865	2.7804	—	19
20	—10.701 861	3.315 794	3.1018	2.8877	2.7807	—	20

Table 5

**Ordinary Annuities Changing in Constant Ratio
(Present Value of Annual Payments Starting at $1
and Changing in Constant Ratio)**

Table 5 - ORDINARY ANNUITIES CHANGING IN CONSTANT RATIO
(Present Value of Annual Payments Starting at $1 and Changing in Constant Ratio)

$$PVF = \frac{1 - (1 + x)^n/(1 + i)^n}{i - x}$$

Where

PVF = Present Value Factor

x = Constant Ratio Change in Income

n = Number of Years

i = Rate of Interest/Yield

(x is positive for increase; negative for decrease)

This Table is used in solving problems dealing with the compound discounting of cash flows that are best represented by an exponential-curve pattern of change (increase/decrease).

Example 1:
Assuming a 15% interest/yield rate, what is the Present Value of an ordinary annuity of ten annual cash flows that start at $10,000 and increase 10% per year compounded?

$10,000 × 7.1773 = $71,773

Same example assuming payments in advance.

$71,773 × 1.150000 = $82,539
         OR
$71,773/.869565 = $82,539

Example 2:
Assuming a 15% interest/yield rate, what is the Present Value of an ordinary annuity of ten annual cash flows that start at $10,000 and decrease 3% per year compounded?

$10,000 × 4.5429 = $45,429

Example 3:

There are 5 years remaining on a lease that provides a level income of $1,000 per year. Inflation over this period will cause purchasing power to decline 10% per year (compound basis). What is the value of the income expressed in constant dollars and discounted at 6%?

$1,000 × .90 × 3.4922 = $3,142.98

PROOF:

Year	Income	×	Inflation Factor	×	PVF @6%	=	Value
1	$1,000	×	.900000	×	.943396	=	$ 849.06
2	1,000	×	.810000	×	.889996	=	720.90
3	1,000	×	.729000	×	.839619	=	612.08
4	1,000	×	.656100	×	.792094	=	519.69
5	1,000	×	.590490	×	.747258	=	441.25
							$3,142.98

6%
ORDINARY ANNUITIES CHANGING IN CONSTANT RATIO
(Present Value of Annual Payments Starting at $1 and Changing in Constant Ratio)

Base: 1.060 000

Annual Percentage INCREASE of:

Years	1%	2%	3%	4%	5%	6%	Years
1	.9434	.9434	.9434	.9434	.9434	.9434	1
2	1.8423	1.8512	1.8601	1.8690	1.8779	1.8868	2
3	2.6988	2.7247	2.7508	2.7771	2.8036	2.8302	3
4	3.5149	3.5653	3.6164	3.6681	3.7205	3.7736	4
5	4.2925	4.3742	4.4574	4.5423	4.6288	4.7170	5
6	5.0334	5.1525	5.2747	5.4000	5.5285	5.6604	6
7	5.7394	5.9015	6.0688	6.2415	6.4198	6.6038	7
8	6.4120	6.6222	6.8404	7.0671	7.3026	7.5472	8
9	7.0530	7.3157	7.5902	7.8772	8.1771	8.4906	9
10	7.6637	7.9830	8.3188	8.6720	9.0434	9.4340	10
11	8.2456	8.6251	9.0268	9.4517	9.9015	10.3774	11
12	8.8000	9.2431	9.7147	10.2168	10.7514	11.3208	12
13	9.3283	9.8377	10.3831	10.9674	11.5934	12.2642	13
14	9.8317	10.4098	11.0327	11.7039	12.4274	13.2075	14
15	10.3114	10.9604	11.6638	12.4265	13.2536	14.1509	15
16	10.7684	11.4902	12.2771	13.1354	14.0720	15.0943	16
17	11.2038	12.0000	12.8730	13.8310	14.8826	16.0377	17
18	11.6187	12.4906	13.4521	14.5134	15.6856	16.9811	18
19	12.0141	12.9626	14.0148	15.1829	16.4810	17.9245	19
20	12.3908	13.4169	14.5615	15.8399	17.2689	18.8679	20

Annual Percentage DECREASE of:

Years	1%	2%	3%	4%	5%	6%	Years
1	.9434	.9434	.9434	.9434	.9434	.9434	1
2	1.8245	1.8156	1.8067	1.7978	1.7889	1.7800	2
3	2.6474	2.6220	2.5967	2.5716	2.5466	2.5219	3
4	3.4160	3.3675	3.3196	3.2724	3.2258	3.1798	4
5	4.1338	4.0567	3.9812	3.9071	3.8344	3.7632	5
6	4.8042	4.6940	4.5865	4.4819	4.3799	4.2806	6
7	5.4303	5.2831	5.1405	5.0024	4.8688	4.7394	7
8	6.0151	5.8278	5.6474	5.4739	5.3069	5.1462	8
9	6.5613	6.3313	6.1113	5.9009	5.6996	5.5070	9
10	7.0714	6.7969	6.5358	6.2876	6.0515	5.8270	10
11	7.5478	7.2273	6.9243	6.6378	6.3669	6.1107	11
12	7.9928	7.6252	7.2798	6.9550	6.6496	6.3624	12
13	8.4083	7.9932	7.6051	7.2423	6.9030	6.5855	13
14	8.7965	8.3333	7.9028	7.5024	7.1300	6.7834	14
15	9.1590	8.6478	8.1752	7.7381	7.3335	6.9588	15
16	9.4975	8.9385	8.4245	7.9515	7.5159	7.1144	16
17	9.8137	9.2073	8.6526	8.1447	7.6793	7.2524	17
18	10.1090	9.4558	8.8613	8.3197	7.8258	7.3748	18
19	10.3849	9.6855	9.0523	8.4783	7.9571	7.4833	19
20	10.6425	9.8980	9.2271	8.6218	8.0747	7.5795	20

ORDINARY ANNUITIES CHANGING IN CONSTANT RATIO

(Present Value of Annual Payments Starting at $1 and Changing in Constant Ratio)

Base: 1.060 000

Annual Percentage INCREASE of:

Years	7%	8%	9%	10%	11%	12%	Years
1	.9434	.9434	.9434	.9434	.9434	.9434	1
2	1.8957	1.9046	1.9135	1.9224	1.9313	1.9402	2
3	2.8570	2.8839	2.9110	2.9383	2.9658	2.9934	3
4	3.8273	3.8817	3.9368	3.9926	4.0491	4.1062	4
5	4.8068	4.8984	4.9916	5.0867	5.1835	5.2821	5
6	5.7956	5.9342	6.0763	6.2220	6.3714	6.5245	6
7	6.7936	6.9896	7.1917	7.4002	7.6153	7.8372	7
8	7.8011	8.0648	8.3386	8.6229	8.9179	9.2242	8
9	8.8181	9.1604	9.5180	9.8916	10.2820	10.6897	9
10	9.8447	10.2766	10.7308	11.2083	11.7104	12.2382	10
11	10.8810	11.4139	11.9779	12.5747	13.2061	13.8743	11
12	11.9270	12.5727	13.2603	13.9926	14.7725	15.6030	12
13	12.9829	13.7533	14.5790	15.4640	16.4127	17.4296	13
14	14.0488	14.9562	15.9350	16.9909	18.1302	19.3596	14
15	15.1247	16.1818	17.3294	18.5755	19.9288	21.3988	15
16	16.2108	17.4305	18.7632	20.2199	21.8123	23.5534	16
17	17.3072	18.7028	20.2376	21.9263	23.7846	25.8301	17
18	18.4138	19.9990	21.7538	23.6971	25.8499	28.2355	18
19	19.5309	21.3198	23.3129	25.5347	28.0126	30.7772	19
20	20.6586	22.6654	24.9161	27.4417	30.2773	33.4627	20

Annual Percentage DECREASE of:

Years	7%	8%	9%	10%	11%	12%	Years
1	.9434	.9434	.9434	.9434	.9434	.9434	1
2	1.7711	1.7622	1.7533	1.7444	1.7355	1.7266	2
3	2.4973	2.4728	2.4486	2.4245	2.4006	2.3768	3
4	3.1344	3.0896	3.0455	3.0019	2.9590	2.9166	4
5	3.6934	3.6250	3.5579	3.4922	3.4278	3.3647	5
6	4.1838	4.0896	3.9978	3.9085	3.8215	3.7367	6
7	4.6141	4.4929	4.3755	4.2619	4.1520	4.0456	7
8	4.9916	4.8429	4.6997	4.5620	4.4295	4.3020	8
9	5.3228	5.1466	4.9781	4.8168	4.6625	4.5149	9
10	5.6134	5.4103	5.2170	5.0331	4.8581	4.6916	10
11	5.8684	5.6391	5.4222	5.2168	5.0224	4.8383	11
12	6.0921	5.8377	5.5983	5.3728	5.1603	4.9601	12
13	6.2883	6.0101	5.7495	5.5052	5.2761	5.0612	13
14	6.4605	6.1597	5.8792	5.6176	5.3733	5.1452	14
15	6.6116	6.2896	5.9907	5.7131	5.4550	5.2148	15
16	6.7441	6.4023	6.0863	5.7941	5.5235	5.2727	16
17	6.8604	6.5001	6.1685	5.8629	5.5811	5.3207	17
18	6.9624	6.5850	6.2390	5.9213	5.6294	5.3606	18
19	7.0520	6.6587	6.2995	5.9710	5.6700	5.3937	19
20	7.1305	6.7226	6.3514	6.0131	5.7040	5.4212	20

7%

ORDINARY ANNUITIES CHANGING IN CONSTANT RATIO

(Present Value of Annual Payments Starting at $1 and Changing in Constant Ratio)

Base: 1.070 000

Annual Percentage INCREASE of:

Years	1%	2%	3%	4%	5%	6%	Years
1	.9346	.9346	.9346	.9346	.9346	.9346	1
2	1.8168	1.8255	1.8342	1.8430	1.8517	1.8604	2
3	2.6495	2.6748	2.7002	2.7259	2.7517	2.7776	3
4	3.4355	3.4844	3.5339	3.5840	3.6348	3.6862	4
5	4.1774	4.2561	4.3363	4.4181	4.5014	4.5864	5
6	4.8777	4.9918	5.1088	5.2288	5.3519	5.4781	6
7	5.5388	5.6931	5.8524	6.0168	6.1864	6.3615	7
8	6.1628	6.3617	6.5682	6.7827	7.0054	7.2366	8
9	6.7518	6.9990	7.2572	7.5271	7.8090	8.1035	9
10	7.3078	7.6065	7.9205	8.2506	8.5976	8.9624	10
11	7.8326	8.1856	8.5590	8.9539	9.3715	9.8132	11
12	8.3279	8.7377	9.1736	9.6374	10.1309	10.6561	12
13	8.7955	9.2640	9.7653	10.3018	10.8761	11.4911	13
14	9.2369	9.7657	10.3348	10.9475	11.6074	12.3182	14
15	9.6535	10.2439	10.8830	11.5752	12.3250	13.1377	15
16	10.0468	10.6998	11.4108	12.1852	13.0292	13.9495	16
17	10.4180	11.1344	11.9188	12.7782	13.7203	14.7537	17
18	10.7684	11.5487	12.4078	13.3545	14.3984	15.5504	18
19	11.0991	11.9436	12.8785	13.9146	15.0639	16.3397	19
20	11.4113	12.3201	13.3317	14.4591	15.7169	17.1215	20

Annual Percentage DECREASE of:

Years	1%	2%	3%	4%	5%	6%	Years
1	.9346	.9346	.9346	.9346	.9346	.9346	1
2	1.7993	1.7905	1.7818	1.7731	1.7643	1.7556	2
3	2.5993	2.5745	2.5499	2.5254	2.5011	2.4769	3
4	3.3396	3.2926	3.2461	3.2003	3.1551	3.1105	4
5	4.0245	3.9502	3.8773	3.8059	3.7359	3.6672	5
6	4.6582	4.5525	4.4496	4.3492	4.2515	4.1562	6
7	5.2445	5.1042	4.9683	4.8367	4.7093	4.5859	7
8	5.7869	5.6094	5.4385	5.2740	5.1157	4.9633	8
9	6.2888	6.0722	5.8648	5.6664	5.4766	5.2948	9
10	6.7532	6.4960	6.2513	6.0185	5.7969	5.5861	10
11	7.1829	6.8842	6.6017	6.3343	6.0814	5.8420	11
12	7.5804	7.2397	6.9193	6.6177	6.3339	6.0668	12
13	7.9482	7.5654	7.2072	6.8720	6.5582	6.2643	13
14	8.2886	7.8636	7.4682	7.1001	6.7573	6.4378	14
15	8.6034	8.1368	7.7048	7.3048	6.9340	6.5902	15
16	8.8948	8.3869	7.9193	7.4884	7.0909	6.7241	16
17	9.1643	8.6161	8.1138	7.6531	7.2303	6.8417	17
18	9.4137	8.8259	8.2901	7.8009	7.3540	6.9451	18
19	9.6445	9.0182	8.4499	7.9335	7.4638	7.0359	19
20	9.8580	9.1942	8.5947	8.0525	7.5613	7.1156	20

ORDINARY ANNUITIES CHANGING IN CONSTANT RATIO

(Present Value of Annual Payments Starting at $1 and Changing in Constant Ratio)

Base: 1.070 000

Annual Percentage INCREASE of:

Years	7%	8%	9%	10%	11%	12%	Years
1	.9346	.9346	.9346	.9346	.9346	.9346	1
2	1.8692	1.8779	1.8866	1.8954	1.9041	1.9128	2
3	2.8037	2.8300	2.8565	2.8831	2.9099	2.9368	3
4	3.7383	3.7911	3.8444	3.8985	3.9532	4.0086	4
5	4.6729	4.7611	4.8509	4.9424	5.0356	5.1305	5
6	5.6075	5.7401	5.8761	6.0155	6.1584	6.3048	6
7	6.5421	6.7284	6.9205	7.1188	7.3232	7.5340	7
8	7.4766	7.7258	7.9845	8.2529	8.5315	8.8207	8
9	8.4112	8.7326	9.0683	9.4189	9.7851	10.1674	9
10	9.3458	9.7488	10.1724	10.6176	11.0854	11.5771	10
11	10.2804	10.7745	11.2971	11.8498	12.4344	13.0527	11
12	11.2150	11.8098	12.4428	13.1167	13.8338	14.5972	12
13	12.1495	12.8547	13.6100	14.4190	15.2856	16.2139	13
14	13.0841	13.9094	14.7990	15.7578	16.7916	17.9061	14
15	14.0187	14.9740	16.0102	17.1342	18.3539	19.6774	15
16	14.9533	16.0485	17.2440	18.5492	19.9746	21.5315	16
17	15.8879	17.1331	18.5009	20.0039	21.6559	23.4723	17
18	16.8224	18.2278	19.7813	21.4993	23.4000	25.5037	18
19	17.7570	19.3327	21.0856	23.0367	25.2094	27.6300	19
20	18.6916	20.4480	22.4143	24.6171	27.0864	29.8557	20

Annual Percentage DECREASE of:

Years	7%	8%	9%	10%	11%	12%	Years
1	.9346	.9346	.9346	.9346	.9346	.9346	1
2	1.7469	1.7381	1.7294	1.7207	1.7119	1.7032	2
3	2.4529	2.4291	2.4054	2.3819	2.3585	2.3353	3
4	3.0665	3.0231	2.9803	2.9380	2.8963	2.8552	4
5	3.5999	3.5339	3.4692	3.4058	3.3437	3.2828	5
6	4.0635	3.9731	3.8850	3.7993	3.7158	3.6345	6
7	4.4664	4.3507	4.2387	4.1302	4.0253	3.9237	7
8	4.8166	4.6753	4.5394	4.4086	4.2827	4.1615	8
9	5.1209	4.9545	4.7952	4.6428	4.4968	4.3571	9
10	5.3855	5.1945	5.0128	4.8397	4.6749	4.5180	10
11	5.6154	5.4009	5.1978	5.0054	4.8231	4.6503	11
12	5.8153	5.5783	5.3551	5.1447	4.9463	4.7592	12
13	5.9890	5.7309	5.4889	5.2619	5.0488	4.8487	13
14	6.1400	5.8621	5.6027	5.3605	5.1340	4.9223	14
15	6.2712	5.9749	5.6995	5.4434	5.2049	4.9828	15
16	6.3852	6.0719	5.7818	5.5131	5.2639	5.0326	16
17	6.4844	6.1552	5.8518	5.5718	5.3130	5.0735	17
18	6.5705	6.2269	5.9114	5.6211	5.3538	5.1072	18
19	6.6454	6.2886	5.9620	5.6626	5.3877	5.1349	19
20	6.7105	6.3416	6.0051	5.6975	5.4160	5.1577	20

8%

ORDINARY ANNUITIES CHANGING IN CONSTANT RATIO

(Present Value of Annual Payments Starting at $1 and Changing in Constant Ratio)

Base: 1.080 000

Annual Percentage INCREASE of:

Years	1%	2%	3%	4%	5%	6%	Years
1	.9259	.9259	.9259	.9259	.9259	.9259	1
2	1.7918	1.8004	1.8090	1.8176	1.8261	1.8347	2
3	2.6016	2.6263	2.6512	2.6762	2.7013	2.7267	3
4	3.3589	3.4063	3.4543	3.5030	3.5522	3.6021	4
5	4.0671	4.1430	4.2204	4.2992	4.3795	4.4613	5
6	4.7295	4.8388	4.9509	5.0659	5.1837	5.3046	6
7	5.3488	5.4959	5.6476	5.8042	5.9657	6.1323	7
8	5.9281	6.1165	6.3121	6.5151	6.7259	6.9447	8
9	6.4698	6.7026	6.9458	7.1997	7.4650	7.7420	9
10	6.9764	7.2562	7.5501	7.8590	8.1836	8.5246	10
11	7.4501	7.7790	8.1265	8.4939	8.8822	9.2926	11
12	7.8932	8.2727	8.6762	9.1052	9.5614	10.0465	12
13	8.3075	8.7391	9.2005	9.6939	10.2217	10.7863	13
14	8.6950	9.1795	9.7004	10.2608	10.8637	11.5125	14
15	9.0573	9.5954	10.1773	10.8067	11.4878	12.2252	15
16	9.3962	9.9883	10.6320	11.3324	12.0947	12.9248	16
17	9.7131	10.3593	11.0657	11.8386	12.6846	13.6114	17
18	10.0095	10.7097	11.4794	12.3260	13.2582	14.2852	18
19	10.2867	11.0407	11.8738	12.7954	13.8158	14.9466	19
20	10.5459	11.3532	12.2500	13.2475	14.3580	15.5957	20

Annual Percentage DECREASE of:

Years	1%	2%	3%	4%	5%	6%	Years
1	.9259	.9259	.9259	.9259	.9259	.9259	1
2	1.7747	1.7661	1.7575	1.7490	1.7404	1.7318	2
3	2.5527	2.5285	2.5045	2.4806	2.4568	2.4333	3
4	3.2659	3.2203	3.1753	3.1309	3.0870	3.0438	4
5	3.9197	3.8481	3.7778	3.7089	3.6414	3.5751	5
6	4.5190	4.4177	4.3190	4.2227	4.1290	4.0376	6
7	5.0683	4.9346	4.8050	4.6795	4.5579	4.4401	7
8	5.5719	5.4036	5.2415	5.0855	4.9352	4.7905	8
9	6.0335	5.8292	5.6336	5.4463	5.2671	5.0954	9
10	6.4566	6.2154	5.9857	5.7671	5.5590	5.3608	10
11	6.8445	6.5658	6.3020	6.0523	5.8158	5.5918	11
12	7.2000	6.8838	6.5861	6.3057	6.0417	5.7929	12
13	7.5260	7.1723	6.8412	6.5310	6.2403	5.9679	13
14	7.8247	7.4341	7.0703	6.7313	6.4151	6.1202	14
15	8.0986	7.6717	7.2761	6.9093	6.5689	6.2528	15
16	8.3496	7.8873	7.4610	7.0675	6.7041	6.3682	16
17	8.5798	8.0829	7.6270	7.2081	6.8230	6.4686	17
18	8.7907	8.2604	7.7761	7.3332	6.9277	6.5560	18
19	8.9841	8.4215	7.9100	7.4443	7.0197	6.6321	19
20	9.1613	8.5677	8.0303	7.5431	7.1007	6.6983	20

ORDINARY ANNUITIES CHANGING IN CONSTANT RATIO

(Present Value of Annual Payments Starting at $1 and Changing in Constant Ratio)

Base: 1.080 000

Annual Percentage INCREASE of:

Years	7%	8%	9%	10%	11%	12%	Years
1	.9259	.9259	.9259	.9259	.9259	.9259	1
2	1.8433	1.8519	1.8604	1.8690	1.8776	1.8861	2
3	2.7521	2.7778	2.8036	2.8295	2.8557	2.8819	3
4	3.6526	3.7037	3.7555	3.8079	3.8609	3.9146	4
5	4.5447	4.6296	4.7162	4.8043	4.8941	4.9855	5
6	5.4285	5.5556	5.6858	5.8192	5.9559	6.0961	6
7	6.3042	6.4815	6.6643	6.8529	7.0473	7.2478	7
8	7.1717	7.4074	7.6520	7.9057	8.1690	8.4421	8
9	8.0313	8.3333	8.6487	8.9780	9.3218	9.6807	9
10	8.8828	9.2593	9.6547	10.0702	10.5067	10.9652	10
11	9.7265	10.1852	10.6701	11.1826	11.7245	12.2973	11
12	10.5624	11.1111	11.6948	12.3157	12.9761	13.6786	12
13	11.3905	12.0370	12.7290	13.4696	14.2625	15.1112	13
14	12.2110	12.9630	13.7728	14.6450	15.5846	16.5968	14
15	13.0238	13.8889	14.8262	15.8421	16.9434	18.1374	15
16	13.8292	14.8148	15.8894	17.0614	18.3400	19.7351	16
17	14.6270	15.7407	16.9625	18.3033	19.7754	21.3919	17
18	15.4175	16.6667	18.0455	19.5682	21.2506	23.1102	18
19	16.2007	17.5926	19.1385	20.8565	22.7668	24.8920	19
20	16.9766	18.5185	20.2416	22.1687	24.3251	26.7399	20

Annual Percentage DECREASE of:

Years	7%	8%	9%	10%	11%	12%	Years
1	.9259	.9259	.9259	.9259	.9259	.9259	1
2	1.7233	1.7147	1.7061	1.6975	1.6890	1.6804	2
3	2.4098	2.3866	2.3635	2.3405	2.3178	2.2951	3
4	3.0011	2.9589	2.9174	2.8764	2.8359	2.7960	4
5	3.5102	3.4465	3.3841	3.3229	3.2629	3.2042	5
6	3.9486	3.8618	3.7773	3.6950	3.6148	3.5367	6
7	4.3261	4.2156	4.1087	4.0051	3.9048	3.8077	7
8	4.6512	4.5170	4.3879	4.2635	4.1438	4.0285	8
9	4.9311	4.7738	4.6231	4.4789	4.3407	4.2084	9
10	5.1722	4.9925	4.8213	4.6583	4.5030	4.3550	10
11	5.3797	5.1788	4.9883	4.8078	4.6367	4.4744	11
12	5.5585	5.3375	5.1291	4.9325	4.7469	4.5718	12
13	5.7124	5.4727	5.2476	5.0363	4.8377	4.6511	13
14	5.8449	5.5878	5.3475	5.1229	4.9126	4.7157	14
15	5.9591	5.6859	5.4317	5.1950	4.9743	4.7683	15
16	6.0573	5.7695	5.5027	5.2551	5.0251	4.8112	16
17	6.1420	5.8407	5.5624	5.3051	5.0670	4.8462	17
18	6.2148	5.9013	5.6128	5.3469	5.1015	4.8747	18
19	6.2776	5.9530	5.6552	5.3817	5.1299	4.8979	19
20	6.3316	5.9970	5.6910	5.4106	5.1534	4.9168	20

9%

ORDINARY ANNUITIES CHANGING IN CONSTANT RATIO

(Present Value of Annual Payments Starting at $1 and Changing in Constant Ratio)

Base: 1.090 000

Annual Percentage INCREASE of:

Years	1%	2%	3%	4%	5%	6%	Years
1	.9174	.9174	.9174	.9174	.9174	.9174	1
2	1.7675	1.7759	1.7844	1.7928	1.8012	1.8096	2
3	2.5552	2.5793	2.6036	2.6280	2.6525	2.6772	3
4	3.2851	3.3311	3.3777	3.4249	3.4726	3.5210	4
5	3.9614	4.0346	4.1092	4.1852	4.2626	4.3415	5
6	4.5881	4.6929	4.8004	4.9106	5.0236	5.1394	6
7	5.1688	5.3090	5.4536	5.6028	5.7567	5.9154	7
8	5.7069	5.8855	6.0708	6.2632	6.4629	6.6700	8
9	6.2055	6.4249	6.6541	6.8934	7.1431	7.4039	9
10	6.6674	6.9298	7.2053	7.4946	7.7984	8.1176	10
11	7.0955	7.4022	7.7261	8.0682	8.4297	8.8116	11
12	7.4922	7.8442	8.2182	8.6155	9.0378	9.4865	12
13	7.8597	8.2579	8.6833	9.1378	9.6235	10.1428	13
14	8.2003	8.6450	9.1227	9.6360	10.1878	10.7811	14
15	8.5159	9.0073	9.5380	10.1114	10.7314	11.4018	15
16	8.8083	9.3462	9.9304	10.5651	11.2550	12.0054	16
17	9.0792	9.6635	10.3012	10.9978	11.7594	12.5924	17
18	9.3303	9.9603	10.6516	11.4108	12.2453	13.1633	18
19	9.5629	10.2381	10.9827	11.8048	12.7134	13.7184	19
20	9.7785	10.4980	11.2956	12.1807	13.1642	14.2583	20

Annual Percentage DECREASE of:

Years	1%	2%	3%	4%	5%	6%	Years
1	.9174	.9174	.9174	.9174	.9174	.9174	1
2	1.7507	1.7423	1.7339	1.7254	1.7170	1.7086	2
3	2.5075	2.4839	2.4604	2.4371	2.4139	2.3909	3
4	3.1949	3.1506	3.1070	3.0639	3.0213	2.9793	4
5	3.8192	3.7501	3.6823	3.6159	3.5507	3.4868	5
6	4.3863	4.2891	4.1944	4.1021	4.0121	3.9244	6
7	4.9013	4.7737	4.6500	4.5302	4.4142	4.3017	7
8	5.3691	5.2094	5.0555	4.9074	4.7647	4.6272	8
9	5.7939	5.6011	5.4164	5.2395	5.0701	4.9078	9
10	6.1798	5.9533	5.7375	5.5321	5.3363	5.1499	10
11	6.5303	6.2699	6.0233	5.7897	5.5684	5.3586	11
12	6.8486	6.5546	6.2776	6.0166	5.7706	5.5386	12
13	7.1377	6.8106	6.5039	6.2165	5.9468	5.6939	13
14	7.4003	7.0407	6.7053	6.3925	6.1005	5.8277	14
15	7.6388	7.2476	6.8846	6.5475	6.2343	5.9432	15
16	7.8554	7.4336	7.0441	6.6840	6.3510	6.0427	16
17	8.0522	7.6009	7.1860	6.8043	6.4527	6.1286	17
18	8.2309	7.7512	7.3123	6.9102	6.5414	6.2027	18
19	8.3932	7.8864	7.4247	7.0035	6.6186	6.2665	19
20	8.5406	8.0080	7.5248	7.0856	6.6860	6.3216	20

9%

ORDINARY ANNUITIES CHANGING IN CONSTANT RATIO

(Present Value of Annual Payments Starting at $1 and Changing in Constant Ratio)

Base: 1.090 000

Annual Percentage INCREASE of:

Years	7%	8%	9%	10%	11%	12%	Years
1	.9174	.9174	.9174	.9174	.9174	.9174	1
2	1.8180	1.8264	1.8349	1.8433	1.8517	1.8601	2
3	2.7021	2.7271	2.7523	2.7776	2.8031	2.8287	3
4	3.5700	3.6195	3.6697	3.7205	3.7720	3.8240	4
5	4.4219	4.5038	4.5872	4.6721	4.7586	4.8467	5
6	5.2582	5.3799	5.5046	5.6324	5.7634	5.8975	6
7	6.0791	6.2479	6.4220	6.6015	6.7865	6.9773	7
8	6.8850	7.1081	7.3394	7.5795	7.8285	8.0867	8
9	7.6761	7.9603	8.2569	8.5665	8.8896	9.2267	9
10	8.4527	8.8047	9.1743	9.5625	9.9701	10.3981	10
11	9.2150	9.6413	10.0917	10.5676	11.0705	11.6017	11
12	9.9634	10.4703	11.0092	11.5820	12.1910	12.8385	12
13	10.6980	11.2917	11.9266	12.6057	13.3322	14.1093	13
14	11.4191	12.1055	12.8440	13.6388	14.4942	15.4150	14
15	12.1270	12.9119	13.7615	14.6814	15.6776	16.7567	15
16	12.8220	13.7109	14.6789	15.7335	16.8827	18.1354	16
17	13.5041	14.5025	15.5963	16.7953	18.1099	19.5519	17
18	14.1738	15.2869	16.5138	17.8668	19.3596	21.0075	18
19	14.8311	16.0641	17.4312	18.9481	20.6323	22.5031	19
20	15.4764	16.8341	18.3486	20.0394	21.9283	24.0399	20

Annual Percentage DECREASE of:

Years	7%	8%	9%	10%	11%	12%	Years
1	.9174	.9174	.9174	.9174	.9174	.9174	1
2	1.7002	1.6918	1.6834	1.6749	1.6665	1.6581	2
3	2.3681	2.3454	2.3228	2.3004	2.2782	2.2561	3
4	2.9379	2.8970	2.8567	2.8169	2.7776	2.7389	4
5	3.4241	3.3626	3.3023	3.2433	3.1854	3.1286	5
6	3.8389	3.7556	3.6744	3.5954	3.5183	3.4433	6
7	4.1928	4.0873	3.9851	3.8861	3.7902	3.6973	7
8	4.4948	4.3673	4.2444	4.1261	4.0122	3.9024	8
9	4.7524	4.6036	4.4609	4.3243	4.1934	4.0680	9
10	4.9723	4.8030	4.6417	4.4880	4.3414	4.2017	10
11	5.1598	4.9713	4.7926	4.6231	4.4623	4.3096	11
12	5.3198	5.1134	4.9186	4.7347	4.5609	4.3968	12
13	5.4564	5.2333	5.0238	4.8268	4.6415	4.4671	13
14	5.5729	5.3346	5.1116	4.9029	4.7073	4.5239	14
15	5.6723	5.4200	5.1849	4.9657	4.7610	4.5698	15
16	5.7571	5.4921	5.2461	5.0175	4.8048	4.6068	16
17	5.8294	5.5530	5.2972	5.0603	4.8407	4.6367	17
18	5.8912	5.6043	5.3399	5.0957	4.8699	4.6608	18
19	5.9438	5.6477	5.3755	5.1249	4.8938	4.6803	19
20	5.9888	5.6843	5.4052	5.1490	4.9133	4.6960	20

10%

ORDINARY ANNUITIES CHANGING IN CONSTANT RATIO

(Present Value of Annual Payments Starting at $1 and Changing in Constant Ratio)

Base: 1.100 000

Annual Percentage INCREASE of:

Years	1%	2%	3%	4%	5%	6%	Years
1	.9091	.9091	.9091	.9091	.9091	.9091	1
2	1.7438	1.7521	1.7603	1.7686	1.7769	1.7851	2
3	2.5102	2.5337	2.5574	2.5812	2.6052	2.6293	3
4	3.2139	3.2586	3.3037	3.3495	3.3959	3.4428	4
5	3.8601	3.9307	4.0026	4.0759	4.1506	4.2267	5
6	4.4533	4.5539	4.6570	4.7627	4.8710	4.9821	6
7	4.9981	5.1318	5.2697	5.4120	5.5587	5.7100	7
8	5.4982	5.6677	5.8435	6.0259	6.2151	6.4115	8
9	5.9575	6.1646	6.3807	6.6063	6.8417	7.0874	9
10	6.3791	6.6253	6.8837	7.1550	7.4398	7.7388	10
11	6.7663	7.0526	7.3548	7.6738	8.0107	8.3664	11
12	7.1218	7.4487	7.7958	8.1644	8.5557	8.9713	12
13	7.4482	7.8161	8.2088	8.6281	9.0759	9.5542	13
14	7.7479	8.1568	8.5955	9.0666	9.5724	10.1158	14
15	8.0230	8.4726	8.9576	9.4811	10.0464	10.6571	15
16	8.2757	8.7655	9.2967	9.8731	10.4989	11.1786	16
17	8.5077	9.0371	9.6142	10.2436	10.9307	11.6812	17
18	8.7207	9.2890	9.9115	10.5940	11.3430	12.1656	18
19	8.9163	9.5225	10.1898	10.9252	11.7365	12.6323	19
20	9.0959	9.7390	10.4505	11.2384	12.1121	13.0820	20

Annual Percentage DECREASE of:

Years	1%	2%	3%	4%	5%	6%	Years
1	.9091	.9091	.9091	.9091	.9091	.9091	1
2	1.7273	1.7190	1.7107	1.7025	1.6942	1.6860	2
3	2.4636	2.4406	2.4177	2.3949	2.3723	2.3498	3
4	3.1264	3.0834	3.0410	2.9992	2.9579	2.9171	4
5	3.7228	3.6561	3.5907	3.5266	3.4636	3.4019	5
6	4.2596	4.1664	4.0755	3.9868	3.9004	3.8162	6
7	4.7428	4.6210	4.5029	4.3885	4.2776	4.1702	7
8	5.1776	5.0259	4.8798	4.7390	4.6034	4.4727	8
9	5.5689	5.3867	5.2122	5.0450	4.8848	4.7312	9
10	5.9211	5.7082	5.5053	5.3120	5.1277	4.9521	10
11	6.2381	5.9946	5.7638	5.5450	5.3376	5.1409	11
12	6.5234	6.2497	5.9917	5.7484	5.5188	5.3022	12
13	6.7801	6.4770	6.1927	5.9259	5.6754	5.4401	13
14	7.0112	6.6795	6.3699	6.0807	5.8105	5.5579	14
15	7.2192	6.8599	6.5262	6.2159	5.9273	5.6586	15
16	7.4063	7.0207	6.6640	6.3339	6.0281	5.7446	16
17	7.5748	7.1639	6.7855	6.4369	6.1152	5.8181	17
18	7.7264	7.2914	6.8927	6.5267	6.1904	5.8809	18
19	7.8629	7.4051	6.9872	6.6051	6.2553	5.9346	19
20	7.9857	7.5064	7.0705	6.6736	6.3114	5.9805	20

ORDINARY ANNUITIES CHANGING IN CONSTANT RATIO

(Present Value of Annual Payments Starting at $1 and Changing in Constant Ratio)

Base: 1.100 000

Annual Percentage INCREASE of:

Years	7%	8%	9%	10%	11%	12%	Years
1	.9091	.9091	.9091	.9091	.9091	.9091	1
2	1.7934	1.8017	1.8099	1.8182	1.8264	1.8347	2
3	2.6536	2.6780	2.7026	2.7273	2.7521	2.7772	3
4	3.4903	3.5384	3.5871	3.6364	3.6863	3.7367	4
5	4.3042	4.3831	4.4636	4.5455	4.6289	4.7138	5
6	5.0959	5.2125	5.3321	5.4545	5.5800	5.7086	6
7	5.8660	6.0269	6.1927	6.3636	6.5398	6.7215	7
8	6.6151	6.8264	7.0455	7.2727	7.5084	7.7528	8
9	7.3438	7.6113	7.8905	8.1818	8.4857	8.8028	9
10	8.0526	8.3820	8.7279	9.0909	9.4720	9.8719	10
11	8.7421	9.1387	9.5576	10.0000	10.4672	10.9605	11
12	9.4127	9.8817	10.3798	10.9091	11.4714	12.0689	12
13	10.0651	10.6111	11.1946	11.8182	12.4848	13.1974	13
14	10.6997	11.3273	12.0019	12.7273	13.5074	14.3465	14
15	11.3170	12.0304	12.8019	13.6364	14.5393	15.5164	15
16	11.9174	12.7208	13.5946	14.5455	15.5805	16.7076	16
17	12.5015	13.3986	14.3801	15.4545	16.6313	17.9205	17
18	13.0696	14.0640	15.1584	16.3636	17.6916	19.1554	18
19	13.6223	14.7174	15.9297	17.2727	18.7615	20.4128	19
20	14.1599	15.3589	16.6940	18.1818	19.8411	21.6930	20

Annual Percentage DECREASE of:

Years	7%	8%	9%	10%	11%	12%	Years
1	.9091	.9091	.9091	.9091	.9091	.9091	1
2	1.6777	1.6694	1.6612	1.6529	1.6446	1.6364	2
3	2.3275	2.3053	2.2833	2.2615	2.2397	2.2182	3
4	2.8769	2.8372	2.7980	2.7594	2.7212	2.6836	4
5	3.3414	3.2820	3.2238	3.1668	3.1108	3.0560	5
6	3.7341	3.6540	3.5761	3.5001	3.4260	3.3539	6
7	4.0661	3.9652	3.8675	3.7728	3.6811	3.5922	7
8	4.3468	4.2254	4.1085	3.9959	3.8874	3.7829	8
9	4.5841	4.4431	4.3080	4.1785	4.0544	3.9354	9
10	4.7847	4.6251	4.4730	4.3278	4.1894	4.0574	10
11	4.9544	4.7774	4.6095	4.4501	4.2987	4.1550	11
12	5.0978	4.9047	4.7224	4.5500	4.3871	4.2331	12
13	5.2190	5.0112	4.8158	4.6319	4.4587	4.2956	13
14	5.3215	5.1003	4.8931	4.6988	4.5166	4.3455	14
15	5.4082	5.1748	4.9570	4.7536	4.5634	4.3855	15
16	5.4815	5.2371	5.0099	4.7984	4.6013	4.4175	16
17	5.5434	5.2892	5.0536	4.8350	4.6320	4.4431	17
18	5.5958	5.3328	5.0898	4.8650	4.6568	4.4636	18
19	5.6401	5.3692	5.1198	4.8896	4.6768	4.4799	19
20	5.6775	5.3997	5.1445	4.9096	4.6931	4.4930	20

11%

ORDINARY ANNUITIES CHANGING IN CONSTANT RATIO

(Present Value of Annual Payments Starting at $1 and Changing in Constant Ratio)

Base: 1.110 000

Annual Percentage INCREASE of:

Years	1%	2%	3%	4%	5%	6%	Years
1	.9009	.9009	.9009	.9009	.9009	.9009	1
2	1.7206	1.7288	1.7369	1.7450	1.7531	1.7612	2
3	2.4665	2.4895	2.5126	2.5358	2.5592	2.5828	3
4	3.1452	3.1885	3.2324	3.2768	3.3218	3.3673	4
5	3.7628	3.8309	3.9003	3.9711	4.0432	4.1166	5
6	4.3247	4.4212	4.5201	4.6216	4.7255	4.8320	6
7	4.8360	4.9636	5.0953	5.2310	5.3710	5.5153	7
8	5.3012	5.4621	5.6289	5.8020	5.9815	6.1677	8
9	5.7245	5.9201	6.1241	6.3370	6.5591	6.7908	9
10	6.1097	6.3410	6.5837	6.8383	7.1055	7.3858	10
11	6.4602	6.7278	7.0101	7.3080	7.6223	7.9540	11
12	6.7791	7.0832	7.4057	7.7480	8.1112	8.4966	12
13	7.0692	7.4098	7.7729	8.1603	8.5736	9.0148	13
14	7.3333	7.7099	8.1136	8.5466	9.0111	9.5096	14
15	7.5735	7.9856	8.4297	8.9085	9.4249	9.9822	15
16	7.7921	8.2391	8.7231	9.2476	9.8164	10.4334	16
17	7.9910	8.4719	8.9953	9.5653	10.1866	10.8644	17
18	8.1720	8.6859	9.2479	9.8630	10.5369	11.2759	18
19	8.3367	8.8826	9.4823	10.1419	10.8683	11.6689	19
20	8.4866	9.0632	9.6998	10.4032	11.1817	12.0441	20

Annual Percentage DECREASE of:

Years	1%	2%	3%	4%	5%	6%	Years
1	.9009	.9009	.9009	.9009	.9009	.9009	1
2	1.7044	1.6963	1.6882	1.6801	1.6719	1.6638	2
3	2.4210	2.3985	2.3762	2.3539	2.3318	2.3099	3
4	3.0602	3.0185	2.9774	2.9367	2.8966	2.8570	4
5	3.6303	3.5659	3.5027	3.4408	3.3800	3.3204	5
6	4.1387	4.0492	3.9619	3.8767	3.7937	3.7127	6
7	4.5922	4.4758	4.3631	4.2537	4.1477	4.0450	7
8	4.9966	4.8525	4.7137	4.5798	4.4508	4.3264	8
9	5.3574	5.1851	5.0200	4.8618	4.7101	4.5647	9
10	5.6791	5.4788	5.2878	5.1057	4.9321	4.7665	10
11	5.9660	5.7380	5.5218	5.3166	5.1221	4.9374	11
12	6.2220	5.9669	5.7262	5.4991	5.2846	5.0821	12
13	6.4502	6.1690	5.9049	5.6569	5.4238	5.2047	13
14	6.6538	6.3474	6.0610	5.7933	5.5429	5.3085	14
15	6.8354	6.5049	6.1975	5.9113	5.6448	5.3964	15
16	6.9973	6.6440	6.3167	6.0134	5.7320	5.4708	16
17	7.1417	6.7667	6.4209	6.1017	5.8067	5.5338	17
18	7.2706	6.8751	6.5120	6.1780	5.8706	5.5872	18
19	7.3855	6.9708	6.5915	6.2441	5.9253	5.6324	19
20	7.4879	7.0553	6.6611	6.3012	5.9721	5.6707	20

ORDINARY ANNUITIES CHANGING IN CONSTANT RATIO

(Present Value of Annual Payments Starting at $1 and Changing in Constant Ratio)

Base: 1.110 000

Annual Percentage INCREASE of:

Years	7%	8%	9%	10%	11%	12%	Years
1	.9009	.9009	.9009	.9009	.9009	.9009	1
2	1.7693	1.7775	1.7856	1.7937	1.8018	1.8099	2
3	2.6065	2.6303	2.6543	2.6784	2.7027	2.7271	3
4	3.4135	3.4601	3.5074	3.5552	3.6036	3.6526	4
5	4.1913	4.2675	4.3451	4.4241	4.5045	4.5864	5
6	4.9412	5.0531	5.1677	5.2851	5.4054	5.5286	6
7	5.6640	5.8174	5.9755	6.1384	6.3063	6.4793	7
8	6.3608	6.5611	6.7687	6.9840	7.2072	7.4386	8
9	7.0325	7.2847	7.5477	7.8220	8.1081	8.4065	9
10	7.6800	7.9887	8.3126	8.6524	9.0090	9.3832	10
11	8.3041	8.6737	9.0637	9.4754	9.9099	10.3686	11
12	8.9058	9.3401	9.8013	10.2909	10.8108	11.3629	12
13	9.4858	9.9886	10.5256	11.0991	11.7117	12.3662	13
14	10.0448	10.6195	11.2368	11.9000	12.6126	13.3785	14
15	10.5838	11.2334	11.9353	12.6937	13.5135	14.3999	15
16	11.1033	11.8307	12.6211	13.4802	14.4144	15.4305	16
17	11.6040	12.4119	13.2946	14.2597	15.3153	16.4704	17
18	12.0868	12.9773	13.9560	15.0321	16.2162	17.5197	18
19	12.5521	13.5275	14.6054	15.7976	17.1171	18.5785	19
20	13.0007	14.0628	15.2432	16.5562	18.0180	19.6467	20

Annual Percentage DECREASE of:

Years	7%	8%	9%	10%	11%	12%	Years
1	.9009	.9009	.9009	.9009	.9009	.9009	1
2	1.6557	1.6476	1.6395	1.6314	1.6232	1.6151	2
3	2.2881	2.2665	2.2450	2.2236	2.2024	2.1814	3
4	2.8180	2.7794	2.7414	2.7038	2.6668	2.6303	4
5	3.2619	3.2046	3.1483	3.0932	3.0392	2.9862	5
6	3.6338	3.5569	3.4820	3.4089	3.3377	3.2683	6
7	3.9455	3.8490	3.7555	3.6649	3.5771	3.4920	7
8	4.2066	4.0911	3.9797	3.8724	3.7690	3.6693	8
9	4.4253	4.2917	4.1636	4.0407	3.9229	3.8099	9
10	4.6086	4.4580	4.3143	4.1771	4.0463	3.9214	10
11	4.7622	4.5958	4.4378	4.2878	4.1452	4.0097	11
12	4.8908	4.7100	4.5391	4.3775	4.2245	4.0798	12
13	4.9986	4.8047	4.6222	4.4502	4.2881	4.1353	13
14	5.0889	4.8832	4.6902	4.5092	4.3391	4.1794	14
15	5.1646	4.9482	4.7461	4.5570	4.3800	4.2143	15
16	5.2280	5.0021	4.7918	4.5958	4.4128	4.2419	16
17	5.2811	5.0468	4.8293	4.6272	4.4391	4.2639	17
18	5.3256	5.0838	4.8601	4.6527	4.4602	4.2813	18
19	5.3629	5.1145	4.8853	4.6733	4.4771	4.2951	19
20	5.3941	5.1400	4.9060	4.6901	4.4906	4.3060	20

12%

ORDINARY ANNUITIES CHANGING IN CONSTANT RATIO

(Present Value of Annual Payments Starting at $1 and Changing in Constant Ratio)

Base: 1.120 000

Annual Percentage INCREASE of:

Years	1%	2%	3%	4%	5%	6%	Years
1	.8929	.8929	.8929	.8929	.8929	.8929	1
2	1.6980	1.7060	1.7140	1.7219	1.7299	1.7379	2
3	2.4241	2.4465	2.4691	2.4918	2.5146	2.5376	3
4	3.0789	3.1209	3.1635	3.2067	3.2503	3.2946	4
5	3.6694	3.7351	3.8022	3.8705	3.9401	4.0109	5
6	4.2018	4.2945	4.3895	4.4869	4.5867	4.6889	6
7	4.6820	4.8039	4.9296	5.0592	5.1928	5.3306	7
8	5.1150	5.2679	5.4264	5.5907	5.7612	5.9379	8
9	5.5055	5.6904	5.8832	6.0842	6.2939	6.5126	9
10	5.8576	6.0752	6.3033	6.5425	6.7934	7.0566	10
11	6.1752	6.4256	6.6896	6.9680	7.2617	7.5714	11
12	6.4616	6.7447	7.0449	7.3632	7.7007	8.0587	12
13	6.7198	7.0354	7.3717	7.7301	8.1123	8.5198	13
14	6.9527	7.3001	7.6722	8.0708	8.4981	8.9562	14
15	7.1627	7.5411	7.9485	8.3872	8.8598	9.3693	15
16	7.3521	7.7607	8.2026	8.6810	9.1989	9.7602	16
17	7.5228	7.9606	8.4364	8.9537	9.5169	10.1302	17
18	7.6768	8.1427	8.6513	9.2070	9.8149	10.4804	18
19	7.8157	8.3085	8.8490	9.4423	10.0943	10.8118	19
20	7.9410	8.4596	9.0307	9.6607	10.3563	11.1254	20

Annual Percentage DECREASE of:

Years	1%	2%	3%	4%	5%	6%	Years
1	.8929	.8929	.8929	.8929	.8929	.8929	1
2	1.6821	1.6741	1.6661	1.6582	1.6502	1.6422	2
3	2.3797	2.3577	2.3358	2.3141	2.2926	2.2711	3
4	2.9963	2.9558	2.9159	2.8764	2.8375	2.7990	4
5	3.5414	3.4792	3.4182	3.3583	3.2996	3.2420	5
6	4.0232	3.9372	3.8533	3.7714	3.6916	3.6138	6
7	4.4491	4.3379	4.2301	4.1255	4.0242	3.9259	7
8	4.8255	4.6885	4.5564	4.4290	4.3062	4.1878	8
9	5.1583	4.9953	4.8390	4.6892	4.5454	4.4076	9
10	5.4524	5.2637	5.0838	4.9121	4.7484	4.5921	10
11	5.7124	5.4986	5.2958	5.1033	4.9205	4.7470	11
12	5.9422	5.7042	5.4794	5.2671	5.0665	4.8769	12
13	6.1453	5.8840	5.6384	5.4075	5.1903	4.9860	13
14	6.3249	6.0414	5.7761	5.5279	5.2954	5.0775	14
15	6.4836	6.1790	5.8954	5.6310	5.3845	5.1543	15
16	6.6239	6.2995	5.9987	5.7194	5.4600	5.2188	16
17	6.7479	6.4049	6.0881	5.7952	5.5241	5.2729	17
18	6.8575	6.4972	6.1656	5.8602	5.5785	5.3184	18
19	6.9544	6.5779	6.2327	5.9159	5.6246	5.3565	19
20	7.0401	6.6485	6.2908	5.9636	5.6637	5.3885	20

ORDINARY ANNUITIES CHANGING IN CONSTANT RATIO

(Present Value of Annual Payments Starting at $1 and Changing in Constant Ratio)

Base: 1.120 000

Annual Percentage INCREASE of:

Years	7%	8%	9%	10%	11%	12%	Years
1	.8929	.8929	.8929	.8929	.8929	.8929	1
2	1.7459	1.7538	1.7618	1.7698	1.7777	1.7857	2
3	2.5608	2.5840	2.6075	2.6310	2.6547	2.6786	3
4	3.3393	3.3846	3.4305	3.4769	3.5239	3.5714	4
5	4.0831	4.1566	4.2314	4.3077	4.3853	4.4643	5
6	4.7937	4.9010	5.0110	5.1236	5.2390	5.3571	6
7	5.4725	5.6188	5.7696	5.9250	6.0851	6.2500	7
8	6.1211	6.3110	6.5079	6.7120	6.9236	7.1429	8
9	6.7407	6.9785	7.2265	7.4850	7.7546	8.0357	9
10	7.3326	7.6221	7.9257	8.2442	8.5782	8.9286	10
11	7.8981	8.2427	8.6063	8.9899	9.3945	9.8214	11
12	8.4384	8.8412	9.2686	9.7222	10.2035	10.7143	12
13	8.9545	9.4183	9.9132	10.4414	11.0052	11.6071	13
14	9.4476	9.9748	10.5405	11.1478	11.7998	12.5000	14
15	9.9187	10.5114	11.1511	11.8416	12.5873	13.3929	15
16	10.3688	11.0289	11.7452	12.5230	13.3678	14.2857	16
17	10.7987	11.5278	12.3235	13.1923	14.1413	15.1786	17
18	11.2095	12.0090	12.8863	13.8495	14.9079	16.0714	18
19	11.6019	12.4729	13.4339	14.4951	15.6677	16.9643	19
20	11.9768	12.9203	13.9670	15.1291	16.4206	17.8571	20

Annual Percentage DECREASE of:

Years	7%	8%	9%	10%	11%	12%	Years
1	.8929	.8929	.8929	.8929	.8929	.8929	1
2	1.6342	1.6263	1.6183	1.6103	1.6024	1.5944	2
3	2.2499	2.2287	2.2077	2.1869	2.1662	2.1456	3
4	2.7610	2.7236	2.6866	2.6502	2.6142	2.5787	4
5	3.1855	3.1301	3.0757	3.0225	2.9702	2.9190	5
6	3.5380	3.4640	3.3919	3.3216	3.2531	3.1863	6
7	3.8306	3.7383	3.6488	3.5620	3.4779	3.3964	7
8	4.0737	3.9636	3.8575	3.7552	3.6566	3.5615	8
9	4.2754	4.1487	4.0271	3.9104	3.7985	3.6911	9
10	4.4430	4.3007	4.1648	4.0352	3.9113	3.7930	10
11	4.5821	4.4256	4.2768	4.1354	4.0010	3.8731	11
12	4.6977	4.5281	4.3678	4.2159	4.0722	3.9360	12
13	4.7936	4.6124	4.4417	4.2807	4.1288	3.9854	13
14	4.8733	4.6816	4.5017	4.3327	4.1738	4.0243	14
15	4.9394	4.7385	4.5505	4.3745	4.2095	4.0548	15
16	4.9943	4.7852	4.5901	4.4081	4.2379	4.0788	16
17	5.0399	4.8235	4.6223	4.4350	4.2605	4.0976	17
18	5.0778	4.8550	4.6485	4.4567	4.2784	4.1124	18
19	5.1092	4.8809	4.6698	4.4742	4.2927	4.1240	19
20	5.1354	4.9022	4.6870	4.4882	4.3040	4.1332	20

13%

ORDINARY ANNUITIES CHANGING IN CONSTANT RATIO

(Present Value of Annual Payments Starting at $1 and Changing in Constant Ratio)

Base: 1.130 000

Annual Percentage INCREASE of:

Years	1%	2%	3%	4%	5%	6%	Years
1	.8850	.8850	.8850	.8850	.8850	.8850	1
2	1.6759	1.6838	1.6916	1.6994	1.7073	1.7151	2
3	2.3829	2.4048	2.4269	2.4490	2.4713	2.4938	3
4	3.0148	3.0557	3.0970	3.1389	3.1813	3.2243	4
5	3.5796	3.6432	3.7079	3.7739	3.8411	3.9095	5
6	4.0844	4.1735	4.2647	4.3583	4.4541	4.5523	6
7	4.5356	4.6522	4.7723	4.8961	5.0237	5.1552	7
8	4.9389	5.0843	5.2349	5.3911	5.5530	5.7208	8
9	5.2994	5.4743	5.6566	5.8467	6.0448	6.2514	9
10	5.6216	5.8263	6.0410	6.2660	6.5018	6.7491	10
11	5.9096	6.1441	6.3913	6.6519	6.9265	7.2160	11
12	6.1670	6.4310	6.7107	7.0070	7.3211	7.6539	12
13	6.3970	6.6899	7.0018	7.3339	7.6877	8.0647	13
14	6.6026	6.9236	7.2671	7.6347	8.0284	8.4501	14
15	6.7864	7.1346	7.5090	7.9116	8.3450	8.8116	15
16	6.9507	7.3251	7.7294	8.1664	8.6391	9.1507	16
17	7.0975	7.4970	7.9303	8.4010	8.9125	9.4688	17
18	7.2288	7.6521	8.1135	8.6168	9.1665	9.7672	18
19	7.3461	7.7922	8.2804	8.8155	9.4025	10.0471	19
20	7.4509	7.9186	8.4326	8.9983	9.6218	10.3097	20

Annual Percentage DECREASE of:

Years	1%	2%	3%	4%	5%	6%	Years
1	.8850	.8850	.8850	.8850	.8850	.8850	1
2	1.6603	1.6524	1.6446	1.6368	1.6289	1.6211	2
3	2.3395	2.3180	2.2967	2.2755	2.2544	2.2335	3
4	2.9346	2.8953	2.8565	2.8181	2.7803	2.7429	4
5	3.4560	3.3959	3.3370	3.2791	3.2223	3.1667	5
6	3.9128	3.8301	3.7494	3.6707	3.5940	3.5192	6
7	4.3130	4.2066	4.1035	4.0035	3.9065	3.8124	7
8	4.6636	4.5332	4.4074	4.2861	4.1692	4.0563	8
9	4.9707	4.8164	4.6683	4.5263	4.3900	4.2593	9
10	5.2399	5.0620	4.8923	4.7303	4.5757	4.4281	10
11	5.4756	5.2750	5.0845	4.9036	4.7318	4.5685	11
12	5.6822	5.4597	5.2495	5.0508	4.8630	4.6853	12
13	5.8632	5.6200	5.3912	5.1759	4.9733	4.7824	13
14	6.0217	5.7589	5.5128	5.2822	5.0660	4.8633	14
15	6.1606	5.8794	5.6172	5.3725	5.1440	4.9305	15
16	6.2823	5.9839	5.7068	5.4492	5.2096	4.9864	16
17	6.3889	6.0745	5.7837	5.5144	5.2647	5.0330	17
18	6.4823	6.1531	5.8497	5.5697	5.3110	5.0717	18
19	6.5642	6.2213	5.9064	5.6168	5.3500	5.1039	19
20	6.6359	6.2804	5.9551	5.6567	5.3827	5.1307	20

ORDINARY ANNUITIES CHANGING IN CONSTANT RATIO

(Present Value of Annual Payments Starting at $1 and Changing in Constant Ratio)

Base: 1.130 000

Annual Percentage INCREASE of:

Years	7%	8%	9%	10%	11%	12%	Years
1	.8850	.8850	.8850	.8850	.8850	.8850	1
2	1.7229	1.7308	1.7386	1.7464	1.7542	1.7621	2
3	2.5164	2.5391	2.5620	2.5850	2.6082	2.6314	3
4	3.2677	3.3117	3.3563	3.4013	3.4469	3.4931	4
5	3.9792	4.0502	4.1224	4.1960	4.2709	4.3472	5
6	4.6529	4.7559	4.8614	4.9695	5.0803	5.1936	6
7	5.2908	5.4304	5.5743	5.7226	5.8753	6.0326	7
8	5.8948	6.0751	6.2619	6.4556	6.6563	6.8642	8
9	6.4667	6.6912	6.9252	7.1692	7.4234	7.6884	9
10	7.0083	7.2801	7.5651	7.8638	8.1770	8.5053	10
11	7.5212	7.8429	8.1822	8.5400	8.9172	9.3150	11
12	8.0068	8.3809	8.7775	9.1982	9.6443	10.1175	12
13	8.4666	8.8950	9.3518	9.8390	10.3586	10.9130	13
14	8.9020	9.3864	9.9057	10.4627	11.0602	11.7013	14
15	9.3143	9.8560	10.4400	11.0699	11.7494	12.4827	15
16	9.7047	10.3048	10.9554	11.6610	12.4264	13.2572	16
17	10.0743	10.7338	11.4526	12.2363	13.0914	14.0249	17
18	10.4244	11.1438	11.9321	12.7964	13.7447	14.7857	18
19	10.7558	11.5357	12.3947	13.3417	14.3864	15.5398	19
20	11.0697	11.9102	12.8409	13.8724	15.0167	16.2873	20

Annual Percentage DECREASE of:

Years	7%	8%	9%	10%	11%	12%	Years
1	.8850	.8850	.8850	.8850	.8850	.8850	1
2	1.6133	1.6055	1.5976	1.5898	1.5820	1.5741	2
3	2.2127	2.1920	2.1715	2.1512	2.1309	2.1108	3
4	2.7060	2.6696	2.6337	2.5983	2.5633	2.5288	4
5	3.1120	3.0585	3.0059	2.9544	2.9038	2.8543	5
6	3.4462	3.3750	3.3056	3.2380	3.1720	3.1078	6
7	3.7212	3.6328	3.5470	3.4639	3.3833	3.3052	7
8	3.9475	3.8426	3.7414	3.6438	3.5497	3.4589	8
9	4.1338	4.0135	3.8979	3.7871	3.6807	3.5786	9
10	4.2871	4.1525	4.0240	3.9012	3.7839	3.6718	10
11	4.4133	4.2658	4.1255	3.9921	3.8652	3.7444	11
12	4.5171	4.3580	4.2073	4.0645	3.9292	3.8010	12
13	4.6026	4.4331	4.2731	4.1222	3.9797	3.8450	13
14	4.6729	4.4942	4.3261	4.1681	4.0194	3.8793	14
15	4.7308	4.5439	4.3688	4.2047	4.0507	3.9060	15
16	4.7785	4.5844	4.4032	4.2338	4.0753	3.9268	16
17	4.8177	4.6174	4.4309	4.2570	4.0947	3.9430	17
18	4.8499	4.6443	4.4532	4.2755	4.1100	3.9556	18
19	4.8765	4.6661	4.4712	4.2902	4.1220	3.9654	19
20	4.8984	4.6839	4.4856	4.3020	4.1315	3.9731	20

14%

ORDINARY ANNUITIES CHANGING IN CONSTANT RATIO

(Present Value of Annual Payments Starting at $1 and Changing in Constant Ratio)

Base: 1.140 000

Annual Percentage INCREASE of:

Years	1%	2%	3%	4%	5%	6%	Years
1	.8772	.8772	.8772	.8772	.8772	.8772	1
2	1.6544	1.6620	1.6697	1.6774	1.6851	1.6928	2
3	2.3429	2.3643	2.3858	2.4075	2.4293	2.4512	3
4	2.9529	2.9926	3.0328	3.0735	3.1147	3.1564	4
5	3.4934	3.5548	3.6174	3.6811	3.7460	3.8121	5
6	3.9722	4.0578	4.1455	4.2354	4.3274	4.4218	6
7	4.3964	4.5079	4.6227	4.7410	4.8630	4.9887	7
8	4.7723	4.9105	5.0538	5.2024	5.3563	5.5158	8
9	5.1053	5.2708	5.4434	5.6232	5.8106	6.0059	9
10	5.4003	5.5932	5.7953	6.0071	6.2291	6.4616	10
11	5.6616	5.8816	6.1133	6.3574	6.6145	6.8854	11
12	5.8932	6.1397	6.4006	6.6769	6.9695	7.2794	12
13	6.0984	6.3706	6.6602	6.9684	7.2965	7.6457	13
14	6.2801	6.5772	6.8948	7.2343	7.5976	7.9864	14
15	6.4412	6.7621	7.1067	7.4769	7.8750	8.3031	15
16	6.5838	6.9275	7.2981	7.6983	8.1305	8.5976	16
17	6.7102	7.0755	7.4711	7.9002	8.3658	8.8715	17
18	6.8222	7.2079	7.6274	8.0844	8.5825	9.1261	18
19	6.9215	7.3263	7.7686	8.2524	8.7822	9.3629	19
20	7.0094	7.4323	7.8962	8.4057	8.9660	9.5830	20

Annual Percentage DECREASE of:

Years	1%	2%	3%	4%	5%	6%	Years
1	.8772	.8772	.8772	.8772	.8772	.8772	1
2	1.6390	1.6313	1.6236	1.6159	1.6082	1.6005	2
3	2.3005	2.2795	2.2587	2.2379	2.2173	2.1969	3
4	2.8750	2.8368	2.7990	2.7618	2.7250	2.6887	4
5	3.3739	3.3158	3.2588	3.2029	3.1480	3.0942	5
6	3.8072	3.7276	3.6501	3.5744	3.5005	3.4285	6
7	4.1834	4.0817	3.9829	3.8872	3.7943	3.7042	7
8	4.5102	4.3860	4.2662	4.1506	4.0391	3.9316	8
9	4.7939	4.6476	4.5072	4.3724	4.2431	4.1190	9
10	5.0403	4.8725	4.7123	4.5593	4.4131	4.2736	10
11	5.2543	5.0658	4.8867	4.7166	4.5548	4.4010	11
12	5.4402	5.2320	5.0352	4.8490	4.6729	4.5061	12
13	5.6015	5.3749	5.1615	4.9606	4.7712	4.5927	13
14	5.7417	5.4977	5.2690	5.0545	4.8532	4.6642	14
15	5.8634	5.6033	5.3605	5.1336	4.9216	4.7231	15
16	5.9691	5.6941	5.4383	5.2003	4.9785	4.7717	16
17	6.0609	5.7721	5.5045	5.2564	5.0259	4.8117	17
18	6.1406	5.8392	5.5609	5.3036	5.0655	4.8448	18
19	6.2098	5.8968	5.6088	5.3434	5.0984	4.8720	19
20	6.2699	5.9464	5.6496	5.3769	5.1259	4.8945	20

14%

ORDINARY ANNUITIES CHANGING IN CONSTANT RATIO

(Present Value of Annual Payments Starting at $1 and Changing in Constant Ratio)

Base: 1.140 000

Annual Percentage INCREASE of:

Years	7%	8%	9%	10%	11%	12%	Years
1	.8772	.8772	.8772	.8772	.8772	.8772	1
2	1.7005	1.7082	1.7159	1.7236	1.7313	1.7390	2
3	2.4733	2.4955	2.5178	2.5403	2.5629	2.5857	3
4	3.1986	3.2414	3.2846	3.3284	3.3727	3.4175	4
5	3.8794	3.9480	4.0177	4.0888	4.1611	4.2347	5
6	4.5184	4.6174	4.7187	4.8225	4.9288	5.0376	6
7	5.1181	5.2515	5.3889	5.5305	5.6763	5.8265	7
8	5.6811	5.8523	6.0298	6.2136	6.4041	6.6014	8
9	6.2094	6.4215	6.6425	6.8728	7.1128	7.3628	9
10	6.7053	6.9607	7.2284	7.5089	7.8028	8.1108	10
11	7.1708	7.4716	7.7885	8.1226	8.4746	8.8457	11
12	7.6077	7.9555	8.3241	8.7148	9.1288	9.5677	12
13	8.0177	8.4140	8.8362	9.2862	9.7658	10.2771	13
14	8.4026	8.8483	9.3259	9.8375	10.3860	10.9740	14
15	8.7638	9.2598	9.7940	10.3696	10.9899	11.6586	15
16	9.1029	9.6497	10.2417	10.8829	11.5778	12.3313	16
17	9.4212	10.0190	10.6696	11.3782	12.1504	12.9921	17
18	9.7199	10.3689	11.0789	11.8562	12.7078	13.6414	18
19	10.0002	10.7003	11.4702	12.3174	13.2506	14.2793	19
20	10.2634	11.0143	11.8443	12.7624	13.7791	14.9060	20

Annual Percentage DECREASE of:

Years	7%	8%	9%	10%	11%	12%	Years
1	.8772	.8772	.8772	.8772	.8772	.8772	1
2	1.5928	1.5851	1.5774	1.5697	1.5620	1.5543	2
3	2.1766	2.1564	2.1364	2.1164	2.0967	2.0770	3
4	2.6528	2.6174	2.5825	2.5481	2.5141	2.4805	4
5	3.0413	2.9895	2.9387	2.8888	2.8399	2.7920	5
6	3.3583	3.2898	3.2230	3.1578	3.0943	3.0324	6
7	3.6168	3.5321	3.4499	3.3702	3.2929	3.2180	7
8	3.8278	3.7277	3.6311	3.5379	3.4480	3.3613	8
9	3.9999	3.8855	3.7757	3.6703	3.5691	3.4718	9
10	4.1402	4.0128	3.8911	3.7748	3.6636	3.5572	10
11	4.2548	4.1156	3.9833	3.8573	3.7373	3.6231	11
12	4.3482	4.1986	4.0568	3.9224	3.7949	3.6740	12
13	4.4244	4.2655	4.1155	3.9738	3.8399	3.7132	13
14	4.4866	4.3195	4.1624	4.0144	3.8750	3.7436	14
15	4.5373	4.3631	4.1998	4.0465	3.9024	3.7670	15
16	4.5787	4.3983	4.2297	4.0718	3.9238	3.7850	16
17	4.6124	4.4267	4.2535	4.0918	3.9405	3.7990	17
18	4.6400	4.4496	4.2725	4.1075	3.9536	3.8097	18
19	4.6624	4.4681	4.2877	4.1200	3.9638	3.8180	19
20	4.6807	4.4830	4.2999	4.1298	3.9717	3.8244	20

15%

ORDINARY ANNUITIES CHANGING IN CONSTANT RATIO

(Present Value of Annual Payments Starting at $1 and Changing in Constant Ratio)

Base: 1.150 000

Annual Percentage INCREASE of:

Years	1%	2%	3%	4%	5%	6%	Years
1	.8696	.8696	.8696	.8696	.8696	.8696	1
2	1.6333	1.6408	1.6484	1.6560	1.6635	1.6711	2
3	2.3040	2.3249	2.3460	2.3671	2.3884	2.4099	3
4	2.8931	2.9317	2.9707	3.0103	3.0503	3.0908	4
5	3.4104	3.4698	3.5303	3.5919	3.6546	3.7185	5
6	3.8648	3.9471	4.0315	4.1179	4.2064	4.2971	6
7	4.2639	4.3705	4.4804	4.5936	4.7102	4.8303	7
8	4.6144	4.7460	4.8824	5.0237	5.1702	5.3219	8
9	4.9222	5.0791	5.2425	5.4128	5.5902	5.7749	9
10	5.1925	5.3745	5.5650	5.7646	5.9736	6.1926	10
11	5.4300	5.6365	5.8539	6.0828	6.3237	6.5775	11
12	5.6385	5.8689	6.1126	6.3705	6.6434	6.9323	12
13	5.8216	6.0750	6.3444	6.6307	6.9353	7.2593	13
14	5.9825	6.2578	6.5519	6.8660	7.2018	7.5608	14
15	6.1237	6.4200	6.7378	7.0789	7.4451	7.8386	15
16	6.2478	6.5638	6.9043	7.2713	7.6673	8.0947	16
17	6.3568	6.6914	7.0534	7.4454	7.8701	8.3308	17
18	6.4525	6.8045	7.1870	7.6028	8.0553	8.5484	18
19	6.5365	6.9049	7.3066	7.7451	8.2244	8.7489	19
20	6.6103	6.9939	7.4137	7.8738	8.3788	8.9338	20

Annual Percentage DECREASE of:

Years	1%	2%	3%	4%	5%	6%	Years
1	.8696	.8696	.8696	.8696	.8696	.8696	1
2	1.6181	1.6106	1.6030	1.5955	1.5879	1.5803	2
3	2.2626	2.2421	2.2217	2.2014	2.1813	2.1613	3
4	2.8174	2.7802	2.7435	2.7073	2.6715	2.6362	4
5	3.2949	3.2388	3.1837	3.1296	3.0765	3.0244	5
6	3.7061	3.6296	3.5549	3.4821	3.4110	3.3417	6
7	4.0600	3.9626	3.8681	3.7763	3.6873	3.6010	7
8	4.3647	4.2464	4.1322	4.0220	3.9156	3.8130	8
9	4.6270	4.4882	4.3550	4.2270	4.1042	3.9863	9
10	4.8528	4.6943	4.5429	4.3982	4.2600	4.1279	10
11	5.0472	4.8699	4.7014	4.5411	4.3887	4.2437	11
12	5.2146	5.0196	4.8351	4.6604	4.4950	4.3383	12
13	5.3586	5.1471	4.9479	4.7600	4.5828	4.4157	13
14	5.4826	5.2558	5.0430	4.8431	4.6554	4.4789	14
15	5.5894	5.3484	5.1232	4.9125	4.7153	4.5306	15
16	5.6813	5.4274	5.1909	4.9705	4.7648	4.5728	16
17	5.7604	5.4946	5.2480	5.0188	4.8057	4.6073	17
18	5.8285	5.5519	5.2961	5.0592	4.8395	4.6356	18
19	5.8872	5.6008	5.3367	5.0929	4.8674	4.6586	19
20	5.9377	5.6424	5.3710	5.1210	4.8905	4.6775	20

ORDINARY ANNUITIES CHANGING IN CONSTANT RATIO

(Present Value of Annual Payments Starting at $1 and Changing in Constant Ratio)

Base: 1.150 000

Annual Percentage INCREASE of:

Years	7%	8%	9%	10%	11%	12%	Years
1	.8696	.8696	.8696	.8696	.8696	.8696	1
2	1.6786	1.6862	1.6938	1.7013	1.7089	1.7164	2
3	2.4314	2.4531	2.4750	2.4969	2.5190	2.5412	3
4	3.1319	3.1734	3.2154	3.2579	3.3010	3.3445	4
5	3.7835	3.8498	3.9172	3.9858	4.0557	4.1268	5
6	4.3899	4.4850	4.5824	4.6821	4.7842	4.8887	6
7	4.9541	5.0816	5.2129	5.3481	5.4874	5.6308	7
8	5.4790	5.6418	5.8105	5.9851	6.1661	6.3534	8
9	5.9674	6.1680	6.3769	6.5945	6.8212	7.0573	9
10	6.4219	6.6621	6.9137	7.1773	7.4535	7.7427	10
11	6.8447	7.1261	7.4226	7.7348	8.0638	8.4103	11
12	7.2381	7.5619	7.9049	8.2681	8.6529	9.0605	12
13	7.6042	7.9712	8.3620	8.7782	9.2215	9.6937	13
14	7.9447	8.3556	8.7953	9.2661	9.7703	10.3104	14
15	8.2616	8.7165	9.2060	9.7328	10.3000	10.9110	15
16	8.5565	9.0555	9.5952	10.1792	10.8113	11.4959	16
17	8.8308	9.3739	9.9642	10.6062	11.3048	12.0656	17
18	9.0861	9.6729	10.3139	11.0146	11.7812	12.6204	18
19	9.3235	9.9537	10.6453	11.4053	12.2410	13.1607	19
20	9.5445	10.2173	10.9595	11.7790	12.6848	13.6870	20

Annual Percentage DECREASE of:

Years	7%	8%	9%	10%	11%	12%	Years
1	.8696	.8696	.8696	.8696	.8696	.8696	1
2	1.5728	1.5652	1.5577	1.5501	1.5425	1.5350	2
3	2.1415	2.1217	2.1021	2.0827	2.0634	2.0442	3
4	2.6014	2.5670	2.5330	2.4995	2.4664	2.4338	4
5	2.9733	2.9231	2.8739	2.8257	2.7784	2.7319	5
6	3.2740	3.2081	3.1437	3.0810	3.0198	2.9601	6
7	3.5173	3.4360	3.3572	3.2808	3.2066	3.1347	7
8	3.7140	3.6184	3.5261	3.4371	3.3512	3.2683	8
9	3.8730	3.7643	3.6598	3.5595	3.4631	3.3705	9
10	4.0017	3.8810	3.7656	3.6552	3.5497	3.4487	10
11	4.1057	3.9744	3.8493	3.7302	3.6167	3.5086	11
12	4.1898	4.0490	3.9155	3.7888	3.6686	3.5544	12
13	4.2579	4.1088	3.9679	3.8348	3.7087	3.5895	13
14	4.3129	4.1566	4.0094	3.8707	3.7398	3.6163	14
15	4.3574	4.1949	4.0422	3.8988	3.7639	3.6368	15
16	4.3934	4.2254	4.0682	3.9208	3.7825	3.6525	16
17	4.4224	4.2499	4.0888	3.9380	3.7969	3.6645	17
18	4.4460	4.2695	4.1050	3.9515	3.8080	3.6737	18
19	4.4650	4.2852	4.1179	3.9620	3.8166	3.6808	19
20	4.4804	4.2977	4.1281	3.9703	3.8233	3.6862	20

16%

ORDINARY ANNUITIES CHANGING IN CONSTANT RATIO

(Present Value of Annual Payments Starting at $1 and Changing in Constant Ratio)

Base: 1.160 000

Annual Percentage INCREASE of:

Years	1%	2%	3%	4%	5%	6%	Years
1	.8621	.8621	.8621	.8621	.8621	.8621	1
2	1.6127	1.6201	1.6275	1.6350	1.6424	1.6498	2
3	2.2662	2.2866	2.3072	2.3279	2.3487	2.3697	3
4	2.8352	2.8727	2.9107	2.9491	2.9881	3.0275	4
5	3.3307	3.3881	3.4466	3.5061	3.5668	3.6285	5
6	3.7620	3.8413	3.9224	4.0055	4.0906	4.1778	6
7	4.1376	4.2397	4.3449	4.4532	4.5648	4.6797	7
8	4.4647	4.5901	4.7200	4.8546	4.9940	5.1384	8
9	4.7494	4.8982	5.0531	5.2145	5.3825	5.5575	9
10	4.9973	5.1691	5.3489	5.5371	5.7341	5.9404	10
11	5.2132	5.4073	5.6115	5.8264	6.0525	6.2904	11
12	5.4011	5.6168	5.8447	6.0857	6.3406	6.6102	12
13	5.5648	5.8010	6.0518	6.3182	6.6014	6.9024	13
14	5.7073	5.9629	6.2356	6.5267	6.8375	7.1695	14
15	5.8313	6.1053	6.3989	6.7136	7.0512	7.4135	15
16	5.9394	6.2305	6.5438	6.8811	7.2446	7.6364	16
17	6.0334	6.3406	6.6725	7.0314	7.4197	7.8402	17
18	6.1153	6.4375	6.7868	7.1661	7.5781	8.0264	18
19	6.1866	6.5226	6.8883	7.2868	7.7216	8.1965	19
20	6.2487	6.5975	6.9784	7.3951	7.8514	8.3520	20

Annual Percentage DECREASE of:

Years	1%	2%	3%	4%	5%	6%	Years
1	.8621	.8621	.8621	.8621	.8621	.8621	1
2	1.5978	1.5904	1.5829	1.5755	1.5681	1.5606	2
3	2.2257	2.2057	2.1857	2.1659	2.1463	2.1267	3
4	2.7616	2.7255	2.6898	2.6546	2.6198	2.5855	4
5	3.2189	3.1646	3.1113	3.0590	3.0076	2.9572	5
6	3.6093	3.5356	3.4638	3.3936	3.3252	3.2584	6
7	3.9424	3.8491	3.7585	3.6706	3.5853	3.5025	7
8	4.2267	4.1139	4.0049	3.8998	3.7983	3.7003	8
9	4.4693	4.3376	4.2110	4.0895	3.9727	3.8606	9
10	4.6764	4.5266	4.3834	4.2465	4.1156	3.9905	10
11	4.8532	4.6862	4.5275	4.3764	4.2326	4.0957	11
12	5.0040	4.8211	4.6480	4.4839	4.3284	4.1810	12
13	5.1327	4.9351	4.7487	4.5729	4.4069	4.2501	13
14	5.2426	5.0314	4.8330	4.6465	4.4712	4.3061	14
15	5.3363	5.1127	4.9034	4.7075	4.5238	4.3515	15
16	5.4164	5.1814	4.9624	4.7579	4.5669	4.3883	16
17	5.4846	5.2395	5.0116	4.7996	4.6022	4.4181	17
18	5.5429	5.2885	5.0528	4.8342	4.6311	4.4423	18
19	5.5927	5.3300	5.0873	4.8628	4.6548	4.4618	19
20	5.6351	5.3650	5.1161	4.8864	4.6742	4.4777	20

ORDINARY ANNUITIES CHANGING IN CONSTANT RATIO

(Present Value of Annual Payments Starting at $1 and Changing in Constant Ratio)

Base: 1.160 000

Annual Percentage INCREASE of:

Years	7%	8%	9%	10%	11%	12%	Years
1	.8621	.8621	.8621	.8621	.8621	.8621	1
2	1.6573	1.6647	1.6721	1.6795	1.6870	1.6944	2
3	2.3907	2.4119	2.4333	2.4547	2.4763	2.4981	3
4	3.0673	3.1077	3.1485	3.1898	3.2317	3.2740	4
5	3.6914	3.7554	3.8206	3.8869	3.9544	4.0232	5
6	4.2671	4.3585	4.4521	4.5479	4.6461	4.7465	6
7	4.7981	4.9200	5.0455	5.1748	5.3079	5.4449	7
8	5.2879	5.4427	5.6031	5.7692	5.9411	6.1192	8
9	5.7397	5.9294	6.1271	6.3328	6.5471	6.7703	9
10	6.1564	6.3826	6.6194	6.8674	7.1270	7.3989	10
11	6.5408	6.8045	7.0820	7.3742	7.6819	8.0058	11
12	6.8954	7.1973	7.5167	7.8549	8.2128	8.5918	12
13	7.2225	7.5630	7.9252	8.3106	8.7209	9.1576	13
14	7.5242	7.9035	8.3090	8.7428	9.2071	9.7039	14
15	7.8025	8.2205	8.6697	9.1527	9.6723	10.2314	15
16	8.0592	8.5156	9.0086	9.5414	10.1174	10.7406	16
17	8.2960	8.7904	9.3270	9.9099	10.5434	11.2323	17
18	8.5144	9.0462	9.6263	10.2594	10.9510	11.7071	18
19	8.7159	9.2844	9.9074	10.5908	11.3411	12.1655	19
20	8.9017	9.5062	10.1716	10.9051	11.7143	12.6080	20

Annual Percentage DECREASE of:

Years	7%	8%	9%	10%	11%	12%	Years
1	.8621	.8621	.8621	.8621	.8621	.8621	1
2	1.5532	1.5458	1.5383	1.5309	1.5235	1.5161	2
3	2.1073	2.0880	2.0689	2.0498	2.0309	2.0122	3
4	2.5516	2.5181	2.4851	2.4525	2.4203	2.3885	4
5	2.9077	2.8592	2.8116	2.7648	2.7190	2.6741	5
6	3.1933	3.1297	3.0677	3.0072	2.9482	2.8907	6
7	3.4222	3.3442	3.2686	3.1952	3.1241	3.0550	7
8	3.6057	3.5144	3.4262	3.3411	3.2590	3.1797	8
9	3.7529	3.6493	3.5499	3.4543	3.3625	3.2742	9
10	3.8708	3.7564	3.6469	3.5422	3.4419	3.3460	10
11	3.9654	3.8413	3.7230	3.6103	3.5028	3.4004	11
12	4.0412	3.9086	3.7827	3.6632	3.5496	3.4417	12
13	4.1020	3.9620	3.8295	3.7042	3.5855	3.4730	13
14	4.1508	4.0043	3.8663	3.7360	3.6130	3.4968	14
15	4.1898	4.0379	3.8951	3.7607	3.6341	3.5148	15
16	4.2212	4.0646	3.9177	3.7798	3.6503	3.5285	16
17	4.2463	4.0857	3.9354	3.7947	3.6627	3.5388	17
18	4.2664	4.1024	3.9494	3.8062	3.6723	3.5467	18
19	4.2826	4.1157	3.9603	3.8152	3.6796	3.5527	19
20	4.2955	4.1263	3.9688	3.8221	3.6852	3.5572	20

17%

ORDINARY ANNUITIES CHANGING IN CONSTANT RATIO

(Present Value of Annual Payments Starting at $1 and Changing in Constant Ratio)

Base: 1.170 000

Annual Percentage INCREASE of:

Years	1%	2%	3%	4%	5%	6%	Years
1	.8547	.8547	.8547	.8547	.8547	.8547	1
2	1.5925	1.5998	1.6071	1.6144	1.6217	1.6290	2
3	2.2294	2.2494	2.2695	2.2898	2.3101	2.3306	3
4	2.7793	2.8157	2.8527	2.8900	2.9279	2.9662	4
5	3.2539	3.3094	3.3660	3.4236	3.4823	3.5420	5
6	3.6636	3.7399	3.8179	3.8979	3.9798	4.0637	6
7	4.0173	4.1151	4.2158	4.3195	4.4263	4.5363	7
8	4.3226	4.4422	4.5660	4.6943	4.8271	4.9645	8
9	4.5862	4.7274	4.8744	5.0274	5.1867	5.3525	9
10	4.8137	4.9760	5.1458	5.3235	5.5094	5.7040	10
11	5.0101	5.1928	5.3848	5.5867	5.7990	6.0224	11
12	5.1797	5.3817	5.5952	5.8207	6.0590	6.3109	12
13	5.3261	5.5465	5.7803	6.0286	6.2922	6.5723	13
14	5.4524	5.6901	5.9434	6.2135	6.5016	6.8091	14
15	5.5615	5.8153	6.0869	6.3778	6.6895	7.0236	15
16	5.6556	5.9244	6.2133	6.5238	6.8581	7.2180	16
17	5.7369	6.0196	6.3245	6.6537	7.0094	7.3940	17
18	5.8071	6.1026	6.4224	6.7691	7.1452	7.5536	18
19	5.8677	6.1749	6.5086	6.8717	7.2670	7.6981	19
20	5.9199	6.2379	6.5845	6.9628	7.3764	7.8291	20

Annual Percentage DECREASE of:

Years	1%	2%	3%	4%	5%	6%	Years
1	.8547	.8547	.8547	.8547	.8547	.8547	1
2	1.5779	1.5706	1.5633	1.5560	1.5487	1.5414	2
3	2.1899	2.1702	2.1508	2.1314	2.1122	2.0931	3
4	2.7077	2.6725	2.6378	2.6036	2.5697	2.5363	4
5	3.1458	3.0932	3.0416	2.9909	2.9412	2.8924	5
6	3.5165	3.4456	3.3764	3.3088	3.2429	3.1785	6
7	3.8302	3.7408	3.6539	3.5696	3.4878	3.4084	7
8	4.0957	3.9880	3.8840	3.7836	3.6867	3.5931	8
9	4.3203	4.1951	4.0748	3.9592	3.8482	3.7414	9
10	4.5103	4.3685	4.2329	4.1033	3.9793	3.8606	10
11	4.6711	4.5138	4.3641	4.2215	4.0857	3.9564	11
12	4.8072	4.6355	4.4728	4.3185	4.1722	4.0334	12
13	4.9223	4.7374	4.5629	4.3981	4.2424	4.0952	13
14	5.0197	4.8228	4.6376	4.4634	4.2994	4.1448	14
15	5.1022	4.8943	4.6996	4.5170	4.3456	4.1847	15
16	5.1719	4.9542	4.7509	4.5609	4.3832	4.2168	16
17	5.2309	5.0044	4.7935	4.5970	4.4137	4.2426	17
18	5.2809	5.0464	4.8288	4.6266	4.4385	4.2633	18
19	5.3231	5.0816	4.8581	4.6509	4.4586	4.2799	19
20	5.3589	5.1111	4.8823	4.6708	4.4749	4.2932	20

ORDINARY ANNUITIES CHANGING IN CONSTANT RATIO

(Present Value of Annual Payments Starting at $1 and Changing in Constant Ratio)

Base: 1.170 000

Annual Percentage INCREASE of:

Years	7%	8%	9%	10%	11%	12%	Years
1	.8547	.8547	.8547	.8547	.8547	.8547	1
2	1.6364	1.6437	1.6510	1.6583	1.6656	1.6729	2
3	2.3512	2.3719	2.3928	2.4138	2.4349	2.4561	3
4	3.0049	3.0442	3.0839	3.1240	3.1647	3.2058	4
5	3.6028	3.6647	3.7277	3.7918	3.8571	3.9235	5
6	4.1496	4.2375	4.3275	4.4197	4.5140	4.6106	6
7	4.6496	4.7662	4.8863	5.0099	5.1372	5.2682	7
8	5.1069	5.2543	5.4069	5.5649	5.7285	5.8978	8
9	5.5251	5.7048	5.8919	6.0867	6.2894	6.5004	9
10	5.9076	6.1207	6.3437	6.5772	6.8216	7.0773	10
11	6.2574	6.5046	6.7647	7.0384	7.3264	7.6296	11
12	6.5773	6.8589	7.1568	7.4720	7.8054	8.1582	12
13	6.8698	7.1860	7.5222	7.8797	8.2599	8.6643	13
14	7.1373	7.4879	7.8626	8.2629	8.6910	9.1487	14
15	7.3820	7.7667	8.1796	8.6233	9.1000	9.6125	15
16	7.6058	8.0239	8.4751	8.9620	9.4880	10.0564	16
17	7.8104	8.2614	8.7503	9.2806	9.8562	10.4813	17
18	7.9975	8.4806	9.0067	9.5800	10.2054	10.8881	18
19	8.1687	8.6830	9.2455	9.8615	10.5368	11.2775	19
20	8.3252	8.8697	9.4680	10.1262	10.8511	11.6503	20

Annual Percentage DECREASE of:

Years	7%	8%	9%	10%	11%	12%	Years
1	.8547	.8547	.8547	.8547	.8547	.8547	1
2	1.5341	1.5268	1.5195	1.5122	1.5049	1.4976	2
3	2.0741	2.0552	2.0365	2.0179	1.9994	1.9811	3
4	2.5033	2.4708	2.4387	2.4069	2.3756	2.3447	4
5	2.8445	2.7975	2.7514	2.7062	2.6618	2.6183	5
6	3.1157	3.0545	2.9947	2.9364	2.8795	2.8240	6
7	3.3313	3.2565	3.1839	3.1135	3.0451	2.9787	7
8	3.5027	3.4154	3.3311	3.2497	3.1710	3.0951	8
9	3.6389	3.5403	3.4455	3.3544	3.2669	3.1826	9
10	3.7471	3.6385	3.5346	3.4350	3.3398	3.2485	10
11	3.8332	3.7158	3.6038	3.4970	3.3952	3.2980	11
12	3.9016	3.7765	3.6577	3.5447	3.4374	3.3353	12
13	3.9560	3.8243	3.6995	3.5814	3.4695	3.3633	13
14	3.9992	3.8618	3.7321	3.6096	3.4939	3.3843	14
15	4.0335	3.8913	3.7575	3.6313	3.5124	3.4002	15
16	4.0609	3.9146	3.7772	3.6480	3.5265	3.4121	16
17	4.0826	3.9328	3.7925	3.6609	3.5373	3.4211	17
18	4.0998	3.9472	3.8044	3.6708	3.5455	3.4278	18
19	4.1135	3.9585	3.8137	3.6784	3.5517	3.4329	19
20	4.1244	3.9673	3.8209	3.6842	3.5564	3.4367	20

18%

ORDINARY ANNUITIES CHANGING IN CONSTANT RATIO

(Present Value of Annual Payments Starting at $1 and Changing in Constant Ratio)

Base: 1.180 000

Annual Percentage INCREASE of:

Years	1%	2%	3%	4%	5%	6%	Years
1	.8475	.8475	.8475	.8475	.8475	.8475	1
2	1.5728	1.5800	1.5872	1.5944	1.6016	1.6087	2
3	2.1937	2.2132	2.2329	2.2527	2.2726	2.2926	3
4	2.7251	2.7606	2.7965	2.8329	2.8697	2.9069	4
5	3.1800	3.2337	3.2885	3.3442	3.4010	3.4587	5
6	3.5693	3.6427	3.7179	3.7949	3.8737	3.9545	6
7	3.9025	3.9962	4.0927	4.1921	4.2944	4.3998	7
8	4.1878	4.3018	4.4199	4.5422	4.6688	4.7998	8
9	4.4319	4.5660	4.7055	4.8508	5.0019	5.1591	9
10	4.6409	4.7943	4.9548	5.1227	5.2983	5.4819	10
11	4.8197	4.9917	5.1724	5.3624	5.5620	5.7719	11
12	4.9728	5.1623	5.3624	5.5736	5.7967	6.0324	12
13	5.1038	5.3098	5.5282	5.7598	6.0056	6.2664	13
14	5.2160	5.4373	5.6729	5.9239	6.1914	6.4766	14
15	5.3120	5.5475	5.7992	6.0685	6.3567	6.6654	15
16	5.3942	5.6427	5.9095	6.1960	6.5039	6.8350	16
17	5.4645	5.7251	6.0057	6.3083	6.6348	6.9874	17
18	5.5247	5.7963	6.0898	6.4073	6.7513	7.1243	18
19	5.5762	5.8578	6.1631	6.4946	6.8550	7.2472	19
20	5.6203	5.9110	6.2271	6.5715	6.9472	7.3577	20

Annual Percentage DECREASE of:

Years	1%	2%	3%	4%	5%	6%	Years
1	.8475	.8475	.8475	.8475	.8475	.8475	1
2	1.5585	1.5513	1.5441	1.5369	1.5297	1.5226	2
3	2.1550	2.1358	2.1168	2.0978	2.0790	2.0603	3
4	2.6554	2.6213	2.5875	2.5542	2.5212	2.4887	4
5	3.0753	3.0244	2.9745	2.9254	2.8773	2.8300	5
6	3.4276	3.3593	3.2926	3.2275	3.1639	3.1019	6
7	3.7232	3.6374	3.5541	3.4732	3.3947	3.3184	7
8	3.9711	3.8683	3.7690	3.6731	3.5805	3.4910	8
9	4.1792	4.0601	3.9457	3.8357	3.7300	3.6284	9
10	4.3537	4.2194	4.0910	3.9681	3.8504	3.7379	10
11	4.5001	4.3517	4.2104	4.0757	3.9474	3.8251	11
12	4.6230	4.4616	4.3085	4.1633	4.0254	3.8946	12
13	4.7261	4.5529	4.3892	4.2345	4.0883	3.9499	13
14	4.8126	4.6286	4.4555	4.2925	4.1389	3.9940	14
15	4.8851	4.6916	4.5101	4.3397	4.1796	4.0291	15
16	4.9460	4.7439	4.5549	4.3780	4.2124	4.0571	16
17	4.9971	4.7873	4.5917	4.4092	4.2388	4.0794	17
18	5.0399	4.8233	4.6220	4.4346	4.2600	4.0971	18
19	5.0758	4.8533	4.6469	4.4553	4.2772	4.1113	19
20	5.1060	4.8781	4.6674	4.4721	4.2909	4.1225	20

ORDINARY ANNUITIES CHANGING IN CONSTANT RATIO

(Present Value of Annual Payments Starting at $1 and Changing in Constant Ratio)

Base: 1.180 000

Annual Percentage INCREASE of:

Years	7%	8%	9%	10%	11%	12%	Years
1	.8475	.8475	.8475	.8475	.8475	.8475	1
2	1.6159	1.6231	1.6303	1.6375	1.6446	1.6518	2
3	2.3127	2.3330	2.3534	2.3739	2.3945	2.4153	3
4	2.9446	2.9827	3.0214	3.0604	3.0999	3.1399	4
5	3.5176	3.5774	3.6384	3.7004	3.7635	3.8277	5
6	4.0371	4.1217	4.2083	4.2970	4.3877	4.4806	6
7	4.5082	4.6199	4.7348	4.8531	4.9749	5.1002	7
8	4.9354	5.0758	5.2211	5.3715	5.5272	5.6883	8
9	5.3228	5.4931	5.6704	5.8548	6.0468	6.2465	9
10	5.6741	5.8751	6.0853	6.3053	6.5355	6.7764	10
11	5.9926	6.2246	6.4687	6.7253	6.9953	7.2793	11
12	6.2814	6.5446	6.8227	7.1168	7.4278	7.7566	12
13	6.5433	6.8374	7.1498	7.4818	7.8346	8.2097	13
14	6.7808	7.1054	7.4520	7.8220	8.2173	8.6397	14
15	6.9962	7.3507	7.7310	8.1392	8.5773	9.0478	15
16	7.1914	7.5752	7.9888	8.4348	8.9159	9.4352	16
17	7.3685	7.7807	8.2270	8.7104	9.2345	9.8029	17
18	7.5291	7.9688	8.4470	8.9673	9.5341	10.1519	18
19	7.6747	8.1409	8.6502	9.2068	9.8160	10.4832	19
20	7.8067	8.2985	8.8379	9.4301	10.0811	10.7976	20

Annual Percentage DECREASE of:

Years	7%	8%	9%	10%	11%	12%	Years
1	.8475	.8475	.8475	.8475	.8475	.8475	1
2	1.5154	1.5082	1.5010	1.4938	1.4866	1.4795	2
3	2.0418	2.0233	2.0050	1.9868	1.9687	1.9508	3
4	2.4567	2.4250	2.3937	2.3628	2.3324	2.3023	4
5	2.7836	2.7381	2.6934	2.6496	2.6066	2.5644	5
6	3.0413	2.9823	2.9246	2.8683	2.8135	2.7599	6
7	3.2444	3.1726	3.1029	3.0352	2.9695	2.9057	7
8	3.4045	3.3210	3.2404	3.1624	3.0871	3.0144	8
9	3.5307	3.4367	3.3464	3.2595	3.1759	3.0955	9
10	3.6301	3.5269	3.4281	3.3335	3.2428	3.1560	10
11	3.7085	3.5973	3.4912	3.3900	3.2933	3.2011	11
12	3.7702	3.6521	3.5398	3.4330	3.3314	3.2347	12
13	3.8189	3.6949	3.5773	3.4659	3.3601	3.2598	13
14	3.8573	3.7282	3.6062	3.4909	3.3818	3.2785	14
15	3.8875	3.7542	3.6285	3.5100	3.3981	3.2924	15
16	3.9114	3.7745	3.6457	3.5246	3.4105	3.3028	16
17	3.9301	3.7903	3.6590	3.5357	3.4198	3.3106	17
18	3.9449	3.8026	3.6692	3.5442	3.4268	3.3164	18
19	3.9566	3.8122	3.6771	3.5506	3.4320	3.3207	19
20	3.9658	3.8197	3.6832	3.5556	3.4360	3.3239	20

19%

ORDINARY ANNUITIES CHANGING IN CONSTANT RATIO

(Present Value of Annual Payments Starting at $1 and Changing in Constant Ratio)

Base: 1.190 000

Annual Percentage INCREASE of:

Years	1%	2%	3%	4%	5%	6%	Years
1	.8403	.8403	.8403	.8403	.8403	.8403	1
2	1.5536	1.5606	1.5677	1.5747	1.5818	1.5889	2
3	2.1589	2.1780	2.1972	2.2166	2.2361	2.2556	3
4	2.6727	2.7072	2.7421	2.7775	2.8133	2.8496	4
5	3.1087	3.1608	3.2138	3.2677	3.3227	3.3786	5
6	3.4789	3.5496	3.6220	3.6962	3.7721	3.8498	6
7	3.7930	3.8828	3.9754	4.0706	4.1687	4.2696	7
8	4.0596	4.1685	4.2812	4.3978	4.5186	4.6435	8
9	4.2859	4.4133	4.5459	4.6838	4.8273	4.9766	9
10	4.4779	4.6232	4.7750	4.9338	5.0997	5.2733	10
11	4.6409	4.8031	4.9733	5.1522	5.3401	5.5375	11
12	4.7793	4.9573	5.1450	5.3431	5.5522	5.7729	12
13	4.8967	5.0894	5.2936	5.5099	5.7393	5.9826	13
14	4.9964	5.2027	5.4222	5.6557	5.9044	6.1694	14
15	5.0809	5.2998	5.5335	5.7832	6.0501	6.3357	15
16	5.1527	5.3830	5.6298	5.8945	6.1787	6.4839	16
17	5.2137	5.4543	5.7132	5.9919	6.2921	6.6159	17
18	5.2654	5.5155	5.7854	6.0769	6.3922	6.7335	18
19	5.3093	5.5679	5.8478	6.1513	6.4805	6.8383	19
20	5.3465	5.6128	5.9019	6.2162	6.5584	6.9316	20

Annual Percentage DECREASE of:

Years	1%	2%	3%	4%	5%	6%	Years
1	.8403	.8403	.8403	.8403	.8403	.8403	1
2	1.5394	1.5324	1.5253	1.5183	1.5112	1.5041	2
3	2.1210	2.1023	2.0837	2.0651	2.0468	2.0285	3
4	2.6049	2.5716	2.5388	2.5063	2.4743	2.4427	4
5	3.0074	2.9582	2.9098	2.8623	2.8156	2.7698	5
6	3.3423	3.2765	3.2122	3.1494	3.0881	3.0283	6
7	3.6209	3.5386	3.4587	3.3810	3.3056	3.2324	7
8	3.8527	3.7545	3.6596	3.5679	3.4793	3.3937	8
9	4.0455	3.9323	3.8233	3.7186	3.6179	3.5211	9
10	4.2059	4.0787	3.9568	3.8402	3.7286	3.6217	10
11	4.3394	4.1992	4.0657	3.9383	3.8169	3.7012	11
12	4.4504	4.2985	4.1544	4.0175	3.8875	3.7639	12
13	4.5428	4.3803	4.2267	4.0813	3.9438	3.8135	13
14	4.6196	4.4476	4.2856	4.1328	3.9887	3.8527	14
15	4.6836	4.5031	4.3336	4.1744	4.0246	3.8836	15
16	4.7367	4.5488	4.3728	4.2079	4.0533	3.9081	16
17	4.7810	4.5864	4.4047	4.2350	4.0761	3.9274	17
18	4.8178	4.6174	4.4307	4.2568	4.0944	3.9427	18
19	4.8484	4.6429	4.4519	4.2744	4.1090	3.9547	19
20	4.8739	4.6639	4.4692	4.2886	4.1206	3.9642	20

ORDINARY ANNUITIES CHANGING IN CONSTANT RATIO

(Present Value of Annual Payments Starting at $1 and Changing in Constant Ratio)

Base: 1.190 000

Annual Percentage INCREASE of:

Years	7%	8%	9%	10%	11%	12%	Years
1	.8403	.8403	.8403	.8403	.8403	.8403	1
2	1.5959	1.6030	1.6101	1.6171	1.6242	1.6312	2
3	2.2753	2.2952	2.3151	2.3352	2.3553	2.3756	3
4	2.8862	2.9233	2.9609	2.9989	3.0373	3.0762	4
5	3.4355	3.4934	3.5524	3.6124	3.6735	3.7356	5
6	3.9294	4.0109	4.0942	4.1795	4.2668	4.3562	6
7	4.3735	4.4804	4.5905	4.7038	4.8203	4.9403	7
8	4.7728	4.9066	5.0451	5.1884	5.3366	5.4900	8
9	5.1319	5.2934	5.4615	5.6363	5.8182	6.0074	9
10	5.4547	5.6444	5.8429	6.0504	6.2674	6.4944	10
11	5.7450	5.9630	6.1922	6.4331	6.6864	6.9527	11
12	6.0060	6.2521	6.5122	6.7869	7.0772	7.3840	12
13	6.2407	6.5146	6.8053	7.1139	7.4418	7.7900	13
14	6.4517	6.7527	7.0737	7.4163	7.7818	8.1721	14
15	6.6414	6.9688	7.3196	7.6957	8.0990	8.5317	15
16	6.8121	7.1650	7.5449	7.9540	8.3949	8.8702	16
17	6.9655	7.3430	7.7512	8.1928	8.6709	9.1888	17
18	7.1034	7.5046	7.9402	8.4135	8.9283	9.4886	18
19	7.2274	7.6512	8.1133	8.6175	9.1684	9.7708	19
20	7.3389	7.7843	8.2718	8.8061	9.3924	10.0364	20

Annual Percentage DECREASE of:

Years	7%	8%	9%	10%	11%	12%	Years
1	.8403	.8403	.8403	.8403	.8403	.8403	1
2	1.4971	1.4900	1.4829	1.4759	1.4688	1.4618	2
3	2.0103	1.9923	1.9744	1.9566	1.9389	1.9213	3
4	2.4114	2.3806	2.3501	2.3201	2.2904	2.2611	4
5	2.7249	2.6808	2.6375	2.5950	2.5533	2.5124	5
6	2.9699	2.9129	2.8572	2.8030	2.7500	2.6983	6
7	3.1613	3.0923	3.0253	2.9602	2.8970	2.8357	7
8	3.3110	3.2310	3.1538	3.0792	3.0070	2.9373	8
9	3.4279	3.3383	3.2521	3.1691	3.0893	3.0125	9
10	3.5193	3.4212	3.3272	3.2371	3.1508	3.0680	10
11	3.5907	3.4853	3.3847	3.2886	3.1968	3.1091	11
12	3.6465	3.5348	3.4286	3.3275	3.2312	3.1395	12
13	3.6901	3.5732	3.4622	3.3569	3.2570	3.1620	13
14	3.7242	3.6028	3.4879	3.3792	3.2762	3.1786	14
15	3.7509	3.6257	3.5076	3.3960	3.2906	3.1909	15
16	3.7717	3.6434	3.5226	3.4088	3.3014	3.2000	16
17	3.7880	3.6571	3.5341	3.4184	3.3094	3.2067	17
18	3.8007	3.6676	3.5429	3.4257	3.3155	3.2117	18
19	3.8106	3.6758	3.5496	3.4312	3.3200	3.2154	19
20	3.8184	3.6822	3.5547	3.4353	3.3233	3.2181	20

20%

ORDINARY ANNUITIES CHANGING IN CONSTANT RATIO

(Present Value of Annual Payments Starting at $1 and Changing in Constant Ratio)

Base: 1.200 000

Annual Percentage INCREASE of:

Years	1%	2%	3%	4%	5%	6%	Years
1	.8333	.8333	.8333	.8333	.8333	.8333	1
2	1.5347	1.5417	1.5486	1.5556	1.5625	1.5694	2
3	2.1251	2.1438	2.1626	2.1815	2.2005	2.2197	3
4	2.6219	2.6555	2.6895	2.7240	2.7588	2.7940	4
5	3.0401	3.0905	3.1418	3.1941	3.2473	3.3014	5
6	3.3921	3.4603	3.5301	3.6015	3.6747	3.7496	6
7	3.6884	3.7746	3.8633	3.9547	4.0487	4.1455	7
8	3.9377	4.0417	4.1494	4.2607	4.3759	4.4952	8
9	4.1476	4.2688	4.3949	4.5260	4.6623	4.8041	9
10	4.3242	4.4618	4.6056	4.7558	4.9128	5.0769	10
11	4.4729	4.6259	4.7865	4.9550	5.1321	5.3179	11
12	4.5980	4.7653	4.9417	5.1277	5.3239	5.5308	12
13	4.7033	4.8839	5.0750	5.2773	5.4917	5.7189	13
14	4.7920	4.9846	5.1894	5.4070	5.6386	5.8850	14
15	4.8666	5.0703	5.2875	5.5194	5.7671	6.0318	15
16	4.9294	5.1430	5.3718	5.6168	5.8796	6.1614	16
17	4.9822	5.2049	5.4441	5.7013	5.9779	6.2759	17
18	5.0267	5.2575	5.5062	5.7744	6.0640	6.3771	18
19	5.0641	5.3022	5.5595	5.8378	6.1394	6.4664	19
20	5.0956	5.3402	5.6052	5.8928	6.2053	6.5453	20

Annual Percentage DECREASE of:

Years	1%	2%	3%	4%	5%	6%	Years
1	.8333	.8333	.8333	.8333	.8333	.8333	1
2	1.5208	1.5139	1.5069	1.5000	1.4931	1.4861	2
3	2.0880	2.0697	2.0514	2.0333	2.0153	1.9975	3
4	2.5560	2.5236	2.4916	2.4600	2.4288	2.3980	4
5	2.9420	2.8942	2.8474	2.8013	2.7561	2.7118	5
6	3.2605	3.1970	3.1350	3.0744	3.0153	2.9576	6
7	3.5232	3.4442	3.3674	3.2929	3.2204	3.1501	7
8	3.7400	3.6461	3.5553	3.4676	3.3828	3.3009	8
9	3.9188	3.8110	3.7072	3.6074	3.5114	3.4190	9
10	4.0664	3.9456	3.8300	3.7193	3.6132	3.5116	10
11	4.1881	4.0556	3.9293	3.8088	3.6938	3.5841	11
12	4.2885	4.1454	4.0095	3.8803	3.7576	3.6409	12
13	4.3713	4.2187	4.0743	3.9376	3.8081	3.6853	13
14	4.4397	4.2786	4.1268	3.9834	3.8481	3.7202	14
15	4.4961	4.3276	4.1691	4.0201	3.8797	3.7475	15
16	4.5426	4.3675	4.2034	4.0494	3.9048	3.7689	16
17	4.5810	4.4001	4.2311	4.0728	3.9246	3.7856	17
18	4.6126	4.4268	4.2534	4.0916	3.9403	3.7987	18
19	4.6388	4.4485	4.2715	4.1066	3.9528	3.8090	19
20	4.6603	4.4663	4.2862	4.1186	3.9626	3.8170	20

ORDINARY ANNUITIES CHANGING IN CONSTANT RATIO

(Present Value of Annual Payments Starting at $1 and Changing in Constant Ratio)

Base: 1.200 000

Annual Percentage INCREASE of:

Years	7%	8%	9%	10%	11%	12%	Years
1	.8333	.8333	.8333	.8333	.8333	.8333	1
2	1.5764	1.5833	1.5903	1.5972	1.6042	1.6111	2
3	2.2389	2.2583	2.2778	2.2975	2.3172	2.3370	3
4	2.8297	2.8658	2.9024	2.9393	2.9767	3.0146	4
5	3.3565	3.4126	3.4697	3.5277	3.5868	3.6469	5
6	3.8262	3.9047	3.9849	4.0671	4.1511	4.2371	6
7	4.2450	4.3475	4.4530	4.5615	4.6731	4.7880	7
8	4.6185	4.7461	4.8781	5.0147	5.1560	5.3021	8
9	4.9515	5.1048	5.2643	5.4301	5.6026	5.7820	9
10	5.2484	5.4277	5.6151	5.8110	6.0158	6.2299	10
11	5.5132	5.7182	5.9337	6.1600	6.3979	6.6479	11
12	5.7492	5.9798	6.2231	6.4800	6.7514	7.0380	12
13	5.9597	6.2151	6.4860	6.7734	7.0784	7.4021	13
14	6.1474	6.4269	6.7248	7.0423	7.3808	7.7420	14
15	6.3148	6.6176	6.9417	7.2887	7.6606	8.0592	15
16	6.4640	6.7891	7.1387	7.5147	7.9194	8.3552	16
17	6.5971	6.9436	7.3176	7.7218	8.1588	8.6316	17
18	6.7157	7.0825	7.4802	7.9116	8.3802	8.8895	18
19	6.8215	7.2076	7.6278	8.0857	8.5850	9.1302	19
20	6.9159	7.3202	7.7619	8.2452	8.7745	9.3548	20

Annual Percentage DECREASE of:

Years	7%	8%	9%	10%	11%	12%	Years
1	.8333	.8333	.8333	.8333	.8333	.8333	1
2	1.4792	1.4722	1.4653	1.4583	1.4514	1.4444	2
3	1.9797	1.9620	1.9445	1.9271	1.9098	1.8926	3
4	2.3676	2.3376	2.3079	2.2786	2.2498	2.2212	4
5	2.6682	2.6255	2.5835	2.5423	2.5019	2.4622	5
6	2.9012	2.8462	2.7925	2.7401	2.6889	2.6390	6
7	3.0818	3.0154	2.9510	2.8884	2.8276	2.7686	7
8	3.2217	3.1451	3.0712	2.9996	2.9305	2.8636	8
9	3.3302	3.2446	3.1623	3.0831	3.0068	2.9333	9
10	3.4142	3.3209	3.2314	3.1456	3.0634	2.9844	10
11	3.4793	3.3793	3.2838	3.1925	3.1053	3.0219	11
12	3.5298	3.4242	3.3236	3.2277	3.1364	3.0494	12
13	3.5689	3.4585	3.3537	3.2541	3.1595	3.0696	13
14	3.5993	3.4849	3.3766	3.2739	3.1767	3.0843	14
15	3.6228	3.5051	3.3939	3.2888	3.1894	3.0952	15
16	3.6410	3.5205	3.4070	3.2999	3.1988	3.1031	16
17	3.6551	3.5324	3.4170	3.3083	3.2058	3.1090	17
18	3.6660	3.5415	3.4246	3.3145	3.2109	3.1132	18
19	3.6745	3.5485	3.4303	3.3192	3.2148	3.1164	19
20	3.6811	3.5539	3.4346	3.3228	3.2176	3.1187	20

21%

ORDINARY ANNUITIES CHANGING IN CONSTANT RATIO

(Present Value of Annual Payments Starting at $1 and Changing in Constant Ratio)

Base: 1.210 000

Annual Percentage INCREASE of:

Years	1%	2%	3%	4%	5%	6%	Years
1	.8264	.8264	.8264	.8264	.8264	.8264	1
2	1.5163	1.5231	1.5300	1.5368	1.5436	1.5504	2
3	2.0921	2.1104	2.1288	2.1473	2.1659	2.1847	3
4	2.5728	2.6055	2.6386	2.6721	2.7060	2.7403	4
5	2.9740	3.0228	3.0725	3.1231	3.1746	3.2270	5
6	3.3088	3.3746	3.4419	3.5108	3.5813	3.6534	6
7	3.5884	3.6711	3.7563	3.8440	3.9342	4.0270	7
8	3.8217	3.9211	4.0240	4.1304	4.2404	4.3542	8
9	4.0165	4.1319	4.2518	4.3765	4.5061	4.6409	9
10	4.1790	4.3095	4.4458	4.5881	4.7367	4.8920	10
11	4.3147	4.4592	4.6108	4.7699	4.9368	5.1120	11
12	4.4280	4.5855	4.7514	4.9262	5.1105	5.3047	12
13	4.5225	4.6919	4.8710	5.0605	5.2611	5.4736	13
14	4.6015	4.7816	4.9728	5.1760	5.3919	5.6215	14
15	4.6673	4.8572	5.0595	5.2752	5.5054	5.7510	15
16	4.7223	4.9210	5.1333	5.3605	5.6038	5.8646	16
17	4.7682	4.9747	5.1961	5.4338	5.6893	5.9640	17
18	4.8065	5.0200	5.2496	5.4969	5.7634	6.0511	18
19	4.8385	5.0582	5.2951	5.5510	5.8278	6.1274	19
20	4.8652	5.0904	5.3339	5.5976	5.8836	6.1943	20

Annual Percentage DECREASE of:

Years	1%	2%	3%	4%	5%	6%	Years
1	.8264	.8264	.8264	.8264	.8264	.8264	1
2	1.5026	1.4958	1.4890	1.4821	1.4753	1.4685	2
3	2.0559	2.0379	2.0201	2.0024	1.9847	1.9672	3
4	2.5085	2.4770	2.4459	2.4151	2.3847	2.3547	4
5	2.8789	2.8326	2.7872	2.7426	2.6987	2.6557	5
6	3.1819	3.1206	3.0608	3.0024	2.9453	2.8896	6
7	3.4298	3.3539	3.2801	3.2085	3.1389	3.0712	7
8	3.6327	3.5428	3.4560	3.3720	3.2908	3.2124	8
9	3.7986	3.6958	3.5969	3.5018	3.4102	3.3220	9
10	3.9344	3.8198	3.7099	3.6047	3.5039	3.4072	10
11	4.0455	3.9201	3.8005	3.6864	3.5774	3.4733	11
12	4.1364	4.0014	3.8732	3.7512	3.6352	3.5247	12
13	4.2108	4.0673	3.9314	3.8026	3.6805	3.5647	13
14	4.2716	4.1206	3.9780	3.8434	3.7161	3.5957	14
15	4.3214	4.1638	4.0155	3.8757	3.7440	3.6198	15
16	4.3621	4.1988	4.0454	3.9014	3.7660	3.6385	16
17	4.3955	4.2271	4.0695	3.9218	3.7832	3.6531	17
18	4.4227	4.2501	4.0888	3.9379	3.7967	3.6644	18
19	4.4451	4.2686	4.1042	3.9508	3.8074	3.6731	19
20	4.4633	4.2837	4.1166	3.9609	3.8157	3.6800	20

ORDINARY ANNUITIES CHANGING IN CONSTANT RATIO

(Present Value of Annual Payments Starting at $1 and Changing in Constant Ratio)

Base: 1.210 000

Annual Percentage INCREASE of:

Years	7%	8%	9%	10%	11%	12%	Years
1	.8264	.8264	.8264	.8264	.8264	.8264	1
2	1.5573	1.5641	1.5709	1.5778	1.5846	1.5914	2
3	2.2035	2.2225	2.2416	2.2608	2.2801	2.2995	3
4	2.7750	2.8102	2.8457	2.8817	2.9181	2.9549	4
5	3.2804	3.3347	3.3899	3.4462	3.5034	3.5616	5
6	3.7273	3.8029	3.8802	3.9593	4.0403	4.1231	6
7	4.1225	4.2207	4.3218	4.4258	4.5328	4.6429	7
8	4.4719	4.5937	4.7197	4.8499	4.9847	5.1240	8
9	4.7810	4.9266	5.0780	5.2355	5.3991	5.5693	9
10	5.0543	5.2238	5.4009	5.5860	5.7794	5.9815	10
11	5.2959	5.4890	5.6917	5.9046	6.1282	6.3630	11
12	5.5096	5.7257	5.9537	6.1943	6.4482	6.7162	12
13	5.6986	5.9370	6.1897	6.4576	6.7417	7.0431	13
14	5.8657	6.1256	6.4023	6.6970	7.0110	7.3457	14
15	6.0135	6.2939	6.5938	6.9146	7.2580	7.6258	15
16	6.1441	6.4441	6.7663	7.1125	7.4846	7.8850	16
17	6.2597	6.5782	6.9217	7.2923	7.6925	8.1250	17
18	6.3619	6.6979	7.0617	7.4558	7.8832	8.3471	18
19	6.4522	6.8048	7.1878	7.6045	8.0582	8.5527	19
20	6.5321	6.9001	7.3014	7.7396	8.2186	8.7430	20

Annual Percentage DECREASE of:

Years	7%	8%	9%	10%	11%	12%	Years
1	.8264	.8264	.8264	.8264	.8264	.8264	1
2	1.4616	1.4548	1.4480	1.4412	1.4343	1.4275	2
3	1.9499	1.9326	1.9154	1.8984	1.8814	1.8646	3
4	2.3251	2.2959	2.2670	2.2385	2.2103	2.1825	4
5	2.6135	2.5721	2.5314	2.4914	2.4522	2.4137	5
6	2.8352	2.7821	2.7302	2.6796	2.6301	2.5819	6
7	3.0055	2.9417	2.8797	2.8195	2.7610	2.7042	7
8	3.1365	3.0631	2.9922	2.9236	2.8573	2.7931	8
9	3.2371	3.1554	3.0768	3.0010	2.9281	2.8578	9
10	3.3145	3.2256	3.1404	3.0586	2.9802	2.9049	10
11	3.3740	3.2790	3.1882	3.1015	3.0185	2.9391	11
12	3.4196	3.3196	3.2242	3.1333	3.0466	2.9640	12
13	3.4548	3.3504	3.2513	3.1570	3.0674	2.9820	13
14	3.4818	3.3739	3.2716	3.1746	3.0826	2.9952	14
15	3.5025	3.3917	3.2869	3.1877	3.0938	3.0048	15
16	3.5185	3.4053	3.2984	3.1975	3.1021	3.0117	16
17	3.5307	3.4156	3.3071	3.2047	3.1081	3.0168	17
18	3.5401	3.4234	3.3136	3.2101	3.1126	3.0205	18
19	3.5474	3.4294	3.3185	3.2142	3.1159	3.0232	19
20	3.5529	3.4339	3.3222	3.2171	3.1183	3.0251	20

22%

ORDINARY ANNUITIES CHANGING IN CONSTANT RATIO

(Present Value of Annual Payments Starting at $1 and Changing in Constant Ratio)

Base: 1.220 000

Annual Percentage INCREASE of:

Years	1%	2%	3%	4%	5%	6%	Years
1	.8197	.8197	.8197	.8197	.8197	.8197	1
2	1.4983	1.5050	1.5117	1.5184	1.5251	1.5318	2
3	2.0600	2.0779	2.0959	2.1141	2.1323	2.1506	3
4	2.5251	2.5570	2.5892	2.6218	2.6548	2.6882	4
5	2.9101	2.9575	3.0056	3.0547	3.1046	3.1554	5
6	3.2289	3.2923	3.3572	3.4236	3.4916	3.5612	6
7	3.4928	3.5722	3.6540	3.7382	3.8248	3.9138	7
8	3.7112	3.8063	3.9046	4.0063	4.1115	4.2202	8
9	3.8921	4.0020	4.1162	4.2349	4.3582	4.4864	9
10	4.0418	4.1656	4.2948	4.4298	4.5706	4.7177	10
11	4.1658	4.3024	4.4456	4.5959	4.7534	4.9187	11
12	4.2684	4.4168	4.5730	4.7374	4.9107	5.0933	12
13	4.3533	4.5124	4.6804	4.8582	5.0461	5.2450	13
14	4.4237	4.5923	4.7712	4.9610	5.1626	5.3768	14
15	4.4819	4.6591	4.8478	5.0488	5.2629	5.4913	15
16	4.5301	4.7150	4.9125	5.1235	5.3492	5.5908	16
17	4.5700	4.7617	4.9671	5.1873	5.4235	5.6773	17
18	4.6030	4.8008	5.0132	5.2416	5.4875	5.7524	18
19	4.6304	4.8335	5.0521	5.2879	5.5425	5.8176	19
20	4.6530	4.8608	5.0850	5.3274	5.5898	5.8743	20

Annual Percentage DECREASE of:

Years	1%	2%	3%	4%	5%	6%	Years
1	.8197	.8197	.8197	.8197	.8197	.8197	1
2	1.4848	1.4781	1.4714	1.4647	1.4579	1.4512	2
3	2.0246	2.0070	1.9895	1.9722	1.9550	1.9378	3
4	2.4626	2.4318	2.4015	2.3716	2.3420	2.3128	4
5	2.8180	2.7731	2.7291	2.6858	2.6433	2.6016	5
6	3.1064	3.0473	2.9895	2.9331	2.8780	2.8242	6
7	3.3404	3.2675	3.1966	3.1277	3.0607	2.9957	7
8	3.5303	3.4444	3.3612	3.2808	3.2030	3.1278	8
9	3.6845	3.5865	3.4921	3.4013	3.3138	3.2296	9
10	3.8095	3.7006	3.5962	3.4961	3.4001	3.3081	10
11	3.9110	3.7923	3.6789	3.5707	3.4673	3.3685	11
12	3.9934	3.8659	3.7447	3.6294	3.5196	3.4151	12
13	4.0602	3.9251	3.7970	3.6756	3.5604	3.4510	13
14	4.1144	3.9726	3.8386	3.7119	3.5921	3.4786	14
15	4.1584	4.0108	3.8717	3.7405	3.6168	3.4999	15
16	4.1941	4.0415	3.8980	3.7631	3.6360	3.5163	16
17	4.2231	4.0661	3.9189	3.7808	3.6510	3.5290	17
18	4.2466	4.0859	3.9355	3.7947	3.6627	3.5387	18
19	4.2657	4.1018	3.9487	3.8057	3.6717	3.5462	19
20	4.2812	4.1145	3.9592	3.8143	3.6788	3.5520	20

ORDINARY ANNUITIES CHANGING IN CONSTANT RATIO

(Present Value of Annual Payments Starting at $1 and Changing in Constant Ratio)

Base: 1.220 000

Annual Percentage INCREASE of:

Years	7%	8%	9%	10%	11%	12%	Years
1	.8197	.8197	.8197	.8197	.8197	.8197	1
2	1.5386	1.5453	1.5520	1.5587	1.5654	1.5722	2
3	2.1691	2.1876	2.2063	2.2251	2.2440	2.2630	3
4	2.7221	2.7563	2.7909	2.8259	2.8613	2.8971	4
5	3.2070	3.2596	3.3132	3.3676	3.4230	3.4793	5
6	3.6324	3.7053	3.7798	3.8560	3.9340	4.0138	6
7	4.0055	4.0997	4.1967	4.2964	4.3990	4.5045	7
8	4.3327	4.4489	4.5692	4.6935	4.8220	4.9549	8
9	4.6196	4.7581	4.9020	5.0515	5.2069	5.3685	9
10	4.8713	5.0317	5.1993	5.3743	5.5571	5.7481	10
11	5.0921	5.2740	5.4649	5.6654	5.8758	6.0966	11
12	5.2857	5.4885	5.7023	5.9278	6.1656	6.4166	12
13	5.4555	5.6783	5.9143	6.1644	6.4294	6.7103	13
14	5.6044	5.8464	6.1038	6.3777	6.6694	6.9799	14
15	5.7350	5.9952	6.2731	6.5701	6.8877	7.2275	15
16	5.8495	6.1269	6.4243	6.7435	7.0864	7.4547	16
17	5.9500	6.2434	6.5594	6.8999	7.2671	7.6634	17
18	6.0381	6.3467	6.6801	7.0409	7.4315	7.8549	18
19	6.1154	6.4380	6.7880	7.1680	7.5812	8.0307	19
20	6.1832	6.5189	6.8843	7.2826	7.7173	8.1921	20

Annual Percentage DECREASE of:

Years	7%	8%	9%	10%	11%	12%	Years
1	.8197	.8197	.8197	.8197	.8197	.8197	1
2	1.4445	1.4378	1.4311	1.4243	1.4176	1.4109	2
3	1.9208	1.9039	1.8871	1.8704	1.8538	1.8374	3
4	2.2839	2.2554	2.2273	2.1995	2.1721	2.1450	4
5	2.5607	2.5205	2.4810	2.4422	2.4042	2.3669	5
6	2.7717	2.7204	2.6703	2.6213	2.5736	2.5269	6
7	2.9325	2.8711	2.8114	2.7534	2.6971	2.6424	7
8	3.0551	2.9848	2.9167	2.8509	2.7872	2.7256	8
9	3.1486	3.0705	2.9953	2.9228	2.8530	2.7857	9
10	3.2198	3.1351	3.0538	2.9758	2.9009	2.8290	10
11	3.2741	3.1839	3.0975	3.0150	2.9359	2.8603	11
12	3.3155	3.2206	3.1301	3.0438	2.9615	2.8828	12
13	3.3471	3.2483	3.1544	3.0651	2.9801	2.8991	13
14	3.3711	3.2692	3.1726	3.0808	2.9937	2.9108	14
15	3.3895	3.2850	3.1861	3.0924	3.0036	2.9193	15
16	3.4034	3.2969	3.1962	3.1010	3.0108	2.9254	16
17	3.4141	3.3058	3.2037	3.1073	3.0161	2.9298	17
18	3.4222	3.3126	3.2093	3.1119	3.0199	2.9330	18
19	3.4284	3.3177	3.2135	3.1153	3.0227	2.9352	19
20	3.4331	3.3215	3.2166	3.1179	3.0248	2.9369	20

23%

ORDINARY ANNUITIES CHANGING IN CONSTANT RATIO

(Present Value of Annual Payments Starting at $1 and Changing in Constant Ratio)

Base: 1.230 000

Annual Percentage INCREASE of:

Years	1%	2%	3%	4%	5%	6%	Years
1	.8130	.8130	.8130	.8130	.8130	.8130	1
2	1.4806	1.4872	1.4938	1.5004	1.5070	1.5136	2
3	2.0288	2.0463	2.0639	2.0817	2.0995	2.1175	3
4	2.4789	2.5099	2.5413	2.5731	2.6053	2.6378	4
5	2.8485	2.8944	2.9411	2.9886	3.0370	3.0862	5
6	3.1521	3.2133	3.2759	3.3400	3.4056	3.4727	6
7	3.4013	3.4777	3.5562	3.6371	3.7202	3.8057	7
8	3.6059	3.6969	3.7910	3.8883	3.9888	4.0927	8
9	3.7740	3.8788	3.9876	4.1006	4.2181	4.3401	9
10	3.9120	4.0295	4.1522	4.2802	4.4138	4.5533	10
11	4.0253	4.1546	4.2901	4.4321	4.5809	4.7369	11
12	4.1183	4.2583	4.4055	4.5604	4.7235	4.8953	12
13	4.1947	4.3443	4.5022	4.6690	4.8453	5.0317	13
14	4.2574	4.4156	4.5831	4.7608	4.9492	5.1493	14
15	4.3090	4.4747	4.6509	4.8384	5.0380	5.2506	15
16	4.3513	4.5237	4.7077	4.9040	5.1137	5.3379	16
17	4.3860	4.5644	4.7552	4.9595	5.1784	5.4131	17
18	4.4145	4.5981	4.7950	5.0064	5.2336	5.4780	18
19	4.4379	4.6261	4.8283	5.0460	5.2807	5.5339	19
20	4.4572	4.6493	4.8562	5.0796	5.3209	5.5820	20

Annual Percentage DECREASE of:

Years	1%	2%	3%	4%	5%	6%	Years
1	.8130	.8130	.8130	.8130	.8130	.8130	1
2	1.4674	1.4608	1.4542	1.4476	1.4409	1.4343	2
3	1.9941	1.9769	1.9598	1.9428	1.9259	1.9092	3
4	2.4180	2.3881	2.3585	2.3293	2.3005	2.2720	4
5	2.7592	2.7157	2.6730	2.6310	2.5898	2.5494	5
6	3.0338	2.9767	2.9210	2.8665	2.8133	2.7613	6
7	3.2549	3.1847	3.1165	3.0503	2.9859	2.9233	7
8	3.4328	3.3504	3.2708	3.1937	3.1192	3.0471	8
9	3.5760	3.4825	3.3924	3.3057	3.2221	3.1417	9
10	3.6912	3.5876	3.4883	3.3930	3.3016	3.2139	10
11	3.7840	3.6715	3.5640	3.4612	3.3631	3.2692	11
12	3.8587	3.7382	3.6236	3.5145	3.4105	3.3114	12
13	3.9188	3.7914	3.6706	3.5560	3.4471	3.3437	13
14	3.9671	3.8338	3.7077	3.5884	3.4754	3.3683	14
15	4.0061	3.8676	3.7370	3.6137	3.4973	3.3872	15
16	4.0374	3.8945	3.7601	3.6335	3.5142	3.4016	16
17	4.0626	3.9160	3.7783	3.6489	3.5272	3.4126	17
18	4.0829	3.9330	3.7926	3.6609	3.5373	3.4210	18
19	4.0993	3.9466	3.8039	3.6703	3.5450	3.4274	19
20	4.1124	3.9575	3.8129	3.6776	3.5510	3.4324	20

23%

ORDINARY ANNUITIES CHANGING IN CONSTANT RATIO

(Present Value of Annual Payments Starting at $1 and Changing in Constant Ratio)

Base: 1.230 000

Annual Percentage INCREASE of:

Years	7%	8%	9%	10%	11%	12%	Years
1	.8130	.8130	.8130	.8130	.8130	.8130	1
2	1.5203	1.5269	1.5335	1.5401	1.5467	1.5533	2
3	2.1355	2.1537	2.1719	2.1903	2.2088	2.2274	3
4	2.6707	2.7040	2.7377	2.7718	2.8063	2.8412	4
5	3.1363	3.1873	3.2391	3.2919	3.3455	3.4001	5
6	3.5414	3.6116	3.6835	3.7570	3.8322	3.9091	6
7	3.8937	3.9842	4.0772	4.1729	4.2713	4.3725	7
8	4.2002	4.3113	4.4261	4.5449	4.6676	4.7945	8
9	4.4668	4.5985	4.7354	4.8775	5.0252	5.1787	9
10	4.6988	4.8508	5.0094	5.1750	5.3480	5.5286	10
11	4.9006	5.0722	5.2522	5.4411	5.6392	5.8471	11
12	5.0761	5.2667	5.4674	5.6790	5.9021	6.1372	12
13	5.2288	5.4374	5.6581	5.8918	6.1393	6.4014	13
14	5.3617	5.5873	5.8271	6.0821	6.3533	6.6419	14
15	5.4772	5.7189	5.9769	6.2523	6.5465	6.8609	15
16	5.5777	5.8345	6.1096	6.4045	6.7208	7.0604	16
17	5.6652	5.9360	6.2272	6.5406	6.8781	7.2420	17
18	5.7413	6.0251	6.3314	6.6623	7.0201	7.4073	18
19	5.8074	6.1033	6.4238	6.7712	7.1482	7.5579	19
20	5.8650	6.1720	6.5056	6.8685	7.2638	7.6950	20

Annual Percentage DECREASE of:

Years	7%	8%	9%	10%	11%	12%	Years
1	.8130	.8130	.8130	.8130	.8130	.8130	1
2	1.4277	1.4211	1.4145	1.4079	1.4013	1.3947	2
3	1.8925	1.8760	1.8595	1.8432	1.8269	1.8108	3
4	2.2439	2.2162	2.1887	2.1617	2.1349	2.1086	4
5	2.5096	2.4706	2.4323	2.3947	2.3578	2.3216	5
6	2.7105	2.6610	2.6125	2.5652	2.5191	2.4740	6
7	2.8624	2.8033	2.7459	2.6900	2.6357	2.5830	7
8	2.9773	2.9098	2.8445	2.7813	2.7202	2.6610	8
9	3.0641	2.9894	2.9175	2.8481	2.7813	2.7168	9
10	3.1298	3.0490	2.9715	2.8970	2.8255	2.7567	10
11	3.1794	3.0936	3.0114	2.9328	2.8575	2.7853	11
12	3.2170	3.1269	3.0410	2.9589	2.8806	2.8058	12
13	3.2454	3.1518	3.0628	2.9781	2.8973	2.8204	13
14	3.2668	3.1705	3.0790	2.9921	2.9095	2.8308	14
15	3.2830	3.1844	3.0910	3.0023	2.9182	2.8383	15
16	3.2953	3.1948	3.0998	3.0098	2.9246	2.8437	16
17	3.3046	3.2027	3.1064	3.0153	2.9292	2.8475	17
18	3.3116	3.2085	3.1112	3.0193	2.9325	2.8503	18
19	3.3169	3.2129	3.1148	3.0223	2.9349	2.8522	19
20	3.3209	3.2161	3.1175	3.0244	2.9366	2.8536	20

24%

ORDINARY ANNUITIES CHANGING IN CONSTANT RATIO

(Present Value of Annual Payments Starting at $1 and Changing in Constant Ratio)

Base: 1.240 000

Annual Percentage INCREASE of:

Years	1%	2%	3%	4%	5%	6%	Years
1	.8065	.8065	.8065	.8065	.8065	.8065	1
2	1.4633	1.4698	1.4763	1.4828	1.4893	1.4958	2
3	1.9983	2.0155	2.0328	2.0501	2.0676	2.0852	3
4	2.4341	2.4644	2.4949	2.5259	2.5572	2.5889	4
5	2.7891	2.8336	2.8789	2.9250	2.9718	3.0196	5
6	3.0782	3.1373	3.1978	3.2596	3.3229	3.3877	6
7	3.3137	3.3871	3.4627	3.5403	3.6202	3.7024	7
8	3.5055	3.5926	3.6827	3.7758	3.8720	3.9714	8
9	3.6618	3.7617	3.8655	3.9732	4.0851	4.2013	9
10	3.7890	3.9007	4.0173	4.1388	4.2656	4.3979	10
11	3.8927	4.0151	4.1434	4.2777	4.4185	4.5660	11
12	3.9771	4.1092	4.2481	4.3942	4.5479	4.7096	12
13	4.0459	4.1866	4.3351	4.4919	4.6575	4.8324	13
14	4.1019	4.2503	4.4074	4.5739	4.7503	4.9374	14
15	4.1475	4.3027	4.4675	4.6426	4.8289	5.0271	15
16	4.1846	4.3457	4.5173	4.7003	4.8954	5.1038	16
17	4.2149	4.3812	4.5587	4.7486	4.9518	5.1694	17
18	4.2396	4.4103	4.5931	4.7891	4.9995	5.2255	18
19	4.2596	4.4343	4.6217	4.8232	5.0399	5.2734	19
20	4.2760	4.4540	4.6455	4.8517	5.0741	5.3143	20

Annual Percentage DECREASE of:

Years	1%	2%	3%	4%	5%	6%	Years
1	.8065	.8065	.8065	.8065	.8065	.8065	1
2	1.4503	1.4438	1.4373	1.4308	1.4243	1.4178	2
3	1.9644	1.9475	1.9308	1.9142	1.8976	1.8812	3
4	2.3748	2.3456	2.3168	2.2884	2.2603	2.2325	4
5	2.7024	2.6603	2.6188	2.5781	2.5381	2.4989	5
6	2.9640	2.9089	2.8550	2.8024	2.7510	2.7008	6
7	3.1729	3.1054	3.0398	2.9761	2.9141	2.8538	7
8	3.3397	3.2607	3.1844	3.1105	3.0390	2.9698	8
9	3.4728	3.3835	3.2975	3.2146	3.1347	3.0578	9
10	3.5791	3.4805	3.3859	3.2952	3.2080	3.1244	10
11	3.6639	3.5572	3.4551	3.3575	3.2642	3.1750	11
12	3.7317	3.6178	3.5092	3.4058	3.3073	3.2133	12
13	3.7858	3.6657	3.5516	3.4432	3.3403	3.2423	13
14	3.8290	3.7035	3.5847	3.4722	3.3655	3.2643	14
15	3.8635	3.7334	3.6106	3.4946	3.3849	3.2810	15
16	3.8910	3.7570	3.6309	3.5119	3.3997	3.2937	16
17	3.9130	3.7757	3.6467	3.5254	3.4111	3.3033	17
18	3.9305	3.7905	3.6591	3.5358	3.4198	3.3106	18
19	3.9445	3.8022	3.6688	3.5438	3.4264	3.3161	19
20	3.9557	3.8114	3.6764	3.5501	3.4315	3.3202	20

ORDINARY ANNUITIES CHANGING IN CONSTANT RATIO

(Present Value of Annual Payments Starting at $1 and Changing in Constant Ratio)

Base: 1.240 000

Annual Percentage INCREASE of:

Years	7%	8%	9%	10%	11%	12%	Years
1	.8065	.8065	.8065	.8065	.8065	.8065	1
2	1.5023	1.5088	1.5153	1.5219	1.5284	1.5349	2
3	2.1028	2.1206	2.1385	2.1565	2.1746	2.1928	3
4	2.6210	2.6534	2.6863	2.7195	2.7530	2.7870	4
5	3.0681	3.1175	3.1678	3.2189	3.2709	3.3238	5
6	3.4539	3.5217	3.5910	3.6619	3.7344	3.8086	6
7	3.7869	3.8737	3.9631	4.0549	4.1494	4.2464	7
8	4.0741	4.1804	4.2901	4.4036	4.5208	4.6419	8
9	4.3220	4.4474	4.5776	4.7128	4.8533	4.9992	9
10	4.5360	4.6800	4.8303	4.9872	5.1509	5.3218	10
11	4.7205	4.8826	5.0525	5.2306	5.4174	5.6133	11
12	4.8798	5.0590	5.2477	5.4465	5.6559	5.8765	12
13	5.0173	5.2127	5.4194	5.6380	5.8694	6.1143	13
14	5.1359	5.3465	5.5702	5.8079	6.0605	6.3290	14
15	5.2382	5.4631	5.7029	5.9586	6.2316	6.5230	15
16	5.3265	5.5646	5.8195	6.0923	6.3847	6.6982	16
17	5.4027	5.6531	5.9220	6.2109	6.5218	6.8564	17
18	5.4685	5.7301	6.0120	6.3162	6.6445	6.9993	18
19	5.5252	5.7972	6.0912	6.4095	6.7544	7.1284	19
20	5.5742	5.8556	6.1608	6.4923	6.8527	7.2450	20

Annual Percentage DECREASE of:

Years	7%	8%	9%	10%	11%	12%	Years
1	.8065	.8065	.8065	.8065	.8065	.8065	1
2	1.4113	1.4048	1.3983	1.3918	1.3853	1.3788	2
3	1.8649	1.8487	1.8326	1.8166	1.8007	1.7849	3
4	2.2051	2.1781	2.1514	2.1250	2.0989	2.0732	4
5	2.4603	2.4224	2.3853	2.3488	2.3129	2.2777	5
6	2.6517	2.6037	2.5569	2.5112	2.4665	2.4229	6
7	2.7952	2.7383	2.6829	2.6291	2.5768	2.5259	7
8	2.9029	2.8381	2.7754	2.7147	2.6559	2.5991	8
9	2.9836	2.9121	2.8432	2.7768	2.7127	2.6509	9
10	3.0441	2.9671	2.8930	2.8219	2.7535	2.6878	10
11	3.0896	3.0078	2.9295	2.8546	2.7827	2.7139	11
12	3.1236	3.0381	2.9564	2.8783	2.8037	2.7324	12
13	3.1492	3.0605	2.9760	2.8956	2.8188	2.7456	13
14	3.1683	3.0771	2.9905	2.9081	2.8296	2.7549	14
15	3.1827	3.0895	3.0011	2.9171	2.8374	2.7616	15
16	3.1935	3.0987	3.0089	2.9237	2.8430	2.7663	16
17	3.2016	3.1055	3.0146	2.9285	2.8470	2.7696	17
18	3.2076	3.1105	3.0188	2.9320	2.8498	2.7720	18
19	3.2122	3.1142	3.0218	2.9345	2.8519	2.7737	19
20	3.2156	3.1170	3.0241	2.9363	2.8534	2.7749	20

25%

ORDINARY ANNUITIES CHANGING IN CONSTANT RATIO

(Present Value of Annual Payments Starting at $1 and Changing in Constant Ratio)

Base: 1.250 000

Annual Percentage INCREASE of:

Years	1%	2%	3%	4%	5%	6%	Years
1	.8000	.8000	.8000	.8000	.8000	.8000	1
2	1.4464	1.4528	1.4592	1.4656	1.4720	1.4784	2
3	1.9687	1.9855	2.0024	2.0194	2.0365	2.0537	3
4	2.3907	2.4202	2.4500	2.4801	2.5106	2.5415	4
5	2.7317	2.7748	2.8188	2.8635	2.9089	2.9552	5
6	3.0072	3.0643	3.1227	3.1824	3.2435	3.3060	6
7	3.2298	3.3004	3.3731	3.4478	3.5245	3.6035	7
8	3.4097	3.4932	3.5794	3.6685	3.7606	3.8558	8
9	3.5550	3.6504	3.7494	3.8522	3.9589	4.0697	9
10	3.6725	3.7787	3.8895	4.0050	4.1255	4.2511	10
11	3.7674	3.8835	4.0050	4.1322	4.2654	4.4049	11
12	3.8440	3.9689	4.1001	4.2380	4.3829	4.5354	12
13	3.9060	4.0386	4.1785	4.3260	4.4817	4.6460	13
14	3.9560	4.0955	4.2431	4.3992	4.5646	4.7398	14
15	3.9965	4.1419	4.2963	4.4602	4.6343	4.8194	15
16	4.0291	4.1798	4.3401	4.5109	4.6928	4.8868	16
17	4.0555	4.2107	4.3763	4.5530	4.7419	4.9440	17
18	4.0769	4.2360	4.4061	4.5881	4.7832	4.9925	18
19	4.0941	4.2565	4.4306	4.6173	4.8179	5.0337	19
20	4.1081	4.2733	4.4508	4.6416	4.8470	5.0685	20

Annual Percentage DECREASE of:

Years	1%	2%	3%	4%	5%	6%	Years
1	.8000	.8000	.8000	.8000	.8000	.8000	1
2	1.4336	1.4272	1.4208	1.4144	1.4080	1.4016	2
3	1.9354	1.9189	1.9025	1.8863	1.8701	1.8540	3
4	2.3328	2.3044	2.2764	2.2486	2.2213	2.1942	4
5	2.6476	2.6067	2.5665	2.5270	2.4882	2.4500	5
6	2.8969	2.8436	2.7916	2.7407	2.6910	2.6424	6
7	3.0944	3.0294	2.9663	2.9049	2.8452	2.7871	7
8	3.2507	3.1751	3.1018	3.0309	2.9623	2.8959	8
9	3.3746	3.2892	3.2070	3.1278	3.0514	2.9777	9
10	3.4727	3.3788	3.2886	3.2021	3.1190	3.0392	10
11	3.5504	3.4490	3.3520	3.2592	3.1705	3.0855	11
12	3.6119	3.5040	3.4011	3.3031	3.2096	3.1203	12
13	3.6606	3.5471	3.4393	3.3368	3.2393	3.1465	13
14	3.6992	3.5809	3.4689	3.3626	3.2618	3.1661	14
15	3.7298	3.6075	3.4919	3.3825	3.2790	3.1809	15
16	3.7540	3.6282	3.5097	3.3978	3.2920	3.1921	16
17	3.7731	3.6445	3.5235	3.4095	3.3019	3.2004	17
18	3.7883	3.6573	3.5342	3.4185	3.3095	3.2067	18
19	3.8004	3.6673	3.5426	3.4254	3.3152	3.2115	19
20	3.8099	3.6752	3.5490	3.4307	3.3196	3.2150	20

25%

ORDINARY ANNUITIES CHANGING IN CONSTANT RATIO

(Present Value of Annual Payments Starting at $1 and Changing in Constant Ratio)

Base: 1.250 000

Annual Percentage INCREASE of:

Years	7%	8%	9%	10%	11%	12%	Years
1	.8000	.8000	.8000	.8000	.8000	.8000	1
2	1.4848	1.4912	1.4976	1.5040	1.5104	1.5168	2
3	2.0710	2.0884	2.1059	2.1235	2.1412	2.1591	3
4	2.5728	2.6044	2.6364	2.6687	2.7014	2.7345	4
5	3.0023	3.0502	3.0989	3.1485	3.1989	3.2501	5
6	3.3700	3.4354	3.5022	3.5706	3.6406	3.7121	6
7	3.6847	3.7681	3.8540	3.9422	4.0328	4.1261	7
8	3.9541	4.0557	4.1606	4.2691	4.3812	4.4969	8
9	4.1847	4.3041	4.4281	4.5568	4.6905	4.8293	9
10	4.3821	4.5187	4.6613	4.8100	4.9651	5.1270	10
11	4.5511	4.7042	4.8646	5.0328	5.2090	5.3938	11
12	4.6957	4.8644	5.0420	5.2289	5.4256	5.6329	12
13	4.8195	5.0029	5.1966	5.4014	5.6180	5.8470	13
14	4.9255	5.1225	5.3314	5.5532	5.7887	6.0389	14
15	5.0163	5.2258	5.4490	5.6868	5.9404	6.2109	15
16	5.0939	5.3151	5.5515	5.8044	6.0751	6.3650	16
17	5.1604	5.3923	5.6409	5.9079	6.1947	6.5030	17
18	5.2173	5.4589	5.7189	5.9989	6.3009	6.6267	18
19	5.2660	5.5165	5.7869	6.0791	6.3952	6.7375	19
20	5.3077	5.5663	5.8462	6.1496	6.4789	6.8368	20

Annual Percentage DECREASE of:

Years	7%	8%	9%	10%	11%	12%	Years
1	.8000	.8000	.8000	.8000	.8000	.8000	1
2	1.3952	1.3888	1.3824	1.3760	1.3696	1.3632	2
3	1.8380	1.8222	1.8064	1.7907	1.7752	1.7597	3
4	2.1675	2.1411	2.1150	2.0893	2.0639	2.0388	4
5	2.4126	2.3759	2.3398	2.3043	2.2695	2.2353	5
6	2.5950	2.5486	2.5033	2.4591	2.4159	2.3737	6
7	2.7307	2.6758	2.6224	2.5706	2.5201	2.4711	7
8	2.8316	2.7694	2.7091	2.6508	2.5943	2.5396	8
9	2.9067	2.8383	2.7722	2.7086	2.6472	2.5879	9
10	2.9626	2.8890	2.8182	2.7502	2.6848	2.6219	10
11	3.0042	2.9263	2.8516	2.7801	2.7116	2.6458	11
12	3.0351	2.9537	2.8760	2.8017	2.7306	2.6626	12
13	3.0581	2.9740	2.8937	2.8172	2.7442	2.6745	13
14	3.0752	2.9888	2.9066	2.8284	2.7539	2.6829	14
15	3.0880	2.9998	2.9160	2.8364	2.7608	2.6887	15
16	3.0975	3.0078	2.9229	2.8422	2.7657	2.6929	16
17	3.1045	3.0138	2.9278	2.8464	2.7692	2.6958	17
18	3.1098	3.0181	2.9315	2.8494	2.7716	2.6978	18
19	3.1137	3.0213	2.9341	2.8516	2.7734	2.6993	19
20	3.1166	3.0237	2.9360	2.8531	2.7747	2.7003	20

26%

ORDINARY ANNUITIES CHANGING IN CONSTANT RATIO

(Present Value of Annual Payments Starting at $1 and Changing in Constant Ratio)

Base: 1.260 000

Annual Percentage INCREASE of:

Years	1%	2%	3%	4%	5%	6%	Years
1	.7937	.7937	.7937	.7937	.7937	.7937	1
2	1.4298	1.4361	1.4424	1.4487	1.4550	1.4613	2
3	1.9398	1.9562	1.9728	1.9894	2.0062	2.0230	3
4	2.3486	2.3773	2.4063	2.4357	2.4655	2.4956	4
5	2.6762	2.7181	2.7607	2.8041	2.8482	2.8931	5
6	2.9389	2.9940	3.0504	3.1081	3.1672	3.2275	6
7	3.1494	3.2174	3.2873	3.3591	3.4329	3.5089	7
8	3.3182	3.3982	3.4809	3.5662	3.6544	3.7456	8
9	3.4535	3.5446	3.6391	3.7372	3.8390	3.9447	9
10	3.5619	3.6631	3.7685	3.8783	3.9928	4.1122	10
11	3.6488	3.7590	3.8742	3.9948	4.1210	4.2531	11
12	3.7185	3.8366	3.9607	4.0910	4.2278	4.3717	12
13	3.7744	3.8995	4.0314	4.1703	4.3168	4.4714	13
14	3.8191	3.9504	4.0891	4.2358	4.3910	4.5553	14
15	3.8550	3.9916	4.1363	4.2899	4.4528	4.6259	15
16	3.8838	4.0249	4.1749	4.3345	4.5043	4.6853	16
17	3.9068	4.0519	4.2065	4.3713	4.5473	4.7352	17
18	3.9253	4.0738	4.2323	4.4017	4.5830	4.7773	18
19	3.9401	4.0915	4.2534	4.4268	4.6129	4.8126	19
20	3.9520	4.1058	4.2706	4.4475	4.6377	4.8424	20

Annual Percentage DECREASE of:

Years	1%	2%	3%	4%	5%	6%	Years
1	.7937	.7937	.7937	.7937	.7937	.7937	1
2	1.4172	1.4109	1.4046	1.3983	1.3920	1.3857	2
3	1.9072	1.8910	1.8750	1.8591	1.8432	1.8275	3
4	2.2922	2.2645	2.2371	2.2101	2.1834	2.1570	4
5	2.5946	2.5549	2.5159	2.4775	2.4398	2.4028	5
6	2.8323	2.7808	2.7305	2.6813	2.6332	2.5862	6
7	3.0190	2.9565	2.8957	2.8365	2.7790	2.7231	7
8	3.1657	3.0931	3.0229	2.9548	2.8889	2.8251	8
9	3.2810	3.1994	3.1208	3.0449	2.9718	2.9013	9
10	3.3716	3.2821	3.1962	3.1136	3.0343	2.9581	10
11	3.4428	3.3464	3.2542	3.1659	3.0814	3.0005	11
12	3.4987	3.3964	3.2989	3.2058	3.1169	3.0321	12
13	3.5426	3.4353	3.3332	3.2362	3.1437	3.0557	13
14	3.5771	3.4655	3.3597	3.2593	3.1639	3.0733	14
15	3.6043	3.4891	3.3801	3.2769	3.1791	3.0864	15
16	3.6256	3.5074	3.3958	3.2904	3.1906	3.0962	16
17	3.6423	3.5216	3.4079	3.3006	3.1993	3.1035	17
18	3.6555	3.5327	3.4172	3.3084	3.2058	3.1090	18
19	3.6658	3.5413	3.4243	3.3143	3.2107	3.1131	19
20	3.6739	3.5480	3.4298	3.3188	3.2144	3.1161	20

26%

ORDINARY ANNUITIES CHANGING IN CONSTANT RATIO

(Present Value of Annual Payments Starting at $1 and Changing in Constant Ratio)

Base: 1.260 000

Annual Percentage INCREASE of:

Years	7%	8%	9%	10%	11%	12%	Years
1	.7937	.7937	.7937	.7937	.7937	.7937	1
2	1.4676	1.4739	1.4802	1.4865	1.4928	1.4991	2
3	2.0400	2.0570	2.0742	2.0914	2.1088	2.1262	3
4	2.5260	2.5568	2.5880	2.6195	2.6514	2.6836	4
5	2.9387	2.9852	3.0324	3.0805	3.1294	3.1791	5
6	3.2893	3.3524	3.4170	3.4830	3.5505	3.6195	6
7	3.5869	3.6671	3.7496	3.8343	3.9215	4.0110	7
8	3.8397	3.9369	4.0373	4.1411	4.2483	4.3590	8
9	4.0543	4.1681	4.2863	4.4089	4.5362	4.6683	9
10	4.2366	4.3663	4.5016	4.6427	4.7898	4.9432	10
11	4.3914	4.5362	4.6879	4.8468	5.0132	5.1876	11
12	4.5229	4.6818	4.8491	5.0250	5.2101	5.4049	12
13	4.6345	4.8067	4.9885	5.1805	5.3835	5.5980	13
14	4.7293	4.9136	5.1091	5.3163	5.5362	5.7696	14
15	4.8098	5.0053	5.2134	5.4349	5.6708	5.9222	15
16	4.8782	5.0840	5.3037	5.5384	5.7894	6.0579	16
17	4.9362	5.1513	5.3817	5.6288	5.8938	6.1784	17
18	4.9855	5.2091	5.4493	5.7077	5.9858	6.2856	18
19	5.0274	5.2586	5.5077	5.7765	6.0669	6.3808	19
20	5.0629	5.3010	5.5583	5.8366	6.1383	6.4655	20

Annual Percentage DECREASE of:

Years	7%	8%	9%	10%	11%	12%	Years
1	.7937	.7937	.7937	.7937	.7937	.7937	1
2	1.3794	1.3731	1.3668	1.3605	1.3542	1.3479	2
3	1.8118	1.7963	1.7808	1.7655	1.7502	1.7351	3
4	2.1309	2.1052	2.0798	2.0547	2.0299	2.0054	4
5	2.3665	2.3308	2.2957	2.2613	2.2275	2.1943	5
6	2.5403	2.4955	2.4517	2.4089	2.3670	2.3262	6
7	2.6687	2.6158	2.5643	2.5143	2.4656	2.4183	7
8	2.7634	2.7036	2.6456	2.5896	2.5352	2.4826	8
9	2.8333	2.7677	2.7044	2.6433	2.5844	2.5275	9
10	2.8849	2.8145	2.7468	2.6817	2.6191	2.5589	10
11	2.9230	2.8487	2.7775	2.7092	2.6437	2.5808	11
12	2.9511	2.8736	2.7996	2.7288	2.6610	2.5961	12
13	2.9718	2.8919	2.8156	2.7428	2.6733	2.6068	13
14	2.9871	2.9052	2.8271	2.7528	2.6819	2.6143	14
15	2.9984	2.9149	2.8355	2.7599	2.6880	2.6195	15
16	3.0068	2.9220	2.8415	2.7650	2.6923	2.6231	16
17	3.0129	2.9272	2.8458	2.7687	2.6954	2.6257	17
18	3.0175	2.9309	2.8490	2.7713	2.6975	2.6275	18
19	3.0208	2.9337	2.8512	2.7731	2.6990	2.6287	19
20	3.0233	2.9357	2.8529	2.7745	2.7001	2.6296	20

27%

ORDINARY ANNUITIES CHANGING IN CONSTANT RATIO

(Present Value of Annual Payments Starting at $1 and Changing in Constant Ratio)

Base: 1.270 000

Annual Percentage INCREASE of:

Years	1%	2%	3%	4%	5%	6%	Years
1	.7874	.7874	.7874	.7874	.7874	.7874	1
2	1.4136	1.4198	1.4260	1.4322	1.4384	1.4446	2
3	1.9116	1.9277	1.9439	1.9602	1.9766	1.9931	3
4	2.3077	2.3356	2.3640	2.3926	2.4216	2.4510	4
5	2.6226	2.6633	2.7046	2.7467	2.7895	2.8331	5
6	2.8731	2.9264	2.9809	3.0367	3.0937	3.1520	6
7	3.0723	3.1377	3.2050	3.2741	3.3452	3.4182	7
8	3.2307	3.3075	3.3867	3.4686	3.5531	3.6404	8
9	3.3567	3.4438	3.5341	3.6278	3.7250	3.8259	9
10	3.4569	3.5533	3.6537	3.7582	3.8671	3.9806	10
11	3.5366	3.6412	3.7506	3.8650	3.9846	4.1098	11
12	3.6000	3.7119	3.8292	3.9524	4.0818	4.2176	12
13	3.6504	3.7686	3.8930	4.0240	4.1621	4.3076	13
14	3.6905	3.8141	3.9447	4.0827	4.2285	4.3828	14
15	3.7223	3.8507	3.9867	4.1307	4.2834	4.4454	15
16	3.7477	3.8801	4.0207	4.1700	4.3288	4.4978	16
17	3.7678	3.9037	4.0483	4.2022	4.3663	4.5415	17
18	3.7839	3.9227	4.0706	4.2286	4.3974	4.5779	18
19	3.7966	3.9379	4.0888	4.2502	4.4230	4.6083	19
20	3.8068	3.9501	4.1035	4.2679	4.4442	4.6337	20

Annual Percentage DECREASE of:

Years	1%	2%	3%	4%	5%	6%	Years
1	.7874	.7874	.7874	.7874	.7874	.7874	1
2	1.4012	1.3950	1.3888	1.3826	1.3764	1.3702	2
3	1.8797	1.8639	1.8481	1.8325	1.8170	1.8016	3
4	2.2527	2.2257	2.1990	2.1726	2.1466	2.1208	4
5	2.5434	2.5048	2.4669	2.4297	2.3931	2.3572	5
6	2.7701	2.7203	2.6716	2.6240	2.5775	2.5321	6
7	2.9467	2.8865	2.8279	2.7709	2.7155	2.6615	7
8	3.0845	3.0148	2.9473	2.8819	2.8187	2.7574	8
9	3.1918	3.1138	3.0385	2.9659	2.8958	2.8283	9
10	3.2755	3.1902	3.1081	3.0293	2.9536	2.8808	10
11	3.3408	3.2491	3.1613	3.0773	2.9968	2.9196	11
12	3.3916	3.2946	3.2020	3.1135	3.0291	2.9484	12
13	3.4313	3.3297	3.2330	3.1409	3.0533	2.9697	13
14	3.4622	3.3568	3.2567	3.1617	3.0713	2.9854	14
15	3.4863	3.3777	3.2748	3.1773	3.0849	2.9971	15
16	3.5050	3.3938	3.2886	3.1892	3.0950	3.0057	16
17	3.5197	3.4062	3.2992	3.1981	3.1025	3.0121	17
18	3.5311	3.4158	3.3073	3.2049	3.1082	3.0168	18
19	3.5400	3.4232	3.3134	3.2100	3.1124	3.0203	19
20	3.5469	3.4290	3.3181	3.2138	3.1156	3.0229	20

27%

ORDINARY ANNUITIES CHANGING IN CONSTANT RATIO

(Present Value of Annual Payments Starting at $1 and Changing in Constant Ratio)

Base: 1.270 000

Annual Percentage INCREASE of:

Years	7%	8%	9%	10%	11%	12%	Years
1	.7874	.7874	.7874	.7874	.7874	.7874	1
2	1.4508	1.4570	1.4632	1.4694	1.4756	1.4818	2
3	2.0097	2.0264	2.0432	2.0601	2.0771	2.0942	3
4	2.4806	2.5107	2.5410	2.5718	2.6028	2.6342	4
5	2.8774	2.9225	2.9683	3.0149	3.0623	3.1105	5
6	3.2117	3.2726	3.3350	3.3987	3.4639	3.5305	6
7	3.4933	3.5704	3.6497	3.7312	3.8149	3.9009	7
8	3.7306	3.8237	3.9198	4.0191	4.1217	4.2276	8
9	3.9305	4.0390	4.1517	4.2685	4.3898	4.5157	9
10	4.0989	4.2222	4.3506	4.4846	4.6242	4.7697	10
11	4.2408	4.3779	4.5214	4.6717	4.8290	4.9938	11
12	4.3604	4.5103	4.6680	4.8337	5.0080	5.1914	12
13	4.4611	4.6230	4.7938	4.9741	5.1645	5.3656	13
14	4.5460	4.7187	4.9018	5.0957	5.3013	5.5193	14
15	4.6175	4.8002	4.9944	5.2010	5.4208	5.6548	15
16	4.6777	4.8695	5.0739	5.2922	5.5253	5.7743	16
17	4.7285	4.9284	5.1422	5.3712	5.6166	5.8797	17
18	4.7712	4.9784	5.2008	5.4396	5.6964	5.9727	18
19	4.8073	5.0210	5.2511	5.4989	5.7661	6.0546	19
20	4.8376	5.0573	5.2942	5.5502	5.8271	6.1269	20

Annual Percentage DECREASE of:

Years	7%	8%	9%	10%	11%	12%	Years
1	.7874	.7874	.7874	.7874	.7874	.7874	1
2	1.3640	1.3578	1.3516	1.3454	1.3392	1.3330	2
3	1.7862	1.7710	1.7559	1.7408	1.7259	1.7111	3
4	2.0954	2.0703	2.0455	2.0211	1.9969	1.9730	4
5	2.3219	2.2872	2.2531	2.2197	2.1868	2.1545	5
6	2.4877	2.4443	2.4018	2.3604	2.3199	2.2803	6
7	2.6091	2.5580	2.5084	2.4601	2.4131	2.3675	7
8	2.6980	2.6405	2.5848	2.5308	2.4785	2.4278	8
9	2.7631	2.7002	2.6395	2.5809	2.5243	2.4697	9
10	2.8108	2.7434	2.6787	2.6164	2.5564	2.4987	10
11	2.8457	2.7748	2.7068	2.6415	2.5789	2.5188	11
12	2.8712	2.7975	2.7269	2.6593	2.5947	2.5327	12
13	2.8900	2.8139	2.7413	2.6720	2.6057	2.5423	13
14	2.9037	2.8258	2.7517	2.6809	2.6134	2.5490	14
15	2.9137	2.8345	2.7591	2.6873	2.6189	2.5537	15
16	2.9211	2.8407	2.7644	2.6918	2.6227	2.5569	16
17	2.9265	2.8452	2.7682	2.6950	2.6253	2.5591	17
18	2.9304	2.8485	2.7709	2.6972	2.6272	2.5606	18
19	2.9333	2.8509	2.7728	2.6988	2.6285	2.5617	19
20	2.9354	2.8526	2.7742	2.6999	2.6294	2.5624	20

28%

ORDINARY ANNUITIES CHANGING IN CONSTANT RATIO

(Present Value of Annual Payments Starting at $1 and Changing in Constant Ratio)

Base: 1.280 000

Annual Percentage INCREASE of:

Years	1%	2%	3%	4%	5%	6%	Years
1	.7813	.7813	.7813	.7813	.7813	.7813	1
2	1.3977	1.4038	1.4099	1.4160	1.4221	1.4282	2
3	1.8841	1.8999	1.9158	1.9318	1.9478	1.9640	3
4	2.2679	2.2952	2.3229	2.3508	2.3791	2.4077	4
5	2.5708	2.6103	2.6504	2.6913	2.7328	2.7751	5
6	2.8098	2.8613	2.9140	2.9679	3.0230	3.0794	6
7	2.9983	3.0614	3.1261	3.1927	3.2611	3.3314	7
8	3.1471	3.2208	3.2968	3.3753	3.4564	3.5400	8
9	3.2645	3.3478	3.4341	3.5237	3.6165	3.7128	9
10	3.3572	3.4490	3.5447	3.6442	3.7479	3.8560	10
11	3.4303	3.5297	3.6336	3.7422	3.8557	3.9745	11
12	3.4879	3.5940	3.7052	3.8218	3.9442	4.0726	12
13	3.5335	3.6452	3.7627	3.8865	4.0167	4.1539	13
14	3.5694	3.6860	3.8091	3.9390	4.0762	4.2212	14
15	3.5977	3.7185	3.8464	3.9817	4.1250	4.2769	15
16	3.6201	3.7445	3.8764	4.0164	4.1650	4.3231	16
17	3.6377	3.7651	3.9005	4.0445	4.1979	4.3613	17
18	3.6516	3.7816	3.9200	4.0674	4.2248	4.3929	18
19	3.6626	3.7947	3.9356	4.0860	4.2469	4.4192	19
20	3.6713	3.8051	3.9482	4.1012	4.2651	4.4409	20

Annual Percentage DECREASE of:

Years	1%	2%	3%	4%	5%	6%	Years
1	.7812	.7812	.7812	.7812	.7812	.7812	1
2	1.3855	1.3794	1.3733	1.3672	1.3611	1.3550	2
3	1.8528	1.8373	1.8219	1.8066	1.7914	1.7763	3
4	2.2143	2.1880	2.1619	2.1362	2.1108	2.0857	4
5	2.4939	2.4564	2.4196	2.3834	2.3479	2.3130	5
6	2.7101	2.6619	2.6149	2.5688	2.5238	2.4798	6
7	2.8774	2.8193	2.7628	2.7079	2.6544	2.6024	7
8	3.0067	2.9398	2.8749	2.8121	2.7513	2.6924	8
9	3.1067	3.0320	2.9599	2.8904	2.8232	2.7585	9
10	3.1841	3.1026	3.0243	2.9490	2.8766	2.8070	10
11	3.2440	3.1567	3.0731	2.9930	2.9162	2.8426	11
12	3.2903	3.1981	3.1101	3.0260	2.9456	2.8688	12
13	3.3261	3.2298	3.1381	3.0508	2.9675	2.8880	13
14	3.3537	3.2541	3.1594	3.0693	2.9837	2.9021	14
15	3.3752	3.2726	3.1754	3.0832	2.9957	2.9125	15
16	3.3917	3.2869	3.1876	3.0937	3.0046	2.9201	16
17	3.4045	3.2978	3.1969	3.1015	3.0112	2.9257	17
18	3.4144	3.3061	3.2039	3.1074	3.0162	2.9298	18
19	3.4221	3.3125	3.2092	3.1118	3.0198	2.9328	19
20	3.4280	3.3174	3.2132	3.1151	3.0225	2.9351	20

ORDINARY ANNUITIES CHANGING IN CONSTANT RATIO

(Present Value of Annual Payments Starting at $1 and Changing in Constant Ratio)

Base: 1.280 000

Annual Percentage INCREASE of:

Years	7%	8%	9%	10%	11%	12%	Years
1	.7813	.7813	.7813	.7813	.7812	.7812	1
2	1.4343	1.4404	1.4465	1.4526	1.4587	1.4648	2
3	1.9803	1.9966	2.0131	2.0296	2.0463	2.0630	3
4	2.4366	2.4659	2.4955	2.5254	2.5557	2.5864	4
5	2.8181	2.8618	2.9063	2.9516	2.9976	3.0443	5
6	3.1370	3.1959	3.2562	3.3177	3.3807	3.4450	6
7	3.4036	3.4778	3.5541	3.6324	3.7129	3.7957	7
8	3.6264	3.7157	3.8078	3.9029	4.0011	4.1024	8
9	3.8127	3.9163	4.0238	4.1353	4.2509	4.3709	9
10	3.9685	4.0857	4.2078	4.3350	4.4676	4.6058	10
11	4.0986	4.2285	4.3644	4.5066	4.6555	4.8113	11
12	4.2074	4.3491	4.4978	4.6542	4.8184	4.9911	12
13	4.2984	4.4508	4.6114	4.7809	4.9597	5.1485	13
14	4.3745	4.5366	4.7082	4.8898	5.0823	5.2862	14
15	4.4380	4.6090	4.7906	4.9835	5.1885	5.4067	15
16	4.4912	4.6701	4.8607	5.0639	5.2807	5.5121	16
17	4.5356	4.7216	4.9204	5.1330	5.3606	5.6043	17
18	4.5727	4.7651	4.9713	5.1925	5.4299	5.6850	18
19	4.6037	4.8018	5.0146	5.2435	5.4900	5.7557	19
20	4.6297	4.8328	5.0515	5.2874	5.5421	5.8174	20

Annual Percentage DECREASE of:

Years	7%	8%	9%	10%	11%	12%	Years
1	.7812	.7812	.7812	.7812	.7812	.7812	1
2	1.3489	1.3428	1.3367	1.3306	1.3245	1.3184	2
3	1.7613	1.7464	1.7315	1.7168	1.7022	1.6876	3
4	2.0609	2.0365	2.0123	1.9884	1.9648	1.9415	4
5	2.2787	2.2450	2.2118	2.1793	2.1474	2.1160	5
6	2.4368	2.3948	2.3537	2.3136	2.2744	2.2360	6
7	2.5518	2.5025	2.4546	2.4080	2.3626	2.3185	7
8	2.6353	2.5799	2.5263	2.4744	2.4240	2.3752	8
9	2.6959	2.6356	2.5773	2.5210	2.4667	2.4142	9
10	2.7400	2.6756	2.6136	2.5539	2.4964	2.4410	10
11	2.7720	2.7043	2.6393	2.5769	2.5170	2.4595	11
12	2.7953	2.7250	2.6576	2.5932	2.5314	2.4721	12
13	2.8122	2.7398	2.6707	2.6046	2.5413	2.4808	13
14	2.8245	2.7505	2.6799	2.6126	2.5483	2.4868	14
15	2.8334	2.7582	2.6865	2.6182	2.5531	2.4909	15
16	2.8399	2.7637	2.6912	2.6222	2.5564	2.4938	16
17	2.8446	2.7676	2.6945	2.6250	2.5588	2.4957	17
18	2.8480	2.7705	2.6969	2.6269	2.5604	2.4971	18
19	2.8505	2.7725	2.6986	2.6283	2.5615	2.4980	19
20	2.8523	2.7740	2.6998	2.6293	2.5623	2.4986	20

29%
ORDINARY ANNUITIES CHANGING IN CONSTANT RATIO
(Present Value of Annual Payments Starting at $1 and Changing in Constant Ratio)

Base: 1.290 000

Annual Percentage INCREASE of:

Years	1%	2%	3%	4%	5%	6%	Years
1	.7752	.7752	.7752	.7752	.7752	.7752	1
2	1.3821	1.3881	1.3941	1.4002	1.4062	1.4122	2
3	1.8573	1.8728	1.8883	1.9040	1.9197	1.9356	3
4	2.2294	2.2560	2.2829	2.3102	2.3378	2.3657	4
5	2.5207	2.5590	2.5980	2.6377	2.6780	2.7191	5
6	2.7487	2.7986	2.8496	2.9017	2.9550	3.0095	6
7	2.9273	2.9880	3.0504	3.1145	3.1804	3.2481	7
8	3.0671	3.1378	3.2108	3.2861	3.3639	3.4442	8
9	3.1766	3.2563	3.3389	3.4245	3.5133	3.6053	9
10	3.2623	3.3499	3.4411	3.5360	3.6348	3.7377	10
11	3.3294	3.4240	3.5227	3.6259	3.7338	3.8465	11
12	3.3819	3.4825	3.5879	3.6984	3.8143	3.9359	12
13	3.4231	3.5288	3.6400	3.7569	3.8799	4.0093	13
14	3.4553	3.5654	3.6815	3.8040	3.9332	4.0697	14
15	3.4805	3.5944	3.7147	3.8420	3.9767	4.1193	15
16	3.5002	3.6172	3.7412	3.8726	4.0120	4.1600	16
17	3.5157	3.6353	3.7624	3.8973	4.0408	4.1935	17
18	3.5278	3.6497	3.7792	3.9172	4.0642	4.2210	18
19	3.5373	3.6610	3.7927	3.9332	4.0833	4.2436	19
20	3.5447	3.6699	3.8035	3.9462	4.0988	4.2622	20

Annual Percentage DECREASE of:

Years	1%	2%	3%	4%	5%	6%	Years
1	.7752	.7752	.7752	.7752	.7752	.7752	1
2	1.3701	1.3641	1.3581	1.3521	1.3461	1.3401	2
3	1.8267	1.8115	1.7964	1.7814	1.7665	1.7517	3
4	2.1771	2.1514	2.1260	2.1009	2.0761	2.0516	4
5	2.4460	2.4096	2.3738	2.3386	2.3041	2.2702	5
6	2.6523	2.6057	2.5601	2.5156	2.4720	2.4294	6
7	2.8107	2.7547	2.7003	2.6473	2.5957	2.5455	7
8	2.9322	2.8679	2.8056	2.7452	2.6867	2.6300	8
9	3.0255	2.9539	2.8848	2.8182	2.7538	2.6917	9
10	3.0971	3.0193	2.9444	2.8724	2.8032	2.7366	10
11	3.1520	3.0689	2.9892	2.9128	2.8396	2.7693	11
12	3.1942	3.1066	3.0229	2.9429	2.8663	2.7931	12
13	3.2266	3.1353	3.0482	2.9652	2.8861	2.8105	13
14	3.2514	3.1570	3.0673	2.9819	2.9006	2.8231	14
15	3.2704	3.1735	3.0816	2.9943	2.9113	2.8324	15
16	3.2851	3.1861	3.0924	3.0035	2.9192	2.8391	16
17	3.2963	3.1956	3.1005	3.0103	2.9250	2.8440	17
18	3.3049	3.2029	3.1065	3.0155	2.9292	2.8476	18
19	3.3115	3.2084	3.1111	3.0193	2.9324	2.8502	19
20	3.3166	3.2126	3.1146	3.0221	2.9347	2.8521	20

ORDINARY ANNUITIES CHANGING IN CONSTANT RATIO

(Present Value of Annual Payments Starting at $1 and Changing in Constant Ratio)

Base: 1.290 000

Annual Percentage INCREASE of:

Years	7%	8%	9%	10%	11%	12%	Years
1	.7752	.7752	.7752	.7752	.7752	.7752	1
2	1.4182	1.4242	1.4302	1.4362	1.4422	1.4482	2
3	1.9515	1.9675	1.9837	1.9999	2.0162	2.0326	3
4	2.3939	2.4224	2.4513	2.4805	2.5100	2.5399	4
5	2.7608	2.8033	2.8465	2.8904	2.9350	2.9804	5
6	3.0652	3.1221	3.1803	3.2398	3.3007	3.3628	6
7	3.3176	3.3891	3.4625	3.5378	3.6153	3.6948	7
8	3.5270	3.6126	3.7008	3.7920	3.8860	3.9831	8
9	3.7007	3.7997	3.9023	4.0087	4.1190	4.2334	9
10	3.8448	3.9563	4.0724	4.1934	4.3194	4.4507	10
11	3.9643	4.0874	4.2163	4.3510	4.4919	4.6394	11
12	4.0634	4.1972	4.3378	4.4853	4.6403	4.8032	12
13	4.1456	4.2892	4.4404	4.5999	4.7680	4.9454	13
14	4.2138	4.3661	4.5272	4.6976	4.8779	5.0689	14
15	4.2704	4.4306	4.6005	4.7809	4.9725	5.1761	15
16	4.3173	4.4845	4.6624	4.8519	5.0538	5.2692	16
17	4.3562	4.5297	4.7148	4.9125	5.1238	5.3500	17
18	4.3885	4.5675	4.7590	4.9641	5.1841	5.4201	18
19	4.4152	4.5991	4.7964	5.0082	5.2359	5.4810	19
20	4.4374	4.6256	4.8279	5.0457	5.2805	5.5339	20

Annual Percentage DECREASE of:

Years	7%	8%	9%	10%	11%	12%	Years
1	.7752	.7752	.7752	.7752	.7752	.7752	1
2	1.3341	1.3280	1.3220	1.3160	1.3100	1.3040	2
3	1.7370	1.7223	1.7078	1.6934	1.6790	1.6647	3
4	2.0274	2.0035	1.9799	1.9566	1.9336	1.9108	4
5	2.2368	2.2041	2.1719	2.1403	2.1092	2.0787	5
6	2.3878	2.3471	2.3073	2.2684	2.2304	2.1932	6
7	2.4966	2.4491	2.4028	2.3578	2.3140	2.2713	7
8	2.5751	2.5218	2.4702	2.4202	2.3717	2.3246	8
9	2.6316	2.5737	2.5177	2.4637	2.4115	2.3610	9
10	2.6724	2.6107	2.5513	2.4940	2.4389	2.3858	10
11	2.7018	2.6371	2.5749	2.5152	2.4579	2.4027	11
12	2.7230	2.6559	2.5916	2.5300	2.4709	2.4143	12
13	2.7383	2.6693	2.6034	2.5403	2.4799	2.4221	13
14	2.7493	2.6789	2.6117	2.5475	2.4862	2.4275	14
15	2.7573	2.6857	2.6176	2.5525	2.4905	2.4312	15
16	2.7630	2.6906	2.6217	2.5560	2.4934	2.4337	16
17	2.7671	2.6941	2.6246	2.5585	2.4955	2.4354	17
18	2.7701	2.6965	2.6267	2.5602	2.4969	2.4365	18
19	2.7722	2.6983	2.6281	2.5614	2.4978	2.4373	19
20	2.7738	2.6996	2.6291	2.5622	2.4985	2.4379	20

30%

ORDINARY ANNUITIES CHANGING IN CONSTANT RATIO

(Present Value of Annual Payments Starting at $1 and Changing in Constant Ratio)

Base: 1.300 000

Annual Percentage INCREASE of:

Years	1%	2%	3%	4%	5%	6%	Years
1	.7692	.7692	.7692	.7692	.7692	.7692	1
2	1.3669	1.3728	1.3787	1.3846	1.3905	1.3964	2
3	1.8312	1.8463	1.8616	1.8769	1.8924	1.9079	3
4	2.1919	2.2179	2.2442	2.2708	2.2977	2.3249	4
5	2.4722	2.5094	2.5473	2.5858	2.6250	2.6649	5
6	2.6899	2.7382	2.7875	2.8379	2.8895	2.9422	6
7	2.8591	2.9176	2.9778	3.0396	3.1030	3.1682	7
8	2.9905	3.0585	3.1285	3.2009	3.2755	3.3525	8
9	3.0926	3.1689	3.2480	3.3299	3.4148	3.5028	9
10	3.1720	3.2556	3.3426	3.4332	3.5274	3.6254	10
11	3.2336	3.3236	3.4176	3.5158	3.6183	3.7253	11
12	3.2815	3.3770	3.4771	3.5818	3.6917	3.8068	12
13	3.3187	3.4189	3.5241	3.6347	3.7510	3.8732	13
14	3.3476	3.4517	3.5614	3.6770	3.7989	3.9274	14
15	3.3701	3.4775	3.5910	3.7108	3.8375	3.9716	15
16	3.3875	3.4977	3.6144	3.7379	3.8688	4.0076	16
17	3.4011	3.5136	3.6329	3.7595	3.8940	4.0370	17
18	3.4116	3.5261	3.6476	3.7769	3.9144	4.0609	18
19	3.4198	3.5358	3.6593	3.7907	3.9309	4.0804	19
20	3.4261	3.5435	3.6685	3.8018	3.9442	4.0964	20

Annual Percentage DECREASE of:

Years	1%	2%	3%	4%	5%	6%	Years
1	.7692	.7692	.7692	.7692	.7692	.7692	1
2	1.3550	1.3491	1.3432	1.3373	1.3314	1.3254	2
3	1.8011	1.7863	1.7715	1.7568	1.7421	1.7276	3
4	2.1409	2.1158	2.0910	2.0665	2.0423	2.0184	4
5	2.3996	2.3642	2.3294	2.2953	2.2617	2.2287	5
6	2.5966	2.5515	2.5074	2.4642	2.4220	2.3808	6
7	2.7466	2.6927	2.6401	2.5890	2.5392	2.4907	7
8	2.8609	2.7991	2.7392	2.6811	2.6248	2.5702	8
9	2.9479	2.8793	2.8131	2.7491	2.6873	2.6277	9
10	3.0142	2.9398	2.8682	2.7993	2.7331	2.6692	10
11	3.0646	2.9854	2.9094	2.8364	2.7665	2.6993	11
12	3.1031	3.0197	2.9401	2.8638	2.7909	2.7210	12
13	3.1323	3.0457	2.9630	2.8841	2.8087	2.7367	13
14	3.1546	3.0652	2.9801	2.8990	2.8218	2.7481	14
15	3.1716	3.0799	2.9928	2.9100	2.8313	2.7563	15
16	3.1845	3.0910	3.0023	2.9182	2.8382	2.7623	16
17	3.1944	3.0994	3.0094	2.9242	2.8433	2.7666	17
18	3.2019	3.1057	3.0147	2.9286	2.8471	2.7697	18
19	3.2076	3.1104	3.0187	2.9319	2.8498	2.7719	19
20	3.2119	3.1140	3.0216	2.9343	2.8518	2.7735	20

30%

ORDINARY ANNUITIES CHANGING IN CONSTANT RATIO

(Present Value of Annual Payments Starting at $1 and Changing in Constant Ratio)

Base: 1.300 000

Annual Percentage INCREASE of:

Years	7%	8%	9%	10%	11%	12%	Years
1	.7692	.7692	.7692	.7692	.7692	.7692	1
2	1.4024	1.4083	1.4142	1.4201	1.4260	1.4320	2
3	1.9235	1.9392	1.9550	1.9709	1.9868	2.0029	3
4	2.3524	2.3802	2.4084	2.4369	2.4657	2.4948	4
5	2.7054	2.7467	2.7886	2.8312	2.8746	2.9186	5
6	2.9960	3.0511	3.1074	3.1649	3.2237	3.2837	6
7	3.2352	3.3040	3.3746	3.4472	3.5217	3.5983	7
8	3.4320	3.5141	3.5987	3.6861	3.7763	3.8693	8
9	3.5941	3.6886	3.7866	3.8882	3.9936	4.1028	9
10	3.7274	3.8336	3.9442	4.0593	4.1791	4.3039	10
11	3.8372	3.9541	4.0763	4.2040	4.3376	4.4772	11
12	3.9275	4.0542	4.1870	4.3265	4.4728	4.6265	12
13	4.0019	4.1373	4.2799	4.4301	4.5883	4.7552	13
14	4.0631	4.2064	4.3578	4.5178	4.6870	4.8660	14
15	4.1135	4.2638	4.4230	4.5920	4.7712	4.9615	15
16	4.1549	4.3114	4.4778	4.6547	4.8431	5.0437	16
17	4.1891	4.3510	4.5237	4.7078	4.9045	5.1146	17
18	4.2171	4.3839	4.5622	4.7528	4.9569	5.1757	18
19	4.2403	4.4113	4.5944	4.7908	5.0017	5.2283	19
20	4.2593	4.4340	4.6215	4.8230	5.0399	5.2736	20

Annual Percentage DECREASE of:

Years	7%	8%	9%	10%	11%	12%	Years
1	.7692	.7692	.7692	.7692	.7692	.7692	1
2	1.3195	1.3136	1.3077	1.3018	1.2959	1.2899	2
3	1.7132	1.6989	1.6846	1.6705	1.6564	1.6424	3
4	1.9948	1.9715	1.9485	1.9257	1.9032	1.8810	4
5	2.1963	2.1644	2.1332	2.1024	2.0722	2.0425	5
6	2.3404	2.3010	2.2624	2.2247	2.1879	2.1519	6
7	2.4435	2.3976	2.3529	2.3094	2.2671	2.2259	7
8	2.5173	2.4660	2.4163	2.3681	2.3213	2.2760	8
9	2.5701	2.5144	2.4606	2.4087	2.3584	2.3099	9
10	2.6078	2.5487	2.4917	2.4368	2.3839	2.3329	10
11	2.6348	2.5729	2.5134	2.4562	2.4013	2.3484	11
12	2.6541	2.5901	2.5286	2.4697	2.4132	2.3589	12
13	2.6680	2.6022	2.5393	2.4790	2.4213	2.3660	13
14	2.6779	2.6108	2.5467	2.4855	2.4269	2.3709	14
15	2.6849	2.6169	2.5519	2.4899	2.4307	2.3741	15
16	2.6900	2.6212	2.5556	2.4930	2.4333	2.3763	16
17	2.6936	2.6242	2.5581	2.4952	2.4351	2.3778	17
18	2.6962	2.6264	2.5599	2.4967	2.4364	2.3788	18
19	2.6980	2.6279	2.5612	2.4977	2.4372	2.3795	19
20	2.6994	2.6290	2.5621	2.4984	2.4378	2.3800	20

Table 6

Sinking Fund Factors
(Periodic Payment to Grow to $1)

Table 6 - SINKING FUND FACTORS (Periodic Payment to Grow to $1)

The level periodic investment or deposit required to accumulate one in a given number of periods including the accumulation of interest at the effective rate. This is commonly known as the *amortization rate* and is reciprocal to the corresponding factor from Table 7.

$$1/S_{\overline{n}} = \frac{i}{S^n - 1}$$

Where

$1/S_{\overline{n}}$ = Sinking Fund Factor

i = Effective Rate of Interest

n = Number of Compounding Periods

S^n = Future Value Factor

This Table is used in solving problems dealing with the calculation of required sinking fund deposits and/or the provision for change in capital value in investment situations where the income/payments are level.

Example 1:
Assuming a 6% interest rate, what monthly, end-of-period deposit is required to provide $10,000 in 10 years?

$10,000 \times .006102 = $61.02

Same example except deposits at the beginning of the period.

$10,000 \times .006102/1.005 = $60.72

Example 2:
Assuming a 6% interest rate, what monthly, end-of-period deposit is required to provide $10,000 in 10 years and 7 months?

$10,000/(1/.006102 + 1.819397*/.140729) = $56.56

* Future Value Factor for 120 months.

Same example except deposits at the beginning of the period.

$56.56/1.005 = $56.28

Example 3:
What is the annual constant for a direct reduction loan, 12% interest, monthly payments for 25 years?

.12 + 12 × .000532 = .126384*

*Actually, loan payments are rounded up to the nearest penny or more and published tables of annual constants will reflect this practice. One common table of annual constants is calculated for $1,000 of loan, which means that the sinking fund factor is rounded up in the 5th decimal place. On this basis, the constant for a 12%, 25-year loan would be:

.12 + 12 × .000540 = .126480

Example 4:
Assuming a 12% interest/yield rate, what monthly payment will provide for interest and 40% amortization of a $100,000 loan in 10 years?

$100,000 × (.12/12 + .4 × .004347) = $1,173.88

Example 5:
A property has an anticipated net operating income of $10,000 per year for the next 5 years and the trend in prices indicates a 15% increase in value over that period of time. What is the calculated value, assuming that a 12% yield rate is appropriate?

$10,000/(.12 − .15 × .157410) = $103,747

3%

SINKING FUND FACTORS
(Periodic Payment to Grow to $1)

Base:	1.002 500	1.007 500	1.015 000	1.030 000	1.030 453	

Frequency of Payments and of Conversions

Months	Monthly	Quarterly	Semiannual	Annual	Annual Payment Daily Conversion	Months
1	1.000 000	—	—	—	—	1
2	.499 376	—	—	—	—	2
3	.332 501	1.000 000	—	—	—	3
4	.249 064	—	—	—	—	4
5	.199 002	—	—	—	—	5
6	.165 628	.498 132	1.000 000	—	—	6
7	.141 789	—	—	—	—	7
8	.123 910	—	—	—	—	8
9	.110 005	.330 846	—	—	—	9
10	.098 880	—	—	—	—	10
11	.089 778	—	—	—	—	11

Years						Years
1	.082 194	.247 205	.496 278	1.000 000	1.000 000	1
2	.040 481	.121 756	.244 445	.492 611	.492 501	2
3	.026 581	.079 951	.160 525	.323 530	.323 385	3
4	.019 634	.059 059	.118 584	.239 027	.238 865	4
5	.015 469	.046 531	.093 434	.188 355	.188 184	5
6	.012 694	.038 185	.076 680	.154 598	.154 422	6
7	.010 713	.032 229	.064 723	.130 506	.130 327	7
8	.009 230	.027 766	.055 765	.112 456	.112 276	8
9	.008 077	.024 300	.048 806	.098 434	.098 252	9
10	.007 156	.021 530	.043 246	.087 231	.087 049	10
11	.006 404	.019 268	.038 703	.078 077	.077 896	11
12	.005 778	.017 385	.034 924	.070 462	.070 281	12
13	.005 249	.015 795	.031 732	.064 030	.063 849	13
14	.004 797	.014 435	.029 001	.058 526	.058 347	14
15	.004 406	.013 258	.026 639	.053 767	.053 588	15
16	.004 064	.012 231	.024 577	.049 611	.049 434	16
17	.003 764	.011 327	.022 762	.045 953	.045 777	17
18	.003 497	.010 526	.021 152	.042 709	.042 534	18
19	.003 259	.009 810	.019 716	.039 814	.039 641	19
20	.003 046	.009 168	.018 427	.037 216	.037 044	20
21	.002 853	.008 589	.017 264	.034 872	.034 702	21
22	.002 679	.008 064	.016 210	.032 747	.032 579	22
23	.002 520	.007 587	.015 251	.030 814	.030 648	23
24	.002 375	.007 150	.014 375	.029 047	.028 883	24
25	.002 242	.006 750	.013 572	.027 428	.027 265	25
26	.002 120	.006 382	.012 833	.025 938	.025 777	26
27	.002 007	.006 043	.012 151	.024 564	.024 405	27
28	.001 903	.005 729	.011 521	.023 293	.023 136	28
29	.001 806	.005 438	.010 937	.022 115	.021 959	29
30	.001 716	.005 168	.010 393	.021 019	.020 865	30
31	.001 632	.004 916	.009 888	.019 999	.019 847	31
32	.001 554	.004 681	.009 415	.019 047	.018 896	32
33	.001 481	.004 461	.008 974	.018 156	.018 008	33
34	.001 413	.004 255	.008 560	.017 322	.017 175	34
35	.001 349	.004 062	.008 172	.016 539	.016 395	35
36	.001 288	.003 880	.007 808	.015 804	.015 661	36
37	.001 231	.003 710	.007 465	.015 112	.014 970	37
38	.001 178	.003 549	.007 141	.014 459	.014 320	38
39	.001 128	.003 397	.006 836	.013 844	.013 706	39
40	.001 080	.003 253	.006 548	.013 262	.013 127	40

Base: 1.002 708   1.008 125   1.016 250   1.032 500   1.033 032

Frequency of Payments and of Conversions

Months	Monthly	Quarterly	Semiannual	Annual	Annual Payment Daily Conversion	Months
1	1.000 000	—	—	—	—	1
2	.499 324	—	—	—	—	2
3	.332 432	1.000 000	—	—	—	3
4	.248 987	—	—	—	—	4
5	.198 920	—	—	—	—	5
6	.165 542	.497 977	1.000 000	—	—	6
7	.141 701	—	—	—	—	7
8	.123 820	—	—	—	—	8
9	.109 913	.330 640	—	—	—	9
10	.098 787	—	—	—	—	10
11	.089 685	—	—	—	—	11

Years	Monthly	Quarterly	Semiannual	Annual	Annual Payment Daily Conversion	Years
1	.082 099	.246 974	.495 970	1.000 000	1.000 000	1
2	.040 384	.121 488	.243 988	.492 005	.491 876	2
3	.026 483	.079 675	.160 023	.322 731	.322 561	3
4	.019 537	.058 779	.118 062	.238 137	.237 948	4
5	.015 372	.046 250	.092 904	.187 416	.187 216	5
6	.012 597	.037 905	.076 145	.153 630	.153 425	6
7	.010 618	.031 950	.064 188	.129 522	.129 313	7
8	.009 135	.027 489	.055 230	.111 463	.111 252	8
9	.007 983	.024 025	.048 273	.097 436	.097 224	9
10	.007 064	.021 258	.042 716	.086 231	.086 020	10
11	.006 312	.018 998	.038 177	.077 079	.076 868	11
12	.005 687	.017 118	.034 402	.069 467	.069 257	12
13	.005 160	.015 530	.031 214	.063 039	.062 830	13
14	.004 708	.014 173	.028 488	.057 542	.057 334	14
15	.004 318	.012 999	.026 131	.052 789	.052 582	15
16	.003 978	.011 975	.024 074	.048 640	.048 435	16
17	.003 678	.011 074	.022 264	.044 990	.044 787	17
18	.003 413	.010 275	.020 659	.041 754	.041 553	18
19	.003 176	.009 563	.019 228	.038 868	.038 669	19
20	.002 964	.008 924	.017 945	.036 279	.036 082	20
21	.002 772	.008 347	.016 787	.033 944	.033 749	21
22	.002 599	.007 825	.015 739	.031 829	.031 637	22
23	.002 441	.007 351	.014 785	.029 906	.029 715	23
24	.002 297	.006 917	.013 915	.028 149	.027 960	24
25	.002 165	.006 520	.013 117	.026 539	.026 353	25
26	.002 044	.006 155	.012 384	.025 060	.024 876	26
27	.001 932	.005 819	.011 708	.023 696	.023 514	27
28	.001 828	.005 508	.011 083	.022 435	.022 256	28
29	.001 733	.005 220	.010 504	.021 267	.021 090	29
30	.001 644	.004 952	.009 966	.020 182	.020 007	30
31	.001 561	.004 703	.009 466	.019 172	.018 999	31
32	.001 484	.004 471	.008 999	.018 230	.018 060	32
33	.001 412	.004 254	.008 563	.017 350	.017 182	33
34	.001 344	.004 051	.008 155	.016 526	.016 360	34
35	.001 281	.003 860	.007 773	.015 753	.015 590	35
36	.001 222	.003 682	.007 414	.015 028	.014 867	36
37	.001 166	.003 514	.007 076	.014 346	.014 188	37
38	.001 113	.003 356	.006 758	.013 704	.013 548	38
39	.001 064	.003 207	.006 459	.013 099	.012 945	39
40	.001 017	.003 066	.006 176	.012 528	.012 376	40

3½%

SINKING FUND FACTORS
(Periodic Payment to Grow to $1)

Base: 1.002 917   1.008 750   1.017 500   1.035 000   1.035 618

Frequency of Payments and of Conversions

Months	Monthly	Quarterly	Semiannual	Annual	Annual Payment Daily Conversion	Months
1	1.000 000	—	—	—	—	1
2	.499 272	—	—	—	—	2
3	.332 363	1.000 000	—	—	—	3
4	.248 909	—	—	—	—	4
5	.198 837	—	—	—	—	5
6	.165 456	.497 822	1.000 000	—	—	6
7	.141 612	—	—	—	—	7
8	.123 730	—	—	—	—	8
9	.109 821	.330 434	—	—	—	9
10	.098 695	—	—	—	—	10
11	.089 591	—	—	—	—	11

Years						Years
1	.082 005	.246 743	.495 663	1.000 000	1.000 000	1
2	.040 286	.121 222	.243 532	.491 400	.491 251	2
3	.026 385	.079 399	.159 523	.321 934	.321 738	3
4	.019 439	.058 500	.117 543	.237 251	.237 033	4
5	.015 275	.045 970	.092 375	.186 481	.186 251	5
6	.012 502	.037 626	.075 614	.152 668	.152 431	6
7	.010 523	.031 673	.063 656	.128 544	.128 304	7
8	.009 041	.027 215	.054 700	.110 477	.110 234	8
9	.007 891	.023 752	.047 745	.096 446	.096 203	9
10	.006 972	.020 988	.042 191	.085 241	.084 998	10
11	.006 222	.018 730	.037 656	.076 092	.075 850	11
12	.005 598	.016 853	.033 886	.068 484	.068 243	12
13	.005 071	.015 269	.030 703	.062 062	.061 822	13
14	.004 621	.013 914	.027 982	.056 571	.056 333	14
15	.004 232	.012 744	.025 630	.051 825	.051 589	15
16	.003 893	.011 723	.023 578	.047 685	.047 451	16
17	.003 594	.010 825	.021 774	.044 043	.043 812	17
18	.003 330	.010 029	.020 175	.040 817	.040 588	18
19	.003 094	.009 320	.018 750	.037 940	.037 714	19
20	.002 883	.008 684	.017 472	.035 361	.035 137	20
21	.002 693	.008 111	.016 321	.033 037	.032 815	21
22	.002 520	.007 592	.015 278	.030 932	.030 713	22
23	.002 363	.007 120	.014 330	.029 019	.028 803	23
24	.002 220	.006 690	.013 466	.027 273	.027 060	24
25	.002 090	.006 296	.012 674	.025 674	.025 464	25
26	.001 969	.005 934	.011 947	.024 205	.023 998	26
27	.001 859	.005 601	.011 277	.022 852	.022 648	27
28	.001 756	.005 293	.010 658	.021 603	.021 401	28
29	.001 662	.005 008	.010 085	.020 445	.020 246	29
30	.001 574	.004 743	.009 553	.019 371	.019 175	30
31	.001 492	.004 498	.009 059	.018 372	.018 179	31
32	.001 416	.004 268	.008 598	.017 442	.017 251	32
33	.001 345	.004 054	.008 168	.016 572	.016 385	33
34	.001 278	.003 854	.007 766	.015 760	.015 575	34
35	.001 216	.003 667	.007 389	.014 998	.014 816	35
36	.001 158	.003 491	.007 036	.014 284	.014 105	36
37	.001 103	.003 326	.006 704	.013 613	.013 437	37
38	.001 052	.003 171	.006 392	.012 982	.012 809	38
39	.001 003	.003 025	.006 098	.012 388	.012 217	39
40	.000 957	.002 887	.005 821	.011 827	.011 659	40

286

Base: 1.003 125   1.009 375   1.018 750   1.037 500   1.038 210

Frequency of Payments and of Conversions

Months	Monthly	Quarterly	Semiannual	Annual	Annual Payment Daily Conversion	Months
1	1.000 000	—	—	—	—	1
2	.499 220	—	—	—	—	2
3	.332 294	1.000 000	—	—	—	3
4	.248 831	—	—	—	—	4
5	.198 754	—	—	—	—	5
6	.165 369	.497 667	1.000 000	—	—	6
7	.141 523	—	—	—	—	7
8	.123 639	—	—	—	—	8
9	.109 729	.330 228	—	—	—	9
10	.098 602	—	—	—	—	10
11	.089 498	—	—	—	—	11

Years						Years
1	.081 911	.246 512	.495 356	1.000 000	1.000 000	1
2	.040 189	.120 956	.243 078	.490 798	.490 627	2
3	.026 288	.079 123	.159 023	.321 140	.320 915	3
4	.019 342	.058 222	.117 025	.236 369	.236 119	4
5	.015 179	.045 692	.091 850	.185 552	.185 289	5
6	.012 407	.037 349	.075 085	.151 712	.151 442	6
7	.010 429	.031 398	.063 127	.127 574	.127 299	7
8	.008 948	.026 942	.054 173	.109 498	.109 222	8
9	.007 799	.023 482	.047 221	.095 465	.095 188	9
10	.006 881	.020 720	.041 671	.084 261	.083 985	10
11	.006 132	.018 466	.037 141	.075 115	.074 840	11
12	.005 509	.016 592	.033 375	.067 512	.067 238	12
13	.004 984	.015 011	.030 198	.061 096	.060 825	13
14	.004 535	.013 660	.027 482	.055 613	.055 344	14
15	.004 147	.012 492	.025 136	.050 876	.050 609	15
16	.003 809	.011 474	.023 090	.046 745	.046 481	16
17	.003 512	.010 580	.021 292	.043 113	.042 852	17
18	.003 249	.009 787	.019 700	.039 897	.039 638	18
19	.003 014	.009 081	.018 281	.037 031	.036 775	19
20	.002 804	.008 449	.017 009	.034 462	.034 210	20
21	.002 615	.007 879	.015 864	.032 149	.031 900	21
22	.002 443	.007 364	.014 828	.030 055	.029 810	22
23	.002 288	.006 896	.013 887	.028 153	.027 911	23
24	.002 146	.006 469	.013 028	.026 419	.026 180	24
25	.002 016	.006 078	.012 243	.024 832	.024 597	25
26	.001 897	.005 719	.011 522	.023 375	.023 143	26
27	.001 788	.005 389	.010 858	.022 033	.021 805	27
28	.001 686	.005 085	.010 246	.020 795	.020 571	28
29	.001 593	.004 803	.009 679	.019 650	.019 429	29
30	.001 506	.004 542	.009 154	.018 588	.018 370	30
31	.001 426	.004 299	.008 666	.017 600	.017 386	31
32	.001 351	.004 073	.008 211	.016 681	.016 470	32
33	.001 281	.003 863	.007 787	.015 824	.015 617	33
34	.001 215	.003 666	.007 391	.015 023	.014 819	34
35	.001 154	.003 482	.007 021	.014 273	.014 073	35
36	.001 097	.003 309	.006 674	.013 571	.013 373	36
37	.001 043	.003 147	.006 348	.012 911	.012 717	37
38	.000 992	.002 995	.006 042	.012 292	.012 101	38
39	.000 945	.002 852	.005 754	.011 709	.011 521	39
40	.000 900	.002 717	.005 483	.011 159	.010 976	40

4%   SINKING FUND FACTORS
(Periodic Payment to Grow to $1)

Base:	1.003 333	1.010 000	1.020 000	1.040 000	1.040 808	
			Frequency of Payments and of Conversions			
Months	Monthly	Quarterly	Semiannual	Annual	Annual Payment Daily Conversion	Months
1	1.000 000	—	—	—	—	1
2	.499 168	—	—	—	—	2
3	.332 225	1.000 000	—	—	—	3
4	.248 753	—	—	—	—	4
5	.198 671	—	—	—	—	5
6	.165 283	.497 512	1.000 000	—	—	6
7	.141 435	—	—	—	—	7
8	.123 549	—	—	—	—	8
9	.109 638	.330 022	—	—	—	9
10	.098 509	—	—	—	—	10
11	.089 404	—	—	—	—	11
Years						**Years**
1	.081 817	.246 281	.495 050	1.000 000	1.000 000	1
2	.040 092	.120 690	.242 624	.490 196	.490 002	2
3	.026 191	.078 849	.158 526	.320 349	.320 093	3
4	.019 246	.057 945	.116 510	.235 490	.235 207	4
5	.015 083	.045 415	.091 327	.184 627	.184 329	5
6	.012 312	.037 073	.074 560	.150 762	.150 456	6
7	.010 335	.031 124	.062 602	.126 610	.126 299	7
8	.008 856	.026 671	.053 650	.108 528	.108 216	8
9	.007 708	.023 214	.046 702	.094 493	.094 180	9
10	.006 791	.020 456	.041 157	.083 291	.082 979	10
11	.006 043	.018 204	.036 631	.074 149	.073 839	11
12	.005 422	.016 334	.032 871	.066 552	.066 244	12
13	.004 898	.014 756	.029 699	.060 144	.059 838	13
14	.004 450	.013 408	.026 990	.054 669	.054 366	14
15	.004 064	.012 244	.024 650	.049 941	.049 642	15
16	.003 727	.011 230	.022 611	.045 820	.045 524	16
17	.003 431	.010 339	.020 819	.042 199	.041 906	17
18	.003 169	.009 550	.019 233	.038 993	.038 705	18
19	.002 935	.008 848	.017 821	.036 139	.035 854	19
20	.002 726	.008 219	.016 556	.033 582	.033 301	20
21	.002 538	.007 653	.015 417	.031 280	.031 003	21
22	.002 368	.007 141	.014 388	.029 199	.028 926	22
23	.002 214	.006 676	.013 453	.027 309	.027 040	23
24	.002 074	.006 253	.012 602	.025 587	.025 322	24
25	.001 945	.005 866	.011 823	.024 012	.023 752	25
26	.001 827	.005 511	.011 109	.022 567	.022 311	26
27	.001 719	.005 184	.010 452	.021 239	.020 987	27
28	.001 619	.004 883	.009 847	.020 013	.019 765	28
29	.001 526	.004 605	.009 287	.018 880	.018 636	29
30	.001 441	.004 347	.008 768	.017 830	.017 591	30
31	.001 361	.004 108	.008 286	.016 855	.016 620	31
32	.001 288	.003 885	.007 839	.015 949	.015 717	32
33	.001 219	.003 678	.007 421	.015 104	.014 877	33
34	.001 154	.003 484	.007 032	.014 315	.014 092	34
35	.001 094	.003 303	.006 668	.013 577	.013 358	35
36	.001 038	.003 134	.006 327	.012 887	.012 672	36
37	.000 986	.002 976	.006 007	.012 240	.012 029	37
38	.000 936	.002 827	.005 708	.011 632	.011 425	38
39	.000 890	.002 687	.005 426	.011 061	.010 858	39
40	.000 846	.002 555	.005 161	.010 523	.010 324	40

SINKING FUND FACTORS

(Periodic Payment to Grow to $1)

4¼%

Base:	1.003 542	1.010 625	1.021 250	1.042 500	1.043 413	
		Frequency of Payments and of Conversions				
Months	Monthly	Quarterly	Semiannual	Annual	Annual Payment Daily Conversion	Months
1	1.000 000	—	—	—	—	1
2	.499 116	—	—	—	—	2
3	.332 156	1.000 000	—	—	—	3
4	.248 676	—	—	—	—	4
5	.198 588	—	—	—	—	5
6	.165 197	.497 358	1.000 000	—	—	6
7	.141 346	—	—	—	—	7
8	.123 459	—	—	—	—	8
9	.109 546	.329 817	—	—	—	9
10	.098 417	—	—	—	—	10
11	.089 311	—	—	—	—	11

Years						Years
1	.081 723	.246 051	.494 743	1.000 000	1.000 000	1
2	.039 995	.120 425	.242 171	.489 596	.489 377	2
3	.026 094	.078 575	.158 030	.319 560	.319 272	3
4	.019 149	.057 669	.115 996	.234 615	.234 296	4
5	.014 988	.045 140	.090 806	.183 707	.183 372	5
6	.012 218	.036 799	.074 037	.149 817	.149 474	6
7	.010 243	.030 853	.062 080	.125 652	.125 304	7
8	.008 764	.026 402	.053 131	.107 565	.107 215	8
9	.007 617	.022 949	.046 187	.093 529	.093 180	9
10	.006 702	.020 193	.040 647	.082 330	.081 981	10
11	.005 956	.017 946	.036 127	.073 193	.072 847	11
12	.005 336	.016 079	.032 373	.065 603	.065 260	12
13	.004 813	.014 504	.029 207	.059 203	.058 863	13
14	.004 366	.013 160	.026 504	.053 738	.053 401	14
15	.003 981	.012 000	.024 171	.049 020	.048 688	15
16	.003 646	.010 990	.022 139	.044 910	.044 582	16
17	.003 351	.010 102	.020 354	.041 300	.040 976	17
18	.003 090	.009 317	.018 775	.038 107	.037 787	18
19	.002 858	.008 619	.017 370	.035 264	.034 949	19
20	.002 651	.007 994	.016 112	.032 720	.032 409	20
21	.002 464	.007 431	.014 981	.030 431	.030 125	21
22	.002 295	.006 923	.013 958	.028 362	.028 062	22
23	.002 142	.006 462	.013 031	.026 486	.026 190	23
24	.002 003	.006 043	.012 187	.024 776	.024 485	24
25	.001 876	.005 659	.011 415	.023 215	.022 929	25
26	.001 759	.005 308	.010 708	.021 783	.021 502	26
27	.001 652	.004 985	.010 058	.020 467	.020 191	27
28	.001 553	.004 688	.009 460	.019 255	.018 984	28
29	.001 462	.004 413	.008 907	.018 135	.017 869	29
30	.001 378	.004 159	.008 395	.017 098	.016 837	30
31	.001 300	.003 923	.007 921	.016 137	.015 880	31
32	.001 227	.003 704	.007 480	.015 243	.014 991	32
33	.001 159	.003 500	.007 069	.014 411	.014 164	33
34	.001 096	.003 310	.006 686	.013 635	.013 393	34
35	.001 037	.003 133	.006 329	.012 910	.012 673	35
36	.000 982	.002 967	.005 995	.012 232	.012 000	36
37	.000 931	.002 812	.005 682	.011 597	.011 370	37
38	.000 882	.002 666	.005 389	.011 002	.010 779	38
39	.000 837	.002 529	.005 113	.010 444	.010 225	39
40	.000 795	.002 401	.004 855	.009 918	.009 705	40

SINKING FUND FACTORS
(Periodic Payment to Grow to $1)

Base: 1.003 750   1.011 250   1.022 500   1.045 000   1.046 025

Frequency of Payments and of Conversions

Months	Monthly	Quarterly	Semiannual	Annual	Annual Payment Daily Conversion	Months
1	1.000 000	—	—	—	—	1
2	.499 064	—	—	—	—	2
3	.332 086	1.000 000	—	—	—	3
4	.248 598	—	—	—	—	4
5	.198 506	—	—	—	—	5
6	.165 111	.497 203	1.000 000	—	—	6
7	.141 258	—	—	—	—	7
8	.123 369	—	—	—	—	8
9	.109 455	.329 611	—	—	—	9
10	.098 324	—	—	—	—	10
11	.089 217	—	—	—	—	11

Years						Years
1	.081 629	.245 821	.494 438	1.000 000	1.000 000	1
2	.039 898	.120 161	.241 719	.488 998	.488 753	2
3	.025 997	.078 302	.157 535	.318 773	.318 452	3
4	.019 053	.057 394	.115 485	.233 744	.233 387	4
5	.014 893	.044 865	.090 288	.182 792	.182 418	5
6	.012 124	.036 527	.073 517	.148 878	.148 495	6
7	.010 150	.030 583	.061 562	.124 701	.124 314	7
8	.008 673	.026 135	.052 617	.106 610	.106 220	8
9	.007 528	.022 685	.045 677	.092 574	.092 185	9
10	.006 614	.019 933	.040 142	.081 379	.080 992	10
11	.005 869	.017 689	.035 628	.072 248	.071 864	11
12	.005 250	.015 826	.031 880	.064 666	.064 285	12
13	.004 729	.014 256	.028 721	.058 275	.057 898	13
14	.004 284	.012 916	.026 025	.052 820	.052 448	14
15	.003 900	.011 760	.023 699	.048 114	.047 746	15
16	.003 566	.010 753	.021 674	.044 015	.043 653	16
17	.003 272	.009 870	.019 897	.040 418	.040 060	17
18	.003 013	.009 089	.018 325	.037 237	.036 885	18
19	.002 783	.008 394	.016 928	.034 407	.034 061	19
20	.002 576	.007 773	.015 677	.031 876	.031 535	20
21	.002 391	.007 215	.014 554	.029 601	.029 266	21
22	.002 224	.006 711	.013 539	.027 546	.027 216	22
23	.002 072	.006 254	.012 619	.025 682	.025 359	23
24	.001 934	.005 838	.011 782	.023 987	.023 670	24
25	.001 808	.005 459	.011 018	.022 439	.022 127	25
26	.001 693	.005 111	.010 319	.021 021	.020 716	26
27	.001 587	.004 792	.009 677	.019 719	.019 419	27
28	.001 490	.004 499	.009 085	.018 521	.018 227	28
29	.001 400	.004 228	.008 540	.017 415	.017 126	29
30	.001 317	.003 977	.008 035	.016 392	.016 109	30
31	.001 240	.003 745	.007 568	.015 443	.015 167	31
32	.001 168	.003 530	.007 134	.014 563	.014 292	32
33	.001 102	.003 330	.006 731	.013 745	.013 479	33
34	.001 040	.003 143	.006 355	.012 982	.012 722	34
35	.000 983	.002 970	.006 005	.012 270	.012 016	35
36	.000 929	.002 807	.005 677	.011 606	.011 357	36
37	.000 878	.002 655	.005 371	.010 984	.010 741	37
38	.000 831	.002 513	.005 085	.010 402	.010 164	38
39	.000 787	.002 380	.004 816	.009 856	.009 623	39
40	.000 746	.002 255	.004 564	.009 343	.009 116	40

SINKING FUND FACTORS

(Periodic Payment to Grow to $1)

4¾%

Base: 1.003 958   1.011 875   1.023 750   1.047 500   1.048 643

Frequency of Payments and of Conversions

Months	Monthly	Quarterly	Semiannual	Annual	Annual Payment Daily Conversion	Months
1	1.000 000	—	—	—	—	1
2	.499 012	—	—	—	—	2
3	.332 017	1.000 000	—	—	—	3
4	.248 521	—	—	—	—	4
5	.198 423	—	—	—	—	5
6	.165 025	.497 049	1.000 000	—	—	6
7	.141 170	—	—	—	—	7
8	.123 278	—	—	—	—	8
9	.109 363	.329 406	—	—	—	9
10	.098 232	—	—	—	—	10
11	.089 124	—	—	—	—	11

Years						Years
1	.081 535	.245 591	.494 132	1.000 000	1.000 000	1
2	.039 801	.119 897	.241 268	.488 400	.488 128	2
3	.025 900	.078 030	.157 042	.317 990	.317 632	3
4	.018 958	.057 120	.114 975	.232 876	.232 480	4
5	.014 799	.044 592	.089 772	.181 881	.181 466	5
6	.012 031	.036 256	.073 001	.147 945	.147 520	6
7	.010 058	.030 315	.061 048	.123 757	.123 328	7
8	.008 583	.025 871	.052 106	.105 662	.105 231	8
9	.007 439	.022 424	.045 171	.091 628	.091 198	9
10	.006 526	.019 676	.039 642	.080 437	.080 010	10
11	.005 783	.017 436	.035 135	.071 313	.070 889	11
12	.005 166	.015 577	.031 394	.063 740	.063 321	12
13	.004 646	.014 011	.028 242	.057 360	.056 945	13
14	.004 202	.012 675	.025 553	.051 916	.051 506	14
15	.003 820	.011 523	.023 235	.047 221	.046 818	15
16	.003 487	.010 521	.021 217	.043 135	.042 738	16
17	.003 195	.009 642	.019 448	.039 551	.039 159	17
18	.002 938	.008 865	.017 884	.036 383	.035 999	18
19	.002 709	.008 175	.016 494	.033 568	.033 189	19
20	.002 504	.007 558	.015 252	.031 050	.030 679	20
21	.002 320	.007 003	.014 136	.028 789	.028 424	21
22	.002 154	.006 503	.013 130	.026 748	.026 390	22
23	.002 004	.006 051	.012 218	.024 900	.024 548	23
24	.001 867	.005 639	.011 389	.023 219	.022 874	24
25	.001 743	.005 264	.010 633	.021 685	.021 348	25
26	.001 629	.004 920	.009 941	.020 282	.019 951	26
27	.001 524	.004 605	.009 306	.018 994	.018 670	27
28	.001 428	.004 316	.008 723	.017 810	.017 493	28
29	.001 340	.004 049	.008 185	.016 718	.016 408	29
30	.001 258	.003 802	.007 688	.015 709	.015 406	30
31	.001 182	.003 574	.007 228	.014 776	.014 478	31
32	.001 112	.003 363	.006 802	.013 909	.013 619	32
33	.001 047	.003 166	.006 406	.013 105	.012 821	33
34	.000 987	.002 983	.006 037	.012 356	.012 078	34
35	.000 930	.002 813	.005 694	.011 658	.011 387	35
36	.000 878	.002 654	.005 374	.011 007	.010 742	36
37	.000 828	.002 506	.005 075	.010 398	.010 140	37
38	.000 783	.002 368	.004 795	.009 829	.009 577	38
39	.000 740	.002 238	.004 533	.009 296	.009 050	39
40	.000 699	.002 116	.004 288	.008 797	.008 556	40

5%

Base: 1.004 167   1.012 500   1.025 000   1.050 000   1.051 267

Frequency of Payments and of Conversions

Months	Monthly	Quarterly	Semiannual	Annual	Annual Payment Daily Conversion	Months
1	1.000 000	—	—	—	—	1
2	.498 960	—	—	—	—	2
3	.331 948	1.000 000	—	—	—	3
4	.248 443	—	—	—	—	4
5	.198 340	—	—	—	—	5
6	.164 939	.496 894	1.000 000	—	—	6
7	.141 081	—	—	—	—	7
8	.123 188	—	—	—	—	8
9	.109 272	.329 201	—	—	—	9
10	.098 139	—	—	—	—	10
11	.089 031	—	—	—	—	11

Years						Years
1	.081 441	.245 361	.493 827	1.000 000	1.000 000	1
2	.039 705	.119 633	.240 818	.487 805	.487 503	2
3	.025 804	.077 758	.156 550	.317 209	.316 814	3
4	.018 863	.056 847	.114 467	.232 012	.231 575	4
5	.014 705	.044 320	.089 259	.180 975	.180 517	5
6	.011 938	.035 987	.072 487	.147 017	.146 549	6
7	.009 967	.030 049	.060 537	.122 820	.122 347	7
8	.008 493	.025 608	.051 599	.104 722	.104 248	8
9	.007 351	.022 165	.044 670	.090 690	.090 218	9
10	.006 440	.019 421	.039 147	.079 505	.079 035	10
11	.005 698	.017 186	.034 647	.070 389	.069 924	11
12	.005 082	.015 331	.030 913	.062 825	.062 366	12
13	.004 564	.013 769	.027 769	.056 456	.056 002	13
14	.004 122	.012 437	.025 088	.051 024	.050 577	14
15	.003 741	.011 290	.022 778	.046 342	.045 902	15
16	.003 410	.010 292	.020 768	.042 270	.041 837	16
17	.003 120	.009 417	.019 007	.038 699	.038 273	17
18	.002 864	.008 645	.017 452	.035 546	.035 128	18
19	.002 636	.007 959	.016 070	.032 745	.032 334	19
20	.002 433	.007 347	.014 836	.030 243	.029 840	20
21	.002 251	.006 797	.013 729	.027 996	.027 601	21
22	.002 086	.006 301	.012 730	.025 971	.025 583	22
23	.001 937	.005 853	.011 827	.024 137	.023 758	23
24	.001 802	.005 445	.011 006	.022 471	.022 100	24
25	.001 679	.005 074	.010 258	.020 952	.020 589	25
26	.001 567	.004 735	.009 574	.019 564	.019 209	26
27	.001 464	.004 424	.008 948	.018 292	.017 944	27
28	.001 369	.004 139	.008 372	.017 123	.016 783	28
29	.001 282	.003 876	.007 842	.016 046	.015 713	29
30	.001 202	.003 633	.007 353	.015 051	.014 727	30
31	.001 127	.003 409	.006 901	.014 132	.013 815	31
32	.001 058	.003 202	.006 482	.013 280	.012 971	32
33	.000 995	.003 009	.006 094	.012 490	.012 188	33
34	.000 935	.002 830	.005 733	.011 755	.011 461	34
35	.000 880	.002 664	.005 397	.011 072	.010 784	35
36	.000 829	.002 509	.005 084	.010 434	.010 154	36
37	.000 781	.002 364	.004 792	.009 840	.009 567	37
38	.000 736	.002 229	.004 520	.009 284	.009 018	38
39	.000 694	.002 103	.004 265	.008 765	.008 505	39
40	.000 655	.001 985	.004 026	.008 278	.008 026	40

SINKING FUND FACTORS

5¼%

(Periodic Payment to Grow to $1)

Frequency of Payments and of Conversions

Months	Monthly	Quarterly	Semiannual	Annual	Annual Payment Daily Conversion	Months
1	1.000 000	—	—	—	—	1
2	.498 909	—	—	—	—	2
3	.331 879	1.000 000	—	—	—	3
4	.248 365	—	—	—	—	4
5	.198 258	—	—	—	—	5
6	.164 853	.496 740	1.000 000	—	—	6
7	.140 993	—	—	—	—	7
8	.123 098	—	—	—	—	8
9	.109 181	.328 996	—	—	—	9
10	.098 047	—	—	—	—	10
11	.088 938	—	—	—	—	11

Years						Years
1	.081 347	.245 132	.493 523	1.000 000	1.000 000	1
2	.039 608	.119 370	.240 369	.487 211	.486 879	2
3	.025 708	.077 488	.156 060	.316 430	.315 996	3
4	.018 768	.056 575	.113 962	.231 151	.230 672	4
5	.014 611	.044 050	.088 748	.180 073	.179 571	5
6	.011 846	.035 719	.071 976	.146 095	.145 582	6
7	.009 877	.029 784	.060 029	.121 889	.121 371	7
8	.008 404	.025 347	.051 096	.103 789	.103 271	8
9	.007 263	.021 909	.044 173	.089 761	.089 244	9
10	.006 354	.019 169	.038 657	.078 582	.078 069	10
11	.005 614	.016 938	.034 164	.069 475	.068 968	11
12	.005 000	.015 087	.030 438	.061 922	.061 421	12
13	.004 483	.013 530	.027 302	.055 564	.055 070	13
14	.004 043	.012 203	.024 629	.050 145	.049 659	14
15	.003 664	.011 060	.022 327	.045 477	.044 999	15
16	.003 334	.010 067	.020 327	.041 419	.040 949	16
17	.003 046	.009 197	.018 574	.037 863	.037 402	17
18	.002 791	.008 429	.017 027	.034 725	.034 273	18
19	.002 565	.007 748	.015 655	.031 939	.031 496	19
20	.002 363	.007 140	.014 429	.029 452	.029 018	20
21	.002 183	.006 595	.013 331	.027 221	.026 796	21
22	.002 020	.006 104	.012 341	.025 212	.024 795	22
23	.001 873	.005 660	.011 446	.023 394	.022 986	23
24	.001 739	.005 257	.010 634	.021 743	.021 345	24
25	.001 617	.004 890	.009 894	.020 241	.019 851	25
26	.001 507	.004 556	.009 219	.018 868	.018 488	26
27	.001 405	.004 249	.008 601	.017 611	.017 240	27
28	.001 312	.003 968	.008 034	.016 457	.016 095	28
29	.001 226	.003 709	.007 512	.015 396	.015 042	29
30	.001 147	.003 471	.007 031	.014 417	.014 072	30
31	.001 074	.003 251	.006 587	.013 513	.013 176	31
32	.001 007	.003 047	.006 176	.012 676	.012 348	32
33	.000 944	.002 859	.005 795	.011 900	.011 581	33
34	.000 886	.002 684	.005 442	.011 180	.010 869	34
35	.000 832	.002 521	.005 113	.010 511	.010 208	35
36	.000 782	.002 370	.004 808	.009 888	.009 593	36
37	.000 736	.002 229	.004 523	.009 307	.009 020	37
38	.000 692	.002 098	.004 258	.008 765	.008 486	38
39	.000 652	.001 975	.004 010	.008 259	.007 988	39
40	.000 614	.001 860	.003 778	.007 786	.007 523	40

5½%

SINKING FUND FACTORS
(Periodic Payment to Grow to $1)

Base: 1.004 583   1.013 750   1.027 500   1.055 000   1.056 536

Frequency of Payments and of Conversions

Months	Monthly	Quarterly	Semiannual	Annual	Annual Payment Daily Conversion	Months
1	1.000 000	—	—	—	—	1
2	.498 857	—	—	—	—	2
3	.331 810	1.000 000	—	—	—	3
4	.248 288	—	—	—	—	4
5	.198 175	—	—	—	—	5
6	.164 767	.496 586	1.000 000	—	—	6
7	.140 905	—	—	—	—	7
8	.123 009	—	—	—	—	8
9	.109 090	.328 792	—	—	—	9
10	.097 955	—	—	—	—	10
11	.088 845	—	—	—	—	11

Years						Years
1	.081 253	.244 902	.493 218	1.000 000	1.000 000	1
2	.039 512	.119 108	.239 921	.486 618	.486 255	2
3	.025 613	.077 218	.155 571	.315 654	.315 179	3
4	.018 673	.056 304	.113 458	.230 294	.229 770	4
5	.014 518	.043 781	.088 240	.179 176	.178 628	5
6	.011 755	.035 452	.071 469	.145 179	.144 619	6
7	.009 787	.029 521	.059 525	.120 964	.120 400	7
8	.008 316	.025 089	.050 597	.102 864	.102 299	8
9	.007 177	.021 654	.043 681	.088 839	.088 278	9
10	.006 269	.018 919	.038 172	.077 668	.077 111	10
11	.005 531	.016 693	.033 686	.068 571	.068 020	11
12	.004 918	.014 847	.029 969	.061 029	.060 486	12
13	.004 403	.013 295	.026 841	.054 684	.054 150	13
14	.003 965	.011 972	.024 177	.049 279	.048 753	14
15	.003 588	.010 835	.021 884	.044 626	.044 109	15
16	.003 260	.009 846	.019 893	.040 583	.040 076	16
17	.002 973	.008 981	.018 149	.037 042	.036 545	17
18	.002 720	.008 218	.016 611	.033 920	.033 433	18
19	.002 496	.007 542	.015 248	.031 150	.030 673	19
20	.002 296	.006 938	.014 032	.028 679	.028 213	20
21	.002 116	.006 398	.012 942	.026 465	.026 009	21
22	.001 955	.005 912	.011 961	.024 471	.024 025	22
23	.001 810	.005 472	.011 075	.022 670	.022 234	23
24	.001 678	.005 074	.010 272	.021 036	.020 611	24
25	.001 558	.004 712	.009 541	.019 549	.019 135	25
26	.001 448	.004 382	.008 874	.018 193	.017 789	26
27	.001 348	.004 079	.008 265	.016 952	.016 558	27
28	.001 256	.003 803	.007 706	.015 814	.015 430	28
29	.001 172	.003 548	.007 193	.014 769	.014 394	29
30	.001 095	.003 314	.006 720	.013 805	.013 441	30
31	.001 023	.003 098	.006 284	.012 917	.012 562	31
32	.000 957	.002 899	.005 881	.012 095	.011 750	32
33	.000 896	.002 714	.005 508	.011 335	.010 999	33
34	.000 839	.002 543	.005 163	.010 630	.010 303	34
35	.000 787	.002 385	.004 842	.009 975	.009 657	35
36	.000 738	.002 237	.004 544	.009 366	.009 058	36
37	.000 693	.002 100	.004 267	.008 800	.008 500	37
38	.000 650	.001 973	.004 009	.008 272	.007 981	38
39	.000 611	.001 854	.003 768	.007 780	.007 498	39
40	.000 574	.001 743	.003 543	.007 320	.007 046	40

SINKING FUND FACTORS

5¾%

(Periodic Payment to Grow to $1)

Base:	1.004 792	1.014 375	1.028 750	1.057 500	1.059 180	
			Frequency of Payments and of Conversions			
Months	Monthly	Quarterly	Semiannual	Annual	Annual Payment Daily Conversion	Months
1	1.000 000	—	—	—	—	1
2	.498 805	—	—	—	—	2
3	.331 741	1.000 000	—	—	—	3
4	.248 210	—	—	—	—	4
5	.198 092	—	—	—	—	5
6	.164 681	.496 432	1.000 000	—	—	6
7	.140 817	—	—	—	—	7
8	.122 919	—	—	—	—	8
9	.108 998	.328 587	—	—	—	9
10	.097 863	—	—	—	—	10
11	.088 752	—	—	—	—	11
Years						Years
1	.081 160	.244 673	.492 914	1.000 000	1.000 000	1
2	.039 416	.118 846	.239 473	.486 027	.485 630	2
3	.025 517	.076 948	.155 083	.314 881	.314 362	3
4	.018 579	.056 034	.112 956	.229 441	.228 870	4
5	.014 425	.043 513	.087 734	.178 284	.177 687	5
6	.011 663	.035 187	.070 964	.144 268	.143 659	6
7	.009 697	.029 260	.059 024	.120 046	.119 433	7
8	.008 228	.024 832	.050 102	.101 946	.101 334	8
9	.007 091	.021 402	.043 192	.087 927	.087 318	9
10	.006 185	.018 672	.037 691	.076 763	.076 160	10
11	.005 448	.016 450	.033 214	.067 677	.067 082	11
12	.004 838	.014 610	.029 505	.060 148	.059 561	12
13	.004 325	.013 062	.026 387	.053 816	.053 240	13
14	.003 888	.011 745	.023 732	.048 426	.047 859	14
15	.003 512	.010 612	.021 448	.043 788	.043 232	15
16	.003 186	.009 629	.019 466	.039 760	.039 216	16
17	.002 901	.008 769	.017 731	.036 236	.035 703	17
18	.002 650	.008 011	.016 204	.033 130	.032 609	18
19	.002 427	.007 339	.014 849	.030 377	.029 867	19
20	.002 229	.006 741	.013 643	.027 923	.027 425	20
21	.002 052	.006 206	.012 562	.025 726	.025 239	21
22	.001 892	.005 724	.011 591	.023 749	.023 274	22
23	.001 748	.005 290	.010 714	.021 965	.021 501	23
24	.001 618	.004 896	.009 920	.020 348	.019 896	24
25	.001 499	.004 539	.009 198	.018 878	.018 438	25
26	.001 392	.004 213	.008 541	.017 539	.017 110	26
27	.001 293	.003 915	.007 940	.016 314	.015 897	27
28	.001 203	.003 643	.007 390	.015 193	.014 787	28
29	.001 120	.003 393	.006 885	.014 163	.013 769	29
30	.001 044	.003 164	.006 421	.013 216	.012 833	30
31	.000 974	.002 952	.005 993	.012 343	.011 971	31
32	.000 909	.002 757	.005 599	.011 538	.011 175	32
33	.000 850	.002 576	.005 234	.010 792	.010 441	33
34	.000 795	.002 409	.004 896	.010 103	.009 761	34
35	.000 743	.002 255	.004 583	.009 463	.009 132	35
36	.000 696	.002 111	.004 293	.008 869	.008 548	36
37	.000 652	.001 978	.004 023	.008 317	.008 006	37
38	.000 611	.001 854	.003 773	.007 803	.007 502	38
39	.000 573	.001 739	.003 539	.007 325	.007 033	39
40	.000 537	.001 631	.003 321	.006 879	.006 596	40

6%

SINKING FUND FACTORS
(Periodic Payment to Grow to $1)

Base: 1.005 000   1.015 000   1.030 000   1.060 000   1.061 831

Frequency of Payments and of Conversions

Months	Monthly	Quarterly	Semiannual	Annual	Annual Payment Daily Conversion	Months
1	1.000 000	—	—	—	—	1
2	.498 753	—	—	—	—	2
3	.331 672	1.000 000	—	—	—	3
4	.248 133	—	—	—	—	4
5	.198 010	—	—	—	—	5
6	.164 595	.496 278	1.000 000	—	—	6
7	.140 729	—	—	—	—	7
8	.122 829	—	—	—	—	8
9	.108 907	.328 383	—	—	—	9
10	.097 771	—	—	—	—	10
11	.088 659	—	—	—	—	11

Years						Years
1	.081 066	.244 445	.492 611	1.000 000	1.000 000	1
2	.039 321	.118 584	.239 027	.485 437	.485 006	2
3	.025 422	.076 680	.154 598	.314 110	.313 547	3
4	.018 485	.055 765	.112 456	.228 591	.227 971	4
5	.014 333	.043 246	.087 231	.177 396	.176 749	5
6	.011 573	.034 924	.070 462	.143 363	.142 703	6
7	.009 609	.029 001	.058 526	.119 135	.118 471	7
8	.008 141	.024 577	.049 611	.101 036	.100 374	8
9	.007 006	.021 152	.042 709	.087 022	.086 365	9
10	.006 102	.018 427	.037 216	.075 868	.075 218	10
11	.005 367	.016 210	.032 747	.066 793	.066 152	11
12	.004 759	.014 375	.029 047	.059 277	.058 646	12
13	.004 247	.012 833	.025 938	.052 960	.052 340	13
14	.003 812	.011 521	.023 293	.047 585	.046 977	14
15	.003 439	.010 393	.021 019	.042 963	.042 367	15
16	.003 114	.009 415	.019 047	.038 952	.038 369	16
17	.002 831	.008 560	.017 322	.035 445	.034 875	17
18	.002 582	.007 808	.015 804	.032 357	.031 799	18
19	.002 361	.007 141	.014 459	.029 621	.029 077	19
20	.002 164	.006 548	.013 262	.027 185	.026 654	20
21	.001 989	.006 018	.012 192	.025 005	.024 487	21
22	.001 831	.005 541	.011 230	.023 046	.022 541	22
23	.001 688	.005 112	.010 363	.021 278	.020 787	23
24	.001 560	.004 723	.009 578	.019 679	.019 201	24
25	.001 443	.004 371	.008 865	.018 227	.017 762	25
26	.001 337	.004 050	.008 217	.016 904	.016 452	26
27	.001 240	.003 757	.007 626	.015 697	.015 258	27
28	.001 151	.003 489	.007 084	.014 593	.014 166	28
29	.001 070	.003 244	.006 588	.013 580	.013 165	29
30	.000 996	.003 019	.006 133	.012 649	.012 247	30
31	.000 927	.002 811	.005 714	.011 792	.011 402	31
32	.000 864	.002 620	.005 328	.011 002	.010 624	32
33	.000 806	.002 444	.004 971	.010 273	.009 906	33
34	.000 752	.002 281	.004 642	.009 598	.009 243	34
35	.000 702	.002 131	.004 337	.008 974	.008 630	35
36	.000 656	.001 991	.004 054	.008 395	.008 062	36
37	.000 613	.001 862	.003 792	.007 857	.007 535	37
38	.000 573	.001 742	.003 548	.007 358	.007 046	38
39	.000 536	.001 630	.003 322	.006 894	.006 592	39
40	.000 502	.001 526	.003 112	.006 462	.006 170	40

SINKING FUND FACTORS
(Periodic Payment to Grow to $1)

6¼%

Base: 1.005 208   1.015 625   1.031 250   1.062 500   1.064 489

Frequency of Payments and of Conversions

Months	Monthly	Quarterly	Semiannual	Annual	Annual Payment Daily Conversion	Months
1	1.000 000	—	—	—	—	1
2	.498 701	—	—	—	—	2
3	.331 603	1.000 000	—	—	—	3
4	.248 055	—	—	—	—	4
5	.197 927	—	—	—	—	5
6	.164 510	.496 124	1.000 000	—	—	6
7	.140 640	—	—	—	—	7
8	.122 739	—	—	—	—	8
9	.108 816	.328 179	—	—	—	9
10	.097 679	—	—	—	—	10
11	.088 566	—	—	—	—	11

Years						Years
1	.080 973	.244 216	.492 308	1.000 000	1.000 000	1
2	.039 225	.118 323	.238 582	.484 848	.484 381	2
3	.025 327	.076 412	.154 113	.313 341	.312 732	3
4	.018 391	.055 497	.111 959	.227 745	.227 075	4
5	.014 241	.042 980	.086 730	.176 513	.175 814	5
6	.011 483	.034 662	.069 963	.142 463	.141 751	6
7	.009 520	.028 744	.058 032	.118 230	.117 515	7
8	.008 055	.024 324	.049 124	.100 133	.099 420	8
9	.006 921	.020 905	.042 229	.086 126	.085 419	9
10	.006 020	.018 185	.036 745	.074 982	.074 283	10
11	.005 287	.015 973	.032 286	.065 919	.065 231	11
12	.004 680	.014 143	.028 595	.058 417	.057 741	12
13	.004 171	.012 607	.025 496	.052 116	.051 452	13
14	.003 738	.011 300	.022 861	.046 757	.046 106	14
15	.003 366	.010 178	.020 597	.042 151	.041 515	15
16	.003 044	.009 206	.018 635	.038 158	.037 536	16
17	.002 762	.008 356	.016 920	.034 668	.034 061	17
18	.002 515	.007 609	.015 412	.031 598	.031 005	18
19	.002 296	.006 948	.014 078	.028 880	.028 303	19
20	.002 101	.006 360	.012 891	.026 462	.025 899	20
21	.001 927	.005 835	.011 830	.024 300	.023 752	21
22	.001 771	.005 363	.010 878	.022 360	.021 827	22
23	.001 630	.004 939	.010 021	.020 611	.020 092	23
24	.001 503	.004 555	.009 246	.019 029	.018 525	24
25	.001 388	.004 208	.008 543	.017 595	.017 105	25
26	.001 284	.003 892	.007 904	.016 290	.015 815	26
27	.001 188	.003 604	.007 322	.015 100	.014 639	27
28	.001 101	.003 341	.006 790	.014 013	.013 566	28
29	.001 022	.003 100	.006 303	.013 017	.012 584	29
30	.000 949	.002 879	.005 856	.012 103	.011 683	30
31	.000 882	.002 676	.005 446	.011 263	.010 856	31
32	.000 820	.002 490	.005 068	.010 489	.010 096	32
33	.000 763	.002 318	.004 720	.009 775	.009 395	33
34	.000 711	.002 159	.004 398	.009 117	.008 749	34
35	.000 662	.002 013	.004 101	.008 507	.008 152	35
36	.000 618	.001 877	.003 827	.007 943	.007 600	36
37	.000 576	.001 752	.003 572	.007 421	.007 089	37
38	.000 538	.001 635	.003 336	.006 936	.006 615	38
39	.000 502	.001 527	.003 117	.006 485	.006 176	39
40	.000 469	.001 427	.002 914	.006 067	.005 768	40

6½%

SINKING FUND FACTORS
(Periodic Payment to Grow to $1)

Base: 1.005 417   1.016 250   1.032 500   1.065 000   1.067 153

Frequency of Payments and of Conversions

Months	Monthly	Quarterly	Semiannual	Annual	Annual Payment Daily Conversion	Months
1	1.000 000	—	—	—	—	1
2	.498 649	—	—	—	—	2
3	.331 534	1.000 000	—	—	—	3
4	.247 978	—	—	—	—	4
5	.197 845	—	—	—	—	5
6	.164 424	.495 970	1.000 000	—	—	6
7	.140 552	—	—	—	—	7
8	.122 649	—	—	—	—	8
9	.108 725	.327 975	—	—	—	9
10	.097 587	—	—	—	—	10
11	.088 474	—	—	—	—	11

Years						Years
1	.080 880	.243 988	.492 005	1.000 000	1.000 000	1
2	.039 130	.118 062	.238 137	.484 262	.483 757	2
3	.025 232	.076 145	.153 630	.312 576	.311 918	3
4	.018 298	.055 230	.111 463	.226 903	.226 180	4
5	.014 149	.042 716	.086 231	.175 635	.174 882	5
6	.011 393	.034 402	.069 467	.141 568	.140 802	6
7	.009 433	.028 488	.057 542	.117 331	.116 563	7
8	.007 970	.024 074	.048 640	.099 237	.098 472	8
9	.006 838	.020 659	.041 754	.085 238	.084 480	9
10	.005 938	.017 945	.036 279	.074 105	.073 357	10
11	.005 207	.015 739	.031 829	.065 055	.064 319	11
12	.004 603	.013 915	.028 149	.057 568	.056 846	12
13	.004 095	.012 384	.025 060	.051 283	.050 574	13
14	.003 664	.011 083	.022 435	.045 940	.045 248	14
15	.003 294	.009 966	.020 182	.041 353	.040 676	15
16	.002 974	.008 999	.018 230	.037 378	.036 717	16
17	.002 695	.008 155	.016 526	.033 906	.033 262	17
18	.002 449	.007 414	.015 028	.030 855	.030 226	18
19	.002 232	.006 758	.013 704	.028 156	.027 544	19
20	.002 039	.006 176	.012 528	.025 756	.025 162	20
21	.001 867	.005 656	.011 478	.023 613	.023 035	21
22	.001 713	.005 190	.010 536	.021 691	.021 129	22
23	.001 574	.004 771	.009 688	.019 961	.019 415	23
24	.001 449	.004 392	.008 923	.018 398	.017 869	24
25	.001 335	.004 050	.008 230	.016 981	.016 468	25
26	.001 233	.003 739	.007 601	.015 695	.015 198	26
27	.001 139	.003 456	.007 028	.014 523	.014 041	27
28	.001 053	.003 197	.006 506	.013 453	.012 987	28
29	.000 975	.002 961	.006 028	.012 474	.012 023	29
30	.000 904	.002 745	.005 590	.011 577	.011 141	30
31	.000 838	.002 547	.005 188	.010 754	.010 332	31
32	.000 778	.002 365	.004 819	.009 997	.009 589	32
33	.000 723	.002 197	.004 479	.009 299	.008 906	33
34	.000 672	.002 043	.004 166	.008 656	.008 276	34
35	.000 625	.001 900	.003 877	.008 062	.007 696	35
36	.000 581	.001 769	.003 610	.007 513	.007 160	36
37	.000 541	.001 647	.003 363	.007 005	.006 665	37
38	.000 504	.001 534	.003 135	.006 535	.006 206	38
39	.000 470	.001 430	.002 923	.006 099	.005 782	39
40	.000 438	.001 334	.002 727	.005 694	.005 389	40

SINKING FUND FACTORS

(Periodic Payment to Grow to $1)

6¾%

Base:	1.005 625	1.016 875	1.033 750	1.067 500	1.069 823	

Frequency of Payments and of Conversions

Months	Monthly	Quarterly	Semiannual	Annual	Annual Payment Daily Conversion	Months
1	1.000 000	—	—	—	—	1
2	.498 598	—	—	—	—	2
3	.331 465	1.000 000	—	—	—	3
4	.247 900	—	—	—	—	4
5	.197 763	—	—	—	—	5
6	.164 338	.495 817	1.000 000	—	—	6
7	.140 464	—	—	—	—	7
8	.122 560	—	—	—	—	8
9	.108 634	.327 771	—	—	—	9
10	.097 495	—	—	—	—	10
11	.088 381	—	—	—	—	11

Years						Years
1	.080 787	.243 760	.491 703	1.000 000	1.000 000	1
2	.039 034	.117 802	.237 694	.483 676	.483 133	2
3	.025 138	.075 879	.153 148	.311 812	.311 105	3
4	.018 205	.054 964	.110 969	.226 064	.225 287	4
5	.014 058	.042 453	.085 735	.174 760	.173 952	5
6	.011 304	.034 143	.068 974	.140 679	.139 858	6
7	.009 346	.028 234	.057 055	.116 439	.115 616	7
8	.007 885	.023 825	.048 161	.098 349	.097 530	8
9	.006 755	.020 416	.041 283	.084 358	.083 548	9
10	.005 857	.017 707	.035 818	.073 237	.072 438	10
11	.005 128	.015 507	.031 378	.064 201	.063 416	11
12	.004 526	.013 689	.027 708	.056 730	.055 960	12
13	.004 021	.012 164	.024 630	.050 461	.049 708	13
14	.003 592	.010 869	.022 016	.045 137	.044 400	14
15	.003 224	.009 758	.019 773	.040 567	.039 849	15
16	.002 906	.008 797	.017 832	.036 611	.035 910	16
17	.002 628	.007 959	.016 139	.033 159	.032 477	17
18	.002 385	.007 223	.014 652	.030 126	.029 463	18
19	.002 170	.006 573	.013 339	.027 447	.026 801	19
20	.001 979	.005 996	.012 173	.025 067	.024 440	20
21	.001 808	.005 482	.011 134	.022 943	.022 335	21
22	.001 656	.005 021	.010 202	.021 040	.020 450	22
23	.001 519	.004 608	.009 365	.019 329	.018 757	23
24	.001 396	.004 234	.008 610	.017 784	.017 230	24
25	.001 284	.003 897	.007 927	.016 387	.015 851	25
26	.001 183	.003 591	.007 308	.015 119	.014 600	26
27	.001 091	.003 313	.006 745	.013 965	.013 463	27
28	.001 007	.003 059	.006 231	.012 913	.012 428	28
29	.000 931	.002 828	.005 763	.011 952	.011 484	29
30	.000 861	.002 617	.005 334	.011 072	.010 620	30
31	.000 797	.002 423	.004 941	.010 266	.009 829	31
32	.000 738	.002 245	.004 581	.009 525	.009 104	32
33	.000 684	.002 082	.004 250	.008 844	.008 438	33
34	.000 635	.001 932	.003 945	.008 216	.007 826	34
35	.000 589	.001 793	.003 664	.007 638	.007 262	35
36	.000 547	.001 666	.003 405	.007 104	.006 742	36
37	.000 508	.001 548	.003 166	.006 611	.006 263	37
38	.000 472	.001 439	.002 945	.006 155	.005 820	38
39	.000 439	.001 339	.002 740	.005 733	.005 411	39
40	.000 409	.001 246	.002 551	.005 342	.005 032	40

7%

SINKING FUND FACTORS
(Periodic Payment to Grow to $1)

Base: 1.005 833   1.017 500   1.035 000   1.070 000   1.072 501

Frequency of Payments and of Conversions

Months	Monthly	Quarterly	Semiannual	Annual	Annual Payment Daily Conversion	Months
1	1.000 000	—	—	—	—	1
2	.498 546	—	—	—	—	2
3	.331 396	1.000 000	—	—	—	3
4	.247 823	—	—	—	—	4
5	.197 680	—	—	—	—	5
6	.164 253	.495 663	1.000 000	—	—	6
7	.140 377	—	—	—	—	7
8	.122 470	—	—	—	—	8
9	.108 544	.327 567	—	—	—	9
10	.097 403	—	—	—	—	10
11	.088 288	—	—	—	—	11

Years	Monthly	Quarterly	Semiannual	Annual	Annual Payment Daily Conversion	Years
1	.080 693	.243 532	.491 400	1.000 000	1.000 000	1
2	.038 939	.117 543	.237 251	.483 092	.482 509	2
3	.025 044	.075 614	.152 668	.311 052	.310 293	3
4	.018 113	.054 700	.110 477	.225 228	.224 396	4
5	.013 968	.042 191	.085 241	.173 891	.173 025	5
6	.011 216	.033 886	.068 484	.139 796	.138 917	6
7	.009 259	.027 982	.056 571	.115 553	.114 673	7
8	.007 800	.023 578	.047 685	.097 468	.096 594	8
9	.006 673	.020 175	.040 817	.083 486	.082 623	9
10	.005 778	.017 472	.035 361	.072 378	.071 527	10
11	.005 051	.015 278	.030 932	.063 357	.062 522	11
12	.004 450	.013 466	.027 273	.055 902	.055 084	12
13	.003 947	.011 947	.024 205	.049 651	.048 852	13
14	.003 521	.010 658	.021 603	.044 345	.043 565	14
15	.003 155	.009 553	.019 371	.039 795	.039 034	15
16	.002 839	.008 598	.017 442	.035 858	.035 118	16
17	.002 563	.007 766	.015 760	.032 425	.031 705	17
18	.002 322	.007 036	.014 284	.029 413	.028 713	18
19	.002 109	.006 392	.012 982	.026 753	.026 074	19
20	.001 920	.005 821	.011 827	.024 393	.023 735	20
21	.001 751	.005 312	.010 798	.022 289	.021 651	21
22	.001 601	.004 857	.009 878	.020 406	.019 788	22
23	.001 466	.004 449	.009 051	.018 714	.018 116	23
24	.001 344	.004 081	.008 306	.017 189	.016 611	24
25	.001 234	.003 749	.007 634	.015 811	.015 252	25
26	.001 135	.003 448	.007 024	.014 561	.014 021	26
27	.001 045	.003 175	.006 471	.013 426	.012 905	27
28	.000 963	.002 926	.005 967	.012 392	.011 889	28
29	.000 888	.002 700	.005 508	.011 449	.010 964	29
30	.000 820	.002 493	.005 089	.010 586	.010 119	30
31	.000 757	.002 304	.004 705	.009 797	.009 347	31
32	.000 700	.002 131	.004 353	.009 073	.008 640	32
33	.000 648	.001 972	.004 030	.008 408	.007 992	33
34	.000 599	.001 826	.003 734	.007 797	.007 396	34
35	.000 555	.001 692	.003 461	.007 234	.006 849	35
36	.000 514	.001 568	.003 210	.006 715	.006 346	36
37	.000 477	.001 454	.002 978	.006 237	.005 882	37
38	.000 442	.001 349	.002 765	.005 795	.005 454	38
39	.000 410	.001 252	.002 567	.005 387	.005 060	39
40	.000 381	.001 163	.002 385	.005 009	.004 696	40

SINKING FUND FACTORS

(Periodic Payment to Grow to $1)

7¼%

Base:	1.006 042	1.018 125	1.036 250	1.072 500	1.075 185	

Frequency of Payments and of Conversions

Months	Monthly	Quarterly	Semiannual	Annual	Annual Payment Daily Conversion	Months
1	1.000 000	—	—	—	—	1
2	.498 494	—	—	—	—	2
3	.331 328	1.000 000	—	—	—	3
4	.247 746	—	—	—	—	4
5	.197 598	—	—	—	—	5
6	.164 167	.495 509	1.000 000	—	—	6
7	.140 289	—	—	—	—	7
8	.122 381	—	—	—	—	8
9	.108 453	.327 364	—	—	—	9
10	.097 311	—	—	—	—	10
11	.088 196	—	—	—	—	11

Years						Years
1	.080 600	.243 305	.491 099	1.000 000	1.000 000	1
2	.038 844	.117 284	.236 809	.482 509	.481 885	2
3	.024 950	.075 349	.152 189	.310 293	.309 482	3
4	.018 021	.054 436	.109 987	.224 396	.223 506	4
5	.013 878	.041 931	.084 750	.173 025	.172 101	5
6	.011 128	.033 630	.067 997	.138 918	.137 981	6
7	.009 174	.027 731	.056 090	.114 674	.113 736	7
8	.007 717	.023 333	.047 213	.096 594	.095 663	8
9	.006 592	.019 936	.040 355	.082 623	.081 704	9
10	.005 698	.017 239	.034 909	.071 527	.070 624	10
11	.004 974	.015 052	.030 491	.062 522	.061 637	11
12	.004 376	.013 246	.026 843	.055 085	.054 219	12
13	.003 875	.011 733	.023 787	.048 852	.048 006	13
14	.003 451	.010 450	.021 196	.043 565	.042 741	14
15	.003 087	.009 352	.018 976	.039 035	.038 232	15
16	.002 773	.008 403	.017 058	.035 118	.034 338	16
17	.002 500	.007 577	.015 388	.031 706	.030 948	17
18	.002 260	.006 853	.013 924	.028 714	.027 979	18
19	.002 049	.006 215	.012 633	.026 074	.025 362	19
20	.001 862	.005 650	.011 489	.023 735	.023 045	20
21	.001 696	.005 147	.010 471	.021 651	.020 984	21
22	.001 547	.004 697	.009 562	.019 788	.019 143	22
23	.001 414	.004 295	.008 746	.018 116	.017 493	23
24	.001 294	.003 932	.008 012	.016 611	.016 009	24
25	.001 186	.003 605	.007 349	.015 252	.014 671	25
26	.001 089	.003 310	.006 750	.014 021	.013 462	26
27	.001 000	.003 042	.006 207	.012 905	.012 366	27
28	.000 920	.002 798	.005 713	.011 890	.011 370	28
29	.000 847	.002 577	.005 263	.010 964	.010 464	29
30	.000 780	.002 375	.004 853	.010 120	.009 639	30
31	.000 719	.002 190	.004 478	.009 347	.008 885	31
32	.000 664	.002 021	.004 135	.008 640	.008 196	32
33	.000 613	.001 867	.003 821	.007 992	.007 565	33
34	.000 566	.001 725	.003 533	.007 396	.006 987	34
35	.000 523	.001 595	.003 268	.006 849	.006 457	35
36	.000 484	.001 475	.003 025	.006 346	.005 969	36
37	.000 447	.001 365	.002 801	.005 882	.005 521	37
38	.000 414	.001 264	.002 594	.005 454	.005 109	38
39	.000 383	.001 171	.002 404	.005 060	.004 729	39
40	.000 355	.001 085	.002 229	.004 696	.004 379	40

7½%

SINKING FUND FACTORS
(Periodic Payment to Grow to $1)

Base: 1.006 250   1.018 750   1.037 500   1.075 000   1.077 876

Frequency of Payments and of Conversions

Months	Monthly	Quarterly	Semiannual	Annual	Annual Payment Daily Conversion	Months
1	1.000 000	—	—	—	—	1
2	.498 442	—	—	—	—	2
3	.331 259	1.000 000	—	—	—	3
4	.247 668	—	—	—	—	4
5	.197 516	—	—	—	—	5
6	.164 081	.495 356	1.000 000	—	—	6
7	.140 201	—	—	—	—	7
8	.122 291	—	—	—	—	8
9	.108 362	.327 161	—	—	—	9
10	.097 220	—	—	—	—	10
11	.088 104	—	—	—	—	11

Years						Years
1	.080 507	.243 078	.490 798	1.000 000	1.000 000	1
2	.038 750	.117 025	.236 369	.481 928	.481 261	2
3	.024 856	.075 085	.151 712	.309 538	.308 671	3
4	.017 929	.054 173	.109 498	.223 568	.222 619	4
5	.013 788	.041 671	.084 261	.172 165	.171 180	5
6	.011 040	.033 375	.067 512	.138 045	.137 048	6
7	.009 088	.027 482	.055 613	.113 800	.112 803	7
8	.007 634	.023 090	.046 745	.095 727	.094 739	8
9	.006 511	.019 700	.039 897	.081 767	.080 793	9
10	.005 620	.017 009	.034 462	.070 686	.069 729	10
11	.004 898	.014 828	.030 055	.061 697	.060 760	11
12	.004 302	.013 028	.026 419	.054 278	.053 362	12
13	.003 804	.011 522	.023 375	.048 064	.047 172	13
14	.003 381	.010 246	.020 795	.042 797	.041 929	14
15	.003 020	.009 154	.018 588	.038 287	.037 443	15
16	.002 708	.008 211	.016 681	.034 391	.033 571	16
17	.002 437	.007 391	.015 023	.031 000	.030 205	17
18	.002 200	.006 674	.013 571	.028 029	.027 259	18
19	.001 991	.006 042	.012 292	.025 411	.024 666	19
20	.001 806	.005 483	.011 159	.023 092	.022 372	20
21	.001 642	.004 986	.010 153	.021 029	.020 333	21
22	.001 495	.004 542	.009 254	.019 187	.018 515	22
23	.001 364	.004 145	.008 449	.017 535	.016 887	23
24	.001 246	.003 788	.007 726	.016 050	.015 425	24
25	.001 140	.003 467	.007 074	.014 711	.014 109	25
26	.001 044	.003 176	.006 485	.013 500	.012 921	26
27	.000 957	.002 914	.005 952	.012 402	.011 845	27
28	.000 879	.002 675	.005 468	.011 405	.010 870	28
29	.000 807	.002 458	.005 028	.010 498	.009 984	29
30	.000 742	.002 261	.004 627	.009 671	.009 177	30
31	.000 683	.002 081	.004 261	.008 916	.008 443	31
32	.000 629	.001 917	.003 927	.008 226	.007 772	32
33	.000 579	.001 767	.003 621	.007 594	.007 159	33
34	.000 534	.001 629	.003 341	.007 015	.006 598	34
35	.000 492	.001 503	.003 085	.006 483	.006 084	35
36	.000 454	.001 388	.002 849	.005 994	.005 612	36
37	.000 419	.001 281	.002 633	.005 545	.005 180	37
38	.000 387	.001 184	.002 434	.005 132	.004 783	38
39	.000 358	.001 094	.002 250	.004 751	.004 418	39
40	.000 331	.001 012	.002 082	.004 400	.004 082	40

302

SINKING FUND FACTORS

7¾%

(Periodic Payment to Grow to $1)

Base:	1.006 458	1.019 375	1.038 750	1.077 500	1.080 573	

Frequency of Payments and of Conversions

Months	Monthly	Quarterly	Semiannual	Annual	Annual Payment Daily Conversion	Months
1	1.000 000	—	—	—	—	1
2	.498 391	—	—	—	—	2
3	.331 190	1.000 000	—	—	—	3
4	.247 591	—	—	—	—	4
5	.197 433	—	—	—	—	5
6	.163 996	.495 203	1.000 000	—	—	6
7	.140 113	—	—	—	—	7
8	.122 202	—	—	—	—	8
9	.108 272	.326 958	—	—	—	9
10	.097 128	—	—	—	—	10
11	.088 011	—	—	—	—	11

Years						Years
1	.080 415	.242 851	.490 497	1.000 000	1.000 000	1
2	.038 655	.116 767	.235 929	.481 348	.480 637	2
3	.024 763	.074 822	.151 236	.308 784	.307 862	3
4	.017 837	.053 911	.109 012	.222 742	.221 733	4
5	.013 699	.041 413	.083 775	.171 308	.170 262	5
6	.010 953	.033 123	.067 031	.137 177	.136 118	6
7	.009 004	.027 235	.055 139	.112 933	.111 876	7
8	.007 552	.022 850	.046 281	.094 867	.093 820	8
9	.006 431	.019 465	.039 443	.080 919	.079 888	9
10	.005 543	.016 781	.034 020	.069 853	.068 842	10
11	.004 823	.014 607	.029 625	.060 882	.059 893	11
12	.004 230	.012 814	.026 000	.053 481	.052 516	12
13	.003 733	.011 314	.022 968	.047 288	.046 348	13
14	.003 313	.010 045	.020 401	.042 041	.041 128	14
15	.002 954	.008 959	.018 206	.037 552	.036 666	15
16	.002 645	.008 023	.016 312	.033 678	.032 818	16
17	.002 376	.007 210	.014 665	.030 308	.029 476	17
18	.002 141	.006 498	.013 225	.027 359	.026 554	18
19	.001 934	.005 873	.011 958	.024 762	.023 984	19
20	.001 751	.005 320	.010 838	.022 465	.021 714	20
21	.001 589	.004 829	.009 843	.020 423	.019 699	21
22	.001 444	.004 391	.008 955	.018 602	.017 904	22
23	.001 315	.004 000	.008 162	.016 971	.016 299	23
24	.001 199	.003 648	.007 449	.015 506	.014 859	24
25	.001 095	.003 333	.006 808	.014 186	.013 565	25
26	.001 001	.003 048	.006 229	.012 995	.012 398	26
27	.000 916	.002 790	.005 706	.011 917	.011 343	27
28	.000 839	.002 557	.005 232	.010 938	.010 388	28
29	.000 769	.002 345	.004 801	.010 050	.009 522	29
30	.000 706	.002 152	.004 410	.009 241	.008 735	30
31	.000 648	.001 977	.004 053	.008 503	.008 019	31
32	.000 595	.001 817	.003 728	.007 830	.007 366	32
33	.000 547	.001 671	.003 431	.007 214	.006 771	33
34	.000 504	.001 538	.003 159	.006 651	.006 227	34
35	.000 463	.001 416	.002 910	.006 135	.005 730	35
36	.000 427	.001 305	.002 683	.005 661	.005 274	36
37	.000 393	.001 202	.002 474	.005 226	.004 857	37
38	.000 362	.001 108	.002 282	.004 827	.004 475	38
39	.000 334	.001 022	.002 106	.004 460	.004 124	39
40	.000 308	.000 943	.001 944	.004 122	.003 802	40

8%

SINKING FUND FACTORS
(Periodic Payment to Grow to $1)

Base: 1.006 667   1.020 000   1.040 000   1.080 000   1.083 277

Frequency of Payments and of Conversions

Months	Monthly	Quarterly	Semiannual	Annual	Annual Payment Daily Conversion	Months
1	1.000 000	—	—	—	—	1
2	.498 339	—	—	—	—	2
3	.331 121	1.000 000	—	—	—	3
4	.247 514	—	—	—	—	4
5	.197 351	—	—	—	—	5
6	.163 910	.495 050	1.000 000	—	—	6
7	.140 025	—	—	—	—	7
8	.122 112	—	—	—	—	8
9	.108 181	.326 755	—	—	—	9
10	.097 037	—	—	—	—	10
11	.087 919	—	—	—	—	11

Years						Years
1	.080 322	.242 624	.490 196	1.000 000	1.000 000	1
2	.038 561	.116 510	.235 490	.480 769	.480 013	2
3	.024 670	.074 560	.150 762	.308 034	.307 053	3
4	.017 746	.053 650	.108 528	.221 921	.220 849	4
5	.013 610	.041 157	.083 291	.170 456	.169 346	5
6	.010 867	.032 871	.066 552	.136 315	.135 193	6
7	.008 920	.026 990	.054 669	.112 072	.110 953	7
8	.007 470	.022 611	.045 820	.094 015	.092 908	8
9	.006 352	.019 233	.038 993	.080 080	.078 991	9
10	.005 466	.016 556	.033 582	.069 029	.067 963	10
11	.004 749	.014 388	.029 199	.060 076	.059 034	11
12	.004 158	.012 602	.025 587	.052 695	.051 680	12
13	.003 664	.011 109	.022 567	.046 522	.045 534	13
14	.003 247	.009 847	.020 013	.041 297	.040 338	14
15	.002 890	.008 768	.017 830	.036 830	.035 900	15
16	.002 583	.007 839	.015 949	.032 977	.032 078	16
17	.002 316	.007 032	.014 315	.029 629	.028 760	17
18	.002 083	.006 327	.012 887	.026 702	.025 862	18
19	.001 878	.005 708	.011 632	.024 128	.023 318	19
20	.001 698	.005 161	.010 523	.021 852	.021 071	20
21	.001 538	.004 676	.009 540	.019 832	.019 080	21
22	.001 395	.004 244	.008 665	.018 032	.017 309	22
23	.001 268	.003 859	.007 882	.016 422	.015 727	23
24	.001 154	.003 513	.007 181	.014 978	.014 310	24
25	.001 051	.003 203	.006 550	.013 679	.013 038	25
26	.000 959	.002 923	.005 982	.012 507	.011 892	26
27	.000 876	.002 671	.005 469	.011 448	.010 859	27
28	.000 801	.002 443	.005 005	.010 489	.009 925	28
29	.000 733	.002 236	.004 584	.009 619	.009 078	29
30	.000 671	.002 048	.004 202	.008 827	.008 311	30
31	.000 615	.001 877	.003 854	.008 107	.007 614	31
32	.000 564	.001 722	.003 538	.007 451	.006 979	32
33	.000 517	.001 581	.003 249	.006 852	.006 401	33
34	.000 475	.001 452	.002 986	.006 304	.005 875	34
35	.000 436	.001 334	.002 745	.005 803	.005 394	35
36	.000 401	.001 226	.002 525	.005 345	.004 954	36
37	.000 368	.001 127	.002 323	.004 924	.004 553	37
38	.000 338	.001 037	.002 139	.004 539	.004 185	38
39	.000 311	.000 954	.001 969	.004 185	.003 849	39
40	.000 286	.000 878	.001 814	.003 860	.003 540	40

SINKING FUND FACTORS

(Periodic Payment to Grow to $1)

8¼%

Base: 1.006 875   1.020 625   1.041 250   1.082 500   1.085 988

Frequency of Payments and of Conversions

Months	Monthly	Quarterly	Semiannual	Annual	Annual Payment Daily Conversion	Months
1	1.000 000	—	—	—	—	1
2	.498 287	—	—	—	—	2
3	.331 052	1.000 000	—	—	—	3
4	.247 437	—	—	—	—	4
5	.197 269	—	—	—	—	5
6	.163 825	.494 896	1.000 000	—	—	6
7	.139 938	—	—	—	—	7
8	.122 023	—	—	—	—	8
9	.108 090	.326 552	—	—	—	9
10	.096 945	—	—	—	—	10
11	.087 827	—	—	—	—	11

Years						Years
1	.080 229	.242 397	.489 896	1.000 000	1.000 000	1
2	.038 466	.116 253	.235 052	.480 192	.479 389	2
3	.024 577	.074 298	.150 289	.307 285	.306 245	3
4	.017 655	.053 390	.108 045	.221 103	.219 967	4
5	.013 521	.040 901	.082 809	.169 609	.168 434	5
6	.010 781	.032 621	.066 076	.135 459	.134 272	6
7	.008 836	.026 746	.054 202	.111 218	.110 035	7
8	.007 389	.022 374	.045 363	.093 169	.092 001	8
9	.006 274	.019 003	.038 548	.079 248	.078 100	9
10	.005 390	.016 333	.033 149	.068 214	.067 091	10
11	.004 675	.014 172	.028 778	.059 280	.058 184	11
12	.004 087	.012 393	.025 179	.051 919	.050 853	12
13	.003 596	.010 907	.022 172	.045 767	.044 732	13
14	.003 181	.009 652	.019 631	.040 564	.039 560	14
15	.002 826	.008 580	.017 461	.036 119	.035 148	15
16	.002 522	.007 657	.015 592	.032 289	.031 350	16
17	.002 257	.006 857	.013 971	.028 964	.028 058	17
18	.002 026	.006 159	.012 556	.026 059	.025 185	18
19	.001 824	.005 546	.011 313	.023 507	.022 666	19
20	.001 646	.005 006	.010 217	.021 254	.020 444	20
21	.001 488	.004 527	.009 246	.019 256	.018 478	21
22	.001 347	.004 101	.008 382	.017 478	.016 730	22
23	.001 222	.003 722	.007 611	.015 889	.015 172	23
24	.001 110	.003 382	.006 921	.014 466	.013 778	24
25	.001 010	.003 077	.006 301	.013 187	.012 528	25
26	.000 919	.002 803	.005 744	.012 036	.011 404	26
27	.000 838	.002 556	.005 241	.010 996	.010 392	27
28	.000 764	.002 333	.004 787	.010 056	.009 479	28
29	.000 698	.002 131	.004 375	.009 204	.008 653	29
30	.000 638	.001 948	.004 003	.008 431	.007 905	30
31	.000 583	.001 782	.003 664	.007 728	.007 226	31
32	.000 533	.001 631	.003 356	.007 089	.006 610	32
33	.000 488	.001 494	.003 076	.006 506	.006 050	33
34	.000 447	.001 369	.002 821	.005 974	.005 540	34
35	.000 410	.001 255	.002 588	.005 488	.005 075	35
36	.000 376	.001 151	.002 376	.005 045	.004 652	36
37	.000 345	.001 057	.002 181	.004 639	.004 265	37
38	.000 316	.000 970	.002 004	.004 267	.003 912	38
39	.000 290	.000 890	.001 841	.003 926	.003 589	39
40	.000 266	.000 818	.001 692	.003 614	.003 294	40

8½%

SINKING FUND FACTORS
(Periodic Payment to Grow to $1)

Base: 1.007 083   1.021 250   1.042 500   1.085 000   1.088 706

Frequency of Payments and of Conversions

Months	Monthly	Quarterly	Semiannual	Annual	Annual Payment Daily Conversion	Months
1	1.000 000	—	—	—	—	1
2	.498 235	—	—	—	—	2
3	.330 983	1.000 000	—	—	—	3
4	.247 359	—	—	—	—	4
5	.197 187	—	—	—	—	5
6	.163 740	.494 743	1.000 000	—	—	6
7	.139 850	—	—	—	—	7
8	.121 934	—	—	—	—	8
9	.108 000	.326 349	—	—	—	9
10	.096 854	—	—	—	—	10
11	.087 735	—	—	—	—	11

Years	Monthly	Quarterly	Semiannual	Annual	Annual Payment Daily Conversion	Years
1	.080 136	.242 171	.489 596	1.000 000	1.000 000	1
2	.038 372	.115 996	.234 615	.479 616	.478 765	2
3	.024 484	.074 037	.149 817	.306 539	.305 438	3
4	.017 565	.053 131	.107 565	.220 288	.219 086	4
5	.013 433	.040 647	.082 330	.168 766	.167 524	5
6	.010 695	.032 373	.065 603	.134 607	.133 354	6
7	.008 753	.026 504	.053 738	.110 369	.109 123	7
8	.007 309	.022 139	.044 910	.092 331	.091 100	8
9	.006 196	.018 775	.038 107	.078 424	.077 216	9
10	.005 315	.016 112	.032 720	.067 408	.066 228	10
11	.004 603	.013 958	.028 362	.058 493	.057 343	11
12	.004 017	.012 187	.024 776	.051 153	.050 036	12
13	.003 528	.010 708	.021 783	.045 023	.043 939	13
14	.003 116	.009 460	.019 255	.039 842	.038 794	14
15	.002 764	.008 395	.017 098	.035 420	.034 407	15
16	.002 462	.007 480	.015 243	.031 614	.030 635	16
17	.002 200	.006 686	.013 635	.028 312	.027 369	17
18	.001 971	.005 995	.012 232	.025 430	.024 522	18
19	.001 771	.005 389	.011 002	.022 901	.022 028	19
20	.001 595	.004 855	.009 918	.020 671	.019 832	20
21	.001 439	.004 382	.008 959	.018 695	.017 890	21
22	.001 301	.003 963	.008 107	.016 939	.016 167	22
23	.001 178	.003 589	.007 348	.015 372	.014 632	23
24	.001 067	.003 255	.006 669	.013 970	.013 262	24
25	.000 969	.002 956	.006 060	.012 712	.012 035	25
26	.000 880	.002 687	.005 513	.011 580	.010 933	26
27	.000 801	.002 446	.005 021	.010 560	.009 943	27
28	.000 729	.002 228	.004 577	.009 639	.009 050	28
29	.000 664	.002 031	.004 175	.008 806	.008 244	29
30	.000 606	.001 853	.003 812	.008 051	.007 515	30
31	.000 553	.001 691	.003 482	.007 365	.006 856	31
32	.000 505	.001 545	.003 183	.006 742	.006 258	32
33	.000 461	.001 412	.002 912	.006 176	.005 715	33
34	.000 421	.001 291	.002 665	.005 660	.005 222	34
35	.000 385	.001 181	.002 440	.005 189	.004 774	35
36	.000 352	.001 081	.002 234	.004 760	.004 365	36
37	.000 323	.000 990	.002 047	.004 368	.003 994	37
38	.000 295	.000 907	.001 877	.004 010	.003 655	38
39	.000 270	.000 831	.001 721	.003 682	.003 346	39
40	.000 248	.000 761	.001 578	.003 382	.003 064	40

SINKING FUND FACTORS

(Periodic Payment to Grow to $1)

8¾%

Base: 1.007 292   1.021 875   1.043 750   1.087 500   1.091 431

Frequency of Payments and of Conversions

Months	Monthly	Quarterly	Semiannual	Annual	Annual Payment Daily Conversion	Months
1	1.000 000	—	—	—	—	1
2	.498 184	—	—	—	—	2
3	.330 915	1.000 000	—	—	—	3
4	.247 282	—	—	—	—	4
5	.197 105	—	—	—	—	5
6	.163 654	.494 590	1.000 000	—	—	6
7	.139 762	—	—	—	—	7
8	.121 845	—	—	—	—	8
9	.107 910	.326 147	—	—	—	9
10	.096 762	—	—	—	—	10
11	.087 643	—	—	—	—	11

Years						Years
1	.080 044	.241 945	.489 297	1.000 000	1.000 000	1
2	.038 278	.115 740	.234 179	.479 042	.478 142	2
3	.024 392	.073 777	.149 347	.305 796	.304 632	3
4	.017 475	.052 874	.107 086	.219 477	.218 208	4
5	.013 346	.040 394	.081 853	.167 927	.166 617	5
6	.010 610	.032 126	.065 133	.133 761	.132 441	6
7	.008 671	.026 264	.053 278	.109 527	.108 215	7
8	.007 229	.021 905	.044 461	.091 499	.090 206	8
9	.006 119	.018 549	.037 670	.077 607	.076 340	9
10	.005 241	.015 893	.032 296	.066 610	.065 372	10
11	.004 532	.013 747	.027 952	.057 715	.056 511	11
12	.003 948	.011 983	.024 379	.050 397	.049 228	12
13	.003 462	.010 512	.021 399	.044 289	.043 158	13
14	.003 052	.009 271	.018 885	.039 132	.038 038	14
15	.002 703	.008 214	.016 742	.034 734	.033 678	15
16	.002 403	.007 305	.014 900	.030 951	.029 933	16
17	.002 143	.006 519	.013 305	.027 673	.026 693	17
18	.001 917	.005 834	.011 916	.024 815	.023 873	18
19	.001 719	.005 235	.010 698	.022 309	.021 405	19
20	.001 545	.004 707	.009 627	.020 102	.019 235	20
21	.001 392	.004 241	.008 680	.018 149	.017 318	21
22	.001 256	.003 828	.007 840	.016 415	.015 620	22
23	.001 134	.003 460	.007 092	.014 870	.014 109	23
24	.001 026	.003 132	.006 425	.013 489	.012 762	24
25	.000 930	.002 839	.005 827	.012 251	.011 558	25
26	.000 843	.002 576	.005 291	.011 140	.010 479	26
27	.000 765	.002 339	.004 809	.010 140	.009 510	27
28	.000 695	.002 127	.004 375	.009 238	.008 638	28
29	.000 632	.001 935	.003 983	.008 423	.007 852	29
30	.000 575	.001 761	.003 629	.007 686	.007 143	30
31	.000 524	.001 605	.003 309	.007 018	.006 502	31
32	.000 477	.001 463	.003 018	.006 412	.005 922	32
33	.000 435	.001 334	.002 755	.005 861	.005 397	33
34	.000 397	.001 217	.002 516	.005 361	.004 920	34
35	.000 362	.001 111	.002 299	.004 905	.004 488	35
36	.000 330	.001 015	.002 101	.004 490	.004 095	36
37	.000 302	.000 927	.001 921	.004 112	.003 738	37
38	.000 276	.000 847	.001 757	.003 767	.003 413	38
39	.000 252	.000 774	.001 607	.003 452	.003 117	39
40	.000 230	.000 708	.001 471	.003 164	.002 848	40

9%

SINKING FUND FACTORS
(Periodic Payment to Grow to $1)

Base: 1.007 500   1.022 500   1.045 000   1.090 000   1.094 162

Frequency of Payments and of Conversions

Months	Monthly	Quarterly	Semiannual	Annual	Annual Payment Daily Conversion	Months
1	1.000 000	—	—	—	—	1
2	.498 132	—	—	—	—	2
3	.330 846	1.000 000	—	—	—	3
4	.247 205	—	—	—	—	4
5	.197 022	—	—	—	—	5
6	.163 569	.494 438	1.000 000	—	—	6
7	.139 675	—	—	—	—	7
8	.121 756	—	—	—	—	8
9	.107 819	.325 945	—	—	—	9
10	.096 671	—	—	—	—	10
11	.087 551	—	—	—	—	11

Years	Monthly	Quarterly	Semiannual	Annual	Annual Payment Daily Conversion	Years
1	.079 951	.241 719	.488 998	1.000 000	1.000 000	1
2	.038 185	.115 485	.233 744	.478 469	.477 518	2
3	.024 300	.073 517	.148 878	.305 055	.303 826	3
4	.017 385	.052 617	.106 610	.218 669	.217 331	4
5	.013 258	.040 142	.081 379	.167 092	.165 713	5
6	.010 526	.031 880	.064 666	.132 920	.131 531	6
7	.008 589	.026 025	.052 820	.108 691	.107 312	7
8	.007 150	.021 674	.044 015	.090 674	.089 317	8
9	.006 043	.018 325	.037 237	.076 799	.075 470	9
10	.005 168	.015 677	.031 876	.065 820	.064 524	10
11	.004 461	.013 539	.027 546	.056 947	.055 687	11
12	.003 880	.011 782	.023 987	.049 651	.048 430	12
13	.003 397	.010 319	.021 021	.043 567	.042 386	13
14	.002 989	.009 085	.018 521	.038 433	.037 294	14
15	.002 643	.008 035	.016 392	.034 059	.032 961	15
16	.002 345	.007 134	.014 563	.030 300	.029 243	16
17	.002 088	.006 355	.012 982	.027 046	.026 031	17
18	.001 864	.005 677	.011 606	.024 212	.023 238	18
19	.001 669	.005 085	.010 402	.021 730	.020 796	19
20	.001 497	.004 564	.009 343	.019 546	.018 652	20
21	.001 346	.004 104	.008 409	.017 617	.016 761	21
22	.001 212	.003 697	.007 581	.015 905	.015 088	22
23	.001 093	.003 336	.006 845	.014 382	.013 602	23
24	.000 987	.003 014	.006 189	.013 023	.012 279	24
25	.000 892	.002 726	.005 602	.011 806	.011 097	25
26	.000 807	.002 468	.005 077	.010 715	.010 041	26
27	.000 731	.002 237	.004 605	.009 735	.009 093	27
28	.000 663	.002 030	.004 181	.008 852	.008 242	28
29	.000 602	.001 843	.003 799	.008 056	.007 476	29
30	.000 546	.001 674	.003 454	.007 336	.006 787	30
31	.000 496	.001 522	.003 143	.006 686	.006 164	31
32	.000 451	.001 384	.002 861	.006 096	.005 602	32
33	.000 410	.001 260	.002 606	.005 562	.005 094	33
34	.000 373	.001 147	.002 375	.005 077	.004 634	34
35	.000 340	.001 045	.002 165	.004 636	.004 217	35
36	.000 310	.000 952	.001 975	.004 235	.003 840	36
37	.000 282	.000 868	.001 802	.003 870	.003 497	37
38	.000 257	.000 791	.001 644	.003 538	.003 186	38
39	.000 234	.000 722	.001 501	.003 236	.002 903	39
40	.000 214	.000 659	.001 371	.002 960	.002 646	40

SINKING FUND FACTORS

9¼%

(Periodic Payment to Grow to $1)

Base:	1.007 708	1.023 125	1.046 250	1.092 500	1.096 900	
			Frequency of Payments and of Conversions			
Months	Monthly	Quarterly	Semiannual	Annual	Annual Payment Daily Conversion	Months
1	1.000 000	—	—	—	—	1
2	.498 080	—	—	—	—	2
3	.330 777	1.000 000	—	—	—	3
4	.247 128	—	—	—	—	4
5	.196 940	—	—	—	—	5
6	.163 484	.494 285	1.000 000	—	—	6
7	.139 587	—	—	—	—	7
8	.121 666	—	—	—	—	8
9	.107 729	.325 742	—	—	—	9
10	.096 580	—	—	—	—	10
11	.087 459	—	—	—	—	11
Years						Years
1	.079 859	.241 493	.488 699	1.000 000	1.000 000	1
2	.038 091	.115 230	.233 309	.477 897	.476 894	2
3	.024 208	.073 259	.148 411	.304 316	.303 022	3
4	.017 296	.052 361	.106 135	.217 864	.216 456	4
5	.013 172	.039 891	.080 907	.166 262	.164 812	5
6	.010 442	.031 636	.064 202	.132 084	.130 625	6
7	.008 508	.025 788	.052 366	.107 860	.106 414	7
8	.007 072	.021 445	.043 573	.089 857	.088 434	8
9	.005 967	.018 104	.036 808	.075 998	.074 607	9
10	.005 095	.015 464	.031 461	.065 039	.063 684	10
11	.004 391	.013 333	.027 145	.056 187	.054 873	11
12	.003 813	.011 584	.023 600	.048 914	.047 642	12
13	.003 332	.010 128	.020 649	.042 854	.041 625	13
14	.002 928	.008 903	.018 163	.037 745	.036 561	14
15	.002 584	.007 860	.016 047	.033 396	.032 256	15
16	.002 289	.006 966	.014 233	.029 661	.028 566	16
17	.002 034	.006 194	.012 666	.026 432	.025 382	17
18	.001 813	.005 524	.011 303	.023 623	.022 616	18
19	.001 620	.004 938	.010 112	.021 165	.020 202	19
20	.001 450	.004 424	.009 066	.019 005	.018 084	20
21	.001 301	.003 971	.008 145	.017 098	.016 219	21
22	.001 169	.003 570	.007 329	.015 409	.014 571	22
23	.001 052	.003 215	.006 605	.013 909	.013 110	23
24	.000 948	.002 899	.005 960	.012 571	.011 810	24
25	.000 855	.002 617	.005 385	.011 376	.010 652	25
26	.000 773	.002 365	.004 870	.010 305	.009 618	26
27	.000 698	.002 139	.004 409	.009 345	.008 692	27
28	.000 632	.001 936	.003 995	.008 481	.007 862	28
29	.000 572	.001 754	.003 622	.007 703	.007 116	29
30	.000 518	.001 590	.003 287	.007 001	.006 446	30
31	.000 470	.001 443	.002 984	.006 368	.005 842	31
32	.000 426	.001 310	.002 711	.005 795	.005 298	32
33	.000 387	.001 189	.002 464	.005 276	.004 807	33
34	.000 351	.001 080	.002 241	.004 806	.004 363	34
35	.000 319	.000 982	.002 039	.004 380	.003 962	35
36	.000 290	.000 893	.001 855	.003 993	.003 599	36
37	.000 264	.000 812	.001 689	.003 642	.003 270	37
38	.000 240	.000 739	.001 538	.003 322	.002 972	38
39	.000 218	.000 672	.001 401	.003 032	.002 702	39
40	.000 198	.000 612	.001 277	.002 767	.002 458	40

9½%

SINKING FUND FACTORS
(Periodic Payment to Grow to $1)

Base: 1.007 917   1.023 750   1.047 500   1.095 000   1.099 645

Frequency of Payments and of Conversions

Months	Monthly	Quarterly	Semiannual	Annual	Annual Payment Daily Conversion	Months
1	1.000 000	—	—	—	—	1
2	.498 029	—	—	—	—	2
3	.330 708	1.000 000	—	—	—	3
4	.247 051	—	—	—	—	4
5	.196 858	—	—	—	—	5
6	.163 398	.494 132	1.000 000	—	—	6
7	.139 500	—	—	—	—	7
8	.121 577	—	—	—	—	8
9	.107 639	.325 541	—	—	—	9
10	.096 489	—	—	—	—	10
11	.087 367	—	—	—	—	11

Years						Years
1	.079 767	.241 268	.488 400	1.000 000	1.000 000	1
2	.037 998	.114 975	.232 876	.477 327	.476 271	2
3	.024 116	.073 001	.147 945	.303 580	.302 218	3
4	.017 206	.052 106	.105 662	.217 063	.215 583	4
5	.013 085	.039 642	.080 437	.165 436	.163 913	5
6	.010 358	.031 394	.063 740	.131 253	.129 724	6
7	.008 427	.025 553	.051 916	.107 036	.105 520	7
8	.006 994	.021 217	.043 135	.089 046	.087 557	8
9	.005 893	.017 884	.036 383	.075 205	.073 751	9
10	.005 023	.015 252	.031 050	.064 266	.062 852	10
11	.004 322	.013 130	.026 748	.055 437	.054 067	11
12	.003 747	.011 389	.023 219	.048 188	.046 863	12
13	.003 269	.009 941	.020 282	.042 152	.040 875	13
14	.002 867	.008 723	.017 810	.037 068	.035 839	14
15	.002 526	.007 688	.015 709	.032 744	.031 562	15
16	.002 233	.006 802	.013 909	.029 035	.027 902	16
17	.001 981	.006 037	.012 356	.025 831	.024 745	17
18	.001 762	.005 374	.011 007	.023 046	.022 008	18
19	.001 572	.004 795	.009 829	.020 613	.019 621	19
20	.001 405	.004 288	.008 797	.018 477	.017 530	20
21	.001 258	.003 841	.007 888	.016 594	.015 691	21
22	.001 128	.003 447	.007 084	.014 928	.014 069	22
23	.001 013	.003 098	.006 372	.013 449	.012 632	23
24	.000 911	.002 788	.005 739	.012 134	.011 357	24
25	.000 820	.002 511	.005 175	.010 959	.010 222	25
26	.000 739	.002 265	.004 671	.009 909	.009 211	26
27	.000 667	.002 044	.004 220	.008 969	.008 306	27
28	.000 602	.001 847	.003 816	.008 124	.007 497	28
29	.000 544	.001 670	.003 453	.007 364	.006 772	29
30	.000 492	.001 511	.003 127	.006 681	.006 120	30
31	.000 445	.001 368	.002 833	.006 064	.005 535	31
32	.000 403	.001 239	.002 569	.005 507	.005 008	32
33	.000 365	.001 122	.002 330	.005 004	.004 534	33
34	.000 330	.001 017	.002 114	.004 549	.004 106	34
35	.000 299	.000 923	.001 919	.004 138	.003 720	35
36	.000 271	.000 837	.001 743	.003 764	.003 371	36
37	.000 246	.000 760	.001 583	.003 426	.003 057	37
38	.000 223	.000 690	.001 439	.003 119	.002 772	38
39	.000 203	.000 626	.001 308	.002 840	.002 514	39
40	.000 184	.000 569	.001 189	.002 587	.002 281	40

SINKING FUND FACTORS

(Periodic Payment to Grow to $1)

9¾%

Base:	1.008 125	1.024 375	1.048 750	1.097 500	1.102 397	
			Frequency of Payments and of Conversions			
					Annual Payment Daily	
Months	Monthly	Quarterly	Semiannual	Annual	Conversion	Months
1	1.000 000	—	—	—	—	1
2	.497 977	—	—	—	—	2
3	.330 640	1.000 000	—	—	—	3
4	.246 974	—	—	—	—	4
5	.196 776	—	—	—	—	5
6	.163 313	.493 980	1.000 000	—	—	6
7	.139 413	—	—	—	—	7
8	.121 488	—	—	—	—	8
9	.107 549	.325 339	—	—	—	9
10	.096 398	—	—	—	—	10
11	.087 276	—	—	—	—	11

Years						Years
1	.079 675	.241 043	.488 103	1.000 000	1.000 000	1
2	.037 905	.114 721	.232 443	.476 758	.475 648	2
3	.024 025	.072 744	.147 481	.302 846	.301 416	3
4	.017 118	.051 852	.105 191	.216 265	.214 712	4
5	.012 999	.039 394	.079 970	.164 615	.163 018	5
6	.010 275	.031 152	.063 281	.130 428	.128 826	6
7	.008 347	.025 320	.051 468	.106 218	.104 632	7
8	.006 917	.020 992	.042 701	.088 241	.086 686	8
9	.005 819	.017 667	.035 963	.074 419	.072 901	9
10	.004 952	.015 043	.030 644	.063 502	.062 028	10
11	.004 254	.012 929	.026 357	.054 696	.053 269	11
12	.003 682	.011 196	.022 842	.047 471	.046 094	12
13	.003 207	.009 756	.019 920	.041 460	.040 134	13
14	.002 807	.008 546	.017 463	.036 402	.035 128	14
15	.002 469	.007 519	.015 377	.032 103	.030 881	15
16	.002 179	.006 641	.013 592	.028 420	.027 249	16
17	.001 929	.005 884	.012 052	.025 241	.024 122	17
18	.001 713	.005 227	.010 717	.022 482	.021 413	18
19	.001 525	.004 656	.009 553	.020 074	.019 054	19
20	.001 360	.004 155	.008 534	.017 962	.016 990	20
21	.001 215	.003 715	.007 638	.016 102	.015 178	21
22	.001 088	.003 328	.006 847	.014 460	.013 581	22
23	.000 975	.002 985	.006 147	.013 004	.012 170	23
24	.000 875	.002 680	.005 525	.011 710	.010 919	24
25	.000 786	.002 410	.004 972	.010 557	.009 808	25
26	.000 707	.002 169	.004 479	.009 527	.008 818	26
27	.000 637	.001 954	.004 039	.008 606	.007 936	27
28	.000 574	.001 761	.003 645	.007 781	.007 147	28
29	.000 517	.001 589	.003 291	.007 040	.006 441	29
30	.000 467	.001 435	.002 974	.006 373	.005 809	30
31	.000 421	.001 296	.002 689	.005 774	.005 242	31
32	.000 380	.001 171	.002 433	.005 233	.004 733	32
33	.000 344	.001 059	.002 202	.004 746	.004 275	33
34	.000 311	.000 958	.001 994	.004 305	.003 863	34
35	.000 281	.000 867	.001 806	.003 908	.003 492	35
36	.000 254	.000 785	.001 637	.003 548	.003 157	36
37	.000 230	.000 710	.001 483	.003 222	.002 856	37
38	.000 208	.000 643	.001 345	.002 927	.002 584	38
39	.000 188	.000 583	.001 220	.002 660	.002 338	39
40	.000 171	.000 528	.001 107	.002 418	.002 117	40

10%

SINKING FUND FACTORS
(Periodic Payment to Grow to $1)

Base: 1.008 333   1.025 000   1.050 000   1.100 000   1.105 156

Frequency of Payments and of Conversions

Months	Monthly	Quarterly	Semiannual	Annual	Annual Payment Daily Conversion	Months
1	1.000 000	—	—	—	—	1
2	.497 925	—	—	—	—	2
3	.330 571	1.000 000	—	—	—	3
4	.246 897	—	—	—	—	4
5	.196 694	—	—	—	—	5
6	.163 228	.493 827	1.000 000	—	—	6
7	.139 325	—	—	—	—	7
8	.121 400	—	—	—	—	8
9	.107 459	.325 137	—	—	—	9
10	.096 307	—	—	—	—	10
11	.087 184	—	—	—	—	11

Years						Years
1	.079 583	.240 818	.487 805	1.000 000	1.000 000	1
2	.037 812	.114 467	.232 012	.476 190	.475 024	2
3	.023 934	.072 487	.147 017	.302 115	.300 614	3
4	.017 029	.051 599	.104 722	.215 471	.213 843	4
5	.012 914	.039 147	.079 505	.163 797	.162 125	5
6	.010 193	.030 913	.062 825	.129 607	.127 932	6
7	.008 268	.025 088	.051 024	.105 405	.103 749	7
8	.006 841	.020 768	.042 270	.087 444	.085 821	8
9	.005 745	.017 452	.035 546	.073 641	.072 059	9
10	.004 882	.014 836	.030 243	.062 745	.061 212	10
11	.004 187	.012 730	.025 971	.053 963	.052 481	11
12	.003 617	.011 006	.022 471	.046 763	.045 334	12
13	.003 145	.009 574	.019 564	.040 779	.039 404	13
14	.002 749	.008 372	.017 123	.035 746	.034 427	14
15	.002 413	.007 353	.015 051	.031 474	.030 211	15
16	.002 126	.006 482	.013 280	.027 817	.026 609	16
17	.001 879	.005 733	.011 755	.024 664	.023 511	17
18	.001 665	.005 084	.010 434	.021 930	.020 831	18
19	.001 479	.004 520	.009 284	.019 547	.018 500	19
20	.001 317	.004 026	.008 278	.017 460	.016 464	20
21	.001 174	.003 593	.007 395	.015 624	.014 679	21
22	.001 049	.003 212	.006 616	.014 005	.013 108	22
23	.000 938	.002 875	.005 928	.012 572	.011 722	23
24	.000 841	.002 577	.005 318	.011 300	.010 495	24
25	.000 754	.002 312	.004 777	.010 168	.009 407	25
26	.000 676	.002 076	.004 294	.009 159	.008 440	26
27	.000 608	.001 867	.003 864	.008 258	.007 579	27
28	.000 546	.001 679	.003 480	.007 451	.006 811	28
29	.000 491	.001 512	.003 136	.006 728	.006 126	29
30	.000 442	.001 362	.002 828	.006 079	.005 512	30
31	.000 398	.001 227	.002 552	.005 496	.004 963	31
32	.000 359	.001 107	.002 304	.004 972	.004 471	32
33	.000 324	.000 999	.002 081	.004 499	.004 029	33
34	.000 292	.000 901	.001 880	.004 074	.003 632	34
35	.000 263	.000 814	.001 699	.003 690	.003 276	35
36	.000 238	.000 735	.001 536	.003 343	.002 955	36
37	.000 215	.000 664	.001 390	.003 030	.002 667	37
38	.000 194	.000 600	.001 257	.002 747	.002 408	38
39	.000 175	.000 542	.001 138	.002 491	.002 174	39
40	.000 158	.000 490	.001 030	.002 259	.001 963	40

SINKING FUND FACTORS

(Periodic Payment to Grow to $1)

10¼%

Base:	1.008 542	1.025 625	1.051 250	1.102 500	1.107 921	

Frequency of Payments and of Conversions

Months	Monthly	Quarterly	Semiannual	Annual	Annual Payment Daily Conversion	Months
1	1.000 000	—	—	—	—	1
2	.497 874	—	—	—	—	2
3	.330 502	1.000 000	—	—	—	3
4	.246 820	—	—	—	—	4
5	.196 612	—	—	—	—	5
6	.163 143	.493 675	1.000 000	—	—	6
7	.139 238	—	—	—	—	7
8	.121 311	—	—	—	—	8
9	.107 369	.324 936	—	—	—	9
10	.096 216	—	—	—	—	10
11	.087 093	—	—	—	—	11

Years						Years
1	.079 491	.240 593	.487 508	1.000 000	1.000 000	1
2	.037 719	.114 214	.231 581	.475 624	.474 401	2
3	.023 843	.072 231	.146 556	.301 386	.299 813	3
4	.016 941	.051 347	.104 255	.214 680	.212 976	4
5	.012 829	.038 901	.079 042	.162 984	.161 236	5
6	.010 110	.030 675	.062 372	.128 792	.127 042	6
7	.008 189	.024 858	.050 583	.104 599	.102 871	7
8	.006 765	.020 547	.041 843	.086 653	.084 962	8
9	.005 673	.017 238	.035 134	.072 870	.071 224	9
10	.004 812	.014 632	.029 845	.061 997	.060 403	10
11	.004 120	.012 534	.025 589	.053 240	.051 700	11
12	.003 554	.010 819	.022 105	.046 065	.044 584	12
13	.003 085	.009 395	.019 214	.040 107	.038 684	13
14	.002 691	.008 202	.016 787	.035 101	.033 738	14
15	.002 358	.007 191	.014 731	.030 855	.029 552	15
16	.002 074	.006 328	.012 975	.027 225	.025 980	16
17	.001 829	.005 586	.011 465	.024 099	.022 912	17
18	.001 618	.004 944	.010 158	.021 391	.020 261	18
19	.001 435	.004 387	.009 022	.019 033	.017 959	19
20	.001 275	.003 900	.008 029	.016 970	.015 951	20
21	.001 135	.003 474	.007 159	.015 159	.014 193	21
22	.001 012	.003 099	.006 393	.013 563	.012 649	22
23	.000 903	.002 769	.005 717	.012 153	.011 288	23
24	.000 807	.002 476	.005 119	.010 903	.010 085	24
25	.000 722	.002 217	.004 588	.009 792	.009 021	25
26	.000 647	.001 987	.004 117	.008 804	.008 076	26
27	.000 580	.001 783	.003 697	.007 922	.007 237	27
28	.000 520	.001 600	.003 322	.007 134	.006 490	28
29	.000 467	.001 438	.002 988	.006 429	.005 823	29
30	.000 419	.001 292	.002 689	.005 798	.005 229	30
31	.000 377	.001 162	.002 421	.005 231	.004 697	31
32	.000 339	.001 046	.002 181	.004 722	.004 222	32
33	.000 305	.000 942	.001 965	.004 265	.003 796	33
34	.000 274	.000 848	.001 772	.003 854	.003 415	34
35	.000 247	.000 764	.001 598	.003 483	.003 072	35
36	.000 222	.000 688	.001 442	.003 149	.002 766	36
37	.000 200	.000 621	.001 301	.002 849	.002 490	37
38	.000 180	.000 559	.001 175	.002 577	.002 242	38
39	.000 163	.000 505	.001 061	.002 332	.002 020	39
40	.000 147	.000 455	.000 958	.002 111	.001 820	40

10½%

SINKING FUND FACTORS
(Periodic Payment to Grow to $1)

Base:

	1.008 750	1.026 250	1.052 500	1.105 000	1.110 694	

Frequency of Payments and of Conversions

Months	Monthly	Quarterly	Semiannual	Annual	Annual Payment Daily Conversion	Months
1	1.000 000	—	—	—	—	1
2	.497 822	—	—	—	—	2
3	.330 434	1.000 000	—	—	—	3
4	.246 743	—	—	—	—	4
5	.196 530	—	—	—	—	5
6	.163 058	.493 523	1.000 000	—	—	6
7	.139 151	—	—	—	—	7
8	.121 222	—	—	—	—	8
9	.107 279	.324 734	—	—	—	9
10	.096 125	—	—	—	—	10
11	.087 001	—	—	—	—	11

Years						Years
1	.079 399	.240 369	.487 211	1.000 000	1.000 000	1
2	.037 626	.113 962	.231 151	.475 059	.473 778	2
3	.023 752	.071 976	.146 095	.300 659	.299 013	3
4	.016 853	.051 096	.103 789	.213 892	.212 110	4
5	.012 744	.038 657	.078 582	.162 175	.160 349	5
6	.010 029	.030 438	.061 922	.127 982	.126 155	6
7	.008 111	.024 629	.050 145	.103 799	.101 997	7
8	.006 690	.020 327	.041 419	.085 869	.084 108	8
9	.005 601	.017 027	.034 725	.072 106	.070 395	9
10	.004 743	.014 429	.029 452	.061 257	.059 602	10
11	.004 054	.012 341	.025 212	.052 525	.050 929	11
12	.003 491	.010 634	.021 743	.045 377	.043 843	12
13	.003 025	.009 219	.018 868	.039 445	.037 975	13
14	.002 634	.008 034	.016 457	.034 467	.033 060	14
15	.002 304	.007 031	.014 417	.030 248	.028 904	15
16	.002 022	.006 176	.012 676	.026 644	.025 364	16
17	.001 781	.005 442	.011 180	.023 545	.022 326	17
18	.001 572	.004 808	.009 888	.020 863	.019 705	18
19	.001 391	.004 258	.008 765	.018 531	.017 432	19
20	.001 234	.003 778	.007 786	.016 493	.015 452	20
21	.001 096	.003 359	.006 929	.014 707	.013 721	21
22	.000 975	.002 990	.006 176	.013 134	.012 203	22
23	.000 869	.002 666	.005 512	.011 747	.010 867	23
24	.000 775	.002 380	.004 925	.010 519	.009 690	24
25	.000 692	.002 126	.004 406	.009 429	.008 648	25
26	.000 618	.001 902	.003 945	.008 461	.007 726	26
27	.000 553	.001 702	.003 536	.007 599	.006 908	27
28	.000 495	.001 525	.003 171	.006 830	.006 181	28
29	.000 443	.001 367	.002 846	.006 143	.005 534	29
30	.000 397	.001 226	.002 555	.005 528	.004 958	30
31	.000 356	.001 100	.002 296	.004 978	.004 444	31
32	.000 320	.000 988	.002 064	.004 485	.003 985	32
33	.000 287	.000 887	.001 856	.004 042	.003 575	33
34	.000 258	.000 797	.001 670	.003 645	.003 209	34
35	.000 231	.000 717	.001 503	.003 288	.002 881	35
36	.000 208	.000 644	.001 353	.002 967	.002 587	36
37	.000 187	.000 580	.001 218	.002 677	.002 324	37
38	.000 168	.000 521	.001 097	.002 417	.002 088	38
39	.000 151	.000 469	.000 988	.002 183	.001 876	39
40	.000 136	.000 422	.000 891	.001 971	.001 686	40

SINKING FUND FACTORS

(Periodic Payment to Grow to $1)

10¾%

Base:	1.008 958	1.026 875	1.053 750	1.107 500	1.113 473	

Frequency of Payments and of Conversions

Months	Monthly	Quarterly	Semiannual	Annual	Annual Payment Daily Conversion	Months
1	1.000 000	—	—	—	—	1
2	.497 770	—	—	—	—	2
3	.330 365	1.000 000	—	—	—	3
4	.246 666	—	—	—	—	4
5	.196 449	—	—	—	—	5
6	.162 973	.493 370	1.000 000	—	—	6
7	.139 064	—	—	—	—	7
8	.121 133	—	—	—	—	8
9	.107 189	.324 533	—	—	—	9
10	.096 035	—	—	—	—	10
11	.086 910	—	—	—	—	11

Years						Years
1	.079 307	.240 145	.486 914	1.000 000	1.000 000	1
2	.037 534	.113 710	.230 722	.474 496	.473 155	2
3	.023 662	.071 722	.145 636	.299 935	.298 214	3
4	.016 766	.050 846	.103 326	.213 108	.211 247	4
5	.012 660	.038 414	.078 123	.161 371	.159 465	5
6	.009 948	.030 203	.061 474	.127 177	.125 273	6
7	.008 033	.024 403	.049 711	.103 004	.101 129	7
8	.006 616	.020 109	.040 999	.085 092	.083 261	8
9	.005 530	.016 818	.034 321	.071 350	.069 574	9
10	.004 676	.014 229	.029 064	.060 525	.058 809	10
11	.003 990	.012 150	.024 839	.051 819	.050 166	11
12	.003 430	.010 451	.021 387	.044 697	.043 111	12
13	.002 966	.009 045	.018 528	.038 793	.037 275	13
14	.002 579	.007 868	.016 133	.033 842	.032 392	14
15	.002 251	.006 874	.014 108	.029 651	.028 268	15
16	.001 972	.006 027	.012 383	.026 075	.024 759	16
17	.001 733	.005 301	.010 902	.023 003	.021 752	17
18	.001 528	.004 674	.009 624	.020 347	.019 161	18
19	.001 349	.004 132	.008 516	.018 041	.016 917	19
20	.001 194	.003 659	.007 550	.016 028	.014 966	20
21	.001 058	.003 246	.006 706	.014 266	.013 262	21
22	.000 940	.002 885	.005 965	.012 718	.011 771	22
23	.000 835	.002 567	.005 314	.011 353	.010 461	23
24	.000 744	.002 286	.004 739	.010 147	.009 307	24
25	.000 663	.002 039	.004 231	.009 079	.008 289	25
26	.000 591	.001 820	.003 780	.008 131	.007 390	26
27	.000 527	.001 625	.003 381	.007 288	.006 593	27
28	.000 471	.001 453	.003 026	.006 538	.005 886	28
29	.000 421	.001 300	.002 710	.005 868	.005 258	29
30	.000 376	.001 163	.002 428	.005 271	.004 700	30
31	.000 337	.001 042	.002 177	.004 737	.004 204	31
32	.000 301	.000 933	.001 953	.004 259	.003 761	32
33	.000 270	.000 836	.001 752	.003 831	.003 366	33
34	.000 242	.000 750	.001 573	.003 447	.003 014	34
35	.000 217	.000 672	.001 413	.003 103	.002 700	35
36	.000 194	.000 603	.001 269	.002 794	.002 419	36
37	.000 174	.000 541	.001 140	.002 516	.002 168	37
38	.000 156	.000 486	.001 025	.002 267	.001 943	38
39	.000 140	.000 436	.000 921	.002 043	.001 742	39
40	.000 126	.000 392	.000 828	.001 841	.001 562	40

11%

SINKING FUND FACTORS
(Periodic Payment to Grow to $1)

Base: 1.009 167   1.027 500   1.055 000   1.110 000   1.116 259

Frequency of Payments and of Conversions

Months	Monthly	Quarterly	Semiannual	Annual	Annual Payment Daily Conversion	Months
1	1.000 000	—	—	—	—	1
2	.497 719	—	—	—	—	2
3	.330 296	1.000 000	—	—	—	3
4	.246 589	—	—	—	—	4
5	.196 367	—	—	—	—	5
6	.162 888	.493 218	1.000 000	—	—	6
7	.138 976	—	—	—	—	7
8	.121 044	—	—	—	—	8
9	.107 099	.324 332	—	—	—	9
10	.095 944	—	—	—	—	10
11	.086 818	—	—	—	—	11

Years						Years
1	.079 215	.239 921	.486 618	1.000 000	1.000 000	1
2	.037 441	.113 458	.230 294	.473 934	.472 532	2
3	.023 572	.071 469	.145 179	.299 213	.297 416	3
4	.016 679	.050 597	.102 864	.212 326	.210 385	4
5	.012 576	.038 172	.077 668	.160 570	.158 584	5
6	.009 867	.029 969	.061 029	.126 377	.124 395	6
7	.007 956	.024 177	.049 279	.102 215	.100 266	7
8	.006 542	.019 893	.040 583	.084 321	.082 420	8
9	.005 459	.016 611	.033 920	.070 602	.068 759	9
10	.004 608	.014 032	.028 679	.059 801	.058 023	10
11	.003 926	.011 961	.024 471	.051 121	.049 412	11
12	.003 369	.010 272	.021 036	.044 027	.042 389	12
13	.002 909	.008 874	.018 193	.038 151	.036 585	13
14	.002 524	.007 706	.015 814	.033 228	.031 735	14
15	.002 199	.006 720	.013 805	.029 065	.027 643	15
16	.001 923	.005 881	.012 095	.025 517	.024 166	16
17	.001 687	.005 163	.010 630	.022 471	.021 190	17
18	.001 484	.004 544	.009 366	.019 843	.018 630	18
19	.001 308	.004 009	.008 272	.017 563	.016 415	19
20	.001 155	.003 543	.007 320	.015 576	.014 493	20
21	.001 022	.003 137	.006 489	.013 838	.012 817	21
22	.000 906	.002 782	.005 761	.012 313	.011 352	22
23	.000 803	.002 470	.005 122	.010 971	.010 067	23
24	.000 714	.002 196	.004 559	.009 787	.008 938	24
25	.000 634	.001 954	.004 061	.008 740	.007 943	25
26	.000 565	.001 741	.003 622	.007 813	.007 066	26
27	.000 503	.001 551	.003 232	.006 989	.006 290	27
28	.000 448	.001 384	.002 887	.006 257	.005 603	28
29	.000 400	.001 235	.002 580	.005 605	.004 995	29
30	.000 357	.001 103	.002 307	.005 025	.004 455	30
31	.000 318	.000 986	.002 064	.004 506	.003 975	31
32	.000 284	.000 881	.001 847	.004 043	.003 548	32
33	.000 254	.000 788	.001 654	.003 629	.003 169	33
34	.000 227	.000 705	.001 482	.003 259	.002 830	34
35	.000 203	.000 631	.001 328	.002 927	.002 529	35
36	.000 181	.000 564	.001 190	.002 630	.002 261	36
37	.000 162	.000 505	.001 067	.002 364	.002 021	37
38	.000 145	.000 452	.000 956	.002 125	.001 807	38
39	.000 130	.000 405·	.000 858	.001 911	.001 617	39
40	.000 116	.000 363	.000 769	.001 719	.001 446	40

SINKING FUND FACTORS
(Periodic Payment to Grow to $1)

11¼%

Base: 1.009 375   1.028 125   1.056 250   1.112 500   1.119 053

<u>**Frequency of Payments and of Conversions**</u>

Months	Monthly	Quarterly	Semiannual	Annual	Annual Payment Daily Conversion	Months
1	1.000 000	—	—	—	—	1
2	.497 667	—	—	—	—	2
3	.330 228	1.000 000	—	—	—	3
4	.246 512	—	—	—	—	4
5	.196 285	—	—	—	—	5
6	.162 803	.493 066	1.000 000	—	—	6
7	.138 889	—	—	—	—	7
8	.120 956	—	—	—	—	8
9	.107 009	.324 132	—	—	—	9
10	.095 853	—	—	—	—	10
11	.086 727	—	—	—	—	11

Years						Years
1	.079 123	.239 697	.486 322	1.000 000	1.000 000	1
2	.037 349	.113 207	.229 867	.473 373	.471 909	2
3	.023 482	.071 216	.144 723	.298 494	.296 619	3
4	.016 592	.050 349	.102 404	.211 548	.209 525	4
5	.012 492	.037 931	.077 214	.159 774	.157 706	5
6	.009 787	.029 736	.060 587	.125 581	.123 521	6
7	.007 879	.023 954	.048 851	.101 432	.099 407	7
8	.006 469	.019 678	.040 170	.083 557	.081 584	8
9	.005 389	.016 406	.033 523	.069 860	.067 951	9
10	.004 542	.013 836	.028 299	.059 085	.057 246	10
11	.003 863	.011 775	.024 108	.050 432	.048 666	11
12	.003 309	.010 094	.020 689	.043 366	.041 676	12
13	.002 852	.008 706	.017 863	.037 518	.035 905	13
14	.002 470	.007 547	.015 501	.032 624	.031 088	14
15	.002 148	.006 569	.013 508	.028 490	.027 030	15
16	.001 875	.005 738	.011 814	.024 969	.023 584	16
17	.001 642	.005 028	.010 363	.021 952	.020 640	17
18	.001 441	.004 417	.009 115	.019 350	.018 110	18
19	.001 268	.003 889	.008 035	.017 096	.015 926	19
20	.001 118	.003 431	.007 097	.015 134	.014 032	20
21	.000 987	.003 032	.006 279	.013 421	.012 384	21
22	.000 872	.002 683	.005 563	.011 920	.010 945	22
23	.000 772	.002 377	.004 936	.010 601	.009 686	23
24	.000 685	.002 109	.004 384	.009 439	.008 581	24
25	.000 607	.001 873	.003 898	.008 413	.007 610	25
26	.000 539	.001 665	.003 469	.007 506	.006 754	26
27	.000 479	.001 481	.003 090	.006 702	.006 000	27
28	.000 426	.001 318	.002 754	.005 988	.005 333	28
29	.000 379	.001 174	.002 456	.005 354	.004 743	29
30	.000 338	.001 046	.002 191	.004 789	.004 220	30
31	.000 301	.000 932	.001 956	.004 286	.003 757	31
32	.000 268	.000 832	.001 747	.003 838	.003 346	32
33	.000 239	.000 742	.001 561	.003 438	.002 981	33
34	.000 213	.000 662	.001 395	.003 081	.002 657	34
35	.000 190	.000 591	.001 247	.002 762	.002 369	35
36	.000 169	.000 528	.001 115	.002 476	.002 112	36
37	.000 151	.000 472	.000 998	.002 221	.001 884	37
38	.000 135	.000 421	.000 893	.001 992	.001 681	38
39	.000 120	.000 376	.000 799	.001 788	.001 500	39
40	.000 108	.000 336	.000 715	.001 604	.001 338	40

11½%

Base: 1.009 583   1.028 750   1.057 500   1.115 000   1.121 853

Frequency of Payments and of Conversions

Months	Monthly	Quarterly	Semiannual	Annual	Annual Payment Daily Conversion	Months
1	1.000 000	—	—	—	—	1
2	.497 616	—	—	—	—	2
3	.330 159	1.000 000	—	—	—	3
4	.246 435	—	—	—	—	4
5	.196 203	—	—	—	—	5
6	.162 718	.492 914	1.000 000	—	—	6
7	.138 802	—	—	—	—	7
8	.120 867	—	—	—	—	8
9	.106 920	.323 931	—	—	—	9
10	.095 763	—	—	—	—	10
11	.086 636	—	—	—	—	11

Years	Monthly	Quarterly	Semiannual	Annual	Annual Payment Daily Conversion	Years
1	.079 032	.239 473	.486 027	1.000 000	1.000 000	1
2	.037 257	.112 956	.229 441	.472 813	.471 286	2
3	.023 393	.070 964	.144 268	.297 776	.295 822	3
4	.016 506	.050 102	.101 946	.210 774	.208 667	4
5	.012 409	.037 691	.076 763	.158 982	.156 831	5
6	.009 708	.029 505	.060 148	.124 791	.122 651	6
7	.007 803	.023 732	.048 426	.100 655	.098 554	7
8	.006 396	.019 466	.039 760	.082 799	.080 755	8
9	.005 320	.016 204	.033 130	.069 126	.067 150	9
10	.004 476	.013 643	.027 923	.058 377	.056 476	10
11	.003 800	.011 591	.023 749	.049 751	.047 929	11
12	.003 250	.009 920	.020 348	.042 714	.040 972	12
13	.002 796	.008 541	.017 539	.036 895	.035 235	13
14	.002 417	.007 390	.015 193	.032 030	.030 452	14
15	.002 099	.006 421	.013 216	.027 924	.026 427	15
16	.001 828	.005 599	.011 538	.024 432	.023 014	16
17	.001 598	.004 896	.010 103	.021 443	.020 102	17
18	.001 400	.004 293	.008 869	.018 868	.017 603	18
19	.001 229	.003 773	.007 803	.016 641	.015 449	19
20	.001 081	.003 321	.006 879	.014 705	.013 584	20
21	.000 952	.002 929	.006 074	.013 016	.011 963	21
22	.000 840	.002 587	.005 372	.011 539	.010 551	22
23	.000 742	.002 288	.004 756	.010 243	.009 318	23
24	.000 657	.002 025	.004 216	.009 103	.008 237	24
25	.000 581	.001 795	.003 741	.008 098	.007 289	25
26	.000 515	.001 592	.003 323	.007 210	.006 455	26
27	.000 457	.001 413	.002 953	.006 425	.005 721	27
28	.000 405	.001 255	.002 626	.005 730	.005 074	28
29	.000 360	.001 115	.002 337	.005 112	.004 502	29
30	.000 320	.000 991	.002 081	.004 564	.003 997	30
31	.000 284	.000 882	.001 854	.004 077	.003 551	31
32	.000 252	.000 785	.001 652	.003 643	.003 155	32
33	.000 225	.000 698	.001 473	.003 257	.002 804	33
34	.000 200	.000 622	.001 313	.002 912	.002 494	34
35	.000 178	.000 554	.001 172	.002 605	.002 218	35
36	.000 158	.000 494	.001 045	.002 331	.001 973	36
37	.000 141	.000 440	.000 933	.002 086	.001 756	37
38	.000 125	.000 392	.000 833	.001 867	.001 562	38
39	.000 112	.000 350	.000 744	.001 672	.001 391	39
40	.000 099	.000 312	.000 664	.001 497	.001 238	40

11¾%

(Periodic Payment to Grow to $1)

Base: 1.009 792 1.029 375 1.058 750 1.117 500 1.124 660

Frequency of Payments and of Conversions

Months	Monthly	Quarterly	Semiannual	Annual	Annual Payment Daily Conversion	Months
1	1.000 000	—	—	—	—	1
2	.497 564	—	—	—	—	2
3	.330 091	1.000 000	—	—	—	3
4	.246 358	—	—	—	—	4
5	.196 121	—	—	—	—	5
6	.162 633	.492 763	1.000 000	—	—	6
7	.138 715	—	—	—	—	7
8	.120 779	—	—	—	—	8
9	.106 830	.323 731	—	—	—	9
10	.095 672	—	—	—	—	10
11	.086 545	—	—	—	—	11

Years						Years
1	.078 940	.239 250	.485 732	1.000 000	1.000 000	1
2	.037 165	.112 706	.229 016	.472 255	.470 664	2
3	.023 303	.070 713	.143 815	.297 062	.295 027	3
4	.016 420	.049 856	.101 490	.210 003	.207 811	4
5	.012 327	.037 453	.076 314	.158 194	.155 959	5
6	.009 629	.029 276	.059 711	.124 006	.121 784	6
7	.007 728	.023 512	.048 004	.099 884	.097 705	7
8	.006 324	.019 255	.039 354	.082 048	.079 931	8
9	.005 252	.016 003	.032 742	.068 399	.066 356	9
10	.004 411	.013 451	.027 552	.057 677	.055 713	10
11	.003 739	.011 409	.023 395	.049 079	.047 200	11
12	.003 192	.009 747	.020 011	.042 071	.040 278	12
13	.002 741	.008 378	.017 219	.036 282	.034 575	13
14	.002 365	.007 236	.014 890	.031 446	.029 826	14
15	.002 050	.006 276	.012 930	.027 369	.025 835	15
16	.001 782	.005 462	.011 267	.023 906	.022 455	16
17	.001 554	.004 767	.009 848	.020 944	.019 575	17
18	.001 359	.004 172	.008 629	.018 397	.017 108	18
19	.001 191	.003 659	.007 578	.016 196	.014 984	19
20	.001 045	.003 215	.006 667	.014 286	.013 148	20
21	.000 919	.002 830	.005 876	.012 623	.011 555	21
22	.000 809	.002 494	.005 186	.011 169	.010 170	22
23	.000 714	.002 201	.004 583	.009 896	.008 962	23
24	.000 630	.001 944	.004 054	.008 778	.007 905	24
25	.000 556	.001 719	.003 590	.007 794	.006 980	25
26	.000 492	.001 521	.003 182	.006 926	.006 168	26
27	.000 435	.001 347	.002 822	.006 159	.005 454	27
28	.000 385	.001 194	.002 504	.005 482	.004 826	28
29	.000 341	.001 059	.002 224	.004 881	.004 273	29
30	.000 302	.000 939	.001 976	.004 349	.003 785	30
31	.000 268	.000 834	.001 756	.003 877	.003 354	31
32	.000 238	.000 740	.001 562	.003 457	.002 974	32
33	.000 211	.000 657	.001 389	.003 084	.002 637	33
34	.000 187	.000 584	.001 236	.002 752	.002 339	34
35	.000 166	.000 519	.001 100	.002 457	.002 076	35
36	.000 148	.000 461	.000 980	.002 194	.001 842	36
37	.000 131	.000 410	.000 872	.001 959	.001 635	37
38	.000 116	.000 365	.000 777	.001 750	.001 452	38
39	.000 104	.000 325	.000 692	.001 564	.001 289	39
40	.000 092	.000 289	.000 617	.001 397	.001 145	40

12% SINKING FUND FACTORS
(Periodic Payment to Grow to $1)

Base:	1.010 000	1.030 000	1.060 000	1.120 000	1.127 474	

Frequency of Payments and of Conversions

Months	Monthly	Quarterly	Semiannual	Annual	Annual Payment Daily Conversion	Months
1	1.000 000	—	—	—	—	1
2	.497 512	—	—	—	—	2
3	.330 022	1.000 000	—	—	—	3
4	.246 281	—	—	—	—	4
5	.196 040	—	—	—	—	5
6	.162 548	.492 611	1.000 000	—	—	6
7	.138 628	—	—	—	—	7
8	.120 690	—	—	—	—	8
9	.106 740	.323 530	—	—	—	9
10	.095 582	—	—	—	—	10
11	.086 454	—	—	—	—	11

Years						Years
1	.078 849	.239 027	.485 437	1.000 000	1.000 000	1
2	.037 073	.112 456	.228 591	.471 698	.470 041	2
3	.023 214	.070 462	.143 363	.296 349	.294 233	3
4	.016 334	.049 611	.101 036	.209 234	.206 957	4
5	.012 244	.037 216	.075 868	.157 410	.155 090	5
6	.009 550	.029 047	.059 277	.123 226	.120 922	6
7	.007 653	.023 293	.047 585	.099 118	.096 862	7
8	.006 253	.019 047	.038 952	.081 303	.079 114	8
9	.005 184	.015 804	.032 357	.067 679	.065 568	9
10	.004 347	.013 262	.027 185	.056 984	.054 959	10
11	.003 678	.011 230	.023 046	.048 415	.046 479	11
12	.003 134	.009 578	.019 679	.041 437	.039 592	12
13	.002 687	.008 217	.016 904	.035 677	.033 925	13
14	.002 314	.007 084	.014 593	.030 871	.029 210	14
15	.002 002	.006 133	.012 649	.026 824	.025 253	15
16	.001 737	.005 328	.011 002	.023 390	.021 907	16
17	.001 512	.004 642	.009 598	.020 457	.019 060	17
18	.001 320	.004 054	.008 395	.017 937	.016 624	18
19	.001 154	.003 548	.007 358	.015 763	.014 530	19
20	.001 011	.003 112	.006 462	.013 879	.012 724	20
21	.000 887	.002 733	.005 683	.012 240	.011 159	21
22	.000 779	.002 404	.005 006	.010 811	.009 800	22
23	.000 686	.002 117	.004 415	.009 560	.008 617	23
24	.000 604	.001 866	.003 898	.008 463	.007 585	24
25	.000 532	.001 647	.003 444	.007 500	.006 683	25
26	.000 470	.001 454	.003 046	.006 652	.005 892	26
27	.000 414	.001 285	.002 696	.005 904	.005 199	27
28	.000 366	.001 136	.002 388	.005 244	.004 590	28
29	.000 324	.001 005	.002 116	.004 660	.004 054	29
30	.000 286	.000 890	.001 876	.004 144	.003 583	30
31	.000 253	.000 788	.001 664	.003 686	.003 168	31
32	.000 224	.000 698	.001 476	.003 280	.002 802	32
33	.000 198	.000 619	.001 310	.002 920	.002 479	33
34	.000 176	.000 548	.001 163	.002 601	.002 194	34
35	.000 155	.000 486	.001 033	.002 317	.001 942	35
36	.000 138	.000 431	.000 918	.002 064	.001 719	36
37	.000 122	.000 383	.000 815	.001 840	.001 523	37
38	.000 108	.000 339	.000 725	.001 640	.001 349	38
39	.000 096	.000 301	.000 644	.001 462	.001 195	39
40	.000 085	.000 267	.000 573	.001 304	.001 059	40

SINKING FUND FACTORS

(Periodic Payment to Grow to $1)

12½%

Base: 1.010 417   1.031 250   1.062 500   1.125 000   1.133 124

Frequency of Payments and of Conversions

Months	Monthly	Quarterly	Semiannual	Annual	Annual Payment Daily Conversion	Months
1	1.000 000	—	—	—	—	1
2	.497 409	—	—	—	—	2
3	.329 885	1.000 000	—	—	—	3
4	.246 127	—	—	—	—	4
5	.195 877	—	—	—	—	5
6	162 379	.492 308	1.000 000	—	—	6
7	.138 455	—	—	—	—	7
8	.120 514	—	—	—	—	8
9	.106 561	.323 130	—	—	—	9
10	.095 402	—	—	—	—	10
11	.086 272	—	—	—	—	11

Years						Years
1	.078 666	.238 582	.484 848	1.000 000	1.000 000	1
2	.036 891	.111 959	.227 745	.470 588	.468 796	2
3	.023 037	.069 963	.142 463	.294 931	.292 646	3
4	.016 163	.049 124	.100 133	.207 708	.205 255	4
5	.012 081	.036 745	.074 982	.155 854	.153 361	5
6	.009 395	.028 595	.058 417	.121 680	.119 209	6
7	.007 505	.022 861	.046 757	.097 603	.095 190	7
8	.006 112	.018 635	.038 158	.079 832	.077 496	8
9	.005 051	.015 412	.031 598	.066 260	.064 014	9
10	.004 221	.012 891	.026 462	.055 622	.053 472	10
11	.003 559	.010 878	.022 360	.047 112	.045 064	11
12	.003 022	.009 246	.019 029	.040 194	.038 248	12
13	.002 581	.007 904	.016 290	.034 496	.032 653	13
14	.002 215	.006 790	.014 013	.029 751	.028 009	14
15	.001 909	.005 856	.012 103	.025 764	.024 122	15
16	.001 650	.005 068	.010 489	.022 388	.020 845	16
17	.001 431	.004 398	.009 117	.019 512	.018 063	17
18	.001 243	.003 827	.007 943	.017 049	.015 691	18
19	.001 083	.003 336	.006 936	.014 928	.013 659	19
20	.000 945	.002 914	.006 067	.013 096	.011 910	20
21	.000 826	.002 549	.005 315	.011 507	.010 402	21
22	.000 722	.002 232	.004 663	.010 125	.009 096	22
23	.000 633	.001 958	.004 096	.008 919	.007 964	23
24	.000 555	.001 719	.003 601	.007 866	.006 979	24
25	.000 487	.001 510	.003 169	.006 943	.006 121	25
26	.000 428	.001 328	.002 791	.006 134	.005 373	26
27	.000 376	.001 168	.002 460	.005 423	.004 720	27
28	.000 330	.001 028	.002 169	.004 797	.004 148	28
29	.000 291	.000 906	.001 914	.004 246	.003 647	29
30	.000 256	.000 798	.001 689	.003 760	.003 208	30
31	.000 225	.000 704	.001 492	.003 331	.002 823	31
32	.000 198	.000 621	.001 318	.002 952	.002 485	32
33	.000 175	.000 547	.001 165	.002 617	.002 189	33
34	.000 154	.000 483	.001 029	.002 321	.001 928	34
35	.000 136	.000 426	.000 910	.002 059	.001 698	35
36	.000 120	.000 376	.000 805	.001 827	.001 497	36
37	.000 106	.000 332	.000 712	.001 621	.001 319	37
38	.000 093	.000 293	.000 630	.001 439	.001 163	38
39	.000 082	.000 259	.000 557	.001 278	.001 025	39
40	.000 073	.000 229	.000 493	.001 134	.000 904	40

13%

SINKING FUND FACTORS
(Periodic Payment to Grow to $1)

Base: 1.010 833   1.032 500   1.065 000   1.130 000   1.138 802

Frequency of Payments and of Conversions

Months	Monthly	Quarterly	Semiannual	Annual	Annual Payment Daily Conversion	Months
1	1.000 000	—	—	—	—	1
2	.497 306	—	—	—	—	2
3	.329 748	1.000 000	—	—	—	3
4	.245 974	—	—	—	—	4
5	.195 713	—	—	—	—	5
6	.162 210	.492 005	1.000 000	—	—	6
7	.138 281	—	—	—	—	7
8	.120 337	—	—	—	—	8
9	.106 383	.322 731	—	—	—	9
10	.095 221	—	—	—	—	10
11	.086 091	—	—	—	—	11

Years						Years
1	.078 484	.238 137	.484 262	1.000 000	1.000 000	1
2	.036 708	.111 463	.226 903	.469 484	.467 552	2
3	.022 861	.069 467	.141 568	.293 522	.291 064	3
4	.015 994	.048 640	.099 237	.206 194	.203 560	4
5	.011 920	.036 279	.074 105	.154 315	.151 643	5
6	.009 241	.028 149	.057 568	.120 153	.117 512	6
7	.007 359	.022 435	.045 940	.096 111	.093 538	7
8	.005 974	.018 230	.037 378	.078 387	.075 902	8
9	.004 920	.015 028	.030 855	.064 869	.062 486	9
10	.004 098	.012 528	.025 756	.054 290	.052 016	10
11	.003 443	.010 536	.021 691	.045 841	.043 681	11
12	.002 913	.008 923	.018 398	.038 986	.036 940	12
13	.002 479	.007 601	.015 695	.033 350	.031 419	13
14	.002 119	.006 506	.013 453	.028 667	.026 848	14
15	.001 819	.005 590	.011 577	.024 742	.023 033	15
16	.001 567	.004 819	.009 997	.021 426	.019 825	16
17	.001 353	.004 166	.008 656	.018 608	.017 110	17
18	.001 171	.003 610	.007 513	.016 201	.014 803	18
19	.001 016	.003 135	.006 535	.014 134	.012 832	19
20	.000 882	.002 727	.005 694	.012 354	.011 142	20
21	.000 768	.002 376	.004 968	.010 814	.009 689	21
22	.000 669	.002 072	.004 341	.009 479	.008 437	22
23	.000 583	.001 809	.003 797	.008 319	.007 354	23
24	.000 509	.001 582	.003 325	.007 308	.006 416	24
25	.000 445	.001 384	.002 914	.006 426	.005 602	25
26	.000 389	.001 211	.002 556	.005 655	.004 896	26
27	.000 340	.001 061	.002 243	.004 979	.004 280	27
28	.000 298	.000 930	.001 969	.004 387	.003 745	28
29	.000 261	.000 815	.001 730	.003 867	.003 277	29
30	.000 229	.000 715	.001 520	.003 411	.002 870	30
31	.000 200	.000 628	.001 337	.003 009	.002 514	31
32	.000 176	.000 551	.001 176	.002 656	.002 202	32
33	.000 154	.000 484	.001 034	.002 345	.001 930	33
34	.000 135	.000 425	.000 910	.002 071	.001 692	34
35	.000 119	.000 373	.000 801	.001 829	.001 484	35
36	.000 104	.000 328	.000 705	.001 616	.001 301	36
37	.000 091	.000 288	.000 621	.001 428	.001 141	37
38	.000 080	.000 253	.000 547	.001 262	.001 001	38
39	.000 070	.000 223	.000 482	.001 116	.000 878	39
40	.000 062	.000 196	.000 424	.000 986	.000 771	40

(Periodic Payment to Grow to $1)

Base:	1.011 250	1.033 750	1.067 500	1.135 000	1.144 508	

Frequency of Payments and of Conversions

Months	Monthly	Quarterly	Semiannual	Annual	Annual Payment Daily Conversion	Months
1	1.000 000	—	—	—	—	1
2	.497 203	—	—	—	—	2
3	.329 611	1.000 000	—	—	—	3
4	.245 821	—	—	—	—	4
5	.195 550	—	—	—	—	5
6	.162 040	.491 703	1.000 000	—	—	6
7	.138 108	—	—	—	—	7
8	.120 161	—	—	—	—	8
9	.106 204	.322 332	—	—	—	9
10	.095 041	—	—	—	—	10
11	.085 910	—	—	—	—	11

Years						Years
1	.078 302	.237 694	.483 676	1.000 000	1.000 000	1
2	.036 527	.110 969	.226 064	.468 384	.466 307	2
3	.022 685	.068 974	.140 679	.292 122	.289 485	3
4	.015 826	.048 161	.098 349	.204 693	.201 874	4
5	.011 760	.035 818	.073 237	.152 791	.149 938	5
6	.009 089	.027 708	.056 730	.118 646	.115 832	6
7	.007 215	.022 016	.045 137	.094 641	.091 905	7
8	.005 838	.017 832	.036 611	.076 966	.074 332	8
9	.004 792	.014 652	.030 126	.063 505	.060 986	9
10	.003 977	.012 173	.025 067	.052 987	.050 590	10
11	.003 330	.010 202	.021 040	.044 602	.042 331	11
12	.002 807	.008 610	.017 784	.037 811	.035 667	12
13	.002 380	.007 308	.015 119	.032 240	.030 222	13
14	.002 027	.006 231	.012 913	.027 621	.025 727	14
15	.001 733	.005 334	.011 072	.023 757	.021 984	15
16	.001 487	.004 581	.009 525	.020 502	.018 846	16
17	.001 279	.003 945	.008 216	.017 743	.016 200	17
18	.001 102	.003 405	.007 104	.015 392	.013 957	18
19	.000 952	.002 945	.006 155	.013 380	.012 048	19
20	.000 824	.002 551	.005 342	.011 651	.010 417	20
21	.000 714	.002 213	.004 642	.010 161	.009 020	21
22	.000 619	.001 922	.004 040	.008 873	.007 819	22
23	.000 538	.001 671	.003 519	.007 757	.006 786	23
24	.000 467	.001 454	.003 069	.006 788	.005 894	24
25	.000 406	.001 267	.002 678	.005 945	.005 123	25
26	.000 354	.001 104	.002 339	.005 211	.004 457	26
27	.000 308	.000 963	.002 044	.004 570	.003 879	27
28	.000 268	.000 840	.001 787	.004 010	.003 378	28
29	.000 234	.000 734	.001 563	.003 521	.002 942	29
30	.000 204	.000 641	.001 368	.003 092	.002 564	30
31	.000 178	.000 560	.001 197	.002 717	.002 236	31
32	.000 155	.000 489	.001 048	.002 388	.001 949	32
33	.000 136	.000 427	.000 918	.002 100	.001 700	33
34	.000 118	.000 374	.000 804	.001 847	.001 484	34
35	.000 103	.000 327	.000 705	.001 624	.001 295	35
36	.000 090	.000 286	.000 618	.001 429	.001 130	36
37	.000 079	.000 250	.000 541	.001 258	.000 986	37
38	.000 069	.000 219	.000 475	.001 107	.000 861	38
39	.000 060	.000 191	.000 416	.000 974	.000 752	39
40	.000 053	.000 167	.000 365	.000 858	.000 656	40

14%

SINKING FUND FACTORS
(Periodic Payment to Grow to $1)

Base: 1.011 667   1.035 000   1.070 000   1.140 000   1.150 242

Frequency of Payments and of Conversions

Months	Monthly	Quarterly	Semiannual	Annual	Annual Payment Daily Conversion	Months
1	1.000 000	—	—	—	—	1
2	.497 100	—	—	—	—	2
3	.329 475	1.000 000	—	—	—	3
4	.245 667	—	—	—	—	4
5	.195 387	—	—	—	—	5
6	.161 871	.491 400	1.000 000	—	—	6
7	.137 934	—	—	—	—	7
8	.119 985	—	—	—	—	8
9	.106 026	.321 934	—	—	—	9
10	.094 862	—	—	—	—	10
11	.085 729	—	—	—	—	11

Years	Monthly	Quarterly	Semiannual	Annual	Annual Payment Daily Conversion	Years
1	.078 120	.237 251	.483 092	1.000 000	1.000 000	1
2	.036 346	.110 477	.225 228	.467 290	.465 064	2
3	.022 511	.068 484	.139 796	.290 731	.287 911	3
4	.015 660	.047 685	.097 468	.203 205	.200 195	4
5	.011 602	.035 361	.072 378	.151 284	.148 244	5
6	.008 939	.027 273	.055 902	.117 157	.114 167	6
7	.007 073	.021 603	.044 345	.093 192	.090 293	7
8	.005 705	.017 442	.035 858	.075 570	.072 785	8
9	.004 667	.014 284	.029 413	.062 168	.059 512	9
10	.003 860	.011 827	.024 393	.051 714	.049 194	10
11	.003 220	.009 878	.020 406	.043 394	.041 014	11
12	.002 705	.008 306	.017 189	.036 669	.034 429	12
13	.002 284	.007 024	.014 561	.031 164	.029 062	13
14	.001 938	.005 967	.012 392	.026 609	.024 644	14
15	.001 651	.005 089	.010 586	.022 809	.020 975	15
16	.001 410	.004 353	.009 073	.019 615	.017 909	16
17	.001 208	.003 734	.007 797	.016 915	.015 331	17
18	.001 037	.003 210	.006 715	.014 621	.013 153	18
19	.000 892	.002 765	.005 795	.012 663	.011 306	19
20	.000 769	.002 385	.005 009	.010 986	.009 733	20
21	.000 663	.002 060	.004 336	.009 545	.008 391	21
22	.000 573	.001 782	.003 758	.008 303	.007 242	22
23	.000 495	.001 543	.003 260	.007 231	.006 257	23
24	.000 428	.001 337	.002 831	.006 303	.005 410	24
25	.000 371	.001 159	.002 460	.005 498	.004 681	25
26	.000 321	.001 006	.002 139	.004 800	.004 053	26
27	.000 279	.000 873	.001 861	.004 193	.003 512	27
28	.000 242	.000 759	.001 620	.003 664	.003 044	28
29	.000 210	.000 659	.001 411	.003 204	.002 639	29
30	.000 182	.000 573	.001 229	.002 803	.002 289	30
31	.000 158	.000 498	.001 071	.002 453	.001 986	31
32	.000 137	.000 434	.000 934	.002 147	.001 724	32
33	.000 119	.000 377	.000 814	.001 880	.001 496	33
34	.000 104	.000 328	.000 710	.001 646	.001 299	34
35	.000 090	.000 286	.000 620	.001 442	.001 128	35
36	.000 078	.000 249	.000 541	.001 263	.000 980	36
37	.000 068	.000 217	.000 472	.001 107	.000 851	37
38	.000 059	.000 189	.000 412	.000 970	.000 739	38
39	.000 051	.000 164	.000 359	.000 850	.000 642	39
40	.000 045	.000 143	.000 314	.000 745	.000 558	40

324

SINKING FUND FACTORS
(Periodic Payment to Grow to $1)

14½%

Base:	1.012 083	1.036 250	1.072 500	1.145 000	1.156 006	

Frequency of Payments and of Conversions

Months	Monthly	Quarterly	Semiannual	Annual	Annual Payment Daily Conversion	Months
1	1.000 000	—	—	—	—	1
2	.496 997	—	—	—	—	2
3	.329 338	1.000 000	—	—	—	3
4	.245 514	—	—	—	—	4
5	.195 225	—	—	—	—	5
6	.161 702	.491 099	1.000 000	—	—	6
7	.137 761	—	—	—	—	7
8	.119 809	—	—	—	—	8
9	.105 848	.321 537	—	—	—	9
10	.094 682	—	—	—	—	10
11	.085 549	—	—	—	—	11

Years						Years
1	.077 939	.236 809	.482 509	1.000 000	1.000 000	1
2	.036 166	.109 987	.224 396	.466 200	.463 821	2
3	.022 338	.067 997	.138 918	.289 350	.286 340	3
4	.015 495	.047 213	.096 594	.201 729	.198 524	4
5	.011 445	.034 909	.071 527	.149 792	.146 563	5
6	.008 791	.026 843	.055 085	.115 688	.112 518	6
7	.006 934	.021 196	.043 565	.091 766	.088 700	7
8	.005 574	.017 058	.035 118	.074 198	.071 262	8
9	.004 544	.013 924	.028 714	.060 858	.058 066	9
10	.003 745	.011 489	.023 735	.050 469	.047 827	10
11	.003 113	.009 562	.019 788	.042 217	.039 729	11
12	.002 605	.008 012	.016 611	.035 559	.033 226	12
13	.002 192	.006 750	.014 021	.030 121	.027 939	13
14	.001 853	.005 713	.011 890	.025 632	.023 598	14
15	.001 572	.004 853	.010 120	.021 896	.020 005	15
16	.001 337	.004 135	.008 640	.018 764	.017 011	16
17	.001 141	.003 533	.007 396	.016 124	.014 502	17
18	.000 975	.003 025	.006 346	.013 886	.012 389	18
19	.000 835	.002 594	.005 454	.011 982	.010 604	19
20	.000 717	.002 229	.004 696	.010 357	.009 089	20
21	.000 616	.001 917	.004 048	.008 964	.007 801	21
22	.000 529	.001 651	.003 494	.007 768	.006 703	22
23	.000 456	.001 423	.003 018	.006 739	.005 765	23
24	.000 392	.001 228	.002 610	.005 851	.004 962	24
25	.000 338	.001 060	.002 258	.005 084	.004 274	25
26	.000 292	.000 916	.001 955	.004 420	.003 684	26
27	.000 252	.000 792	.001 694	.003 846	.003 177	27
28	.000 217	.000 685	.001 468	.003 348	.002 740	28
29	.000 188	.000 592	.001 273	.002 915	.002 365	29
30	.000 162	.000 512	.001 104	.002 539	.002 042	30
31	.000 140	.000 444	.000 958	.002 213	.001 763	31
32	.000 121	.000 384	.000 832	.001 929	.001 523	32
33	.000 105	.000 333	.000 722	.001 682	.001 316	33
34	.000 091	.000 288	.000 627	.001 467	.001 137	34
35	.000 078	.000 250	.000 544	.001 279	.000 982	35
36	.000 068	.000 216	.000 473	.001 116	.000 849	36
37	.000 059	.000 187	.000 411	.000 974	.000 734	37
38	.000 051	.000 162	.000 357	.000 850	.000 634	38
39	.000 044	.000 141	.000 310	.000 742	.000 549	39
40	.000 038	.000 122	.000 269	.000 647	.000 474	40

15%

SINKING FUND FACTORS
(Periodic Payment to Grow to $1)

Base:	1.012 500	1.037 500	1.075 000	1.150 000	1.161 798	

Frequency of Payments and of Conversions

Months	Monthly	Quarterly	Semiannual	Annual	Annual Payment Daily Conversion	Months
1	1.000 000	—	—	—	—	1
2	.496 894	—	—	—	—	2
3	.329 201	1.000 000	—	—	—	3
4	.245 361	—	—	—	—	4
5	.195 062	—	—	—	—	5
6	.161 534	.490 798	1.000 000	—	—	6
7	.137 589	—	—	—	—	7
8	.119 633	—	—	—	—	8
9	.105 671	.321 140	—	—	—	9
10	.094 503	—	—	—	—	10
11	.085 368	—	—	—	—	11

Years						Years
1	.077 758	.236 369	.481 928	1.000 000	1.000 000	1
2	.035 987	.109 498	.223 568	.465 116	.462 578	2
3	.022 165	.067 512	.138 045	.287 977	.284 773	3
4	.015 331	.046 745	.095 727	.200 265	.196 861	4
5	.011 290	.034 462	.070 686	.148 316	.144 893	5
6	.008 645	.026 419	.054 278	.114 237	.110 886	6
7	.006 797	.020 795	.042 797	.090 360	.087 127	7
8	.005 445	.016 681	.034 391	.072 850	.069 762	8
9	.004 424	.013 571	.028 029	.059 574	.056 645	9
10	.003 633	.011 159	.023 092	.049 252	.046 490	10
11	.003 009	.009 254	.019 187	.041 069	.038 476	11
12	.002 509	.007 726	.016 050	.034 481	.032 056	12
13	.002 103	.006 485	.013 500	.029 110	.026 851	13
14	.001 770	.005 468	.011 405	.024 688	.022 589	14
15	.001 496	.004 627	.009 671	.021 017	.019 073	15
16	.001 268	.003 927	.008 226	.017 948	.016 151	16
17	.001 077	.003 341	.007 015	.015 367	.013 711	17
18	.000 917	.002 849	.005 994	.013 186	.011 664	18
19	.000 782	.002 434	.005 132	.011 336	.009 940	19
20	.000 668	.002 082	.004 400	.009 761	.008 483	20
21	.000 571	.001 783	.003 778	.008 417	.007 249	21
22	.000 489	.001 529	.003 247	.007 266	.006 201	22
23	.000 419	.001 312	.002 794	.006 278	.005 309	23
24	.000 359	.001 127	.002 405	.005 430	.004 549	24
25	.000 308	.000 969	.002 072	.004 699	.003 900	25
26	.000 265	.000 833	.001 787	.004 070	.003 346	26
27	.000 227	.000 717	.001 541	.003 526	.002 871	27
28	.000 195	.000 617	.001 330	.003 057	.002 465	28
29	.000 168	.000 532	.001 148	.002 651	.002 118	29
30	.000 144	.000 458	.000 991	.002 300	.001 819	30
31	.000 124	.000 395	.000 856	.001 996	.001 564	31
32	.000 107	.000 340	.000 740	.001 733	.001 344	32
33	.000 092	.000 293	.000 639	.001 505	.001 155	33
34	.000 079	.000 253	.000 553	.001 307	.000 994	34
35	.000 068	.000 218	.000 478	.001 135	.000 854	35
36	.000 059	.000 188	.000 413	.000 986	.000 735	36
37	.000 050	.000 162	.000 357	.000 857	.000 632	37
38	.000 043	.000 140	.000 309	.000 744	.000 544	38
39	.000 037	.000 121	.000 267	.000 647	.000 468	39
40	.000 032	.000 104	.000 231	.000 562	.000 403	40

SINKING FUND FACTORS   15½%

(Periodic Payment to Grow to $1)

Base: 1.012 917   1.038 750   1.077 500   1.155 000   1.167 619

Frequency of Payments and of Conversions

Months	Monthly	Quarterly	Semiannual	Annual	Annual Payment Daily Conversion	Months
1	1.000 000	—	—	—	—	1
2	.496 792	—	—	—	—	2
3	.329 065	1.000 000	—	—	—	3
4	.245 208	—	—	—	—	4
5	.194 900	—	—	—	—	5
6	.161 365	.490 497	1.000 000	—	—	6
7	.137 416	—	—	—	—	7
8	.119 458	—	—	—	—	8
9	.105 493	.320 744	—	—	—	9
10	.094 324	—	—	—	—	10
11	.085 189	—	—	—	—	11

Years						Years
1	.077 578	.235 929	.481 348	1.000 000	1.000 000	1
2	.035 808	.109 012	.222 742	.464 037	.461 336	2
3	.021 994	.067 031	.137 177	.286 613	.283 210	3
4	.015 168	.046 281	.094 867	.198 814	.195 205	4
5	.011 137	.034 020	.069 853	.146 855	.143 236	5
6	.008 501	.026 000	.053 481	.112 804	.109 269	6
7	.006 662	.020 401	.042 041	.088 976	.085 575	7
8	.005 319	.016 312	.033 678	.071 526	.068 285	8
9	.004 307	.013 225	.027 359	.058 316	.055 251	9
10	.003 524	.010 838	.022 465	.048 063	.045 182	10
11	.002 908	.008 955	.018 602	.039 951	.037 254	11
12	.002 415	.007 449	.015 506	.033 433	.030 919	12
13	.002 017	.006 229	.012 995	.028 132	.025 798	13
14	.001 691	.005 232	.010 938	.023 777	.021 617	14
15	.001 423	.004 410	.009 241	.020 171	.018 177	15
16	.001 201	.003 728	.007 830	.017 165	.015 329	16
17	.001 016	.003 159	.006 651	.014 643	.012 958	17
18	.000 862	.002 683	.005 661	.012 520	.010 976	18
19	.000 732	.002 282	.004 827	.010 723	.009 313	19
20	.000 622	.001 944	.004 122	.009 199	.007 913	20
21	.000 530	.001 658	.003 524	.007 901	.006 731	21
22	.000 451	.001 415	.003 017	.006 795	.005 732	22
23	.000 385	.001 209	.002 584	.005 848	.004 885	23
24	.000 329	.001 034	.002 216	.005 038	.004 166	24
25	.000 281	.000 885	.001 901	.004 343	.003 556	25
26	.000 240	.000 758	.001 632	.003 746	.003 036	26
27	.000 205	.000 649	.001 401	.003 233	.002 593	27
28	.000 175	.000 556	.001 204	.002 791	.002 216	28
29	.000 150	.000 477	.001 035	.002 411	.001 894	29
30	.000 129	.000 409	.000 890	.002 083	.001 620	30
31	.000 110	.000 351	.000 765	.001 800	.001 385	31
32	.000 094	.000 301	.000 658	.001 556	.001 185	32
33	.000 081	.000 258	.000 566	.001 345	.001 014	33
34	.000 069	.000 221	.000 487	.001 164	.000 868	34
35	.000 059	.000 190	.000 419	.001 006	.000 743	35
36	.000 051	.000 163	.000 361	.000 871	.000 636	36
37	.000 043	.000 140	.000 311	.000 753	.000 544	37
38	.000 037	.000 120	.000 267	.000 652	.000 466	38
39	.000 032	.000 103	.000 230	.000 564	.000 399	39
40	.000 027	.000 089	.000 198	.000 488	.000 341	40

16%

SINKING FUND FACTORS
(Periodic Payment to Grow to $1)

Base:	1.013 333	1.040 000	1.080 000	1.160 000	1.173 469	

Frequency of Payments and of Conversions

Months	Monthly	Quarterly	Semiannual	Annual	Annual Payment Daily Conversion	Months
1	1.000 000	—	—	—	—	1
2	.496 689	—	—	—	—	2
3	.328 928	1.000 000	—	—	—	3
4	.245 055	—	—	—	—	4
5	.194 737	—	—	—	—	5
6	.161 197	.490 196	1.000 000	—	—	6
7	.137 244	—	—	—	—	7
8	.119 283	—	—	—	—	8
9	.105 316	.320 349	—	—	—	9
10	.094 146	—	—	—	—	10
11	.085 009	—	—	—	—	11

Years						Years
1	.077 398	.235 490	.480 769	1.000 000	1.000 000	1
2	.035 630	.108 528	.221 921	.462 963	.460 094	2
3	.021 824	.066 552	.136 315	.285 258	.281 651	3
4	.015 007	.045 820	.094 015	.197 375	.193 558	4
5	.010 985	.033 582	.069 029	.145 409	.141 591	5
6	.008 359	.025 587	.052 695	.111 390	.107 669	6
7	.006 529	.020 013	.041 297	.087 613	.084 041	7
8	.005 195	.015 949	.032 977	.070 224	.066 832	8
9	.004 192	.012 887	.026 702	.057 082	.053 883	9
10	.003 418	.010 523	.021 852	.046 901	.043 902	10
11	.002 810	.008 665	.018 032	.038 861	.036 063	11
12	.002 325	.007 181	.014 978	.032 415	.029 816	12
13	.001 934	.005 982	.012 507	.027 184	.024 779	13
14	.001 615	.005 005	.010 489	.022 898	.020 679	14
15	.001 354	.004 202	.008 827	.019 358	.017 317	15
16	.001 138	.003 538	.007 451	.016 414	.014 542	16
17	.000 959	.002 986	.006 304	.013 952	.012 241	17
18	.000 809	.002 525	.005 345	.011 885	.010 324	18
19	.000 684	.002 139	.004 539	.010 142	.008 721	19
20	.000 579	.001 814	.003 860	.008 667	.007 377	20
21	.000 491	.001 541	.003 287	.007 416	.006 247	21
22	.000 417	.001 310	.002 802	.006 353	.005 295	22
23	.000 354	.001 114	.002 390	.005 447	.004 492	23
24	.000 301	.000 949	.002 040	.004 673	.003 814	24
25	.000 256	.000 808	.001 743	.004 013	.003 239	25
26	.000 217	.000 689	.001 490	.003 447	.002 753	26
27	.000 185	.000 587	.001 274	.002 963	.002 340	27
28	.000 157	.000 501	.001 090	.002 548	.001 991	28
29	.000 134	.000 427	.000 932	.002 192	.001 693	29
30	.000 114	.000 365	.000 798	.001 886	.001 441	30
31	.000 097	.000 311	.000 683	.001 623	.001 226	31
32	.000 083	.000 266	.000 585	.001 397	.001 044	32
33	.000 071	.000 227	.000 501	.001 203	.000 889	33
34	.000 060	.000 194	.000 429	.001 036	.000 757	34
35	.000 051	.000 166	.000 368	.000 892	.000 645	35
36	.000 044	.000 142	.000 315	.000 769	.000 549	36
37	.000 037	.000 121	.000 270	.000 662	.000 468	37
38	.000 032	.000 103	.000 231	.000 571	.000 398	38
39	.000 027	.000 088	.000 198	.000 492	.000 339	39
40	.000 023	.000 075	.000 170	.000 424	.000 289	40

328

Base: 1.013 750   1.041 250   1.082 500   1.165 000   1.179 349

Frequency of Payments and of Conversions

Months	Monthly	Quarterly	Semiannual	Annual	Annual Payment Daily Conversion	Months
1	1.000 000	—	—	—	—	1
2	.496 586	—	—	—	—	2
3	.328 792	1.000 000	—	—	—	3
4	.244 902	—	—	—	—	4
5	.194 575	—	—	—	—	5
6	.161 029	.489 896	1.000 000	—	—	6
7	.137 072	—	—	—	—	7
8	.119 108	—	—	—	—	8
9	.105 139	.319 954	—	—	—	9
10	.093 967	—	—	—	—	10
11	.084 830	—	—	—	—	11

Years						Years
1	.077 218	.235 052	.480 192	1.000 000	1.000 000	1
2	.035 452	.108 045	.221 103	.461 894	.458 853	2
3	.021 654	.066 076	.135 459	.283 911	.280 095	3
4	.014 847	.045 363	.093 169	.195 948	.191 919	4
5	.010 835	.033 149	.068 214	.143 979	.139 958	5
6	.008 218	.025 179	.051 919	.109 993	.106 084	6
7	.006 398	.019 631	.040 564	.086 270	.082 528	7
8	.005 074	.015 592	.032 289	.068 946	.065 401	8
9	.004 079	.012 556	.026 059	.055 874	.052 542	9
10	.003 314	.010 217	.021 254	.045 766	.042 651	10
11	.002 714	.008 382	.017 478	.037 799	.034 903	11
12	.002 237	.006 921	.014 466	.031 426	.028 744	12
13	.001 854	.005 744	.012 036	.026 266	.023 793	13
14	.001 542	.004 787	.010 056	.022 049	.019 776	14
15	.001 287	.004 003	.008 431	.018 575	.016 492	15
16	.001 077	.003 356	.007 089	.015 694	.013 791	16
17	.000 904	.002 821	.005 974	.013 292	.011 559	17
18	.000 760	.002 376	.005 045	.011 281	.009 706	18
19	.000 639	.002 004	.004 267	.009 590	.008 163	19
20	.000 539	.001 692	.003 614	.008 165	.006 874	20
21	.000 455	.001 431	.003 064	.006 960	.005 795	21
22	.000 384	.001 211	.002 601	.005 938	.004 889	22
23	.000 325	.001 026	.002 209	.005 071	.004 129	23
24	.000 275	.000 869	.001 878	.004 334	.003 489	24
25	.000 232	.000 737	.001 597	.003 707	.002 949	25
26	.000 197	.000 626	.001 359	.003 172	.002 495	26
27	.000 167	.000 531	.001 157	.002 715	.002 111	27
28	.000 141	.000 451	.000 985	.002 325	.001 787	28
29	.000 120	.000 383	.000 840	.001 992	.001 513	29
30	.000 101	.000 325	.000 715	.001 707	.001 281	30
31	.000 086	.000 276	.000 610	.001 463	.001 085	31
32	.000 073	.000 235	.000 520	.001 254	.000 919	32
33	.000 062	.000 200	.000 443	.001 075	.000 779	33
34	.000 053	.000 170	.000 378	.000 922	.000 660	34
35	.000 045	.000 144	.000 322	.000 791	.000 559	35
36	.000 038	.000 123	.000 275	.000 678	.000 474	36
37	.000 032	.000 104	.000 234	.000 582	.000 402	37
38	.000 027	.000 089	.000 200	.000 499	.000 341	38
39	.000 023	.000 075	.000 171	.000 428	.000 289	39
40	.000 020	.000 064	.000 146	.000 368	.000 245	40

17%

SINKING FUND FACTORS
(Periodic Payment to Grow to $1)

Base: 1.014 167   1.042 500   1.085 000   1.170 000   1.185 257

Frequency of Payments and of Conversions

Months	Monthly	Quarterly	Semiannual	Annual	Annual Payment Daily Conversion	Months
1	1.000 000	—	—	—	—	1
2	.496 483	—	—	—	—	2
3	.328 655	1.000 000	—	—	—	3
4	.244 750	—	—	—	—	4
5	.194 413	—	—	—	—	5
6	.160 861	.489 596	1.000 000	—	—	6
7	.136 900	—	—	—	—	7
8	.118 933	—	—	—	—	8
9	.104 962	.319 560	—	—	—	9
10	.093 789	—	—	—	—	10
11	.084 651	—	—	—	—	11

Years						Years
1	.077 038	.234 615	.479 616	1.000 000	1.000 000	1
2	.035 276	.107 565	.220 288	.460 829	.457 612	2
3	.021 486	.065 603	.134 607	.282 574	.278 544	3
4	.014 688	.044 910	.092 331	.194 533	.190 288	4
5	.010 686	.032 720	.067 408	.142 564	.138 337	5
6	.008 079	.024 776	.051 153	.108 615	.104 516	6
7	.006 269	.019 255	.039 842	.084 947	.081 034	7
8	.004 955	.015 243	.031 614	.067 690	.063 993	8
9	.003 970	.012 232	.025 430	.054 691	.051 225	9
10	.003 213	.009 918	.020 671	.044 657	.041 428	10
11	.002 622	.008 107	.016 939	.036 765	.033 773	11
12	.002 153	.006 669	.013 970	.030 466	.027 704	12
13	.001 776	.005 513	.011 580	.025 378	.022 840	13
14	.001 472	.004 577	.009 639	.021 230	.018 906	14
15	.001 223	.003 812	.008 051	.017 822	.015 701	15
16	.001 020	.003 183	.006 742	.015 004	.013 073	16
17	.000 852	.002 665	.005 660	.012 662	.010 910	17
18	.000 713	.002 234	.004 760	.010 706	.009 121	18
19	.000 597	.001 877	.004 010	.009 067	.007 636	19
20	.000 501	.001 578	.003 382	.007 690	.006 401	20
21	.000 421	.001 329	.002 856	.006 530	.005 372	21
22	.000 354	.001 119	.002 414	.005 550	.004 512	22
23	.000 298	.000 944	.002 042	.004 721	.003 792	23
24	.000 251	.000 796	.001 728	.004 019	.003 189	24
25	.000 211	.000 672	.001 463	.003 423	.002 684	25
26	.000 178	.000 568	.001 240	.002 917	.002 259	26
27	.000 150	.000 480	.001 051	.002 487	.001 902	27
28	.000 127	.000 406	.000 891	.002 121	.001 602	28
29	.000 107	.000 343	.000 756	.001 810	.001 350	29
30	.000 090	.000 290	.000 641	.001 545	.001 138	30
31	.000 076	.000 245	.000 544	.001 318	.000 959	31
32	.000 064	.000 207	.000 462	.001 126	.000 808	32
33	.000 054	.000 175	.000 392	.000 961	.000 682	33
34	.000 046	.000 148	.000 333	.000 821	.000 575	34
35	.000 039	.000 126	.000 282	.000 701	.000 485	35
36	.000 033	.000 106	.000 240	.000 599	.000 409	36
37	.000 028	.000 090	.000 204	.000 512	.000 345	37
38	.000 023	.000 076	.000 173	.000 437	.000 291	38
39	.000 020	.000 064	.000 147	.000 373	.000 245	39
40	.000 017	.000 055	.000 125	.000 319	.000 207	40

(Periodic Payment to Grow to $1)

Base:	1.014 583	1.043 750	1.087 500	1.175 000	1.191 196	
		Frequency of Payments and of Conversions				
Months	Monthly	Quarterly	Semiannual	Annual	Annual Payment Daily Conversion	Months
1	1.000 000	—	—	—	—	1
2	.496 381	—	—	—	—	2
3	.328 519	1.000 000	—	—	—	3
4	.244 597	—	—	—	—	4
5	.194 251	—	—	—	—	5
6	.160 693	.489 297	1.000 000	—	—	6
7	.136 728	—	—	—	—	7
8	.118 758	—	—	—	—	8
9	.104 786	.319 166	—	—	—	9
10	.093 612	—	—	—	—	10
11	.084 472	—	—	—	—	11

Years						Years
1	.076 859	.234 179	.479 042	1.000 000	1.000 000	1
2	.035 100	.107 086	.219 477	.459 770	.456 372	2
3	.021 319	.065 133	.133 761	.281 245	.276 997	3
4	.014 531	.044 461	.091 499	.193 130	.188 666	4
5	.010 539	.032 296	.066 610	.141 163	.136 728	5
6	.007 943	.024 379	.050 397	.107 254	.102 964	6
7	.006 142	.018 885	.039 132	.083 645	.079 560	7
8	.004 838	.014 900	.030 951	.066 456	.062 609	8
9	.003 862	.011 916	.024 815	.053 531	.049 935	9
10	.003 115	.009 627	.020 102	.043 573	.040 233	10
11	.002 532	.007 840	.016 415	.035 757	.032 672	11
12	.002 071	.006 425	.013 489	.029 533	.026 696	12
13	.001 702	.005 291	.011 140	.024 518	.021 920	13
14	.001 404	.004 375	.009 238	.020 440	.018 069	14
15	.001 162	.003 629	.007 686	.017 098	.014 942	15
16	.000 965	.003 018	.006 412	.014 343	.012 388	16
17	.000 802	.002 516	.005 361	.012 060	.010 293	17
18	.000 669	.002 101	.004 490	.010 159	.008 567	18
19	.000 558	.001 757	.003 767	.008 572	.007 140	19
20	.000 466	.001 471	.003 164	.007 243	.005 959	20
21	.000 390	.001 233	.002 661	.006 126	.004 977	21
22	.000 326	.001 034	.002 239	.005 187	.004 161	22
23	.000 273	.000 868	.001 886	.004 395	.003 481	23
24	.000 229	.000 729	.001 589	.003 726	.002 914	24
25	.000 192	.000 613	.001 340	.003 161	.002 440	25
26	.000 161	.000 515	.001 130	.002 683	.002 044	26
27	.000 135	.000 433	.000 954	.002 278	.001 713	27
28	.000 113	.000 365	.000 805	.001 935	.001 436	28
29	.000 095	.000 307	.000 680	.001 644	.001 204	29
30	.000 080	.000 258	.000 574	.001 398	.001 010	30
31	.000 067	.000 217	.000 485	.001 188	.000 847	31
32	.000 056	.000 183	.000 410	.001 010	.000 711	32
33	.000 047	.000 154	.000 346	.000 859	.000 596	33
34	.000 040	.000 130	.000 293	.000 730	.000 500	34
35	.000 033	.000 109	.000 247	.000 621	.000 420	35
36	.000 028	.000 092	.000 209	.000 528	.000 352	36
37	.000 024	.000 078	.000 177	.000 450	.000 296	37
38	.000 020	.000 065	.000 149	.000 382	.000 248	38
39	.000 017	.000 055	.000 126	.000 325	.000 208	39
40	.000 014	.000 046	.000 107	.000 277	.000 175	40

18%

SINKING FUND FACTORS
(Periodic Payment to Grow to $1)

Base:	1.015 000	1.045 000	1.090 000	1.180 000	1.197 164	

Frequency of Payments and of Conversions

Months	Monthly	Quarterly	Semiannual	Annual	Annual Payment Daily Conversion	Months
1	1.000 000	—	—	—	—	1
2	.496 278	—	—	—	—	2
3	.328 383	1.000 000	—	—	—	3
4	.244 445	—	—	—	—	4
5	.194 089	—	—	—	—	5
6	.160 525	.488 998	1.000 000	—	—	6
7	.136 556	—	—	—	—	7
8	.118 584	—	—	—	—	8
9	.104 610	.318 773	—	—	—	9
10	.093 434	—	—	—	—	10
11	.084 294	—	—	—	—	11

Years						Years
1	.076 680	.233 744	.478 469	1.000 000	1.000 000	1
2	.034 924	.106 610	.218 669	.458 716	.455 132	2
3	.021 152	.064 666	.132 920	.279 924	.275 454	3
4	.014 375	.044 015	.090 674	.191 739	.187 051	4
5	.010 393	.031 876	.065 820	.139 778	.135 131	5
6	.007 808	.023 987	.049 651	.105 910	.101 428	6
7	.006 018	.018 521	.038 433	.082 362	.078 106	7
8	.004 723	.014 563	.030 300	.065 244	.061 247	8
9	.003 757	.011 606	.024 212	.052 395	.048 670	9
10	.003 019	.009 343	.019 546	.042 515	.039 066	10
11	.002 444	.007 581	.015 905	.034 776	.031 601	11
12	.001 991	.006 189	.013 023	.028 628	.025 718	12
13	.001 630	.005 077	.010 715	.023 686	.021 030	13
14	.001 340	.004 181	.008 852	.019 678	.017 264	14
15	.001 104	.003 454	.007 336	.016 403	.014 215	15
16	.000 913	.002 861	.006 096	.013 710	.011 735	16
17	.000 756	.002 375	.005 077	.011 485	.009 707	17
18	.000 627	.001 975	.004 235	.009 639	.008 043	18
19	.000 521	.001 644	.003 538	.008 103	.006 674	19
20	.000 433	.001 371	.002 960	.006 820	.005 544	20
21	.000 361	.001 144	.002 478	.005 746	.004 609	21
22	.000 300	.000 955	.002 077	.004 846	.003 835	22
23	.000 250	.000 798	.001 742	.004 090	.003 194	23
24	.000 209	.000 667	.001 461	.003 454	.002 661	24
25	.000 174	.000 558	.001 227	.002 919	.002 217	25
26	.000 146	.000 467	.001 030	.002 467	.001 849	26
27	.000 122	.000 391	.000 866	.002 087	.001 542	27
28	.000 101	.000 328	.000 728	.001 765	.001 286	28
29	.000 085	.000 274	.000 612	.001 494	.001 073	29
30	.000 071	.000 230	.000 514	.001 264	.000 896	30
31	.000 059	.000 193	.000 432	.001 070	.000 748	31
32	.000 049	.000 161	.000 364	.000 906	.000 624	32
33	.000 041	.000 135	.000 306	.000 767	.000 521	33
34	.000 035	.000 113	.000 257	.000 650	.000 435	34
35	.000 029	.000 095	.000 216	.000 550	.000 363	35
36	.000 024	.000 080	.000 182	.000 466	.000 303	36
37	.000 020	.000 067	.000 153	.000 395	.000 253	37
38	.000 017	.000 056	.000 129	.000 335	.000 212	38
39	.000 014	.000 047	.000 109	.000 284	.000 177	39
40	.000 012	.000 039	.000 091	.000 240	.000 148	40

(Periodic Payment to Grow to $1)

Base:	1.015 833	1.047 500	1.095 000	1.190 000	1.209 189	
			Frequency of Payments and of Conversions			
					Annual Payment Daily	
Months	Monthly	Quarterly	Semiannual	Annual	Conversion	Months
1	1.000 000	—	—	—	—	1
2	.496 073	—	—	—	—	2
3	.328 111	1.000 000	—	—	—	3
4	.244 140	—	—	—	—	4
5	.193 766	—	—	—	—	5
6	.160 190	.488 400	1.000 000	—	—	6
7	.136 214	—	—	—	—	7
8	.118 236	—	—	—	—	8
9	.104 258	.317 990	—	—	—	9
10	.093 080	—	—	—	—	10
11	.083 938	—	—	—	—	11

Years						Years
1	.076 323	.232 876	.477 327	1.000 000	1.000 000	1
2	.034 575	.105 662	.217 063	.456 621	.452 655	2
3	.020 823	.063 740	.131 253	.277 308	.272 381	3
4	.014 067	.043 135	.089 046	.188 991	.183 846	4
5	.010 107	.031 050	.064 266	.137 050	.131 975	5
6	.007 543	.023 219	.048 188	.103 274	.098 404	6
7	.005 775	.017 810	.037 068	.079 855	.075 255	7
8	.004 501	.013 909	.029 035	.062 885	.058 590	8
9	.003 554	.011 007	.023 046	.050 192	.046 215	9
10	.002 834	.008 797	.018 477	.040 471	.036 813	10
11	.002 277	.007 084	.014 928	.032 891	.029 545	11
12	.001 840	.005 739	.012 134	.026 896	.023 851	12
13	.001 494	.004 671	.009 909	.022 102	.019 343	13
14	.001 218	.003 816	.008 124	.018 235	.015 745	14
15	.000 995	.003 127	.006 681	.015 092	.012 854	15
16	.000 816	.002 569	.005 507	.012 523	.010 518	16
17	.000 670	.002 114	.004 549	.010 414	.008 623	17
18	.000 551	.001 743	.003 764	.008 676	.007 081	18
19	.000 453	.001 439	.003 119	.007 238	.005 822	19
20	.000 374	.001 189	.002 587	.006 045	.004 792	20
21	.000 308	.000 983	.002 148	.005 054	.003 947	21
22	.000 254	.000 814	.001 785	.004 229	.003 254	22
23	.000 210	.000 674	.001 484	.003 542	.002 684	23
24	.000 174	.000 558	.001 234	.002 967	.002 214	24
25	.000 143	.000 463	.001 027	.002 487	.001 828	25
26	.000 119	.000 384	.000 855	.002 086	.001 509	26
27	.000 098	.000 318	.000 712	.001 750	.001 247	27
28	.000 081	.000 264	.000 593	.001 468	.001 030	28
29	.000 067	.000 219	.000 494	.001 232	.000 851	29
30	.000 056	.000 182	.000 412	.001 034	.000 703	30
31	.000 046	.000 151	.000 343	.000 869	.000 581	31
32	.000 038	.000 125	.000 286	.000 729	.000 481	32
33	.000 032	.000 104	.000 238	.000 612	.000 397	33
34	.000 026	.000 086	.000 199	.000 514	.000 328	34
35	.000 022	.000 072	.000 166	.000 432	.000 272	35
36	.000 018	.000 060	.000 138	.000 363	.000 224	36
37	.000 015	.000 049	.000 115	.000 305	.000 186	37
38	.000 012	.000 041	.000 096	.000 256	.000 153	38
39	.000 010	.000 034	.000 080	.000 215	.000 127	39
40	.000 008	.000 028	.000 067	.000 181	.000 105	40

20%

SINKING FUND FACTORS
(Periodic Payment to Grow to $1)

Base: 1.016 667 1.050 000 1.100 000 1.200 000 1.221 335

Frequency of Payments and of Conversions

Months	Monthly	Quarterly	Semiannual	Annual	Annual Payment Daily Conversion	Months
1	1.000 000	—	—	—	—	1
2	.495 868	—	—	—	—	2
3	.327 839	1.000 000	—	—	—	3
4	.243 836	—	—	—	—	4
5	.193 444	—	—	—	—	5
6	.159 856	.487 805	1.000 000	—	—	6
7	.135 872	—	—	—	—	7
8	.117 889	—	—	—	—	8
9	.103 908	.317 209	—	—	—	9
10	.092 727	—	—	—	—	10
11	.083 584	—	—	—	—	11

Years						Years
1	.075 968	.232 012	.476 190	1.000 000	1.000 000	1
2	.034 229	.104 722	.215 471	.454 545	.450 180	2
3	.020 497	.062 825	.129 607	.274 725	.269 324	3
4	.013 764	.042 270	.087 444	.186 289	.180 675	4
5	.009 827	.030 243	.062 745	.134 380	.128 868	5
6	.007 286	.022 471	.046 763	.100 706	.095 444	6
7	.005 540	.017 123	.035 746	.077 424	.072 483	7
8	.004 287	.013 280	.027 817	.060 609	.056 022	8
9	.003 360	.010 434	.021 930	.048 079	.043 858	9
10	.002 659	.008 278	.017 460	.038 523	.034 665	10
11	.002 120	.006 616	.014 005	.031 104	.027 600	11
12	.001 699	.005 318	.011 300	.025 265	.022 099	12
13	.001 369	.004 294	.009 159	.020 620	.017 772	13
14	.001 106	.003 480	.007 451	.016 893	.014 343	14
15	.000 896	.002 828	.006 079	.013 882	.011 607	15
16	.000 728	.002 304	.004 972	.011 436	.009 414	16
17	.000 592	.001 880	.004 074	.009 440	.007 649	17
18	.000 483	.001 536	.003 343	.007 805	.006 224	18
19	.000 394	.001 257	.002 747	.006 462	.005 070	19
20	.000 322	.001 030	.002 259	.005 357	.004 134	20
21	.000 263	.000 844	.001 860	.004 444	.003 374	21
22	.000 215	.000 692	.001 532	.003 690	.002 755	22
23	.000 176	.000 568	.001 263	.003 065	.002 250	23
24	.000 144	.000 466	.001 041	.002 548	.001 839	24
25	.000 118	.000 383	.000 859	.002 119	.001 504	25
26	.000 097	.000 315	.000 709	.001 762	.001 230	26
27	.000 079	.000 259	.000 585	.001 467	.001 006	27
28	.000 065	.000 213	.000 483	.001 221	.000 823	28
29	.000 053	.000 175	.000 399	.001 016	.000 673	29
30	.000 044	.000 144	.000 330	.000 846	.000 551	30
31	.000 036	.000 118	.000 272	.000 705	.000 451	31
32	.000 029	.000 097	.000 225	.000 587	.000 369	32
33	.000 024	.000 080	.000 186	.000 489	.000 302	33
34	.000 020	.000 066	.000 153	.000 407	.000 247	34
35	.000 016	.000 054	.000 127	.000 339	.000 202	35
36	.000 013	.000 044	.000 105	.000 283	.000 166	36
37	.000 011	.000 037	.000 087	.000 235	.000 136	37
38	.000 009	.000 030	.000 072	.000 196	.000 111	38
39	.000 007	.000 025	.000 059	.000 163	.000 091	39
40	.000 006	.000 020	.000 049	.000 136	.000 074	40

(Periodic Payment to Grow to $1)

Base:	1.017 500	1.052 500	1.105 000	1.210 000	1.233 603	
		Frequency of Payments and of Conversions				
Months	Monthly	Quarterly	Semiannual	Annual	Annual Payment Daily Conversion	Months
1	1.000 000	—	—	—	—	1
2	.495 663	—	—	—	—	2
3	.327 567	1.000 000	—	—	—	3
4	.243 532	—	—	—	—	4
5	.193 121	—	—	—	—	5
6	.159 523	.487 211	1.000 000	—	—	6
7	.135 531	—	—	—	—	7
8	.117 543	—	—	—	—	8
9	.103 558	.316 430	—	—	—	9
10	.092 375	—	—	—	—	10
11	.083 230	—	—	—	—	11

Years						Years
1	.075 614	.231 151	.475 059	1.000 000	1.000 000	1
2	.033 886	.103 789	.213 892	.452 489	.447 707	2
3	.020 175	.061 922	.127 982	.272 175	.266 285	3
4	.013 466	.041 419	.085 869	.183 632	.177 537	4
5	.009 553	.029 452	.061 257	.131 765	.125 811	5
6	.007 036	.021 743	.045 377	.098 203	.092 548	6
7	.005 312	.016 457	.034 467	.075 067	.069 787	7
8	.004 081	.012 676	.026 644	.058 415	.053 543	8
9	.003 175	.009 888	.020 863	.046 053	.041 598	9
10	.002 493	.007 786	.016 493	.036 665	.032 621	10
11	.001 972	.006 176	.013 134	.029 411	.025 762	11
12	.001 568	.004 925	.010 519	.023 730	.020 457	12
13	.001 252	.003 945	.008 461	.019 234	.016 312	13
14	.001 003	.003 171	.006 830	.015 647	.013 051	14
15	.000 806	.002 555	.005 528	.012 766	.010 469	15
16	.000 649	.002 064	.004 485	.010 441	.008 415	16
17	.000 523	.001 670	.003 645	.008 555	.006 775	17
18	.000 423	.001 353	.002 967	.007 020	.005 462	18
19	.000 342	.001 097	.002 417	.005 769	.004 408	19
20	.000 276	.000 891	.001 971	.004 745	.003 561	20
21	.000 224	.000 724	.001 609	.003 906	.002 878	21
22	.000 181	.000 588	.001 314	.003 218	.002 328	22
23	.000 147	.000 478	.001 074	.002 652	.001 883	23
24	.000 119	.000 389	.000 878	.002 187	.001 524	24
25	.000 097	.000 317	.000 718	.001 804	.001 234	25
26	.000 078	.000 258	.000 587	.001 489	.000 999	26
27	.000 064	.000 210	.000 480	.001 229	.000 810	27
28	.000 052	.000 171	.000 393	.001 015	.000 656	28
29	.000 042	.000 139	.000 322	.000 838	.000 531	29
30	.000 034	.000 113	.000 263	.000 692	.000 431	30
31	.000 028	.000 092	.000 216	.000 572	.000 349	31
32	.000 022	.000 075	.000 176	.000 472	.000 283	32
33	.000 018	.000 061	.000 145	.000 390	.000 229	33
34	.000 015	.000 050	.000 118	.000 322	.000 186	34
35	.000 012	.000 041	.000 097	.000 266	.000 151	35
36	.000 010	.000 033	.000 079	.000 220	.000 122	36
37	.000 008	.000 027	.000 065	.000 182	.000 099	37
38	.000 006	.000 022	.000 053	.000 150	.000 080	38
39	.000 005	.000 018	.000 044	.000 124	.000 065	39
40	.000 004	.000 015	.000 036	.000 103	.000 053	40

22%

SINKING FUND FACTORS
(Periodic Payment to Grow to $1)

Base:	1.018 333	1.055 000	1.110 000	1.220 000	1.245 993	
			Frequency of Payments and of Conversions			

Months	Monthly	Quarterly	Semiannual	Annual	Annual Payment Daily Conversion	Months
1	1.000 000	—	—	—	—	1
2	.495 458	—	—	—	—	2
3	.327 296	1.000 000	—	—	—	3
4	.243 229	—	—	—	—	4
5	.192 800	—	—	—	—	5
6	.159 190	.486 618	1.000 000	—	—	6
7	.135 190	—	—	—	—	7
8	.117 198	—	—	—	—	8
9	.103 210	.315 654	—	—	—	9
10	.092 025	—	—	—	—	10
11	.082 878	—	—	—	—	11

Years						Years
1	.075 261	.230 294	.473 934	1.000 000	1.000 000	1
2	.033 545	.102 864	.212 326	.450 450	.445 237	2
3	.019 857	.061 029	.126 377	.269 658	.263 262	3
4	.013 173	.040 583	.084 321	.181 020	.174 432	4
5	.009 286	.028 679	.059 801	.129 206	.122 803	5
6	.006 793	.021 036	.044 027	.095 764	.089 716	6
7	.005 093	.015 814	.033 228	.072 782	.067 167	7
8	.003 884	.012 095	.025 517	.056 299	.051 149	8
9	.002 999	.009 366	.019 843	.044 111	.039 432	9
10	.002 336	.007 320	.015 576	.034 895	.030 676	10
11	.001 833	.005 761	.012 313	.027 807	.024 029	11
12	.001 446	.004 559	.009 787	.022 285	.018 920	12
13	.001 145	.003 622	.007 813	.017 939	.014 957	13
14	.000 909	.002 887	.006 257	.014 491	.011 862	14
15	.000 724	.002 307	.005 025	.011 738	.009 430	15
16	.000 578	.001 847	.004 043	.009 530	.007 512	16
17	.000 462	.001 482	.003 259	.007 751	.005 993	17
18	.000 370	.001 190	.002 630	.006 313	.004 786	18
19	.000 296	.000 956	.002 125	.005 148	.003 827	19
20	.000 237	.000 769	.001 719	.004 202	.003 062	20
21	.000 190	.000 619	.001 391	.003 432	.002 451	21
22	.000 153	.000 499	.001 126	.002 805	.001 964	22
23	.000 123	.000 402	.000 912	.002 294	.001 573	23
24	.000 098	.000 324	.000 739	.001 877	.001 261	24
25	.000 079	.000 261	.000 599	.001 536	.001 011	25
26	.000 064	.000 211	.000 486	.001 258	.000 811	26
27	.000 051	.000 170	.000 394	.001 030	.000 650	27
28	.000 041	.000 137	.000 320	.000 843	.000 522	28
29	.000 033	.000 111	.000 259	.000 691	.000 419	29
30	.000 027	.000 089	.000 210	.000 566	.000 336	30
31	.000 021	.000 072	.000 171	.000 464	.000 269	31
32	.000 017	.000 058	.000 138	.000 380	.000 216	32
33	.000 014	.000 047	.000 112	.000 311	.000 173	33
34	.000 011	.000 038	.000 091	.000 255	.000 139	34
35	.000 009	.000 031	.000 074	.000 209	.000 112	35
36	.000 007	.000 025	.000 060	.000 171	.000 090	36
37	.000 006	.000 020	.000 049	.000 140	.000 072	37
38	.000 005	.000 016	.000 040	.000 115	.000 058	38
39	.000 004	.000 013	.000 032	.000 094	.000 046	39
40	.000 003	.000 010	.000 026	.000 077	.000 037	40

SINKING FUND FACTORS 23%
(Periodic Payment to Grow to $1)

Base: 1.019 167   1.057 500   1.115 000   1.230 000   1.258 508

Frequency of Payments and of Conversions

Months	Monthly	Quarterly	Semiannual	Annual	Annual Payment Daily Conversion	Months
1	1.000 000	—	—	—	—	1
2	.495 254	—	—	—	—	2
3	.327 025	1.000 000	—	—	—	3
4	.242 926	—	—	—	—	4
5	.192 479	—	—	—	—	5
6	.158 857	.486 027	1.000 000	—	—	6
7	.134 851	—	—	—	—	7
8	.116 853	—	—	—	—	8
9	.102 862	.314 881	—	—	—	9
10	.091 675	—	—	—	—	10
11	.082 528	—	—	—	—	11

Years	Monthly	Quarterly	Semiannual	Annual	Annual Payment Daily Conversion	Years
1	.074 910	.229 441	.472 813	1.000 000	1.000 000	1
2	.033 207	.101 946	.210 774	.448 430	.442 770	2
3	.019 543	.060 148	.124 791	.267 173	.260 257	3
4	.012 885	.039 760	.082 799	.178 451	.171 361	4
5	.009 024	.027 923	.058 377	.126 700	.119 844	5
6	.006 556	.020 348	.042 714	.093 389	.086 947	6
7	.004 881	.015 193	.032 030	.070 568	.064 623	7
8	.003 695	.011 538	.024 432	.054 259	.048 841	8
9	.002 831	.008 869	.018 868	.042 249	.037 359	9
10	.002 188	.006 879	.014 705	.033 208	.028 829	10
11	.001 703	.005 372	.011 539	.026 289	.022 394	11
12	.001 332	.004 216	.009 103	.020 926	.017 483	12
13	.001 046	.003 323	.007 210	.016 728	.013 702	13
14	.000 823	.002 626	.005 730	.013 418	.010 770	14
15	.000 650	.002 081	.004 564	.010 791	.008 485	15
16	.000 514	.001 652	.003 643	.008 697	.006 697	16
17	.000 407	.001 313	.002 912	.007 021	.005 293	17
18	.000 323	.001 045	.002 331	.005 676	.004 188	18
19	.000 256	.000 833	.001 867	.004 593	.003 317	19
20	.000 203	.000 664	.001 497	.003 720	.002 629	20
21	.000 162	.000 530	.001 201	.003 016	.002 084	21
22	.000 128	.000 423	.000 964	.002 446	.001 654	22
23	.000 102	.000 338	.000 774	.001 984	.001 312	23
24	.000 081	.000 270	.000 622	.001 611	.001 042	24
25	.000 065	.000 215	.000 500	.001 308	.000 827	25
26	.000 051	.000 172	.000 402	.001 062	.000 657	26
27	.000 041	.000 138	.000 323	.000 863	.000 521	27
28	.000 033	.000 110	.000 260	.000 701	.000 414	28
29	.000 026	.000 088	.000 209	.000 570	.000 329	29
30	.000 021	.000 070	.000 168	.000 463	.000 261	30
31	.000 016	.000 056	.000 135	.000 376	.000 208	31
32	.000 013	.000 045	.000 109	.000 306	.000 165	32
33	.000 010	.000 036	.000 087	.000 249	.000 131	33
34	.000 008	.000 029	.000 070	.000 202	.000 104	34
35	.000 007	.000 023	.000 056	.000 164	.000 083	35
36	.000 005	.000 018	.000 045	.000 133	.000 066	36
37	.000 004	.000 015	.000 037	.000 109	.000 052	37
38	.000 003	.000 012	.000 029	.000 088	.000 041	38
39	.000 003	.000 009	.000 024	.000 072	.000 033	39
40	.000 002	.000 007	.000 019	.000 058	.000 026	40

24%
SINKING FUND FACTORS
(Periodic Payment to Grow to $1)

Base: 1.020 000   1.060 000   1.120 000   1.240 000   1.271 147

Frequency of Payments and of Conversions

Months	Monthly	Quarterly	Semiannual	Annual	Annual Payment Daily Conversion	Months
1	1.000 000	—	—	—	—	1
2	.495 050	—	—	—	—	2
3	.326 755	1.000 000	—	—	—	3
4	.242 624	—	—	—	—	4
5	.192 158	—	—	—	—	5
6	.158 526	.485 437	1.000 000	—	—	6
7	.134 512	—	—	—	—	7
8	.116 510	—	—	—	—	8
9	.102 515	.314 110	—	—	—	9
10	.091 327	—	—	—	—	10
11	.082 178	—	—	—	—	11

Years						Years
1	.074 560	.228 591	.471 698	1.000 000	1.000 000	1
2	.032 871	.101 036	.209 234	.446 429	.440 306	2
3	.019 233	.059 277	.123 226	.264 718	.257 270	3
4	.012 602	.038 952	.081 303	.175 926	.168 325	4
5	.008 768	.027 185	.056 984	.124 248	.116 935	5
6	.006 327	.019 679	.041 437	.091 074	.084 242	6
7	.004 676	.014 593	.030 871	.068 422	.062 153	7
8	.003 513	.011 002	.023 390	.052 293	.046 616	8
9	.002 671	.008 395	.017 937	.040 465	.035 375	9
10	.002 048	.006 462	.013 879	.031 602	.027 076	10
11	.001 581	.005 006	.010 811	.024 852	.020 856	11
12	.001 226	.003 898	.008 463	.019 648	.016 142	12
13	.000 954	.003 046	.006 652	.015 598	.012 540	13
14	.000 745	.002 388	.005 244	.012 423	.009 769	14
15	.000 583	.001 876	.004 144	.009 919	.007 626	15
16	.000 457	.001 476	.003 280	.007 936	.005 964	16
17	.000 358	.001 163	.002 601	.006 359	.004 670	17
18	.000 281	.000 918	.002 064	.005 102	.003 660	18
19	.000 221	.000 725	.001 640	.004 098	.002 871	19
20	.000 174	.000 573	.001 304	.003 294	.002 254	20
21	.000 137	.000 453	.001 037	.002 649	.001 770	21
22	.000 108	.000 358	.000 825	.002 132	.001 390	22
23	.000 085	.000 283	.000 657	.001 716	.001 093	23
24	.000 067	.000 224	.000 523	.001 382	.000 859	24
25	.000 053	.000 177	.000 417	.001 113	.000 675	25
26	.000 042	.000 140	.000 332	.000 897	.000 531	26
27	.000 033	.000 111	.000 264	.000 723	.000 417	27
28	.000 026	.000 088	.000 211	.000 583	.000 328	28
29	.000 020	.000 070	.000 168	.000 470	.000 258	29
30	.000 016	.000 055	.000 134	.000 379	.000 203	30
31	.000 013	.000 044	.000 107	.000 305	.000 160	31
32	.000 010	.000 035	.000 085	.000 246	.000 126	32
33	.000 008	.000 027	.000 068	.000 198	.000 099	33
34	.000 006	.000 022	.000 054	.000 160	.000 078	34
35	.000 005	.000 017	.000 043	.000 129	.000 061	35
36	.000 004	.000 014	.000 034	.000 104	.000 048	36
37	.000 003	.000 011	.000 027	.000 084	.000 038	37
38	.000 002	.000 009	.000 022	.000 068	.000 030	38
39	.000 002	.000 007	.000 017	.000 055	.000 023	39
40	.000 001	.000 005	.000 014	.000 044	.000 018	40

338

SINKING FUND FACTORS

25%

(Periodic Payment to Grow to $1)

Base:	1.020 833	1.062 500	1.125 000	1.250 000	1.283 914	

Frequency of Payments and of Conversions

Months	Monthly	Quarterly	Semiannual	Annual	Annual Payment Daily Conversion	Months
1	1.000 000	—	—	—	—	1
2	.494 845	—	—	—	—	2
3	.326 484	1.000 000	—	—	—	3
4	.242 322	—	—	—	—	4
5	.191 838	—	—	—	—	5
6	.158 195	.484 848	1.000 000	—	—	6
7	.134 174	—	—	—	—	7
8	.116 167	—	—	—	—	8
9	.102 170	.313 341	—	—	—	9
10	.090 979	—	—	—	—	10
11	.081 830	—	—	—	—	11

Years						Years
1	.074 211	.227 745	.470 588	1.000 000	1.000 000	1
2	.032 538	.100 133	.207 708	.444 444	.437 845	2
3	.018 926	.058 417	.121 680	.262 295	.254 301	3
4	.012 324	.038 158	.079 832	.173 442	.165 322	4
5	.008 518	.026 462	.055 622	.121 847	.114 075	5
6	.006 104	.019 029	.040 194	.088 819	.081 600	6
7	.004 478	.014 013	.029 751	.066 342	.059 757	7
8	.003 339	.010 489	.022 388	.050 399	.044 473	8
9	.002 519	.007 943	.017 049	.038 756	.033 479	9
10	.001 916	.006 067	.013 096	.030 073	.025 413	10
11	.001 466	.004 663	.010 125	.023 493	.019 409	11
12	.001 128	.003 601	.007 866	.018 448	.014 892	12
13	.000 870	.002 791	.006 134	.014 543	.011 466	13
14	.000 673	.002 169	.004 797	.011 501	.008 851	14
15	.000 522	.001 689	.003 760	.009 117	.006 847	15
16	.000 405	.001 318	.002 952	.007 241	.005 305	16
17	.000 315	.001 029	.002 321	.005 759	.004 115	17
18	.000 245	.000 805	.001 827	.004 586	.003 194	18
19	.000 191	.000 630	.001 439	.003 656	.002 482	19
20	.000 149	.000 493	.001 134	.002 916	.001 929	20
21	.000 116	.000 386	.000 895	.002 327	.001 500	21
22	.000 090	.000 303	.000 706	.001 858	.001 167	22
23	.000 071	.000 237	.000 557	.001 485	.000 908	23
24	.000 055	.000 186	.000 440	.001 186	.000 707	24
25	.000 043	.000 146	.000 347	.000 948	.000 550	25
26	.000 034	.000 114	.000 274	.000 758	.000 428	26
27	.000 026	.000 090	.000 216	.000 606	.000 334	27
28	.000 020	.000 070	.000 171	.000 485	.000 260	28
29	.000 016	.000 055	.000 135	.000 387	.000 202	29
30	.000 012	.000 043	.000 107	.000 310	.000 158	30
31	.000 010	.000 034	.000 084	.000 248	.000 123	31
32	.000 008	.000 027	.000 067	.000 198	.000 096	32
33	.000 006	.000 021	.000 053	.000 159	.000 074	33
34	.000 005	.000 016	.000 042	.000 127	.000 058	34
35	.000 004	.000 013	.000 033	.000 101	.000 045	35
36	.000 003	.000 010	.000 026	.000 081	.000 035	36
37	.000 002	.000 008	.000 020	.000 065	.000 027	37
38	.000 002	.000 006	.000 016	.000 052	.000 021	38
39	.000 001	.000 005	.000 013	.000 042	.000 017	39
40	.000 001	.000 004	.000 010	.000 033	.000 013	40

26%

SINKING FUND FACTORS
(Periodic Payment to Grow to $1)

Base: 1.021 667   1.065 000   1.130 000   1.260 000   1.296 808

Frequency of Payments and of Conversions

Months	Monthly	Quarterly	Semiannual	Annual	Annual Payment Daily Conversion	Months
1	1.000 000	—	—	—	—	1
2	.494 641	—	—	—	—	2
3	.326 214	1.000 000	—	—	—	3
4	.242 020	—	—	—	—	4
5	.191 519	—	—	—	—	5
6	.157 865	.484 262	1.000 000	—	—	6
7	.133 837	—	—	—	—	7
8	.115 825	—	—	—	—	8
9	.101 825	.312 576	—	—	—	9
10	.090 633	—	—	—	—	10
11	.081 482	—	—	—	—	11

Years						Years
1	.073 863	.226 903	.469 484	1.000 000	1.000 000	1
2	.032 208	.099 237	.206 194	.442 478	.435 387	2
3	.018 624	.057 568	.120 153	.259 902	.251 350	3
4	.012 051	.037 378	.078 387	.170 999	.162 354	4
5	.008 274	.025 756	.054 290	.119 496	.111 265	5
6	.005 887	.018 398	.038 986	.086 623	.079 019	6
7	.004 288	.013 453	.028 667	.064 326	.057 434	7
8	.003 173	.009 997	.021 426	.048 573	.042 411	8
9	.002 374	.007 513	.016 201	.037 119	.031 668	9
10	.001 791	.005 694	.012 354	.028 616	.023 838	10
11	.001 360	.004 341	.009 479	.022 207	.018 050	11
12	.001 036	.003 325	.007 308	.017 319	.013 728	12
13	.000 793	.002 556	.005 655	.013 559	.010 475	13
14	.000 608	.001 969	.004 387	.010 647	.008 013	14
15	.000 467	.001 520	.003 411	.008 379	.006 141	15
16	.000 359	.001 176	.002 656	.006 606	.004 713	16
17	.000 277	.000 910	.002 071	.005 216	.003 621	17
18	.000 213	.000 705	.001 616	.004 122	.002 785	18
19	.000 165	.000 547	.001 262	.003 261	.002 143	19
20	.000 127	.000 424	.000 986	.002 581	.001 650	20
21	.000 098	.000 329	.000 771	.002 045	.001 270	21
22	.000 076	.000 256	.000 603	.001 620	.000 979	22
23	.000 059	.000 199	.000 472	.001 284	.000 754	23
24	.000 045	.000 154	.000 369	.001 018	.000 581	24
25	.000 035	.000 120	.000 289	.000 807	.000 448	25
26	.000 027	.000 093	.000 226	.000 640	.000 345	26
27	.000 021	.000 072	.000 177	.000 508	.000 266	27
28	.000 016	.000 056	.000 139	.000 403	.000 205	28
29	.000 012	.000 044	.000 109	.000 320	.000 158	29
30	.000 010	.000 034	.000 085	.000 254	.000 122	30
31	.000 007	.000 026	.000 067	.000 201	.000 094	31
32	.000 006	.000 021	.000 052	.000 160	.000 073	32
33	.000 004	.000 016	.000 041	.000 127	.000 056	33
34	.000 003	.000 012	.000 032	.000 101	.000 043	34
35	.000 003	.000 010	.000 025	.000 080	.000 033	35
36	.000 002	.000 007	.000 020	.000 063	.000 026	36
37	.000 002	.000 006	.000 015	.000 050	.000 020	37
38	.000 001	.000 005	.000 012	.000 040	.000 015	38
39	.000 001	.000 004	.000 009	.000 032	.000 012	39
40	.000 001	.000 003	.000 007	.000 025	.000 009	40

SINKING FUND FACTORS

(Periodic Payment to Grow to $1)

27%

Base: | 1.022 500 | 1.067 500 | 1.135 000 | 1.270 000 | 1.309 832

Frequency of Payments and of Conversions

Months	Monthly	Quarterly	Semiannual	Annual	Annual Payment Daily Conversion	Months
1	1.000 000	—	—	—	—	1
2	.494 438	—	—	—	—	2
3	.325 945	1.000 000	—	—	—	3
4	.241 719	—	—	—	—	4
5	.191 200	—	—	—	—	5
6	.157 535	.483 676	1.000 000	—	—	6
7	.133 500	—	—	—	—	7
8	.115 485	—	—	—	—	8
9	.101 482	.311 812	—	—	—	9
10	.090 288	—	—	—	—	10
11	.081 136	—	—	—	—	11

Years						Years
1	.073 517	.226 064	.468 384	1.000 000	1.000 000	1
2	.031 880	.098 349	.204 693	.440 529	.432 932	2
3	.018 325	.056 730	.118 646	.257 539	.248 417	3
4	.011 782	.036 611	.076 966	.168 598	.159 421	4
5	.008 035	.025 067	.052 987	.117 196	.108 505	5
6	.005 677	.017 784	.037 811	.084 484	.076 501	6
7	.004 104	.012 913	.027 621	.062 374	.055 182	7
8	.003 014	.009 525	.020 502	.046 814	.040 426	8
9	.002 237	.007 104	.015 392	.035 551	.029 940	9
10	.001 674	.005 342	.011 651	.027 231	.022 347	10
11	.001 260	.004 040	.008 873	.020 991	.016 775	11
12	.000 952	.003 069	.006 788	.016 260	.012 645	12
13	.000 722	.002 339	.005 211	.012 641	.009 561	13
14	.000 549	.001 787	.004 010	.009 856	.007 247	14
15	.000 418	.001 368	.003 092	.007 701	.005 502	15
16	.000 318	.001 048	.002 388	.006 027	.004 183	16
17	.000 243	.000 804	.001 847	.004 723	.003 183	17
18	.000 186	.000 618	.001 429	.003 705	.002 425	18
19	.000 142	.000 475	.001 107	.002 909	.001 848	19
20	.000 108	.000 365	.000 858	.002 285	.001 409	20
21	.000 083	.000 281	.000 665	.001 796	.001 074	21
22	.000 063	.000 216	.000 515	.001 412	.000 819	22
23	.000 049	.000 166	.000 400	.001 111	.000 625	23
24	.000 037	.000 128	.000 310	.000 874	.000 477	24
25	.000 028	.000 098	.000 241	.000 688	.000 364	25
26	.000 022	.000 076	.000 187	.000 541	.000 278	26
27	.000 017	.000 058	.000 145	.000 426	.000 212	27
28	.000 013	.000 045	.000 112	.000 335	.000 162	28
29	.000 010	.000 035	.000 087	.000 264	.000 124	29
30	.000 007	.000 027	.000 068	.000 208	.000 094	30
31	.000 006	.000 021	.000 053	.000 164	.000 072	31
32	.000 004	.000 016	.000 041	.000 129	.000 055	32
33	.000 003	.000 012	.000 032	.000 101	.000 042	33
34	.000 003	.000 009	.000 025	.000 080	.000 032	34
35	.000 002	.000 007	.000 019	.000 063	.000 024	35
36	.000 002	.000 006	.000 015	.000 049	.000 019	36
37	.000 001	.000 004	.000 011	.000 039	.000 014	37
38	.000 001	.000 003	.000 009	.000 031	.000 011	38
39	.000 001	.000 003	.000 007	.000 024	.000 008	39
40	.000 001	.000 002	.000 005	.000 019	.000 006	40

28% SINKING FUND FACTORS
(Periodic Payment to Grow to $1)

Base:	1.023 333	1.070 000	1.140 000	1.280 000	1.322 986	
		Frequency of Payments and of Conversions				
Months	Monthly	Quarterly	Semiannual	Annual	Annual Payment Daily Conversion	Months
1	1.000 000	—	—	—	—	1
2	.494 234	—	—	—	—	2
3	.325 675	1.000 000	—	—	—	3
4	.241 418	—	—	—	—	4
5	.190 882	—	—	—	—	5
6	.157 206	.483 092	1.000 000	—	—	6
7	.133 165	—	—	—	—	7
8	.115 145	—	—	—	—	8
9	.101 139	.311 052	—	—	—	9
10	.089 944	—	—	—	—	10
11	.080 792	—	—	—	—	11

Years						Years
1	.073 173	.225 228	.467 290	1.000 000	1.000 000	1
2	.031 555	.097 468	.203 205	.438 596	.430 480	2
3	.018 030	.055 902	.117 157	.255 206	.245 503	3
4	.011 519	.035 858	.075 570	.166 236	.156 522	4
5	.007 802	.024 393	.051 714	.114 944	.105 793	5
6	.005 473	.017 189	.036 669	.082 400	.074 044	6
7	.003 927	.012 392	.026 609	.060 482	.053 001	7
8	.002 861	.009 073	.019 615	.045 119	.038 519	8
9	.002 107	.006 715	.014 621	.034 049	.028 291	9
10	.001 563	.005 009	.010 986	.025 912	.020 937	10
11	.001 167	.003 758	.008 303	.019 842	.015 579	11
12	.000 874	.002 831	.006 303	.015 265	.011 638	12
13	.000 657	.002 139	.004 800	.011 785	.008 720	13
14	.000 495	.001 620	.003 664	.009 123	.006 548	14
15	.000 373	.001 229	.002 803	.007 077	.004 925	15
16	.000 282	.000 934	.002 147	.005 499	.003 709	16
17	.000 213	.000 710	.001 646	.004 277	.002 796	17
18	.000 161	.000 541	.001 263	.003 331	.002 109	18
19	.000 122	.000 412	.000 970	.002 595	.001 591	19
20	.000 092	.000 314	.000 745	.002 023	.001 201	20
21	.000 070	.000 239	.000 573	.001 578	.000 907	21
22	.000 053	.000 182	.000 440	.001 232	.000 685	22
23	.000 040	.000 139	.000 338	.000 961	.000 518	23
24	.000 030	.000 106	.000 260	.000 750	.000 391	24
25	.000 023	.000 081	.000 200	.000 586	.000 296	25
26	.000 017	.000 062	.000 154	.000 458	.000 223	26
27	.000 013	.000 047	.000 118	.000 357	.000 169	27
28	.000 010	.000 036	.000 091	.000 279	.000 128	28
29	.000 008	.000 027	.000 070	.000 218	.000 096	29
30	.000 006	.000 021	.000 054	.000 170	.000 073	30
31	.000 004	.000 016	.000 042	.000 133	.000 055	31
32	.000 003	.000 012	.000 032	.000 104	.000 042	32
33	.000 003	.000 009	.000 025	.000 081	.000 031	33
34	.000 002	.000 007	.000 019	.000 063	.000 024	34
35	.000 001	.000 005	.000 015	.000 050	.000 018	35
36	.000 001	.000 004	.000 011	.000 039	.000 014	36
37	.000 001	.000 003	.000 009	.000 030	.000 010	37
38	.000 001	.000 002	.000 007	.000 024	.000 008	38
39	.000 000	.000 002	.000 005	.000 018	.000 006	39
40	.000 000	.000 001	.000 004	.000 014	.000 004	40

SINKING FUND FACTORS

(Periodic Payment to Grow to $1)

29%

Base:	1.024 167	1.072 500	1.145 000	1.290 000	1.336 271	
			Frequency of Payments and of Conversions			
Months	Monthly	Quarterly	Semiannual	Annual	Annual Payment Daily Conversion	Months
1	1.000 000	—	—	—	—	1
2	.494 030	—	—	—	—	2
3	.325 406	1.000 000	—	—	—	3
4	.241 118	—	—	—	—	4
5	.190 564	—	—	—	—	5
6	.156 878	.482 509	1.000 000	—	—	6
7	.132 830	—	—	—	—	7
8	.114 806	—	—	—	—	8
9	.100 798	.310 293	—	—	—	9
10	.089 601	—	—	—	—	10
11	.080 448	—	—	—	—	11

Years						Years
1	.072 829	.224 396	.466 200	1.000 000	1.000 000	1
2	.031 233	.096 594	.201 729	.436 681	.428 032	2
3	.017 739	.055 085	.115 688	.252 902	.242 607	3
4	.011 260	.035 118	.074 198	.163 913	.153 658	4
5	.007 575	.023 735	.050 469	.112 739	.103 131	5
6	.005 276	.016 611	.035 559	.080 371	.071 648	6
7	.003 757	.011 890	.025 632	.058 649	.050 890	7
8	.002 716	.008 640	.018 764	.043 487	.036 686	8
9	.001 984	.006 346	.013 886	.032 612	.026 721	9
10	.001 460	.004 696	.010 357	.024 657	.019 604	10
11	.001 080	.003 494	.007 768	.018 755	.014 459	11
12	.000 802	.002 610	.005 851	.014 331	.010 704	12
13	.000 597	.001 955	.004 420	.010 987	.007 947	13
14	.000 446	.001 468	.003 348	.008 445	.005 912	14
15	.000 333	.001 104	.002 539	.006 504	.004 405	15
16	.000 249	.000 832	.001 929	.005 017	.003 285	16
17	.000 187	.000 627	.001 467	.003 874	.002 453	17
18	.000 140	.000 473	.001 116	.002 994	.001 832	18
19	.000 105	.000 357	.000 850	.002 316	.001 369	19
20	.000 079	.000 269	.000 647	.001 792	.001 024	20
21	.000 059	.000 203	.000 493	.001 387	.000 765	21
22	.000 044	.000 154	.000 376	.001 074	.000 572	22
23	.000 033	.000 116	.000 287	.000 832	.000 428	23
24	.000 025	.000 088	.000 218	.000 644	.000 320	24
25	.000 019	.000 066	.000 167	.000 499	.000 240	25
26	.000 014	.000 050	.000 127	.000 387	.000 179	26
27	.000 011	.000 038	.000 097	.000 300	.000 134	27
28	.000 008	.000 029	.000 074	.000 232	.000 100	28
29	.000 006	.000 022	.000 056	.000 180	.000 075	29
30	.000 004	.000 016	.000 043	.000 140	.000 056	30
31	.000 003	.000 012	.000 033	.000 108	.000 042	31
32	.000 003	.000 009	.000 025	.000 084	.000 031	32
33	.000 002	.000 007	.000 019	.000 065	.000 024	33
34	.000 001	.000 005	.000 015	.000 050	.000 018	34
35	.000 001	.000 004	.000 011	.000 039	.000 013	35
36	.000 001	.000 003	.000 008	.000 030	.000 010	36
37	.000 001	.000 002	.000 006	.000 023	.000 007	37
38	.000 000	.000 002	.000 005	.000 018	.000 006	38
39	.000 000	.000 001	.000 004	.000 014	.000 004	39
40	.000 000	.000 001	.000 003	.000 011	.000 003	40

30%

SINKING FUND FACTORS
(Periodic Payment to Grow to $1)

Base:	1.025 000	1.075 000	1.150 000	1.300 000	1.349 690	
			Frequency of Payments and of Conversions			
Months	Monthly	Quarterly	Semiannual	Annual	Annual Payment Daily Conversion	Months
1	1.000 000	—	—	—	—	1
2	.493 827	—	—	—	—	2
3	.325 137	1.000 000	—	—	—	3
4	.240 818	—	—	—	—	4
5	.190 247	—	—	—	—	5
6	.156 550	.481 928	1.000 000	—	—	6
7	.132 495	—	—	—	—	7
8	.114 467	—	—	—	—	8
9	.100 457	.309 538	—	—	—	9
10	.089 259	—	—	—	—	10
11	.080 106	—	—	—	—	11
Years						Years
1	.072 487	.223 568	.465 116	1.000 000	1.000 000	1
2	.030 913	.095 727	.200 265	.434 783	.425 588	2
3	.017 452	.054 278	.114 237	.250 627	.239 730	3
4	.011 006	.034 391	.072 850	.161 629	.150 829	4
5	.007 353	.023 092	.049 252	.110 582	.100 518	5
6	.005 084	.016 050	.034 481	.078 394	.069 313	6
7	.003 593	.011 405	.024 688	.056 874	.048 846	7
8	.002 577	.008 226	.017 948	.041 915	.034 927	8
9	.001 867	.005 994	.013 186	.031 235	.025 225	9
10	.001 362	.004 400	.009 761	.023 463	.018 346	10
11	.000 999	.003 247	.007 266	.017 729	.013 411	11
12	.000 735	.002 405	.005 430	.013 454	.009 838	12
13	.000 542	.001 787	.004 070	.010 243	.007 237	13
14	.000 401	.001 330	.003 057	.007 818	.005 333	14
15	.000 297	.000 991	.002 300	.005 978	.003 936	15
16	.000 220	.000 740	.001 733	.004 577	.002 908	16
17	.000 163	.000 553	.001 307	.003 509	.002 150	17
18	.000 121	.000 413	.000 986	.002 692	.001 590	18
19	.000 090	.000 309	.000 744	.002 066	.001 177	19
20	.000 067	.000 231	.000 562	.001 587	.000 871	20
21	.000 050	.000 173	.000 425	.001 219	.000 645	21
22	.000 037	.000 129	.000 321	.000 937	.000 478	22
23	.000 027	.000 097	.000 242	.000 720	.000 354	23
24	.000 020	.000 072	.000 183	.000 554	.000 262	24
25	.000 015	.000 054	.000 139	.000 426	.000 194	25
26	.000 011	.000 041	.000 105	.000 327	.000 144	26
27	.000 008	.000 030	.000 079	.000 252	.000 107	27
28	.000 006	.000 023	.000 060	.000 194	.000 079	28
29	.000 005	.000 017	.000 045	.000 149	.000 058	29
30	.000 003	.000 013	.000 034	.000 115	.000 043	30
31	.000 003	.000 010	.000 026	.000 088	.000 032	31
32	.000 002	.000 007	.000 020	.000 068	.000 024	32
33	.000 001	.000 005	.000 015	.000 052	.000 018	33
34	.000 001	.000 004	.000 011	.000 040	.000 013	34
35	.000 001	.000 003	.000 008	.000 031	.000 010	35
36	.000 001	.000 002	.000 006	.000 024	.000 007	36
37	.000 000	.000 002	.000 005	.000 018	.000 005	37
38	.000 000	.000 001	.000 004	.000 014	.000 004	38
39	.000 000	.000 001	.000 003	.000 011	.000 003	39
40	.000 000	.000 001	.000 002	.000 008	.000 002	40

Table 7

Sinking Fund Accumulation Factors
(Future Value of Periodic Payments of $1)

Table 7 - SINKING FUND ACCUMULATION FACTORS (Future Value of Periodic Payments of $1)

The total accumulation of principal and interest of a series of deposits or installments of one per period for a given number of periods with interest at the effective rate per period. This factor is also known as the *amount of one per period*. It is reciprocal to the corresponding factor from Table 6.

$$S_{\overline{n}|} = \frac{S^n - 1}{i}$$

Where $S_{\overline{n}|}$ = Sinking Fund Accumulation Factor

i = Effective Rate of Interest

S^n = Future Value Factor

This Table is used in solving problems dealing with the growth of sinking funds and/or the calculation of capital recovery in investment situations where the income/payments are level.

Example 1:
Assuming a 6% nominal interest rate, how much money would be accumulated if month-end deposits of $100 were made for a period of 10 years?

$100 × 163.879347 = $16,387.93

Same example except deposits made at the beginning of each month.

$16,387.93 × 1.005 = $16,469.87

Example 2:
Assuming a 6% nominal interest rate, how much money would be accumulated if month-end deposits of $100 were made for a period of 10 years and 7 months?

$100 × (163.879347 + 7.105879 × 1.819397*) = $17,680.78

* Future Value Factor for 120 months
OR
$100 × (7.105879 + 163.879347 × 1.035529*) = $17,680.77

* Future Value Factor for 7 months

346

Example 3:
Assuming a 6% nominal interest rate and daily compounding, how much money would be accumulated in a Keogh Retirement Plan if year-end deposits of $1,200 were made for 10 years?

$1,200 × 13.294699 = $15,953.64

Same example except deposits made at the beginning of each year.

$15,953.64 × 1.061831 = $16,940.07

Example 4:
Given a $100,000 loan with monthly payments of $908.71 including nominal interest at 10%, how much will be paid off in 10 years?

[$908.71 − ($100,000 × .10/12)] × 204.844979 = $15,440.53

3% SINKING FUND ACCUMULATION FACTORS
(Future Value of Periodic Payments of $1)

Base: 1.002 500   1.007 500   1.015 000   1.030 000   1.030 453

Frequency of Payments and of Conversions

Months	Monthly	Quarterly	Semiannual	Annual	Annual Payment Daily Conversion	Months
1	1.000 000	—	—	—	—	1
2	2.002 500	—	—	—	—	2
3	3.007 506	1.000 000	—	—	—	3
4	4.015 025	—	—	—	—	4
5	5.025 063	—	—	—	—	5
6	6.037 625	2.007 500	1.000 000	—	—	6
7	7.052 719	—	—	—	—	7
8	8.070 351	—	—	—	—	8
9	9.090 527	3.022 556	—	—	—	9
10	10.113 253	—	—	—	—	10
11	11.138 536	—	—	—	—	11

Years	Monthly	Quarterly	Semiannual	Annual	Annual Payment Daily Conversion	Years
1	12.166 383	4.045 225	2.015 000	1.000 000	1.000 000	1
2	24.702 818	8.213 180	4.090 903	2.030 000	2.030 453	2
3	37.620 560	12.507 586	6.229 551	3.090 900	3.092 287	3
4	50.931 208	16.932 282	8.432 839	4.183 627	4.186 457	4
5	64.646 713	21.491 219	10.702 722	5.309 136	5.313 949	5
6	78.779 387	26.188 471	13.041 211	6.468 410	6.475 776	6
7	93.341 920	31.028 233	15.450 382	7.662 462	7.672 984	7
8	108.347 387	36.014 830	17.932 370	8.892 336	8.906 651	8
9	123.809 259	41.152 716	20.489 376	10.159 106	10.177 888	9
10	139.741 419	46.446 482	23.123 667	11.463 879	11.487 837	10
11	156.158 171	51.900 856	25.837 580	12.807 796	12.837 679	11
12	173.074 254	57.520 711	28.633 521	14.192 030	14.228 628	12
13	190.504 855	63.311 068	31.513 969	15.617 790	15.661 936	13
14	208.465 626	69.277 100	34.481 479	17.086 324	17.138 893	14
15	226.972 690	75.424 137	37.538 681	18.598 914	18.660 828	15
16	246.042 664	81.757 670	40.688 288	20.156 881	20.229 111	16
17	265.692 670	88.283 357	43.933 092	21.761 588	21.845 153	17
18	285.940 350	95.007 028	47.275 969	23.414 435	23.510 409	18
19	306.803 882	101.934 689	50.719 885	25.116 868	25.226 377	19
20	328.301 998	109.072 531	54.267 894	26.870 374	26.994 602	20
21	350.454 000	116.426 928	57.923 141	28.676 486	28.816 675	21
22	373.279 777	124.004 453	61.688 868	30.536 780	30.694 236	22
23	396.799 821	131.811 873	65.568 414	32.452 884	32.628 976	23
24	421.035 250	139.856 164	69.565 219	34.426 470	34.622 634	24
25	446.007 823	148.144 512	73.682 828	36.459 264	36.677 005	25
26	471.739 961	156.684 322	77.924 892	38.553 042	38.793 939	26
27	498.254 766	165.483 223	82.295 171	40.709 634	40.975 341	27
28	525.576 044	174.549 075	86.797 543	42.930 923	43.223 173	28
29	553.728 325	183.889 979	91.435 999	45.218 850	45.539 459	29
30	582.736 885	193.514 277	96.214 652	47.575 416	47.926 283	30
31	612.627 767	203.430 569	101.137 740	50.002 678	50.385 794	31
32	643.427 810	213.647 713	106.209 628	52.502 759	52.920 205	32
33	675.164 665	224.174 837	111.434 814	55.077 841	55.531 797	33
34	707.866 827	235.021 346	116.817 931	57.730 177	58.222 920	34
35	741.563 657	246.196 929	122.363 753	60.462 082	60.995 997	35
36	776.285 408	257.711 570	128.077 197	63.275 944	63.853 523	36
37	812.063 254	269.575 556	133.963 331	66.174 223	66.798 070	37
38	848.929 318	281.799 485	140.027 372	69.159 449	69.832 288	38
39	886.916 698	294.394 279	146.274 700	72.234 233	72.958 908	39
40	926.059 501	307.371 189	152.710 852	75.401 260	76.180 744	40

SINKING FUND ACCUMULATION FACTORS 3¼%

(Future Value of Periodic Payments of $1)

Base: 1.002 708   1.008 125   1.016 250   1.032 500   1.033 032

Frequency of Payments and of Conversions

Months	Monthly	Quarterly	Semiannual	Annual	Annual Payment Daily Conversion	Months
1	1.000 000	—	—	—	—	1
2	2.002 708	—	—	—	—	2
3	3.008 132	1.000 000	—	—	—	3
4	4.016 279	—	—	—	—	4
5	5.027 157	—	—	—	—	5
6	6.040 772	2.008 125	1.000 000	—	—	6
7	7.057 132	—	—	—	—	7
8	8.076 245	—	—	—	—	8
9	9.098 119	3.024 441	—	—	—	9
10	10.122 759	—	—	—	—	10
11	11.150 175	—	—	—	—	11

Years						Years
1	12.180 374	4.049 015	2.016 250	1.000 000	1.000 000	1
2	24.762 560	8.231 235	4.098 561	2.032 500	2.033 032	2
3	37.759 813	12.551 042	6.249 096	3.098 556	3.100 188	3
4	51.185 827	17.012 964	8.470 092	4.199 259	4.202 595	4
5	65.054 745	21.621 676	10.763 856	5.335 735	5.341 417	5
6	79.381 177	26.382 005	13.132 774	6.509 147	6.517 856	6
7	94.180 218	31.298 942	15.579 307	7.720 694	7.733 157	7
8	109.467 457	36.377 636	18.105 999	8.971 616	8.988 601	8
9	125.258 999	41.623 411	20.715 475	10.263 194	10.285 516	9
10	141.571 480	47.041 763	23.410 448	11.596 748	11.625 271	10
11	158.422 086	52.638 369	26.193 719	12.973 642	13.009 281	11
12	175.828 569	58.419 093	29.068 182	14.395 285	14.439 009	12
13	193.809 265	64.389 994	32.036 823	15.863 132	15.915 964	13
14	212.383 118	70.557 326	35.102 730	17.378 684	17.441 706	14
15	231.569 695	76.927 553	38.269 088	18.943 491	19.017 847	15
16	251.389 208	83.507 349	41.539 189	20.559 155	20.646 051	16
17	271.862 537	90.303 608	44.916 431	22.227 327	22.328 040	17
18	293.011 252	97.323 453	48.404 326	23.949 715	24.065 588	18
19	314.857 630	104.574 238	52.006 498	25.728 081	25.860 531	19
20	337.424 688	112.063 562	55.726 693	27.564 244	27.714 766	20
21	360.736 200	119.799 271	59.568 775	29.460 082	29.630 251	21
22	384.816 724	127.789 471	63.536 741	31.417 534	31.609 009	22
23	409.691 629	136.042 534	67.634 712	33.438 604	33.653 129	23
24	435.387 120	144.567 109	71.866 950	35.525 359	35.764 772	24
25	461.930 267	153.372 128	76.237 853	37.679 933	37.946 168	25
26	489.349 032	162.466 816	80.751 965	39.904 531	40.199 620	26
27	517.672 302	171.860 704	85.413 978	42.201 428	42.527 509	27
28	546.929 915	181.563 634	90.228 737	44.572 975	44.932 294	28
29	577.152 692	191.585 773	95.201 247	47.021 596	47.416 514	29
30	608.372 474	201.937 623	100.336 676	49.549 798	49.982 794	30
31	640.622 150	212.630 031	105.640 363	52.160 167	52.633 845	31
32	673.935 695	223.674 200	111.117 821	54.855 372	55.372 466	32
33	708.348 204	235.081 703	116.774 742	57.638 172	58.201 550	33
34	743.895 931	246.864 492	122.617 007	60.511 412	61.124 086	34
35	780.616 324	259.034 915	128.650 688	63.478 033	64.143 160	35
36	818.548 069	271.605 724	134.882 057	66.541 069	67.261 961	36
37	857.731 125	284.590 090	141.317 592	69.703 654	70.483 783	37
38	898.206 772	298.001 618	147.963 980	72.969 023	73.812 030	38
39	940.017 650	311.854 363	154.828 131	76.340 516	77.250 217	39
40	983.207 807	326.162 838	161.917 180	79.821 583	80.801 975	40

3½% SINKING FUND ACCUMULATION FACTORS
(Future Value of Periodic Payments of $1)

Base: 1.002 917   1.008 750   1.017 500   1.035 000   1.035 618

Frequency of Payments and of Conversions

Months	Monthly	Quarterly	Semiannual	Annual	Annual Payment Daily Conversion	Months
1	1.000 000	—	—	—	—	1
2	2.002 917	—	—	—	—	2
3	3.008 759	1.000 000	—	—	—	3
4	4.017 534	—	—	—	—	4
5	5.029 252	—	—	—	—	5
6	6.043 921	2.008 750	1.000 000	—	—	6
7	7.061 549	—	—	—	—	7
8	8.082 145	—	—	—	—	8
9	9.105 718	3.026 327	—	—	—	9
10	10.132 276	—	—	—	—	10
11	11.161 829	—	—	—	—	11

Years	Monthly	Quarterly	Semiannual	Annual	Annual Payment Daily Conversion	Years
1	12.194 384	4.052 807	2.017 500	1.000 000	1.000 000	1
2	24.822 485	8.249 335	4.106 230	2.035 000	2.035 618	2
3	37.899 729	12.594 680	6.268 706	3.106 225	3.108 122	3
4	51.442 091	17.094 120	8.507 530	4.214 943	4.218 827	4
5	65.466 113	21.753 120	10.825 399	5.362 466	5.369 093	5
6	79.988 927	26.577 337	13.225 104	6.550 152	6.560 329	6
7	95.028 273	31.572 631	15.709 533	7.779 408	7.793 995	7
8	110.602 523	36.745 069	18.281 677	9.051 687	9.071 601	8
9	126.730 702	42.100 932	20.944 635	10.368 496	10.394 713	9
10	143.432 510	47.646 724	23.701 611	11.731 393	11.764 951	10
11	160.728 352	53.389 182	26.555 926	13.141 992	13.183 995	11
12	178.639 353	59.335 280	29.511 016	14.601 962	14.653 581	12
13	197.187 395	65.492 238	32.570 440	16.113 030	16.175 512	13
14	216.395 133	71.867 534	35.737 880	17.676 986	17.751 650	14
15	236.286 033	78.468 912	39.017 150	19.295 681	19.383 928	15
16	256.884 391	85.304 388	42.412 200	20.971 030	21.074 343	16
17	278.215 370	92.382 265	45.927 115	22.705 016	22.824 968	17
18	300.305 027	99.711 137	49.566 129	24.499 691	24.637 947	18
19	323.180 345	107.299 906	53.333 624	26.357 180	26.515 500	19
20	346.869 269	115.157 789	57.234 134	28.279 682	28.459 928	20
21	371.400 736	123.294 329	61.272 357	30.269 471	30.473 612	21
22	396.804 712	131.719 406	65.453 154	32.328 902	32.559 019	22
23	423.112 231	140.443 255	69.781 559	34.460 414	34.718 705	23
24	450.355 427	149.476 469	74.262 784	36.666 528	36.955 314	24
25	478.567 582	158.830 020	78.902 225	38.949 857	39.271 586	25
26	507.783 156	168.515 266	83.705 466	41.313 102	41.670 359	26
27	538.037 840	178.543 972	88.678 292	43.759 060	44.154 572	27
28	569.368 590	188.928 316	93.826 690	46.290 627	46.727 267	28
29	601.813 680	199.680 910	99.156 859	48.910 799	49.391 596	29
30	635.412 742	210.814 814	104.675 216	51.622 677	52.150 824	30
31	670.206 821	222.343 548	110.388 405	54.429 471	55.008 329	31
32	706.238 420	234.281 115	116.303 306	57.334 502	57.967 613	32
33	743.551 552	246.642 013	122.427 039	60.341 210	61.032 300	33
34	782.191 799	259.441 254	128.766 979	63.453 152	64.206 145	34
35	822.206 362	272.694 383	135.330 758	66.674 013	67.493 036	35
36	863.644 121	286.417 494	142.126 280	70.007 603	70.897 000	36
37	906.555 694	300.627 256	149.161 726	73.457 869	74.422 205	37
38	950.993 502	315.340 925	156.445 567	77.028 895	78.072 972	38
39	997.011 827	330.576 371	163.986 573	80.724 906	81.853 770	39
40	1044.666 884	346.352 097	171.793 824	84.550 278	85.769 234	40

SINKING FUND ACCUMULATION FACTORS   3¾%
(Future Value of Periodic Payments of $1)

Base: 1.003 125   1.009 375   1.018 750   1.037 500   1.038 210

Frequency of Payments and of Conversions

Months	Monthly	Quarterly	Semiannual	Annual	Annual Payment Daily Conversion	Months
1	1.000 000	—	—	—	—	1
2	2.003 125	—	—	—	—	2
3	3.009 385	1.000 000	—	—	—	3
4	4.018 789	—	—	—	—	4
5	5.031 348	—	—	—	—	5
6	6.047 071	2.009 375	1.000 000	—	—	6
7	7.065 968	—	—	—	—	7
8	8.088 049	—	—	—	—	8
9	9.113 324	3.028 213	—	—	—	9
10	10.141 803	—	—	—	—	10
11	11.173 496	—	—	—	—	11

Years						Years
1	12.208 414	4.056 602	2.018 750	1.000 000	1.000 000	1
2	24.882 594	8.267 480	4.113 913	2.037 500	2.038 210	2
3	38.040 311	12.638 500	6.288 381	3.113 906	3.116 090	3
4	51.700 011	17.175 753	8.545 156	4.230 678	4.235 156	4
5	65.880 847	21.885 560	10.887 353	5.389 328	5.396 981	5
6	80.602 700	26.774 484	13.318 207	6.591 428	6.603 199	6
7	95.886 211	31.849 338	15.841 072	7.838 607	7.855 507	7
8	111.752 808	37.117 191	18.459 431	9.132 554	9.155 666	8
9	128.224 735	42.585 384	21.176 899	10.475 025	10.505 504	9
10	145.325 088	48.261 537	23.997 228	11.867 838	11.906 919	10
11	163.077 842	54.153 556	26.924 311	13.312 882	13.361 882	11
12	181.507 886	60.269 654	29.962 188	14.812 116	14.872 439	12
13	200.641 060	66.618 350	33.115 053	16.367 570	16.440 714	13
14	220.504 190	73.208 491	36.387 260	17.981 354	18.068 913	14
15	241.125 123	80.049 260	39.783 325	19.655 654	19.759 326	15
16	262.532 772	87.150 188	43.307 936	21.392 742	21.514 329	16
17	284.757 150	94.521 168	46.965 959	23.194 960	23.336 391	17
18	307.829 417	102.172 472	50.762 444	25.064 781	25.228 074	18
19	331.781 921	110.114 759	54.702 631	27.004 710	27.192 038	19
20	356.648 243	118.359 097	58.791 961	29.017 387	29.231 045	20
21	382.463 248	126.916 973	63.036 079	31.105 539	31.347 962	21
22	409.263 129	135.800 310	67.440 843	33.271 996	33.545 767	22
23	437.085 460	145.021 486	72.012 334	35.519 696	35.827 550	23
24	465.969 249	154.593 349	76.756 864	37.851 685	38.196 519	24
25	495.954 992	164.529 237	81.680 981	40.271 123	40.656 007	25
26	527.084 730	174.842 992	86.791 484	42.781 290	43.209 472	26
27	559.402 107	185.548 987	92.095 427	45.385 588	45.860 504	27
28	592.952 434	196.662 137	97.600 133	48.087 548	48.612 833	28
29	627.782 750	208.197 928	103.313 200	50.890 831	51.470 328	29
30	663.941 886	220.172 433	109.242 516	53.799 237	54.437 007	30
31	701.480 541	232.602 335	115.396 266	56.816 709	57.517 044	31
32	740.451 344	245.504 955	121.782 945	59.947 335	60.714 768	32
33	780.908 934	258.898 270	128.411 370	63.195 360	64.034 678	33
34	822.910 033	272.800 941	135.290 691	66.565 186	67.481 441	34
35	866.513 528	287.232 340	142.430 405	70.061 381	71.059 904	35
36	911.780 552	302.212 574	149.840 369	73.688 682	74.775 101	36
37	958.774 572	317.762 516	157.530 811	77.452 008	78.632 256	37
38	1007.561 475	333.903 833	165.512 348	81.356 458	82.636 792	38
39	1058.209 662	350.659 014	173.795 999	85.407 326	86.794 341	39
40	1110.790 142	368.051 406	182.393 199	89.610 100	91.110 750	40

4% SINKING FUND ACCUMULATION FACTORS
(Future Value of Periodic Payments of $1)

Base: 1.003 333   1.010 000   1.020 000   1.040 000   1.040 808

Frequency of Payments and of Conversions

Months	Monthly	Quarterly	Semiannual	Annual	Annual Payment Daily Conversion	Months
1	1.000 000	—	—	—	—	1
2	2.003 333	—	—	—	—	2
3	3.010 011	1.000 000	—	—	—	3
4	4.020 044	—	—	—	—	4
5	5.033 445	—	—	—	—	5
6	6.050 223	2.010 000	1.000 000	—	—	6
7	7.070 390	—	—	—	—	7
8	8.093 958	—	—	—	—	8
9	9.120 938	3.030 100	—	—	—	9
10	10.151 341	—	—	—	—	10
11	11.185 179	—	—	—	—	11

Years						Years
1	12.222 463	4.060 401	2.020 000	1.000 000	1.000 000	1
2	24.942 888	8.285 671	4.121 608	2.040 000	2.040 808	2
3	38.181 562	12.682 503	6.308 121	3.121 600	3.124 091	3
4	51.959 601	17.257 864	8.582 969	4.246 464	4.251 580	4
5	66.298 978	22.019 004	10.949 721	5.416 323	5.425 080	5
6	81.222 564	26.973 465	13.412 090	6.632 975	6.646 470	6
7	96.754 159	32.129 097	15.973 938	7.898 294	7.917 702	7
8	112.918 536	37.494 068	18.639 285	9.214 226	9.240 811	8
9	129.741 474	43.076 878	21.412 312	10.582 795	10.617 914	9
10	147.249 805	48.886 373	24.297 370	12.006 107	12.051 215	10
11	165.471 452	54.931 757	27.298 984	13.486 351	13.543 007	11
12	184.435 477	61.222 608	30.421 862	15.025 805	15.095 676	12
13	204.172 126	67.768 892	33.670 906	16.626 838	16.711 707	13
14	224.712 876	74.580 982	37.051 210	18.291 911	18.393 686	14
15	246.090 488	81.669 670	40.568 079	20.023 588	20.144 304	15
16	268.339 057	89.046 187	44.227 030	21.824 531	21.966 362	16
17	291.494 067	96.722 220	48.033 802	23.697 512	23.862 776	17
18	315.592 448	104.709 931	51.994 367	25.645 413	25.836 579	18
19	340.672 634	113.021 975	56.114 940	27.671 229	27.890 930	19
20	366.774 626	121.671 522	60.401 983	29.778 079	30.029 116	20
21	393.940 053	130.672 274	64.862 223	31.969 202	32.254 558	21
22	422.212 242	140.038 494	69.502 657	34.247 970	34.570 817	22
23	451.636 283	149.785 019	74.330 564	36.617 889	36.981 599	23
24	482.259 105	159.927 293	79.353 519	39.082 604	39.490 761	24
25	514.129 547	170.481 383	84.579 401	41.645 908	42.102 318	25
26	547.298 441	181.464 012	90.016 409	44.311 745	44.820 449	26
27	581.818 687	192.892 579	95.673 072	47.084 214	47.649 503	27
28	617.745 341	204.785 192	101.558 264	49.967 583	50.594 005	28
29	655.135 702	217.160 693	107.681 218	52.966 286	53.658 669	29
30	694.049 404	230.038 689	114.051 539	56.084 938	56.848 397	30
31	734.548 511	243.439 584	120.679 222	59.328 335	60.168 292	31
32	776.697 613	257.384 608	127.574 662	62.701 469	63.623 668	32
33	820.563 935	271.895 856	134.748 679	66.209 527	67.220 052	33
34	866.217 439	286.996 319	142.212 525	69.857 909	70.963 199	34
35	913.730 937	302.709 922	149.977 911	73.652 225	74.859 098	35
36	963.180 208	319.061 559	158.057 019	77.598 314	78.913 982	36
37	1014.644 119	336.077 139	166.462 522	81.702 246	83.134 340	37
38	1068.204 748	353.783 620	175.207 608	85.970 336	87.526 925	38
39	1123.947 521	372.209 054	184.305 996	90.409 150	92.098 764	39
40	1181.961 340	391.382 635	193.771 958	95.025 516	96.857 173	40

(Future Value of Periodic Payments of $1)

Base:	1.003 542	1.010 625	1.021 250	1.042 500	1.043 413	

Frequency of Payments and of Conversions

Months	Monthly	Quarterly	Semiannual	Annual	Annual Payment Daily Conversion	Months
1	1.000 000	—	—	—	—	1
2	2.003 542	—	—	—	—	2
3	3.010 638	1.000 000	—	—	—	3
4	4.021 300	—	—	—	—	4
5	5.035 542	—	—	—	—	5
6	6.053 377	2.010 625	1.000 000	—	—	6
7	7.074 816	—	—	—	—	7
8	8.099 872	—	—	—	—	8
9	9.128 559	3.031 988	—	—	—	9
10	10.160 890	—	—	—	—	10
11	11.196 876	—	—	—	—	11

Years						Years
1	12.236 532	4.064 203	2.021 250	1.000 000	1.000 000	1
2	25.003 367	8.303 907	4.129 316	2.042 500	2.043 413	2
3	38.323 487	12.726 690	6.327 926	3.129 306	3.132 125	3
4	52.220 871	17.340 459	8.620 971	4.262 302	4.268 101	4
5	66.720 536	22.153 460	11.012 505	5.443 450	5.453 394	5
6	81.848 584	27.174 297	13.506 759	6.674 796	6.690 145	6
7	97.632 246	32.411 944	16.108 146	7.958 475	7.980 587	7
8	114.099 936	37.875 764	18.821 266	9.296 710	9.327 052	8
9	131.281 298	43.575 524	21.650 918	10.691 820	10.731 971	9
10	149.207 262	49.521 412	24.602 109	12.146 223	12.197 883	10
11	167.910 095	55.724 056	27.680 058	13.662 437	13.727 435	11
12	187.423 467	62.194 543	30.890 210	15.243 091	15.323 390	12
13	207.782 504	68.944 441	34.238 243	16.890 922	16.988 631	13
14	229.023 855	75.985 813	37.730 079	18.608 786	18.726 166	14
15	251.185 757	83.331 247	41.371 895	20.399 660	20.539 133	15
16	274.308 106	90.993 872	45.170 132	22.266 645	22.430 808	16
17	298.432 525	98.987 386	49.131 510	24.212 978	24.404 606	17
18	323.602 440	107.326 078	53.263 035	26.242 029	26.464 094	18
19	349.863 163	116.024 852	57.572 016	28.357 316	28.612 992	19
20	377.261 965	125.099 258	62.066 074	30.562 501	30.855 180	20
21	405.848 169	134.565 516	66.753 158	32.861 408	33.194 710	21
22	435.673 233	144.440 547	71.641 561	35.258 018	35.635 806	22
23	466.790 848	154.742 004	76.739 928	37.756 483	38.182 879	23
24	499.257 029	165.488 300	82.057 278	40.361 134	40.840 529	24
25	533.130 220	176.698 644	87.603 016	43.076 482	43.613 557	25
26	568.471 398	188.393 075	93.386 952	45.907 233	46.506 971	26
27	605.344 181	200.592 497	99.419 318	48.858 290	49.525 999	27
28	643.814 948	213.318 716	105.710 783	51.934 767	52.676 093	28
29	683.952 949	226.594 480	112.272 476	55.141 995	55.962 943	29
30	725.830 439	240.443 521	119.116 005	58.485 530	59.392 487	30
31	769.522 805	254.890 593	126.253 473	61.971 165	62.970 919	31
32	815.108 697	269.961 520	133.697 507	65.604 939	66.704 703	32
33	862.670 178	285.683 243	141.461 274	69.393 149	70.600 584	33
34	912.292 866	302.083 864	149.558 507	73.342 358	74.665 598	34
35	964.066 087	319.192 699	158.003 528	77.459 408	78.907 088	35
36	1018.083 041	337.040 330	166.811 276	81.751 433	83.332 716	36
37	1074.440 967	355.658 660	175.997 331	86.225 869	87.950 476	37
38	1133.241 316	375.080 970	185.577 942	90.890 468	92.768 709	38
39	1194.589 938	395.341 977	195.570 054	95.753 313	97.796 117	39
40	1258.597 270	416.477 898	205.991 344	100.822 829	103.041 783	40

4½% SINKING FUND ACCUMULATION FACTORS
(Future Value of Periodic Payments of $1)

Base:	1.003 750	1.011 250	1.022 500	1.045 000	1.046 025	
			Frequency of Payments and of Conversions			
					Annual Payment Daily	
Months	Monthly	Quarterly	Semiannual	Annual	Conversion	Months
1	1.000 000	—	—	—	—	1
2	2.003 750	—	—	—	—	2
3	3.011 264	1.000 000	—	—	—	3
4	4.022 556	—	—	—	—	4
5	5.037 641	—	—	—	—	5
6	6.056 532	2.011 250	1.000 000	—	—	6
7	7.079 244	—	—	—	—	7
8	8.105 791	—	—	—	—	8
9	9.136 188	3.033 877	—	—	—	9
10	10.170 449	—	—	—	—	10
11	11.208 588	—	—	—	—	11

Years						Years
1	12.250 620	4.068 008	2.022 500	1.000 000	1.000 000	1
2	25.064 031	8.322 188	4.137 036	2.045 000	2.046 025	2
3	38.466 089	12.771 061	6.347 797	3.137 025	3.140 193	3
4	52.483 834	17.423 538	8.659 162	4.278 191	4.284 720	4
5	67.145 552	22.288 935	11.075 708	5.470 710	5.481 924	5
6	82.480 827	27.376 998	13.602 222	6.716 892	6.734 229	6
7	98.520 602	32.697 916	16.243 708	8.019 152	8.044 172	7
8	115.297 241	38.262 347	19.005 398	9.380 014	9.414 404	8
9	132.844 596	44.081 434	21.892 763	10.802 114	10.847 701	9
10	151.198 074	50.166 832	24.911 520	12.288 209	12.346 966	10
11	170.394 707	56.530 730	28.067 650	13.841 179	13.915 234	11
12	190.473 230	63.185 871	31.367 403	15.464 032	15.555 681	12
13	211.474 157	70.145 585	34.817 316	17.159 913	17.271 630	13
14	233.439 862	77.423 812	38.424 222	18.932 109	19.066 555	14
15	256.414 669	85.035 127	42.195 264	20.784 054	20.944 092	15
16	280.444 934	92.994 775	46.137 912	22.719 337	22.908 042	16
17	305.579 145	101.318 696	50.259 976	24.741 707	24.962 383	17
18	331.868 018	110.023 563	54.569 619	26.855 084	27.111 275	18
19	359.364 596	119.126 808	59.075 377	29.063 562	29.359 069	19
20	388.124 363	128.646 665	63.786 176	31.371 423	31.710 318	20
21	418.205 348	138.602 198	68.711 346	33.783 137	34.169 782	21
22	449.668 249	149.013 347	73.860 642	36.303 378	36.742 444	22
23	482.576 549	159.900 964	79.244 262	38.937 030	39.433 512	23
24	516.996 652	171.286 853	84.872 872	41.689 196	42.248 436	24
25	552.998 007	183.193 818	90.757 618	44.565 210	45.192 917	25
26	590.653 259	195.645 707	96.910 157	47.570 645	48.272 917	26
27	630.038 387	208.667 457	103.342 674	50.711 324	51.494 674	27
28	671.232 860	222.285 149	110.067 912	53.993 333	54.864 712	28
29	714.319 800	236.526 055	117.099 190	57.423 033	58.389 856	29
30	759.386 147	251.418 698	124.450 435	61.007 070	62.077 245	30
31	806.522 833	266.992 905	132.136 208	64.752 388	65.934 345	31
32	855.824 971	283.279 866	140.171 731	68.666 245	69.968 967	32
33	907.392 041	300.312 201	148.572 921	72.756 226	74.189 283	33
34	961.328 092	318.124 022	157.356 417	77.030 256	78.603 839	34
35	1017.741 957	336.751 003	166.539 618	81.496 618	83.221 574	35
36	1076.747 464	356.230 450	176.140 711	86.163 966	88.051 841	36
37	1138.463 674	376.601 375	186.178 714	91.041 344	93.104 419	37
38	1203.015 116	397.904 577	196.673 509	96.138 205	98.389 543	38
39	1270.532 040	420.182 722	207.645 883	101.464 424	103.917 913	39
40	1341.150 680	443.480 428	219.117 569	107.030 323	109.700 727	40

SINKING FUND ACCUMULATION FACTORS   4¾%
(Future Value of Periodic Payments of $1)

Base: 1.003 958   1.011 875   1.023 750   1.047 500   1.048 643

Frequency of Payments and of Conversions

Months	Monthly	Quarterly	Semiannual	Annual	Annual Payment Daily Conversion	Months
1	1.000 000	—	—	—	—	1
2	2.003 958	—	—	—	—	2
3	3.011 891	1.000 000	—	—	—	3
4	4.023 813	—	—	—	—	4
5	5.039 740	—	—	—	—	5
6	6.059 689	2.011 875	1.000 000	—	—	6
7	7.083 676	—	—	—	—	7
8	8.111 715	—	—	—	—	8
9	9.143 824	3.035 766	—	—	—	9
10	10.180 018	—	—	—	—	10
11	11.220 314	—	—	—	—	11

Years						Years
1	12.264 728	4.071 816	2.023 750	1.000 000	1.000 000	1
2	25.124 882	8.340 515	4.144 770	2.047 500	2.048 643	2
3	38.609 370	12.815 618	6.367 734	3.144 756	3.148 295	3
4	52.748 501	17.507 105	8.697 543	4.294 132	4.301 437	4
5	67.574 057	22.425 439	11.139 333	5.498 103	5.510 672	5
6	83.119 362	27.581 587	13.698 484	6.759 263	6.778 727	6
7	99.419 359	32.987 051	16.380 639	8.080 328	8.108 464	7
8	116.510 687	38.653 883	19.191 709	9.464 144	9.502 883	8
9	134.431 762	44.594 723	22.137 890	10.913 691	10.965 131	9
10	153.222 867	50.822 819	25.225 677	12.432 091	12.498 507	10
11	172.926 240	57.352 060	28.461 876	14.022 615	14.106 471	11
12	193.586 171	64.197 010	31.853 619	15.688 690	15.792 651	12
13	215.249 097	71.372 931	35.408 384	17.433 902	17.560 851	13
14	237.963 713	78.895 829	39.134 004	19.262 013	19.415 062	14
15	261.781 075	86.782 480	43.038 694	21.176 958	21.359 467	15
16	286.754 719	95.050 473	47.131 058	23.182 864	23.398 454	16
17	312.940 781	103.718 246	51.420 118	25.284 050	25.536 623	17
18	340.398 121	112.805 130	55.915 328	27.485 042	27.778 799	18
19	369.188 457	122.331 391	60.626 596	29.790 582	30.130 041	19
20	399.376 502	132.318 274	65.564 306	32.205 635	32.595 654	20
21	431.030 113	142.788 050	70.739 343	34.735 402	35.181 201	21
22	464.220 440	153.764 070	76.163 114	37.385 334	37.892 518	22
23	499.022 087	165.270 811	81.847 572	40.161 137	40.735 720	23
24	535.513 280	177.333 935	87.805 249	43.068 791	43.717 224	24
25	573.776 043	189.980 345	94.049 276	46.114 559	46.843 757	25
26	613.896 382	203.238 244	100.593 416	49.305 000	50.122 374	26
27	655.964 479	217.137 201	107.452 094	52.646 988	53.560 473	27
28	700.074 893	231.708 211	114.640 429	56.147 720	57.165 810	28
29	746.326 774	246.983 770	122.174 263	59.814 736	60.946 522	29
30	794.824 085	262.997 946	130.070 205	63.655 936	64.911 139	30
31	845.675 839	279.786 451	138.345 657	67.679 593	69.068 606	31
32	898.996 337	297.386 729	147.018 862	71.894 374	73.428 304	32
33	954.905 433	315.838 029	156.108 935	76.309 357	78.000 071	33
34	1013.528 796	335.181 502	165.635 915	80.934 051	82.794 221	34
35	1074.998 200	355.460 286	175.620 800	85.778 419	87.821 574	35
36	1139.451 813	376.719 606	186.085 599	90.852 894	93.093 471	36
37	1207.034 513	399.006 874	197.053 379	96.168 406	98.621 809	37
38	1277.898 209	422.371 794	208.548 315	101.736 405	104.419 061	38
39	1352.202 188	446.866 473	220.595 744	107.568 884	110.498 309	39
40	1430.113 467	472.545 539	233.222 222	113.678 406	116.873 269	40

5% SINKING FUND ACCUMULATION FACTORS
(Future Value of Periodic Payments of $1)

Base: 1.004 167   1.012 500   1.025 000   1.050 000   1.051 267

Frequency of Payments and of Conversions

Months	Monthly	Quarterly	Semiannual	Annual	Annual Payment Daily Conversion	Months
1	1.000 000	—	—	—	—	1
2	2.004 167	—	—	—	—	2
3	3.012 517	1.000 000	—	—	—	3
4	4.025 070	—	—	—	—	4
5	5.041 841	—	—	—	—	5
6	6.062 848	2.012 500	1.000 000	—	—	6
7	7.088 110	—	—	—	—	7
8	8.117 644	—	—	—	—	8
9	9.151 467	3.037 656	—	—	—	9
10	10.189 599	—	—	—	—	10
11	11.232 055	—	—	—	—	11

Years						Years
1	12.278 855	4.075 627	2.025 000	1.000 000	1.000 000	1
2	25.185 921	8.358 888	4.152 516	2.050 000	2.051 267	2
3	38.753 336	12.860 361	6.387 737	3.152 500	3.156 431	3
4	53.014 885	17.591 164	8.736 116	4.310 125	4.318 253	4
5	68.006 083	22.562 979	11.203 382	5.525 631	5.539 639	5
6	83.764 259	27.788 084	13.795 553	6.801 913	6.823 642	6
7	100.328 653	33.279 384	16.518 953	8.142 008	8.173 472	7
8	117.740 512	39.050 441	19.380 225	9.549 109	9.592 506	8
9	136.043 196	45.115 505	22.386 349	11.026 564	11.084 289	9
10	155.282 279	51.489 557	25.544 658	12.577 893	12.652 552	10
11	175.505 671	58.188 337	28.862 856	14.206 787	14.301 216	11
12	196.763 730	65.228 388	32.349 038	15.917 127	16.034 403	12
13	219.109 391	72.627 097	36.011 708	17.712 983	17.856 446	13
14	242.598 299	80.402 736	39.859 801	19.598 632	19.771 900	14
15	267.288 944	88.574 508	43.902 703	21.578 564	21.785 555	15
16	293.242 809	97.162 593	48.150 278	23.657 492	23.902 445	16
17	320.524 523	106.188 201	52.612 885	25.840 366	26.127 862	17
18	349.202 021	115.673 621	57.301 413	28.132 385	28.467 371	18
19	379.346 715	125.642 280	62.227 297	30.539 004	30.926 820	19
20	411.033 669	136.118 795	67.402 554	33.065 954	33.512 359	20
21	444.341 787	147.129 040	72.839 808	35.719 252	36.230 452	21
22	479.354 011	158.700 206	78.552 323	38.505 214	39.087 895	22
23	516.157 528	170.860 868	84.554 034	41.430 475	42.091 832	23
24	554.843 982	183.641 059	90.859 582	44.501 999	45.249 772	24
25	595.509 708	197.072 342	97.484 349	47.727 099	48.569 613	25
26	638.255 971	211.187 886	104.444 494	51.113 454	52.059 653	26
27	683.189 213	226.022 551	111.756 996	54.669 126	55.728 618	27
28	730.421 325	241.612 973	119.439 694	58.402 583	59.585 682	28
29	780.069 922	257.997 654	127.511 329	62.322 712	63.640 488	29
30	832.258 635	275.217 058	135.991 590	66.438 848	67.903 173	30
31	887.117 422	293.313 711	144.901 164	70.760 790	72.384 395	31
32	944.782 889	312.332 304	154.261 786	75.298 829	77.095 359	32
33	1005.398 630	332.319 805	164.096 289	80.063 771	82.047 841	33
34	1069.115 587	353.325 577	174.428 663	85.066 959	87.254 224	34
35	1136.092 425	375.401 494	185.284 114	90.320 307	92.727 525	35
36	1206.495 925	398.602 077	196.689 122	95.836 323	98.481 429	36
37	1280.501 402	422.984 621	208.671 509	101.628 139	104.530 320	37
38	1358.293 140	448.609 342	221.260 504	107.709 546	110.889 323	38
39	1440.064 850	475.539 523	234.486 818	114.095 023	117.574 335	39
40	1526.020 156	503.841 671	248.382 713	120.799 774	124.602 071	40

SINKING FUND ACCUMULATION FACTORS 5¼%
(Future Value of Periodic Payments of $1)

Base: 1.004 375   1.013 125   1.026 250   1.052 500   1.053 899

Frequency of Payments and of Conversions

Months	Monthly	Quarterly	Semiannual	Annual	Annual Payment Daily Conversion	Months
1	1.000 000	—	—	—	—	1
2	2.004 375	—	—	—	—	2
3	3.013 144	1.000 000	—	—	—	3
4	4.026 327	—	—	—	—	4
5	5.043 942	—	—	—	—	5
6	6.066 009	2.013 125	1.000 000	—	—	6
7	7.092 548	—	—	—	—	7
8	8.123 578	—	—	—	—	8
9	9.159 118	3.039 547	—	—	—	9
10	10.199 190	—	—	—	—	10
11	11.243 811	—	—	—	—	11

Years						Years
1	12.293 003	4.079 441	2.026 250	1.000 000	1.000 000	1
2	25.247 146	8.377 307	4.160 274	2.052 500	2.053 899	2
3	38.897 988	12.905 291	6.407 805	3.160 256	3.164 601	3
4	53.282 998	17.675 717	8.774 881	4.326 170	4.335 168	4
5	68.441 661	22.701 563	11.267 858	5.553 294	5.568 827	5
6	84.415 585	27.996 506	13.893 435	6.844 842	6.868 979	6
7	101.248 617	33.574 955	16.658 664	8.204 196	8.239 207	7
8	118.986 962	39.452 089	19.570 973	9.634 916	9.683 288	8
9	137.679 308	45.643 901	22.638 184	11.140 749	11.205 203	9
10	157.376 963	52.167 238	25.868 538	12.725 638	12.809 147	10
11	178.133 996	59.039 853	29.270 711	14.393 734	14.499 541	11
12	200.007 381	66.280 445	32.853 843	16.149 405	16.281 045	12
13	223.057 158	73.908 718	36.627 558	17.997 249	18.158 569	13
14	247.346 595	81.945 430	40.601 994	19.942 105	20.137 289	14
15	272.942 365	90.412 448	44.787 826	21.989 065	22.222 659	15
16	299.914 723	99.332 813	49.196 298	24.143 491	24.420 428	16
17	328.337 705	108.730 798	53.839 253	26.411 025	26.736 653	17
18	358.289 329	118.631 976	58.729 162	28.797 603	29.177 719	18
19	389.851 808	129.063 290	63.879 162	31.309 478	31.750 355	19
20	423.111 776	140.053 124	69.303 084	33.953 225	34.461 653	20
21	458.160 528	151.631 383	75.015 500	36.735 769	37.319 085	21
22	495.094 269	163.829 573	81.031 754	39.664 397	40.330 529	22
23	534.014 375	176.680 887	87.368 008	42.746 778	43.504 285	23
24	575.027 679	190.220 294	94.041 280	45.990 984	46.849 102	24
25	618.246 755	204.484 637	101.069 497	49.405 511	50.374 200	25
26	663.790 234	219.512 732	108.471 539	52.999 300	54.089 295	26
27	711.783 128	235.345 470	116.267 289	56.781 763	58.004 628	27
28	762.357 171	252.025 936	124.477 687	60.762 806	62.130 992	28
29	815.651 180	269.599 518	133.124 788	64.952 853	66.479 761	29
30	871.811 442	288.114 037	142.231 821	69.362 878	71.062 923	30
31	930.992 109	307.619 872	151.823 248	74.004 429	75.893 110	31
32	993.355 624	328.170 102	161.924 834	78.889 662	80.983 636	32
33	1059.073 166	349.820 646	172.563 715	84.031 369	86.348 535	33
34	1128.325 122	372.630 417	183.768 467	89.443 016	92.002 594	34
35	1201.301 579	396.661 485	195.569 189	95.138 774	97.961 399	35
36	1278.202 847	421.979 241	207.997 581	101.133 560	104.241 374	36
37	1359.240 010	448.652 576	221.087 027	107.443 071	110.859 830	37
38	1444.635 505	476.754 073	234.872 689	114.083 833	117.835 012	38
39	1534.623 731	506.360 199	249.391 597	121.073 234	125.186 146	39
40	1629.451 693	537.551 516	264.682 753	128.429 579	132.933 495	40

5½% SINKING FUND ACCUMULATION FACTORS
(Future Value of Periodic Payments of $1)

Base:	1.004 583	1.013 750	1.027 500	1.055 000	1.056 536	
			Frequency of Payments and of Conversions			
Months	Monthly	Quarterly	Semiannual	Annual	Annual Payment Daily Conversion	Months
1	1.000 000	—	—	—	—	1
2	2.004 583	—	—	—	—	2
3	3.013 771	1.000 000	—	—	—	3
4	4.027 584	—	—	—	—	4
5	5.046 044	—	—	—	—	5
6	6.069 172	2.013 750	1.000 000	—	—	6
7	7.096 989	—	—	—	—	7
8	8.129 516	—	—	—	—	8
9	9.166 777	3.041 439	—	—	—	9
10	10.208 791	—	—	—	—	10
11	11.255 581	—	—	—	—	11

Years						Years
1	12.307 170	4.083 259	2.027 500	1.000 000	1.000 000	1
2	25.308 560	8.395 771	4.168 046	2.055 000	2.056 536	2
3	39.043 331	12.950 409	6.427 940	3.168 025	3.172 805	3
4	53.552 852	17.760 766	8.813 838	4.342 266	4.352 183	4
5	68.880 823	22.841 200	11.332 765	5.581 091	5.598 239	5
6	85.073 412	28.206 874	13.992 137	6.888 051	6.914 742	6
7	102.179 391	33.873 802	16.799 786	8.266 894	8.305 675	7
8	120.250 282	39.858 899	19.763 979	9.721 573	9.775 246	8
9	139.340 512	46.180 028	22.893 445	11.256 260	11.327 901	9
10	159.507 582	52.856 056	26.197 398	12.875 354	12.968 337	10
11	180.812 233	59.906 908	29.685 566	14.583 498	14.701 518	11
12	203.318 634	67.353 629	33.368 222	16.385 591	16.532 685	12
13	227.094 572	75.218 444	37.256 209	18.286 798	18.467 380	13
14	252.211 661	83.524 828	41.360 975	20.292 572	20.511 455	14
15	278.745 550	92.297 573	45.694 608	22.408 663	22.671 094	15
16	306.776 160	101.562 861	50.269 868	24.641 140	24.952 831	16
17	336.387 916	111.348 348	55.100 228	26.996 403	27.363 569	17
18	367.670 008	121.683 238	60.199 910	29.481 205	29.910 600	18
19	400.716 657	132.598 379	65.583 931	32.102 671	32.601 631	19
20	435.627 395	144.126 349	71.268 145	34.868 318	35.444 803	20
21	472.507 374	156.301 554	77.269 289	37.786 076	38.448 717	21
22	511.467 674	169.160 334	83.605 035	40.864 310	41.622 460	22
23	552.625 640	182.741 067	90.294 039	44.111 847	44.975 635	23
24	596.105 240	197.084 288	97.355 996	47.537 998	48.518 385	24
25	642.037 430	212.232 807	104.811 701	51.152 588	52.261 429	25
26	690.560 558	228.231 836	112.683 108	54.965 981	56.216 091	26
27	741.820 771	245.129 128	120.993 396	58.989 109	60.394 333	27
28	795.972 463	262.975 115	129.767 034	63.233 510	64.808 798	28
29	853.178 736	281.823 062	139.029 857	67.711 354	69.472 840	29
30	913.611 893	301.729 222	148.809 140	72.435 478	74.400 568	30
31	977.453 954	322.753 011	159.133 680	77.419 429	79.606 892	31
32	1044.897 210	344.957 176	170.033 877	82.677 498	85.107 561	32
33	1116.144 795	368.407 990	181.541 829	88.224 760	90.919 217	33
34	1191.411 305	393.175 445	193.691 420	94.077 122	97.059 442	34
35	1270.923 437	419.333 464	206.518 427	100.251 364	103.546 812	35
36	1354.920 678	446.960 120	220.060 621	106.765 189	110.400 953	36
37	1443.656 024	476.137 870	234.357 876	113.637 274	117.642 600	37
38	1537.396 741	506.953 798	249.452 292	120.887 324	125.293 663	38
39	1636.425 171	539.499 881	265.388 316	128.536 127	133.377 288	39
40	1741.039 583	573.873 258	282.212 873	136.605 614	141.917 930	40

SINKING FUND ACCUMULATION FACTORS 5¾%
(Future Value of Periodic Payments of $1)

Base: 1.004 792   1.014 375   1.028 750   1.057 500   1.059 180

Frequency of Payments and of Conversions

Months	Monthly	Quarterly	Semiannual	Annual	Annual Payment Daily Conversion	Months
1	1.000 000	—	—	—	—	1
2	2.004 792	—	—	—	—	2
3	3.014 398	1.000 000	—	—	—	3
4	4.028 842	—	—	—	—	4
5	5.048 147	—	—	—	—	5
6	6.072 336	2.014 375	1.000 000	—	—	6
7	7.101 432	—	—	—	—	7
8	8.135 460	—	—	—	—	8
9	9.174 443	3.043 332	—	—	—	9
10	10.218 403	—	—	—	—	10
11	11.267 367	—	—	—	—	11

Years						Years
1	12.321 356	4.087 080	2.028 750	1.000 000	1.000 000	1
2	25.370 163	8.414 282	4.175 830	2.057 500	2.059 180	2
3	39.189 369	12.995 716	6.448 142	3.175 806	3.181 044	3
4	53.824 459	17.846 317	8.852 990	4.358 415	4.369 299	4
5	69.323 602	22.981 899	11.398 104	5.609 024	5.627 876	5
6	85.737 812	28.419 205	14.091 666	6.931 543	6.960 936	6
7	103.121 114	34.175 964	16.942 335	8.330 107	8.372 887	7
8	121.530 723	40.270 941	19.959 273	9.809 088	9.868 398	8
9	141.027 233	46.724 010	23.152 179	11.373 110	11.452 414	9
10	161.674 813	53.556 208	26.531 316	13.027 064	13.130 172	10
11	183.541 423	60.789 809	30.107 546	14.776 120	14.907 221	11
12	206.699 033	68.448 397	33.892 366	16.625 747	16.789 436	12
13	231.223 866	76.556 941	37.897 941	18.581 728	18.783 042	13
14	257.196 640	85.141 877	42.137 148	20.650 177	20.894 630	14
15	284.702 842	94.231 192	46.623 613	22.837 562	23.131 183	15
16	313.833 006	103.854 521	51.371 758	25.150 722	25.500 096	16
17	344.683 010	114.043 237	56.396 846	27.596 888	28.009 202	17
18	377.354 392	124.830 558	61.715 030	30.183 710	30.666 798	18
19	411.954 688	136.251 654	67.343 406	32.919 273	33.481 671	19
20	448.597 780	148.343 759	73.300 065	35.812 131	36.463 130	20
21	487.404 273	161.146 296	79.604 156	38.871 329	39.621 033	21
22	528.501 895	174.701 006	86.275 943	42.106 430	42.965 822	22
23	572.025 914	189.052 078	93.336 872	45.527 550	46.508 557	23
24	618.119 583	204.246 302	100.809 641	49.145 384	50.260 952	24
25	666.934 615	220.333 213	108.718 271	52.971 243	54.235 416	25
26	718.631 679	237.365 258	117.088 184	57.017 090	58.445 090	26
27	773.380 928	255.397 966	125.946 285	61.295 573	62.903 894	27
28	831.362 563	274.490 128	135.321 049	65.820 068	67.626 572	28
29	892.767 425	294.703 988	145.242 610	70.604 722	72.628 740	29
30	957.797 619	316.105 448	155.742 862	75.664 493	77.926 939	30
31	1026.667 185	338.764 282	166.855 558	81.015 202	83.538 687	31
32	1099.602 799	362.754 362	178.616 419	86.673 576	89.482 540	32
33	1176.844 518	388.153 901	191.063 251	92.657 307	95.778 153	33
34	1258.646 576	415.045 709	204.236 064	98.985 102	102.446 344	34
35	1345.278 214	443.517 458	218.177 201	105.676 745	109.509 160	35
36	1437.024 569	473.661 972	232.931 477	112.753 158	116.989 957	36
37	1534.187 613	505.577 530	248.546 320	120.236 464	124.913 470	37
38	1637.087 147	539.368 184	265.071 922	128.150 061	133.305 900	38
39	1746.061 852	575.144 098	282.561 406	136.518 690	142.194 997	39
40	1861.470 405	613.021 910	301.070 992	145.368 514	151.610 155	40

6% SINKING FUND ACCUMULATION FACTORS

(Future Value of Periodic Payments of $1)

Base:	1.005 000	1.015 000	1.030 000	1.060 000	1.061 831	

Frequency of Payments and of Conversions

Months	Monthly	Quarterly	Semiannual	Annual	Annual Payment Daily Conversion	Months
1	1.000 000	—	—	—	—	1
2	2.005 000	—	—	—	—	2
3	3.015 025	1.000 000	—	—	—	3
4	4.030 100	—	—	—	—	4
5	5.050 251	—	—	—	—	5
6	6.075 502	2.015 000	1.000 000	—	—	6
7	7.105 879	—	—	—	—	7
8	8.141 409	—	—	—	—	8
9	9.182 116	3.045 225	—	—	—	9
10	10.228 026	—	—	—	—	10
11	11.279 167	—	—	—	—	11

Years						Years
1	12.335 562	4.090 903	2.030 000	1.000 000	1.000 000	1
2	25.431 955	8.432 839	4.183 627	2.060 000	2.061 831	2
3	39.336 105	13.041 211	6.468 410	3.183 600	3.189 317	3
4	54.097 832	17.932 370	8.892 336	4.374 616	4.386 516	4
5	69.770 031	23.123 667	11.463 879	5.637 093	5.657 740	5
6	86.408 856	28.633 521	14.192 030	6.975 319	7.007 565	6
7	104.073 927	34.481 479	17.086 324	8.393 838	8.440 851	7
8	122.828 542	40.688 288	20.156 881	9.897 468	9.962 760	8
9	142.739 900	47.275 969	23.414 435	11.491 316	11.578 769	9
10	163.879 347	54.267 894	26.870 374	13.180 795	13.294 699	10
11	186.322 629	61.688 868	30.536 780	14.971 643	15.116 727	11
12	210.150 163	69.565 219	34.426 470	16.869 941	17.051 413	12
13	235.447 328	77.924 892	38.553 042	18.882 138	19.105 723	13
14	262.304 766	86.797 543	42.930 923	21.015 066	21.287 053	14
15	290.818 712	96.214 652	47.575 416	23.275 970	23.603 258	15
16	321.091 337	106.209 628	52.502 759	25.672 528	26.062 677	16
17	353.231 110	116.817 931	57.730 177	28.212 880	28.674 164	17
18	387.353 194	128.077 197	63.275 944	30.905 653	31.447 123	18
19	423.579 854	140.027 372	69.159 449	33.759 992	34.391 538	19
20	462.040 895	152.710 852	75.401 260	36.785 591	37.518 009	20
21	502.874 129	166.172 636	82.023 196	39.992 727	40.837 794	21
22	546.225 867	180.460 482	89.048 409	43.392 290	44.362 846	22
23	592.251 446	195.625 082	96.501 457	46.995 828	48.105 855	23
24	641.115 782	211.720 235	104.408 396	50.815 577	52.080 300	24
25	692.993 962	228.803 043	112.796 867	54.864 512	56.300 489	25
26	748.071 876	246.934 114	121.696 197	59.156 383	60.781 618	26
27	806.546 875	266.177 771	131.137 495	63.705 766	65.539 821	27
28	868.628 484	286.602 288	141.153 768	68.528 112	70.592 229	28
29	934.539 150	308.280 125	151.780 033	73.639 798	75.957 034	29
30	1004.515 042	331.288 191	163.053 437	79.058 186	81.653 552	30
31	1078.806 895	355.708 115	175.013 391	84.801 677	87.702 292	31
32	1157.680 906	381.626 531	187.701 707	90.889 778	94.125 033	32
33	1241.419 693	409.135 393	201.162 741	97.343 165	100.944 900	33
34	1330.323 306	438.332 297	215.443 551	104.183 755	108.186 449	34
35	1424.710 299	469.320 826	230.594 064	111.434 780	115.875 751	35
36	1524.918 875	502.210 922	246.667 242	119.120 867	124.040 492	36
37	1631.308 097	537.119 271	263.719 277	127.268 119	132.710 069	37
38	1744.259 173	574.169 720	281.809 781	135.904 206	141.915 697	38
39	1864.176 824	613.493 716	301.001 997	145.058 458	151.690 520	39
40	1991.490 734	655.230 772	321.363 019	154.761 966	162.069 733	40

SINKING FUND ACCUMULATION FACTORS   6¼%
(Future Value of Periodic Payments of $1)

Base:	1.005 208	1.015 625	1.031 250	1.062 500	1.064 489	

Frequency of Payments and of Conversions

Months	Monthly	Quarterly	Semiannual	Annual	Annual Payment Daily Conversion	Months
1	1.000 000	—	—	—	—	1
2	2.005 208	—	—	—	—	2
3	3.015 652	1.000 000	—	—	—	3
4	4.031 359	—	—	—	—	4
5	5.052 355	—	—	—	—	5
6	6.078 670	2.015 625	1.000 000	—	—	6
7	7.110 329	—	—	—	—	7
8	8.147 362	—	—	—	—	8
9	9.189 797	3.047 119	—	—	—	9
10	10.237 660	—	—	—	—	10
11	11.290 981	—	—	—	—	11

Years						Years
1	12.349 788	4.094 730	2.031 250	1.000 000	1.000 000	1
2	25.493 938	8.451 442	4.191 437	2.062 500	2.064 489	2
3	39.483 542	13.086 897	6.488 745	3.191 406	3.197 625	3
4	54.372 984	18.018 929	8.931 878	4.390 869	4.403 835	4
5	70.220 141	23.266 514	11.530 093	5.665 298	5.687 833	5
6	87.086 617	28.849 840	14.293 234	7.019 380	7.054 634	6
7	105.037 974	34.790 387	17.231 769	8.458 091	8.509 578	7
8	124.143 996	41.111 012	20.356 832	9.986 722	10.058 349	8
9	144.478 951	47.836 032	23.680 264	11.610 892	11.706 999	9
10	166.121 888	54.991 319	27.214 656	13.336 572	13.461 968	10
11	189.156 938	62.604 403	30.973 399	15.170 108	15.330 113	11
12	213.673 643	70.704 574	34.970 734	17.118 240	17.318 732	12
13	239.767 308	79.322 994	39.221 805	19.188 130	19.435 594	13
14	267.539 365	88.492 823	43.742 721	21.387 388	21.688 970	14
15	297.097 771	98.249 338	48.550 608	23.724 100	24.087 663	15
16	328.557 427	108.630 077	53.663 684	26.206 856	26.641 044	16
17	362.040 625	119.674 977	59.101 320	28.844 784	29.359 090	17
18	397.677 524	131.426 532	64.884 119	31.647 583	32.252 419	18
19	435.606 652	143.929 953	71.033 990	34.625 557	35.332 336	19
20	475.975 451	157.233 345	77.574 233	37.789 655	38.610 871	20
21	518.940 844	171.387 891	84.529 629	41.151 508	42.100 836	21
22	564.669 849	186.448 046	91.926 529	44.723 477	45.815 863	22
23	613.340 227	202.471 753	99.792 959	48.518 695	49.770 468	23
24	665.141 172	219.520 659	108.158 723	52.551 113	53.980 100	24
25	720.274 047	237.660 356	117.055 517	56.835 558	58.461 206	25
26	778.953 169	256.960 635	126.517 049	61.387 780	63.231 292	26
27	841.406 639	277.495 748	136.579 167	66.224 516	68.308 995	27
28	907.877 229	299.344 702	147.279 993	71.363 549	73.714 152	28
29	978.623 328	322.591 555	158.660 070	76.823 771	79.467 880	29
30	1053.919 945	347.325 745	170.762 516	82.625 256	85.592 659	30
31	1134.059 777	373.642 433	183.633 184	88.789 335	92.112 417	31
32	1219.354 348	401.642 867	197.320 837	95.338 668	99.052 626	32
33	1310.135 221	431.434 773	211.877 335	102.297 335	106.440 400	33
34	1406.755 284	463.132 770	227.357 830	109.690 918	114.304 601	34
35	1509.590 125	496.858 810	243.820 974	117.546 601	122.675 954	35
36	1619.039 489	532.742 648	261.329 141	125.893 263	131.587 165	36
37	1735.528 836	570.922 339	279.948 667	134.761 592	141.073 048	37
38	1859.510 988	611.544 773	299.750 096	144.184 192	151.170 664	38
39	1991.467 898	654.766 237	320.808 451	154.195 704	161.919 461	39
40	2131.912 515	700.753 018	343.203 519	164.832 935	173.361 434	40

6½% SINKING FUND ACCUMULATION FACTORS
(Future Value of Periodic Payments of $1)

Base: 1.005 417   1.016 250   1.032 500   1.065 000   1.067 153

Frequency of Payments and of Conversions

Months	Monthly	Quarterly	Semiannual	Annual	Annual Payment Daily Conversion	Months
1	1.000 000	—	—	—	—	1
2	2.005 417	—	—	—	—	2
3	3.016 279	1.000 000	—	—	—	3
4	4.032 618	—	—	—	—	4
5	5.054 461	—	—	—	—	5
6	6.081 839	2.016 250	1.000 000	—	—	6
7	7.114 782	—	—	—	—	7
8	8.153 321	—	—	—	—	8
9	9.197 485	3.049 014	—	—	—	9
10	10.247 304	—	—	—	—	10
11	11.302 811	—	—	—	—	11

Years	Monthly	Quarterly	Semiannual	Annual	Annual Payment Daily Conversion	Years
1	12.364 034	4.098 561	2.032 500	1.000 000	1.000 000	1
2	25.556 111	8.470 092	4.199 259	2.065 000	2.067 153	2
3	39.631 685	13.132 774	6.509 147	3.199 225	3.205 968	3
4	54.649 927	18.105 999	8.971 616	4.407 175	4.421 257	4
5	70.673 968	23.410 448	11.596 748	5.693 641	5.718 157	5
6	87.771 168	29.068 182	14.395 285	7.063 728	7.102 147	6
7	106.013 400	35.102 730	17.378 684	8.522 870	8.579 076	7
8	125.477 348	41.539 189	20.559 155	10.076 856	10.155 185	8
9	146.244 833	48.404 326	23.949 715	11.731 852	11.837 133	9
10	168.403 154	55.726 693	27.564 244	13.494 423	13.632 029	10
11	192.045 460	63.536 741	31.417 534	15.371 560	15.547 458	11
12	217.271 134	71.866 950	35.525 359	17.370 711	17.591 513	12
13	244.186 218	80.751 965	39.904 531	19.499 808	19.772 831	13
14	272.903 856	90.228 737	44.572 975	21.767 295	22.100 632	14
15	303.544 767	100.336 676	49.549 798	24.182 169	24.584 750	15
16	336.237 756	111.117 821	54.855 372	26.754 010	27.235 684	16
17	371.120 256	122.617 007	60.511 412	29.493 021	30.064 635	17
18	408.338 901	134.882 057	66.541 069	32.410 067	33.083 559	18
19	448.050 147	147.963 980	72.969 023	35.516 722	36.305 211	19
20	490.420 930	161.917 180	79.821 583	38.825 309	39.743 206	20
21	535.629 362	176.799 685	87.126 797	42.348 954	43.412 072	21
22	583.865 486	192.673 389	94.914 566	46.101 636	47.327 313	22
23	635.332 073	209.604 307	103.216 767	50.098 242	51.505 473	23
24	690.245 473	227.662 852	112.067 379	54.354 628	55.964 208	24
25	748.836 525	246.924 124	121.502 630	58.887 679	60.722 359	25
26	811.351 528	267.468 229	131.561 138	63.715·378	65.800 033	26
27	878.053 277	289.380 604	142.284 074	68.856 877	71.218 687	27
28	949.222 165	312.752 378	153.715 326	74.332 574	77.001 219	28
29	1025.157 366	337.680 750	165.901 684	80.164 192	83.172 063	29
30	1106.178 087	364.269 392	178.893 027	86.374 864	89.757 297	30
31	1192.624 917	392.628 880	192.742 530	92.989 230	96.784 748	31
32	1284.861 251	422.877 155	207.506 879	100.033 530	104.284 111	32
33	1383.274 822	455.140 015	223.246 505	107.535 710	112.287 077	33
34	1488.279 333	489.551 633	240.025 832	115.525 531	120.827 464	34
35	1600.316 191	526.255 119	257.913 538	124.034 690	129.941 362	35
36	1719.856 364	565.403 117	276.982 839	133.096 945	139.667 284	36
37	1847.402 364	607.158 247	297.311 787	142.748 247	150.046 328	37
38	1983.490 356	651.694 724	318.983 589	153.026 883	161.122 354	38
39	2128.692 413	699.197 202	342.086 948	163.973 630	172.942 165	39
40	2283.618 920	749.863 421	366.716 429	175.631 916	185.555 709	40

SINKING FUND ACCUMULATION FACTORS 6¾%
(Future Value of Periodic Payments of $1)

Base: 1.005 625   1.016 875   1.033 750   1.067 500   1.069 823

Frequency of Payments and of Conversions

Months	Monthly	Quarterly	Semiannual	Annual	Annual Payment Daily Conversion	Months
1	1.000 000	—	—	—	—	1
2	2.005 625	—	—	—	—	2
3	3.016 907	1.000 000	—	—	—	3
4	4.033 877	—	—	—	—	4
5	5.056 567	—	—	—	—	5
6	6.085 010	2.016 875	1.000 000	—	—	6
7	7.119 239	—	—	—	—	7
8	8.159 284	—	—	—	—	8
9	9.205 180	3.050 910	—	—	—	9
10	10.256 960	—	—	—	—	10
11	11.314 655	—	—	—	—	11

Years	Monthly	Quarterly	Semiannual	Annual	Annual Payment Daily Conversion	Years
1	12.378 300	4.102 394	2.033 750	1.000 000	1.000 000	1
2	25.618 475	8.488 788	4.207 095	2.067 500	2.069 823	2
3	39.780 537	13.178 843	6.529 616	3.207 056	3.214 346	3
4	54.928 673	18.193 580	9.011 552	4.423 533	4.438 783	4
5	71.131 543	23.555 477	11.663 847	5.722 121	5.748 714	5
6	88.462 585	29.288 567	14.498 192	7.108 364	7.150 109	6
7	107.000 353	35.418 547	17.527 085	8.588 179	8.649 355	7
8	126.828 866	41.972 892	20.763 877	10.167 881	10.253 283	8
9	148.037 998	48.980 981	24.222 841	11.854 213	11.969 203	9
10	170.723 878	56.474 225	27.919 224	13.654 372	13.804 934	10
11	194.989 330	64.486 211	31.869 323	15.576 042	15.768 843	11
12	220.944 334	73.052 850	36.090 553	17.627 425	17.869 879	12
13	248.706 532	82.212 539	40.601 525	19.817 276	20.117 616	13
14	278.401 755	92.006 334	45.422 126	22.154 942	22.522 298	14
15	310.164 594	102.478 133	50.573 608	24.650 401	25.094 884	15
16	344.139 015	113.674 872	56.078 683	27.314 303	27.847 096	16
17	380.479 004	125.646 738	61.961 621	30.158 019	30.791 478	17
18	419.349 272	138.447 391	68.248 359	33.193 685	33.941 446	18
19	460.925 996	152.134 207	74.966 612	36.434 259	37.311 356	19
20	505.397 622	166.768 532	82.146 000	39.893 571	40.916 565	20
21	552.965 715	182.415 960	89.818 175	43.586 387	44.773 503	21
22	603.845 877	199.146 628	98.016 960	47.528 468	48.899 745	22
23	658.268 719	217.035 524	106.778 502	51.736 640	53.314 096	23
24	716.480 912	236.162 830	116.141 428	56.228 863	58.036 672	24
25	778.746 299	256.614 280	126.147 017	61.024 311	63.088 995	25
26	845.347 097	278.481 541	136.839 380	66.143 452	68.494 089	26
27	916.585 171	301.862 626	148.265 657	71.608 135	74.276 586	27
28	992.783 404	326.862 334	160.476 223	77.441 684	80.462 836	28
29	1074.287 164	353.592 720	173.524 910	83.668 998	87.081 032	29
30	1161.465 863	382.173 594	187.469 247	90.316 655	94.161 334	30
31	1254.714 634	412.733 062	202.370 710	97.413 030	101.736 007	31
32	1354.456 125	445.408 098	218.294 996	104.988 409	109.839 570	32
33	1461.142 410	480.345 157	235.312 310	113.075 127	118.508 952	33
34	1575.257 040	517.700 836	253.497 677	121.707 698	127.783 661	34
35	1697.317 238	557.642 570	272.931 269	130.922 967	137.705 962	35
36	1827.876 234	600.349 386	293.698 766	140.760 268	148.321 073	36
37	1967.525 785	646.012 705	315.891 724	151.261 586	159.677 368	37
38	2116.898 845	694.837 199	339.607 986	162.471 743	171.826 599	38
39	2276.672 443	747.041 711	364.952 109	174.438 586	184.824 132	39
40	2447.570 748	802.860 231	392.035 830	187.213 190	198.729 198	40

7% SINKING FUND ACCUMULATION FACTORS
(Future Value of Periodic Payments of $1)

Base: 1.005 833   1.017 500   1.035 000   1.070 000   1.072 501

Frequency of Payments and of Conversions

Months	Monthly	Quarterly	Semiannual	Annual	Annual Payment Daily Conversion	Months
1	1.000 000	—	—	—	—	1
2	2.005 833	—	—	—	—	2
3	3.017 534	1.000 000	—	—	—	3
4	4.035 136	—	—	—	—	4
5	5.058 675	—	—	—	—	5
6	6.088 184	2.017 500	1.000 000	—	—	6
7	7.123 698	—	—	—	—	7
8	8.165 253	—	—	—	—	8
9	9.212 883	3.052 806	—	—	—	9
10	10.266 625	—	—	—	—	10
11	11.326 514	—	—	—	—	11

Years	Monthly	Quarterly	Semiannual	Annual	Annual Payment Daily Conversion	Years
1	12.392 585	4.106 230	2.035 000	1.000 000	1.000 000	1
2	25.681 032	8.507 530	4.214 943	2.070 000	2.072 501	2
3	39.930 101	13.225 104	6.550 152	3.214 900	3.222 759	3
4	55.209 236	18.281 677	9.051 687	4.439 943	4.456 412	4
5	71.592 902	23.701 611	11.731 393	5.750 739	5.779 506	5
6	89.160 944	29.511 016	14.601 962	7.153 291	7.198 525	6
7	107.998 981	35.737 880	17.676 986	8.654 021	8.720 424	7
8	128.198 821	42.412 200	20.971 030	10.259 803	10.352 663	8
9	149.858 909	49.566 129	24.499 691	11.977 989	12.103 240	9
10	173.084 807	57.234 134	28.279 682	13.816 448	13.980 736	10
11	197.989 707	65.453 154	32.328 902	15.783 599	15.994 351	11
12	224.694 985	74.262 784	36.666 528	17.888 451	18.153 956	12
13	253.330 789	83.705 466	41.313 102	20.140 643	20.470 134	13
14	284.036 677	93.826 690	46.290 627	22.550 488	22.954 237	14
15	316.962 297	104.675 216	51.622 677	25.129 022	25.618 439	15
16	352.268 112	116.303 306	57.334 502	27.888 054	28.475 798	16
17	390.126 188	128.766 979	63.453 152	30.840 217	31.540 319	17
18	430.721 027	142.126 280	70.007 603	33.999 033	34.827 020	18
19	474.250 470	156.445 567	77.028 895	37.378 965	38.352 010	19
20	520.926 660	171.793 824	84.550 278	40.995 492	42.132 564	20
21	570.977 075	188.244 992	92.607 371	44.865 177	46.187 212	21
22	624.645 640	205.878 326	101.238 331	49.005 739	50.535 826	22
23	682.193 909	224.778 773	110.484 031	53.436 141	55.199 718	23
24	743.902 347	245.037 388	120.388 257	58.176 671	60.201 746	24
25	810.071 693	266.751 768	130.997 910	63.249 038	65.566 426	25
26	881.024 427	290.026 522	142.363 236	68.676 470	71.320 050	26
27	957.106 339	314.973 777	154.538 058	74.483 823	77.490 817	27
28	1038.688 219	341.713 718	167.580 031	80.697 691	84.108 969	28
29	1126.167 659	370.375 165	181.550 919	87.346 529	91.206 944	29
30	1219.970 996	401.090 196	196.516 883	94.460 786	98.819 528	30
31	1320.555 383	434.024 811	212.548 798	102.073 041	106.984 031	31
32	1428.411 024	469.319 643	229.722 586	110.218 154	115.740 467	32
33	1544.063 557	507.150 729	248.119 577	118.933 425	125.131 754	33
34	1668.076 622	547.700 319	267.826 894	128.258 765	135.203 916	34
35	1801.054 601	591.163 764	288.937 865	138.236 878	146.006 320	35
36	1943.645 569	637.750 450	311.552 464	148.913 460	157.591 907	36
37	2096.544 450	687.684 809	335.777 788	160.337 402	170.017 459	37
38	2260.496 403	741.207 404	361.728 561	172.561 020	183.343 875	38
39	2436.300 456	798.576 080	389.527 678	185.640 292	197.636 468	39
40	2624.813 398	860.067 214	419.306 787	199.635 112	212.965 286	40

SINKING FUND ACCUMULATION FACTORS 7¼%
(Future Value of Periodic Payments of $1)

Base:	1.006 042	1.018 125	1.036 250	1.072 500	1.075 185	

Frequency of Payments and of Conversions

Months	Monthly	Quarterly	Semiannual	Annual	Annual Payment Daily Conversion	Months
1	1.000 000	—	—	—	—	1
2	2.006 042	—	—	—	—	2
3	3.018 162	1.000 000	—	—	—	3
4	4.036 396	—	—	—	—	4
5	5.060 783	—	—	—	—	5
6	6.091 358	2.018 125	1.000 000	—	—	6
7	7.128 160	—	—	—	—	7
8	8.171 226	—	—	—	—	8
9	9.220 594	3.054 704	—	—	—	9
10	10.276 302	—	—	—	—	10
11	11.338 388	—	—	—	—	11

Years						Years
1	12.406 891	4.110 070	2.036 250	1.000 000	1.000 000	1
2	25.743 781	8.526 320	4.222 804	2.072 500	2.075 185	2
3	40.080 381	13.271 558	6.570 756	3.222 756	3.231 208	3
4	55.491 629	18.370 293	9.092 020	4.456 406	4.474 146	4
5	72.058 078	23.848 858	11.799 389	5.779 496	5.810 534	5
6	89.866 319	29.735 550	14.706 600	7.198 509	7.247 399	6
7	109.009 436	36.060 770	17.828 404	8.720 401	8.792 295	7
8	129.587 488	42.857 188	21.180 641	10.352 630	10.453 343	8
9	151.708 036	50.159 905	24.780 320	12.103 196	12.239 277	9
10	175.486 703	58.006 638	28.645 706	13.980 677	14.159 486	10
11	201.047 778	66.437 914	32.796 412	15.994 276	16.224 067	11
12	228.524 868	75.497 277	37.253 499	18.153 861	18.443 873	12
13	258.061 593	85.231 518	42.039 581	20.470 016	20.830 574	13
14	289.812 342	95.690 912	47.178 943	22.954 093	23.396 720	14
15	323.943 072	106.929 478	52.697 663	25.618 264	26.155 802	15
16	360.632 184	119.005 262	58.623 741	28.475 588	29.122 325	16
17	400.071 449	131.980 631	64.987 248	31.540 069	32.311 885	17
18	442.467 014	145.922 601	71.820 470	34.826 724	35.741 253	18
19	488.040 479	160.903 178	79.158 081	38.351 661	39.428 458	19
20	537.030 053	176.999 733	87.037 311	42.132 156	43.392 885	20
21	589.691 802	194.295 401	95.498 138	46.186 738	47.655 377	21
22	646.300 986	212.879 511	104.583 494	50.535 276	52.238 344	22
23	707.153 498	232.848 044	114.339 476	55.199 084	57.165 882	23
24	772.567 411	254.304 134	124.815 587	60.201 017	62.463 896	24
25	842.884 639	277.358 595	136.064 983	65.565 591	68.160 242	25
26	918.472 727	302.130 499	148.144 742	71.319 096	74.284 867	26
27	999.726 770	328.747 786	161.116 157	77.489 731	80.869 971	27
28	1087.071 477	357.347 929	175.045 045	84.107 736	87.950 177	28
29	1180.963 395	388.078 640	190.002 081	91.205 547	95.562 707	29
30	1281.893 291	421.098 635	206.063 157	98.817 949	103.747 585	30
31	1390.388 720	456.578 456	223.309 766	106.982 251	112.547 843	31
32	1507.016 781	494.701 347	241.829 416	115.738 464	122.009 748	32
33	1632.387 084	535.664 203	261.716 078	125.129 503	132.183 046	33
34	1767.154 931	579.678 588	283.070 655	135.201 392	143.121 222	34
35	1912.024 747	626.971 826	306.001 500	146.003 492	154.881 785	35
36	2067.753 757	677.788 174	330.624 964	157.588 746	167.526 566	36
37	2235.155 949	732.390 087	357.065 986	170.013 930	181.122 044	37
38	2415.106 324	791.059 570	385.458 727	183.339 940	195.739 697	38
39	2608.545 473	854.099 638	415.947 251	197.632 085	211.456 378	39
40	2816.484 491	921.835 877	448.686 258	212.960 411	228.354 717	40

7½% SINKING FUND ACCUMULATION FACTORS
(Future Value of Periodic Payments of $1)

Base: 1.006 250   1.018 750   1.037 500   1.075 000   1.077 876

Frequency of Payments and of Conversions

Months	Monthly	Quarterly	Semiannual	Annual	Annual Payment Daily Conversion	Months
1	1.000 000	—	—	—	—	1
2	2.006 250	—	—	—	—	2
3	3.018 789	1.000 000	—	—	—	3
4	4.037 656	—	—	—	—	4
5	5.062 892	—	—	—	—	5
6	6.094 535	2.018 750	1.000 000	—	—	6
7	7.132 626	—	—	—	—	7
8	8.177 205	—	—	—	—	8
9	9.228 312	3.056 602	—	—	—	9
10	10.285 989	—	—	—	—	10
11	11.350 277	—	—	—	—	11

Years						Years
1	12.421 216	4.113 913	2.037 500	1.000 000	1.000 000	1
2	25.806 723	8.545 156	4.230 678	2.075 000	2.077 876	2
3	40.231 382	13.318 207	6.591 428	3.230 625	3.239 692	3
4	55.775 864	18.459 431	9.132 554	4.472 922	4.491 985	4
5	72.527 105	23.997 228	11.867 838	5.808 391	5.841 802	5
6	90.578 789	29.962 188	14.812 116	7.244 020	7.296 736	6
7	110.031 871	36.387 260	17.981 354	8.787 322	8.864 975	7
8	130.995 147	43.307 936	21.392 742	10.446 371	10.555 342	8
9	153.585 857	50.762 444	25.064 781	12.229 849	12.377 346	9
10	177.930 342	58.791 961	29.017 387	14.147 087	14.341 241	10
11	204.164 753	67.440 843	33.271 996	16.208 119	16.458 076	11
12	232.435 809	76.756 864	37.851 685	18.423 728	18.739 761	12
13	262.901 620	86.791 484	42.781 290	20.805 508	21.199 133	13
14	295.732 572	97.600 133	48.087 548	23.365 921	23.850 031	14
15	331.112 276	109.242 516	53.799 237	26.118 365	26.707 370	15
16	369.238 599	121.782 945	59.947 335	29.077 242	29.787 226	16
17	410.324 767	135.290 691	66.565 186	32.258 035	33.106 928	17
18	454.600 560	149.840 369	73.688 682	35.677 388	36.685 154	18
19	502.313 599	165.512 348	81.356 458	39.353 192	40.542 037	19
20	553.730 725	182.393 199	89.610 100	43.304 681	44.699 278	20
21	609.139 496	200.576 169	98.494 372	47.552 532	49.180 267	21
22	668.849 794	220.161 699	108.057 458	52.118 972	54.010 216	22
23	733.195 558	241.257 975	118.351 223	57.027 895	59.216 301	23
24	802.536 650	263.981 530	129.431 496	62.304 987	64.827 814	24
25	877.260 872	288.457 887	141.358 371	67.977 862	70.876 328	25
26	957.786 129	314.822 249	154.196 534	74.076 201	77.395 873	26
27	1044.562 771	343.220 248	168.015 613	80.631 916	84.423 134	27
28	1138.076 109	373.808 752	182.890 556	87.679 310	91.997 647	28
29	1238.849 131	406.756 727	198.902 037	95.255 258	100.162 031	29
30	1347.445 425	442.246 172	216.136 896	103.399 403	108.962 222	30
31	1464.472 331	480.473 126	234.688 606	112.154 358	118.447 735	31
32	1590.584 340	521.648 749	254.657 782	121.565 935	128.671 939	32
33	1726.486 751	566.000 490	276.152 728	131.683 380	139.692 360	33
34	1872.939 621	613.773 341	299.290 023	142.559 633	151.571 005	34
35	2030.762 007	665.231 192	324.195 151	154.251 606	164.374 708	35
36	2200.836 555	720.658 289	351.003 187	166.820 476	178.175 508	36
37	2384.114 432	780.360 802	379.859 524	180.332 012	193.051 056	37
38	2581.620 647	844.668 521	410.920 666	194.856 913	209.085 048	38
39	2794.459 783	913.936 672	444.355 073	210.471 181	226.367 699	39
40	3023.822 174	988.547 881	480.344 078	227.256 520	244.996 249	40

366

SINKING FUND ACCUMULATION FACTORS   7¾%

(Future Value of Periodic Payments of $1)

Base: 1.006 458   1.019 375   1.038 750   1.077 500   1.080 573

Frequency of Payments and of Conversions

Months	Monthly	Quarterly	Semiannual	Annual	Annual Payment Daily Conversion	Months
1	1.000 000	—	—	—	—	1
2	2.006 458	—	—	—	—	2
3	3.019 417	1.000 000	—	—	—	3
4	4.038 917	—	—	—	—	4
5	5.065 002	—	—	—	—	5
6	6.097 713	2.019 375	1.000 000	—	—	6
7	7.137 094	—	—	—	—	7
8	8.183 188	—	—	—	—	8
9	9.236 038	3.058 500	—	—	—	9
10	10.295 687	—	—	—	—	10
11	11.362 180	—	—	—	—	11

Years						Years
1	12.435 561	4.117 759	2.038 750	1.000 000	1.000 000	1
2	25.869 859	8.564 039	4.238 564	2.077 500	2.080 573	2
3	40.383 106	13.365 050	6.612 168	3.238 506	3.248 212	3
4	56.061 955	18.549 094	9.173 289	4.489 490	4.509 931	4
5	73.000 020	24.146 729	11.936 743	5.837 426	5.873 310	5
6	91.298 431	30.190 952	14.918 515	7.289 827	7.346 542	6
7	111.066 443	36.717 392	18.135 851	8.854 788	8.938 476	7
8	132.422 083	43.764 523	21.607 361	10.541 034	10.658 678	8
9	155.492 858	51.373 884	25.353 127	12.357 964	12.517 482	9
10	180.416 517	59.590 332	29.394 813	14.315 707	14.526 056	10
11	207.341 869	68.462 302	33.755 799	16.425 174	16.696 467	11
12	236.429 677	78.042 091	38.461 310	18.698 125	19.041 755	12
13	267.853 614	88.386 171	43.538 564	21.147 229	21.576 011	13
14	301.801 302	99.555 518	49.016 928	23.786 140	24.314 459	14
15	338.475 430	111.615 973	54.928 092	26.629 566	27.273 553	15
16	378.094 967	124.638 631	61.306 248	29.693 357	30.471 071	16
17	420.896 468	138.700 256	68.188 287	32.994 592	33.926 224	17
18	467.135 486	153.883 740	75.614 018	36.551 673	37.659 769	18
19	517.088 099	170.278 587	83.626 394	40.384 428	41.694 138	19
20	571.052 555	187.981 440	92.271 759	44.514 221	46.053 569	20
21	629.351 059	207.096 654	101.600 123	48.964 073	50.764 253	21
22	692.331 690	227.736 911	111.665 441	53.758 788	55.854 492	22
23	760.370 484	250.023 880	122.525 935	58.925 095	61.354 869	23
24	833.873 678	274.088 938	134.244 426	64.491 789	67.298 428	24
25	913.280 134	300.073 945	146.888 695	70.489 903	73.720 879	25
26	999.063 960	328.132 076	160.531 882	76.952 870	80.660 807	26
27	1091.737 343	358.428 730	175.252 901	83.916 718	88.159 908	27
28	1191.853 602	391.142 498	191.136 904	91.420 264	96.263 236	28
29	1300.010 499	426.466 222	208.275 768	99.505 334	105.019 475	29
30	1416.853 800	464.608 129	226.768 629	108.216 997	114.481 232	30
31	1543.081 137	505.793 057	246.722 455	117.603 815	124.705 353	31
32	1679.446 170	550.263 784	268.252 665	127.718 110	135.753 265	32
33	1826.763 088	598.282 456	291.483 794	138.616 264	147.691 343	33
34	1985.911 468	650.132 133	316.550 220	150.359 024	160.591 310	34
35	2157.841 533	706.118 459	343.596 932	163.011 849	174.530 669	35
36	2343.579 816	766.571 462	372.780 376	176.645 267	189.593 167	36
37	2544.235 297	831.847 501	404.269 358	191.335 275	205.869 298	37
38	2761.006 022	902.331 366	438.246 019	207.163 759	223.456 851	38
39	2995.186 253	978.438 544	474.906 889	224.218 950	242.461 489	39
40	3248.174 201	1060.617 674	514.464 026	242.595 919	262.997 391	40

8% SINKING FUND ACCUMULATION FACTORS
(Future Value of Periodic Payments of $1)

Base: 1.006 667   1.020 000   1.040 000   1.080 000   1.083 277

Frequency of Payments and of Conversions

Months	Monthly	Quarterly	Semiannual	Annual	Annual Payment Daily Conversion	Months
1	1.000 000	—	—	—	—	1
2	2.006 667	—	—	—	—	2
3	3.020 044	1.000 000	—	—	—	3
4	4.040 178	—	—	—	—	4
5	5.067 113	—	—	—	—	5
6	6.100 893	2.020 000	1.000 000	—	—	6
7	7.141 566	—	—	—	—	7
8	8.189 176	—	—	—	—	8
9	9.243 771	3.060 400	—	—	—	9
10	10.305 396	—	—	—	—	10
11	11.374 099	—	—	—	—	11

Years						Years
1	12.449 926	4.121 608	2.040 000	1.000 000	1.000 000	1
2	25.933 190	8.582 969	4.246 464	2.080 000	2.083 277	2
3	40.535 558	13.412 090	6.632 975	3.246 400	3.256 767	3
4	56.349 915	18.639 285	9.214 226	4.506 112	4.527 983	4
5	73.476 856	24.297 370	12.006 107	5.866 601	5.905 062	5
6	92.025 325	30.421 862	15.025 805	7.335 929	7.396 820	6
7	112.113 308	37.051 210	18.291 911	8.922 803	9.012 808	7
8	133.868 583	44.227 030	21.824 531	10.636 628	10.763 372	8
9	157.429 535	51.994 367	25.645 413	12.487 558	12.659 718	9
10	182.946 035	60.401 983	29.778 079	14.486 562	14.713 987	10
11	210.580 392	69.502 657	34.247 970	16.645 487	16.939 330	11
12	240.508 387	79.353 519	39.082 604	18.977 126	19.349 994	12
13	272.920 390	90.016 409	44.311 745	21.495 297	21.961 412	13
14	308.022 574	101.558 264	49.967 583	24.214 920	24.790 302	14
15	346.038 222	114.051 539	56.084 938	27.152 114	27.854 775	15
16	387.209 149	127.574 662	62.701 469	30.324 283	31.174 449	16
17	431.797 244	142.212 525	69.857 909	33.750 226	34.770 577	17
18	480.086 128	158.057 019	77.598 314	37.450 244	38.666 182	18
19	532.382 966	175.207 608	85.970 336	41.446 263	42.886 203	19
20	589.020 416	193.771 958	95.025 516	45.761 964	47.457 656	20
21	650.358 746	213.866 607	104.819 598	50.422 921	52.409 808	21
22	716.788 127	235.617 701	115.412 877	55.456 755	57.774 363	22
23	788.731 114	259.161 785	126.870 568	60.893 296	63.585 664	23
24	866.645 333	284.646 659	139.263 206	66.764 759	69.880 915	24
25	951.026 395	312.232 306	152.667 084	73.105 940	76.700 419	25
26	1042.411 042	342.091 897	167.164 718	79.954 415	84.087 833	26
27	1141.380 571	374.412 879	182.845 359	87.350 768	92.090 453	27
28	1248.564 521	409.398 150	199.805 540	95.338 830	100.759 510	28
29	1364.644 687	447.267 331	218.149 672	103.965 936	110.150 504	29
30	1490.359 449	488.258 152	237.990 685	113.283 211	120.323 556	30
31	1626.508 474	532.627 934	259.450 725	123.345 868	131.343 794	31
32	1773.957 801	580.655 213	282.661 904	134.213 537	143.281 768	32
33	1933.645 350	632.641 484	307.767 116	145.950 620	156.213 907	33
34	2106.586 886	688.913 096	334.920 912	158.626 670	170.223 002	34
35	2293.882 485	749.823 299	364.290 459	172.316 804	185.398 737	35
36	2496.723 526	815.754 461	396.056 560	187.102 148	201.838 270	36
37	2716.400 273	887.120 471	430.414 776	203.070 320	219.646 844	37
38	2954.310 082	964.369 336	467.576 621	220.315 945	238.938 471	38
39	3211.966 288	1047.985 991	507.770 873	238.941 221	259.836 655	39
40	3491.007 831	1138.495 348	551.244 977	259.056 519	282.475 186	40

SINKING FUND ACCUMULATION FACTORS 8¼%
(Future Value of Periodic Payments of $1)

Base: 1.006 875   1.020 625   1.041 250   1.082 500   1.085 988

Frequency of Payments and of Conversions

Months	Monthly	Quarterly	Semiannual	Annual	Annual Payment Daily Conversion	Months
1	1.000 000	—	—	—	—	1
2	2.006 875	—	—	—	—	2
3	3.020 672	1.000 000	—	—	—	3
4	4.041 439	—	—	—	—	4
5	5.069 224	—	—	—	—	5
6	6.104 075	2.020 625	1.000 000	—	—	6
7	7.146 041	—	—	—	—	7
8	8.195 170	—	—	—	—	8
9	9.251 512	3.062 300	—	—	—	9
10	10.315 116	—	—	—	—	10
11	11.386 032	—	—	—	—	11

Years						Years
1	12.464 311	4.125 460	2.041 250	1.000 000	1.000 000	1
2	25.996 716	8.601 946	4.254 376	2.082 500	2.085 988	2
3	40.688 741	13.459 326	6.653 852	3.254 306	3.265 359	3
4	56.639 757	18.730 008	9.255 366	4.522 787	4.546 142	4
5	73.957 650	24.449 160	12.075 933	5.895 916	5.937 058	5
6	92.759 550	30.654 941	15.133 995	7.382 330	7.447 576	6
7	113.172 626	37.388 758	18.449 551	8.991 372	9.087 981	7
8	135.334 941	44.695 538	22.044 282	10.733 160	10.869 442	8
9	159.396 393	52.624 036	25.941 695	12.618 646	12.804 088	9
10	185.519 722	61.227 150	30.167 276	14.659 684	14.905 091	10
11	213.881 614	70.562 283	34.748 658	16.869 108	17.186 757	11
12	244.673 898	80.691 720	39.715 799	19.260 809	19.664 618	12
13	278.104 839	91.683 046	45.101 182	21.849 826	22.355 548	13
14	314.400 549	103.609 599	50.940 022	24.652 436	25.277 866	14
15	353.806 515	116.550 953	57.270 501	27.686 262	28.451 469	15
16	396.589 263	130.593 457	64.134 017	30.970 379	31.897 966	16
17	443.038 156	145.830 804	71.575 451	34.525 435	35.640 821	17
18	493.467 354	162.364 660	79.643 466	38.373 784	39.705 518	18
19	548.217 938	180.305 343	88.390 820	42.539 621	44.119 733	19
20	607.660 217	199.772 555	97.874 716	47.049 140	48.913 518	20
21	672.196 232	220.896 187	108.157 170	51.930 694	54.119 514	21
22	742.262 475	243.817 178	119.305 422	57.214 976	59.773 165	22
23	818.332 845	268.688 461	131.392 375	62.935 212	65.912 964	23
24	900.921 848	295.675 983	144.497 068	69.127 366	72.580 715	24
25	990.588 079	324.959 809	158.705 197	75.830 374	79.821 815	25
26	1087.938 001	356.735 326	174.109 673	83.086 380	87.685 566	26
27	1193.630 046	391.214 546	190.811 229	90.941 006	96.225 509	27
28	1308.379 069	428.627 521	208.919 083	99.443 639	105.499 787	28
29	1432.961 180	469.223 876	228.551 646	108.647 740	115.571 546	29
30	1568.218 999	513.274 479	249.837 302	118.611 178	126.509 359	30
31	1715.067 350	561.073 243	272.915 243	129.396 600	138.387 698	31
32	1874.499 451	612.939 090	297.936 383	141.071 820	151.287 436	32
33	2047.593 628	669.218 079	325.064 342	153.710 245	165.296 402	33
34	2235.520 617	730.285 712	354.476 518	167.391 340	180.509 976	34
35	2439.551 470	796.549 445	386.365 244	182.201 126	197.031 742	35
36	2661.066 164	868.451 402	420.939 052	198.232 719	214.974 188	36
37	2901.562 926	946.471 324	458.424 028	215.586 918	234.459 476	37
38	3162.668 369	1031.129 776	499.065 297	234.372 839	255.620 274	38
39	3446.148 496	1122.991 615	543.128 625	254.708 598	278.600 654	39
40	3753.920 642	1222.669 758	590.902 154	276.722 058	303.557 081	40

369

8½% SINKING FUND ACCUMULATION FACTORS
(Future Value of Periodic Payments of $1)

Base:	1.007 083	1.021 250	1.042 500	1.085 000	1.088 706	

Frequency of Payments and of Conversions

Months	Monthly	Quarterly	Semiannual	Annual	Annual Payment Daily Conversion	Months
1	1.000 000	—	—	—	—	1
2	2.007 083	—	—	—	—	2
3	3.021 300	1.000 000	—	—	—	3
4	4.042 701	—	—	—	—	4
5	5.071 337	—	—	—	—	5
6	6.107 259	2.021 250	1.000 000	—	—	6
7	7.150 519	—	—	—	—	7
8	8.201 168	—	—	—	—	8
9	9.259 260	3.064 202	—	—	—	9
10	10.324 846	—	—	—	—	10
11	11.397 980	—	—	—	—	11

Years						Years
1	12.478 716	4.129 316	2.042 500	1.000 000	1.000 000	1
2	26.060 437	8.620 971	4.262 302	2.085 000	2.088 706	2
3	40.842 659	13.506 759	6.674 796	3.262 225	3.273 987	3
4	56.931 495	18.821 266	9.296 710	4.539 514	4.564 410	4
5	74.442 437	24.602 109	12.146 223	5.925 373	5.969 301	5
6	93.501 188	30.890 210	15.243 091	7.429 030	7.498 815	6
7	114.244 559	37.730 079	18.608 786	9.060 497	9.164 006	7
8	136.821 455	45.170 132	22.266 645	10.830 639	10.976 909	8
9	161.393 943	53.263 035	26.242 029	12.751 244	12.950 629	9
10	188.138 416	62.066 074	30.562 501	14.835 099	15.099 429	10
11	217.246 858	71.641 561	35.258 018	17.096 083	17.438 841	11
12	248.928 220	82.057 278	40.361 134	19.549 250	19.985 774	12
13	283.409 927	93.386 952	45.907 233	22.210 936	22.758 634	13
14	320.939 504	105.710 783	51.934 767	25.098 866	25.777 465	14
15	361.786 353	119.116 005	58.485 530	28.232 269	29.064 085	15
16	406.243 693	133.697 507	65.604 939	31.632 012	32.642 248	16
17	454.630 657	149.558 507	73.342 358	35.320 733	36.537 815	17
18	507.294 589	166.811 276	81.751 433	39.322 995	40.778 944	18
19	564.613 533	185.577 942	90.890 468	43.665 450	45.396 287	19
20	626.998 951	205.991 344	100.822 829	48.377 013	50.423 217	20
21	694.898 672	228.195 980	111.617 381	53.489 059	55.896 066	21
22	768.800 112	252.349 028	123.348 967	59.035 629	61.854 390	22
23	849.233 766	278.621 457	136.098 928	65.053 658	68.341 254	23
24	936.777 024	307.199 238	149.955 666	71.583 219	75.403 544	24
25	1032.058 310	338.284 660	165.015 255	78.667 792	83.092 301	25
26	1135.761 595	372.097 766	181.382 110	86.354 555	91.463 099	26
27	1248.631 307	408.877 902	199.169 711	94.694 692	100.576 438	27
28	1371.477 676	448.885 420	218.501 387	103.743 741	110.498 185	28
29	1505.182 546	492.403 517	239.511 173	113.561 959	121.300 053	29
30	1650.705 711	539.740 238	262.344 740	124.214 725	133.060 113	30
31	1809.091 800	591.230 659	287.160 403	135.772 977	145.863 363	31
32	1981.477 780	647.239 261	314.130 221	148.313 680	159.802 339	32
33	2169.101 112	708.162 502	343.441 187	161.920 343	174.977 788	33
34	2373.308 640	774.431 634	375.296 529	176.683 572	191.499 393	34
35	2595.566 257	846.515 747	409.917 113	192.701 675	209.486 566	35
36	2837.469 426	924.925 095	447.542 980	210.081 318	229.069 311	36
37	3100.754 635	1010.214 702	488.435 008	228.938 230	250.389 166	37
38	3387.311 862	1102.988 299	532.876 720	249.397 979	273.600 224	38
39	3699.198 142	1203.902 590	581.176 249	271.596 808	298.870 244	39
40	4038.652 333	1313.671 904	633.668 480	295.682 536	326.381 871	40

SINKING FUND ACCUMULATION FACTORS 8¾%

(Future Value of Periodic Payments of $1)

Base:	1.007 292	1.021 875	1.043 750	1.087 500	1.091 431	
			Frequency of Payments and of Conversions			

Months	Monthly	Quarterly	Semiannual	Annual	Annual Payment Daily Conversion	Months
1	1.000 000	—	—	—	—	1
2	2.007 292	—	—	—	—	2
3	3.021 928	1.000 000	—	—	—	3
4	4.043 963	—	—	—	—	4
5	5.073 450	—	—	—	—	5
6	6.110 444	2.021 875	1.000 000	—	—	6
7	7.155 000	—	—	—	—	7
8	8.207 171	—	—	—	—	8
9	9.267 015	3.066 104	—	—	—	9
10	10.334 587	—	—	—	—	10
11	11.409 944	—	—	—	—	11

Years						Years
1	12.493 141	4.133 175	2.043 750	1.000 000	1.000 000	1
2	26.124 355	8.640 043	4.270 240	2.087 500	2.091 431	2
3	40.997 316	13.554 391	6.695 809	3.270 156	3.282 652	3
4	57.225 142	18.913 061	9.338 259	4.556 295	4.582 787	4
5	74.931 254	24.756 226	12.216 981	5.954 971	6.001 794	5
6	94.250 319	31.127 690	15.353 101	7.476 031	7.550 542	6
7	115.329 271	38.075 218	18.769 634	9.130 183	9.240 893	7
8	138.328 427	45.650 895	22.491 653	10.929 074	11.085 794	8
9	163.422 710	53.911 513	26.546 473	12.885 368	13.099 375	9
10	190.802 977	62.918 999	30.963 851	15.012 838	15.297 060	10
11	220.677 472	72.740 881	35.776 205	17.326 461	17.695 680	11
12	253.273 409	83.450 791	41.018 850	19.842 527	20.313 608	12
13	288.838 699	95.129 018	46.730 262	22.578 748	23.170 894	13
14	327.643 839	107.863 111	52.952 355	25.554 388	26.289 424	14
15	369.983 965	121.748 534	59.730 790	28.790 397	29.693 084	15
16	416.181 099	136.889 382	67.115 313	32.309 557	33.407 942	16
17	466.586 599	153.399 162	75.160 116	36.136 643	37.462 452	17
18	521.583 830	171.401 645	83.924 237	40.298 600	41.887 669	18
19	581.591 078	191.031 790	93.471 994	44.824 727	46.717 486	19
20	647.064 737	212.436 758	103.873 455	49.746 891	51.988 897	20
21	718.502 772	235.777 018	115.204 952	55.099 744	57.742 276	21
22	796.448 513	261.227 546	127.549 645	60.920 971	64.021 690	22
23	881.494 785	288.979 137	140.998 127	67.251 556	70.875 236	23
24	974.288 418	319.239 838	155.649 092	74.136 067	78.355 405	24
25	1075.535 163	352.236 505	171.610 060	81.622 973	86.519 492	25
26	1186.005 063	388.216 507	188.998 162	89.764 984	95.430 026	26
27	1306.538 310	427.449 575	207.941 006	98.619 420	105.155 256	27
28	1438.051 632	470.229 831	228.577 606	108.248 619	115.769 671	28
29	1581.545 267	516.877 986	251.059 408	118.720 373	127.354 568	29
30	1738.110 574	567.743 749	275.551 400	130.108 406	139.998 680	30
31	1908.938 325	623.208 449	302.233 320	142.492 891	153.798 852	31
32	2095.327 771	683.687 889	331.300 979	155.961 019	168.860 783	32
33	2298.696 516	749.635 469	362.967 696	170.607 608	185.299 836	33
34	2520.591 305	821.545 579	397.465 862	186.535 774	203.241 922	34
35	2762.699 781	899.957 313	435.048 649	203.857 654	222.824 465	35
36	3026.863 328	985.458 501	475.991 866	222.695 199	244.197 453	36
37	3315.091 070	1078.690 125	520.595 983	243.181 029	267.524 588	37
38	3629.575 155	1180.351 118	569.188 335	265.459 369	292.984 537	38
39	3972.707 426	1291.203 606	622.125 526	289.687 064	320.772 307	39
40	4347.097 613	1412.078 621	679.796 047	316.034 682	351.100 731	40

9% SINKING FUND ACCUMULATION FACTORS
(Future Value of Periodic Payments of $1)

Base: 1.007 500   1.022 500   1.045 000   1.090 000   1.094 162

Frequency of Payments and of Conversions

Months	Monthly	Quarterly	Semiannual	Annual	Annual Payment Daily Conversion	Months
1	1.000 000	—	—	—	—	1
2	2.007 500	—	—	—	—	2
3	3.022 556	1.000 000	—	—	—	3
4	4.045 225	—	—	—	—	4
5	5.075 565	—	—	—	—	5
6	6.113 631	2.022 500	1.000 000	—	—	6
7	7.159 484	—	—	—	—	7
8	8.213 180	—	—	—	—	8
9	9.274 779	3.068 006	—	—	—	9
10	10.344 339	—	—	—	—	10
11	11.421 922	—	—	—	—	11

Years						Years
1	12.507 586	4.137 036	2.045 000	1.000 000	1.000 000	1
2	26.188 471	8.659 162	4.278 191	2.090 000	2.094 162	2
3	41.152 716	13.602 222	6.716 892	3.278 100	3.291 352	3
4	57.520 711	19.005 398	9.380 014	4.573 129	4.601 273	4
5	75.424 137	24.911 520	12.288 209	5.984 711	6.034 538	5
6	95.007 028	31.367 403	15.464 032	7.523 335	7.602 762	6
7	116.426 928	38.424 222	18.932 109	9.200 435	9.318 653	7
8	139.856 164	46.137 912	22.719 337	11.028 474	11.196 115	8
9	165.483 223	54.569 619	26.855 084	13.021 036	13.250 364	9
10	193.514 277	63.786 176	31.371 423	15.192 930	15.498 044	10
11	224.174 837	73.860 642	36.303 378	17.560 293	17.957 371	11
12	257.711 590	84.872 872	41.689 196	20.140 720	20.648 272	12
13	294.394 279	96.910 157	47.570 645	22.953 385	23.592 554	13
14	334.518 079	110.067 912	53.993 333	26.019 189	26.814 076	14
15	378.405 769	124.450 435	61.007 070	29.360 916	30.338 942	15
16	426.410 427	140.171 731	68.666 245	33.003 399	34.195 717	16
17	478.918 252	157.356 417	77.030 256	36.973 705	38.415 653	17
18	536.351 674	176.140 711	86.163 966	41.301 338	43.032 947	18
19	599.172 747	196.673 509	96.138 205	46.018 458	48.085 014	19
20	667.886 870	219.117 569	107.030 323	51.160 120	53.612 794	20
21	743.046 852	243.650 796	118.924 789	56.764 530	59.661 081	21
22	825.257 358	270.467 657	131.913 842	62.873 338	66.278 886	22
23	915.179 777	299.780 720	146.098 214	69.531 939	73.519 837	23
24	1013.537 539	331.822 341	161.587 902	76.789 813	81.442 610	24
25	1121.121 937	366.846 502	178.503 028	84.700 896	90.111 408	25
26	1238.798 495	405.130 828	196.974 769	93.323 977	99.596 476	26
27	1367.513 924	446.978 787	217.146 373	102.723 135	109.974 677	27
28	1508.303 750	492.722 092	239.174 268	112.968 217	121.330 110	28
29	1662.300 631	542.723 336	263.229 280	124.135 356	133.754 793	29
30	1830.743 483	597.378 862	289.497 954	136.307 539	147.349 408	30
31	2014.987 436	657.121 905	318.184 003	149.575 217	162.224 120	31
32	2216.514 743	722.426 029	349.509 886	164.036 987	178.499 464	32
33	2436.946 701	793.808 878	383.718 533	179.800 315	196.307 326	33
34	2678.056 697	871.836 279	421.075 231	196.982 344	215.792 012	34
35	2941.784 474	957.126 730	461.869 680	215.710 755	237.111 414	35
36	3230.251 735	1050.356 299	506.418 237	236.124 723	260.438 293	36
37	3545.779 215	1152.263 986	555.066 375	258.375 948	285.961 678	37
38	3890.905 350	1263.657 578	608.191 358	282.629 783	313.888 394	38
39	4268.406 696	1385.420 056	666.205 168	309.066 463	344.444 746	39
40	4681.320 273	1518.516 589	729.557 699	337.882 445	377.878 344	40

SINKING FUND ACCUMULATION FACTORS 9¼%

(Future Value of Periodic Payments of $1)

Base: 1.007 708   1.023 125   1.046 250   1.092 500   1.096 900

Frequency of Payments and of Conversions

Months	Monthly	Quarterly	Semiannual	Annual	Annual Payment Daily Conversion	Months
1	1.000 000	—	—	—	—	1
2	2.007 708	—	—	—	—	2
3	3.023 184	1.000 000	—	—	—	3
4	4.046 488	—	—	—	—	4
5	5.077 680	—	—	—	—	5
6	6.116 820	2.023 125	1.000 000	—	—	6
7	7.163 971	—	—	—	—	7
8	8.219 193	—	—	—	—	8
9	9.282 549	3.069 910	—	—	—	9
10	10.354 102	—	—	—	—	10
11	11.433 915	—	—	—	—	11

Years						Years
1	12.522 052	4.140 901	2.046 250	1.000 000	1.000 000	1
2	26.252 784	8.678 329	4.286 155	2.092 500	2.096 900	2
3	41.308 863	13.650 253	6.738 043	3.286 056	3.300 090	3
4	57.818 217	19.098 280	9.421 975	4.590 016	4.619 869	4
5	75.921 123	25.068 001	12.359 912	6.014 593	6.067 535	5
6	95.771 396	31.609 372	15.575 892	7.570 943	7.655 480	6
7	117.537 700	38.777 135	19.096 230	9.271 255	9.397 296	7
8	141.404 978	46.631 271	22.949 729	11.128 846	11.307 895	8
9	167.576 024	55.237 505	27.167 920	13.158 264	13.403 632	9
10	196.273 209	64.667 859	31.785 317	15.375 404	15.702 445	10
11	227.740 365	75.001 248	36.839 699	17.797 629	18.224 014	11
12	262.244 861	86.324 144	42.372 424	20.443 909	20.989 923	12
13	300.079 874	98.731 303	48.428 761	23.334 971	24.023 848	13
14	341.566 880	112.326 551	55.058 263	26.493 456	27.351 762	14
15	387.058 383	127.223 657	62.315 175	29.944 100	31.002 151	15
16	436.940 915	143.547 285	70.258 875	33.713 930	35.006 262	16
17	491.638 316	161.434 037	78.954 359	37.832 468	39.398 373	17
18	551.615 338	181.033 595	88.472 776	42.331 972	44.216 080	18
19	617.381 589	202.509 974	98.892 006	47.247 679	49.500 623	19
20	689.495 873	226.042 895	110.297 303	52.618 089	55.297 238	20
21	768.570 926	251.829 291	122.781 987	58.485 262	61.655 547	21
22	855.278 631	280.084 948	136.448 209	64.895 149	68.629 976	22
23	950.355 723	311.046 321	151.407 789	71.897 951	76.280 228	23
24	1054.610 051	344.972 503	167.783 130	79.548 511	84.671 790	24
25	1168.927 439	382.147 401	185.708 219	87.906 748	93.876 496	25
26	1294.279 215	422.882 105	205.329 720	97.038 122	103.973 139	26
27	1431.730 465	467.517 498	226.808 183	107.014 149	115.048 147	27
28	1582.449 079	516.427 101	250.319 346	117.912 958	127.196 325	28
29	1747.715 679	570.020 207	276.055 585	129.819 906	140.521 663	29
30	1928.934 497	628.745 301	304.227 476	142.828 247	155.138 227	30
31	2127.645 307	693.093 812	335.065 529	157.039 860	171.171 138	31
32	2345.536 509	763.604 230	368.822 067	172.566 047	188.757 640	32
33	2584.459 472	840.866 609	405.773 292	189.528 407	208.048 276	33
34	2846.444 272	925.527 506	446.221 546	208.059 784	229.208 177	34
35	3133.716 930	1018.295 390	490.497 784	228.305 315	252.418 474	35
36	3448.718 338	1119.946 573	538.964 285	250.423 556	277.877 851	36
37	3794.124 987	1231.331 706	592.017 609	274.587 735	305.804 245	37
38	4172.871 720	1353.382 894	650.091 851	300.987 101	336.436 710	38
39	4588.176 657	1487.121 503	713.662 184	329.828 407	370.037 463	39
40	5043.568 550	1633.666 699	783.248 754	361.337 535	406.894 134	40

9½% SINKING FUND ACCUMULATION FACTORS
(Future Value of Periodic Payments of $1)

Base: 1.007 917   1.023 750   1.047 500   1.095 000   1.099 645

Frequency of Payments and of Conversions

Months	Monthly	Quarterly	Semiannual	Annual	Annual Payment Daily Conversion	Months
1	1.000 000	—	—	—	—	1
2	2.007 917	—	—	—	—	2
3	3.023 813	1.000 000	—	—	—	3
4	4.047 751	—	—	—	—	4
5	5.079 796	—	—	—	—	5
6	6.120 011	2.023 750	1.000 000	—	—	6
7	7.168 461	—	—	—	—	7
8	8.225 211	—	—	—	—	8
9	9.290 328	3.071 814	—	—	—	9
10	10.363 876	—	—	—	—	10
11	11.445 923	—	—	—	—	11

Years						Years
1	12.536 537	4.144 770	2.047 500	1.000 000	1.000 000	1
2	26.317 295	8.697 543	4.294 132	2.095 000	2.099 645	2
3	41.465 760	13.698 484	6.759 263	3.294 025	3.308 864	3
4	58.117 673	19.191 709	9.464 144	4.606 957	4.638 576	4
5	76.422 249	25.225 677	12.432 091	6.044 618	6.100 788	5
6	96.543 509	31.853 619	15.688 690	7.618 857	7.708 701	6
7	118.661 756	39.134 004	19.262 013	9.342 648	9.476 835	7
8	142.975 186	47.131 058	23.182 864	11.230 200	11.421 155	8
9	169.701 665	55.915 328	27.485 042	13.297 069	13.559 217	9
10	199.080 682	65.564 306	32.205 635	15.560 291	15.910 326	10
11	231.375 495	76.163 114	37.385 334	18.038 518	18.495 712	11
12	266.875 491	87.805 249	43.068 791	20.752 178	21.338 718	12
13	305.898 776	100.593 416	49.305 000	23.723 634	24.465 017	13
14	348.795 027	114.640 429	56.147 720	26.977 380	27.902 835	14
15	395.948 628	130.070 205	63.655 936	30.540 231	31.683 215	15
16	447.782 110	147.018 862	71.894 374	34.441 553	35.840 291	16
17	504.759 939	165.635 915	80.934 051	38.713 500	40.411 600	17
18	567.392 681	186.085 599	90.852 894	43.391 283	45.438 417	18
19	636.241 570	208.548 315	101.736 405	48.513 454	50.966 131	19
20	711.923 546	233.222 222	113.678 406	54.122 233	57.044 655	20
21	795.116 775	260.324 986	126.781 842	60.263 845	63.728 874	21
22	886.566 731	290.095 699	141.159 669	66.988 910	71.079 142	22
23	987.092 874	322.796 990	156.935 829	74.352 856	79.161 828	23
24	1097.595 994	358.717 340	174.246 319	82.416 378	88.049 914	24
25	1219.066 282	398.173 627	193.240 362	91.245 934	97.823 655	25
26	1352.592 202	441.513 923	214.081 695	100.914 297	108.571 300	26
27	1499.370 247	489.120 564	236.949 978	111.501 156	120.389 895	27
28	1660.715 659	541.413 520	262.042 344	123.093 766	133.386 155	28
29	1838.074 212	598.854 105	289.575 100	135.787 673	147.677 428	29
30	2033.035 174	661.949 042	319.785 589	149.687 502	163.392 757	30
31	2247.345 541	731.254 936	352.934 236	164.907 815	180.674 040	31
32	2482.925 693	807.383 183	389.306 796	181.574 057	199.677 318	32
33	2741.886 607	891.005 364	429.216 815	199.823 593	220.574 179	33
34	3026.548 765	982.859 168	473.008 333	219.806 834	243.553 309	34
35	3339.462 955	1083.754 903	521.058 849	241.688 483	268.822 197	35
36	3683.433 122	1194.582 640	573.782 579	265.648 889	296.609 004	36
37	4061.541 498	1316.320 069	631.634 021	291.885 534	327.164 631	37
38	4477.176 216	1450.041 121	695.111 877	320.614 659	360.764 974	38
39	4934.061 676	1596.925 443	764.763 352	352.073 052	397.713 427	39
40	5436.291 914	1758.268 805	841.188 868	386.519 992	438.343 610	40

SINKING FUND ACCUMULATION FACTORS 9¾%
(Future Value of Periodic Payments of $1)

Base: 1.008 125   1.024 375   1.048 750   1.097 500   1.102 397

Frequency of Payments and of Conversions

Months	Monthly	Quarterly	Semiannual	Annual	Annual Payment Daily Conversion	Months
1	1.000 000	—	—	—	—	1
2	2.008 125	—	—	—	—	2
3	3.024 441	1.000 000	—	—	—	3
4	4.049 015	—	—	—	—	4
5	5.081 913	—	—	—	—	5
6	6.123 203	2.024 375	1.000 000	—	—	6
7	7.172 954	—	—	—	—	7
8	8.231 235	—	—	—	—	8
9	9.298 113	3.073 719	—	—	—	9
10	10.373 661	—	—	—	—	10
11	11.457 947	—	—	—	—	11

Years						Years
1	12.551 042	4.148 641	2.048 750	1.000 000	1.000 000	1
2	26.382 005	8.716 806	4.302 122	2.097 500	2.102 397	2
3	41.623 411	13.746 917	6.780 553	3.302 006	3.317 676	3
4	58.419 093	19.285 690	9.506 522	4.623 952	4.657 395	4
5	76.927 553	25.384 560	12.504 750	6.074 787	6.134 298	5
6	97.323 453	32.100 167	15.802 432	7.667 079	7.762 431	6
7	119.799 271	39.494 877	19.429 474	9.414 619	9.557 280	7
8	144.567 109	47.637 364	23.418 773	11.332 544	11.535 916	8
9	171.860 704	56.603 244	27.806 510	13.437 468	13.717 158	9
10	201.937 623	66.475 782	32.632 479	15.747 621	16.121 752	10
11	235.081 703	7.7.346 662	37.940 449	18.283 014	18.772 569	11
12	271.605 724	89.316 839	43.778 560	21.065 607	21.694 822	12
13	311.854 363	102.497 478	50.199 762	24.119 504	24.916 304	13
14	356.207 446	117.010 984	57.262 292	27.471 156	28.467 656	14
15	405.083 533	132.992 142	65.030 203	31.149 594	32.382 656	15
16	458.943 868	150.589 364	73.573 946	35.186 679	36.698 539	16
17	518.296 730	169.966 072	82.971 009	39.617 380	41.456 355	17
18	583.702 232	191.302 213	93.306 618	44.480 075	46.701 357	18
19	655.777 606	214.795 932	104.674 512	49.816 882	52.483 431	19
20	735.203 025	240.665 409	117.177 792	55.674 028	58.857 571	20
21	822.728 028	269.150 888	130.929 858	62.102 246	65.884 403	21
22	919.178 587	300.516 909	146.055 432	69.157 215	73.630 761	22
23	1025.464 906	335.054 759	162.691 696	76.900 043	82.170 322	23
24	1142.590 009	373.085 184	180.989 534	85.397 797	91.584 307	24
25	1271.659 204	414.961 365	201.114 896	94.724 083	101.962 255	25
26	1413.890 516	461.072 196	223.250 310	104.959 681	113.402 873	26
27	1570.626 183	511.845 899	247.596 534	116.193 249	126.014 974	27
28	1743.345 316	567.753 997	274.374 375	128.522 091	139.918 516	28
29	1933.677 867	629.315 697	303.826 694	142.052 995	155.245 736	29
30	2143.420 002	697.102 708	336.220 610	156.903 162	172.142 417	30
31	2374.551 057	771.744 554	371.849 919	173.201 221	190.769 265	31
32	2629.252 215	853.934 416	411.037 760	191.088 340	211.303 444	32
33	2909.927 088	944.435 574	454.139 549	210.719 453	233.940 259	33
34	3219.224 404	1044.088 492	501.546 196	232.264 599	258.895 014	34
35	3560.063 001	1153.818 625	553.687 656	255.910 398	286.405 058	35
36	3935.659 371	1274.645 011	611.036 826	281.861 661	316.732 045	36
37	4349.558 013	1407.689 740	674.113 833	310.343 173	350.164 421	37
38	4805.664 889	1554.188 367	743.490 756	341.601 633	387.020 168	38
39	5308.284 276	1715.501 393	819.796 807	375.907 792	427.649 830	39
40	5862.159 390	1893.126 897	903.724 044	413.558 802	472.439 842	40

10% SINKING FUND ACCUMULATION FACTORS
(Future Value of Periodic Payments of $1)

Base: 1.008 333   1.025 000   1.050 000   1.100 000   1.105 156

Frequency of Payments and of Conversions

Months	Monthly	Quarterly	Semiannual	Annual	Annual Payment Daily Conversion	Months
1	1.000 000	—	—	—	—	1
2	2.008 333	—	—	—	—	2
3	3.025 069	1.000 000	—	—	—	3
4	4.050 278	—	—	—	—	4
5	5.084 031	—	—	—	—	5
6	6.126 398	2.025 000	1.000 000	—	—	6
7	7.177 451	—	—	—	—	7
8	8.237 263	—	—	—	—	8
9	9.305 907	3.075 625	—	—	—	9
10	10.383 456	—	—	—	—	10
11	11.469 985	—	—	—	—	11

Years	Monthly	Quarterly	Semiannual	Annual	Annual Payment Daily Conversion	Years
1	12.565 568	4.152 516	2.050 000	1.000 000	1.000 000	1
2	26.446 915	8.736 116	4.310 125	2.100 000	2.105 156	2
3	41.781 821	13.795 553	6.801 913	3.310 000	3.326 524	3
4	58.722 492	19.380 225	9.549 109	4.641 000	4.676 327	4
5	77.437 072	25.544 658	12.577 893	6.105 100	6.168 069	5
6	98.111 314	32.349 038	15.917 127	7.715 610	7.816 676	6
7	120.950 418	39.859 801	19.598 632	9.487 171	9.638 643	7
8	146.181 076	48.150 278	23.657 492	11.435 888	11.652 200	8
9	174.053 713	57.301 413	28.132 385	13.579 477	13.877 493	9
10	204.844 979	67.402 554	33.065 954	15.937 425	16.336 789	10
11	238.860 493	78.552 323	38.505 214	18.531 167	19.054 693	11
12	276.437 876	90.859 582	44.501 999	21.384 284	22.058 401	12
13	317.950 102	104.444 494	51.113 454	24.522 712	25.377 964	13
14	363.809 201	119.439 694	58.402 583	27.974 983	29.046 599	14
15	414.470 346	135.991 590	66.438 848	31.772 482	33.101 010	15
16	470.436 376	154.261 786	75.298 829	35.949 730	37.581 766	16
17	532.262 780	174.428 663	85.066 959	40.544 703	42.533 698	17
18	600.563 216	196.689 122	95.836 323	45.599 173	48.006 353	18
19	676.015 601	221.260 504	107.709 546	51.159 090	54.054 489	19
20	759.368 836	248.382 713	120.799 774	57.274 999	60.738 620	20
21	851.450 244	278.320 556	135.231 751	64.002 499	68.125 624	21
22	953.173 779	311.366 333	151.143 006	71.402 749	76.289 413	22
23	1065.549 097	347.842 687	168.685 164	79.543 024	85.311 670	23
24	1189.691 580	388.105 758	188.025 393	88.497 327	95.282 667	24
25	1326.833 403	432.548 654	209.347 996	98.347 059	106.302 170	25
26	1478.335 767	481.605 296	232.856 165	109.181 765	118.480 436	26
27	1645.702 407	535.754 648	258.773 922	121.099 942	131.939 313	27
28	1830.594 523	595.525 404	287.348 249	134.209 936	146.813 467	28
29	2034.847 258	661.501 133	318.851 445	148.630 930	163.251 721	29
30	2260.487 925	734.325 993	353.583 718	164.494 023	181.418 550	30
31	2509.756 117	814.711 013	391.876 049	181.943 425	201.495 721	31
32	2785.125 947	903.441 034	434.093 344	201.137 767	223.684 118	32
33	3089.330 596	1001.382 375	480.637 912	222.251 544	248.205 750	33
34	3425.389 447	1109.491 289	531.953 298	245.476 699	275.305 967	34
35	3796.638 052	1228.823 303	588.528 511	271.024 368	305.255 923	35
36	4206.761 236	1360.543 518	650.902 683	299.126 805	338.355 284	36
37	4659.829 677	1505.937 989	719.670 208	330.039 486	374.935 228	37
38	5160.340 305	1666.426 280	795.486 404	364.043 434	415.361 756	38
39	5713.260 935	1843.575 325	879.073 761	401.447 778	460.039 359	39
40	6324.079 581	2039.114 724	971.228 821	442.592 556	509.415 060	40

SINKING FUND ACCUMULATION FACTORS 10¼%

(Future Value of Periodic Payments of $1)

Base: 1.008 542   1.025 625   1.051 250   1.102 500   1.107 921

Frequency of Payments and of Conversions

Months	Monthly	Quarterly	Semiannual	Annual	Annual Payment Daily Conversion	Months
1	1.000 000	—	—	—	—	1
2	2.008 542	—	—	—	—	2
3	3.025 698	1.000 000	—	—	—	3
4	4.051 542	—	—	—	—	4
5	5.086 149	—	—	—	—	5
6	6.129 594	2.025 625	1.000 000	—	—	6
7	7.181 951	—	—	—	—	7
8	8.243 296	—	—	—	—	8
9	9.313 708	3.077 532	—	—	—	9
10	10.393 262	—	—	—	—	10
11	11.482 038	—	—	—	—	11

Years						Years
1	12.580 114	4.156 393	2.051 250	1.000 000	1.000 000	1
2	26.512 026	8.755 474	4.318 141	2.102 500	2.107 921	2
3	41.940 993	13.844 392	6.823 342	3.318 006	3.335 410	3
4	59.027 882	19.475 318	9.591 907	4.658 102	4.695 372	4
5	77.950 846	25.705 980	12.651 521	6.135 557	6.202 102	5
6	98.907 179	32.600 256	16.032 782	7.764 452	7.871 439	6
7	122.115 378	40.228 823	19.769 503	9.560 308	9.720 934	7
8	147.817 417	48.669 891	23.899 053	11.540 240	11.770 028	8
9	176.281 272	58.009 997	28.462 728	13.723 114	14.040 263	9
10	207.803 714	68.344 895	33.506 167	16.129 734	16.555 504	10
11	242.713 406	79.780 538	39.079 805	18.783 031	19.342 193	11
12	281.374 322	92.434 163	45.239 381	21.708 292	22.429 625	12
13	324.189 554	106.435 496	52.046 491	24.933 392	25.850 255	13
14	371.605 502	121.928 076	59.569 210	28.489 065	29.640 044	14
15	424.116 537	139.070 734	67.882 766	32.409 194	33.838 832	15
16	482.270 153	158.039 215	77.070 298	36.731 136	38.490 757	16
17	546.672 673	179.027 983	87.223 684	41.496 078	43.644 723	17
18	617.995 576	202.252 213	98.444 460	46.749 426	49.354 911	18
19	696.982 491	227.950 001	110.844 837	52.541 242	55.681 350	19
20	784.456 956	256.384 797	124.548 824	58.926 719	62.690 544	20
21	881.331 002	287.848 115	139.693 464	65.966 708	70.456 179	21
22	988.614 662	322.662 514	156.430 207	73.728 295	79.059 890	22
23	1107.426 503	361.184 912	174.926 427	82.285 446	88.592 123	23
24	1239.005 287	403.810 236	195.367 091	91.719 704	99.153 086	24
25	1384.722 888	450.975 481	217.956 612	102.120 974	110.853 800	25
26	1546.098 594	503.164 181	242.920 891	113.588 373	123.817 268	26
27	1724.814 949	560.911 374	270.509 580	126.231 182	138.179 769	27
28	1922.735 295	624.809 081	300.998 572	140.169 878	154.092 287	28
29	2141.923 199	695.512 378	334.692 767	155.537 290	171.722 102	29
30	2384.663 970	773.746 112	371.929 117	172.479 862	191.254 547	30
31	2653.488 485	860.312 332	413.079 997	191.159 048	212.894 955	31
32	2951.199 576	956.098 511	458.556 927	211.752 851	236.870 821	32
33	3280.901 254	1062.086 643	508.814 690	234.457 518	263.434 189	33
34	3646.031 071	1179.363 315	564.355 880	259.489 414	292.864 307	34
35	4050.395 965	1309.130 842	625.735 923	287.087 078	325.470 556	35
36	4498.211 944	1452.719 594	693.568 640	317.513 504	361.595 709	36
37	4994.148 053	1611.601 637	768.532 377	351.058 638	401.619 529	37
38	5543.375 045	1787.405 821	851.376 794	388.042 148	445.962 766	38
39	6151.619 301	1981.934 484	942.930 359	428.816 469	495.091 575	39
40	6825.222 528	2197.181 924	1044.108 637	473.770 157	549.522 421	40

10½% SINKING FUND ACCUMULATION FACTORS
(Future Value of Periodic Payments of $1)

Base: 1.008 750   1.026 250   1.052 500   1.105 000   1.110 694

Frequency of Payments and of Conversions

Months	Monthly	Quarterly	Semiannual	Annual	Annual Payment Daily Conversion	Months
1	1.000 000	—	—	—	—	1
2	2.008 750	—	—	—	—	2
3	3.026 327	1.000 000	—	—	—	3
4	4.052 807	—	—	—	—	4
5	5.088 269	—	—	—	—	5
6	6.132 791	2.026 250	1.000 000	—	—	6
7	7.186 453	—	—	—	—	7
8	8.249 335	—	—	—	—	8
9	9.321 516	3.079 439	—	—	—	9
10	10.403 080	—	—	—	—	10
11	11.494 107	—	—	—	—	11

Years						Years
1	12.594 680	4.160 274	2.052 500	1.000 000	1.000 000	1
2	26.577 337	8.774 881	4.326 170	2.105 000	2.110 694	2
3	42.100 932	13.893 435	6.844 842	3.326 025	3.344 334	3
4	59.335 280	19.570 973	9.634 916	4.675 258	4.714 530	4
5	78.468 912	25.868 538	12.725 638	6.166 160	6.236 399	5
6	99.711 137	32.853 843	16.149 405	7.813 606	7.926 728	6
7	123.294 329	40.601 994	19.942 105	9.634 035	9.804 166	7
8	149.476 469	49.196 298	24.143 491	11.645 609	11.889 425	8
9	178.543 972	58.729 162	28.797 603	13.868 398	14.205 508	9
10	210.814 814	69.303 084	33.953 225	16.324 579	16.777 967	10
11	246.642 013	81.031 754	39.664 397	19.038 660	19.635 181	11
12	286.417 494	94.041 280	45.990 984	22.037 720	22.808 670	12
13	330.576 371	108.471 539	52.999 300	25.351 680	26.333 443	13
14	379.601 707	124.477 687	60.762 806	29.013 607	30.248 387	14
15	434.029 805	142.231 821	69.362 878	33.060 035	34.596 690	15
16	494.456 068	161.924 834	78.889 662	37.531 339	39.426 323	16
17	561.541 512	183.768 467	89.443 016	42.472 130	44.790 564	17
18	636.020 005	207.997 581	101.133 560	47.931 703	50.748 594	18
19	718.706 284	234.872 689	114.083 833	53.964 532	57.366 138	19
20	810.504 876	264.682 753	128.429 579	60.630 808	64.716 203	20
21	912.419 990	297.748 290	144.321 169	67.997 043	72.879 873	21
22	1025.566 501	334.424 821	161.925 176	76.136 732	81.947 209	22
23	1151.182 148	375.106 694	181.426 126	85.131 089	92.018 241	23
24	1290.641 073	420.231 321	203.028 425	95.069 854	103.204 072	24
25	1445.468 853	470.283 882	226.958 507	106.052 188	115.628 103	25
26	1617.359 188	525.802 543	253.467 205	118.187 668	129.427 394	26
27	1808.192 431	587.384 241	282.832 380	131.597 373	144.754 180	27
28	2020.056 156	655.691 105	315.361 837	146.415 097	161.777 542	28
29	2255.267 995	731.457 570	351.396 546	162.788 683	180.685 281	29
30	2516.400 990	815.498 278	391.314 220	180.881 494	201.685 986	30
31	2806.311 742	908.716 837	435.533 273	200.874 051	225.011 336	31
32	3128.171 659	1012.115 534	484.517 205	222.965 827	250.918 652	32
33	3485.501 649	1126.806 113	538.779 462	247.377 238	279.693 742	33
34	3882.210 638	1254.021 730	598.888 816	274.351 848	311.654 051	34
35	4322.638 325	1395.130 208	665.475 329	304.158 792	347.152 162	35
36	4811.602 664	1551.648 748	739.236 955	337.095 466	386.579 686	36
37	5354.452 560	1725.260 239	820.946 857	373.490 489	430.371 586	37
38	5957.126 387	1917.831 356	911.461 512	413.706 991	479.010 969	38
39	6626.216 950	2131.432 625	1011.729 687	458.146 225	533.034 420	39
40	7369.043 601	2368.360 691	1122.802 384	507.251 579	593.037 922	40

378

SINKING FUND ACCUMULATION FACTORS 10¾%

(Future Value of Periodic Payments of $1)

Base: | 1.008 958 | 1.026 875 | 1.053 750 | 1.107 500 | 1.113 473

Frequency of Payments and of Conversions

Months	Monthly	Quarterly	Semiannual	Annual	Annual Payment Daily Conversion	Months
1	1.000 000	—	—	—	—	1
2	2.008 958	—	—	—	—	2
3	3.026 955	1.000 000	—	—	—	3
4	4.054 072	—	—	—	—	4
5	5.090 389	—	—	—	—	5
6	6.135 991	2.026 875	1.000 000	—	—	6
7	7.190 959	—	—	—	—	7
8	8.255 378	—	—	—	—	8
9	9.329 333	3.081 347	—	—	—	9
10	10.412 908	—	—	—	—	10
11	11.506 190	—	—	—	—	11

Years						Years
1	12.609 266	4.164 158	2.053 750	1.000 000	1.000 000	1
2	26.642 850	8.794 335	4.334 212	2.107 500	2.113 473	2
3	42.261 640	13.942 683	6.866 411	3.334 056	3.353 295	3
4	59.644 698	19.667 192	9.678 138	4.692 467	4.733 804	4
5	78.991 310	26.032 340	12.800 248	6.196 908	6.270 962	5
6	100.523 278	33.109 824	16.267 006	7.863 075	7.982 547	6
7	124.487 454	40.979 361	20.116 455	9.708 356	9.888 351	7
8	151.158 576	49.729 592	24.390 842	11.752 004	12.010 412	8
9	180.842 414	59.459 076	29.137 074	14.015 344	14.373 269	9
10	213.879 280	70.277 405	34.407 238	16.521 994	17.004 247	10
11	250.647 925	82.306 431	40.259 171	19.298 108	19.933 769	11
12	291.569 882	95.681 647	46.757 093	22.372 655	23.195 714	12
13	337.114 303	110.553 707	53.972 315	25.777 715	26.827 801	13
14	387.803 331	127.090 125	61.984 018	29.548 820	30.872 032	14
15	444.218 090	145.477 163	70.880 126	33.725 318	35.375 174	15
16	507.005 349	165.921 927	80.758 267	38.350 789	40.389 301	16
17	576.884 931	188.654 700	91.726 846	43.473 499	45.972 395	17
18	654.657 972	213.931 538	103.906 236	49.146 900	52.189 021	18
19	741.216 102	242.037 151	117.430 098	55.430 192	59.111 065	19
20	837.551 665	273.288 113	132.446 847	62.388 938	66.818 574	20
21	944.769 102	308.036 425	149.121 280	70.095 749	75.400 678	21
22	1064.097 607	346.673 482	167.636 388	78.631 042	84.956 619	22
23	1196.905 224	389.634 479	188.195 362	88.083 879	95.596 900	23
24	1344.714 524	437.403 318	211.023 822	98.552 895	107.444 567	24
25	1509.220 069	490.518 051	236.372 294	110.147 332	120.636 623	25
26	1692.307 834	549.576 947	264.518 960	122.988 170	135.325 622	26
27	1896.076 828	615.245 228	295.772 710	137.209 398	151.681 425	27
28	2122.863 162	688.262 563	330.476 532	152.959 408	169.893 170	28
29	2375.266 830	769.451 395	369.011 276	170.402 545	190.171 457	29
30	2656.181 515	859.726 213	411.799 835	189.720 818	212.750 781	30
31	2968.827 763	960.103 844	459.311 783	211.115 806	237.892 249	31
32	3316.789 910	1071.714 912	512.068 530	234.810 756	265.886 594	32
33	3704.057 170	1195.816 571	570.649 045	261.052 912	297.057 542	33
34	4135.069 369	1333.806 666	635.696 208	290.116 100	331.765 550	34
35	4614.767 848	1487.239 474	707.923 866	322.303 581	370.411 979	35
36	5148.652 114	1657.843 219	788.124 668	357.951 215	413.443 735	36
37	5742.842 886	1847.539 528	877.178 761	397.430 971	461.358 433	37
38	6404.152 265	2058.465 084	976.063 452	441.154 801	514.710 155	38
39	7140.161 837	2292.995 691	1085.863 932	489.578 942	574.115 857	39
40	7959.309 586	2553.773 031	1207.785 183	543.208 678	640.262 501	40

11% SINKING FUND ACCUMULATION FACTORS
(Future Value of Periodic Payments of $1)

Base: 1.009 167   1.027 500   1.055 000   1.110 000   1.116 259

Frequency of Payments and of Conversions

Months	Monthly	Quarterly	Semiannual	Annual	Annual Payment Daily Conversion	Months
1	1.000 000	—	—	—	—	1
2	2.009 167	—	—	—	—	2
3	3.027 584	1.000 000	—	—	—	3
4	4.055 337	—	—	—	—	4
5	5.092 511	—	—	—	—	5
6	6.139 192	2.027 500	1.000 000	—	—	6
7	7.195 468	—	—	—	—	7
8	8.261 427	—	—	—	—	8
9	9.337 156	3.083 256	—	—	—	9
10	10.422 747	—	—	—	—	10
11	11.518 289	—	—	—	—	11

Years	Monthly	Quarterly	Semiannual	Annual	Annual Payment Daily Conversion	Years
1	12.623 873	4.168 046	2.055 000	1.000 000	1.000 000	1
2	26.708 566	8.813 838	4.342 266	2.110 000	2.116 259	2
3	42.423 123	13.992 137	6.888 051	3.342 100	3.362 294	3
4	59.956 151	19.763 979	9.721 573	4.709 731	4.753 192	4
5	79.518 080	26.197 398	12.875 354	6.227 801	6.305 795	5
6	101.343 692	33.368 222	16.385 591	7.912 860	8.038 902	6
7	125.694 940	41.360 975	20.292 572	9.783 274	9.973 500	7
8	152.864 085	50.269 868	24.641 140	11.859 434	12.133 012	8
9	183.177 212	60.199 910	29.481 205	14.163 972	14.543 588	9
10	216.998 139	71.268 145	34.868 318	16.722 009	17.234 415	10
11	254.732 784	83.605 035	40.864 310	19.561 430	20.238 077	11
12	296.834 038	97.355 996	47.537 998	22.713 187	23.590 941	12
13	343.807 200	112.683 108	54.965 981	26.211 638	27.333 608	13
14	396.216 042	129.767 034	63.233 510	30.094 918	31.511 395	14
15	454.689 575	148.809 140	72.435 478	34.405 359	36.174 888	15
16	519.929 596	170.033 877	82.677 498	39.189 948	41.380 555	16
17	592.719 117	193.691 420	94.077 122	44.500 843	47.191 430	17
18	673.931 757	220.060 621	106.765 189	50.395 936	53.677 874	18
19	764.542 228	249.452 292	120.887 324	56.939 488	60.918 427	19
20	865.638 038	282.212 873	136.605 614	64.202 832	69.000 761	20
21	978.432 537	318.728 514	154.100 464	72.265 144	78.022 742	21
22	1104.279 485	359.429 624	173.572 669	81.214 309	88.093 613	22
23	1244.689 295	404.795 946	195.245 719	91.147 884	99.335 316	23
24	1401.347 165	455.362 213	219.368 367	102.174 151	111.883 972	24
25	1576.133 301	511.724 449	246.217 476	114.413 307	125.891 526	25
26	1771.145 485	574.546 995	276.101 207	127.998 771	141.527 588	26
27	1988.724 252	644.570 341	309.362 546	143.078 636	158.981 489	27
28	2231.480 981	722.619 851	346.383 247	159.817 286	178.464 568	28
29	2502.329 236	809.615 495	387.588 214	178.397 187	200.212 736	29
30	2804.519 736	906.582 688	433.450 372	199.020 878	224.489 332	30
31	3141.679 369	1014.664 383	484.496 100	221.913 174	251.588 307	31
32	3517.854 723	1135.134 539	541.311 272	247.323 624	281.837 792	32
33	3937.560 650	1269.413 135	604.547 978	275.529 222	315.604 060	33
34	4405.834 459	1419.082 913	674.932 013	306.837 437	353.295 972	34
35	4928.296 368	1585.908 029	753.271 204	341.589 555	395.369 920	35
36	5511.216 962	1771.854 851	840.464 682	380.164 406	442.335 355	36
37	6161.592 447	1979.115 131	937.513 203	422.982 490	494.760 961	37
38	6887.228 628	2210.131 846	1045.530 633	470.510 564	553.281 531	38
39	7696.834 582	2467.627 987	1165.756 732	523.266 726	618.605 663	39
40	8600.127 195	2754.638 660	1299.571 387	581.826 066	691.524 333	40

SINKING FUND ACCUMULATION FACTORS 11¼%

(Future Value of Periodic Payments of $1)

Base: 1.009 375   1.028 125   1.056 250   1.112 500   1.119 053

Frequency of Payments and of Conversions

Months	Monthly	Quarterly	Semiannual	Annual	Annual Payment Daily Conversion	Months
1	1.000 000	—	—	—	—	1
2	2.009 375	—	—	—	—	2
3	3.028 213	1.000 000	—	—	—	3
4	4.056 602	—	—	—	—	4
5	5.094 633	—	—	—	—	5
6	6.142 395	2.028 125	1.000 000	—	—	6
7	7.199 980	—	—	—	—	7
8	8.267 480	—	—	—	—	8
9	9.344 988	3.085 166	—	—	—	9
10	10.432 597	—	—	—	—	10
11	11.530 402	—	—	—	—	11

Years						Years
1	12.638 500	4.171 936	2.056 250	1.000 000	1.000 000	1
2	26.774 484	8.833 390	4.350 334	2.112 500	2.119 053	2
3	42.585 384	14.041 798	6.909 762	3.350 156	3.371 331	3
4	60.269 654	19.861 339	9.765 223	4.727 049	4.772 697	4
5	80.049 260	26.363 719	12.950 958	6.258 842	6.340 899	5
6	102.172 472	33.629 061	16.505 168	7.962 962	8.095 799	6
7	126.916 973	41.746 887	20.470 473	9.858 795	10.059 625	7
8	154.593 349	50.817 224	24.894 421	11.967 909	12.257 250	8
9	185.548 987	60.951 836	29.830 061	14.314 299	14.716 507	9
10	220.172 433	72.275 599	35.336 577	16.924 657	17.468 545	10
11	258.898 270	84.928 044	41.479 999	19.828 681	20.548 221	11
12	302.212 574	99.065 072	48.333 995	23.059 408	23.994 540	12
13	350.659 014	114.860 879	55.980 751	26.653 592	27.851 152	13
14	404.845 676	132.510 098	64.511 962	30.652 121	32.166 904	14
15	465.452 695	152.230 200	74.029 927	35.100 484	36.996 457	15
16	533.240 794	174.264 175	84.648 780	40.049 289	42.400 981	16
17	609.060 830	198.883 522	96.495 851	45.554 834	48.448 927	17
18	693.864 473	226.391 597	109.713 203	51.679 752	55.216 898	18
19	788.716 155	257.127 352	124.459 328	58.493 725	62.790 612	19
20	894.806 428	291.469 508	140.911 050	66.074 269	71.265 998	20
21	1013.466 907	329.841 226	159.265 644	74.507 624	80.750 399	21
22	1146.186 983	372.715 316	179.743 206	83.889 731	91.363 943	22
23	1294.632 522	420.620 069	202.589 285	94.327 326	103.241 057	23
24	1460.666 770	474.145 759	228.077 835	105.939 150	116.532 173	24
25	1646.373 742	533.951 924	256.514 494	118.857 305	131.405 630	25
26	1854.084 378	600.775 487	288.240 252	133.228 752	148.049 810	26
27	2086.405 804	675.439 841	323.635 541	149.216 986	166.675 523	27
28	2346.254 051	758.864 990	363.124 792	167.003 897	187.518 676	28
29	2636.890 662	852.078 888	407.181 531	186.791 836	210.843 260	29
30	2961.963 624	956.230 104	456.334 051	208.805 917	236.944 697	30
31	3325.553 160	1072.601 977	511.171 751	233.296 583	266.153 576	31
32	3732.222 944	1202.628 427	572.352 202	260.542 448	298.839 849	32
33	4187.077 378	1347.911 622	640.609 033	290.853 474	335.417 507	33
34	4695.825 666	1510.241 724	716.760 727	324.574 489	376.349 830	34
35	5264.853 472	1691.618 943	801.720 434	362.089 120	422.155 252	35
36	5901.303 071	1894.278 187	896.506 926	403.824 145	473.413 928	36
37	6613.162 997	2120.716 597	1002.256 810	450.254 362	530.775 082	37
38	7409.368 314	2373.724 318	1120.238 154	501.907 978	594.965 231	38
39	8299.912 764	2656.418 879	1251.865 700	559.372 625	666.797 382	39
40	9295.974 209	2972.283 608	1398.717 822	623.302 045	747.181 338	40

11½% SINKING FUND ACCUMULATION FACTORS
(Future Value of Periodic Payments of $1)

Base: 1.009 583   1.028 750   1.057 500   1.115 000   1.121 853

Frequency of Payments and of Conversions

Months	Monthly	Quarterly	Semiannual	Annual	Annual Payment Daily Conversion	Months
1	1.000 000	—	—	—	—	1
2	2.009 583	—	—	—	—	2
3	3.028 842	1.000 000	—	—	—	3
4	4.057 868	—	—	—	—	4
5	5.096 756	—	—	—	—	5
6	6.145 600	2.028 750	1.000 000	—	—	6
7	7.204 495	—	—	—	—	7
8	8.273 538	—	—	—	—	8
9	9.352 827	3.087 077	—	—	—	9
10	10.442 458	—	—	—	—	10
11	11.542 531	—	—	—	—	11

Years						Years
1	12.653 147	4.175 830	2.057 500	1.000 000	1.000 000	1
2	26.840 607	8.852 990	4.358 415	2.115 000	2.121 853	2
3	42.748 428	14.091 666	6.931 543	3.358 225	3.380 407	3
4	60.585 221	19.959 273	9.809 088	4.744 421	4.792 319	4
5	80.584 891	26.531 316	13.027 064	6.290 029	6.376 276	5
6	103.009 708	33.892 366	16.625 747	8.013 383	8.153 244	6
7	128.153 744	42.137 148	20.650 177	9.934 922	10.146 740	7
8	156.346 728	51.371 758	25.150 722	12.077 438	12.383 149	8
9	187.958 374	61.715 030	30.183 710	14.466 343	14.892 070	9
10	223.403 228	73.300 065	35.812 131	17.129 972	17.706 711	10
11	263.146 100	86.275 943	42.106 430	20.099 919	20.864 324	11
12	307.708 167	100.809 641	49.145 384	23.411 410	24.406 701	12
13	357.673 800	117.088 184	57.017 090	27.103 722	28.380 727	13
14	413.698 232	135.321 049	65.820 068	31.220 650	32.838 999	14
15	476.516 149	155.742 862	75.664 493	35.811 025	37.840 524	15
16	546.951 324	178.616 419	86.673 576	40.929 293	43.451 500	16
17	625.927 421	204.236 064	98.985 102	46.636 161	49.746 188	17
18	714.480 107	232.931 477	112.753 158	52.999 320	56.807 902	18
19	813.770 632	265.071 922	128.150 061	60.094 242	64.730 106	19
20	925.101 060	301.070 992	145.368 514	68.005 080	73.617 653	20
21	1049.931 340	341.391 934	164.624 018	76.825 664	83.588 173	21
22	1189.898 456	386.553 611	186.157 568	86.660 615	94.773 629	22
23	1346.837 891	437.137 178	210.238 672	97.626 586	107.322 064	23
24	1522.807 696	493.793 562	237.168 721	109.853 643	121.399 562	24
25	1720.115 481	557.251 834	267.284 763	123.486 812	137.192 443	25
26	1941.348 676	628.328 595	300.963 721	138.687 796	154.909 731	26
27	2189.408 459	707.938 486	338.627 110	155.636 892	174.785 921	27
28	2467.547 806	797.105 951	380.746 314	174.535 135	197.084 081	28
29	2779.414 142	896.978 426	427.848 482	195.606 675	222.099 335	29
30	3129.097 181	1008.841 102	480.523 132	219.101 443	250.162 769	30
31	3521.182 550	1134.133 464	539.429 522	245.298 109	281.645 812	31
32	3960.811 927	1274.467 815	605.304 906	274.507 391	316.965 153	32
33	4453.750 468	1431.650 023	678.973 759	307.075 741	356.588 255	33
34	5006.462 404	1607.702 758	761.358 098	343.389 451	401.039 545	34
35	5626.195 819	1804.891 524	853.489 020	383.879 238	450.907 351	35
36	6321.077 691	2025.753 809	956.519 605	429.025 351	506.851 690	36
37	7100.220 473	2273.131 742	1071.739 353	479.363 266	569.613 006	37
38	7973.841 584	2550.208 660	1200.590 316	535.490 042	640.021 966	38
39	8953.397 405	2860.550 078	1344.685 155	598.071 396	719.010 457	39
40	10051.733 506	3208.149 571	1505.827 313	667.849 607	807.623 920	40

SINKING FUND ACCUMULATION FACTORS 11¾%

(Future Value of Periodic Payments of $1)

Base: 1.009 792   1.029 375   1.058 750   1.117 500   1.124 660

Frequency of Payments and of Conversions

Months	Monthly	Quarterly	Semiannual	Annual	Annual Payment Daily Conversion	Months
1	1.000 000	—	—	—	—	1
2	2.009 792	—	—	—	—	2
3	3.029 471	1.000 000	—	—	—	3
4	4.059 134	—	—	—	—	4
5	5.098 880	—	—	—	—	5
6	6.148 807	2.029 375	1.000 000	—	—	6
7	7.209 014	—	—	—	—	7
8	8.279 602	—	—	—	—	8
9	9.360 673	3.088 988	—	—	—	9
10	10.452 330	—	—	—	—	10
11	11.554 675	—	—	—	—	11

Years						Years
1	12.667 815	4.179 727	2.058 750	1.000 000	1.000 000	1
2	26.906 933	8.872 639	4.366 509	2.117 500	2.124 660	2
3	42.912 258	14.141 743	6.953 395	3.366 306	3.389 520	3
4	60.902 867	20.057 786	9.853 169	4.761 847	4.812 058	4
5	81.125 014	26.700 198	13.103 675	6.321 364	6.411 930	5
6	103.855 497	34.158 161	16.747 335	8.064 125	8.211 241	6
7	129.405 446	42.531 809	20.831 702	10.011 659	10.234 855	7
8	158.124 586	51.933 569	25.410 079	12.188 029	12.510 733	8
9	190.406 019	62.489 672	30.542 217	14.620 123	15.070 322	9
10	226.691 611	74.341 849	36.295 096	17.337 987	17.948 989	10
11	267.478 031	87.649 229	42.743 795	20.375 200	21.186 511	11
12	313.323 559	102.590 482	49.972 474	23.769 287	24.827 623	12
13	364.855 722	119.366 215	58.075 472	27.562 178	28.922 636	13
14	422.779 884	138.201 664	67.158 541	31.800 734	33.528 134	14
15	487.888 901	159.349 719	77.340 222	36.537 320	38.707 754	15
16	561.073 978	183.094 321	88.753 393	41.830 455	44.533 065	16
17	643.336 860	209.754 273	101.547 004	47.745 533	51.084 560	17
18	735.803 550	239.687 520	115.888 023	54.355 634	58.452 765	18
19	839.739 717	273.295 956	131.963 610	61.742 420	66.739 491	19
20	956.568 025	311.030 817	149.983 565	69.997 155	76.059 240	20
21	1087.887 601	353.398 746	170.183 062	79.221 821	86.540 790	21
22	1235.495 930	400.968 586	192.825 719	89.530 384	98.328 971	22
23	1401.413 451	454.379 027	218.207 041	101.050 205	111.586 667	23
24	1587.911 219	514.347 173	246.658 274	113.923 604	126.497 069	24
25	1797.541 987	581.678 178	278.550 727	128.309 627	143.266 202	25
26	2033.175 151	657.276 047	314.300 623	144.386 008	162.125 777	26
27	2298.036 022	742.155 784	354.374 524	162.351 364	183.336 387	27
28	2595.749 977	837.457 011	399.295 427	182.427 650	207.191 114	28
29	2930.392 078	944.459 273	449.649 583	204.862 898	234.019 572	29
30	3306.542 859	1064.599 216	506.094 152	229.934 289	264.192 468	30
31	3729.351 014	1199.489 879	569.365 781	257.951 568	298.126 719	31
32	4204.603 879	1350.942 347	640.290 212	289.260 877	336.291 217	32
33	4738.806 645	1520.990 070	719.793 063	324.249 030	379.213 303	33
34	5339.271 398	1711.916 164	808.911 909	363.348 291	427.486 059	34
35	6014.217 212	1926.284 063	908.809 818	407.041 715	481.776 501	35
36	6772.882 645	2166.971 942	1020.790 536	455.869 117	542.834 792	36
37	7625.652 195	2437.211 353	1146.315 496	510.433 738	611.504 615	37
38	8584.198 445	2740.630 617	1287.022 896	571.409 702	688.734 822	38
39	9661.641 835	3081.303 541	1444.749 076	639.550 343	775.592 552	39
40	10872.730 247	3463.804 108	1621.552 485	715.697 508	873.277 973	40

12% SINKING FUND ACCUMULATION FACTORS
(Future Value of Periodic Payments of $1)

Base: 1.010 000   1.030 000   1.060 000   1.120 000   1.127 474

Frequency of Payments and of Conversions

Months	Monthly	Quarterly	Semiannual	Annual	Annual Payment Daily Conversion	Months
1	1.000 000	—	—	—	—	1
2	2.010 000	—	—	—	—	2
3	3.030 100	1.000 000	—	—	—	3
4	4.060 401	—	—	—	—	4
5	5.101 005	—	—	—	—	5
6	6.152 015	2.030 000	1.000 000	—	—	6
7	7.213 535	—	—	—	—	7
8	8.285 671	—	—	—	—	8
9	9.368 527	3.090 900	—	—	—	9
10	10.462 213	—	—	—	—	10
11	11.566 835	—	—	—	—	11

Years						Years
1	12.682 503	4.183 627	2.060 000	1.000 000	1.000 000	1
2	26.973 465	8.892 336	4.374 616	2.120 000	2.127 474	2
3	43.076 878	14.192 030	6.975 319	3.374 400	3.398 673	3
4	61.222 608	20.156 881	9.897 468	4.779 328	4.831 916	4
5	81.669 670	26.870 374	13.180 795	6.352 847	6.447 861	5
6	104.709 931	34.426 470	16.869 941	8.115 189	8.269 798	6
7	130.672 274	42.930 923	21.015 066	10.089 012	10.323 985	7
8	159.927 293	52.502 759	25.672 528	12.299 693	12.640 027	8
9	192.892 579	63.275 944	30.905 653	14.775 656	15.251 306	9
10	230.038 689	75.401 260	36.785 591	17.548 735	18.195 456	10
11	271.895 856	89.048 409	43.392 290	20.654 583	21.514 909	11
12	319.061 559	104.408 396	50.815 577	24.133 133	25.257 507	12
13	372.209 054	121.696 197	59.156 383	28.029 109	29.477 190	13
14	432.096 982	141.153 768	68.528 112	32.392 602	34.234 775	14
15	499.580 198	163.053 437	79.058 186	37.279 715	39.598 829	15
16	575.621 974	187.701 707	90.889 778	42.753 280	45.646 662	16
17	661.307 751	215.443 551	104.183 755	48.883 674	52.465 439	17
18	757.860 630	246.667 242	119.120 867	55.749 715	60.153 434	18
19	866.658 830	281.809 781	135.904 206	63.439 681	68.821 451	19
20	989.255 365	321.363 019	154.761 966	72.052 442	78.594 418	20
21	1127.400 210	365.880 536	175.950 545	81.698 736	89.613 187	21
22	1283.065 279	415.985 393	199.758 032	92.502 584	102.036 566	22
23	1458.472 574	472.378 852	226.508 125	104.602 894	116.043 606	23
24	1656.125 905	535.850 186	256.564 529	118.155 241	131.836 185	24
25	1878.846 626	607.287 733	290.335 905	133.333 870	149.641 911	25
26	2129.813 909	687.691 320	328.281 422	150.333 934	169.717 410	26
27	2412.610 125	778.186 267	370.917 006	169.374 007	192.352 019	27
28	2731.271 980	880.039 126	418.822 348	190.698 887	217.871 960	28
29	3090.348 134	994.675 416	472.648 790	214.582 754	246.645 037	29
30	3494.964 133	1123.699 571	533.128 181	241.332 684	279.085 942	30
31	3950.895 567	1268.917 394	601.082 824	271.292 606	315.662 229	31
32	4464.650 520	1432.361 333	677.436 661	304.847 719	356.901 052	32
33	5043.562 459	1616.318 927	763.227 832	342.429 446	403.396 767	33
34	5695.894 923	1823.364 819	859.622 792	384.520 979	455.819 490	34
35	6430.959 471	2056.396 794	967.932 170	431.663 496	514.924 763	35
36	7259.248 603	2318.676 336	1089.628 586	484.463 116	581.564 441	36
37	8192.585 529	2613.874 271	1226.366 679	543.598 690	656.669 965	37
38	9244.292 939	2946.122 147	1380.005 601	609.830 533	741.411 210	38
39	10429.383 172	3320.070 059	1552.634 293	684.010 197	836.922 090	39
40	11764.772 510	3740.951 728	1746.599 891	767.091 420	944.608 153	40

Table 8

Direct Reduction Loan Factors
(Monthly Payment and Annual Constant per $1 of Loan)

Table 8 - DIRECT REDUCTION LOAN FACTORS (Monthly Payment and Annual Constant per $1 of Loan)

Payment: $$1/a_{\overline{n}|} = \frac{i}{1 - 1/S^n}$$

Annual Constant: $R_M = 12/a_n$

Where

$1/a_{\overline{n}|}$ = Direct Reduction Loan Factor

$1/S^n$ = Present Value Factor

i = Effective Rate of Interest

R_M = Annual Constant

Part Paid Off: $$P = \frac{R_M - 12i}{R_{Mp} - 12i}$$

Where

R_M = Actual Annual Constant

R_{Mp} = Annual Constant for Projection Period

i = Effective Rate of Interest

This Table is used in solving problems dealing with monthly payment, direct reduction loans. (Payments and constants for quarterly, semi-annual, and annual payment loans can be obtained by calculating reciprocals of factors from Table 3.)

Example 1:
What is the level monthly payment and annual debt service for a direct reduction loan in the amount of $100,000 assuming nominal interest at 10% and full amortization over 25 years?

$100,000 × .0090870 = $ 908.70*
$100,000 × .1090441 = $10,904.41*

*In actual practice, the payment would be rounded up to $908.71 and the debt service would be: $908.71 × 12 = $10,904.52

Example 2:
In ten years, how much would be paid off of the loan in Example 1?

$100,000 × .1544 = $15,440

OR

$100,000 × [($10,904.52/$100,000 − .10)/(.1585809 − .10)] = $15,440.53

Example 3:
For the loan in Example 1, what discounted price would achieve a 14% yield?

Assuming Full Term:

$10,904.41/.1444513 = $75,488.49

Assuming a 10-Year Call:

$10,904.52/.1863197   = $58,525.86
($100,000 − $15,440.53) × .248603* = 21,021.74
                                       $79,547.60

* Present Value Factor for 120 months.

Example 4:
What is the level monthly payment and annual debt service for a direct reduction loan in the amount of $100,000 assuming nominal interest at 10% and full amortization over 25 years and 7 months?

$100,000/(1/.0090870 + .082940*/.1476586) = $904.09

$904.09 × 12 = $10,849.08

* Present Value Factor for 300 months.

Example 5:
In 10 years, how much would be paid off of the loan in Example 4?

$100,000 × [($10,849.08/$100,000 − .10)/(.1585809 − .10)] = $14,494.14

6% DIRECT REDUCTION LOAN FACTORS
(Monthly Payment and Annual Constant per $1 of Loan)

Base: 1.005 000

Months	Payment	Annual Constant	Part Paid Off Projection				Months
			1 Year	5 Years	10 Years	15 Years	
1	1.005 0000	—	—	—	—	—	1
2	.503 7531	—	—	—	—	—	2
3	.336 6722	—	—	—	—	—	3
4	.253 1328	—	—	—	—	—	4
5	.203 0100	—	—	—	—	—	5
6	.169 5955	—	—	—	—	—	6
7	.145 7285	—	—	—	—	—	7
8	.127 8289	—	—	—	—	—	8
9	.113 9074	—	—	—	—	—	9
10	.102 7706	—	—	—	—	—	10
11	.093 6590	—	—	—	—	—	11

Years	Payment	Annual Constant	1 Year	5 Years	10 Years	15 Years	Years
1	.086 0664	1.032 7972	1.0000	—	—	—	1
2	.044 3206	.531 8473	.4850	—	—	—	2
3	.030 4219	.365 0632	.3136	—	—	—	3
4	.023 4850	.281 8203	.2280	—	—	—	4
5	.019 3328	.231 9936	.1768	1.0000	—	—	5
6	.016 5729	.198 8747	.1428	.8074	—	—	6
7	.014 6086	.175 3027	.1185	.6704	—	—	7
8	.013 1414	.157 6972	.1004	.5680	—	—	8
9	.012 0057	.144 0690	.0864	.4888	—	—	9
10	.011 1021	.133 2246	.0753	.4257	1.0000	—	10
11	.010 3670	.124 4044	.0662	.3745	.8795	—	11
12	.009 7585	.117 1020	.0587	.3320	.7798	—	12
13	.009 2472	.110 9668	.0524	.2963	.6960	—	13
14	.008 8124	.105 7483	.0470	.2660	.6248	—	14
15	.008 4386	.101 2628	.0424	.2399	.5635	1.0000	15
16	.008 1144	.097 3725	.0384	.2173	.5104	.9057	16
17	.007 8310	.093 9721	.0349	.1975	.4639	.8233	17
18	.007 5816	.090 9795	.0318	.1801	.4231	.7508	18
19	.007 3608	.088 3300	.0291	.1647	.3869	.6866	19
20	.007 1643	.085 9717	.0267	.1510	.3547	.6294	20
21	.006 9886	.083 8628	.0245	.1387	.3259	.5783	21
22	.006 8307	.081 9689	.0226	.1277	.3000	.5324	22
23	.006 6885	.080 2617	.0208	.1178	.2767	.4910	23
24	.006 5598	.078 7174	.0192	.1088	.2556	.4536	24
25	.006 4430	.077 3162	.0178	.1007	.2365	.4197	25
26	.006 3368	.076 0412	.0165	.0933	.2191	.3888	26
27	.006 2399	.074 8782	.0153	.0865	.2032	.3606	27
28	.006 1512	.073 8149	.0142	.0803	.1887	.3348	28
29	.006 0700	.072 8406	.0132	.0747	.1754	.3112	29
30	.005 9955	.071 9461	.0123	.0695	.1631	.2895	30
31	.005 9269	.071 1234	.0114	.0647	.1519	.2696	31
32	.005 8638	.070 3656	.0107	.0603	.1416	.2512	32
33	.005 8055	.069 6664	.0099	.0562	.1320	.2343	33
34	.005 7517	.069 0204	.0093	.0524	.1232	.2186	34
35	.005 7019	.068 4228	.0087	.0490	.1150	.2041	35
36	.005 6558	.067 8693	.0081	.0458	.1075	.1907	36
37	.005 6130	.067 3561	.0076	.0428	.1005	.1783	37
38	.005 5733	.066 8797	.0071	.0400	.0940	.1667	38
39	.005 5364	.066 4372	.0066	.0374	.0879	.1560	39
40	.005 5021	.066 0256	.0062	.0350	.0823	.1460	40

DIRECT REDUCTION LOAN FACTORS 6¼%

(Monthly Payment and Annual Constant per $1 of Loan)

| | Base: | 1.005 208 | | | Part Paid Off | | | |
| | | | Annual | | | Projection | | |
Months	Payment		Constant	1 Year	5 Years	10 Years	15 Years	Months
1	1.005 2083		—	—	—	—	—	1
2	.503 9096		—	—	—	—	—	2
3	.336 8116		—	—	—	—	—	3
4	.253 2637		—	—	—	—	—	4
5	.203 1358		—	—	—	—	—	5
6	.169 7180		—	—	—	—	—	6
7	.145 8488		—	—	—	—	—	7
8	.127 9474		—	—	—	—	—	8
9	.114 0247		—	—	—	—	—	9
10	.102 8869		—	—	—	—	—	10
11	.093 7746		—	—	—	—	—	11

Years								Years
1	.086 1814		1.034 1766	1.0000	—	—	—	1
2	.044 4333		.533 2001	.4844	—	—	—	2
3	.030 5353		.366 4241	.3128	—	—	—	3
4	.023 5998		.283 1978	.2271	—	—	—	4
5	.019 4493		.233 3911	.1759	1.0000	—	—	5
6	.016 6912		.200 2938	.1418	.8063	—	—	6
7	.014 7287		.176 7444	.1176	.6685	—	—	7
8	.013 2635		.159 1619	.0995	.5656	—	—	8
9	.012 1298		.145 5571	.0855	.4860	—	—	9
10	.011 2280		.134 7361	.0743	.4227	1.0000	—	10
11	.010 4949		.125 9394	.0653	.3712	.8782	—	11
12	.009 8884		.118 6604	.0578	.3286	.7775	—	12
13	.009 3790		.112 5485	.0515	.2929	.6928	—	13
14	.008 9461		.107 3532	.0462	.2625	.6209	—	14
15	.008 5742		.102 8907	.0416	.2364	.5591	1.0000	15
16	.008 2519		.099 0233	.0376	.2137	.5056	.9042	16
17	.007 9705		.095 6455	.0341	.1940	.4588	.8206	17
18	.007 7229		.092 6752	.0311	.1766	.4177	.7471	18
19	.007 5040		.090 0478	.0284	.1612	.3814	.6820	19
20	.007 3093		.087 7114	.0259	.1475	.3490	.6242	20
21	.007 1353		.085 6240	.0238	.1353	.3201	.5725	21
22	.006 9793		.083 7514	.0219	.1244	.2942	.5261	22
23	.006 8387		.082 0650	.0201	.1145	.2708	.4844	23
24	.006 7118		.080 5413	.0186	.1056	.2498	.4467	24
25	.006 5967		.079 1603	.0171	.0975	.2306	.4125	25
26	.006 4921		.077 9053	.0159	.0901	.2133	.3814	26
27	.006 3968		.076 7618	.0147	.0835	.1974	.3531	27
28	.006 3098		.075 7176	.0136	.0773	.1830	.3272	28
29	.006 2302		.074 7621	.0126	.0718	.1698	.3036	29
30	.006 1572		.073 8861	.0117	.0666	.1576	.2819	30
31	.006 0901		.073 0815	.0109	.0619	.1465	.2620	31
32	.006 0284		.072 3413	.0101	.0576	.1362	.2437	32
33	.005 9716		.071 6594	.0094	.0536	.1268	.2268	33
34	.005 9192		.071 0303	.0088	.0499	.1181	.2112	34
35	.005 8708		.070 4492	.0082	.0465	.1100	.1968	35
36	.005 8260		.069 9118	.0076	.0434	.1026	.1835	36
37	.005 7845		.069 4143	.0071	.0405	.0957	.1712	37
38	.005 7461		.068 9533	.0066	.0378	.0893	.1598	38
39	.005 7105		.068 5257	.0062	.0353	.0834	.1492	39
40	.005 6774		.068 1287	.0058	.0329	.0779	.1394	40

6½% DIRECT REDUCTION LOAN FACTORS
(Monthly Payment and Annual Constant per $1 of Loan)

Base: 1.005 417

Months	Payment	Annual Constant	1 Year	5 Years	10 Years	15 Years	Months
				Part Paid Off Projection			
1	1.005 4167	—	—	—	—	—	1
2	.504 0662	—	—	—	—	—	2
3	.336 9509	—	—	—	—	—	3
4	.253 3946	—	—	—	—	—	4
5	.203 2617	—	—	—	—	—	5
6	.169 8406	—	—	—	—	—	6
7	.145 9691	—	—	—	—	—	7
8	.128 0661	—	—	—	—	—	8
9	.114 1420	—	—	—	—	—	9
10	.103 0033	—	—	—	—	—	10
11	.093 8902	—	—	—	—	—	11

Years	Payment	Annual Constant	1 Year	5 Years	10 Years	15 Years	Years
1	.086 2964	1.035 5570	1.0000	—	—	—	1
2	.044 5463	.534 5550	.4838	—	—	—	2
3	.030 6490	.367 7880	.3120	—	—	—	3
4	.023 7150	.284 5794	.2262	—	—	—	4
5	.019 5661	.234 7938	.1749	1.0000	—	—	5
6	.016 8099	.201 7192	.1409	.8052	—	—	6
7	.014 8494	.178 1932	.1166	.6667	—	—	7
8	.013 3862	.160 6348	.0985	.5632	—	—	8
9	.012 2545	.147 0542	.0845	.4833	—	—	9
10	.011 3548	.136 2576	.0734	.4197	1.0000	—	10
11	.010 6238	.127 4852	.0644	.3680	.8769	—	11
12	.010 0192	.120 2305	.0569	.3253	.7751	—	12
13	.009 5119	.114 1428	.0506	.2894	.6897	—	13
14	.009 0810	.108 9715	.0453	.2590	.6171	—	14
15	.008 7111	.104 5329	.0407	.2328	.5548	1.0000	15
16	.008 3908	.100 6890	.0368	.2102	.5008	.9028	16
17	.008 1112	.097 3345	.0333	.1904	.4538	.8179	17
18	.007 8656	.094 3874	.0303	.1731	.4124	.7434	18
19	.007 6486	.091 7827	.0276	.1577	.3759	.6775	19
20	.007 4557	.089 4688	.0252	.1441	.3434	.6189	20
21	.007 2836	.087 4036	.0231	.1319	.3144	.5667	21
22	.007 1294	.085 5527	.0212	.1210	.2884	.5199	22
23	.006 9906	.083 8878	.0195	.1112	.2651	.4778	23
24	.006 8654	.082 3851	.0179	.1024	.2440	.4398	24
25	.006 7521	.081 0249	.0165	.0944	.2249	.4054	25
26	.006 6492	.079 7901	.0152	.0871	.2076	.3741	26
27	.006 5555	.078 6666	.0141	.0805	.1918	.3457	27
28	.006 4702	.077 6419	.0130	.0745	.1774	.3198	28
29	.006 3921	.076 7055	.0121	.0689	.1643	.2961	29
30	.006 3207	.075 8482	.0112	.0639	.1522	.2744	30
31	.006 2552	.075 0618	.0104	.0593	.1412	.2545	31
32	.006 1950	.074 3395	.0096	.0550	.1311	.2362	32
33	.006 1396	.073 6751	.0089	.0511	.1217	.2194	33
34	.006 0886	.073 0630	.0083	.0475	.1132	.2040	34
35	.006 0415	.072 4985	.0077	.0442	.1052	.1897	35
36	.005 9981	.071 9773	.0072	.0411	.0979	.1765	36
37	.005 9580	.071 4956	.0067	.0383	.0912	.1643	37
38	.005 9208	.071 0499	.0062	.0356	.0849	.1530	38
39	.005 8864	.070 6373	.0058	.0332	.0791	.1426	39
40	.005 8546	.070 2548	.0054	.0309	.0737	.1329	40

DIRECT REDUCTION LOAN FACTORS   6¾%

(Monthly Payment and Annual Constant per $1 of Loan)

Base: 1.005 625

Months	Payment	Annual Constant	Part Paid Off Projection 1 Year	5 Years	10 Years	15 Years	Months
1	1.005 6250	—	—	—	—	—	1
2	.504 2227	—	—	—	—	—	2
3	.337 0903	—	—	—	—	—	3
4	.253 5255	—	—	—	—	—	4
5	.203 3876	—	—	—	—	—	5
6	.169 9633	—	—	—	—	—	6
7	.146 0895	—	—	—	—	—	7
8	.128 1848	—	—	—	—	—	8
9	.114 2595	—	—	—	—	—	9
10	.103 1198	—	—	—	—	—	10
11	.094 0060	—	—	—	—	—	11

Years	Payment	Annual Constant	1 Year	5 Years	10 Years	15 Years	Years
1	.086 4115	1.036 9385	1.0000	—	—	—	1
2	.044 6593	.535 9120	.4832	—	—	—	2
3	.030 7629	.369 1551	.3112	—	—	—	3
4	.023 8304	.285 9651	.2254	—	—	—	4
5	.019 6835	.236 2015	.1740	1.0000	—	—	5
6	.016 9292	.203 1506	.1399	.8041	—	—	6
7	.014 9708	.179 6492	.1157	.6648	—	—	7
8	.013 5096	.162 1157	.0976	.5608	—	—	8
9	.012 3800	.148 5603	.0836	.4805	—	—	9
10	.011 4824	.137 7889	.0725	.4166	1.0000	—	10
11	.010 7535	.129 0418	.0635	.3648	.8756	—	11
12	.010 1510	.121 8123	.0560	.3219	.7727	—	12
13	.009 6458	.115 7496	.0498	.2860	.6864	—	13
14	.009 2169	.110 6032	.0445	.2555	.6132	—	14
15	.008 8491	.106 1891	.0399	.2293	.5504	1.0000	15
16	.008 5308	.102 3696	.0360	.2067	.4961	.9013	16
17	.008 2533	.099 0392	.0325	.1870	.4487	.8152	17
18	.008 0096	.096 1158	.0295	.1696	.4071	.7396	18
19	.007 7945	.093 5345	.0269	.1543	.3704	.6729	19
20	.007 6036	.091 2437	.0245	.1407	.3378	.6137	20
21	.007 4334	.089 2012	.0224	.1286	.3087	.5609	21
22	.007 2811	.087 3726	.0205	.1178	.2827	.5136	22
23	.007 1441	.085 7296	.0188	.1081	.2594	.4712	23
24	.007 0207	.084 2485	.0173	.0993	.2383	.4329	24
25	.006 9091	.082 9094	.0159	.0913	.2192	.3983	25
26	.006 8079	.081 6954	.0146	.0841	.2020	.3669	26
27	.006 7160	.080 5921	.0135	.0776	.1863	.3384	27
28	.006 6323	.079 5872	.0125	.0716	.1720	.3124	28
29	.006 5558	.078 6702	.0115	.0662	.1589	.2887	29
30	.006 4860	.077 8318	.0107	.0612	.1470	.2670	30
31	.006 4220	.077 0639	.0099	.0567	.1361	.2472	31
32	.006 3633	.076 3596	.0091	.0525	.1260	.2290	32
33	.006 3094	.075 7128	.0085	.0487	.1168	.2123	33
34	.006 2598	.075 1178	.0079	.0452	.1084	.1969	34
35	.006 2142	.074 5700	.0073	.0419	.1006	.1827	35
36	.006 1721	.074 0650	.0068	.0389	.0934	.1697	36
37	.006 1333	.073 5990	.0063	.0362	.0868	.1576	37
38	.006 0974	.073 1687	.0058	.0336	.0806	.1465	38
39	.006 0642	.072 7709	.0054	.0312	.0750	.1362	39
40	.006 0336	.072 4028	.0051	.0291	.0698	.1267	40

7% DIRECT REDUCTION LOAN FACTORS
(Monthly Payment and Annual Constant per $1 of Loan)

Base: 1.005 833

Months	Payment	Annual Constant	Part Paid Off Projection 1 Year	5 Years	10 Years	15 Years	Months
1	1.005 8333	—	—	—	—	—	1
2	.504 3792	—	—	—	—	—	2
3	.337 2298	—	—	—	—	—	3
4	.253 6564	—	—	—	—	—	4
5	.203 5136	—	—	—	—	—	5
6	.170 0859	—	—	—	—	—	6
7	.146 2099	—	—	—	—	—	7
8	.128 3035	—	—	—	—	—	8
9	.114 3770	—	—	—	—	—	9
10	.103 2363	—	—	—	—	—	10
11	.094 1218	—	—	—	—	—	11

Years	Payment	Annual Constant	1 Year	5 Years	10 Years	15 Years	Years
1	.086 5267	1.038 3210	1.0000	—	—	—	1
2	.044 7726	.537 2709	.4826	—	—	—	2
3	.030 8771	.370 5252	.3104	—	—	—	3
4	.023 9462	.287 3549	.2245	—	—	—	4
5	.019 8012	.237 6144	.1731	1.0000	—	—	5
6	.017 0490	.204 5881	.1390	.8030	—	—	6
7	.015 0927	.181 1122	.1147	.6629	—	—	7
8	.013 6337	.163 6046	.0967	.5585	—	—	8
9	.012 5063	.150 0753	.0827	.4777	—	—	9
10	.011 6108	.139 3302	.0716	.4136	1.0000	—	10
11	.010 8841	.130 6092	.0626	.3616	.8742	—	11
12	.010 2838	.123 4057	.0552	.3186	.7703	—	12
13	.009 7807	.117 3689	.0489	.2826	.6832	—	13
14	.009 3540	.112 2481	.0436	.2521	.6094	—	14
15	.008 9883	.107 8594	.0391	.2259	.5461	1.0000	15
16	.008 6721	.104 0650	.0352	.2032	.4913	.8998	16
17	.008 3966	.100 7593	.0318	.1835	.4437	.8125	17
18	.008 1550	.097 8603	.0288	.1662	.4018	.7359	18
19	.007 9419	.095 3031	.0261	.1510	.3650	.6683	19
20	.007 7530	.093 0359	.0238	.1374	.3323	.6085	20
21	.007 5847	.091 0166	.0217	.1254	.3031	.5551	21
22	.007 4342	.089 2109	.0198	.1146	.2771	.5074	22
23	.007 2992	.087 5903	.0182	.1049	.2537	.4646	23
24	.007 1776	.086 1311	.0167	.0962	.2327	.4261	24
25	.007 0678	.084 8135	.0153	.0884	.2137	.3913	25
26	.006 9684	.083 6205	.0141	.0813	.1965	.3598	26
27	.006 8781	.082 5378	.0129	.0748	.1808	.3312	27
28	.006 7961	.081 5530	.0119	.0689	.1666	.3052	28
29	.006 7213	.080 6556	.0110	.0636	.1537	.2815	29
30	.006 6530	.079 8363	.0102	.0587	.1419	.2598	30
31	.006 5906	.079 0871	.0094	.0542	.1311	.2400	31
32	.006 5334	.078 4009	.0087	.0501	.1212	.2219	32
33	.006 4810	.077 7717	.0080	.0464	.1121	.2053	33
34	.006 4328	.077 1939	.0074	.0429	.1038	.1900	34
35	.006 3886	.076 6628	.0069	.0398	.0961	.1760	35
36	.006 3478	.076 1740	.0064	.0368	.0891	.1631	36
37	.006 3103	.075 7237	.0059	.0341	.0826	.1512	37
38	.006 2757	.075 3086	.0055	.0317	.0766	.1402	38
39	.006 2438	.074 9255	.0051	.0294	.0710	.1301	39
40	.006 2143	.074 5718	.0047	.0273	.0659	.1208	40

DIRECT REDUCTION LOAN FACTORS 7¼%
(Monthly Payment and Annual Constant per $1 of Loan)

Base: 1.006 042

Months	Payment	Annual Constant	1 Year	Part Paid Off Projection			Months
				5 Years	10 Years	15 Years	
1	1.006 0417	—	—	—	—	—	1
2	.504 5358	—	—	—	—	—	2
3	.337 3692	—	—	—	—	—	3
4	.253 7874	—	—	—	—	—	4
5	.203 6396	—	—	—	—	—	5
6	.170 2087	—	—	—	—	—	6
7	.146 3303	—	—	—	—	—	7
8	.128 4223	—	—	—	—	—	8
9	.114 4945	—	—	—	—	—	9
10	.103 3529	—	—	—	—	—	10
11	.094 2376	—	—	—	—	—	11

Years							Years
1	.086 6420	1.039 7045	1.0000	—	—	—	1
2	.044 8860	.538 6320	.4819	—	—	—	2
3	.030 9915	.371 8984	.3096	—	—	—	3
4	.024 0624	.288 7488	.2236	—	—	—	4
5	.019 9194	.239 0323	.1722	1.0000	—	—	5
6	.017 1693	.206 0317	.1381	.8018	—	—	6
7	.015 2152	.182 5822	.1138	.6610	—	—	7
8	.013 7585	.165 1015	.0957	.5561	—	—	8
9	.012 6333	.151 5993	.0818	.4750	—	—	9
10	.011 7401	.140 8812	.0707	.4106	1.0000	—	10
11	.011 0156	.132 1873	.0617	.3584	.8729	—	11
12	.010 4176	.125 0107	.0543	.3153	.7679	—	12
13	.009 9167	.119 0005	.0481	.2792	.6800	—	13
14	.009 4922	.113 9061	.0428	.2486	.6055	—	14
15	.009 1286	.109 5435	.0383	.2224	.5417	1.0000	15
16	.008 8146	.105 7749	.0344	.1998	.4866	.8983	16
17	.008 5412	.102 4946	.0310	.1801	.4386	.8097	17
18	.008 3017	.099 6207	.0280	.1629	.3966	.7321	18
19	.008 0907	.097 0881	.0254	.1476	.3596	.6638	19
20	.007 9038	.094 8451	.0231	.1342	.3268	.6032	20
21	.007 7375	.092 8496	.0210	.1222	.2976	.5493	21
22	.007 5889	.091 0672	.0192	.1115	.2715	.5012	22
23	.007 4558	.089 4694	.0175	.1019	.2482	.4581	23
24	.007 3361	.088 0326	.0161	.0933	.2271	.4193	24
25	.007 2281	.086 7368	.0147	.0855	.2082	.3843	25
26	.007 1304	.085 5652	.0135	.0785	.1911	.3527	26
27	.007 0419	.084 5033	.0124	.0721	.1755	.3240	27
28	.006 9616	.083 5388	.0114	.0663	.1614	.2980	28
29	.006 8884	.082 6612	.0105	.0610	.1486	.2743	29
30	.006 8218	.081 8612	.0097	.0562	.1369	.2527	30
31	.006 7609	.081 1307	.0089	.0518	.1262	.2330	31
32	.006 7052	.080 4628	.0082	.0478	.1164	.2150	32
33	.006 6543	.079 8512	.0076	.0441	.1075	.1984	33
34	.006 6075	.079 2906	.0070	.0408	.0993	.1833	34
35	.006 5647	.078 7761	.0065	.0377	.0918	.1694	35
36	.006 5253	.078 3034	.0060	.0348	.0849	.1567	36
37	.006 4891	.077 8688	.0056	.0322	.0785	.1449	37
38	.006 4557	.077 4687	.0051	.0298	.0727	.1341	38
39	.006 4250	.077 1003	.0048	.0276	.0673	.1242	39
40	.006 3967	.076 7606	.0044	.0256	.0623	.1150	40

7½% DIRECT REDUCTION LOAN FACTORS
(Monthly Payment and Annual Constant per $1 of Loan)

Base: 1.006 250

Months	Payment	Annual Constant	1 Year	5 Years	Part Paid Off Projection 10 Years	15 Years	Months
1	1.006 2500	—	—	—	—	—	1
2	.504 6924	—	—	—	—	—	2
3	.337 5087	—	—	—	—	—	3
4	.253 9184	—	—	—	—	—	4
5	.203 7656	—	—	—	—	—	5
6	.170 3314	—	—	—	—	—	6
7	.146 4508	—	—	—	—	—	7
8	.128 5412	—	—	—	—	—	8
9	.114 6122	—	—	—	—	—	9
10	.103 4696	—	—	—	—	—	10
11	.094 3536	—	—	—	—	—	11

Years	Payment	Annual Constant	1 Year	5 Years	10 Years	15 Years	Years
1	.086 7574	1.041 0890	1.0000	—	—	—	1
2	.044 9996	.539 9951	.4813	—	—	—	2
3	.031 1062	.373 2746	.3087	—	—	—	3
4	.024 1789	.290 1468	.2227	—	—	—	4
5	.020 0379	.240 4554	.1713	1.0000	—	—	5
6	.017 2901	.207 4813	.1371	.8007	—	—	6
7	.015 3383	.184 0593	.1129	.6591	—	—	7
8	.013 8839	.166 6064	.0948	.5537	—	—	8
9	.012 7610	.153 1322	.0809	.4722	—	—	9
10	.011 8702	.142 4421	.0698	.4076	1.0000	—	10
11	.011 1480	.133 7761	.0608	.3552	.8715	—	11
12	.010 5523	.126 6272	.0534	.3120	.7655	—	12
13	.010 0537	.120 6445	.0472	.2759	.6768	—	13
14	.009 6314	.115 5772	.0420	.2452	.6017	—	14
15	.009 2701	.111 2415	.0375	.2190	.5374	1.0000	15
16	.008 9583	.107 4993	.0336	.1964	.4819	.8967	16
17	.008 6871	.104 2451	.0303	.1768	.4336	.8070	17
18	.008 4497	.101 3968	.0273	.1595	.3914	.7284	18
19	.008 2408	.098 8895	.0247	.1444	.3542	.6592	19
20	.008 0559	.096 6712	.0224	.1310	.3213	.5980	20
21	.007 8917	.094 6999	.0204	.1191	.2921	.5436	21
22	.007 7451	.092 9412	.0186	.1084	.2660	.4950	22
23	.007 6139	.091 3667	.0169	.0989	.2427	.4516	23
24	.007 4960	.089 9526	.0155	.0904	.2217	.4126	24
25	.007 3899	.088 6789	.0142	.0827	.2028	.3774	25
26	.007 2941	.087 5289	.0130	.0757	.1858	.3457	26
27	.007 2073	.086 4881	.0119	.0694	.1703	.3170	27
28	.007 1287	.085 5441	.0109	.0637	.1563	.2909	28
29	.007 0572	.084 6864	.0100	.0585	.1436	.2673	29
30	.006 9921	.083 9057	.0092	.0538	.1321	.2457	30
31	.006 9328	.083 1941	.0085	.0495	.1215	.2261	31
32	.006 8787	.082 5444	.0078	.0456	.1119	.2082	32
33	.006 8292	.081 9505	.0072	.0420	.1031	.1918	33
34	.006 7839	.081 4070	.0066	.0387	.0950	.1768	34
35	.006 7424	.080 9091	.0061	.0357	.0876	.1630	35
36	.006 7044	.080 4525	.0056	.0330	.0808	.1504	36
37	.006 6694	.080 0333	.0052	.0304	.0746	.1389	37
38	.006 6374	.079 6482	.0048	.0281	.0689	.1283	38
39	.006 6079	.079 2942	.0044	.0260	.0637	.1185	39
40	.006 5807	.078 9685	.0041	.0240	.0588	.1095	40

DIRECT REDUCTION LOAN FACTORS   7¾%

(Monthly Payment and Annual Constant per $1 of Loan)

Base:	1.006 458						
		Annual		Part Paid Off Projection			
Months	Payment	Constant	1 Year	5 Years	10 Years	15 Years	Months

Months	Payment	Annual Constant	1 Year	5 Years	10 Years	15 Years	Months
1	1.006 4583	—	—	—	—	—	1
2	.504 8489	—	—	—	—	—	2
3	.337 6481	—	—	—	—	—	3
4	.254 0495	—	—	—	—	—	4
5	.203 8916	—	—	—	—	—	5
6	.170 4542	—	—	—	—	—	6
7	.146 5714	—	—	—	—	—	7
8	.128 6601	—	—	—	—	—	8
9	.114 7299	—	—	—	—	—	9
10	.103 5864	—	—	—	—	—	10
11	.094 4696	—	—	—	—	—	11

Years							Years
1	.086 8729	1.042 4746	1.0000	—	—	—	1
2	.045 1134	.541 3603	.4807	—	—	—	2
3	.031 2212	.374 6540	.3079	—	—	—	3
4	.024 2957	.291 5489	.2218	—	—	—	4
5	.020 1570	.241 8835	.1704	1.0000	—	—	5
6	.017 4114	.208 9371	.1362	.7996	—	—	6
7	.015 4620	.185 5434	.1120	.6573	—	—	7
8	.014 0099	.168 1193	.0939	.5513	—	—	8
9	.012 8895	.154 6740	.0800	.4695	—	—	9
10	.012 0011	.144 0128	.0689	.4046	1.0000	—	10
11	.011 2813	.135 3754	.0600	.3521	.8701	—	11
12	.010 6879	.128 2550	.0526	.3088	.7631	—	12
13	.010 1917	.122 3006	.0464	.2725	.6736	—	13
14	.009 7718	.117 2613	.0412	.2419	.5978	—	14
15	.009 4128	.112 9531	.0367	.2157	.5330	1.0000	15
16	.009 1032	.109 2381	.0329	.1931	.4772	.8952	16
17	.008 8342	.106 0106	.0295	.1734	.4286	.8042	17
18	.008 5990	.103 1885	.0266	.1563	.3862	.7246	18
19	.008 3922	.100 7069	.0240	.1412	.3489	.6546	19
20	.008 2095	.098 5138	.0218	.1278	.3159	.5927	20
21	.008 0473	.096 5673	.0198	.1160	.2867	.5378	21
22	.007 9027	.094 8327	.0180	.1054	.2606	.4889	22
23	.007 7735	.093 2818	.0164	.0960	.2373	.4451	23
24	.007 6576	.091 8907	.0149	.0875	.2164	.4059	24
25	.007 5533	.090 6395	.0136	.0799	.1975	.3706	25
26	.007 4593	.089 5112	.0124	.0731	.1806	.3388	26
27	.007 3743	.088 4917	.0114	.0669	.1653	.3100	27
28	.007 2974	.087 5684	.0104	.0612	.1514	.2840	28
29	.007 2276	.086 7307	.0096	.0562	.1388	.2604	29
30	.007 1641	.085 9695	.0088	.0515	.1273	.2389	30
31	.007 1064	.085 2766	.0081	.0473	.1169	.2194	31
32	.007 0538	.084 6452	.0074	.0435	.1074	.2015	32
33	.007 0057	.084 0690	.0068	.0400	.0988	.1853	33
34	.006 9619	.083 5426	.0063	.0368	.0908	.1704	34
35	.006 9218	.083 0611	.0058	.0338	.0836	.1569	35
36	.006 8850	.082 6204	.0053	.0311	.0770	.1444	36
37	.006 8514	.082 2165	.0049	.0287	.0709	.1330	37
38	.006 8205	.081 8462	.0045	.0264	.0653	.1226	38
39	.006 7922	.081 5064	.0042	.0244	.0602	.1130	39
40	.006 7662	.081 1944	.0038	.0225	.0555	.1042	40

8% DIRECT REDUCTION LOAN FACTORS
(Monthly Payment and Annual Constant per $1 of Loan)

Base:	1.006 667	Annual	Part Paid Off Projection				
Months	Payment	Constant	1 Year	5 Years	10 Years	15 Years	Months
1	1.006 6667	—	—	—	—	—	1
2	.505 0055	—	—	—	—	—	2
3	.337 7876	—	—	—	—	—	3
4	.254 1805	—	—	—	—	—	4
5	.204 0177	—	—	—	—	—	5
6	.170 5771	—	—	—	—	—	6
7	.146 6920	—	—	—	—	—	7
8	.128 7791	—	—	—	—	—	8
9	.114 8476	—	—	—	—	—	9
10	.103 7032	—	—	—	—	—	10
11	.094 5857	—	—	—	—	—	11

Years							Years
1	.086 9884	1.043 8611	1.0000	—	—	—	1
2	.045 2273	.542 7275	.4801	—	—	—	2
3	.031 3364	.376 0364	.3071	—	—	—	3
4	.024 4129	.292 9551	.2209	—	—	—	4
5	.020 2764	.243 3167	.1694	1.0000	—	—	5
6	.017 5332	.210 3989	.1353	.7984	—	—	6
7	.015 5862	.187 0346	.1110	.6554	—	—	7
8	.014 1367	.169 6402	.0930	.5489	—	—	8
9	.013 0187	.156 2246	.0791	.4667	—	—	9
10	.012 1328	.145 5931	.0681	.4016	1.0000	—	10
11	.011 4154	.136 9854	.0591	.3489	.8688	—	11
12	.010 8245	.129 8943	.0518	.3055	.7607	—	12
13	.010 3307	.123 9689	.0456	.2692	.6703	—	13
14	.009 9132	.118 9582	.0404	.2385	.5939	—	14
15	.009 5565	.114 6783	.0360	.2123	.5287	1.0000	15
16	.009 2493	.110 9910	.0322	.1898	.4725	.8937	16
17	.008 9826	.107 7908	.0288	.1702	.4237	.8014	17
18	.008 7496	.104 9955	.0259	.1530	.3811	.7208	18
19	.008 5450	.102 5402	.0234	.1380	.3436	.6500	19
20	.008 3644	.100 3728	.0211	.1247	.3106	.5875	20
21	.008 2043	.098 4514	.0191	.1130	.2813	.5321	21
22	.008 0618	.096 7413	.0174	.1025	.2552	.4828	22
23	.007 9345	.095 2143	.0158	.0932	.2319	.4387	23
24	.007 8205	.093 8465	.0144	.0848	.2111	.3993	24
25	.007 7182	.092 6179	.0131	.0773	.1924	.3639	25
26	.007 6260	.091 5118	.0119	.0705	.1755	.3320	26
27	.007 5428	.090 5136	.0109	.0644	.1603	.3032	27
28	.007 4676	.089 6110	.0100	.0588	.1465	.2771	28
29	.007 3995	.088 7935	.0091	.0538	.1341	.2536	29
30	.007 3376	.088 0517	.0084	.0493	.1228	.2322	30
31	.007 2815	.087 3778	.0077	.0452	.1125	.2127	31
32	.007 2304	.086 7645	.0070	.0414	.1031	.1951	32
33	.007 1838	.086 2059	.0064	.0380	.0946	.1790	33
34	.007 1414	.085 6964	.0059	.0349	.0868	.1643	34
35	.007 1026	.085 2313	.0054	.0320	.0798	.1509	35
36	.007 0672	.084 8063	.0050	.0294	.0733	.1386	36
37	.007 0348	.084 4176	.0046	.0270	.0673	.1274	37
38	.007 0052	.084 0619	.0042	.0249	.0619	.1171	38
39	.006 9780	.083 7360	.0039	.0229	.0570	.1077	39
40	.006 9531	.083 4374	.0036	.0210	.0524	.0991	40

DIRECT REDUCTION LOAN FACTORS   8¼%

(Monthly Payment and Annual Constant per $1 of Loan)

Base:	1.006 875			Part Paid Off Projection				
Months	Payment	Annual Constant	1 Year	5 Years	10 Years	15 Years	Months
1	1.006 8750	—	—	—	—	—	1
2	.505 1621	—	—	—	—	—	2
3	.337 9271	—	—	—	—	—	3
4	.254 3116	—	—	—	—	—	4
5	.204 1438	—	—	—	—	—	5
6	.170 7000	—	—	—	—	—	6
7	.146 8126	—	—	—	—	—	7
8	.128 8981	—	—	—	—	—	8
9	.114 9654	—	—	—	—	—	9
10	.103 8201	—	—	—	—	—	10
11	.094 7019	—	—	—	—	—	11

Years							Years
1	.087 1041	1.045 2488	1.0000	—	—	—	1
2	.045 3414	.544 0968	.4795	—	—	—	2
3	.031 4518	.377 4219	.3063	—	—	—	3
4	.024 5304	.294 3653	.2201	—	—	—	4
5	.020 3963	.244 7550	.1685	1.0000	—	—	5
6	.017 6556	.211 8667	.1344	.7973	—	—	6
7	.015 7111	.188 5327	.1101	.6535	—	—	7
8	.014 2641	.171 1689	.0921	.5465	—	—	8
9	.013 1487	.157 7840	.0782	.4640	—	—	9
10	.012 2653	.147 1832	.0672	.3987	1.0000	—	10
11	.011 5505	.138 6058	.0583	.3458	.8674	—	11
12	.010 9621	.131 5449	.0509	.3023	.7582	—	12
13	.010 4708	.125 6492	.0448	.2659	.6671	—	13
14	.010 0557	.120 6679	.0396	.2352	.5901	—	14
15	.009 7014	.116 4168	.0352	.2090	.5244	1.0000	15
16	.009 3965	.112 7580	.0314	.1865	.4678	.8921	16
17	.009 1321	.109 5857	.0281	.1669	.4187	.7986	17
18	.008 9015	.106 8177	.0253	.1499	.3760	.7170	18
19	.008 6991	.104 3891	.0227	.1349	.3384	.6454	19
20	.008 5207	.102 2479	.0205	.1217	.3053	.5822	20
21	.008 3627	.100 3519	.0185	.1100	.2760	.5263	21
22	.008 2222	.098 6668	.0168	.0996	.2499	.4767	22
23	.008 0970	.097 1640	.0152	.0904	.2267	.4324	23
24	.007 9850	.095 8197	.0138	.0821	.2059	.3927	24
25	.007 8845	.094 6140	.0126	.0747	.1873	.3572	25
26	.007 7942	.093 5300	.0115	.0680	.1705	.3252	26
27	.007 7128	.092 5534	.0104	.0620	.1554	.2964	27
28	.007 6393	.091 6717	.0095	.0565	.1418	.2704	28
29	.007 5729	.090 8743	.0087	.0516	.1295	.2469	29
30	.007 5127	.090 1520	.0079	.0472	.1183	.2256	30
31	.007 4581	.089 4968	.0073	.0431	.1082	.2063	31
32	.007 4085	.088 9017	.0066	.0395	.0990	.1887	32
33	.007 3634	.088 3605	.0061	.0361	.0906	.1728	33
34	.007 3223	.087 8679	.0056	.0331	.0830	.1583	34
35	.007 2849	.087 4189	.0051	.0303	.0760	.1450	35
36	.007 2508	.087 0095	.0047	.0278	.0697	.1330	36
37	.007 2196	.086 6357	.0043	.0255	.0639	.1219	37
38	.007 1912	.086 2943	.0039	.0234	.0587	.1119	38
39	.007 1652	.085 9821	.0036	.0215	.0538	.1027	39
40	.007 1414	.085 6967	.0033	.0197	.0494	.0942	40

8½% DIRECT REDUCTION LOAN FACTORS
(Monthly Payment and Annual Constant per $1 of Loan)

Base: 1.007 083

Months	Payment	Annual Constant	1 Year	5 Years	10 Years	15 Years	Months
				Part Paid Off Projection			
1	1.007 0833	—	—	—	—	—	1
2	.505 3187	—	—	—	—	—	2
3	.338 0667	—	—	—	—	—	3
4	.254 4427	—	—	—	—	—	4
5	.204 2700	—	—	—	—	—	5
6	.170 8229	—	—	—	—	—	6
7	.146 9333	—	—	—	—	—	7
8	.129 0172	—	—	—	—	—	8
9	.115 0833	—	—	—	—	—	9
10	.103 9371	—	—	—	—	—	10
11	.094 8182	—	—	—	—	—	11

Years							Years
1	.087 2198	1.046 6374	1.0000	—	—	—	1
2	.045 4557	.545 4681	.4788	—	—	—	2
3	.031 5675	.378 8104	.3055	—	—	—	3
4	.024 6483	.295 7796	.2192	—	—	—	4
5	.020 5165	.246 1984	.1676	1.0000	—	—	5
6	.017 7784	.213 3406	.1335	.7962	—	—	6
7	.015 8365	.190 0378	.1092	.6516	—	—	7
8	.014 3921	.172 7055	.0912	.5441	—	—	8
9	.013 2794	.159 3522	.0773	.4612	—	—	9
10	.012 3986	.148 7828	.0663	.3957	1.0000	—	10
11	.011 6864	.140 2367	.0574	.3427	.8660	—	11
12	.011 1006	.133 2067	.0501	.2991	.7558	—	12
13	.010 6118	.127 3415	.0440	.2627	.6638	—	13
14	.010 1992	.122 3902	.0389	.2320	.5862	—	14
15	.009 8474	.118 1687	.0345	.2058	.5200	1.0000	15
16	.009 5449	.114 5389	.0307	.1832	.4631	.8906	16
17	.009 2829	.111 3951	.0274	.1637	.4138	.7958	17
18	.009 0546	.108 6549	.0246	.1467	.3709	.7132	18
19	.008 8545	.106 2535	.0221	.1318	.3332	.6408	19
20	.008 6782	.104 1388	.0199	.1187	.3001	.5770	20
21	.008 5224	.102 2687	.0180	.1071	.2707	.5206	21
22	.008 3841	.100 6087	.0162	.0968	.2447	.4706	22
23	.008 2609	.099 1304	.0147	.0877	.2215	.4260	23
24	.008 1508	.097 8099	.0133	.0795	.2008	.3862	24
25	.008 0523	.096 6273	.0121	.0721	.1823	.3505	25
26	.007 9638	.095 5656	.0110	.0655	.1656	.3185	26
27	.007 8842	.094 6105	.0100	.0596	.1507	.2897	27
28	.007 8125	.093 7497	.0091	.0543	.1372	.2638	28
29	.007 7477	.092 9725	.0083	.0495	.1250	.2404	29
30	.007 6891	.092 2696	.0076	.0451	.1140	.2192	30
31	.007 6361	.091 6332	.0069	.0411	.1040	.2000	31
32	.007 5880	.091 0561	.0063	.0376	.0949	.1826	32
33	.007 5444	.090 5322	.0058	.0343	.0867	.1668	33
34	.007 5047	.090 0562	.0053	.0314	.0793	.1524	34
35	.007 4686	.089 6233	.0048	.0287	.0725	.1394	35
36	.007 4358	.089 2291	.0044	.0262	.0663	.1275	36
37	.007 4058	.088 8700	.0040	.0240	.0607	.1167	37
38	.007 3786	.088 5426	.0037	.0220	.0555	.1068	38
39	.007 3537	.088 2439	.0034	.0201	.0509	.0978	39
40	.007 3309	.087 9713	.0031	.0184	.0466	.0896	40

DIRECT REDUCTION LOAN FACTORS   8¾%

(Monthly Payment and Annual Constant per $1 of Loan)

Base:	1.007 292		Part Paid Off Projection				
Months	Payment	Annual Constant	1 Year	5 Years	10 Years	15 Years	Months
1	1.007 2917	—	—	—	—	—	1
2	.505 4754	—	—	—	—	—	2
3	.338 2062	—	—	—	—	—	3
4	.254 5738	—	—	—	—	—	4
5	.204 3962	—	—	—	—	—	5
6	.170 9459	—	—	—	—	—	6
7	.147 0541	—	—	—	—	—	7
8	.129 1363	—	—	—	—	—	8
9	.115 2013	—	—	—	—	—	9
10	.104 0541	—	—	—	—	—	10
11	.094 9345	—	—	—	—	—	11

Years							Years
1	.087 3356	1.048 0270	1.0000	—	—	—	1
2	.045 5701	.546 8415	.4782	—	—	—	2
3	.031 6835	.380 2021	.3047	—	—	—	3
4	.024 7665	.297 1980	.2183	—	—	—	4
5	.020 6372	.247 6468	.1667	1.0000	—	—	5
6	.017 9017	.214 8205	.1326	.7950	—	—	6
7	.015 9625	.191 5499	.1083	.6497	—	—	7
8	.014 5208	.174 2501	.0903	.5417	—	—	8
9	.013 4108	.160 9292	.0764	.4585	—	—	9
10	.012 5327	.150 3921	.0655	.3927	1.0000	—	10
11	.011 8232	.141 8780	.0566	.3396	.8646	—	11
12	.011 2400	.134 8796	.0493	.2959	.7533	—	12
13	.010 7538	.129 0457	.0433	.2594	.6606	—	13
14	.010 3438	.124 1251	.0381	.2287	.5823	—	14
15	.009 9945	.119 9338	.0338	.2025	.5157	1.0000	15
16	.009 6945	.116 3336	.0300	.1800	.4585	.8890	16
17	.009 4349	.113 2187	.0268	.1606	.4089	.7930	17
18	.009 2089	.110 5068	.0240	.1437	.3658	.7093	18
19	.009 0111	.108 1331	.0215	.1288	.3281	.6362	19
20	.008 8371	.106 0453	.0193	.1158	.2949	.5718	20
21	.008 6834	.104 2014	.0174	.1043	.2656	.5149	21
22	.008 5472	.102 5669	.0157	.0941	.2396	.4645	22
23	.008 4261	.101 1132	.0142	.0850	.2165	.4197	23
24	.008 3181	.099 8167	.0128	.0769	.1958	.3797	24
25	.008 2214	.098 6572	.0116	.0697	.1774	.3440	25
26	.008 1348	.097 6180	.0105	.0632	.1609	.3120	26
27	.008 0570	.096 6846	.0096	.0574	.1460	.2832	27
28	.007 9871	.095 8446	.0087	.0521	.1327	.2573	28
29	.007 9240	.095 0875	.0079	.0474	.1206	.2339	29
30	.007 8670	.094 4040	.0072	.0431	.1098	.2129	30
31	.007 8155	.093 7862	.0065	.0393	.1000	.1938	31
32	.007 7689	.093 2270	.0060	.0358	.0911	.1766	32
33	.007 7267	.092 7203	.0054	.0326	.0830	.1610	33
34	.007 6884	.092 2608	.0050	.0297	.0757	.1468	34
35	.007 6536	.091 8436	.0045	.0271	.0691	.1339	35
36	.007 6220	.091 4645	.0041	.0248	.0630	.1222	36
37	.007 5933	.091 1198	.0038	.0226	.0576	.1116	37
38	.007 5672	.090 8062	.0034	.0206	.0526	.1019	38
39	.007 5434	.090 5206	.0031	.0189	.0480	.0931	39
40	.007 5217	.090 2605	.0029	.0172	.0439	.0851	40

9% DIRECT REDUCTION LOAN FACTORS
(Monthly Payment and Annual Constant per $1 of Loan)

Base: 1.007 500

Months	Payment	Annual Constant	1 Year	5 Years	10 Years	15 Years	Months
				Part Paid Off Projection			
1	1.007 5000	—	—	—	—	—	1
2	.505 6320	—	—	—	—	—	2
3	.338 3458	—	—	—	—	—	3
4	.254 7050	—	—	—	—	—	4
5	.204 5224	—	—	—	—	—	5
6	.171 0689	—	—	—	—	—	6
7	.147 1749	—	—	—	—	—	7
8	.129 2555	—	—	—	—	—	8
9	.115 3193	—	—	—	—	—	9
10	.104 1712	—	—	—	—	—	10
11	.095 0509	—	—	—	—	—	11

Years	Payment	Annual Constant	1 Year	5 Years	10 Years	15 Years	Years
1	.087 4515	1.049 4177	1.0000	—	—	—	1
2	.045 6847	.548 2169	.4776	—	—	—	2
3	.031 7997	.381 5968	.3039	—	—	—	3
4	.024 8850	.298 6205	.2174	—	—	—	4
5	.020 7584	.249 1003	.1658	1.0000	—	—	5
6	.018 0255	.216 3064	.1316	.7939	—	—	6
7	.016 0891	.193 0689	.1074	.6478	—	—	7
8	.014 6502	.175 8024	.0894	.5393	—	—	8
9	.013 5429	.162 5149	.0756	.4558	—	—	9
10	.012 6676	.152 0109	.0646	.3898	1.0000	—	10
11	.011 9608	.143 5296	.0558	.3365	.8632	—	11
12	.011 3803	.136 5637	.0485	.2927	.7509	—	12
13	.010 8968	.130 7617	.0425	.2562	.6573	—	13
14	.010 4894	.125 8725	.0374	.2255	.5785	—	14
15	.010 1427	.121 7120	.0331	.1993	.5114	1.0000	15
16	.009 8452	.118 1419	.0293	.1769	.4538	.8874	16
17	.009 5880	.115 0565	.0261	.1575	.4041	.7901	17
18	.009 3644	.112 3734	.0233	.1406	.3608	.7055	18
19	.009 1690	.110 0276	.0209	.1259	.3230	.6315	19
20	.008 9973	.107 9671	.0187	.1129	.2897	.5666	20
21	.008 8458	.106 1497	.0168	.1015	.2604	.5093	21
22	.008 7117	.104 5409	.0152	.0914	.2345	.4585	22
23	.008 5927	.103 1122	.0137	.0824	.2114	.4135	23
24	.008 4866	.101 8397	.0123	.0744	.1909	.3734	24
25	.008 3920	.100 7036	.0112	.0673	.1726	.3375	25
26	.008 3072	.099 6868	.0101	.0609	.1562	.3055	26
27	.008 2313	.098 7750	.0091	.0552	.1415	.2767	27
28	.008 1630	.097 9560	.0083	.0500	.1283	.2509	28
29	.008 1016	.097 2189	.0075	.0454	.1164	.2276	29
30	.008 0462	.096 5547	.0068	.0412	.1057	.2067	30
31	.007 9963	.095 9554	.0062	.0374	.0960	.1878	31
32	.007 9512	.095 4139	.0056	.0340	.0873	.1707	32
33	.007 9103	.094 9242	.0051	.0310	.0794	.1553	33
34	.007 8734	.094 4809	.0047	.0282	.0723	.1413	34
35	.007 8399	.094 0792	.0043	.0256	.0658	.1286	35
36	.007 8096	.093 7149	.0039	.0233	.0599	.1171	36
37	.007 7820	.093 3843	.0035	.0213	.0546	.1067	37
38	.007 7570	.093 0841	.0032	.0194	.0497	.0973	38
39	.007 7343	.092 8114	.0029	.0177	.0453	.0887	39
40	.007 7136	.092 5634	.0027	.0161	.0413	.0808	40

DIRECT REDUCTION LOAN FACTORS 9¼%

(Monthly Payment and Annual Constant per $1 of Loan)

Base: 1.007 708

Months	Payment	Annual Constant	Part Paid Off Projection 1 Year	5 Years	10 Years	15 Years	Months
1	1.007 7083	—	—	—	—	—	1
2	.505 7886	—	—	—	—	—	2
3	.338 4854	—	—	—	—	—	3
4	.254 8362	—	—	—	—	—	4
5	.204 6487	—	—	—	—	—	5
6	.171 1920	—	—	—	—	—	6
7	.147 2957	—	—	—	—	—	7
8	.129 3748	—	—	—	—	—	8
9	.115 4374	—	—	—	—	—	9
10	.104 2884	—	—	—	—	—	10
11	.095 1674	—	—	—	—	—	11

Years							Years
1	.087 5675	1.050 8094	1.0000	—	—	—	1
2	.045 7995	.549 5944	.4770	—	—	—	2
3	.031 9162	.382 9946	.3031	—	—	—	3
4	.025 0039	.300 0470	.2166	—	—	—	4
5	.020 8799	.250 5588	.1649	1.0000	—	—	5
6	.018 1499	.217 7984	.1307	.7927	—	—	6
7	.016 2162	.194 5949	.1065	.6459	—	—	7
8	.014 7802	.177 3626	.0886	.5369	—	—	8
9	.013 6758	.164 1093	.0747	.4531	—	—	9
10	.012 8033	.153 6393	.0638	.3868	1.0000	—	10
11	.012 0993	.145 1916	.0550	.3334	.8618	—	11
12	.011 5216	.138 2588	.0477	.2895	.7484	—	12
13	.011 0408	.132 4894	.0417	.2530	.6541	—	13
14	.010 6360	.127 6322	.0367	.2223	.5746	—	14
15	.010 2919	.123 5031	.0324	.1961	.5071	1.0000	15
16	.009 9970	.119 9637	.0287	.1738	.4492	.8858	16
17	.009 7423	.116 9082	.0255	.1544	.3992	.7873	17
18	.009 5212	.114 2543	.0227	.1376	.3558	.7017	18
19	.009 3281	.111 9369	.0203	.1230	.3179	.6269	19
20	.009 1587	.109 9040	.0182	.1101	.2847	.5614	20
21	.009 0094	.108 1134	.0163	.0988	.2554	.5036	21
22	.008 8775	.106 5305	.0146	.0888	.2295	.4526	22
23	.008 7606	.105 1269	.0132	.0799	.2065	.4073	23
24	.008 6566	.103 8786	.0119	.0720	.1861	.3670	24
25	.008 5638	.102 7658	.0107	.0649	.1679	.3311	25
26	.008 4810	.101 7716	.0097	.0587	.1516	.2991	26
27	.008 4068	.100 8815	.0087	.0530	.1371	.2703	27
28	.008 3403	.100 0832	.0079	.0480	.1240	.2446	28
29	.008 2805	.099 3661	.0072	.0434	.1123	.2215	29
30	.008 2268	.098 7211	.0065	.0394	.1018	.2007	30
31	.008 1783	.098 1400	.0059	.0357	.0922	.1819	31
32	.008 1347	.097 6161	.0053	.0324	.0837	.1650	32
33	.008 0953	.097 1431	.0048	.0294	.0759	.1498	33
34	.008 0596	.096 7158	.0044	.0267	.0690	.1360	34
35	.008 0274	.096 3293	.0040	.0242	.0626	.1235	35
36	.007 9983	.095 9796	.0036	.0220	.0569	.1122	36
37	.007 9719	.095 6628	.0033	.0200	.0517	.1020	37
38	.007 9480	.095 3757	.0030	.0182	.0470	.0928	38
39	.007 9263	.095 1154	.0027	.0165	.0428	.0844	39
40	.007 9066	.094 8793	.0025	.0151	.0389	.0767	40

9½% DIRECT REDUCTION LOAN FACTORS
(Monthly Payment and Annual Constant per $1 of Loan)

Months	Payment	Annual Constant	Part Paid Off Projection				Months
			1 Year	5 Years	10 Years	15 Years	
1	1.007 9167	—	—	—	—	—	1
2	.505 9453	—	—	—	—	—	2
3	.338 6250	—	—	—	—	—	3
4	.254 9674	—	—	—	—	—	4
5	.204 7750	—	—	—	—	—	5
6	.171 3151	—	—	—	—	—	6
7	.147 4166	—	—	—	—	—	7
8	.129 4941	—	—	—	—	—	8
9	.115 5555	—	—	—	—	—	9
10	.104 4057	—	—	—	—	—	10
11	.095 2840	—	—	—	—	—	11

Base: 1.007 917

Years	Payment	Annual Constant	1 Year	5 Years	10 Years	15 Years	Years
1	.087 6835	1.052 2021	1.0000	—	—	—	1
2	.045 9145	.550 9739	.4764	—	—	—	2
3	.032 0329	.384 3954	.3023	—	—	—	3
4	.025 1231	.301 4776	.2157	—	—	—	4
5	.021 0019	.252 0223	.1640	1.0000	—	—	5
6	.018 2747	.219 2963	.1299	.7916	—	—	6
7	.016 3440	.196 1278	.1056	.6440	—	—	7
8	.014 9109	.178 9306	.0877	.5345	—	—	8
9	.013 8094	.165 7123	.0739	.4503	—	—	9
10	.012 9398	.155 2771	.0630	.3839	1.0000	—	10
11	.012 2386	.146 8637	.0542	.3303	.8604	—	11
12	.011 6637	.139 9648	.0470	.2864	.7460	—	12
13	.011 1857	.134 2287	.0410	.2498	.6508	—	13
14	.010 7837	.129 4042	.0359	.2191	.5708	—	14
15	.010 4422	.125 3070	.0317	.1930	.5028	1.0000	15
16	.010 1499	.121 7987	.0280	.1707	.4446	.8842	16
17	.009 8978	.118 7737	.0248	.1514	.3944	.7844	17
18	.009 6791	.116 1494	.0221	.1347	.3509	.6978	18
19	.009 4884	.113 8608	.0197	.1201	.3129	.6223	19
20	.009 3213	.111 8557	.0176	.1073	.2796	.5562	20
21	.009 1743	.110 0921	.0158	.0961	.2504	.4980	21
22	.009 0446	.108 5354	.0141	.0862	.2246	.4466	22
23	.008 9297	.107 1569	.0127	.0774	.2017	.4011	23
24	.008 8277	.105 9330	.0114	.0696	.1814	.3607	24
25	.008 7370	.104 8436	.0103	.0627	.1633	.3248	25
26	.008 6560	.103 8719	.0093	.0565	.1472	.2927	26
27	.008 5836	.103 0034	.0084	.0510	.1328	.2641	27
28	.008 5188	.102 2258	.0075	.0460	.1199	.2384	28
29	.008 4607	.101 5286	.0068	.0416	.1083	.2154	29
30	.008 4085	.100 9025	.0062	.0376	.0979	.1948	30
31	.008 3616	.100 3396	.0056	.0340	.0886	.1762	31
32	.008 3194	.099 8330	.0050	.0308	.0802	.1595	32
33	.008 2814	.099 3765	.0046	.0279	.0726	.1444	33
34	.008 2471	.098 9649	.0041	.0253	.0658	.1308	34
35	.008 2161	.098 5934	.0038	.0229	.0596	.1186	35
36	.008 1882	.098 2578	.0034	.0207	.0540	.1075	36
37	.008 1629	.097 9545	.0031	.0188	.0490	.0975	37
38	.008 1400	.097 6803	.0028	.0171	.0445	.0884	38
39	.008 1193	.097 4321	.0025	.0155	.0403	.0802	39
40	.008 1006	.097 2074	.0023	.0141	.0366	.0728	40

DIRECT REDUCTION LOAN FACTORS 9¾%

(Monthly Payment and Annual Constant per $1 of Loan)

Base: 1.008 125

Months	Payment	Annual Constant	Part Paid Off Projection 1 Year	5 Years	10 Years	15 Years	Months
1	1.008 1250	—	—	—	—	—	1
2	.506 1020	—	—	—	—	—	2
3	.338 7646	—	—	—	—	—	3
4	.255 0987	—	—	—	—	—	4
5	.204 9013	—	—	—	—	—	5
6	.171 4382	—	—	—	—	—	6
7	.147 5376	—	—	—	—	—	7
8	.129 6135	—	—	—	—	—	8
9	.115 6737	—	—	—	—	—	9
10	.104 5230	—	—	—	—	—	10
11	.095 4007	—	—	—	—	—	11

Years							Years
1	.087 7997	1.053 5959	1.0000	—	—	—	1
2	.046 0296	.552 3555	.4757	—	—	—	2
3	.032 1499	.385 7993	.3015	—	—	—	3
4	.025 2427	.302 9123	.2148	—	—	—	4
5	.021 1242	.253 4909	.1632	1.0000	—	—	5
6	.018 4000	.220 8002	.1290	.7904	—	—	6
7	.016 4723	.197 6676	.1048	.6421	—	—	7
8	.015 0422	.180 5064	.0868	.5321	—	—	8
9	.013 9437	.167 3240	.0730	.4476	—	—	9
10	.013 0770	.156 9243	.0622	.3809	1.0000	—	10
11	.012 3788	.148 5461	.0534	.3272	.8590	—	11
12	.011 8068	.141 6817	.0462	.2832	.7435	—	12
13	.011 3316	.135 9795	.0402	.2467	.6475	—	13
14	.010 9324	.131 1882	.0352	.2160	.5669	—	14
15	.010 5936	.127 1235	.0310	.1899	.4985	1.0000	15
16	.010 3039	.123 6470	.0273	.1676	.4400	.8826	16
17	.010 0544	.120 6528	.0242	.1484	.3896	.7816	17
18	.009 8382	.118 0584	.0215	.1318	.3460	.6940	18
19	.009 6499	.115 7989	.0191	.1173	.3079	.6177	19
20	.009 4852	.113 8220	.0171	.1046	.2747	.5510	20
21	.009 3405	.112 0856	.0153	.0935	.2454	.4924	21
22	.009 2129	.110 5551	.0137	.0837	.2197	.4407	22
23	.009 1002	.109 2020	.0122	.0750	.1969	.3950	23
24	.009 0002	.108 0025	.0110	.0673	.1767	.3545	24
25	.008 9114	.106 9365	.0099	.0605	.1588	.3185	25
26	.008 8323	.105 9872	.0089	.0544	.1428	.2865	26
27	.008 7617	.105 1403	.0080	.0490	.1286	.2579	27
28	.008 6986	.104 3833	.0072	.0441	.1158	.2324	28
29	.008 6421	.103 7058	.0065	.0398	.1044	.2095	29
30	.008 5915	.103 0985	.0059	.0359	.0942	.1890	30
31	.008 5461	.102 5536	.0053	.0324	.0850	.1706	31
32	.008 5053	.102 0640	.0048	.0293	.0768	.1541	32
33	.008 4687	.101 6238	.0043	.0264	.0694	.1392	33
34	.008 4356	.101 2276	.0039	.0239	.0627	.1258	34
35	.008 4059	.100 8707	.0035	.0216	.0567	.1138	35
36	.008 3791	.100 5490	.0032	.0195	.0513	.1029	36
37	.008 3549	.100 2589	.0029	.0177	.0464	.0931	37
38	.008 3331	.099 9971	.0026	.0160	.0420	.0843	38
39	.008 3134	.099 7606	.0024	.0145	.0380	.0763	39
40	.008 2956	.099 5470	.0021	.0131	.0344	.0691	40

10% DIRECT REDUCTION LOAN FACTORS
(Monthly Payment and Annual Constant per $1 of Loan)

Base: 1.008 333

Months	Payment	Annual Constant	1 Year	5 Years	10 Years	15 Years	Months
			Part Paid Off Projection				
1	1.008 3333	—	—	—	—	—	1
2	.506 2586	—	—	—	—	—	2
3	.338 9043	—	—	—	—	—	3
4	.255 2299	—	—	—	—	—	4
5	.205 0277	—	—	—	—	—	5
6	.171 5614	—	—	—	—	—	6
7	.147 6586	—	—	—	—	—	7
8	.129 7329	—	—	—	—	—	8
9	.115 7920	—	—	—	—	—	9
10	.104 6404	—	—	—	—	—	10
11	.095 5174	—	—	—	—	—	11

Years							Years
1	.087 9159	1.054 9906	1.0000	—	—	—	1
2	.046 1449	.553 7391	.4751	—	—	—	2
3	.032 2672	.387 2062	.3007	—	—	—	3
4	.025 3626	.304 3510	.2140	—	—	—	4
5	.021 2470	.254 9645	.1623	1.0000	—	—	5
6	.018 5258	.222 3101	.1281	.7893	—	—	6
7	.016 6012	.199 2142	.1039	.6402	—	—	7
8	.015 1742	.182 0900	.0860	.5297	—	—	8
9	.014 0787	.168 9442	.0722	.4449	—	—	9
10	.013 2151	.158 5809	.0613	.3780	1.0000	—	10
11	.012 5199	.150 2385	.0526	.3242	.8576	—	11
12	.011 9508	.143 4094	.0455	.2801	.7410	—	12
13	.011 4785	.137 7418	.0395	.2436	.6443	—	13
14	.011 0820	.132 9843	.0345	.2129	.5631	—	14
15	.010 7461	.128 9526	.0303	.1868	.4942	1.0000	15
16	.010 4590	.125 5082	.0267	.1646	.4354	.8810	16
17	.010 2121	.122 5453	.0236	.1455	.3849	.7787	17
18	.009 9984	.119 9812	.0209	.1289	.3411	.6901	18
19	.009 8126	.117 7511	.0186	.1145	.3030	.6131	19
20	.009 6502	.115 8026	.0165	.1020	.2698	.5458	20
21	.009 5078	.114 0936	.0148	.0909	.2406	.4868	21
22	.009 3825	.112 5895	.0132	.0812	.2149	.4348	22
23	.009 2718	.111 2618	.0118	.0727	.1922	.3890	23
24	.009 1739	.110 0866	.0106	.0651	.1722	.3484	24
25	.009 0870	.109 0441	.0095	.0584	.1544	.3124	25
26	.009 0098	.108 1172	.0085	.0524	.1386	.2804	26
27	.008 9410	.107 2917	.0076	.0471	.1245	.2519	27
28	.008 8796	.106 5552	.0069	.0423	.1119	.2264	28
29	.008 8248	.105 8972	.0062	.0381	.1007	.2037	29
30	.008 7757	.105 3086	.0056	.0343	.0906	.1834	30
31	.008 7318	.104 7813	.0050	.0309	.0816	.1651	31
32	.008 6924	.104 3086	.0045	.0278	.0735	.1488	32
33	.008 6570	.103 8843	.0041	.0251	.0663	.1342	33
34	.008 6253	.103 5033	.0037	.0226	.0598	.1210	34
35	.008 5967	.103 1607	.0033	.0204	.0540	.1092	35
36	.008 5710	.102 8526	.0030	.0184	.0487	.0985	36
37	.008 5479	.102 5752	.0027	.0166	.0440	.0889	37
38	.008 5271	.102 3254	.0024	.0150	.0397	.0803	38
39	.008 5084	.102 1004	.0022	.0136	.0359	.0725	39
40	.008 4915	.101 8975	.0020	.0122	.0324	.0655	40

DIRECT REDUCTION LOAN FACTORS   10¼%
(Monthly Payment and Annual Constant per $1 of Loan)

Base: 1.008 542

Months	Payment	Annual Constant	1 Year	5 Years	10 Years	15 Years	Months
				Part Paid Off Projection			
1	1.008 5417	—	—	—	—	—	1
2	.506 4153	—	—	—	—	—	2
3	.339 0439	—	—	—	—	—	3
4	.255 3612	—	—	—	—	—	4
5	.205 1541	—	—	—	—	—	5
6	.171 6846	—	—	—	—	—	6
7	.147 7796	—	—	—	—	—	7
8	.129 8524	—	—	—	—	—	8
9	.115 9103	—	—	—	—	—	9
10	.104 7578	—	—	—	—	—	10
11	.095 6342	—	—	—	—	—	11

Years	Payment	Annual Constant	1 Year	5 Years	10 Years	15 Years	Years
1	.088 0322	1.056 3864	1.0000	—	—	—	1
2	.046 2604	.555 1248	.4745	—	—	—	2
3	.032 3847	.388 6163	.2999	—	—	—	3
4	.025 4828	.305 7938	.2131	—	—	—	4
5	.021 3703	.256 4432	.1614	1.0000	—	—	5
6	.018 6522	.223 8259	.1272	.7881	—	—	6
7	.016 7306	.200 7677	.1030	.6383	—	—	7
8	.015 3068	.183 6812	.0851	.5273	—	—	8
9	.014 2144	.170 5730	.0714	.4422	—	—	9
10	.013 3539	.160 2468	.0605	.3751	1.0000	—	10
11	.012 6618	.151 9410	.0518	.3212	.8562	—	11
12	.012 0957	.145 1478	.0447	.2770	.7385	—	12
13	.011 6263	.139 5154	.0388	.2404	.6410	—	13
14	.011 2327	.134 7923	.0339	.2098	.5592	—	14
15	.010 8995	.130 7941	.0297	.1838	.4900	1.0000	15
16	.010 6152	.127 3823	.0261	.1616	.4309	.8794	16
17	.010 3709	.124 4510	.0230	.1426	.3801	.7758	17
18	.010 1598	.121 9176	.0204	.1261	.3363	.6863	18
19	.009 9764	.119 7171	.0180	.1118	.2981	.6085	19
20	.009 8164	.117 7972	.0160	.0994	.2649	.5406	20
21	.009 6763	.116 1158	.0143	.0884	.2358	.4812	21
22	.009 5532	.114 6382	.0127	.0788	.2102	.4290	22
23	.009 4447	.113 3359	.0114	.0704	.1876	.3830	23
24	.009 3488	.112 1852	.0102	.0629	.1677	.3423	24
25	.009 2638	.111 1660	.0091	.0563	.1501	.3063	25
26	.009 1885	.110 2615	.0081	.0504	.1344	.2743	26
27	.009 1214	.109 4573	.0073	.0452	.1205	.2459	27
28	.009 0618	.108 7411	.0065	.0405	.1081	.2206	28
29	.009 0085	.108 1024	.0059	.0364	.0970	.1980	29
30	.008 9610	.107 5322	.0053	.0327	.0871	.1779	30
31	.008 9185	.107 0223	.0047	.0294	.0783	.1598	31
32	.008 8805	.106 5661	.0043	.0264	.0704	.1437	32
33	.008 8465	.106 1575	.0038	.0238	.0633	.1293	33
34	.008 8159	.105 7913	.0035	.0214	.0570	.1163	34
35	.008 7886	.105 4627	.0031	.0192	.0513	.1047	35
36	.008 7640	.105 1677	.0028	.0173	.0462	.0943	36
37	.008 7419	.104 9028	.0025	.0156	.0416	.0849	37
38	.008 7221	.104 6647	.0023	.0141	.0375	.0765	38
39	.008 7042	.104 4507	.0020	.0127	.0338	.0689	39
40	.008 6882	.104 2582	.0018	.0114	.0304	.0621	40

10½% DIRECT REDUCTION LOAN FACTORS
(Monthly Payment and Annual Constant per $1 of Loan)

Base: 1.008 750

Months	Payment	Annual Constant	1 Year	5 Years	10 Years	15 Years	Months
				Part Paid Off Projection			
1	1.008 7500	—	—	—	—	—	1
2	.506 5720	—	—	—	—	—	2
3	.339 1836	—	—	—	—	—	3
4	.255 4926	—	—	—	—	—	4
5	.205 2805	—	—	—	—	—	5
6	.171 8079	—	—	—	—	—	6
7	.147 9007	—	—	—	—	—	7
8	.129 9719	—	—	—	—	—	8
9	.116 0287	—	—	—	—	—	9
10	.104 8754	—	—	—	—	—	10
11	.095 7511	—	—	—	—	—	11

Years	Payment	Annual Constant	1 Year	5 Years	10 Years	15 Years	Years
1	.088 1486	1.057 7832	1.0000	—	—	—	1
2	.046 3760	.556 5125	.4739	—	—	—	2
3	.032 5024	.390 0293	.2992	—	—	—	3
4	.025 6034	.307 2406	.2123	—	—	—	4
5	.021 4939	.257 9268	.1605	1.0000	—	—	5
6	.018 7790	.225 3476	.1263	.7870	—	—	6
7	.016 8607	.202 3281	.1022	.6364	—	—	7
8	.015 4400	.185 2802	.0843	.5250	—	—	8
9	.014 3509	.172 2103	.0705	.4395	—	—	9
10	.013 4935	.161 9220	.0597	.3722	1.0000	—	10
11	.012 8045	.153 6535	.0511	.3181	.8547	—	11
12	.012 2414	.146 8969	.0440	.2740	.7360	—	12
13	.011 7750	.141 3002	.0381	.2374	.6377	—	13
14	.011 3843	.136 6121	.0332	.2067	.5554	—	14
15	.011 0540	.132 6479	.0290	.1808	.4857	1.0000	15
16	.010 7724	.129 2691	.0255	.1587	.4264	.8778	16
17	.010 5308	.126 3697	.0224	.1397	.3754	.7729	17
18	.010 3223	.123 8673	.0198	.1234	.3315	.6824	18
19	.010 1414	.121 6967	.0175	.1092	.2933	.6039	19
20	.009 9838	.119 8056	.0155	.0968	.2601	.5355	20
21	.009 8460	.118 1518	.0138	.0860	.2311	.4757	21
22	.009 7251	.116 7009	.0123	.0765	.2056	.4232	22
23	.009 6187	.115 4241	.0109	.0682	.1831	.3770	23
24	.009 5248	.114 2977	.0098	.0608	.1633	.3363	24
25	.009 4418	.113 3018	.0087	.0543	.1458	.3003	25
26	.009 3683	.112 4195	.0078	.0485	.1303	.2684	26
27	.009 3030	.111 6365	.0070	.0434	.1166	.2400	27
28	.009 2450	.110 9404	.0062	.0388	.1044	.2149	28
29	.009 1934	.110 3209	.0056	.0348	.0935	.1925	29
30	.009 1474	.109 7687	.0050	.0312	.0838	.1725	30
31	.009 1063	.109 2761	.0045	.0280	.0751	.1547	31
32	.009 0697	.108 8361	.0040	.0251	.0674	.1387	32
33	.009 0369	.108 4428	.0036	.0225	.0605	.1245	33
34	.009 0076	.108 0910	.0032	.0202	.0543	.1118	34
35	.008 9813	.107 7761	.0029	.0182	.0488	.1004	35
36	.008 9578	.107 4940	.0026	.0163	.0438	.0902	36
37	.008 9368	.107 2411	.0024	.0147	.0394	.0811	37
38	.008 9179	.107 0144	.0021	.0132	.0354	.0729	38
39	.008 9009	.106 8110	.0019	.0118	.0318	.0655	39
40	.008 8857	.106 6284	.0017	.0106	.0286	.0589	40

DIRECT REDUCTION LOAN FACTORS 10¾%

(Monthly Payment and Annual Constant per $1 of Loan)

Base:	1.008 958	Annual			Part Paid Off Projection			
Months	Payment	Constant	1 Year	5 Years	10 Years	15 Years	Months
1	1.008 9583	—	—	—	—	—	1
2	.506 7287	—	—	—	—	—	2
3	.339 3233	—	—	—	—	—	3
4	.255 6239	—	—	—	—	—	4
5	.205 4070	—	—	—	—	—	5
6	.171 9312	—	—	—	—	—	6
7	.148 0218	—	—	—	—	—	7
8	.130 0915	—	—	—	—	—	8
9	.116 1471	—	—	—	—	—	9
10	.104 9930	—	—	—	—	—	10
11	.095 8681	—	—	—	—	—	11

Years	Payment	Constant	1 Year	5 Years	10 Years	15 Years	Years
1	.088 2651	1.059 1811	1.0000	—	—	—	1
2	.046 4919	.557 9023	.4733	—	—	—	2
3	.032 6205	.391 4454	.2984	—	—	—	3
4	.025 7243	.308 6914	.2114	—	—	—	4
5	.021 6180	.259 4154	.1596	1.0000	—	—	5
6	.018 9063	.226 8753	.1254	.7858	—	—	6
7	.016 9913	.203 8953	.1013	.6345	—	—	7
8	.015 5739	.186 8868	.0834	.5226	—	—	8
9	.014 4880	.173 8561	.0697	.4368	—	—	9
10	.013 6339	.163 6064	.0590	.3693	1.0000	—	10
11	.012 9480	.155 3759	.0503	.3151	.8533	—	11
12	.012 3880	.148 6565	.0432	.2709	.7335	—	12
13	.011 9247	.143 0962	.0374	.2343	.6344	—	13
14	.011 5370	.138 4435	.0325	.2037	.5515	—	14
15	.011 2095	.134 5138	.0284	.1778	.4815	1.0000	15
16	.010 9307	.131 1684	.0249	.1558	.4218	.8762	16
17	.010 6918	.128 3014	.0219	.1369	.3707	.7700	17
18	.010 4858	.125 8302	.0193	.1207	.3267	.6785	18
19	.010 3075	.123 6896	.0170	.1066	.2886	.5993	19
20	.010 1523	.121 8275	.0151	.0943	.2554	.5304	20
21	.010 0168	.120 2015	.0133	.0836	.2264	.4702	21
22	.009 8981	.118 7772	.0118	.0742	.2010	.4175	22
23	.009 7938	.117 5259	.0105	.0660	.1787	.3711	23
24	.009 7020	.116 4238	.0094	.0587	.1591	.3303	24
25	.009 6209	.115 4511	.0084	.0523	.1417	.2943	25
26	.009 5492	.114 5909	.0075	.0467	.1264	.2625	26
27	.009 4857	.113 8289	.0067	.0417	.1128	.2343	27
28	.009 4294	.113 1527	.0059	.0372	.1008	.2093	28
29	.009 3793	.112 5521	.0053	.0333	.0900	.1870	29
30	.009 3348	.112 0178	.0047	.0297	.0805	.1672	30
31	.009 2952	.111 5420	.0042	.0266	.0720	.1496	31
32	.009 2598	.111 1180	.0038	.0238	.0645	.1339	32
33	.009 2283	.110 7397	.0034	.0213	.0577	.1199	33
34	.009 2002	.110 4020	.0030	.0191	.0517	.1074	34
35	.009 1750	.110 1003	.0027	.0171	.0463	.0963	35
36	.009 1526	.109 8307	.0024	.0153	.0415	.0863	36
37	.009 1325	.109 5896	.0022	.0138	.0372	.0774	37
38	.009 1145	.109 3738	.0020	.0123	.0334	.0694	38
39	.009 0984	.109 1806	.0018	.0111	.0300	.0622	39
40	.009 0840	.109 0077	.0016	.0099	.0269	.0558	40

11% DIRECT REDUCTION LOAN FACTORS
(Monthly Payment and Annual Constant per $1 of Loan)

Base: 1.009 167

Months	Payment	Annual Constant	Part Paid Off Projection 1 Year	5 Years	10 Years	15 Years	Months
1	1.009 1667	—	—	—	—	—	1
2	.506 8855	—	—	—	—	—	2
3	.339 4630	—	—	—	—	—	3
4	.255 7553	—	—	—	—	—	4
5	.205 5335	—	—	—	—	—	5
6	.172 0545	—	—	—	—	—	6
7	.148 1430	—	—	—	—	—	7
8	.130 2111	—	—	—	—	—	8
9	.116 2657	—	—	—	—	—	9
10	.105 1107	—	—	—	—	—	10
11	.095 9851	—	—	—	—	—	11

Years	Payment	Annual Constant	1 Year	5 Years	10 Years	15 Years	Years
1	.088 3817	1.060 5799	1.0000	—	—	—	1
2	.046 6078	.559 2941	.4727	—	—	—	2
3	.032 7387	.392 8646	.2976	—	—	—	3
4	.025 8455	.310 1463	.2106	—	—	—	4
5	.021 7424	.260 9091	.1588	1.0000	—	—	5
6	.019 0341	.228 4089	.1246	.7846	—	—	6
7	.017 1224	.205 4692	.1004	.6326	—	—	7
8	.015 7084	.188 5011	.0826	.5202	—	—	8
9	.014 6259	.175 5103	.0689	.4341	—	—	9
10	.013 7750	.165 3000	.0582	.3664	1.0000	—	10
11	.013 0923	.157 1082	.0496	.3122	.8519	—	11
12	.012 5356	.150 4266	.0425	.2679	.7310	—	12
13	.012 0753	.144 9033	.0367	.2313	.6312	—	13
14	.011 6905	.140 2865	.0319	.2007	.5477	—	14
15	.011 3660	.136 3916	.0278	.1749	.4772	1.0000	15
16	.011 0900	.133 0800	.0243	.1529	.4174	.8745	16
17	.010 8538	.130 2457	.0213	.1342	.3661	.7671	17
18	.010 6505	.127 8060	.0187	.1180	.3220	.6747	18
19	.010 4746	.125 6957	.0165	.1040	.2838	.5947	19
20	.010 3219	.123 8626	.0146	.0919	.2507	.5253	20
21	.010 1887	.122 2645	.0129	.0813	.2218	.4647	21
22	.010 0722	.120 8668	.0114	.0720	.1965	.4118	22
23	.009 9701	.119 6410	.0101	.0639	.1743	.3653	23
24	.009 8803	.118 5632	.0090	.0567	.1548	.3245	24
25	.009 8011	.117 6136	.0080	.0505	.1377	.2885	25
26	.009 7313	.116 7753	.0071	.0449	.1225	.2567	26
27	.009 6695	.116 0340	.0063	.0400	.1091	.2286	27
28	.009 6148	.115 3776	.0057	.0356	.0972	.2038	28
29	.009 5663	.114 7955	.0050	.0318	.0867	.1817	29
30	.009 5232	.114 2788	.0045	.0284	.0774	.1621	30
31	.009 4850	.113 8196	.0040	.0253	.0691	.1447	31
32	.009 4509	.113 4112	.0036	.0226	.0617	.1293	32
33	.009 4206	.113 0476	.0032	.0202	.0551	.1155	33
34	.009 3936	.112 7237	.0029	.0180	.0493	.1032	34
35	.009 3696	.112 4349	.0026	.0161	.0440	.0923	35
36	.009 3481	.112 1774	.0023	.0144	.0394	.0825	36
37	.009 3290	.111 9475	.0020	.0129	.0352	.0738	37
38	.009 3119	.111 7424	.0018	.0115	.0315	.0660	38
39	.009 2966	.111 5591	.0016	.0103	.0282	.0591	39
40	.009 2829	.111 3953	.0015	.0092	.0252	.0529	40

DIRECT REDUCTION LOAN FACTORS 11¼%

(Monthly Payment and Annual Constant per $1 of Loan)

Base: 1.009 375

Months	Payment	Annual Constant	Part Paid Off Projection 1 Year	5 Years	10 Years	15 Years	Months
1	1.009 3750	—	—	—	—	—	1
2	.507 0422	—	—	—	—	—	2
3	.339 6028	—	—	—	—	—	3
4	.255 8867	—	—	—	—	—	4
5	.205 6600	—	—	—	—	—	5
6	.172 1779	—	—	—	—	—	6
7	.148 2643	—	—	—	—	—	7
8	.130 3308	—	—	—	—	—	8
9	.116 3842	—	—	—	—	—	9
10	.105 2284	—	—	—	—	—	10
11	.096 1022	—	—	—	—	—	11

Years	Payment	Annual Constant	1 Year	5 Years	10 Years	15 Years	Years
1	.088 4983	1.061 9798	1.0000	—	—	—	1
2	.046 7240	.560 6879	.4720	—	—	—	2
3	.032 8572	.394 2868	.2968	—	—	—	3
4	.025 9671	.311 6052	.2097	—	—	—	4
5	.021 8673	.262 4077	.1579	1.0000	—	—	5
6	.019 1624	.229 9485	.1237	.7835	—	—	6
7	.017 2542	.207 0500	.0996	.6307	—	—	7
8	.015 8436	.190 1230	.0818	.5178	—	—	8
9	.014 7644	.177 1729	.0681	.4314	—	—	9
10	.013 9169	.167 0027	.0574	.3636	1.0000	—	10
11	.013 2375	.158 8503	.0488	.3092	.8504	—	11
12	.012 6839	.152 2071	.0418	.2649	.7285	—	12
13	.012 2268	.146 7213	.0360	.2283	.6279	—	13
14	.011 8451	.142 1409	.0312	.1977	.5438	—	14
15	.011 5234	.138 2814	.0272	.1720	.4730	1.0000	15
16	.011 2503	.135 0039	.0237	.1501	.4129	.8729	16
17	.011 0169	.132 2025	.0208	.1314	.3615	.7642	17
18	.010 8162	.129 7944	.0182	.1154	.3173	.6708	18
19	.010 6429	.127 7146	.0160	.1015	.2792	.5901	19
20	.010 4926	.125 9107	.0141	.0895	.2461	.5202	20
21	.010 3617	.124 3405	.0125	.0790	.2172	.4593	21
22	.010 2475	.122 9695	.0110	.0698	.1921	.4061	22
23	.010 1474	.121 7690	.0098	.0618	.1701	.3595	23
24	.010 0596	.120 7154	.0087	.0548	.1507	.3187	24
25	.009 9824	.119 7887	.0077	.0486	.1337	.2827	25
26	.009 9143	.118 9722	.0068	.0432	.1187	.2510	26
27	.009 8543	.118 2515	.0061	.0384	.1055	.2231	27
28	.009 8012	.117 6145	.0054	.0341	.0938	.1984	28
29	.009 7542	.117 0508	.0048	.0304	.0835	.1765	29
30	.009 7126	.116 5514	.0043	.0270	.0743	.1571	30
31	.009 6757	.116 1084	.0038	.0241	.0662	.1400	31
32	.009 6429	.115 7152	.0034	.0214	.0590	.1247	32
33	.009 6138	.115 3660	.0030	.0191	.0526	.1112	33
34	.009 5880	.115 0555	.0027	.0170	.0469	.0991	34
35	.009 5649	.114 7793	.0024	.0152	.0418	.0884	35
36	.009 5445	.114 5334	.0021	.0136	.0373	.0789	36
37	.009 5262	.114 3146	.0019	.0121	.0333	.0704	37
38	.009 5100	.114 1196	.0017	.0108	.0297	.0628	38
39	.009 4955	.113 9458	.0015	.0096	.0265	.0561	39
40	.009 4826	.113 7909	.0014	.0086	.0237	.0501	40

11½% DIRECT REDUCTION LOAN FACTORS
(Monthly Payment and Annual Constant per $1 of Loan)

Base: 1.009 583

Months	Payment	Annual Constant	Part Paid Off Projection				Months
			1 Year	5 Years	10 Years	15 Years	
1	1.009 5833	—	—	—	—	—	1
2	.507 1989	—	—	—	—	—	2
3	.339 7425	—	—	—	—	—	3
4	.256 0181	—	—	—	—	—	4
5	.205 7866	—	—	—	—	—	5
6	.172 3014	—	—	—	—	—	6
7	.148 3856	—	—	—	—	—	7
8	.130 4506	—	—	—	—	—	8
9	.116 5029	—	—	—	—	—	9
10	.105 3462	—	—	—	—	—	10
11	.096 2194	—	—	—	—	—	11

Years							Years
1	.088 6151	1.063 3806	1.0000	—	—	—	1
2	.046 8403	.562 0838	.4714	—	—	—	2
3	.032 9760	.395 7121	.2960	—	—	—	3
4	.026 0890	.313 0681	.2088	—	—	—	4
5	.021 9926	.263 9113	.1570	1.0000	—	—	5
6	.019 2912	.231 4939	.1228	.7823	—	—	6
7	.017 3865	.208 6375	.0987	.6288	—	—	7
8	.015 9794	.191 7525	.0809	.5154	—	—	8
9	.014 9037	.178 8439	.0673	.4287	—	—	9
10	.014 0595	.168 7145	.0566	.3607	1.0000	—	10
11	.013 3835	.160 6020	.0481	.3062	.8490	—	11
12	.012 8332	.153 9980	.0411	.2619	.7260	—	12
13	.012 3792	.148 5501	.0354	.2253	.6246	—	13
14	.012 0006	.144 0067	.0306	.1948	.5400	—	14
15	.011 6819	.140 1828	.0266	.1691	.4688	1.0000	15
16	.011 4116	.136 9398	.0231	.1473	.4085	.8712	16
17	.011 1810	.134 1716	.0202	.1287	.3569	.7613	17
18	.010 9830	.131 7954	.0177	.1128	.3127	.6669	18
19	.010 8122	.129 7462	.0155	.0990	.2745	.5856	19
20	.010 6643	.127 9716	.0137	.0871	.2415	.5151	20
21	.010 5358	.126 4293	.0121	.0768	.2128	.4539	21
22	.010 4237	.125 0849	.0106	.0677	.1877	.4005	22
23	.010 3258	.123 9098	.0094	.0598	.1659	.3538	23
24	.010 2400	.122 8802	.0083	.0529	.1467	.3129	24
25	.010 1647	.121 9763	.0074	.0468	.1299	.2770	25
26	.010 0984	.121 1813	.0065	.0415	.1151	.2455	26
27	.010 0401	.120 4809	.0058	.0368	.1020	.2176	27
28	.009 9886	.119 8631	.0051	.0327	.0905	.1931	28
29	.009 9431	.119 3175	.0046	.0290	.0804	.1714	29
30	.009 9029	.118 8350	.0040	.0258	.0714	.1523	30
31	.009 8673	.118 4079	.0036	.0229	.0634	.1353	31
32	.009 8358	.118 0297	.0032	.0203	.0564	.1203	32
33	.009 8079	.117 6944	.0028	.0181	.0502	.1070	33
34	.009 7831	.117 3969	.0025	.0161	.0446	.0952	34
35	.009 7611	.117 1329	.0022	.0143	.0397	.0847	35
36	.009 7415	.116 8984	.0020	.0127	.0353	.0754	36
37	.009 7242	.116 6901	.0018	.0113	.0315	.0671	37
38	.009 7087	.116 5049	.0016	.0101	.0280	.0598	38
39	.009 6950	.116 3403	.0014	.0090	.0250	.0532	39
40	.009 6828	.116 1938	.0013	.0080	.0222	.0474	40

DIRECT REDUCTION LOAN FACTORS 11¾%

(Monthly Payment and Annual Constant per $1 of Loan)

Base: 1.009 792

Months	Payment	Annual Constant	1 Year	5 Years	10 Years	15 Years	Months
				Part Paid Off Projection			
1	1.009 7917	—	—	—	—	—	1
2	.507 3557	—	—	—	—	—	2
3	.339 8823	—	—	—	—	—	3
4	.256 1496	—	—	—	—	—	4
5	.205 9132	—	—	—	—	—	5
6	.172 4248	—	—	—	—	—	6
7	.148 5069	—	—	—	—	—	7
8	.130 5704	—	—	—	—	—	8
9	.116 6216	—	—	—	—	—	9
10	.105 4641	—	—	—	—	—	10
11	.096 3367	—	—	—	—	—	11

Years							Years
1	.088 7319	1.064 7825	1.0000	—	—	—	1
2	.046 9568	.563 4817	.4708	—	—	—	2
3	.033 0950	.397 1404	.2952	—	—	—	3
4	.026 2113	.314 5351	.2080	—	—	—	4
5	.022 1183	.265 4199	.1562	1.0000	—	—	5
6	.019 4204	.233 0452	.1220	.7811	—	—	6
7	.017 5193	.210 2318	.0979	.6269	—	—	7
8	.016 1158	.193 3895	.0801	.5130	—	—	8
9	.015 0436	.180 5232	.0665	.4261	—	—	9
10	.014 2029	.170 4354	.0559	.3579	1.0000	—	10
11	.013 5303	.162 3635	.0474	.3033	.8475	—	11
12	.012 9833	.155 7991	.0404	.2589	.7235	—	12
13	.012 5325	.150 3897	.0347	.2223	.6213	—	13
14	.012 1570	.145 8836	.0300	.1919	.5362	—	14
15	.011 8413	.142 0958	.0260	.1663	.4646	1.0000	15
16	.011 5740	.138 8876	.0226	.1446	.4040	.8696	16
17	.011 3461	.136 1527	.0197	.1261	.3524	.7584	17
18	.011 1507	.133 8087	.0172	.1103	.3081	.6631	18
19	.010 9825	.131 7901	.0151	.0966	.2700	.5810	19
20	.010 8371	.130 0448	.0132	.0848	.2370	.5100	20
21	.010 7109	.128 5306	.0116	.0746	.2084	.4485	21
22	.010 6011	.127 2127	.0103	.0657	.1835	.3949	22
23	.010 5052	.126 0628	.0090	.0579	.1618	.3481	23
24	.010 4214	.125 0571	.0080	.0511	.1428	.3073	24
25	.010 3480	.124 1758	.0070	.0451	.1261	.2714	25
26	.010 2835	.123 4021	.0062	.0399	.1115	.2400	26
27	.010 2268	.122 7219	.0055	.0353	.0986	.2123	27
28	.010 1769	.122 1229	.0049	.0313	.0873	.1880	28
29	.010 1329	.121 5950	.0043	.0277	.0774	.1665	29
30	.010 0941	.121 1292	.0038	.0245	.0686	.1476	30
31	.010 0598	.120 7177	.0034	.0218	.0608	.1308	31
32	.010 0295	.120 3540	.0030	.0193	.0539	.1160	32
33	.010 0027	.120 0323	.0027	.0171	.0478	.1030	33
34	.009 9790	.119 7475	.0024	.0152	.0425	.0914	34
35	.009 9579	.119 4953	.0021	.0135	.0377	.0811	35
36	.009 9393	.119 2718	.0019	.0120	.0335	.0720	36
37	.009 9228	.119 0736	.0017	.0106	.0297	.0640	37
38	.009 9082	.118 8979	.0015	.0095	.0264	.0568	38
39	.009 8952	.118 7420	.0013	.0084	.0235	.0505	39
40	.009 8836	.118 6037	.0012	.0075	.0208	.0449	40

12% DIRECT REDUCTION LOAN FACTORS
(Monthly Payment and Annual Constant per $1 of Loan)

Base: 1.010 000

Months	Payment	Annual Constant	Part Paid Off Projection				Months
			1 Year	5 Years	10 Years	15 Years	
1	1.010 0000	—	—	—	—	—	1
2	.507 5124	—	—	—	—	—	2
3	.340 0221	—	—	—	—	—	3
4	.256 2811	—	—	—	—	—	4
5	.206 0398	—	—	—	—	—	5
6	.172 5484	—	—	—	—	—	6
7	.148 6283	—	—	—	—	—	7
8	.130 6903	—	—	—	—	—	8
9	.116 7404	—	—	—	—	—	9
10	.105 5821	—	—	—	—	—	10
11	.096 4541	—	—	—	—	—	11

Years	Payment	Annual Constant	1 Year	5 Years	10 Years	15 Years	Years
1	.088 8488	1.066 1855	1.0000	—	—	—	1
2	.047 0735	.564 8817	.4702	—	—	—	2
3	.033 2143	.398 5717	.2944	—	—	—	3
4	.026 3338	.316 0060	.2072	—	—	—	4
5	.022 2444	.266 9334	.1553	1.0000	—	—	5
6	.019 5502	.234 6023	.1211	.7800	—	—	6
7	.017 6527	.211 8328	.0971	.6250	—	—	7
8	.016 2528	.195 0341	.0793	.5107	—	—	8
9	.015 1842	.182 2108	.0657	.4234	—	—	9
10	.014 3471	.172 1651	.0551	.3550	1.0000	—	10
11	.013 6779	.164 1345	.0466	.3004	.8461	—	11
12	.013 1342	.157 6103	.0397	.2560	.7210	—	12
13	.012 6867	.152 2399	.0341	.2194	.6180	—	13
14	.012 3143	.147 7715	.0294	.1890	.5324	—	14
15	.012 0017	.144 0202	.0254	.1635	.4605	1.0000	15
16	.011 7373	.140 8470	.0220	.1419	.3996	.8679	16
17	.011 5122	.138 1459	.0192	.1235	.3479	.7554	17
18	.011 3195	.135 8340	.0167	.1078	.3035	.6592	18
19	.011 1539	.133 8463	.0146	.0942	.2654	.5764	19
20	.011 0109	.132 1303	.0128	.0826	.2325	.5050	20
21	.010 8870	.130 6440	.0112	.0724	.2040	.4431	21
22	.010 7794	.129 3526	.0099	.0637	.1793	.3894	22
23	.010 6856	.128 2278	.0087	.0560	.1577	.3425	23
24	.010 6038	.127 2458	.0077	.0493	.1389	.3017	24
25	.010 5322	.126 3869	.0068	.0435	.1224	.2659	25
26	.010 4695	.125 6343	.0060	.0383	.1080	.2346	26
27	.010 4145	.124 9739	.0053	.0339	.0953	.2071	27
28	.010 3661	.124 3936	.0046	.0299	.0842	.1829	28
29	.010 3236	.123 8831	.0041	.0264	.0744	.1617	29
30	.010 2861	.123 4335	.0036	.0234	.0658	.1429	30
31	.010 2531	.123 0373	.0032	.0207	.0582	.1264	31
32	.010 2240	.122 6878	.0028	.0183	.0515	.1119	32
33	.010 1983	.122 3793	.0025	.0162	.0456	.0991	33
34	.010 1756	.122 1068	.0022	.0143	.0404	.0877	34
35	.010 1555	.121 8660	.0020	.0127	.0358	.0777	35
36	.010 1378	.121 6531	.0017	.0113	.0317	.0688	36
37	.010 1221	.121 4647	.0015	.0100	.0281	.0610	37
38	.010 1082	.121 2981	.0014	.0088	.0249	.0540	38
39	.010 0959	.121 1506	.0012	.0078	.0221	.0479	39
40	.010 0850	.121 0200	.0011	.0069	.0196	.0425	40

(Monthly Payment and Annual Constant per $1 of Loan)

Base:	1.010 208	Annual	Part Paid Off Projection				
Months	Payment	Constant	1 Year	5 Years	10 Years	15 Years	Months
1	1.010 2083	—	—	—	—	—	1
2	.507 6692	—	—	—	—	—	2
3	.340 1619	—	—	—	—	—	3
4	.256 4126	—	—	—	—	—	4
5	.206 1665	—	—	—	—	—	5
6	.172 6719	—	—	—	—	—	6
7	.148 7497	—	—	—	—	—	7
8	.130 8102	—	—	—	—	—	8
9	.116 8592	—	—	—	—	—	9
10	.105 7001	—	—	—	—	—	10
11	.096 5715	—	—	—	—	—	11

Years							Years
1	.088 9658	1.067 5894	1.0000	—	—	—	1
2	.047 1903	.566 2837	.4696	—	—	—	2
3	.033 3338	.400 0061	.2936	—	—	—	3
4	.026 4568	.317 4810	.2063	—	—	—	4
5	.022 3710	.268 4518	.1544	1.0000	—	—	5
6	.019 6804	.236 1653	.1203	.7788	—	—	6
7	.017 7867	.213 4405	.0962	.6231	—	—	7
8	.016 3905	.196 6862	.0785	.5083	—	—	8
9	.015 3256	.183 9066	.0650	.4207	—	—	9
10	.014 4920	.173 9038	.0544	.3522	1.0000	—	10
11	.013 8263	.165 9151	.0459	.2975	.8446	—	11
12	.013 2860	.159 4316	.0391	.2530	.7185	—	12
13	.012 8417	.154 1007	.0334	.2165	.6148	—	13
14	.012 4725	.149 6705	.0287	.1862	.5286	—	14
15	.012 1630	.145 9558	.0248	.1607	.4563	1.0000	15
16	.011 9015	.142 8180	.0215	.1392	.3953	.8662	16
17	.011 6792	.140 1507	.0187	.1209	.3434	.7525	17
18	.011 4893	.137 8713	.0163	.1053	.2990	.6553	18
19	.011 3262	.135 9143	.0142	.0919	.2610	.5719	19
20	.011 1856	.134 2278	.0124	.0804	.2281	.5000	20
21	.011 0641	.132 7693	.0109	.0704	.1998	.4378	21
22	.010 9587	.131 5043	.0095	.0617	.1752	.3839	22
23	.010 8670	.130 4044	.0084	.0542	.1538	.3370	23
24	.010 7872	.129 4460	.0073	.0476	.1351	.2961	24
25	.010 7174	.128 6093	.0065	.0419	.1188	.2605	25
26	.010 6565	.127 8775	.0057	.0368	.1046	.2293	26
27	.010 6030	.127 2366	.0050	.0325	.0921	.2019	27
28	.010 5562	.126 6746	.0044	.0286	.0812	.1780	28
29	.010 5151	.126 1812	.0039	.0252	.0716	.1569	29
30	.010 4790	.125 7476	.0034	.0223	.0632	.1385	30
31	.010 4472	.125 3662	.0030	.0196	.0558	.1222	31
32	.010 4192	.125 0305	.0027	.0173	.0492	.1079	32
33	.010 3946	.124 7349	.0024	.0153	.0435	.0953	33
34	.010 3729	.124 4743	.0021	.0135	.0384	.0842	34
35	.010 3537	.124 2445	.0018	.0120	.0339	.0744	35
36	.010 3368	.124 0418	.0016	.0106	.0300	.0657	36
37	.010 3219	.123 8630	.0014	.0093	.0265	.0581	37
38	.010 3088	.123 7050	.0013	.0083	.0234	.0514	38
39	.010 2971	.123 5656	.0011	.0073	.0207	.0454	39
40	.010 2869	.123 4423	.0010	.0065	.0183	.0402	40

12½% DIRECT REDUCTION LOAN FACTORS
(Monthly Payment and Annual Constant per $1 of Loan)

Base: 1.010 417

Months	Payment	Annual Constant	Part Paid Off Projection 1 Year	5 Years	10 Years	15 Years	Months
1	1.010 4167	—	—	—	—	—	1
2	.507 8260	—	—	—	—	—	2
3	.340 3018	—	—	—	—	—	3
4	.256 5441	—	—	—	—	—	4
5	.206 2932	—	—	—	—	—	5
6	.172 7955	—	—	—	—	—	6
7	.148 8712	—	—	—	—	—	7
8	.130 9302	—	—	—	—	—	8
9	.116 9781	—	—	—	—	—	9
10	.105 8182	—	—	—	—	—	10
11	.096 6890	—	—	—	—	—	11

Years	Payment	Annual Constant	1 Year	5 Years	10 Years	15 Years	Years
1	.089 0829	1.068 9944	1.0000	—	—	—	1
2	.047 3073	.567 6877	.4690	—	—	—	2
3	.033 4536	.401 4435	.2928	—	—	—	3
4	.026 5800	.318 9600	.2055	—	—	—	4
5	.022 4979	.269 9753	.1536	1.0000	—	—	5
6	.019 8112	.237 7341	.1194	.7776	—	—	6
7	.017 9212	.215 0549	.0954	.6212	—	—	7
8	.016 5288	.198 3457	.0777	.5059	—	—	8
9	.015 4676	.185 6106	.0642	.4181	—	—	9
10	.014 6376	.175 6514	.0537	.3494	1.0000	—	10
11	.013 9754	.167 7051	.0452	.2946	.8431	—	11
12	.013 4386	.161 2629	.0384	.2501	.7159	—	12
13	.012 9977	.155 9719	.0328	.2136	.6115	—	13
14	.012 6317	.151 5802	.0282	.1833	.5248	—	14
15	.012 3252	.147 9026	.0243	.1580	.4522	1.0000	15
16	.012 0667	.144 8004	.0210	.1366	.3909	.8645	16
17	.011 8473	.142 1671	.0182	.1184	.3389	.7496	17
18	.011 6600	.139 9201	.0158	.1029	.2946	.6515	18
19	.011 4995	.137 9941	.0138	.0896	.2565	.5674	19
20	.011 3614	.136 3369	.0120	.0782	.2238	.4950	20
21	.011 2422	.134 9062	.0105	.0683	.1956	.4325	21
22	.011 1390	.133 6675	.0092	.0598	.1711	.3784	22
23	.011 0494	.132 5924	.0080	.0524	.1499	.3315	23
24	.010 9714	.131 6573	.0071	.0459	.1314	.2907	24
25	.010 9035	.130 8425	.0062	.0403	.1153	.2551	25
26	.010 8443	.130 1313	.0054	.0354	.1013	.2240	26
27	.010 7925	.129 5096	.0048	.0311	.0890	.1969	27
28	.010 7471	.128 9656	.0042	.0274	.0783	.1731	28
29	.010 7074	.128 4889	.0037	.0241	.0689	.1523	29
30	.010 6726	.128 0709	.0033	.0212	.0606	.1341	30
31	.010 6420	.127 7041	.0029	.0187	.0534	.1181	31
32	.010 6152	.127 3819	.0025	.0164	.0470	.1040	32
33	.010 5916	.127 0987	.0022	.0145	.0414	.0916	33
34	.010 5708	.126 8496	.0020	.0128	.0365	.0808	34
35	.010 5525	.126 6305	.0017	.0112	.0322	.0712	35
36	.010 5365	.126 4377	.0015	.0099	.0284	.0628	36
37	.010 5223	.126 2679	.0013	.0087	.0250	.0554	37
38	.010 5099	.126 1183	.0012	.0077	.0221	.0488	38
39	.010 4989	.125 9865	.0010	.0068	.0195	.0431	39
40	.010 4892	.125 8703	.0009	.0060	.0172	.0380	40

(Monthly Payment and Annual Constant per $1 of Loan)

			Part Paid Off Projection				
Months	Payment	Annual Constant	1 Year	5 Years	10 Years	15 Years	Months
1	1.010 6250	—	—	—	—	—	1
2	.507 9828	—	—	—	—	—	2
3	.340 4416	—	—	—	—	—	3
4	.256 6757	—	—	—	—	—	4
5	.206 4199	—	—	—	—	—	5
6	.172 9192	—	—	—	—	—	6
7	.148 9927	—	—	—	—	—	7
8	.131 0502	—	—	—	—	—	8
9	.117 0971	—	—	—	—	—	9
10	.105 9364	—	—	—	—	—	10
11	.096 8066	—	—	—	—	—	11

Years							Years
1	.089 2000	1.070 4003	1.0000	—	—	—	1
2	.047 4245	.569 0938	.4683	—	—	—	2
3	.033 5737	.402 8840	.2921	—	—	—	3
4	.026 7036	.320 4430	.2046	—	—	—	4
5	.022 6253	.271 5036	.1527	1.0000	—	—	5
6	.019 9424	.239 3088	.1186	.7764	—	—	6
7	.018 0563	.216 6759	.0946	.6193	—	—	7
8	.016 6677	.200 0127	.0769	.5035	—	—	8
9	.015 6102	.187 3228	.0634	.4154	—	—	9
10	.014 7840	.177 4078	.0529	.3466	1.0000	—	10
11	.014 1254	.169 5046	.0445	.2917	.8416	—	11
12	.013 5920	.163 1040	.0378	.2472	.7134	—	12
13	.013 1545	.157 8535	.0322	.2108	.6082	—	13
14	.012 7917	.153 5006	.0276	.1806	.5210	—	14
15	.012 4884	.149 8604	.0237	.1553	.4480	1.0000	15
16	.012 2328	.146 7939	.0205	.1340	.3866	.8629	16
17	.012 0162	.144 1948	.0177	.1159	.3345	.7466	17
18	.011 8317	.141 9804	.0154	.1006	.2901	.6476	18
19	.011 6738	.140 0853	.0133	.0874	.2522	.5628	19
20	.011 5381	.138 4574	.0116	.0761	.2196	.4900	20
21	.011 4212	.137 0544	.0101	.0663	.1914	.4273	21
22	.011 3202	.135 8419	.0088	.0579	.1671	.3731	22
23	.011 2326	.134 7914	.0077	.0506	.1461	.3261	23
24	.011 1566	.133 8794	.0068	.0443	.1278	.2853	24
25	.011 0905	.133 0863	.0059	.0388	.1119	.2498	25
26	.011 0329	.132 3953	.0052	.0340	.0981	.2189	26
27	.010 9827	.131 7926	.0046	.0298	.0860	.1920	27
28	.010 9388	.131 2662	.0040	.0262	.0755	.1684	28
29	.010 9005	.130 8059	.0035	.0230	.0662	.1478	29
30	.010 8669	.130 4032	.0031	.0202	.0582	.1298	30
31	.010 8375	.130 0505	.0027	.0177	.0511	.1141	31
32	.010 8118	.129 7413	.0024	.0156	.0449	.1002	32
33	.010 7892	.129 4702	.0021	.0137	.0395	.0881	33
34	.010 7694	.129 2324	.0018	.0120	.0347	.0775	34
35	.010 7520	.129 0235	.0016	.0106	.0305	.0681	35
36	.010 7367	.128 8402	.0014	.0093	.0269	.0599	36
37	.010 7233	.128 6790	.0013	.0082	.0236	.0527	37
38	.010 7115	.128 5375	.0011	.0072	.0208	.0464	38
39	.010 7011	.128 4130	.0010	.0063	.0183	.0408	39
40	.010 6920	.128 3036	.0009	.0056	.0161	.0359	40

Base: 1.010 625

13% DIRECT REDUCTION LOAN FACTORS
(Monthly Payment and Annual Constant per $1 of Loan)

Base: 1.010 833

Months	Payment	Annual Constant	Part Paid Off Projection 1 Year	5 Years	10 Years	15 Years	Months
1	1.010 8333	—	—	—	—	—	1
2	.508 1396	—	—	—	—	—	2
3	.340 5815	—	—	—	—	—	3
4	.256 8073	—	—	—	—	—	4
5	.206 5467	—	—	—	—	—	5
6	.173 0429	—	—	—	—	—	6
7	.149 1143	—	—	—	—	—	7
8	.131 1703	—	—	—	—	—	8
9	.117 2161	—	—	—	—	—	9
10	.106 0546	—	—	—	—	—	10
11	.096 9243	—	—	—	—	—	11

Years	Payment	Annual Constant	1 Year	5 Years	10 Years	15 Years	Years
1	.089 3173	1.071 8073	1.0000	—	—	—	1
2	.047 5418	.570 5019	.4677	—	—	—	2
3	.033 6940	.404 3274	.2913	—	—	—	3
4	.026 8275	.321 9300	.2038	—	—	—	4
5	.022 7531	.273 0369	.1519	1.0000	—	—	5
6	.020 0741	.240 8893	.1177	.7752	—	—	6
7	.018 1920	.218 3036	.0938	.6173	—	—	7
8	.016 8073	.201 6871	.0761	.5012	—	—	8
9	.015 7536	.189 0431	.0627	.4128	—	—	9
10	.014 9311	.179 1729	.0522	.3438	1.0000	—	10
11	.014 2761	.171 3133	.0439	.2888	.8402	—	11
12	.013 7463	.164 9550	.0371	.2444	.7109	—	12
13	.013 3121	.159 7452	.0316	.2080	.6049	—	13
14	.012 9526	.155 4316	.0270	.1778	.5172	—	14
15	.012 6524	.151 8291	.0232	.1526	.4439	1.0000	15
16	.012 3999	.148 7985	.0200	.1314	.3823	.8612	16
17	.012 1861	.146 2337	.0172	.1135	.3301	.7437	17
18	.012 0043	.144 0519	.0149	.0982	.2858	.6437	18
19	.011 8490	.142 1878	.0129	.0852	.2479	.5583	19
20	.011 7158	.140 5891	.0112	.0740	.2153	.4851	20
21	.011 6011	.139 2137	.0098	.0644	.1874	.4221	21
22	.011 5023	.138 0272	.0085	.0561	.1632	.3677	22
23	.011 4168	.137 0011	.0074	.0489	.1424	.3207	23
24	.011 3427	.136 1120	.0065	.0427	.1243	.2800	24
25	.011 2784	.135 3402	.0057	.0373	.1086	.2446	25
26	.011 2224	.134 6693	.0050	.0326	.0950	.2139	26
27	.011 1738	.134 0851	.0043	.0286	.0831	.1871	27
28	.011 1313	.133 5760	.0038	.0250	.0727	.1638	28
29	.011 0943	.133 1318	.0033	.0219	.0637	.1435	29
30	.011 0620	.132 7439	.0029	.0192	.0558	.1257	30
31	.011 0337	.132 4050	.0026	.0168	.0489	.1102	31
32	.011 0090	.132 1085	.0022	.0147	.0429	.0966	32
33	.010 9874	.131 8492	.0020	.0129	.0376	.0847	33
34	.010 9685	.131 6221	.0017	.0113	.0330	.0743	34
35	.010 9519	.131 4232	.0015	.0099	.0289	.0652	35
36	.010 9374	.131 2489	.0013	.0087	.0254	.0572	36
37	.010 9247	.131 0961	.0012	.0077	.0223	.0502	37
38	.010 9135	.130 9622	.0010	.0067	.0196	.0441	38
39	.010 9037	.130 8447	.0009	.0059	.0172	.0387	39
40	.010 8951	.130 7417	.0008	.0052	.0151	.0340	40

DIRECT REDUCTION LOAN FACTORS 13¼%

(Monthly Payment and Annual Constant per $1 of Loan)

Base: 1.011 042

Months	Payment	Annual Constant	Part Paid Off Projection 1 Year	5 Years	10 Years	15 Years	Months
1	1.011 0417	—	—	—	—	—	1
2	.508 2964	—	—	—	—	—	2
3	.340 7214	—	—	—	—	—	3
4	.256 9389	—	—	—	—	—	4
5	.206 6735	—	—	—	—	—	5
6	.173 1666	—	—	—	—	—	6
7	.149 2359	—	—	—	—	—	7
8	.131 2905	—	—	—	—	—	8
9	.117 3352	—	—	—	—	—	9
10	.106 1729	—	—	—	—	—	10
11	.097 0420	—	—	—	—	—	11

Years							Years
1	.089 4346	1.073 2153	1.0000	—	—	—	1
2	.047 6593	.571 9120	.4671	—	—	—	2
3	.033 8145	.405 7739	.2905	—	—	—	3
4	.026 9517	.323 4209	.2030	—	—	—	4
5	.022 8813	.274 5751	.1510	1.0000	—	—	5
6	.020 2063	.242 4755	.1169	.7741	—	—	6
7	.018 3282	.219 9378	.0929	.6154	—	—	7
8	.016 9474	.203 3688	.0753	.4988	—	—	8
9	.015 8976	.190 7714	.0619	.4101	—	—	9
10	.015 0789	.180 9467	.0515	.3410	1.0000	—	10
11	.014 4276	.173 1313	.0432	.2860	.8387	—	11
12	.013 9013	.166 8157	.0365	.2415	.7083	—	12
13	.013 4706	.161 6471	.0310	.2052	.6016	—	13
14	.013 1144	.157 3731	.0264	.1751	.5134	—	14
15	.012 8174	.153 8084	.0227	.1500	.4398	1.0000	15
16	.012 5678	.150 8140	.0195	.1289	.3780	.8595	16
17	.012 3570	.148 2836	.0168	.1111	.3258	.7407	17
18	.012 1779	.146 1344	.0145	.0960	.2814	.6399	18
19	.012 0251	.144 3012	.0125	.0831	.2436	.5538	19
20	.011 8943	.142 7317	.0109	.0720	.2112	.4802	20
21	.011 7820	.141 3838	.0094	.0625	.1834	.4169	21
22	.011 6853	.140 2231	.0082	.0544	.1594	.3624	22
23	.011 6018	.139 2212	.0071	.0473	.1387	.3154	23
24	.011 5296	.138 3547	.0062	.0412	.1208	.2748	24
25	.011 4670	.137 6041	.0054	.0359	.1054	.2395	25
26	.011 4127	.136 9527	.0047	.0313	.0919	.2090	26
27	.011 3656	.136 3869	.0041	.0274	.0802	.1824	27
28	.011 3246	.135 8947	.0036	.0239	.0701	.1593	28
29	.011 2888	.135 4662	.0032	.0209	.0612	.1392	29
30	.011 2577	.135 0928	.0028	.0182	.0535	.1217	30
31	.011 2306	.134 7672	.0024	.0160	.0468	.1064	31
32	.011 2069	.134 4831	.0021	.0140	.0409	.0931	32
33	.011 1863	.134 2351	.0018	.0122	.0358	.0814	33
34	.011 1682	.134 0184	.0016	.0107	.0313	.0713	34
35	.011 1524	.133 8291	.0014	.0094	.0274	.0624	35
36	.011 1386	.133 6635	.0012	.0082	.0240	.0546	36
37	.011 1266	.133 5188	.0011	.0072	.0210	.0478	37
38	.011 1160	.133 3922	.0009	.0063	.0184	.0419	38
39	.011 1068	.133 2814	.0008	.0055	.0161	.0367	39
40	.011 0987	.133 1844	.0007	.0048	.0141	.0321	40

13½% DIRECT REDUCTION LOAN FACTORS
(Monthly Payment and Annual Constant per $1 of Loan)

Base: 1.011 250

Months	Payment	Annual Constant	Part Paid Off Projection 1 Year	5 Years	10 Years	15 Years	Months
1	1.011 2500	—	—	—	—	—	1
2	.508 4532	—	—	—	—	—	2
3	.340 8613	—	—	—	—	—	3
4	.257 0706	—	—	—	—	—	4
5	.206 8003	—	—	—	—	—	5
6	.173 2903	—	—	—	—	—	6
7	.149 3576	—	—	—	—	—	7
8	.131 4107	—	—	—	—	—	8
9	.117 4543	—	—	—	—	—	9
10	.106 2913	—	—	—	—	—	10
11	.097 1598	—	—	—	—	—	11

Years	Payment	Annual Constant	1 Year	5 Years	10 Years	15 Years	Years
1	.089 5520	1.074 6243	1.0000	—	—	—	1
2	.047 7770	.573 3242	.4665	—	—	—	2
3	.033 9353	.407 2234	.2897	—	—	—	3
4	.027 0763	.324 9159	.2021	—	—	—	4
5	.023 0098	.276 1182	.1502	1.0000	—	—	5
6	.020 3390	.244 0675	.1161	.7729	—	—	6
7	.018 4649	.221 5787	.0921	.6135	—	—	7
8	.017 0882	.205 0579	.0746	.4964	—	—	8
9	.016 0423	.192 5078	.0612	.4075	—	—	9
10	.015 2274	.182 7291	.0508	.3382	1.0000	—	10
11	.014 5799	.174 9584	.0425	.2832	.8372	—	11
12	.014 0572	.168 6861	.0359	.2387	.7058	—	12
13	.013 6299	.163 5590	.0304	.2024	.5984	—	13
14	.013 2771	.159 3248	.0259	.1724	.5096	—	14
15	.012 9832	.155 7982	.0221	.1474	.4358	1.0000	15
16	.012 7367	.152 8402	.0190	.1264	.3738	.8578	16
17	.012 5287	.150 3443	.0163	.1087	.3215	.7378	17
18	.012 3523	.148 2278	.0141	.0937	.2771	.6360	18
19	.012 2021	.146 4254	.0122	.0810	.2394	.5493	19
20	.012 0737	.144 8850	.0105	.0700	.2071	.4753	20
21	.011 9637	.143 5644	.0091	.0607	.1794	.4118	21
22	.011 8691	.142 4293	.0079	.0526	.1557	.3572	22
23	.011 7876	.141 4514	.0069	.0457	.1352	.3102	23
24	.011 7173	.140 6072	.0060	.0397	.1175	.2696	24
25	.011 6564	.139 8774	.0052	.0346	.1022	.2345	25
26	.011 6038	.139 2454	.0045	.0301	.0889	.2041	26
27	.011 5581	.138 6975	.0039	.0262	.0775	.1778	27
28	.011 5185	.138 2219	.0034	.0228	.0675	.1549	28
29	.011 4841	.137 8087	.0030	.0199	.0588	.1350	29
30	.011 4541	.137 4495	.0026	.0174	.0513	.1178	30
31	.011 4281	.137 1369	.0023	.0151	.0448	.1027	31
32	.011 4054	.136 8647	.0020	.0132	.0391	.0897	32
33	.011 3856	.136 6276	.0017	.0115	.0341	.0783	33
34	.011 3684	.136 4210	.0015	.0101	.0298	.0683	34
35	.011 3534	.136 2409	.0013	.0088	.0260	.0597	35
36	.011 3403	.136 0837	.0012	.0077	.0227	.0521	36
37	.011 3289	.135 9466	.0010	.0067	.0198	.0455	37
38	.011 3189	.135 8270	.0009	.0059	.0173	.0398	38
39	.011 3102	.135 7225	.0008	.0051	.0151	.0347	39
40	.011 3026	.135 6313	.0007	.0045	.0132	.0304	40

DIRECT REDUCTION LOAN FACTORS 13¾%

(Monthly Payment and Annual Constant per $1 of Loan)

Base:	1.011 458		Part Paid Off Projection				
Months	Payment	Annual Constant	1 Year	5 Years	10 Years	15 Years	Months
1	1.011 4583	—	—	—	—	—	1
2	.508 6101	—	—	—	—	—	2
3	.341 0012	—	—	—	—	—	3
4	.257 2023	—	—	—	—	—	4
5	.206 9272	—	—	—	—	—	5
6	.173 4141	—	—	—	—	—	6
7	.149 4794	—	—	—	—	—	7
8	.131 5310	—	—	—	—	—	8
9	.117 5735	—	—	—	—	—	9
10	.106 4098	—	—	—	—	—	10
11	.097 2777	—	—	—	—	—	11

Years							Years
1	.089 6695	1.076 0344	1.0000	—	—	—	1
2	.047 8949	.574 7384	.4659	—	—	—	2
3	.034 0563	.408 6760	.2889	—	—	—	3
4	.027 2012	.326 4148	.2013	—	—	—	4
5	.023 1388	.277 6661	.1493	1.0000	—	—	5
6	.020 4721	.245 6653	.1152	.7717	—	—	6
7	.018 6022	.223 2262	.0913	.6116	—	—	7
8	.017 2295	.206 7543	.0738	.4941	—	—	8
9	.016 1877	.194 2521	.0605	.4049	—	—	9
10	.015 3767	.184 5202	.0501	.3355	1.0000	—	10
11	.014 7329	.176 7947	.0419	.2803	.8357	—	11
12	.014 2138	.170 5659	.0352	.2359	.7032	—	12
13	.013 7901	.165 4808	.0298	.1996	.5951	—	13
14	.013 4406	.161 2868	.0253	.1697	.5059	—	14
15	.013 1499	.157 7985	.0216	.1448	.4317	1.0000	15
16	.012 9064	.154 8769	.0185	.1240	.3696	.8561	16
17	.012 7013	.152 4155	.0159	.1064	.3172	.7348	17
18	.012 5276	.150 3317	.0137	.0915	.2729	.6321	18
19	.012 3800	.148 5601	.0118	.0789	.2352	.5449	19
20	.012 2541	.147 0486	.0102	.0681	.2031	.4704	20
21	.012 1463	.145 7552	.0088	.0589	.1756	.4067	21
22	.012 0538	.144 6455	.0076	.0510	.1520	.3520	22
23	.011 9743	.143 6913	.0066	.0442	.1317	.3050	23
24	.011 9058	.142 8693	.0057	.0383	.1142	.2645	24
25	.011 8467	.142 1599	.0050	.0332	.0991	.2296	25
26	.011 7956	.141 5469	.0043	.0289	.0861	.1994	26
27	.011 7514	.141 0166	.0037	.0251	.0748	.1732	27
28	.011 7131	.140 5572	.0033	.0218	.0650	.1506	28
29	.011 6799	.140 1590	.0028	.0190	.0566	.1310	29
30	.011 6511	.139 8135	.0025	.0165	.0492	.1140	30
31	.011 6261	.139 5135	.0021	.0144	.0428	.0992	31
32	.011 6044	.139 2530	.0019	.0125	.0373	.0864	32
33	.011 5855	.139 0265	.0016	.0109	.0325	.0752	33
34	.011 5691	.138 8295	.0014	.0095	.0283	.0655	34
35	.011 5549	.138 6582	.0012	.0083	.0246	.0571	35
36	.011 5424	.138 5091	.0011	.0072	.0215	.0497	36
37	.011 5316	.138 3793	.0009	.0063	.0187	.0433	37
38	.011 5222	.138 2664	.0008	.0055	.0163	.0378	38
39	.011 5140	.138 1680	.0007	.0048	.0142	.0329	39
40	.011 5069	.138 0822	.0006	.0042	.0124	.0287	40

14% DIRECT REDUCTION LOAN FACTORS
(Monthly Payment and Annual Constant per $1 of Loan)

Base: 1.011 667

Months	Payment	Annual Constant	Part Paid Off Projection 1 Year	5 Years	10 Years	15 Years	Months
1	1.011 6667	—	—	—	—	—	1
2	.508 7669	—	—	—	—	—	2
3	.341 1412	—	—	—	—	—	3
4	.257 3340	—	—	—	—	—	4
5	.207 0541	—	—	—	—	—	5
6	.173 5380	—	—	—	—	—	6
7	.149 6011	—	—	—	—	—	7
8	.131 6513	—	—	—	—	—	8
9	.117 6928	—	—	—	—	—	9
10	.106 5283	—	—	—	—	—	10
11	.097 3957	—	—	—	—	—	11

Years	Payment	Annual Constant	1 Year	5 Years	10 Years	15 Years	Years
1	.089 7871	1.077 4454	1.0000	—	—	—	1
2	.048 0129	.576 1546	.4653	—	—	—	2
3	.034 1776	.410 1316	.2882	—	—	—	3
4	.027 3265	.327 9177	.2005	—	—	—	4
5	.023 2683	.279 2190	.1485	1.0000	—	—	5
6	.020 6057	.247 2689	.1144	.7705	—	—	6
7	.018 7400	.224 8801	.0905	.6097	—	—	7
8	.017 3715	.208 4580	.0730	.4917	—	—	8
9	.016 3337	.196 0044	.0597	.4023	—	—	9
10	.015 5266	.186 3197	.0494	.3327	1.0000	—	10
11	.014 8867	.178 6399	.0412	.2775	.8342	—	11
12	.014 3713	.172 4553	.0346	.2331	.7007	—	12
13	.013 9510	.167 4124	.0292	.1969	.5918	—	13
14	.013 6049	.163 2588	.0248	.1671	.5021	—	14
15	.013 3174	.159 8090	.0211	.1423	.4277	1.0000	15
16	.013 0770	.156 9239	.0181	.1216	.3654	.8544	16
17	.012 8748	.154 4971	.0155	.1041	.3130	.7318	17
18	.012 7038	.152 4460	.0133	.0894	.2687	.6283	18
19	.012 5588	.150 7051	.0114	.0769	.2311	.5404	19
20	.012 4352	.149 2225	.0098	.0662	.1991	.4656	20
21	.012 3297	.147 9561	.0085	.0571	.1718	.4016	21
22	.012 2393	.146 8715	.0073	.0494	.1483	.3469	22
23	.012 1617	.145 9408	.0063	.0427	.1283	.2999	23
24	.012 0950	.145 1405	.0055	.0369	.1110	.2595	24
25	.012 0376	.144 4513	.0047	.0320	.0961	.2247	25
26	.011 9881	.143 8570	.0041	.0277	.0833	.1947	26
27	.011 9453	.143 3439	.0036	.0240	.0722	.1688	27
28	.011 9084	.142 9004	.0031	.0208	.0626	.1464	28
29	.011 8764	.142 5167	.0027	.0181	.0543	.1270	29
30	.011 8487	.142 1846	.0023	.0157	.0472	.1103	30
31	.011 8247	.141 8969	.0020	.0136	.0410	.0958	31
32	.011 8040	.141 6475	.0018	.0118	.0356	.0832	32
33	.011 7859	.141 4313	.0015	.0103	.0309	.0723	33
34	.011 7703	.141 2436	.0013	.0089	.0268	.0628	34
35	.011 7567	.141 0808	.0012	.0078	.0233	.0546	35
36	.011 7450	.140 9394	.0010	.0067	.0203	.0474	36
37	.011 7347	.140 8166	.0009	.0059	.0176	.0412	37
38	.011 7258	.140 7100	.0008	.0051	.0153	.0358	38
39	.011 7181	.140 6173	.0007	.0044	.0133	.0312	39
40	.011 7114	.140 5368	.0006	.0039	.0116	.0271	40

DIRECT REDUCTION LOAN FACTORS 14¼%

(Monthly Payment and Annual Constant per $1 of Loan)

Base: 1.011 875

Months	Payment	Annual Constant	Part Paid Off Projection 1 Year	5 Years	10 Years	15 Years	Months
1	1.011 8750	—	—	—	—	—	1
2	.508 9238	—	—	—	—	—	2
3	.341 2812	—	—	—	—	—	3
4	.257 4657	—	—	—	—	—	4
5	.207 1811	—	—	—	—	—	5
6	.173 6619	—	—	—	—	—	6
7	.149 7230	—	—	—	—	—	7
8	.131 7717	—	—	—	—	—	8
9	.117 8122	—	—	—	—	—	9
10	.106 6469	—	—	—	—	—	10
11	.097 5138	—	—	—	—	—	11

Years	Payment	Annual Constant	1 Year	5 Years	10 Years	15 Years	Years
1	.089 9048	1.078 8575	1.0000	—	—	—	1
2	.048 1311	.577 5729	.4646	—	—	—	2
3	.034 2992	.411 5901	.2874	—	—	—	3
4	.027 4520	.329 4246	.1996	—	—	—	4
5	.023 3981	.280 7768	.1477	1.0000	—	—	5
6	.020 7398	.248 8781	.1136	.7693	—	—	6
7	.018 8784	.226 5406	.0898	.6078	—	—	7
8	.017 5141	.210 1689	.0723	.4894	—	—	8
9	.016 4804	.197 7646	.0590	.3997	—	—	9
10	.015 6773	.188 1277	.0487	.3300	1.0000	—	10
11	.015 0412	.180 4942	.0406	.2748	.8327	—	11
12	.014 5295	.174 3539	.0340	.2304	.6981	—	12
13	.014 1128	.169 3537	.0287	.1942	.5885	—	13
14	.013 7701	.165 2407	.0243	.1645	.4984	—	14
15	.013 4858	.161 8296	.0206	.1398	.4236	1.0000	15
16	.013 2484	.158 9811	.0176	.1192	.3612	.8526	16
17	.013 0491	.156 5890	.0150	.1019	.3088	.7289	17
18	.012 8809	.154 5704	.0129	.0873	.2645	.6245	18
19	.012 7384	.152 8602	.0111	.0749	.2271	.5360	19
20	.012 6172	.151 4063	.0095	.0644	.1952	.4608	20
21	.012 5139	.150 1666	.0082	.0554	.1680	.3966	21
22	.012 4256	.149 1070	.0071	.0478	.1448	.3418	22
23	.012 3500	.148 1994	.0061	.0412	.1249	.2949	23
24	.012 2851	.147 4206	.0053	.0356	.1078	.2546	24
25	.012 2293	.146 7513	.0045	.0307	.0932	.2199	25
26	.012 1813	.146 1753	.0039	.0266	.0805	.1901	26
27	.012 1399	.145 6790	.0034	.0230	.0697	.1645	27
28	.012 1043	.145 2510	.0029	.0199	.0603	.1423	28
29	.012 0735	.144 8816	.0025	.0172	.0522	.1232	29
30	.012 0469	.144 5625	.0022	.0149	.0452	.1067	30
31	.012 0239	.144 2866	.0019	.0129	.0392	.0924	31
32	.012 0040	.144 0481	.0017	.0112	.0339	.0801	32
33	.011 9868	.143 8417	.0014	.0097	.0294	.0694	33
34	.011 9719	.143 6630	.0012	.0084	.0255	.0602	34
35	.011 9590	.143 5083	.0011	.0073	.0221	.0522	35
36	.011 9479	.143 3743	.0009	.0063	.0192	.0452	36
37	.011 9382	.143 2582	.0008	.0055	.0166	.0392	37
38	.011 9298	.143 1576	.0007	.0048	.0144	.0340	38
39	.011 9225	.143 0704	.0006	.0041	.0125	.0295	39
40	.011 9162	.142 9948	.0005	.0036	.0108	.0256	40

14½% DIRECT REDUCTION LOAN FACTORS
(Monthly Payment and Annual Constant per $1 of Loan)

Base: 1.012 083

Months	Payment	Annual Constant	Part Paid Off Projection 1 Year	5 Years	10 Years	15 Years	Months
1	1.012 0833	—	—	—	—	—	1
2	.509 0806	—	—	—	—	—	2
3	.341 4211	—	—	—	—	—	3
4	.257 5974	—	—	—	—	—	4
5	.207 3080	—	—	—	—	—	5
6	.173 7858	—	—	—	—	—	6
7	.149 8448	—	—	—	—	—	7
8	.131 8921	—	—	—	—	—	8
9	.117 9316	—	—	—	—	—	9
10	.106 7655	—	—	—	—	—	10
11	.097 6319	—	—	—	—	—	11

Years	Payment	Annual Constant	1 Year	5 Years	10 Years	15 Years	Years
1	.090 0225	1.080 2706	1.0000	—	—	—	1
2	.048 2494	.578 9931	.4640	—	—	—	2
3	.034 4210	.413 0517	.2866	—	—	—	3
4	.027 5780	.330 9354	.1988	—	—	—	4
5	.023 5283	.282 3394	.1468	1.0000	—	—	5
6	.020 8744	.250 4931	.1128	.7681	—	—	6
7	.019 0173	.228 2077	.0890	.6059	—	—	7
8	.017 6573	.211 8871	.0715	.4870	—	—	8
9	.016 6277	.199 5326	.0583	.3971	—	—	9
10	.015 8287	.189 9441	.0481	.3272	1.0000	—	10
11	.015 1964	.182 3573	.0399	.2720	.8312	—	11
12	.014 6885	.176 2619	.0334	.2276	.6956	—	12
13	.014 2754	.171 3045	.0281	.1915	.5853	—	13
14	.013 9360	.167 2324	.0238	.1619	.4947	—	14
15	.013 6550	.163 8601	.0202	.1373	.4196	1.0000	15
16	.013 4207	.161 0484	.0172	.1169	.3571	.8509	16
17	.013 2242	.158 6909	.0146	.0997	.3046	.7259	17
18	.013 0587	.156 7049	.0125	.0852	.2604	.6206	18
19	.012 9188	.155 0252	.0107	.0730	.2231	.5316	19
20	.012 8000	.153 5997	.0092	.0626	.1913	.4560	20
21	.012 6989	.152 3866	.0079	.0538	.1644	.3917	21
22	.012 6126	.151 3517	.0068	.0462	.1413	.3368	22
23	.012 5389	.150 4670	.0058	.0398	.1216	.2899	23
24	.012 4758	.149 7094	.0050	.0343	.1048	.2497	24
25	.012 4216	.149 0595	.0043	.0296	.0903	.2152	25
26	.012 3751	.148 5015	.0037	.0255	.0779	.1857	26
27	.012 3351	.148 0217	.0032	.0220	.0672	.1602	27
28	.012 3007	.147 6088	.0028	.0190	.0580	.1383	28
29	.012 2711	.147 2532	.0024	.0164	.0501	.1195	29
30	.012 2456	.146 9467	.0021	.0142	.0433	.1032	30
31	.012 2235	.146 6824	.0018	.0122	.0374	.0892	31
32	.012 2045	.146 4543	.0016	.0106	.0324	.0771	32
33	.012 1881	.146 2574	.0013	.0092	.0280	.0667	33
34	.012 1739	.146 0874	.0012	.0079	.0242	.0577	34
35	.012 1617	.145 9405	.0010	.0068	.0209	.0499	35
36	.012 1511	.145 8135	.0009	.0059	.0181	.0431	36
37	.012 1420	.145 7038	.0008	.0051	.0157	.0373	37
38	.012 1341	.145 6089	.0007	.0044	.0135	.0323	38
39	.012 1272	.145 5269	.0006	.0038	.0117	.0279	39
40	.012 1213	.145 4560	.0005	.0033	.0101	.0242	40

DIRECT REDUCTION LOAN FACTORS 14¾%

(Monthly Payment and Annual Constant per $1 of Loan)

Base:	1.012 292		Part Paid Off Projection				
Months	Payment	Annual Constant	1 Year	5 Years	10 Years	15 Years	Months
1	1.012 2917	—	—	—	—	—	1
2	.509 2375	—	—	—	—	—	2
3	.341 5611	—	—	—	—	—	3
4	.257 7292	—	—	—	—	—	4
5	.207 4351	—	—	—	—	—	5
6	.173 9098	—	—	—	—	—	6
7	.149 9667	—	—	—	—	—	7
8	.132 0126	—	—	—	—	—	8
9	.118 0510	—	—	—	—	—	9
10	.106 8843	—	—	—	—	—	10
11	.097 7501	—	—	—	—	—	11
Years							**Years**
1	.090 1404	1.081 6846	1.0000	—	—	—	1
2	.048 3680	.580 4154	.4634	—	—	—	2
3	.034 5430	.414 5163	.2858	—	—	—	3
4	.027 7042	.332 4502	.1980	—	—	—	4
5	.023 6589	.283 9068	.1460	1.0000	—	—	5
6	.021 0095	.252 1138	.1120	.7669	—	—	6
7	.019 1568	.229 8811	.0882	.6039	—	—	7
8	.017 8010	.213 6124	.0708	.4847	—	—	8
9	.016 7757	.201 3085	.0576	.3945	—	—	9
10	.015 9807	.191 7689	.0474	.3245	1.0000	—	10
11	.015 3524	.184 2292	.0393	.2693	.8297	—	11
12	.014 8483	.178 1790	.0328	.2249	.6930	—	12
13	.014 4387	.173 2648	.0276	.1889	.5820	—	13
14	.014 1028	.169 2338	.0233	.1593	.4909	—	14
15	.013 8250	.165 9005	.0197	.1349	.4157	1.0000	15
16	.013 5938	.163 1255	.0167	.1146	.3530	.8492	16
17	.013 4002	.160 8027	.0142	.0975	.3005	.7230	17
18	.013 2374	.158 8491	.0121	.0832	.2564	.6168	18
19	.013 1000	.157 1998	.0104	.0711	.2191	.5271	19
20	.012 9836	.155 8026	.0089	.0609	.1876	.4512	20
21	.012 8847	.154 6159	.0076	.0522	.1607	.3867	21
22	.012 8004	.153 6054	.0065	.0448	.1379	.3318	22
23	.012 7286	.152 7432	.0056	.0384	.1184	.2850	23
24	.012 6672	.152 0064	.0048	.0330	.1018	.2449	24
25	.012 6146	.151 3758	.0041	.0284	.0876	.2106	25
26	.012 5696	.150 8353	.0036	.0245	.0753	.1813	26
27	.012 5310	.150 3717	.0031	.0211	.0649	.1561	27
28	.012 4978	.149 9735	.0026	.0181	.0559	.1344	28
29	.012 4693	.149 6313	.0023	.0156	.0481	.1158	29
30	.012 4448	.149 3371	.0020	.0135	.0415	.0998	30
31	.012 4237	.149 0839	.0017	.0116	.0358	.0861	31
32	.012 4055	.148 8659	.0015	.0100	.0309	.0742	32
33	.012 3898	.148 6782	.0013	.0086	.0266	.0640	33
34	.012 3764	.148 5164	.0011	.0075	.0230	.0552	34
35	.012 3647	.148 3770	.0009	.0064	.0198	.0477	35
36	.012 3547	.148 2568	.0008	.0055	.0171	.0411	36
37	.012 3461	.148 1531	.0007	.0048	.0148	.0355	37
38	.012 3386	.148 0637	.0006	.0041	.0127	.0306	38
39	.012 3322	.147 9866	.0005	.0036	.0110	.0264	39
40	.012 3267	.147 9201	.0004	.0031	.0095	.0228	40

15% DIRECT REDUCTION LOAN FACTORS
(Monthly Payment and Annual Constant per $1 of Loan)

Base:	1.012 500			Part Paid Off Projection			
Months	Payment	Annual Constant	1 Year	5 Years	10 Years	15 Years	Months
1	1.012 5000	—	—	—	—	—	1
2	.509 3944	—	—	—	—	—	2
3	.341 7012	—	—	—	—	—	3
4	.257 8610	—	—	—	—	—	4
5	.207 5621	—	—	—	—	—	5
6	.174 0338	—	—	—	—	—	6
7	.150 0887	—	—	—	—	—	7
8	.132 1331	—	—	—	—	—	8
9	.118 1706	—	—	—	—	—	9
10	.107 0031	—	—	—	—	—	10
11	.097 8684	—	—	—	—	—	11
Years							**Years**
1	.090 2583	1.083 0997	1.0000	—	—	—	1
2	.048 4866	.581 8398	.4628	—	—	—	2
3	.034 6653	.415 9839	.2851	—	—	—	3
4	.027 8307	.333 9690	.1972	—	—	—	4
5	.023 7899	.285 4792	.1452	1.0000	—	—	5
6	.021 1450	.253 7402	.1112	.7657	—	—	6
7	.019 2968	.231 5611	.0874	.6020	—	—	7
8	.017 9454	.215 3449	.0700	.4823	—	—	8
9	.016 9243	.203 0920	.0569	.3919	—	—	9
10	.016 1335	.193 6019	.0467	.3218	1.0000	—	10
11	.015 5091	.186 1098	.0387	.2665	.8282	—	11
12	.015 0088	.180 1052	.0323	.2222	.6905	—	12
13	.014 6029	.175 2345	.0270	.1863	.5787	—	13
14	.014 2704	.171 2448	.0228	.1568	.4872	—	14
15	.013 9959	.167 9505	.0192	.1325	.4117	1.0000	15
16	.013 7677	.165 2124	.0163	.1123	.3489	.8475	16
17	.013 5770	.162 9241	.0139	.0954	.2964	.7200	17
18	.013 4169	.161 0029	.0118	.0812	.2523	.6130	18
19	.013 2820	.159 3838	.0101	.0693	.2152	.5228	19
20	.013 1679	.158 0147	.0086	.0592	.1838	.4465	20
21	.013 0712	.156 8541	.0073	.0506	.1572	.3818	21
22	.012 9890	.155 8677	.0063	.0433	.1346	.3269	22
23	.012 9190	.155 0278	.0054	.0371	.1153	.2801	23
24	.012 8593	.154 3115	.0046	.0318	.0989	.2402	24
25	.012 8083	.153 6997	.0040	.0273	.0849	.2061	25
26	.012 7647	.153 1765	.0034	.0234	.0729	.1770	26
27	.012 7274	.152 7285	.0029	.0201	.0626	.1520	27
28	.012 6954	.152 3448	.0025	.0173	.0538	.1306	28
29	.012 6680	.152 0157	.0022	.0149	.0462	.1123	29
30	.012 6444	.151 7333	.0019	.0128	.0398	.0966	30
31	.012 6242	.151 4909	.0016	.0110	.0342	.0831	31
32	.012 6069	.151 2826	.0014	.0095	.0294	.0715	32
33	.012 5920	.151 1037	.0012	.0081	.0253	.0615	33
34	.012 5792	.150 9499	.0010	.0070	.0218	.0529	34
35	.012 5681	.150 8176	.0009	.0060	.0188	.0455	35
36	.012 5587	.150 7038	.0008	.0052	.0161	.0392	36
37	.012 5505	.150 6060	.0006	.0045	.0139	.0338	37
38	.012 5435	.150 5218	.0006	.0039	.0120	.0291	38
39	.012 5374	.150 4493	.0005	.0033	.0103	.0250	39
40	.012 5322	.150 3869	.0004	.0029	.0089	.0216	40

DIRECT REDUCTION LOAN FACTORS 15¼%
(Monthly Payment and Annual Constant per $1 of Loan)

			Part Paid Off Projection				
Base:	1.012 708	Annual					
Months	Payment	Constant	1 Year	5 Years	10 Years	15 Years	Months
1	1.012 7083	—	—	—	—	—	1
2	.509 5513	—	—	—	—	—	2
3	.341 8412	—	—	—	—	—	3
4	.257 9929	—	—	—	—	—	4
5	.207 6892	—	—	—	—	—	5
6	.174 1579	—	—	—	—	—	6
7	.150 2107	—	—	—	—	—	7
8	.132 2537	—	—	—	—	—	8
9	.118 2901	—	—	—	—	—	9
10	.107 1219	—	—	—	—	—	10
11	.097 9868	—	—	—	—	—	11

Years							Years
1	.090 3763	1.084 5159	1.0000	—	—	—	1
2	.048 6055	.583 2661	.4622	—	—	—	2
3	.034 7879	.417 4546	.2843	—	—	—	3
4	.027 9576	.335 4917	.1963	—	—	—	4
5	.023 9214	.287 0563	.1444	1.0000	—	—	5
6	.021 2810	.255 3722	.1104	.7645	—	—	6
7	.019 4373	.233 2474	.0866	.6001	—	—	7
8	.018 0904	.217 0844	.0693	.4800	—	—	8
9	.017 0736	.204 8833	.0562	.3893	—	—	9
10	.016 2869	.195 4432	.0461	.3191	1.0000	—	10
11	.015 6666	.187 9991	.0381	.2638	.8267	—	11
12	.015 1700	.182 0404	.0317	.2195	.6879	—	12
13	.014 7678	.177 2134	.0265	.1837	.5755	—	13
14	.014 4388	.173 2651	.0223	.1543	.4835	—	14
15	.014 1675	.170 0100	.0188	.1301	.4077	1.0000	15
16	.013 9424	.167 3087	.0159	.1101	.3448	.8457	16
17	.013 7546	.165 0549	.0135	.0933	.2924	.7170	17
18	.013 5972	.163 1660	.0114	.0793	.2484	.6091	18
19	.013 4647	.161 5769	.0097	.0675	.2114	.5184	19
20	.013 3530	.160 2358	.0083	.0575	.1801	.4418	20
21	.013 2584	.159 1010	.0071	.0491	.1537	.3770	21
22	.013 1782	.158 1385	.0060	.0419	.1313	.3220	22
23	.013 1100	.157 3205	.0052	.0358	.1123	.2753	23
24	.013 0520	.156 6244	.0044	.0307	.0960	.2355	24
25	.013 0026	.156 0310	.0038	.0262	.0822	.2017	25
26	.012 9604	.155 5246	.0032	.0225	.0704	.1727	26
27	.012 9243	.155 0921	.0028	.0193	.0604	.1480	27
28	.012 8935	.154 7223	.0024	.0165	.0517	.1269	28
29	.012 8672	.154 4059	.0020	.0142	.0444	.1088	29
30	.012 8446	.154 1350	.0018	.0122	.0381	.0934	30
31	.012 8252	.153 9030	.0015	.0104	.0327	.0801	31
32	.012 8087	.153 7042	.0013	.0089	.0280	.0688	32
33	.012 7945	.153 5337	.0011	.0077	.0241	.0590	33
34	.012 7823	.153 3875	.0010	.0066	.0207	.0507	34
35	.012 7718	.153 2621	.0008	.0057	.0177	.0435	35
36	.012 7629	.153 1544	.0007	.0049	.0152	.0374	36
37	.012 7552	.153 0621	.0006	.0042	.0131	.0321	37
38	.012 7486	.152 9828	.0005	.0036	.0112	.0276	38
39	.012 7429	.152 9147	.0004	.0031	.0097	.0237	39
40	.012 7380	.152 8563	.0004	.0026	.0083	.0203	40

15½% DIRECT REDUCTION LOAN FACTORS
(Monthly Payment and Annual Constant per $1 of Loan)

Base: 1.012 917

Months	Payment	Annual Constant	Part Paid Off Projection				Months
			1 Year	5 Years	10 Years	15 Years	
1	1.012 9167	—	—	—	—	—	1
2	.509 7082	—	—	—	—	—	2
3	.341 9813	—	—	—	—	—	3
4	.258 1247	—	—	—	—	—	4
5	.207 8163	—	—	—	—	—	5
6	.174 2820	—	—	—	—	—	6
7	.150 3328	—	—	—	—	—	7
8	.132 3744	—	—	—	—	—	8
9	.118 4098	—	—	—	—	—	9
10	.107 2409	—	—	—	—	—	10
11	.098 1052	—	—	—	—	—	11

Years	Payment	Annual Constant	1 Year	5 Years	10 Years	15 Years	Years
1	.090 4944	1.085 9330	1.0000	—	—	—	1
2	.048 7245	.584 6945	.4616	—	—	—	2
3	.034 9107	.418 9282	.2835	—	—	—	3
4	.028 0849	.337 0183	.1955	—	—	—	4
5	.024 0532	.288 6383	.1436	1.0000	—	—	5
6	.021 4175	.257 0099	.1096	.7633	—	—	6
7	.019 5783	.234 9402	.0859	.5982	—	—	7
8	.018 2359	.218 8311	.0686	.4776	—	—	8
9	.017 2235	.206 6823	.0555	.3867	—	—	9
10	.016 4411	.197 2926	.0454	.3165	1.0000	—	10
11	.015 8247	.189 8969	.0375	.2611	.8251	—	11
12	.015 3320	.183 9845	.0311	.2169	.6853	—	12
13	.014 9335	.179 2015	.0260	.1811	.5722	—	13
14	.014 6079	.175 2948	.0218	.1519	.4799	—	14
15	.014 3399	.172 0788	.0183	.1278	.4038	1.0000	15
16	.014 1179	.169 4144	.0155	.1079	.3408	.8440	16
17	.013 9329	.167 1951	.0131	.0913	.2884	.7140	17
18	.013 7782	.165 3383	.0111	.0774	.2444	.6053	18
19	.013 6483	.163 7791	.0094	.0657	.2076	.5140	19
20	.013 5388	.162 4657	.0080	.0559	.1765	.4371	20
21	.013 4464	.161 3564	.0068	.0476	.1503	.3722	21
22	.013 3681	.160 4174	.0058	.0405	.1281	.3172	22
23	.013 3018	.159 6211	.0050	.0346	.1093	.2706	23
24	.013 2454	.158 9447	.0042	.0295	.0933	.2310	24
25	.013 1975	.158 3694	.0036	.0252	.0797	.1973	25
26	.013 1566	.157 8796	.0031	.0215	.0681	.1686	26
27	.013 1218	.157 4620	.0026	.0184	.0582	.1442	27
28	.013 0922	.157 1058	.0023	.0158	.0498	.1233	28
29	.013 0668	.156 8018	.0019	.0135	.0426	.1055	29
30	.013 0452	.156 5420	.0017	.0115	.0365	.0903	30
31	.013 0267	.156 3201	.0014	.0099	.0312	.0773	31
32	.013 0109	.156 1303	.0012	.0085	.0267	.0662	32
33	.012 9973	.155 9679	.0010	.0072	.0229	.0567	33
34	.012 9858	.155 8290	.0009	.0062	.0196	.0485	34
35	.012 9758	.155 7102	.0008	.0053	.0168	.0416	35
36	.012 9674	.155 6084	.0007	.0046	.0144	.0356	36
37	.012 9601	.155 5213	.0006	.0039	.0123	.0305	37
38	.012 9539	.155 4466	.0005	.0033	.0106	.0262	38
39	.012 9486	.155 3827	.0004	.0029	.0090	.0224	39
40	.012 9440	.155 3280	.0004	.0025	.0078	.0192	40

DIRECT REDUCTION LOAN FACTORS 15¾%

(Monthly Payment and Annual Constant per $1 of Loan)

Base: 1.013 125

Months	Payment	Annual Constant	Part Paid Off Projection 1 Year	5 Years	10 Years	15 Years	Months
1	1.013 1250	—	—	—	—	—	1
2	.509 8651	—	—	—	—	—	2
3	.342 1214	—	—	—	—	—	3
4	.258 2566	—	—	—	—	—	4
5	.207 9435	—	—	—	—	—	5
6	.174 4061	—	—	—	—	—	6
7	.150 4549	—	—	—	—	—	7
8	.132 4951	—	—	—	—	—	8
9	.118 5295	—	—	—	—	—	9
10	.107 3599	—	—	—	—	—	10
11	.098 2237	—	—	—	—	—	11

Years	Payment	Annual Constant	1 Year	5 Years	10 Years	15 Years	Years
1	.090 6126	1.087 3511	1.0000	—	—	—	1
2	.048 8437	.586 1249	.4610	—	—	—	2
3	.035 0337	.420 4048	.2827	—	—	—	3
4	.028 2124	.338 5489	.1947	—	—	—	4
5	.024 1854	.290 2251	.1427	1.0000	—	—	5
6	.021 5544	.258 6532	.1088	.7621	—	—	6
7	.019 7199	.236 6393	.0851	.5963	—	—	7
8	.018 3821	.220 5848	.0678	.4753	—	—	8
9	.017 3741	.208 4889	.0548	.3842	—	—	9
10	.016 5958	.199 1502	.0448	.3138	1.0000	—	10
11	.015 9836	.191 8033	.0369	.2585	.8236	—	11
12	.015 4948	.185 9374	.0306	.2143	.6828	—	12
13	.015 0999	.181 1985	.0255	.1786	.5690	—	13
14	.014 7778	.177 3336	.0213	.1494	.4762	—	14
15	.014 5131	.174 1569	.0179	.1255	.3999	1.0000	15
16	.014 2941	.171 5293	.0151	.1057	.3368	.8423	16
17	.014 1120	.169 3444	.0127	.0892	.2844	.7111	17
18	.013 9600	.167 5196	.0108	.0755	.2406	.6015	18
19	.013 8325	.165 9901	.0091	.0640	.2038	.5097	19
20	.013 7253	.164 7040	.0077	.0543	.1730	.4325	20
21	.013 6350	.163 6200	.0066	.0461	.1469	.3674	21
22	.013 5587	.162 7043	.0056	.0392	.1250	.3124	22
23	.013 4941	.161 9292	.0048	.0334	.1063	.2659	23
24	.013 4394	.161 2723	.0041	.0284	.0906	.2265	24
25	.013 3929	.160 7147	.0035	.0242	.0772	.1930	25
26	.013 3534	.160 2410	.0029	.0207	.0658	.1646	26
27	.013 3198	.159 8381	.0025	.0176	.0561	.1404	27
28	.013 2913	.159 4951	.0021	.0150	.0479	.1198	28
29	.013 2669	.159 2030	.0018	.0128	.0409	.1022	29
30	.013 2462	.158 9541	.0016	.0110	.0349	.0873	30
31	.013 2285	.158 7418	.0013	.0094	.0298	.0746	31
32	.013 2134	.158 5607	.0011	.0080	.0255	.0637	32
33	.013 2005	.158 4062	.0010	.0068	.0218	.0544	33
34	.013 1895	.158 2743	.0008	.0058	.0186	.0465	34
35	.013 1801	.158 1616	.0007	.0050	.0159	.0397	35
36	.013 1721	.158 0655	.0006	.0043	.0136	.0339	36
37	.013 1653	.157 9833	.0005	.0036	.0116	.0290	37
38	.013 1594	.157 9131	.0004	.0031	.0099	.0248	38
39	.013 1544	.157 8531	.0004	.0027	.0085	.0212	39
40	.013 1502	.157 8019	.0003	.0023	.0072	.0181	40

16% DIRECT REDUCTION LOAN FACTORS
(Monthly Payment and Annual Constant per $1 of Loan)

Base: 1.013 333

Months	Payment	Annual Constant	Part Paid Off Projection				Months
			1 Year	5 Years	10 Years	15 Years	
1	1.013 3333	—	—	—	—	—	1
2	.510 0221	—	—	—	—	—	2
3	.342 2615	—	—	—	—	—	3
4	.258 3885	—	—	—	—	—	4
5	.208 0706	—	—	—	—	—	5
6	.174 5303	—	—	—	—	—	6
7	.150 5771	—	—	—	—	—	7
8	.132 6159	—	—	—	—	—	8
9	.118 6493	—	—	—	—	—	9
10	.107 4790	—	—	—	—	—	10
11	.098 3423	—	—	—	—	—	11

Years	Payment	Annual Constant	1 Year	5 Years	10 Years	15 Years	Years
1	.090 7309	1.088 7703	1.0000	—	—	—	1
2	.048 9631	.587 5573	.4603	—	—	—	2
3	.035 1570	.421 8844	.2820	—	—	—	3
4	.028 3403	.340 0834	.1939	—	—	—	4
5	.024 3181	.291 8167	.1419	1.0000	—	—	5
6	.021 6918	.260 3021	.1080	.7609	—	—	6
7	.019 8621	.238 3448	.0844	.5943	—	—	7
8	.018 5288	.222 3454	.0671	.4730	—	—	8
9	.017 5253	.210 3030	.0542	.3816	—	—	9
10	.016 7513	.201 0157	.0442	.3112	1.0000	—	10
11	.016 1432	.193 7181	.0363	.2558	.8221	—	11
12	.015 6583	.187 8990	.0300	.2117	.6802	—	12
13	.015 2670	.183 2045	.0250	.1760	.5657	—	13
14	.014 9485	.179 3815	.0209	.1470	.4725	—	14
15	.014 6870	.176 2441	.0175	.1232	.3960	1.0000	15
16	.014 4711	.173 6532	.0147	.1036	.3329	.8405	16
17	.014 2919	.171 5026	.0124	.0873	.2804	.7081	17
18	.014 1425	.169 7096	.0105	.0737	.2367	.5977	18
19	.014 0175	.168 2096	.0088	.0623	.2002	.5054	19
20	.013 9126	.166 9507	.0075	.0527	.1695	.4279	20
21	.013 8243	.165 8917	.0063	.0447	.1436	.3627	21
22	.013 7499	.164 9988	.0054	.0379	.1219	.3077	22
23	.013 6871	.164 2447	.0046	.0322	.1035	.2613	23
24	.013 6339	.163 6069	.0039	.0274	.0879	.2220	24
25	.013 5889	.163 0667	.0033	.0233	.0748	.1888	25
26	.013 5507	.162 6087	.0028	.0198	.0636	.1606	26
27	.013 5183	.162 2200	.0024	.0168	.0541	.1367	27
28	.013 4908	.161 8899	.0020	.0143	.0461	.1163	28
29	.013 4674	.161 6094	.0017	.0122	.0392	.0991	29
30	.013 4476	.161 3708	.0015	.0104	.0334	.0844	30
31	.013 4307	.161 1679	.0013	.0089	.0285	.0719	31
32	.013 4163	.160 9952	.0011	.0076	.0243	.0613	32
33	.013 4040	.160 8482	.0009	.0064	.0207	.0522	33
34	.013 3936	.160 7230	.0008	.0055	.0176	.0445	34
35	.013 3847	.160 6163	.0007	.0047	.0150	.0379	35
36	.013 3771	.160 5255	.0006	.0040	.0128	.0323	36
37	.013 3707	.160 4480	.0005	.0034	.0109	.0276	37
38	.013 3652	.160 3820	.0004	.0029	.0093	.0235	38
39	.013 3605	.160 3258	.0004	.0025	.0079	.0201	39
40	.013 3565	.160 2778	.0003	.0021	.0068	.0171	40

DIRECT REDUCTION LOAN FACTORS   16¼%

(Monthly Payment and Annual Constant per $1 of Loan)

			Part Paid Off Projection				
Base:	**1.013 542**	Annual					
Months	Payment	Constant	1 Year	5 Years	10 Years	15 Years	Months
1	1.013 5417	—	—	—	—	—	1
2	.510 1790	—	—	—	—	—	2
3	.342 4016	—	—	—	—	—	3
4	.258 5205	—	—	—	—	—	4
5	.208 1979	—	—	—	—	—	5
6	.174 6545	—	—	—	—	—	6
7	.150 6993	—	—	—	—	—	7
8	.132 7367	—	—	—	—	—	8
9	.118 7691	—	—	—	—	—	9
10	.107 5981	—	—	—	—	—	10
11	.098 4610	—	—	—	—	—	11

Years							Years
1	.090 8492	1.090 1905	1.0000	—	—	—	1
2	.049 0826	.588 9918	.4597	—	—	—	2
3	.035 2806	.423 3670	.2812	—	—	—	3
4	.028 4685	.341 6218	.1931	—	—	—	4
5	.024 4511	.293 4131	.1411	1.0000	—	—	5
6	.021 8297	.261 9566	.1072	.7597	—	—	6
7	.020 0047	.240 0566	.0836	.5924	—	—	7
8	.018 6761	.224 1131	.0664	.4706	—	—	8
9	.017 6771	.212 1247	.0535	.3791	—	—	9
10	.016 9074	.202 8893	.0435	.3085	1.0000	—	10
11	.016 3034	.195 6412	.0357	.2532	.8205	—	11
12	.015 8224	.189 8693	.0295	.2091	.6776	—	12
13	.015 4349	.185 2193	.0245	.1735	.5625	—	13
14	.015 1199	.181 4382	.0204	.1447	.4689	—	14
15	.014 8617	.178 3402	.0171	.1210	.3922	1.0000	15
16	.014 6488	.175 7860	.0143	.1015	.3289	.8388	16
17	.014 4725	.173 6696	.0120	.0853	.2765	.7051	17
18	.014 3257	.171 9083	.0101	.0719	.2329	.5939	18
19	.014 2031	.170 4374	.0086	.0606	.1965	.5011	19
20	.014 1005	.169 2055	.0072	.0512	.1660	.4233	20
21	.014 0143	.168 1711	.0061	.0433	.1404	.3580	21
22	.013 9417	.167 3008	.0052	.0367	.1189	.3031	22
23	.013 8806	.166 5673	.0044	.0311	.1007	.2568	23
24	.013 8290	.165 9482	.0037	.0263	.0854	.2177	24
25	.013 7854	.165 4250	.0032	.0223	.0724	.1847	25
26	.013 7485	.164 9823	.0027	.0190	.0615	.1567	26
27	.013 7173	.164 6075	.0023	.0161	.0522	.1330	27
28	.013 6908	.164 2899	.0019	.0137	.0443	.1130	28
29	.013 6684	.164 0206	.0016	.0116	.0376	.0960	29
30	.013 6493	.163 7922	.0014	.0099	.0320	.0816	30
31	.013 6332	.163 5982	.0012	.0084	.0272	.0693	31
32	.013 6195	.163 4336	.0010	.0071	.0231	.0589	32
33	.013 6078	.163 2938	.0009	.0061	.0197	.0501	33
34	.013 5979	.163 1750	.0007	.0052	.0167	.0426	34
35	.013 5895	.163 0740	.0006	.0044	.0142	.0362	35
36	.013 5823	.162 9882	.0005	.0037	.0121	.0308	36
37	.013 5763	.162 9152	.0004	.0032	.0103	.0262	37
38	.013 5711	.162 8532	.0004	.0027	.0087	.0223	38
39	.013 5667	.162 8005	.0003	.0023	.0074	.0190	39
40	.013 5630	.162 7556	.0003	.0020	.0063	.0161	40

16½% DIRECT REDUCTION LOAN FACTORS
(Monthly Payment and Annual Constant per $1 of Loan)

Base: 1.013 750

Months	Payment	Annual Constant	Part Paid Off Projection 1 Year	5 Years	10 Years	15 Years	Months
1	1.013 7500	—	—	—	—	—	1
2	.510 3360	—	—	—	—	—	2
3	.342 5417	—	—	—	—	—	3
4	.258 6524	—	—	—	—	—	4
5	.208 3251	—	—	—	—	—	5
6	.174 7788	—	—	—	—	—	6
7	.150 8216	—	—	—	—	—	7
8	.132 8576	—	—	—	—	—	8
9	.118 8891	—	—	—	—	—	9
10	.107 7174	—	—	—	—	—	10
11	.098 5797	—	—	—	—	—	11

Years	Payment	Annual Constant	1 Year	5 Years	10 Years	15 Years	Years
1	.090 9676	1.091 6116	1.0000	—	—	—	1
2	.049 2024	.590 4282	.4591	—	—	—	2
3	.035 4044	.424 8526	.2804	—	—	—	3
4	.028 5970	.343 1641	.1923	—	—	—	4
5	.024 5845	.295 0143	.1403	1.0000	—	—	5
6	.021 9681	.263 6167	.1064	.7585	—	—	6
7	.020 1479	.241 7747	.0829	.5905	—	—	7
8	.018 8240	.225 8877	.0657	.4683	—	—	8
9	.017 8295	.213 9538	.0528	.3765	—	—	9
10	.017 0642	.204 7708	.0429	.3059	1.0000	—	10
11	.016 4644	.197 5726	.0352	.2505	.8190	—	11
12	.015 9873	.191 8480	.0290	.2065	.6751	—	12
13	.015 6036	.187 2428	.0240	.1711	.5593	—	13
14	.015 2920	.183 5037	.0200	.1423	.4653	—	14
15	.015 0371	.180 4450	.0167	.1188	.3884	1.0000	15
16	.014 8273	.177 9276	.0140	.0994	.3251	.8370	16
17	.014 6538	.175 8451	.0117	.0834	.2727	.7022	17
18	.014 5096	.174 1153	.0098	.0701	.2292	.5902	18
19	.014 3894	.172 6734	.0083	.0590	.1929	.4968	19
20	.014 2890	.171 4681	.0070	.0497	.1626	.4188	20
21	.014 2048	.170 4581	.0059	.0420	.1372	.3534	21
22	.014 1342	.169 6100	.0050	.0355	.1159	.2985	22
23	.014 0747	.168 8967	.0042	.0300	.0980	.2523	23
24	.014 0247	.168 2960	.0036	.0254	.0829	.2134	24
25	.013 9824	.167 7894	.0030	.0215	.0701	.1806	25
26	.013 9468	.167 3617	.0025	.0182	.0594	.1529	26
27	.013 9167	.167 0004	.0022	.0154	.0503	.1295	27
28	.013 8912	.166 6949	.0018	.0130	.0426	.1097	28
29	.013 8697	.166 4365	.0016	.0110	.0361	.0930	29
30	.013 8515	.166 2178	.0013	.0094	.0306	.0788	30
31	.013 8360	.166 0325	.0011	.0079	.0260	.0669	31
32	.013 8230	.165 8756	.0009	.0067	.0220	.0567	32
33	.013 8119	.165 7427	.0008	.0057	.0187	.0481	33
34	.013 8025	.165 6300	.0007	.0048	.0158	.0408	34
35	.013 7945	.165 5345	.0006	.0041	.0134	.0346	35
36	.013 7878	.165 4535	.0005	.0035	.0114	.0294	36
37	.013 7821	.165 3848	.0004	.0030	.0097	.0249	37
38	.013 7772	.165 3265	.0004	.0025	.0082	.0211	38
39	.013 7731	.165 2771	.0003	.0021	.0070	.0179	39
40	.013 7696	.165 2351	.0003	.0018	.0059	.0152	40

DIRECT REDUCTION LOAN FACTORS 16¾%
(Monthly Payment and Annual Constant per $1 of Loan)

			Part Paid Off Projection				
Base:	1.013 958	Annual					
Months	Payment	Constant	1 Year	5 Years	10 Years	15 Years	Months
1	1.013 9583	—	—	—	—	—	1
2	.510 4929	—	—	—	—	—	2
3	.342 6819	—	—	—	—	—	3
4	.258 7844	—	—	—	—	—	4
5	.208 4524	—	—	—	—	—	5
6	.174 9031	—	—	—	—	—	6
7	.150 9439	—	—	—	—	—	7
8	.132 9785	—	—	—	—	—	8
9	.119 0090	—	—	—	—	—	9
10	.107 8367	—	—	—	—	—	10
11	.098 6986	—	—	—	—	—	11
Years							**Years**
1	.091 0862	1.093 0338	1.0000	—	—	—	1
2	.049 3222	.591 8667	.4585	—	—	—	2
3	.035 5284	.426 3412	.2797	—	—	—	3
4	.028 7259	.344 7104	.1915	—	—	—	4
5	.024 7184	.296 6202	.1395	1.0000	—	—	5
6	.022 1069	.265 2824	.1056	.7573	—	—	6
7	.020 2916	.243 4990	.0821	.5886	—	—	7
8	.018 9724	.227 6691	.0650	.4660	—	—	8
9	.017 9825	.215 7903	.0522	.3740	—	—	9
10	.017 2217	.206 6601	.0423	.3033	1.0000	—	10
11	.016 6260	.199 5122	.0346	.2479	.8175	—	11
12	.016 1529	.193 8352	.0285	.2040	.6725	—	12
13	.015 7729	.189 2749	.0235	.1686	.5560	—	13
14	.015 4648	.185 5779	.0195	.1400	.4616	—	14
15	.015 2132	.182 5585	.0163	.1166	.3845	1.0000	15
16	.015 0065	.180 0776	.0136	.0974	.3212	.8352	16
17	.014 8358	.178 0290	.0114	.0815	.2689	.6992	17
18	.014 6942	.176 3305	.0095	.0684	.2255	.5864	18
19	.014 5764	.174 9173	.0080	.0574	.1894	.4926	19
20	.014 4782	.173 7383	.0067	.0483	.1593	.4143	20
21	.014 3960	.172 7524	.0057	.0407	.1341	.3488	21
22	.014 3272	.171 9262	.0048	.0343	.1130	.2939	22
23	.014 2694	.171 2328	.0040	.0289	.0953	.2479	23
24	.014 2208	.170 6500	.0034	.0244	.0804	.2092	24
25	.014 1800	.170 1596	.0029	.0206	.0679	.1766	25
26	.014 1456	.169 7466	.0024	.0174	.0574	.1492	26
27	.014 1165	.169 3984	.0021	.0147	.0485	.1261	27
28	.014 0921	.169 1047	.0017	.0124	.0410	.1066	28
29	.014 0714	.168 8568	.0015	.0105	.0346	.0901	29
30	.014 0540	.168 6475	.0012	.0089	.0293	.0762	30
31	.014 0392	.168 4706	.0010	.0075	.0248	.0645	31
32	.014 0268	.168 3211	.0009	.0064	.0210	.0545	32
33	.014 0162	.168 1948	.0008	.0054	.0177	.0461	33
34	.014 0073	.168 0879	.0006	.0046	.0150	.0390	34
35	.013 9998	.167 9976	.0005	.0039	.0127	.0330	35
36	.013 9934	.167 9211	.0005	.0033	.0108	.0280	36
37	.013 9880	.167 8565	.0004	.0028	.0091	.0237	37
38	.013 9835	.167 8017	.0003	.0023	.0077	.0200	38
39	.013 9796	.167 7554	.0003	.0020	.0065	.0170	39
40	.013 9764	.167 7162	.0002	.0017	.0055	.0144	40

17%   DIRECT REDUCTION LOAN FACTORS
(Monthly Payment and Annual Constant per $1 of Loan)

Base: 1.014 167

Months	Payment	Annual Constant	Part Paid Off Projection 1 Year	5 Years	10 Years	15 Years	Months
1	1.014 1667	—	—	—	—	—	1
2	.510 6499	—	—	—	—	—	2
3	.342 8221	—	—	—	—	—	3
4	.258 9164	—	—	—	—	—	4
5	.208 5797	—	—	—	—	—	5
6	.175 0274	—	—	—	—	—	6
7	.151 0662	—	—	—	—	—	7
8	.133 0995	—	—	—	—	—	8
9	.119 1291	—	—	—	—	—	9
10	.107 9560	—	—	—	—	—	10
11	.098 8175	—	—	—	—	—	11

Years	Payment	Annual Constant	1 Year	5 Years	10 Years	15 Years	Years
1	.091 2048	1.094 4570	1.0000	—	—	—	1
2	.049 4423	.593 3072	.4579	—	—	—	2
3	.035 6527	.427 8327	.2789	—	—	—	3
4	.028 8550	.346 2605	.1907	—	—	—	4
5	.024 8526	.298 2309	.1387	1.0000	—	—	5
6	.022 2461	.266 9536	.1049	.7561	—	—	6
7	.020 4358	.245 2297	.0814	.5867	—	—	7
8	.019 1215	.229 4574	.0643	.4637	—	—	8
9	.018 1362	.217 6343	.0515	.3715	—	—	9
10	.017 3798	.208 5572	.0417	.3007	1.0000	—	10
11	.016 7883	.201 4599	.0340	.2453	.8159	—	11
12	.016 3192	.195 8308	.0279	.2014	.6699	—	12
13	.015 9430	.191 3154	.0231	.1662	.5528	—	13
14	.015 6384	.187 6606	.0191	.1377	.4580	—	14
15	.015 3900	.184 6805	.0159	.1145	.3807	1.0000	15
16	.015 1863	.182 2361	.0132	.0954	.3173	.8335	16
17	.015 0184	.180 2212	.0111	.0797	.2651	.6962	17
18	.014 8795	.178 5537	.0093	.0667	.2218	.5827	18
19	.014 7641	.177 1690	.0078	.0559	.1859	.4883	19
20	.014 6680	.176 0161	.0065	.0469	.1560	.4098	20
21	.014 5878	.175 0538	.0055	.0394	.1311	.3443	21
22	.014 5208	.174 2492	.0046	.0331	.1102	.2894	22
23	.014 4646	.173 5753	.0039	.0279	.0927	.2435	23
24	.014 4175	.173 0101	.0033	.0235	.0781	.2050	24
25	.014 3780	.172 5356	.0027	.0198	.0658	.1727	25
26	.014 3447	.172 1368	.0023	.0167	.0554	.1456	26
27	.014 3168	.171 8014	.0019	.0140	.0467	.1227	27
28	.014 2933	.171 5191	.0016	.0118	.0394	.1035	28
29	.014 2734	.171 2813	.0014	.0100	.0332	.0873	29
30	.014 2568	.171 0810	.0012	.0084	.0280	.0736	30
31	.014 2427	.170 9122	.0010	.0071	.0237	.0621	31
32	.014 2308	.170 7699	.0008	.0060	.0200	.0524	32
33	.014 2208	.170 6498	.0007	.0051	.0169	.0443	33
34	.014 2124	.170 5486	.0006	.0043	.0142	.0374	34
35	.014 2053	.170 4631	.0005	.0036	.0120	.0315	35
36	.014 1993	.170 3910	.0004	.0030	.0101	.0266	36
37	.014 1942	.170 3302	.0004	.0026	.0086	.0225	37
38	.014 1899	.170 2788	.0003	.0022	.0072	.0190	38
39	.014 1863	.170 2354	.0003	.0018	.0061	.0160	39
40	.014 1832	.170 1988	.0002	.0016	.0052	.0135	40

(Monthly Payment and Annual Constant per $1 of Loan)

	Base:	1.014 375			Part Paid Off Projection			
Months	Payment	Annual Constant	1 Year	5 Years	10 Years	15 Years	Months

Months	Payment	Annual Constant	1 Year	5 Years	10 Years	15 Years	Months
1	1.014 3750	—	—	—	—	—	1
2	.510 8069	—	—	—	—	—	2
3	.342 9623	—	—	—	—	—	3
4	.259 0485	—	—	—	—	—	4
5	.208 7071	—	—	—	—	—	5
6	.175 1518	—	—	—	—	—	6
7	.151 1886	—	—	—	—	—	7
8	.133 2206	—	—	—	—	—	8
9	.119 2492	—	—	—	—	—	9
10	.108 0755	—	—	—	—	—	10
11	.098 9364	—	—	—	—	—	11

Years	Payment	Annual Constant	1 Year	5 Years	10 Years	15 Years	Years
1	.091 3234	1.095 8812	1.0000	—	—	—	1
2	.049 5625	.594 7497	.4573	—	—	—	2
3	.035 7773	.429 3273	.2781	—	—	—	3
4	.028 9845	.347 8146	.1899	—	—	—	4
5	.024 9872	.299 8464	.1379	1.0000	—	—	5
6	.022 3859	.268 6303	.1041	.7549	—	—	6
7	.020 5805	.246 9665	.0806	.5848	—	—	7
8	.019 2710	.231 2526	.0636	.4614	—	—	8
9	.018 2905	.219 4855	.0509	.3690	—	—	9
10	.017 5385	.210 4620	.0411	.2981	1.0000	—	10
11	.016 9513	.203 4156	.0335	.2428	.8144	—	11
12	.016 4862	.197 8345	.0274	.1989	.6674	—	12
13	.016 1137	.193 3643	.0226	.1638	.5496	—	13
14	.015 8126	.189 7517	.0187	.1355	.4544	—	14
15	.015 5676	.186 8108	.0155	.1124	.3770	1.0000	15
16	.015 3669	.184 4028	.0129	.0935	.3135	.8317	16
17	.015 2018	.182 4214	.0107	.0779	.2614	.6933	17
18	.015 0654	.180 7847	.0090	.0651	.2182	.5789	18
19	.014 9524	.179 4283	.0075	.0544	.1825	.4841	19
20	.014 8584	.178 3010	.0063	.0456	.1528	.4054	20
21	.014 7802	.177 3622	.0053	.0382	.1281	.3398	21
22	.014 7149	.176 5787	.0044	.0320	.1074	.2850	22
23	.014 6603	.175 9240	.0037	.0269	.0902	.2393	23
24	.014 6147	.175 3760	.0031	.0226	.0758	.2010	24
25	.014 5764	.174 9170	.0026	.0190	.0637	.1689	25
26	.014 5443	.174 5320	.0022	.0160	.0535	.1420	26
27	.014 5174	.174 2090	.0019	.0134	.0450	.1194	27
28	.014 4948	.173 9378	.0016	.0113	.0379	.1005	28
29	.014 4758	.173 7099	.0013	.0095	.0319	.0845	29
30	.014 4599	.173 5183	.0011	.0080	.0268	.0712	30
31	.014 4464	.173 3572	.0009	.0067	.0226	.0599	31
32	.014 4351	.173 2217	.0008	.0057	.0190	.0504	32
33	.014 4256	.173 1077	.0007	.0048	.0160	.0425	33
34	.014 4176	.173 0118	.0006	.0040	.0135	.0358	34
35	.014 4109	.172 9310	.0005	.0034	.0114	.0301	35
36	.014 4053	.172 8630	.0004	.0029	.0096	.0254	36
37	.014 4005	.172 8058	.0003	.0024	.0081	.0214	37
38	.014 3965	.172 7576	.0003	.0020	.0068	.0180	38
39	.014 3931	.172 7170	.0002	.0017	.0057	.0152	39
40	.014 3902	.172 6828	.0002	.0014	.0048	.0128	40

17½% DIRECT REDUCTION LOAN FACTORS
(Monthly Payment and Annual Constant per $1 of Loan)

Base: 1.014 583

Months	Payment	Annual Constant	Part Paid Off Projection				Months
			1 Year	5 Years	10 Years	15 Years	
1	1.014 5833	—	—	—	—	—	1
2	.510 9639	—	—	—	—	—	2
3	.343 1025	—	—	—	—	—	3
4	.259 1806	—	—	—	—	—	4
5	.208 8344	—	—	—	—	—	5
6	.175 2762	—	—	—	—	—	6
7	.151 3111	—	—	—	—	—	7
8	.133 3417	—	—	—	—	—	8
9	.119 3693	—	—	—	—	—	9
10	.108 1950	—	—	—	—	—	10
11	.099 0555	—	—	—	—	—	11

Years							Years
1	.091 4422	1.097 3065	1.0000	—	—	—	1
2	.049 6828	.596 1942	.4567	—	—	—	2
3	.035 9021	.430 8248	.2774	—	—	—	3
4	.029 1144	.349 3725	.1891	—	—	—	4
5	.025 1222	.301 4666	.1371	1.0000	—	—	5
6	.022 5260	.270 3126	.1033	.7537	—	—	6
7	.020 7258	.248 7095	.0799	.5828	—	—	7
8	.019 4212	.233 0545	.0629	.4591	—	—	8
9	.018 4453	.221 3440	.0502	.3665	—	—	9
10	.017 6979	.212 3745	.0405	.2955	1.0000	—	10
11	.017 1149	.205 3792	.0329	.2402	.8128	—	11
12	.016 6539	.199 8464	.0269	.1965	.6648	—	12
13	.016 2851	.195 4215	.0221	.1615	.5464	—	13
14	.015 9876	.191 8510	.0183	.1332	.4509	—	14
15	.015 7458	.188 9494	.0151	.1103	.3732	1.0000	15
16	.015 5481	.186 5775	.0126	.0915	.3098	.8300	16
17	.015 3858	.184 6295	.0104	.0761	.2576	.6903	17
18	.015 2519	.183 0234	.0087	.0634	.2147	.5752	18
19	.015 1412	.181 6949	.0073	.0529	.1791	.4799	19
20	.015 0494	.180 5930	.0061	.0442	.1496	.4010	20
21	.014 9731	.179 6772	.0051	.0370	.1251	.3353	21
22	.014 9095	.178 9146	.0042	.0310	.1047	.2806	22
23	.014 8565	.178 2786	.0036	.0259	.0877	.2350	23
24	.014 8123	.177 7475	.0030	.0217	.0735	.1970	24
25	.014 7753	.177 3036	.0025	.0182	.0616	.1651	25
26	.014 7443	.176 9321	.0021	.0153	.0517	.1385	26
27	.014 7184	.176 6211	.0018	.0128	.0434	.1162	27
28	.014 6967	.176 3606	.0015	.0108	.0364	.0975	28
29	.014 6785	.176 1422	.0012	.0090	.0306	.0819	29
30	.014 6633	.175 9590	.0010	.0076	.0257	.0688	30
31	.014 6504	.175 8054	.0009	.0064	.0215	.0577	31
32	.014 6397	.175 6764	.0007	.0053	.0181	.0485	32
33	.014 6307	.175 5682	.0006	.0045	.0152	.0407	33
34	.014 6231	.175 4773	.0005	.0038	.0128	.0342	34
35	.014 6168	.175 4010	.0004	.0032	.0107	.0287	35
36	.014 6114	.175 3370	.0004	.0027	.0090	.0242	36
37	.014 6069	.175 2831	.0003	.0022	.0076	.0203	37
38	.014 6032	.175 2379	.0003	.0019	.0064	.0171	38
39	.014 6000	.175 1999	.0002	.0016	.0053	.0143	39
40	.014 5973	.175 1680	.0002	.0013	.0045	.0120	40

DIRECT REDUCTION LOAN FACTORS 17¾%
(Monthly Payment and Annual Constant per $1 of Loan)

Months	Payment	Annual Constant	Part Paid Off Projection 1 Year	5 Years	10 Years	15 Years	Months
1	1.014 7917	—	—	—	—	—	1
2	.511 1209	—	—	—	—	—	2
3	.343 2427	—	—	—	—	—	3
4	.259 3127	—	—	—	—	—	4
5	.208 9619	—	—	—	—	—	5
6	.175 4007	—	—	—	—	—	6
7	.151 4336	—	—	—	—	—	7
8	.133 4628	—	—	—	—	—	8
9	.119 4895	—	—	—	—	—	9
10	.108 3145	—	—	—	—	—	10
11	.099 1746	—	—	—	—	—	11

Years	Payment	Annual Constant	1 Year	5 Years	10 Years	15 Years	Years
1	.091 5611	1.098 7327	1.0000	—	—	—	1
2	.049 8034	.597 6407	.4561	—	—	—	2
3	.036 0271	.432 3253	.2766	—	—	—	3
4	.029 2445	.350 9343	.1883	—	—	—	4
5	.025 2576	.303 0915	.1363	1.0000	—	—	5
6	.022 6667	.272 0003	.1026	.7524	—	—	6
7	.020 8716	.250 4587	.0792	.5809	—	—	7
8	.019 5719	.234 8632	.0623	.4567	—	—	8
9	.018 6008	.223 2097	.0496	.3640	—	—	9
10	.017 8579	.214 2946	.0399	.2930	1.0000	—	10
11	.017 2792	.207 3508	.0324	.2377	.8113	—	11
12	.016 8222	.201 8664	.0264	.1940	.6622	—	12
13	.016 4572	.197 4868	.0217	.1591	.5432	—	13
14	.016 1632	.193 9585	.0179	.1310	.4473	—	14
15	.015 9247	.191 0960	.0148	.1083	.3695	1.0000	15
16	.015 7300	.188 7602	.0122	.0897	.3060	.8282	16
17	.015 5704	.186 8454	.0101	.0744	.2540	.6874	17
18	.015 4391	.185 2695	.0084	.0619	.2112	.5715	18
19	.015 3307	.183 9686	.0070	.0515	.1758	.4758	19
20	.015 2410	.182 8919	.0059	.0429	.1465	.3966	20
21	.015 1666	.181 9987	.0049	.0358	.1223	.3309	21
22	.015 1047	.181 2566	.0041	.0299	.1021	.2763	22
23	.015 0532	.180 6390	.0034	.0250	.0853	.2309	23
24	.015 0104	.180 1244	.0028	.0209	.0713	.1930	24
25	.014 9746	.179 6952	.0024	.0175	.0597	.1615	25
26	.014 9447	.179 3369	.0020	.0146	.0499	.1351	26
27	.014 9198	.179 0376	.0017	.0122	.0418	.1131	27
28	.014 8989	.178 7874	.0014	.0103	.0350	.0947	28
29	.014 8815	.178 5781	.0012	.0086	.0293	.0793	29
30	.014 8669	.178 4031	.0010	.0072	.0245	.0664	30
31	.014 8547	.178 2566	.0008	.0060	.0206	.0556	31
32	.014 8445	.178 1339	.0007	.0050	.0172	.0466	32
33	.014 8359	.178 0312	.0006	.0042	.0144	.0391	33
34	.014 8288	.177 9452	.0005	.0035	.0121	.0327	34
35	.014 8228	.177 8731	.0004	.0030	.0101	.0274	35
36	.014 8177	.177 8127	.0003	.0025	.0085	.0230	36
37	.014 8135	.177 7621	.0003	.0021	.0071	.0193	37
38	.014 8100	.177 7197	.0002	.0017	.0060	.0162	38
39	.014 8070	.177 6842	.0002	.0015	.0050	.0135	39
40	.014 8045	.177 6544	.0002	.0012	.0042	.0114	40

Base: 1.014 792

18% DIRECT REDUCTION LOAN FACTORS
(Monthly Payment and Annual Constant per $1 of Loan)

Base: 1.015 000

Months	Payment	Annual Constant	Part Paid Off Projection 1 Year	5 Years	10 Years	15 Years	Months
1	1.015 0000	—	—	—	—	—	1
2	.511 2779	—	—	—	—	—	2
3	.343 3830	—	—	—	—	—	3
4	.259 4448	—	—	—	—	—	4
5	.209 0893	—	—	—	—	—	5
6	.175 5252	—	—	—	—	—	6
7	.151 5562	—	—	—	—	—	7
8	.133 5840	—	—	—	—	—	8
9	.119 6098	—	—	—	—	—	9
10	.108 4342	—	—	—	—	—	10
11	.099 2938	—	—	—	—	—	11

Years	Payment	Annual Constant	1 Year	5 Years	10 Years	15 Years	Years
1	.091 6800	1.100 1599	1.0000	—	—	—	1
2	.049 9241	.599 0892	.4555	—	—	—	2
3	.036 1524	.433 8287	.2759	—	—	—	3
4	.029 3750	.352 5000	.1875	—	—	—	4
5	.025 3934	.304 7211	.1355	1.0000	—	—	5
6	.022 8078	.273 6935	.1018	.7512	—	—	6
7	.021 0178	.252 2141	.0785	.5790	—	—	7
8	.019 7232	.236 6786	.0616	.4544	—	—	8
9	.018 7569	.225 0827	.0490	.3615	—	—	9
10	.018 0185	.216 2222	.0394	.2904	1.0000	—	10
11	.017 4442	.209 3301	.0319	.2352	.8097	—	11
12	.016 9912	.203 8943	.0260	.1916	.6597	—	12
13	.016 6300	.199 5601	.0213	.1568	.5400	—	13
14	.016 3395	.196 0740	.0175	.1289	.4438	—	14
15	.016 1042	.193 2505	.0144	.1062	.3658	1.0000	15
16	.015 9126	.190 9507	.0119	.0878	.3023	.8264	16
17	.015 7557	.189 0687	.0099	.0727	.2504	.6844	17
18	.015 6269	.187 5230	.0082	.0603	.2077	.5677	18
19	.015 5208	.186 2494	.0068	.0501	.1725	.4716	19
20	.015 4331	.185 1974	.0056	.0417	.1435	.3922	20
21	.015 3605	.184 3266	.0047	.0347	.1194	.3265	21
22	.015 3004	.183 6045	.0039	.0289	.0995	.2720	22
23	.015 2504	.183 0049	.0033	.0241	.0830	.2268	23
24	.015 2089	.182 5064	.0027	.0201	.0692	.1892	24
25	.015 1743	.182 0916	.0023	.0168	.0577	.1578	25
26	.015 1455	.181 7461	.0019	.0140	.0482	.1318	26
27	.015 1215	.181 4581	.0016	.0117	.0403	.1100	27
28	.015 1015	.181 2179	.0013	.0098	.0336	.0919	28
29	.015 0848	.181 0175	.0011	.0082	.0281	.0768	29
30	.015 0709	.180 8502	.0009	.0068	.0235	.0642	30
31	.015 0592	.180 7106	.0008	.0057	.0196	.0536	31
32	.015 0495	.180 5939	.0006	.0048	.0164	.0448	32
33	.015 0414	.180 4965	.0005	.0040	.0137	.0375	33
34	.015 0346	.180 4151	.0005	.0033	.0115	.0313	34
35	.015 0289	.180 3470	.0004	.0028	.0096	.0262	35
36	.015 0242	.180 2902	.0003	.0023	.0080	.0219	36
37	.015 0202	.180 2426	.0003	.0019	.0067	.0183	37
38	.015 0169	.180 2029	.0002	.0016	.0056	.0153	38
39	.015 0141	.180 1697	.0002	.0014	.0047	.0128	39
40	.015 0118	.180 1419	.0002	.0011	.0039	.0107	40

(Monthly Payment and Annual Constant per $1 of Loan)

Base: 1.015 208

Months	Payment	Annual Constant	Part Paid Off Projection 1 Year	5 Years	10 Years	15 Years	Months
1	1.015 2083	—	—	—	—	—	1
2	.511 4349	—	—	—	—	—	2
3	.343 5232	—	—	—	—	—	3
4	.259 5769	—	—	—	—	—	4
5	.209 2168	—	—	—	—	—	5
6	.175 6498	—	—	—	—	—	6
7	.151 6788	—	—	—	—	—	7
8	.133 7053	—	—	—	—	—	8
9	.119 7302	—	—	—	—	—	9
10	.108 5539	—	—	—	—	—	10
11	.099 4131	—	—	—	—	—	11

Years	Payment	Annual Constant	1 Year	5 Years	10 Years	15 Years	Years
1	.091 7990	1.101 5882	1.0000	—	—	—	1
2	.050 0450	.600 5398	.4548	—	—	—	2
3	.036 2779	.435 3352	.2751	—	—	—	3
4	.029 5058	.354 0696	.1867	—	—	—	4
5	.025 5296	.306 3555	.1348	1.0000	—	—	5
6	.022 9493	.275 3922	.1011	.7500	—	—	6
7	.021 1646	.253 9755	.0778	.5771	—	—	7
8	.019 8751	.238 5006	.0609	.4521	—	—	8
9	.018 9136	.226 9627	.0484	.3590	—	—	9
10	.018 1798	.218 1573	.0388	.2879	1.0000	—	10
11	.017 6098	.211 3172	.0314	.2327	.8082	—	11
12	.017 1608	.205 9301	.0255	.1892	.6571	—	12
13	.016 8034	.201 6413	.0208	.1545	.5368	—	13
14	.016 5165	.198 1974	.0171	.1267	.4402	—	14
15	.016 2844	.195 4128	.0140	.1043	.3621	1.0000	15
16	.016 0957	.193 1487	.0116	.0860	.2986	.8247	16
17	.015 9416	.191 2995	.0096	.0710	.2468	.6815	17
18	.015 8153	.189 7835	.0079	.0588	.2043	.5641	18
19	.015 7114	.188 5369	.0066	.0487	.1693	.4675	19
20	.015 6258	.187 5093	.0055	.0404	.1405	.3879	20
21	.015 5550	.186 6605	.0045	.0336	.1167	.3222	21
22	.015 4965	.185 9582	.0038	.0279	.0970	.2678	22
23	.015 4480	.185 3762	.0031	.0232	.0807	.2227	23
24	.015 4078	.184 8935	.0026	.0193	.0671	.1854	24
25	.015 3744	.184 4926	.0022	.0161	.0559	.1543	25
26	.015 3466	.184 1595	.0018	.0134	.0465	.1285	26
27	.015 3235	.183 8825	.0015	.0112	.0388	.1071	27
28	.015 3043	.183 6520	.0013	.0093	.0323	.0892	28
29	.015 2883	.183 4602	.0010	.0078	.0269	.0744	29
30	.015 2750	.183 3004	.0009	.0065	.0224	.0620	30
31	.015 2639	.183 1673	.0007	.0054	.0187	.0517	31
32	.015 2547	.183 0564	.0006	.0045	.0156	.0431	32
33	.015 2470	.182 9640	.0005	.0037	.0130	.0359	33
34	.015 2406	.182 8870	.0004	.0031	.0109	.0300	34
35	.015 2352	.182 8227	.0004	.0026	.0091	.0250	35
36	.015 2308	.182 7692	.0003	.0022	.0075	.0208	36
37	.015 2270	.182 7245	.0002	.0018	.0063	.0174	37
38	.015 2239	.182 6873	.0002	.0015	.0053	.0145	38
39	.015 2214	.182 6562	.0002	.0013	.0044	.0121	39
40	.015 2192	.182 6303	.0001	.0011	.0037	.0101	40

18½%   DIRECT REDUCTION LOAN FACTORS
(Monthly Payment and Annual Constant per $1 of Loan)

Base: 1.015 417

Months	Payment	Annual Constant	1 Year	5 Years	10 Years	15 Years	Months
				Part Paid Off Projection			
1	1.015 4167	—	—	—	—	—	1
2	.511 5920	—	—	—	—	—	2
3	.343 6635	—	—	—	—	—	3
4	.259 7091	—	—	—	—	—	4
5	.209 3443	—	—	—	—	—	5
6	.175 7744	—	—	—	—	—	6
7	.151 8014	—	—	—	—	—	7
8	.133 8266	—	—	—	—	—	8
9	.119 8506	—	—	—	—	—	9
10	.108 6737	—	—	—	—	—	10
11	.099 5325	—	—	—	—	—	11

Years	Payment	Annual Constant	1 Year	5 Years	10 Years	15 Years	Years
1	.091 9181	1.103 0174	1.0000	—	—	—	1
2	.050 1660	.601 9923	.4542	—	—	—	2
3	.036 4037	.436 8446	.2743	—	—	—	3
4	.029 6369	.355 6430	.1859	—	—	—	4
5	.025 6662	.307 9945	.1340	1.0000	—	—	5
6	.023 0914	.277 0963	.1003	.7488	—	—	6
7	.021 3119	.255 7430	.0771	.5752	—	—	7
8	.020 0274	.240 3293	.0603	.4499	—	—	8
9	.019 0708	.228 8498	.0478	.3565	—	—	9
10	.018 3417	.220 0998	.0382	.2854	1.0000	—	10
11	.017 7760	.213 3119	.0308	.2302	.8066	—	11
12	.017 3311	.207 9737	.0250	.1868	.6545	—	12
13	.016 9775	.203 7304	.0204	.1523	.5336	—	13
14	.016 6941	.200 3286	.0167	.1246	.4367	—	14
15	.016 4652	.197 5828	.0137	.1023	.3585	1.0000	15
16	.016 2795	.195 3543	.0113	.0842	.2950	.8229	16
17	.016 1281	.193 5375	.0093	.0694	.2432	.6785	17
18	.016 0042	.192 0510	.0077	.0573	.2009	.5604	18
19	.015 9026	.190 8311	.0064	.0474	.1661	.4634	19
20	.015 8190	.189 8276	.0053	.0393	.1375	.3837	20
21	.015 7500	.189 0004	.0044	.0325	.1140	.3179	21
22	.015 6931	.188 3174	.0036	.0270	.0945	.2636	22
23	.015 6461	.187 7527	.0030	.0224	.0784	.2188	23
24	.015 6071	.187 2853	.0025	.0186	.0651	.1816	24
25	.015 5748	.186 8981	.0021	.0154	.0541	.1508	25
26	.015 5481	.186 5770	.0017	.0128	.0449	.1253	26
27	.015 5259	.186 3107	.0014	.0107	.0373	.1042	27
28	.015 5075	.186 0895	.0012	.0089	.0310	.0866	28
29	.015 4922	.185 9059	.0010	.0074	.0258	.0720	29
30	.015 4794	.185 7533	.0008	.0061	.0215	.0599	30
31	.015 4689	.185 6266	.0007	.0051	.0179	.0498	31
32	.015 4601	.185 5212	.0006	.0042	.0148	.0414	32
33	.015 4528	.185 4336	.0005	.0035	.0124	.0345	33
34	.015 4467	.185 3607	.0004	.0029	.0103	.0287	34
35	.015 4417	.185 3001	.0003	.0024	.0086	.0239	35
36	.015 4375	.185 2497	.0003	.0020	.0071	.0198	36
37	.015 4340	.185 2078	.0002	.0017	.0059	.0165	37
38	.015 4311	.185 1729	.0002	.0014	.0049	.0137	38
39	.015 4287	.185 1439	.0002	.0012	.0041	.0114	39
40	.015 4266	.185 1197	.0001	.0010	.0034	.0095	40

DIRECT REDUCTION LOAN FACTORS 18¾%
(Monthly Payment and Annual Constant per $1 of Loan)

Base: 1.015 625

Months	Payment	Annual Constant	Part Paid Off Projection 1 Year	5 Years	10 Years	15 Years	Months
1	1.015 6250	—	—	—	—	—	1
2	.511 7490	—	—	—	—	—	2
3	.343 8038	—	—	—	—	—	3
4	.259 8413	—	—	—	—	—	4
5	.209 4719	—	—	—	—	—	5
6	.175 8990	—	—	—	—	—	6
7	.151 9241	—	—	—	—	—	7
8	.133 9480	—	—	—	—	—	8
9	.119 9711	—	—	—	—	—	9
10	.108 7935	—	—	—	—	—	10
11	.099 6519	—	—	—	—	—	11

Years	Payment	Annual Constant	1 Year	5 Years	10 Years	15 Years	Years
1	.092 0373	1.104 4477	1.0000	—	—	—	1
2	.050 2872	.603 4469	.4536	—	—	—	2
3	.036 5297	.438 3569	.2736	—	—	—	3
4	.029 7684	.357 2203	.1851	—	—	—	4
5	.025 8032	.309 6382	.1332	1.0000	—	—	5
6	.023 2338	.278 8058	.0996	.7476	—	—	6
7	.021 4597	.257 5166	.0764	.5733	—	—	7
8	.020 1804	.242 1646	.0596	.4476	—	—	8
9	.019 2287	.230 7439	.0472	.3541	—	—	9
10	.018 5041	.222 0497	.0377	.2829	1.0000	—	10
11	.017 9428	.215 3142	.0303	.2277	.8050	—	11
12	.017 5021	.210 0249	.0246	.1844	.6520	—	12
13	.017 1523	.205 8272	.0200	.1501	.5305	—	13
14	.016 8723	.202 4674	.0163	.1225	.4332	—	14
15	.016 6467	.199 7603	.0134	.1004	.3549	1.0000	15
16	.016 4639	.197 5671	.0110	.0824	.2914	.8211	16
17	.016 3152	.195 7825	.0090	.0678	.2397	.6756	17
18	.016 1938	.194 3253	.0074	.0559	.1975	.5567	18
19	.016 0943	.193 1317	.0061	.0461	.1630	.4593	19
20	.016 0127	.192 1519	.0051	.0381	.1346	.3794	20
21	.015 9455	.191 3460	.0042	.0315	.1113	.3137	21
22	.015 8902	.190 6820	.0035	.0261	.0921	.2595	22
23	.015 8445	.190 1342	.0029	.0216	.0762	.2149	23
24	.015 8068	.189 6818	.0024	.0179	.0631	.1780	24
25	.015 7757	.189 3078	.0020	.0148	.0523	.1475	25
26	.015 7499	.188 9985	.0016	.0123	.0434	.1222	26
27	.015 7285	.188 7424	.0014	.0102	.0360	.1013	27
28	.015 7109	.188 5303	.0011	.0084	.0298	.0840	28
29	.015 6962	.188 3546	.0009	.0070	.0247	.0697	29
30	.015 6841	.188 2090	.0008	.0058	.0205	.0578	30
31	.015 6740	.188 0882	.0006	.0048	.0170	.0480	31
32	.015 6657	.187 9881	.0005	.0040	.0141	.0398	32
33	.015 6588	.187 9051	.0004	.0033	.0117	.0330	33
34	.015 6530	.187 8362	.0004	.0028	.0097	.0274	34
35	.015 6483	.187 7790	.0003	.0023	.0081	.0228	35
36	.015 6443	.187 7316	.0003	.0019	.0067	.0189	36
37	.015 6410	.187 6922	.0002	.0016	.0056	.0157	37
38	.015 6383	.187 6596	.0002	.0013	.0046	.0130	38
39	.015 6360	.187 6325	.0001	.0011	.0038	.0108	39
40	.015 6342	.187 6100	.0001	.0009	.0032	.0090	40

19% DIRECT REDUCTION LOAN FACTORS
(Monthly Payment and Annual Constant per $1 of Loan)

Base: 1.015 833

Months	Payment	Annual Constant	Part Paid Off Projection				Months
			1 Year	5 Years	10 Years	15 Years	
1	1.015 8333	—	—	—	—	—	1
2	.511 9061	—	—	—	—	—	2
3	.343 9442	—	—	—	—	—	3
4	.259 9736	—	—	—	—	—	4
5	.209 5995	—	—	—	—	—	5
6	.176 0237	—	—	—	—	—	6
7	.152 0469	—	—	—	—	—	7
8	.134 0694	—	—	—	—	—	8
9	.120 0916	—	—	—	—	—	9
10	.108 9135	—	—	—	—	—	10
11	.099 7715	—	—	—	—	—	11

Years	Payment	Annual Constant	1 Year	5 Years	10 Years	15 Years	Years
1	.092 1566	1.105 8789	1.0000	—	—	—	1
2	.050 4086	.604 9034	.4530	—	—	—	2
3	.036 6560	.439 8722	.2728	—	—	—	3
4	.029 9001	.358 8014	.1843	—	—	—	4
5	.025 9406	.311 2866	.1324	1.0000	—	—	5
6	.023 3767	.280 5207	.0988	.7463	—	—	6
7	.021 6080	.259 2962	.0757	.5713	—	—	7
8	.020 3339	.244 0064	.0590	.4453	—	—	8
9	.019 3871	.232 6450	.0466	.3516	—	—	9
10	.018 6672	.224 0068	.0371	.2804	1.0000	—	10
11	.018 1103	.217 3239	.0298	.2253	.8035	—	11
12	.017 6736	.212 0838	.0241	.1821	.6494	—	12
13	.017 3276	.207 9315	.0196	.1478	.5273	—	13
14	.017 0511	.204 6137	.0160	.1205	.4297	—	14
15	.016 8288	.201 9451	.0130	.0985	.3513	1.0000	15
16	.016 6489	.199 7871	.0107	.0807	.2878	.8193	16
17	.016 5029	.198 0345	.0088	.0662	.2363	.6726	17
18	.016 3838	.196 6061	.0072	.0545	.1943	.5530	18
19	.016 2866	.195 4386	.0059	.0448	.1599	.4553	19
20	.016 2068	.194 4822	.0049	.0370	.1318	.3752	20
21	.016 1414	.193 6971	.0040	.0305	.1087	.3095	21
22	.016 0876	.193 0517	.0033	.0252	.0897	.2555	22
23	.016 0434	.192 5204	.0028	.0208	.0741	.2110	23
24	.016 0069	.192 0827	.0023	.0172	.0612	.1744	24
25	.015 9768	.191 7216	.0019	.0142	.0506	.1441	25
26	.015 9520	.191 4236	.0016	.0117	.0419	.1192	26
27	.015 9315	.191 1775	.0013	.0097	.0346	.0986	27
28	.015 9145	.190 9742	.0011	.0080	.0286	.0816	28
29	.015 9005	.190 8061	.0009	.0066	.0237	.0675	29
30	.015 8889	.190 6671	.0007	.0055	.0196	.0558	30
31	.015 8793	.190 5522	.0006	.0046	.0162	.0462	31
32	.015 8714	.190 4571	.0005	.0038	.0134	.0383	32
33	.015 8649	.190 3784	.0004	.0031	.0111	.0317	33
34	.015 8594	.190 3133	.0003	.0026	.0092	.0262	34
35	.015 8549	.190 2594	.0003	.0021	.0076	.0217	35
36	.015 8512	.190 2148	.0002	.0018	.0063	.0180	36
37	.015 8482	.190 1778	.0002	.0015	.0052	.0149	37
38	.015 8456	.190 1472	.0002	.0012	.0043	.0123	38
39	.015 8435	.190 1219	.0001	.0010	.0036	.0102	39
40	.015 8417	.190 1010	.0001	.0008	.0030	.0085	40

DIRECT REDUCTION LOAN FACTORS 19¼%
(Monthly Payment and Annual Constant per $1 of Loan)

Base: 1.016 042

Months	Payment	Annual Constant	Part Paid Off Projection				Months
			1 Year	5 Years	10 Years	15 Years	
1	1.016 0417	—	—	—	—	—	1
2	.512 0632	—	—	—	—	—	2
3	.344 0845	—	—	—	—	—	3
4	.260 1058	—	—	—	—	—	4
5	.209 7271	—	—	—	—	—	5
6	.176 1484	—	—	—	—	—	6
7	.152 1697	—	—	—	—	—	7
8	.134 1909	—	—	—	—	—	8
9	.120 2122	—	—	—	—	—	9
10	.109 0334	—	—	—	—	—	10
11	.099 8911	—	—	—	—	—	11

Years	Payment	Annual Constant	1 Year	5 Years	10 Years	15 Years	Years
1	.092 2759	1.107 3112	1.0000	—	—	—	1
2	.050 5302	.606 3620	.4524	—	—	—	2
3	.036 7825	.441 3905	.2721	—	—	—	3
4	.030 0322	.360 3864	.1835	—	—	—	4
5	.026 0783	.312 9397	.1317	1.0000	—	—	5
6	.023 5201	.282 2410	.0981	.7451	—	—	6
7	.021 7568	.261 0818	.0750	.5694	—	—	7
8	.020 4879	.245 8547	.0583	.4430	—	—	8
9	.019 5461	.234 5530	.0460	.3492	—	—	9
10	.018 8309	.225 9712	.0366	.2779	1.0000	—	10
11	.018 2784	.219 3411	.0293	.2229	.8019	—	11
12	.017 8458	.214 1501	.0237	.1798	.6468	—	12
13	.017 5036	.210 0433	.0192	.1457	.5241	—	13
14	.017 2306	.206 7675	.0156	.1185	.4263	—	14
15	.017 0114	.204 1372	.0127	.0966	.3477	1.0000	15
16	.016 8345	.202 0142	.0104	.0790	.2842	.8176	16
17	.016 6911	.200 2932	.0085	.0647	.2328	.6697	17
18	.016 5745	.198 8934	.0070	.0531	.1910	.5494	18
19	.016 4793	.197 7516	.0057	.0436	.1569	.4513	19
20	.016 4015	.196 8182	.0047	.0359	.1290	.3711	20
21	.016 3378	.196 0536	.0039	.0295	.1062	.3054	21
22	.016 2855	.195 4265	.0032	.0243	.0874	.2515	22
23	.016 2426	.194 9113	.0026	.0200	.0720	.2072	23
24	.016 2073	.194 4878	.0022	.0165	.0594	.1708	24
25	.016 1783	.194 1393	.0018	.0136	.0490	.1409	25
26	.016 1544	.193 8523	.0015	.0112	.0404	.1162	26
27	.016 1347	.193 6159	.0012	.0093	.0333	.0959	27
28	.016 1184	.193 4209	.0010	.0076	.0275	.0791	28
29	.016 1050	.193 2602	.0008	.0063	.0227	.0653	29
30	.016 0940	.193 1276	.0007	.0052	.0188	.0539	30
31	.016 0849	.193 0182	.0006	.0043	.0155	.0445	31
32	.016 0773	.192 9279	.0005	.0036	.0128	.0368	32
33	.016 0711	.192 8534	.0004	.0029	.0106	.0304	33
34	.016 0660	.192 7919	.0003	.0024	.0087	.0251	34
35	.016 0618	.192 7411	.0003	.0020	.0072	.0207	35
36	.016 0583	.192 6991	.0002	.0017	.0059	.0171	36
37	.016 0554	.192 6645	.0002	.0014	.0049	.0141	37
38	.016 0530	.192 6359	.0001	.0011	.0041	.0117	38
39	.016 0510	.192 6122	.0001	.0009	.0034	.0096	39
40	.016 0494	.192 5927	.0001	.0008	.0028	.0080	40

19½% DIRECT REDUCTION LOAN FACTORS
(Monthly Payment and Annual Constant per $1 of Loan)

Base: 1.016 250

Months	Payment	Annual Constant	Part Paid Off Projection 1 Year	5 Years	10 Years	15 Years	Months
1	1.016 2500	—	—	—	—	—	1
2	.512 2202	—	—	—	—	—	2
3	.344 2249	—	—	—	—	—	3
4	.260 2381	—	—	—	—	—	4
5	.209 8548	—	—	—	—	—	5
6	.176 2731	—	—	—	—	—	6
7	.152 2925	—	—	—	—	—	7
8	.134 3125	—	—	—	—	—	8
9	.120 3328	—	—	—	—	—	9
10	.109 1535	—	—	—	—	—	10
11	.100 0107	—	—	—	—	—	11

Years	Payment	Annual Constant	1 Year	5 Years	10 Years	15 Years	Years
1	.092 3954	1.108 7445	1.0000	—	—	—	1
2	.050 6519	.607 8225	.4518	—	—	—	2
3	.036 9093	.442 9117	.2713	—	—	—	3
4	.030 1646	.361 9752	.1827	—	—	—	4
5	.026 2164	.314 5973	.1309	1.0000	—	—	5
6	.023 6639	.283 9666	.0974	.7439	—	—	6
7	.021 9061	.262 8734	.0743	.5675	—	—	7
8	.020 6425	.247 7095	.0577	.4407	—	—	8
9	.019 7057	.236 4679	.0454	.3467	—	—	9
10	.018 9952	.227 9427	.0361	.2754	1.0000	—	10
11	.018 4471	.221 3655	.0289	.2205	.8003	—	11
12	.018 0186	.216 2238	.0232	.1775	.6443	—	12
13	.017 6802	.212 1625	.0188	.1435	.5210	—	13
14	.017 4107	.208 9285	.0152	.1165	.4228	—	14
15	.017 1947	.206 3364	.0124	.0948	.3441	1.0000	15
16	.017 0207	.204 2481	.0101	.0773	.2807	.8158	16
17	.016 8799	.202 5585	.0083	.0632	.2294	.6667	17
18	.016 7656	.201 1870	.0068	.0517	.1878	.5458	18
19	.016 6725	.200 0706	.0055	.0424	.1539	.4473	19
20	.016 5966	.199 1598	.0046	.0348	.1263	.3669	20
21	.016 5346	.198 4153	.0037	.0286	.1037	.3013	21
22	.016 4838	.197 8060	.0031	.0235	.0852	.2475	22
23	.016 4422	.197 3067	.0025	.0193	.0700	.2035	23
24	.016 4081	.196 8970	.0021	.0159	.0576	.1673	24
25	.016 3801	.196 5607	.0017	.0130	.0474	.1377	25
26	.016 3570	.196 2844	.0014	.0107	.0390	.1133	26
27	.016 3381	.196 0573	.0012	.0088	.0321	.0933	27
28	.016 3225	.195 8705	.0010	.0073	.0264	.0768	28
29	.016 3097	.195 7169	.0008	.0060	.0218	.0632	29
30	.016 2992	.195 5904	.0006	.0049	.0179	.0521	30
31	.016 2905	.195 4863	.0005	.0041	.0148	.0429	31
32	.016 2834	.195 4006	.0004	.0033	.0122	.0353	32
33	.016 2775	.195 3300	.0004	.0028	.0100	.0291	33
34	.016 2727	.195 2719	.0003	.0023	.0083	.0240	34
35	.016 2687	.195 2240	.0002	.0019	.0068	.0198	35
36	.016 2654	.195 1846	.0002	.0015	.0056	.0163	36
37	.016 2627	.195 1521	.0002	.0013	.0046	.0134	37
38	.016 2604	.195 1253	.0001	.0010	.0038	.0111	38
39	.016 2586	.195 1033	.0001	.0009	.0031	.0091	39
40	.016 2571	.195 0851	.0001	.0007	.0026	.0075	40

DIRECT REDUCTION LOAN FACTORS 19¾%

(Monthly Payment and Annual Constant per $1 of Loan)

Base: 1.016 458

Months	Payment	Annual Constant	Part Paid Off Projection				Months
			1 Year	5 Years	10 Years	15 Years	
1	1.016 4583	—	—	—	—	—	1
2	.512 3773	—	—	—	—	—	2
3	.344 3653	—	—	—	—	—	3
4	.260 3704	—	—	—	—	—	4
5	.209 9825	—	—	—	—	—	5
6	.176 3979	—	—	—	—	—	6
7	.152 4154	—	—	—	—	—	7
8	.134 4341	—	—	—	—	—	8
9	.120 4536	—	—	—	—	—	9
10	.109 2736	—	—	—	—	—	10
11	.100 1305	—	—	—	—	—	11

Years	Payment	Annual Constant	1 Year	5 Years	10 Years	15 Years	Years
1	.092 5149	1.110 1788	1.0000	—	—	—	1
2	.050 7738	.609 2851	.4512	—	—	—	2
3	.037 0363	.444 4359	.2706	—	—	—	3
4	.030 2973	.363 5679	.1820	—	—	—	4
5	.026 3550	.316 2597	.1301	1.0000	—	—	5
6	.023 8081	.285 6976	.0966	.7427	—	—	6
7	.022 0559	.264 6710	.0736	.5656	—	—	7
8	.020 7976	.249 5708	.0571	.4385	—	—	8
9	.019 8658	.238 3896	.0448	.3443	—	—	9
10	.019 1601	.229 9212	.0355	.2730	1.0000	—	10
11	.018 6164	.223 3972	.0284	.2181	.7988	—	11
12	.018 1921	.218 3048	.0228	.1752	.6417	—	12
13	.017 8574	.214 2890	.0184	.1414	.5178	—	13
14	.017 5914	.211 0966	.0149	.1145	.4194	—	14
15	.017 3785	.208 5426	.0121	.0930	.3406	1.0000	15
16	.017 2074	.206 4887	.0098	.0757	.2772	.8140	16
17	.017 0692	.204 8303	.0080	.0617	.2261	.6638	17
18	.016 9572	.203 4867	.0066	.0504	.1847	.5421	18
19	.016 8663	.202 3953	.0054	.0412	.1510	.4433	19
20	.016 7922	.201 5067	.0044	.0337	.1236	.3628	20
21	.016 7318	.200 7821	.0036	.0276	.1012	.2972	21
22	.016 6825	.200 1903	.0029	.0227	.0830	.2436	22
23	.016 6422	.199 7063	.0024	.0186	.0681	.1998	23
24	.016 6092	.199 3102	.0020	.0152	.0558	.1639	24
25	.016 5821	.198 9858	.0016	.0125	.0458	.1345	25
26	.016 5600	.198 7198	.0013	.0103	.0376	.1105	26
27	.016 5418	.198 5017	.0011	.0084	.0309	.0907	27
28	.016 5269	.198 3228	.0009	.0069	.0254	.0745	28
29	.016 5147	.198 1759	.0007	.0057	.0208	.0612	29
30	.016 5046	.198 0553	.0006	.0047	.0171	.0503	30
31	.016 4964	.197 9563	.0005	.0038	.0141	.0413	31
32	.016 4896	.197 8750	.0004	.0032	.0116	.0340	32
33	.016 4840	.197 8082	.0003	.0026	.0095	.0279	33
34	.016 4794	.197 7533	.0003	.0021	.0078	.0229	34
35	.016 4757	.197 7082	.0002	.0018	.0064	.0189	35
36	.016 4726	.197 6711	.0002	.0014	.0053	.0155	36
37	.016 4701	.197 6406	.0002	.0012	.0043	.0127	37
38	.016 4680	.197 6156	.0001	.0010	.0036	.0105	38
39	.016 4663	.197 5950	.0001	.0008	.0029	.0086	39
40	.016 4648	.197 5781	.0001	.0007	.0024	.0071	40

20% DIRECT REDUCTION LOAN FACTORS
(Monthly Payment and Annual Constant per $1 of Loan)

Base: 1.016 667

Months	Payment	Annual Constant	1 Year	5 Years	10 Years	15 Years	Months
				Part Paid Off Projection			
1	1.016 6667	—	—	—	—	—	1
2	.512 5344	—	—	—	—	—	2
3	.344 5057	—	—	—	—	—	3
4	.260 5028	—	—	—	—	—	4
5	.210 1102	—	—	—	—	—	5
6	.176 5228	—	—	—	—	—	6
7	.152 5383	—	—	—	—	—	7
8	.134 5557	—	—	—	—	—	8
9	.120 5744	—	—	—	—	—	9
10	.109 3938	—	—	—	—	—	10
11	.100 2503	—	—	—	—	—	11

Years	Payment	Annual Constant	1 Year	5 Years	10 Years	15 Years	Years
1	.092 6345	1.111 6141	1.0000	—	—	—	1
2	.050 8958	.610 7496	.4506	—	—	—	2
3	.037 1636	.445 9630	.2698	—	—	—	3
4	.030 4304	.365 1643	.1812	—	—	—	4
5	.026 4939	.317 9266	.1294	1.0000	—	—	5
6	.023 9528	.287 4339	.0959	.7414	—	—	6
7	.022 2062	.266 4744	.0729	.5637	—	—	7
8	.020 9532	.251 4384	.0564	.4362	—	—	8
9	.020 0265	.240 3180	.0442	.3419	—	—	9
10	.019 3256	.231 9068	.0350	.2706	1.0000	—	10
11	.018 7863	.225 4361	.0279	.2157	.7972	—	11
12	.018 3661	.220 3930	.0224	.1729	.6391	—	12
13	.018 0352	.216 4227	.0180	.1393	.5147	—	13
14	.017 7727	.213 2718	.0146	.1125	.4160	—	14
15	.017 5630	.210 7556	.0118	.0912	.3371	1.0000	15
16	.017 3947	.208 7359	.0096	.0741	.2738	.8122	16
17	.017 2590	.207 1083	.0078	.0603	.2228	.6609	17
18	.017 1494	.205 7924	.0064	.0491	.1815	.5385	18
19	.017 0605	.204 7256	.0052	.0401	.1481	.4394	19
20	.016 9882	.203 8590	.0042	.0327	.1209	.3588	20
21	.016 9295	.203 1537	.0035	.0267	.0988	.2932	21
22	.016 8816	.202 5790	.0028	.0219	.0808	.2398	22
23	.016 8425	.202 1101	.0023	.0179	.0661	.1962	23
24	.016 8106	.201 7272	.0019	.0146	.0541	.1606	24
25	.016 7845	.201 4142	.0016	.0120	.0443	.1315	25
26	.016 7632	.201 1583	.0013	.0098	.0363	.1077	26
27	.016 7457	.200 9489	.0010	.0080	.0297	.0882	27
28	.016 7315	.200 7775	.0009	.0066	.0244	.0723	28
29	.016 7198	.200 6372	.0007	.0054	.0200	.0592	29
30	.016 7102	.200 5222	.0006	.0044	.0164	.0486	30
31	.016 7023	.200 4281	.0005	.0036	.0134	.0398	31
32	.016 6959	.200 3509	.0004	.0030	.0110	.0326	32
33	.016 6906	.200 2877	.0003	.0024	.0090	.0267	33
34	.016 6863	.200 2359	.0003	.0020	.0074	.0219	34
35	.016 6828	.200 1934	.0002	.0016	.0061	.0180	35
36	.016 6799	.200 1586	.0002	.0013	.0050	.0147	36
37	.016 6775	.200 1300	.0001	.0011	.0041	.0121	37
38	.016 6756	.200 1066	.0001	.0009	.0033	.0099	38
39	.016 6740	.200 0874	.0001	.0007	.0027	.0081	39
40	.016 6726	.200 0717	.0001	.0006	.0022	.0067	40

DIRECT REDUCTION LOAN FACTORS 20¼%

(Monthly Payment and Annual Constant per $1 of Loan)

Base: 1.016 875

Months	Payment	Annual Constant	1 Year	5 Years	10 Years	15 Years	Months
				Part Paid Off Projection			
1	1.016 8750	—	—	—	—	—	1
2	.512 6915	—	—	—	—	—	2
3	.344 6461	—	—	—	—	—	3
4	.260 6351	—	—	—	—	—	4
5	.210 2379	—	—	—	—	—	5
6	.176 6477	—	—	—	—	—	6
7	.152 6613	—	—	—	—	—	7
8	.134 6774	—	—	—	—	—	8
9	.120 6952	—	—	—	—	—	9
10	.109 5141	—	—	—	—	—	10
11	.100 3702	—	—	—	—	—	11

Years	Payment	Annual Constant	1 Year	5 Years	10 Years	15 Years	Years
1	.092 7542	1.113 0504	1.0000	—	—	—	1
2	.051 0180	.612 2162	.4500	—	—	—	2
3	.037 2911	.447 4931	.2691	—	—	—	3
4	.030 5637	.366 7646	.1804	—	—	—	4
5	.026 6332	.319 5982	.1286	1.0000	—	—	5
6	.024 0980	.289 1755	.0952	.7402	—	—	6
7	.022 3570	.268 2837	.0722	.5618	—	—	7
8	.021 1094	.253 3124	.0558	.4339	—	—	8
9	.020 1878	.242 2532	.0437	.3395	—	—	9
10	.019 4916	.233 8993	.0345	.2681	1.0000	—	10
11	.018 9568	.227 4820	.0274	.2133	.7956	—	11
12	.018 5407	.222 4884	.0220	.1707	.6366	—	12
13	.018 2136	.218 5634	.0176	.1372	.5116	—	13
14	.017 9545	.215 4540	.0142	.1106	.4126	—	14
15	.017 7479	.212 9753	.0115	.0895	.3336	1.0000	15
16	.017 5825	.210 9896	.0093	.0725	.2704	.8104	16
17	.017 4494	.209 3925	.0076	.0589	.2195	.6580	17
18	.017 3420	.208 1038	.0062	.0479	.1785	.5350	18
19	.017 2551	.207 0613	.0050	.0390	.1453	.4354	19
20	.017 1847	.206 2163	.0041	.0317	.1184	.3548	20
21	.017 1275	.205 5300	.0033	.0259	.0965	.2893	21
22	.017 0810	.204 9720	.0027	.0211	.0787	.2360	22
23	.017 0432	.204 5178	.0022	.0172	.0643	.1926	23
24	.017 0123	.204 1477	.0018	.0141	.0525	.1573	24
25	.016 9872	.203 8460	.0015	.0115	.0429	.1285	25
26	.016 9666	.203 5998	.0012	.0094	.0350	.1050	26
27	.016 9499	.203 3988	.0010	.0077	.0286	.0858	27
28	.016 9362	.203 2347	.0008	.0063	.0234	.0701	28
29	.016 9251	.203 1006	.0007	.0051	.0191	.0573	29
30	.016 9159	.202 9911	.0005	.0042	.0156	.0469	30
31	.016 9085	.202 9016	.0004	.0034	.0128	.0383	31
32	.016 9024	.202 8284	.0004	.0028	.0105	.0313	32
33	.016 8974	.202 7686	.0003	.0023	.0086	.0256	33
34	.016 8933	.202 7196	.0002	.0019	.0070	.0210	34
35	.016 8900	.202 6797	.0002	.0015	.0057	.0171	35
36	.016 8872	.202 6469	.0002	.0013	.0047	.0140	36
37	.016 8850	.202 6202	.0001	.0010	.0038	.0115	37
38	.016 8832	.202 5983	.0001	.0008	.0031	.0094	38
39	.016 8817	.202 5804	.0001	.0007	.0026	.0077	39
40	.016 8805	.202 5658	.0001	.0006	.0021	.0063	40

20½% DIRECT REDUCTION LOAN FACTORS
(Monthly Payment and Annual Constant per $1 of Loan)

Base: 1.017 083

Months	Payment	Annual Constant	1 Year	5 Years	10 Years	15 Years	Months
				Part Paid Off Projection			
1	1.017 0833	—	—	—	—	—	1
2	.512 8487	—	—	—	—	—	2
3	.344 7865	—	—	—	—	—	3
4	.260 7675	—	—	—	—	—	4
5	.210 3657	—	—	—	—	—	5
6	.176 7726	—	—	—	—	—	6
7	.152 7844	—	—	—	—	—	7
8	.134 7992	—	—	—	—	—	8
9	.120 8161	—	—	—	—	—	9
10	.109 6345	—	—	—	—	—	10
11	.100 4902	—	—	—	—	—	11

Years							Years
1	.092 8740	1.114 4877	1.0000	—	—	—	1
2	.051 1404	.613 6847	.4494	—	—	—	2
3	.037 4188	.449 0260	.2683	—	—	—	3
4	.030 6974	.368 3687	.1796	—	—	—	4
5	.026 7729	.321 2743	.1278	1.0000	—	—	5
6	.024 2435	.290 9224	.0945	.7390	—	—	6
7	.022 5082	.270 0989	.0716	.5599	—	—	7
8	.021 2661	.255 1927	.0552	.4317	—	—	8
9	.020 3496	.244 1950	.0431	.3371	—	—	9
10	.019 6582	.235 8988	.0340	.2657	1.0000	—	10
11	.019 1279	.229 5350	.0270	.2110	.7940	—	11
12	.018 7159	.224 5907	.0215	.1685	.6340	—	12
13	.018 3926	.220 7110	.0173	.1351	.5085	—	13
14	.018 1369	.217 6429	.0139	.1087	.4092	—	14
15	.017 9335	.215 2016	.0112	.0877	.3302	1.0000	15
16	.017 7708	.213 2496	.0091	.0709	.2670	.8087	16
17	.017 6402	.211 6827	.0073	.0575	.2163	.6551	17
18	.017 5351	.210 4210	.0060	.0466	.1754	.5314	18
19	.017 4502	.209 4024	.0048	.0379	.1425	.4315	19
20	.017 3815	.208 5785	.0039	.0308	.1158	.3508	20
21	.017 3259	.207 9109	.0032	.0250	.0942	.2853	21
22	.017 2808	.207 3693	.0026	.0204	.0767	.2322	22
23	.017 2441	.206 9294	.0021	.0166	.0624	.1891	23
24	.017 2143	.206 5718	.0017	.0135	.0509	.1541	24
25	.017 1901	.206 2808	.0014	.0110	.0415	.1256	25
26	.017 1703	.206 0440	.0011	.0090	.0338	.1023	26
27	.017 1543	.205 8512	.0009	.0073	.0275	.0834	27
28	.017 1412	.205 6941	.0008	.0060	.0225	.0680	28
29	.017 1305	.205 5661	.0006	.0049	.0183	.0555	29
30	.017 1218	.205 4617	.0005	.0040	.0149	.0453	30
31	.017 1147	.205 3766	.0004	.0032	.0122	.0369	31
32	.017 1089	.205 3073	.0003	.0026	.0099	.0301	32
33	.017 1042	.205 2507	.0003	.0022	.0081	.0246	33
34	.017 1004	.205 2045	.0002	.0018	.0066	.0200	34
35	.017 0972	.205 1669	.0002	.0014	.0054	.0164	35
36	.017 0947	.205 1362	.0001	.0012	.0044	.0133	36
37	.017 0926	.205 1111	.0001	.0010	.0036	.0109	37
38	.017 0909	.205 0906	.0001	.0008	.0029	.0089	38
39	.017 0895	.205 0740	.0001	.0006	.0024	.0073	39
40	.017 0884	.205 0604	.0001	.0005	.0020	.0059	40

DIRECT REDUCTION LOAN FACTORS 20¾%

(Monthly Payment and Annual Constant per $1 of Loan)

Base: 1.017 292

Months	Payment	Annual Constant	Part Paid Off Projection 1 Year	5 Years	10 Years	15 Years	Months
1	1.017 2917	—	—	—	—	—	1
2	.513 0058	—	—	—	—	—	2
3	.344 9270	—	—	—	—	—	3
4	.260 8999	—	—	—	—	—	4
5	.210 4936	—	—	—	—	—	5
6	.176 8976	—	—	—	—	—	6
7	.152 9075	—	—	—	—	—	7
8	.134 9210	—	—	—	—	—	8
9	.120 9371	—	—	—	—	—	9
10	.109 7549	—	—	—	—	—	10
11	.100 6102	—	—	—	—	—	11

Years	Payment	Annual Constant	1 Year	5 Years	10 Years	15 Years	Years
1	.092 9938	1.115 9260	1.0000	—	—	—	1
2	.051 2629	.615 1553	.4487	—	—	—	2
3	.037 5468	.450 5620	.2676	—	—	—	3
4	.030 8314	.369 9766	.1789	—	—	—	4
5	.026 9129	.322 9550	.1271	1.0000	—	—	5
6	.024 3895	.292 6746	.0938	.7377	—	—	6
7	.022 6600	.271 9199	.0709	.5580	—	—	7
8	.021 4233	.257 0793	.0546	.4294	—	—	8
9	.020 5120	.246 1434	.0425	.3347	—	—	9
10	.019 8254	.237 9050	.0335	.2633	1.0000	—	10
11	.019 2996	.231 5949	.0265	.2087	.7925	—	11
12	.018 8917	.226 7000	.0211	.1663	.6315	—	12
13	.018 5721	.222 8655	.0169	.1331	.5054	—	13
14	.018 3199	.219 8385	.0136	.1069	.4058	—	14
15	.018 1195	.217 4344	.0109	.0860	.3267	1.0000	15
16	.017 9596	.215 5158	.0088	.0694	.2636	.8069	16
17	.017 8316	.213 9788	.0071	.0561	.2131	.6522	17
18	.017 7286	.212 7436	.0058	.0454	.1725	.5278	18
19	.017 6457	.211 7486	.0047	.0368	.1397	.4277	19
20	.017 5788	.210 9455	.0038	.0298	.1133	.3468	20
21	.017 5247	.210 2962	.0031	.0242	.0920	.2815	21
22	.017 4809	.209 7706	.0025	.0197	.0747	.2286	22
23	.017 4454	.209 3446	.0020	.0160	.0607	.1857	23
24	.017 4166	.208 9991	.0017	.0130	.0493	.1509	24
25	.017 3932	.208 7188	.0013	.0106	.0401	.1227	25
26	.017 3743	.208 4910	.0011	.0086	.0326	.0998	26
27	.017 3588	.208 3061	.0009	.0070	.0265	.0811	27
28	.017 3463	.208 1557	.0007	.0057	.0216	.0660	28
29	.017 3361	.208 0335	.0006	.0046	.0175	.0537	29
30	.017 3278	.207 9341	.0005	.0038	.0143	.0437	30
31	.017 3211	.207 8532	.0004	.0031	.0116	.0356	31
32	.017 3156	.207 7874	.0003	.0025	.0095	.0289	32
33	.017 3112	.207 7339	.0003	.0020	.0077	.0235	33
34	.017 3075	.207 6904	.0002	.0016	.0063	.0192	34
35	.017 3046	.207 6550	.0002	.0013	.0051	.0156	35
36	.017 3022	.207 6261	.0001	.0011	.0041	.0127	36
37	.017 3002	.207 6027	.0001	.0009	.0034	.0103	37
38	.017 2986	.207 5836	.0001	.0007	.0027	.0084	38
39	.017 2973	.207 5680	.0001	.0006	.0022	.0068	39
40	.017 2963	.207 5554	.0001	.0005	.0018	.0056	40

21% DIRECT REDUCTION LOAN FACTORS
(Monthly Payment and Annual Constant per $1 of Loan)

Base: 1.017 500

Months	Payment	Annual Constant	Part Paid Off Projection 1 Year	5 Years	10 Years	15 Years	Months
1	1.017 5000	—	—	—	—	—	1
2	.513 1629	—	—	—	—	—	2
3	.345 0675	—	—	—	—	—	3
4	.261 0324	—	—	—	—	—	4
5	.210 6214	—	—	—	—	—	5
6	.177 0226	—	—	—	—	—	6
7	.153 0306	—	—	—	—	—	7
8	.135 0429	—	—	—	—	—	8
9	.121 0581	—	—	—	—	—	9
10	.109 8753	—	—	—	—	—	10
11	.100 7304	—	—	—	—	—	11

Years	Payment	Annual Constant	1 Year	5 Years	10 Years	15 Years	Years
1	.093 1138	1.117 3653	1.0000	—	—	—	1
2	.051 3857	.616 6278	.4481	—	—	—	2
3	.037 6751	.452 1008	.2668	—	—	—	3
4	.030 9657	.371 5883	.1781	—	—	—	4
5	.027 0534	.324 6403	.1263	1.0000	—	—	5
6	.024 5360	.294 4320	.0931	.7365	—	—	6
7	.022 8122	.273 7467	.0703	.5561	—	—	7
8	.021 5810	.258 9721	.0540	.4272	—	—	8
9	.020 6749	.248 0984	.0420	.3323	—	—	9
10	.019 9932	.239 9180	.0330	.2610	1.0000	—	10
11	.019 4718	.233 6616	.0261	.2064	.7909	—	11
12	.019 0680	.228 8161	.0207	.1641	.6289	—	12
13	.018 7522	.225 0267	.0166	.1311	.5023	—	13
14	.018 5034	.222 0407	.0133	.1050	.4025	—	14
15	.018 3061	.219 6735	.0107	.0844	.3233	1.0000	15
16	.018 1490	.217 7880	.0086	.0679	.2603	.8051	16
17	.018 0234	.216 2805	.0069	.0548	.2099	.6493	17
18	.017 9226	.215 0716	.0056	.0442	.1695	.5243	18
19	.017 8417	.214 0999	.0045	.0358	.1370	.4238	19
20	.017 7764	.213 3172	.0037	.0289	.1109	.3429	20
21	.017 7238	.212 6857	.0030	.0234	.0898	.2776	21
22	.017 6813	.212 1758	.0024	.0190	.0727	.2249	22
23	.017 6470	.211 7634	.0019	.0154	.0589	.1823	23
24	.017 6191	.211 4297	.0016	.0125	.0478	.1478	24
25	.017 5966	.211 1595	.0013	.0101	.0388	.1199	25
26	.017 5784	.210 9406	.0010	.0082	.0314	.0972	26
27	.017 5636	.210 7632	.0008	.0067	.0255	.0789	27
28	.017 5516	.210 6193	.0007	.0054	.0207	.0640	28
29	.017 5419	.210 5027	.0006	.0044	.0168	.0520	29
30	.017 5340	.210 4080	.0004	.0036	.0136	.0422	30
31	.017 5276	.210 3312	.0004	.0029	.0111	.0342	31
32	.017 5224	.210 2689	.0003	.0023	.0090	.0278	32
33	.017 5182	.210 2183	.0002	.0019	.0073	.0226	33
34	.017 5148	.210 1772	.0002	.0015	.0059	.0183	34
35	.017 5120	.210 1439	.0002	.0013	.0048	.0149	35
36	.017 5097	.210 1168	.0001	.0010	.0039	.0121	36
37	.017 5079	.210 0949	.0001	.0008	.0032	.0098	37
38	.017 5064	.210 0770	.0001	.0007	.0026	.0080	38
39	.017 5052	.210 0626	.0001	.0005	.0021	.0065	39
40	.017 5042	.210 0508	.0001	.0004	.0017	.0053	40

DIRECT REDUCTION LOAN FACTORS   21¼%
(Monthly Payment and Annual Constant per $1 of Loan)

Base:	1.017 708	Annual	Part Paid Off Projection				
Months	Payment	Constant	1 Year	5 Years	10 Years	15 Years	Months
1	1.017 7083	—	—	—	—	—	1
2	.513 3201	—	—	—	—	—	2
3	.345 2080	—	—	—	—	—	3
4	.261 1648	—	—	—	—	—	4
5	.210 7493	—	—	—	—	—	5
6	.177 1476	—	—	—	—	—	6
7	.153 1538	—	—	—	—	—	7
8	.135 1649	—	—	—	—	—	8
9	.121 1792	—	—	—	—	—	9
10	.109 9959	—	—	—	—	—	10
11	.100 8506	—	—	—	—	—	11

Years							Years
1	.093 2338	1.118 8056	1.0000	—	—	—	1
2	.051 5085	.618 1023	.4475	—	—	—	2
3	.037 8035	.453 6426	.2661	—	—	—	3
4	.031 1003	.373 2038	.1773	—	—	—	4
5	.027 1942	.326 3302	.1256	1.0000	—	—	5
6	.024 6829	.296 1946	.0923	.7353	—	—	6
7	.022 9649	.275 5793	.0696	.5542	—	—	7
8	.021 7393	.260 8711	.0534	.4249	—	—	8
9	.020 8383	.250 0599	.0414	.3300	—	—	9
10	.020 1615	.241 9377	.0325	.2586	1.0000	—	10
11	.019 6446	.235 7351	.0256	.2041	.7893	—	11
12	.019 2449	.230 9390	.0203	.1620	.6264	—	12
13	.018 9329	.227 1946	.0162	.1291	.4992	—	13
14	.018 6874	.224 2493	.0130	.1032	.3991	—	14
15	.018 4932	.221 9188	.0104	.0827	.3200	1.0000	15
16	.018 3388	.220 0661	.0083	.0665	.2570	.8033	16
17	.018 2157	.218 5879	.0067	.0535	.2068	.6464	17
18	.018 1171	.217 4049	.0054	.0431	.1666	.5208	18
19	.018 0380	.216 4559	.0044	.0348	.1344	.4200	19
20	.017 9744	.215 6933	.0035	.0281	.1085	.3390	20
21	.017 9233	.215 0794	.0028	.0227	.0876	.2739	21
22	.017 8821	.214 5847	.0023	.0183	.0708	.2213	22
23	.017 8488	.214 1856	.0019	.0148	.0573	.1790	23
24	.017 8219	.213 8634	.0015	.0120	.0463	.1448	24
25	.017 8003	.213 6031	.0012	.0097	.0375	.1171	25
26	.017 7827	.213 3927	.0010	.0078	.0303	.0948	26
27	.017 7685	.213 2226	.0008	.0063	.0245	.0767	27
28	.017 7571	.213 0849	.0006	.0051	.0199	.0621	28
29	.017 7478	.212 9736	.0005	.0042	.0161	.0503	29
30	.017 7403	.212 8835	.0004	.0034	.0130	.0407	30
31	.017 7342	.212 8105	.0003	.0027	.0105	.0330	31
32	.017 7293	.212 7515	.0003	.0022	.0085	.0267	32
33	.017 7253	.212 7037	.0002	.0018	.0069	.0216	33
34	.017 7221	.212 6650	.0002	.0014	.0056	.0175	34
35	.017 7195	.212 6336	.0001	.0012	.0045	.0142	35
36	.017 7174	.212 6082	.0001	.0010	.0037	.0115	36
37	.017 7156	.212 5877	.0001	.0008	.0030	.0093	37
38	.017 7143	.212 5710	.0001	.0006	.0024	.0075	38
39	.017 7131	.212 5575	.0001	.0005	.0020	.0061	39
40	.017 7122	.212 5466	.0001	.0004	.0016	.0049	40

21½% DIRECT REDUCTION LOAN FACTORS
(Monthly Payment and Annual Constant per $1 of Loan)

Base: 1.017 917

Months	Payment	Annual Constant	Part Paid Off Projection 1 Year	5 Years	10 Years	15 Years	Months
1	1.017 9167	—	—	—	—	—	1
2	.513 4773	—	—	—	—	—	2
3	.345 3485	—	—	—	—	—	3
4	.261 2973	—	—	—	—	—	4
5	.210 8772	—	—	—	—	—	5
6	.177 2727	—	—	—	—	—	6
7	.153 2770	—	—	—	—	—	7
8	.135 2868	—	—	—	—	—	8
9	.121 3004	—	—	—	—	—	9
10	.110 1165	—	—	—	—	—	10
11	.100 9709	—	—	—	—	—	11

Years	Payment	Annual Constant	1 Year	5 Years	10 Years	15 Years	Years
1	.093 3539	1.120 2469	1.0000	—	—	—	1
2	.051 6316	.619 5789	.4469	—	—	—	2
3	.037 9323	.455 1873	.2653	—	—	—	3
4	.031 2353	.374 8231	.1766	—	—	—	4
5	.027 3354	.328 0246	.1249	1.0000	—	—	5
6	.024 8302	.297 9624	.0916	.7340	—	—	6
7	.023 1181	.277 4176	.0690	.5522	—	—	7
8	.021 8980	.262 7763	.0528	.4227	—	—	8
9	.021 0023	.252 0278	.0409	.3276	—	—	9
10	.020 3303	.243 9640	.0320	.2563	1.0000	—	10
11	.019 8179	.237 8153	.0252	.2019	.7877	—	11
12	.019 4224	.233 0685	.0200	.1599	.6238	—	12
13	.019 1141	.229 3690	.0159	.1271	.4961	—	13
14	.018 8720	.226 4643	.0127	.1014	.3958	—	14
15	.018 6808	.224 1702	.0101	.0811	.3166	1.0000	15
16	.018 5292	.222 3500	.0081	.0650	.2538	.8015	16
17	.018 4084	.220 9007	.0065	.0522	.2037	.6435	17
18	.018 3119	.219 7432	.0052	.0420	.1638	.5172	18
19	.018 2347	.218 8167	.0042	.0338	.1318	.4162	19
20	.018 1728	.218 0738	.0034	.0272	.1061	.3352	20
21	.018 1231	.217 4770	.0027	.0219	.0855	.2701	21
22	.018 0831	.216 9972	.0022	.0177	.0690	.2178	22
23	.018 0509	.216 6110	.0018	.0143	.0556	.1757	23
24	.018 0250	.216 3000	.0014	.0115	.0449	.1418	24
25	.018 0041	.216 0493	.0012	.0093	.0362	.1144	25
26	.017 9873	.215 8471	.0009	.0075	.0292	.0924	26
27	.017 9737	.215 6840	.0008	.0061	.0236	.0746	27
28	.017 9627	.215 5524	.0006	.0049	.0191	.0602	28
29	.017 9538	.215 4462	.0005	.0039	.0154	.0487	29
30	.017 9467	.215 3604	.0004	.0032	.0124	.0393	30
31	.017 9409	.215 2911	.0003	.0026	.0101	.0317	31
32	.017 9363	.215 2352	.0003	.0021	.0081	.0256	32
33	.017 9325	.215 1900	.0002	.0017	.0066	.0207	33
34	.017 9295	.215 1535	.0002	.0014	.0053	.0167	34
35	.017 9270	.215 1240	.0001	.0011	.0043	.0135	35
36	.017 9250	.215 1002	.0001	.0009	.0035	.0109	36
37	.017 9234	.215 0810	.0001	.0007	.0028	.0088	37
38	.017 9221	.215 0654	.0001	.0006	.0023	.0071	38
39	.017 9211	.215 0529	.0001	.0005	.0018	.0058	39
40	.017 9202	.215 0427	.0000	.0004	.0015	.0047	40

DIRECT REDUCTION LOAN FACTORS 21¾%
(Monthly Payment and Annual Constant per $1 of Loan)

| Base: | 1.018 125 | | Part Paid Off Projection | | | | |
Months	Payment	Annual Constant	1 Year	5 Years	10 Years	15 Years	Months
1	1.018 1250	—	—	—	—	—	1
2	.513 6344	—	—	—	—	—	2
3	.345 4890	—	—	—	—	—	3
4	.261 4299	—	—	—	—	—	4
5	.211 0052	—	—	—	—	—	5
6	.177 3978	—	—	—	—	—	6
7	.153 4003	—	—	—	—	—	7
8	.135 4089	—	—	—	—	—	8
9	.121 4216	—	—	—	—	—	9
10	.110 2372	—	—	—	—	—	10
11	.101 0912	—	—	—	—	—	11

Years							Years
1	.093 4741	1.121 6892	1.0000	—	—	—	1
2	.051 7548	.621 0574	.4463	—	—	—	2
3	.038 0612	.456 7349	.2646	—	—	—	3
4	.031 3705	.376 4461	.1758	—	—	—	4
5	.027 4770	.329 7235	.1241	1.0000	—	—	5
6	.024 9779	.299 7354	.0909	.7328	—	—	6
7	.023 2718	.279 2616	.0683	.5503	—	—	7
8	.022 0573	.264 6876	.0522	.4205	—	—	8
9	.021 1668	.254 0021	.0404	.3253	—	—	9
10	.020 4997	.245 9969	.0315	.2539	1.0000	—	10
11	.019 9918	.239 9021	.0248	.1996	.7861	—	11
12	.019 6004	.235 2046	.0196	.1578	.6213	—	12
13	.019 2958	.231 5499	.0155	.1252	.4930	—	13
14	.019 0571	.228 6854	.0124	.0997	.3925	—	14
15	.018 8690	.226 4275	.0099	.0796	.3133	1.0000	15
16	.018 7200	.224 6396	.0079	.0636	.2505	.7997	16
17	.018 6016	.223 2188	.0063	.0510	.2007	.6406	17
18	.018 5072	.222 0865	.0051	.0409	.1609	.5138	18
19	.018 4318	.221 1821	.0041	.0328	.1292	.4124	19
20	.018 3715	.220 4584	.0033	.0264	.1038	.3314	20
21	.018 3232	.219 8785	.0026	.0212	.0835	.2664	21
22	.018 2844	.219 4133	.0021	.0170	.0671	.2143	22
23	.018 2533	.219 0396	.0017	.0137	.0540	.1725	23
24	.018 2283	.218 7394	.0014	.0110	.0435	.1388	24
25	.018 2082	.218 4980	.0011	.0089	.0350	.1118	25
26	.018 1920	.218 3037	.0009	.0072	.0282	.0900	26
27	.018 1790	.218 1474	.0007	.0058	.0227	.0725	27
28	.018 1685	.218 0216	.0006	.0046	.0183	.0584	28
29	.018 1600	.217 9203	.0005	.0037	.0147	.0471	29
30	.018 1532	.217 8386	.0004	.0030	.0119	.0379	30
31	.018 1477	.217 7729	.0003	.0024	.0096	.0306	31
32	.018 1433	.217 7199	.0002	.0020	.0077	.0246	32
33	.018 1398	.217 6772	.0002	.0016	.0062	.0199	33
34	.018 1369	.217 6429	.0002	.0013	.0050	.0160	34
35	.018 1346	.217 6151	.0001	.0010	.0040	.0129	35
36	.018 1327	.217 5928	.0001	.0008	.0033	.0104	36
37	.018 1312	.217 5748	.0001	.0007	.0026	.0084	37
38	.018 1300	.217 5603	.0001	.0005	.0021	.0068	38
39	.018 1291	.217 5486	.0001	.0004	.0017	.0054	39
40	.018 1283	.217 5392	.0000	.0003	.0014	.0044	40

22% DIRECT REDUCTION LOAN FACTORS
(Monthly Payment and Annual Constant per $1 of Loan)

Base: 1.018 333

Months	Payment	Annual Constant	Part Paid Off Projection 1 Year	5 Years	10 Years	15 Years	Months
1	1.018 3333	—	—	—	—	—	1
2	.513 7916	—	—	—	—	—	2
3	.345 6296	—	—	—	—	—	3
4	.261 5624	—	—	—	—	—	4
5	.211 1332	—	—	—	—	—	5
6	.177 5230	—	—	—	—	—	6
7	.153 5236	—	—	—	—	—	7
8	.135 5310	—	—	—	—	—	8
9	.121 5429	—	—	—	—	—	9
10	.110 3580	—	—	—	—	—	10
11	.101 2117	—	—	—	—	—	11

Years							Years
1	.093 5944	1.123 1326	1.0000	—	—	—	1
2	.051 8782	.622 5379	.4457	—	—	—	2
3	.038 1905	.458 2854	.2638	—	—	—	3
4	.031 5061	.378 0729	.1750	—	—	—	4
5	.027 6189	.331 4269	.1234	1.0000	—	—	5
6	.025 1261	.301 5135	.0903	.7315	—	—	6
7	.023 4259	.281 1113	.0677	.5484	—	—	7
8	.022 2171	.266 6050	.0516	.4183	—	—	8
9	.021 3319	.255 9828	.0398	.3229	—	—	9
10	.020 6697	.248 0363	.0310	.2516	1.0000	—	10
11	.020 1663	.241 9954	.0244	.1974	.7845	—	11
12	.019 7789	.237 3472	.0192	.1557	.6187	—	12
13	.019 4781	.233 7371	.0152	.1233	.4900	—	13
14	.019 2427	.230 9128	.0121	.0979	.3892	—	14
15	.019 0576	.228 6907	.0096	.0780	.3100	1.0000	15
16	.018 9112	.226 9347	.0077	.0622	.2473	.7979	16
17	.018 7952	.225 5421	.0061	.0497	.1977	.6377	17
18	.018 7029	.224 4346	.0049	.0398	.1582	.5103	18
19	.018 6293	.223 5520	.0039	.0319	.1267	.4087	19
20	.018 5706	.222 8472	.0032	.0256	.1016	.3276	20
21	.018 5236	.222 2837	.0025	.0205	.0815	.2628	21
22	.018 4861	.221 8326	.0020	.0164	.0654	.2109	22
23	.018 4559	.221 4713	.0016	.0132	.0525	.1693	23
24	.018 4318	.221 1815	.0013	.0106	.0421	.1360	24
25	.018 4124	.220 9491	.0011	.0085	.0339	.1092	25
26	.018 3969	.220 7625	.0008	.0068	.0272	.0877	26
27	.018 3844	.220 6128	.0007	.0055	.0219	.0705	27
28	.018 3744	.220 4925	.0005	.0044	.0176	.0567	28
29	.018 3663	.220 3958	.0004	.0036	.0141	.0455	29
30	.018 3598	.220 3182	.0004	.0029	.0113	.0366	30
31	.018 3546	.220 2558	.0003	.0023	.0091	.0294	31
32	.018 3505	.220 2056	.0002	.0018	.0073	.0237	32
33	.018 3471	.220 1653	.0002	.0015	.0059	.0190	33
34	.018 3444	.220 1329	.0001	.0012	.0047	.0153	34
35	.018 3422	.220 1069	.0001	.0010	.0038	.0123	35
36	.018 3405	.220 0859	.0001	.0008	.0031	.0099	36
37	.018 3391	.220 0691	.0001	.0006	.0025	.0079	37
38	.018 3380	.220 0556	.0001	.0005	.0020	.0064	38
39	.018 3371	.220 0447	.0000	.0004	.0016	.0051	39
40	.018 3363	.220 0359	.0000	.0003	.0013	.0041	40

(Monthly Payment and Annual Constant per $1 of Loan)

Months	Payment	Annual Constant	Part Paid Off Projection 1 Year	5 Years	10 Years	15 Years	Months
Base:	1.018 542						
1	1.018 5417	—	—	—	—	—	1
2	.513 9488	—	—	—	—	—	2
3	.345 7701	—	—	—	—	—	3
4	.261 6950	—	—	—	—	—	4
5	.211 2612	—	—	—	—	—	5
6	.177 6482	—	—	—	—	—	6
7	.153 6470	—	—	—	—	—	7
8	.135 6532	—	—	—	—	—	8
9	.121 6643	—	—	—	—	—	9
10	.110 4788	—	—	—	—	—	10
11	.101 3322	—	—	—	—	—	11

Years	Payment	Annual Constant	1 Year	5 Years	10 Years	15 Years	Years
1	.093 7147	1.124 5769	1.0000	—	—	—	1
2	.052 0017	.624 0203	.4451	—	—	—	2
3	.038 3199	.459 8389	.2631	—	—	—	3
4	.031 6420	.379 7035	.1743	—	—	—	4
5	.027 7612	.333 1349	.1226	1.0000	—	—	5
6	.025 2747	.303 2968	.0896	.7303	—	—	6
7	.023 5806	.282 9667	.0670	.5465	—	—	7
8	.022 3774	.268 5283	.0510	.4160	—	—	8
9	.021 4975	.257 9698	.0393	.3206	—	—	9
10	.020 8402	.250 0820	.0306	.2493	1.0000	—	10
11	.020 3413	.244 0952	.0239	.1952	.7829	—	11
12	.019 9580	.239 4962	.0188	.1536	.6162	—	12
13	.019 6609	.235 9305	.0149	.1214	.4869	—	13
14	.019 4288	.233 1461	.0118	.0962	.3860	—	14
15	.019 2466	.230 9596	.0094	.0765	.3067	1.0000	15
16	.019 1029	.229 2352	.0075	.0609	.2442	.7962	16
17	.018 9892	.227 8705	.0060	.0485	.1947	.6348	17
18	.018 8990	.226 7874	.0048	.0388	.1554	.5068	18
19	.018 8272	.225 9261	.0038	.0310	.1242	.4050	19
20	.018 7700	.225 2399	.0030	.0248	.0993	.3239	20
21	.018 7244	.224 6925	.0024	.0198	.0795	.2592	21
22	.018 6879	.224 2553	.0019	.0159	.0636	.2075	22
23	.018 6588	.223 9058	.0016	.0127	.0510	.1662	23
24	.018 6355	.223 6262	.0012	.0102	.0408	.1331	24
25	.018 6169	.223 4025	.0010	.0082	.0327	.1067	25
26	.018 6019	.223 2234	.0008	.0065	.0262	.0855	26
27	.018 5900	.223 0799	.0006	.0052	.0210	.0685	27
28	.018 5804	.222 9649	.0005	.0042	.0169	.0550	28
29	.018 5727	.222 8728	.0004	.0034	.0135	.0441	29
30	.018 5666	.222 7989	.0003	.0027	.0108	.0353	30
31	.018 5616	.222 7397	.0003	.0022	.0087	.0283	31
32	.018 5577	.222 6922	.0002	.0017	.0070	.0227	32
33	.018 5545	.222 6542	.0002	.0014	.0056	.0182	33
34	.018 5520	.222 6237	.0001	.0011	.0045	.0146	34
35	.018 5499	.222 5992	.0001	.0009	.0036	.0117	35
36	.018 5483	.222 5796	.0001	.0007	.0029	.0094	36
37	.018 5470	.222 5638	.0001	.0006	.0023	.0075	37
38	.018 5459	.222 5512	.0001	.0005	.0019	.0060	38
39	.018 5451	.222 5411	.0000	.0004	.0015	.0049	39
40	.018 5444	.222 5329	.0000	.0003	.0012	.0039	40

22½% DIRECT REDUCTION LOAN FACTORS
(Monthly Payment and Annual Constant per $1 of Loan)

Base: 1.018 750

Months	Payment	Annual Constant	1 Year	5 Years	10 Years	15 Years	Months
				Part Paid Off Projection			
1	1.018 7500	—	—	—	—	—	1
2	.514 1060	—	—	—	—	—	2
3	.345 9107	—	—	—	—˅	—	3
4	.261 8276	—	—	—	—	—	4
5	.211 3893	—	—	—	—	—	5
6	.177 7734	—	—	—	—	—	6
7	.153 7704	—	—	—	—	—	7
8	.135 7754	—	—	—	—	—	8
9	.121 7857	—	—	—	—	—	9
10	.110 5997	—	—	—	—	—	10
11	.101 4528	—	—	—	—	—	11

Years							Years
1	.093 8352	1.126 0222	1.0000	—	—	—	1
2	.052 1254	.625 5048	.4445	—	—	—	2
3	.038 4496	.461 3952	.2624	—	—	—	3
4	.031 7782	.381 3378	.1735	—	—	—	4
5	.027 9039	.334 8473	.1219	1.0000	—	—	5
6	.025 4238	.305 0852	.0889	.7291	—	—	6
7	.023 7356	.284 8276	.0664	.5446	—	—	7
8	.022 5381	.270 4577	.0505	.4138	—	—	8
9	.021 6636	.259 9630	.0388	.3183	—	—	9
10	.021 0112	.252 1342	.0301	.2470	1.0000	—	10
11	.020 5168	.246 2014	.0235	.1930	.7814	—	11
12	.020 1376	.241 6514	.0185	.1516	.6137	—	12
13	.019 8442	.238 1300	.0146	.1195	.4839	—	13
14	.019 6154	.235 3853	.0115	.0945	.3827	—	14
15	.019 4362	.233 2342	.0091	.0750	.3035	1.0000	15
16	.019 2951	.231 5410	.0073	.0595	.2411	.7944	16
17	.019 1836	.230 2038	.0058	.0474	.1918	.6320	17
18	.019 0954	.229 1448	.0046	.0377	.1528	.5034	18
19	.019 0254	.228 3044	.0037	.0301	.1218	.4013	19
20	.018 9697	.227 6364	.0029	.0240	.0972	.3202	20
21	.018 9254	.227 1047	.0023	.0192	.0776	.2556	21
22	.018 8901	.226 6810	.0019	.0153	.0620	.2041	22
23	.018 8619	.226 3431	.0015	.0122	.0495	.1631	23
24	.018 8395	.226 0734	.0012	.0098	.0396	.1304	24
25	.018 8215	.225 8581	.0010	.0078	.0316	.1042	25
26	.018 8072	.225 6861	.0008	.0062	.0253	.0833	26
27	.018 7957	.225 5487	.0006	.0050	.0202	.0666	27
28	.018 7866	.225 4388	.0005	.0040	.0162	.0533	28
29	.018 7793	.225 3510	.0004	.0032	.0129	.0426	29
30	.018 7734	.225 2808	.0003	.0026	.0103	.0341	30
31	.018 7687	.225 2246	.0002	.0020	.0083	.0273	31
32	.018 7650	.225 1797	.0002	.0016	.0066	.0218	32
33	.018 7620	.225 1438	.0002	.0013	.0053	.0175	33
34	.018 7596	.225 1150	.0001	.0010	.0042	.0140	34
35	.018 7577	.225 0920	.0001	.0008	.0034	.0112	35
36	.018 7561	.225 0736	.0001	.0007	.0027	.0089	36
37	.018 7549	.225 0589	.0001	.0005	.0022	.0072	37
38	.018 7539	.225 0471	.0001	.0004	.0017	.0057	38
39	.018 7531	.225 0377	.0000	.0003	.0014	.0046	39
40	.018 7525	.225 0302	.0000	.0003	.0011	.0037	40

DIRECT REDUCTION LOAN FACTORS 22¾%

(Monthly Payment and Annual Constant per $1 of Loan)

Base: 1.018 958

Months	Payment	Annual Constant	1 Year	5 Years	10 Years	15 Years	Months
				Part Paid Off Projection			
1	1.018 9583	—	—	—	—	—	1
2	.514 2633	—	—	—	—	—	2
3	.346 0513	—	—	—	—	—	3
4	.261 9602	—	—	—	—	—	4
5	.211 5174	—	—	—	—	—	5
6	.177 8987	—	—	—	—	—	6
7	.153 8939	—	—	—	—	—	7
8	.135 8976	—	—	—	—	—	8
9	.121 9071	—	—	—	—	—	9
10	.110 7207	—	—	—	—	—	10
11	.101 5735	—	—	—	—	—	11

Years	Payment	Annual Constant	1 Year	5 Years	10 Years	15 Years	Years
1	.093 9557	1.127 4685	1.0000	—	—	—	1
2	.052 2493	.626 9912	.4439	—	—	—	2
3	.038 5795	.462 9545	.2616	—	—	—	3
4	.031 9147	.382 9759	.1728	—	—	—	4
5	.028 0470	.336 5643	.1212	1.0000	—	—	5
6	.025 5732	.306 8787	.0882	.7278	—	—	6
7	.023 8912	.286 6942	.0658	.5427	—	—	7
8	.022 6994	.272 3931	.0499	.4116	—	—	8
9	.021 8302	.261 9624	.0383	.3160	—	—	9
10	.021 1827	.254 1927	.0297	.2447	1.0000	—	10
11	.020 6928	.248 3139	.0231	.1908	.7798	—	11
12	.020 3177	.243 8129	.0181	.1496	.6111	—	12
13	.020 0280	.240 3356	.0143	.1177	.4809	—	13
14	.019 8025	.237 6303	.0113	.0929	.3795	—	14
15	.019 6262	.235 5142	.0089	.0735	.3002	1.0000	15
16	.019 4877	.233 8520	.0071	.0582	.2380	.7926	16
17	.019 3785	.232 5419	.0056	.0462	.1889	.6291	17
18	.019 2922	.231 5066	.0045	.0367	.1501	.4999	18
19	.019 2239	.230 6868	.0035	.0292	.1194	.3976	19
20	.019 1697	.230 0366	.0028	.0233	.0950	.3165	20
21	.019 1267	.229 5202	.0022	.0185	.0757	.2521	21
22	.019 0925	.229 1097	.0018	.0148	.0603	.2009	22
23	.019 0653	.228 7831	.0014	.0118	.0481	.1601	23
24	.019 0436	.228 5230	.0011	.0094	.0383	.1276	24
25	.019 0263	.228 3158	.0009	.0075	.0306	.1018	25
26	.019 0126	.228 1508	.0007	.0060	.0244	.0812	26
27	.019 0016	.228 0191	.0006	.0048	.0194	.0648	27
28	.018 9929	.227 9142	.0005	.0038	.0155	.0517	28
29	.018 9859	.227 8305	.0004	.0030	.0124	.0412	29
30	.018 9803	.227 7637	.0003	.0024	.0099	.0329	30
31	.018 9759	.227 7105	.0002	.0019	.0079	.0263	31
32	.018 9723	.227 6680	.0002	.0015	.0063	.0210	32
33	.018 9695	.227 6341	.0001	.0012	.0050	.0167	33
34	.018 9672	.227 6070	.0001	.0010	.0040	.0134	34
35	.018 9654	.227 5854	.0001	.0008	.0032	.0107	35
36	.018 9640	.227 5682	.0001	.0006	.0026	.0085	36
37	.018 9629	.227 5544	.0001	.0005	.0020	.0068	37
38	.018 9620	.227 5434	.0000	.0004	.0016	.0054	38
39	.018 9612	.227 5347	.0000	.0003	.0013	.0043	39
40	.018 9606	.227 5277	.0000	.0003	.0010	.0035	40

23% DIRECT REDUCTION LOAN FACTORS
(Monthly Payment and Annual Constant per $1 of Loan)

Base: 1.019 167

Months	Payment	Annual Constant	1 Year	Part Paid Off Projection 5 Years	10 Years	15 Years	Months
1	1.019 1667	—	—	—	—	—	1
2	.514 4205	—	—	—	—	—	2
3	.346 1920	—	—	—	—	—	3
4	.262 0929	—	—	—	—	—	4
5	.211 6455	—	—	—	—	—	5
6	.178 0241	—	—	—	—	—	6
7	.154 0174	—	—	—	—	—	7
8	.136 0200	—	—	—	—	—	8
9	.122 0287	—	—	—	—	—	9
10	.110 8417	—	—	—	—	—	10
11	.101 6942	—	—	—	—	—	11

Years	Payment	Annual Constant	1 Year	5 Years	10 Years	15 Years	Years
1	.094 0763	1.128 9159	1.0000	—	—	—	1
2	.052 3733	.628 4797	.4433	—	—	—	2
3	.038 7097	.464 5167	.2609	—	—	—	3
4	.032 0515	.384 6177	.1720	—	—	—	4
5	.028 1905	.338 2857	.1205	1.0000	—	—	5
6	.025 7231	.308 6773	.0875	.7266	—	—	6
7	.024 0472	.288 5663	.0652	.5409	—	—	7
8	.022 8612	.274 3343	.0493	.4094	—	—	8
9	.021 9973	.263 9679	.0378	.3137	—	—	9
10	.021 3548	.256 2574	.0292	.2425	1.0000	—	10
11	.020 8694	.250 4326	.0227	.1887	.7782	—	11
12	.020 4984	.245 9805	.0178	.1476	.6086	—	12
13	.020 2123	.242 5471	.0140	.1159	.4779	—	13
14	.019 9901	.239 8810	.0110	.0912	.3763	—	14
15	.019 8166	.237 7996	.0087	.0720	.2970	1.0000	15
16	.019 6807	.236 1679	.0069	.0570	.2349	.7908	16
17	.019 5737	.234 8846	.0054	.0451	.1860	.6263	17
18	.019 4894	.233 8727	.0043	.0358	.1475	.4965	18
19	.019 4228	.233 0732	.0034	.0284	.1170	.3940	19
20	.019 3700	.232 4404	.0027	.0225	.0929	.3129	20
21	.019 3283	.231 9390	.0022	.0179	.0738	.2486	21
22	.019 2951	.231 5413	.0017	.0142	.0587	.1976	22
23	.019 2688	.231 2256	.0014	.0113	.0467	.1571	23
24	.019 2479	.230 9749	.0011	.0090	.0371	.1250	24
25	.019 2313	.230 7756	.0009	.0072	.0295	.0994	25
26	.019 2181	.230 6171	.0007	.0057	.0235	.0791	26
27	.019 2076	.230 4911	.0005	.0045	.0187	.0630	27
28	.019 1992	.230 3909	.0004	.0036	.0149	.0501	28
29	.019 1926	.230 3112	.0003	.0029	.0119	.0399	29
30	.019 1873	.230 2477	.0003	.0023	.0094	.0318	30
31	.019 1831	.230 1972	.0002	.0018	.0075	.0253	31
32	.019 1797	.230 1570	.0002	.0014	.0060	.0201	32
33	.019 1771	.230 1250	.0001	.0012	.0048	.0160	33
34	.019 1750	.230 0995	.0001	.0009	.0038	.0128	34
35	.019 1733	.230 0792	.0001	.0007	.0030	.0102	35
36	.019 1719	.230 0631	.0001	.0006	.0024	.0081	36
37	.019 1709	.230 0502	.0001	.0005	.0019	.0064	37
38	.019 1700	.230 0400	.0000	.0004	.0015	.0051	38
39	.019 1693	.230 0318	.0000	.0003	.0012	.0041	39
40	.019 1688	.230 0254	.0000	.0002	.0010	.0033	40

DIRECT REDUCTION LOAN FACTORS $23\frac{1}{4}$%

(Monthly Payment and Annual Constant per $1 of Loan)

Base: 1.019 375

Months	Payment	Annual Constant	Part Paid Off Projection				Months
			1 Year	5 Years	10 Years	15 Years	
1	1.019 3750	—	—	—	—	—	1
2	.514 5777	—	—	—	—	—	2
3	.346 3326	—	—	—	—	—	3
4	.262 2256	—	—	—	—	—	4
5	.211 7737	—	—	—	—	—	5
6	.178 1494	—	—	—	—	—	6
7	.154 1410	—	—	—	—	—	7
8	.136 1423	—	—	—	—	—	8
9	.122 1503	—	—	—	—	—	9
10	.110 9628	—	—	—	—	—	10
11	.101 8150	—	—	—	—	—	11

Years	Payment	Annual Constant	1 Year	5 Years	10 Years	15 Years	Years
1	.094 1970	1.130 3642	1.0000	—	—	—	1
2	.052 4975	.629 9701	.4427	—	—	—	2
3	.038 8401	.466 0817	.2602	—	—	—	3
4	.032 1886	.386 2632	.1713	—	—	—	4
5	.028 3343	.340 0115	.1197	1.0000	—	—	5
6	.025 8734	.310 4809	.0869	.7253	—	—	6
7	.024 2037	.290 4440	.0645	.5390	—	—	7
8	.023 0235	.276 2814	.0488	.4072	—	—	8
9	.022 1650	.265 9795	.0373	.3114	—	—	9
10	.021 5274	.258 3282	.0288	.2402	1.0000	—	10
11	.021 0465	.252 5574	.0223	.1866	.7766	—	11
12	.020 6795	.248 1541	.0174	.1456	.6061	—	12
13	.020 3970	.244 7644	.0137	.1141	.4748	—	13
14	.020 1781	.242 1373	.0107	.0896	.3731	—	14
15	.020 0075	.240 0903	.0085	.0706	.2939	1.0000	15
16	.019 8741	.238 4889	.0067	.0557	.2319	.7890	16
17	.019 7693	.237 2320	.0053	.0440	.1832	.6234	17
18	.019 6869	.236 2430	.0042	.0348	.1449	.4931	18
19	.019 6219	.235 4633	.0033	.0276	.1147	.3904	19
20	.019 5706	.234 8476	.0026	.0218	.0909	.3093	20
21	.019 5301	.234 3609	.0021	.0173	.0720	.2452	21
22	.019 4980	.233 9757	.0016	.0137	.0571	.1944	22
23	.019 4726	.233 6706	.0013	.0109	.0453	.1542	23
24	.019 4524	.233 4289	.0010	.0086	.0360	.1224	24
25	.019 4364	.233 2372	.0008	.0069	.0285	.0971	25
26	.019 4238	.233 0852	.0007	.0054	.0227	.0771	26
27	.019 4137	.232 9646	.0005	.0043	.0180	.0612	27
28	.019 4057	.232 8689	.0004	.0034	.0143	.0486	28
29	.019 3994	.232 7929	.0003	.0027	.0113	.0386	29
30	.019 3944	.232 7326	.0003	.0022	.0090	.0306	30
31	.019 3904	.232 6847	.0002	.0017	.0072	.0243	31
32	.019 3872	.232 6467	.0002	.0014	.0057	.0193	32
33	.019 3847	.232 6165	.0001	.0011	.0045	.0154	33
34	.019 3827	.232 5925	.0001	.0009	.0036	.0122	34
35	.019 3811	.232 5735	.0001	.0007	.0028	.0097	35
36	.019 3799	.232 5584	.0001	.0005	.0023	.0077	36
37	.019 3789	.232 5464	.0001	.0004	.0018	.0061	37
38	.019 3781	.232 5368	.0000	.0003	.0014	.0049	38
39	.019 3774	.232 5293	.0000	.0003	.0011	.0039	39
40	.019 3769	.232 5232	.0000	.0002	.0009	.0031	40

23½% DIRECT REDUCTION LOAN FACTORS
(Monthly Payment and Annual Constant per $1 of Loan)

Base: 1.019 583

Months	Payment	Annual Constant	1 Year	5 Years	10 Years	15 Years	Months
				Part Paid Off Projection			
1	1.019 5833	—	—	—	—	—	1
2	.514 7350	—	—	—	—	—	2
3	.346 4733	—	—	—	—	—	3
4	.262 3583	—	—	—	—	—	4
5	.211 9019	—	—	—	—	—	5
6	.178 2749	—	—	—	—	—	6
7	.154 2646	—	—	—	—	—	7
8	.136 2648	—	—	—	—	—	8
9	.122 2719	—	—	—	—	—	9
10	.111 0840	—	—	—	—	—	10
11	.101 9359	—	—	—	—	—	11

Years	Payment	Annual Constant	1 Year	5 Years	10 Years	15 Years	Years
1	.094 3178	1.131 8135	1.0000	—	—	—	1
2	.052 6219	.631 4625	.4421	—	—	—	2
3	.038 9708	.467 6497	.2594	—	—	—	3
4	.032 3260	.387 9124	.1705	—	—	—	4
5	.028 4785	.341 7418	.1190	1.0000	—	—	5
6	.026 0241	.312 2896	.0862	.7241	—	—	6
7	.024 3606	.292 3271	.0639	.5371	—	—	7
8	.023 1862	.278 2343	.0482	.4050	—	—	8
9	.022 3331	.267 9971	.0368	.3091	—	—	9
10	.021 7004	.260 4052	.0283	.2380	1.0000	—	10
11	.021 2240	.254 6883	.0220	.1844	.7750	—	11
12	.020 8611	.250 3337	.0171	.1437	.6036	—	12
13	.020 5823	.246 9875	.0134	.1123	.4719	—	13
14	.020 3666	.244 3990	.0105	.0881	.3700	—	14
15	.020 1988	.242 3861	.0082	.0692	.2907	1.0000	15
16	.020 0679	.240 8146	.0065	.0545	.2289	.7872	16
17	.019 9653	.239 5837	.0051	.0429	.1804	.6206	17
18	.019 8848	.238 6174	.0040	.0339	.1424	.4898	18
19	.019 8214	.237 8572	.0032	.0268	.1125	.3868	19
20	.019 7715	.237 2582	.0025	.0212	.0889	.3057	20
21	.019 7321	.236 7858	.0020	.0167	.0703	.2418	21
22	.019 7011	.236 4128	.0016	.0132	.0556	.1913	22
23	.019 6765	.236 1180	.0012	.0105	.0440	.1514	23
24	.019 6571	.235 8850	.0010	.0083	.0348	.1198	24
25	.019 6417	.235 7007	.0008	.0066	.0276	.0949	25
26	.019 6296	.235 5549	.0006	.0052	.0218	.0751	26
27	.019 6200	.235 4395	.0005	.0041	.0173	.0595	27
28	.019 6123	.235 3481	.0004	.0033	.0137	.0471	28
29	.019 6063	.235 2757	.0003	.0026	.0109	.0373	29
30	.019 6015	.235 2184	.0002	.0020	.0086	.0296	30
31	.019 5978	.235 1730	.0002	.0016	.0068	.0234	31
32	.019 5948	.235 1371	.0002	.0013	.0054	.0186	32
33	.019 5924	.235 1086	.0001	.0010	.0043	.0147	33
34	.019 5905	.235 0861	.0001	.0008	.0034	.0117	34
35	.019 5890	.235 0682	.0001	.0006	.0027	.0092	35
36	.019 5878	.235 0540	.0001	.0005	.0021	.0073	36
37	.019 5869	.235 0428	.0000	.0004	.0017	.0058	37
38	.019 5862	.235 0339	.0000	.0003	.0013	.0046	38
39	.019 5856	.235 0269	.0000	.0003	.0011	.0036	39
40	.019 5851	.235 0213	.0000	.0002	.0008	.0029	40

(Monthly Payment and Annual Constant per $1 of Loan)

			Part Paid Off Projection				
Base:	1.019 792						
Months	Payment	Annual Constant	1 Year	5 Years	10 Years	15 Years	Months
1	1.019 7917	—	—	—	—	—	1
2	.514 8922	—	—	—	—	—	2
3	.346 6140	—	—	—	—	—	3
4	.262 4910	—	—	—	—	—	4
5	.212 0301	—	—	—	—	—	5
6	.178 4003	—	—	—	—	—	6
7	.154 3882	—	—	—	—	—	7
8	.136 3873	—	—	—	—	—	8
9	.122 3937	—	—	—	—	—	9
10	.111 2052	—	—	—	—	—	10
11	.102 0569	—	—	—	—	—	11

Years							Years
1	.094 4387	1.133 2638	1.0000	—	—	—	1
2	.052 7464	.632 9568	.4415	—	—	—	2
3	.039 1017	.469 2205	.2587	—	—	—	3
4	.032 4638	.389 5654	.1698	—	—	—	4
5	.028 6230	.343 4765	.1183	1.0000	—	—	5
6	.026 1753	.314 1033	.0855	.7228	—	—	6
7	.024 5180	.294 2157	.0633	.5352	—	—	7
8	.023 3494	.280 1931	.0477	.4029	—	—	8
9	.022 5017	.270 0207	.0363	.3069	—	—	9
10	.021 8740	.262 4882	.0279	.2358	1.0000	—	10
11	.021 4021	.256 8253	.0216	.1824	.7734	—	11
12	.021 0433	.252 5191	.0168	.1417	.6010	—	12
13	.020 7680	.249 2163	.0131	.1106	.4689	—	13
14	.020 5555	.246 6661	.0102	.0865	.3668	—	14
15	.020 3906	.244 6870	.0080	.0678	.2876	1.0000	15
16	.020 2621	.243 1450	.0063	.0533	.2259	.7854	16
17	.020 1617	.241 9399	.0050	.0419	.1777	.6178	17
18	.020 0830	.240 9957	.0039	.0330	.1399	.4864	18
19	.020 0212	.240 2546	.0031	.0260	.1102	.3833	19
20	.019 9727	.239 6720	.0024	.0205	.0869	.3022	20
21	.019 9345	.239 2136	.0019	.0162	.0686	.2384	21
22	.019 9044	.238 8524	.0015	.0128	.0541	.1882	22
23	.019 8806	.238 5677	.0012	.0101	.0427	.1486	23
24	.019 8619	.238 3431	.0009	.0080	.0337	.1173	24
25	.019 8472	.238 1660	.0007	.0063	.0267	.0927	25
26	.019 8355	.238 0261	.0006	.0050	.0211	.0732	26
27	.019 8263	.237 9156	.0005	.0039	.0166	.0578	27
28	.019 8190	.237 8284	.0004	.0031	.0131	.0457	28
29	.019 8133	.237 7595	.0003	.0024	.0104	.0361	29
30	.019 8088	.237 7051	.0002	.0019	.0082	.0285	30
31	.019 8052	.237 6621	.0002	.0015	.0065	.0226	31
32	.019 8023	.237 6281	.0001	.0012	.0051	.0178	32
33	.019 8001	.237 6012	.0001	.0010	.0041	.0141	33
34	.019 7983	.237 5800	.0001	.0008	.0032	.0111	34
35	.019 7969	.237 5632	.0001	.0006	.0025	.0088	35
36	.019 7958	.237 5500	.0001	.0005	.0020	.0070	36
37	.019 7950	.237 5395	.0000	.0004	.0016	.0055	37
38	.019 7943	.237 5312	.0000	.0003	.0012	.0043	38
39	.019 7937	.237 5247	.0000	.0002	.0010	.0034	39
40	.019 7933	.237 5195	.0000	.0002	.0008	.0027	40

24% DIRECT REDUCTION LOAN FACTORS
(Monthly Payment and Annual Constant per $1 of Loan)

Base: 1.020 000

Months	Payment	Annual Constant	Part Paid Off Projection 1 Year	5 Years	10 Years	15 Years	Months
1	1.020 0000	—	—	—	—	—	1
2	.515 0495	—	—	—	—	—	2
3	.346 7547	—	—	—	—	—	3
4	.262 6238	—	—	—	—	—	4
5	.212 1584	—	—	—	—	—	5
6	.178 5258	—	—	—	—	—	6
7	.154 5120	—	—	—	—	—	7
8	.136 5098	—	—	—	—	—	8
9	.122 5154	—	—	—	—	—	9
10	.111 3265	—	—	—	—	—	10
11	.102 1779	—	—	—	—	—	11

Years	Payment	Annual Constant	1 Year	5 Years	10 Years	15 Years	Years
1	.094 5596	1.134 7152	1.0000	—	—	—	1
2	.052 8711	.634 4532	.4409	—	—	—	2
3	.039 2329	.470 7942	.2580	—	—	—	3
4	.032 6018	.391 2220	.1690	—	—	—	4
5	.028 7680	.345 2156	.1176	1.0000	—	—	5
6	.026 3268	.315 9220	.0849	.7216	—	—	6
7	.024 6758	.296 1097	.0627	.5333	—	—	7
8	.023 5131	.282 1575	.0471	.4007	—	—	8
9	.022 6708	.272 0502	.0358	.3046	—	—	9
10	.022 0481	.264 5772	.0275	.2336	1.0000	—	10
11	.021 5807	.258 9681	.0212	.1803	.7718	—	11
12	.021 2259	.254 7103	.0164	.1398	.5985	—	12
13	.020 9542	.251 4505	.0128	.1088	.4659	—	13
14	.020 7449	.248 9385	.0100	.0850	.3637	—	14
15	.020 5827	.246 9928	.0078	.0665	.2845	1.0000	15
16	.020 4567	.245 4800	.0061	.0521	.2230	.7837	16
17	.020 3584	.244 3002	.0048	.0409	.1750	.6149	17
18	.020 2815	.243 3779	.0038	.0321	.1374	.4830	18
19	.020 2213	.242 6555	.0030	.0252	.1080	.3797	19
20	.020 1741	.242 0890	.0023	.0199	.0850	.2987	20
21	.020 1370	.241 6441	.0018	.0156	.0669	.2351	21
22	.020 1079	.241 2945	.0014	.0123	.0527	.1851	22
23	.020 0850	.241 0195	.0011	.0097	.0415	.1458	23
24	.020 0669	.240 8032	.0009	.0076	.0327	.1149	24
25	.020 0527	.240 6329	.0007	.0060	.0257	.0905	25
26	.020 0416	.240 4987	.0006	.0047	.0203	.0713	26
27	.020 0328	.240 3931	.0004	.0037	.0160	.0562	27
28	.020 0258	.240 3098	.0003	.0029	.0126	.0443	28
29	.020 0204	.240 2442	.0003	.0023	.0099	.0349	29
30	.020 0160	.240 1925	.0002	.0018	.0078	.0275	30
31	.020 0126	.240 1518	.0002	.0014	.0062	.0217	31
32	.020 0100	.240 1197	.0001	.0011	.0049	.0171	32
33	.020 0079	.240 0943	.0001	.0009	.0038	.0135	33
34	.020 0062	.240 0744	.0001	.0007	.0030	.0106	34
35	.020 0049	.240 0586	.0001	.0006	.0024	.0084	35
36	.020 0039	.240 0462	.0001	.0004	.0019	.0066	36
37	.020 0030	.240 0365	.0000	.0003	.0015	.0052	37
38	.020 0024	.240 0287	.0000	.0003	.0012	.0041	38
39	.020 0019	.240 0227	.0000	.0002	.0009	.0032	39
40	.020 0015	.240 0179	.0000	.0002	.0007	.0026	40

Table 9

J-Factors
(Adjustment Factors for Changes in Income)

Table 9 - J-FACTORS (Adjustment Factors for Changes in Income)

Ellwood:	$J = 1/S_{\overline{n}} [n/ (1 - 1/S^n) - (1/Y_E)]$
Straight-Line:	$J = (1/n - 1/S_{\overline{n}})/Y_E$
Where	J = Factor
	$1/S_{\overline{n}}$ = SFF at Equity Yield Rate for Projection
	n = Projection
	$1/S^n$ = Reversion Factor at Y_E for Projection
	Y_E = Equity Yield Rate

This Table is used in solving mortgage/equity problems dealing with changing income: specifically, the factors can be substituted in any of the "J-Factor, Changing Income" formulas which solve for Overall Rates, Change in Property Values, or Equity Yield Rates.

The Ellwood Premise J-Factors reflect curvilinear income which changes from time zero in relation to a Sinking Fund Accumulation curve; the Straight-Line premise J-Factors reflect income changing in equal annual amounts after the first year.

Facts for the examples: Change in both Income and Value = $+25\%$ in 5 years; Mortgage terms = 70% ratio, 12% nominal interest, and 25-year term; desired Equity Yield = 18%.

$$C = Y_E + P\, 1/S_{\overline{n}} - R_M$$

$$C = .18 + .0435 \times .139778 - .1263869$$

$$C = .05969344 \text{ say, } .0597$$

Example 1:
Assuming income at time zero is \$10,000, what is the calculated value using the Ellwood premise?

$$R_0 = (Y_E - MC - \Delta_0\, 1/S_{\overline{n}})/(1 + \Delta_I J)$$

$$R_0 = (.18 - .70 \times .0597 - .25 \times .139778)/(1 + .25 \times .4651)$$

$$R_0 = .092509$$

$$V_0 = I_0/R_0$$

$$V_0 = \$10,000/.092509$$

$$V_0 = \$108,098$$

PROOF: Debt Service = \$108,098 × .70 = \$75,668

$$\$\,75{,}668 \times .1263869 = \$\,9{,}563$$

Reversion = \$108,098 × 1.25 − \$75,668 × (1 − .0435) = \$62,746

Equity = \$108,098 × .30 = \$32,429

Time	Income	−	Debt Service	=	Cash to Equity	×	PVF @18%	=	Value
1	\$10,349	−	\$9,563	=	\$ 786	×	.847458	=	\$ 666
2	10,762	−	9,563	=	1,199	×	.718184	=	861
3	11,248	−	9,563	=	1,685	×	.608631	=	1,026
4	11,823	−	9,563	=	2,260	×	.515789	=	1,166
5	12,500	−	9,563	=	2,937	×	.437109	=	1,284
Reversion:					62,746	×	.437109	=	27,427
Total Equity									\$32,430

Example 2:

Assuming Income at the end of year one is \$10,000, what is the calculated value using the Straight-Line premise?

$$R_0 = (Y_E - MC - \Delta_0\, 1/S_{\overline{n}})/(1 + \Delta_I J)$$

$$R_0 = (.18 - .70 \times .0597 - .25 \times .139778)/(1 + .25 \times .3346)$$

$$R_0 = .095294$$

$$V_0 = I_0/R_0$$

$$V_0 = \$10{,}000/.095294$$

$$V_0 = \$104{,}938$$

PROOF: Debt Service = \$104,938 × .70 = \$73,457

$$\$\,73{,}457 \times .1263869 = \$\,9{,}284$$

Reversion = \$104,938 × 1.25 − \$73,457 × (1 − .0435) = \$60,911

Equity = \$104,938 × .30 = \$31,481

Time	Income	−	Debt Service	=	Cash to Equity	×	PVF @18%	=	Value
1	\$10,000	−	\$9,284	=	\$ 716	×	.847458	=	\$ 607
2	10,500	−	9,284	=	1,216	×	.718184	=	873
3	11,000	−	9,284	=	1,716	×	.608631	=	1,044
4	11,500	−	9,284	=	2,216	×	.515789	=	1,143
5	12,000	−	9,284	=	2,716	×	.437109	=	1,187
Reversion:					60,911	×	.437109	=	26,625
Total Equity									\$31,479

J - FACTORS

(Adjustment Factors for Changes in Income)

	6.0%		6.5%		7.0%		7.5%		
YEARS	ELLWOOD	STRAIGHT LINE	ELLWOOD	STRAIGHT LINE	ELLWOOD	STRAIGHT LINE	ELLWOOD	STRAIGHT LINE	YEARS
1	1.0000	.0000	1.0000	.0000	1.0000	.0000	1.0000	.0000	1
2	.7352	.2427	.7340	.2421	.7328	.2415	.7316	.2410	2
3	.6404	.3204	.6383	.3193	.6361	.3183	.6340	.3173	3
4	.5881	.3568	.5851	.3553	.5821	.3539	.5791	.3524	4
5	.5528	.3767	.5490	.3749	.5452	.3730	.5413	.3711	5
6	.5261	.3884	.5214	.3861	.5168	.3839	.5122	.3816	6
7	.5042	.3954	.4988	.3927	.4934	.3901	.4880	.3874	7
8	.4855	.3994	.4792	.3963	.4731	.3933	.4669	.3903	8
9	.4688	.4015	.4618	.3980	.4549	.3946	.4480	.3913	9
10	.4535	.4022	.4458	.3984	.4382	.3946	.4306	.3909	10
11	.4394	.4019	.4310	.3978	.4226	.3936	.4143	.3895	11
12	.4261	.4009	.4170	.3964	.4079	.3919	.3990	.3874	12
13	.4135	.3994	.4037	.3945	.3940	.3896	.3844	.3848	13
14	.4014	.3974	.3910	.3921	.3806	.3869	.3704	.3817	14
15	.3898	.3951	.3787	.3894	.3678	.3839	.3570	.3784	15
16	.3786	.3925	.3669	.3865	.3554	.3806	.3440	.3748	16
17	.3678	.3896	.3554	.3833	.3433	.3771	.3315	.3710	17
18	.3572	.3867	.3443	.3800	.3317	.3735	.3194	.3670	18
19	.3470	.3835	.3335	.3766	.3204	.3697	.3076	.3629	19
20	.3369	.3803	.3230	.3730	.3094	.3658	.2961	.3588	20
21	.3272	.3769	.3127	.3693	.2987	.3619	.2851	.3545	21
22	.3176	.3735	.3027	.3656	.2883	.3578	.2743	.3502	22
23	.3083	.3700	.2930	.3618	.2781	.3538	.2638	.3459	23
24	.2992	.3665	.2835	.3580	.2683	.3497	.2536	.3416	24
25	.2903	.3629	.2742	.3541	.2587	.3456	.2438	.3372	25
26	.2816	.3593	.2651	.3503	.2493	.3414	.2342	.3328	26
27	.2731	.3557	.2563	.3464	.2402	.3373	.2249	.3285	27
28	.2648	.3520	.2477	.3425	.2314	.3332	.2158	.3241	28
29	.2566	.3484	.2393	.3386	.2228	.3291	.2071	.3198	29
30	.2486	.3447	.2311	.3347	.2144	.3250	.1986	.3155	30
31	.2409	.3411	.2231	.3308	.2063	.3209	.1904	.3112	31
32	.2333	.3375	.2153	.3270	.1984	.3168	.1824	.3070	32
33	.2258	.3338	.2077	.3231	.1907	.3128	.1747	.3028	33
34	.2186	.3302	.2003	.3193	.1832	.3088	.1673	.2986	34
35	.2115	.3266	.1931	.3155	.1760	.3048	.1601	.2945	35
36	.2046	.3230	.1862	.3118	.1690	.3009	.1531	.2904	36
37	.1978	.3195	.1794	.3080	.1622	.2970	.1464	.2864	37
38	.1913	.3160	.1728	.3043	.1557	.2932	.1399	.2825	38
39	.1849	.3125	.1663	.3007	.1493	.2893	.1337	.2785	39
40	.1786	.3090	.1601	.2970	.1431	.2856	.1277	.2747	40

J - FACTORS

(Adjustment Factors for Changes in Income)

	8.0%		8.5%		9.0%		9.5%		
YEARS	ELLWOOD	STRAIGHT LINE	ELLWOOD	STRAIGHT LINE	ELLWOOD	STRAIGHT LINE	ELLWOOD	STRAIGHT LINE	YEARS
1	1.0000	.0000	1.0000	.0000	1.0000	.0000	1.0000	.0000	1
2	.7304	.2404	.7292	.2398	.7280	.2392	.7268	.2387	2
3	.6319	.3162	.6297	.3152	.6276	.3142	.6255	.3132	3
4	.5761	.3510	.5731	.3496	.5702	.3481	.5672	.3467	4
5	.5375	.3693	.5338	.3675	.5300	.3656	.5262	.3638	5
6	.5076	.3794	.5030	.3772	.4985	.3750	.4940	.3728	6
7	.4826	.3848	.4773	.3822	.4720	.3796	.4667	.3771	7
8	.4608	.3873	.4548	.3843	.4487	.3814	.4428	.3785	8
9	.4412	.3879	.4344	.3846	.4277	.3812	.4210	.3780	9
10	.4231	.3871	.4156	.3834	.4082	.3798	.4009	.3761	10
11	.4061	.3854	.3980	.3814	.3900	.3774	.3821	.3734	11
12	.3902	.3830	.3814	.3786	.3728	.3743	.3643	.3700	12
13	.3750	.3800	.3656	.3753	.3565	.3706	.3474	.3660	13
14	.3604	.3766	.3505	.3716	.3408	.3666	.3313	.3617	14
15	.3464	.3730	.3360	.3676	.3258	.3623	.3158	.3571	15
16	.3329	.3690	.3220	.3634	.3113	.3578	.3009	.3523	16
17	.3199	.3649	.3085	.3590	.2974	.3531	.2866	.3473	17
18	.3073	.3607	.2955	.3544	.2840	.3483	.2729	.3422	18
19	.2951	.3563	.2829	.3498	.2711	.3433	.2596	.3370	19
20	.2833	.3518	.2708	.3450	.2586	.3384	.2469	.3318	20
21	.2718	.3473	.2590	.3403	.2466	.3334	.2347	.3266	21
22	.2607	.3428	.2476	.3355	.2350	.3283	.2229	.3213	22
23	.2500	.3382	.2366	.3307	.2238	.3233	.2116	.3161	23
24	.2395	.3336	.2260	.3258	.2131	.3183	.2007	.3109	24
25	.2295	.3290	.2158	.3210	.2027	.3133	.1902	.3057	25
26	.2197	.3244	.2059	.3163	.1927	.3083	.1802	.3005	26
27	.2102	.3199	.1963	.3115	.1831	.3034	.1706	.2955	27
28	.2011	.3153	.1871	.3068	.1739	.2985	.1614	.2904	28
29	.1922	.3108	.1782	.3021	.1650	.2936	.1526	.2855	29
30	.1837	.3063	.1697	.2974	.1565	.2889	.1442	.2806	30
31	.1755	.3019	.1615	.2929	.1484	.2841	.1362	.2757	31
32	.1675	.2975	.1536	.2883	.1406	.2795	.1285	.2710	32
33	.1598	.2931	.1460	.2838	.1331	.2749	.1212	.2663	33
34	.1524	.2888	.1387	.2794	.1259	.2704	.1142	.2617	34
35	.1453	.2846	.1317	.2751	.1191	.2660	.1076	.2572	35
36	.1385	.2804	.1250	.2708	.1126	.2616	.1013	.2528	36
37	.1319	.2763	.1185	.2666	.1064	.2573	.0953	.2484	37
38	.1255	.2722	.1124	.2624	.1004	.2531	.0896	.2442	38
39	.1194	.2682	.1065	.2583	.0948	.2489	.0842	.2400	39
40	.1136	.2642	.1009	.2543	.0894	.2449	.0791	.2359	40

J - FACTORS

(Adjustment Factors for Changes in Income)

YEARS	10.0% ELLWOOD	10.0% STRAIGHT LINE	10.5% ELLWOOD	10.5% STRAIGHT LINE	11.0% ELLWOOD	11.0% STRAIGHT LINE	11.5% ELLWOOD	11.5% STRAIGHT LINE	YEARS
1	1.0000	.0000	1.0000	.0000	1.0000	.0000	1.0000	.0000	1
2	.7256	.2381	.7244	.2375	.7233	.2370	.7221	.2364	2
3	.6234	.3122	.6213	.3112	.6192	.3102	.6171	.3092	3
4	.5643	.3453	.5613	.3439	.5584	.3425	.5555	.3411	4
5	.5225	.3620	.5188	.3602	.5151	.3585	.5114	.3567	5
6	.4895	.3706	.4850	.3684	.4805	.3663	.4761	.3641	6
7	.4615	.3745	.4563	.3720	.4511	.3695	.4460	.3670	7
8	.4368	.3756	.4309	.3727	.4251	.3698	.4193	.3670	8
9	.4144	.3747	.4079	.3715	.4014	.3683	.3950	.3651	9
10	.3937	.3725	.3865	.3690	.3795	.3654	.3725	.3619	10
11	.3743	.3695	.3666	.3656	.3589	.3617	.3514	.3579	11
12	.3559	.3657	.3477	.3615	.3395	.3573	.3315	.3532	12
13	.3385	.3614	.3298	.3569	.3211	.3525	.3127	.3481	13
14	.3219	.3568	.3127	.3520	.3036	.3473	.2948	.3426	14
15	.3060	.3519	.2963	.3468	.2869	.3418	.2778	.3369	15
16	.2907	.3468	.2807	.3415	.2710	.3362	.2615	.3310	16
17	.2761	.3416	.2658	.3360	.2558	.3305	.2460	.3251	17
18	.2620	.3363	.2515	.3304	.2412	.3247	.2313	.3190	18
19	.2485	.3308	.2377	.3248	.2273	.3188	.2172	.3130	19
20	.2356	.3254	.2246	.3191	.2140	.3129	.2038	.3069	20
21	.2231	.3199	.2120	.3135	.2014	.3071	.1911	.3009	21
22	.2112	.3145	.2000	.3078	.1893	.3013	.1790	.2949	22
23	.1998	.3091	.1885	.3022	.1778	.2955	.1675	.2890	23
24	.1888	.3037	.1776	.2966	.1668	.2898	.1566	.2832	24
25	.1784	.2983	.1671	.2911	.1564	.2842	.1463	.2774	25
26	.1684	.2930	.1571	.2857	.1465	.2786	.1365	.2717	26
27	.1588	.2878	.1476	.2804	.1372	.2732	.1273	.2662	27
28	.1497	.2826	.1386	.2751	.1283	.2678	.1186	.2607	28
29	.1410	.2775	.1301	.2699	.1199	.2625	.1104	.2554	29
30	.1327	.2725	.1219	.2648	.1119	.2574	.1027	.2502	30
31	.1248	.2676	.1142	.2598	.1045	.2523	.0954	.2451	31
32	.1173	.2628	.1069	.2549	.0974	.2473	.0886	.2401	32
33	.1102	.2580	.1000	.2501	.0907	.2425	.0822	.2352	33
34	.1034	.2534	.0935	.2454	.0845	.2378	.0762	.2304	34
35	.0970	.2488	.0874	.2408	.0786	.2331	.0706	.2258	35
36	.0909	.2443	.0816	.2363	.0730	.2286	.0653	.2213	36
37	.0852	.2400	.0761	.2319	.0679	.2242	.0604	.2169	37
38	.0798	.2357	.0709	.2276	.0630	.2199	.0559	.2126	38
39	.0747	.2315	.0661	.2234	.0585	.2157	.0516	.2084	39
40	.0698	.2274	.0616	.2193	.0542	.2116	.0477	.2044	40

J - FACTORS

(Adjustment Factors for Changes in Income)

YEARS	12.0% ELLWOOD	12.0% STRAIGHT LINE	12.5% ELLWOOD	12.5% STRAIGHT LINE	13.0% ELLWOOD	13.0% STRAIGHT LINE	13.5% ELLWOOD	13.5% STRAIGHT LINE	YEARS
1	1.0000	.0000	1.0000	.0000	1.0000	.0000	1.0000	.0000	1
2	.7209	.2358	.7197	.2353	.7186	.2347	.7174	.2342	2
3	.6150	.3082	.6130	.3072	.6109	.3062	.6088	.3053	3
4	.5526	.3397	.5497	.3383	.5469	.3370	.5440	.3356	4
5	.5077	.3549	.5041	.3532	.5004	.3514	.4968	.3497	5
6	.4717	.3620	.4673	.3599	.4630	.3578	.4587	.3557	6
7	.4409	.3645	.4359	.3620	.4309	.3596	.4259	.3572	7
8	.4136	.3641	.4079	.3613	.4022	.3586	.3966	.3558	8
9	.3887	.3619	.3824	.3588	.3761	.3557	.3700	.3526	9
10	.3656	.3585	.3587	.3550	.3520	.3516	.3453	.3482	10
11	.3440	.3541	.3367	.3504	.3294	.3467	.3223	.3430	11
12	.3236	.3491	.3159	.3451	.3082	.3411	.3007	.3372	12
13	.3044	.3437	.2962	.3394	.2882	.3352	.2804	.3310	13
14	.2861	.3380	.2776	.3334	.2693	.3289	.2612	.3245	14
15	.2688	.3320	.2600	.3272	.2514	.3225	.2431	.3178	15
16	.2523	.3259	.2433	.3209	.2345	.3160	.2260	.3111	16
17	.2366	.3197	.2274	.3145	.2185	.3093	.2098	.3043	17
18	.2217	.3135	.2123	.3081	.2033	.3027	.1946	.2975	18
19	.2075	.3072	.1981	.3016	.1890	.2961	.1803	.2908	19
20	.1940	.3010	.1846	.2952	.1755	.2896	.1668	.2841	20
21	.1813	.2948	.1718	.2889	.1628	.2831	.1542	.2775	21
22	.1692	.2887	.1598	.2826	.1508	.2767	.1423	.2710	22
23	.1577	.2827	.1484	.2765	.1396	.2705	.1312	.2646	23
24	.1469	.2767	.1377	.2704	.1290	.2643	.1208	.2584	24
25	.1367	.2708	.1277	.2645	.1192	.2583	.1111	.2523	25
26	.1271	.2651	.1182	.2586	.1099	.2524	.1021	.2463	26
27	.1181	.2594	.1094	.2529	.1013	.2466	.0937	.2405	27
28	.1095	.2539	.1011	.2473	.0932	.2410	.0859	.2348	28
29	.1016	.2485	.0934	.2419	.0857	.2355	.0787	.2293	29
30	.0941	.2432	.0861	.2366	.0788	.2302	.0720	.2240	30
31	.0871	.2381	.0794	.2314	.0723	.2250	.0658	.2188	31
32	.0805	.2331	.0731	.2264	.0663	.2200	.0601	.2138	32
33	.0744	.2282	.0672	.2215	.0607	.2151	.0548	.2089	33
34	.0687	.2234	.0618	.2167	.0556	.2103	.0500	.2042	34
35	.0633	.2188	.0568	.2121	.0509	.2057	.0455	.1996	35
36	.0584	.2143	.0521	.2076	.0465	.2012	.0414	.1952	36
37	.0538	.2099	.0478	.2032	.0424	.1969	.0376	.1909	37
38	.0495	.2056	.0438	.1990	.0387	.1927	.0342	.1867	38
39	.0455	.2015	.0401	.1949	.0353	.1887	.0310	.1827	39
40	.0418	.1975	.0367	.1909	.0322	.1847	.0282	.1788	40

J - FACTORS

(Adjustment Factors for Changes in Income)

YEARS	14.0% ELLWOOD	STRAIGHT LINE	14.5% ELLWOOD	STRAIGHT LINE	15.0% ELLWOOD	STRAIGHT LINE	15.5% ELLWOOD	STRAIGHT LINE	YEARS
1	1.0000	.0000	1.0000	.0000	1.0000	.0000	1.0000	.0000	1
2	.7162	.2336	.7151	.2331	.7139	.2326	.7127	.2320	2
3	.6068	.3043	.6047	.3033	.6027	.3024	.6007	.3014	3
4	.5411	.3343	.5383	.3329	.5355	.3316	.5326	.3302	4
5	.4932	.3480	.4896	.3463	.4861	.3446	.4825	.3429	5
6	.4544	.3536	.4501	.3516	.4458	.3495	.4416	.3475	6
7	.4209	.3547	.4160	.3524	.4112	.3500	.4063	.3476	7
8	.3911	.3531	.3856	.3504	.3802	.3477	.3748	.3450	8
9	.3639	.3496	.3579	.3466	.3519	.3436	.3461	.3406	9
10	.3388	.3449	.3323	.3416	.3259	.3383	.3196	.3351	10
11	.3153	.3394	.3084	.3358	.3017	.3323	.2950	.3288	11
12	.2934	.3333	.2861	.3295	.2790	.3257	.2720	.3219	12
13	.2727	.3269	.2652	.3228	.2578	.3188	.2506	.3148	13
14	.2533	.3201	.2455	.3158	.2379	.3116	.2305	.3074	14
15	.2350	.3133	.2270	.3088	.2193	.3043	.2118	.3000	15
16	.2177	.3063	.2097	.3016	.2019	.2970	.1943	.2925	16
17	.2015	.2993	.1934	.2945	.1856	.2897	.1780	.2850	17
18	.1862	.2924	.1781	.2874	.1703	.2825	.1628	.2777	18
19	.1719	.2855	.1638	.2803	.1561	.2753	.1487	.2704	19
20	.1585	.2787	.1505	.2734	.1429	.2683	.1355	.2632	20
21	.1459	.2720	.1381	.2666	.1306	.2613	.1234	.2562	21
22	.1342	.2654	.1265	.2599	.1192	.2546	.1122	.2494	22
23	.1232	.2589	.1157	.2534	.1086	.2480	.1019	.2428	23
24	.1131	.2526	.1057	.2470	.0988	.2416	.0923	.2363	24
25	.1036	.2464	.0965	.2408	.0898	.2353	.0836	.2300	25
26	.0948	.2404	.0879	.2348	.0816	.2293	.0756	.2240	26
27	.0866	.2346	.0801	.2289	.0739	.2234	.0682	.2181	27
28	.0791	.2289	.0728	.2232	.0670	.2177	.0616	.2124	28
29	.0722	.2234	.0661	.2177	.0606	.2122	.0554	.2069	29
30	.0657	.2181	.0600	.2124	.0547	.2069	.0499	.2016	30
31	.0598	.2129	.0544	.2072	.0494	.2017	.0448	.1965	31
32	.0544	.2079	.0492	.2022	.0445	.1968	.0403	.1916	32
33	.0494	.2030	.0445	.1974	.0401	.1920	.0361	.1868	33
34	.0449	.1983	.0403	.1927	.0361	.1874	.0324	.1822	34
35	.0407	.1938	.0363	.1882	.0325	.1829	.0290	.1778	35
36	.0369	.1894	.0328	.1839	.0292	.1786	.0259	.1736	36
37	.0334	.1851	.0296	.1797	.0262	.1745	.0231	.1695	37
38	.0302	.1810	.0266	.1756	.0235	.1705	.0207	.1656	38
39	.0273	.1771	.0240	.1717	.0210	.1666	.0184	.1618	39
40	.0246	.1732	.0215	.1679	.0188	.1629	.0164	.1581	40

J - FACTORS

(Adjustment Factors for Changes in Income)

YEARS	16.0% ELLWOOD	16.0% STRAIGHT LINE	16.5% ELLWOOD	16.5% STRAIGHT LINE	17.0% ELLWOOD	17.0% STRAIGHT LINE	17.5% ELLWOOD	17.5% STRAIGHT LINE	YEARS
1	1.0000	.0000	1.0000	.0000	1.0000	.0000	1.0000	.0000	1
2	.7116	.2315	.7104	.2309	.7093	.2304	.7082	.2299	2
3	.5986	.3005	.5966	.2995	.5946	.2986	.5926	.2977	3
4	.5298	.3289	.5270	.3276	.5242	.3263	.5215	.3250	4
5	.4790	.3412	.4755	.3395	.4720	.3379	.4685	.3362	5
6	.4374	.3455	.4333	.3435	.4291	.3415	.4250	.3395	6
7	.4015	.3453	.3968	.3430	.3921	.3406	.3874	.3384	7
8	.3695	.3423	.3642	.3397	.3590	.3371	.3538	.3345	8
9	.3403	.3377	.3345	.3348	.3289	.3319	.3233	.3290	9
10	.3134	.3319	.3072	.3287	.3012	.3255	.2952	.3224	10
11	.2884	.3253	.2820	.3219	.2756	.3185	.2694	.3152	11
12	.2652	.3182	.2585	.3146	.2519	.3110	.2454	.3074	12
13	.2435	.3109	.2366	.3070	.2299	.3032	.2233	.2995	13
14	.2233	.3033	.2163	.2993	.2095	.2953	.2028	.2914	14
15	.2045	.2957	.1974	.2915	.1905	.2873	.1838	.2832	15
16	.1870	.2880	.1799	.2837	.1730	.2794	.1663	.2752	16
17	.1707	.2804	.1636	.2759	.1568	.2715	.1502	.2672	17
18	.1555	.2729	.1486	.2683	.1419	.2638	.1354	.2594	18
19	.1415	.2656	.1347	.2609	.1281	.2563	.1219	.2518	19
20	.1286	.2583	.1219	.2535	.1155	.2489	.1095	.2443	20
21	.1166	.2513	.1101	.2464	.1040	.2417	.0981	.2371	21
22	.1056	.2444	.0994	.2395	.0934	.2347	.0879	.2301	22
23	.0955	.2377	.0895	.2328	.0838	.2280	.0785	.2233	23
24	.0862	.2312	.0805	.2263	.0751	.2215	.0700	.2168	24
25	.0778	.2249	.0723	.2200	.0672	.2152	.0624	.2105	25
26	.0700	.2188	.0648	.2139	.0600	.2091	.0555	.2044	26
27	.0630	.2130	.0581	.2080	.0535	.2032	.0493	.1986	27
28	.0565	.2073	.0519	.2024	.0477	.1976	.0437	.1930	28
29	.0507	.2018	.0464	.1969	.0424	.1922	.0387	.1876	29
30	.0455	.1965	.0414	.1917	.0377	.1870	.0343	.1825	30
31	.0407	.1915	.0369	.1866	.0334	.1820	.0303	.1775	31
32	.0364	.1866	.0328	.1818	.0296	.1772	.0267	.1728	32
33	.0325	.1819	.0292	.1771	.0262	.1726	.0236	.1683	33
34	.0290	.1773	.0259	.1727	.0232	.1682	.0208	.1639	34
35	.0258	.1730	.0230	.1684	.0205	.1639	.0183	.1597	35
36	.0230	.1688	.0204	.1642	.0181	.1599	.0161	.1557	36
37	.0205	.1648	.0181	.1603	.0160	.1560	.0141	.1519	37
38	.0182	.1609	.0160	.1565	.0141	.1522	.0124	.1482	38
39	.0162	.1572	.0142	.1528	.0124	.1486	.0109	.1447	39
40	.0143	.1536	.0125	.1493	.0109	.1452	.0095	.1413	40

J - FACTORS

(Adjustment Factors for Changes in Income)

	18.0%		19.0%		20.0%		21.0%		
YEARS	ELLWOOD	STRAIGHT LINE	ELLWOOD	STRAIGHT LINE	ELLWOOD	STRAIGHT LINE	ELLWOOD	STRAIGHT LINE	YEARS
1	1.0000	.0000	1.0000	.0000	1.0000	.0000	1.0000	.0000	1
2	.7070	.2294	.7047	.2283	.7025	.2273	.7002	.2262	2
3	.5906	.2967	.5866	.2949	.5827	.2930	.5787	.2912	3
4	.5187	.3237	.5132	.3211	.5078	.3186	.5024	.3160	4
5	.4651	.3346	.4582	.3313	.4514	.3281	.4448	.3249	5
6	.4210	.3375	.4129	.3336	.4050	.3298	.3971	.3260	6
7	.3828	.3361	.3736	.3316	.3647	.3272	.3558	.3228	7
8	.3487	.3320	.3386	.3269	.3288	.3220	.3191	.3171	8
9	.3177	.3262	.3069	.3206	.2963	.3152	.2861	.3098	9
10	.2894	.3194	.2779	.3133	.2668	.3074	.2561	.3016	10
11	.2632	.3118	.2513	.3054	.2398	.2990	.2288	.2928	11
12	.2391	.3039	.2269	.2970	.2152	.2903	.2039	.2838	12
13	.2168	.2958	.2044	.2885	.1926	.2815	.1814	.2747	13
14	.1963	.2875	.1838	.2800	.1720	.2727	.1609	.2656	14
15	.1773	.2792	.1649	.2714	.1533	.2639	.1423	.2567	15
16	.1599	.2711	.1477	.2630	.1363	.2553	.1256	.2479	16
17	.1439	.2630	.1319	.2548	.1209	.2469	.1106	.2394	17
18	.1292	.2551	.1176	.2467	.1070	.2388	.0972	.2311	18
19	.1159	.2474	.1047	.2389	.0944	.2308	.0851	.2232	19
20	.1037	.2399	.0929	.2313	.0832	.2232	.0744	.2155	20
21	.0926	.2326	.0824	.2240	.0732	.2159	.0650	.2082	21
22	.0826	.2256	.0729	.2170	.0642	.2088	.0566	.2011	22
23	.0735	.2188	.0643	.2102	.0563	.2021	.0491	.1944	23
24	.0653	.2123	.0567	.2037	.0492	.1956	.0426	.1880	24
25	.0579	.2060	.0499	.1974	.0429	.1894	.0369	.1819	25
26	.0513	.2000	.0438	.1915	.0374	.1835	.0319	.1761	26
27	.0454	.1942	.0385	.1857	.0326	.1779	.0275	.1705	27
28	.0401	.1886	.0337	.1802	.0283	.1725	.0237	.1652	28
29	.0354	.1833	.0295	.1750	.0245	.1673	.0204	.1602	29
30	.0312	.1782	.0258	.1700	.0213	.1624	.0175	.1554	30
31	.0274	.1733	.0225	.1652	.0184	.1578	.0150	.1509	31
32	.0241	.1686	.0196	.1606	.0159	.1533	.0129	.1466	32
33	.0212	.1641	.0171	.1563	.0137	.1491	.0110	.1424	33
34	.0186	.1598	.0148	.1521	.0118	.1450	.0094	.1385	34
35	.0163	.1557	.0129	.1481	.0102	.1412	.0081	.1348	35
36	.0142	.1517	.0112	.1443	.0088	.1375	.0069	.1312	36
37	.0125	.1480	.0097	.1406	.0075	.1340	.0059	.1278	37
38	.0109	.1443	.0084	.1372	.0065	.1306	.0050	.1246	38
39	.0095	.1409	.0073	.1338	.0056	.1274	.0043	.1215	39
40	.0083	.1376	.0063	.1306	.0048	.1243	.0036	.1186	40

J - FACTORS

(Adjustment Factors for Changes in Income)

YEARS	22.0% ELLWOOD	STRAIGHT LINE	23.0% ELLWOOD	STRAIGHT LINE	24.0% ELLWOOD	STRAIGHT LINE	25.0% ELLWOOD	STRAIGHT LINE	YEARS
1	1.0000	.0000	1.0000	.0000	1.0000	.0000	1.0000	.0000	1
2	.6980	.2252	.6958	.2242	.6936	.2232	.6914	.2222	2
3	.5748	.2894	.5710	.2877	.5671	.2859	.5633	.2842	3
4	.4970	.3135	.4918	.3111	.4865	.3086	.4813	.3062	4
5	.4381	.3218	.4316	.3187	.4252	.3156	.4188	.3126	5
6	.3894	.3223	.3818	.3186	.3743	.3150	.3670	.3114	6
7	.3472	.3185	.3387	.3143	.3304	.3101	.3223	.3061	7
8	.3097	.3123	.3006	.3076	.2916	.3029	.2829	.2984	8
9	.2761	.3045	.2664	.2994	.2570	.2944	.2479	.2894	9
10	.2457	.2959	.2356	.2904	.2260	.2850	.2166	.2797	10
11	.2181	.2868	.2079	.2810	.1981	.2752	.1887	.2697	11
12	.1932	.2775	.1830	.2713	.1732	.2654	.1639	.2595	12
13	.1707	.2681	.1606	.2617	.1510	.2555	.1419	.2495	13
14	.1504	.2588	.1405	.2522	.1312	.2459	.1224	.2397	14
15	.1321	.2497	.1225	.2429	.1136	.2364	.1053	.2302	15
16	.1158	.2408	.1066	.2339	.0981	.2274	.0902	.2210	16
17	.1012	.2321	.0925	.2252	.0845	.2186	.0771	.2123	17
18	.0882	.2238	.0800	.2169	.0725	.2102	.0657	.2039	18
19	.0767	.2158	.0690	.2089	.0621	.2022	.0558	.1959	19
20	.0665	.2082	.0594	.2012	.0531	.1946	.0473	.1883	20
21	.0576	.2008	.0510	.1939	.0452	.1874	.0400	.1812	21
22	.0498	.1939	.0437	.1870	.0384	.1805	.0338	.1744	22
23	.0429	.1872	.0374	.1804	.0326	.1740	.0284	.1680	23
24	.0369	.1809	.0319	.1742	.0276	.1679	.0239	.1619	24
25	.0317	.1748	.0272	.1682	.0233	.1620	.0200	.1562	25
26	.0272	.1691	.0231	.1626	.0197	.1565	.0167	.1508	26
27	.0233	.1637	.0196	.1573	.0166	.1513	.0140	.1457	27
28	.0199	.1585	.0166	.1522	.0139	.1464	.0117	.1409	28
29	.0170	.1536	.0141	.1474	.0117	.1417	.0097	.1364	29
30	.0144	.1489	.0119	.1429	.0098	.1373	.0081	.1321	30
31	.0123	.1445	.0100	.1386	.0082	.1331	.0067	.1280	31
32	.0105	.1403	.0085	.1345	.0069	.1292	.0056	.1242	32
33	.0089	.1363	.0071	.1307	.0057	.1254	.0046	.1206	33
34	.0075	.1325	.0060	.1270	.0048	.1219	.0038	.1171	34
35	.0064	.1289	.0050	.1235	.0040	.1185	.0031	.1139	35
36	.0054	.1255	.0042	.1202	.0033	.1153	.0026	.1108	36
37	.0046	.1222	.0035	.1170	.0028	.1123	.0021	.1078	37
38	.0039	.1191	.0030	.1140	.0023	.1094	.0018	.1051	38
39	.0033	.1161	.0025	.1112	.0019	.1066	.0015	.1024	39
40	.0027	.1133	.0021	.1084	.0016	.1040	.0012	.0999	40

J - FACTORS

(Adjustment Factors for Changes in Income)

	26.0%		27.0%		28.0%		29.0%		
YEARS	ELLWOOD	STRAIGHT LINE	ELLWOOD	STRAIGHT LINE	ELLWOOD	STRAIGHT LINE	ELLWOOD	STRAIGHT LINE	YEARS
1	1.0000	.0000	1.0000	.0000	1.0000	.0000	1.0000	.0000	1
2	.6892	.2212	.6870	.2203	.6848	.2193	.6827	.2183	2
3	.5595	.2824	.5557	.2807	.5520	.2790	.5483	.2773	3
4	.4762	.3038	.4711	.3015	.4660	.2992	.4610	.2969	4
5	.4125	.3096	.4063	.3067	.4001	.3038	.3941	.3009	5
6	.3597	.3079	.3526	.3044	.3456	.3010	.3387	.2976	6
7	.3143	.3020	.3065	.2981	.2988	.2942	.2913	.2904	7
8	.2744	.2940	.2661	.2896	.2580	.2853	.2501	.2811	8
9	.2390	.2846	.2304	.2799	.2221	.2752	.2141	.2707	9
10	.2076	.2746	.1989	.2695	.1906	.2646	.1825	.2598	10
11	.1797	.2642	.1711	.2590	.1629	.2538	.1550	.2488	11
12	.1551	.2539	.1466	.2484	.1386	.2431	.1311	.2379	12
13	.1333	.2437	.1252	.2381	.1176	.2326	.1104	.2274	13
14	.1142	.2338	.1065	.2280	.0993	.2225	.0926	.2172	14
15	.0975	.2242	.0903	.2184	.0836	.2128	.0773	.2075	15
16	.0830	.2150	.0763	.2092	.0701	.2036	.0644	.1982	16
17	.0704	.2062	.0642	.2004	.0585	.1948	.0534	.1895	17
18	.0595	.1978	.0539	.1920	.0488	.1865	.0441	.1812	18
19	.0502	.1899	.0451	.1842	.0405	.1787	.0364	.1735	19
20	.0422	.1824	.0376	.1767	.0335	.1713	.0299	.1662	20
21	.0354	.1753	.0313	.1697	.0277	.1644	.0245	.1594	21
22	.0296	.1686	.0260	.1631	.0228	.1579	.0200	.1530	22
23	.0247	.1623	.0215	.1569	.0188	.1518	.0163	.1471	23
24	.0206	.1563	.0178	.1511	.0154	.1461	.0133	.1415	24
25	.0171	.1507	.0147	.1456	.0126	.1408	.0108	.1362	25
26	.0142	.1455	.0121	.1404	.0103	.1357	.0087	.1313	26
27	.0118	.1405	.0099	.1356	.0084	.1310	.0071	.1267	27
28	.0098	.1358	.0082	.1310	.0068	.1266	.0057	.1224	28
29	.0081	.1314	.0067	.1267	.0055	.1224	.0046	.1183	29
30	.0066	.1272	.0055	.1227	.0045	.1184	.0037	.1145	30
31	.0055	.1233	.0045	.1189	.0036	.1147	.0030	.1109	31
32	.0045	.1196	.0036	.1153	.0030	.1112	.0024	.1075	32
33	.0037	.1161	.0030	.1119	.0024	.1079	.0019	.1043	33
34	.0030	.1127	.0024	.1086	.0019	.1048	.0015	.1012	34
35	.0025	.1096	.0020	.1056	.0016	.1019	.0012	.0984	35
36	.0020	.1066	.0016	.1027	.0013	.0991	.0010	.0957	36
37	.0017	.1038	.0013	.1000	.0010	.0964	.0008	.0931	37
38	.0014	.1011	.0011	.0974	.0008	.0939	.0006	.0907	38
39	.0011	.0985	.0009	.0949	.0007	.0915	.0005	.0884	39
40	.0009	.0961	.0007	.0925	.0005	.0892	.0004	.0862	40

J - FACTORS

(Adjustment Factors for Changes in Income)

YEARS	30.0% ELLWOOD	30.0% STRAIGHT LINE	31.0% ELLWOOD	31.0% STRAIGHT LINE	32.0% ELLWOOD	32.0% STRAIGHT LINE	33.0% ELLWOOD	33.0% STRAIGHT LINE	YEARS
1	1.0000	.0000	1.0000	.0000	1.0000	.0000	1.0000	.0000	1
2	.6805	.2174	.6784	.2165	.6763	.2155	.6742	.2146	2
3	.5446	.2757	.5409	.2740	.5373	.2724	.5337	.2708	3
4	.4561	.2946	.4512	.2923	.4463	.2901	.4415	.2879	4
5	.3881	.2981	.3822	.2953	.3764	.2925	.3707	.2898	5
6	.3320	.2942	.3253	.2910	.3188	.2877	.3124	.2845	6
7	.2840	.2866	.2769	.2829	.2699	.2793	.2630	.2757	7
8	.2425	.2769	.2350	.2729	.2278	.2689	.2207	.2650	8
9	.2063	.2663	.1987	.2619	.1915	.2577	.1844	.2535	9
10	.1748	.2551	.1673	.2506	.1602	.2461	.1533	.2418	10
11	.1474	.2439	.1403	.2392	.1334	.2346	.1268	.2301	11
12	.1238	.2329	.1170	.2281	.1105	.2234	.1044	.2188	12
13	.1036	.2223	.0972	.2173	.0912	.2126	.0855	.2079	13
14	.0862	.2120	.0803	.2071	.0748	.2023	.0697	.1976	14
15	.0715	.2023	.0662	.1973	.0612	.1926	.0566	.1880	15
16	.0591	.1931	.0543	.1881	.0498	.1834	.0457	.1789	16
17	.0486	.1844	.0443	.1795	.0404	.1748	.0368	.1703	17
18	.0399	.1762	.0361	.1714	.0326	.1668	.0295	.1624	18
19	.0326	.1686	.0293	.1638	.0263	.1593	.0236	.1550	19
20	.0266	.1614	.0237	.1568	.0211	.1524	.0188	.1482	20
21	.0216	.1547	.0191	.1502	.0169	.1459	.0149	.1418	21
22	.0176	.1484	.0154	.1440	.0135	.1398	.0118	.1359	22
23	.0142	.1425	.0124	.1382	.0108	.1342	.0094	.1303	23
24	.0115	.1370	.0099	.1329	.0086	.1289	.0074	.1252	24
25	.0092	.1319	.0079	.1279	.0068	.1240	.0058	.1204	25
26	.0074	.1271	.0063	.1232	.0054	.1195	.0046	.1159	26
27	.0060	.1226	.0050	.1188	.0042	.1152	.0036	.1118	27
28	.0048	.1184	.0040	.1147	.0034	.1112	.0028	.1079	28
29	.0038	.1144	.0032	.1108	.0026	.1074	.0022	.1042	29
30	.0031	.1107	.0025	.1072	.0021	.1039	.0017	.1008	30
31	.0024	.1072	.0020	.1038	.0016	.1006	.0013	.0976	31
32	.0019	.1039	.0016	.1006	.0013	.0975	.0010	.0946	32
33	.0015	.1008	.0012	.0976	.0010	.0946	.0008	.0917	33
34	.0012	.0979	.0010	.0948	.0008	.0918	.0006	.0891	34
35	.0010	.0951	.0008	.0921	.0006	.0892	.0005	.0865	35
36	.0008	.0925	.0006	.0895	.0005	.0868	.0004	.0841	36
37	.0006	.0900	.0005	.0871	.0004	.0844	.0003	.0819	37
38	.0005	.0877	.0004	.0849	.0003	.0822	.0002	.0797	38
39	.0004	.0854	.0003	.0827	.0002	.0801	.0002	.0777	39
40	.0003	.0833	.0002	.0806	.0002	.0781	.0001	.0757	40